The History of Chinese Legal Civilization

Jinfan Zhang

The History of Chinese Legal Civilization

Ancient China—From About 21st Century B.C. to 1840 A.D.

Volume 1

 Springer

Jinfan Zhang
China University of Political Science and Law
Beijing, China

Chief Translator: Lixin Zhang
Other Translators: Ruiying Liu
China University of Political Science and Law, Beijing, China

Xing Li
China University of Political Science and Law, Beijing, China

Yue Wang
China University of Political Science and Law, Beijing, China

Xiaoqi Ou
China University of Political Science and Law, Beijing, China

Chen Yan
China University of Political Science and Law, Beijing, China

Qichen Liao
China University of Political Science and Law, Beijing, China

Sponsored by Chinese Fund for the Humanities and Social Sciences (本书获中华社会科学基金中华外译项目资助)

ISBN 978-981-10-1027-9   ISBN 978-981-10-1029-3   (eBook)
https://doi.org/10.1007/978-981-10-1029-3

© Springer Nature Singapore Pte Ltd. 2020
This work is subject to copyright. All rights are reserved by the Publisher, whether the whole or part of the material is concerned, specifically the rights of translation, reprinting, reuse of illustrations, recitation, broadcasting, reproduction on microfilms or in any other physical way, and transmission or information storage and retrieval, electronic adaptation, computer software, or by similar or dissimilar methodology now known or hereafter developed.
The use of general descriptive names, registered names, trademarks, service marks, etc. in this publication does not imply, even in the absence of a specific statement, that such names are exempt from the relevant protective laws and regulations and therefore free for general use.
The publisher, the authors, and the editors are safe to assume that the advice and information in this book are believed to be true and accurate at the date of publication. Neither the publisher nor the authors or the editors give a warranty, expressed or implied, with respect to the material contained herein or for any errors or omissions that may have been made. The publisher remains neutral with regard to jurisdictional claims in published maps and institutional affiliations.

This Springer imprint is published by the registered company Springer Nature Singapore Pte Ltd.
The registered company address is: 152 Beach Road, #21-01/04 Gateway East, Singapore 189721, Singapore

Introduction

The Origin and Main Features of Chinese Legal Civilization

Early in the era of "Huang Di" (Yellow Emperor, a legendary ruler) as was recorded in historical documents, Chinese legal civilization dawned on the land of China. It was recorded that after defeating and exterminating the whole clan of San Miao, "Huang Di" (Yellow Emperor) adopted its criminal penalty, inheriting, and passing on the "Five Cruel Penalties" created by Chi You, the leader of San Miao, which ushered in the prelude of Chinese legal history. In Xia Dynasty, around the twenty-first century B.C., a relatively stable and united country came into being, and "Xia Xing" (The Penal Code of Xia), also called "Yu Xing" (The Penal Code of Yu) containing over 3000 articles based on the "Five Cruel Penalties" was developed. During the more than 4000 years of development since Xia Dynasty, Chinese legal civilization was passed down from generation to generation without interruption, and its continuity, systematicness, and integrity were unrivalled among the ancient civilizations. Moreover, the people in the Han, Tang, Song, and Ming dynasties had exerted such a great influence on the neighboring countries with their advanced legal civilization that it had made it possible for Chinese law to stand proudly in the family of legal systems in the world.

The economic pattern of agrarianism, the political system of despotism, the social structure of family-centered patriarchy, the stable blood and geographical relationships, the unified and multi-ethnic national composition and the Confucianism-dominated ideology in ancient China have constituted a unique national condition which has further determined the main feature of Chinese legal civilization.

Introducing "Li" (Rites) Into Law and Integrating "Li" (Rites) with Law

"Li" (rites) originated from the religious ceremonies at the last stage of clan society. Because it not only fitted in with the national conditions of the ancient society which was dominated by patriarchal ethics but also performed the function of governance in accordance with social customs and exercised the power of spiritual deterrent, after entering the class society, "Li" (rites) was transformed by the rulers into a code of conduct which had reflected the hierarchical order and become an effective means of government. As a social phenomenon, "Li" (rites) had not only originated early, but also run throughout the whole ancient society, influenced every field of social life and adjusted the behavioral relations between individuals, between man and society, and between man and the state. The mutual penetration and integration of "Li" (rites) and "Fa" (law) constitutes the main feature of Chinese legal civilization.

Because the major function of "Li" (rites) was to "distinguish the noble from the humble, the superior from the inferior," and to establish a patriarchal and hierarchical order of "Zun Zun" (showing respect to nobility represented by the emperor), "Qin Qin" (showing respect to relatives represented by parents), "Zhang Zhang" (showing respect to the seniors) and "Nan Nv You Bie" (giving different treatments to males and females), it was accepted and guaranteed by the state. Thus, a systematic project to integrate "Li" (rites) with "Fa" (law) under the guidance of Confucianism was conducted. If it could be regarded as the beginning of the combination of "Li" (rites) and "Fa" (law) for the Confucian scholars in Han Dynasty to introduce "Li" (rites) into law through interpreting, annotating and making reference to Confucian classics when hearing cases, an inseparable relationship of "Ben" (the essence) and "Yong" (application) between "Li" (rites) and "Fa" (law) had formed in Tang Dynasty. Just as was recorded in *Tang Lv Shu Yi* (*The Comments on Tang Code*), "'De' (virtue) and 'Li' (rites) are the essence of administration while punishment is only a supplementary method, just as day and night are mutually interdependent to be a whole day and spring and autumn are mutually interdependent to be a whole year." The principle of "Gang Chang" (the Chinese ethical tradition) in "Li" (rites) had guided the enactment of "Fa" (law), meanwhile, the codes of "Li" (rites) were constantly legalized, codified, and finally became the mandatory rules for the regulation of people's conducts as well as the criteria for people to tell the right from the wrong.

The hierarchy of "Li" (rites) was consistent with the privilege of "Fa" (law), which was mutually complementary to achieve a lasting political stability of a country: to take "Li" (rites) as the guidance and "Fa" (law) as the criterion; to gain popular support by applying "Li" (rites) prudently and to distinguish the good from the evil by enforcing "Fa" (law) explicitly; to use "Li" (rites) to overstate the benevolent governance and to use "Fa" (law) to demonstrate the equity of administration; to execute "Fa" (law) with the guidance of "Li" (rites) to reduce the opposition in its enforcement, and to reinforce "Li" (rites) with "Fa" (law) to endow "Li" (rites) with more powerful authority; to introduce "Li" (rites) into

"Fa" (law) to make "Fa" (law) more moralized, so that not only the evil could be punished but also "Fa" (law) could be greatly promoted; to attach "Fa" (law) to "Li" (rites) to make morality legalized, so that "Fa" (law) could be resorted to when the principles of "Li" (rites) were violated. All this have proved that the operation of state apparatus could be promoted effectively by the integration of "Li" (rites) and "Fa" (law), which is of great significance in maintaining social stability. For this reason, "Li Zhu Xing Fu" (employing rites as the primary means, punishment as the supplement) and their integration in practice had always been an established policy in every feudal dynasty. Therefore, the combination of "Li" (rites) and "Fa" (law) and the unification of family and legal obligation embodied therein had exerted a great and extensive influence ever since.

"Yi Ren Wei Ben" (People-Oriented) and "Ming De Shen Fa" (Promoting Virtue and Being Prudent in the Enforcement of Punishment)

Humanism is the philosophical foundation of ancient Chinese legal civilization. Early at the beginning of Western Zhou Dynasty, the rulers learned from the downfall of the Shang Dynasty the importance of "Min Xin" (popular support) and "Min Qing" (the condition of the people) in ruling the country, so put forward the immortal theory that "man should not take water as a mirror but the people"[1] and connected worshiping "Tian" (Heaven) with protection of the people. The pre-Qin Confucian scholars had not only developed the theory of humanism and Confucius' theory that "the benevolent love the others," but also affirmed the status, value, and dignity of human beings and emphasized that "Ren" (benevolence) should be regarded as a basic principle in dealing with interpersonal relationships. Later, Confucius' theory of benevolence was further developed by Meng Zi (Mencius), who had put forward the theory of benevolent governance by attaching great importance to the people and advocated that "the people are the most important, next comes the country, so the ruler is the least important."[2]

The Confucian humanism is reflected in law in the following aspects: (1) emphasizing "De Zhu Xing Fu" (employing moral teaching as the primary means, punishment as the supplement) and stressing education; (2) helping and caring about the old, the young, women and the disabled; and (3) attaching importance to people's lives by implementing the reviewing system for death penalty.

Therefore, the legalization of humanism has been passed down and developed from generation to generation, which is another important feature of Chinese legal civilization.

---

[1]"Jiu Gao" (Announcement to Ban Alcohol) in *Shang Shu* (*The Book of Historical Document*).
[2]"Jin Xin" (With all One's Heart) (Part 2) in *Meng Zi* (*Mencius*).

Following "Tian Li" (Heavenly Principles) and Enforcing Laws According to Specific Circumstances

Dong Zhongshu, a Confucian scholar in Han Dynasty, based on the interaction between "Tian" (Heaven) and man, not only proposed that "'San Gang' (three cardinal guides) of 'Wang Dao' (the benevolent government) relied on 'Tian' (heaven)", but also even ethicized "Tian" (Heaven) itself. The Confucian scholars in Song Dynasty took a further step and even regarded "San Gang" (three cardinal guides, namely, ruler as the guide of subjects, father as the guide of son, and husband the guide of wife) as "Tian Li" (heavenly principles), so "Tian Li" (heavenly principles) was embodied as the national law, which had given "Guo Fa" (national law) a sense of irresistible mystery. Thus, enforcing law in accordance with "Min Qing" (the condition of the people) had harmonized both "Guo Fa" (national law) and "Ren Qing" (human feeling), which had not only given "Guo Fa" (national law) a touch of ethics, but also made it possible for "Guo Fa" (national law) to gain public support besides guaranteeing the state power, so that when "Guo Fa" (national law) was enforced, it would be more effective. That was exactly the starting point and the end-result of the unification of "Tian Li" (heavenly principles), "Guo Fa" (national law), and "Ren Qing" (human feeling). The harmony and mutual complementation of the three elements had constituted the essential connotation of ancient Chinese legal civilization, which was not accidental, but was determined by the ancient Chinese patriarchal social structure, the long-lasting cultural accumulation, the national mindset, and the political and legal consciousness.

The harmony of "Tian Li" (heavenly principles), "Guo Fa" (national law), and "Ren Qing" (human feeling), the integration of "Tian Li" (heavenly principles) and "Ren Qing" (human feeling), the combination of ethics and law, and the unification of family and legal obligation, etc. had exerted a great influence not only on the development of ancient Chinese law but also on the law of other countries in the cultural circle of Confucianism in the east, such as ancient Korea, Japan and Vietnam.

The Family-Oriented Principle and the Ethical Legal System

In ancient Chinese law, the family-oriented social structure was protected and patriarchal system was affirmed, which not only was the foundation of the stability of the country, but also a necessary condition for the existence and development of feudal natural economy. Therefore, patriarchy was also introduced into the administrative and legal areas and it was often preached that the emperor was "Tian Zi" (the son of Heaven), the parent of the people and the embodiment of national patriarchy. In addition, the local officials of "Zhou" (subprefecture) and "Xian" (county) were also called parenting magistrates to strengthen imperial and administrative power.

The core in ethical legislation was the legalization of family obligation and the differentiation of punishments for the same crimes committed by people of different classes. As for the family rules employed to regulate the domestic relations, they were in a subordinate position in feudal legal system; but they were important supplementary parts to state law. All the behaviors against the national law would be forbidden by family rules, so the family members who disobeyed family rules would naturally not be tolerated by the national law. Therefore, such family rules supported by state law had a great regulating function, which was unique in ancient China.

Because of family orientation, the law of "Zu Zhu" (killing of the whole clan of a criminal) was made and the emphasis on ethics and kinship had led to more severe punishment for the infringement of the rights of kinsmen. The long-standing patriarchal system had laid a solid foundation for the family-oriented and ethical legal system. In addition, The Confucian doctrines of "Li Xue" (Neo-Confucianism: a Confucian school of idealist philosophy of the Song and Ming Dynasties) had provided the theoretical basis for the ethical legal system of family-orientation, and the despotic political system had in turn asserted a special claim to the patriarchal system. Thus, the legal relationship of rights and obligations expressed by the identification of the family, the nation, and "Fu Zhi" (mourning apparel system) was unique to Chinese legal civilization.

Pursuing No Litigation and Settling Conflicts by Mediation

Under the despotic rule of monarchs in ancient China, the primary task of the law was to safeguard the public power, i.e., the right of ruling by the state, thus the criminal law, which was used primarily for the punishment of the violation of state interests, was especially emphasized. However, the awareness of private rights was relatively weak, and property disputes among individuals were regarded as trivial matters, therefore there had lacked necessary legal mediation in this respect. As a result, civil law was sporadic and not systematic.

Moreover, the value of individual persons was determined by their ranking in ethical order and social status, and there was no extensive development of contractual relations or any movement for the freedom of individuals. As for the lawsuits for private rights, the rulers regarded them as no more than trivial disputes and paid little attention. In practice, what those officials pursued was to reduce or even to eliminate litigation, because it would be regarded as the evidence of their good reputation and their achievements in officialdom.

It had been the goal of administration since Confucius "to make sure that there were no litigations."[3] Thus, it not only became the value orientation of officials "to eliminate litigation," it also exerted an extensive influence on the public. This was

---

[3] "Yan Yuan" (Yan Yuan, one of Confucius' disciples) in *Lun Yu* (*The Analects*).

not incidental because it resulted from the profound sediment of traditional Chinese culture in which the members of the society were closely related because of the blood relationship of living together of the whole family, the geographical relationship of being neighbors from generation to generation, the national psychology of pursuing harmony and the economic structure of agricultural society in particular, so it was regarded as the guideline to live in harmony without conflict. Even when there were disputes, they were expected to be mediated by the patriarchs and their neighbors, so the civil mediation system in ancient China had reached to a very advanced degree, which was unique in the ancient world. As mediation was based on "Li" (rites), customs and "Fa" (law), its popularity not only promoted the development of legal culture featured by the combination of "Li" (rites) and "Fa" (law), but also reduced people's burden of litigation, and ultimately facilitated the formation of the general mood of society. However, the mediation system with the cooperation in and out of court had also resulted in the negative consequence that the public had little notion of the rights of litigation.

The World Position of Chinese Legal Civilization

In the history of world legal system, ancient Chinese legal system not only had an earlier origin, it also was in the vanguard of development for a long time. *Yun Meng Qin Jian* (*Amounts of Bamboo Writing Slips in Qin Dynasty Excavated in Yunmeng*) which was unearthed has proved that "everything had certain rules to regulate" even in the state of Qin around the fourth century B.C. Therefore, compared with the early feudal laws of the western countries, *Qin Lv* (*Qin Code*) was made over 1000 years earlier than *Lex Salics,* which was made in the Frankish Kingdom. In contents, it was no match for *Yun Meng Qin Jian* (*Amounts of Bamboo Writing Slips in Qin Dynasty Excavated in Yunmeng*) because it was still a customary law.

As a model of Chinese feudal codes, *Tang Lv* (*Tang Code*) in particular, was applied for reference as the parent law by the neighboring countries and regions for a long time. Taking Japan as an example, *Jin Jiang Ling* (*The Ōmi Code*) enacted in the reign of Emperor Tenji and *Tian Wu Lv Ling* (*The Temmu Decree*) enacted in the reign of Emperor Temmu were both modeled on the "Ling" (decree) during the reign of Zhenguan in the Tang Dynasty. *Taihō Lv Ling* (*Taihō Code*), which had an epoch-making significance in Japanese legal history, had copied *Tang Lv Shu Yi* (*The Comments on Tang Code*) both in terms of the titles of chapters and contents, with just some deletion and combination made. For instance, "Yi Qin" (the Diligence: including military and civil officials who have displayed great diligence in their work through thorough occupation of public affairs) and "Yi Bin" (the Guests of the State: to treat the descendants of previous dynasties as guests of the state who could enjoy a legal privilege) in "Ba Yi" (The Eight Deliberations) were omitted and "Ba Yi" (The Eight Deliberations) was reduced to "Liu Yi" (Six Deliberations), so was *Yanglao Lv* (*Yoro Code*) which was made after *Taihō Lv Ling* (*Taihō Code*). Doctor Kuwabara Jitsuzoh, a Japanese scholar of legal history, had pointed out that "all the codes of the imperial society from the Nara Age to the Heian Age were based on *Tang Lv* (*Tang Code*) both in form and contents."[4] Doctor Hozumi Nobushige also said that *Xing Lv Gang Ling* (*The Programme for the New Code*) issued in December of the 3rd year of Meiji (1870) "was based on the codes of Tang, Ming and Qing dynasties in China."[5]

Besides Japan, Korea also drew reference from *Tang Lv* (*Tang Code*) during its 447 years of ruling. It was stated in "Xing Fa Zhi" (The Record of the Criminal Law) in volume eighty-four of *Gao Li Shi* (*The History of Korea*) that "almost all the systems of Korea were made by following those of the Tang Dynasty. As for the criminal law, those from *Tang Lv* (*Tang Code*) were also adopted and applied in accordance with the actual conditions of Korea."

Tang Lv (*Tang Code*) also had a great influence on the feudal codes of Vietnam. *Xing Shu* (*The Criminal Book*) enacted in the reign of the Emperor Li Taizun and *Guo Chao Xing Lv* (*The National Criminal Codes*) enacted during the reign of Chen Taizun were both adopted from *Tang Lv* (*Tang Code*). It was noted in *Xing Lv Zhi* (*The Record of Criminal Code*) in volume thirty-three of *Li Chao Xian Zhang Lei Zhi* (*The Record of Laws and Regulations of the Past Dynasties*) written by a Vietnamese scholar named Pan Hui in the nineteenth century that "according to the criminal laws of Li and Chen…when laws were made at the time, the laws of Tang and Song dynasties were also followed with the leniency and severeness of the punishment deliberated on."[6]

To the time of Ming Dynasty, *Ming Lv* (*Ming Code*) became another Chinese law that had had an important influence on Southeast Asian countries besides *Tang Lv* (*Tang Code*). In *Xing Dian* (*The Criminal Code*) and *Xing Fa Da Quan* (*Encyclopedia of Criminal Laws*) in *Jing Guo Da Dian* (*Gyeongguk Daejeon* or *Complete Code of Law*), *Da Dian Xu Lu* (*A Extended Record to the Great Code*) and *Xu Da Dian* (*A Sequel to the Great Code*) which were enacted in the reign of Li Guicheng, the founder of Korea, the key provisions in the *Ming Lv* (*Ming Code*) were all adopted. Moreover, many other laws were all directly influenced by *Ming Lv* (*Ming Code*), such as *Jia Long Huang Yue Lv Li* (*The Laws and Precedents of Jialong*) made in the reign of Nguyễn Phúc Ánh, Emperor Gao of Vietnam, *Qin Ding Da Na Nan Hui Shi Li* (*The Vietnamese Codes and Laws Made by Imperial Order*) made in the reign of Nguyễn Phúc Tuyền, Emperor Xianzu of Vietnam, *Xin Lv Gang Ling*

---

[4] Kuwabara Jitsuzoh (Japan), *Zhong Guo Fa Zhi Shi Lun Cong* (*The Review on Chinese Legal History*), p. 213, quoted from Yang Honglie's *Zhong Guo Fa Lv Dui Dong Ya Zhu Guo Zhi Ying Xiang* (*The Influence of Chinese Law on the East Asian Countries*), China University of Political Science and Law Press, 1999, p. 4.

[5] Hozumi Nobushige (Japan), *Ri Ben Xin Min Fa* (*The New Civil Law of Japan*), quoted from Yang Honglie's *Zhong Guo Fa Lv Dui Dong Ya Zhu Guo Zhi Ying Xiang* (*The Influence of Chinese Law on the East Asian Countries*), China University of Political Science and Law Press, 1999, p. 274.

[6] Quoted from Yang Honglie, *Zhong Guo Fa Lv Dui Dong Ya Zhu Guo Zhi Ying Xiang* (*The Influence of Chinese Law on the East Asian Countries*), China University of Political Science and Law Press, 1999, p. 420.

(*The Guiding Principles of New Law*), and *Gai Ding Lv Li* (*The Revised Laws and Precedents*) made in Japanese Meiji period.

As the laws of the neighboring countries were attached to the Chinese legal system for a long time, and more importantly, because Chinese law not only had its own uniqueness but also its progressiveness in legal culture, it is universally acknowledged in the world as one of the most important legal systems, namely, the Chinese legal system.

To sum up, the ancient Chinese legal civilization has had an important position in the history of world legal civilization, which has manifested the great contribution made by Chinese nation to the development of world legal system.

Contents

1	**The Origin of Chinese Legal Civilization: The Legal Systems of the Xia and Shang Dynasties**.............................		1
	1.1	The Earliest Dawn of Chinese Legal Civilization: The Legal System of the Xia Dynasty...............................	1
		1.1.1 The Disintegration of Clan Society and the Emergence of Legal System................................	2
		1.1.2 The Pathway for China to Move Towards Legal Civilization...................................	7
		1.1.3 From the Primitive Customs to the Law in Class Society.......................................	10
		1.1.4 The State Structure and Legal System of Xia Dynasty.......................................	19
	1.2	The Legal System of Shang Dynasty Under the Ruling of Theocracy....................................	28
		1.2.1 The Unity of Kingship Rights, Family Authority and Theocracy.................................	28
		1.2.2 The Extension of the Scope of the State Management and Division of the Duties of Officials...............	31
		1.2.3 The More Enriched Contents of Legislation...........	33
		1.2.4 The Judicial System Under the Influence of Theocratic Law................................	43
2	**The Early Developed Form of the Chinese Legal Civilization: The Legal System of Western Zhou Dynasty**..................		45
	2.1	Setting Up the Administrative Management System Protected by Dukes and Princes and Dominated by Royal Families.......	46
	2.2	Implementing the Comprehensive Strategy of Ruling by "Li" (Rites), "Yue" (Music), "Zheng" (Government) and "Xing" (Punishment)...............................	52

		2.3	Establishing the Guiding Principle of "Jing Tian Bao Ming" (Respecting Heaven and Protecting the People) and "Ming De Shen Fa" (Promoting Virtue and Being Prudent in the Enforcement of Punishment)..................................	59

2.3 Establishing the Guiding Principle of "Jing Tian Bao Ming" (Respecting Heaven and Protecting the People) and "Ming De Shen Fa" (Promoting Virtue and Being Prudent in the Enforcement of Punishment)............................ 59
2.4 The Legal Contents of *Lv Xing* (*The Penal Code of Lv*) and *Jiu Xing* (*The Code Nine Penalties*).................... 62
    2.4.1 The Administrative Laws in Inscriptions and Documentary Records........................... 66
    2.4.2 The Criminal Law: Emphasizing Public Rights and Being Cautious with Patriarchal Clan System........ 69
    2.4.3 The Civil Law Beginning to Take Shape.............. 84
2.5 The Judicial Activities with the Initial Differentiation of Criminal and Civil Litigation.......................... 99

3 The Legal System of the Spring and Autumn and Warring States Period Featured by Social Transformation and Legal Reform..... 113
3.1 The Reform Adaptable to Social Transformation.............. 114
3.2 The Collapse of the System of "Shi Qing" (Inheritance of Noble Titles) and the Formation of Bureaucratic System..... 119
3.3 Confucianism and Legalism in "Bai Jia Zheng Ming" (The Contention of a Hundred Schools of Thought)........... 124
3.4 The Legal Reform Adaptable to Social Transformation......... 144
    3.4.1 The Issuing of the Statute Laws in the Vassal States and the Legislative Activities in the Spring and Autumn Period.............................. 144
    3.4.2 Legislations in Each State in the Warring States Period and *Fa Jing* (*Canon of Laws*) Written by Li Kui.. 149

4 The Legal System of Qin Dynasty with "Laws Made in Every Field"... 157
4.1 The Legal System of Qin Dynasty Recorded in *Yun Meng Qin Jian* (*Amounts of Bamboo Writing Slips in Qin Dynasty Excavated in Yunmeng*)................................... 158
    4.1.1 The Nature of *Qin Lv* (*Qin Code*) Recorded in *Yun Meng Qin Jian* (*Amounts of Bamboo Writing Slips in Qin Dynasty Excavated in Yunmeng*).......... 158
    4.1.2 The Main Contents of *Qin Lv* (*Qin Code*) in *Qin Jian*....................................... 162
    4.1.3 The Judicial System Stressing the Responsibility of Officials..................................... 225
4.2 The Legal System of Qin Dynasty After Its Unification........ 231
    4.2.1 The State System Reflecting Despotism and the Centralization of State Power..................... 232

| | | 4.2.2 | "Ming Fa Du" (Make Law Known to the People) and "Ding Lv Ling" (Making Laws and Decrees) . . . . | 237 |

5 The Confucianization of the Legal Systems in Western and Eastern Han Dynasties 249

5.1 The Establishment of Western Han Dynasty and the Change of the Legislative Policy 250
5.2 The Legislative Activities and the Forms of Law 266
5.3 The Enriching and Development of Administrative Law 276
    5.3.1 The Establishment of the Operation Mechanism of State Institutions Headed by the Emperor 276
    5.3.2 The Strengthening of Official Management 283
5.4 The Criminal Law in Documents and *Han Jian* (*The Bamboo Slip of Han Dynasty*) 298
    5.4.1 The Main Accusation in the Laws of Han Dynasty 299
    5.4.2 The Penalty System Reform of Abolishing Corporal Punishment 320
    5.4.3 The Criminal Principle Under the Influence of Confucianism 334
5.5 The Development of Civil Legal Relationship and Civil Legislation 343
    5.5.1 Identity and Civil Rights 343
    5.5.2 The Ownership and Legal Protection 345
    5.5.3 The Legal Adjustment and Protection of Debt 347
    5.5.4 Marriage, Family and Inheritance 351
5.6 The Economic Laws of "Zhong Nong Yi Shang" (Encouraging Agriculture and Restraining Commerce) 355
5.7 The Judicial System Under the Influence of Confucianism 360
    5.7.1 The Judicial System 361
    5.7.2 The Litigation and Jurisdiction 363
    5.7.3 Trial 364
5.8 The Rising of the Private Law Annotation 376

6 The Legal Systems of Wei, Jin, Southern and Northern Dynasty: The Legislative Progress and Cultural Amalgamation 381

6.1 The Legislative Achievements in Wei, Jin, Southern and Northern Dynasty 382
    6.1.1 The Legislative Achievement of "San Guo" (Three Kingdoms) Represented by *Wei Lv* (*Wei Code*) 385
    6.1.2 The Legislative Achievements of Western and Eastern Jin and Southern Dynasty Represented by *Jin Lv* (*Jin Code*) 393
    6.1.3 The Legislative Achievements in Northern Dynasty Represented by *Bei Wei Lv* (*Bei Wei Code*) and *Bei Qi Lv* (*Bei Qi Code*) 403

	6.2	The Basic Contents of the Laws in Different Dynasties.	418
		6.2.1 The Strengthening of the Tendency of the Codification of Administrative Law.	418
		6.2.2 The Tendency of Applying Severe Punishments and the Drafting of "Zhong Zui Shi Tiao" (Ten Felonies).	436
		6.2.3 The Civil Law Under the Privileged System of "Shi Zu" (the Gentry).	454
	6.3	Inheriting the Judicial System of Han Dynasty.	466
7	**The Legal Systems of Sui and Tang Dynasties: The Finalization of the Forms of Chinese Legal Civilization**.	471
	7.1	The Legal System of Sui Dynasty Made by Adopting the Strong Points of the Laws of Southern and Northern Dynasties.	471
		7.1.1 Legislation in the Early Period of Sui Dynasty and the Historical Role of *Kai Huang Lv* (*The Code Made in the Year of Kai Huang*).	472
		7.1.2 The Management System and the System of "Kai Ke Qu Shi" (To Recruit Talents Through Imperial Examination) in Sui Dynasty.	479
		7.1.3 The Establishment of the Basic Framework of Feudal Criminal Law.	482
		7.1.4 The Civil and Economic Laws Centered on "Jun Tian Zhi" (The System of Land Equalization) and "Zu Yong Diao Fa" (Law on Farmland Rent, Handicraft Tax, and Corvée).	487
		7.1.5 The Judicial System of the Centralized Government.	489
	7.2	The Legal System of Tang Dynasty Symbolizing the Establishment of Chinese Legal System.	495
		7.2.1 The Legislative Ideology Drawn from the Lessons of the Extinction of Sui Dynasty.	496
		7.2.2 The Legislative Activities and the Major Legislative Achievements.	509
		7.2.3 The Organic Law of the Administrative Organs and the Official Administration Law.	518
		7.2.4 The Finalized Criminal Law.	550
		7.2.5 The More Complicated Civil Law.	567
		7.2.6 The Strengthening of the Legal Adjustment of Economic Relationships.	600
		7.2.7 The Judicial System Tending To Be Perfect.	609
		7.2.8 The Characteristics of *Tang Lv* (*Tang Code*) and Its World Position.	627
	7.3	The Legal Systems of "Wu Dai Shi Guo" (Five Dynasties and Ten Kingdoms).	642

Contents for Volume 2

8	**The Legal Civilization of Northern and Southern Song Dynasties Fostered by Commercial Economy**		**649**
	8.1 The National Policy and Characteristics of the Legislation of the Early Song Dynasty		651
		8.1.1 The National Policy of Strengthening the Centralization of Authority	651
		8.1.2 The Characteristics of the Legislation	653
	8.2 The Administrative Law for Strengthening the Centralization of Authority		662
		8.2.1 The System Reform for Strengthening the Centralization of Authority	664
		8.2.2 The Enrichment of the Official Administrative Law	671
	8.3 Criminal Law Aiming to Maintain the Centralization of Authority		699
		8.3.1 "Dao Zei Zhong Fa" (Severe Punishment for Robbery and Theft)	700
		8.3.2 The Changes of the Penal System Shown by "She Zhang Fa"	712
	8.4 Civil Law Adapting to the Development of Commodity Economy		716
		8.4.1 The Expansion of Household Registration and the Changes of People's Identities	717
		8.4.2 New Development of Property Rights	723
		8.4.3 The New Achievements of the Law of Obligation	730
		8.4.4 Marriage and Inheritance for the Improvement of Women's Social Status	739
	8.5 The Economic and Financial Law Made with the Spirit of Reform		748
		8.5.1 Agricultural, Industrial, and Commercial Legislation	748
		8.5.2 The Financial Legislation	760

	8.6	The Judicial System of "Ju Yan Fen Si" (The Separation of Interrogation and Conviction)......................	772
		8.6.1 The Change of Judicial System.................	772
		8.6.2 Perfection of the Judicial Proceedings of Civil Procedure............................	775
		8.6.3 The Creation of the System of "Ju Yan Fen Si" (The Separation of Interrogation and Conviction).....	780
	8.7	The Historical Role of the Legal System and the Achievement of "Lv Xue" (The Study of Statutory Laws) in the Southern and Northern Song Dynasties..........................	788
	8.8	The Legal Systems of Liao, Western Xia, and Jin Dynasties Compared with That of the Song Dynasty.................	792
		8.8.1 The Legal System of the Liao Dynasty.............	793
		8.8.2 The Legal System of Western Xia Dynasty..........	799
		8.8.3 The Legal System of the Jin Dynasty..............	813
9	**The Legal System of "Zu Shu Bian Tong" in the Yuan Dynasty**....		833
	9.1	The Legislative Achievements of "Fu Hui Han Fa" (Sticking to and Integrating the Laws of the Han Nationality)....	835
	9.2	The Administrative Legislation and Management System with National Characteristics...........................	846
		9.2.1 The Administrative Law of "Zu Shu Bian Tong"......	846
		9.2.2 The Management System with Its Distinctive Features..................................	848
		9.2.3 The Official Administration Law Focused on Supervision..............................	855
	9.3	Criminal Law Made by Combining Reference to the Old Systems of the Tang and Song Dynasties and Innovation......	868
		9.3.1 Executing Penalties According to "Fu Zhi" (Mourning Apparel System)....................	869
		9.3.2 Changing "Shi E" (The Ten Abominations) to "Zhu E" (Various Abominations).......................	870
		9.3.3 The Penalty System and the Principle of Making Criminal Law with National Characteristics..........	873
	9.4	The Civil Law with National Differences..................	880
		9.4.1 Classifying the People According to Their Ethnic Identities.................................	880
		9.4.2 The Characteristics of the Times of the Protection of Property Rights...........................	882
		9.4.3 The Making of Debt Contract...................	887
		9.4.4 Marriage and Inheritance Law with the Integration of the Laws of Mongolian and Han Nationalities......	893
	9.5	The Trial System with Diverse Jurisdiction................	900
		9.5.1 The Diversified Judicial Organization System........	900

| | | 9.5.2 | Concurrency of Regional Jurisdiction and Ethnic and Religious Jurisdiction | 902 |

| | | 9.5.3 | Mediation Extensively Practiced in Civil Trials | 904 |

10 The Legal System of the Ming Dynasty: The Final Form of Chinese Legal Civilization 909

    10.1 Legislative Ideology and Achievements of the Ming Dynasty . . 911

        10.1.1 Zhu Yuanzhang's Legislative Ideology in the Early Ming Dynasty 911

        10.1.2 The Making of *Da Ming Lv* (*The Great Ming Code*), the Amendment of *Wen Xing Tiao Li* (*The Ordinance for Inquisition*), and the Issuing of *Ming Hui Dian* (*The Collected Statutes of Ming Dynasty*) 924

    10.2 The Administrative Legislation for the Strengthening of Absolutism 946

        10.2.1 The Major Changes of the Central Administrative System 947

        10.2.2 The Law on the State Officials to Maintain the Operation of Bureaucracy 958

        10.2.3 The Change of the Supervisory System and Enriching of Supervision Law 968

    10.3 Criminal Law Reflecting the Thoughts of Ruling the Country with Severe Penalties 977

        10.3.1 The Ideology of "Bringing Order Out of the Troubled Times by Enforcing Severe Penalties" and Its Influence on the Legislation of Criminal Law 978

        10.3.2 The Penal System Focusing on the Punishment of Treacherous People and the Applicable Principles of Criminal Law 995

    10.4 Further Development of Civil Law 1001

        10.4.1 "Ren Hu Fen Bian" (Separation of Registered and Actual Residence) and the Subjects of Civil Rights 1002

        10.4.2 The Usufruct of Estate Rights and the Expansion of Guarantee 1005

        10.4.3 The New Development of the Law of Obligation 1011

        10.4.4 Marriage and Inheritance Law Adapted from That of the Tang and Song Dynasties 1016

    10.5 Economic Legislation Adapting to the Economic Development 1022

        10.5.1 The Agricultural Legislation Encouraging Land Reclamation 1023

        10.5.2 The Government-Run Handicraft Industry with the Promotion of the System of "Jiang Ji" (The Craftsman Household Registration) 1026

		10.5.3	The Strengthening of "Jin Que Zhi Du" (The System of State Monopoly for Some Important Goods) in Commerce	1029
		10.5.4	The Making of the Laws on Metallic and Paper Money	1035
	10.6	The Change of Jurisdiction and the Joint Trial System		1038
		10.6.1	The Change of the Administration of "San Fa Si" (Three Judicial Departments)	1039
		10.6.2	The Judicial Procedures Emphasizing Judicial Jurisdiction	1046
		10.6.3	The Newly Created "Hui Shen Zhi Du" (The Joint Trial System)	1049
	10.7	The Achievement of "Lv Xue" (The Study of Statutory Laws) and the World Position of *Da Ming Lv* (*The Great Ming Code*)		1057
		10.7.1	The Achievement of "Lv Xue" (The Study of Statutory Laws)	1057
		10.7.2	The World Position of *Da Ming Lv* (*The Great Ming Code*)	1062
11	**The Legal System of the Qing Dynasty: The Final Form of Chinese Legal Civilization**			**1071**
	11.1	The Foundation of the Legal System Before Entering Shanhaiguan		1072
		11.1.1	The Transition from Jurchen Customary Law to Statute Law	1073
		11.1.2	Initiation of the Legal System of "Can Han Zhuo Jin"	1077
		11.1.3	Characteristics of the Legal System in the Early Period	1088
	11.2	The Complete Implementation of the Legislative Principle of "Can Han Zhuo Jin"		1097
		11.2.1	*Da Qing Lv Li* (*The Laws and Precedents of Great Qing*): The Main Achievements of "Can Han Zhuo Jin"	1098
		11.2.2	*Da Qing Hui Dian* (*The Collected Statutes of Great Qing*) and the Making of Departmental Regulations	1107
		11.2.3	The National Legislation Made according to *Li Fan Yuan Ze Li* (*The Regulation for the Bureau of National Minority Affairs*)	1114
	11.3	The Legalization of the Administrative System and the System of Official Management		1129
		11.3.1	The Change of Administrative System	1129
		11.3.2	The Legalization of Official Management	1156

11.4	The Criminal Law Made to Strengthen the Autocratic Ruling...		1166
	11.4.1	The Main Crimes in *Da Qing Xing Lv* (*The Criminal Law of Great Qing*)...............	1166
	11.4.2	The Penalty System and the Principle for the Application of Criminal Law................	1182
11.5	Codification of Civil Law.............................		1189
	11.5.1	Social Structure and Identity....................	1190
	11.5.2	The Further Enrichment of Property Rights.........	1205
	11.5.3	The Perfection of "Zhai Fa" (Law of Obligation)....	1224
	11.5.4	Marriage, Family, and Inheritance Mixed with the Custom of the Jurchen Nationality...............	1235
11.6	Enriching of the System of Economic Law................		1251
	11.6.1	The New Development of Tax Legislation..........	1251
	11.6.2	The Industrial and Commercial Legislation of Secluding the Country from the Outside World....	1253
	11.6.3	The Legislation Ensuring Water Transportation......	1259
11.7	The More Complete Judicial System....................		1261
	11.7.1	Reform of the Judicial System..................	1261
	11.7.2	The More Specific Criminal and Civil Litigation.....	1269
	11.7.3	The Criminal Trial and "Hui Shen Zhi Du" (The Joint Trial System).......................	1276
	11.7.4	The Civil Trial with the a Combination of Judgment and Mediation...............................	1291
11.8	The New Achievement of "Lv Xue" (The Study of Statutory Laws) and Its Impact on Legislation and the Judiciary...................................		1301

Chapter 1
The Origin of Chinese Legal Civilization: The Legal Systems of the Xia and Shang Dynasties

(About 21st Century B.C.–11th Century B.C.)

1.1 The Earliest Dawn of Chinese Legal Civilization: The Legal System of the Xia Dynasty

Chinese legal civilization has developed for over 4000 years without interruption. Its continuity, systematicness, and integrity are very rare among the ancient civilizations. The Chinese legal civilization is the fruit of the wisdom and rationality of the Chinese nation and it has reflected the great creativity of the nation and the profound background of legal culture.

The origin of Chinese legal civilization is diversified. San Miao nationality living in the Yangtze River basin was the first to have private property and class differentiation. According to historical records, "the Miao people made use of penalties rather than spirits in the regulation of society and they made 'Wu Xing' (Five Penalties) which was called 'Fa' (law)." Therefore, it had indicated that the Miao people had shaken off the control of religious gods and spirits and made laws to meet the needs of the ruling class.

The "Hua Xia" nationality (an ancient name for China), living in the Yellow River basin, had set up the first class society, namely, the Xia Dynasty around the twenty-first century B.C. Thus, they made "Xia Xing" (The Penal Code of Xia), which had lifted the great curtain of the history of Chinese legal civilization. "Hua Xia" nationality became a significant promoter of the continuous development of Chinese legal civilization for its progressiveness, inclusiveness, and comprehensiveness.

1.1.1 The Disintegration of Clan Society and the Emergence of Legal System

China is one of the earliest countries with advanced civilization in the world, and it has a long and uninterrupted history and splendid culture. The discovery of underground relics proved that our ancestors had labored and lived on this vast and fertile land around one million years ago. In the period of Yangshao culture, about 6000 or 7000 years ago, the clan society centered by matriarchy had reached its zenith and begun to be changed to patriarchal society. In the later period of Longshan culture and Hemudu culture, the patriarchal society had been completely established. The replacement of matriarchy by patriarchy was an inevitable result of the transformation of the status in production between men and women, so it was "one of the most radical revolutions" in human history.

In a clan society, with extremely low level of productivity, it had to rely on the clan members' collective labor to maintain the production of scanty means of material subsistence. Accordingly, the basis of the relationship of production was the public ownership of the means of production by the clan: the products were owned by all clan members and were distributed equally without private ownership or exploitation, which was so-called "Tian Xia Wei Gong" (the whole world as one community).[1] Thus, under such situations, "there is no private plantation or weaving, and the people have to cope with the problems of coldness and hunger together."[2] Furthermore, all clan members were equal and there was no such phenomenon of the exploitation of man by man. To organize clan members to conduct production, to fight against natural disasters, and to protect and ensure the survival of the whole clan, clan institutions by which the public affairs were managed gradually came into being. The leaders were elected by all clan members to fulfill their responsibilities endowed by the clan community. Therefore, when there were major events or disputes, a meeting of all the clan members would be held to have them settled collectively, and the head of the clan would be replaced if he were incompetent. The legend of "Yao Shun Shan Rang" (Yao's abdicating and passing on the crown to Shun) was an example of the primitive democratic system. The state and law, which had functioned as the ruling of classes, did not exist at that time, so everything was done in accordance with the primitive customs, which had a traditional and universal restraining force. The primitive democratic system and the ruling of customs were depicted in some ancient books: "in Archaean time, the ancient people lived in a perfect order without the distinction of the upper and the lower, so there was no 'Tian' (Heaven) or monarch."[3] Moreover, "people were obedient even without laws or decrees in the period of Shennong (the patron of

---

[1] "Li Yun" (The Rites in the Pre-Qin Dynasties) in *Li Ji* (*The Book of Rites*).
[2] "Zhi Ben" (Getting at the Root) in *Wei Liao Zi* (*On the Art of War*).
[3] "Ban Lu" (Ranks and Salaries) in *Qian Fu Lun* (*On Hermits*).

agriculture)",[4] "so the society operated peacefully without penalties and the leaders ruled successfully without fighting a single battle."[5]

The customs in a clan society were a kind of collective consciousness which had come into being gradually, and at first they manifested in the worship of nature, totem, gods and ancestors, then later they developed into a code of conduct to constrain people's behaviors and to maintain the social order of the clan, such as the punishment for the violation of public interests of the clan, the vengeance for kinsmen, the maintenance of public ownership and the distribution of property, on the basis of which, these customs were further evolved into customary laws of clan society.

However, the democratic clan system was a primitive democratic system in keeping with the extremely low level of productivity, so it was bound to collapse and to be replaced by new social institutions and systems with the development of productivity.

The patriarchal period at the end of primitive society was also a time when private ownership and polarization of the rich and the poor dramatically developed. As productivity continued to develop, the basis of clannish public ownership was constantly impacted. When there was surplus for the products of labor created by human being after basic needs were met, private property inevitably appeared and developed. Therefore, the previous notion that "although people hate to see property abandoned, they would not necessarily pick it up and keep it to themselves" was gradually replaced by new concepts that "property and labor were privately owned", "people tried their best to make personal gains", and "everyone just regarded his relatives as loved ones so treated their own children as children."[6] The development of private property also brought about polarization of the rich and the poor within the clan. A few tribal leaders in the clan had taken possession of the surplus products and accumulated great fortune by taking the advantage of their official positions, so they became the wealthy and the exploiters. It was stated in "Jin Xin" (With all One's Heart) in *Meng Zi* (*Mencius*) that when Shun was an ordinary member in the tribe, "he just ate wild plants," but "when he became the monarch later, he wore gorgeous clothes and played music with two maids serving him." In some of the tombs of the Xia Dynasty unearthed in Erlitou, more than twenty one funerary objects were found and except the various wine containers like "Gu", "Jue", "Jia", and "He" (all are wine containers in ancient China), there were also decorations like shells, jewelries, and turquoises; while in other tombs just one or two pieces of crude pottery were found or nothing was found at all. The evident difference of burial objects indicated that the polarization of the rich and the poor had already become a common social phenomenon.

To plunder and expand the possession of social wealth, predatory wars were often waged against other clans. It was recorded in "Huang Wang Bu" (The Section of

---

[4]"Si Lun Xun" (Instructions of Si Lun) in *Huai Nan Zi* (*Masters from Huainan*).
[5]"Hua Ce" (Policies) in *Shang Jun Shu* (*The Book of Lord Shang*).
[6]"Li Yun" (The Rites in the Pre-Qin Dynasties) in *Li Ji* (*The Book of Rites*).

Emperors) in *Tai Ping Yu Lan* (*Imperial Readings of the Taiping Era*) quoted from "Wan Ji Lun" (On a Myriad of State Affairs) in *Jiang Zi* (*Essays by Jiang Ji*) that "at the beginning of his reign, 'Huang Di' (Yellow Emperor) had paid more attention to self-cultivation, loved his people and hated war, while the other four emperors had instead conferred themselves titles, become rebellious by using different colors representing their domains and conspired against 'Huang Di' (Yellow Emperor). Consequently, the border towns were constantly plundered by the armies, so 'Huang Di' (Yellow Emperor) sighed: 'The emperor is already in danger, but the common people are indifferent and just indulgent in enjoying themselves; the ruler has lost his empire, but his subjects have betrayed him by following others. The reason for the disaster is that lenient attitudes have been adopted toward the bandits. Now I'm the master of the people but the four traitors have revolted against me and attacked me with armies, therefore I shall send troops to wipe them out." The war at that time was more a plundering than a simple revenge for relatives, as was stated in "Wu Di Ben Ji" (The Chronicles of Five Emperors) in *Shi Ji* (*The Records of the Grand Historian*) that, "if there were rebellious people, 'Huang Di' (Yellow Emperor) would send troops to have them suppressed by cutting through the mountains to make paths without taking a rest." Through military campaigns, "finally the vassals all came over and pledged allegiance." Apart from the war between "Huang Di" (Yellow Emperor) and Chi You, the wars between Zhuan Xu and Gong Gong, between Yao Shun and Jiu Li, and between Yao Shun and San Miao were all carried on a large scale and had lasted for a long time. During the reign of Yu, wars were more frequent. For example, it was recorded that "Yu had attacked You Hu",[7] "Yu had crusaded against Gong Gong",[8] "Yu had fought against You Miao",[9] and "Yu had conquered Cao, Wei, Quao, and You Hu to put his doctrines into practice."[10] These wars not only enabled Yu "to expand his territory and make himself the emperor"[11] but also changed most of the conquered into slaves, as was recorded that "the descendants of 'Li Miao' (Jiu Li and San Miao nationalities)... were going to be slaves and their social status was much lower than the common people."[12] All these had led to the formation of slavery society, so it was in a series of rampant and violent wars that Xia Dynasty started to build the state.

The wars of plundering had accelerated the class polarization within the clan and changed the nature of armed forces. Thus, they were changed from the representatives of the interests of the whole clan to the privately owned ones protecting the

---

[7]"Ren Jian Shi" (Human World) in *Zhuang Zi* (*Zhuang Zi*).

[8]"Yi Bing" (On Military Affairs) in *Xun Zi* (*Xun Zi*).

[9]"Fei Gong" (Opposing Aggression) in *Mo Zi* (*Mo Zi*) (Book 2).

[10]"Zhao Lei" (Attraction of the Kindred) in *Lv Shi Chun Qiu* (*Spring and Autumn Annals of Master Lv*).

[11]"Zi Chan Bu" (Assets), quoted from "Sui Chao Zi" (a follower of *Mo Zi*) in *Tai Ping Yu Lan* (*Imperial Readings of the Taiping Era*), Vol. 823.

[12]"Zhou Yu" (The Historical Records of Zhou Dynasty) in *Guo Yu* (*The Historical Records of Various States*), Vol. 2.

interests of a few clan leaders. The clan leader, once a public servant, finally became the authority ruling the whole clan. For example, on the oath-taking rally before the war, Yu had issued orders in the tone of a king, "all of you gentlemen, please listen to what I am saying: I do not dare to start rampant chaos, but the people of Miao have acted in a foolhardy manner, so God has imposed the punishment. Now I lead you and confer upon you titles to fight against You Miao."[13] Another example: when meeting vassals in Kuai Ji, Yu had killed Fang Feng for his being late to warn those who dared to challenge his authority, as was written in "Shi Xie" (punishments on the evils and evil-doings) in *Han Fei Zi* (*Han Feizi*): "When Yu made the rulers of each states assemble in Kuai Ji, he killed Fang Feng for his being late." Along with the disintegration of clannish democratic system, the blood ties also lost their binding force on the new relationships within the clan. Furthermore, the position of the clan leader became what the dignitary families tried to struggle for. During the time of Xia Qi, the traditional clan election system, which was also called the system of "Shan Rang" (abdicating and handing over the crown to another person) in *Meng Zi* (*Mencius*), was finally abolished, the system of hereditary kingship was established, and the first "family-governed" dynasty was set up. Thus, Xia Qi became the first king of China.

The system of hereditary kingship was an inevitable result of the private ownership and the formation of classes, by which the privilege of noble families to monopolize the leading positions hereditarily was institutionally established, which had surely had a great impact on the clannish democratic tradition and had finally caused the armed rebellion of Bo Yi and You Hu, who were the leaders of Dong Yi nationality (a clan living at the lower stretches of Yellow River). It was stated in the ancient book of *Zhu Shu Ji Nian* (the bomboo *Annals*) that "Bo Yi fought against Qi to get his position," which implied that the purpose of this war was to usurp Qi's throne. In the end, Xia Qi defeated You Hu, sentenced him to be a shepherd slave, and killed Bo Yi. Although it marked the first victory of the monarchical power, yet his dominion was not strengthened, because after Xia Qi, King Taikang had even "lost his kingdom." It was not until after Shaokang's nearly half a century of fighting that the rebellion of those who had cast greedy eyes on the throne was finally suppressed. From then on, the private ownership of kingship was legalized, because "the hereditary titles of monarchs are regarded as being in accordance with 'Li' (rites)."[14] This tendency was closely related to the need of continuously strengthening the power of the supreme military leaders in the wars of plundering and in the establishment of patriarchal system. Engels once said, "The war of plundering has reinforced the power of the supreme and junior military leaders who had habitually chose their successors within the same family. Especially after the establishment of patriarchal system, the hereditary system gradually came into being. So people's attitude towards the system changed: at the beginning they

---

[13]"Jian Ai" (Universal Love) in *Mo Zi* (*Mo Zi*), quoted from *Yu Shi* (*Oath of Yu*).
[14]"Li Yun" (The Rites in the Pre-Qin Dynasties) in *Li Ji* (*The Book of Rites*).

were tolerant, then they began to require, finally swarmed to usurp the hereditary system, which had laid the foundation of the hereditary kingship and nobility."[15]

From this we can see that, the superficial conflict between "passing the throne on to the son" and "passing the throne on to the capable" was, in essence, a conflict between the maintenance and the struggle for the right to rule, which was a stark-naked struggle for power. The nature of the struggle had made it impossible to be settled in a peaceful way within the clan, therefore, it must be settled by way of bloody wars. Because the system of hereditary kingship, which was based on private ownership, was in accordance with historical trend, it was irreversible. Consequently, "the people did not come to Yi but came to Qi instead to pay homage or to file lawsuits," and "songs of praise were not written for Yi but for Qi."[16] As was written in ancient books, from Xia Yu to Jie of the Xia Dynasty, there were fourteen generations and seventeen kings. The clear-cut system had proved that the slavery system centered on the noble family of Xia had already been firmly established.

During the transitional time from clannish democratic system to state system, the primitive customary law which had been used to deal with the relationships among clan members and which had been consciously obeyed were gradually evolved into compulsory codes of conduct—the law.

Archaeological discoveries in recent years have proved that the origin of Chinese civilization is diversified. Thus, besides the Central Plains it also includes the cultural origin of the Yangtze River Basin and Yan and Liao districts. Especially, the geographical environment in Yangtze River Basin has led to the advanced agricultural economy dominated by rice plantation, so the Yangtze River Basin has achieved legal civilization at an earlier time than the Central Plains. Among the nationality of San Miao (also called Youmiao or the Miaoshi) in the Yangtze River Basin, the private ownership of property and drastic class differentiation appeared very early. In the annotation of "Wen Gong Shi Ba Nian" (The 18th Year of the Duke of Wen) in *Zuo Shi Chun Qiu* (or *Zuo Zhuan, The Chronicle of Zuo*), Du Yu had pointed out that "Miao people are as greedy as 'Tao Tie' (a mythical and ferocious animal in ancient China) for obtaining property and food" and that "they were all treacherous and perfidious." To suppress the rebellion of the exploited people, the earliest penalties were made, as was recorded that "the Miao people made use of penalties rather than spirits in the regulation of society, and they made 'Wu Xing' (Five Penalties) which was called 'Fa' (law)." They killed innocent people and abused penalties such as "Yi" (to cut down the nose), "Yue" (to amputate the feet), "Zhuo" (castration), and "Qing" (to tattoo on the face)."[17] It was annotated that "the leaders of San Miao had inherited the evilness of Chi You..., put much emphasis on penalties, created 'Wu Xing' (Five Penalties), and

---

[15](Germany) Engels, "The Origin of the Family, Private Property and the State" in *Ma Ke Si En Ge Si Xuan Ji (The Selected Works of Marx and Engels)*, Vol. 4, The People's Publishing House, 1972, pp. 160–161.

[16]"Wan Zhang" (a student of Mencius) in *Meng Zi (Mencius)* (Book 1).

[17]"Lv Xing" (The Penal Code of Lv) in *Shang Shu (The Book of Historical Document)*.

called them 'Fa' (law)." It was thus clear that the people of San Miao were earlier than "Hua Xia" nationality (an ancient name for China) in the Central Basin in making preliminary "Wu Xing" (Five Penalties). Chi You, the forefather of San Miao, was the first ancestor who had created the legal system, and the rulers of San Miao had just developed the penalties made by him.

After many years of war with "Huang Di" (Yellow Emperor), San Miao nationality was finally defeated by the joint forces of "Huang Di" (Yellow Emperor) and "Yan Di" (Yan Emperor). Those defeated people of Miao were either expelled to remote and dangerous areas or degraded to be slaves. As to the penalties made by Miao nationality, it was inherited by the people of "Hua Xia" nationality (an ancient name for China) by "adopting its penalties after exterminating the clan." Therefore, it was based on the old penalties of Miao, namely, "Yi" (to cut down the nose), "Yue" (to amputate the feet), "Zhuo" (castration), and "Qing" (to tattoo on the face) that the penal system of "Wu Xing" (Five Penalties) including "Mo" (tattooing on the face or forehead of the offenders with indelible ink), "Yi" (to cut down the nose), "Yue" (to amputate the feet), "Gong" (castration), and "Bi" (capital punishment) was developed, which had been universally used by the three dynasties of Xia, Shang, and Zhou. Thus, it had been used for a long time until the early Han Dynasty and it had become the mainstream of Chinese legal civilization. The diversity and unity of legal civilization was a prominent feature in the early development of Chinese legal civilization.

1.1.2 The Pathway for China to Move Towards Legal Civilization

Compared with ancient eastern countries, such as ancient Greece and ancient Rome, although there are some similarities in China's pathway to legal civilization, it has its own particularity. Thus, it can also be called its typicality.

First, China is an inland country and locates in a relative enclosed situation largely isolated from the outer world, which has shaped the typical psychology and concepts of continental nation. Taking "Hua Xia" people (an ancient name for China) living in the Yellow River Basin as an example, the moderate climate with abundant rainfall and the soft and fertile soil is good for primitive agriculture, so it is possible that the "Hua Xia" people (an ancient name for China) had already developed primitive agriculture, produced surplus products and owned private property around the twenty-first century B.C., while still employing woods and stones as their production tools. Thus, the class differentiation between the poor and the rich emerged, which had provided the material basis for Xia nationality to enter a new phase of civilization. In ancient Greece and ancient Rome, under the condition of relatively advanced commodity economy, the class of slaves consisted largely of debt slaves; however, in ancient China, the majority was ethnic slaves with very few debt slaves. Furthermore, ancient Greece and ancient Rome were geographically surrounded on three sides by the sea and had excellent harbors, so seafaring and seaborne trades developed early, which had stimulated the production and circulation of commodities. Thus, commodity economy was exactly the strongest weapon that destroyed the blood relations within the clan. With the development of industry and commerce, a group of industrial and commercial slaveholders gradually came into being, and they were not only a great power fighting against the clan system, but also the main force changing the traditional clannish relations. Nevertheless, in China, there was neither the production nor the circulation of commodities, which was the strongest weapon to destroy the clannish relationship, nor the outside social forces, which were opposites of the clan system. Therefore, China's pathway towards civilization was not a "revolution" in which the clan system was thoroughly eliminated, but a gradual transformation and a "reform" within the clan. For example, the clannish public ownership of land was turned into state ownership, the dignitary families within a clan was turned into royal bureaucrats, the ruling power of certain families was turned into that of the state, and the customs adjusting the internal relationships of the clan were turned into the laws of the state. The blood ties among kinsmen of the clan were not loosened because of the disintegration of clan system but on the contrary, they continued to serve as a bridge of blood relationship linking family and state, family and clan.

Second, for the limitation of the disintegration of clan system, the patriarchal clan system, which originated from the patriarchal system, was retained and it had acted as the state political system on the way towards civilization. The inheritance law of noble families was also applicable for the inheritance of the throne, so kingship and clan authority were unified on a new basis. The new rulers of the country clung to the old ideology and conception that "those who do not belong to the same clan think differently,"[18] so that the ranks of official positions of the state were decided by the closeness and remoteness of family blood relationships; at the same time, the form of state structure in building the country was also completed through patriarchal enfeoffment, and the networks of the ruling of the country had become the connection of the centers of all noble families. The statement that "it is better to appoint old acquaintances, but to use new utensils" in "Pan Geng" (one of the rulers of Shang Dynasty) in *Shang Shu* (*The Book of Historical Document*) had reflected the unification of the royal relatives and the nobilities as well as the family and the state in the transformation of power.

It was just because the state was an amplification of the family that the capital of the country had also become the location of the ancestral temples, just as what was said that "all 'Yi'(vassal state) with the ancestral temple of the emperor was called 'Du'(capital), if without, they are called 'Cheng'(cities). So it was called 'Zhu' to build the city and 'Cheng' to build the capital."[19] The army, as an important part of

---

[18]"Cheng Gong Si Nian" (The 4th Year of the Duke of Cheng) in *Zuo Zhuan* (*The Chronicle of Zuo*).

[19]"Zhuang Gong Er Shi Ba Nian" (The 28th Year of the Duke of Zhuang) in *Zuo Zhuan* (*The Chronicle of Zuo*).

the state apparatus, was made up of the members of noble families; the officials who violated the state law would be executed at the ancestral temple, which was described as "being slain at the temple,"[20] to show that they were abandoned by the clan as well as the state. The external punitive wars and the offering of sacrifices to the gods or the spirits of the dead at the temple were of the same significance, as was reflected in the statement, "the main affairs of a country were offering sacrifices to the gods or the spirits of the dead at the temple and fighting wars."[21] In the classics of pre-Qin period, the subjugation of a state was the same as the subjugation of a family, so the head of the subjugated state would often surrendered on the battlefield by carrying "Shen Zhu" (the long and narrow wooden board on which the names of the dead are inscribed and is used when offering sacrifice).

After entering the feudal society, the political nature of patriarchal system was obviously weakened, but the patriarchal spirit and belief still dominated and constrained the state and society.

Contrary to China, although ancient Greece and ancient Rome also experienced the period in which blood relationship dominated social life, this dominant power was gradually weakened along with the development of commodity economy and the reform of the old clan system. In 594 B.C., after Solon's reform, the rights and obligations of Greek citizens were decided by the amount of their landed property. As the wealth and power of propertied class increased, the old communities bound by blood ties were gradually repelled. In 509 B.C., Cleisthenes' reform of dividing electoral districts entirely by regional principles had completely destroyed the clan organizations based on blood ties.

In the sixth century B.C., through Servius Tullius' reform, three primitive tribes bound by blood relations were abolished and the principle of dividing residents by regions was established in ancient Rome. "Thus, also in Rome, before royal politics was abolished, the ancient social system which was based on individual kinship was destroyed and replaced by a real new state system based on regional difference and wealth."[22]

Third, frequent wars among tribes in late clan society had a direct influence on the development of legal civilization in China. Wars required strict disciplines to restrain the army and to establish the commander's absolute power in making the troops obey his orders and deciding the life and death of subordinates. Thus, the earliest law was made to meet this need, as was manifested in the statement that "penalty originated from the army." While in ancient Greece and Rome, it was mainly the struggle between the civilians and the nobles within a clan that gradually destroyed the basis of old clan system and accelerated the process of civilization.

---

[20]"Cheng Gong San Nian" (The 3rd Year of the Duke of Cheng) in *Zuo Zhuan* (*The Chronicle of Zuo*).

[21]"Cheng Gong Shi San Nian" (The 13th Year of the Duke of Cheng) in *Zuo Zhuan* (*The Chronicle of Zuo*).

[22](Germany) Engels, "The Origin of Family, Private Ownership and State" in *Ma Ke Si En Ge Si Xuan Ji* (*The Selected Works of Marx and Engels*), Vol. 4, The People's Publishing House, 1972, p.126.

Finally, after entering class society, autocracy developed in China with the king as the supreme authority. Because the king was the embodiment of the state, the interests of noble families represented by the king were consistent with state interests. Therefore, it was the primary task of law to protect the supremacy of the state and the public rights, and criminal law had become the most advanced form of law. While in ancient Greece and Rome, the concept of private property and private ownership was formed earlier, and the law adjusting and protecting private rights, namely, the private law, was significantly developed. Thus, in ancient Roman legal system, there was the division of public law and private law from the very beginning.

The pathway of China towards legal civilization was different not only from ancient Greece and ancient Rome, but also from ancient Egypt and Babylon in the East. In ancient Egypt and Babylon, water control was a great event for the survival and the rise and fall of the state, so public works department for water control was one of the most important institutions. Although there were records of water control by Xia Yu in China, it did not have a decisive influence on the emergence of the state, so no special state institution was set up because of water control.

1.1.3 From the Primitive Customs to the Law in Class Society

1.1.3.1 From "Xiang Xing" (Xiang Penalty) to the Criminal Law with Class Characteristics

"Xing" in ancient Chinese classics meant both law and punishment. In "Shi Gu" (The Meaning and Usages of Words) in *Er Ya* (*Using Graceful and Elegant Languages*), it was thus defined, "'Xing' refers to principles and laws." It was explained in *Shuo Wen Jie Zi* (*The Origin of Chinese Characters*) by quoting from the book *Yi* (*The Book of Changes*) that, "'Jing' (well or 'Xing') means laws." It was defined in *Feng Su Tong* (*Comprehensive Meaning of Customs and Habits*) that "Jing (well or 'Xing') refers to laws and 'Jie' (restriction)." The so-called "Yu Xing" (*The Penal Code of Yu*), "Tang Xing" (*The Penal Code of Tang*), "Jiu Xing" (*The Code Nine Penalties*), and "Lv Xing" (*The Penal Code of Lv*) were all typical laws made during the three dynasties of Xia, Shang, and Zhou. Therefore, it refers to the same thing to investigate the origin of "Fa" (law) and the origin of "Xing" (punishment).

In China, like in other nations of the world, during the long history of clan society in which there was no class, no state, nor penalty, only clan customs were accepted by all members as the principles adjusting the interpersonal relations and the standards guiding people's conducts, so they had a universal binding effect. At that time, there was still no conception of law.

Under the rule of clan customs, the behaviors which violated the rules of common life would be condemned and punished by what was called "Xiang Xing" (Xiang Penalty: a punishment on spirits and personality). The phrase "Xiang Xing" originated from the sentence that "'Xiang' was employed to implement punishment" in

1.1 The Earliest Dawn of Chinese Legal Civilization: The Legal System of the Xia...

"Shun Dian" (Shun Code) in *Shang Shu* (*The Book of Historical Document*). In fact, there were many interpretations about "Xiang Xing" (Xiang Penalty). In *Shuo Wen Jie Zi* (*The Origin of Chinese Characters*), it was interpreted that "'Xiang' means 'decorations'", namely, to implement punishment by putting on special decorations. Moreover, it was recorded in *Shang Shu Da Zhuan* (*Interpretations of Shang Shu*) that "people dared not commit crimes because of the enforcement of 'Xiang Xing' (Xiang Penalty) in the period of Tang Yu (Yao and Shun)." "Aa for the enforcement of 'Xiang Xing' (Xiang Penalty) in Tang Yu (Yao and Shun) period, the most severe punishment was for criminals to wear reddish-brown clothes instead of death penalty, the less severe punishment was for criminals to wear hemp shoes instead of the penalty of cutting off the feet and the least severe punishment was for criminals to paint his face with ink instead of humiliating tattoo penalty." In *Tai Ping Yu Lan* (*Imperial Readings of the Taiping Era*), Shenzi's statement was quoted and it was recorded that "as for the punishment in the time of Yu (Shun), the punishment of 'Mo' (tattooing on the face or forehead of the offenders with indelible ink) was replaced by covering the face with a towel, the punishment of 'Yi' (to cut down the nose) was replaced by wearing a hat made of grass, the punishment of 'Yue' (to amputate the feet) was replaced by wearing hemp shoes, the punishment of 'Gong' (castration) was replaced by cutting off the hem of the dress, and the punishment of 'Bi' (capital punishment) was replaced by wearing a collarless dress." Similar expressions could also be found in "Xing Fa Zhi" (The Record of the Criminal Law) in *Jin Shu* (*The History of Jin Dynasty*): "Those who should be punished by 'Qing' (to tattoo on the face) would have their scarves colored black; those who should be punished by "Yi' (to cut down the nose) would have the part between the nose and the upper lip colored red; those who should be punished by 'Yue' (to amputate the feet) would have their bodies painted black; those who should be punished by 'Gong' (castration) would have their shoes painted in different colors; those who should be punished by 'Bi' (capital punishment) would wear plain clothes without a collar."

Another interpretation of "Xiang Xing" (Xiang Penalty) was "drawing pictures to show punishment," which meant to portray five pictures illustrating five different corporal penalties on utilities so that other people could see what the man was punished for. It was explained in "Da Si Kou" (The Senior Minister of Justice) in "Qiu Guan" (Ministry of Penalty) in *Zhou Li* (*The Rites of Zhou Dynasty*) that "the picture of penalty was posted on tall buildings in front of the palace for all people to watch." In *Tang Lv Shu Yi* (*The Comments on Tang Code*), it was defined in the following way: "by 'Xiang Xing' (Xiang Penalty) the convicts were made feel guilty by drawing the pictures of penalty. In volume sixty-seven of *Yu Hai* (a great reference book in ancient China) Zhu Xi's words were quoted and it was stated, "'Xiang Xing' means portraying five pictures of corporal punishment on objects and showing them to people." Cheng Dachang in Song Dynasty said in *Kao Gu Bian* (*A Collection of Archaeology*) that "'Xing' means portraying pictures of five corporal penalties on objects to make people feel guilty and terrified."

Some people interpreted "Xiang" in "Xiang Xing" as a law. It was stated in Kong Anguo's *Shang Shu Zhu Shu* (*Annotation of Shang Shu*) that "'Xiang' referred to the law by which certain penalty was executed, beyond which penalties should not be enforced." Therefore, "Xiang Yi Dian Xing" meant enforcing punishments according to law.

After the Warring States Period, Confucian scholars often interpreted "Xiang Xing" (Xiang Penalty) as a symbolic punishment to preach the customs of lenient punishment at the times of Yao and Shun. Zheng Xuan, a great Confucian scholar in Han Dynasty, thought that "Ming Xing" mentioned in "Si Yuan" (official in charge of prison) in *Zhou Li* (*The Rites of Zhou Dynasty*) referred to a variety of "Xiang Xing" (Xiang Penalty) in ancient China. He said in the annotating text: "Wasn't it like the ancient 'Xiang Xing' to force criminals to wear just black towel without wearing hats?" There were other interpretations among the Confucian scholars of Han Dynasty. For example, Ban Gu said: "'Xiang Xing' (Xiang Penalty) which represents Heaven's will has been made to have the criminals punished, that is why there are people wearing hemp shoes and reddish brown clothes."[23] Dong Yue in Ming Dynasty had made use of the laws of the State of Wei in the Warring States Period to prove his traditional Confucian views by quoting *Ban Gu Da Ren Shu* (*Ban Gu's Reply to People*) in his *Qi Guo Kao* (*Investigations of the Seven Countries*), and he said that "in the Warring States Period, according to the law of the State of Wei, criminals committing minor crimes were supposed to wear red towel, to paint the collar and to put on clothes with special marks to distinguish themselves." The rulers who were influenced by Confucian thoughts in early Han Dynasty also praised "Xiang Xing" (Xiang Penalty) because they thought it was a good way of government. In 167 B.C., the 13th year of Emperor Wen of Han, it was stated in an imperial edict that "it was said that in the period of Shun, the punishment was embodied by drawings and changes of clothes. Consequently, fewer crimes were committed. How effective it was!"[24] However, there had been criticism for these opinions since ancient times. Xun Zi had pointed out "it was said that there were no corporal punishments except 'Xiang Xing' (Xiang Penalty) in the period of Yao and Shun. The punishment of 'Mo' (tattooing on the face or forehead of the offenders with indelible ink) and the punishment of 'Qing' (to tattoo on the face) were replaced by wearing hat made of grass, the punishment of 'Gong' (castration) was replaced by cutting off the hem of the dress, the punishment of 'Fei' (to amputate the feet) was replaced by wearing hemp shoes, and the punishment of 'Sha' (death) was replaced by wearing collarless clothes. But it was not true. How could the society operate successfully? If nobody commits crime, neither corporal punishment nor 'Xiang Xing' (Xiang Penalty) shall be implemented; if penalty is mitigated, a killer won't be killed, and a man who hurts others won't be punished; if serious offenses receive lenient punishments, nobody will know what wickedness is. Therefore, it would lead to great disorder."[25]

---

[23]"Xing Fa Zhi" (The Record of the Criminal Law) in *Han Shu* (*The History of Han Dynasty*).
[24]"Xing Fa Zhi" (The Record of the Criminal Law) in *Han Shu* (*The History of Han Dynasty*).
[25]"Zheng Lun" (Correcting Wrong Ideas) in *Xun Zi* (*Xun Zi*).

Wang Mingsheng in Qing Dynasty thought that with regard to "Xiang Xing" (Xiang Penalty), many people had made far-fetched interpretations by using "Wu Xing" (Five Penalties), so their opinion that "Xiang Xing" meant enforcing the punishments by making use of the changes of clothes and symbols on clothes was just arbitrary. According to historical books, the ancient custom of "Xiang Xing" (Xiang Penalty) even existed in the Spring and Autumn Period. Shen Jiaben thought that "Wu Xing" (Five Penalties) and "Xiang Xing" (Xiang Penalty) coexisted in the time of Shun, and that they were applied to different objects. "Wu Xing" (Five Penalties) "was used to punish the barbarians . . .and the evil people, while 'Xiang Xing' (Xiang Penalty) was used to punish the common people." Thus, the purpose of "Xiang Xing" (Xiang Penalty) was "moralization."[26]

In my opinion, "Xiang Xing" (Xiang Penalty) can be explained as the rules of customs applicable to all members in a clan. For those who had violated the common principles of the clan, they adopted the way of making their clothes different to show their difference from other members to intensify their feelings of regret and guilt. Therefore, its real purpose was to have people humiliated rather than punished with the support of the state, from which the penalty of humiliation in early class society evolved. Besides, we can also find some traces of "Xiang Xing" (Xiang Penalty) in the customary laws of some minority groups. For example, a case similar to "Xiang Xing" (Xiang Penalty) was recorded in "Tubo Zhuan" (Annals of Tubo) in *Xin Tang Shu* (*The New Book of Tang Dynasty*): "The soldier's self-sacrifice in battles was highly valued by Tubo people, and the families with lost members in battles were regarded as heroes for many generations; meanwhile the cowards were humiliated by hanging a fox's tail on their heads and they were forbidden to be ranked among 'Jun Zi' (gentlemen)." The rules of clan customs were necessary for maintaining the existence and development of the clan, so it was unanimously approved. In addition, it was a representation of the common will of all the clan members.

1.1.3.2 The Main Points of View on the Origin of Chinese Law

1.1.3.2.1 The Upper Limits of the Emergence of Law

According to one opinion, law originated in the period of "Huang Di" (Yellow Emperor). It was recorded in "Hua Ce" (Policies) in *Shang Jun Shu* (*The Book of Lord Shang*) that "the obligations of the monarchs and his officials, the etiquettes between father and son and those among brothers, and the ethics related to husband and wife were all formulated and implemented by 'Huang Di' (Yellow Emperor) who had handled domestic affairs with knives and saws and foreign affairs with armed forces." Sima Qian held the same view and he stated in "Wu Di Ben Ji" (The

---

[26]Shen Jiaben (Qing Dynasty), "Tang Yu" (Yao and Shun) in "Xing Zhi Zong Kao" (*A General Textual Research of the Criminal Systems*) in *Li Dai Xing Fa Kao* (*A Textual Research of the Criminal Laws in the Past Dynasties*).

Chronicles of Five Emperors) in *Shi Ji* (*The Records of the Grand Historian*): "In the period of Xuanyuan, because of the decline of Shennong, the vassal states fought against each other and treated the people cruelly, but Shennong was helpless in changing the situation. And then Xuanyuan started to make them subordinated by force and they all came over and pledge allegiance." "All the vassals respected Xuanyuan as the son of 'Tian' (Heaven), so he finally replaced Shennong and was called 'Huang Di' (Yellow Emperor). If anyone dared to disobey, 'Huang Di' (Yellow Emperor) would send an army to have him suppressed." It was more clearly stated in "Lan Ming Xun" (Instructions of Lan Ming) in *Huai Nan Zi* (*Masters from Huainan*) that "Yellow Emperor ruled the world…with clear-cut laws." According to *Tong Jian Qian Bian Wai Ji* (*A Supplementary Collection of the First Part of the General Survey of History*), "Huang Di" (Yellow Emperor) had set up an institution called "Li Guan" (judges in ancient China) to deal with the affairs of criminal law, which "was referred to as the position of 'Da Li'." There might also be "Li Fa" (law), but "it is difficult to find the contents," so it was hard to be proven. Therefore, in view of the theory and practice that "the law originated in the army" recorded in ancient times, it might be reasonable to consider the period of "Huang Di" (Yellow Emperor) as the upper limit of the origin of law.

According to another opinion, the law originated in the times of Tang Yu (Yao and Shun). It was recorded in "Xiang Xing Dian" (Prudent Settlement of Lawsuits) in *Gu Jin Tu Shu Ji Cheng* (*A Complete Collection of Ancient and Modern Books*) that "emperor Yao commanded Shun to make five kinds of penalties and regulations about "Liu" (exile), "You" (pardoning), "Bian" (whipping), "Pu" (corporal punishment including "Chi", "Bian", and "Zhang"), "Shu" (atonement), and "She" (absolution). Gong Gong was exiled to Youzhou, Huan Dou to Chongshan, San Miao to Sanwei, and Gun to Yushan. After having these four convicts punished, the people in the world submitted themselves to the supremacy of Emperor Yao." It was recorded in *Tong Jian Qian Bian* (*The First Part of the General Survey of History*) that "Emperor Yao made 'Wu Xing' (Five Penalties) at the age of seventy six." The story about Shun's requiring Gao Yao to make law was often read in classics. In "Shun Dian" (Shun Code) in *Shang Shu* (*The Book of Historical Document*), it was recorded that "Emperor Yao said, 'GaoYao, the savages have invaded our country, committed theft, robbery, and murder, so you, as the head of army, should enact the five kinds of penalties, and execute them in three different places in accordance with the status of the convicts; the five kinds of exiles should be confined to three different places." It was recorded in *Zhu Shu Ji Nian* (the bomboo *Annals*) that "in the 3rd year of Emperor Shun, Gao Yao was ordered to make laws." In "Zhao Gong Shi Si Nian" (The 14th Year of the Duke of Zhao) in *Zuo Zhuan* (*The Chronicle of Zuo*), it was recorded that "in the historical records of Xia Dynasty it was mentioned that the law of 'Hun' (hanging), 'Mo' (tattooing on the face or forehead of the offenders with indelible ink), 'Zei' (putting the criminal to death), and 'Sha' (death penalty) were enacted by Gao Yao." Moreover, it was recorded in *Ji Jiu Zhang* (*Hurriedly-Written Essay*) that "prisons were built and the penalties were enacted by GaoYao." It was stated in "Zhang Min Zhuan" (The Biography of Zhang Min) in *Latter Han Shu* (*The History of Latter Han Dynasty*) that "it was to prevent ordinary people from conducting illegal behaviors that classic books were written by Confucius and laws were enacted by GaoYao." In *Tai Ping Yu Lan* (*Imperial Readings of the Taiping Era*), it was also recorded that "the law was in fact the teaching of late Jiu Yao (Gao Yao), so Xiao He was ordered to popularize it in the Han Dynasty." Thus, Gao Yao was often regarded as the creator of laws in ancient books.

Some people held the view that the law had existed in Xia Dynasty. It was stated in *Shang Shu Da Zhuan* (*Interpretations of Shang Shu*) that, "over 3,000 articles were made in Xia Dynasty." It was recorded in "Zhao Gong Liu Nian" (The 6th Year of the Duke of Zhao) in *Zuo Zhuan* (*The Chronicle of Zuo*) that "Xia *Yu Xing* (*The Penal Code of Yu*) was enacted because of the chaotic situation." Besides, it was recorded in "Xing Fa Zhi" (The Record of the Criminal Law) in *Han Shu* (*The History of Han Dynasty*) that "after Yao and Shun, people's morality degraded, so corporal punishment was made by Yu." In "Jing Ji Zhi" (The Record of Classic Books) in *Sui Shu* (*The History of Sui Dynasty*), there was the following record: "In Xia Dynasty, there were 5 kinds of penalties with 3,000 articles."

According to the underground archaeological excavation in recent years, in the times of Xia Yu, China had undoubtedly entered class society, with the state built and laws enacted. In ancient China, the level of productivity was extremely low and the society developed quite slowly, so it took a long time to reach the national and legal state of Xia Dynasty. This was also the process of the transformation from "Xiang Xing" (Xiang Penalty) in the late clan society to the laws in class society. Therefore, in late clan society when "Huang Di" (Yellow Emperor), Yao and Shun were in power, it was quite possible to establish the compulsive legal norms. Therefore, the relevant legal records in ancient documents should not be neglected for their uncertainty and doubts; instead, they should be studied comprehensively with the discovery of underground cultural relics. In conclusion, Xia Dynasty was already an established form of state, but the state was surely formed at a much earlier time than Xia Dynasty, so the upper limit of Chinese legal history must be earlier than Xia Dynasty.

1.1.3.2.2 The Causes of the Creation of Law

First, the penalties originated from the army. In ancient China, law and penalty were not separated, nor were the army and penalty. It was recorded that "the most severe penalty was enforced with armor and weaponry; the less severe penalty was enforced with axe-shaped Yue; the lighter penalty was enforced with knife and saw, next with drill and the lightest penalty was enforced with whips."[27] On the threshold of class society, there were several large-scale battles in China, such as the war between Gong Gong and Chi You, the war between "Huang Di" (Yellow Emperor) and Chi You, the war between "Huang Di" (Yellow Emperor) and "Yan Di" (Yan Emperor), and the war between Xia and Youhu. To win the war, the army needed to be strictly

---

[27]"Xing Fa Zhi" (The Record of the Criminal Law) in *Han Shu* (*The History of Han Dynasty*).

disciplined, for which military laws with the nature of criminal law were made. Before attacking Youhu clan, a law in the form of a military order was issued by Xia Qi: "If being asked to attack in the left direction and you fail to do so, you disobey the order; if being asked to attack in the right direction and you fail to do so, you disobey the order; if you fail to drive a carriage in the right way, you disobey the order. Obey the order, you will be rewarded at the temple; disobey the order; you will be punished at the temple. I will kill you or make you slaves."[28] Thus, it indicated that wars had not only enhanced the power of military leaders but also contributed to the law making. It was stated in *Yi Jing* (*The Book of Changes*) that "army should be disciplined." Moreover, it was recorded in *Zheng Yi* (*The Annotation of Confucians' Classics and the Books of History*) that "the discipline for the army is law. ...so it is to regulate the army. Since it is to command the army, it should be implemented when the troops are dispatched. Hence, the army should be regulated by law." In "Tong Dian" (The General Codes) in *Xing Fa* (*The Criminal Law*), there was the following record: "'Huang Di' (Yellow Emperor) brought peace to the world by the army, which is the highest form of 'Xing' (penalty)." It was stated in "Liao Shi" (The History of Liao) in *Xing Fa Zhi* (*The Record of the Criminal Law*) that "'Xing' originated from the army ...Chi You started rebellion and the people had committed all kinds of crimes so they were all evil. Should they be exempted from the penalty?" In ancient China, judges were usually entitled with different military ranks, such as "Shi Shi" (the official in charge of criminal affairs), "Si Kou" (the minister of justice) and "Ting Wei" (the supreme official in charge of judicature), which had reflected the close relationship between the army and penalty, so in "Pan Shui" (Pan River) in "Lu Song" (Odes of the Lu State) in *Shi* (*Poetry*), the two events, namely, Hu Chen's offering of the left ear of the captives and Gao Yao's offering of the slave prisoners, were mentioned together. Just because the prisoners of war were no longer killed according to the past customs but were made racial slaves to be exploited, criminal laws were needed to be made to have them suppressed and controlled. Therefore, the opinion that laws originated from army was very influential in ancient times.

Second, the penalty originated from the punishment of "Tian" (Heaven). In ancient times, because of the low level of productivity, people lacked the power of conquering nature, thus a sense of reverence towards all kinds of natural phenomena prevailed. Under this condition, "Tian" (Heaven) was worshipped as the origin of everything, so likewise the law was bestowed by "Tian" (Heaven). Apart from the ignorance of knowledge, the rulers had intentionally connected penalty with "Tian" (Heaven) and had done their utmost to propagate this theory to justify that judiciary punishment was in reality the execution of the will of "Tian" (Heaven). It was stated in "Gao Yao Mo" (Gao Yao's Planning Government Affairs) in *Shang Shu* (*The Book of Historical Document*) that "the duties of 'Tian' (Heaven) is fulfilled by men" and that "the guilty is punished by 'Tian' (Heaven) with 'Wu Xing' (five penalties)." It was written in *Kong Zhuan* (*The Biography of Confucius*) that "those defied by the

---

[28]"Gan Shi" (The Military Order Issued at Gan) in *Shang Shu* (*The Book of Historical Document*).

1.1 The Earliest Dawn of Chinese Legal Civilization: The Legal System of the Xia... 17

people are punished by 'Tian' (Heaven)." According to the annotation in *Xiang Xing Yao Lan* (*A Survey of Prudent Settlement of Lawsuits*), "punishments originated from 'Tian' (Heaven) and they should not be implemented in private." Thus, most rulers in Xia and Shang dynasties had conducted the so-called "Tian Tao" (Heavenly condemnation) and "Tian Fa" (Heavenly punishment) in the name of 'Tian' (Heaven) to argue in favor of their state activities. For example, when attacking You Hu, Xia Qi had declared in the military order that "he (You Hu) was ordered to be killed by 'Tian' (Heaven), so I am just executing the penalty of 'Tian' (Heaven)."[29] When attacking Xia Jie, Tang in Shang Dynasty had declared: "Xia is guilty of many crimes, so he is ordered to be killed by 'Tian' (Heaven)....You should help me execute heaven's penalty."[30] It was concluded in "Xing Fa Zhi" (The Record of the Criminal Law) in *Han Shu* (*The History of Han Dynasty*) that "'Wu Xing' (Five Penalties) was made by saints to have heavenly punishment implemented."

In addition, the rulers had whipped up public opinion that their power was endowed by "Tian" (Heaven) deliberately to enhance their authorities, as was said in the saying that "'Tian' (Heaven) is in favor of me and has entrusted me with the responsibility of ruling the world and acting as the emperor."[31] This opinion had prevailed throughout ancient Chinese society, so even Puyi, the puppet emperor of Manchurian state had said that he was "subservient to heavenly mandate" in his imperial edict of enthronement.

Third, the penalty was made in the process of "Ding Fen Zhi Zheng" (establishing status and preventing conflicts). "Ding Fen" means differentiating the senior and the junior, and the noble and the humble. Guan Zi said, "In ancient times there was no differentiation of the ruler and his subjects, of the upper and the lower, of the husband and wife, so people lived together like animals. They competed by strength and force. Therefore, the clever cheats the slow-witted, the stronger bullied the weaker. The old, the young, the orphans, and the lonely had no shelter. Therefore, the wise stopped the calamity with the help of the masses with the brutish people wiped out. Moreover, the wise had brought benefit to the people, eradicated the evilness for them, and redressed the people's morality, so they were regarded by the people as teachers....Therefore, the differentiation of the upper and the lower was established with people's livelihood protected and the state capital built in the end."[32] Thus, "'Fa' (law) is made to reward the good and to punish the evil; and 'Lv' (criminal law) is made is to establish the order and to prevent conflicts."[33] Shang Yang also thought that "in ancient time when there was no differentiation between the monarchs and the subjects, the society was in disorder. Therefore, the

---

[29]"Gan Shi" (The Military Order Issued at Gan) in *Shang Shu* (*The Book of Historical Document*).
[30]"Tang Shi" (Oath of Tang) in *Shang Shu* (*The Book of Historical Document*).
[31]"Da Yu Mo" (Da Yu's Planning Government Affairs) in *Shang Shu* (*The Book of Historical Document*).
[32]"Jun Chen" (The Monarch and his Subjects) in *Guan Zi* (*The Book of Master Guan*).
[33]"Qi Chen Qi Zhu" (Seven Ministers and Seven Rulers) in *Guan Zi* (*The Book of Master Guan*).

saint differentiated the noble and the humble, established the ranks and titles, made the names and aliases and implemented the order of ruler and subject, the senior and junior."[34] In ancient time, "the lack of means of production had brought about competition, which in turn led to riots, which finally led to poverty. The earlier kings worried about the social disorder, so "Li" (rites) was established to differentiate the people so that there was difference between the rich and the poor, between the noble and the humble."[35] Du You in the Tang Dynasty said, "The wisest among humans didn't have claws to obtain what they desired, nor ran faster to shun danger, nor had feather to avoid the heat and cold. They must take advantage of others and depend on wisdom rather than strength. So without love, one can't live in a group; without being in a group, one can't defeat others, all in all, it was a monarch's business to get people to live together, and it was a king's business to attract people to him and to have them united. Living in groups, it would be very likely that people would feel unhappy or angry, which might not only cause conflicts and fighting, but also lead to lenient and severe penalties. So among the many systems, penalties were enforced the earliest"[36] and it was to confine the "conflicts" within certain limits that led to the making of law.

Fourth, the penalty was made because of the evilness of human nature. Xun Kuang insisted on the evil nature of human beings and explained the origin of law from the viewpoint of humanity. He said, "The ancient saints thought that human beings were evil by nature because they were biased, unjust, rebellious, and disobedient. So the monarchs were selected to deal with the human beings, to show them 'Li' (rites) and justice to have them educated, to make laws to have them ruled, to implement severe penalties to have them restricted (preventing them from committing crimes), that was why they were all well-governed and behaved in a proper way."[37]

The theories mentioned above are all products of certain historical background, some of which are quite reasonable to some extent. Take the theory of "Ding Fen Zhi Zheng" (establishing status and preventing conflicts) as an example, because economy was stressed in the theory, it was accepted by generations of progressive thinkers. However, in this theory, the nature of "conflicts" was not analyzed and it was simply regarded it as a competition among different groups. Meanwhile, they had attributed the competition among different groups to people's "evil nature," which had made the tendency of plain materialism which was contained in the theory of conflict preventing slide to idealism.

Examined from the reality of Chinese legal history, the law was surely not only an outcome of certain historical background, but also an inevitable historical result of private ownership and class differentiation. To protect their privileges, the patriarchs of noble families who had entered the class society had collected the rules of customs

---

[34]"Jun Chen" (The Monarch and his Subjects) in *Shang Jun Shu* (*The Book of Lord Shang*).
[35]"Wang Zhi" (The Royal Regulations) in *Xun Zi* (*Xun Zi*).
[36]"Xing Fa" (Criminal Law) in *Tong Dian* (*The General Codes*).
[37]"Xing E" (Evil Nature) in *Xun Zi* (*Xun Zi*).

in clan society which were in their favor and established them in the form of law. In addition, at this time, "there was a need to make general rules for the production, distribution and exchange of goods which were performed repeatedly every day so that they could be obeyed by the individuals in the production and exchange of goods. At the beginning, the rules were expressed in the form of customs and later they became established laws."[38] The original law was made in the form of family rules, namely, the domestic rules of big families in the patriarchal period, so it was closely related to the customs of clan society. Clan customs represented the interests and will of the whole clan, while family regulations were mainly used to confirm the patriarchal privileges and codes of conduct in their favor. Therefore, with the development of society and emergence of the state, family regulations were partially transformed into the laws of slavery system.

1.1.4 The State Structure and Legal System of Xia Dynasty

1.1.4.1 The State Structure

At the time of Xia Yu, Yu had already possessed special power not owned by other clan leaders. To the time of Qi, the king's orders relevant to the person's life and death were not only strictly implemented, but also regarded as the most authoritative laws. According to "Gan Shi" (The Military Order Issued at Gan) in *Shang Shu* (*The Book of Historical Document*), when fighting with You Hu in Gan, Qi announced the words of oath-taking: "I warn you, the six generals: You Hu has violated 'Wu Xing' (the five elements, including metal, wood, water, fire and earth, held by the ancients to compose the physical universe) and humiliated "San Zheng" (the right way of Heaven, Earth and Man), therefore, he is ordered to be killed by 'Tian' (Heaven) and I am just executing his penalty....Obey the order, you will be rewarded at the temple; disobey the order, you will be punished at the temple. I will kill you or make you slaves."

The power of the king of Xia originated not only from the support of the family of Xia Yu, but also from the armed forces with advanced weapons, as was recorded in following in ancient books: "It has discovered from the tomb of Yu that copper had been used for weaponry"[39] and "reed had been used for armor".[40] At the site of early Erlitou culture in Yanshi, Henan province, some copper weapons like "Ge" (dagger-axe), "Qi" (battle-axe), and "Jian Zu" (arrowhead) have been unearthed in recent years.

---

[38] (Germany) Engels, "Lun Zhu Zhai Wen Ti" (On Homestead) in *Ma Ke Si En Ge Si Xuan Ji* (*The Selected Works of Marx and Engels*), Vol. 2, The People's Publishing House, 1972, p. 539.

[39] "Ji Bao Jian" (On Treasured Swords) in *Yue Jue Shu* (*Local Chronicles*).

[40] "Fei Shi" (The Military Order Issued at Fei) in *Shang Shu Zheng Yi* (*The Proper Meaning of the Book of Historical Document*), quoted from *Shi Ben* (*The Origin of Genealogy*).

To perform the state functions, preliminary administrative organs were established in Xia Dynasty to handle the state affairs. According to ancient books, "San Zheng" (the right way of Heaven, Earth and Man) and "Liu Shi Zhi Ren" (men in charge of six businesses) were officials in charge of managing the government affairs, among whom "San Lao" (local officials in charge of education), "Wu Geng" (local officials in charge of retired officials), "Si Fu" (four assistants of the ruler), "Si Yue" (official in charge of dukes) were in charge of consulting and "Liu Qing" (six officials) were in charge of agriculture, education, prison, construction, fishing, and pasturing. Besides, "Che Zheng" was in charge of making chariots; "Pao Zheng" was in charge of the kitchen affairs of the royal family; "Mu Zheng" was in charge of pasturing; "Qiu Ren" was in charge of announcing imperial orders; "Se Fu "under "Si Kong" (the minister of public works) was in charge of public works; "Zhi Zong" and "Xi He" were in charge of religious matters and calendar compilation. In addition, all of these officials constituted the main body of "the hundreds of officials of Xia." From the grandiose site of the remains of the palace unearthed in Erlitou and the historical records that showed that Xia Jie had about 500 attendants with him when exiled by Shang Tang,[41] it can be seen that the state structure of Xia had reached to a considerable scale.

According to some records of the Spring and Autumn Period, after replacing Bo Yi, Xia Qi divided the area under his rule into "Jiu Zhou" (the nine states), as was described in the saying that "the area Yu traveled through was divided into 'Jiu Zhou' (the nine states) with roads built in the nine states at the time of Qi."[42] The position of "Jiu Mu" was set as the chief of the nine states to regulate the management of the residents.[43] He also ordered "nine tripods casted as the symbols of nine states.[44] It was said that the copper used was the tribute paid by the nine states, as was illustrated in the statement that "the copper contributed by 'Jiu Mu' was made into nine tripods to symbolize the nine states."[45] Although this view about nine states was not evident enough to be the proof of local administrative divisions of Xia Dynasty, it had shown that after the old forces were defeated by Qi, with the expansion of the ruling area and the increase of the number of clan slaves, it was no longer possible to regulate the citizens according to the standard of blood relations. Thus, some conquered tribal leaders were appointed officials administrating the local affairs, which had shown the establishment of new relationships between the conqueror and the conquered, the central and the local. If we say that the cause for the prosperity of Xia Dynasty was the support provided by many tribes,

---

[41]"Yin Zhu Jie" (Best Wishes for Yin Shang) in *Yi Zhou Shu* (*The History of Zhou Dynasty*).

[42]"Xiang Gong Si Nian" (The 4th Year of the Duke of Xiang) in *Zuo Zhuan* (*The Chronicle of Zuo*).

[43]"Xuan Gong San Nian" (The 3rd Year of the Duke of Xuan) in *Zuo Zhuan* (*The Chronicle of Zuo*).

[44]"Jiao Si Zhi" (The Record of Offering Sacrifice to Heaven and Earth in Suburbs) in *Han Shu* (*The History of Han Dynasty*) (Book 1).

[45]"Xuan Gong San Nian" (The 3rd Year of the Duke of Xuan) in *Zuo Zhuan* (*The Chronicle of Zuo*).

then the cause for its downfall was because "'Jiu Yi' (the nine Tribes of the East) had not shown their support by sending out the armies."[46] After studying the history of ancient Greece and ancient Rome, Engels drew a conclusion that it was one of the most important symbols of state to divide residents by regions. However, in China, the blood relations of clan were not totally destroyed. Moreover, there was not a great impact from the powerful exterior social forces, so the principle of dividing residents by regions was not an important prerequisite of moving toward civilization. Therefore, it could not be simply used in studying the origin of the Chinese state.

To cover the expenses necessarily used in state activities, tax was begun to be levied on the conquered tribes nearby in Xia Dynasty, and all the tribes, which had recognized Xia as their common master, had the obligation to pay tribute. It was written in "Xia Ben Ji" (The Records of the Xia Dynasty) in *Shi Ji* (*The Records of the Grand Historian*) that "from the period of Yu and Xia, the system of paying tributes was established." It was described in *Meng Zi* (*Mencius*) that "residents in Xia had paid one tenth of the grain production of their fifty *mu* of land (*mu*: a unit of area, one *mu* is about 0.0667 hectares)",[47] so the amount mentioned referred to what the civilians had to pay to the nobles. Although the tax system was simple in Xia Dynasty, it was of great social significance because "tax was the economic embodiment of the existence of state."[48]

In conclusion, according to the principle of unification of relatives and nobles, the organization which was made up of hundreds of officials at all levels who were respectively in charge of political affairs, military affairs, taxation, religions, litigation, carriages and horses, calendar, archives, food, astronomical phenomena and measuring vessels was established in Xia Dynasty. In addition, the judiciary organs and prisons were also started to be set up.

The judiciary organs of Xia Dynasty were not systematic, and there were only preliminary central and the local divisions. The judicial officials presiding over the central affairs were called "Da Li" and those presiding over the local were called "Shi" or "Li". Under "Shi" and "Li", there were "Zheng" and "Shi", who were in charge of the trials and the measurement of penalty respectively. Because "Tian Fa" (Heavenly punishment) was favored, the officials in charge of the religious affairs had exerted a greater influence on the judiciary practice.

The prison, "the physical appurtenance" of the state, had been built in Xia Dynasty. It was recorded in *Ji Jiu Zhang* (*Hurriedly-Written Essay*) which was written in Han Dynasty that "prisons were built by Gao Yao and the laws were made." It was also recorded in *Guang Yun* (*Dictionary of Vowel System*) that "the prison system was established by Gao Yao." Gao Yao, a judiciary official in the time of Yu Shun, was famous for his efficiency at handling lawsuits. When Yu took the power, Gao Yao continued to be put in important positions. It was written in "Xia

---

[46]Liu Xiang (Han Dynasty), "Quan Mou" (Tactics) in *Shuo Yuan* (*Collection of Stories*).

[47]"Teng Wen Gong" (The Duke of Teng Wen) in *Meng Zi* (*Mencius*) (Book 1).

[48]*Ma Ke Si En Ge Si Quan Ji* (*The Complete Works of Marx and Engels*), Vol. 1, The People's Publishing House, 1972, p. 181.

Ben Ji" (The Records of Xia Dynasty) in *Shi Ji* (*The Records of the Grand Historian*) that "Yu recommended Gao Yao and entrusted him with administration of government affairs." The story that the law and prison were both made by Gao Yao was recorded in ancient documents, which had reflected the close connection of legislation and judiciary at the beginning of class society.

According to "Shang Liu" (the 6th place of negative trigram in the Eight Diagrams) in "Kan Gua" (one of the divinatory symbols of the Eight Diagrams) in *Yi Jing* (*The Book of Changes*), "it is ill omen to be tied with strings and put in thorns for three years." Moreover, what was said in *Zheng Yi* (*The Annotation of Confucians' Classics and the Books of History*) that "the place where the prisoners are jailed is overgrown with thorny bushes, so it is forbidden for people to enter" might refer to an early form of prison. It was recorded clearly in the current version of *Zhu Shu Ji Nian* (the bamboo *Annals*) that "in the 36th year of King Fen of the Xia Dynasty, 'Huan Tu was made." The so-called "Huan Tu" was defined in "Shi Gong Shi" (Palace Construction) in *Shi Ming* (*The Origin of the Word Meaning*) in the following way: "'Yu' (prison)...or 'Huan Tu' referred to a wall built like a circle." According to Zheng's annotation of "Da Si Kou" (The Senior Minister of Justice) in "Qiu Guan" (Ministry of Penalty) in *Zhou Li* (*The Rites of Zhou Dynasty*), "'Huan Tu' is the wall of a prison" and it was similar to a dungeon. Fen was the 7th king after Qi. In his time, the state was powerful and prosperous, with the expanding of its territory and the constant increasing of slaves and criminals captured in battles, and prisons were built. Besides "Huan Tu", prisons built within the capital of Xia were called "Xia Tai" and "Jun Tai". It was recorded in "Xia Ben Ji" (The Records of Xia Dynasty) in *Shi Ji* (*The Records of the Grand Historian*) that "so he summoned Tang and imprisoned him in 'Xia Tai'." It was also recorded in "Lu Zhao Gong Si Nian" (The 4th Year of Duke Zhao of Lu) in *Zuo Zhuan* (*The Chronicle of Zuo*) that, "Xia Qi had built 'Jun Tai'." "Xia Tai" and "Jun Tai" might be the names of prisons directly under the jurisdiction of Xia. "Xia Tai" was in the south of Yu County and "Jun Tai" was in Zhai County in Nan Yang, Henan province.

Although it is difficult to prove the existence of prisons in Xia Dynasty, the statement in ancient books that "prisons began to appear at the time of 'San Wang' (three dynasties of Xia, Shang, and Zhou)"[49] was believable because it is in accordance with the reality of Chinese society in ancient time.

1.1.4.2 "Yu Xing" (The Penal Code of Yu)

The customs of clan society, which were meticulously selected by the ruling class, were either abolished or retained as customary law or transformed into state law. The statement in "Lv Xing" (The Penal Code of Lv) in *Shang Shu* (*The Book of Historical Document*) that "law was made and used by Bo Yi to regulate people's behaviors" had reflected the slow process of transformation of law from the specific

---

[49]Ying Shao (Han Dynasty), *Feng Su Tong* (*Comprehensive Meaning of Customs and Habits*).

adjustment of individuals to that of the general public. It was written in "Lu Zhao Gong Si Nian" (The 4th Year of Duke Zhao of Lu) in *Zuo Zhuan* (*The Chronicle of Zuo*) that "Xia suffered from chaotic political situation, so 'Yu Xing' (The Penal Code of Yu) was made." In "Xing Fa Zhi" (The Record of the Criminal Law) in *Han Shu* (*The History of Han Dynasty*), there were similar records: "after Yao and Shun, the people's morality degraded, so corporal punishment was made by Yu." Therefore, the "moral degeneration" and "political chaos" mentioned above could be understood as following:

(a) The slaves' revolt against slave owners.
(b) The struggles of the groups sticking to old clan tradition against the new nobles who supported the class system. The establishment of penalty system was out of need to change the chaotic political situation, which was in accordance with the rules of historical development. "Yu Xing" (The Penal Code of Yu) might not refer to the criminal laws made at the time of Yu, but rather to a general legal term in Xia Dynasty. The use of Yu's name just showed people's cherishment of and respect to the excellent ancestors of the Xia nation and the founders of the state itself. As to the records in the classical books that "there were 3000 articles in Xia penalty,"[50] "there were five normal penalties with 300 articles in Xia Penalty,"[51] and that "there were 3,000 articles of corporal punishments in Xia Penalty,"[52] etc., they just meant that there were numerous penalties in Xia Dynasty in general. In fact, many of the opinions were just conclusions wrongly drawn by the people of later ages based on their own understanding of *Lv Xing* (*The Penal Code of Lv*).

Apart from "Yu Xing" (The Penal Code of Yu), the kings' orders were also important forms of law. For example, Xia Qi's military orders with regard to oath taking mentioned above were also a form of law.

For the lack of historical materials, the contents of "Yu Xing" (The Penal Code of Yu) can only be listed roughly according to documentary records.

1.1.4.2.1 Accusation

According to the quotation of *Xia Shu* (*History of Xia Dynasty*) in "Zhao Gong Shi Si Nian" (The 14th Year of the Duke of Zhao) in *Zuo Zhuan* (*The Chronicle of Zuo*), the penalties of "Hun" (hanging), "Mo" (tattooing on the face or forehead of the offenders with indelible ink), "Zei" (putting the criminal to death), "Sha" (death penalty) were made by Gao Yao." "Whoever had done anything evil or and had claimed credit and merit belonging to others would be charged by 'Hun' (hanging); the officials who were greedy and corrupted would be charged by "Mo" (tattooing on

---

[50] *Shang Shu Da Zhuan* (*Interpretations of Shang Shu*).

[51] "Jing Ji Zhi" (The Record of Classic Books) in *Sui Shu* (*The History of Sui Dynasty*).

[52] Yang Xiong (Han Dynasty), "Xian Zhi" (Prophet) in *Yang Zi Fa Yan* (*Essays of Yang Xiong*).

the face or forehead of the offenders with indelible ink) and whoever had killed people recklessly would be charged by 'Zei' (putting the criminal to death)." It showed that punishments were already enforced for the crime of robbery, corruption and homicide in the Xia Dynasty, and all those who had committed such crimes would be sentenced to death.

As blood relations still had a strong binding power, "Bu Xiao" (being unfilial) was considered as a felony, as was described in the saying that "there were 300 crimes in 'Wu Xing' (Five Penalties), among which the most severe was 'Bu Xiao' (being unfilial)."[53] As for this record, Zhang Taiyan, the prominent modern scholar, had proved that it was a penalty enforced in the period of Xia and he had even written a book entitled *Xiao Jing Ben Xia Fa Shuo* (*The Classics of Filial Piety Being the Law of Xia Dynasty*).

Besides, there were also the crimes of disobeying 'Wu Xing' (the five elements, including metal, wood, water, fire, and earth, held by the ancients to compose the physical universe) and abandoning "San Zheng" (the right way of Heaven, Earth, and Man). The crime of disobeying "Wu Xing" meant violating the holy virtue represented by the king; while abandoning "San Zheng" meant abandoning the right way of Heaven, Earth, and Man, which had become an important reason for Xia Qi to attack You Hu, because he claimed that he was "implementing 'Tian Fa' (Heavenly punishment)" and "he had exterminated You Hu by obeying Heaven's command."[54] It was thus clear that both of the crimes belonged to felonies. In *Zheng Dian* (*Policies and Systems*) written in Xia Dynasty, it was recorded that "the man who has done his work ahead of time would be punished by death penalty without pardoning, and the man who has not done his work in time would also be punished by death penalty without pardoning,"[55] so it generally referred to the duty-related crimes of Xia Dynasty, and those involved would certainly be severely punished.

1.1.4.2.2 The Criminal Law and the Principles of Penalty

The records about the origin of "Wu Xing" (Five Penalties) of Xia Dynasty were first read in "Yao Dian" (Yao Code) in *Shang Shu* (*The Book of Historical Document*): "Replacing 'Wu Xing' (Five Penalties) with 'Liu' (exile)." In "Da Yu Mo" (Da Yu's Planning Government Affairs) and "Gao Yao Mo" (Gao Yao's Planning Government Affairs) in *Shang Shu* (*The Book of Historical Document*), there were the records like "drafting 'Wu Xing' (Five Penalties) and making it known to the public" and "Wu Xing Wu Yong" (five penalties for five different purposes). It was recorded in *Xiao Jing Zhu Shu* (*Annotation for the Classic of Filial Piety*) that "the names for 'Wu Xing' (Five Penalties) were already used in Confucian classics and the commentaries since Tang Yu (Yao and Shun) period, but it was not known when they

---

[53]"Wu Xing Zhang" (The Chatper of Five Penalites) in *Xiao Jing* (*The Classic of Filial Piety*).
[54]"Gan Shi" (The Military Order Issued at Gan) in *Shang Shu* (*The Book of Historical Document*).
[55]"Yin Zheng" (Punitive Expedition by Yin) in *Shang Shu* (*The Book of Historical Document*).

were first used in ancient times." In terms of the origin of "Wu Xing" (Five Penalties), there were three kinds of opinions in ancient books: according to the first, it originated from the "five cruel penalties" of Miao clan; according to the second, "'Wu Xing' (Five Penalties) was made by Gao Yao for the sake of 'Tian Fa' (Heavenly punishment)"; according to the third, "Wu Xing" (Five Penalties) was created by the ancient people according to the mutual promotion and restriction of "Wu Xing" (the five elements), among which the most popular was that it was made based on the corporal punishment of "Yi" (to cut down the nose), "Er" (to cut down the ears), "Zhuo" (castration), and "Qing" (to tattoo on the face) created by Miao people, with "Er" (to cut down the ears) changed into "Bin" (to cut down the knee cap) and "Zhuo" changed into "Gong" (castration). Therefore, the five "formal penalties" were finally made including "Mo" (tattooing on the face or forehead of the offenders with indelible ink), "Yi" (cutting off the nose), "Fei" (cutting off the left or right foot or both feet), "Gong" (castration), and "Bi" (capital punishment). Among these penalties, there were both death and corporal punishments. According to historical records, "200 people were punished by 'Da Bi' (capital punishment); 300 people were punished by 'Bin Bi' (to cut down the knee cap); 500 people were punished by 'Gong Bi' (castration); 1000 people were punished by 'Yi' (to cut down the nose), and 1000 people were punished by 'Mo' (tattooing on the face or forehead of the offenders with indelible ink)."[56] "Wu Xing" (Five Penalties) in Xia Dynasty was applicable only to the captives and slaves, while the kinsmen were just punished by "Liu" (exile), "Shu" (atonement), "Bian" (whipping), and "Pu" (corporal punishment including "Chi", "Bian", and "Zhang"). With the sharpening of social conflicts, "Wu Xing" (Five Penalties) gradually was applied to the kinsmen who were degraded to the social status of common people. The last king Xia Jie was both wicked and cruel and he had abused torture in inquisition. Thus, according to "Chu Zhen Xun" (Instructions of Chu Zhen) in *Huai Nan Zi* (*Masters from Huainan*), at the time of King Jie, the punishments similar to "burning a person alive" and "killing the remonstrators" which were enforced by King Zhou of Shang Dynasty had been established.

It is noteworthy that the system of penalty redeeming had already existed in Xia Dynasty. It was said that, when King Mu of Zhou had commanded Marquis Lv to make *Lv Xing* (*The Penal Code of Lv*) to establish the system of penalty redeeming, he referred to the penalty redeeming system of Xia, as was described in the saying that: "the penalty redeeming system of Xia was taken as a model."[57] In "Ping Zhun Shu" (On Fair Trade) in *Shi Ji* (*The Records of the Grand Historian*), Sima Zhen said in *Suo Yin* (*Index*) by citing *Shang Shu Da Zhuan* (*Interpretations of Shang Shu*) that "in Xia Dynasty, no death penalty and other punishments were imposed, so death penalty could be redeemed by 2000 *zhuan* (one *zhuan* is about 300 grams of bronze)." It was also stated in "Hou Ji" (Postscript) in *Lu Shi* (*Grand History*) that

---

[56]"Xing Fa Zhi" (The Record of the Criminal Law) in *Wei Shu* (*The History of Northern Wei Dynasty*).
[57]"Lv Xing" (The Penal Code of Lv) in *Shang Shu* (*The Book of Historical Document*).

"in Xia Dynasty, the principle of 'Zui Yi Wei Qing' (in dubio pro reo) was established, so death penalty could be redeemed by 1000 *zhuan*, the less serious crimes could be redeemed by 500 *zhuan* and the minor crimes could be redeemed by 200 *zhuan*." It was thus clear that the penalties ranging from corporal punishment to death penalty could all be redeemed. In Xia Dynasty, bronze was smelted to cast sacrificial utensils and weapons, so it was written in volume eleven of *Yue Jue Shu* (*Local Chronicles*) that "in the time of Yu, copper was used to make weapons." Now the site of bronze smelting in Xia Dynasty has been discovered, so it is probably true that in Xia Dynasty one's crime can be redeemed with bronze, which has shown that the goal of law making in Xia Dynasty is to protect the interests of nobles and slave owners.

To sum up, "Fa" (law) was different from the traditional customs of clans, so it was not the common will of clan members but the will of the ruling class of slave owners. The king of Xia Dynasty had possessed supreme power of legislation and the enforcement of penalty. Furthermore, the law was a kind of violence that the people were forced to obey, and which was backed by the mandatory forces of the state, so anyone who had violated it would be punished or would have his family members implicated. At the site of Erlitou, the discovered bones with heads and bodies separated or with hands tied up were clear evidence of the punishments enforced. To reinforce the deterrent effect of the law, the rulers of Xia Dynasty had conducted "Tian Tao" (Heavenly condemnation) and "Tian Fa" (Heavenly punishment) in the name of "Tian" (Heaven).

Based on punishing crimes according to the system of penalty, some preliminary principles of criminal law were summarized in Xia Dynasty. For example, the principle of "Yu Qi Sha Bu Gu, Ning Shi Bu Jing" was stated by quoting *Xia Shu* (*History of Xia Dynasty*) in "Xiang Gong Er Shi Liu Nian" (The 26th Year of the Duke of Xiang) in *Zuo Zhuan* (*The Chronicle of Zuo*). In this sentence, "Gu" means "crimes", and "Jing" means "law", so the sentence means that "we would rather violate the law than kill the innocent." This principle was continually praised by later generations for its discretion in applying punishments without being restrained by legal articles. Another principle of criminal law is "Sheng Zai Si She, Hu Zhong Zei Xing" mentioned in "Shun Dian" (Shun Code) in *Shang Shu* (*The Book of Historical Document*), and it meant that "those who have committed the crimes caused by faults and force majeure should be remitted, while those who are steeped in evil deeds and refuse to repent should be severely punished." Although "Shun Dian" (Shun Code) in *Shang Shu* (*The Book of Historical Document*) was only a faked book of ancient Chinese prose and was not suitable to be referred to as evidence, yet, in view of the principle of enforcing different punishments for criminal negligence, and intentional, habitual and casual crimes in early Zhou Dynasty, we can guess that the above mentioned principles of criminal law might have been put forward in Xia Dynasty.

Besides law, in Xia Dynasty a new way of governing people, namely, "Xia Li" (the rites of Xia Dynasty) was created. The original meaning of "Li" (rites) referred to a sacrificial ceremony of praying to gods, as was stated in the following statements: "'Li (rites)' was an activity to pay tribute to gods and to pray for good luck."[58] Originally, "'Li' originated from the god worshiping activities and was later extended to include all 'Li Yi' (etiquette)."[59] After entering class society, under the control of theocracy, state activities were usually closely related to worshiping gods, which had endowed "Li" (rites) with a new feature, so it became a new way of governing people in class society. "Xia Li" (the rites of Xia Dynasty) was a newly formed norm to fit in with the new order of class differentiation based on the transformation of old traditional customs, which was not only a process full of struggles, but also a gradual progress of cultural development. No doubt, "Xia Li" (the rites of Xia Dynasty) had a crucial historical influence Shang and Zhou dynasties, so the statement of Confucius was probably true that "'Yin' (Shang Dynasty) followed the 'Li' (rites) of Xia, so what was added to and deleted were evident; Zhou followed the 'Li' (rites) of 'Yin' (Shang Dynasty), so what was added to and deleted was also evident."[60]

The main contents of "Li" (rites) are as follows: "worshipping 'Tian' (Heaven) up above, worshipping 'Di' (Earth) down below and showing respect to the ancestors and the monarchs."[61] To make "Li" (rites) a new norm to adjust the class order, the power of gods was resorted, so they had listed "worshipping 'Tian' (Heaven) up above" as the most important element. Then the class order, which was adjusted by "Li" (rites), was compared to "the order of 'Tian' (Heaven) and 'Di' (Earth)." In Xia Dynasty, which was characterized by a strong color of patriarchal politics with the unification of the relatives, the nobles, the family, and the state, it was the most practical goal of "Li" (rites) "to show respect to ancestors and monarchs." The very fact that death penalty for felony would be executed at the ancestral temple and altar had reflected the earliest tendency of the combination of "Li" (rites) and "Xing" (punishment), as was indicated in the statement that "obedience of the order would be awarded at the ancestral temple, while the violation of the order would also be punished at the altar."[62]

Therefore, the history of legal civilization of Xia Dynasty had shown eloquently that it was the outcome of the society that had developed to a certain degree, and it was achieved by partially transforming the old clan customs and partially setting up the new standards. According to the records in ancient books and the discoveries of underground ruins, the outline of legal civilization of the Xia Dynasty can be basically depicted. Seen from the historical process of development, and seen from the relatively definite forms of legal system of Shang Dynasty, which was inherited from Xia Dynasty, it is obvious that Xia Dynasty had entered the gate of legal civilization.

---

[58] Xu Shen (Han Dynasty), *Shuo Wen Jie Zi* (*The Origin of Chinese Characters*).

[59] Xu Hao (Qing Dynasty), *Shuo Wen Jie Zi Zhu Jian* (*The Annotation of the Origin of Chinese Characters*).

[60] "Wei Zheng" (Handling Political Affairs) in *Lun Yu* (*The Analects*).

[61] "Li Shu" (On Rites) in *Shi Ji* (*The Record of the Grand Historian*).

[62] "Gan Shi" (The Military Order Issued at Gan) in *Shang Shu* (*The Book of Historical Document*).

1.2 The Legal System of Shang Dynasty Under the Ruling of Theocracy

After annihilating Xia Dynasty, Shang Dynasty was established by Shang Tang. Compared with Xia Dynasty, Shang Dynasty was more developed in economy, politics, and culture, so it had finally become a great slavery state. Moreover, the inscriptions on bones or tortoise shells have provided reliable evidence for the state affairs of Shang Dynasty. Shang Dynasty was one of the few dynasties in ancient China when the ruling of theocracy was established, so the gods in "Tian" (Heaven) and the kings on "Di" (Earth) were integrated to demonstrate the sacred dignity of kingship and irresistibility of state activities, legislation, and execution. Therefore, the interrelation of kingship and theocracy was a prominent feature of the legal civilization of Shang Dynasty.

1.2.1 The Unity of Kingship Rights, Family Authority and Theocracy

From the time when the state was founded by Xia Dynasty to Shang Dynasty, through several hundred years of development, the state had taken a relatively established form, so an autocratic kingdom with Chinese characteristics of the unity of kingship rights, family authority, and theocracy came into being.

The king of Shang was the chief representative of the slave owners and an embodiment of the supreme power of the state. In ancient books of Shang Dynasty, the king of Shang called himself "Yu Yi Ren" (I alone: a self-proclaimed name by kings in ancient China), which was a title used only by the kings and which had symbolized the imperial privilege since the time of King Tang. Many important state activities, such as wars and sacrifices were called "Wang Shi" (the king's events). Records in the oracle inscriptions on tortoise shells or animal bones, such as "Wang Ming" (king's order), "Wang Ling" (king's command), and "Wang Hu" (Oh, Kings) implied that important state affairs were all decided by the king of Shang. Therefore, the king of Shang not only had military, economic, and judicial power, but also had the power of managing the theocratic affairs like praying and divining.

In Shang Dynasty, family authority and theocracy were the two very important backbones of autocratic kingship of slavery system.

The important position of family authority in the state of Shang Dynasty was closely related to the pathway of China's civilization. According to the principle of "the unity of relatives and nobles," only members of noble families had the qualification to be appointed as officials of the state offices, so the senior leaders of the largest noble family were naturally the king of Shang. This principle had insured the monopoly of state power by nobles and reflected the prominent feature of aristocratic politics in ancient China.

1.2 The Legal System of Shang Dynasty Under the Ruling of Theocracy

In his instruction to mobilize nobles to move the capital to Yin, Pan Geng, the king of Shang pointed out that their ancestors and late kings of Shang had ruled jointly because they had "worked and rested together", so he promised the nobles that they would obtain the privilege of holding state offices for generations, as was expressed in the statement that "you are chosen as officials for generations."[63] The custom of hereditary holding of the official positions even influenced the Western Zhou Dynasty and the Spring and Autumn Period. According to "Shang Xian" (On Appointment of Officials) in *Mo Zi* (*Mo Zi*) (Book 2), "at present, the rich and privileged nobles are all those who have blood ties with the king, so they are rich and privileged without any other reasons."

For the reason that the family organizations of nobles and the state organizations were mutually infiltrated and closely related, there were elements of the ruling of the family in the ruling of the state. Moreover, family authority was used by nobles as a means of political rule, therefore, the notion of "respecting forefathers and ancestors" was propagated by the slave owners and sacrifices were listed in the ancestral temples as a great state event to take the advantage of the blood relations to cover up the antagonistic relations between the noble and the humble and to make the common people the tools of war.

There were already records about "Da Zong" (the main clan) in the inscriptions on bones or tortoise shells. According to the patriarchal clan system of the Shang Dynasty, "Da Zong" (the main clan) referred to the direct relatives of the royal family, and only after the son had inherited the throne was it possible for the family to match up with the condition of the direct relatives. Therefore, the king of the state was also the chief of "Da Zong" (the main clan), so kingship and family authority were unified, and the law of the inheritance of the throne was consistent with the patriarchal clan system of the nobles. In late Shang Dynasty, from the period of Kangding to that of Zhou, the throne was not only passed on from father to son, but also to "Di Zi" (the son born of the legal wife). The establishment of the patriarchal clan system centered by the inheritance of "Di Zi" (the son born of the legal wife) was the result of the further enhancement of kingship. The closeness and remoteness of blood relations to the king also determined the relative superiority and inferiority of the power and the positions inside the ruling class.

As a political means, the patriarchal family authority was started from Xia and Shang dynasties, and then was further systematized in Western Zhou Dynasty. Thus, it had influenced the later dynasties for a long time ever since and had become a unique historical tradition in Chinese legal civilization.

Besides the clan authority, the ruler of the Shang Dynasty also preached the thought of theocracy, which had mixed the religious belief and superstitions with political ruling and controlled and intimidated slaves and civilians in spirit. Thus, they made up an almighty and supreme god called "Di" (the Supreme Being), who determined not only the rewards and punishments, good harvests and bad harvests,

---

[63]"Pan Geng" (one of the rulers of Shang Dynasty) in *Shang Shu* (*The Book of Historical Document*) (Book 1).

victory and defeat, but also the construction of cities and dismissal and promotion of officials on earth. The establishment of monotheism represented by "Di" (the Supreme Being) was a reflection of the despotic political system of the Shang Dynasty in religion. "Di" (the Supreme Being) in "Tian" (Heaven) was just a projection of the king on earth. Therefore, like the king on the earth, "Di" (the Supreme Being) also had his own officials and imperial courts.

To strengthen the kingship by means of theocracy, the king of Shang had combined the worship of gods with the worship of ancestors of the royal families, preaching that "Di" (the Supreme Being) was the king's ancestral god and the king was the legitimate son of "Di" (the Supreme Being) to unify theocracy and kingship, which had given aristocracy with mysterious color, so the kings of Shang had often threatened people by carrying out "Tian Fa" (Heavenly punishment). In late Shang Dynasty, the king had attempted to overcome the ruling crisis by making use of theocracy, and called himself "Di" (the Supreme Being). Therefore, there were the Chinese characters of "Wang Di" and "Xia Di" in inscriptions on bones or tortoise shells. Thus, it was clear that the religion in Shang Dynasty was not only the religion of nobles, but also the spiritual pillar of autocratic politics and the ideological weapon in ruling the slaves and civilians. The kings' frequent sacrificial activities for ghosts, gods, and ancestors were, in essence, political activities covered up under the religious outerwear, and their devout appearance was just the need to serve political purpose. In addition, the king of Shang also expressed his own will in the name of God through divination. Therefore, only authorized historians and the king himself had the right to divine and interpret the messages. For this reason, the officials in charge of religious affairs had a crucial position in the state of Shang Dynasty.

The major officials in charge of religious affairs recorded in inscriptions included "Zha Ce", "Bu Wu", and "Shi", etc., and they were collectively called "Shi Guan" (official in charge of recording and compiling history). Specifically speaking, they were in charge of administrating sacrifices, divining and recording of the important events, so they were not only the media between gods and human being and the masters of theocratic knowledge, but also important government officials. Therefore, they had exerted a great influence on the state activities and sometimes they even intervened in the royal affairs under the guise of god's will. Wang Guowei pointed out in *Shi Shi* (*The Interpretation of History*) that "before Yin Shang, most of the officials were appointed by "Shi", which had fully reflected his honor and importance." "Shi Guan" (official in charge of recording and compiling history) was also the monopolist and administrator of documents and files, and he was even in charge of drafting and issuing political orders. The statement made by the people of Zhou Dynasty was probably true that "only the ancestors of Yin had books and canons."[64] In late Shang Dynasty, as the king's power was further strengthened, the power of "Shi Guan" (official in charge of recording and compiling history) was relatively undermined. After Wuyi, the king of Shang had obtained the right to divine, so the

---

[64]"Duo Shi" (The Ministers) in *Shang Shu* (*The Book of Historical Document*).

power of "Shi Guan" (official in charge of recording and compiling history) was further weakened. Read from the oracle inscriptions on tortoise shells or animal bones, we can see that the diviner's name was usually recorded before rather than after Wuyi, which was not accidental. During the reign of Di Yi and Di Xin, the divination of "Shi Guan" (official in charge of recording and compiling history) was largely replaced by that of kings.

1.2.2 The Extension of the Scope of the State Management and Division of the Duties of Officials

Ten generations after the establishment of Shang Dynasty, Pan Geng, the king of Shang moved the capital to Yin. Since then, the national power was rapidly strengthened, and its dominion extended to both sides of the Yellow River in modern Henan and the majority of Shandong and part of Hebei and Shanxi province, which was known in history as "having an extent of thousands of li (unit of length: one li is equal to 500 meters)" and "people coming over from the whole world to pay tribute."[65] Along with the extension of the scope of state management, the division of officials' duties was preliminarily defined, and a system of official management centered on the king came into being. As what was written in "Jiu Gao" (Announcement to Ban Alcohol) in *Shang Shu* (*The Book of Historical Document*) that "in terms of 'Nei Fu' (official in the capital), there were hundreds of officials like 'Bai Liao', 'Shu Yin', 'Wei Ya', 'Wei Fu', and 'Zong Gong'"; while "in terms of 'Wai Fu' (official outside the capital), there were 'Hou', 'Dian', 'Nan', 'Wei', and 'Bang Bo'." Moreover, the inscriptions like "Yin Bian Hou Dian" (general terms for officials outside the capital) and "Yin Zheng Bai Bi" (general terms for officials inside the capital)[66] could also be found on bronze utilities.

The so-called "Nei Fu" was a general name used for the officials of the central government of the Shang Dynasty, many of whom were the eminent assistant ministers of the king. It was recorded in "Jun Shi" (Duke of Zhao) in *Shang Shu* (*The Book of Historical Document*) that "when Tang accepted Heaven's will to be the king, there was Yi Yin acting as the spokesman of 'Tian' (Heaven); in the period of Taijia, there was Bao Heng acting as the spokesman of 'Tian' (Heaven); in the period of Taiwu, there were Yi Zhi and Chen Hu acting as the spokesmen of "Tian" (Heaven) and Wu Xian helping with the management of the kingdom; in the period of Zuyi, there was Wu Xian; in the period of Wu Ding, there was Gan Pan." Those people mentioned above and the other people as Zhong Hui and Fu Yue mentioned in "Yin Ben Ji" (The Records of Yin Dynasty) in *Shi Ji* (*The Records of the Grand Historian*) were all important assistant ministers of the kings of Shang. In addition,

---

[65]"Xuan Niao" (a god bird like swallow) in "Shang Song" (Ode to Shang) in *Shi Jing* (*Book of Songs*).
[66]Inscriptions of *Da Xu Ding* (*Great Yu Tripod*).

there were other important officials such as the ministers in charge of labor recruitment (Si Tu), the ministers in charge of public works (Si Kong), and the ministers in charge of penalties (Si Kou). "Xiao Ji Chen" and "Xiao Zhong Ren Chen" mentioned in the inscriptions on bones or tortoise shells referred to the officials in charge of agriculture, and the officials in charge of foreign affairs were called "Bin". Besides, the officials in charge of handling the affairs in the palace such as "Zai" and "Xiao Chen" were also begun to be appointed. As for the duties and status of "Shi Guan" (official in charge of recording and compiling history), we have explained in previous passages.

Although these officials of central government discussed above have reached a certain scale in number, yet in general, the structure was not so strict and the division of duties was not so clear, which was a very natural phenomenon at that time.

A preliminary local management system was also established in Shang Dynasty. Under their direct ruling, two different systems were set up by the kings of Shang, which were respectively called "Bai Xing" and "Li Jun". "Bai Xing" referred to an official position for the hereditary nobles whose surnames were the same as or different from that of the king; while "Li Jun" referred to an official position in the basic administrative district. The coexistence of these two local management systems had reflected that in Shang Dynasty on the one hand the residents were organized and managed according to regional principle; on the other hand, the governance was maintained by blood relationship passed down from clan systems.

The vassals established outside the regions under the king's direct rule were collectively called "Wai Fu", such as "Hou, Dian, Nan, Wei, and Bang Bo."[67] Besides, King Wen of Zhou was once called "Xi Bo", and "Mei Bo" was mentioned in "Tian Wen" (Questions about the Heavens) in *Chu Ci* (*The Song of Chu*), and "Nan Yan" (On the Difficulty of Offering Advice) in *Han Feizi*. Moreover, the titles like "Jiu Hou", "E Hou", and "Chong Hou Hu" could be found in "Yin Ben Ji" (The Records of Yin Dynasty) in *Shi Ji* (*The Records of the Grand Historian*). Among these officials, "Hou" (dukes) and "Bo" (marquises) had relatively higher social status. It was stated in "Zhao Ce" (Strategy of Zhao) in *Zhan Guo Ce* (*Stratagems of the Warring States*) that "in the past, Gui Hou, E Hou, and King Wen were all three ministers of King Zhou," some of them were the king's sons who were born of his concubines and who were later enfeoffed to local areas. It was written in historical books that "he (the king) enfeoffed them after that, so they took the names of their states as their surnames, such as Yin, Lai, Song, Kongtong, Zhi, Beiyin, and Muyi."[68] The enfeoffment system implemented in early Zhou Dynasty actually had originated from this practice, and the others were leaders of various vassal states or tribes affiliated to the Shang Dynasty. Moreover, all nobles and dukes dispatched by the king of Shang to border regions or fortified points had their own political organizations and forces, and they acknowledged the king's supremacy, accepted the titles conferred upon them by him, and acted as agents of the king of Shang to control

---

[67]"Jiu Gao" (Announcement to Ban Alcohol) in *Shang Shu* (*The Book of Historical Document*).
[68]"Yin Ben Jin" (The Record of Yin Dynasty) in *Shi Ji* (*The Record of the Grand Historian*).

local areas. They also had the duty to pay tribute, to fight battles on behalf of the king of Shang and to report to the king regularly. It was stated in "Yin Wu" (Heroic King of Yin) in "Shang Song" (Ode to Shang) in *Shi Jing* (*Book of Songs*) that "when Shang Dynasty was established by Tang, no one was bold enough to fail to pay tribute or to acknowledge allegiance to him, including the Diqiang clan in the remote areas. The king of Shang was actually the leader of the whole China." Besides, the king of Shang had to protect the "Hou" (dukes) and "Bo" (marquises) against being attacked and to pray for good harvest for them in person, as was described in the sayings like "Quan Shou Nian" (there is a good harvest in Quan) and "Zhi Shou Nian" (there is a good harvest in Zhi) in oracle inscriptions on bones. However, the land and people possessed by allegiant vassal states and tribes were not granted by the king of Shang, so they had very weak subordinative relations with Shang. For example, although Zhou had respected Shang as "a grand state" or "grand Shang" and called itself "affiliated state", it called itself "grand state" to the tribes around Zhou. The double identities of "Hou" (dukes) and "Bo" (marquises) had shown their own independence. Especially for those vassal states conquered by Shang Dynasty by force, they often obeyed or betrayed along with Shang's prosperity or decline. Furthermore, some rulers of the vassal states tried to expand their power, which had led to constant wars between Shang and many vassal states. "To sue some state" often read in the divinations of oracle inscriptions on bones meant that when a vassal state rebelled, the king of Shang sent an army to have it suppressed and prayed to "Tian" (Heaven) and "Di" (Earth) for blessing. There were also records of employing the conquered dukes as sacrifices for the king's ancestors and gods.

In addition, the character of "Yi" (cities) found in inscriptions on bones or tortoise shells referred to a unit made up of a certain number of slaves and land, which could be used for awards and exchanges. Some of the "Yi" (cities) were equivalent to grassroots organizations in its nature. Seen from their establishment, some were set for the king's inspection tour, and others were set in newly conquered places. In a word, cities were built obviously for political purposes and they were primary strongholds to strengthen the rule of the Shang Dynasty. Therefore, according to the oracle inscriptions written on bones that "Tu state seized ten of my slaves and plundered two eastern cities," it showed that two cities had been lost, so it should be reported to the emperor. The capital of Shang Dynasty was called "Tian Yi" (the heavenly city), as was shown in the expression of "heavenly city of Shang". In early Shang Dynasty, Jiu Dan, who was "Si Kong" (the minister of public works), had made laws for the residence of people, moreover he also made regulations to make people settled by dividing the residential areas.

1.2.3 The More Enriched Contents of Legislation

It was stated in historical books that when Xia was annihilated by Shang, Zhong Gu, "Tai Shi Ling" (Imperial Astronomer) of Xia Dynasty "took out his law books...and left for Shang," so "Tang announced to the vassals happily that the king of Xia treated his civilians cruelly...so the law-abiding officials had come over and pledged allegiance to Shang by themselves."[69] "The law-abiding official's surrender and pledging allegiance to Shang by themselves" had brought great joy to Tang, because it had fully shown his emphasis on legal documents. His announcement to all the vassals showed that the extinguishing of Xia by Shang not only accorded with Heaven's will, but also accorded with the aspirations of the people. It was because of the strengthening of the ruler's legal consciousness that he had commenced the work of legislation to cope with the new situation soon after Xia Dynasty was wiped out. It was recorded in "Shao Gong Liu Nian" (The 6th Year of the Duke of Shao) in *Zuo Zhuan* (*The Chronicle of Zuo*) that "'Tang Xing' (The Penal Code of Tang) was made because of the political corruption of Shang." Thus, similar to "Yu Xing" (The Penal Code of Yu), "Tang Xing" (The Penal Code of Tang) was a general name of the law of Shang Dynasty. It was just to express people's remembrance of and respect to this excellent leader of the Shang clan and the founder of the state that the name of Tang was adopted.

When the throne was passed on to Tang's eldest grandson Tai Jia, "'Tang Xing' (The Penal Code of Tang) was completely abandoned and morality was trampled"[70]; moreover, Tai Jia had acted recklessly and cruelly, so it had resulted in the wane of national power and the turmoil of social order. To stabilize his rule, in the 24th year of Zujia, "'Tang Xing' (The Penal Code of Tang) was reenacted,"[71] which meant that to recover the weakened national power and to rectify social disorder, the law made in early Shang Dynasty was amended by the rulers.

The record of "Zuo Bi" (making law) in oracle inscriptions on bones and tortoise shells also referred to legislation, and "Bi" not only referred to criminal law but also the law in general.

In addition, the rulers of early Shang Dynasty had learned a lesson from the downfall of Xia Dynasty caused by "the indulgence of the activities related to ghosts, gods and licentiousness"[72] since King Kongjia, so "bureaucratic system was established to conduct supervision over those in power." It was stated in *Kong Zhuan* (*The Biography of Confucius*) that "criminal laws were made by Tang to regulate and to warn all officials." The main contents of the law are as follows:

> It is the practice of 'Wu Feng' (sorcery) to dance often in the court and sing in the room; it is practice of 'Yin Feng' (licentious) to lust for fortune and sex and indulge in hunting; it is the practice of 'Luan Feng' (violation of social customs) to challenge the sages' words, to fail to be loyal and just, to alienate oneself from virtue and to act like naïve children. An official committing any one of these three malpractices will lose his family and a king committing any one of these three malpractices will lose his state. If an official doesn't admonish the king, he will be sentenced to the penalty of 'Mo' (tattooing on the face or forehead of the

---

[69]"Xian Shi" (Foresight and Sagacity) in *Lv Shi Chun Qiu* (*Spring and Autumn Annals of Master Lv*).
[70]"Yin Ben Ji" (The Record of Yin Dynasty) in *Shi Ji* (*The Record of the Grand Historian*).
[71]*Zhu Shu Ji Nian* (the bomboo *Annals*).
[72]"Xia Ben Ji" (The Record of Xia Dynasty) in *Shi Ji* (*The Record of the Grand Historian*).

1.2 The Legal System of Shang Dynasty Under the Ruling of Theocracy

offenders with indelible ink), and what is mentioned above should be imparted to lower officials.[73]

Although "Yi Xun" (Warnings of Yi Yin in the Shang Dynasty) in *Shang Shu* (*The Book of Historical Document*) was not evident enough of the bureaucratic penalty in Shang Dynasty, in *Mo Zi Fei Yue* (*Mo Zi's Theory against Music*) (Book 1) a record can be found and it was stated that: "it was recorded in "the books of former kings" in *Tang Zhi Guan Xing* (*Penalties for the Officials of Tang Dynasty*) that 'if the officials are indulgent in dancing in the palace, it is 'Wu Feng' (sorcery). So 'Jun Zi' (gentlemen) would be imposed with a fine of two *wei* of silk (*wei*: one *wei* is about one *chi*) and 'Xiao Ren' (common people) would be exempted from punishment.'" To a certain extent, what was described in the "books of former kings" was not totally groundless. The rulers of Shang and Zhou dynasties had attached much importance to the historical experience of the rise and fall of the previous dynasties, so the downfall of Xia Dynasty had served as a warning and enlightenment to Tang, so he had realized the necessity and significance of regulating officials by strict laws.

With the expansion of royal power, the orders and decrees of the kings of Shang became the main sources of law. It was recorded in "Tang Shi" (*Oath of Tang*) in *Shang Shu* (*The Book of Historical Document*) that "if you do not follow my order, I will kill you." It was also stated in "Pan Geng" (one of the rulers of Shang Dynasty) in *Shang Shu* (*The Book of Historical Document*) that "what I have said is just the order to obey…abide only by my law…only I have the power to enforce punishment" and "I will kill them all with no descendant of theirs surviving."

In terms of the contents of "Tang Xing" (The Penal Code of Tang), "Bu Xiao" (being unfilial) was still regarded as a felony according to the patriarchal system, in "Xiao Xing" (Filial Conduct) in *Lv Shi Chun Qiu* (*Spring and Autumn Annals of Master Lv*), *Shang Shu* (*The Book of Historical Document*) was quoted and it was stated that "among the 300 penalties, none was severer than that for the crime of 'Bu Xiao' (being unfilial)." According to Gao Xiu's annotation, "it was a law made in Shang Dynasty." It was said that one of the reasons for Taijia to be exiled by Yi Yin was that he did not follow the rituals of mourning. In keeping with the expansion of royal power, any actions like disobeying the king's orders, infringing upon kingship or arbitrarily changing the law would be punished severely. Shang Tang announced in the order of oath taking for attacking Xia that "if you do not follow my order, I will kill you," and "no one is to be forgiven."[74] That is to say, they would never be exempted from punishment. Pan Geng once declared clearly that the crime of "Dian Yue Bu Gong" (to transgress the law and to disrespect the superior) and "Zan Yu Jian Gui" (to be harmful to the state) were two felonies.[75] "Dian Yue Bu Gong"

---

[73]"Yi Xun" (Warnings of Yi Yin in Shang Dynasty) in *Shang Shu* (*The Book of Historical Document*).

[74]"Tang Shi" (Oath of Tang) in *Shang Shu* (*The Book of Historical Document*).

[75]"Pan Geng" (one of the rulers of Shang Dynasty) in *Shang Shu* (*The Book of Historical Document*) (Book 2).

meant that people were arrogant and unbridled without obeying laws and regulations and without showing respect to the king; "Zan Yu Jian Gui" meant that people had endangered the state power and staged illegal armed rebellions. Generally speaking, the rebellion started from abroad was called "Jian", and that started from home was called "Gui". With regard to these crimes, "the criminals and all their descendants would be killed so that they could not have any evil influence on the decent people in the city,"[76] which meant that every family members should be killed with no descendants left, so the authority of the king of Shang and the referent of criminal law were clearly indicated.

It was also recorded in "Wang Zhi" (The Royal Regulations) in *Li Ji* (*Book of Rites*) that "those who violate regulations with empty talks, who change the systems with different names, and who bring corruption to politics with heretical beliefs would all be sentenced to death; those who behave lasciviously, wear weird clothes, engage in odd arts and use strange objects to make the public confused would all be killed; those who have done wrong and being obstinate, who express wrong ideas and indulge in sophistry, who learn too many heretical thoughts, who accept wrong thoughts and even elaborate on them to make the public confused will all be killed; those who make the public confused in the name of ghosts and gods or make comments on current affairs by way of fortune telling and divination will all be killed." These four examples mentioned above were called "Si Zhu" (four killings), and the violators would all be killed immediately. "Wang Zhi" (The Royal Regulations) in *Li Ji* (*Book of Rites*) was compiled by the scholars in the period of Emperor Wen of Han Dynasty, in which the system of Shang was described in detail, so it could be used as a reference for discussing the systems of Shang and Zhou dynasties. The accusation of "Si Zhu" (four killings) was all closely related to the maintenance of the royal power of extreme autocratic despotism.

Besides, the following two accusations were recorded in the documents and files of the Shang Dynasty:

The crime of giving up farming: when attacking Xia Dynasty, Shang Tang announced a crime committed by Xia Jie: "The king didn't understand and sympathize with the people; in addition he had neglected agriculture...the king of Xia dynasty had wasted the wealth of the state and exploited its people."[77] In ancient China, a state was founded based on agriculture, so it would have endangered the survival of the people and social stability to give up farming and to fail to engage in agricultural production timely. Therefore, it was aimed at gaining the support of Xia people for Shang Tang to launch a punitive expedition against Xia Jie for this reason.

The crime of littering ash on public roads: according to "Nei Chu Shuo" (The Inner Categories of Sayings) in *Han Fei Zi* (*Han Feizi*), "a law was made in Shang dynasty" and if "a man has littered ash on public roads, he will be punished by cutting off his hands." Public roads were the main means of transportation, so it

---

[76]"Pan Geng" (one of the rulers of Shang Dynasty) in *Shang Shu* (*The Book of Historical Document*) (Book 2).

[77]"Tang Shi" (Oath of Tang) in *Shang Shu* (*The Book of Historical Document*).

would be sentenced to the penalty of cutting off one's hands to litter ash on the road. It was said that this strict law was supported by Confucius and he said: "This is the way to govern, because ashes littered on the road are sure to affect other people, so they will get angry, which will not only lead to disputes, but also to killing of each other by three clans. Thus, the behavior that may lead to mass killing should be forbidden. Although severe penalties are disliked by everyone, yet comparatively speaking, it is much easier to persuade people to stop littering. It is the way to rule the world to make people do what is easier without forcing them to do what they dislike. Some agree that anyone who litters ashes on public roads should be punished by cut off his hands. Zigong asks, 'the severe penalty of cutting off one's hands for the minor offences of littering ashes! Aren't the ancient people too cruel?' Confucius answers, 'it is easier to give up littering ashes, but it is disliked to have one's hands cut off. So do what is easier without doing what one dislikes, because the ancient people thought it was easier for them to do so, they just do it.'"[78]

There were different opinions about the law of prohibiting littering ashes in the Warring States Period. Shen Jiaben in the Qing Dynasty had stated in "Lv Ling" (*The Laws and Decrees*) in *Li Dai Xing Fa Kao* (*A Textual Research of the Criminal Laws in the Past Dynasties*) that "this penalty is too severe to be true, so there are different accounts about it." It can be seen from the ruins of the Shang Dynasty that public roads of Shang are not very wide; therefore, it not only affected public traffic, but also hampered the timely expedition or suppression of slaves' rebellions to litter ashes on public roads, so anyone who committed this crime would be punished by cutting off his hands.

According to the records of ancient books, the penalties of Shang Dynasty originated from "Wu Xing" (Five Penalties) of the Xia Dynasty with some addition and deletion. "When the Xia families ruled the world, there were over 3000 articles in 'Wu Xing' (Five Penalties), and in Shang and Zhou dynasties some articles were either added or deleted."[79] The so-called "Wu Xing" (Five Penalties) referred to "Mo" (tattooing on the face or forehead of the offenders with indelible ink), "Yi" (to cut down the nose), "Yue" (to amputate the feet), "Gong" (castration) and "Da Bi" (capital punishment). However, in Xia Dynasty, "Wu Xing" (Five Penalties) was not established statutory penalties; moreover, it was unpractical for them to formulate 3000 systematic punitive regulations. In Shang Dynasty, there were already records of "Wu Xing" (Five Penalties) in both classic books and inscriptions on bones and tortoise shells. According to the records in inscriptions on bones, the penalties at the time included "Yi" (to cut down the nose), "Yue" (in Shang Dynasty, there was only one kind of punishment of having the feet amputated, and there was no difference), "Sha" (death penalty), "Bi" (capital punishment), and "Yi" (also cutting down the nose). Besides, there were also the penalties symbolizing burning, the penalties symbolizing manacling the two hands of the convicted and the penalties of "putting the convict in prison with his hands manacled." In ancient books, there

---

[78]"Nei Chu Shuo" (The Inner Categories of Sayings) in *Han Fei Zi* (*Han Feizi*) (Book 1).
[79]"Xing Fa Zhi" in *Jin Shu* (*The History of Jin Dynasty*).

were also the records of cruel penalties such as "Tian Xing" (Heavenly Penalty, or 'Qing E': tattooing on the forehead), "Zui Ren Yi Zu", namely, the penalty of "Yi Tian" (exterminating all family members of the criminal together with him) and the penalty of making one's wife a slave for sacrifice, etc.

Zhou, the king of the later period of Shang Dynasty was extremely brutal and oppressive. To avoid the collapsing of the regime, extremely brutal extrajudicial penalties were implemented "without following the conventional ones." It was recorded in "Yin Ben Ji" (The Records of Yin Dynasty) in *Shi Ji* (*The Records of the Grand Historian*) that "severe penalties such as 'Pao Luo Penalty' (an ancient torture or punishment by ordering a prisoner to walk on a slippery metal being kept hot by coal underneath) were implemented by King Zhou." At the same time, "Jiu Hou was seared with his body minced . . .E Hou's body was dried up into meat" and "Bi Gan's heart was dug out to have an examination of his heart." The so-called "Pao Luo Penalty" was a brutal punishment: a copper pillar was coated with oil, burnt hot with charcoals under it, and then the criminal was ordered to walk on it, in the end the criminal fell into the charcoal and was burned to death. It was said that before King Zhou conquered Shang, King Wen of Zhou had "offered to give King Zhou the land west of Luo River and a territory of 1000 *li* in exchange for the abolishment of this penalty." Confucius once praised King Wen of Zhou and said: "How benevolent King Wen was to give up a territory of 1000 *li* in exchange for the abolishment of the penalty of 'Pao Luo'; how wise King Wen was to win the support of the world by giving up a territory of 1000 *li*."[80]

It was written in "Yin Ben Ji" (The Records of Yin Dynasty) in *Shi Ji* (*The Records of the Grand Historian*) that "Jiu Hou had a beautiful daughter who was married to King Zhou. She disliked wantonness, so Zhou was angry and he killed her and minced Jiu Hou." "E Hou was competitive and eloquent, so he was air-dried."

Besides death and corporal penalties, there was "Tu Xing" (penal servitude), a punishment of having the offenders imprisoned and forced to labor. It was recorded in "Yin Ben Ji" (The Records of Yin Dynasty) in *Shi Ji* (*The Records of the Grand Historian*) that "Wu Ding dreamed of a sage named Yue one night. He looked around at his officials but found none of them was Yue; therefore, he asked many people to look for him in the wilderness, so he was finally found in Fu Xian. At the time, Yue was a slave building roads at Fu Xian; he went to present himself before Wu Ding and was thus recognized. Then Wu Ding talked with him and found out that he was really a sage, so he was appointed the prime minister and Shang Dynasty became prosperous under his leadership." What Kong Anguo said was quoted in *Ji Jie* (*Collected Interpretations*): "Fu Xian was on the border of Yu and Guo State, and there was a road through it. The road was often blocked by mountain streams, so slaves were asked to have it rebuilt." The above records imply that in the place of Fu Xian, prisoners and slaves were forced to build roads. The implementation of "Tu Xing" (penal servitude) had reflected the progress of legal civilization.

---

[80]"Nan Er" (Questions) (Part 2) in *Han Fei Zi* (*Han Feizi*).

1.2 The Legal System of Shang Dynasty Under the Ruling of Theocracy

The progress of legal civilization in Shang Dynasty was also reflected in the drafting of civil and economic legal regulation.

Along with the formation of private ownership and class differentiation, the property and personal relationship which had not existed in clan society were bound to appear, and surely, such relationship needed to be adjusted by law, so it had led to the making of civil legal regulation. The main contents the civil regulation included the confirmation of class identity, the protection of ownership, the adjustment of creditor's rights and debts, the establishment of marriage and inheritance system and so on. Meanwhile, legal regulations were also made to adjust the economic relationship.

Although the civil and economic laws of Shang Dynasty were simple in content and incomplete in system, yet as a legal norm adjusting special objects, their existence was beyond question.

Under slavery system, the society was divided into two opposite classes, namely, the class of slaves and the class of slave owners. Most of the slaves were prisoners of war; however, after some civilians committed crimes they also became slaves known as "Zui Li" (criminal slaves). Slaves were a class which was ruled and exploited, so they had just lived a dog's life without any life guarantee, so they were often killed as "Ren Xun" (human buried alive with the dead) and "Ren Sheng" (human sacrifices). However, at the same time, slaves were also the class that had created great social wealth. In one of the nobles' mausoleums of the Shang Dynasty unearthed, around 400 people were buried alive as "Ren Xun" (human buried alive with the dead). In "Sang Zhong" (mourning masses) and "Ni Zhong" (rebelling masses) in the inscriptions on bones and tortoise shells, the slaves' rebellions and struggles were recorded.

Apart from slaves, "Xiao Ren" (common people) was a civilian class in the Shang society who had enjoyed complete civil rights and who could get land from the nobles. Besides, they had their freedom, so they were the principal members of the army of the Shang Dynasty. The political tendency of "Xiao Ren" (common people) had influenced the state activities of Shang to some extent, and they had to pay tribute to aristocrats and were often used as tools of war. In addition, their social status was not stable because they often went broke easily because of military service, tax and natural or man-made disasters, or became slaves because of the crimes they had committed. In late Shang Dynasty, the revolt of the common people against aristocracy gradually combined with the slave uprisings, which had shown that the rule of Shang Dynasty was in a deep crisis.

In opposition to the vast masses of slaves were aristocratic slave holders, namely, the "royal vassals", "royal clans", "nobilities", "state lords", "military leaders and hundreds of ministers", and "monarchs" who were mentioned in ancient codes and books. They were originally chiefs at different levels in tribal confederation, and the leaders of military organizations, so they possessed state power and had played certain positive roles in the organization of production under slavery system and in the elimination of the remaining backward forces of clan system.

Land, the basic means of production in Shang Dynasty, was state-owned. The king of Shang Dynasty enjoyed paramount ownership of the land, so he distributed land to aristocrats who only had the right of owning, cultivating, and managing the land, while he had the ownership and right of disposition of the land. Zhi Ga was an important general in the period of Wu Ding. After getting the land, Zhi Ga was invaded by Tu State and Ji State, so he reported to the king of Shang Dynasty timely: "On the day of Guisi, divination was practiced by a person named Zhen. When asked whether there would be disaster in the next ten days, the king answered (in accordance with the cracks on turtle shells) that there was going to be misfortune. So on the 5th day of the year of Dingyou, disasters really stroke in the west. Zhi Ga reported that Tu State had attacked the people in the east and occupied two cities and that Ji State had invaded the land in the west." It showed that Zhi Ga only had the right of the management of the land, so when the right of ownership was infringed upon, he had to report to the king of Shang for help immediately. The aristocrats who had gained the right of owning and cultivating the land had to pay tax and tribute to the king of Shang.

It should be noted that the ownership of some vassal states, which had accepted the ruling of the king of Shang, was different from that of the areas under the king's direct rule. It was recorded in "Yin Ben Ji" (The Records of Yin Dynasty) in *Shi Ji* (*The Records of the Grand Historian*) that "during the reign of king Zhou (King Zhou of the Shang Dynasty), Xi Bo (King Wen of the Zhou Dynasty) offered the land west of Luo to persuade the king to abolish "Pao Luo Penalty" (An ancient torture or punishment by ordering a prisoner to walk on a slippery metal being kept hot by coal underneath). King Zhou agreed and gave him bows, arrows, hatchets, and axes to help him to go on a punitive expedition." This indicated that although Xi Bo had pledged allegiance to Shang, the ownership of his land was not changed and it still belonged to the king himself.

Besides land, slaves were also important objects of ownership. Like livestock and tools, they was the property of the aristocrats and could be exchanged as objects of trade or awards, or even be killed at their owner's will. On and around an altar south of the ancestral temple in Xiaotun, Anyang, many remains of men and livestock were found as sacrifices.

There were also records of constant infringement of plundering land, livestock and slaves in the inscriptions on bones and tortoise shells, such as "ten of my slaves having been seized by Tu state." Such cases were often reported to the king of Shang to request him to have them settled by force.

With regard to marriage and inheritance, the dominant form of marriage in the Shang Dynasty was monogamy. Historical records and oracle inscriptions proved that among the thirty-one kings of Shang Dynasty, most of them followed the custom of monogamy. For example, Tang was married to Bi Bing and Da Jia was married to Bi Xin. It was the case with the kings, so was it with other common people. However, the kings and nobles often took many concubines. For example, Wu Ding had up to sixty-four concubines. It was recorded in "Yin Ben Ji" (The Records of Yin Dynasty) in *Shi Ji* (*The Records of the Grand Historian*) that king Zhou of Shang had "bestowed favor on women". To make sure that a nobleman could own a number of concubines, the system of "Teng Jia" (following the wife together to marry the husband of the woman) was carried out in Shang Dynasty, by which the company of the wife's younger sisters was allowed in the marriage. The

1.2 The Legal System of Shang Dynasty Under the Ruling of Theocracy

number of wives and concubines in Shang Dynasty was in direct proportion to the status, power, and property of the aristocrats. However, a woman could only have one husband. It was recorded in "Jiu San" (nine and three: one of the trigrams in *The Book of Changes*) in "Jian" (The 53rd Diagram: Gradually) in *Yi* (*The Book of Changes*) that "if the husband has not come back from his military duty but his wife is pregnant, the baby born will not be raised up, because it is an ill omen." This statement proved that it was illegal for a wife to have sexual intercourse with another man while her husband was away in the army.

Following the establishment of patriarchal system, the inheritance of the throne changed from the inheritance by the younger brother to that by the son. More specifically, before Kang Ding, various forms of inheritance alternated, including the inheritance of the throne by younger brother or by the son. Kang Ding, Wu Ding, Wen Ding, Di Yi, and Di Xin all inherited the throne from their fathers. Under the dual function of royal power and patriarchy, the system of the inheritance of the younger brother was replaced by the system of the inheritance of "Di Zhang Zi" (the eldest son born of the legal wife). In the period of the reign of Di Yi, it was already strictly regulated as a law that "when the legitimate wife has a son, it is not lawful to choose the son of the concubine as the heir."[81] "Di Yi's eldest son was named Weizi Qi, because Qi's mother's social status was humble, he could not be the heir. Di Yi's youngest son was Xin, whose mother was the legitimate wife, so Xin became the heir. After Di Yi's death, Xin ascended the throne and was called Di Xin, who was later called Zhou by the people."[82] Zhou's succession to the throne was given a more detailed account in "Dang Wu" (Urgent Affairs) in *Lv Shi Chun Qiu* (*Spring and Autumn Annals of Master Lv*):

> Zhou had two brothers born of the same mother. The eldest one was called Weizi Qi and the second one was called Zhong Yan. Zhou was the youngest of the brothers. When the first two sons were born, the mother was still a concubine. After she became the legitimate wife, Zhou was born. Both Zhou's father and mother wanted to make Qi the heir, but "Tai Shi" (ancient senior official in charge of state affairs) argued that 'according to law when the legitimate wife has a son, it is not lawful to choose the concubine's son as the heir.' So Zhou became the heir.

The issue of the inheritance of the throne of the Shang Dynasty was also mentioned in Duke of Zhou's warning to King Cheng, which was recorded in "Wu Yi" (No Enjoying Ease and Comfort) in *Shang Shu* (*The Book of Historical Document*): "it was unjust for Zu Jia to be the king." Ma Rong explained, "Zu Jia had an elder brother called Zu Geng, but Zu Jia was more capable. Thus, Wu Ding wanted to make him the heir. However, Zu Jia thought it unjust to depose the elder but enthrone the younger."[83] It can be seen from above that the succession to the throne by the eldest legitimate son was universally acknowledged. This system of

---

[81] "Dang Wu" (Urgent Affairs) in *Lv Shi Chun Qiu* (*Spring and Autumn Annals of Master Lv*).
[82] "Yin Ben Ji" (The Record of Yin Dynasty) in *Shi Ji* (*The Record of the Grand Historian*).
[83] "Lu Zhou Gong Shi Jia" (The Aristocratic Family of the Duke of Lu) in *Shi Ji* (*The Record of the Grand Historian*) (index interpreted by Ma Rong).

inheritance was established by the ruling class to prevent their property right and political privilege from being infringed upon and to keep the interior order. Thus, it was legalized in Zhou Dynasty and was followed by most of the later feudal dynasties.

The economic law of Shang Dynasty was still simple, and it mainly consisted of regulations on tax and currency.

The tax of Shang Dynasty mainly consisted of land tax. It was stated in "Teng Wen Gong" (The Duke of Tengwen) (Part 1) in *Meng Zi* (*Mencius*) that "the residents in Xia would be taxed for their fifty *mu* of land by 'Gong' (paying tribute), the residents of Yin would be taxed for their seventy *mu* of land by 'Zhu' (the rent of service provided by civic who cultivated the public land), and the residents of Zhou would be taxed for their one hundred *mu* of land by 'Che' (land grant paid to the country for the harvest of one hundred *mu* of land). Actually, the tax rate of all of the three dynasties was about one-tenth." Fifty *mu*, seventy *mu*, and one hundred *mu* were land units used to calculate tax and "Zhu" referred to an exploiting system to use slaves to cultivate public land. However, the records related to tax in Xia and Shang dynasties were quite rare.

The basic currency of Shang Dynasty was "Bei" (shell). Shell was a kind of decorating object, and then with the expansion of trade, it was developed into a universal equivalent, namely, currency. Pan Geng called shell "a good commodity" and "a treasure of commodity". He even ordered that when people moved to new houses, they should "have shells and jades".[84] Moreover, the kings and aristocrats of Shang Dynasty often awarded their subjects with shells. The Chinese characters in inscriptions on bones and tortoise shells like "Bao" (treasure), "Zhu" (save), and "Mai" (buy) all have the component of "Bei" (shell) as symbols of property. In most of the tombs around Yin ruins, one to over twenty shells was found among the burial objects. According to inscriptions on ancient bronze utilities and bones and tortoise shells, the unit of "Bei" (shell) was *peng*. As to the number of shells in one *peng* (*peng*: unit of measurement), no one could give a definite answer today. According to Guo Moruo's study, "one *peng* equals to ten shells."[85] At least one *peng* or at most twenty *peng* was awarded to his subjects by the king of Shang, for example, "in the year of Gengxu...one *peng* was awarded to Duonv by the king,"[86] and "in the year of Bingwu, twenty *peng* was awarded to Shu Sizi by the king."[87]

It can be seen from above that as a great slavery country, the legal civilization of Shang was not only more developed than that of Xia Dynasty, but also had exerted a greater influence on later Zhou Dynasty. When Duke of Zhou (named Dan), a

---

[84]"Pan Geng" (one of the rulers of Shang Dynasty) in *Shang Shu* (*The Book of Historical Document*).

[85]Guo Moruo, "A Study of Characters on Shells and Bones: Interpretation of Peng" in *Guo Mo Ruo Quan Ji* (*The Collected Works of Guo Moruo*) (Archaeology), Vol. 1, Science Press, 1962, p. 110.

[86]Guo Moruo, "A Study of Characters on Shells and Bones: Interpretation of Peng" in *Guo Mo Ruo Quan Ji* (*The Collected Works of Guo Moruo*) (Archaeology), Vol. 1, Science Press, 1962, p. 112.

[87]*Shu Si Zi Ding* (*Shu Sizi Tripod*).

politician in early Zhou Dynasty, admonished his followers how to govern the subjects of Shang Dynasty, he often mentioned that "only the ancestors of Yin had compiled books and codes,"[88] so "punishments should be enforced according to the regulations of Yin because they are just and righteous."[89] In the Warring States Period, when talking about the evolution of law Xun Zi pointed out: "'Xing Ming' (law) of Shang should be followed."[90] In Han Dynasty, Dong Zhongshu also held the view that "'Wu Xing' (Five Penalties) was implemented in Yin Dynasty to supervise the treacherousness and corporal penalties were made to enforce punishment."[91]

1.2.4 The Judicial System Under the Influence of Theocratic Law

In judicial trial, for both conviction and measurement of penalty, usually the judgment of God was obtained through divination. The question "whether this person should be punished or not",[92] which was described in inscriptions, was a record of questions about whether corporal penalty was to be enforced or not which the diviners had raised to gods. But on the other hand, as the representative of god on earth, the king of Shang had the supreme judicial authority, as was illustrated in the statement that "only I, the king, had the right to punish."[93] Sometimes, the king's judgment was endowed with a greater power of intimidating by means of oracles. For example, it was recorded in inscriptions: "making divination: the monarch enforces punishments"; "making divination: the monarch doesn't enforce punishments."[94] However, as theocracy weakened, the realistic tendency of attaching importance to man in judicial trial was enhanced.

Below the king of Shang, "Si Kou" (the minister of justice) was the chief of central judiciary office. Within the area of capital, "Shi" and "Meng Shi" were in charge of the jurisdiction and hearing of the various cases, and outside the area of capital, local judges called "Zheng" and "Shi" were appointed. When there were important cases, these officials should not make judgment by themselves, but instead

---

[88]"Duo Fang" (In Many Ways) in *Shang Shu* (*The Book of Historical Document*).

[89]"Kang Gao" (The Orders of Duke Zhou to Kang Shu) in *Shang Shu* (*The Book of Historical Document*).

[90]"Zheng Ming" (Rectification of the Name) in *Xun Zi* (*Xun Zi*).

[91]"Dong Zhong Shu Zhuan" (The Biography of Dong Zhongshu) in *Han Shu* (*The History of Han Dynasty*).

[92]*Yin Qi Yi Cun* (*Collections of Contracts in Qin Dynasty*), p. 850.

[93]"Pan Geng" (one of the rulers of Shang Dynasty) in *Shang Shu* (*The Book of Historical Document*) (Book 1).

[94]*Yin Xu Wen Zi Yi Bian* (*The Second Collection of the Characters of the Ruins of Yin Dynasty*), p. 4604.

they should report to "Si Kou" (the minister of justice) for reviewing, which showed that a preliminary division of trials had already established in Shang Dynasty. As to the enfeoffed vassals, they had a relatively greater judicial power.

The prison of Shang Dynasty was called "Huan Tu", a round dungeon dug out underground or a circle wall built above the ground to imprison criminals. It was recorded in "Shang Xian" (On Appointment of Officials) in *Mo Zi* (*Mo Zi*) (Book 2) that "in the past, Fu Yue was imprisoned in 'Huan Tu' in the North Sea State." Fu Yue was once a criminal imprisoned in such a kind of dungeon. It was recorded in "Yin Ben Ji" (The Records of Yin Dynasty) in *Shi Ji* (*The Records of the Grand Historian*) that "King Zhou imprisoned Xi Bo (King Wen of the Zhou Dynasty) in Li" and made him wear shackles for seven years. It was also stated in *Zheng Yi* (*The Annotation of Confucians' Classics and the Books of History*) that "'牖' (pronounced 'You') also means '羑' [the same pronunciation with 酉(You)"] (both names of places). Thus, "Youli" was the location of the prison in Shang Dynasty, which is now in the north of Tangyin County in Henan province. There is a Chinese character "圉" (yu) in inscriptions on bones, which symbolizes that a criminal wearing an instrument of punishment was imprisoned in a square dungeon. According to the research of Duan Yucai, a scholar in Qing Dynasty, the Chinese character "'圉' is made up of the component '囗' plus component '幸'. Therefore, the character of '幸' symbolizes the guilty person, and the component '囗' symbolizes imprisonment." "Xun Yu", "Bing Yu", and "Yao Yu" are all prisons at different places. The Chinese character "圉" looks like placing an instrument of punishment like shackles in a prison. Another example, the Chinese character "婞" (pronounced 'Xing') in inscriptions on shells is like a criminal wearing a hand shackle in prison, and dungeons unearthed in Yin ruins are good evidence of the prison of Shang Dynasty.

The land ownership of "Jing Tian Zhi" (the "nine squares" system of land ownership in China) had not only enhanced agricultural production, but also stimulated animal husbandry. In addition, there was also the division of labor in handicraft industry. With the gradual expansion of the scale of production and the promotion of the exchange of commodities, currency finally emerged. The cast of bronze wares, in particular, had marked the level at which the social productive forces reached in Shang Dynasty.

Chapter 2
The Early Developed Form of the Chinese Legal Civilization: The Legal System of Western Zhou Dynasty

(The 11th Century B.C.–770 B.C.)

Zhou, originally an affiliated state to Shang Dynasty in the northwest, had maintained a relationship that was either rebellious or obedient in different periods with Shang Dynasty, according to the record of oracle inscriptions such as "the appointed vassal of Zhou" or "the rebels of Zhou". Before taking the place of Shang Dynasty, Zhou had completed the transition from the primitive tribal system to the early slavery state and become the leader of a number of small northwestern states that threatened the rule of Shang Dynasty. After King Wu of Zhou exterminated Shang Dynasty, a famous slavery state was established in Chinese history, which had symbolized the developed form of legal civilization of slavery system.

At the beginning of Zhou Dynasty, with "Hua Xia" (an ancient name for China) culture as the principal, the quintessence of other ethnic cultures was also adopted. Zhou Gong (Duke of Zhou), the prominent thinker and politician had learned from the lessons of Shang Dynasty and realized that Shang Dynasty was doomed because of its overemphasis on cruel punishments. Thus, he put forward the principle of "Ming De Shen Fa" (promoting virtue and being prudent in the enforcement of punishment), by which the respecting of "Tian" (Heaven) was integrated with the protection of the people. He also made "Li" (rites) and "Yue" (music) and formulated the strategy of the comprehensive governance of "Li" (rites), "Yue" (music), "Xing" (punishment), and "Zheng" (government). The coordinative government of "Ming De Shen Fa" (promoting virtue and being prudent in the enforcement of punishment) and "Li" (rites), "Yue" (music), "Xing" (punishment), and "Zheng" (government) constituted the core of the legal civilization of Western Zhou Dynasty, and it had exerted a great influence on the later generations with its important theoretical value and practical effect.

2.1 Setting Up the Administrative Management System Protected by Dukes and Princes and Dominated by Royal Families

In the Western Zhou Dynasty, the despotic political system of slave owning class of aristocracy headed by the king was established by imitating of the old system of Xia and Shang dynasties. The important affairs of the state were presided over by the king himself, as was stated in the statement, "'Li' (Rites), "Yue" (music), and orders for expedition were all issued by the king."[1] The title of "Yu Yi Ren" (I alone: a self-proclaimed name by kings in ancient China) which symbolized the absolute monarchic rule of in Shang Dynasty was still the only privilege which the king had in Western Zhou Dynasty, as was illustrated in the inscriptions of *Da Yu Ding* (*Great Yu Tripod*): "Day and night only assist me myself in ruling the world" and the inscriptions of *Mao Gong Ding* (*Duke Mao Tripod*): "Sincerely hope day and night only benefit me myself." It was also recorded in *Shang Shu* (*The Book of Historical Document*) that the rulers of Zhou often called themselves "Yu Yi Ren" (I alone: a self-proclaimed name by kings in ancient China).

To establish the rule of the whole country by the royal family centered by the clan of Zhou, enfeoffment was implemented on a large scale for "Yi Fan Ping Zhou" (protecting Zhou with vassal states) in early Zhou Dynasty. The ruler awarded land and people to the children bearing the same surnames, the in-laws, and those who had rendered outstanding service, which was properly elaborated as "awarding people and land"[2] and "bequeathing land and titles."[3] According to ancient books, King Wu, Duke of Zhou, and King Cheng had set up altogether seventy-one states and almost all the Zhou aristocrats received land as well as the titles of dukes and princes. The administrative system, which was protected by dukes and princes and dominated by the royal families, was established by the policy of enfeoffment. The vassal states regarded the king of Zhou as the master of all states and assumed the due obligations of protecting the royal families, defending the land, paying tribute, and reporting their work to imperial courts. Meanwhile, the governing bodies of the vassal states and the system of "Li" (rites), "Yue" (music), "Xing" (punishment), and "Zheng" (government) were all established according to the model of Luoyi (now Luoyang) and the legal system of Zhou Dynasty.

The record that King Cheng had ordered the important officials of the vassal states to "be dedicated to their work" in "San Shi Ling" (orders for three offices handling governmental affairs) and "Si Fang Ling" (orders for other dukes and princes) in "Jin Wen" (inscriptions on ancient bronze objects) had proved that the government decrees of Zhou Dynasty had been delivered to all vassal states.

---

[1] "Ji Shi" (Ji Kang, the Prime Minister of the State of Lu) in *Lun Yu* (*The Analects*).
[2] Inscriptions on *Da Yu Ding* (*Great Yu Tripod*).
[3] "Yin Gong Ba Nian" (The 8th Year of the Duke of Yin) in *Zuo Zhuan* (*The Chronicle of Zuo*).

All the vassal states, however, were relatively independent in economic, political, and military affairs. The vassals donated part of their land and people to the senior officials as "Cai Yi" (fief), and the senior officials then in turn donated part of theirs to the scholars as "Lu Tian" (the farmland as salary). Thus, there had formed certain rights and obligations between the king and the vassals and between the vassals and their senior officials, which had then constituted the main relationship of class affiliation and overlapping administrative networks. Enfeoffment in early Zhou Dynasty was a most important political measure for the aristocrats of Zhou Dynasty to establish its ruling nationwide. The state structure set up through enfeoffment reflected the formation of a unified country with only one king, which was a great progress compared to Shang Dynasty, which was made up of so many small countries. Fifty-three of the seventy-one states set up in early Zhou through enfeoffment were governed by rulers with the same surnames, so it had reflected the close relationship of enfeoffment and patriarchal clan system. Therefore, the relationship between vassal states and Zhou Dynasty was the relationship of patriarchal in blood ties as well as that of political affiliation; thereby a typical patriarchal country was established under the action of the dual principles of blood ties and politics.

As early as in late Shang Dynasty, the succession to the throne and the patriarchal relationship had begun to be integrated, thus endowing the patriarchal system with an obvious political nature. After Zhou Dynasty was established to meet the political needs of setting up states through enfeoffment, a patriarchal clan system more complete than that of Shang Dynasty was constructed. Thus, it was recorded in detail in "Da Zhuan" (or Shang Shu Da Zhuan) in *Li Ji* (*Book of Rites*):

> If 'Bie Zi' (other sons rather than the eldest) is an ancestor, the offsprings of 'Bie Zi' are 'Zong' (clan), and the offsprings of other brothers of 'Bie Zi" are 'Xiao Zong' (the minor clan). Some 'Zong' (clan) honor the same ancestor for one hundred generations, some change after five generations. Those who honor the same ancestor for one hundred generations are the offsprings of 'Bie Zi' (other sons rather than the eldest) and those offsprings of 'Bie Zi' (other sons rather than the eldest) who have not changed for one hundred generations are 'Zong' and those who have changed after five generations are the offsprings of Gaozu. Therefore, it means showing respect to 'Zong' (clan) to show respect to ancestors, and it is showing respect to one's ancestors to show respect to 'Zong' (clan).

The king of Zhou claimed himself the eldest son of God, so he belonged to "Da Zong" (the senior clan), and the vassals with the same surnames belonged to "Xiao Zong" (the minor clan). Meanwhile, the vassal was "Da Zong" (the senior clan) in his vassal state while the senior officials were "Xiao Zong" (the minor clan). The senior officials, however, were "Xiao Zong" (the minor clan) in his "Cai Yi" (fief). The titles of the king, vassals and senior officials would be inherited by "Di Zhang Zi" (the eldest son born of the legal wife), who were always "Da Zong" (the senior clan) in different classes. "Da Zong" (the senior clan) had the right to rule the clan members and enjoyed the privileges in politics. Therefore, the consistency of ranks in patriarchal clan and politics was an outstanding feature of the political system of Western Zhou Dynasty.

The patriarchal clan system was not only the inheritance law of aristocrats at various levels but also the standard to distinguish the classes of aristocrats. The blood relationship determined the superiority and inferiority of the ranks in politics, which had contributed to the formation of the political caste featured by "the king ruling the dukes, the dukes ruling 'Da Fu' (senior officials in ancient China) and 'Da Fu' (senior officials in ancient China) ruling 'Shi' (scholars)."[4] Moreover, it was also featured by the phenomenon that "'Tian Zi' (the son of Heaven) was in charge of founding the states, the vassals were in charge of setting up homes, the ministers were in charge of establishing siderooms, and the senior officials were served by junior clans and the scholars were served by their followers."[5]

Thus, it can be seen that the patriarchal clan system, under the cloak of blood relationships, had served as an important tool in strengthening the power of the royal families and in ruling the people. The differentiation of classes in patriarchal clan system had enjoyed more certainty and binding force because of the verification and demonstration of "Li" (rites), which had further consolidated the social hierarchy of different ranks of the superior and inferior, the high and the low, the honorable and the humble. In this political system, The king of Zhou was not only the supreme land owner in name who possessed large amounts of territory called "Wang Ji" (the empire) by himself; he was also the supreme military commander of the national army who controlled the most powerful military forces of "Liu Jun" (six units of army directly under the control of the king). In addition, he also had the supreme legislative and judicial power. Thus, the mighty economic and military power held by the king of Zhou had made up the important pillars of kingship.

Below the king was the central administrative system with "Qing Shi Liao" (an ancient government office handling national affairs) and "Tai Shi Liao" (secretariat) as the main framework. The head of "Qing Shi Liao" was called "Qing Shi", which was often held by "Tai Shi" (ancient senior official in charge of state affairs) and "Tai Bao" (ancient senior official in charge of state affairs). He was the king's prime minister who was knowledgeable and skillful at 'Yin Yang' (the two opposing principles in nature, the former feminine and negative, the latter masculine and positive)"[6] and who had rich experience in ruling as a nobility of higher ranks. For example, when King Cheng came into power, he appointed Zhao Gong (Duke of Zhao) as 'Tai Bao' (ancient senior official in charge of state affairs) and Zhou Gong (Duke of Zhou) as 'Tai Shi' (ancient senior official in charge of state affairs)"[7] to assist him in the management. It was also recorded in the bronze inscriptions of the Western Zhou Dynasty that "Tai Bao" (ancient senior official in charge of state affairs) and "Tai Shi" (ancient senior official in charge of state affairs) had even commanded troops in the war. However, the titles of "Tai Bao" (ancient senior official in charge of state affairs) and "Tai Shi" (ancient senior official in charge of

---

[4] "Zhao Gong Qi Nian" (The 7th Year of the Duke of Zhao) in *Zuo Zhuan* (*The Chronicle of Zuo*).
[5] "Huan Gong Er Nian" (The 2nd Year of the Duke of Huan) in *Zuo Zhuan* (*The Chronicle of Zuo*).
[6] "Zhou Guan" (The Official System of Zhou Dynasty) in *Shang Shu* (*The Book of Historical Document*).
[7] "Zhou Ben Ji" (Chronicles of Zhou) in *Shi Ji* (*The Record of the Grand Historian*).

2.1 Setting Up the Administrative Management System Protected by Dukes and Princes...

state affairs) often referred to "certain people rather than fixed positions."[8] Bo Qin, the eldest son of Zhou Gong (Duke of Zhou), was appointed "Qing Shi" (the head of "Qing Shi Liao") of the Zhou Dynasty, while at the same time he was the duke of Lu state. It was recorded in the bronze inscription *Ling Yi* (the bronze ware in earlier Western Zhou Dynasty) that "Zhou Gong's son Ming Bao was in charge of 'San Shi' (three officials in charge of important governmental affairs: 'Tai Shi', 'Tai Fu' and 'Tai Bao') and 'Si Fang' (the affairs of other dukes and princes). Meanwhile, he was appointed as 'Qing Shi' (the head of "Qing Shi Liao")...so he issued 'San Shi Ling' (orders for three offices handling governmental affairs). Besides, he was in charge of 'Qing Shi Liao' (an ancient government office handling national affairs), 'Yin' (official in charge of capital affairs), 'Li Jun' (leader of a neighborhood), 'Bai Gong' (craftsmen), and 'Zhu Hou' (dukes or princes). He issued 'Si Fang Ling' (orders for other dukes and princes) to 'Hou' (marquis), 'Dian' (one of the five degrees of official mourning attire in dynastic China), 'Nan' (the lowest rank of nobility), and 'She' (a unit in ancient army)."

In addition, the administrative officials of "Qing Shi Liao" (an ancient government office handling national affairs) also included "Si Tu" (the minister of civil affairs), "Si Ma" (the minister of military affairs), "Si Kong" (the minister of public works) and "Si Kou" (the minister of justice). "Si Tu" (the minister of civil affairs), also called "Zuo Tu" in "Jin Wen" (inscriptions on ancient bronze objects), was mainly in charge of "Ji Tian" (the ceremonies of plowing held by emperor before spring plowing), as was described in the record that "you are ordered to be in charge of land and field."[9] Moreover, he was also in charge of the matters of agriculture, forestry, and tax. "Si Ma" (the minister of military affairs) was mainly in charge of military and political matters, as well as military tax and orders; "Si Kong" (the minister of public works), also called "Gong" in "Jin Wen" (inscriptions on ancient bronze objects), was mainly in charge of the construction of city walls, ancestral temples and palaces, and the division of labor that was referred to as "Si Bai Gong (craftsmen)."[10] "Si Tu" (the minister of civil affairs), "Si Ma" (the minister of military affairs), and "Si Kong" (the minister of public works) were collectively called "San You Si". "Si Kou" (the minister of justice) was mainly in charge of juridical matters. The establishment of a special judicial organ in the central government proved that jurisdiction had become an important aspect of state activities. The title "Si Kou" (the minister of justice) was once taken by Kang Shu, the younger brother of King Wu in early Zhou Dynasty, which had shown its importance in the government offices. "San Si" (The Three Departments) and "Si Kou" (the minister of justice) were held by influential aristocrats as adjunct positions.

The other administrative system in parallel with "Qing Shi Liao" (an ancient government office handling national affairs) was "Tai Shi Liao" (secretariat) which

---

[8]"Zhou Guan" (The Official System of Zhou Dynasty) in *Shang Shu* (*The Book of Historical Document*).

[9]*XieYin Ming* (*Inscriptions on the Bronze Ware in Western Zhou Dynasty*).

[10]Inscriptions on *Cai Gui* (*The Bronze Ware in Earlier Xi Zhou Dynasty*).

consisted of "Tai Shi" (ancient senior official in charge of state affairs), "Tai Zhu" (ancient official in charge of sacrifice), "Tai Bu" (ancient official in charge of divination), "Tai Zai" (ancient official in charge of royal affairs), and "Tai Zong" (ancient official in charge of ancestral temple sacrifice). "Tai Shi" (ancient senior official in charge of state affairs) was known as "Liu Tai" (six senior officials). "Tai Shi Liao" (secretariat) referred to the assistant officials around "Tian Zi" (the son of Heaven), among whom "Tai Zai" (ancient official in charge of royal affairs) was the head, and he was responsible for the management of slaves and finance of the royal family. Moreover, "Tai Zai" (ancient official in charge of royal affairs) could issue orders on behalf of the king of the Zhou Dynasty, serving as the confidant and right-hand assistant of the king of Zhou Dynasty, who was often taken by "Tai Shi" (ancient senior official in charge of state affairs) and "Shi Bao" (ancient official in charge of the affairs of teaching kings and the children in royal families) as adjunct positions. Both Zhou Gong (Duke of Zhou) and Zhao Gong (Duke of Zhao) had once held the position of "Tai Zai" (ancient official in charge of royal affairs). "Tai Shi" (ancient senior official in charge of state affairs), an important position in the Zhou Dynasty, was charge of drafting writs, recording historical events, keeping state books and arranging astronomy, calendar, worship, and other things; "Tai Zong" (ancient official in charge of ancestral temple sacrifice), also called "Zong Bo" was the predecessor of "Zong Zheng" (official in charge of the royal affairs) in Western Han Dynasty and was in charge of the sacrificial etiquette of ancestral temple; "Tai Zhu" was in charge of sacrifice and the etiquette of "She" (the god of land), "Ji" (the god of grain); "Tai Bu" was in charge of divination and pray; "Tai Shi" (ancient official in charge of the affairs of god worshipping and judicial affairs) was in charge of judicial system. Among the officials of "Liu Tai" (six senior officials), although "Tai Zhu" (ancient official in charge of sacrifice), "Tai Bu" (ancient official in charge of divination), "Tai Zong" (ancient official in charge of ancestral temple sacrifice) still had religious functions, their authority as well as their roles in the state affairs were undermined in comparison with the historiographer in Shang Dynasty.

In addition to "Liu Tai" (six senior officials), other positions were set up including "Zuo Ce", which was responsible for title-conferring affairs, "Nei Shi" which was responsible for passing and reading the orders from the king, "Hu Chen" which was responsible for the safety of the palace, "Shan Fu" which was responsible for the diet of the king, "Qu Ma" which was responsible for the management of the king's horses. The other officials included "Xiao Yin" (petty officials), "Zhui Yi" (official in charge of emperor's clothes), "Zuo You Xie Pu" (emperor's attendants), "Bai Si" (all ranks of officials) and "Shu Fu" (government departments), etc. The officials who held these posts all served the king of Zhou by participating in and handling the state affairs at different degrees. For example, "Tai Zai" (ancient official in charge of royal affairs) was an important administrative official as well as the leader of imperial organs. Because he had a close relation to and was trusted by the king of Zhou, his position was more eminent than that of all the others.

In Zhou Dynasty, the preliminary local administrative management system was also formed. According to ancient books such as *Zhou Li (The Rites of Zhou*

2.1 Setting Up the Administrative Management System Protected by Dukes and Princes...   51

Dynasty) and *Shang Shu* (*The Book of Historical Document*), the land within about thirty miles of the capital was called "Jiao" with "Xiang" (townships) set up inside the capital and "Sui" (local organization outskirts) set up outside. "Xiang Da Fu" (village official), as the leader of "Xiang" (townships), was in charge of the political and religious matters of "Xiang"[11] and "Sui Da Fu" (local magistrate in outskirts), as the leader of "Sui" (local organization outskirts), was in charge of the political and religious matters of "Sui".[12] There were six "Xiang" (townships) and "Sui" (local organization outskirts) respectively within the "Wang Ji" (the empire) of the kingdom.

"Yi" (cities) was set up often on a small scale as the primary-level organization beneath "Xiang" (townships) and "Sui" (local organization outskirts). For example, "'Yi' (cities) consisting of ten households was set up." In addition, "Yi" (cities) was governed by "Li Xu" (public errand for the management of village affairs) and "Lin Zhang" (leader of a neighborhood).

Owing to the separate management of slaves and civilians, administrative regions were divided between "Guo", "Ye", "Du", and "Bi". Aristocrats, civilians, and the slaves directly serving the aristocrats lived in "Guo" or "Du", namely, "Da Yi" (big cities), but most slaves lived in "Bi" and "Ye" (remote places), as was recorded in the saying that "Jun Zi (gentlemen) lived in 'Guo' and slaves in 'Ye'", so "there are different customs and habits between 'Du' and 'Bi' as those between the superior and the inferior."[13] The slaves were arranged according to the division of labor to live in different places like "the village of industry and commerce" and "the village of common people" where full-time officials were appointed to have them administered, but mixed residence and free migration were prohibited.

To sum up, with the establishment of the position of joint master by the king of Zhou, the central government headed by the king of Zhou handled the national activities effectively. Along with this, the imperial court, which had provided services to the king of Zhou, gradually became systematic and was put the charge of the administrative power to some degree. The establishment of the patriarchal system strengthened the ties between the government power, clan power and the monarchal power, so the king of Zhou had not only controlled the state organs, but also the clan organizations for the sake of political rule under the pretense of religion. Therefore, the country seemed to be an amplification of the family of "Ji" (the royal families) and the principle of the clans, which had guided the important state activities, had become in fact a basic principle of administration. Accordingly, the government office in charge of religious affairs had lost the control of the state affairs with the weakening of theocracy. To adjust the rights and obligations of Zhou

---

[11] "Xiang Dai Fu" (Village Officials) in "Di Guan Si Tu" (The Official of Internal Affairs) in *Zhou Li* (*The Rites of Zhou Dynasty*).

[12] "Sui Dai Fu" (Local Magistrate Outskirts) in "Di Guan Si Tu" (The Official of Internal Affairs) in *Zhou Li* (*The Rites of Zhou Dynasty*).

[13] "Xiang Gong Shi San Nian" (The 13th Year of the Duke of Xiang) in *Zuo Zhuan* (*The Chronicle of Zuo*).

Dynasty and the vassal states, "Li" (rites) and "Fa" (law) began to perform the function of the administrative measures, which had finally led to the establishment of a great slavery country centered on by many other states.

2.2 Implementing the Comprehensive Strategy of Ruling by "Li" (Rites), "Yue" (Music), "Zheng" (Government) and "Xing" (Punishment)

Over 1000 years had passed from the founding of Xia Dynasty to that of Zhou Dynasty, so rich experience of governing the country had been accumulated. Faced with extremely fierce, complicated, and dangerous situation after the extermination of Shang Dynasty, to consolidate the political power of Zhou Dynasty, Duke of Zhou (named Dan), the great politician and thinker, took a series of important measures to put down revolts and to set up the various systems. It was written in historical books that "he suppressed the rebellion in the first year, conquered Yin (the capital of Shang Dynasty) in the second year, crushed Yan (a city in today's Henan province) in the third year, established "Hou Wei" (five regions around the capital varying from Hou to Wei) in the fourth year, built Chengzhou (the city of Luoyang) in the fifth year, made "Li" (rites) and "Yue" (music) in the sixth year and handed the power of administration over to Cheng Wang (the second monarch of Western Zhou Dynasty) in the seventh year."[14] So Duke of Zhou's measures of making "Li" (rites) and "Yue" (music), establishing administration and instituting penalty were closely interwoven, which was a great pioneering work in setting up the overall superstructure and which had set a precedent for ruling the country comprehensively by using all kinds of methods. The so-called making "Li" (rites) meant to tease out the popular standard of "Li" (rites) (including institutional and ceremonious ones) according to the principles of "Zun Zun" (showing respect to nobility represented by the emperor) and "Qin Qin" (showing respect to relatives represented by parents) to make it systematic and institutionalized. Thus, its core was to establish a hierarchical etiquette and a code system of "king subjecting ministers, ministers subjecting 'Da Fu' (senior officials in ancient China), and 'Da Fu' subjecting 'Shi' (member of the senior ministerial class)" among the aristocrats.[15] The rule that "'Li' (rites) is not applied to the common people" had manifested its privileged nature. Through making the rules of "Li" (rites), a pyramidal hierarchical structure was established with the king of Zhou at the core, by which the country was smoothly operated and the ruling was effectively consolidated. Therefore, "Li" (Rites) was regarded as the most important among the four measures of governing the country.

Besides the codes of conduct, the rights and obligations of the aristocrats and the aspects like politics, economy, military affairs, administration, law, society, religion,

---

[14] "Da Zhuan" (Shang Shu Da Zhuan) in *Shang Shu* (*The Book of Historical Document*).
[15] "Zhao Gong Qi Nian" (The 7th Year of the Duke of Zhao) in *Zuo Zhuan* (*The Chronicle of Zuo*).

2.2 Implementing the Comprehensive Strategy of Ruling by "Li" (Rites), "Yue"...

education, ethics and custom were also regulated by "Li" (rites), ranging from "the hierarchical order of king and courts to the differentiation of vehicles, clothing, housing, food, wedding and funeral among ordinary people."[16] With "Li" (rites), order and hierarchy came into being with the differentiation of the king and the officials, the respectable and the humble, the noble and the lowly, the old and the young. Therefore, "Li" (rites) was regarded as the basic means of stabilizing the country. Confucius had once said, "nothing is better than 'Li' (rites) to reassure the monarchs and to rule the public."[17] In the Spring and Autumn Period, "Li" (rites) made by Duke of Zhou was still used by the state of Lu. When recollecting the merits and virtues of Duke of Zhou, Ji Wenzi said:

> "Li" (rites) was made by the reverend Duke of Zhou in Zhou Dynasty, and he said that 'regulations are drafted to have an examination of 'De' (virtue), by which the daily affairs are coped with, which in turn are used to have an assessment of one's achievements, according to which rewards are given to the people.' So (Duke of Zhou) had made an oath and said that 'those who break the regulations have committed the crime of 'Zei'; those who hide the thieves have committed the crime of 'Cang' (covering up a criminal); those who take bribery have committed the crime of 'Dao' (theft) and those who steal the equipment have committed the crime of 'Jian' (betrayal). These felonies must be severely punished and never pardoned.' These are recorded in *Jiu Xing* (*The Code Nine Penalties*) and will never be forgotten.[18]

"Yue" (music) was one of the six classics, and the establishment of "Li" (rites) was closely related to the composing of "Yue" (music), which had reflected that "Yue" (music) not only provided service to "Li" (rites), but also functioned to carry out "Li" (rites). Because the content of "Li" (rites) was the etiquette and code system within the aristocratic group, there was not only "Yue" (music) for the king and the imperial court, but also that for nobles, dukes, and ministers respectively in accordance with their status. *Da Ya* (*Major Court Hymns*) was a kind of ancient music; *Xiao Ya* (*Minor Court Hymns*) was a kind of new music, *Song* (*Eulogies*) was a kind of song for the royal temple, *Ya* (*Grace*) was a kind of court music and *Guo Feng* (*Custom of the State*) was a kind of folk music. Through music, prevailing habits and customs were transformed to enhance the centripetal forces and the affinity of the conquered states and tribes. Confucius said, "nothing is better than music in transforming the prevailing habits and customs."[19] Besides, it could also help people to cultivate and purify their inner world, "to seek a common ground" toward the virtuous realm to compose "Yue" (music) to lead the society to peace and the country to stability. Confucius expressed his respect to Duke of Zhou by his dreaming of him, so he once said: "After listening to 'Shao' (ancient Chinese

---

[16]"Li Shu" (On Rites) in *Shi Ji* (*The Record of the Grand Historian*).

[17]"Guang Yao Dao" (Popularizing Filial Piety) in *Xiao Jing* (*The Classic of Filial Piety*).

[18]"Wen Gong Shi Ba Nian" (The 18th Year of the Duke of Wen) in *Zuo Zhuan* (*The Chronicle of Zuo*).

[19]"Guang Yao Dao" (Popularizing Filial Piety) in *Xiao Jing* (*The Classic of Filial Piety*).

music) in the State of Qi, I do not know the taste of meat for three months,"[20] which had fully shown the charisma of "Yue" (music).

In addition, "Yue" (music) also reflected the trend of the times and the rise and fall of different dynasties, so there was "Yue" (music) for peaceful and prosperous times, "Yue" (music) for troubled times and "Yue" (music) for the conquered nations. "'Yue' (music) for the peaceful and prosperous times is full of peace and joy, which indicates that the state is harmonious; 'Yue' (music) for the troubled times is full of bitterness and anger, which indicates that the ruling is against the will of the people; 'Yue' (music) for a conquered nation is full of sorrow and sadness, which indicates the frustration of the people. Thus, the way of 'Yue' (music) is related to that of the administration."[21] Consequently, the relationship of "Li" (rites) and "Yue" (music) can be summarized as the following:

> "Li" (rites) was used to distinguish the difference, namely, to distinguish the classes of the noble and the humble; "Yue" (music) was used to seek the things in common, namely, to ease the conflicts between the upper and the lower classes, as was said in the saying that "'Yue' (music) was to seek the things in common, while 'Li' (rites) was to distinguish the difference. So people are attached to each other because of the things in common and people are respectful to each other because of their distinction."[22] With the combination of "Yue" (music) and "Li" (rites), the ideal state could be achieved in which "the mobs would abide by the law, the dukes would acknowledge allegiance, the civilians have no worries, and the emperor is pleased, so there are no needs to set up armies and to implement 'Five Penalties'."[23] Therefore, Confucius proposed, "making a country prosperous by *Shi Jing* (*The Book of Songs*), making a country strong by "Li" (rites), and making a country successful by 'Yue' (music)."[24]

Zhou Gong's achievement in making "Li" (rites) and composing "Yue" (music) was highly praised in historical books, and it was regarded as great classic legal code by the Western Zhou Dynasty in establishing its state system and operational mechanism, and which had exerted a great influence on the later generations.

Although "Li" (rites) and "Yue" (music) had contributed to the ruling of the country by establishing the systems, setting up standards and evoking people's inner benevolent sentiments, it could not function well without the protection of the autocratic regime and the compulsory laws. Therefore, Zhou Gong (Duke of Zhou) also paid great attention to the establishment of the regime and the making of the law, which was also reflected in Ji Wenzi's recollections aforesaid.

"Zheng" (government) mainly referred to the establishment of the official positions, the division of duties, and the setting up of regime institutions. In "Li Zheng" (Establishment of Proper Governance of a State) in *Shang Shu* (*The Book of Historical Document*), there is the following record:

---

[20]"Shu Er" (Narration) in *Lun Yu* (*The Analects*).
[21]"Yue Ji" (The Record of Music) in *Li Ji* (*The Book of Rites*).
[22]"Yue Ji" (The Record of Music) in *Li Ji* (*The Book of Rites*).
[23]"Yue Ji" (The Record of Music) in *Li Ji* (*The Book of Rites*).
[24]"Tai Bo" (one virtuous ancestor of the kings of Zhou Dynasty) in *Lun Yu* (*The Analects*).

2.2 Implementing the Comprehensive Strategy of Ruling by "Li" (Rites), "Yue"...

As far as 'Li Zheng' (Establishment of Proper Governance of a State) was concerned, three officials were appointed (by King Wen and King Wu), including 'Ren Ren' (official dealing with affairs), 'Zhun Fu' (official dealing with the law) and 'Mu' (official dealing with the people) to handle the administrative, judicial and governmental affairs respectively. Besides, other officials were also appointed, including 'Hu Ben' (the guards of the king), 'Zhui Yi' (official in charge of emperor's clothes), 'Qu Ma Xiao Yin' (official in charge of horses), 'Zuo You Xie Pu' (low-level officials close to the king), 'Bai Si Shu Fu' (various officials serving the king), 'Da Du Xiao Bo' (local officials responsible for the areas surrounding the capital), 'Yi Ren' (official close to the king), 'Biao Chen Bai Si' (official in the vassal states and various officials), 'Tai Shi' (ancient senior official in charge of state affairs), 'Yin Bo' (head official of each office) and 'Shu Chang Ji Shi' (those selected from "Jin Shi" to be courtiers of emperor). The positions of 'Si Tu' (the minister of civil affairs), 'Si Ma' (the minister of military affairs), 'Si Kong' (the minister of public works), and 'Ya Lv' (official lower than the ministers) were set up. 'Yi' (ethnic group in the east), 'Wei' (ethnic group in the south), and 'Lu' (ethnic group in the west) each have their own monarchs. The officials were also appointed for the old capitals of the Xia and Shang dynasties.

It can be seen that in the Western Zhou Dynasty state institutions such as chamber courtiers, political officials and the officials dealing with the affairs of vassal states and border areas were all established with the king of Zhou as the supreme leader. Dominated by the patriarchal system, the government organization principle of "the unity of relatives and nobles" was still followed in Western Zhou Dynasty. Moreover, the offsprings of nobles and ministers had the privilege of being appointed as officials for generations, which was called "the hereditary-official system".

Through the enfeoffment system implemented in early Zhou Dynasty, a state structure centered on Zhou Dynasty and was protected by all vassal states was formed, under which the vassal states undertook mutual legal rights and obligations.

"Xing" (punishment) was a general term for law and it did not just refer to penalty. Legislation was carried out under the guidance of "Ming De Shen Fa" (promoting virtue and being prudent in the enforcement of punishment). As was recorded by Ji Wenzi of Lu state, "'those who break the regulations have committed the crime of 'Zei'; those who hide the thieves have committed the crime of 'Cang' (covering up a criminal); those who take bribery have committed the crime of 'Dao' (theft) and those who steal the equipment have committed the crime of 'Jian' (betrayal). These felonies must be severely punished and never pardoned.' These are recorded in *Jiu Xing* (*The Code Nine Penalties*) and will never be forgotten."[25] The so-called "Jiu Xing" (Nine Penalties) was recorded in "Zhao Gong Liu Nian" (The 6th Year of the Duke of Zhao) in *Zuo Zhuan* (*The Chronicle of Zuo*): "there were chaotic political situations, so 'Jiu Xing' (Nine Penalties) was made." In the Period of "San Guo" (Three Kingdoms), a native of Wu named Wei Zhao said when annotating *Zuo Zhuan* (*The Chronicle of Zuo*): "'Jiu Xing' (Nine Penalties) referred to the five formal penalties (Mo, Yi, Fei, Gong, Da Bi) and 'Liu' (exile), 'Shu' (ransom), 'Bian' (whipping), 'Pu' (corporal punishment including 'Chi', 'Bian' and

---

[25] "Wen Gong Shi Ba Nian" (The 18th Year of the Duke of Wen) in *Zuo Zhuan* (*The Chronicle of Zuo*).

'Zhang')." "Jiu Xing" (Nine Penalties) referred to both the nine types of penalties and the nine articles of penalties.

To implement the policy of "Ming De Shen Fa" (promoting virtue and being prudent in the enforcement of punishment), the legislative principle of executing penalties in accordance with different circumstances was developed, and a series of guidelines for prudent punishment such as enforcing punishment according to reality and enforcing punishment according to different situations were established, which had surely exerted a far-reaching influence.

All this has proved that "Li" (rites), "Yue" (music), "Zheng" (government), and "Xing" (punishment) are not only an interconnected unity in a dynamic condition, but also a complete system of superstructure, which has symbolized the progress of the institutional construction of the nation.

After the overthrowing of Shang Dynasty and establishment of the state, it had become an urgent need for Zhou Dynasty to build a hierarchical order to differentiate the noble and the humble, the old and the young, the superior and the inferior to stabilize the social basis of ruling and to consolidate the unified state. It was under this historical background that it was possible for Zhou Gong to make "Li" (rites) successful. Therefore, "Li" (rites) was not only ranked above "Yue" (music), "Zheng" (government), and "Xing" (punishment); it also ran through their activities and determined the direction of their operation.

When people of later generations made comments on Zhou Gong's making of "Li" (rites), they had also revealed the relationship between "Li" (rites), "Yue" (music), "Zheng" (government), and "Xing" (punishment).

The relation of "Li" (rites) to "Yue" (music) was summarized as the following: "'Yue' (music) expresses the invariable emotion, while 'Li' (rites) expresses the invariable reason; 'Yue' (music) seeks the common ground, while 'Li' (rites) focuses on distinguishing the difference; so the theory of 'Li' (rites) and 'Yue' (music) are about 'Ren Qing' (human feeling)." According to the annotation of Kong Yingda, "'Yue' (music) is created for harmony and affinity, hence it has made the people far and near united together; 'Li' (rites) is created for respection and courtesy, hence it has brought about the hierarchy between the noble and the humble."[26] According to the annotation of Gao You, "'Li' (rites) is made to govern the state, to stabilize the country and to benefit the people, while 'Yue' (music) is made to transform the outmoded habits and customs, to remove human evil and to preserve the integrity of man."[27] "'Yue' (music) is made for the things in common, while 'Li' (rites) is made for distinction. People are attached to each other because of the things in common and people are respectful to each other because of the distinction." "So 'Yue' (music) comes from inside, while 'Li' (rites) is made from outside."[28] It can be seen that "Li" (rites) is made to regulate from without, while

---

[26]"Yue Ji" (The Record of Music) in *Li Ji* (*The Book of Rites*).
[27]"Yue Ji" (The Record of Music) in *Li Ji* (*The Book of Rites*).
[28]"Yue Ji" (The Record of Music) in *Li Ji* (*The Book of Rites*).

"Yue" (music) is made to harmonize from within, so they coordinates with each other to achieve a kind of moderation and love.

The relationship between "Li" (rites) and "Zheng" (government) can be summarized as the following: not only policies should be made in accordance with "Li" (rites), the country should also be ruled in the same way, so "Li" (rites) should be taken as the major law and principle of the country. Guo, who was "Nei Shi" (official in charge of passing and reading the orders from the king) in Zhou Dynasty said: "'Li' (rites) is the backbone of the country, while 'Jing' (being reverent) is the carrier of 'Li' (rites). Without 'Jing' (being reverent), 'Li' (rites) could not be implemented; if 'Li' (rites) is not implemented, the whole country would be corrupted, so how could it last for generations?"[29] Confucius said: "People should learn 'Li' (rites) before administrating political affairs, because 'Li' (rites) is the basis of politics!"[30] Therefore, only by following "Li" (rites) could the politics of the country be on the right track; without "Li" (rites), the politics of the country is bound to be chaotic. Jia Yi in the Han Dynasty said, "Without 'Li' (rites), moral, virtue, humanity and righteousness cannot be realized; without 'Li' (rites), the teaching of right and wrong is not complete; without 'Li' (rites), disputes and argument cannot be settled; without 'Li' (rites), the relationship between the monarch and his subordinates and that between father and son cannot be ascertained; without 'Li' (rites), the learning of statecraft cannot be conducted with intimacy; without 'Li' (rites), there is no authority in ranking officials, handling affairs and practicing law, and without 'Li' (rites), one cannot be pious and solemn in praying and making sacrifices to God and ghosts."[31] It was more explicitly stated in "Jing Jie" (Explanations of the Classics) in *Li Ji* (*The Book of Rites*): "the relationship between 'Li' (rites) and 'Zheng' (government) is like that between scale and weight, between carpenter's line marker and straightness, between compass and circle, between carpenter's square and rectangle. Therefore, with scale, one can't be dishonest with weight; with carpenter's line marker, one can't be dishonest with crookedness and straightness; with compass and carpenter's square, one can't be dishonest with circle and rectangle, so a gentleman who has a good knowledge of 'Li' (rites) may keep away from treacherousness. Those who show respect to and abide by 'Li' (rites) are called gentlemen with virtue; while those who fail to do so are called ill-mannered people." As can be seen, "Li" (rites) had provided a spiritual support for a country to avoid losing the support of its people, for a monarch to avoid losing the support of his officials, for the noble to avoid becoming lowly, and for the respectable to avoid becoming humble.

The relationship between "Li" (rites) and "Xing" (punishment) can be summarized as the following: the brutal ruling of misusing the cruel penalties by King Zhou in the late Shang Dynasty had resulted in the perishing of the country, which had served as a lesson for Zhou Gong (Duke of Zhou), so he carried out the policy of "Ming De Shen Fa" (promoting virtue and being prudent in the enforcement of

---

[29]"Xi Gong Shi Yi Nian" (The 11th Year of Xi Gong) in *Zuo Zhuan* (*The Chronicle of Zuo*).

[30]"Ai Gong Wen" (The Questions of Duke Ai) in *Li Ji* (*The Book of Rites*).

[31]Jia Yi (Han Dynasty), "Li" (Rites) in *Xin Shu* (*New Writings*).

punishment) and "Jing Tian Bao Ming" (respecting Heaven and protecting the people) instead. The rulers of early Zhou Dynasty had integrated the education of "Li" (rites) with the suppression of "Xing" (punishment) skillfully and explicitly put forward and put into practice the criminal policy that "'Li' (rites) prevents what has not been committed, and the law punishes what has been committed."[32] That is to say, "Li" (rites) was the positive and preventive measure to stop crimes before it was committed, while "Xing" (punishment) was the negative punishment after the crime was committed; "Li Jiao" (feudal ethical code) was "Ben" (the essence), while "Xing" (punishment) was "Yong" (application) and they were complementary with each other. "Where 'Li' (rites) lacks, 'Xing' (punishment) is carried out; where there is no 'Li' (rites), 'Xing' (punishment) is applied instead; so they are the inside and outside of one thing."[33] Confucius also thought that "Li" (rites), "Yue" (music), and "Xing" (punishment) were closely related so according to him, "if 'Li' (rites) and 'Yue' (music) are not promoted, 'Xing' (punishment) would be inappropriately enforced, if so, people would be at a loss for what to do."[34] If the people were confused about what was right and what was wrong, it may lead to the disorder and upheaval of the society. In the Warring States Period, Xun Zi, who had always advocated the principle of "Li" (rites) and stressed the importance of "Fa" (law) had made comments on the relationship between "Li" (rites) and "Fa" (law): "'Li' (rites) is not only the basis of 'Fa' (law), it is also the general guideline of all things."[35]

On the relationship between "Li" (rites), "Yue" (music), "Zheng" (government), and "Xing" (punishment), there are the following arguments in "Yue Ji" (The Record of Music) in *Shi Ji* (*The Records of the Grand Historian*):

- "Li" (rites) is to guide the mind, "Yue" (music) to harmonize the voice, "Zheng" (government) to regulate the behavior and "Xing" (punishment) to prevent evilness. The purpose of "Li" (Rites), "Yue" (music), "Xing" (punishment), and "Zheng" (government) are the same; so they are the instruments to unite people's mind and to get the suitable ways of administration.
- "Li" (rites) is to regulate people's mind, "Yue" (music) is to harmonize their voices, "Zheng" (government) is to supervise the administration, and "Xing" (punishment) is to provide the preventive measures. Thus, if the four are in harmony, the kingcraft is complete.
- "Yue" (music) is made for the things in common, while 'Li' (rites) is made for distinction. People are attached to each other because of the things in common and people are respectful to each other because of the distinction. Therefore, overemphasis on "Yue" (music) will lead to inappropriateness; while

---

[32]"Li Cha Pian" (On Rites) in *Da Dai Li Ji* (*The Rites of Da Dai*). Also see "Jia Yi Zhuan" (The Biography of Jia Yi) in *Han Shu* (*The History of Han Dynasty*).

[33]"Chen Chong Zhuan" (The Biography of Chen Chong) in *Latter Han Shu* (*The History of Latter Han Dynasty*).

[34]"Zi Lu" (Zi Lu, one of Confucius' disciples) in *Lun Yu* (*The Analects*).

[35]"Quan Xue" (On Study) in *Xun Zi* (*Xun Zi*).

overemphasis on "Li" (rites) would lead to estrangement; it is the goal of "Li" (rites) and "Yue" (music) to make people love each other wholeheartedly and to respect each other politely.
- If "Li" (rites) is established, the noble and the humble would be differentiated; if "Yue" (music) is harmonious, the superior and the inferior would live in peace; if the good and the evil are clearly defined, the worthy and the unworthy are differentiated; if violence is prevented by penalty and the worthy are awarded with official titles, there would be justice. Love the people with benevolence and punish them with justice, then they are obedient.

The accounts about the comprehensive ruling of the country by "Li" (rites), "Yue" (music), "Zheng" (government) and "Xing" (punishment) resulted from Zhou Gong's making "Li" (rites) and "Yue" (music) is not only a successful summary of the experience of governance, but also a great contribution to the ancient jurisprudence, which has constituted an important part of Chinese legal civilization. The history of Eastern and Western Zhou and Qin and Han dynasties had proved that the integration of these four measures would bring about the prosperity of the nation and the development of the society, as was shown in "Cheng Kang Zhi Zhi" (the excellent administration of Emperor Cheng Kang) and "Wen Jing Zhi Zhi" (the excellent administration of Emperors Wen and Jing). Thus, "Zhou Song" (Praise of Zhou) in *Shi Jing* (*The Book of Songs*) can be regarded as a reliable resource to sing the praise of this achievement. On the contrary, the violation of "Li" (rites), the deterioration of "Yue" (music), the mispractice of "Zheng" (government), and the injustice of "Xing" (punishment) might lead to the turmoil of the society and the extinguishing of ancient dynasties. Therefore, generations of rulers after Zhou Dynasty had paid much attention to drawing the lessons from history, so they had taken comprehensive measures to govern the country.

2.3 Establishing the Guiding Principle of "Jing Tian Bao Ming" (Respecting Heaven and Protecting the People) and "Ming De Shen Fa" (Promoting Virtue and Being Prudent in the Enforcement of Punishment)

The rulers of Zhou Dynasty learned that it was "the misuse of severe punishment" in the late Shang Dynasty that had led to its extinction; they also learned many lessons from the experience of the suppression of the rebellion of "San Jian" (three important officials appointed by the king of Zhou Dynasty to be guardians of the son of King Zhou, the last king of Shang Dynasty), for example, "it is difficult to get the support of the common people," "it often helps the sincere people no matter how awful the Heaven is," and "the monarch should not regard water but the people as the mirror."[36] They had connected "Tian" (Heaven) with the people, so they concluded that "the rulers must listen to the people and meet their needs,"[37] so the foothold of running the country was shifted to getting the support of the people. Consequently, the status of the people was raised, while the authority of "Tian" (Heaven) became declined; the value of morality was emphasized, while the role of religion was depreciated. To consolidate the rule of Zhou Dynasty, Zhou Gong (Duke of Zhou) said in "Kang Gao" (The Orders of Duke Zhou to Kang Shu) in *Shang Shu* (*The Book of Historical Document*) that, "it is your distinguished father, King Wen, who is able to carry out the policy of 'Ming De Shen Fa' (promoting virtue and being prudent in the enforcement of punishment)." "Ming De" (promoting virtue) meant advocating and respecting virtue, and valuing the people. The overthrowing of Shang Dynasty by Zhou was naturally the result of "matching 'De' (virtue) with 'Tian' (Heaven)" by the rulers of Zhou Dynasty. "Shen Fa" (to inflict penalty with prudence) referred to being prudent with punishment without "imposing punishment upon the innocent" to avoid "the general complaint because it may be directed against the ruler personally."[38] "Ming De" (promoting virtue) was the spiritual core of "Shen Fa" (to inflict penalty with prudence), whereas the latter was the embodiment of the former in the field of law. It was recorded in "Li Zheng" (Establishment of Proper Governance of a State) in *Shang Shu* (*The Book of Historical Document*) that Zhou Gong (Duke of Zhou) praised the Duke of Su, who was "Si Kou" (the minister of justice) at the time, because he had set a good example of enforcing appropriate punishment: "Duke of Su, 'Si Kou' (the minister of justice), has dealt with all the criminal matters that he is in charge of reverently, who thereby has perpetuated the fortunes of our kingdom. He is extremely prudent and is one of those who enforce punishment appropriately." The change from advocating the punishment of "Tian" (Heaven) to "Ming De Shen Fa" (promoting virtue and being prudent in the enforcement of punishment) had reflected the influence which the changes of historical circumstances had on the rulers' legislative thinking and the progress of legal civilization, by which a series of legal principles about "Shen Xing" (prudent punishment) and "Xu Xing" (penalty reduction) were formed at that time. However, the rulers of Zhou Dynasty had not and would never give up the idea of "Tian Fa" (Heavenly punishment) completely. On the contrary, they continued to advocate it on many occasions. For example, Zhou Gong (Duke of Zhou) consoled the survivors of Shang Dynasty in the name of "making evident the punishment of 'Tian' (Heaven)."[39] In "Duo Fang" (In Many Ways) in *Shang Shu* (*The Book of Historical Document*), it was depicted in detail that Dan, Zhou Gong (Duke of Zhou), had warned the people of Shang and the people of the country under the guise of the will of "Tian" (Heaven):

[36]"Kang Gao" (The Orders of Duke Zhou to Kang Shu) in *Shang Shu* (*The Book of Historical Document*).
[37]"Tai Shi" (The Great Declaration) in *Shang Shu* (*The Book of Historical Document*).
[38]"Wu Yi" (No Enjoying Ease and Comfort) in *Shang Shu* (*The Book of Historical Document*).
[39]"Duo Shi" (The Ministers) in *Shang Shu* (*The Book of Historical Document*).

2.3 Establishing the Guiding Principle of "Jing Tian Bao Ming" (Respecting Heaven... 61

You now still dwell in your houses, and cultivate your fields; why don't you obey our kings and follow the decree of 'Tian' (Heaven)? You are disobedient, you have no love in your heart, you refuse so determinedly to obey the ordinance of 'Tian' (Heaven), you rejected the decree contemptuously and pursued unlawful courses... So I have imprisoned the chief criminals of war— I have done so twice and then three times. But if you do not cherish the leniency with which I have spared your lives, I will proceed to apply severe punishments, and put you to death.

"Ming De Shen Fa" (promoting virtue and being prudent in the enforcement of punishment) does not mean undermining punishments. Instead, it means to enforce punishment with more efficiency and accuracy to avoid conflicts caused by the abuse of penalty. When admonishing Kang Shu of Wei, Zhou Gong (Duke of Zhou) expressed himself explicitly: "I proclaim to you about the use of virtue in enforcing punishment."[40] So on the one hand, the rulers of Zhou Dynasty implemented laws with the guidance of virtue to reduce resistance and to make more achievement; on the other hand, they strengthened virtue through punishment. By "prudent and justified punishment," they could not only "eliminate punishment" but also enhance the authority of virtue. In "Lv Xing" (The Penal Code of Lv) in *Shang Shu* (*The Book of Historical Document*), it was recorded that "'Wu Xing' (Five Penalties) should be respected to fully exhibit 'San De' (three virtues)." "San De" (three virtues) referred to what were termed as "perseverance, flexibility, and integrity" in "Hong Fan" (Models) in *Shang Shu* (*The Book of Historical Document*), which had demonstrated that the rulers of Western Zhou Dynasty had endeavored to make virtue and punishment mutually complementary and interoperable.

As "Yi De Pei Tian" [matching 'De' (virtue) with 'Tian' (Heaven)] was advocated by the rulers of Zhou Dynasty, "Ming De" (promoting virtue) meant respecting "Tian" (Heaven), so the principle of "Yi De Shi Xing" (enforcing the laws with virtue) was in fact another form of enforcing punishments on behalf of "Tian" (Heaven). Under the guidance of the legislative principle of "Ming De Shen Fa" (promoting virtue and being prudent in the enforcement of punishment), in Zhou Dynasty, it was the key of the enforcement of the criminal law to punish the felonies like "robbery, theft, villainy and treachery, to punish the murderers, robbers" and to punish those "unfilial and unfriendly". The law-executors were demanded to "show respect to the statutes," which implied that they were forbidden to make judgments arbitrarily by "using intimidation, coercion and torture" according to their own preference. Instead, they should "meditate for five or six days, even up to ten days"[41] before making judgment, which indeed had eased the serious situation faced in the early Zhou Dynasty, and to some extent, prevented the slave-owning aristocracy from misusing punishments.

No doubt, "Ming De Shen Fa" (promoting virtue and being prudent in the enforcement of punishment) best reflected the characteristics of the times in

---

[40]"Kang Gao" (The Orders of Duke Zhou to Kang Shu) in *Shang Shu* (*The Book of Historical Document*).

[41]"Kang Gao" (The Orders of Duke Zhou to Kang Shu) in *Shang Shu* (*The Book of Historical Document*).

legislative civilization of the Zhou Dynasty and the outstanding statesmanship of the rulers in early Zhou Dynasty. It not only had much greater political appeal, but also more extensive social permeability to replace "Tian Fa" (Heavenly punishment) with "Ming De Shen Fa" (promoting virtue and being prudent in the enforcement of punishment). Therefore, the legalization of "Ming De Shen Fa" (promoting virtue and being prudent in the enforcement of punishment) had brought about both good legal order and "the Reign of Cheng Kang" (a period of stability and prosperity) in early Zhou Dynasty. It was recorded in "Zhou Ben Ji" (Chronicles of Chou) in *Shi Ji* (*The Records of the Grand Historian*) that "during the Reign of Chengkang, the world was in peace, so no punishment was enforced for forty years." The relatively stable situation constituted the necessary condition for the development of production and the progress of the society. Thus, this legislative ideology was applied until *Lv Xing* (*The Penal Code of Lv*) was formulated in the period of King Mu of Zhou. In addition, the historical lesson of the ancient tribe You Miao being punished by "Tian Fa" (Heavenly punishment) because of their misuse of penalty was often used to prove the significance of "Ming De Shen Fa" (promoting virtue and being prudent in the enforcement of punishment).

2.4 The Legal Contents of *Lv Xing* (*The Penal Code of Lv*) and *Jiu Xing* (*The Code Nine Penalties*)

Before Shang Dynasty was defeated by Zhou, King Wen of Zhou had already started "replacing both the legal system and calendar of the Yin Dynasty with the new ones"[42] and made famous laws and decrees like "searching for the runaway slaves on a large scale" and "having only the law offenders punished instead of the whole family." It was recorded in "Zhao Gong Qi Nian" (The 7th Year of the Duke of Zhao) in *Zuo Zhuan* (*The Chronicle of Zuo*) that "the law was made by King Wen of Zhou to require to 'search for the escaping slaves on a large scale.'" Du Yu noted that "'Huang' refers to 'something big'; 'Yue' means 'searching'; so it means that if the slaves have escaped, they should be searched and caught by the public." That is to say, it was the legal obligation of the noblemen to search for the escaping slaves together to protect the slaveholders' interests. Therefore, this law had won the support of the slave owners, which was a sharp contrast to King Zhou of the Shang Dynasty who "tried every means to capture the slaves and forced them to fight for him,"[43] and which had become one of the crucial reasons for King Wen of Zhou to "conquer and occupy the entire country."[44] Besides, according to "Liang Hui Wang" (King Hui of Liang, Part 2) in *Meng Zi* (*Mencius*), "tax is not collected when the markets and customs passes are checked and fishing in lakes and rivers is

---

[42]"Zhou Ben Ji" (Chronicles of Chou) in *Shi Ji* (*The Record of the Grand Historian*).
[43]"Zhao Gong Qi Nian" (The 7th Year of the Duke of Zhao) in *Zuo Zhuan* (*The Chronicle of Zuo*).
[44]"Zhao Gong Qi Nian" (The 7th Year of the Duke of Zhao) in *Zuo Zhuan* (*The Chronicle of Zuo*).

2.4 The Legal Contents of *Lv Xing* (*The Penal Code of Lv*) and *Jiu Xing*...

not forbidden, meanwhile, only law offenders are punished instead of the whole family," which was contrary to the law made by King Zhou of the Shang Dynasty, in which it was stipulated that "those who have committed an offense should be punished together with their family members." Although it was undoubtedly a political strategy to "get rid of the influence of the Shang Dynasty," it had surely reflected the need of social development and the progress of legal civilization, so it was of great historical significance to the legislation in the early Zhou Dynasty, as was stated in historical records, "the political and legal systems of King Wen of Zhou were inherited and adopted in Western Zhou Dynasty."[45]

After the extinction of Shang Dynasty, with the social development and progress of legal civilization, the customary law was gradually transformed into statute law in Zhou Dynasty and *Jiu Xing* (*The Code Nine Penalties*) and *Lv Xing* (*The Penal Code of Lv*) were finally formulated.

In "Zhao Gong Liu Nian" (The 6th Year of the Duke of Zhao) in *Zuo Zhuan* (*The Chronicle of Zuo*), it was recorded that "in Zhou Dynasty, the political situation was in turmoil, so *Jiu Xing* (*The Code Nine Penalties*) was formulated." According to "Wen Gong Shi Ba Nian" (The 18th Year of the Duke of Wen) in *Zuo Zhuan* (*The Chronicle of Zuo*), "the late Zhou Gong (Duke of Zhou) wrote in 'Shi Ming' (Vigilance) that 'those who break the regulations have committed the crime of 'Zei'; those who hide the thieves have committed the crime of 'Cang' (covering up a criminal); those who take bribery have committed the crime of 'Dao' (theft) and those who steal the equipment have committed the crime of 'Jian' (betrayal). These felonies must be severely punished and never pardoned. They are recorded in *Jiu Xing* (*The Code Nine Penalties*) and will never be forgotten.'" This can be said to be the main content of *Jiu Xing* (*The Code Nine Penalties*). *Jiu Xing* (*The Code Nine Penalties*) might also be referred to as "the criminal laws in nine chapters." According to "Chang Mai Jie" (Tasting the New Wheat) in *Zhou Shu* (*The History of Zhou Dynasty*), during the reign of King Cheng, "in April, the King requested 'Da Zheng' (minister of justice) to have the criminal book revised, so the court historian presented nine chapters of criminal law to 'Da Zheng'." *Jiu Xing* (*The Code Nine Penalties*) could also be considered to be made up mainly of five formal punishments, namely, "Mo" (tattooing on the face or forehead of the offenders with indelible ink), "Yi" (to cut down the nose), "Yue" (to amputate the feet), "Gong" (castration) and "Bi" (capital punishment) and another four complementary punishments, namely, "Liu" (exile), "Shu" (atonement), "Bian" (whipping), and "Pu" (corporal punishment including "Chi", "Bian", and "Zhang"). *Jiu Xing* (*The Code Nine Penalties*) had been revised repeatedly in accordance with the concrete needs of different times.

During "The Reign of Cheng Kang" (a period of stability and prosperity), the country was in peace so punishment was not enforced for forty years",[46] but since

---

[45]"Wen Gong Jiu Nian" (The 9th Year of the Duke of Wen) in *Chun Qiu Gong Yang Zhuan (Annotation to Chun Qiu by Master Gong Yang)*.

[46]"Zhou Ben Ji" (Chronicles of Zhou) in *Shi Ji* (*The Record of the Grand Historian*).

the reign of King Zhao, the country declined because of the lack of "Wang Dao" (the benevolent government). By the reign of King Mu, it was already about one hundred years since the founding of the state, so the king was fond of traveling and lived a very extravagant life, which had led to serious financial crisis and acute social conflicts. "King Mu lamented over the loss of benevolent civil and military government once practiced by King Wen and King Wu"[47] and ordered Lv Hou (or Fu Hou), "Si Kou" (the minister of justice) at the time, to "make new laws in line with the then current circumstances."[48] Thus, *Lv Xing* (*The Penal Code of Lv*) was drafted, which was also called "Fu Xing" in "Zhou Ben Ji" (Chronicles of Zhou) in *Shi Ji* (*The Records of the Grand Historian*). This masterpiece was the best example of the codes made in the middle of Western Zhou Dynasty. But the original copy was already lost, and only a chapter called "Lv Xing" (The Penal Code of Lv) was remained in *Shang Shu* (*The Book of Historical Document*). Although *Lv Xing* (*The Penal Code of Lv*) was not written by Lv Hou himself, it indeed was a historical document filed by the official record of the Western Zhou Dynasty. The main contents of this masterpiece were not only in line with the background of the period of reigning by King Mu, but also in line with the consistent guidelines of the criminal law since early Zhou Dynasty.

As *Lv Xing* (*The Penal Code of Lv*) was drafted to solve the financial crisis and to reduce the social contradiction, a comprehensive set of rules for the punishment of "Shu Xing" (atonement) were laid down. Copper money varying from 100 to 1000 *huan* (ancient monetary unit, one *huan* is about 300 g) could be used to atone for the five punishments (Mo, Yi, Fei, Gong, Da Bi). The establishment of the system had made it more convenient for nobles to escape penalties.

The guiding principle of "Ming De Shen Fa" (promoting virtue and being prudent in the enforcement of punishment), which was carried out in the early Zhou Dynasty, was followed in *Lv Xing* (*The Penal Code of Lv*), so it demonstrated the importance of respecting virtue in punishment and teaching morality through punishments through the example of the Miao people's destruction because of their moral degradation and abuse of punishment. Thus "fair punishments were enforced by the judicial officials to teach ordinary people the importance of virtue," and "'San De' (three virtues) was promoted by showing reverence for 'Wu Xing' (five penalties)." To carry out the policy of "Ming De Shen Fa" (promoting virtue and being prudent in the enforcement of punishment), it was emphasized in *Lv Xing* (*The Penal Code of Lv*) to be "fair (Zhong) with penalty". The so-called "Zhong" had the implication of fairness, accuracy, and leniency, and it could only be achieved through "Ming De Shen Fa" (promoting virtue and being prudent in the enforcement of punishment).

In *Lv Xing* (*The Penal Code of Lv*), the record of "Wu Xing" (five penalties), principles of criminal law, and some regulations about judicial system were also included, which had shown an obvious development of legal civilization. Therefore,

---

[47]"Zhou Ben Ji" (Chronicles of Zhou) in *Shi Ji* (*The Record of the Grand Historian*).

[48]"Xing Fa Zhi" (The Record of the Criminal Law) in *Han Shu* (*The History of Han Dynasty*).

2.4 The Legal Contents of *Lv Xing* (*The Penal Code of Lv*) and *Jiu Xing*... 65

Lv Xing (*The Penal Code of Lv*) had become a model for others to follow and it was often quoted in the criminal laws of later dynasties since Han Dynasty, from which we can see the influence of this monumental work.

Apart from *Jiu Xing* (*The Code Nine Penalties*) and *Lv Xing* (*The Penal Code of Lv*), the most frequent legislative activities and the most significant legal documents were "Gao" (imperial mandate), "Shi" (oath), and "Ming" (command) issued by the monarchs of Zhou, which were of the supreme legal authority. The written admonishment referred to the king's instructions to the nobles and his subordinates. For example, after the revolt was suppressed by Zhou Gong (Duke of Zhou), he appointed Kang Shu to rule the subjects of the former Yin Dynasty by issuing "Kang Gao" (The Orders of Duke Zhou to Kang Shu). Therefore, some important criminal legal principles and policies were included in "Kang Gao" and it had acted as the guideline for the legislation and judiciary of the Western Zhou Dynasty. "Shi" (oath), namely, pledges, referred to the "military orders" released by the king and vassals to their subjects. For example, "Mu Shi" (Oath Taken at Mu) was the pledge given by King Wu to the tribe leaders and the officials before launching the attack against King Zhou of the Shang Dynasty in Muye in the suburbs of Shang. He declared that anyone who was brave and who had killed the enemies would be awarded; anyone who was afraid of the enemies would be put to death; the enemies who had surrendered themselves would not be killed. Moreover, the nobles also had the right to announce "oaths" which were legally binding in his vassal state. For instance, "Fei Shi" (The Military Order Issued at Fei) was the vow made by Duke of Lu called Bo Qin to his soldiers at the place "Bi" when they defeated the Huaiyi People and the Xurong people. As for "Ming" (command), it was the important basis on which the national activities were conducted and the reason that the principle of "no violation of His Majesty's directives" was constantly stressed by the kings of Zhou.[49] So "Ming" (command) issued by the vassals and officials in their fiefs was also legally binding. Fan Muzhong (a nobleman in the Western Zhou Dynasty) told Lu Xiaogong (the 12th Duke of Lu) that, "the rules and laws of the late kings must be consulted before punishment is enforced."[50] Of course, the orders of the vassals of previous generations should also be consulted.

In addition, some customs and regulations in line with the interests of nobles had played the role of legal adjustment in practice and became crucial supplements for the statute law of the Western Zhou Dynasty.

Some applicable laws were also inherited by the rulers of the Western Zhou Dynasty from the Shang Dynasty. Zhou Gong (Duke of Zhou) admonished Kang Shu repeatedly that "the reasonable penal laws of 'Yin Fa' should be inherited" and that "the justified and righteous as for the criminal laws of 'Yin Bi' should be

---

[49] Inscriptions on *Da Yu Ding* (*Great Yu Tripod*).
[50] "Zhou Yu" (The Historical Records of Zhou Dynasty) in *Guo Yu* (*The Historical Records of Various States*) (Book 1).

adopted."[51] The "Yin Fa" and "Yin Bi" mentioned above referred to the laws of Shang Dynasty. Because of the similarity of the laws of Shang and Zhou dynasties, they were interchangeable in practice. In particular, when punishments were enforced by the rulers of Zhou Dynasty, the laws of the Shang Dynasty were usually applied, because those punished were mostly the adherents of the former Shang Dynasty, which obviously reflected the policy of "an eye for an eye, and a tooth for a tooth" in Zhou Dynasty.

2.4.1 The Administrative Laws in Inscriptions and Documentary Records

The development of Western Zhou Dynasty had markedly enriched the administrative law, and its main task was to ensure the proper function of the state institutions, to protect the administrative management mechanism under the supreme leadership of the kings of Zhou Dynasty, and to adjust the relationship between the sovereign state and the vassal states. Besides, the structure, duty, power, the procedure of performing duties, and the legal liability of the officials were also formulated.

The administrative law of the Western Zhou Dynasty was mostly found in bronze inscriptions. For example, the litigation judgment for the violation of the administrative orders of one's superior were recorded in the inscriptions on *Shi Lv Ding* (*Tripod for Military Purpose*), while an account of King Kang's admonition to a senior nobleman called Yu was recorded in the inscriptions on *Da Yu Ding* (*Great Yu Tripod*), which included some regulations about some duties performed by officials. In the inscriptions on *Da Ke Ding* (*Great Yu Tripod*), the king's appointment of Ke and the code of conduct which he should obey were recorded; while in the inscriptions on *Xun Gui* (container of food owned by Xun), the king of Zhou's commanding Xun to inherit the post and duties of his ancestors was recorded. An ancient book called *Zhou Guan* (*The Official System of Zhou Dynasty*) completed in the Eastern Zhou Dynasty showed that the rulers of Zhou Dynasty had tried to legally confirm the establishment of positions, the appointment of officials and the relations of rights and obligations between the sovereign state and the vassal states, so it is very valuable and it should be cherished and further studied. Furthermore, in the administrative laws of Western Zhou Dynasty, official appointments and their appraisal were also specified. Under the aristocratic system, the successor still needed to be appointed according to the orders of the monarchs. From the establishment of the official positions in charge of making appointment, we can see the frequency of the official appointment. Official appointment was usually held in palaces or temples with grand ceremonies not only to show the mission of the officials and the importance of their power but also to strengthen the holy authority

---

[51]"Kang Gao" (The Orders of Duke Zhou to Kang Shu) in *Shang Shu* (*The Book of Historical Document*).

of the monarchs. Meanwhile, it was held to show that the officials appointed by monarchs were endowed with missions granted by Heaven.

Officials at the grassroots levels were selected through local recommendation and examination: "any outstanding people who is recognized by the 'Lao Ren' (the elder) of "Xiang" (townships) shall be promoted to be 'Si Tu' (the minister of civil affairs), which is called 'Xuan Shi'; anyone who is considered excellent by the group of "Si Tu" (the minister of civil affairs) shall be promoted to be 'Zhu Xue' (an official post), which is called 'Jun Shi'; anyone who has been promoted but not appointed is called 'Zao Shi'; anyone who is excellent among 'Zao Shi' shall be recommend by 'Da Yue Zheng' to be "Si Ma" (the minister of military affairs), which is called 'Jin Shi'."[52] "'Si Ma' (the minister of military affairs) is in charge of selecting those who are outstanding in terms of political talent among 'Jin Shi' (those who passed the imperial examination at the national level in ancient China) and recommending them to the king."[53] However, this method of selection was not applicable to the nobles and the officials of higher ranks.

There seemed to be certain standards for the official selection in the Western Zhou Dynasty, as was recorded in *Tong Dian* (*The General Codes*): "first, 'Liu De' (six virtue); second, 'Liu Xing' (six behaviors); third, 'Liu Yi' (six skills)…so it takes nine years to master 'Si Shu' (four techniques), including 'Shi' (poetry), 'Shu' (writing), 'Li' (rites) and 'Yue' (music)."[54] The so-called "Liu De" (six virtue) referred to "Zhi" (knowledge), "Ren" (benevolence), "Sheng" (holiness), "Yi" (justice), "He" (harmony), and "Zhong" (temperance); "Liu Xing" (six behaviors) included "Xiao" (being filial), "You" (friendliness), "Mu" (harmonious), "Yin" (marriage), "Ren" (responsibility), and "Xu" (sympathy); "Liu Yi" (six skills) referred to "Li" (rites), "Yue" (music), "She" (archery), "Yu" (driving), "Shu" (writing) and "Shu" (arithmetic). It can be inferred that in the slavery society of China, besides the precondition of patriarchal ranks, virtue and ability were also very important in the official-selecting system.

In Zhou Dynasty, not only systems were established for selecting officials and scholars, the assessment of the officials' performance were also recorded in many documents. As far back in "Shun Dian" (Shun Code) in *Shang Shu* (*The Book of Historical Document*), it was already written that "every three years an examination of merits was held, and after three examinations the incompetent ones were demoted, and the competent ones were promoted." Besides, it was also recorded in "Si Tu" (the minister of civil affairs) in "Di Guan" (Land Official) in *Zhou Li* (*The Rites of Zhou Dynasty*) that "every three years a large scale examination was held, in which the virtue and talents of the officials were evaluated, while the competent ones were promoted." In addition, it was recorded in "Da Zai" (name of an ancient official) in "Tian Guan" (The Ministers) in *Zhou Li* (*The Rites of Zhou Dynasty*) that "at the end of a year, the local authorities were demanded to have the documents filed according

---

[52]"Xuan Ju" (Election) in *Tong Dian* (*The General Codes*) (Book 1).

[53]"Wang Zhi" (The Royal Regulations) in *Li Ji* (*Book of Rites*).

[54]"Xuan Ju" (Election) in *Tong Dian* (*The General Codes*) (Book 1).

to facts and to have the general ledgers prepared and reported to the emperor, so their achievements would be evaluated for the king to make decisions about the demotion and promotion of the officials; every three years, the achievements of all officials were examined to help the king to decide the punishments and awards. 'Tai Zai' (title of senior official in ancient time) was in charge of the large-scale achievement assessment, while 'Xiao Zai' (title of petty official in ancient time) was in charge of the specific examination. There were "six criteria" to evaluate the officials: "Lian Shan" (kindness), "Lian Neng" (talented), "Lian Jing" (loyal), "Lian Zheng" (uncorrupted), "Lian Fa" (justice), and "Lian Bian" (prudential). Besides, the form of "Yao Hui" (briefing) was usually taken in evaluation and it was held every month, every year, or every three years, respectively.

"Xiang Da Fu" (village official) was responsible for the evaluation of officials outside the capital and it was held once every three years. The contents of the examinations included: "education, administration, land, population, the livestock, the weapons, and the number of apparatus. Those being assessed should wait for government decrees."[55]

Other ways of evaluation included the king's inspection tours and the reporting of the vassals on their work. It was recorded in "Liang Hui Wang" (King Liang Hui) in *Meng Zi* (*Mencius*) (Book 2) that "the reporting of the work by the officials to the king is called 'Shu Zhi'" and that "'Shu Zhi' means the officials reporting on their work." Thus, the nobleman should accept the assessment of the king, if anyone had "failed to make the report," he would be punished either by being deprived of his title, or by deprived of his land or by being suppressed by the army. It was stated in "Gao Zi" (a student of Mencius) in *Meng Zi* (*Mencius*) (Book 2) that "if any nobleman fails to make report for once, he shall be demoted; if he fails to make report for twice, his land shall be confiscated; if he fails to make report for three times, he will be attacked by the troops sent by the king." It is thus obvious that it is a rule that the noblemen must obey to report about his work to the king.

After examination, award and punishment were conducted. According to "Da Zai" (title of an ancient official) in "Tian Guan Zhong Zhai" (Executive Ministers) in *Zhou Li* (*The Rites of Zhou Dynasty*), both punishments and awards were included in "the eight methods which were applied by the rulers to control the officials, namely, 'Jue' (titles of nobility), 'Lu' (salaries), 'Yu' (endowment), 'Zhi' (settlement), 'Sheng' (livelihood), 'Duo' (deprivation), 'Fei' (dismissal), 'Zhu' (punishment)." Moreover, there are also many records in the bronze inscriptions about the promotion of excellent officials who had done very well in their positions.

The performance rating system previously mentioned as was recorded in *Zhou Li* (*The Rites of Zhou Dynasty*) might have been misinterpreted by people's false analogy in later ages. It was not until the Warring States Period that the performance rating system was institutionalized with the establishment of bureaucratic system.

---

[55]"Xiao Si Tu" (The Assistant of "Si Tu") in "Di Guan Si Tu" (The Official of Internal Affairs) in *Zhou Li* (*The Rites of Zhou Dynasty*).

In Zhou Dynasty, the hereditary official system was correlated with hereditary salary system. The officials at all levels met their economic needs by levying tax on the inhabitants in their vassals, so "the vassals live on tributes; 'Da Fu' (senior officials in ancient China) live on their own fiefs; while 'Shi' (scholars) live on their land."[56] The salary system of the Warring States Period did not exist in Western Zhou Dynasty.

2.4.2 The Criminal Law: Emphasizing Public Rights and Being Cautious with Patriarchal Clan System

After China entered class society, the political system of autocracy was carried out and the supremacy of the state and the king was highly praised, thus public rights were stressed and private rights were neglected. Thus, any action that endangered the state or the king would be severely punished by law. Under this background, the criminal law was relatively more developed. In Western Zhou Dynasty, more than 3000 provisions were included in "Wu Xing" (Five Penalties) and the regulations about crimes and punishments were elaborated on in great detail.

2.4.2.1 The Accusation Reflecting the Principle of Emphasizing Public Rights and Being Cautious with Patriarchal Clan System

"Bu Xiao" (Being Unfilial) or "Bu You" (Being Unfriendly) The establishment of patriarchal clan system in the Western Zhou Dynasty not only made "Bu Xiao"(being unfilial) the most serious crime, but also gave rise to such new crimes as "Bu Ti" (not loving brothers), "Bu You" (being unfriendly), "Bu Mu" (inharmonious), "Bu Yin" (being unmarried) and "Bu Jing Zu" (showing no reverence for ancestors). These crimes were regarded as "the most serious crimes abhorred by people," so they would be punished severely by both the state law and the patriarchal rules without remittance. It was recorded in "Kang Gao" (The Orders of Duke Zhou to Kang Shu) in *Shang Shu* (*The Book of Historical Document*) that "these abominable criminals are extremely abhorred, and how (detestable) are 'Bu Xiao' (being unfilial) and 'Bu You' (being unfriendly)?...so they should be punished severely with no pardoning." Therefore, anyone who had murdered his relatives would be sentenced to capital punishment, as it was said in the saying that "the criminals who have killed their families shall be definitely punished by death penalty,"[57] and

---

[56]"Jin Yu" (The Historical Records of Jin State) in *Guo Yu* (*The Historical Records of Various States*), Vol. 4.
[57]"Si Ma" (The Minister of Military Affairs) in "Xia Guan" (Ministry of Military Affairs) in *Zhou Li* (*The Rites of Zhou Dynasty*).

"anyone who has murdered his family members shall be punished by burning."[58] Even those who were irreverent, impolite, or disobedient when worshiping in the ancestral temples would be punished for "Bu Jing" (being irreverent). Therefore, nobilities used brutal punishments to punish the civilians who dared to disobey them, to have them tightly chained to the clan chiefs.

Disobeying the King's Orders Under the autocratic regime with the king as the supreme authority, it was considered a felony to disobey the king's orders, so "anyone who is not obedient to the king shall be punished by the law."[59] In the early Zhou Dynasty, the Duke Dan of Zhou Dynasty once announced to all of the nobles on behalf of King Cheng: "If you do not take the advantage of the leniency by which I have spared your lives, I will put you to death by applying severe punishments."[60] During the reign of King Xuan of Zhou, the father of Fan Zhongshan said, "Anyone who has violated the king's orders shall be killed, so all instructions should be obeyed."[61] Furthermore, the king's orders were endowed with the mysteriousness of the Heaven's will, as was reflected in the statement, "the kings' instructions are equal to those of 'Tian' (Heaven)." Therefore, disobeying the king's orders meant defying "Tian" (Heaven), so it was often used as the excuse by the big countries to attack the smaller ones. A notable example was that "Xu Jiafu was exiled to the state of Wei by the people of Jin for disobeying the king's orders and Xu Ke was chosen to succeed the throne instead."[62]

Defaming or Murdering the King Anyone who had defamed the king would be found guilty of "slandering". According to "Zhou Ben Ji" (Chronicles of Zhou) in *Shi Ji* (*The Records of the Grand Historian*), during the reign of King Li, "he demanded Wei Wu to have an investigation of the people who had defamed him and to have them killed." If anyone had killed the king, he would be punished by the cruelest penalty. It was recorded in "Si Ma" (The Minister of Military Affairs) in "Xia Guan" (Ministry of Military Affairs) in *Zhou Li* (*The Rites of Zhou Dynasty*) that "anyone who intends to exile or kill the king will be sentenced to death." Besides, it was also recorded in "Tan Gong" (Duke of Tan) in *Li Ji* (*The Book of Rites*) that anyone who killed the king "will be sentenced to death with his house destroyed and his palace flooded by water." According to "Zhuang Gong Shi Er Nian" (The 12th Year of the Duke of Zhuang) in *Zuo Zhuan* (*The Chronicle of Zuo*), "Song Wan killed the Duke Min of Song at a place called Meng Ze. Hence he was chopped into pieces by the Song People." Even when the relatives of the king were

---

[58]"Zhang Lu" (The Office of Execution) in "Qiu Guan" (Ministry of Penalty) in *Zhou Li* (*Rites of Zhou Dynasty*).

[59]"Zhao Gong San Shi Yi Nian" (The 31st Year of the Duke of Zhao) in *Zuo Zhuan* (*The Chronicle of Zuo*).

[60]"Duo Fang" (In Many Ways) in *Shang Shu* (*The Book of Historical Document*).

[61]"Zhou Yu" (The Historical Records of Zhou Dynasty) in *Guo Yu* (*The Historical Records of Various States*), Vol.1.

[62]"Xuan Gong Yuan Nian" (The 1st Year of the Duke of Xuan) in *Zuo Zhuan* (*The Chronicle of Zuo*).

killed, the killers would receive the most severe penalty. It was recorded in "Zhang Lu" (The Office of Execution) in "Qiu Guan" (Ministry of Penalty) in *Zhou Li* (*The Rites of Zhou Dynasty*) that "anyone who kills the king's family shall be punished by 'Gu'." According to Zheng Xuan's annotation, "'辜' means '枯', which means "Zhe" (to open and split, breaking apart the criminal's body), so it means cutting one's body into pieces."

Endangering the Regime In Western Zhou Dynasty, the crime of doing harm to the regime included "Fan" (plotting rebellion), "Ni" (sedition), and "Luan" (disturbance). Anyone who did not "follow the king's orders" was guilty of "Ni" (sedition), which was the same as the crime of "Fan" (plotting rebellion). Thus, they were two different words but they had the same meaning. As to "Luan" (disturbance), it meant "internal turmoil", as was explained that "the warfare started within the state means 'Luan'". During the reign of King Li of Zhou Dynasty, anyone who dared to make comments on the state affairs would be arrested and killed for committing the crime of endangering the regime, so that "the people in the country were even afraid of speaking and they just communicated with each other by eye contact when they met in the streets."[63] In the end, a riot broke out, so the king was forced to be exiled. Moreover, "anyone who dares to spread rumors, or to break the law, or to change the given names without authorization, or to practice witchcraft to disturb the state order"[64] would be sentenced to death for the crime of endangering the regime.

To prevent the slaves from gathering to plot rebellion, "both male and female slaves would be supervised and punished if they had ganged together, and they would be killed if they had violated the injunctions."[65]

Changing the Class Ranks and Titles In Western Zhou Dynasty, the king, nobles, vassals and scholars had their own class identities and titles respectively. If anyone of them had transgressed the boundary, he would be punished. For instance, "the orders for 'Li' (Rites), "Yue" (music) and expedition were all issued by the king," so it meant disobedience to the king "to change 'Li' (rites) and 'Yue' (music) randomly and the violator would be punished by 'Liu' (exile)." "Changing the regulations for clothes without authorization meant 'Pan' (treason) and the violator would be suppressed."[66] It was recorded in "Yin Gong Yuan Nian" (The 1st Year of the Duke of Yin) in *Zuo Zhuan* (*The Chronicle of Zuo*) that the reason for Zheng Bo's sending a punitive expedition against Duan was that he dared to be on an equal footing with the king, because "according to the system of former kings, the biggest city in the country should not be more than one third of the capital; and the medium-sized should not be more than one-fifth; the small-sized one should not be more than

---

[63]"Zhou Ben Ji" (Chronicles of Zhou) in *Shi Ji* (*The Record of the Grand Historian*).

[64]"Wang Zheng" (The King's Order) in *Li Ji* (*Book of Rites*).

[65]"Jin Bao Shi" (Peace Officers) in "Qiu Guan" (Ministry of Penalty) in *Zhou Li* (*The Rites of Zhou Dynasty*).

[66]"Wang Zhi" (The Royal Regulations) in *Li Ji* (*Book of Rites*).

one-ninth. The construction of the capital was not in conformity to the rule," so Duan was attacked and suppressed.

In the early Zhou Dynasty, the vassal states were of different size, so certain obligations and rights were regulated between them. If a small vassal did not perform its duties, it would be attacked by the bigger ones. For example, "the Duke of Song did not show respect to the king of Zhou, so Zheng Bo went on a punitive expedition against him in the name of the king."[67]

The crime of killing "Di Zi" (the son born of the legal wife) and appointing "Shu Zi" (the son born of a concubine) as the inheritor was also related to the identities and status of the patriarchal clan system, and the offenders would be severely punished.

Breaching the Oath of Alliance According to "Qu Li" (The Summary of the Rules of Propriety) in *Li Ji* (*The Book of Rites*), "it is called 'Shi' to make a contract for both parties to abide by and it is called 'Meng' to read out the written contract with a sacrifice before the celestial beings." "Meng Shi" (oath) was a manifestation of the agreement between the vassals and nobles during the theocratic ruling. The breaching of the oath of alliance, therefore, was regarded as a criminal conduct that could not be tolerated by "Tian" (Heaven). In many oaths in *Zuo Zhuan* (*The Chronicle of Zuo*) it was declared that "either of the two parties who breaks the promise shall be killed by the gods,"[68] which had shown the importance of keeping promises.

Drinking Together In early Zhou Dynasty, the rulers had learned from a lesson from Shang Dynasty. The people in Shang Dynasty were so addicted to alcohol that they were finally trapped in corruption, which had led to the extinction of the nation, therefore drinking together was prohibited. Zhou Gong (Duke of Zhou) once gave explicit orders to Kang Shu of Wei that if Zhou people "drink alcohol in groups, you should arrest them all and send them to the capital. Do not let anyone escape. I will decide who should be sentenced to death."[69] The purpose of making this rule was also to prevent the drinkers from making trouble, because it might pose a great threat to social order. However, during Shang Dynasty, the penalty for drinking in groups was in fact not so severe, and the drinkers would be educated rather than killed. It was recorded that "there was no need to kill them (the survivors of the Shang Dynasty) for being addicted to alcohol, it was enough to have them educated."[70] But if the Shang people did not listen to the admonishment and "continued to commit the offence", they "would be put to death", which had shown Duke of Zhou's different treatment to the people of Zhou Dynasty and the survivors of Shang Dynasty in terms of criminal law.

---

[67]"Yin Gong Jiu Nian" (The 9th Year of the Duke of Yin) in *Zuo Zhuan* (*The Chronicle of Zuo*).
[68]"Xi Gong Er Shi Ba Nian" (The 28th Year of the Duke of Xi) in *Zuo Zhuan* (*The Chronicle of Zuo*).
[69]"Jiu Gao" (Announcement to Ban Alcohol) in *Shang Shu* (*The Book of Historical Document*).
[70]"Jiu Gao" (Announcement to Ban Alcohol) in *Shang Shu* (*The Book of Historical Document*).

2.4 The Legal Contents of *Lv Xing* (*The Penal Code of Lv*) and *Jiu Xing*...

Murder Since Xia Dynasty, "anyone who killed other people would be regarded as a 'Zei' (banditry)" and be executed. In the documents of pre-Qin dynasties, "Zei" (banditry) and "Dao" (robbery) were different in meaning. Generally, "Zei" referred to assaulting people, while "Dao" referred to stealing other people's possessions. Zhou Gong (Duke of Zhou) once made it clear that "those who break the regulations have committed the crime of 'Zei'; those who hide the thieves have committed the crime of 'Cang' (covering up a criminal); those who take bribery have committed the crime of 'Dao' (theft) and those who steal the equipment have committed the crime of 'Jian' (betrayal). These felonies must be severely punished and never pardoned."[71] In Zhou Dynasty, there were also crimes of robbery and homicide. It was recorded in "Kang Gao" (The Orders of Duke Zhou to Kang Shu) in *Shang Shu* (*The Book of Historical Document*) that "those who have killed other people or have violently assaulted them to take their property…have committed crimes." This is the origin of the phrase "Sha Ren Yue Huo" (killing the people and robbing their goods). As to the murderers, they should not only be put to death, but also "had their bodies exposed at the market for three days" to warn the public.[72]

Injuring People The crime of causing injury included both injury by negligence and intentional injury, which were punished by different penalties. For example, it was recorded in "Xiang She Li" (an archery contest) in *Yi Li* (*Etiquette and Ceremony*) that "if the shooter is guilty, he will be whipped." According to Zheng's annotation, "(although he) is guilty because his arrow has injured someone… he does not do it on purpose," so he was just whipped for negligent injury. However, for intentional injury, severe sentence would be inflicted. It was recorded in "Jin Sha Lu" (forbidding killing) in "Qiu Guan" (Ministry of Penalty) in *Zhou Li* (*The Rites of Zhou Dynasty*) that "anyone who hurts other people or has made them bleeding without reporting, or any official who has harbored the criminal or does not accept the case, or any official who has prevented the victim from filing a litigation, will be reported to the supervisors of judicial affairs and be put to death after investigation."

Property Torts It was recorded in "Kang Gao" (The Orders of Zhou Gong (Duke of Zhou) to Kang Shu) in *Shang Shu* (*The Book of Historical Document*) that "all those who are involved in "Kou" (robbing), "Rang" (stealing), "Jian" (villainy) and "Gui" (evil-deeds) have committed crimes, so they should be punished." It was recorded in "Lv Xing" (The Penal Code of Lv) in *Shang Shu* (*The Book of Historical Document*) that "there are no robbers and murderers…traitors and villains, robbing and stealing." In the above quotation, "Kou" means robbing, "Rang" means stealing, both of which are committed to infringe property, despite the difference of their means. "Kou" referred to the crime of robbery, and "Rang" referred to the crime of stealing. While "Jian" and "Gui" had the implication of "Kou", or robbery, as was

---

[71]"Wen Gong Shi Ba Nian" (The 18th Year of the Duke of Wen) in *Zuo Zhuan* (*The Chronicle of Zuo*).

[72]"Zhang Lu" (The Office of Execution) in "Qiu Guan" (The Ministry of Penalty) in *Zhou Li* (*The Rites of Zhou Dynasty*).

recorded in "Shi Gu" (The Meaning and Usages of Words) in *Guang Ya* (the first encyclopedia in ancient China) that "'Jian' and 'Gui' means 'Dao' and 'Qie' (theft)." It was recorded in "Fei Shi" (The Military Order Issued at Fei) in *Shang Shu* (*The Book of Historical Document*) that "let none of you to presume to commit any robbery or detain any creature that comes in your way, to jump over enclosures and walls to steal (people's) horses or oxen, or to seduce their servants or female attendants. If you do so, you shall be punished according to the law." Different punishments were enforced to the crime of robbery and theft: "anyone who breaks through the strategic passes, or climbs over the city walls to rob (other people) shall have their feet cut off...anyone who commits such crime as villainy, treachery or theft shall have their nose cut off."[73] Although the sentences quoted above from "Fei Shi" (The Military Order Issued at Fei) in *Shang Shu* (*The Book of Historical Document*) are just military orders, they are also applied to ordinary people. The basic purpose of criminal law was to protect the private possession of the slave owners from being infringed. In the annotation of "Kang Gao" (The Orders of Duke Zhou to Kang Shu) in *Shang Shu* (*The Book of Historical Document*), Wang Mingsheng of the Qing Dynasty said that in Zhou Dynasty those who had infringed upon the private rights "shall be punished by death penalty without pardoning."

In addition, anyone who had committed the crime of the infringement of unclaimed objects would be punished without pardoning. It was stated in "Zhong Dong" (Months in the Midwinter) in "Yue Ling" (Monthly Orders) in *Li Ji* (*The Book of Rites*) that "the crop with no one to harvest or the livestock with no one to attend to can be taken by people for their own without inquiring..., nevertheless, those who fight over the property with one another shall be severely punished."

Licentiousness According to chapter five of *Lu Shi* (*Grand History*), during the reign of You Chao, "the youngest son of Shi was licentious and had sexual intercourse with women at the market in daytime. The king was infuriated and had him exiled to the southwest." This can be said to be the earliest crime of indecent exposure recorded. By the reign of Yellow Emperor, siblings were forbidden to marry each other, and anyone who offended the rule would be expelled from the community, which had reflected the gradual establishment of patriarchial system. In Zhou Dynasty, "any inappropriate relationship between a male and a female is called promiscuity; an affair with one's senior is called 'Zheng', with one's junior is called 'Bao' and with one's peer is called 'Tong'."[74] The people who committed the crime of adultery would be punished by castration, as was recorded in *Shang Shu Da Zhuan* (*Interpretations of Shang Shu*): "Any male or female who has an improper relationship shall be castrated."

Failing to Do What Should Be Done During Farming Season Zhou Dynasty was agriculture-oriented, so the agricultural affairs should be conducted on time;

---

[73] *Shang Shu Da Zhuan* (*Interpretations of Shang Shu*).
[74] "Guang Yi" in *Er Ya* (*Using Graceful and Elegant Languages*).

otherwise, the farmers involved should be punished. It was recorded in "Yue Ling" (Monthly Orders) in *Li Ji* (*The Book of Rites*) that "in mid-autumn ... (the peasants) were told to grow wheat and anyone who delayed in the farming season would be punished undoubtedly."

Making Lascivious Sounds and Wearing Bizarre Clothes It was written in "Wang Zhi" (The Royal Regulations) in Li Ji (Book of Rites) that "anyone who made lascivious sounds, wore bizarre clothes, performed strange skills or showed odd instruments to make the public deceived would be put to death." The capital punishment was enforced for this crime to prevent the confusion of people's mind, the degradation of public morality and the disruption of social order.

Dereliction of Duty "Wei Guan" (being warped by the influence of power), "Wei Fan" (by private grudge), "Wei Nei" (by secret control), "Wei Huo" (by blackmail), or "Wei Lai" (by bribes) were classified as "five cases of misbehavior" in "*Lv Xing*" (The Penal Code of Lv) in *Shang Shu* (*The Book of Historical Document*), "so the same punishment would be enforced for the offenders of these crimes" and "careful investigations should be conducted for these cases." In "Meng Dong Zhi Yue" (The First Month of Winter) in "Yue Ling" (Monthly Orders) in *Li Ji* (*The Book of Rites*), the punishment for officials' dereliction of duty was recorded, according to which, "'Gong Shi' (an ancient official position) was asked to work efficiently, ...and the names of the craftsmen must be carved on the products to insure the quality. If there was any misconduct, the officials would be investigated and punished."

2.4.2.2 The System of "Wu Xing" (Five Penalties)

In Zhou Dynasty, "Wu Xing" (Five Penalties) was made more systematic based on the penalty systems of Xia and Shang dynasties. According to "Lv Xing" (The Penal Code of Lv) in *Shang Shu* (*The Book of Historical Document*), "altogether, there are 3000 crimes in 'Wu Xing' (Five Penalties), including 1000 crimes punishable by 'Mo' (tattooing on the face or forehead of the offenders with indelible ink); 500 punishable by 'Fei' (cutting off the left or right foot or both feet); 300 punishable by 'Gong' (castration) and 200 punishable by 'Da Bi' (capital punishment)." According to "Si Xing" (Overseer of Penalty Affairs) in "Qiu Guan" (Ministry of Penalty) in *Zhou Li* (*The Rites of Zhou Dynasty*), "there are 500 cases respectively for the crimes punishable by 'Mo' (tattooing on the face or forehead of the offenders with indelible ink), 'Yi' (to cut down the nose), 'Gong' (castration), 'Yue' (to amputate the feet), and 'Sha' (death penalty)."

The Punishment of "Mo" (Tattooing on the Face or Forehead of the Offenders with Indelible Ink) "Mo" was the lightest of the five forms of punishments, so it ranked the first. It was recorded in "Zheng Yi" (*The Annotation of Confucians' Classics and the Books of History*) in *Lv Xing* (*The Penal Code of Lv*) that "'Mo' is also known as 'Qing'". It was recorded in "Si Xing" (Overseer of Penalty Affairs) in *Zhou Li* (*The Rites of Zhou Dynasty*) that "there are about 500 crimes punishable by

'Mo'". Zheng Xuan noted that "'Mo' is also called 'Qing' (to tattoo on the face). Carve the face first with knife, and then color it with ink. Namely, to engrave on the forehead and then use ink to fill in the wound to change its color." Kong Anguo also explained that "'Mo' means carving the forehead first and then coloring it with dyes." In Han Dynasty, it was stated in "Wu Xing" (Five Penalties) in *Bai Hu Tong* (*The Virtuous Discussions in White Tiger Hall*) that "'Mo' refers to coloring the forehead with ink." "Mo" was also called "Tian Xing" (heavenly penalty), so it was recorded in "Kui Liu San" (one of the trigrams in *The Book of Changes*) in *Yi* (*The Book of Changes*) that "this person should be sentenced to the punishment of 'Tian' with his ears cut off at the same time." Besides, it was also written in *Shi Wen* (*Explanation of Words and Phrases*) that "'Tian' means 'Qing' (to tattoo on the face)." In *Ji Jie* (*Collected Interpretations*) Yu Fan's interpretation was quoted and it was stated that "the tattooing of the forehead is called 'Tian' (to tattoo on the face)."

As was recorded in the ancient books of Shang Dynasty, the crime punishable by "Mo" (tattooing on the face or forehead of the offenders with indelible ink) included the crime of "the dereliction of their duties by officials."[75] Cai Zhu explained, "the officials who refuse to provide service to the sovereign shall be punished with 'Mo' (tattooing on the face or forehead of the offenders with indelible ink)." Thus, it can be inferred that "Mo" is one of the penalties applicable to officials.

In addition, according to "Si Yue" (official in charge of dukes) in "Qiu Guan" (Ministry of Penalty) in *Zhou Li* (*The Rites of Zhou Dynasty*), "the people who fail to keep their promises shall also be punished by 'Mo' (tattooing on the face or forehead of the offenders with indelible ink)," which indicated that those who broke their promises were punished by "Mo". In "Da Zhuan" (or Shang Shu Da Zhuan) in *Shang Shu* (*The Book of Historical Document*), it was also recorded that "anyone who argues with others with abusive words or spreads rumors against morality and justice shall be punished by 'Mo' (tattooing on the face or forehead of the offenders with indelible ink)."

In 1975, a brassware of the Age of King Li called "Zhen Yi" (Washbasin Entitled Zhen) was unearthed in Qishan in Shan'xi province, which had provided enough material evidence for the enforcement of the punishment of "Mo" (tattooing on the face or forehead of the offenders with indelible ink). In the inscription, the punishment of "Mo" was called "Wu". Therefore, the discovery was of great significance because it had not only explained the levels and targets of the penalty but also rectified some relevant historical accounts. The main contents of the inscriptions are as follows:

A low rank nobleman Mu Niu had broken his promise and committed the crime of false accusations against the senior authorities. Originally, he was punished by "Bian" (whipping) for 1000 stokes with the punishment of "Chu Wu". Later, he was excused and was punished by "Bian" (whipping) for 1000 strokes. In "Da Zhuan" (or Shang Shu Da Zhuan) in *Shang Shu* (*The Book of Historical Document*) it was

---

[75]"Yi Xun" (Warnings of Yi Yin in the Shang Dynasty) in *Shang Shu* (*The Book of Historical Document*).

recorded that "the penalty of 'Mo Meng'" meant that after the person was tattooed, his head was covered with a piece of black cloth, which was the most severe punishment of "Mo". "Chu Wu" meant having the official dismissed after he was tattooed, which was the lightest form of the penalty of "Mo". From the inscriptions, it could be inferred that, normally, those who had committed the crime of breaching contract and defying the superiors would be punished by "Chu Wu". The penalty of "Mo" could be aggravated or mitigated according to concrete situations, and it could be atoned by paying money. For "Chu Wu", the ransom was about 300 *huan* of copper money. However, this was inconsistent with the amount recorded in "Lv Xing" (The Penal Code of Lv) in *Shang Shu* (*The Book of Historical Document*), in which it was recorded that "if the case is doubtful, the punishment of 'Mo' can be exempted," however, it was proved by evidence that the penalty of "Mo" could be atoned.

In Zhou Dynasty, the people who was punished by "Mo" could still be employed as palace guards, because it was recorded in "Zhang Lu" (The Office of Execution) in Qiu Guan (Ministry of Penalty) in *Zhou Li* (*The Rites of Zhou Dynasty*) that "the people who have been punished by 'Mo' shall be recruited to guard the palace gate." The corporal punishment was obviously not abolished until in the reign of Emperor Wen of the Han Dynasty.

The Punishment of "Yi" (to Cut Down the Nose) The punishment of "Yi" (to cut down the nose) was a regular punishment that was much severer than "Mo" (tattooing on the face or forehead of the offenders with indelible ink), but it was less severe than the punishment of "Yue" (to amputate the feet). It was stated in "Kun Jiu Wu" (Trapped by Nine and Five: one of the trigrams in *The Book of Changes*) in *Yi* (*The Book of Changes*) that "he was trapped in his office because his nose and feet were cut off." It was also recorded in *Shi Wen* (*Explanation of Words and Phrases*) that "the punishment of 'Yi' (to cut down the nose) meant having one's nose cut down." Similar statements could also be found in such ancient books as "Lv Xing" (The Penal Code of Lv) in *Shang Shu* (*The Book of Historical Document*) (annotated by Kong Anguo) and *Shuo Wen* (*The Origin of Chinese Characters*). Thus, the punishment of "Yi" (to cut down the nose) was usually applied to comparatively serious crimes. Zheng Xuan, a renowned thinker in late Eastern Han Dynasty stated in the chapter of "Zhang Lu" (The Office of Execution) in "Qiu Guan" (Ministry of Penalty) in *Zhou Li* (*The Rites of Zhou Dynasty*) that "it was recorded in the book of *Shang Shu* (*The Book of Historical Document*) that anyone who defied the king, or violated the rules and regulations, or committed adultery and robbery or inflicted physical injury on other people would be sentenced to the punishment of 'Yi' (to cut off the nose)." In addition, in Zhou Dynasty, "the people who were sentenced to 'Yi' (to cut off the nose) would often be assigned to guard the borders."

The Punishment of "Fei" (Cutting Off the Left or Right Foot or Both Feet) It was explained in *Shi Gu* (explaining the different meaning and usages of words in ancient times) that "'Fei' means 'Yue'". In *Shuo Wen* (*The Origin of Chinese Characters*), it was interpreted that "'Yue' means 'cutting off'. Therefore, 'Yue

Zu' (cutting off one's foot) is called 'Fei'". In the chapter of "Si Xing" (Overseer of Penalty Affairs) in "Qiu Guan" (Ministry of Penalty) in *Zhou Li* (*The Rites of Zhou Dynasty*), Zheng Xuan annotated that: "'Fei' means cutting off the feet." In Xia Dynasty, this punishment was called "Bin", which was originally a severe punishment among the Miao people". While in Shang Dynasty, this punishment was called "Yue". There was a character in the inscriptions of bones and tortoise shells that resembled the action of cutting off the feet. In early Zhou Dynasty, this punishment was also called "Yue", and it was not until when *Lv Xing* (*The Penal Code of Lv*) was written that "Yue" was replaced by "Fei" (cutting off the left or right foot or both feet). In fact, "Bin", "Yue", and "Fei" (cutting off the left or right foot or both feet) imply exactly the same thing. In *Qi Guo Kao* (*Investigations of the Seven Countries*), Dong Shuo quoted a line from *Fa Jing* (*Canon of Laws*), the first relatively systematic written code of the Chinese history, and said, "anyone who spied on the palace would be sentenced to 'Bin'." After that, he added a note, which was quoted from Ying Shao, a well-known jurist from the Eastern Han Dynasty, and in the note, he explained, "'Bin' means cutting off the feet."

In Zhou Dynasty, there were three categories for punishment of "Yue" (to amputate the feet): cutting off the right, left or both feet. A figure of gatekeeper with his left foot cut off was inscribed on a bronze cooking vessel called "Yue Xing Nu Li Shou Men Tong Fang Ge" (Square Bronze Cooking Vessel with a Slave Watchman being Punished with the penalty of "Yue"), which was unearthed in Fufeng, Shaanxi province in December 1976. The punishment of "Yue" included not only cutting down the feet, but also the hands. In *Shuo Wen* (*The Origin of Chinese Characters*), it was thus defined that "'Yue' means cutting off. As a penalty, it means cutting off one's hands or feet." The punishment of cutting off both hands and feet was enforced after the Age of King Li of Zhou Dynasty, which had reflected the brutality of punishment in suppression. "Yue" was applied to serious crimes like the crime of defying the kings and the crime of robbery. It was recorded in *Han Fei Zi* (*Han Feizi*) that "a person with the surname of 'He' in Chu state had gotten a jade in Mount Chu, so he presented it to King Li, who then asked a jade expert to have an examination of it. However, the expert said that 'it's an ordinary stone'. The king thought he was deceived, so he ordered to have He's left foot cut off. Later, King Li died and King Wu succeeded to the throne. He dedicated the jade to King Wu, who again asked a jade expert to examine whether it was a real one. The jade expert again said that 'it's an ordinary stone'. The king thought he was deceived, so he ordered to have He's right foot cut off." This not only illustrated that the punishment of "Yue" was applied to the crime of defying the king, but also showed that the principle of accumulative penalty was applied to habitual criminals. It was stated in "Da Zhuan" (or Shang Shu Da Zhuan) in *Shang Shu* (*The Book of Historical Document*) that "anyone who breaks through the strategic passes, or climbs over the city walls to rob (other people) shall be punished by having their feet cut off."

When King Mu of Zhou drafted *Lv Xing* (*The Penal Code of Lv*), for the first time, it was stipulated that the punishment of "Yue" was less severe than the punishment of "Gong" (castration). In fact, before the Sui and Tang dynasties, the penalties of

"Yue" and "Gong" were only less severe than the punishment of death. According to *Si Ma Fa* (*The Law of Si Ma*), "for minor offenses, the criminal's ears should be pierced by an arrow; for medium offenses, the criminal's feet should be cut off; for serious crimes, the criminal's head should be cut off." In early Han Dynasty, it was proposed that the penalty of cutting off the right feet should be replaced by the punishment of "Qi Shi" (exposing the executed body publicly at markets), which had fully shown the cruelty of the punishment. In early Tang Dynasty, Wei Zheng and Dai Zhou once proposed that people should be exempted from death penalty and should be punished by cutting off their feet instead.

In Zhou Dynasty, it was stipulated that "anyone who was sentenced to 'Yue' should be ordered to guard the animal farm."[76] It was recorded in "Xiang Gong Er Shi Jiu Nian" (The 29th Year of the Duke of Xiang) in *Gong Yang Zhuan* (*The Biography of Gongyang*) that "what is 'Hun' (gate keeper)? It refers to criminal offenders who guard the gate." This meant that the people who were punished by "Yue" had become guilty slaves, so they had to guard the animal farms, to suffer from drudgery and "to live among beasts."

The Punishment of "Gong" (Castration) "Gong" (castration) originated from the punishment of "Zhuo" among Miao People and it was also called "Yin". In "Lv Xing" (The Penal Code of Lv) in *Shang Shu* (*The Book of Historical Document*), Kong Anguo noted that "'Gong' (castration) was also referred to as 'Yin', which means cutting off the reproductive organs of males or shutting females' vaginal orifice. So this is a penalty only less severe than death sentence." Zheng Xuan also made similar notes in the chapter of "Si Xing" (Overseer of Penalty Affairs) in "Qiu Guan" (Ministry of Penalty) in *Zhou Li* (*The Rites of Zhou Dynasty*): "The man would have his genitals cut off like the eunuchs while the woman would have her vaginal orifice clogged." "Gong" (castration) was applied to both men and women who had committed adultery. Jia Gongyan noted that "men and women having committed adultery would be sentenced to castration." However, the punishment of "Gong" (castration) did not apply to noblemen because the king "could not bear to destroy his own clan."[77] In Zhou Dynasty, "those who were punished by "Gong" (castration) would be ordered to guard the palace."[78] By the Spring and Autumn Period, "Gong" (castration) was applied not just to people committing adultery. "During the period of Qin Shi Huang (the first emperor of Qin), there were about

---

[76]"Zhang Lu" (The Office of Execution) in "Qiu Guan" (Ministry of Penalty) in "Zhou Li" (*The Rites of Zhou Dynasty*).

[77]Shen Jiaben (Qing Dynasty), "Gong" (Castration) in "Xing Fa Fen Kao" (Separate Textual Research on Penal Law) in *Li Dai Xing Fa Kao* (*A Textual Research of the Criminal Laws in the Past Dynasties*).

[78]"Zhang Lu" (The Office of Execution) in "Qiu Guan" (Ministry of Penalty) in *Zhou Li* (*The Rites of Zhou*).

720,000 cases of castration."[79] Apparently, not all of them were punished just because of adultery.

"Da Bi" (Capital Punishment) In "Lv Xing" (The Penal Code of Lv) in *Shang Shu (The Book of Historical Document)*, Zheng Xuan noted that "death sentence is the most severe penalty, thus it is called 'Da Bi' (meaning "big" or "severe")." It was recorded in "Shi Gu" (The Meaning and Usages of Words) in *Er Ya (Using Graceful and Elegant Languages*: an ancient book containing commentaries on classics, names, etc.) that "'Bi' means 'a crime'" and it was stated in *Bai Hu Tong (The Virtuous Discussions in White Tiger Hall)* that "'Da Bi' refers to death." This punishment was usually applied to serious crimes and its execution was usually carried out at the court if the offenders were senior officials; and its execution was usually carried out at the market if the offenders were ordinary persons. Moreover, the dead bodies of those executed would be exposed in public to show that "they were abandoned by the public." However, "anyone with a title or from the royal family would be sent to "Dian Shi Shi" (official in charge of the land) to wait to be sentenced to death,"[80] and "the noblemen who are sentenced to death penalty would be taken to 'Dian Ren' (official in charge of land and the death penalty for royal families) to be executed."[81] "Dian Shi Shi" and "Dian Ren'" referred to the local officials in the countryside.

2.4.2.3 The Applicable Principle of the Discriminatory Application of Criminal Law

Differentiating Manslaughter and Intentional Homicide; The Casual Offense and Habitual Offense In the early Zhou Dynasty, a preliminary differentiation between these four types of offences was established according to the guiding principle of "Ming De Shen Fa" (promoting virtue and being prudent in the enforcement of punishment). In the admonishment of Zhou Gong (Duke of Zhou) to Kang Shu, he explicitly stated, "if someone has committed a crime intentionally or habitually instead of accidentally, he shall be sentenced to death, even though it is a minor crime." He also said that "if someone commits a major crime but just for once and not on purpose ... he shall be exempted from death penalty."[82] This criminal principle had not only reflected the key target of the criminal law of Zhou Dynasty, but also shown that the subjective motivation of the offenders should be considered in settling cases. "The people who have committed crimes with goodwill shall be

---

[79]Yuan Mei (Qing Dynasty), "Sui Yuan Sui Bi" (Notes in Sui Yuan) (Part 2) in *Zhu Shi Lei (Various Histories)*.

[80]"Zhang Qiu" (Jailor) in "Qiu Guan" (Ministry of Penalty) in *Zhou Li (The Rites of Zhou)*.

[81]"Wen Wang Shi Zi" (King Wen and the Way of being the Crown Prince) in *Li Ji (The Book of Rites)*.

[82]"Kang Gao" (The Orders of Duke Zhou to Kang Shu) in *Shang Shu (The Book of Historical Document)*.

exempted from the punishment, while those with ill intention shall be sentenced to death."[83] This was the principle of "Lun Xin Ding Zui" (executing convictions according to intentions) which was called by later generations.

After titles and territories were subinfeudated, different laws were applied to different states. It was stated in "Da Si Kou" (The Senior Minister of Justice) in "Qiu Guan" (Ministry of Penalty) in *Zhou Li* (*The Rites of Zhou Dynasty*) that "lenient punishments should be executed for the newly established vassal states, moderate punishments should be executed for the peaceful vassal states and severe punishments should be executed for the turbulent vassal states." For example, the Duke Dan of Zhou ordered Kang Shu who was in charge of "Yin Xu" (the ruins of Yin Dynasty) and Bo Qin who was in charge of the Yan State (which was once submitted to the rule of Shang Dynasty) to "continue to have the people of Zhou Dynasty governed by applying the law of Shang Dynasty," whilst ordered Tang Shu who was in charge of "Xia Xu" (the ruins of Xia Dynasty) to "to have the Rong people governed by applying the laws of Xia Dynasty."[84] Surely, it had exerted a favorable influence on the stabilization of the new order and the consolidation of the country to apply different laws according to the concrete situations. This principle of criminal law had shown a kind of plain materialism based on actuality, so it had had a great influence on the later dynasties.

Enforcing Punishments by Analogy The principle of "enforcing punishments by analogy" originated from "Lv Xing" (The Penal Code of Lv) in *Shang Shu* (*The Book of Historical Document*). Cai Shen explained in his book *Ji Zhuan* (or *Shu Jing Ji Zhuan*: Interpretation of Shang Shu): "If there are no established laws for certain offenses, we should enforce punishments according to the previous ones by 'Bi Fu' (legal analogy)." To be more specific, "for those who have committed serious crimes, if they should be punished leniently, they should get lenient punishment, and for those who have committed minor crimes, if they should be punished severely, they should get severe punishment. So the judicial officials had the right to decide whether severe or lenient punishments should be enforced." "Shun said that even if those have committed serious crimes, but if they are not intentional or out of reasons of mischance and misfortune, they should be punished leniently; however even if those have committed minor crimes, but if they are intentional, they should be punished severely. Besides, it was described in 'Kang Gao' (The Orders of Zhou Gong (Duke of Zhou) to Kang Shu) that 'even though it is a minor crime, if it is committed deliberately, or if it is habitually committed, the offender should be punished severely; on the other hand, even though it is a serious crime, if it is committed negligently, the offender should be punished leniently." According to "Zheng Yi" (The Annotation of Confucians' Classics and the Books of History) in *Li Ji* (*The Book of Rites*), "when there are no available legal articles, convictions should be made by 'Bi Fu' (legal analogy)", namely, "convictions should be made by

---

[83]"Xing De" (The Penal Morality) in *Yan Tie Lun* (*Debates on Salt and Iron*).

[84]"Ding Gong Si Nian" (The 4th Year of the Duke of Ding) in *Zuo Zhuan* (*The Chronicle of Zuo*).

making reference to the severe punishment for major crimes, and making reference to the light punishments for the minor crimes." Therefore, it can be inferred that when there were no explicit written regulations, the method of analogy was often applied in Zhou Dynasty, just as Xun Zi in the Warring States Period had said that "punishments should be enforced in accordance with the law, but if there are no laws to follow, 'Bi Fu' (legal analogy) should be applied."[85] In enforcing punishment by "Bi Fu" (legal analogy), the focus was not only on "Zhi Fa" (enforcing laws) but also on "Yuan Qing" (enforcing laws according to specific circumstances). Thus, not only the crimes were punished, the ideology of prudent penalty and morality was also publicized.

"Zui Yi Cong Qing" (Enforcing Lenient Punishment for the Doubtful Cases) and "Zui Yi Cong She" (Remitting the Punishment for the Doubtful Cases)

The theory was first put forward in "Da Yu Mo" (Da Yu's Planning Government Affairs) in *Shang Shu* (*The Book of Historical Document*) and it was stated that "in the case of doubtful crimes, they should be dealt with leniently." In "Xiang Gong Er Shi Liu Nian" (the 26th Year of the Duke of Xiang) in *Zuo Zhuan* (*The Chronicle of Zuo*) in *Xia Shu* (*History of Xia Dynasty*) it was stated that "in the case of doubtful crimes, the offenders should be dealt with leniently to avoid killing the innocent." Therefore, to some extent, this was a specific reflection of the principle of "Zui Yi Cong She" (remitting the punishment for the doubtful cases). In Shang Dynasty, it was stipulated that public opinion should be stressed, so "in the case of doubtful crimes, the offender should be pardoned if the public have misgivings." This principle was further developed in the Western Zhou Dynasty and it was stated in "Lv Xing" (The Penal Code of Lv) in *Shang Shu* (*The Book of Historical Document*) that "when there are doubts concerning 'Wu Xing' (Five Penalties) or 'Wu Fa' (Five Fines), the offenders should be pardoned." When making annotation to "Zheng Yi" (The Annotation of Confucians' Classics and the Books of History) in *Li Ji* (*The Book of Rites*), Kong Yingda pointed out that "in the case of doubtful criminal penalties, the offenders should be pardoned and lenient punishment should be enforced; in the case of doubtful fines, the offenders should be pardoned." Meanwhile, "if the crime can be punished either leniently or severely, lenient punishment should be applied, and those who have committed major crimes should also be exempted from punishment."[86] Therefore, lenient punishment should be applied in the judgment and the offenders of the major crimes should be pardoned when handling the doubtful cases to show benevolence. However, this system of penalty reduction should be reviewed by the process of "San Ci" (one of the ways for the ancient Chinese court officials to make conviction. In other words, in handling the major and difficult cases, first it should be discussed by a group of ministers, if it cannot be decided after that, then it should be handed over to a group of officials to discuss. If it cannot be decided either, it should be discussed by all the people) in

---

[85]"Da Lue" (The Great Strategy) in *Xun Zi* (*Xun Zi*).

[86]"Wang Zhi" (The Royal Regulations) in *Li Ji* (*Book of Rites*).

2.4 The Legal Contents of *Lv Xing* (*The Penal Code of Lv*) and *Jiu Xing*... 83

judicial litigation. It was written in "Si Ci" (the assistant to senior minister of justice in charge of inquiries) in "Qiu Guan" (Ministry of Penalty) in *Zhou Li* (*The Rites of Zhou Dynasty*) that "(there were the regulations of) 'San Ci': inquiring the nobles, the officials, and the common people...so as to decide what punishment should be enforced." What was related to the principle of "Zui Yi Cong She" (remitting the punishment for the doubtful cases) was the punishment redemption system, which was applied to any penalties such as "Mo" (tattooing on the face or forehead of the offenders with indelible ink), "Yi" (to cut down the nose), "Fei" (cutting off the left or right foot or both feet), "Gong" (castration) and "Da Bi" (capital punishment). After the offenders paid a certain amount of money, their penalties, if doubtful, could be absolved. According to "Lv Xing" (The Penal Code of Lv) in *Shang Shu* (*The Book of Historical Document*), "when handling doubtful cases punishable by 'Mo', the punishment should be cancelled, and it could be atoned by paying 100 *huan* of copper money;...when handling the doubtful cases punishable by 'Yi', the ransom must be doubled;...when handling the doubtful cases punishable by 'Fei', the ransom is more than doubled;...when handling the doubtful cases punishable by 'Gong', the ransom is 600 *huan* of copper money; ...when handling the doubtful cases punishable by 'Da Bi', the ransom is 1000 *huan* of copper money."

This remitting principle for "Wu Xing" (Five Penalties) and "Wu Fa" (Five Fines), in effect, is the same as the principle of the presumption of innocence in the criminal law of modern times, so it had exemplified the spirit of "Fa Zhi" (the rule of law) in the criminal law of Zhou Dynasty 3000 years ago. For any offenders, if they were proved innocent after investigation, their penalties could be ransomed with different amount of money, and any doubtful crimes punishable by "Wu Fa" (Five Fines) could also be pardoned.

Different Punishments Applied to the Same Crime This is a principle of criminal law which has embodied the patriarchal clan system. "Ba Bi" (the eight conditions for mitigating punishments) depicted in *Zhou Li* (*The Rites of Zhou Dynasty*) had publicly provided people of the special social status with the privileges of commutation or being exempted from penalties. The system of "Ba Yi" (The Eight Deliberations) in the later ages had originated from the rules of "Ba Bi" made in Zhou Dynasty. Moreover, if the relatives of nobles and senior officials had committed crimes and were punishable by castration, they could be pardoned, just as was illustrated in the statement that "the punishment of castration does not apply to nobles because it is stipulated that it is forbidden to have their reproductive organs cut off."[87] If "Da Fu" (senior officials in ancient China) or anyone above their ranks had committed crimes punishable by death penalty, they could be executed in some specific places: "Da Fu" (senior officials in ancient China) would be executed in the court, while "Shi" (scholars) at the market. In addition, the nobles could be pardoned by paying the ransom.

---

[87]"Xing Kao" (A Textual Research of the Criminal Penalties) in *Wen Xian Tong Kao* (*A General Examination of Documents*).

"**The Father, Sons and Brothers of the Criminal Should Not Be Punished for His Crime**" Learning the lessons from the late Shang Dynasty that "the punishment of the whole clan of the criminal" might provoke fierce struggle, which in the end, might lead to the destruction of the country, the rulers of Zhou Dynasty emphasized that "only the offender himself should be punished" and none of his relatives should be implicated for his crime arbitrarily. "Kang Gao" (The Orders of Duke Zhou to Kang Shu) in *Shang Shu* (*The Book of Historical Document*) was quoted in "Zhao Gong Er Shi Nian" (The 20th Year of the Duke of Zhao) in *Zuo Zhuan* (*The Chronicle of Zuo*) and it was stated that "it is forbidden for the criminal's father, sons or brothers to be punished, let alone the officials in charge." In "Xiang Gong Er Shi Yi Nian" (The 21st Year of the Duke of Xiang) in *Zuo Zhuan* (*The Chronicle of Zuo*), the story of Yu and his father was also cited as a historical evidence to show that no implication should be inflicted between father and son. According to the story, "although Yu's father was sentenced to death for failing to control the flood, Yu was still enthroned for his success." This was completely different from the principle of "Nu Lu" (implication of the sons and grandsons in the punishment) and "Zui Ren Yi Zu", namely, "Yi Tian" (exterminating all family members of the criminal together with him) carried out in the Xia and Shang dynasties, so it is obviously a great progress of legal civilization.

In addition, it was not guilty for people to kill the thieves or robbers who broke into their houses, and it was recorded in the chapter of "Chao Shi" (an ancient official position in charge of the ranking of officials in the outer court and justice) in "Qiu Guan" (Ministry of Penalty) in *Zhou Li* (*The Rites of Zhou Dynasty*) that "anyone who kills the robbers, thieves or the families of the robbers and thieves is not guilty." It was noted by Zheng Xuan that "if the thieves and robbers have organized gangs and robbed people and their families, it is lawful for them to be killed by the victims; if anyone has invaded other people's residences, farmhouses, carriages and boats or has kidnapped people and violated the law, it is lawful for him to be killed by the victims." This principle, which was put forward more than 3000 years ago, was similar to the principle of justifiable defense in modern times, which had fully proved that the people of Zhou Dynasty were good at summarizing the practical judicial experience and developing it into theories.

2.4.3 The Civil Law Beginning to Take Shape

2.4.3.1 The Capacity for Civil Rights and Civil Acts

In the Western Zhou Dynasty, the hierarchy system was enforced strictly, so the legal status, the capacity for civil rights, and civil acts of different classes were completely unequal.

The slave owners enjoyed full capacity for legal rights and legal acts. Although the peasants of the civilians were attached to the nobles to some extent, they enjoyed personal freedom and had their own families and possessions. Therefore, they also had the capacity for civil rights and independent action. The merchants "who travel a long way with their carts and oxen to do business"[88] also had independent personalities and the qualifications for the civil subjects in legal relations.

Only slaves were treated as objects, just like horses and oxen. Therefore, they had no civil rights, and they had to do labor work for their masters without any payment. As the objects of the proprietary rights, they could be disposed of randomly at the owners' will, either as compensation, gifts, or as sacrifices at the altar.

According to "Da Si Kou" (The Senior Minister of Justice) in "Qiu Guan" (Ministry of Penalty) in *Zhou Li* (*The Rites of Zhou Dynasty*), there were the following rules concerning the obtaining of the capacity for rights: "'Si Min' (a government post) was in charge of the registration of the number of population. They registered people's names, recorded their addresses, and specified the details such as their sex and the places whether they were born: in the capital, fief or in the suburbs. Besides, the number of new born babies and the people who died were also recorded." In ancient times, the babies grew teeth when they were seven (female) or eight month (male) old. Thus, "Si Min" was in charge of having the names of the babies who had grown teeth registered, by which it meant that they had obtained the capacity for civil rights. However, the cancellation of household registration meant the end of the capacity.

As to the capacity for civil acts, it was recorded in "Qu Li" (The Summary of the Rules of Propriety) in *Li Ji* (*The Book of Rites*) that "a boy gets a formal name when he is twenty years old by attending a capping ceremony"; while "a girl gets a formal name when she is betrothed by attending a hair-pinning ceremony." It was further explained in *Zheng Yi* (*The Annotation of Confucians' Classics and the Books of History*) that "any boy who has gotten a formal name by attending a capping ceremony has become an adult"; while "if a girl is betrothed, then she attends the hair-pinning ceremony at the age of 15; if not, then at 20. This meant that she has become an adult." It was thus clear that males and females boasted the capacity for legal action when they were 20 and 15 respectively.

Because of the underdevelopment of civil laws in Western Zhou Dynasty, there were still not clear and definite concepts or rules for the capacity for civil rights and legal actions.

2.4.3.2 The Division of Personal Property and Real Estate and the Ownership Relationship

With the development of the right of private ownership, the people in Zhou Dynasty had already had initial conceptual differentiation between personal property and real estate. All farmland, land, and houses were real estate, while wealth, goods, and wares were personal property. The ownership of these two was not only the core of

---

[88]"Jiu Gao" (Announcement to Ban Alcohol) in *Shang Shu* (*The Book of Historical Document*).

all property rights but also an important component part of the property rights in early modern civil law.

In Western Zhou Dynasty, the object of real estate was land. Because the society was founded on agriculture, land was the lifeline for the existence and development of a country. The king enjoyed the highest degree and the most complete ownership of the land, as was reflected in the saying that "all the land in the world belongs to the king."[89] The ownership of land for the king of Zhou Dynasty was the blessing of "Tian" (Heaven), and "'Tian' (Heaven) awards all the land and people to the late kings of this country,"[90] thus only the king was entitled to "award people and land to the feudatory kings."[91] There were many records in the books of Western Zhou Dynasty such as "awarding him land, water, and slaves working on the land."[92] More records of the awards for nobles who had won great honors in wars were discovered in the inscriptions on copper wares. For example, it was recorded in *Shi Yong Yu* (wide-mouthed jar entitled "Shi Yong") that Yi Gong delivered the message of "awarding land" issued by the king of Zhou to Shi Yong and invited Jing Bo and other four people to attend the ceremony to show the importance of this event. According to the event recorded in the inscriptions on *Da Gui* (big food container made of bronze), the king of Zhou Dynasty had dispatched "Shan Fu" (official in charge of the king's food and drinks) to send the message of awarding Kui's land to Da. However, the ownership of the land was not changed after the awarding. All the nobles, dukes, and officials were just the holders and cultivators of the land, and they had not the capacity to sell or buy them, which was called "Tian Li Bu Yu" (no selling the land).[93] Moreover, the king of Zhou had the right to take the land back at any time, which was called "Xue Di" (reducing the enfeoffed land). The copper ware *Yi Hou Ce Gui*, which was unearthed in Yandun Mountain, Dantu, Jiangsu province in 1954 had provided sufficient evidence that the king had the power to change the ownership of the land awarded to vassals.

As to the plebeians, they were the main forces for agricultural production, so they needed to pay land tax to the authority. Based on "Jing Tian Zhi" (the "nine squares" system of land ownership), the system of "Che Fa" was carried out in the Zhou Dynasty, so according to the system, "tax was paid by the people of Zhou Dynasty in proportion to the income of their land." Some scholars had different explanations for "Che". Zhu Xi thought it meant "fair share", so he wrote that, "in Zhou Dynasty, each farmer was awarded one hundred *mu* of land...eight households worked together on the same land and divided the harvest equally, which was why this

---

[89]"Bei Shan" (Northern Mountains) in "Xiao Ya" (Minor Odes of the Kingdom) in *Shi Jing* (*The Book of Songs*).
[90]"Zi Cai" (High Quality Wood) in *Shang Shu* (*The Book of Historical Document*).
[91]Inscriptions on *Da Yu Ding* (*Great Yu Tripod*).
[92]"Bi Guan" (The Palace of Bi) in "Lu Song" (Odes to Lu) in *Shi Jing* (*The Book of Songs*).
[93]"Wang Zhi" (The Royal Regulations) in *Li Ji* (*The Book of Rites*).

2.4 The Legal Contents of *Lv Xing* (*The Penal Code of Lv*) and *Jiu Xing*...

method was called 'Che'."[94] "So the people kept nine tenths of the harvest and paid the rest to the government."[95] Thus, the one tenth of the harvest was called land tax.

Since Western Zhou Dynasty, the authority started recruiting military and labor service, so the military recruiting was carried out on a national scale, while the labor service recruiting was carried out on both national and local scale. According to *Zhou Li* (*The Rites of Zhou Dynasty*), "any city dweller aged twenty to sixty or countryman aged fifteen to sixty-five should be recruited to provide the service for the country. Yet the privileged, the noble, the capable, the civil servants, the old, and the sick could be exempted from it."[96] With the development of private economy, the ordinary people obtained the ownership of a small portion of the land they had cultivated. Therefore, the description that "it rains on the public land, as well as my private land" in "Da Tian" of "Xiao Ya" in *Shi Jing* (*The Book of Songs*) has reflected the plebeians' concern over the production of their private land.

Apart from the real estate, the land, there was also personal property, including slaves, subjects, concubines, boy servants, servants, horses, oxen and so on. The king of Zhou enjoyed the supreme ownership of slaves, which was reflected in the statement, "everyone in the country is the king's subject."[97]

People could obtain the ownership not only by the awards from the king, but also by some other significant means like claiming private land, making interests, exchanging commodities, inheriting and so on. Besides, people could claim anything that was not owned by others. As was recorded in "Zhong Dong Zhi Yue" (The Month of Midwinter) in "Yue Ling" (Monthly Orders) in *Li Ji* (*The Book of Rites*) that "this month, any harvests which had not been collected or any livestock which had no one to pasture could be claimed without being investigated." It was also recorded in "Chao Shi" (an ancient official position in charge of the ranking of officials in the outer court and justice) in "Qiu Guan" (Ministry of Penalty) in *Zhou Li* (*The Rites of Zhou Dynasty*) that "any goods, slaves, and livestock collected should be reported to the imperial court and made known to the public. If nobody claims the article within ten days, and if they are of large amount, they shall be confiscated by the government, but if they are of small amount, they can be possessed by the plebeians."

The male head of a household enjoyed the ownership of both personal and real estate. Nevertheless, children did not enjoy the ownership, just as what was said in "Qu Li" (The Summary of the Rules of Propriety) in *Li Ji* (*The Book of Rites*), "if the parents are alive, ...the children are forbidden to keep private wealth."

---

[94]Zhu Xi (Song Dynasty), "Meng Zi" (Mencius) (Part 5) in *Si Shu Zhang Ju Ji Zhu* (*Collected Notes to The Four Great Classics*).

[95]Zhu Xi (Song Dynasty), "Lun Yu" (The Analects) (Part 6) in *Si Shu Zhang Ju Ji Zhu* (*Collected Notes to The Four Great Classics*).

[96]"Xiang Dai Fu" (Village Officials) in "Di Guan" (Ministry of Land) in *Zhou Li* (*The Rites of Zhou Dynasty*).

[97]"Bei Shan" (Northern Mountains) in "Xiao Ya" (Minor Odes of the Kingdom) in *Shi Jing* (*The Book of Songs*).

2.4.3.3 "Ze" (Debt)

In Western Zhou Dynasty, debts were called "Ze". It was stated in the chapter of "Chao Shi" (an ancient official position in charge of the ranking of officials in the outer court and justice) in "Qiu Guan" (Ministry of Penalty) in *Zhou Li* (*The Rites of Zhou Dynasty*) that "if there are disputes over debts and if loan contracts have been signed, the case shall be accepted" and that "the case of 'Ze' (debt) shall be accepted if there is a loan contract." It was recorded in "Xiao Zai" (name of petty official in ancient time) in "Tian Guan" (The Ministers) in *Zhou Li* (*The Rites of Zhou Dynasty*) that "the litigation about loan is handled according to contracts."

In Western Zhou Dynasty, debts were categorized into tort claims, illegal benefit, and contractual debt.

Tort Claims Tort claims resulted from the infringement upon other people's property rights. In the early times, the revengeful measure of "tit for tat" was taken. For example, "if an ox had trampled on other people's farmland, the ox shall be confiscated." With the development of economy and legal culture, the indemnity about the infringement gradually went beyond the scope of customary law. In the inscriptions of *Hu Ding* (*Hu Tripod*) in the later years of King Gong of the Western Zhou Dynasty and *Shi Ren Pan* (*San Family Plate*) in the reign of King Li in late Western Zhou Dynasty, two cases concerning the payments for infringement were described in detail. According to *Hu Ding* (*Hu Tripod*), Kuang Ji, a nobleman with lower social status, had ordered his men to take away ten zi of Hu's rice crop (one zi is about one billion). In the end, twenty zi were paid back as compensation. According to the inscriptions of *Shi Ren Pan* (*San Family Plate*), there was a lawsuit for Shi's infringement of the right of San, and San demanded payment. Shi agreed to pay the debt by "Mei Tian" (sloping fields) and "Jing Yi Tian" (a square piece of land). Thus, according to the record "Shi infringed upon San's domain, so he should pay the debt with his land." With the mediation of the government, both parties sent people to make a measurement of land, sign the contract, and complete the transaction procedures of land. In addition, Shi made a pledge to show his determination to fulfill the contract. The two examples above showed that, civil liability compensation was already emphasized at that time, and it was punitive to pay more than the damages caused.

Debts Resulting from Illegal Benefit According to regulation, "all goods, slaves, and livestock that had been obtained should be reported to the imperial court within ten days and the major cases relevant should be made known to the public while the minor ones should be settled by the parties themselves."[98] If anyone had appropriated to oneself what belonged to others, it would be taken as illegal benefit, so he would be punished according to the criminal law; yet if anyone had handed in all the unclaimed property to the government, he would be duly awarded.

---

[98]"Chao Shi" (Official in Charge of Official Assessment and Justice) in "Qiu Guan" (Ministry of Penalty) in *Zhou Li* (*The Rites of Zhou Dynasty*).

2.4 The Legal Contents of *Lv Xing* (*The Penal Code of Lv*) and *Jiu Xing*...

Contractual Debt In Western Zhou Dynasty, contracts were called "Pan Shu", "Qi Yue", "Fu Bie", "Yue Ji", "Zhi Ji", and so on. After the middle of the Western Zhou Dynasty, contracts which were regarded as credit vouchers and the proof of civil action began to be used more frequently and became the main form of debts. Among the common contracts are contracts for goods exchanges, sale contracts, loan contracts, lease contracts and so on, which will be elaborated as follows:

Contracts for the Exchanges of Goods During the reign of King Gong, it was recorded on the copper ware *Wu Si Wei Ding* (*Wu Si Wei Tripod*) that Qiu Wei had exchanged land with Bang Junli. The relevant officials and witnesses were invited to attend and participate in the ceremony when the exchange contract was signed. Qiu Wei, to legalize the exchange and to protect his newly obtained right to the 500 *mu* of land through contract, had inscribed the entire process of the deal on a vessel.

It was recorded in *Jiu Nian Wei Ding* (*Wei Tripod of the 9th Year of King Kong*) that in the 9th year of King Gong, Qiu Wei got Ju Bo's land in exchange for his carriages, horses, and clothes. After the exchanging ceremony, Qiu Wei carved the statement on a vessel on which it was written that "Wei can own this land for 1000 years" to insure his ownership of the land he had obtained.

Besides, it was recorded in the inscriptions of *Bo Ge Gui* (*Bo Ge's Food Vessel*) that a good horse could be sold in exchange for 3000 *mu* of farmland. It was also written in *Hu Ding* (*Hu Tripod*) that five slaves could be sold in exchange for a horse and a bunch of silk.

Sale contract referred to the contract signed by both parties of the deal. Owing to the development of merchandise economy in the early Zhou Dynasty, business became an indispensable social economic sector and markets appeared in some cities, so slaves, as well as oxen, horses, weaponry and jewelry, were all sold at the markets.

To ensure and protect the purchaser's ownership, the "Qi Juan" (contract), which was signed after the sale, must be received from "Zhi Ren" (the officials in charge of the markets). According to "Zhi Ren" (the officials in charge of the markets) in "Di Guan" (Land Official) in *Zhou Li* (*The Rites of Zhou Dynasty*), "'Zhi Ren' (the officials in charge of the markets) is in charge of 'Zhi Ji' (sale contract) of goods, people, oxen and horses, weaponry, jewelry at the market." "Zhi Ji" referred to written contracts for exchanges. Zheng Xuan also annotated that "'Zhi Ji' referred to coupons which need to be collected. At the big markets, long-term contracts were needed in the dealing of people, oxen, and horses, while at the smaller ones, only short-term contracts were needed in the dealing of weaponry and jewelry."[99] So the expressions like "administering transactions with 'Zhi Ji'" could be found in "Xiao Zai" (name of petty official in ancient time) in "Tian Guan" (The Ministers) in *Zhou Li* (*The Rites of Zhou Dynasty*), in which full expressions about the popularity of sale contracts were recorded. Therefore, the function of contracts was to "prevent people

---

[99]"Zhi Ren" (Official in Charge of Markets) in "Di Guan" (Ministry of Land) in *Zhou Li* (*The Rites of Zhou Dynasty*), annotated by Zheng Xuan.

from fighting with each other"[100] and to maintain the normal trade relations, so it was just for this reason that "all major sale contracts were often carved on bronze sacrificial utensils, while the minor sale contracts were recorded in red on bamboo tablets and textiles."[101]

During the reign of King Gong, it was recorded on the bronze ware *Bo Ge Gui* (*Bo Ge's Food Vessel*) that Bo Ge exchanged four good horses for 3000 *mu* of farmland on discount (termed 'Jue Jia' in ancient Chinese language). This agreement had involved witnesses and pledges. Besides, the contracts were written on wooden slips, which was divided into two parts (also called "Xi" in Chinese), with one kept in the government and the other kept by the purchaser himself, which could be used as evidence if a lawsuit was filed. After the purchase, inscriptions were carved by Bo Ge on a bronze vessel as proof. *Wei He* (*Wei's Wine Vessel*), which has been unearthed in recent years, has a record of a purchase conducted in the 3rd year of the reign of King Gong. Ju Bo tried to buy "Jin Zhang" (an object to carry when meeting the king) from Qiu Wei. Qiu demanded eighty *peng* of shells, so Ju exchanged with forty *mu* of land. Afterwards, Ju bought two pieces of red tiger skin, two pieces of deerskin for decoration, and two pieces of underwear, which were worth twenty *peng* with "three *mu* of farmland". In both purchases, *peng* (ancient unit of currency) was used as measure of the value of goods and the sales were carved on vessels. Because the farmland owned by Ju was originally a public one, this deal was reckoned as a major event. Thus, the king of Zhou sent "Si Tu" (the minister of civil affairs), "Si Ma" (the minister of military affairs), and "Si Kong" (the minister of public works) to attend the land transaction ceremony. The sale contracts became legal documents, which had shown the development of the role of the law in regulating ownership. If one party broke the contract, the other party could sue to the government and ask the officials for verdicts.

In the land purchase contract, it was a crucial part to mark off the boundary. For instance, in *Wu Si Wei Ding* (*Wu Si Wei Tripod*) the dividing of the border of the newly bought land of Qiu Wei was recorded: the farmland extended northward to Li's land, eastward to San's land, southward to Fu's land and westward to Li's land. In the inscription on *San Shi Pan* (*San Family Plate*), the lakes, rivers, hills, mountains, and towns involved in the boundary division were all described in great detail, so were the methods of planting trees and making signs. Further, after dividing the boundary, it was stipulated that "it should be written down" and recorded in inscriptions. Moreover, a map on which the boundaries were marked clearly should be drawn up.

As the transfer of land was closely related to the change of ownership, both the "buyer" and the "seller" should ask the relevant people to witness the delivering of the land. To name only a few, on both *Wei He* (*Wei's Wine Vessel*) and *Wu Si Wei Ding* (*Wu Si Wei Tripod*) there were the records of "Si Tu" (the minister of civil

---

[100]"Shou Dao" (Sticking to the Law) in *Han Fei Zi* (*HanFeizi*).

[101]"Zhi Ren" (Official in Charge of Markets) in "Qiu Guan" (Ministry of Penalty) in *Zhou Li* (*The Rites of Zhou Dynasty*).

2.4 The Legal Contents of *Lv Xing* (*The Penal Code of Lv*) and *Jiu Xing*...

affairs), "Si Ma" (the minister of military affairs) and "Si Kong" (the minister of public works) attending the civil activity of land transference.

Loan Contract Loan contract was also a common kind of contract in Zhou Dynasty. In this relationship, the creditor had the right of asking the debtor to perform his duties, whereas the debtor should take the legal responsibility for the creditor. It was stated in "Xiao Zai" (name of petty official in ancient time) in "Qiu Guan" (Ministry of Penalty) in *Zhou Li* (*The Rites of Zhou Dynasty*) that "the lawsuit about loan is judged according to 'Fu Bie' (contracts)." According to the annotation of Zheng Xuan, "'Fu Bie' refers to documents of agreement... 'Fu' means recording the purchase in written records, while 'Bie' means dividing 'Fu' in two parts for both sides to hold." Namely, debts, rights, and obligations were described in the contract and it was then divided into two parts, one of which was kept by the government, the other of which by the debtor. Debt contracts were also called "Qi Quan", "Shu Qi", "Quan Qi", and "Yue Ji". According to "Xiao Zai" (name of petty official in ancient time) in "Tian Guan" (The Ministers) in *Zhou Li* (*The Rites of Zhou Dynasty*), "loan was administered with contracts." In "Qi Ce" (Strategies of Qi) in *Zhan Guo Ce* (*Stratagems of the Warring States*), Feng Yuan, to help Meng Changjun, went to Xue's house to collect debt: "he traveled there with the loan contract in hand." As to "Yue Ji" (debt contract), it was usually applied to the debt relationship between common people, and it was kept by the government to show its importance. If disputes occurred, "Yue Ji" could be used as evidence just like "Fu Bie". It was recorded in "Shi Shi" (The Interpretation of History) in "Qiu Guan" (Ministry of Penalty) in *Zhou Li* (*The Rites of Zhou Dynasty*) that "when a dispute over property occurred, 'Fu Bie' and 'Yue Ji' should be referred to in making proper judgment." It was also recorded in "Chao Shi" (an ancient official position in charge of the ranking of officials in the outer court and justice) in "Qiu Guan" (Ministry of Penalty) in *Zhou Li* (*The Rites of Zhou Dynasty*) that "Pan Shu' should be handed in by those who are involved in disputes of debt in 'the trial of court." "'Pan' refers to the combination of the two halves," which had demonstrated that "Pan Shu" referred to the same thing as "Fu Bie" and "Yue Ji".

With the continuous development of private ownership and the prevalence of loan relationship, laws were started to be applied by the state to maintain proper loan contract relationships, and anyone who had violated the law would be punished. Therefore, "it is a duty for everyone who has reached a trade agreement to carry it out according to the law of the country, and those against the law shall be punished"[102]; "if anyone has disputes over contracts with others, then a ceremony will be held when opening the storage sites of the contract (to check the original version of the contract) to make sure which party has broken the contract, the swindler shall be

---

[102]"Chao Shi" (Official in Charge of Official Assessment and Justice) in "Qiu Guan" (Ministry of Penalty) in *Zhou Li* (*The Rights of Zhou Dynasty*).

sentenced to the punishment of 'Mo' (tattooing on the face or forehead of the offenders with indelible ink)."[103]

Lease Contract After the middle period of the Western Zhou Dynasty, with the development of commodity economy, a new relationship of property circulation called "leasing" appeared. It was recorded in the inscriptions on *Ge You Cong Ding* (*Ge Cong and You Tripod*) of King Li's reign that You Weimu rented land from Ge for planting, but a dispute was caused for his delaying of paying the full rent. In the end, Ge won the lawsuit and You Weimu was ordered by the officials to take a pledge: "if I don't pay Ge the rent, I am willing to be punished by 'Liu' (exile)."

Moreover, the event of noblemen Xing Bo and others renting farmland from King Li was also recorded in the inscriptions of *Wu Si Wei Ding* (*Wu Si Wei Tripod*), in which not only pledges, but also witnesses were included.

The two cases above indicate that lease relationship starts from the time when the lease contract takes effect, and anyone who has broken the contract will be punished in accordance with the criminal law. However, the law tended to be partial to the leasers. The occurrence of farmland leasehold in the late Western Zhou Dynasty could be demostrated by the phenomenon of "employing laborers in the countryside,"[104] which was popular in the Spring and Autumn Period.

In summary, it can be concluded that in Western Zhou Dynasty, it was an essential precondition for the establishment of a contract to meet the needs of both parties. There were both oral agreement and written contract, with the former applied in small economic activities, and the latter applied in bulk commodity transactions and exchanges. In the existent contracts, the ones with farmland and slaves as the subject matter often took up the major part, which had reflected the loosening of the king's ownership resulted from the development of merchandise economy. In terms of varieties, the contracts for exchanging, purchasing, and loaning were the most common; whereas leasehold and employment contracts were rare. Generally, the contents of the contracts included the time, location, the names, and subject matter of both parties, the witnesses, and the oaths, which in fact, was a form of guarantee with strong religious color. Besides, the contracts were not restricted to individuals, so the government could also negotiate contracts with individuals as creditors to earn the interests that the country needed. To ensure the implementation of the contract, the document was divided into two parts, with one kept by the government, and the other by the creditor. When a dispute arose, the contract could be used to ensure the payment of debts. Just as it was recorded in "Si Meng" (The Official in charge of Dealing with Agreements) in "Qiu Guan" (Ministry of Penalty) in *Zhou Li* (*The Rites of Zhou Dynasty*) that "if anyone has reached an agreement with the others, then a copy shall be kept by 'Si Meng' (The Official in charge of Dealing with

---

[103]"Si Yue" (Official in Charge of Dukes) in "Qiu Guan" (Ministry of Penalty) in *Zhou Li* (*The Rights of Zhou Dynasty*).
[104]"Xiang Gong Er Shi Qi Nian" (The 27th Year of the Duke of Xiang) in *Zuo Zhuan* (*The Chronicle of Zuo*).

2.4 The Legal Contents of *Lv Xing* (*The Penal Code of Lv*) and *Jiu Xing*... 93

Agreements).'' As far as the signing of important contracts and transferring of bulk possessions was concerned, not only witnesses were needed, the king was also needed to hear the report and send officials to attend the ceremony to show his concern over the change of ownership and to conduct necessary supervision.

It was not coincidence that after a transference contract was signed or a civil lawsuit was settled, the new owner of the transferred object or the party that won the lawsuit often carved the process on bronze wares. In Western Zhou Dynasty, the bronze vessels were called "Zhong Qi" (important instruments) and were reckoned as the symbols of state power. In fact, Chu people had inquired about the bronze vessel to replace the regime of Zhou, so the inscriptions on the wares were either records of state affairs, or signals of important power transference, or reflection of certain knowledge of state power, thus they were of precious value. That is why it was publicly acknowledged that "only titles and sacrificial vessels were not to be lent to others."[105] Therefore, it had fully reflected that great the importance was attached by the Zhou people to the transference of ownership relations by carving the contracts about the transfer of ownership and the judgments of civil litigation on the bronze vessels. From the ancient times to the present time, no one, regardless of his class and caste, has ignored the property relationship concerning his interests, so the purpose of making civil laws in ancient China was just to protect people's property rights.

2.4.3.4 Marriage and Inheritance

In ancient China, it was thought that "the Heaven and the Earth were made before all things; all things were made before males and females; males and females were made before couples; couples were made before fathers and sons; then at last the monarchs and his subjects, the superior and the inferior and the etiquette were made."[106] Therefore, the ancient Chinese people attached great importance to the legal adjustment of marriage, family, and order.

Monogamy was dominant in the Western Zhou Dynasty, however, polygamy was practiced and even institutionalized among nobles. It was explicitly provided that "the son of 'Tian' (heaven) shall descendants, have 'Fu Ren' (female attendants), have 'Shi Fu' (female officials in palace), have 'Pin' (maid of honor), have 'Qi' (wives), and have 'Qie' (concubines)," "so shall the nobles."[107] According to "Gui Mei" (The 54th Diagram: Marry off One's Daughter) in *Yi* (*The Book of Changes*), "when a lady gets married, her sister will marry the same man as a concubine," which had shown the social reality of polygamy at the time. Because of the establishment of patriarchal clan system in Western Zhou Dynasty, there was great

---

[105]"Da Gao" (The Great Imperial Mandate) in *Shang Shu* (*The Book of Historical Document*), annotated by Zheng Xuan.

[106]"Xu Gua" (Introduction to Divinatory Symbols) in *Zhou Yi* (*The Book of Changes*).

[107]"Qu Li" (The Summary of the Rules of Propriety) in *Li Ji* (*The Book of Rites*) (Book 2).

difference for the inheritance rights of "Di Zi" (the son born of the legal wife) and "Shu Zi" (the son born of a concubine). Hence, the division between wife and concubines was strictly marked, as was shown in the statement that "if the woman has a formal license of marriage, she is the wife; if the woman elopes with the man, then she is the concubine."[108] If a vassal had treated a concubine as legal wife, he would be attacked and condemned.

The Establishment of Marital Relationship First, the male and female were not allowed to get married until they reached the legal age for marriage. According to "Mei Shi" (Office of Marriage) in "Di Guan" (Land Official) in *Zhou Li* (*The Rites of Zhou Dynasty*), "men were required to marry after they reached to the age of thirty, while women after twenty." It was also recorded in "Nei Ze" (The Pattern of the Family) in *Li Ji* (*The Book of Rites*) that "males become grown-ups as they turn to twenty, so they start to learn 'Li' (rites) afterwards...and after the age of thirty, they begin to have a family and take the responsibility as a man. Females become grown-ups as they turn to fifteen and get married after twenty; should any accident happen, they can get married at the age of twenty three." In reality, at the age of twenty, the ceremony of "Guan" (the ceremony of crowning of adulthood for man) was held for the male; at the age of fifteen, the ceremony of "Ji" (the ceremony of crowning of adulthood for woman) was held for female, so they could get married officially.

Second, young people were not allowed to get married until they had gotten the permission of their parents. As was recorded in "Nan Shan" (Southern Mountain) in *Shi Jing* (*Book of Songs*) that "information about the woman whom the man is going to marry should be made known to his parents." In Western Zhou Dynasty, the power of the parents in determining the marriage was not as great as that in the later times, so it was recorded that "in February of spring, young men and young women are required to meet each other, so private dating are not forbidden during this time of the year," which has shown a relatively much freer form of marriage.

As it was regarded as "Li" (rites) for "both males and females to reject seeking marriage alliance by their own," matchmakers played a very important role. "If the matchmaker does not come and propose marriage, the male and female even don't know each other's name."[109] "So men and women don't get married without matchmakers."[110] "How to marry a woman? It can only be arranged by a matchmaker."[111] Therefore, a special official position called "Mei Shi" (office of marriage) was set up to "take charge of the affairs of marriage in the country."[112]

---

[108]"Mei Shi" (Office of Marriage) in "Di Guan" (Ministry of Land) in *Zhou Li* (*Rites of Zhou Dynasty*).

[109]"Qu Li" (The Summary of the Rules of Propriety) in *Li Ji* (*The Book of Rites*) (Book 1).

[110]"Fang Ji" (The Record of Neighborhood) in *Li Ji* (*The Book of Rites*).

[111]"Nan Shan" (Southern Mountains) in *Shi Jing* (*The Book of Songs*).

[112]"Mei Shi" (Office of Marriage) in "Di Guan" (Ministry of Land) in *Zhou Li* (*Rites of Zhou Dynasty*).

2.4 The Legal Contents of *Lv Xing* (*The Penal Code of Lv*) and *Jiu Xing*...

At last, a series of legal ceremony should be held for the marriage, including matchmaking, inquiring about family members, engagement, presenting dowries, selecting the auspicious date for wedding and the wedding itself, which were called "Liu Li" (six kinds of etiquette in feudal marriage). Although in this customs of marriage there were still the traces of mercenary marriage, it had shown the progress of civilization because marriage by force, which was prevalent in ancient time, had been stopped. The order of the "Liu Li" (six kinds of etiquette in feudal marriage) and the amount of betrothal money were determined by the status of both parties.

It should be noted that the widows and widowers were allowed to remarry. It was recorded in "Da Guo" (Overmuch) in *Yi* (*The Book of Changes*) that "if an elderly man marries a young woman, it is just like an old tree growing new branches. Isn't it good?" and it was also stated that "the blooming of an old poplar just resembles an elderly lady married to a young husband, so there is nothing to be blamed or praised."

The Taboos of Marriage First, people with the same family names were not allowed to get married, no matter how distant or close their relationship was, or how many generations were there between them. It was stated in "Qu Li" (The Summary of the Rules of Propriety) in *Li Ji* (*The Book of Rites*) that "don't marry a woman who has the same family name with you. Yet because when a concubine is bought, her name is unknown, divination was often used (forecast the name)." It was also recorded in "Xiao Te Sheng" (Sacrificial Animal) in *Li Ji* (*The Book of Rites*) that "since marriage is the root of all things, it was forbidden to have intermarriage inside the same clan to avoid social disorder, but it was encouraged to establish kinship relationship between two different and distant families." Wang Guowei pointed out in *Yin Zhou Zhi Du Kao* (*The Investigation of the Systems of Yin and Zhou*) that "the third difference between Zhou and Shang dynasties was the system by which the marriages between the people with the same family names were forbidden." This was because it was against morality and ethics for people in the same clan to get married under patriarchal clan system. Moreover, the nobles tried to enlarge the scope of their power and strengthen the alliance with each other by marriage bonds. Besides, according to the account of "Xi Gong Er Shi San Nian" (The 23rd Year of the Duke of Xi) in *Zuo Zhuan* (*The Chronicle of Zuo*), "if the husband and the wife share the same family names, it is harmful for their offspring." People in Zhou Dynasty seemed to understand that the closeness of the kinship of a couple would exert a bad influence on the health of later generations. By quoting Morgan, Engles said in *The Origin of the Family, Private Property and the State* that "the marriages between the members of different blood ties will produce human species that are stronger both mentally and physically. When two advanced clans mix, the skull and brains of a new generation will naturally be increased and it will not stop until they combine with those of the two groups. Thus, the groups who have implemented the clan system must defeat the less developed one or make them follow their example." Out of patriarchal and political consideration, the policy of the prohibition of the marriage between relatives was implemented by the people of

Zhou Dynasty, which had brought about a physically and mentally stronger generation, so it had exerted a great influence on the multiplication of Chinese nation.

Second, the people from different social status were forbidden to marry each other. The strict caste system of the Zhou Dynasty had had a great influence on the marriage relationship. It can be inferred from the inscriptions on bronze vessels like *Zong Fu Ding* (*Zong Fu Tripod*), *Qin Gong Zhong* (*Qin Gong Bell*), *Qin Gong You* (*Qin Gong Window*), *Shu Ji Gui* (*Food Vessel Entitled Shu Ji*), *Fan Peng Sheng Hu* (*Kettle Entitled Fan Peng Sheng*), *Shi Wang Gui* (*Food Vessel Entitled Shi Wang*) and *KeXu* (*Grain Container Entitled Ke*) that there were intermarriages between the royal families and the vassals, and between the vassals and the nobles. However, intermarriage between the nobles and the ordinary folks was forbidden, so the ordinary folks could only marry ordinary folks. These hierarchical restrictions on marriage had a lasting influence, although it was not applicable to concubines.

Lastly, marriage was forbidden within three years after the death of one's parents. According to "Sang Fu" (Mourning Apparel) in *Yi Li* (*Etiquette and Ceremony*), a man "should not get married within three years after his father's death, which is the standard of being a filial son."

The Dissolution of Marriage First, it was up to the parents' preference, besides the elder brother also had the rights to interfere. It was described in "Jiang Zhong Zi" (My Dear Zhongzi) in *Shi Jing* (*Book of Songs*) that, "How can I love him? I am afraid of my parents;...how can I love him? I am afraid of my elder brother." It was recorded in "Nei Ze" (The Pattern of the Family) in *Li Ji* (*The Book of Rites*) that "even if a man loves his wife very much, he may be demanded to have her divorced if his parents don't like her. If he doesn't love her, but his parents do, they would say, 'she takes good care of us'. Thus, he would never divorce her but had to treat her as his wife."

Second, if the wife could not bear a child within three years after marriage, the husband could file for a divorce. It was stated in "Jian" (The 53rd Diagram: Gradually) in *Yi* (*The Book of Changes*) that "if the wife hasn't been pregnant for three years, something must be done and things will turn out all right (she will get pregnant eventually)." If the wife had an affair, then the kids born hence were illegal and could not be accepted. As was stated in *Yi* (*The Book of Changes*), "if the wife gets pregnant when the husband is away in the army, the child will be abandoned."

Lastly, if either of the couple passed away, a divorce was permitted. "Qi Chu" (Seven Reasons to Repudiate the Wife) was recorded in "Ben Ming" (Sexagenary Cycle of one's Birth) in *Da Dai Li Ji* (*The Rites of Da Dai*): "the divorce of a wife is permitted for the following seven circumstances: "failing to bear a male offspring", "being lascivious", "being unfilial to parents-in-law", "gossiping", "committing theft", "being jealous", and "having severe illness". The wives of the king or nobles would not be divorced if they could not bear sons; but if they commit the other six offenses, they would be divorced, too." The regulations for "Qi Chu" (Seven Reasons to Repudiate the Wife) might not have been necessarily practiced in Western Zhou Dynasty, but most probably, they were made by people of the Han

2.4 The Legal Contents of *Lv Xing* (*The Penal Code of Lv*) and *Jiu Xing*...

Dynasty. Besides, according to "Xiao Kuang" (Personal Writing) in *Guan Zi* (*The Book of Master Guan*), "if a man divorces more than three times, he shall be exiled out of the country," from which we can see that frequent divorce was forbidden in law.

Under the patriarchal clan system, patriarchy was also practiced in families, just as was described in the saying that "there are not two suns in the sky, nor two kings in one country, nor two heads in one family, so there should be only one person in control."[113] The rights and obligations of the husband and wife were unequal. After the wedding ceremony, the wife would leave the patrilineal family and joined her husband's family. It was prescribed in law that the husband enjoyed the dominant role, and the wife was only in a subordinate position so she had no rights at all, as was described in the saying that "the man guides the woman, and the woman follows the man. Thus, it is where the harmony between husband and wife begins. Accordingly, women should always be obedient. When she was young, she should be obedient to her father and elder brothers; after getting married, she should be obedient to her husband; after her husband passes away, she should be obedient to her son."[114] Women enjoyed civil rights despite the fact that they were subordinate to their husbands in the family, which could be proved by the inscriptions on *Diao Sheng Gui* (*Food Vessel Entitled Diao Sheng*), in which it was recorded that "Yu sends 'Fu' (a married woman) a pot"; which could also be proved by the inscriptions on *Ling Gui* (*Food Vessel Entitled Ling*), in which it was recorded that Wang Jiang "has awarded Ling ten *peng* of shells, ten households of subjects and one hundred servants."

As for children, they were at the mercy of their parents and had low social positions in the family. In "Nei Ze" (The Pattern of the Family) in *Li Ji* (*The Book of Rites*), it was recorded that "the children dared not complain even if the parents had whipped them to bleeding when they are not happy; instead, the children had to stand up to show obedience and respect." Besides, the sons and daughters were forbidden to go to the government to file lawsuit against their father, as it was ruled that "even if the father or the son has violated the law, it is forbidden for them to report the other to the government because it might destroy the patriarchal system."[115]

In terms of inheritance system, the succession of "Di Zhang Zi" (the eldest son born of the legal wife) was gradually institutionalized. "It is 'Di Zhang Zi' (the eldest son born of the legal wife) but not the virtuous one who has the right to inherit; and it is 'Di Zi' (the son born of the legal wife) but not the eldest one who has the right to inherit,"[116] which was not only the rule of the clan, but also the law of the state.

---

[113]"Fang Ji" (The Record of Neighborhood) in *Li Ji* (*The Book of Rites*).

[114]"Xiao Te Sheng" (Sacrificial Animals) in *Li Ji* (*The Book of Rites*).

[115]"Zhou Yu" (The Historical Records of Zhou Dynasty) in *Guo Yu* (*The Historical Records of Various States*), Vol. 2.

[116]"Yin Gong Yuan Nian" (The 1st Year of Yin Gong) in *Chun Qiu Gong Yang Zhuan* (*Annotation to Chun Qiu by Master Gong Yang*).

Therefore, its goal was to prevent the political prerogative, titles and property of the noblemen from being embezzled or undermined. Meanwhile, it had helped to maintain the interior order and the continuation of the reigning of the ruling class. In principle, this system could be applied to anyone ranging from the king to ordinary people. For example, during the reign of King Xuan of Zhou, Duke Wu of Lu took his eldest son Kuo and the youngest son Xi to the court. King Xuan planned to let Xi inherit his father's title and property, but he was opposed to by the officials. The reason was that if the king did not grant the eldest son the title of vassal, it meant that he was "teaching people to revolt". However, whether with or without the family name Ji, some of the younger sons did inherit titles in some vassal states. For example, in "Xiang Gong San Shi Yi Nian" (The 31st Year of the Duke of Xiang) in *Zuo Zhuan* (*The Chronicle of Zuo*), Lu Mu Shu said, "since the eldest son has passed away, his younger brother shall inherit." In "Jin Yu" (The Historical Records of Jin State) in *Guo Yu* (*The Historical Records of Various States*), Duke Xian of Jin said: "There are three ways to decide who will be the crown prince: if all of the princes are of noble birth, the eldest one shall inherit; if they are of the same age, the favored one shall inherit; but if the king loves them equally, then divination shall be used to decide." In the vassal state of Chu, in particular, "the younger son always succeeded to the throne."[117] Therefore, the system of the succession of "Di Zhang Zi" (the eldest son born of the legal wife) did not apply universally. Although the common people did not have any titles or property to inherit, they were also restricted by the patriarchal principle of the system of primogeniture.

The above marriage and family system which were developed from the core spirit of patriarchal clan system were established to establish the dominance of fathers and husbands by adjusting the relationship between parents and children and between husband and wife and to maintain the national order of aristocratic dictatorship. As was stated by You Zi in "Xue Er" (On Study) in *Lun Yu* (*The Analects*), "among those who are filial and fraternal, there are few offenders of their superiors; among those who never offend their superiors, there are few trouble makers."

If a comparison is made between the marriage and family systems of the Western Zhou Dynasty and those of ancient Rome, great difference can be found. For example, the marriage in ancient Rome was based on family interests to inherit the lineage and bear sacrifice. As was said by the famous jurist Modestinus, "marriage means lifelong union of husband and wife and the joint adventure of God's affairs and human affairs."[118] However, in the empire period, the definition of marriage was changed and it referred to "the union of a man and a woman to live together forever" in the well-known *The Institutes of Justinian* written by Justinianus. Apparently, emphasis was put on the common interests of both sides. In a family, the relationship between husband and wife was equal, which meant both sides had their own

---

[117]"Wen Gong Yuan Nian" (The 1st Year of the Duke of Wen) in *Zuo Zhuan* (*The Chronicle of Zuo*).

[118]Quoted from Zhou Xiang, et al., *Luo Ma Fa* (*Roman Law*), Qun Zhong Publishing House, 1983. p. 98.

independent property and shared the responsibility of mutual loyalty and help, so any of the two parties could file for a divorce. On the contrary, in "Hun Yi" (The Significance of Marriage) in *Li Ji* (*The Book of Rites*), it was stated that "marriage is to unite two families, to pay homage to ancestors in the clan temples and to maintain the family lineage," which had totally ignored the interests of the man and the woman concerned. The relationship between wife and husband in a family was always that of man superior to woman and woman obedient to man, so that the husband took the complete initiative to end the marriage.

As children's personality was legally accepted, the marriage relationship in ancient Rome was established firstly by inquiring about the opinions of parties involved and then by getting the permission of the parents.

The differences aforesaid were made by the different national circumstances of the two countries. Since ancient Rome entered commodity economy in an earlier era, the prosperity of seaborne commerce and the integration with foreigners had enabled its single and enclosed civil law to develop into that of the coexistence of the civil law and the law of different peoples (jus gentium), which had determined the progress of marriage and family system. However, in Western Zhou Dynasty, the autocratic royalty and the patriarchal clan system based on unitary small-scale peasant economy as well as the conservative rule of "Li" (rites) shaped by the isolated environment had undoubtedly exerted a profound influence on the marriage and family relations of the country.

It can be inferred from the civil law of the Western Zhou Dynasty that in the process of the transformation of land ownership from state to individual, the property law and the law of obligation were also developed to some extent. With the comprehensive establishment of the patriarchal clan system, the family property, the inheritance of "Di Zhang Zi" (the eldest son born of the legal wife), and the dominance of the father and the husband were initially legalized. Except for a handful of codes, "Li" (rites) gradually became the origin of civil law in the adjustment of civil legal relationship. To maintain the hierarchy and social stability, the government authorities had intervened in the local civil legal activities.

2.5 The Judicial Activities with the Initial Differentiation of Criminal and Civil Litigation

The continuing discovery of the inscriptions on bronze wares and the classic records represented by *Zhou Li* (*The Rites of Zhou Dynasty*) had provided a much accurate evidence for the scale and the contents of the legal system of the Western Zhou Dynasty.

Under the political system of Western Zhou Dynasty, the king was the supreme judge with the right of final jurisdiction. It was recorded in "Zhang Qiu" (Jailor) in "Qiu Guan" (Ministry of Penalty) in *Zhou Li* (*The Rites of Zhou Dynasty*) that "upon the day of execution, (the jailor) reports the criminal's name to the king and takes the criminal to 'Chao Shi' (an ancient official position in charge of the ranking of officials in the outer court and justice)." This has demonstrated that the king is also in charge of settling the legal disputes among nobles. It was recorded in the inscriptions on *Hu Ding* (*Hu Tripod*) that the Eastern Palace also had the judicial authority of the settlement of the disputes among the nobles.

Under the king of Zhou, "Da Si Kou" (The Senior Minister of Justice) "was not only in charge of implementing 'San Dian' (three codes) of the state, but also in charge of helping the king to punish the vassals who violated the law and in conducting interrogation." The so-called "San Dian" (three codes) included: "lenient punishment for the newly established vassal states; moderate punishment for peaceful vassal states; and severe punishment for the turbulent vassal states." At the same time, "Da Si Kou" (The Senior Minister of Justice) took the charge of the entire judicial work by taking the following measures: "'Wu Xing' (Five Penalties) was used to punish the offenders"; "both parties of the litigation were required to be present at the court to prevent false accusation and to bring with them relevant proof materials to prevent imputation"; "'Huan Tu' (prison) was set up to imprison people who idled about"; "'Jia Shi' (a stone placed on the left side of the court gate) was used to help villains to repent and to make a new start" and "'Fei Shi' (a stone placed outside the court gate) was set up to allow the helpless people to lodge their complaints."[119]

"Xiao Si Kou" (The Junior Minister of Justice) was a secondary judiciary. Thus, he "was not only in charge of the matters outside the court" but also responsible for hearing the trials in the territories governed directly by the central government and "the cases of the ordinary people according to 'Wu Xing' (Five Penalties)."[120] In 'Li Zheng" (Establishment of Proper Governance of a State) in *Shang Shu* (*The Book of Historical Document*), "Si Kou Su" was regarded as a model and he was praised because he had "dealt with all the criminal matters that he was in charge of reverently, thereby he has perpetuated the fortunes of the kingdom." According to the record in "Ding Gong Si Nian" (The 4th Year of the Duke of Ding) in *Zuo Zhuan* (*The Chronicle of Zuo*), Kang Shu was once a "Si Kou" (the minister of justice). And the discovery of bronze vessels like *Si Kou Liang Fu Gui* (*Food Vessel Entitled Si Kou Named Liang Fu*), *Yu Si Kou Hu* (*Kettle Entitled Si Kou of the State of Yu*) and *Da Liang Si Kou Ding* (*Tripod Entitled Si Kou of Da Liang*) have shown that this official post was established both in the early Zhou Dynasty and the Warring States Period.

Below "Xiao Si Kou" (The Junior Minister of Justice) was "Shi Shi" (the official in charge of criminal affairs), who took the charge of "Wu Jin" (the five prohibitions), namely, "Gong Jin" (palace prohibition), "Guan Jin" (official prohibition), "Guo Jin" (state prohibition), "Ye Jin" (field prohibition) and "Jun Jin" (military

---

[119]"Da Si Kou" (The Senior Minister of Justice) in "Qiu Guan" (Ministry of Penalty) in *Zhou Li* (*The Rites of Zhou Dynasty*).

[120]"Xiao Si Kou" (The Junior Minister of Justice) in "Qiu Guan" (Ministry of Penalty) in *Zhou Li* (*The Rites of Zhou Dynasty*).

2.5 The Judicial Activities with the Initial Differentiation of Criminal and Civil...

prohibition), and "Wu Jie" (five commandments), namely, "Shi" (standard), "Gao" (imperial mandate) "Jin" (prohibition), "Jiu" (correction), and "Xian" (constitution), which were used in sequence to enforce "punishment". Besides, "rules and regulations were also posted on the doors and gates of alleys" by "Shi Shi" (the official in charge of criminal affairs)[121] to give publicity to the law and to prevent crimes.

In addition, officials were appointed to be in charge of specific judicial affairs such as "Si Xing" who was "in charge of enforcing the punishment of 'Wu Xing' (Five Penalties)"[122]; "Si Ci" who was "in charge of enforcing the punishment of 'San Ci' (one of the ways for the ancient Chinese court officials to make conviction. In other words, in handling the major and difficult cases, first it should be discussed by a group of ministers, if it cannot be decided after that, then it should be handed over to a group of officials to discuss. If it cannot be decided either, it should be discussed by all the people), 'San You' (the three kinds of circumstances for lenient treatment) and 'San She' (amnesty to three kinds of people: the young and weak, the old, and the foolish)"[123]; "Si Huan" (official in charge of prison) who was in charge of the jail and prisoners and who was responsible for the execution of the penalties. Many other officials who were in charge of legal affairs affiliated to "Si Kou" (the minister of justice) were also appointed, which showed that judicial judgment had become the major state activities.

According to "Xiang Shi" (Judicial Official in Charge of the Capital and the Surrounding Areas) in "Qiu Guan" (Ministry of Penalty) in *Zhou Li* (*The Rites of Zhou Dynasty*), the regional judicial system in the Western Zhou Dynasty is as follows:

> 'Xiang Shi' is in charge of the administration of the people in the local district to prevent them from doing bad deeds. Moreover, he is also in charge of accepting lawsuits, collecting testimonies, making judgments about the nature of the crimes, differentiating death penalty from other ones and noting down his opinions about the judgment. Ten days later, the details of the case shall be publicized outside the court. After 'Xiao Si Kou' (The Junior Minister of Justice) hears the lawsuit, he will make judgments and report it to the imperial court....after the trial, 'Shi Shi' (the official in charge of criminal affairs) receives and keeps the written verdict, and then a suitable date will be chosen to have the criminal punished or executed or have the criminal's body exposed in public for three days. If the emperor wants to pardon the criminals, 'San Gong' (the three councilors) will be sent to jointly attend the court trial to set the final date.

Apart from "Xiang Shi" (judicial official in charge of the capital and the surrounding areas), "Sui Shi" (official in charge of the legal affairs in the area between 100 and 200 *li* from the capital), "Gao Shi" (official in charge of the legal affairs of the area of marshland), "Fang Shi" (official in charge of the legal affairs of the 3rd level fiefs), "Ya Shi" (official in charge of the legal affairs of the vassal states) were responsible for the civil and criminal cases in their districts ("Sui", "Gao", "Yi", etc.,

---

[121] "Shi Shi" (The Interpretation of History) in "Qiu Guan" in *Zhou Li* (*The Rites of Zhou Dynasty*).
[122] "Si Xing" (Overseer of Penalty Affairs) in "Qiu Guan" in *Zhou Li* (*The Rites of Zhou Dynasty*).
[123] "Si Ci" (The Assistant of the Minister of Justice in Charge of Inquiry) in "Qiu Guan" in *Zhou Li* (*The Rites of Zhou Dynasty*).

respectively). The ordinary cases could be dealt with by local authorities, but in the case of major crimes, "Si Kou" (the minister of justice) should "make judgments" by himself. Thus, it can be seen that the trial system at different levels in Western Zhou Dynasty tended to be more complex than that of the Shang Dynasty.

In the vassal states, the vassal assumed the supreme judicial rights in his fief and the judicial authorities had also established their own judicial posts of "Shi Shi" (the official in charge of criminal affairs) and "Si Kou" (the minister of justice), which could be certified by the inscriptions on bronze wares like *Si Kou Liang Fu Gui* (*Food Vessel Entitled Si Kou Named Liang Fu*). In some vassal states, the judicial ministers were not called "Si Kou" but were called "Da Li" or "Si Bai".

It should be noted that under the restriction of the strict hierarchal system, the disputes between the vassals of lower ranks were settled by the vassals of higher ranks. It was recorded in the inscriptions of *Hu Ding* (*Hu Tripod*) that when Vassal Hu and Vassal Xian filed a lawsuit, it was heard and settled by a noble of higher ranks called Jing Shu. The head of a noble household also had the power to judge the family members and even to sentence them to death penalty.

In Western Zhou Dynasty, there was already initial differentiation between criminal and civil litigation. It was recorded in "Da Si Kou" (The Senior Minister of Justice) in "Qiu Guan" (Ministry of Penalty) in *Zhou Li* (*The Rites of Zhou Dynasty*) that "both parties of the litigation were required to be present at the court to prevent false accusation and to bring with them relevant proof materials to prevent imputation." According to the notes of Zheng Xuan, "if both parties have accused the other of having committed a crime, then this is called "Yu" (a criminal case), while if the two parties have disputes over money, then this is called "Song" (a civil case)." He also said that "it is called 'Yu' to file a lawsuit of crimes and it is called 'Song' to file a lawsuit of property."[124] "Although it is a general term for hearing civil and criminal cases to make judgment after hearing the debate at court," yet this classification was not so scientific in theory and practice.

In both civil and criminal action, the form of direct appeal by the plaintiff was taken. According to *Zhou Li* (*The Rites of Zhou Dynasty*), in Zhou Dynasty, the system of "Lu Gu" and "Fei Shi" were used. The former one meant that the claimant could beat the drum outside the innermost gate in the palace and state his grievances; the latter one meant the claimant was demanded "to stand on 'Fei Shi' (a stone placed outside the court gate) for three days" "so that his testimony can be heard and reported."[125] Both "Lu Gu" and "Fei Shi" were mainly established for the helpless and the poor. Besides, the plaintiffs could lodge their complaints orally if it was a minor case, whilst they could present the statements in written form if it was a serious one. Both parties of the criminal litigation should hand in "Jun Jin" (copper money: thirty *jin* for each *Jun*) (*jin*: unit of weight, one *jin* is about 500 g), while

---

[124]"Da Si Kou" (The Senior Minister of Justice) in "Qiu Guan" (Ministry of Penalty) in *Zhou Li* (*The Rites of Zhou Dynasty*).
[125]"Da Si Kou" (The Senior Minister of Justice) in "Qiu Guan" (Ministry of Penalty) in *Zhou Li* (*The Rites of Zhou Dynasty*).

both sides of the civil litigation should hand in "Shu Shi" (one hundred arrows as a bunch), which are similar to the litigation cost in later ages. If either party had failed to hand in "Jun Jin" or "Shu Shi", he would be taken to confess his own fault but his case would not be accepted, or he would simply lose the lawsuit. It was recorded in "Qi Yu" (The Historical Records of Qi State) in *Guo Yu* (*The Historical Records of Various States*) that "both parties of the case shall bring with them 'Shu Shi' (one hundred arrows as a bunch)." Wei noted that "both parties of the civil litigation shall bring 'Shu Shi' (one hundred arrows as a bunch) with them to the court to hear the trial. If two persons file a lawsuit, but just one of them brings 'Shu Shi' (one hundred arrows as a bunch), it is unfair, so the one who fails to bring 'Shu Shi' (one hundred arrows as a bunch) with him would lose the case. The trial is not held until both parties hand in 'Shu Shi' (one hundred arrows as a bunch)." In *Zhou Li* (*The Rites of Zhou Dynasty*) there were also similar accounts: "let both parties of the litigation be present at the court to prevent false accusation, and then the case will be heard after each of them bring 'Shu Shi' (one hundred arrows as a bunch) with him." Proof could be found in bronze inscriptions as well, so it was recorded in *Yang Gui* (*Food Vessel Entitled Yang*) that "the king said, 'Yang . . . as 'Si Kong' (the minister of public works) . . . and "Si Kou" (the minister of justice) was paid five *lue* (ancient measurement: one *lue* is about 50 g) of bronze to make the verdict'." In *Fu Chu Gui* (*Food Vessel Entitled Gui*) "the king said, 'Fu Chu, you are to be in charge of the people of Chengzhou and the vassals; Da Ya holds a civil trial and gets five *lue* of bronze." These inscriptions show that the king ordered Yang and Fu Chu to hear the lawsuits and allowed them to get five *lue* of bronze as payment. This system of paying "Jun Jin" (copper money: thirty *jin* for each *Jun*) and "Shu Shi" (one hundred arrows as a bunch) had obviously imposed restrictions on the litigation filed by the populace.

Under the patriarchal system, the litigation between fathers and sons was forbidden, "if the father or the son has violated the law, it is forbidden for either one of them to report to the government, because if so, the patriarchal system would be destroyed."[126]

To protect the interests of the privileged class, the junior officials were not allowed to contest in a lawsuit with the senior ones. On *Ying Yi* (*Washbasin Entitled Zhen*), a bronze ware of the later years of the Western Zhou Dynasty, inscriptions about a case between Mu Niu and his superior official were recorded. The case was heard by a judicial official Bo Yangfu. In the end, Mu Niu was convicted of having broken his promise, so was sentenced to the punishment of "Bian" (whipping) for 1000 strokes with the punishment of "Mo" (tattooing on the face or forehead of the offenders with indelible ink). Finally, this punishment was reduced to "Bian" (whipping) for 500 strokes with the rest of the 500 ones ransomed by 300 *huan* of copper money. Mu Niu was also required to promise that he would not interfere with any business of the superior anymore; otherwise, he would be punished by "Bian"

---

[126]"Zhou Yu" (The Historical Records of Zhou Dynasty) in *Guo Yu* (*The Historical Records of Various States*), Vol. 2.

(whipping) and "Mo" (tattooing on the face or forehead of the offenders with indelible ink). The case was closed after Mu Niu paid the fine, accepted the verdict, and swore an oath. Thus, it can be concluded that the hierarchal system of the Western Zhou was fairly rigid and those who had breached the contract would be punished according to the criminal law.

During the trial, both parties should attend the session of the court, which was called "Liang Zao Ju Bei" (the presence of both parties).[127] If any nobleman was involved in the case, then he could send his subordinates, sons, or brothers instead to attend the court trial, no matter how serious the case was. It was stated in "Si Kou" (the minister of justice) in "Qiu Guan" (Ministry of Penalty) in *Zhou Li* (*The Rites of Zhou Dynasty*) that "the nobilities like "Ming Fu" (Da Fu: senior official in ancient China) and "Ming Fu" (his wife) shall not be present at the court" to "prevent them from being offended by the judges." A case was recorded in the inscriptions on *Hu Ding* (*Hu Tripod*), and according to the record, both parties involved in the case were nobilities so they had sent their subordinates to court instead of attending the trial by themselves. During the trial, the judge "heard the testimonies from both sides without prejudice," "examined the differences of their presentation,"[128] and pointed out the contradiction of their confessions. In the meanwhile, the judge also carefully observed what both sides said and did, as was illustrated in the statement that "he settles the cases according to five kinds of observations to find out the truth and to make judgments: words, expressions, breaths, sense of hearing and expressions in the eyes."[129] This had not only reflected their accumulated experience in judicial work, but also their deep understanding of criminal psychology, which was a great step forward compared with the method of settling cases by referring to supernatural beings in Xia and Shang Dynasties, and which has exerted a relatively profound influence on later generations. Thus, it is a progress of legal system worthy to be affirmed.

In criminal litigation, it was allowed to extort confessions by torture, as was illustrated in the saying that "people's lawsuits were heard by applying 'Wu Xing' (Five Penalties)."[130] It was stated in "Yue Ling" (Monthly Orders) in *Li Ji* (*The Book of Rites*) that "in the mid-spring..., 'You Si' (official) is ordered to release the prisoners, to get rid of their hand and foot cuffs, to stop arbitrary whipping, and to prevent litigation." Thus, it implied that arbitrary whipping was not forbidden except mid-spring. Besides, it was proved by the bronze inscriptions that the punishment of "Bian" (whipping) was used to coerce statements.

Apart from oral confessions, documentary evidence, testimony of a witness, and physical evidence were of great significance as well. "Dao Zei Zhi Ren Qi Huo Hui"

---

[127]"Lv Xing" (The Penal Code of Lv) in *Shang Shu* (*The Book of Historical Document*).

[128]"Lv Xing" (The Penal Code of Lv) in *Shang Shu* (*The Book of Historical Document*).

[129]"Xiao Si Kou" (The Junior Minister of Justice) in "Qiu Guan" (Ministry of Penalty) in *Zhou Li* (*The Rites of Zhou Dynasty*).

[130]"Xiao Si Kou" (The Junior Minister of Justice) in "Qiu Guan" (Ministry of Penalty) in *Zhou Li* (*The Rites of Zhou Dynasty*).

2.5 The Judicial Activities with the Initial Differentiation of Criminal and Civil...

(The Weapons and Booty), which was recorded in "Si Li" (official in charge of the Weapons and Property of the Rebels and Thieves) in "Qiu Guan" (Ministry of Penalty) in *Zhou Li* (*The Rites of Zhou Dynasty*), referred to tools or weapons for criminal purposes, which was a very important evidence for fair judgment. Further, the judges had the obligation to check the body of the victims and to investigate the scene of crime. It was recorded in "Yue Ling" (Monthly Orders) in *Li Ji* (*The Book of Rites*) that "at the beginning of autumn, the judge is ordered to check the bruises, hurts or wounds of the criminals; moreover, the judgment of cases should be fair and just, and anyone guilty of murder shall be punished severely."

Documentary evidence was crucial in civil litigation. It was written in "Xiao Si Tu" (The Assistant of 'Si Tu') in "Qiu Guan" (Ministry of Penalty) in *Zhou Li* (*The Rites of Zhou Dynasty*) that, "when disputes arise, the people living nearby are the witnesses; when a dispute over land arises, the 'Tu' (contract) will serve as evidence for fair judgment." It was recorded in "Shi Shi" (The Interpretation of History) in "Qiu Guan" (Ministry of Penalty) in *Zhou Li* (*The Rites of Zhou Dynasty*) that "when a dispute over money occurs, 'Fu Bie' and 'Yue Ji' (contracts) shall be checked." The contract documents like "Tu", "Fu Bie", and "Yue Ji" mentioned here are the most crucial physical evidence to confirm property relationship and to divide the boundaries of farmland.

Different laws were applied to different parties according to their status in trials. "Lawsuits involved nobles were judged according to "Bang Dian" (the state code); lawsuits involved officials were judged according to "Bang Fa" (the state law); lawsuits involved common people were judged by "Ba Cheng" (the statute law)."[131] The "Dian", "Fa", and "Cheng" here, according to *Shuo Wen Jie Zi* (*Origin of Chinese Characters*), refers to three different books of laws. Besides statute laws, case laws also played an important role in judicial practice. The principle of "Shang Xia Bi Zui" (making convictions by the comparison of the legal punishments) recorded in "Lv Xing" (The Penal Code of Lv) in *Shang Shu* (*The Book of Historical Document*) and the principle of "figuring out the nature of the crime to make fair judgments by referring to the cases in the past" recorded in "Wang Zhi" (The Royal Regulations) in *Li Ji* (*The Book of Rites*) both demonstrated that the established precedents in the past could be used as references for analogy when there were no statute laws.

To exempt the nobles from punishment, it was clearly stipulated in *Zhou Li* (*The Rites of Zhou Dynasty*) that "'Ba Bi' (the eight conditions for mitigating punishments) should be used as a supplement to the criminal law to reduce punishments." The so-called "Ba Bi" (the eight conditions for mitigating punishments) included: "Yi Qin" (the cases which involved "Huang Qin": the relatives of the Emperor), "Yi Gu" (the old retainers of the Emperor: including those who had been in the emperor's service for a long time), "Yi Xian" (the morally worthy: including worthy men or superior men whose speech and conduct were greatly virtuous and may be taken as a

---

[131]"Si Kou" (The Minister of Justice) in "Qiu Guan" (Ministry of Penalty) in *Zhou Li* (*The Rites of Zhou Dynasty*).

model for the country), "Yi Neng" (the great ability: including people of great talent), "Yi Gong" (great achievement: including those of great achievement and glory), "Yi Gui" (the high status: including all active duty officials of the third rank and above), "Yi Qin" (diligent: including military and civil officials who have displayed great diligence in their work through thorough occupation of public affairs), and "Yi Bin" (the guests of the state: to treat the descendants of previous dynasties as guests of the state who could enjoy a legal privilege)"[132] "Ba Bi" (the eight conditions for mitigating punishments) is a manifestation of the legal privilege of the aristocracy and it has become the historical origin of "Ba Yi" (The Eight Deliberations) in the feudal laws of later ages.

"Ming De Shen Fa" (promoting virtue and being prudent in the enforcement of punishment) was the state policy carried out in the early Zhou Dynasty, so before judgment, the system of "San Ci" (one of the ways for the ancient Chinese court officials to make conviction. In other words, in handling the major and difficult cases, first it should be discussed by a group of ministers, if it cannot be decided after that, then it should be handed over to a group of officials to discuss. If it cannot be decided either, it should be discussed by all the people) were carried out, "the first refers to consulting the nobles, the second refers to consulting the officials, and the third refers to consulting the common people...so as to decide the execution of the punishment."[133] It remained unknown whether this procedure was implemented comprehensively or was implemented with the mixture of the ideal of later generations, but in the inscriptions of bronze wares, there indeed were the records like "consulting officials concerned". By "examining and deliberating over the prisoner's confessions" and carrying out the system of "San Ci", the judicial principles such as "Wu Ci Jian Fu, Zheng Yu Wu Xing" [verifying both parties' statements and making judgment in accordance with "Wu Xing" (five penalties)], "'Shang Xia Bi Zui' (making convictions by the comparison of the legal punishments), 'Wu Jian Luan Ci' (no admitting the assumptive and false pleadings), 'Wu Yong Bu Xing' (no using the obsolete laws) and 'Wei Cha Wei Fa' (making careful examination and making conviction in accordance with law)" could be carried out in making convictions.[134]

Because of the crudeness and simplicity of the law, the judges were allowed to apply the method of "Shang Xia Bi Zui" (making convictions by the comparison of the legal punishments)[135] in bringing a verdict. In doubtful cases, the principle of the presumption of innocence might be put into practice, so "when there are doubts

---

[132]"Xiao Si Kou" (The Junior Minister of Justice) in "Qiu Guan" (Ministry of Penalty) in *Zhou Li* (*The Rites of Zhou Dynasty*).

[133]"Xiao Si Kou" (The Junior Minister of Justice) in "Qiu Guan" (Ministry of Penalty) in *Zhou Li* (*The Rites of Zhou Dynasty*).

[134]"Lv Xing" (The Penal Code of Lv) in *Shang Shu* (*The Book of Historical Document*).

[135]"Lv Xing" (The Penal Code of Lv) in *Shang Shu* (*The Book of Historical Document*).

about 'Wu Xing' (Five Penalties), remit them; when there are doubts about 'Wu Fa' (Five Punishments), remit them."[136]

In Zhou Dynasty, the verdict of the judicial authority was called "He", and the written legal documents were called "Cheng He". For example, it was recorded in the inscriptions of *Ying Yi* (*Washbasin Entitled Zhen*) that "Bo Yangfu thus drafted 'He'." Moreover, the verdict should be read out to the litigants, so it was written in "Xiao Si Kou" (The Junior Minister of Justice) in "Qiu Guan" (Ministry of Penalty) in *Zhou Li* (*The Rites of Zhou Dynasty*) that "when passing a sentence, the crime should be announced." Zheng annotated that "it is just similar to the way of reading the verdict which we use now (in Han Dynasty) when making a conviction." The Duke of Jia elaborated it this way: "'Du Shu Ze Yong Fa' means when passing a sentence, relevant laws and facts about the crime should be read aloud to show that punishment is enforced in accordance with law." Sometimes, the parties who lost the lawsuits would be ordered to make a pledge to show fair statement and resolute execution. The inscriptions of *Ge You Cong Ding* (*Ge Cong and You Tripod*) and *Ying Yi* (*Washbasin Entitled Zhen*) that were unearthed also took records of the pledge activities of both parties. However, the pledges mentioned here are with less religious color, so they are more significant legally.

After the judgment was announced, the litigant was allowed to lodge an appeal again if he was not satisfied with the decision. There were different time limits for appeals in different regions: "ten days within the capital, twenty days in the suburbs, thirty days in the countryside, three months in "Du" (ancient administrative region), and no more than a year in vassal states. The appeals shall only be accepted within the time limit."[137]

As to death penalty, the criminal would be executed at the market with his body displayed for three days, which was called "Yu Zhong Gong Qi". In the chapter of "Zhang Lu" (The Office of Execution) in "Qiu Guan" (Ministry of Penalty) in *Zhou Li* (*The Rites of Zhou Dynasty*), it was stated that "all the murderers would be put to death with their bodies exhibited at the market for three days," which was similar to "Qi Shi" (exposing the executed body publicly at markets) in bronze inscriptions and both of them referred to putting the criminal to death at the market. Besides, the female criminals "shall be punished but the punishment will not be enforced at the market."[138] In Zhou Dynasty, the execution of death penalty was closely related to the climate and other natural phenomena. In "Xiang Gong Er Shi Liu Nian" (The 26th Year of the Duke of Xiang) in *Zuo Zhuan* (*The Chronicle of Zuo*), there were also the records of "carrying out executions in autumn and winter by following Heaven's threatening and frightening power." Thus, it can be inferred that the

---

[136]"Lv Xing" (The Penal Code of Lv) in *Shang Shu* (*The Book of Historical Document*).

[137]"Chao Shi" (Official in Charge of Official Assessment and Justice) in "Qiu Guan" (Ministry of Penalty) in *Zhou Li* (*The Rites of Zhou Dynasty*).

[138]"Xiang Gong Shi Jiu Nian" (The 19th Year of the Duke of Xiang) in *Zuo Zhuan* (*The Chronicle of Zuo*).

tradition of carrying out execution in autumn and winter began in Western Zhou Dynasty.

After the corporal punishments ("Mo": tattooing on the face or forehead of the offenders with indelible ink; "Yi": to cut down the nose; "Yue": to amputate the feet; "Gong": castration), the criminals should also do forced labor at certain places. For example, "the people who are sentenced to the punishment of 'Mo' shall be ordered to guard the gate; the people who are sentenced to the punishment of 'Yi' shall be ordered to guard the state border; the people who are sentenced to the punishment of 'Gong' shall be ordered to guard the palace; the people who are sentenced to the punishment of 'Yue' shall be ordered to guard the animal farm and the people who are sentenced to the punishment of 'Kun' (having the criminal's long hair cut short) shall be ordered to guard the barn."[139]

The enforcement of "Tu" (imprisonment) was called "Zhi Zhi Huan Tu" and the convicts were forced to do labor work for one to three years. Moreover, "Ju Xi" (custody) was established. This term first appeared in "Meng" (The 4th Diagram) in *Yi* (*The Book of Changes*), and it was described that "catch him, tie him tightly, and force him to follow." For minor crimes, the convicts would be sentenced to hard labor after being caught and imprisoned.

Because the redeeming system was established, the nobles could atone for their crimes by paying copper money or silk, unless they had committed major crimes like endangering the country or the king of Zhou Dynasty. This system was not only an important development of the legal system of the Western Zhou Dynasty; it was also a reflection of the social and economic development and private property ownership in the penal system. Only when the society and economy develop to a certain degree can the redeeming system be carried out in punishment.

In civil litigation, the settlement of cases by mediation was already put into practice. It was recorded in the inscriptions of *Hu Ding* (*Hu Tripod*) that Xian broke the contract with Hu, so the case was reported to Jing Shu, who criticized Xian for the breaching of contract as a royal member. Through the mediation of Jing Shu, Xian agreed to keep his promise, so the litigation was settled. This was one of the typical cases.

Although theocracy was not so evident in the Western Zhou Dynasty, it was still one form of judgment to pledge to "Tian" (Heaven) in judicial activities. This practice was applied to civil or even the criminal cases, which was called "trial by oath."

It was recorded in "Si Meng" (The Official in charge of Dealing with Agreement) in *Zhou Li* (*The Rites of Zhou Dynasty*) that "the public would be assembled to condemn anyone who has disobeyed the monarch or broken his promise." According to another account, "anyone who is involved in a lawsuit shall make a pledge," which means that the litigant should make a vow when filing a lawsuit.

---

[139]"Zhang Lu" (The Office of Execution) in "Qiu Guan" (Ministry of Penalty) in *Zhou Li* (*The Rites of Zhou Dynasty*).

2.5 The Judicial Activities with the Initial Differentiation of Criminal and Civil...

In *Ge You Cong Ding* (*Ge Cong and You Tripod*) the litigation between Ge Cong and You Weimu over the land rent was recorded. The latter lost the lawsuit for his breaching of the contract, so afterwards he had to go to the government office to receive punishment. Finally, the case was settled with the pledges of the both parties. It was also recorded in *Ying Yi* (*Washbasin Entitled Zhen*) that Mu Niu had taken an oath when accepting the judgment.

"Meng Shi" (oath) was frequently adopted in the litigation to settle the cases with the help of god, but it was completely different from the trials held in the name of god in Xia and Shang dynasties, in which "Tian" (Heaven) (which was in fact the so-called soothsayer who could communicate with Heaven) was endowed with complete judicial authority. As far as "Meng Shi" (oath) in the Western Zhou Dynasty was concerned, the authority of judgment was already shifted to the judges of the secular world, and it was only through the protection of "Tian" (Heaven) that the judgment was carried out. Therefore, in this sense, remarkable progress had undoubtedly been made in the litigation system of the Western Zhou Dynasty.

In the judicial construction of the Western Zhou Dynasty, what should be noted were the explicit requirements for judicial officials. It was recorded in "Kang Gao" (The Orders of Duke Zhou to Kang Shu) in *Shang Shu* (*The Book of Historical Document*) that Zhou Gong (Duke of Zhou) once admonished Kangshu who used to be a "Si Kou" (the minister of justice) that he should be "Jing Ming Nai Fa", which means that "one should be prudent and fair in the infliction of punishments." In "Lv Xing" (The Penal Code of Lv) in *Shang Shu* (*The Book of Historical Document*), the following statements were recorded: "'Wu Xing (the five penalties) should be prudently applied"; "the law should be enforced fairly without showing fear to the powerful or the wealthy by the officials who were in charge of the criminal cases." Besides, the principle like "Shang Xia Bi Zui" (making convictions by the comparison of the legal punishments) and "Wu Jian Luan Ci" (no admitting the assumptive and false pleadings) all referred to the legal rules the officials should obey. Thus, it was forbidden for officials to deliberately increase or reduce the punishment when making sentences by abusing their power. "Wu Guo Zhi Ci" (five cases of malpractice) stipulated by King Mu of Zhou was in reality the specific standard to evaluate the judicial officials. The so-called "Wu Guo Zhi Ci" (five cases of malpractice) included relying on the influence of the powerful, showing private gratitude or revenging by taking the advantage of trial, bending the law for relatives, blackmailing the litigants or taking bribes in settling lawsuits, which were obviously made for the judicial officials. Thus, anyone who had violated these rules "would be regarded as the violation of law." In this way, the judicial officials were encouraged to take state affairs seriously and to be prudent when executing punishments.

As for prison, as "Tu Xing" (penal servitude) became a major punishment, the jail and jail management had been developed to some extent compared with Xia and Shang dynasties. "Huan Tu", which was used in Xia and Shang dynasties, still referred to jail in Zhou Dynasty. In the annotation of "Si Huan" (Official in charge of Prison) in "Qiu Guan" (Ministry of Penalty) in *Zhou Li* (*The Rites of Zhou Dynasty*), Zheng Sinong stated that "'Huan Tu' refers to jails" and that "'Huan Tu' was set up to imprison people who idled about." In Zhou Dynasty, "Ling Yu" was also used to refer to jails. According to *Xu Bo Wu Zhi* (*Sequel to the Record of Natural Objects*), "it was called 'Ling Yu' in the Zhou Dynasty." It was stated in "Wu Fu" (Relatives within the Five Degrees of Mourning) in *Guan Zhong* that "when the capable officials are in office, the barn is filled with grain and 'Ling Yu' is empty, but when incompetent officials are in office, the barn is empty but 'Ling Yu' crowded" In *Shi Ming* (*The Origin of the Word Meaning*) the following definition was provided for "Ling Yu": "jails are also called 'Ling Yu'; 'Ling' means 'guiding', while 'Yu' means 'stopping'; so 'Ling Yu' means guiding the prisoners and stopping them (from running away)." "Ling Tai", "Ji Liu", and "Han Yu" were other names for jail. Clearly, the various names for jails showed that there were more jails built in the country. It was stated in *Wei Liao Zi* (*On the Art of War*) that "nowadays as far as imprisonment is concerned, there are more than ten smaller jails, more than one hundred medium jails and over one thousand bigger jails." Some distinguished officials had even built prisons on a large scale in their own fiefs. For example, Huang Xie, also known as Chun Shenjun, had built a prison with three *li* in circumference.[140]

In Western Zhou Dynasty, the systems of jail management were already established and special officials were assigned to take charge of the prisoners.

As for the term of imprisonment, it was no more than three years. "For felony, the criminals shall be released after three years of imprisonment; for less serious crimes, two years; for minor crimes, one year."[141] As for the criminals who could not mend their ways after three years of imprisonment, they would be put to death. It was recorded in "Da Si Kou" (The Senior Minister of Justice) in "Qiu Guan" (Ministry of Penalty) in *Zhou Li* (*The Rites of Zhou Dynasty*) that "'Huan Tu' was set up to imprison people who idled about, and anyone who had committed murder would be imprisoned, be forced to do corvée and to be humiliated by bearing a board marked with his crime on his back. If he had mended his way, he would be sent back to his hometown within three years. If not, he would be killed."

In conclusion, in Western Zhou Dynasty the principle of "Tian Dao" (The Way of Heaven) featured by "You Ming Zai Tian" (having the destiny controlled by Heaven) was replaced by "Yi De Pei Tian" [matching 'De' (virtue) with 'Tian' (Heaven)], so the legislative guideline of "Ming De Shen Fa" (promoting virtue and being prudent in the enforcement of punishment) and the strategy of running a state with the integration of "Li" (rites), "Yue" (music), "Xing" (punishment), and "Zheng" (government) were formed. In addition, detailed departmental laws and regulations were made and a primary differentiation of civil and criminal legal activities was initiated. As the dual standards of blood relationship and politics were adopted in the state structure, the state laws were consistent with the family laws. Furthermore, the secrecy of law was kept within a certain scope, because it was thought that the power of law was unfathomable if it was kept unpredictable. But as a

---

[140]*Yue Jue Shu* (*Local Chronicles*), Vol. 3.

[141]"Si Huan" (Official in Charge of Prison) in "Qiu Guan" (Ministry of Penalty) in *Zhou Li* (*The Rites of Zhou Dynasty*).

whole, extraordinary political and legal wisdom of the Chinese nation has been shown in the legal system of the Western Zhou Dynasty, so it has best represented the legal system of the three dynasties—Xia, Shang and Zhou and it has exerted a great influence on the legal development of the later ages.

Chapter 3
The Legal System of the Spring and Autumn and Warring States Period Featured by Social Transformation and Legal Reform

(770 B.C.–221 B.C.)

The Spring and Autumn and the Warring States Period refers to the time starting from the year 770 B.C. when King Ping of the Zhou Dynasty moved the capital eastward to Luoyi to the year 211 B.C. when the nation was unified by Qin Dynasty. This is also the time of great transition from the slavery to the feudal society. Thus, sharp contradiction between the new and the old and between the reformative and the conservative has existed in almost all areas, such as politics, economy, culture, and ideology. The fundamental reason for the social upheaval is the improvement of the level of productive forces.

In the Spring and Autumn Period, iron tools were widely used in agriculture, which had not only raised the level of productivity rapidly but also made household production possible. The emergence of private land had accelerated the destabilization of the state ownership of land. Thus, it had become the inherent requirement of social development to reform the existent productive relations. Accordingly, class relationship changed significantly, and some of the big nobilities declined, while some other new social forces or some forces with weak traditional blood relations started to lease a portion of the land to the direct producers with a certain amount of rent. This new force was the initial representative of feudal landlord class. Simultaneously, the ordinary people and businessmen who specialized in individual operation were transformed to farmers who were attached to the feudal production relationship. Besides, "Shi" (scholar), who was at the bottom of the pyramid of the power structure, also developed and became an independent social group, and they had played an indispensable role in the bloody wars of annexation.

The development of local economy strengthened the political independence of the vassals and the officials, so the situation of the coexistence of the vassal states and the sole dominance of the royal family and the hierarchal system in which the king ruled over "Gong" (duke), who in turn ruled over "Da Fu" (senior officials in ancient China), who in turn ruled over "Shi" (scholar) in the early Zhou Dynasty were all destroyed. "Li" (Rites), "Yue" (music), and the order for battles and punitive expeditions were not issued by the king anymore but by the vassals and officials. "Li" (rites), which had regulated the hierarchy in the past, had lost its dominant role in the contention for power, so endless wars of annexation for territory expansion and wealth plundering were waged by the vassal states. Moreover, the system of "Jun Gong Jue" (the Military Glory System) was enforced, so it was possible for people of humble birth, such as Guan Zhong, Ning Qi, and Bai Lixi to fully display their talents to win the favor of the king and to take the charge of national political affairs, which had not only symbolized the collapse of "Shi Qing System" (Inheritance of Noble Titles) featured by the combination of blood relations and politics but also the emergence of bureaucracy. The new power group demanded statute laws to be made to safeguard their own great interests, which had finally become an irreversible historical trend. Thus, *Fa Jing* (*Canon of Laws*), which epitomized all the statute laws, was made in the end. Meanwhile, the major change of the society had led to the phenomenon of "Bai Jia Zheng Ming" (the contention of a hundred schools of thought) in the ideological sphere, and Confucianism and Legalism, the two prominent schools of thought, were woven into a colorful cultural curtain of "De Zhi" (the ruling of virtue), "Li Zhi" (the ruling of rites), "Fa Zhi" (the ruling of law), and "Ren Zhi" (the ruling of man), which had not only given a full play to the wisdom and exquisite rational thinking of the Chinese nation but also broken the new grounds for legal civilization.

3.1 The Reform Adaptable to Social Transformation

To adapt to the great changes caused by social transformation, to gain space for survival and to win the wars of annexation, reforms mainly focused on land and military system were carried out by the rulers of the states of Qi, Jin, Lu, Zheng, and Chu.

In 645 B.C., the policy of "Zuo Yuan Tian" (changing the ownership of the land) was carried out in the state of Jin to award farmland to its people to encourage them to serve in the army and fight for the king. Therefore, at the same time, the policy of "Zuo Zhou Bing" (making weapons by each state) was formulated, the restrictions in recruiting soldiers were abolished, and state military forces were enlarged,[1] which had created a precedent for later generations to grant land and houses according to military achievements.

In 594 B.C., the system of "Chu Shui Mu" (taxation in accordance with the size of the land) was put into practice by Duke Xuan of Lu, according to which private land was legally accepted with tax levied. Four years thereafter, the system of "Zuo Qiu Jia"[2] was established, according to which military service and tax would be rendered according to "Qiu" (a piece of land separated by water from other pieces of land).

---

[1]"Xi Gong Shi Wu Nian" (The 15th Year of the Duke of Xi) in *Zuo Zhuan* (*The Chronicle of Zuo*).
[2]"Cheng Gong Yuan Nian" (The 1st Year of the Duke of Cheng) in *Zuo Zhuan* (*The Chronicle of Zuo*).

3.1 The Reform Adaptable to Social Transformation

In 552 B.C., in the state of Chu, the land and military systems were begun to be adjusted and military tax was collected according to the land revenue, as was stated in the saying that "tax should be paid according to land revenue to cover the expenses on military carriages, horses, weapons and armors."[3]

In 538 B.C., the policy of "Zuo Qiu Fu" was carried out in the state of Zheng[4] and its basic contents were similar to those in "Zuo Qiu Jia."

The policy of "levying tax according to land conditions," as was called "An Tian Er Shui"[5] was also carried out by Guan Zhong in the state of Qi.[6] Simultaneously, relevant reforms were also carried out by the grass-roots organizations. For example, it was recorded in "Qi Yu" (The Historical Records of Qi State) in *Guo Yu* (*The Historical Records of Various States*) that the state was ruled by Guan Zhong in the following ways:

> The group of five households constituted one 'Gui' with 'Gui' as the head; ten 'Gui' constituted one 'Li' with 'Si' as the head; four 'Li' constituted one 'Lian' with 'Lian' as the head; ten 'Lian' constituted one 'Xiang' with 'Liang Ren' as the head. At the same time, military orders were issued: five households constituted one 'Gui', so five people formed one 'Wu' (a grassroot unit of five families) with 'Gui' as the head; ten 'Gui' constituted one 'Li', so 50 people constituted one 'Xiao Rong' with 'Li You Si' as the head; four 'Li' constituted one 'Lian', so 200 people constituted one 'Zu' with 'Lian' as the head; ten 'Lian' constituted one 'Xiang', so 2000 people constituted one 'Lv' with 'Liang Ren' as the head; five 'Xiang' constituted one 'Shuai', so 10,000 people constituted one 'Jun', with the head of the five 'Xiang' as the head…In both spring and autumn, military training was carried out in the way of hunting. 'Zu' and 'Wu' (a grassroot unit of five families) were trained in 'Li' (a basic resident organization consisting of five neighborhoods) and 'Jun' and 'Lv' were trained in the suburbs of the capital. Once established, this system of training soldiers is forbidden to be changed.

When Zi Chan of the state of Zheng was in power, the traditional system that "the cities and rural areas are ruled according to regulations, and the people of different classes are ruled according to "Fu Zhi" (mourning apparel system)"[7] was followed, besides, he also created the method of "dividing land with ditches and setting up the grassroots unit on the basis of five households,"[8] and organized the peasants according to "Shi Wu" (a basic level organization grouped by five or ten households) based on recognizing the legitimacy of individual farmers.

---

[3]"Xiang Gong Er Shi Wu Nian" (The 25th Year of the Duke of Xiang) in *Zuo Zhuan* (*The Chronicle of Zuo*).

[4]"Zhao Gong Si Nian" (The 4th Year of the Duke of Zhao) in *Zuo Zhuan* (*The Chronicle of Zuo*).

[5]"Da Kuang" (Assistance to the Monarch, Official Version of the State of Qi) in *Guan Zi* (*The Book of Master Guan*).

[6]"Qi Yu" (The Historical Records of Qi State) in *Guo Yu* (*The Historical Records of Various States*).

[7]"Xiang Gong San Shi Nian" (The 30th Year of the Duke of Xiang) in *Zuo Zhuan* (*The Chronicle of Zuo*).

[8]"Xiang Gong San Shi Nian" (The 30th Year of the Duke of Xiang) in *Zuo Zhuan* (*The Chronicle of Zuo*).

"Shi Wu" (a basic level organization grouped by five or ten households) was both grassroots organization of the residents and the undertaker of military service and taxation. The establishment of this system had tightened the rule of the state so it was adopted by the later generations for a long time.

In the Warring States Period, aggressive reformers were employed in different states to take charge of state politics. Li Kui Ximen Bao and Yue Yang were appointed by Wei state; Shen Buhai was appointed by Han state; Niu Chu and Xun Xin were appointed by Zhao state; Wu Qi was appointed by Chu state, Zou Ji was appointed by Qi state, and Shang Yang were appointed by Qin state, so different reforms were carried out. For instance, the reform of "giving food to anyone who works hard and paying salary to anyone who has made contribution" was carried out by Li Kui,[9] which had deprived the privileges of "Yin Min" (dawdler) who had gotten rewards without working hard in the past. This had created a favorable condition for the landlord class to enter the political stage and for officials to become landlords. *Fa Jing* (*Canon of Laws*) formulated by Li Kui, in particular, had laid the foundation of the feudal legal system.

The reforms previously mentioned had touched some aspect of the economic foundation and superstructure; whilst Shang Yang's political reform had best reflected the nature and orientation of reform.

In 356 B.C., the tendency of feudalization of the reform in each state was most comprehensively and systematically shown by Shang Yang's political reform carried out in the state of Qin. Shang Yang, who was born in Wei state, was awarded a fief called "Shang" after rendering a great service in the reform, so his family name was changed from the original name Gongsun to Shang. Shang Yang "was interested in criminal law since he was young"[10] and he was once a disciple of Li Kui. In 361 B.C., after Duke Xiao of Qin took office, he issued orders to recruit the talented people to make the country strong and prosperous. Thus, Shang Yang took *Fa Jing* (*Canon of Laws*) to Qin state and persuaded Duke Xiao of Qin to accept his "idea of making the state powerful," which had won him the trust and support of Duke Xiao, soon, reform was carried out on a large scale.

The main contents of Shang Yang's reform are as follows:

First, "Jing Tian Zhi" (the "nine squares" system of land ownership) was abolished, the footpaths between fields were built, and the common people were allowed to do business. Moreover, the new land ownership system and land sales were acknowledged legally. To develop feudal agricultural economy as well as to ensure the financial and military resources of the state, those "who are devoted themselves to agricultural production to have a good harvest of grain, or produce enough cloth and silk could be exempted from corvée. Anyone who makes no profit

---

[9] (Han Dynasty) Liu Xiang, "Zheng Li" (The Principles of Government) in *Shuo Yuan* (*Collection of Stories*).

[10] "Shang Jun Lie Zhuan" (The Collected Biographies of Shang Yang) in *Shi Ji* (*The Record of the Grand Historian*).

3.1 The Reform Adaptable to Social Transformation

in business or who is lazy shall become official slaves."[11] "If two men live together in one household without registering separately, the taxation shall be doubled."[12]

Second, "any nobleman who has no military merits shall not be listed in the genealogy books and anyone who has military merits shall be granted titles and be awarded accordingly."[13] Moreover, "Shi Qing System" (Inheritance of Noble Titles) was abolished, which had further stimulated to the formation of bureaucracy. To award people with military achievements, *Jun Jue Lv* (*Statutes on Military Exploit and Official Titles*) was made, and twenty ranks of military merit titles were established, ranging from "Gong Shi" (the lowest rank of nobility) to "Che Hou" (the highest rank of nobility in the state and empire of Qin and Han Dynasty) with each enjoying corresponding rights. It was stated in "Shang Jun Lie Zhuan" (The Collected Biographies of Shang Yang) in *Shi Ji* (*The Records of the Grand Historian*) that rules were made by Shang Yang, according to which "anyone who has military merits shall be conferred upon titles and awarded accordingly," "the levels of different titles of nobility will be affirmed, and the size of land, the number of houses, wives and clothes should also be conferred upon accordingly." "If anyone enjoying a title above 'Yi Pin' (the first-rank) has committed a crime, he shall be remitted"; on the contrary, if anyone of the common people "has committed a crime, he shall be punished accordingly"[14]; if the legitimate boundary of the ranks was transgressed, the person involved would be punished for the crime of breaking through the boundary of the social status.

Third, the households were organized into groups of "Shi Wu" (a basic level organization grouped by five or ten households), and the people within the same group were mutually responsible for their activities; "anyone who has informed against the traitors shall receive the same award as those who have killed enemies in battlefields; while anyone who has collided with traitors shall receive the same punishment as those who have surrendered themselves to the enemy in battlefields."[15]

Fourth, "Fa" (law) was transformed to "Lv" (criminal law), and the unitary application and abiding of law was emphasized. To establish the authority of law, he opened up the path of reform by employing law. Moreover, the opponents who were against reform were cracked down, and Gongsun Jia and Gongzi Qian, who were the teachers of the prince were punished with "Qing" (tattooing on the face or forehead) and "Yi" (cutting off the nose) respectively for violating the law by themselves, as was illustrated in the record that "the prince was punished for his

---

[11]"Shang Jun Lie Zhuan" (The Collected Biographies of Shang Yang) in *Shi Ji* (*The Record of the Grand Historian*).

[12]"Shang Jun Lie Zhuan" (The Collected Biographies of Shang Yang) in *Shi Ji* (*The Record of the Grand Historian*).

[13]"Shang Jun Lie Zhuan" (The Collected Biographies of Shang Yang) in *Shi Ji* (*The Record of the Grand Historian*).

[14]Wei Hong (The Han Dynasty), *Han Jiu Yi* (*Traditional Rituals of Han Dynasty*).

[15]"Shang Jun Lie Zhuan" (The Collected Biographies of Shang Yang) in *Shi Ji* (*The Record of the Grand Historian*).

violation of law, so were his teachers (sentenced to 'Qing' or 'Bi')."[16] Shang Yang also declared that anyone who dared to change the new law randomly "shall be sentenced to death without pardoning, even with one word added or deleted."[17] Consequently, "the officials do not dare to treat the common people illegally, nor do the common people dare to offend the officials by violating the law,"[18] so that "the law was fully implemented and the people of Qin were well governed."[19]

As a representative of Legalism and a practitioner, Shang Yang was expert not only at opening up the path of reform and clearing away roadblocks by the way of law, but also at safeguarding the fruits of his reform. Although Shang Yang became a martyr of reform, the laws he made in Qin Dynasty were continued to be applied even after his death.

Since Shang Yang's political reform was in conformity to historical trends, even though "at first, it was criticized (about his changing of laws) by the common people, yet after three years, it was praised."[20] Although Shang Yang died as a martyr, the laws of Qin were continued to be applied. Wang Anshi from Song Dynasty once made a fair comment on Shang Yang's political reform, and he said, "since old times, faith has been the best way to inspire people, so a word is worth more than hundreds of *jin* of gold. So people nowadays should not blame Shang Yang, because he could make government decrees carried out effectively."[21]

Although Shang Yang's political reform was carried out much later than those of other countries in the east, much experience was absorbed from them. In addition, the foundation of conservative forces in Qin state was weak, so the reform was carried out more completely. After the reform, Qin state was changed from a backward state to the strongest one at that time both economically and politically in a short time, which had laid a solid foundation for its annexation of other six states in the later period.

Therefore, from above, we can have a general idea about the reforms carried out in the Spring and Autumn as well as the Warring States Period. If reform merely meant a kind of improvement in the Spring and Autumn Period, then it had become a devastating revolution in the Warring States Period. Gu Yanwu wrote in "Zhou Mo Feng Su" (The Customs of Weekends) in *Ri Zhi Lu* (*The Record of Daily Reading*) that "in the Spring and Autumn Period, 'Li' (rites) and 'Xin' (integrity) were valued and respected, but they were neglected by the rulers of the seven states in the Warring States Period; in the Spring and Autumn Period, the king of Zhou was respected, but in the seven states of the Warring States Period, the king was even

---

[16]"Qin Ce" (The Strategy of the State of Qin) (Part 1) in *Zhan Guo Ce* (*Stratagems of the Warring States*).
[17]"Yi Xing" (Unitary Punishment) in *Shang Jun Shu* (*The Book of Lord Shang*).
[18]"Ding Fen" (Defining a Person's Social Status) in *Shang Jun Shu* (*The Book of Lord Shang*).
[19]"Qin Ben Ji" (The History of the State of Qin) in *Shi Ji* (*The Record of the Grand Historian*).
[20]"Qin Ben Ji" (The History of the State of Qin) in *Shi Ji* (*The Record of the Grand Historian*).
[21]Wang Anshi (Song Dynasty), *Lin Chuan Xian Sheng Wen Ji* (*Collected Works of Wang Anshi*), Vol. 32.

never mentioned; sacrificial ceremonies, state visits as well as banquets for the visitors were stressed in the Spring and Autumn Period, but they were abolished in the seven states in the Warring States Period; clans and families were emphasized in the Spring and Autumn Period, but they were never mentioned in the seven states in the Warring States Period." Because the reforms carried out in the Warring States Period were aimed at overthrowing the old systems, each measure and decree to be carried out was challenged by the stubborn resistance of the old power of nobilities and was struggled for by bloodshed. Therefore, the reforms in some of the seven states were carried out repeatedly and some even failed, yet the wheels of history cannot be stopped, so they marched forward with unstoppable forces.

3.2 The Collapse of the System of "Shi Qing" (Inheritance of Noble Titles) and the Formation of Bureaucratic System

In the Spring and Autumn Period, it was not coincidental that the system of "Shi Qing" (Inheritance of Noble Titles) was toppled down and that of bureaucracy was set up. On one hand, the destruction of "Jing Tian Zhi" (the "nine squares" system of land ownership in China) and the collapse of the patriarchal clan system had shaken the foundation of the system of "Shi Qing" (Inheritance of Noble Titles); on the other hand, "Jun Gong Jue" (the Military Glory System) was universally practiced in each state as part of the reform, which had dealt a devastating blow to the hereditary privilege of the old nobles. When making a mass pledge, Zhang Yang from the state of Jin said, "Those who have defeated the enemy will be rewarded: the senior officials will be awarded the tax collected from 'Xian' (county), the junior officials will be awarded the tax collected from 'Jun' (shire), the soldiers will be awarded 667 *qing* of land (*qing*: a unit of area, one *qing* is about 6.6667 hectares), the common people and businessmen will be awarded titles of 'Shi' (senior officials) if they have military merits, and the slaves shall get freedom."[22] The first two awards mentioned above are not the traditional rewards of fiefs, but the tax collected from "Xian" (county) and "Jun" (shire). Besides, the solders would be awarded 667 *qing* of land, the common people and businessmen would be awarded titles of "Shi" (senior officials) if they had military merits, and the slaves would get freedom. All these policies and measures were of great appeal at that time, for it not only won the favor of the masses, but also won the support of a group of officials for the new regime. Guan Zhong used to be a guilty slave; Ning Qi used to be a peasant, Bai Lixi used to be a beggar, and Xuan Gao used to be a businessman, but they were all promoted to be in charge of important state affairs, which had shown that the bureaucratic system was more effective in selecting talents and imbuing vitality to the political regime than the system of "Shi Qing" (Inheritance of Noble Titles). At

---

[22] "Ai Gong Er Nian" (The 2nd Year of the Duke of Ai) in *Zuo Zhuan* (*The Chronicle of Zuo*).

the same time, it was prevalent in all the states to recruit and employ "Shi" (scholars), so it had made a full preparation for the formation of bureaucrat class. "Shi" (scholars) came from complex background, such as "wanderers," "disputers," "warriors," "hermits," and "heroes," all of whom had boasted of special skills and knowledge that enabled them to maneuver among various political groups. Thus, they were valued and employed by the kings and nobilities even in the turbulent times of Spring and Autumn Period. As early as in the first half of the Spring and Autumn Period, Duke Huan of Qi had recruited eighty "Shi" (scholars). By the end of Spring and Autumn Period, "Shi" (scholars) were recruited by both the government and individuals, so their status and roles were improved markedly. According to a proverb popular in that period, "anyone who has lost 'Shi' (scholars) shall perish, but anyone who has recruited 'Shi' (scholars) shall prosper."[23] It was recorded that Tian Chengzi from the state of Qi "had killed an ox, eaten a small part of it, but left the rest to 'Shi' (scholars)"[24] to win their support. Therefore, the phenomenon of appointing "Shi" (scholars) as officials indicated that the state organizational principle of "the combination of relatives and nobles" was in declining under patriarchal clan system.

In the Warring States Period, the officials in both central and local government and the chief generals of the army were all appointed and dismissed by the king. Besides, the officials at all levels were also selected by the king not only according to their virtues and but also according to the principle of "awarding those who make contribution and granting titles to those who are talented."[25] "... for the enlightened rulers, their prime ministers must have been selected from the local officials of 'Zhou' (subprefecture), and their valiant generals must have been selected from the soldiers."[26] The well-known statesmen and strategists Shang Yang, Su Qin, Zhang Yi, Fan Ju, Sun Bin, Bai Qi, Lian Po, and Wang Jian were all promoted to ministers from the common people. Apart from being appointed to important positions by the kings for their military achievements and talents, it was also a significant way to be appointed as officials in the government by recommendation.

Relevant to the appointment system was the seal and tally system. Seals and tallies, the tokens of power, were granted or taken back from the subordinates when they were appointed or dismissed. The officials needed to give the seal back to the king when they resigned, so it was recorded in "Wai Chu Shuo Zuo" (The Outer Categories of Sayings) (Part 1) in *Han Fei Zi* (*Han Feizi*) (Book 2) that "when making judgments, Liang Che was impartial to his relatives or nobles, so Cheng Hou took away his seal (because Liang Che thought he was not kind)." It was also

---

[23]"Gou Jian Yin Mou Wai Zhuan" (The Unauthorized Record of Gou Jian's Plot) in *Wu Yue Chun Qiu* (*A History of the State of Wu and the State of Yue in the Spring and Autumn Period*).

[24]"Wai Chu Shuo You" (The Outer Categories of Sayings) (Part 2) in *Han Fei Zi* (*Han Feizi*) (Book 1).

[25]Li Zhi (Ming Dynasty), "Jun Chen" (The Monarch and his Subjects) (Part 1) in *Chu Tan Ji* (*The Collected Works of Li Zhi Published Right After he Arrived at Long Tan Pond*), Vol. 21.

[26]"Xian Xue" (Noted School of Thought) in *Han Fei Zi* (*Han Feizi*).

recorded in "Fan Ju Cai Ze Lie Zhuan" (The Collected Biographies of Fan Ju and Cai Ze) in *Shi Ji* (*The Records of the Grand Historian*) that "Fan Ju (thus) made the excuse that he was ill and asked (King Zhao) to take back the seal." Seals were not only used in appointing officials, but also in the exchange of official documents. For major events, the king's seal was needed. Lao Ai, the Marquis of Changxin of the state of Qin wanted to stage a rebellion, so he forged a fake seal to recruit soldiers in the king's name.

At the same time, the commanders' tallies were also used. Each tally was divided into two parts, one for the king, and the other was kept by the commander himself. Only when the two matched with each other could the generals maneuver the troops. The well-known story of Xinlingjun of the state of Wei stealing the tallies to save the state of Zhao and the unearthed "Xin Qi's Tally," which bore the characters of "Zuo Zai Wang, You Zai Xin Qi" (the left part kept by the king, the right part kept by Xin Qi), were both solid evidence. The universal establishment of seal and tally system had reflected the complete establishment of the bureaucratic system and further concentration of the king's power.

Because the work of appointment, dismissal, award, and punishment of the officials were all conducted by the king, the system of "Shang Ji" (local officials regularly write the budget revenue, the increase of registration, land and treasury on a wooden board and report to higher authorities), which was used to evaluate the work performance of the officials, was set up. The so-called "Shang Ji" meant that the officials wrote the budget revenue, the increase of registration, land and treasury on a wooden board, which would be divided into two parts, the right part for the king while the left part for the officials. At the end of the year, the king would evaluate the officials' work according to what had been written on the wooden board and decided on whether they should be promoted or demoted, just as what was said, "when the two parts of the board were joined together, awards and punishments were accordingly distributed."[27] The ledger used for "Shang Ji" (local officials regularly write the budget revenue, the increase of registration, land, and treasury on a wooden board and report to higher authorities) was called "Ji Shu" (accounting book). It was recorded in "Jin Shi" (Forbidding to Use) in *Shang Jun Shu* (*The Book of Lord Shang*) that "in December, the events of the past year were registered in the accounting books, so it was checked by the king once every year." Duke Wen of Wei evaluated the officials' work by making use of "Shang Ji" successfully, as was illustrated in the following statement: "Xie Bian was the official in the eastern border city. He reported to the king in the accounting document and the income by the end of the year was three times more than the amount expected."[28] "Li Dui was the official of Zhong Shan. In the annual accounting book, more income has been reported by Ku Jing county than that predicted in 'Shang Ji'."[29] After "Shang Ji" (local officials regularly write the budget revenue, the increase of registration, land

---

[27]"Zhu Dao" (The Way of Ruling the State) in *Han Fei Zi* (*Han Feizi*).

[28]"Ren Jian Xun" (Instruction on Human World) in *Huai Nan Zi* (*Masters from Huainan*).

[29]"Nan" (Crisis) in *Han Fei Zi* (*Han Feizi*) (Book 2).

and treasury on a wooden board and report to higher authorities), the outstanding officials would be rewarded, the poorly-performed ones would be demoted, and the worst ones would be sentenced to jail. In "Shang Ji," taxation, land, registration, and public security were mainly focused on, which had fully demonstrated that the maintenance of bureaucracy and military activities was greatly influenced by economic and financial situation; at the same time, it also reflected that in the early stage of feudal regime, the ability of the officials in administration was greatly stressed and the central government's control over local areas were strengthened proactively. The system of "Shang Ji" was set up the Warring States Period and it was carried on through the entire feudal society, which had testified that it was not only a very important system to supervise and encourage officials, but also a very important way to maintain the official administration.

With the establishment of bureaucracy, "Feng Lu," a salary system, took the place of feudal fiefdom. In the Warring States Period, "Feng Lu" (salary) was in the form of material objects and because of the difference of measurements in different states, the unit of "Feng Lu" was different too. "*dan*" ("担"a unit of weight, one *dan* is about 50 kg) was used by the state of Chu state; "*zhong*" (a unit of weight, without universal standard) was used by Qi state; and "*dan*" ("石," a unit of weight, one *dan* is about 60 kg) was used by Han, Zhao, Wei, and Qin state. The maximum of "Feng Lu" might be 10,000 *dan* (担), 10,000 *zhong*, or 10,000 *dan* (石), but the minimum might be one *dou* (a unit of measurement, one *dou* is about one decalitre). In addition to the fixed amount of "Feng Lu," extra award was also granted by the king based on the officials' performance.

The system of "Feng Lu" (salary) was the epitome of the feudal employment relationship in the state system, as is stated in the saying that "the master sells titles, and the officials sell wisdom."[30] "Feng Lu" (salary), in actuality, was a redistribution of the accumulated wealth, therefore, the officials could not only enjoy privileges, but also get wealth (legally or illegally). To ensure the implementation of the system of "Feng Lu" (salary) permanently, abundant material wealth must be obtained by the state. For this purpose, in the Warring States Period, in almost all countries heavy tax was levied on cloth, grain, and money to support a large group of officials.

To sum up, the official appointment and dismissal system, the seal and tally system, the system of "Shang Ji" and "Feng Lu" (salary) carried out in all the states were the basic contents of feudal bureaucracy and the primal form of feudal official management, which had played an important role in strengthening the centralized autocracy, in clearing away the remainders of heredity system, in consolidating the economic foundation of feudalism as well as in unifying the entire country.

With the establishment of bureaucracy, the system of "Jun" (shire) and "Xian" (county) was also set up. "Jun" (shire) and "Xian" (county) were set up initially in the newly conquered remote areas, so it was at fist an expedient method to control the newly conquered regions, but it gradually became a permanent local system. Among

---

[30]"Wai Chu Shuo You" (The Outer Categories of Sayings) (Part 2) in *Han Fei Zi* (*Han Feizi*) (Book 2).

all the states, there was the largest "Xian" (county) in Chu state, some of which could even provide several thousand soldiers and carriages, whereas in the state of Jin, there were forty to fifty "Xian" (county), which was the largest in number. "Xian" (county) was different from feudal fiefdom in that it was the local authority directly controlled by the king with a set of administrative and military organizations directly subordinate to it. The senior official (called "Xian Ling" or "Xian Yin") was the head of a "Xian" (county), who was appointed by the king and who could be transferred or replaced at any time. "Jun Shou" (governor) was the head of "Jun" (shire), which was bigger than "Xian" (county); but at the beginning, "Jun Shou" (governor) was a post lower than the county magistrate, just as was illustrated in the statement that "among those who have defeated the enemies, the senior officials shall be granted the tax collected from 'Xian' (county), while the junior officials shall be granted the tax collected from 'Jun' (shire)."[31] However, with frequent wars of annexation, the king endowed greater power to "Jun Shou" (governor), so his jurisdiction expanded even beyond his "Xian" (county) to deal with the urgent matters even without asking permission from the monarch. At the beginning of Warring States Period, the border areas were getting more and more prosperous, and wars of annexation were getting fiercer, so the status of "Jun" (shire) became higher than that of "Xian" (county), and the latter became a subordinate to the former. Hence, the two-level system of "Jun" (shire) and "Xian" (county), which had lasted for a long time, came into being.

"Jun Shou" (governor) and "Xian Ling" (county magistrate) were not hereditary, and they were appointed and dismissed by the king, so they were in charge of the administrative matters in their areas, including levying tax, resolving disputes, and at the same time, they were also in charge of part of the military responsibilities. Moreover, they just received salaries and fulfilled the duty of guarding the land instead of owning it. When confronting with more severe military and political affairs, the king would be in charge and the local authorities had no right to handle the affairs on their own. In this way, the local areas were tightly controlled by the central government.

The establishment of the system of "Jun" (shire) and "Xian" (county) contributed to the deprivation of the power of nobilities, brought a closer connection between the central government and local authorities, helped to implement the policies of the central government, and improved the efficiency of local management, so it was quickly established nationwide. The establishment of the system of "Jun" (shire) and "Xian" (county) also marked a major progress of the local administrative management system.

---

[31]"Ai Gong Er Nian" (The 2nd Year of the Duke of Ai) in *Zuo Zhuan* (*The Chronicle of Zuo*).

3.3 Confucianism and Legalism in "Bai Jia Zheng Ming" (The Contention of a Hundred Schools of Thought)

The social upheaval in the Spring and Autumn Period exerted a huge influence on the theocratic law since Xia and Shang Dynasty, and the system of "Li" (rites), which was established by Zhou Gong (Duke of Zhou) had lost its prestige under the background of the destruction of the rituals of Zhou Dynasty. The original hierarchal order was dislocated after this struggle between the rulers and the common people, so it was urgent for the newly appeared and more complex social relationship to be demonstrated by new theories and to be adjusted by new regulations. Hence, the phenomenon of "Bai Jia Zheng Ming" (the contention of a hundred schools of thought) arose in the ideological sphere. As was said by Sima Qian, "All people worried about the same thing so they tried to achieve the same goal by a variety of ways and strategies. Moreover, they took different measures, and the school of "Yin Yang Xue" (School of Yin Yang Theory), Confucianists, Mohists, Logicians, Legalists, and Taoists were all devoted to attaining a peaceful world. They had different opinions and tried all means."[32] It was the common goal of all the schools of thoughts to formulate new and effective state plans, among which Confucianism and Legalism were the most famous ones, because they both contained rich contents with grand scale of academic team and profound influence.

Confucius was the founder of the school of Confucianism. Later, his thoughts were succeeded and developed by Meng Zi (Mencius) and Xun Zi (Xuncius). As for the strategy of running a state, Confucianists insisted that "of all the methods for ruling the people, none is more important than the application of 'Li' (rites)"[33], so "the country should be ruled with 'Li' (rites)."[34] "Fa" (law) is guided by "Li" (rites), and "when 'Li' (rites) and 'Yue' (music) have declined, it is impossible for punishment to be properly carried out; if punishments are not properly enforced, people will be at a loss as to how to behave."[35] This theory not only showed the relationship between "Li" (rites) and "Fa" (law), but also proved that "Li" (rites) was of great importance to social stability.

Apart from the rule of "Li" (rites), the rule of "De" (virtue) was also the core of Confucianism. Confucianists advocated educating the common people with virtue and was against "suppressing the people with power," because they thought that it could not prevent people from committing crimes fundamentally to rely on punishment alone. He said, "If the people are guided by politics and disciplined by law, they will try to avoid committing crimes, but they have no sense of shame; if they are guided by 'De' (virtue) and governed by 'Li' (rites), they will have the sense of

---

[32]"Tai Shi Gong Zi Xu" (Preface by Tai Shi Gong himself) in *Shi Ji* (*The Record of the Grand Historian*).
[33]"Ji Tong" (The Customs of Sacrifice) in *Li Ji* (*The Book of Rites*).
[34]"Xian Jin" (The Example) in *Lun Yu* (*The Analects*).
[35]"Zi Lu" (Zi Lu, one of Confucius' disciples) in *Lun Yu* (*The Analects*).

shame, and become 'Jun Zi' (gentlemen)."[36] Guiding people with "De" (virtue) meant educating people with virtue, making them give up evilness and follow good examples; integrating people by "Li" (rites) meant regulating people's behaviors and making them follow tradition. The rule of "De" (virtue) originated from the principle of "Ming De Shen Fa" (promoting virtue and being prudent in the enforcement of punishment) put forward by Zhou Gong (Duke of Zhou), which was further developed and summarized in the theory of "De Zhu Xing Fu" (employing moral teaching as the primary means, punishment as the supplement), which was carried out in the process of the 2000 years of legislation.

Taking the position of safeguarding the hierarchal system, Confucius insisted that "the penal statutes should not be applied to high-ranking officials, and 'Li' (rites) should not be applied to the common people,"[37] and he emphasized that "'Li' (rites) is made to regulate the virtuous men, while punishment is used to regulate 'Xiao Ren' (common people)" and that "'Jun Zi' (gentlemen) show more concern to law and penalty, while 'Xiao Ren' (common people) show more concern to their personal interests."[38] Confucius insisted that anyone who violated the interests of the ruling class should be suppressed. For example, troops were sent by the state of Zheng "to attack bandits near the mashes and have them all killed." Confucius praised this atrocious act and said, "Well done! Lenient policies will lead to people's negligence, which will lead to more severe punishments, which in turn will bring suffering to the people, so lenient policies will be carried out again to show concern to the suffering people. Lenient policies were used to complement the severe policies, and severe policies were in turn used to supplement the lenient policies, because only in this way is it possible for the country to be ruled effectively."[39] It can be concluded that Confucius took the combination of "Xing" (punishment) and "De" (virtue) as well as the integration of leniency and severity as the principle of administration and jurisdiction, but he was against the enforcement of death penalty without moral education, because he thought it was a kind of "slaughtering."[40] He supported "Ren Zheng" (benevolent administration) and opposed high-handed ruling and tough laws.

Confucius also put forward the principle of "Ren Xue" (the doctrine of benevolence). He thought that "the benevolent love others," so "Ren" (benevolence) was the basic principle in adjusting interpersonal relationship, by which the status, value and dignity of human were fully confirmed. "Ren Xue" (the doctrine of benevolence) was a people-oriented philosophy with historical significance, which had offered the basic principles of humanitarianism for politics, jurisdiction, and governance. This thought was success and developed by Meng Zi (Mencius). Thus,

---

[36]"Wei Zheng" (Handling Political Affairs) in *Lun Yu* (*The Analects*).

[37]"Qu Li" (The Summary of the Rules of Propriety) in *Li Ji* (*The Book of Rites*).

[38]"Li Ren" (Benevolent Neighbors) in *Lun Yu* (*The Analects*).

[39]"Zhao Gong Er Shi Nian" (The 20th Year of the Duke of Zhao) in *Zuo Zhuan* (*The Chronicle of Zuo*).

[40]"Yao Yue" (Yao's Words) in *Lun Yu* (*The Analects*).

based on the epistemological view that "men are good in nature," Meng Zi (Mencius) crystallized the principle of "Ai Ren" (loving others) and embodied it by a more practical political proposal: "One should love his family and the people, one should love the people and all creatures."[41] The thought of people-orientation was thus developed to a systematic theory of "Ren Zheng" (benevolent administration), and its core was "valuing people." Moreover, it was advocated that "'Tian' (Heaven) sees as my people see and 'Tian' (Heaven) hears as my people hear,"[42] and "the people are the most important factor in a nation, 'She Ji' (the country) comes the next, and the ruler is the least important."[43] Confucius also said, "it is human to be benevolent," which showed that people possessed the inherent quality of kindness. Therefore, only when people were morally cultivated could they display their values and achieve the ideal state of "showing universal love for all," "being benevolent to all under 'Tian' (Heaven)." The theory that "do not do to others what you don't want others to do to you"[44] and "if 'Jun Zi' (gentlemen) wants to be successful by oneself, one wants to others to be successful immediately; if one wants to realize one's dream, he will immediately think about helping others to realize it"[45] advocated by Confucian, and the theory that "when supporting and showing reverence to your elders, you should not forget the other old people who are not related to you; while raising and educating your own children, you should not forget the other children who are not related to you,"[46] which was advocated by Meng Zi (Mencius) were also aimed to demonstrate that people should not only have themselves morally cultivated but also to promote it to adjust the interpersonal relationship. This has not only reflected the tenet that "the benevolent are all full of love to other people" but also reflected the goal that "all are benevolent under 'Tian' (Heaven)."

As to the notion of "Ren Zhi" (the rule of man) advocated by Confucianism, it was mainly embodied by glorifying and upholding the autocratic monarchy, the core of which meant that "Li" (rites), "Yue" (music) and punitive expedition all depended on the monarch. It was because of this that Confucius had called for "rectifying names" to save the world at the times of "Li Beng Yue Huai" (the disintegration of rites and collapse of rituals) and serious violation of social hierarchy in the Spring and Autumn Period. He said that "what is necessary is 'Zheng Ming' (to rectify the social status and relevant responsibilities) ..., if 'Ming' (social status and relevant responsibilities) is not correct, people would be unworthy of the titles; if people are unworthy of the titles, things cannot be completed...."[47] What he meant by "Zheng Ming" (to rectify the social status and relevant responsibilities) was to recover the hierarchal system in which "the king is being the king, the minister being the

---

[41]"Jin Xin Shang" (With all One's Heart) (Part 1) in *Meng Zi* (*Mencius*).
[42]"Tai Shi" (Grand Oath) in *Meng Zi* (*Mencius*).
[43]"Jin Xin Xia" (With all One's Heart) (Part 2) in *Meng Zi* (*Mencius*).
[44]"Yan Yuan" (Yan Yuan, one of Confucius' disciples) in *Lun Yu* (*The Analects*).
[45]"Yong Ye" (Ran Yong, one of Confucius' disciples) in *Lun Yu* (*The Analects*).
[46]"Liang Hui Wang Shang" (The King of Liang Hui) (Part 1) in *Meng Zi* (*Mencius*).
[47]"Zi Lu" (Zi Lu, one of Confucius' disciples) in *Lun Yu* (*The Analects*).

minister, the father being the father, and the son being the son." As to what Confucius proclaimed in the theory of "Wei Zheng Zai Ren" (the administration of government lies in getting the proper men) and "with the gifted men, the administration will be in good order; without the gifted men, the administration will be in chaos,"[48] he meant to argue that the kings, sagacious officials and law executors have played important roles in state ruling and law enforcement, which is a summary of the universal experience of all times and in all countries.

Xun Kuang was born in the state of Zhao in the Warring States Period. He was, for the most part, a Confucianist. However, in the late Warring States Period, the changing social situation and the cultural environment of a hundred schools of thoughts had inspired him to form a new type of Confucianism, which was a mixture of Confucianism and legalism, so it had become a distinct and a long-lasting school of thought after Confucius and Meng Zi (Mencius).

Xun Kuang criticized the theory that "human beings are virtuous in nature" put forward by Meng Zi (Mencius), but he went the opposite way instead. He thought human beings were born evil, and he said that "human beings are evil by nature, and their virtuousness is just a disguise."[49] He also claimed that all "atrocities," promiscuity" and other behaviors that had destroyed social order originated from the evil human nature. Thus, to "transform human nature," "Li" (rites) and "Fa" (law) should be regulated, educated, and reformed. He said: "Therefore, the evil nature of human beings has been reformed and the morals cultivated by the sages, which has resulted in 'Li' (rites) and 'Fa' (law). Hence, 'Li' (rites) and 'Fa' (law) are made by the sages."[50] He also said that "because the ancient sages think human beings are evil and they are prejudiced and rebellious by nature, the authority of king is established to have them governed, 'Li' (rites) is publicized to have them educated, and 'Fa' (law) is made to have them punished. Moreover, severe punishments are enforced to prohibit the violations of law, because only in this way can the whole world be in peace and order. This is the administration of a sagacious king and the education of 'Li' (rites)."[51] It can be seen that, the conception of evil human nature had laid the theoretic basis for the origin, function, and relation of "Li" (rites) and "Fa" (law). Besides, the shackles of traditional theory of "Tian Ming" (the Mandate of Heaven) were abolished and the initiatives in making laws of human beings were stressed, which had contributed to the progress of ancient humanistic thoughts. In Xun Zi's legal thinking, the core was the comprehensive and unified rule of "Li" (rites) and "Fa" (law). He maintained "the method of ruling a country lies in nothing but 'Li' (rites) and 'Xing' (punishments)",[52] "therefore, without 'Li' (rites), there would be no 'Fa' (law)."[53] As for the relationship between "Li" (rites) and "Fa" (law), "Li"

---

[48]"Zhong Yong" (The Doctrine of Mean) in *Li Ji* (*The Book of Rites*).
[49]"Xing E" (Evil Nature) in *Xun Zi* (*Xun Zi*).
[50]"Xing E" (Evil Nature) in *Xun Zi* (*Xun Zi*).
[51]"Xing E" (Evil Nature) in *Xun Zi* (*Xun Zi*).
[52]"Cheng Xiang" (an ancient art form) in *Xun Zi* (*Xun Zi*).
[53]"Xiu Shen" (Cultivating One's Morality and Character) in *Xun Zi* (*Xun Zi*).

(rites) was the essence, and "'Li' (rites) is not only the general principle of 'Fa' (law), but also the foundation of legal settlements,"[54] yet "the proper application of 'Fa' (law) is very important in the proper management of a state."[55] Therefore, "Li" (rites) and "Fa" (law) played different roles in running a state, in handling government affairs, and in ruling and educating the people. This is why he has focused on advocating both "Li" (rites) and "Fa" (law): "if the king holds 'Li' (rites) in esteem and values sagacious people, he shall dominate the world; if he emphasizes "Fa Zhi" (the rule of law) and cares for people, he shall be the sovereign of all nobles."[56] Xun Kuang also said, "it can ensure the long lasting prosperity of a country to stress both 'Li' (rites) and 'Fa' (law)."[57]

The emphasis on 'Li' (rites) and 'Fa' (law) shows that the confrontation of Confucianism and Legalism in the Spring and Autumn Period has been changed to collaboration, which is the inevitable result of the historical development. Because in the constantly changing world, the value of law is more practical than the empty theory of "Ren Zheng" (benevolent administration), which has fully explained why Xun Zi is regarded as "the most sagacious people at that time."

As to the opinion of stressing the power of authority by use of laws held by Shen Dao, Xun Kuang stressed the importance of people instead. He said, "There is the person who can make the country stable, but there is no law that can make the country stable automatically,"[58] so "law cannot stand alone by itself and rules cannot be practiced automatically. With talented people, law may exist; without them, law may perish."[59] This is why Xun Zi is regarded as one of the pioneers of "Ren Zhi" (the rule of man) and is criticized by those who are for the theory of "Fa Zhi" (the rule of law). In modern times, Liang Qichao pointed out explicitly that "Xun's theory of 'Zhi Ren' (the rule of man) rather than 'Zhi Fa' (the rule of law) has misled the whole nation, which has resulted in the phenomenon that for several thousand years, China has been a country without laws, and Chinese people have been a people without laws."[60] In actuality, this criticism is not fair in that Xun Kuang never talked about "Zhi Ren" (the rule of man) without mentioning "Zhi Fa" (the rule of law). Thus, he was more a supporter of those who stressed the importance of people in enforcing the laws rather than the supporter of "Ren Zhi" (the rule of man).

"Zhi Ren" (the rule of man) and "Zhi Fa" (the rule of law) held by Xun Kuang focused on how to deal with the relationship between law and man. He deemed that there were good laws and bad laws, so were there "Jun Zi" (gentlemen) and "Xiao Ren" (common people). Good laws were the ones that were effective in ruling,

---

[54]"Quan Xue" (On Study) in *Xun Zi* (*Xun Zi*).
[55]"Jun Dao" (On the Way of a Lord) in *Xun Zi* (*Xun Zi*).
[56]"Qiang Guo" (On Building a Prosperous Country) in *Xun Zi* (*Xun Zi*).
[57]"Jun Dao" (On the Way of a Lord) in *Xun Zi* (*Xun Zi*).
[58]"Jun Dao" (On the Way of a Lord) in *Xun Zi* (*Xun Zi*).
[59]"Jun Dao" (On the Way of a Lord) in *Xun Zi* (*Xun Zi*).
[60]Liang Qichao, "Lun Li Fa Quan" (On the Right of Legislation) in *Yin Bing Shi Wen Ji* (*Collected Works of Yin Bing Shi*).

whilst gentlemen were those who could effectively run a state. In the chapter "Jun Dao" (On the Way of a Lord), he made clear the relationship between talented people and good laws. He said, "Only a bad king can mess up a state, and a state cannot mess up itself; there is the person who can make the country stable, but there is no law that can make the country stable automatically. The shooting skill of Hou Yi had been handed down, but he could not help the later generations shoot without any misses; the laws of Da Yu still existed, but his offspring of Xia Dynasty did not rule forever. Therefore, laws cannot stand alone by itself and rules cannot be practiced automatically; with talented people, laws may exist; without them, laws may perish. 'Fa' (law) is the origin of good administration, and sages are the origin of good administration. Hence, even with simple laws, the sages could use them effectively, but without sages, even the most complete laws could not be implemented properly and might fail to deal with different situations. This is disaster already. People who do not understand the essence of laws but merely memorize the rules shall be confused when faced with specific matters, no matter how many rules they know. That's why the sagacious kings are eager to recruit talented people while the fatuous ones are thirsty for power. If the talented people are recruited, the rulers can rule the country easily, and they will make great achievements and gain good reputations. In favorable conditions, they could be the king, and at least they could be the ruler of an area. If the talented people are not recruited, the rulers have to toil and moil and his state would be in chaos. What's more, they will achieve nothing, they will have their fame ruined, and the state will be at stake as well." It is evident that the theory that "there is the person who can make the country stable, but there is no law that can make the country stable automatically," which was put forward by Xun Kuang, was directed at the overemphasis on power by some rulers with "Zhi Fa" (the rule of law) as a prerequisite. He never talked about "Zhi Ren" (the rule of man) without talking about "Zhi Fa" (the rule of law), let alone ignored the role that good laws played in running a state. He just put much emphasis on human initiative in the relationship between law and man. Comparing Xun Kuang's theory of laws being enforced by sagacious people and Legalists' theory of "Zhi Fa" (the rule of law), it can be seen that they are the same in that the law is the tool to govern the nation. As for the implementation of laws, Xun depended on the sages, while the latter relied on the kings; so it can be concluded that they have different approaches but equally satisfactory results. Xun's opinions had exerted a great impact on the later generations. In Tang Dynasty, Bai Juyi said, "If we only have laws of Zhen Guan period, but without the officials at that time, it will be rather difficult to enforce punishment correctly."[61] In the late Ming and early Qing Dynasty, Wang Fuzhi also suggested that "the officials should be selected and taught about law so they will observe it by themselves,"[62] and that "it is important to choose senior people to take charge of

---

[61](Tang) Bai Juyi, "Lun Xing Fa Zhi Bi Sheng Fa Ke Xuan Fa Li" (On the Malpractice of Criminal Law and the Emphasis on Legal Subject and Election of Law Experts as Officials) in *Bai Shi Chang Qing Ji* (*Collection of Works by Bai Juyi in the Year of Changqing*) ,Vol. 48.

[62]Wang Fuzhi (Ming Dynasty), *Du Tong Jian Lun* (*Notes on Zi Zhi Tong Jian*), Vol. 10.

legal affairs and to make people obey the same law."[63] He further pointed out that only in this way could "the state be effectively administered."

It can be seen from the above that the legal thought of Xun Kuang was comprehensively formed from selectively absorbing and criticizing the theories of hundred schools. The scope of theories like "Li" (rites) and "Fa" (law), "Zhi Ren" (the rule of man) and "Zhi Fa" (the rule of law) put forward by him had opened up a new page of ancient legal culture and gone beyond the barrier of Confucianism as well as that of Legalism. We can say that the trend of the integration of Confucianism outside and Legalism inside had all originated from Xun Zi. Thus, the richness and temporal spirit of his theory have made him the undisputable founder of new Confucianism, and his contribution to Chinese legal civilization is tremendous and is of great historical significance.

In the Spring and Autumn and the Warring States Period, another notable school of thought coexisting with Confucianism was Legalism. Guan Zi, an early legalist, had compared the objectivity of laws with that of measurement apparatus. He said, "Sizes, line markers, rules, scales, and angles are called laws." Later, he used explicit words to explain his own theory of "Fa Zhi" (the rule of law): "Monarchical power does not belong to two families; nor does political decrees. 'Fa Zhi' (the rule of law) merely means that everything is dealt with by law."[64] He demanded that laws should be applied to both the kings and the common people to check their behaviors, as was stated in his saying that "the rules and regulations should be used to regulate the officials and common people"[65] and "it requires the knowledge of law to govern and unite the people."[66] In addition, he said that "all people including the superior like the king and the inferior like the common citizens should be abided by laws"[67] and "the rules should not be changed according to the king's preferences, since the former is superior to the latter."[68] Because the principle of ruling by "Li" (rites) characterized by the combination of the king's relatives and superiors was destroyed by the application of "Fa Zhi" (the rule of law), it is helpful to "recruit the sagacious and talented people"[69] to promote the relationship of feudal production. Consequently, the so-called reform of the "revision of the old laws"[70] had made "all the people of the state of Qi pleased."[71] It should be noted that the masterpiece *Guan Zi* (*The Book of Master Guan*) was written by someone in the middle of Warring States

---

[63]Wang Fuzhi (Ming Dynasty), *Du Tong Jian Lun* (*Notes on Zi Zhi Tong Jian*), Vol. 3.

[64]"Ming Fa" (Make Law Known to the People) in *Guan Zi* (*The Book of Master Guan*).

[65]"Qi Zhu Qi Chen" (Seven Types of Monarchs and Seven Types of Officials) in *Guan Zi* (*The Book of Master Guan*).

[66]"Qi Fa" (Seven Laws) in *Guan Zi* (*The Book of Master Guan*).

[67]"Ren Fa" (Relying on Laws) in *Guan Zi* (*The Book of Master Guan*).

[68]"Fa Fa" (Enforce Law by Means of Law) in *Guan Zi* (*The Book of Master Guan*).

[69]"Qi Tai Gong Shi Jia" (The Family of Qi) in *Shi Ji* (*The Record of the Grand Historian*).

[70]"Qi Yu" (The Historical Records of Qi State) in *Guo Yu* (*The Historical Records of Various States*).

[71]"Qi Tai Gong Shi Jia" (The Family of Qi) in *Shi Ji* (*The Record of the Grand Historian*).

Period in Guan Zhong's name, but its main idea, undoubtedly was closely connected with Guan Zhong himself.

Deng Xi, another representative of early Legalism also proposed that "things should be settled in accordance with law."[72] He believed that "the law, etiquettes, and rites of the former kings could be revised,"[73] so he not only challenged the tradition of the ruling of "Li" (rites), but also criticized the book about criminal law written by Zi Chan. Instead, he compiled a book called *Zhu Xing* (the bamboo *Punishment*) by himself. Du Yu in Jin Dynasty had made notes about it in *Zuo Zhuan* (*The Chronicle of Zuo*), according to him, Deng Xi "wants to change the old rules without following the mandate of the king. So he makes new laws on bamboo slips by himself, that is why it is called *Zhu Xing* (the bamboo *Punishment*)." Deng Xi also recruited disciples in private and taught laws by himself, "so there were large numbers of law students," which had greatly facilitated the trend of "making comments on laws by civilians."[74] In the end, even the authorities were afraid of him, so he was killed by Zheng Sichuan. Although he was killed, his *Zhu Xing* (the bamboo *Punishment*) were adopted, which had fully shown the value of the book.

After Guan Zhong and Deng Xi, the people like Li Kui, Shen Buhai, Shang Yang, and Han Fei all rose up like bright stars and they all came forth in succession. These people were all active advocators and practitioners of "Fa Zhi" (the rule of law) in the feudal times. They not only discussed nomology, but also closely combined the theory of laws with legislation and justice, which had not only guided the reform of law and politics, but also broken the ground for the formation of feudal legal system. The legalists' contributions to law and their passion for changing the realities had no rivals in other schools of thoughts.

In late Warring States Period, Han Fei was the epitome of the thoughts of the legalist school. He was born in a downfallen noble family of slave owners and was a son of a feudal prince. Living in a turbulent era, he faced with the collapse of old systems and the economic, political, and cultural transformation. Even when he was a small boy, he had begun to seek for new ways and theoretical explanations for the future and the strategies of running a state. Han Fei was influenced by his teacher Xun Kuang, so he had the character of facing reality with bravery and courage, which had played an important role in the formation of his conception of history to carry out reforms without following the old tracks. On the other hand, living under the historical background of the late Warring States Period, Han Fei was able to criticize Confucianism, Mohism, and Taoism among others with new knowledge and experience. He even summarized the legal theory of mid-Warring States Period in a critical way.

Han Fei's theory of "Yi Fa Wei Ben" (law-orientedness) and his combination of "Fa" (law), "Shu" (tactics) and "Shi" (power) was a new comprehensive notion

---

[72]"Zhuan Ci" (Euphemism) in *Deng Xi Zi* (*Deng Xizi*).
[73]"Fei Shi Er Zi" (The Twelve False Philosophers) in *Xun Zi* (*Xun Zi*).
[74]"Li Wei" (Inconsistency between Words and Thoughts) in *Lv Shi Chun Qiu* (*Spring and Autumn Annals of Master Lv*).

formed from critically absorbing legalism. This was why he had become a master of legalism and had created a sound and perfect theoretical system of "Fa Zhi" (the rule of law). His historical conception of keeping pace with times, his empirical spirit formed from experience, his theoretical system of "Yi Fa Wei Ben" (law-orientedness), and the combination of "Fa" (law), "Shu" (tactics), and "Shi" (power) along with the blueprint of building a country with "Fa Zhi" (the rule of law) should all be regarded as outstanding achievements. His sharp argument, rigorous thought, concrete evidence, and profound analysis had all made him a great ideologist in history. Since "Fa Zhi" (the rule of law), he had advocated was not only related to dictatorship but also was a tool for the realization of dictatorship, it was indeed "the instrument" of the king. The paradox of beginning with "Fa Zhi" (the rule of law) but ending up "Jun Zhi" (the rule of the king) had exactly shown that "Fa Zhi" (the rule of law) pursued by Han Fei was that carried out under the system of feudal autocracy, which was determined by the historical conditions of his times.

The ideological characteristics of the legalists in the Spring and Autumn Period and the Warring States Period can be summarized as follows:

First, "Xing" (punishment) was changed to "Fa" (law), and "Fa" (law) to "Lv" (criminal law), and the unitary application of law was emphasized.

In the ancient Chinese legal history, it was not merely the evolution of Chinese characters to change "Xing" (punishment) to "Fa" (law) and "Fa" (law) to "Lv" (criminal law), it was also a reflection of the legal progress under certain historical conditions. In Xia, Shang, and Western Zhou Dynasties, the Chinese character for penalties or "Xing" had the implication of punitive expedition, killing, and punishment. According to *Shuo Wen Jie Zi (The Origin of Chinese Characters)*, "'Xing' refers to punishment and sin, so it has the component of 'well' and 'knife edge' in Chinese character." With social development, *Yu Xing (The Penal Code of Yu)* in Xia Dynasty, *Tang Xing (The Penal Code of Tang)* in Shang Dynasty and *Jiu Xing (The Code Nine Penalties)* in Zhou Dynasty all referred to "Xing" in criminal punishment and they had become the antonomasia of "Fa" (law).

The transformation of "Xing" (punishment) to "Fa" (law) was caused by the great changes of social relationship in the Spring and Autumn and Warring States Period. Statute laws were made extensively, at the same time, many legalists began to be in power successively, and they had put forward their explanations about nomology, all of which had played important roles. The Chinese character of "Fa" was read for the first time in bronze inscriptions on *Da Yu Ding Ming (Inscriptions on Great Yu Tripod)*, "so originally it refers to laws safeguarding the former kings." In *Shuo Wen Jie Zi (Origin of Chinese Characters)*, it was explained in the following way: "'Fa' (rules) is equal to 'Xing' (punishments). It has the component of 'water', so it means as fair as water. Besides, the word has the component of the animal 'Zhi' (an ancient legendary animals of unicorn which can tell the right from the wrong), so it can attack the evil person and drive him away." Li Kui, an early representative of Legalism had written *Fa Jing (Canon of Laws)* and he had replaced "Fa" (law) with "Xing" (punishment) and used it as the names of codes, which was inseparable from the development of statute laws in all vassal states in the Spring and Autumn Period and the Warring States Period as well as the development of the concept of law. If "Xing" (punishment) mentioned in the principle that "the penal statutes should not be applied to high-ranking officials" reflected the privilege, which was characteristic of patriarchal hierarchy, then "Fa" (law) stood for objective justice. Shen Dao said, "'Fa' (law) is the best system to regulate people's behaviors and to achieve justice."[75] Therefore, legalists often compared "Fa" (law) to the instruments of weights and measures.

According to the notes of *Tang Lv Shu Yi* (*The Comments on Tang Code*) and *Tang Liu Dian* (*The Six Statutes of Tang Dynasty*), the change of "Xing" (punishment) to "Fa" (law) started from Shang Yang's being appointed as the prime minister of the state of Qin. It was recorded that "Shang Yang taught *Fa Jing* (*Canon of Laws*) and changed "Xing" (punishment) to "Fa" (law)." The Chinese character "Lv" (criminal law) was discovered early in the inscriptions of tortoise shells, and it meant military laws and disciplines. "Hu Lv" (Statutes on Households) and "Ben Ming Lv" (Statutes on Fugitives) made in the 25th year (252 B.C.) of the King An of Wei, which were included in *Yun Meng Qin Jian* (*Amounts of Bamboo Writing Slips in Qin Dynasty Excavated in Yunmeng*), had proved that it was not later than that time that the legal documents containing the name of "Lv" (criminal law) had existed, at the same time, it also proved that by that time it had experienced the process of changing "Fa" (law) to "Lv" (criminal law). This was because it was impossible for "Lv" (criminal law) to appear in a fixed form overnight because of the slow development of ancient legal culture.

Before Shang Yang changed "Fa" (law) to "Lv" (criminal law), the form of the "Lv" (criminal law) had already existed, and Shang Yang had only declared it formally in Qin state with the authority of a reformer. It was not by coincidence that the Chinese character "Lv" appeared in *Yun Meng Qin Jian* (*Amounts of Bamboo Writing Slips in Qin Dynasty Excavated in Yunmeng*) for 88 times, since "Lv" (criminal law) had the function of standardization, it was recorded in "Shi" (Army Division) in *Yi* (*The Book of Changes*) that "an army must have 'Lv' (criminal law)." Moreover, "Lv" was also related to metrical patterns, and the term "Lv Lv" (pitch-pipes to regulate the pitch of musical instruments) indicated that "Lv" (criminal law) had the function of fixing the temperaments of music. In the Warring States Period, to ensure the success of reform, the rulers of new landlord class especially emphasized the unitary application of law, therefore, it was easy to understand the historical necessity of changing "Fa" (law) to "Lv" (criminal law). However, the diversity of legal adjustment was decided by the complexity of social relationship. When "Fa" (law) was changed to "Lv" (criminal law) in the Warring States Period, the form of "Ling" (decree) also appeared frequently. For example, *Kai Qian Mo Feng Jiang Ling* (*The Order on Abolishing the Boundary of Fields*) was issued in 350 B.C. and *Chu Wei Fu Ling* (*The Order on the first Taxation*) was issued in 348 B.C., in which the order about levying tax according to land and family members was promulgated. Thereafter, *Ken Cao Ling* (*The Order for Reclaiming Grass*), *Tong Yi Du Liang Heng Ling* (*The Order for Unifying Weights and*

---

[75]"Yi Wen" (The Lost and Scattered Articles) in *Shen Zi* (*Master Shen*).

Measures), and *Shi Wu Ling* (*The Order for Military Units*) were enacted one after another one.

Second, to rule the country and the people by law.

Since the policy of "Fa Zhi" (the rule of law) was put forward by Guan Zhong, it had become the goal of the struggle of the legalists of the later generations, so new progress was made in both theory and practice.

Han Fei inherited the legal thoughts from the earlier legalists, and he not only did his best to advocate "Fa Zhi" (the rule of law) but also designed an ideal state of "Fa Zhi" (the rule of law) in which "there will be no essays in ancient books, instead laws and rules will be used as textbooks; there will be no words of the former kings, instead the petty officials will become teachers; there will be no assassins for individual service, instead there will be bravery killing of enemies and military achievements. Thus, all people within the state shall be abided by law when they make comments; all laborers shall contribute to the country and all the brave men shall serve in the army. So it is because of this that the state will become prosperous in peaceful times and will have strong military forces in war times. . . ."[76] Moreover, in this country of "Fa Zhi" (the rule of law), "there would be no other equally honorable statements besides the orders of the kings, and there would be no laws which can cater to both state and individuals; therefore, any word or action against law shall be forbidden."[77] He drew a lesson from the malpractice of Shen Buhai for the "disunity of the law": "the old laws of Jin are not abolished whereas new laws of Han are made; the orders of previous kings are not taken back whereas the orders of the new king are already issued. So Shen Buhai is not expert at enforcing the new laws, nor has he unified the new laws of Han Dynasty, that is why there are many evil people."[78]

This was why he related the enforcement of "Fa Zhi" (the rule of law) with the poverty and prosperity of the state. He said, "No country can be powerful forever, nor can any country be poor forever; if the law-executor act in accordance with the law, the country will be powerful, and vice versa."[79]

It should be noted that during the legal reform of the state of Qin, Shang Yang showed his ambition of ruling the state by law, issued laws and orders with great authority, established new legal order, strengthened the dominant position of the king and achieved the goal of "Fu Guo Qiang Bin" (making the country rich and its military forces strong), which had brought peace and prosperity to Qin state and laid a solid foundation for the unification of the other six states by Qin Shi Huang (the first emperor of Qin). Although Shang Yang sacrificed his life for the realization of "Fa Zhi" (the rule of law), the laws he made were inherited by the later generations, which showed that the cause he had undertaken was in conformity to the historical trend of development.

---

[76]"Wu Du" (Five Pests, referring to people from five trades) in *Han Fei Zi* (*Han Feizi*).
[77]"Wen Bian" (Ask and Debate) in *Han Fei Zi* (*Han Feizi*).
[78]"Ding Fa" (Law Making) in *Han Fei Zi* (*Han Feizi*).
[79]"You Du" (Being Lawful) in *Han Fei Zi* (*Han Feizi*).

Third, the legalists put emphasis on the justice of law and opposed the hierarchical privilege asserted by the principle that "the penal statutes should not be applied to high-ranking officials."

Shen Dao said, "Law is the best system to regulate people's behaviors and to achieve justice",[80] which was explained by Shang Yang in a more determined tone: "there are no differentiation for punishment, so anyone, from ministers, senior officials and generals to the common people, should obey the laws of the country and anyone who disobeys or violates the law shall be sentenced to death without pardoning."[81] He not only talked about it, but also put it into practice. Even if the prince violated the law, he would still be punished, "so one of the teachers of the prince, Gongsun Qian was punished by death penalty and the other, Gongsun Jia was punished by 'Qing' (to tattoo on the face)."[82] According to Han Fei's understanding of "Fa Zhi" (the rule of law), "even if 'Da Fu' (senior officials in ancient China) shall not be exempted from punishment, and even if the common people shall be awarded likewise," because the value of laws lay in the fact that "what is ruled in the law should not be violated by the wise people nor challenged by the reckless people."[83] Moreover, the legalists also compared the fairness of law to the tools of weights and measures. Apart from some comments by Guan Zi quoted in the previous text, Shen Dao also said in "Wei De" (The Virtue of Authority) in *Shen Zi* (*Master Shen*) that "so divination is used to establish common sense, scale is used to establish the standard of righteousness, contract is used to establish public credit, the tools for weights and measures are used to establish public supervision and rules and rites are used to establish morality. All are established for the public, so selfishness is eliminated." He also said in *Yi Lin* (*Excerpts from Ancient Classics*), "Scales are made to prevent people from cheating about weights; rulers are made to prevent people from cheating about sizes; laws are made to prevent people from committing the crime of fraud and forgery."[84] Han Fei said, "Therefore, even if a wise craftsman's estimate is accurate and he can accord with the line of ink marker with his naked eye, first he should use established rules as the standard for the measurement; even if a wise man could handle the business properly in a short time, first he should use the rules made by the former kings as the standard; if the line is straight, then the crooked wood shall be made straight by cutting; if the gradienter is accurate, then the high ridges shall be levelled; if the scale is used, shortage of weight or measurement should be avoided; if *dou* and *dan* are used, insufficiency of quantity should be made up. Hence, to rule the country with "Fa Zhi" (the rule of law) just means working out measures to carry them out. Laws shall not show partiality for the noblemen just like the line of ink marker shall not accommodate itself to the crooked

---

[80]"Yi Wen" (The Lost and Scattered Articles) in *Shen Zi* (*Master Shen*).

[81]"Yi Xing" (Unitary Punishment) in *Shang Jun Shu* (*The Book of Lord Shang*).

[82]"Shang Jun Lie Zhuan" (The Collected Biographies of Shang Yang) in *Shi Ji* (*The Record of the Grand Historian*).

[83]"You Du" (Being Lawful) in *Han Fei Zi* (*Han Feizi*).

[84]*Yi Lin* (*Excerpts from Ancient Classics*), Vol. 2.

wood."[85] Therefore, the justice stressed by legalists was not only the inherent value orientation of law, but also a way to protect the new regime and to safeguard the political and the economic interests of landlord class by fighting against the authority of the old nobility.

Fourth, to advocate the flexibility of law by using the concept of historical evolution.

In fact, at a very early time, it was proposed in "Lv Xing" (The Penal Code of Lv) in *Shang Shu* (*The Book of Historical Document*) that "'Xing' (punishment) and "Fa" (law) should be enforced leniently or severely in accordance with concrete situations," which meant that punishment should vary with times. Han Fei was one of the representatives in this area.

Han Fei's theory of "Fa Zhi" (the rule of law) was formed based on the plain concept of historical evolution. He regarded history as evolutionary, so he thought that it had gone through four stages: "remote times," "medieval times," "ancient times nearest to the present" and "present times." "In the remote ages, people contended with each other with morality; in medieval times, people contended with each other with wisdom and strategies; at present, people contended with each other with power." "Customs are different between the past and the present, so different political measures are enforced in the new and old ages,"[86] which was an objective law of historical development. Therefore, he opposed conservatism and the idea of returning to ancients but insisted on reform, and he proposed that "time changes, so circumstances and politics will change as well."[87] He also emphasized that "even the sages have not expected to follow the old rules, nor have they clung to the old traditions or customs. However, they take political measures in accordance with the current social situation."[88] Han Fei's conception of history was both a part of his theoretical basis of legal reform and the foothold of the theory of "Fa Zhi" (the rule of law), so he thought, "law rather than virtue should be relied on."[89] Although Han Fei regarded "De" (virtue) and "Fa" (law) as "two important methods" "that the kings have employed to take control of the subordinates,"[90] he also maintained that in a turbulent world, "violence can be prevented by power and force, but chaos cannot be prevented by 'De' (virtue)," so "a sagacious king will rule the country by applying different methods of awards and punishments without relying on people's virtue, why? Because the state law should not be neglected, and the king does not rule only one person."[91] Hence, if a sagacious king rule the state, then "(he should) make people abide by law and have the criminals severely punished, so that the

---

[85]"You Du" (Being Lawful) in *Han Fei Zi* (*Han Feizi*).

[86]"Wu Du" (Five Pests, referring to people from five trades) in *Han Fei Zi* (*Han Feizi*).

[87]"Wu Du" (Five Pests, referring to people from five trades) in *Han Fei Zi* (*Han Feizi*).

[88]"Wu Du" (Five Pests, referring to people from five trades) in *Han Fei Zi* (*Han Feizi*).

[89]"Xian Xue" (Noted School of Thought) in *Han Fei Zi* (*Han Feizi*).

[90]"Er Bing" (Two Handles) in *Han Fei Zi* (*Han Feizi*).

[91]"Xian Xue" (Noted School of Thought) in *Han Fei Zi* (*Han Feizi*).

common people avoid doing evil things out of the deterrence of law instead of out of integrity."[92]

The society was developing and advancing, which has decided the changeability of law. Thus, only the law that changes with times can be effective and can be applied in ruling the state. Han Fei said, "So, there are no unalterable conventions to govern the common people. Law is the only way to rule the world, so good government can only be ensured by the laws which are changing with times, and only the government which is ruled in accordance with concrete social condition can be effective... if time changes but the way of running a state remains unchanged, the society will be in chaos; if the wise people rule, but if the rules and regulations remain unchanged, then the state shall be at stake. So if a sagacious king rules the people, he first must make laws that change with the times and the prohibitions that change with the historical conditions."[93] This is a historical conclusion applicable to all times and all countries.

Fifth, Han Fei suggested that statute laws should be made and issued to public, so he was against the old tradition that "punishment should be kept secret so that its power shall be unfathomable."

He stressed that it was the prerequisite for "Yi Fa Zhi Guo" (the ruling the country according to law) to draft statute laws. Therefore, the laws can be made more practical and authoritative if they are ensured by the compulsive enforcement of judicial departments and based on the explicit awards and punishments to common people. Han Fei said, "Laws, maps and household registration are written and compiled by the authorities, and then publicized to the common people...so the more they are made public, the better...therefore, when the sagacious kings talk about laws, even the servants and the common people in the country know them"[94]; "the so-called laws are made by the government so the awards and punishment should be conducted to win the support of the people; the people who obey laws shall be awarded, while the ones who violate laws shall be punished. This is what the subordinates should follow."[95] Since "the more the laws are made public, the better," and laws should be announced to the public, then they should be made stable and unified for the common people to abide by without disorientation. Consequently, Han Fei added, "Laws should be made consistent for people to understand"[96] and "there would be no other equally honorable statements besides the orders of the kings, and there would be no laws which can cater to both state and individuals; therefore, any word or action against law shall be forbidden..."[97] He cited the example of the malpractice of Shen Buhai for his "disunity of the law": "the old laws of Jin are not abolished whereas new laws of Han are made; the orders of

---

[92] "Liu Fan" (Six Oppositions) in *Han Fei Zi* (*Han Feizi*).
[93] "Xin Du" (Mind) in *Han Fei Zi* (*Han Feizi*).
[94] "Nan" (Crisis) in *Han Fei Zi* (*Han Feizi*) (Book 3).
[95] "Ding Fa" (Law Making) in *Han Fei Zi* (*Han Feizi*).
[96] "Wu Du" (Five Pests, referring to people from five trades) in *Han Fei Zi* (*Han Feizi*).
[97] "Wen Bian" (Ask and Debate) in *Han Fei Zi* (*Han Feizi*).

previous kings are not taken back whereas the orders of the new king are already issued. So Shen Buhai is not expert at enforcing the new laws, nor has he unified the new laws of Han Dynasty, that is why there are many evil people."[98] From this statement, it can be seen that Han Fei paid more attention to common people and had endeavored to win "the people's support" through "due rewards and punishments." To let common people understand laws, it was stressed that laws must be "unified and remain consistent all the time." During Shang Yang's political reform, it was emphasized that the common people should be educated to learn and obey the rules by propagating "Fa Zhi" (the rule of law). It was recorded in history book that "women and children in Qin are all talking about laws made by Shang."[99] Consequently, "the officials do not dare to treat the common people illegally, nor do the common people dare to offend the officials by violating the law,"[100] so that "the law was fully implemented and the people of Qin were well governed."[101] It was also specially pointed out by Shang Yang that people's condition should be taken into consideration in legislation, and he explained, "If the specific conditions of the common people are not taken into consideration in the making laws, then it is impossible for the laws to be effectively applied."[102] The theory of stressing people put forward by legalists and the human-oriented ideology put forward by Confucianists were just to achieve the same goal through different means.

Sixth, Han Fei proposed that due punishment should be carried out and "Xing" (punishment) should be eliminated by employing "Xing" (punishment) itself.

In the early stage, the legalists Guan Zhong and Zi Chan were both representatives who suggested that the regulations for punishments and awards should be carried out rigorously to ensure the implementation of reform and the practice of "Fa Zhi" (the rule of law). Guan Zhong said that (a king should) "encourage people by awards and rectify them by punishment."[103] Zi Chan stressed that "the common people may become obedient with lenient punishment only under the rule of the people with noble character; nevertheless, in the second place, no punishments are more effective than the ones as frightening as the burning fire, because it may intimidate the common people, that is why there are not many deaths caused by fire; water is not so dangerous, so people often get close to and play in it, therefore, many are drown in it."[104] Hence, "satisfactory results can be achieved" only by

---

[98]"Ding Fa" (Law Making) in *Han Fei Zi* (*Han Feizi*).
[99]"Qi Ce Yi" (Strategies of Qi) (Part 1) in *Zhan Guo Ce* (*Stratagems of the Warring States*).
[100]"Ding Fen" (Defining a Person's Social Status) in *Shang Jun Shu* (*The Book of Lord Shang*).
[101]"Qin Ben Ji" (The History of the State of Qin) in *Shi Ji* (*The Record of the Grand Historian*).
[102]"Yi Yan" (Unification of Words) in *Shang Jun Shu* (*The Book of Lord Shang*).
[103]"Qi Yu" (The Historical Records of Qi State) in *Guo Yu* (*The Historical Records of Various States*).
[104]"Zhao Gong Er Shi Nian" (The 20th Year of the Duke of Zhao) in *Zuo Zhuan* (*The Chronicle of Zuo*).

severe punishments, which should be clearly stated.[105] During the time of Shang Yang's political reform, he strongly supported that "due punishments should be carried out" with "generous awards and severe punishments conducted at proper time." Whether awards or punishments, they were conducted to get "trustworthiness" and to get rid of "selfishness." He said, "If people believe in the king's awards, then things will be successfully handled; if they believe in the king's punishments, then crimes will be avoided."[106] In "Qin Ce" (The Strategy of the State of Qin) in *Zhan Guo Ce* (*Stratagems of the Warring States*) the unselfishness and bravery of Shang Yang, which was shown in his execution of awards and punishments, was highly praised:

> When the king Shang ran the state of Qin, the laws were all strictly carried out and he had shown great integrity and unselfishness; he was not afraid of the powerful nobles in carrying out punishment; he shows no favor to his relatives in giving rewards; even the prince was punished according to law with his teachers punished by 'Qing' (to tattoo on the face) and 'Yi' (to cut down the nose).

In terms of awards and punishments, Shang Yang advocated that "more punishments and fewer awards should be conducted."[107] He insisted that "punishments should be executed before awards"[108] and "if punishments are aggravated and awards are reduced, then even if the king shows love and protection to the common people, he is still hated by them; if awards are increased and punishments are mitigated, then even if the king shows no love and protection to the common people, he is not hated by them."[109] Meanwhile, He was also an advocator of severe punishment, and he thought, "(therefore) there is nothing better than severe punishment in preventing evilness and crimes"[110]; so in particular, he put forward the idea of "enforcing severe punishment for minor crimes" and suggested that "'Xing' (punishment) should be eliminated by employing 'Xing' (punishment)."[111] He said, "it is impossible to prevent crimes to enforce severe punishment for severe crimes and light punishment for minor crimes, because it is impossible for minor crimes to be prevented by light punishments, let alone major crimes."[112] Consequently, "the state will decline."[113] Thus, the only practical method was to apply severe punishments for minor offenses. The reason is as follows: "if severe punishments are executed for minor offenses, then neither minor nor severe crimes will be committed." Thus, in the end, "punishments can be eliminated by employing

---

[105]"Xiang Gong Er Shi Wu Nian" (The 25th Year of the Duke of Xiang) in *Zuo Zhuan* (*The Chronicle of Zuo*).
[106]"Xiu Quan" (On the Usage of Power) in *Shang Jun Shu* (*The Book of Lord Shang*).
[107]"Ding Fa" (Law Making) in *Han Fei Zi* (*Han Feizi*).
[108]"Wu Du" (Five Pests, referring to people from five trades) in *Han Fei Zi* (*Han Feizi*).
[109]"Wen Bian" (Ask and Debate) in *Han Fei Zi* (*Han Feizi*).
[110]"Nan" (Crisis) in *Han Fei Zi* (*Han Feizi*) (Book 3).
[111]"Hua Ce" (Policies) in *Shang Jun Shu* (*The Book of Lord Shang*).
[112]"Ding Fa" (Law Making) in *Han Fei Zi* (*Han Feizi*).
[113]"Qi Ce Yi" (Strategies of Qi) (Part 1) in *Shang Jun Shu* (*The Book of Lord Shang*).

punishments, and when punishments are eliminated, then the state affairs will be handled effectively." He especially was objected to enforcing lenient punishments for severe crimes, because "if lenient punishments are enforced for severe crimes, more crimes will be committed randomly, so this is in fact increasing punishments by employing punishments, and the country will definitely decline with such practices."[114]

On the one hand, Han Fei pointed out that "De Zhi" (the rule of virtue) was impractical by itself. He said, "major crimes can be prevented by power and force, but chaos cannot be prevented by 'De' (virtue) alone;" "when a sagacious king was on the throne, the common people are constrained by law instead of integrity or 'De' (virtue)"[115]; on the other hand, he demonstrated what social effect would be achieved through "due punishments and awards": "Generous awards should be given to meet people's needs; rigorous and definite punishments should be enforced to deter people...so awards should be given according to rules, and punishments should be enforced without remission; after awards, praise should be given, and after punishment, condemnation should be followed. In this way, anyone, whether talented or not, will try their best."[116] "Generous awards will bring what the king expects; severe punishments will prevent what the king dislikes...hence generous awards will be given to the people by those who hope to run the state well and severe punishments will be imposed upon the people by those who dislike chaos."[117]

According to Han Fei's understanding of "Fa Zhi" (the rule of law), awards, and punishments were very important measures, and as part of the theories of legalists, the severe punishment mentioned by him was closely connected with Shang Yang's theory of "eliminating punishments with punishments." By his ideology of granting generous awards and executing severe punishments, Han Fei showed the inclination of stressing material gains while neglecting education; stressing the state while neglecting individuals; stressing the public power while neglecting the private rights. This was the inevitable result of the philosophical perception of the legalists, according to which people were born evil and human beings were selfish. Just as Han Fei said, "It depends on 'Ren Qing' (human feelings) to run the state. Because it's human nature to have likes and dislikes, awards and punishments should be conducted accordingly, so only in this way is it possible for laws to be made and state policies to be carried out."[118] Thus, it was for this reason that Ban Gu from Han Dynasty had made the following criticism: "legalism may all come from 'Li Guan' (judicial officials), who suggested that anyone who had made contribution should be rewarded and anyone who had committed crimes should be punished, so the rule of 'Li' (rites) should be used as a supplementary method in ruling. It is stated in *Yi* (*The Book of Changes*) that 'Fa' (law) is enforced by the deceased kings with severe

---

[114]"Ding Fen" (Defining a Person's Social Status) in *Shang Jun Shu* (*The Book of Lord Shang*).
[115]"Liu Fan" (Six Oppositions) in *Han Fei Zi* (*Han Feizi*).
[116]"Wu Du" (Five Pests, referring to people from five trades) in *Han Fei Zi* (*Han Feizi*).
[117]"Liu Fan" (Six Oppositions) in *Han Fei Zi* (*Han Feizi*).
[118]"Ba Jing" (Eight Canons) in *Han Fei Zi* (*Han Feizi*).

punishments', so it is one of their advantages. On the contrary, when brutal officials are in office, education is neglected, benevolence is abandoned, and severe punishments are solely applied to achieve order and peace, so that even the relatives are harmed and kindness is paid back by ingratitude."[119]

Seventh, once the laws are made, they should not be interfered with by any individuals.

The importance of maintaining the authority of law was emphasized by a legalist named Deng Xi in a much earlier period: "what is the most important for 'Fa Zhi' (the rule of law) is that it should not be interfered with by any individuals....Now law is made for personal ends and is perverted by people, so the disorder caused is worse than the state in which the law is not made, ... so when law is made, no favoritism should be pursued"; otherwise, "the rulers would grant awards as they like and refuse granting awards to those who have done outstanding service; they would kill people when they are unhappy, regardless of what the victim has done; they would reward and punish people as they please and require the officials to carry out their orders blindly. In the end, it would lead to the subjugation of the nation and the ceaseless killing of kings."[120] Shen Dao held similar opinions: "What is most important to law is to prevent people from pursuing selfish ends..., and from being perverted by people, because the disorder caused is worse than the state in which the law is not made....In a country with moral integrity, as soon as laws are made, individual annotations should be prohibited....So it is one of the most important affairs of a country to make judgments in accordance with law."[121]

Shang Yang made even more insightful comments on this topic and he said that "if private comments are made without following the law, then the treacherous officials will play favoritism by accepting bribery, and the ordinary officials will conceal the truth from the king and exploit the people. As the old saying goes, 'too many moths can break trees and big cracks can destroy walls', so if officials just play favoritism for self-interests but don't care about the common people, then the civilians will be estranged from the king, which is like the cracks in a wall; moreover, the government officials who conceal the truth and encroach upon people's interests are like moths. No country with moths and cracks can survive, therefore, laws are made by the sagacious kings to restrain the private interests to make sure that there will be no moths or cracks."[122] "Hence, laws should be made and responsibilities should be clearly defined between the public and the private to prevent the laws from being violated by private interests."[123]

The opinion that "if the laws made are not enforced, then it's no better than the state in which the law is not made" proposed by legalists had focused on safeguarding the authority of laws, which was a comprehensive summary of the

---

[119]"Yi Wen Zhi" (Books and Records) in *Han Shu* (*The History of Han Dynasty*).

[120]"Zhuan Ci" (Euphemism) in *Deng Xi Zi* (*Deng Xi*).

[121]"Yi Wen" (The Lost and Scattered Articles) in *Shen Zi* (*Master Shen*).

[122]"Xiu Quan" (On the Usage of Power) in *Shang Jun Shu* (*The Book of Lord Shang*).

[123]"Xiu Quan" (On the Usage of Power) in *Shang Jun Shu* (*The Book of Lord Shang*).

experience. Thus, the sarcastic statement, profound thinking, and clear target still function as a warning to the people today.

Eighth, it is the foundation of making a state powerful to enforce and obey the law.

The legalists maintained that laws are the weights and measurements of a state. If there are no laws or the laws cannot be enforced, then the state will lose its weights and measurements and cannot function properly, so it is unavoidable for the decline of the state. At the same time, laws are also "rules regulating people's behaviors." Han Fei said, "All comments in the country should be made in accordance with rules, all behaviors should be beneficial to the state and all brave people should serve in the army because in this way the state can be prosperous in peaceful time and its military force can be powerful in wartime."[124] He then added, "What is ruled in the law should not be violated by the wise people nor challenged by the reckless people."[125] So he concluded that "no country can be powerful forever, nor can any country be poor forever; if the law-executor act in accordance with the law, the country will be powerful, and vice versa."[126]

This conclusion has had universal values transcending time and space after the historical test of later generations. Of course, the laws enforced must be good laws.

Ninth, the king's power is strengthened and "Fa" (law), "Shu" (tactics), and "Shi" (power) should be unified.

Han Fei was a supporter of monarchical power, and the combination of "Fa" (law), "Shu" (tactics), and "Shi" (power) was put forward by him to strengthen the monarchical power. He criticized Shang Yang's idea of "merely stressing 'Fa' (law) while neglecting 'Shu' (tactics)," because although it could only make the state of Qin "wealthy and militarily powerful," still "the king didn't have any 'Shu' (tactics) to know the treacherous officials" so that "an official was often honored only after he won a military victory and fiefdom was often granted after he had more obtained land."[127] Consequently, it was more difficult to make greater achievements in the political reforms. He also reprimanded Shen Buhai because he only talked about and "stressed 'Shu' (tactics) but ignored 'Fa' (law)"[128] so he had lost the criteria not only for distinguishing the loyal and the treacherous and but also for giving awards and enforcing punishments, which had made "the friendly people compete to flatter each other, and made the hostile people slander each other by forming cliques. So slander and flattery were mixed so that the king got confused."[129]

From the critical summery of Shen Buhai's theories of tactics, Han Fei formed the "law oriented" ideological system with the combination of "Fa" (law), "Shu" (tactics), and "Shi" (power). On the one hand, he spoke in defense of Shen Dao's

---

[124]"Wu Du" (Five Pests, referring to people from five trades) in *Han Fei Zi* (*Han Feizi*).
[125]"You Du" (Being Lawful) in *Han Fei Zi* (*Han Feizi*).
[126]"You Du" (Being Lawful) in *Han Fei Zi* (*Han Feizi*).
[127]"Ding Fa" (Law Making) in *Han Fei Zi* (*Han Feizi*).
[128]"Ding Fa" (Law Making) in *Han Fei Zi* (*Han Feizi*).
[129]"Nan Mian" (Facing the South) in *Han Fei Zi* (*Han Feizi*).

3.3 Confucianism and Legalism in "Bai Jia Zheng Ming" (The Contention of...

emphasis on "authority" by explaining that "the authority can be the king's abyss,"[130] and that the king's authority comes from power, as was illustrated in the statement that "the reason why the king is respected lies in his power."[131] Therefore, "authority" and "power" should only be enjoyed by the king instead of being shared by officials. On the other hand, he stressed that "the order of the country can be guaranteed by getting hold of 'Shi' (power) and carrying out 'Fa' (law), while chaos may arise by abandoning 'Fa' (law) and losing the authority."[132] He suggested that "Fa" (law) should be combined with "Shi" (power), "Fa" (law) should be enforced with the help of "Shi" (power), and "Shi" (power) should be consolidated with the help of "Fa" (law). He thus concluded that "if the king takes control of political power, then the orders and prohibitions should be strictly enforced. Moreover, political power can decide the life and death of the people, and authority is the basis for ruling the common people."[133]

To maintain power and privilege, apart from "Fa Zhi" (the rule of law), the king had to master "Shu" (tactics) about how to control officials, which was also called "the way of running the state." He said, "The so-called 'Shu' (tactics) means the ability to confer official titles in accordance with their talents, to investigate and assign the tasks according to titles, to decide life and death of the people and to evaluate the performances of officials,"[134] so "'Shu' (tactics), which is hidden in the king's mind are used to deal with various affairs and to control the officials in private. So the more publicized 'Fa' (law), the better, yet 'Shu' (tactics) should not be revealed;...when 'Shu' (tactics) is employed, even the most trusted followers of the king are not in the know."[135] When criticizing Shang Yang for his "merely stressing 'Fa' (law) while neglecting 'Shu' (tactics)" and Shen Buhai for his "merely stressing 'Shu' (tactics) while neglecting 'Fa' (law)," Han Fei, at the same time, endeavored to unite the two together and insisted that "'Shu' (tactics) should be controlled by the king while 'Fa' (law) should be obeyed by the officials,"[136] and he thought that "the king without 'Shu' (tactics) can be deceived and the officials disobeying 'Fa' (law) will make trouble, so neither 'Shu' (tactics) nor 'Fa' (law) can be neglected, because they are all an integral part of the king's measures to rule the country."[137]

The purpose of Han Fei's theory of the unification of "Fa" (law), "Shu" (tactics) and "Shi" (power) was to reinforce the king's power, to realize the rule of the autocrat monarchy and to complete the great task of "Fu Guo Qiang Bin" (making

---

[130]"Nei Chu Shuo" (The Inner Categories of Sayings) in *Han Fei Zi* (*Han Feizi*) (Book 2).

[131]"Xin Du" (Mind) in *Han Fei Zi* (*Han Feizi*).

[132]"Nan Shi" (Difficult Situation) in *Han Fei Zi* (*Han Feizi*).

[133]"Ba Jing" (Eight Canons) in *Han Fei Zi* (*Han Feizi*).

[134]"Ding Fa" (Law Making) in *Han Fei Zi* (*Han Feizi*).

[135]"Nan" (Crisis) in *Han Fei Zi* (*Han Feizi*) (Book 3).

[136]"Shuo Yi" (On Suspicion) in *Han Fei Zi* (*Han Feizi*).

[137]"Yi Wen" (The Lost and Scattered Articles) in *Shen Zi* (*Master Shen*).

the country rich and its military forces strong). His thoughts had provided a theoretic basis for China's two thousand years of feudal autocratic system.

As Han Fei's teacher, Xun Kuang once said, "That's why the sagacious kings are eager to recruit the talented people while the fatuous ones are thirsty for power; if the talented people are recruited, the rulers can rule the country easily, and they will make great achievements and get good reputation. In favorable conditions, they could be the king; while in unfavorable conditions they at least could be the ruler of a local area. If the talented people are not recruited, the rulers will suffer and his state would be in chaos. What's more, they will achieve nothing, and their fame will be ruined and the state will be at stake as well."[138] It can be inferred that the most important thing is to obtain talents who can help to enforce laws and to rule the state. Han Fei's focus is on the monarchs, that is, to practice "Fa Zhi" (the rule of law) by virtue of the power of monarchs. If Xun Kuang's "Ren Zhi" (the rule of man) is focused on law enforcement by the sagacious people, then Han Fei's theory is focused on the monarchical power by which the law is enforced.

3.4 The Legal Reform Adaptable to Social Transformation

3.4.1 The Issuing of the Statute Laws in the Vassal States and the Legislative Activities in the Spring and Autumn Period

In the early Spring and Autumn Period, the laws of the Western Zhou Dynasty were followed by almost all vassal states. Around the middle era, the profound social transformation had fostered the making of new laws by some countries, so it had reflected the demand of times.

In 685 B.C., Guan Zhong was the prime minister of Qi state, so "he relied on the formulation of domestic politics to renovate military orders," which "had helped him to repel the invading minority groups, to establish the authority of the king at home and to pacify the nobles."[139]

In 636 B.C., the Duke Wen of Jin state took office. He carried out reforms with keen determination and drafted *Bei Lu Zhi Fa* (*Laws of Bei Lu*). In "Xing Fa Zhi" (The Record of the Criminal Law) in *Han Shu* (*The History of Han Dynasty*), Ying Shao annotated that "in the place called Beilu, the law was made to govern the officials of six departments, so the law was thus entitled." *Bei Lu Zhi Fa* (*Laws of Bei Lu*) was about the selection of talents and the establishment of bureaucracy, but the details could not be proven now. Thus, Jin state became powerful since then.

In 621 B.C., Zhao Dun inherited the throne of Jin state from Zhao Xuanzi, and he began to take the following measures to rectify the country: "Zhi Shi Dian" (making

---

[138]"Jun Dao" (On the Way of a Lord) in *Xun Zi* (*Xun Zi*).

[139]"Xing Fa Zhi" (The Record of the Criminal Law) in *Han Shu* (*The History of Han Dynasty*).

3.4 The Legal Reform Adaptable to Social Transformation 145

regulations for handling state affairs); "Zheng Fa Zui" (revising the laws and decrees); "Pi Xing Yu" (enforcing penalties); "Dong Bu Tao"(catching the escaped prisoners); "You Zhi Yao" (making contracts); "Zhi Jiu Wu"(rectifying the old customs); "Ben Zhi Li" (maintaining hierarchal order); "Xu Chang Zhi" (continuing the original official positions) and "Chu Zhi Yan"(inviting the virtuous and able people to be officials). After the rules and regulations were made, they were handed over to Jia Tuo, who was the teacher of the prince, so they were issued in Jin state and used as common laws."[140]

The so-called "Zhi Shi Dian" refers to making regulations for officials to follow in handling state affairs; "Zheng Fa Zui" refers to revising the laws and decrees of punishments; "Pi Xing Yu" refers to making judgments and settling lawsuits; "Dong Bu Tao" refers to catching the escaped prisoners; "You Zhi Yao" refers to using contracts and accounts as the certificate in handling property relations; "Zhi Jiu Wu" refers to rectifying the old customs that were harmful to the people and state; "Ben Zhi Li" refers to maintaining the hierarchal order; "Xu Chang Zhi" and "Chu Zhi Yan" refers to appointing the talents as officials.

In 593 B.C., Fan Wuzi came into power and "the laws of Fan Wuzi" was issued, which was mainly about the revision of the official posts and titles.

In 513 B.C., the criminal laws formulated by Fan Xuanzi were inscribed on a bronze vessel cast in the state of Jin, which was not only the fourth legislation in Jin state, but also a major measure taken by the newly emerged forces after they attained the political power (as is shown in the next passages), In more than one hundred years, four major legislative activities were carried out in the state of Jin, which had demonstrated that legislation should be made timely to be adjusted to the changes caused by social upheaval.

Just like Jin state, the second legislation was made in Chu state. During the reign of the Duke Wen of Chu, *Pu Qu Fa* (*Pu Qu La*) was formulated. Wu Yu, "Yu Yin" (anient official) at the time stated in "Zhao Gong Qi Nian" (The 7th Year of the Duke of Zhao) in *Zuo Zhuan* (*The Chronicle of Zuo*) that "laws were laid down by our former kings to punish the crime of harboring the escaped prisoners." Du Yu noted, "'Pu Qu' is a book of criminal law." While according to Fu Qian, "'Pu' means hiding, and 'Qu' means harboring, so this is a law about hiding and harboring the escaped prisoners." It was said that it was laid down by imitating the provision of "searching for the escaping slaves" in the laws made by Duke Wen. However, it was stipulated in *Pu Qu Fa* (*Pu Qu Law*) that "anyone who conceals the possessions stolen by thieves shall be punished by the same penalty for the criminals," which had shown that the law was made to punish the escaped criminals who had stolen the others' possessions. Therefore, these two laws were fundamentally different.

During the period of the Duke Zhuang of Chu state, *Mao Men Fa* (*Mao Men Law*) was drafted. According to "Wai Chu Shuo You" (The Outer Categories of Sayings) (Part 2) in *Han Fei Zi* (*Han Feizi*) (Book 1), "when nobles, scholars and princes went to the imperial courts, if their horses had threaded on the drainage ditches of the

---

[140]"Wen Gong Liu Nian" (The 6th Year of the Duke of Wen) in *Zuo Zhuan* (*The Chronicle of Zuo*).

palace, their carriage shaft will be cut off and the carriage will be destroyed." "Mao Men," or "Zhi Men," was one of the palace gates. Thus, *Mao Men Fa* (*Mao Men Law*) was a legislation made for the guarding of the special palace gates. According to the law, when nobles, scholars and princes went to the imperial courts, it was forbidden for their carriages to enter the palace gates; otherwise, they shall be punished, which had fully shown that the king of the vassal state had tried to establish his authority through law under this historical background of "Li Beng Yue Huai" (the disintegration of rites and collapse of rituals). Therefore, *Mao Men Fa* (*Mao Men Law*) was the predecessor of the law on guarding the palace gate in the later ages.

From 543 B.C. to 522 B.C., Zi Chan took office in the state of Zheng and he began to actively carry out reforms. He divided land by building ditches between land, and levied military tax on private landowners. In the initial stage of the reform, he was sharply criticized, so according to the records in "Xiang Gong San Shi Nian" (The 30th Year of the Duke of Xiang) in *Zuo Zhuan* (*The Chronicle of Zuo*), "at the beginning, people sang the song: 'my possessions are calculated and my farmland is measured to levy tax, so I will lend a hand to anyone who wants to kill Zi Chan'." However, three years later, when his policy of "Fu Guo Qiang Bin" (making the country rich and its military forces strong) carried on based on protecting the private property achieved success, people's opinion changed accordingly, so they said: "I have sons and younger brothers who are educated by Zi Chan; I have farmland whose output of grain is increased by Zi Chan. If he dies, who will take his place?" Therefore, it is under these circumstances that it is possible to carry out the activity of casting laws on bronze vessels, which is of great historical significance.

Although the legislative activities mentioned above added new contents that reflected the characteristics of the time, they were not publicized to the outside world, and the promulgation of statute laws started in the state of Zheng and Jin in late Spring and Autumn Period.

It was recorded in "Zhao Gong Liu Nian" (The 6th Year of the Duke of Zhao) in *Zuo Zhuan* (*The Chronicle of Zuo*) that "criminal laws were cast on bronze vessels by Zheng people." Du Yu noted that "the criminal laws were cast on bronze vessels and were used as statue laws." Since Zi Chan had "cast criminal laws on bronze vessels," he had broken the old tradition that "punishments should be enforced temporarily instead of being publicized in advance," because "punishment should be kept secret so that its power shall be unfathomable."[141] This had prevented nobles from arbitrarily persecuting the innocent by false accusation, or changing the verdicts of guilty to that of innocence, so it caused a great shock and was flatly rejected by old nobles like Shu Xiang. Shu Xiang wrote a letter to Zi Chan and criticized him because "in the past, the king made judgments by discussing the state affairs rather than making laws to prevent the common people from revolting... because if people know the laws, they will not show reverence to the king anymore.

---

[141]"Zhao Gong Liu Nian" (The 6th Year of the Duke of Zhao) in *Chun Qiu Zuo Zhuan Zheng Yi* (*Interpretation of the Chronicle of Zuo*).

3.4 The Legal Reform Adaptable to Social Transformation

If the criminal laws are used as evidence, then it is hard to manage them...now you help Zheng state to build ditches between the borders of the farmland, to set up rules about politics, to draft three kinds of laws and cast criminal laws on bronze vessels to pacify the common people, isn't it hard too?... If people know they can fight for their rights at court, they will abandon 'Li' (rites) and employ 'Fa' (law). So the details of the law shall be argued about, the criminal cases will increase, and bribery will be prevalent in society. So if you are alive, it is probable that the state of Zheng will perish! I heard that 'when a state is going to perish, more laws will be made', so I am afraid this is what's about!"[142] The so-called "system" in "handling affairs according to the established system" is similar to the "stories" and "precedents" in later ages, which were in fact controlled by nobles secretly to make arbitrary judgment. This not only added a sense of mystery to law, but also demonstrated the power and authority of the nobilities. This was why they condemned the activities of depriving them of their privileges by issuing the statute laws to establish the rule of hearing cases by law. Though faced with condemnation, Zi Chan stuck to his cause and he even said: "I could save the world." The so-called "saving the world" referred to changing the conception of the power and the legal system that are not suitable to the transforming society. Therefore, the power of new landlord officials was protected and social reform was pushed forward through making statute laws, which had surely brought new looks to the state of Zheng.

Following Zi Chan's activity of casting criminal laws on bronze vessels, Deng Xi, the scholar of Zheng state revised the state laws on his own in 502 B.C., inscribed them on bamboos, and named it *Zhu Xing* (the bamboo *Punishment*). Deng Xi called for "making judgment according to law" and publicizing the legal knowledge to the common people, thus he was envied and hated by the rulers of Zheng state. Although "Deng Xi was killed by Zheng Si in 501 B.C., bamboo punishment was adopted,"[143] which showed that bamboo punishment was already acknowledged to some degree at that time.

It is true that history has developed without following the will of any individuals. Twenty-three years after criminal law was cast by Zheng state, it was also issued in the state of Jin by "casting it on bronze vessels." In "Zhao Gong Er Shi Jiu Nian" (The 29th Year of the Duke of Zhao) in *Zuo Zhuan* (*The Chronicle of Zuo*), there were the following records: "in winter, Zhao Yang and Xun Yin of Jin led troops to build a city along the bank of River Ru and then they collected one *gu* (ancient Chinese measurement, one *gu* is about 240 kilograms) of iron from the people to cast a bronze vessel and carved the criminal law which was made by Fan Xuanzi on it." According to Du Yu's comments in "Zhao Gong Er Shi Jiu Nian" (The 29th Year of the Duke of Zhao) in *Chun Qiu Zuo Zhuan Ji Jie* (*Collected Commentaries on the Spring and Autumn Annals and the Chronicle of Zuo*), "the punishments employed by Fan Xuan Zi were drafted in Yi." Moreover, Confucius made similar comments:

---

[142] "Zhao Gong Liu Nian" (The 6th Year of the Duke of Zhao) in *Zuo Zhuan* (*The Chronicle of Zuo*).
[143] "Ding Gong Jiu Nian" (The 9th Year of the Duke of Ding) in *Zuo Zhuan* (*The Chronicle of Zuo*).

"the law of Xuan Zi was made in Yizhisou."[144] Therefore, it can be seen that the criminal laws carved on bronze vessels were "continued to be used by the imperial court" when Fan Xuanzi took office, but "were not publicized to the common people," so were the laws made by Zhao Dun. It was not until the 29th year of the Duke Zhao that "the criminal laws were shown to the common people by being carved on bronze vessels."[145]

If casting criminal law on bronze vessels in Zheng was the fruit of Zi Chan's reform, then it was not by coincidence that the same thing was done by the Jin people. In the Spring and Autumn Period, the economy of the Jin state was fairly developed, the reform was carried out very successfully, and at the same time, the patriarchal system and the old family organization were destroyed to a certain degree, which had provided a favorable condition for legal reform. Besides, to maintain the social order under the new circumstances, to suppress the hostile forces and to ensure the victory of the wars of annexation, it was necessary to promulgate statute laws and to replace the arbitrary measurement of judgment by the routinization law enforcement.

Confucius, in the first place, criticized the act of publicizing the law of Zhao Dun by casting them on bronze vessels, he said, "Fan Xuanzi's so-called laws were formulated when he inspected Yizhisou and they were the chaotic systems of Jin state, therefore, they could not be regarded as laws."[146] Therefore, he made sharp criticism on the activities of the publishing of the statute laws: "I am afraid that the state of Jin will perish because 'Li' (rites) was abandoned. So in Jin state, the laws of Tang Shu should be followed to control its people so that they can be abided by the senior officials who in turn will be respected by the common people. What is important is that everyone, whether the noble or the humble can all fulfill their duties, so that there will be no violation of social status, which is called 'Du' (rule)... If we abandon these rules and cast laws on bronze vessels, people will show no reverence to nobles anymore, because they can read the laws by themselves. If there is no difference between the noble and the humble, then how can the state be ruled?"[147] What Confucius talked about in the sentence that "people will show no reverence to nobles anymore, because they can read the laws by themselves" was similar to Shu Xiang's words that "people will not show respect to those who are superior to themselves once they know the laws." However, Confucius raised this question to the high level of "ruling the state," so it had reflected the fierceness of the struggle, which could be proved by what was written in *Zheng Yi (The Annotation of Confucians' Classics and the Books of History)* by Kong Yingda:

---

[144]"Zhao Gong Er Shi Jiu Nian" (The 29th Year of the Duke of Zhao) in *Chun Qiu Zuo Zhuan Zheng Yi (Interpretation of the Chronicle of Zuo)*.

[145]"Zhao Gong Er Shi Jiu Nian" (The 29th Year of the Duke of Zhao) in *Chun Qiu Zuo Zhuan Zheng Yi (Interpretation of the Chronicle of Zuo)*.

[146]"Zhao Gong Er Shi Jiu Nian" (The 29th Year of the Duke of Zhao) in *Chun Qiu Zuo Zhuan Zheng Yi (Interpretation of the Chronicle of Zuo)*.

[147]"Zhao Gong Er Shi Jiu Nian" (The 29th Year of the Duke of Zhao) in *Chun Qiu Zuo Zhuan Zheng Yi (Interpretation of the Chronicle of Zuo)*.

When the old laws are followed, it is difficult to predict what the people will do, so it is advisable to make temporary laws, because in this way, it is impossible for people to know what punishment they will get, so they will be deterred by the law by showing respect to it. This is called 'Xing' (punishment). The law is made by the government, which will be respected by the people, so they can perform their duties accordingly with the official positions and salaries of nobilities protected. The noble people will be given the right to control the humble so the humble will show reverence to the noble, so that the social order of the noble and the humble, the superior and the inferior will be maintained. This is called 'Du' or 'Fa Du' generally.

So after the criminal laws were made, "'Li' (rites) will be abandoned and laws will be followed," and when there were disputes, "people will know that punishments should be enforced according to the laws inscribed on bronze vessels, so the noble people dare not aggravate or mitigate punishment randomly anymore."[148] Because the authority lies in the laws inscribed on bronze vessels, the people "are not afraid of or would not show reverence to their superiors anymore,"[149] so it was difficult to keep the old systems.

In the Spring and Autumn Period, the publicity of statute laws reflected the demands of the feudal productive relationship that was taking shape and the determination of new landlord class. To protect the developing private ownership, to affirm the changing social relationship, to adjust the political structure caused by the loosen patriarchal clan system and to reinforce the insecure political power already obtained, the statesmen representing new landlord classes had promulgated the statute laws with great courage and resolution. Thus, it can be seen that the argument over the publicity of statute law was not only the power struggle between the new and the old, but also an important step in the process of replacing the slavery legal system by the feudal one. For this reason, the publicity of statute laws began in the state of Zheng and Jin, and was followed by other states. With Li Kui's *Fa Jing* (*Canon of Laws*) written in the Warring States Period, the publicity of statute laws in all states of the Spring and Autumn Period was summarized perfectly.

3.4.2 Legislations in Each State in the Warring States Period and Fa Jing (Canon of Laws) Written by Li Kui

In the Warring States Period, the trend of making statute laws in the Spring and Autumn Period was continue and feudal laws were formulated one after another in each state.

In approximately 403 B.C., reforms centering on the selection of talents, appointment of virtuous officials and improvement of legal systems were carried out by

---

[148]"Zhao Gong Er Shi Jiu Nian" (The 29th Year of the Duke of Zhao) in *Chun Qiu Zuo Zhuan Zheng Yi* (*Interpretation of the Chronicle of Zuo*).

[149]"Zhao Gong Er Shi Jiu Nian" (The 29th Year of the Duke of Zhao) in *Chun Qiu Zuo Zhuan Zheng Yi* (*Interpretation of the Chronicle of Zuo*).

Gongzhong Lian of in the state of Zhao and the statute law called *Guo Lv* (*The State Law*) was made. The enforcement of this law had brought about great prosperity to Zhao state, but its abolishment had brought about its declination instead. Han Fei therefore commented that "after *Guo Lv* (*The State Law*) was issued in Zhao state, a great and strong army was set up and the country was prosperous and powerful, which had helped them to defeat the state of Qi and Yan; when *Guo Lv* (*The State Law*) was abolished and the rulers became weak, the state declined day by day."[150] This is a historical experience worthy of attention.

In around 390 B.C., Wu Qi was appointed "Ling Yin" (senior official in charge of state affairs) in Chu state and was put in charge of reform focused on "Fa Zhi" (the ruling of law). He carried out reforms to "prevent the officials from playing favoritism in their work and to have the customs of Chu unified."[151] Besides, Qu Yuan was ordered to draft *Xian Ling* (*Constitution*). According to "Qu Yuan Lie Zhuan" (The Biography of Qu Yuan) in *Shi Ji* (*The Records of the Grand Historian*), "King Huai required Qu Yuan to formulate laws, but before he finished the final draft, another senior official wanted to take it away from him. Qu Yuan refused. So the official spoke ill of Qu before the king and said, 'Your majesty has asked Qu Yuan to draft the law and everyone knows about it. However, Qu Yuan has boasted of his own contribution whenever an article of law is made, claiming that no one else can do it.' The king was thus infuriated and began to keep a distance from Qu Yuan." Although Qu Yuan was demoted by the king, *Xian Ling* (*Constitution*) was adopted.

Besides, another influential code *Ji Ci Zhi Fa* (*Ji Ci Code*) was made in Chu state. According to "Chu Ce" (The Strategies of Chu) in *Zhan Guo Ce* (*Stratagems of the Warring States*), "Wu and Chu were fighting a battle in Boju. The Wu army launched three attacks and occupied the capital of Chu…then Meng Gu came to the palace of Chu, took away the code of Chu and escaped to Yunmeng by boat; later, King Zhao of Chu went back to the capital, but the people was in chaos because the law was lost. Meng Gu presented the code, so the law was established and the people were well governed in the end."

In 357 B.C., in the state of Qi, Zou Ji was appointed as the prime minister, and he advocated the revision of laws and the supervision of the evil officials. Under the guidance of Guan Zi's thoughts of "Ze" (natural law), "Xiang" (phenomenon), "Fa" (regulation), "Hua" (education), "Jue Se" (prohibition), "Xin Shu" (intention), "Ji Shu" (measurement), he made *Qi Fa* (*Seven Laws*), which had ensured the implementation of the reform in the state of Qi.

In about 355 B.C., a reform was carried out by the famous legalist Shen Buhai in the State of Han. He proposed that "Shu" (tactics) should be considered as the most important thing so that "Fa Zhi" (the rule of law) could be strengthened by the rulers in their administration. Under the guidance of this legal ideology, the statute law *Xing Fu* (*Criminal Law*) was drafted.

---

[150]"Shi Xie" (The Punishment of the Evil Deeds) in *Han Fei Zi* (*Han Feizi*).
[151]"Qin Ce" (The Strategy of the State of Qin) in *Zhan Guo Ce* (*Stratagems of the Warring States*) (Book 3).

3.4 The Legal Reform Adaptable to Social Transformation

In Wei state, *Da Fu Zhi Xian* (*Constitution of Da Fu*) was made, and it was called *Wei Xian* (*The Constitution of Wei State*). According to "Wei Ce" (The Strategies of Wei) in *Zhan Guo Ce* (*Stratagems of the Warring States*), "Mr. An Ling said, 'my father was ordered by King Xiang to be in charge of the management of the land, so he accepted the laws in *Da Fu Zhi Xian* (*Constitution of Da Fu*). It was ruled in the first chapter that a son who killed his father or any official who killed the king should be punished without pardoning. Even in the case of an amnesty, those who gave up or deserted their cities should not be pardoned.'"

The legislation mentioned above was both the product and the driving forces of the reform carried out in all states, among which *Fa Jing* (*Canon of Laws*) written by Li Kui during the reign of Duke Wen of Wei was the most representative.

Li Kui was a well-known statesman and a representative of early legalists at the beginning of Warring States Period. In 445 B.C., Duke Wen of Wei took office and put Li Kui in charge of an important position to carry out reforms. At that time, it was the main task of Wei state to develop the feudal economy, to clear away the remains of the hereditary system and to reinforce the feudal regime. Therefore, the reform mainly includes the following contents: first, the economic policy of "encouraging farming" and "purchasing grain at a fair price" was practiced to develop feudal economy[152]; second, the political measure of "enforcing due punishment and granting due awards"[153] was carried out and privileges enjoyed by "Yin Min" (dawdler) who obtained much interests without making any contribution were abolished to break the path for the establishment of feudal autocracy. As for *Fa Jing* (*Canon of Laws*) written by Li Kui, it was both an important part and a protection of the reform. Laws were laid down based on social and material life, whether public or private laws, they should all reflect the demands of the economic relationship, so eventually, they should be reformed in accordance with social reform. After half a century of the implementation of "Chu Shui Mu" (taxation in accordance with the size of the land) in Lu state, "Xing Shu" (Criminal Punishment) was issued by Zi Chan in Zheng state, "Zhu Xing" (the bamboo Punishment) was issued by Deng Xi and "Zhu Xing Ding" (inscriptions of laws on casted bronze vessel) was issued by Jin state respectively. It was more than 190 years since "Chu Shui Mu" (taxation in accordance with the size of the land) was issued when Li Kui wrote *Fa Jing* (*Canon of Laws*), so it was after the basic establishment of the feudal economic and political system that the code such as *Fa Jing* (*Canon of Laws*) was written.

It was a common trend that "Xing" (punishment) was changed to "Fa" (law) in *Fa Jing* (*Canon of Laws*). Thus, it was not merely a change of one word, but a reflection of two different legal systems. The laws in slavery times were mostly customary laws kept in private. However, the feudal laws were statute laws, which were made known to the public and were universally applicable. Some legalists said that "laws

---

[152]"Shi Huo Zhi" (The Records of National Finance and Economy) in *Han Shu* (*The History of Han Dynasty*).

[153]"Zheng Li" (The Principles of Government) in *Shuo Yuan* (*Collection of Stories*).

are written works which are compiled by the rulers and made known to the public later"[154] and that "people from all classes should be abided by laws."[155] In *Fa Jing* (*Canon of Laws*), the revolutionary spirit of the author and the development of history were revealed in the name of law.

Fa Jing (*Canon of Laws*) was completed in the 19th year of King Wei Lie of Eastern Zhou Dynasty (407 B.C.), but as early as in the Han Dynasty, it was already lost and so was not passed down. In "Yi Wen Zhi" (Books and Records) in *Han Shu* (*The History of Han Dynasty*), thirty-three chapters of *Li Zi* (*Master Li*) were included, which ranked the first among all legalists. Ban Gu merely explained in his comments that Li Zi "was also called Kui, and he was the prime minister of Wei. So he had devoted himself to making the state rich and the military strong." Afterwards, the origin and contents of *Fa Jing* (*Canon of Laws*) were introduced in a general way in "Xing Fa Zhi" (The Record of the Criminal Law) in *Jin Shu* (*The History of Jin Dynasty*) in commenting on the evolution of the laws of Qin and Han Dynasties: "at that time (before the new laws were made by Emperor Ming of Wei), the old laws of Qin and Han Dynasties, which were drafted by Li Kui, the teacher of Wei Wen Hou, were still in use. Li Kui made *Fa Jing* (*Canon of Laws*) by referring to the laws of all states. He thought that it was the most urgent thing to have the bandits and thieves punished, so the criminal law was started with chapters of "Dao" (robbery) and "Zei" (banditry). Bandits and thieves must be caught and arrested, so the two chapters of "Wang" (net) (suspected of being a mistake for Qiu: prisoners) and "Bu" (arresting) were drafted. Deception, climbing over the city walls, gambling, promiscuity, and transgression of social status were included in *Za Lv* (*Miscellaneous Laws*). In *Ju Lv* (*Specific Laws*), the circumstances where penalty should be aggravated or alleviated were made clear. Moreover, it was only consisted of six chapters, all of which were concerned with crimes. So Shang Jun learned of it and assisted the king." According to *Tang Lv Shu Yi* (*The Comments on Tang Code*) and *Tang Liu Dian* (*The Six Statutes of Tang Dynasty*) made in Tang Dynasty, the structure and origin of *Fa Jing* (*Canon of Laws*) was similar to "Xing Fa Zhi" (The Record of the Criminal Law) in *Jin Shu* (*The History of Jin Dynasty*). According to "Shu" in *Ming Li Lv* (*Statutes and Terms*) in *Tang Lv Shu Yi* (*The Comments on Tang Code*), "Duke of Wei became a student of Li Kui, so he collected the criminal codes of all states, wrote *Fa Jing* (*Canon of Laws*) which was made up of six parts: 'Dao Fa' (Laws on Theft), 'Zei Fa' (Laws on Banditry), 'Qiu Lv' (Statutes on Imprisonment), 'Bu Fa'(Laws on Arresting),'Za Fa' (Miscellaneous Laws), and 'Ju Fa' (Specific Laws). The laws were taught and changed into "Lv" (statutes) by Shang Yang." Li Linfu, "Yuan Wai Lang" (deputy head of a subministry department) of "Xing Bu" (The Department of Punishment) noted in the 6th volume of *Tang Liu Dian* (*The Six Statutes of Tang Dynasty*): "Duke of Wei became a student of Li Kui. He collected the criminal codes of all states and wrote *Fa Jing* (*Canon of Laws*) consisting of six parts: 'Dao Fa' (Laws on Theft), 'Zei Fa' (Laws on

---

[154]"Nan" (Crisis) in *Han Fei Zi* (*Han Feizi*) (Book 3).

[155]"Ren Fa" (Relying on Laws) in *Guan Zi* (*The Book of Master Guan*).

3.4 The Legal Reform Adaptable to Social Transformation

Banditry), 'Qiu Lv' (Statutes on Imprisonment), 'Bu Fa' (Laws on Arresting), 'Za Fa' (Miscellaneous Laws), and 'Ju Fa' (Specific Laws). So the laws were taught and changed into "Lv" (criminal law) by Shang Yang."

In the late Ming Dynasty, Dong Shuo made the following comments on *Fa Jing* (*Canon of Laws*) in "Wei Xing Fa" (The Criminal Law of the State of Wei) in *Qi Guo Kao* (*Investigations of the Seven Countries*) by quoting Huan Tan's *Xin Lun* (*New Theory*):

> According to Huan Tan's *Xin Shu* (*New Book*), 'Li Kui was ordered by Duke Wen of Wei to compile *Fa Jing* (*Canon of Laws*), who thought that for the ruler nothing was more urgent than the prevention of 'Dao' (theft) and 'Zei' (banditry), so this book began with the chapter of 'Dao' and 'Zei'. Thieves and bandits must be arrested, so the criminal laws which he made started with the chapters of "Dao" (robbery) and "Zei" (banditry);bandits and thieves must be caught and arrested, so the two chapters of "Wang" (net) (suspected of being a mistake for Qiu: prisoners) and "Bu" (arresting) were drafted. Deception, climbing over the city walls, gambling, promiscuity, and transgression of social status were included in *Za Lv* (*Miscellaneous Laws*). In *Ju Lv* (*Specific Laws*), the circumstances where penalty could be aggravated or alleviated were made clear. Wei Yang from the state of Wei accepted these laws and became the prime minister of Qin state, therefore, the brutality of the laws of Qin state was quite similar to that of Wei state.' It was stated in *Zheng Lv* (*Official Law*) that 'the murderer shall be sentenced to death, so shall be his family and the family of his wife. The principal thieves shall be sent to guard the border regions but if they have committed major crimes, they shall be sentenced to death; those who peeps into the palace shall be punished by 'Bin' (to cut down the knee cap) and those who pick up the lost property shall be punished by 'Yue' (to amputate the feet). It was stated in *Za Lv* (*Miscellaneous Laws*) that 'the penalty for a man with one wife and two concubines is 'Ni', for one with two wives, death; the penalty for a woman with extramarital sexual relationship is 'Gong' (castration), which is called 'Yin Jin'. Those who steal a 'Fu' (symbol-assumpsit, an authoritative piece of paper to give orders in ancient China) shall be sentenced to death, so shall be his family; those who make comments on laws shall be sentenced to death, so shall his family and the family of his wife, which is called 'Jiao Jin'; those who climb over the city walls shall be executed, but if ten or more people have climbed the city walls, their families and neighbors should be punished, which is called 'Cheng Jin'; the crime of gambling shall be imposed with a fine of three *dan*; if the crown prince gambles, he will be punished by 'Chi' (flogging with light sticks); if he doesn't mend his way, he will be punished more severely; if he still gambles, his title will be deprived, which is called 'Xi Jin'; if a group of people have gathered for more than one day, they shall be interrogated, for three, four or five days, they shall be punished by death penalty, which is called 'Tu Jin'; if the prime minister takes bribes, he and his subordinates shall be killed with those subordinate generals sentenced to death for taking bribes; those who take no more than *yi* (a unit of weight in ancient China, one *yi* is about one kilogram) shall be imposed with a fine rather than killed, which is called 'Jin Jin'; if the objects possessed by 'Hou' (dukes) are found in the home of 'Da Fu' (senior officials in ancient China), the entire family of 'Da Fu' (senior officials in ancient China) shall be executed.

Moreover, it was recorded in *Jian Lv* (*Laws on Mitigation*) that 'if the criminal is five years old or younger, the penalty shall be three levels lighter than the normal one in the case of a major crime and one level lighter in the case of a minor one. If the criminal is sixty years old or older, the penalty shall be alleviated for emotional consideration in the case of a minor crime, and the penalty shall be executed according to concrete situations in the case of a major crime.' So it has been taken as the law of the state since Wu Hou."[156]

The contents and main idea of *Fa Jing* (*Canon of Laws*), which was quoted in *Xin Lun* (*New Theory*) and *Qi Guo Kao* (*Investigations of the Seven Countries*) successively, were basically the same as those in "Xing Fa Zhi" (The Record of the Criminal Law) in *Jin Shu* (*The History of Jin Dynasty*), meanwhile, they were also in line with the historical background at that time, so they are worthy to be studied further.

From the general introduction to *Fa Jing* (*Canon of Laws*), the following points can be seen:

First, the fundamental guiding principle of this book was to punish the bandits and thieves, as was reflected in the statement, "there is nothing more urgent than the problems of having the bandits and thieves punished for the king." In pre-Qin era, "Dao (theft) refers to those who steal things" and "Zei (banditry) refers to those who hurt the good people."[157] Therefore, the thieves and bandits referred to those who robbed others' possessions and broken the life and social order. The primary goal of punishing bandits and thieves showed that *Fa Jing* (*Canon of Laws*) was made to protect the private ownership and to strengthen the feudal economy and autocracy. According to *Fa Jing* (*Canon of Laws*), the bandits who committed major crimes were usually sent to border areas or sentenced to death while the people who picked up money on the road would have their feet cut off to curb the tendency of banditry. Thus, it was not by coincidence that it was proposed in *Fa Jing* (*Canon of Laws*) that "there is nothing more urgent than the problem of having the bandits and thieves punished." Yet it was also closely related to the class struggles at that time. Since the farmers were suppressed and exploited by the feudal forces in the Warring States Period, they revolted by "escaping" or other means. According to records, "more than 10,000 people had fled and evaded taxation by relying on the prestigious family relationship."[158] After the reform, the state of Wei ranked among one of the most powerful nations, but it was still faced with severe situation surrounded by big powers. Therefore, it became the main task of *Fa Jing* (*Canon of Laws*) to protect and reinforce the regime, by which its legal system centering on the criminal law with the adopting of various other laws was formed. That was why the criminal laws that he made started with the chapters of "Dao" (robbery) and "Zei" (banditry). Bandits and thieves must be caught and arrested, so the two chapters of "Wang" (net) (suspected of being a mistake for Qiu: prisoners) and "Bu" (arresting) were drafted. Deception, climbing over the city walls, gambling, promiscuity, and transgression of social status were included in *Za Lv* (*Miscellaneous Laws*). In *Ju Lv* (*Specific Laws*),

---

[156]Dong Shuo (Ming Dynasty), "Wei Xing Fa" (The Criminal Law of the State of Wei) in *Qi Guo Kao* (*Investigations of the Seven Countries*), Vol.12.
[157]"Xiu Shen" (Cultivating One's Morality and Character) in *Xun Zi* (*Xun Zi*).
[158]"Gui Shi" (Curious Motivation) in *Han Fei Zi* (*Han Feizi*).

3.4 The Legal Reform Adaptable to Social Transformation

the circumstances where penalty could be aggravated or alleviated were made clear. So it was consisted of only six chapters."[159]

Second, according to *Fa Jing* (*Canon of Laws*), anyone who violated the rules of the state and the king should be punished severely, and those who peeped into the palace, stole a 'Fu' (symbol-assumpsit, an authoritative piece of paper to give orders in ancient China), climbed over the city walls or lived in groups illegally should be punished severely with even their families and neighbors executed. To insure the implementation of law, anyone who made comments on the state laws would be punished by death penalty. In feudal criminal law, as it were, the enforcement of punishment for one's speech and ideology started from *Fa Jing* (*Canon of Laws*).

The regulations for the punishment of murderers in *Fa Jing* (*Canon of Laws*) also carried political implication for the struggle with the old noble forces. The provision that anyone who committed murder should be punished by death penalty could be applied at any time and at any place. However, according to *Fa Jing* (*Canon of Laws*), not only those who had committed murder should be punished by death penalty, their family members should also be punished, which was not coincident, because the aristocracy dominated the rights of killing during the period of slavery, they could kill the slaves, the common people and the newly appeared landlords as they wished. In the state of Wei where Li Kui lived, the declining aristocracy also had great power, so they made troubles continuously. According to *Fa Jing* (*Canon of Laws*), the murderers were punished severely to counterattack the remaining aristocratic forces.

Third, the legal principle of "the people at all levels, whether the close or distant relatives or whether the superior or the inferior, should be judged according to the law"[160] ran through *Fa Jing* (*Canon of Laws*) itself. It was proposed that the privilege of the hierarchical slavery system should be eliminated and the boundary between "Li" (rites) and "Xing" (punishment) should be abolished. Moreover, Even the prince would be punished by "Chi" (flogging with light sticks) if he had committed crimes; if the prime minister took bribes, he would be punished by death penalty with his subordinates; if a general took bribes, he would be put to death. Yet as a feudal code, at the time of negating the slavery system, the feudal hierarchical system was affirmed in *Fa Jing* (*Canon of Laws*). Therefore, it was ruled that if "Da Fu" (senior officials in ancient China) had objects in his family that should be owned by vassals, then he had committed the crime of transgressing the social boundaries, so should be severely punished.

Fourth, *Fa Jing* (*Canon of Laws*) reflected the thoughts of stressing penalties. Anyone who peeped at the palace would have his patella cut off, and anyone who picked up money on the street would have his feet cut off, which had reflected the theory of "eliminating punishment by punishment" held by legalists. Han Fei once said, "It is not for the single purpose of punishment to enforce severe punishments,

---

[159]"Xing Fa Zhi" (The Record of Criminal Law) in *Jin Shu* (*The History of Jin Dynasty*).

[160]"Tai Shi Gong Zi Xu" (Preface by Tai Shi Gong himself) in *Shi Ji* (*The Record of the Grand Historian*).

because it is the code of conduct of the wise kings."[161] "If the punishments are severe, then the humble dare not violate the noble; if the law is strict, then the monarchs shall be respected without being humiliated."[162] "So it is the way of governance to have one evil person severely punished to prevent evil deeds in the state. Besides, if the bandits and thieves are severely punished, the decent people will be afraid of committing crimes. That is why severe punishments are usually used by the rulers."[163]

To sum up, *Fa Jing* (*Canon of Laws*) drafted by Li Kui is the first systematic feudal code in the history of our country and it is one of the epitome of all of the laws in the Spring and Autumn Period. The guiding principles of *Fa Jing* (*Canon of Laws*), the layout of *Zheng Lv* (*Official Law*), *Za Lv* (*Miscellaneous Laws*) and *Ju Lv* (*Specific Laws*) and the specific regulations about crime and punishment had all laid the foundation for the development of legal systems of later ages. For example, Shang Yang was greatly influenced by *Fa Jing Canon of Laws*), so he was appointed as the prime minister of the state of Qin to carry out his reforms. His practice of "Lian Zuo Fa" (being punished for being related to somebody who committed an offence) was developed from "Tu Jin" (ganging together) in *Fa Jing* (*Canon of Laws*). The well-known *Jiu Zhang Lv* (*The Code in Nine Chapters*) made in Han Dynasty was also developed from *Fa Jing* (*Canon of Laws*) with other three chapters added, including, "Hu Lv" (Statutes on Households), "Xing Lv" (The Penal Code) and "Jiu Lv" (Statutes on Livestock Breeding).

---

[161]"Liu Fan" (Six Oppositions) in *Han Fei Zi* (*Han Feizi*).
[162]"You Du" (Being Lawful) in *Han Fei Zi* (*Han Feizi*).
[163]"Liu Fan" (Six Oppositions) in *Han Fei Zi* (*Han Feizi*).

Chapter 4
The Legal System of Qin Dynasty with "Laws Made in Every Field"

(The 4th Century B.C.–206 B.C.)

The discovery of *Shui Hu Di Qin Jian* (the bamboo writing slips found in the tomb of Qin in Shuihudi) unearthed in Yunmeng county in Hubei province in 1975 revealed us the law of the state of Qin in Warring States Period. Although it did not include all the laws of the state of Qin, it was evident that the book was theoretically based on the theories of legalists and it had played the function of adjustment to the social life, state activities and the families and individuals in many aspects.

It was proved in this book that the state of Qin was regulated by law in every aspect. The elaborate items, concise expressions and especially the scientificity shown in judicial inspections had spoken eloquently of the brilliancy of the legal civilization of the state of Qin. Thus, we have a comparison between *Lex Salics*, the representative legal code in the early western countries, with the law of the state of Qin recorded on bamboo slips, although the latter was made more than one thousand years earlier than the former, there is no comparability between them in contents because *Lex Salics* was just made up of customary law and was not systematic. Nevertheless, the law of the state of Qin recorded on bamboo slips was a statue law consisting of all types of laws and it was systematic. The discovery of the law of the state of Qin recorded on bamboo slips had eloquently proved the long history and the progressiveness of Chinese legal civilization.

To the time of Qin Shi Huang (The First Emperor of Qin), he "defeated other states, united the country"[1] and established the first autocratic regime characterized by the centralization of power by complying with the historical trend of the time. The unification of Qin had positively promoted the economic, political, and cultural development and made great contribution to legal civilization. The fall of Qin state during the reign of the second emperor had served as a lesson and it showed that if the legal system is established, the country will be strong and prosperous, but if it is abolished, the country will perish.

---

[1]"Qin Shi Huang Ben Ji" (The Biography of Qin Shi Huang) in *Shi Ji* (*The Record of the Grand Historian*).

4.1 The Legal System of Qin Dynasty Recorded in *Yun Meng Qin Jian* (*Amounts of Bamboo Writing Slips in Qin Dynasty Excavated in Yunmeng*)

4.1.1 The Nature of Qin Lv (Qin Code) Recorded in Yun Meng Qin Jian (Amounts of Bamboo Writing Slips in Qin Dynasty Excavated in Yunmeng)

The legal system of Qin Dynasty was not widely known before the discovery of *Yun Meng Qin Jian* (*Amounts of Bamboo Writing Slips in Qin Dynasty Excavated in Yunmeng*), because its relevant materials were scattered in ancient literature. Its discovery has provided the most valuable first-hand information for the research of the legal systems in the Qin Dynasty, filled in the gaps of the research materials and shown the splendid legal civilization of ancient China to the whole world.

In December 1975, twelve tombs were unearthed in Shuihudi of Yunmeng county in Hubei province, and the occupants of the tombs lived between the time of late Warring States Period and the time of the unification of Qin Dynasty. About 1155 bamboo slips were discovered in the Tomb No. 11, among which, *Bian Nian Ji* (*The Chronicle*) recorded the events which occurred from the 1st year of King Zhao of Qin (306 B.C.) to the 30th year of Qin Shi Huang (The First Emperor of Qin) (217 B.C.), while *Qin Lv Shi Ba Zhong* (*Eighteen Kinds of Laws of Qin Dynasty*) recorded the laws on administration, economy and management of prisoners. The stipulations concerning the appointment and removal of officials and the military regulations were recorded in *Qin Lv Za Chao* (*Miscellaneous Copies of Decrees of the State of Qin*), while the official explanations and descriptions of criminal provisions were recorded in *Fa Lv Da Wen* (*Legal Questions and Answers*). Moreover, the general requirements for judges during "Zhi Yu" (trial of cases) and "Xun Yu" (interrogating the accused), the matters about investigation and inspection that ought to be noted and the patterns of the documents and reports were recorded in *Feng Zhen Shi* (*Judicial Principles, Methods, and Cases*). In addition, there were other records such as *Yu Shu* (*Official Notice*), *Wei Lv Zhi Dao* (*How to Behave As an Official*), and so on.

Numerous slips with transcriptions of laws of Qin unearthed in the No. 11 tomb are closely connected with the identity of the occupant named Xi (262 B.C.–217 B.C.), who had served as an official and held the position of "Yu Shi" (the censor) of Anlu, "Ling Shi" (assistant officials to the magistrate) of Anlu and of Yan, the warder of Yan, and some other judicial positions. It is a reflection of the life of the dead to bury such a great number of sacrificial legal documents with him. However, undoubtedly, the funerary laws and documents are the most effective and valuable parts of them. Although the laws written on the bamboo slips are not the complete records of the laws of Qin state, they did provide us with sufficient information, basically as a reproduction of the general conditions of laws of Qin during the turbulent times from the period of the feudal separatism to the unification of the six states. In terms of legal forms, there were "Lv" (criminal law), "Ling" (decree), "Cheng" (procedure), "Shi" (standard), "Ke" (rule), and some other forms, which had reflected a higher level and more completed system of legislation compared with those of Western Zhou Dynasty. Qin state was once a backward country, which was "secluded in" in the northwest with slow economic development. Therefore, except the promulgation of "Zhi Cong Si" (forbid burying people with the dead)[2] in the 1st year of King of Xian in the State of Qin (384 B.C.) and the promulgation of a decree about "establishing household registration with every five households as a group"[3] in the 10th year, there were almost no other legislative activities. And successful reforms were carried out by Shang Yang with the support of King of Xiao of the State of Qin to making the country rich and its military forces strong, by which Qin state was made a prosperous and powerful country overnight where "Fa Zhi" (the ruling of law) was greatly stressed.

There were about twenty-nine types of laws in *Yun Meng Qin Jian* (*Amounts of Bamboo Writing Slips in Qin Dynasty Excavated in Yunmeng*), which had proved the credibility of the annotation of *Tang Liu Dian* (*The Six Statutes of Tang Dynasty*) in which it was recorded that "Shang Yang had propagated *Fa Jing* (*Canon of Laws*) written by Li Kui and adopted it into the laws of Qin to help to govern the country." After the unification of Qin Dynasty, a criminal law, namely, *Xie Shu Lv* (*Statutes Forbidding the Possession of Books*) was enacted, so it was shown that "Lv" (criminal law) was the most important legal form in the legal systems of Qin Dynasty at that time.

"Ling" (decree) was an important complementary form of "Lv" (criminal law). For example, legal orders were issued on the land apart from land decrees and some single criminal laws were promulgated in the form of "Ling" (decree). However, in Qin Dynasty, there was still no clear distinction between "Lv" (criminal law) and "Ling" (decree). In *Yu Shu* (*Official Notice*) in *Yun Meng Qin Jian* (*Amounts of Bamboo Writing Slips in Qin Dynasty Excavated in Yunmeng*), "Fa" (law), "Lv" (criminal law) and "Ling" (decree) were usually mentioned together, such as "amending 'Fa' (law), 'Lv' (criminal law) and 'Ling' (decree)," "'Fa' (law), 'Lv' (criminal law) and 'Ling' (decree) having been made" and "'Fa' (law), 'Lv' (criminal law) and 'Ling' (decree) having been promulgated," and so on.

"Shi" (standard) referred to rules and formulas. According to *Shuo Wen Jie Zi* (*The Origin of Chinese Characters*), "'Shi' (standard) is a kind of law." As one of the legal forms, "Shi" first appeared in the state of Qin. *Feng Zhen Shi* (*Judicial Principles, Methods and Cases*) recorded in *Yun Meng Qin Jian* (*Amounts of Bamboo Writing Slips in Qin Dynasty Excavated in Yunmeng*) was a formula of legal documents about inquest, investigation and trial.

It should be noted that *Fa Lv Da Wen* (*Legal Questions and Answers*) on the bamboo slips was mainly the official interpretation of *Qin Lv* (*Qin Code*). Besides,

---

[2]"Qin Ben Ji" (The History of the State of Qin) in *Shi Ji* (*The Record of the Grand Historian*).
[3]"Qin Shi Huang Ben Ji" (The Biography of Qin Shi Huang) in *Shi Ji* (*The Record of the Grand Historian*).

some specific accounts were made in the following aspects: convictions, measurement of penalties, and the application of laws and litigation systems. This document was legally effective like the law itself, so it was regarded as a precedent for interpreting laws by making comments by the later generations.

The laws written on the bamboo slips covered many fields, such as economy, politics, military affairs, judicial work and culture, so it had reached the highest level of legislation in the world at that time for its extensive ranges, comprehensive entries, exhaustive contents, rigorous procedures, meticulous judicial inquests and wide application of forensic medicine, which had eloquently proved the progressiveness of Chinese legal system.

The laws written on the bamboo slips were a collection of laws featured by early Chinese feudalism, which was determined by the economic, political, social and some other conditions of Qin Dynasty at that time. As for the economic condition, since the reform carried out by Shang Yang, the old land system was abolished and the reclamation of ownerless wasteland was encouraged, so the system of "Jing Tian Zhi" (the "nine squares" system of land ownership in China) which was carried out in slavery period was changed, at the same time, the private ownership of land which had been continuously developed since the late Western Zhou Dynasty was gradually established. Accordingly, the transaction of land was allowed according to law, so "the common people can buy and sell land freely." Although a large proportion of land was state-owned, the key economic relationship, which was with the prospect of development, was still feudal. Therefore, it was inevitable the requirements of feudal economic relations were reflected in *Qin Lv* (*Qin Code*) to confirm, protect, and promote the development of economic relationship through its special functions, because it was a very important component of new superstructure, which was illustrated by the specific provisions in *Qin Lv* (*Qin Code*).

In terms of political condition, based on the patriarchal clan and consanguinity system, "Shi Qing system" (Inheritance of Noble Titles) by which the kinship and state power was tightly bound together had suffered a great blow, so it gradually withdrew itself from the political and historical stages. Instead, a feudal bureaucratic system, which had broken through the kinship restrictions, appeared, by which the king was allowed to freely appoint and dismiss government officials according to their military exploits and talents. In particular, the official system of Qin Dynasty, which had broken through the restrictions of blood relationship, symbolized that "Shi Qing system" (Inheritance of Noble Titles) was abolished at a much larger scale than that in the Warring States Period. Thus, to adapt to the new political relationship, the appointment, removal, assessment, and the matters such as salary, seal, and some other officials systems were all acknowledged by legal forms in *Qin Lv* (*Qin Code*).

In terms of social relationship, under the historical condition of the collapsing of the slavery system and gradual establishment of the feudal system, the emancipation of slaves was supported and the development of slavery was restricted in *Qin Lv* (*Qin Code*). For instance, slaves could exchange for the personal liberty for themselves and their family by using military credits or serving corvée for guarding the frontiers. In *Jun Jue Lv* (*Statutes on Military Exploit and Official Titles*), it was ruled that, "it was allowed for a person to willingly give up two ranks of his title of nobility in exchange for the exemption of his mother or father who was punished to be official slaves. And for a slave who had killed enemies in battles or who was supposed to be awarded the title of 'Gong Shi' (the lowest rank of nobility), he was allowed to give up the rank in exchange for the freedom of his wife and he would then be regarded as a common people. But the official slaves, who had killed enemies in battles or were exempted from slavery because of his bravery, should still be ordered to work as an artisan." In *Si Kong Lv (Statutes on National Projects)*, it was stipulated that "for a person whose mother or brothers were punished by government servitude, if the accused was not sentenced to the punishment of guarding the frontier as a demotion or exile, but if the person was willing to guard the frontier for five years in exchange for one of them to beexempted and freed as a common people, he was allowed to do so."

In addition, it was stipulated in *Fa Lv Da Wen (Legal Questions and Answers)* that "it is forbidden for people in debt relationship to settle debts by using mortgages, so anyone who proposes or accepts it will be imposed with a fine of two *jia* (armor)," which obviously is a kind of restriction on debt slaves. Especially, it was declared in *Qin Lv (Qin Code)* by definite forms that it was forbidden for slaves to be killed randomly and they were even allowed to testify as litigants in courts. The restriction of slavery and conditional liberation of slaves in *Qin Lv (Qin Code)* was out of the consideration of the social development and national interest, which had shown a great difference from the laws of Shang and Zhou Dynasties. In the meanwhile, according to *Qin Lv (Qin Code)*, it was allowed to own official and private slaves, so if the children of slaves had changed their social identities without permission, they would be punished accordingly. Moreover, the criminals who were punished by "Ji Mo" (the cancellation of a household registration) and their families became new sources of slaves. According to *Qin Lv (Qin Code)*, "the enemy soldiers who surrender themselves will serve as official slaves."[4] In terms of legal status, the slaves were still the property of their owners, so they could be traded or awarded as objects. If a slave was "arrogant and aggressive," or "slow in performing farm labor" or involved in crimes, his punishment would be more severe than that for the common people, and his master still had the right to decide the slave's life or death, although he could not kill a slave at his will after the case was reported to the government. As a country newly breaking away from slavery society, it was inevitable that some remnants of slavery retained in Qin Dynasty, which had exactly reflected the transitional feature of the early feudal system. Thus, *Qin Lv (Qin Code)*, which was a law with the nature of early feudalism.

Certainly, as a law made in the third century B.C., it was inevitable that there were still some shortcomings in *Qin Lv (Qin Code)*, such as redundant entries, implicit boundaries between laws and legal orders, repetitive contents; moreover, there were even some contradictory points, for example there were even some provisions on

---

[4]"Qin Lv Za Chao" (Miscellaneous Copies of Decrees of the State of Qin) in *Qin Jian (The Bamboo Writing Slips in Qin Dynasty)*.

trivial things like wearing shoes. It was stated in *Fa Lv Da Wen* (*Legal Questions and Answers*) that "the common people are not allowed to wear brocade shoes. What are brocade shoes like? According to the law, the shoes, which are made with different colors of silk in patterns, are called brocade shoes. But if just the uppers of shoes are made of silk, they are not regarded as brocade shoes. However, with regard to case law, they can be treated as brocade shoes."

4.1.2 The Main Contents of Qin Lv (Qin Code) in Qin Jian

4.1.2.1 The Administrative Law on Promoting Bureaucracy

Among *Qin Lv* (*Qin Code*) contained in *Qin Jian* (*The Bamboo Writing Slips in Qin Dynasty*), some were about the appointment, selection, official transference, investigation, and the responsibilities of the officials, such as *Zhi Li Lv* (*Statutes on the Regulation of Officials*), *Chu Li Lv* (*Statutes on the Removal of Officials*), *Chu Di Zi Lv* (*Statutes on the Expulsion of Apprentices*), *Nei Shi Za* (*Statutes on State Offices in the Capital*), *Si Kong* (*Statutes on the Minister of Public works*), and *Xiao Lv* (*Statutes on the Inspection of the Supplies and Property of State Offices*).

The laws concerning the management of the household registering, tax and service include *Fu Lv* (*Statutes on the Household Registration*), *Yao Lv* (*Statutes on Corvée and Tax*), *Xu Lv* (*Statutes on Military Service*).

The laws concerning economic administrative management include *Ken Cao Ling* (*Decrees on Grassland Reclamation*), *Tian Lv* (*Statutes on Farming and Forest Protection*), *Cang Lv* (*Statutes on Storage of* Forage), *Jiu Yuan Lv* (*Statutes on Livestock Breeding and Gardening*), *Niu Yang Ke Lv* (*Statutes on Cows and Sheep Management*), *Guan Shi Lv* (*Statutes on Border Market*), *Jin Bu Lv* (*Statutes on Currency and Property*), *Gong Lv* (*Statutes on Handicraft Industry*), *Jun Gong Lv* (*Statutes on Controlling Handicraftsmen*), *Gong Ren Cheng* (*Statutes on Handicraft Production*), and *Si Kong* (*Statutes on the Minister of Public works*).

The laws concerning the regulation of military and judicial administration include *Jun Jue Lv* (*Statutes on Military Exploit and Official Titles*), *Zhong Lao Lv* (*Statutes on Workers*), *Dun Biao Lv* (*Statutes on Military Stationing*), *Gong Che Si Ma Lie Lv* (*Statutes on the Hunting Activities Organized by the Officials of Palace Guards*), *Yu Za Lv* (*Statutes on Junior Officials*), *Bu Dao Lv* (*Statutes on Catching the Thieves*), *Feng Zhen Shi* (*Judicial Principles, Methods and Cases*).

As the legalists' theory that enlightened kings should govern their officials instead of their people was followed in Qin Dynasty, the rules for the appointment and management of officials became the main contents of administrative law. According to *Qin Lv* (*Qin Code*), it was the most important thing to select officials according to their ability and those incompetent officials would be dismissed. In *Chu Li Lv* (*Statutes on the Removal of Officials*), it was stipulated that "if the officials and the archer or 'Se Fu' (a minor official in the county) are appointed illegally, they should be removed. If the archer cannot hit the target, 'Xian Wei' should be imposed a fine of two *Jia*, and the archer who cannot hit the target shall be imposed a fine of two *Jia* and shall be dismissed." In addition, "if the official who has been employed to drive carts for the officials for four years still does not know how to drive, then the coach of this person shall be imposed with a fine of one *dun*, be dismissed and serve 'Yao Xu' (labor service) for four years."[5]

The legalists advocated that "an official should be loyal to his king,"[6] which meant that officials must be loyal to their rulers and meanwhile they need to be familiar with the law. Shang Yang once pointed out that "if an official dares to forget the provisions of an important law, he would be accused and punished according to the provision that he has forgotten."[7]

Wei Li Zhi Dao (*The Way of Being an Official*) contained in *Qin Jian* (*The Bamboo Writing Slips in Qin Dynasty*) was similar to the official mottoes in the later times "which could be used as the standard for being officials" in its nature. Moreover, it not only contained all kinds of requirements for officials and the standards for official appointment and evaluation, but also recorded the tactics of the ruling and the philosophy of life. As *Wei Li Zhi Dao* (*The Way of Being an Official*) was buried in the tombs together with *Qin Lv* (*Qin Code*), it can be inferred that it was of great practical value so great importance was attached to it by officials.

In *Wei Li Zhi Dao* (*The Way of Being an Official*), the standard for the appointment of officials was listed, and "the candidate's ability to serve the people" was stressed. The so-called "ability," according to the annotation of Yan Shigu (historian and linguist of Tang Dynasty), "refers to one's competence."[8] The requirement for ability was different in different periods and the ability mentioned in *Wei Li Zhi Dao* (*The Way of Being an Official*) mainly referred to the talents needed in the war of annexation. For this reason, when Fan Ju was the prime minister of Qin, he proposed that "Ke Shi" (foreigners) should be appointed to hold important positions, namely, the talented people who were expert at military and state affairs in the various countries in the east should be appointed as officials. Thus, this policy had played a significant role in making Qin state strong and prosperous and in achieving its final unification.

In this legal document, the importance of officials in governing the country was also demonstrated and it was stated that the officials should be cautiously and regularly examined to distinguish the good officials from the bad ones, and that they should be appointed and their salaries should be paid according to their merits so that no one dared to deceive the senior officials and the state was greatly consolidated.

In *Wei Li Zhi Dao* (*The Way of Being an Official*), the codes of conduct that should be followed by officials were specified. "As to the laws on the behaviors of

---

[5] *Shui Hu Di Qin Mu Zhu Jian* (*The Bamboo Slips from the Tombs of Qin in Shuihudi*), p. 128.
[6] *Shui Hu Di Qin Mu Zhu Jian* (*The Bamboo Slips from the Tombs of Qin in Shuihudi*), p. 285.
[7] "Ding Fen" (Defining a Person's Social Status) in *Shang Jun Shu* (*The Book of Lord Shang*).
[8] "Gao Di Ji" (The Record of the First Emperor of Han Dynasty) in *Han Shu* (*The History of Han Dynasty*) (Book 1).

the officials, it was stipulated that the officials must maintain their moral integrity and remain cautious with strong minds. Moreover, they should conduct investigations impartially, do researches carefully, making sentences leniently and enforcing rewards and punishments prudently." So these rules were summarized as "Wu Shan" (five good conducts: referring to the five standards in morality) and "Wu Shi" (five misconducts: referring to the five shortcoming in morality). "Wu Shan" (five good conducts: referring to the five standards in morality) included the following aspects: first, officials should be loyal to the imperial court, to respect and obey their seniors; second, they must be honest, upright without slandering others; third, they must remain prudent and handle affairs appropriately; fourth, they were supposed to do good deeds to benefit the nation and people; fifth, they should always be modest and respectful. "Wu Shi" (five misconducts: referring to the five Shortcomings in morality) mainly included the following aspects: first, boasting without being practical; second, flattering the superiors; third, acting beyond one's authority; fourth, defying their superiors and plotting a rebellion; fifth, showing despise to scholars and being greedy for monetary interests. Given these above rules, there were two important points in *Wei Li Zhi Dao* (*The Way of Being an Official*): first, officials must be loyal to the king. Therefore, the primary merit of the officials was that they should be obedient to the imperial court, to show respect to and obey their seniors. In the state of Qin, which was a newly founded feudal regime, kingship was the symbol of the concentration of state power and the pivot to adjust the relationship inside the ruling class, therefore, the loyalty to the king and the state were unified, and the king and officials were integrated. It was stated in this law that "it is the essence of politics for the monarchs to be ambitious and the officials to be loyal" and "it is the foundation of the ruling of the state for the officials to be strictly administered and for the rulers to be enlightened and people to be virtuous." Second, the law should be enforced strictly, impartially, and prudently, without being bent for personal interests, let alone "make profits by taking advantage of one's official position," "prioritize money over meritous people" or "delay in carrying out orders." Shang Yang once pointed out that "law is the life of the people and the foundation of ruling"[9] and that "the wise monarchs and honest officials who want to run the state well mustn't forget the laws for a single minute."[10] These thoughts of Shang Yang mentioned above had had a long-term impact on the state and the empire of Qin Dynasty. According to *Yu Shu* (*Official Notice*) which was issued by Teng, the governor of Southern Sun in 227 B.C. and which was recorded in *Yun Meng Qin Jian* (*Amounts of Bamboo Writing Slips in Qin Dynasty Excavated in Yunmeng*), it was a standard to distinguish the good officials from the bad ones whether the officials are familiar with laws and regulations.

In *Wei Li Zhi Dao* (*The Way of Being an Official*), the standards for officials' personality and the styles in handling state affairs were also stipulated: "being strict without showing brutality; acting uprightly without hurting others; showing no

---

[9]"Ding Fen" (Defining a Person's Social Status) in *Shang Jun Shu* (*The Book of Lord Shang*).
[10]"Shen Fa" (Prudent Enforcement of Law) in *Shang Jun Shu* (*The Book of Lord Shang*).

4.1 The Legal System of Qin Dynasty Recorded in *Yun Meng Qin Jian (Amounts...*

jealousy or aggressiveness without making random judgments"; "being tolerant and faithful; being moderate without complaining; no over repenting; showing kindness to the subordinates without humiliating them; respecting the superiors without offending them; accepting remonstration, conducting investigations to know the ability of the people, being expert at assessing people's competence, working hard as examples for other people, and being upright to have people rectified." It was required that the officials should be strict, honest and sticking to principles, while at the same time, they should not be brutal or make decisions emotionally. They should not only show tolerance, moderation, benevolence to the subordinates, they should also correct and rectify their misconducts by strict management and necessary sanctions. The personality and style mentioned above is exactly the continuation and application of the tactics of ruling used by legalists which is featured by the use of the two methods of "De" (virtue) and "Xing" (punishment), and its starting point was not "showing benevolence to the subordinates" but "regulating subordinates"; so the purpose of "examining the ability of the people by conducting investigations" was to have a better governance of people and the purpose of "being good at assessing people's competence" was to have a more effective exploitation.

What needs to be pointed out is that to win the support of the peasants, to win a complete victory over the old aristocracy, and to lay a solid foundation for the long-term stability, efforts were made by Qin state mainly in two aspects: on the one hand, necessary restrictions were imposed upon officials who were the concrete agents of state functions, so it was regulated that they were forbidden to exceed the jurisdiction stipulated in law or to blindly seek for power and property, because "if the desire for wealth is exceedingly strong, then it would lead to the poverty of the common people; if the desire for power is exceedingly strong, then it would lose the support of the people of lower social status." On the other hand, it advocated the feudal concept that "the rulers should be ambitious, the officials should be loyal, the fathers should be kind and the sons should be obedient" by portraying officials as "generous," "benevolent," "self-controlled" and "temperate" people to establish a stable ruling order. However, as for the issues concerning national interests such as tax collection, corvée, and military service, it had required the officials "to administer according to law" and "to try their best to fulfill their duties" with no negligence or carelessness.

To conclude, *Wei Li Zhi Dao (The Way of Being an Official)* was a real record of the feudal bureaucracy of Qin Dynasty, which had truly shown the efforts made by the rulers to try to establish and consolidate the feudal regime at that time. Although the feudal bureaucracy reflected the dictatorship of landlord class, it was indeed full of vitality at the early stage of feudal society, and its general practice had played a progressive role in history in clearing away the residual of hereditary system and in consolidating the feudal system. Even the kingship maintained by *Wei Li Zhi Dao (The Way of Being an Official)* represented a new order, so it became a progressive factor in the chaos of conflicts between the upper and the lower classes.

The assessment of officials in Qin Dynasty was called "Ke" (appraisal), and according to *Ke Lv (The Statute of Appraisal)*, the first month in lunar calendar every year was scheduled for officials' assessment; the standard of assessment included "Zui" and "Dian." "Zui" meant "excellence," and those who were considered excellent would be rewarded or promoted, while "Dian" meant "inferiority," and those who were considered inferior would be punished by "Chi" (flogging with light sticks). Regulations about how to examine officials who were in charge of animal husbandry were also stipulated:

> Cattle competitions are held in April, July, October and the first month of lunar calendar every year. After a full year, there will be a major assessment in the first month of the lunar year, and anyone whose cattle win the match will be awarded a bottle of good wine and ten strips of dried meat. Moreover, the person who has raised the cattle will be exempted from a year's service of night guard and will be rewarded an extra salary of thirty days. However, for those whose cattle get poor grades in the match, they will be reprimanded and the breeder of the cattle will also be imposed a fine of two months' salary. If a cattle gets thinner after ploughing in the field, the owner will be punished by 'Chi' (flogging with light sticks) for ten strokes for every inch thinner of the waist. In addition, examinations will also be held in the village, the excellent performers will get award with an extra salary of ten days and the poor ones will be punished by 'Chi' (flogging with light sticks) for thirty strokes.

In addition, there are rules about "Ci Lao," which meant to let people to be on leave for a few days as a reward for their contribution and merits. This method was still in use in Han Dynasty, and it was recorded in *Ju Yan Han Jian* (*Ju Yan Bamboo Slips of Han Dynasty*) that "according to No. 45 decree on awards, 'Shang Li' (local official), 'Hou Zhang' (local supervisory official), and 'Feng Sui Zhang' (in charge of signal fire) often held autumn archery test to determine awards, and six was used as a standard. If more than six shots hit the target, the winner would be awarded." "As for the border officials and patrolmen like 'Hou Zhang' and 'Hou Shi', they can be given preferential treatment in the calculation of credit. For example, two days may be counted as three days."[11]

In Qin Dynasty, strict assessment system was also implemented in the army. According to "Jing Nei" (Within the Territory) in *Shang Jun Shu* (*The Book of Lord Shang*), "when an enemy site is besieged…the general makes a wooden platform and steps onto it with "Guo Zheng Jian" (a supervisory official) and 'Yu Shi' (the censors) to supervise the battle. The first soldier who breaks into the besieged enemy city shall be regarded as the excellent one and the last one will be regarded as the worse."

As for the assessment of officials in the state of Qin, the relatively specific criteria and necessary procedures and the strict systems of reward and punishment were set up to encourage officials to fulfill their duties with due diligence. According to *Wei Li Zhi Dao* (*The Way of Being an Official*), if an official could completely achieve 'Wu Shan' (five good conducts: referring to the five standards in morality), he would definitely get great awards, but among all 'Wu Shi' (five misconducts: referring to the five shortcomings in morality), the very misconduct of "being irreverent to seniors" would be punished by death penalty, which was of universal significance and which had reflected the legalistic thoughts of applying harsh punishments and generous rewards. Shang Yang once said, "Rewarding is a civilized method, but penalty is a military one, and the combination of civilized and military methods is the

---

[11] *Ju Yan Han Jian* (*Ju Yan Bamboo Slips of Han Dynasty*).

basic restriction of law."[12] Han Fei once praised Shang Yang and said, "the ruling of Qin state by Shang Yang's methods...in which generous awards and severe penalties were emphasized, was carried out in accordance with law."[13] So we can see from the provisions in *Qin Lv* (*Qin Code*) that the regulations on performance appraisal, rewards and punishments covered many departments, such as agriculture, handicraft, military, finance, justice and administration, to name just a few, which had not only laid a solid foundation for the official inspection system of later dynasties, but also symbolized the formation of Chinese civil service system and the progress of legal civilization.

Apart from the assessment of the achievements, many rules about the supervision of officials were also recorded in *Qin Jian* (*The Bamboo Writing Slips in Qin Dynasty*). For example, *Yu Shu* (*Official Notice*) which was issued in the 20th year of Qin Shi Huang (the first emperor of Qin) (227 B.C.), was an important document with the nature of the law of official surveillance before the unification of Qin Dynasty.

It was recorded in *Yu Shu* (*Official Notices*) that "the aldermen must send people to oversee the work in the region and have the law breakers punished accordingly. If any county official had violated the law, or if his seniors failed to have him reported, those in charge would be punished. So "Jun Shou" (governor) would be sent to the local counties to conduct careful investigation, if those petty officials had violated law, they would be punished according to law. If the officials in the county had violated law but the county magistrate and other officials had failed to investigate and or have them punished according to the law, they would be reported to the imperial court to be punished for their malfeasance.

Some specific rules on supervisory officials were also stipulated in *Yu Shu* (*Official Notices*):

"For the competent officials who are familiar with law, there is nothing that they cannot handle. Besides, they are usually honest and loyal to the emperor, and they know that it is not allowed to make arbitrary decisions in government offices, so each of them is righteous. Moreover, they can often have self-criticism and they dislike to argue with others, so they seldom quarrel with others." "On the other hand, for the incompetent officials who are ignorant of law, they do not carry out orders. Besides, they know nothing about their work and are often dishonest. As a result, they cannot work effectively for the emperor. Moreover, they are often lazy and easily satisfied; they avoid responsibilities, sow discords among colleagues and blaspheme and insult others shamelessly; they are prejudiced so they often handle the matters offensively; they are also good at arguing and are often aggressive in cooperation. When they compete with others, they usually like to show off their power threateningly (by staring and clenching their fists); they just tell all sorts of lies, pretending they are good at governance by speaking arrogantly; they pretend to be apologetic for their ignorance to speak against common sense to show that they can control themselves; they are just conceited, rude and stubborn and are good at showing off their ability and merits, but their superiors mistakenly think they have talents and capacities. So such people must be punished."

---

[12]"Xiu Quan" (On the Usage of Power) in *Shang Jun Shu* (*The Book of Lord Shang*).
[13]"Ding Fa" (Law Making) in *Shang Jun Shu* (*The Book of Lord Shang*).

These regulations prove that as far as the official supervision of the state of Qin is concerned, the focus is to let people understand the law, abide by the law and carry out the law, which had closely integrated the enforcement of law with the supervision of officials, which was a basic feature of the feudal legal system and which had fully reflected the thoughts of legalists. During the supervision process of officials, great attention was paid to appointing officials according to their respective abilities and to choosing officials according to their talents to consolidate their power. The officials with serious misconducts were required to be punished severely with their misdeeds recorded and made known to the people in the county as a warning to other officials.

To improve the efficiency of administration, Shang Yang strictly required that officials must settle the problems on the spot. He said: "It is a weak country for the regional affairs to be decided and solved within ten miles and it is a powerful country to do so within five miles. In a country where the daily affairs are handled within the day, its leader deserves to be a king; in a country where the daily affairs are delayed to be handled in the evening, the country is weak; in a country where the daily affairs are delayed to be handled until the next day, the country will decline."[14] Moreover, special provisions concerning document transferring called *Xing Shu Lv* (*Statutes on the Delivery of Documents*) were also made. One thing worthy of particular attention is that the areas ruled by Qin state were inhabited by different ethnic groups, so *Shu Bang Lv* (*Statutes on the Management of Vassal States*) was especially made for the regulation of the affairs for minority groups.

To sum up, although the administrative law of Qin Dynasty was still simple and imperfect, it was prominently practicable.

4.1.2.2 The Criminal Law Under the Guidance of the Ideology of Legalists

4.1.2.2.1 Legalism had already become a very famous school of study in the Warring States Period, so, consequently, in the state of Qin, which was influenced by the doctrine of legalism, the following legalist thoughts are included into its criminal law:

Explicit Regulations and Unified Punishments Shang Yang once pointed out that "laws have to be made easier and clearer enough for people to understand," because "when people know the law, they will refrain from violating it."[15] Unified punishments meant that the criminal penalty should be enforced without being affected by the criminals' social status, as was said that "if anyone has disobeyed the king and

---

[14]"Qu Qiang" (Getting Rid of the Disobedient) in *Shang Jun Shu* (*The Book of Lord Shang*).
[15]"Ding Fen" (Defining a Person's Social Status) in *Shang Jun Shu* (*The Book of Lord Shang*).

violated the state law, they will be sentenced to death without being pardoned whether they are ministers or generals, senior officials, or ordinary people."[16]

Severe Penalties for Misdemeanor Legalists favored severe punishments because they thought that the crimes would not be prevented or controlled without severe punishments, and "there are no other effective methods than the strict criminal law to eradicate crimes."[17] The legalists also thought that severe penalties should be imposed for misdemeanor and punishment should be utilized to deter punishment. "it is impossible to prevent crimes to enforce severe punishment for severe crimes and light punishment for minor crimes, because it is impossible for minor crimes to be prevented by light punishments, let alone major crimes. So things illegal just continue to happen, so the country will be become weaker constantly."[18] "If punishments are executed after the crimes are committed, then the crimes will never be eliminated,...therefore, if punishment are imposed just before the crime is committed, then there will not be felonies anymore."[19] To implement the idea of severe penalties, Shang Yang restored the punishment of "Yi Zu" (implicating the nine generations of a family). It was recorded in "Xing Fa Zhi" (The Record of the Criminal Law) in *Han Shu* (*The History of Han Dynasty*) that "the king of Qin appointed Shang Yang...who restored the penalty of 'Yi Zu' (implicating the nine generations of a family)," so the officials who did not abide by the law would be "punished by death penalty" and "their relatives involved would also be punished." According to the annotation of Ru Chun, the relatives referred to "the three respective clans of their fathers, mothers, and their wives."

No Pardoning and Forgiving; Being Rewarded for Merits and Being Punished for Crimes Legalists believed that it would make people have fluke minds to pardon and forgive the offenders, as was described in the saying that, "if the person subject to penalties were not punished, then the wicked people would not take the penalties seriously, and they would take a chance and counting on get away with it."[20] Consequently, "even the senior officials in high positions would not be pardoned in spite of their prior achievements and glories, so they would not be exempted from punishment just because they have made great achievements before or have committed crimes afterwards." "As long as those loyal officials and dutiful sons have violated the law, they will still be punished accordingly."[21]

Besides the principle of offering no pardoning, the legalists also believed that the rule of giving rewards for merits and enforcing punishment for misconducts must be carried out. Shang Yang concluded from his experience that "unless the people are

---

[16]"Shang Xing" (Rewards and Punishments) in *Shang Jun Shu* (*The Book of Lord Shang*).
[17]"Kai Sai" (Reform) in *Shang Jun Shu* (*The Book of Lord Shang*).
[18]"Qu Qiang" (Getting Rid of the Disobedient) in *Shang Jun Shu* (*The Book of Lord Shang*).
[19]"Kai Sai" (Reform) in *Shang Jun Shu* (*The Book of Lord Shang*).
[20]"Suan Di" (Measuring Land) in *Shang Jun Shu* (*The Book of Lord Shang*).
[21]"Shang Xing" (Rewards and Punishments) in *Shang Jun Shu* (*The Book of Lord Shang*).

intimidated by penalties and motivated by rewards, it is impossible for them to fulfill their duties for the rulers."[22] "So awards have to be generous and penalties have to be severe; when people see the generous rewards they will forget the fear of death, similarly, when people see the severity of penalties, they will be scared and will obey the law."[23]

Encouraging People to Inform Against Misconducts and Crimes The legalists thought that "nothing is more important than eliminating the evil people in the law enforcement."[24] During Shang Yang's reform, it was stipulated that "people who do wrong or steal things will be sentenced to death."[25] To prevent crimes, people were encouraged to inform against the misconducts and crimes in a collateral system. "Anyone who has known of a crime but has failed to report it will be punished by 'Yao Zhan' (cutting at waist); anyone who has done so will be awarded according to the regulation on soldiers' killing the enemies; anyone who has helped to hide the criminals will be punished according to the regulation on those surrendering to the enemies."[26] As a punishment, "Lian Zuo" (being punished for being related to somebody who committed an offense) was different from "Zu Xing" (killing of the whole clan of a criminal). For "Zu Xing" (killing of the whole clan of a criminal), those involved were usually executed, but for "Lian Zuo" (being punished for being related to somebody who committed an offense), only the relatives of the criminal who had committed felonies would be sentenced to death, while the others were usually punished by paying fines or being forced to move to other places.

The principles mentioned above reflected a distinctive theory of criminal law during the period of social transition, which had provided a guidance for the criminal legislation in Qin state. However, these principles had been criticized by the later generations. For example, it was criticized in "Fei Yang" (Against Shang Yang) in *Yan Tie Lun (Debates on Salt and Iron)* by the people of Han Dynasty that, "people's resentment to the vicious and cruel laws of Qin Dynasty was even stronger than personal hatred" and "the accumulation of hatred was as great as the high mountain." Sima Qian, the famous historian even criticized that Shang Yang's principle of severe penalties were executed because of "his inborn acerb nature."[27] However, severe penalty was a necessary measure for the emerging landlords to establish and consolidate their power, and it was determined by the historical conditions. Take Qin Dynasty as an example, if such policies were not adopted, it would not have been possible to succeed in sweeping away the power of old nobilities and the old customs

---

[22]"Shen Fa" (Prudent Enforcement of Law) in *Shang Jun Shu (The Book of Lord Shang)*.

[23]"Wai Nei" (The Outer and the Inner) in *Shang Jun Shu (The Book of Lord Shang)*.

[24]"Kai Sai" (Reform) in *Shang Jun Shu (The Book of Lord Shang)*.

[25]"Hua Ce" (Policies) in *Shang Jun Shu (The Book of Lord Shang)*.

[26]"Shang Jun Lie Zhuan" (The Collected Biographies of Shang Yang) in *Shi Ji (The Record of the Grand Historian)*.

[27]"Shang Jun Lie Zhuan" (The Collected Biographies of Shang Yang) in *Shi Ji (The Record of the Grand Historian)*.

and in developing and consolidating the basis of feudal system. Consequently, the laws of Qin Dynasty were inherited even after Shang Yang died later. "So since Shang Yang's reform carried out in the period of Duke Xiao of Qin, the state of Qin had gradually become a powerful country in the world and the laws of Qin state were abided by the Qin people had for hundreds of years, namely, the laws applied by their ancestors were laid down by Shang Yang'"[28] As to the arbitrary killing conducted by Qin Shi Huang (the first emperor of Qin) in his later years, the original meaning of Shang Yang's notion of enforcing severe penalties for minor crimes was lost because it had been carried to extremes.

4.1.2.2.2 In *Qin Lv* (*Qin Code*), a series of new accusation for the punishment of the offenses of endangering the autocratic ruling and social order was established. Moreover, a penal system characterized by severe penalties was beginning to take shape.

In Qin Dynasty, rebellion was the most serious crime. King Hui of Qin who succeeded the throne after the death of Duke Xiao of Qin killed Shang Yang for the accusation of "Mou Fan" (plotting rebellion or plotting to endanger the country). In "Shang Jun Lie Zhuan" (The Collected Biographies of Shang Yang) in *Shi Ji* (*The Records of the Grand Historian*), there are the following records: "The followers of Prince Qian accused Shang Yang of rebellion, so the king sent people to have Shang Yang arrested…and King Hui of Qin ordered to have Shang Yang punished by 'Che Lie' (tearing a person asunder with carts) to warn people that they are forbidden to rebel like Shang Yang. Later he asked soldiers to kill the whole family of Shang Yang."

In the 9th year of King Zheng of Qin Dynasty (238 B.C.), "Duke of Chang Xin, Lao Ai revolted against King Zheng of Qin and plotted to attack the king's palace," but he was "severely suppressed and sentenced to death by 'Che Lie' (tearing a person asunder with carts) with all people of his clan killed." Twenty of other principal criminals such as Wei Wei, etc., were all "punished by 'Xiao Shou' (the penalty of hanging the head of the criminal on top of a pole for public display) and 'Che Lie' (tearing a person asunder with carts) with the people of their clans all killed." "…the rest of the convicts were also punished, and the minimum sentence was 'Gui Xin' (The male criminal was sentenced go up the mountain to cut firewood for sacrificial ceremony). More than 4000 aristocrats were deprived of their titles and forced to leave their homes."

To reward agriculture and military exploits, those who surrendered themselves were punished by Qin rulers according to the same penalty for the crime of hiding criminals. It was recorded in *Suo Yin* (*Index*) for the annotation of "Shang Jun Lie Zhuan" (The Collected Biographies of Shang Yang) in *Shi Ji* (*The Records of the Grand Historian*) that "those who surrender themselves will be sentenced to death with their family fortune all confiscated." According to "Fan Ju Cai Ze Lie Zhuan"

---

[28]Shen Jiaben (Qing Dynasty), "Zi Xu" (The Author's Preface) to *Ha Lv Zhi Yi* (*Collections of Laws in Han Dynasty*).

(The Biographies of Fan Ju and Cai Ze) in *Shi Ji* (*The Records of the Grand Historian*), Duke of Ying, Fan Ju, "ordered Zheng Anping to attack the state of Zhao, but Zheng was surrounded by the troops of Zhao, so under such urgent conditions, Zheng surrendered himself to Zhao with 20,000 soldiers. Xi Gao, the duke of Ying pleaded guilty and asked himself to be punished…so he should be punished with three generations of his clan people arrested and put in prison." In the 8th year of King Zheng of Qin Dynasty (239 B.C.), "a general called Cheng Jiao attacked Zhao and surrendered himself." "Even though the soldiers who had surrendered themselves had died, they were punished by 'Lu Shi' (an ancient form of torture. In order to punish the deceased's behavior, digging graves open the coffin, the body will be displayed)."[29] From this, we can see the severity of the punishment for surrender.

Apart from surrendering themselves to the enemy, the people who preached the powerfulness of enemy and shook the morale of the army would also be beheaded to warn the public. It was recorded in "Fa Lv Da Wen" (Legal Questions and Answers) in *Qin Jian* (*The Bamboo Writing Slips in Qin Dynasty*) that "those who praised the enemy and intimidated the public by spreading fallacies would be punished by death penalty.

In Qin Dynasty, it was encouraged to report law breakers to the government since Shang Yang's reform, but to prevent framing-up accusations to disturb social stability, the punishment for the crime of "Tou Shu Zui" (delivery of false accusation letters) was formulated, which referred to writing letters anonymously to frame the innocent people and to give vent to the author's private anger. While there were not specific rules for the punishment of those letter writers in *Fa Lv Da Wen* (*Legal Questions and Answers*), there were indeed rules about how to award those who had successfully caught those false accusers: more award was given to them than that given to those who had arrested the criminals of "Zei Sha" (premeditated murder) or "Zei Sha" (premeditated hurting). Therefore, it can be inferred that the punishment for filing the frame-up accusation must be more severe than that for those who kill or hurt others intentionally. Its purpose was to put an end to deception and framing-up accusation to offset the negative impact of encouraging to report crimes. After Qin Dynasty, the accusation such as "Fei Shu" (anonymous letters) and "Wu Wang" (slandering) was established in the law of Han Dynasty, so the accusation like "delivering anonymous letters to frame up others" in the law of Tang Dynasty had originated from provision of "Tou Shu Zui" (delivery of false accusation letters) made in the Qin Dynasty.

To establish the authority of monarchical power, according to the laws of Qin Dynasty, those who showed no respect to the monarchs would be severely punished. In light of the law, those who did not stand up when listening to the emperor speeches would be punished with a fine for irreverence. If anyone did not follow the king's command or violated it, he would be given administrative punishment

---

[29]"Qin Shi Huang Ben Ji" (The Biography of Qin Shi Huang) in *Shi Ji* (*The Record of the Grand Historian*).

4.1 The Legal System of Qin Dynasty Recorded in *Yun Meng Qin Jian* (Amounts...)

such as dismissal from his position or being transferred to a lower rank. Moreover, he would be held accountable or even convicted for the crime of being irreverent.

Punishments were also enforced for hurting the king's horses, or using inappropriate methods in raising and taming the horses. In *Qin Lv Za Chao* (*Miscellaneous Copies of Laws of Qin*), the following rules are recorded:

> If anyone hurts the horses of the ruler, for a wound in the skin which is one *cun* long (*cun*: a unit of length, one *cun* is about 1/3 decimeter), he will be imposed with a fine of one *dun*; for two *cun* long, the fine is two *dun* (shield); for over two *dun*, the fine will be one *jia*. When inspecting mules, if the number of mules that have been tamed is more than one but fewer than six, the person in charge shall be imposed with a fine of one *dun*. Besides, the special horses should be kept behind other horses when drawing a cart, and they should not be whipped; anyone who violates of this rule will be imposed with a fine of one *dun*. And for the running horses, if they are not unharnessed in time, the cart driver will be imposed with a fine of one *dun*.

The crimes of assaulting and offending against individuals accounted for the largest portion of criminal law of Qin Dynasty, including the crimes of murdering, injuring somebody in fighting, raping, and so on. According to the criminal law of Qin Dynasty, there were different accusation for different types of killing, including "Zei Sha" (premeditated murder), "Dao Sha" (killing in stealing), "Shan Sha" (unauthorized killing), and "Dou Sha" (killing during fighting). "Zei Sha" (premeditated murder) means "Gu Sha" (intentional homicide). If a "Nu Bi" (the slave girls and maidservants) had attempted to kill his or her master, even unsuccessful, he or she would be sued and punished for trying to "murder the master." If a criminal had resisted the arrest and killed the official who tried to catch him, although this belonged to "Dou Sha" (killing during fighting), he would be considered as a murder and would be punished accordingly.

During Qin Dynasty, much emphasis was put on rescuing the victims of killing or murder. It was stated in *Fa Lv Da Wen* (*Legal Questions and Answers*) that if a person intends to kill someone in the street, the on-lookers within a hundred feet who did not try to rescue or help the victim would be imposed with a fine of two *jia*. Another case in *Fa Lv Da Wen* (*Legal Questions and Answers*) also showed the responsibility of rescuing: "if a thief breaks into A's house and hurts A, and A shouts loudly for help, A's neighbors, Dian and Lao (both were local official) are all not at home and have not heard the cries, should these people be punished? When neighbors are not at home, they could be exempted from punishment; yet for the local officials, even if they are not at home, they shall still be punished." The regulations on the rescuing responsibility were helpful to maintain a good social order, at the same time the grassroots officials' responsibility of safeguarding the public security was stressed.

"Dao Sha" (killing in stealing) referred to killing committed in stealing. Since it had combined the crimes of "Dao" (robbery) and "Zei" (banditry), it was more severely punished. In *Fa Lv Da Wen* (*Legal Questions and Answers*), the following case is recorded: "if A asks B to kill a person and gives him ten *qian* (a unit of weight, one *qian* is about five grams) for that in return, but B is still a juvenile, how should A be convicted and punished? A should be sentenced to the penalty of 'Zhe' (to open and split, breaking apart the criminal's body)." The reason for A to be severe punished in this case had fully shown the government's intention to enforce severe punishment on those who instigated juveniles to commit crimes.

"Shan Sha" (unauthorized killing) specifically referred to the crime of the noble killing the humble or a master killing his slaves or servants. This kind of crime was only limited to the cases involved in hierarchy system. Consequently, although it was the crime of "Gu Sha" (intentional homicide), it would be dealt with as the crime of "Shan Sha" (unauthorized killing) instead of "Zei Sha" (premeditated murder). For example, "if parents kill their children, they shall be punished with 'Cheng Dan Chong' (the punishment of men building cities and women thrashing rice for lifetime), which means that they will be punished by getting shameful tattoos on their faces and then punished by penal servitude, with men building cities and women thrashing rice for lifetime."[30] If parents killed their children because they had too many children to take care of, they would be convicted of "Sha Zi" (killing the child), but if the killed child was born with malformation, his parents would be exempted from punishment; if an adopted child living together was killed by his parents, the parents should be punished by "Qi Shi" (exposing the executed body publicly at markets), which was much severer than the unauthorized killing of the adopted children; if the slaves killed their kids, they should be punished by "Cheng Dan" (the punishment of men building cities) and "Qing" (to tattoo on the face), and then be returned to their masters. Even the nobles and the chiefs of the minority groups subject to the rule of Qin would be punished if they had randomly killed their legal successors.

The rules about "Shan Sha" (unauthorized killing) in the criminal law of Qin Dynasty were made to prevent the privileged people from killing others at will. It showed that in Qin Dynasty the influence of feudal relationship on law was not as great as that in the later dynasties. In addition, the fact that masters were forbidden to randomly kill the slaves also reflected the changes of slaves' social status in the transitional period from slavery to feudal system.

Injury from fighting belonged to an ordinary crime in *Qin Lv* (*Qin Code*). As it was quite common, it was ruled with rather specific provisions. For instance, as for hurting people, it was divided into "Dou Shang" (hurting from fighting) and "Zei Shang" (premeditated hurting).

Those who fought with weapons and hurt others would get much severer punishment than the ordinary ones. If people fought with needles or awls, they would be imposed with a fine of two *jia*; if anyone was hurt by these weapons, the offender should be punished by "Qing" (to tattoo on the face) and "Cheng Dan" (the punishment of men building cities). If people fought with swords, they would be punished by "Cheng Dan Chong" (the punishment of men building cities and women thrashing rice for lifetime) for all their lives, although they just cut the hair of the other party.

---

[30]"Fa Lv Da Wen" (Legal Questions and Answers) in *Qin Jian* (*The Bamboo Writing Slips in Qin Dynasty*).

If officials hurt others, they would be sentenced with much severe penalties. It was recorded in "Fan Li Teng Guan Lie Zhuan" (The Biographies of Fan, Li, Teng, and Guan) in *Shi Ji* (*The Records of the Grand Historian*) that "the first emperor of Han Dynasty once hurt Duke of Xia in a fighting, and he was reported by someone. At that time, he was just a local official, but he was punished more severely because of this...." According to Ru Chun's interpretation in *Ji Jie* (*Collected Interpretations*), "if an official hurts others, he will get much severer punishment."

During the times of Qin Dynasty, if the immigrants of other states fought with the citizens of the state of Qin, even if they hurt others with knives, sticks or by fists, they would just be leniently punished by handing in a certain amount of cloth as a fine. This was because they wanted to attract more new immigrants to Qin state to strengthen its state power.

In the fighting between couples, although the wife was more ferocious, if the husband hurt his wife, he would be sentenced to the penalty of "Nai" (having the criminal's beard shaven for two years), which was prescribed in *Fa Lv Da Wen* (*Legal Questions and Answers*): "if a wife is ferocious and tough and her husband beats her and hurts her ear or other parts of her body, he shall be sentenced to 'Nai' (having the criminal's beard shaven for two years)." This rule was similar to the criminal laws in later times, according to which if a husband hurt his wife or actually caused a certain degree of injury, he would be punished more severely. Thus, it indicated that the feudal moral orders and ethic rules were not yet so strict in the Qin Dynasty.

As to the crime of raping, there was only one case recorded in *Fa Lv Da Wen* (*Legal Questions and Answers*) about a male slave who had raped his female master: "if a slave rapes the master, what is the punishment? He should be punished the same as that for the slave who hurts his master." In the law of Qin Dynasty, the slaves who hurt their masters would be sentenced to death, so the slaves who committed the crime of raping would also be put to death. There were two cases about adultery in *Qin Jian* (*The Bamboo Writing Slips in Qin Dynasty*): one was about ordinary people, and both the adulterer and the adulteress were arrested and tied with wooden shackles; the other one was about a brother and his half sister who had the same father but different mother, and both of them were punished by "Qi Shi" (exposing the executed body publicly at markets). The reason for enforcing severe punishment for the crimes in the latter case was that the rulers of Qin Dynasty were trying to maintain the feudal ethic relationship.

With a large-scale establishment of private ownership, quite specific and concrete rules were made concerning the punishment for the crime of infringing upon others' private property. In *Fa Lv Da Wen* (*Legal Questions and Answers*), cases of stealing cows were recorded. For example, "A stole a cow which was one year old and around 1.2 meters tall in the burglary. But afterwards, when the case was settled, the cow was found and measured again, but it became around 1.6 meters tall, then what punishment should A get? A should be punished by 'Cheng Dan' (the punishment of men building cities)." In the other case, slaves A and B stole their master's cow together and tried to escape to abroad, but they were arrested, then how to punish them? They should be punished by "Qing" (to tattoo on the face) and "Cheng Dan" (the punishment of men building cities).

If a person stole a hundred *qian* but surrendered himself to the government, he would be punished by "Nai" (having the criminal's beard shaven for two years) and serving as a slave, or he would be imposed a fine of two *jia*.

As for stealing the sacrificial offerings in public places, although the amount is no more than one *qian*, because the booty is sacrificial, the person should also be punished by "Nai" (having the criminal's beard shaven for two years) and serving as a slave" to show that god should never be profaned.

To establish the concept that private property was inviolable, the crimes of attempted theft and minor theft were also punished. For example, "if a person had stolen mulberry worth less than one *qian*, how should he be punished? He should be sentenced to penal servitude for thirty days"; "A had plotted to persuade B to be involved in stealing… before they came off, they were arrested and both were punished by 'Qing' (to tattoo on the face)." Besides, ethic orders were also taken into consideration in punishment, so "if a father steals from his children, it shall not be taken as theft"; but if an adoptive father stole from his adopted child, he would be punished for theft. In addition, the wife would always undertake joint criminal responsibility for her husband's theft, whether she was aware of her husband's crime. For example, "if a husband stole 300 *qian* and told his wife about it, but his wife spent the money together with him, how should the wife be punished? She did not join in the previous plot of theft, so she should be punished for accepting the stolen money." Nevertheless, if she had conspired together with her husband beforehand, she should be punished the same as her husband.

If anyone had smuggled jewelry or jade to another country and sold them to foreigners, he should be punished by a much severer punishment than "Nai" (having the criminal's beard shaven for two years) or be sentenced to a payment of fine.

If an official whose job was to arrest thieves had committed the crime of theft, he should be punished more severely.

If a person escaped with the official property that he borrowed, he should be punished according to the rules for the crime of theft; if a person misappropriates public funds of "Shao Nei" (the government office in charge of collecting and storing money) in a county without permission, he should be punished for the crime of theft.

Although there was no concept of robbery in *Qin Lv* (*Qin Code*), there was a case similar to robbery. It was recorded in "Qun Dao Yuan Shu" (The Confession of Gang Robbery) that "a local official with his two subordinates named B and C sent a man named D, a chopped-off head, two crossbows and twenty arrows to the superior officials and reported that 'D and the man who was killed belong to a robbery gang. Yesterday when A led B and C to patrol a mountain, he found D and the man who was killed robbing people with weapons. So they arrested them.'" For people who robbed others with a gang, they would be punished by cutting off their left toe and be punished by "Cheng Dan" (the punishment of men building cities). If the crime was serious, besides the punishment of cutting off their left toe and "Cheng Dan" (the punishment of men building cities), they would also be punished by "Qing" (to tattoo on the face).

To urge its department officials and staff at all levels to fulfill their duties conscientiously, very detailed provisions about professional crimes were stipulated in Qin Dynasty.

Because the role of officials was stressed in Qin Dynasty, the system of "Lian Zuo" (being punished for being related to somebody who committed an offense) was adopted in the officials' recommendation process. If "an official has recommended a person who is not capable and who has failed to perform his duties, both the official and the one who is recommended will be punished accordingly."[31] It was recorded in *Xiao Lv* (*Statutes on the Inspection of the Supplies and Property of State Offices*) that if a county accountant and his subordinates had committed crimes, the county magistrate and his colleague would be punished. According to *Zhi Li Lv* (*Statutes on the Regulation of Officials*), there was a fixed time in Qin Dynasty for the appointment or dismissal of the local officials and their subordinates. The appointment usually started from December 1st to the end of March, but if there were any exceptional circumstances, the time was not limited. Moreover, the appointed officials should not take their offices and perform their duties until they got the official appointment. If a person exercised his power before he was appointed officially, or had privately plotted with others to take office beforehand, he would be punished according to the law.

In addition, it was forbidden for a transferred "Se Fu" (a minor official in the county) to take his subordinates who used to work with him to his new office. Thus, it was stipulated that "'Se Fu' (a minor official in the county) who has been transferred to another position shall not take his ex-subordinates away with him or appoint them to new posts."[32] If "Se Fu" (a minor official in the county) was dismissed but a new one was not appointed after two months, the county magistrate and his colleague would be punished for violating the law and should hold responsibility for this; "if an official was permanently dismissed, but he took office again, he should be punished"[33]; if anyone had recommended a permanently dismissed official to take office again, he would be imposed with a fine of two *jia*. In *Chu Di Zi Lv* (*Statutes on the Expulsion of Apprentices*), the following rule was made: "Anyone who has made inappropriate appointments shall be sentenced to 'Nai' (having the criminal's beard shaven for two years) and be exiled to remote areas."

In *Qin Jian* (*The Bamboo Writing Slips in Qin Dynasty*), "Fan Ling" (The Breach of Orders) referred to "doing what is forbidden by the imperial order" and "Fei Ling" (Failure to Obey Orders) referred to "failing to do what is required to do," both of

---

[31] "Fan Ju Cai Ze Lie Zhuan" (The Record of the Historian Collected biographies of Fan Ju and Cai Ze) in *Shi Ji* (*The Record of the Grand Historian*).

[32] "Zhi Li Lv" (Statutes on the Regulation of Officials) in "Qin Lv Shi Ba Zhong" (Eighteen Kinds of Laws of Qin Dynasty) in *Qin Jian* (*The Bamboo Writing Slips in Qin Dynasty*).

[33] "Nei Shi Za" (Statutes on State Offices in the Capital) in "Qin Lv Shi Ba Zhong" (Eighteen Kinds of Laws of Qin Dynasty) in *Qin Jian* (*The Bamboo Writing Slips in Qin Dynasty*).

which referred to unlawful acts. In the state of Qin where officials were required to "fully understand the laws, regulations and orders," if anyone had committed the crime of "Fan Ling" (The Breach of Orders) or "Fei Ling" (Failure to Obey Orders), all the relevant officials were legally responsible, even the officials who had been dismissed or transferred to somewhere else would be punished. Apart from these two kinds of crimes, the accusation of "Bu Cong Ling" (Disobeying Orders) was also established to punish the officials who did not act strictly in accordance with the law. To make officials fully understand the laws, it was stipulated in *Nei Shi Za* (*Statutes on State Offices in the Capital*) that "it is required that in each 'Xian' (county) which was under the direct control of the capital, 'Du Guan' (feudal officials in the capital district) should be respectively notified to have the laws copied," which meant that in each 'Xian' (county) within the jurisdiction of "Jing Shi" (the capital city), "Du Guan" (feudal officials in the capital district) should be informed to copy the laws which they usually applied.

If an official pretended to obey an imperial order, but in reality delayed carrying it out, he would be sentenced to the punishment of "Nai" (having the criminal's beard shaven for two years) and would not be appointed anymore, which was described as "Zhi Shu." As for the delivery of orders, specific rules were also made: "the urgent orders should be delivered instantly"; "the less urgent ones should be delivered within the day"; if the order was delayed and overstocked, "the one who is responsible shall be punished according to the law." "If the official had delivered fake imperial orders unintentionally," "he shall be imposed with a fine of two *jia*."[34]

If an official lost the official seals or "Bing Fu" (A vouchers used in ancient times to convey a command or a general), even if the lost ones were found again, in view of the seriousness of his behavior, it was forbidden for him to be exempted from punishment. According to the principle of penalty relief for the elimination of the consequences of crime, he would still be punished according to the original conviction.

For the officials who did not perform their duties well but who had spent all day seeking for their own profits, they should be exiled according to *Fa Lv Da Wen* (*Legal Questions and Answers*).

The officials would be sentenced to severe penalties for the crime of "Tong Qian" (the crime of taking bribes by bending the law), "even if an official only accepts one *qian* of bribery, he shall punished by 'Qing' (to tattoo on the face) and 'Cheng Dan' (the punishment of men building cities)." If a person had helped to hide the bribery without reporting to officials, even if "the money has been returned to its owner," he would still be punished when his crime was discovered. In accordance with the provisions of the law, the officials who took charge of the storage of grain must prevent the irrelevant personnel from living in the barn and should keep close watch at night. When they closed the gate, they should extinguish the fire or smoke nearby. If anyone had violated the above rules and caused the loss and damage of grain, or

---

[34]"Xing Shu Lv" (The Law of Executing the Commands) in *Qin Jian* (*The Bamboo Writing Slips in Qin Dynasty*).

fire, the officials in charge would be punished with severe penalties. Besides, the senior "Se Fu" (a minor official in the county) and "Cheng" (the assistant of county magistrate) would also be held responsible. If the granary leaked or if rain dropped in, which had resulted in moldy and rotten grain, or if the grain had become inedible because of inappropriate management, the officials involved would be punished. If the loss was less than 100 *dan*, "Se Fu" (a minor official in the county) would be scolded; if it was more than 100 *dan* and less than 1000 *dan*, "Se Fu" (a minor official in the county) would be imposed with a fine of one *jia*, and if more than 1000 *dan*, two *jia*. At the same time, "Se Fu" (a minor official in the county) and all the officials should share their responsibilities in the compensation of the losses. If there were one or two rat holes, the official in charge would be reprimanded; if there were three or more rat holes, the official would be imposed with a fine of one *dun*; if the grain leaked out of the barn because of loose doors, the official would be imposed with a fine of one *jia*; if stored leather was bitten by insects, "Se Fu" (a minor official in the county) who was in charge would be imposed with a fine of one *jia* and the "Ling" (magistrate) and "Cheng" (the assistant of county magistrate) would be sentenced to a fine of one *dun*.

If the officials of "Xian" (county) and "Jun" (shire) had used cattle for driving carts, but more than one third of the cattle (with the total number exceeding ten) or more than three (of the total number below ten) died in one year, "Tu" (an ancient official), "Ling" (magistrate) and "Cheng" (the assistant of county magistrate) who were in charge or who were responsible for feeding cattle would be found guilty. Because "cattle were used for ploughing in the state of Qin,"[35] they were strictly protected for the development of agriculture.

In addition, it was forbidden for the officials to borrow official property without permission; otherwise, they would be punished. And the officials should compensate for the damages of the official property, if an official in charge of the public property had taken the advantage of his position and seek for personal gains, he would be demoted; if an official was punished by paying a certain sum of money to the government to atone for his crime, but he failed to do so within the year, or did not pay in accordance with the law after its due time, he should be punished all the same according to the law.

The above duty-related crimes stipulated in *Qin Lv* (*Qin Code*) had concretized the idea that "a wise monarch manages his officials," which had brought about a more strict and rigorous management of officials: "in the national capital and local authorities, all the officials appear respectful, upright, loyal and trustful...,"[36] which was very significant not only for the prosperity of the state of Qin, but also for the efficient functioning of the state machine and the unification of six other states.

As tax and corvée were the basic condition for the existence and development of a country, Marx once said, "tax is the source of life of bureaucracy, military troops,

---

[35]"Zhao Ce" (The Strategies of the State of Zhao) in *Zhan Guo Ce* (*Stratagems of the Warring States*).
[36]"Qiang Guo" (On Building a Prosperous Country) in *Xun Zi* (*Xun Zi*).

priests, and royal court. So to sum it up, it is the source of the whole administrative organization."[37] Therefore, the crimes concerning the evasion of tax or corvée accounted for a large part in *Qin Lv* (*Qin Code*).

In Qin Dynasty, there were several kinds of tax collected by the state, including "Tian Fu" (land tax), "Hu Fu" (household tax), and "Kou Fu" (poll tax). Dong Zhongshu in the Han Dynasty once said, "in Qin Dynasty, the land rent, poll tax, and tax for salt and iron industry were about twenty times higher than those of ancient times."[38]

Tian Fu" (land tax) was collected according to the amount of land, whether it was cultivated or not. It was stipulated in *Tian Lv* (*Statutes on Farming and Forest Protection*) that "tax shall be collected according to the land owned by the landlord, whether cultivated or not, and three *dan* of 'Chu' (grass for feeding animals) and two *dan* of "Gao" (hay) shall be collected for every *qing* (a unit of area, one *qing* is about 6.6667 hectares) of land." Besides, a lot of provisions concerning "crops collected," "crops packed in barns," and so on were recorded in *Cang Lv* (*Statutes on Storage of Forage*) and *Xiao Lv* (*Statutes on the Inspection of the Supplies and Property of State Offices*), which showed that there was a legally prescribed amount of grain to pay for every *qing* of land. If the officials in charge of collecting land tax did not report the tax income, they would be convicted of "the crime of concealing land tax," so would be punished according to the law. In *Tian Fa* (*The Land Law*) inscribed in the bamboo slips unearthed from the tombs of Han Dynasty in Mountain Yi, the punishment for people who paid less land tax than their due amount in the state of Qi was recorded: "Anyone who pays 100 *dou* less will be punished by working for the government for a year; 200 *dou*, for two years; 300 *dou*, will be punished by 'Qing' (to tattoo on the face) and 'Cheng Dan' (the punishment of men building cities)."[39]

"Hu Fu" (household tax) referred to the tax collected per household. During the period of Shang Yang's reform, it was decided that "if there are two men in a household and they do not live separately as two families, the household tax should be doubled."[40] At that time, household tax evasion was convicted as the crime of "Ni Hu." "What is 'Ni Hu'? ...according to *Fa Lv Da Wen* (*Legal Questions and Answers*), it means evading corvée, labor service and household tax as is required by law."

"Kou Fu" (poll tax) meant tax collected per person. It was recorded in "Si Lun Xun" (Instructions of Si Lun) in *Huai Nan Zi* (*Masters from Huainan*) in Han Dynasty that "in the Qin Dynasty...a heavy poll tax was collected and all the

---

[37]*Ma Ke Si En Ge Si Xuan Ji* (*The Selected Works of Marx and Engels*), Vol.1, The People's Publishing House, 1972, p. 697.

[38]"Shi Huo Zhi" (The Records of National Finance and Economy) in *Han Shu* (*The History of Han Dynasty*).

[39]"Yin Que Shan Zhu Shu Shou Fa Shou Ling Deng Shi San Pian" (Thirteen Articles of Bamboo Slips from Mountain Yunque, such as Abiding by the law, Abiding by the Command and so on) in *Wen Wu* (*Cultural relic*), V.4, 1985.

[40]"Shang Jun Lie Zhuan" (The Collected Biographies of Shang Yang) in *Shi Ji* (*The Record of the Grand Historian*).

money was transported into the Emperor's exchequer for personal enjoyment." An annotation was made by Gao: "'Tou Hui' means collecting tax according to the number of people and the tax for ordinary people is very heavy." As "Kou Fu" (poll tax) was collected according to the unit of per head, emigration was forbidden in Qin Dynasty. It was stated in *Fa Lv Da Wen* (*Legal Questions and Answers*) that "the minority groups were forbidden to leave their hometown for the state of Xia." Besides, there were similar rules in *You Shi Lv* (*Laws for Lobbyists*) in *Qin Lv Za Chao* (*Miscellaneous Copies of Decrees of the State of Qin*): "if people whose titles are above 'Shang Zao' (title of nobility) help the inhabitants of Qin to move out of the state or cancel their household registration, they will be punished by 'Gui Xin' (The male criminal was sentenced go up the mountain to cut firewood for sacrificial ceremony) and those lower than 'Gong Shi' (the lowest rank of nobility) will be punished by 'Cheng Dan' (the punishment of men building cities)." It was stated in *Fu Lv* (*Statutes on the Household Registration*) in *Qin Lv Za Chao* (*Miscellaneous Copies of Decrees of the State of Qin*) that if parents had concealed the fact that their children had become adults or had made a false report of their disability, or had been exempted from tax fraudulently without reporting to the government, "Dian" (the people in charge) and the leader of "Wu" (a grassroot unit of five families), sometimes even all the people of "Wu" (a grassroot unit of five families), would be punished. "If the number of servants are concealed or the number of diseased are falsely reported, 'Dian' (the people in charge) and the leader of 'Wu' (a grassroot unit of five families) shall be sentenced to 'Nai' (having the criminal's beard shaven for two years); if the people who are not old enough are exempted from labor service by making false report, they shall be imposed with a fine of two *jia*; if 'Dian' (the people in charge) and the leader of 'Wu' (a grassroot unit of five families) have failed to report this, they shall be imposed with a fine of one *jia* respectively, and the people who live within the 'Wu' (a grassroot unit of five families) shall be imposed with a fine of one *dun*, with all of them moved away to other places.

Qin Dynasty was at the early stage of feudal society, so its super-economic exploitation, which was mainly conducted by corvée labor, was extremely serious. According to "Shi Huo Zhi" (The Records of National Finance and Economy) in *Han Shu* (*The History of Han Dynasty*), "the amount of corvée service in Qin Dynasty was thirty times more than that in ancient times." Many world-famous grand buildings were completed by making a requisition of great amount of corvée service in a short time, so many provisions were made to prevent people from resisting to provide corvée service. It was recorded in *Fa Lv Da Wen* (*Legal Questions and Answers*) that "if people do not report their arrivals in corvée service...they shall be punished by 'Chi' (flogging with light sticks) for fifty strokes;...now A does not report his arrival in 'Wu Jia' (neighborhood organization), so he shall be punished by 'Chi' (flogging with light sticks) for fifty strokes; if he escapes and gets caught within a year, he shall also be punished by 'Chi' (flogging with light sticks). Should the punishment be aggravated? Yes." The so-called "Hui" meant reporting one's arrival in serving corvée; if one had failed to report his arrival, he would be punished by 'Chi' (flogging with light sticks) for fifty strokes; if he escaped and was caught within a year, he would not only be punished but also would be severely punished by 'Chi' (flogging with light sticks). The crime of "Bu Hui" (evading corvée) was the same as "Fu Shi," as was noted in *Fa Lv Da Wen* (*Legal Questions and Answers*), "what is the crime 'Fu Shi'? According to law, if a person should provide obligatory corvée service and the officials in charge (Yao, Li, Dian) have already notified him, but he refuses and intentionally ignores it or even escapes, then it has constituted the crime of 'Fu Shi'."

In *Qin Lv* (*Qin Code*), the crimes such as "Bu Hui," "Fu Shi," and "Fa Yao" (all crimes refer to the evasion of corvée service) reflected both the heavy corvée service and the struggle of the peasants to avoid the heavy corvée service. In addition, in *Yao Lv* (*Statutes on Corvée and Tax*) rules for the punishment of grassroots officials who delayed levying corvée service or failed to provide corvée service on time were also stipulated: "As for corvée service demanded by the court, if the local officials do not take actions, they shall be imposed with a fine of two *jia*; for a delay of three to five days, the official shall be rebuked; six to ten days, fined a *dun*; more than ten days, one *jia*." "If people fail to provide corvée service before deadline, they shall get beheaded according to the law,"[41] which had in fact become the direct cause of the uprising of Chen Sheng and Wu Guang. Moreover, if the project built by peasants collapsed within one year, it had to be repaired by the builders and the time spent would not be included in their service time.

According to "Bian Nian Ji" (The Chronicle) in *Qin Jian* (*The Bamboo Writing Slips in Qin Dynasty*), boys should be registered when they turned seventeen years old, which was called "Fu Ji." "'Fu' means registering, which means that it is the time for them to provide corvée service for the government,"[42] and they should not be exempted from providing corvée service until they were after sixty years old. Even the disabled people had to do some corvée service. In *Fa Lv Da Wen* (*Legal Questions and Answers*), it was recorded that "if the disabled people who act as guards of the local government have escaped and are captured later, should they get the same punishment as that for those ordinary guards? The answer is yes, and they should be handled in the same way," which indicated that even the disabled people were also required to provide the corvée service of guarding the local government. If anyone had concealed the "grown-up boy" who was between fifteen and twenty, or had given false report about his age, "Li Dian" and "Wu Lao" (both local village officials) would be punished by "Nai" penalty (having the criminal's beard shaven for two years). The people under sixty were called "Bu Dang Lao" (not old yet). If there was any false reporting of one's age or "Li Dian" and "Wu Lao" (both local village officials) had failed to report, the officials would be imposed with a fine of one *jia* and the neighbors living in the same "Wu" (a grassroot unit of five families) would be imposed with a fine of one *dun* per household and be exiled together.[43]

---

[41]"Chen She Shi Jia" (The Family of Chen She) in *Shi Ji* (*The Record of the Grand Historian*).

[42]"Gao Di Ji" (The Record of the First Emperor of Han Dynasty) in *Han Shu* (*The History of Han Dynasty*).

[43]"Fu Lv" (Statutes on the Household Registration) in "Qin Lv Za Chao" (Miscellaneous Copies of Decrees of the State of Qin) in *Qin Jian* (*The Bamboo Writing Slips in Qin Dynasty*).

From this, we can see the severity of the punishment and the range and scope of the people implicated.

As for the peasants serving corvée, they should prepare their own clothes. According to the evidence discovered in the two bamboo slips unearthed from No. 4 tomb in Yunmeng, the people serving corvée had asked their families to mail their clothes to them. Besides, three Chinese characters "urgent" were written in the letter and it was recorded that "they would die" if their families did not deliver the clothes. Obviously, heavy tax, frequent and compulsory corvée labor, and military service had become people's unbearable burden.

To keep the great number of peasants on the land and make them pay heavy land tax and fulfill their obligatory corvée service, severe punishments were enforced in Qin Dynasty for the escaped peasants, slaves and criminals and the people were authorized to have them arrested and punished in addition to the grassroots registration system of "Shi" (a grassroot unit of ten families) and "Wu" (a grassroot unit of five families). Since Shang Yang's reform, it was forbidden for hotels to accept guests who did not have authorized certificates; otherwise, the hotel owners would be punished, so "the hotel owners who failed to check the authorized certificates of guests would be punished."[44] It was recorded in *You Shi Lv* (*Laws for Lobbyists*) that "if a guest do not have certificate, the magistrate of the county where he lives would be imposed with a fine of one *jia*; if the person has lived in the county for one year without certificate, the magistrate shall be punished according to law." Besides security reasons, this rule was made to restrict the activities of the lobbyists.

In addition, if anyone had secretly used the seal of county magistrate, or forged documents and then escaped, he would be punished by "Nai" (having the criminal's beard shaven for two years)[45]; if any official had helped the people to escape from the state of Qin, the officials concerned would be punished; if the prisoner in custody had escaped, the jailer would be found guilty, and on serious occasions, he would be punished the same as the escaped prisoner. Only when the official involved had captured or given clues for the capture of fugitives could his punishment be exempted; if the imprisoned criminal had escaped, his wife and children would be punished by "Ji Mo" (the cancellation of a household registration) and be taken as slaves.

4.1.2.2.3 From summarizing and absorbing the systems of criminal law of Xia, Shang, and Western Zhou Dynasties, some measures of new penalties were created in Qin Dynasty, so a penalty system characterized by stressing criminal laws was formed. However, because it was still right at the beginning of the transition to feudal system, some remnants of the penalties used under the slavery system were retained.

---

[44]"Shang Jun Lie Zhuan" (The Collected Biographies of Shang Yang) in *Shi Ji* (*The Record of the Grand Historian*).

[45]"Fa Lv Da Wen" (Legal Questions and Answers) in *Qin Jian* (*The Bamboo Writing Slips in Qin Dynasty*).

Death Penalty Totally, more than ten kinds of death penalties were recorded in *Qin Jian* (*The Bamboo Writing Slips in Qin Dynasty*) and in other historical documents:
"Lu." It was stated in *Fa Lv Da Wen* (*Legal Questions and Answers*) that "anyone who sing the praise of the enemy to intimidate our own people shall be punished with 'Lu'. What is 'Lu'? It refers to insulting the criminal before he is beheaded." It meant having the person humiliated before putting him to death. Sometimes, the dead body was exposed in public after the criminal was executed. According to annotations in "Jin Yu" (The Historical Records of Jin State) in *Guo Yu* (*The Historical Records of Various States*), "'Lu' means exposing the dead body in the public places. Cheng Jiao had led the army to attack Zhao state but he revolted in Tunliu and failed, as a result, all his men were killed and…their bodies were exposed in the streets and markets."[46]

"Qi Shi" (exposing the executed body publicly at markets). It was mentioned twice in *Fa Lv Da Wen* (*Legal Questions and Answers*). For the first time: "a man in 'Wu Jia' (neighborhood organization) was childless, therefore, he adopted his nephew as his heir, and they lived together. But he kills his nephew without authorization, so he should be punished by 'Qi Shi' (exposing the executed body publicly at markets)"; for the second time, "if two people who are half-brother and sister had commit adultery, how should they be punished? They should be punished by 'Qi Shi' (exposing the executed body publicly at markets)." This penalty can also be found in historical records. For example, in "Qin Shi Huang Ben Ji" (The Biography of Qin Shi Huang) in *Shi Ji* (*The Records of the Grand Historian*), it was stipulated that "anyone who dares to talk about Confucian classics shall be punished by 'Qi Shi' (exposing the executed body publicly at markets)." According to Yan Shi's annotations in "Jing Di Ji" (The Biography of Emperor Jing) in *Han Shu* (*The History of Han Dynasty*), "'Qi Shi' refers to killing the criminal in the street and then abandoning the body there." According to Hu Sansheng's annotation of *Zi Zhi Tong Jian* (*History as a Mirror*), "'Qi Shi' has been prescribed in *Qin Lv* (*Qin Code*), and it refers to the penalty of execution in the street with the body abandoned there," the purpose of which was to intimidate and warn the public.

"Zhe" was another death penalty recorded in *Fa Lv Da Wen* (*Legal Questions and Answers*): "A asked B to kill another person and gave B ten *qian* for this, but B was less than six *chi* (a unit of length, one *chi* is about 1/3 meter) tall (under age), how should A be punished? A should be punished with 'Zhe'." According to *Shuo Wen Jie Zi* (*The Origin of Chinese Characters*), "'Zhe' means 'Gu' (being punished according to ancient customs)." An annotation was given by Zheng who said that "'Zhe' means opening and splitting, so it means breaking apart the criminal's body." As a brutal death penalty, "Zhe" was only applied to serious crimes. Many bodies unearthed in the prison cemetery of Qin Dynasty in the village of Zhaobeihu in Xi'an were not complete with the heads and limbs separated from the bodies, which had further proved the existence of the punishment of "Zhe."

---

[46]"Qin Shi Huang Ben Ji" (The Biography of Qin Shi Huang) in *Shi Ji* (*The Record of the Grand Historian*).

4.1 The Legal System of Qin Dynasty Recorded in *Yun Meng Qin Jian (Amounts...* 185

"Ding Sha" was recorded in *Fa Lv Da Wen* (*Legal Questions and Answers*): "people infected with epidemic disease shall be sentenced to death by 'Ding Sha'. What is 'Ding Sha'? It refers to drowning the patients alive in water, or burying the patients alive, which is something special." Therefore "Ding Sha" referred to throwing a specific object into the water to be drowned, which was first recorded in *Qin Jian* (*The Bamboo Writing Slips in Qin Dynasty*), but it was not recorded in the existing historical records or ancient legal codes.

"She Sha" (killing by archery) was usually applied to convicts sentenced to death. On the right side of the temporal bone of the body unearthed from tombs of Qin Dynasty in Shangjiao county, Lintong, Xi'an, there was an arrow stuck in the bone, so the man was probably killed by the arrow. In Han Dynasty, "She Sha" (killing by archery) was more widely used, and the criminal who had committed the crime of "Bu Xiao" (being unfilial) would be punished by this penalty.

"Yao Zhan" (cutting people in two at the waist). It was stated in *Shi Ming* (*The Origin of the Word Meaning*) that "'Yao Zhan' means cutting people in two at the waist." In Shen Jiaben's "Xing Fa Fen Kao"(Separate Textual Research on Penal Law) in *Li Dai Xing Fa Kao* (*A Textual Research of the Criminal Laws in the Past Dynasties*) (Book 3), "Yao Zhan" was explained in detail: "the criminal lies on the wood and the executor cuts his waist with an ax." According to the laws of Qin Dynasty, "the people who do not report the criminals to the government shall be punished by 'Yao Zhan'." For example, Li Si was punished by "Yao Zhan" after being punished by 'Ju Wu Xing' (a brutal punishment in ancient China), "he was cut in two at the waist in the street of 'Xian Yang'." "Yao Zhan" was rather commonly used in Qin Dynasty.

"Che Lie" (tearing a person asunder with carts) is also called "Huan Xing." It was annotated in *Shi Ming* (*The Origin of the Word Meaning*) that "'Huan' means being dismembered and it refers to splitting the bodies apart." In the period of King Hui of Qin Dynasty, "Shang Yang was killed by 'Che Lie' to warn people not to follow his example."[47] Another example, in the 9th year of the reign of Qin Shi Huang (the first emperor of Qin), Lao Ai was "killed by 'Che Lie' (tearing a person asunder with carts) to warn the public."[48]

"Xiao Shou." "The penalty of hanging the head of the criminal up as a warning to others is called 'Xiao Shou'."[49] It was enforced to show the seriousness of the crime. Gu Yewang was cited in *Qin Hui Yao Bu Ding* (*Supplements to the Collections of Historical Records in Song Dynasty*): "It is a penalty of Qin Dynasty to hang the

---

[47]"Shang Jun Lie Zhuan" (The Collected Biographies of Shang Yang) in *Shi Ji* (*The Record of the Grand Historian*).
[48]"Qin Shi Huang Ben Ji" (The Biography of Qin Shi Huang) in *Shi Ji* (*The Record of the Grand Historian*).
[49]"Xing" (Punishment) (Part 1) in *Tong Dian* (*The General Codes*), Vol. 163.

heads on top of the woods to show the seriousness of crime." In 238 B.C., Lao Ai and his gang of "around twenty people were all killed by 'Xiao Shou'."[50]

"Nang Pu" (the penalty of putting people in a sack and then hitting them to death).[51] This penalty was implemented since Duke Xiao in Qin Dynasty, and there were records of the king of Qin Dynasty killing his two brothers by this method in "Qin Shi Huang Ben Ji" (The Biography of Qin Shi Huang) in *Shi Ji* (*The Records of the Grand Historian*) and *Zheng Yi* (*The Annotation of Confucians' Classics and the Books of History*).

"Zao Dian" was another penalty implemented during Shang Yang's Reform. It was recorded in "Xing Fa Zhi" (The Record of the Criminal Law) in *Han Shu* (*The History of Han Dynasty*) that "Shang Yang was appointed in Qin Dynasty…to increase corporal punishments and death penalties including 'Zao Dian', 'Chou Lei' (the punishment of removing people's ribs) and 'Huo Peng' (the punishment of boil people in cauldrons)." "Zao Dian" was also referred to as "Zao Ding." According to *Shuo Wen Jie Zi* (*The Origin of Chinese Characters*), "'Dian' means 'Ding', namely the top of things."

"Keng" meant burying people alive. In 228 B.C., "when Ying Zheng made himself king of Qin in Han Dan, he killed all the people who used to be the enemies of his mother by burying them all alive."[52]

"Jiao" was a method of executing death penalty by keeping the body complete. "The duke of Ying wanted to attack Zhao, but Wu Anjun deliberately made things difficult for him, therefore when Wu An Jun was seven *li* away from Xianyang, he was killed by 'Jiao'."[53]

"Zu" (killing of the whole clan of a criminal) was the cruelest punishment by which the innocent people were implicated ever since the slavery system. As early as in the 20th year of the Duke Wen of Qin Dynasty, "the punishment of 'Zu' (extermination of the entire family) was implemented." When Shang Yang carried out his reform, he "implemented the punishment of the killing of 'San Yi' (three kinds of family members: parents, brothers and sisters and wife)," and adopted the penalties practiced among the minority groups into the laws of Qin Dynasty. In the 48th year of King Zhao of Qin, Duke of Ying was convicted of the crime of "appointing the incompetent persons" so was "punished by having his 'San Yi' (three kinds of family members: parents, brothers and sisters and wife) killed."[54] In addition, all the people who were included in the penalty of "Zu" (killing of the whole clan of a criminal) were punished by death penalty.

---

[50]"Qin Shi Huang Ben Ji" (The Biography of Qin Shi Huang) in *Shi Ji* (*The Record of the Grand Historian*).

[51]*Zi Zhi Tong Jian* (*History as a Mirror*), Vol. 6, annotated by Hu Sansheng.

[52]"Qin Shi Huang Ben Ji" (The Biography of Qin Shi Huang) in *Shi Ji* (*The Record of the Grand Historian*).

[53]"Qin Ce" (The Strategy of the State of Qin) in *Zhan Guo Ce* (*Strategems of the Warring States*).

[54]"Fan Ju Cai Ze Lie Zhuan" (The Collected Biographies of Fan Ju and Cai Ze) in *Shi Ji* (*The Record of the Grand Historian*).

4.1 The Legal System of Qin Dynasty Recorded in *Yun Meng Qin Jian (Amounts...*

"Rou Xing" meant "cutting the criminals' limbs off and chisel their skin,"[55] so it refers to the punishment of harming the body. Although "Rou Xing" was applied independently in Qin Dynasty, in most cases, it was used together with "Zuo Xing" (imprisonment and labor service), so it had gradually lost its original independence and became a subsidiary punishment to "Zuo Xing" (imprisonment and labor service).

The widespread application of the punishment of "Qing" (to tattoo on the face) was documented in detail not only in the historical documents of Qin Dynasty but also in *Qin Lv* (*Code of Qin*). Among the corporal punishments of Qin Dynasty, "Qing" (to tattoo on the face) was a relatively light penalty and it could be used alone as a principal penalty. For example, Qing Bu "was a civilian during the Qin Dynasty. In his childhood, a guest looked at his face and said: 'before you become a king you will be punished by the penalty of 'Qing.' In his prime of life, he broke the law and was sentenced to 'Qing'."[56] Moreover, "Qing" (to tattoo on the face) could also be applied in combination with other penalties, so it was often used as a supplementary punishment to "Cheng Dan" (the punishment of men building cities). It was recorded in *Fa Lv Da Wen* (*Legal Questions and Answers*) that "people who beat their parents shall be additionally punished by 'Cheng Dan' (the punishment of men building cities) after being punished by 'Qing' (to tattoo on the face)." "Anyone who kills his or her child shall be punished by 'Qing' (to tattoo on the face) and 'Cheng Dan' (the punishment of men building cities)." For some specific crimes, there were special requirements for the positions of the tattooing. According to *Zuo Zhuan* (*The Chronicle of Zuo*), in the 19th year of the Duke of Xiang, "women were usually not subjected to corporal punishments, so even when they were sentenced to be punished by 'Qing', it would not be executed in public." Nevertheless, if women broke the law, they might also be punished with "Qing" (to tattoo on the face). For example, "a woman named A ran away from home and a man named B also left home secretly, and then the two got married. So they should be punished by 'Qing' and 'Cheng Dan Chong' (the punishment of men building cities and women thrashing rice for lifetime)."

"Yi" refers to the penalty of cutting one's nose, which was one of the widely used corporal punishments in Qin Dynasty and which could be applied alone. For example, "Prince Qian broke the law again, so he was punished by 'Yi'."[57] The punishment of "Yi" was mentioned twice in *Qin Jian* (*The Bamboo Writing Slips in Qin Dynasty*), and both were used together with the penalty of "Qing" (to tattoo on the face). A case was recorded in *Fa Lv Da Wen* (*Legal Questions and Answers*): "if theft was committed together by fewer than five people but the money stolen was more than 660 *qian*, the thieves must be punished by 'Qing' (to tattoo on the face),

---

[55]"Wai Pian" (Supplementary Essays) in *Shen Zi* (*Master Shen*).

[56]"Qing Bu Lie Zhuan" (The Collected Biographies of Qing Bu) in *Shi Ji* (*The Record of the Grand Historian*).

[57]"Shang Jun Lie Zhuan" (The Collected Biographies of Shang Yang) in *Shi Ji* (*The Record of the Grand Historian*).

their noses must be cut off and at the same time they must be punished by 'Cheng Dan' (the punishment of men building cities). But if money stolen was more than 220 and less than 660 *qian*, they should be punished by 'Qing' (to tattoo on the face) and 'Cheng Dan' (the punishment of men building cities)." "if a person was supposed to be punished by 'Qing' (to tattoo on the face) and "Cheng Dan" (the punishment of men building cities), but he lied that he had completed the punishment, how to handle this case? He should be punished with 'Qing' (to tattoo on the face) and 'Yi' (to cut down the nose)."

The penalty of cutting off the toes of left and right feet or cutting off the left and right feet was similar to the penalty of "Yue" (to amputate the feet) in Zhou Dynasty. According to "Zhang Er Chen Yu Lie Zhuan" (The Collected biographies of Zhang Er and Chen Yu) in *Shi Ji Shi Ji* (*The Records of the Grand Historian*), Kuai Tong tried to persuade the magistrate of Fanyang, so he said: "The laws of Qin are very severe and cruel. Since you have been the magistrate of Fanyang for about ten years, you have killed countless fathers, orphaned countless children, and cut off countless feet...." According to "Zhao Sheng" (Imperial Edict) in *Yan Tie Lun* (*Debates on Salt and Iron*), "so many feet were cut off in Qin Dynasty that they can fill up many carts," but in *Qin Jian* (*The Bamboo Writing Slips in Qin Dynasty*), there were only the records of cutting off the left foot: "Five people have committed theft together, and if they have stolen more than one *qian*, they shall all have their left foot cut off and be punished by 'Qing' (to tattoo on the face) and 'Cheng Dan' (the punishment of men building cities)." The penalty of cutting off feet was not used frequently and it was only applied to felonies such as "stealing together," which was different from the prevalence of the application of the penalty of "Yue" (to amputate the feet) in the Spring and Autumn period, during which "the shoes for the disabled people whose feet had been cut off were much more expensive than the shoes for the ordinary people" (because of overuse of severe punishment). This is because a lot of labor force is needed in the successive wars and in the large-scale construction projects in Qin Dynasty because the prisoners were the main undertakers of corvée labor.

"Gong" (castration) is the severest and cruelest penalty "next only to death penalty among the corporal punishments." It was recorded in "Qin Shi Huang Ben Ji" (The Biography of Qin Shi Huang) in *Shi Ji* (*The Records of the Grand Historian*) that, "after the penalty of 'Gong' (castration), the criminal needs one hundred days' rest in a dark room to wait for his body to heal, so it is also called 'Ying Gong'." It was recorded in "Lv Bu Wei Lie Zhuan" (The Collected Biographies of Lv Buwei) in *Shi Ji* (*The Records of the Grand Historian*) that Lv Buwei brought Lao Ai to the queen, and "accused Lao Ai of a crime punishable by 'Gong'." In *Fa Lv Da Wen* (*Legal Questions and Answers*), there were also records of the punishment of "Gong." For example, "for the leaders of the subjugated states of the minorities, preferential treatments are prescribed for atonement. If the rank of him is above 'Shang Zao' (title of nobility), and if his crime is about stealing together with others, he can atone for his crime by 'Gui Xin' (The male criminal was sentenced go up the mountain to cut firewood for sacrificial ceremony) and 'Wu Zu' (cutting off the criminal's feet); if he is punished by 'Gong', he can also atone for it by paying ransom." However, whether in the historical documents and codes of Qin Dynasty or *Qin Lv* (*Qin Code*), there were no records of women being punished by this penalty.

As for the combination of corporal punishment and "Zuo Xing" (imprisonment and labor service), apart from the above examples, there were the following punishments: cutting off the left foot with "Qing" (to tattoo on the face) and "Cheng Dan" (the punishment of men building cities); cutting off the left foot with "Cheng Dan" (the punishment of men building cities); "Cheng Dan" (the punishment of men building cities) with criminal punishment; "Gui Xin" (The male criminal was sentenced go up the mountain to cut firewood for sacrificial ceremony) with criminal punishment and "Gui Xin" (The male criminal was sentenced go up the mountain to cut firewood for sacrificial ceremony) with "Wu Zu" (cutting off the criminal's feet) and so on.

As a penalty, "Chi" (flogging with light sticks) had a long history. It was recorded in "Yan Ce" (Strategy of Yan) in *Zhan Guo Ce* (*Stratagems of the Warring States*) that "(a man) had tied his concubine and punished her by 'Chi' (flogging with light sticks)." In "Zheng Lun" (Correcting Wrong Ideas) in *Xun Zi* (*Xun Zi*), there were records like "hitting with a hammer, whipping, and slashing the kneecap." Thus, the penalty was just continued to be used in Qin Dynasty from the earlier time. "Chi" (flogging with light sticks) actually was also one of the corporal punishments, but it was different from "Rou Xing" (corporal punishment) because "Rou Xing" (corporal punishment) mainly referred to "cutting off the criminals' limbs and chiseling their skin." Therefore, "Rou Xing" (corporal punishment) was abolished by King Wen of Han Dynasty and was replaced by "Chi" (flogging with light sticks). There were many regulations about "Chi" (flogging with light sticks), such as "if people serving 'Cheng Dan' (the punishment of men building cities) broke the pottery, iron or wood ware, they shall be punished by "Chi." If the value is one *qian*, he shall be punished by 'Chi' (flogging with light sticks) for ten strokes; more than twenty *qian*, he shall be severely punished by 'Chi' (flogging with light sticks)." It was also stated in *Qin Lv Za Chao* (*Miscellaneous Copies of Decrees of the State of Qin*) that "if the workmanship for 'Cheng Dan' (the punishment of men building cities) was rated inferior, the person involved shall be punished by 'Chi' (flogging with light sticks) for one hundred strokes." Here "Chi" (flogging with light sticks) appeared as a penalty, which had a different meaning from "Chi" in interrogation for confession, namely, "flogging to intimidate" in *Feng Zhen Shi* (*Judicial Principles, Methods and Cases*).

"Zuo Xing" (imprisonment and labor service) refers to "Tu Xing" (penal servitude) called in later ages, which meant imprisoning the criminals for a certain time and forcing them to provide free labor. Since Warring States Period, it had been widely used in civil engineering, so the officials in charge of the projects were also responsible for managing the criminals. In *Qin Lv* (*Qin Code*), several kinds of "Zuo Xing" (imprisonment and labor service) were recorded: "Cheng Dan Chong" (the punishment of men building cities and women thrashing rice for lifetime), "Gui Xin Bai Can" (The male criminal went up the mountain to cut firewood, and the woman criminal was sentenced to choose grains of rice), "Li Chen Qie" ('Li Chen': male servants and 'Li Qie': female servants), "Si Kou" (forcing criminals to serve penal servitude), "Hou" (the punishment of relegating officials to remote border areas to be scouts), and so on. It was classified into different levels according to the variation of the accessory corporal punishments and the difference between "Kun" (having his long hair cut short) and "Nai" (having the criminal's beard shaven for two years).

"Cheng Dan" (the punishment of men building cities) was one of the severest punishments of "Zuo Xing" (imprisonment and labor service), often coupled with corporal punishments, such as "Cheng Dan" (the punishment of men building cities) with the punishment of "Qing" (to tattoo on the face). There were some categories of "Cheng Dan" (the punishment of men building cities) without corporal punishments, such as "Wan Cheng Dan" (the punishment of men building cities without other corporal punishments). It was recorded in *Qin Jian* (*The Bamboo Writing Slips in Qin Dynasty*) that "five people had stolen things worth more than one *qian*, they should have their left feet cut off and then be punished by 'Cheng Dan' (the punishment of men building cities) and 'Qing' (to tattoo on the face)"[58]; "A stole a cow which was six *chi* in height, and after a year, when the cow was measured again, it turned out to be six *chi* and seven *cun*, ... so A should be punished by 'Wan Cheng Dan' (the punishment of men building cities without other corporal punishments)."[59]

"Gui Xin Bai Can" (The male criminal went up the mountain to cut firewood, and the woman criminal was sentenced to choose grains of rice) was a type of "Zuo Xing" (imprisonment and labor service) slightly lighter than "Cheng Dan" (the punishment of men building cities). It was stated in the *You Shi Lv* (*Laws for Lobbyists*) that "anyone who helps people of Qin to leave the country shall be punished by 'Ji Mo' (the cancellation of a household registration); if the person involved is an official above 'Shang Zao' (title of nobility), he shall be punished by 'Gui Xin' (The male criminal went up the mountain to cut firewood)." In the 9th year of King Zheng of Qin Dynasty, after the failure of Lao Ai, "all his followers were punished, and the lightest punishment was 'Gui Xin' (The male criminal was sentenced go up the mountain to cut firewood for sacrificial ceremony)."[60] Moreover, there were various levels of the punishment for 'Gui Xin' in accordance with its combination with other penalties, such as "Nai" (having the criminal's beard shaven for two years) with 'Gui Xin'; "Nai" (having the criminal's beard shaven for two years) with "Gui Xin Wu Zu" (The male criminal was sentenced go up the mountain to cut firewood for sacrificial ceremony and was punished by having his feet cut off) and criminal penalty with "Gui Xin." Therefore, "Gui Xin" was definitely not just limited to the interpretation of fetching wood for the ancestral temples in Han Dynasty. As for "Bai Can" (The woman criminal was sentenced to

---

[58] "Fa Lv Da Wen" (Legal Questions and Answers) in *Qin Jian* (*The Bamboo Writing Slips in Qin Dynasty*).

[59] "Fa Lv Da Wen" (Legal Questions and Answers) in *Qin Jian* (*The Bamboo Writing Slips in Qin Dynasty*).

[60] "Qin Shi Huang Ben Ji" (The Biography of Qin Shi Huang) in *Shi Ji* (*The Record of the Grand Historian*).

choose grains of rice for sacrificial ceremony), relevant records can be found in *Qin Jian* (*The Bamboo Writing Slips in Qin Dynasty*): "those who were sentenced to the punishment of 'Bai Can' (The woman criminal was sentenced to choose grains of rice for sacrificial ceremony) and 'Tu Gong' (labor involved in civil engineering) shall have three *sheng* (a unit of weight, one *sheng* is about one-tenth of *dou*) of rice for meal, while those serving 'Bai Can' (The woman criminal was sentenced to choose grains of rice for sacrificial ceremony) without 'Tu Gong' (labor involved in civil engineering) shall have their meal in accordance with relevant regulations",[61] which indicated that the punishment of "Bai Can" (The woman criminal was sentenced to choose grains of rice for sacrificial ceremony) was not just limited to choosing grains of rice for sacrificial ceremony, as was interpreted by the people in Han Dynasty.

"Li Chen Qie" ('Li Chen': male servants and 'Li Qie': female servants) was a kind of the punishment of "Zuo" (imprisonment and labor service) which was lighter than "Gui Xin Bai Can" (The male criminal went up the mountain to cut firewood, and the woman criminal was sentenced to choose grains of rice), with different names for the same penalty for male and female wrongdoers. In "Xing Fa Zhi" (The Record of the Criminal Law) in *Han Shu* (*The History of Han Dynasty*), annotations were made by Yan Shigu: "Men were 'Li Chen' (male servants) and women were 'Li Qie' (female servants). The slaves like "Li Chen" (male servants) or "Li Qie" (female servants) were criminals who were forced to work in the fields of the government, to serve the labor service in manual workshops, or to do chores in the government. In addition, "Li Chen Qie" could also be applied as a supplementary punishment, such as "being punished by criminal penalties and 'Li Chen' (male servants)," "suffering the penalty of "Nai" (having the criminal's beard shaven for two years) and 'Li Qie' (female servants)" or "being tattooed on the face with slaves as 'Chen Qie' (female servants)." Besides, this punishment was also recorded in *Qin Jian* (*The Bamboo Writing Slips in Qin Dynasty*), for example, it was noted in *Fa Lv Da Wen* that "soldier A stole things…worth 110 *qian*…so he should be punished with 'Nai' (having the criminal's beard shaven for two years) and enslaved as 'Chen' (male servants)." It was also recorded in the book that "a woman who was the wife of 'Chen' (male servants) had a son. After 'Chen' (male servants) died, his wife cheated her son and said that he was not the son of 'Chen' (male servants). How should the woman be punished? She could be punished by serving as 'Li Qie' (female servants)." In Qin Dynasty, "Li Chen Qie" ('Li Chen': male servants and 'Li Qie': female servants) was a kind of the punishment of "Zuo" (imprisonment and labor service) without fixed period.

"Si Kou" (forcing criminals to serve penal servitude), according to *Han Jiu Yi* (*Traditional Rituals of Han Dynasty*), "referred to male criminals working as guards and females as 'Zuo Ru Si Kou' (a punishment similar to 'Si Kou'), both of which would last for two years." The punishment referred to forcing the male criminals to

---

[61] "Cang Lv" (Statutes on Storage of Forage) in "Qin Lv Shi Ba Zhong" (Eighteen Kinds of Laws of Qin Dynasty) in *Qin Jian* (*The Bamboo Writing Slips in Qin Dynasty*).

serve labor service in remote areas and also to work as guards on borderland, as was explained by Shen Jiaben, "'Si' means observing...'Si Kou' (forcing criminals to serve penal servitude) means monitoring and supervising the criminals who guard the borderland, which may be the meaning of 'Si Kou'." However "as to 'Zuo Ru Si Kou' (a punishment similar to 'Si Kou'), we do not know what they do."[62] In *Fa Lv Da Wen* (*Legal Questions and Answers*), it was recorded that "if an official who was sentenced to the penalty of 'Hou' (the punishment of relegating officials to remote border areas to be scouts) and "Nai" (having the criminal's beard shaven for two years) had framed a case against others, how should he be punished? He should be punished by 'Si Kou' (forcing criminals to serve penal servitude) together with the penalty of "Nai" (having the criminal's beard shaven for two years)." It was recorded in "Si Kong Lv" (Statutes on National Projects) in "Qin Lv Shi Ba Zhong" (Eighteen Kinds of Laws of Qin Dynasty) that "'Si Kou' (forcing criminals to serve penal servitude) does not refer to servants or cooks or guards of the government office. If there are orders which are in conflict with these regulations, the official in charge should have them checked." In *Qin Lv* (*Qin Code*), the original punishment of "Cheng Dan Si Kou," "Chong Si Kou," "Xi Cheng Chong Dan" were all changed into "Si Kou" (forcing criminals to serve penal servitude). As far as the term of imprisonment was concerned, it was not reduced and the difference only lay in the categories of labor and the living conditions during the service period.

"Hou" (the punishment of relegating officials to remote border areas to be scouts) was the lightest punishment of "Zuo" (imprisonment and labor service). It was recorded in "Chu Di Zi Lv" (Statutes on the Expulsion of Apprentices) in *Qin Lv Za Chao* (*Miscellaneous Copies of Decrees of the State of Qin*) that "if the registration of 'Di Zi' (disciple) should be cancelled but the official in charge refused to investigate into the matter, then both of them should be sentenced to 'Nai' (having the criminal's beard shaven for two years) and 'Hou' (the punishment of relegating officials to remote border areas to be scouts)." It was recorded in *Fa Lv Da Wen* (*Legal Questions and Answers*) that "if an official who was sentenced to the penalty of 'Hou' (the punishment of relegating officials to remote border areas to be scouts) and 'Nai' (having the criminal's beard shaven for two years) had framed a case against others, how should he be punished? He should be punished by 'Si Kou' (forcing criminals to serve penal servitude) together with the penalty of 'Nai' (having the criminal's beard shaven for two years)." The punishment of "Nai" (having the criminal's beard shaven for two years) and 'Hou' referred to the punishment of relegating officials to remote border areas to serve as "Chi Hou" (ancient scouts).

It can be inferred from the previous passages that the number of the punishment of "Zuo" (imprisonment and labor service) in Qin Dynasty was increased greatly, which had shown the urgent need for labor force at that time. Therefore, the penalties

---

[62](Qing Dynasty) Shen Jiaben, "Si Kou" (The Minister of Justice) in "Xing Fa Fen Kao" (Separate Textual Research on Penal Law) in *Li Dai Xing Fa Kao* (*A Textual Research of the Criminal Laws in the Past Dynasties*).

of "Tu" (imprisonment) and "Chong Jun" (to be forced to join the army) in later generations were an evolution and development of the punishment of "Zuo" (imprisonment and labor service) in Qin Dynasty.

Although the penalty of "Tu Xing" (penal servitude) was mentioned more than 100 times *Qin Jian* (*The Bamboo Writing Slips in Qin Dynasty*), there were no specific rules about the term. This indicated that the system of the punishment of "Zuo" (imprisonment and labor service) was still not complete and it was not until in Han Dynasty that the term of "Tu Xing" (penal servitude) was adopted. Zhang Fei (Jin Dynasty) stated in *Zhu Lv Biao* (*Table of Annotations for Codes*) that "the punishment of 'Tu' (imprisonment) may not be more than six years and 'Qiu' (putting under arrest) may not be more than five years. So the total term of penalty is not more than eleven years."[63] Based on the records in *Qin Jian* (*The Bamboo Writing Slips in Qin Dynasty*), "Xing Fa Zhi" (The Record of the Criminal Law) in *Han Shu* (*The History of Han Dynasty*) and *Han Jiu Yi* (*Traditional Rituals of Han Dynasty*), it can be inferred that the general terms of the punishments of "Zuo" (imprisonment and labor service) in Qin Dynasty are as follows: "Cheng Dan" (the punishment of men building cities), five to six years; "Gui Xin Bai Can" (The male criminal went up the mountain to cut firewood, and the woman criminal was sentenced to choose grains of rice), four years; "Li Chen Qie" ('Li Chen': male servants and 'Li Qie': female servants), three years; "Si Kou" (forcing criminals to serve penal servitude), two years and "Hou" (the punishment of relegating officials to remote border areas to be scouts), one year.

In Qin Dynasty, there were not only different types of penalties for different categories of "Tu Xing" (penal servitude), but also different clothing, management and instruments for torture for the criminals, which had shown the different levels of penalties. The criminals could give up their titles, guard in borderland, or even atone for their crimes by finding someone else to replace them. Certainly, the chance of remission was a good opportunity for them to be exempted from criminal punishment. For example, King of Zhao Xiang had offered amnesties for seven times, so the criminals were made resettled in the newly occupied territories.

The punishment of "Kun" (having the criminal's long hair cut short), "Nai" (having the criminal's beard shaven for two years), and "Wan Xing" (forced labor). The punishment of "Kun"(having the criminal's long hair cut short) originated from Zhou Dynasty, so if anyone in the royal family had committed crimes punishable by "Gong Xing" (castration), he would be punished by "Kun"(having the criminal's long hair cut short) instead to have his long hair cut short with generally the length of two *cun*. According to *Shuo Wen Jie Zi* (*The Origin of Chinese Characters*), "'Kun' (having the criminal's long hair cut short) means having the hair cut." If "Kun" (having the criminal's long hair cut short) was said to be a substitute penalty for the royal nobilities in Zhou Dynasty, its nature had been changed in Qin Dynasty. It was recorded in *Fa Lv Da Wen* (*Legal Questions and Answers*) that "anyone who had committed unauthorized killing, or had maltreated

---

[63]"Xing Fa Zhi" (The Record of Criminal Law) in *Jin Shu* (*The History of Jin Dynasty*).

his stepchild or had had his stepchild's hair cut, he would be so punished." This penalty was usually used as a supplementary punishment. Zheng Xuan wrote in *Li Ji Zhu Shu* (*Annotation for Book of Rites*) that "'Nai' (having the criminal's beard shaven for two years) refers to cutting the beard off...in ancient age, criminals were punished by having their beard cut off, which is called 'Nai' (having the criminal's beard shaven for two years)." According to the annotation in "Lian Po Lin Xiang Ru Lie Zhuan" (The Collected Biographies of Lian Po and Lin Xiangru) in *Shi Ji* (*The Records of the Grand Historian*) by quoting the laws of Han Dynasty, "it refers to 'Nai' (having the criminal's beard shaven for two years) to keep the hair intact." The punishment of "Nai" meant keeping the criminal's hair intact by only shaving his beard, so it was also called "Wan Xing." In *Qin Lv* (*Qin Code*), "Nai" (having the criminal's beard shaven for two years) was often used as the principal penalty. For instance, it was recorded in *Qin Lv Za Chao* (*Miscellaneous Copies of Decrees of the State of Qin*) that "in hunting, if one army was dispatched but it was falsely reported as two, the people would be punished by 'Nai' (having the criminal's beard shaven for two years)." Besides, it was also used as supplementary punishment, such as "Nai" (having the criminal's beard shaven for two years) with "Li Chen" (punished as male servants), "Nai" (having the criminal's beard shaven for two years) with "Hou" (the punishment of relegating officials to remote border areas to be scouts) and "Nai" (having the criminal's beard shaven for two years) with "Wan Cheng Dan" (the punishment of men building cities without other corporal punishments). So "Nai" (having the criminal's beard shaven for two years) had lost its original meaning of humiliation and it meant having the offenders imprisoned to serve a certain period of labor service.

"Qian Xing" (the penalty of banishing the criminals to do forced labor in remote areas) was similar to "Liu Xing" (exile) in the later dynasties, but it was with some distinctive differences. As for the penalty of "Qian" (the penalty of banishing the criminals to do forced labor in remote areas), sometimes, not only the offender himself, his family members were also executed. As for the level of punishment, it was more lenient than "Cheng Dan" (the punishment of men building cities), but the penalty of "Liu" (exile) in later generations was a much severe penalty only next to death penalty. Moreover, occasionally "Qian Xing" (the penalty of banishing the criminals to do forced labor in remote areas) might be widely applied as a political measure rather than as a kind of penalty. A case in point was in 239 B. C., "Duke of Chang'an rebelled and died in Tunliu..., so all his people were punished with the penalty of 'Qian' (the penalty of banishing the criminals to do forced labor in remote areas) and were forced to move to Lintiao."[64] However, it was more than a kind of penalty, as was illustrated in the statement that, "being exempted from death penalty but forced to serve the penalty of 'Liu' (exile)." For example, in the 9th year of Qin Shi Huang (the first emperor of Qin), all the followers of Lao Ai were punished and "more than 4000 families were deprived of their titles and were forced to move to

---

[64]"Qin Shi Huang Ben Ji" (The Biography of Qin Shi Huang) in *Shi Ji* (*The Record of the Grand Historian*).

Sichuan province."⁶⁵ According to Ru Chun's annotation in "Gao Di Ji" (The Record of the First Emperor of Han Dynasty) in *Han Shu* (*The History of Han Dynasty*), "the offenders should be forced to move to Sichuan province according to the laws of Qin Dynasty." It was recorded in "Fu Lv" (Statutes on the Household Registration) in *Qin Lv Za Chao* (*Miscellaneous Copies of Decrees of the State of Qin*) that "as for the people who are not old enough or too old, if the crime of frauds or deceit are committed in this regard...every family of the whole 'Wu' (a grassroot unit of five families) would be imposed a fine of one *dun* and all of them would be moved to other areas."

"Zi Fa" (The Law on Atonement). "Zi" (atoning for the punishment), according to *Yu Pian* (*The Chapter on Jade*), referred to "property and goods." According to *Shuo Wen Jie Zi* (*The Origin of Chinese Characters*), "'Zi' (atoning for the punishment) refers to the self-redemption for the minor offenses by using money." Therefore, "Zi Fa" (The Law on Atonement) was a kind of economic sanction to atone for the punishment by using money. In *Qin Lv* (*Qin Code*), the regulations about "Zi Fa" (The Law on the Atonement) were both rigorous and extensive. Thus, the offenders were forced to pay a certain amount of fine to the country to achieve the aim of punishing crimes.

One category of "Zi Fa" (The Law on the Atonement) included "Zi Jia" (atoning for the punishment by paying *jia*), "Zi Dun" (atoning for the punishment by paying *dun*) or "Zi Bu" (atoning for the punishment by paying cloth). For example, it was recorded in *Xiao Lv* (*Statutes on the Inspection of the Supplies and Property of State Offices*) that "if the scale (instrument for measuring weight) is not accurate, which had led to an error of more than 16 *liang* (a unit of weight, one *liang* is equal to 50 grams), "Guan Se Fu" (a minor official in the county) shall be imposed with a fine of one *jia*; if the error is more than eight *liang* but less than sixteen *liang*, the fine shall be one *dun*." It was recorded in *Qin Lv Za Chao* (*Miscellaneous Copies of Decrees of the State of Qin*) that "if anyone has hurt the horses of the emperor's cart and if the scratch of the skin is one *cun* long, he will be punished by a fine of one *dun*; two *cun* long, two *dun*; more than two *cun*, the fine will be one *jia*." According to *Fa Lv Da Wen* (*Legal Questions and Answers*), "if foreigners fight with the citizens of Qin state by using weapons like knives and sticks or if they hit the Qin people with fists, the foreigners shall be punished by paying a certain amount of cloth as a fine or compensation. And the cloth should be expropriated by the authority." The offenders who were required to pay the fine could serve labor service for the atonement or pay some fine and serve the sentence of "Cheng Dan" (the punishment of men building cities). As for the latter penalty, "Qian" (clamps) would be put around the offender's neck and chains be put around his ankles. As far as the historical development of instruments of torture is concerned, "Gu" (hand shackle) was often used in Shang Dynasty, while "Zhi" (foot shackle) and "Gu" (hand shackle) were simultaneously used in West Zhou Dynasty. When it came to Qin Dynasty, "Gu" (hand shackle) was

---

⁶⁵"Qin Shi Huang Ben Ji" (The Biography of Qin Shi Huang) in *Shi Ji* (*The Record of the Grand Historian*).

often replaced by "Qian" (clamps), because a large number of civil engineering projects were under construction and many offenders were needed to provide labor service.

Another category of "Zi" (atoning for the punishment) included "Zi Yao" (labor service) and "Zi Shu" (garrisoning the frontiers). It was recorded in *Fa Lv Da Wen* (*Legal Questions and Answers*) that "if someone steals mulberry leaves from others, and the value is less than one *qian*, how should he be punished? He should be punished by thirty days' labor service." According to *Qin Lv Za Chao* (*Miscellaneous Copies of Decrees of the State of Qin*), "if a soldier sells or buys 'Bing' (grain) at the place where he receives it or at the places where he passes by, he should be punished by guarding borders for two years." Therefore, it was obvious that "Zi Yao" or "Zi Shu" referred to serving labor service or guarding the frontiers for minor offenses. Atoning for the penalty by paying the fine of *jia* and *dun* was clearly out of the needs of the wars of annexation. Guan Zhong in Qi Dynasty said that "because in Qi Dynasty there lacks soldiers and armor…the offenses of people can be atoned by paying armor and weapons instead,"[66] which was evidently a kind of exploitation in addition to punishment.

According to *Qin Lv* (*Qin Code*), minor negligence or dereliction of duty by government officials, such as rotten grain caused by leakage of rain in the barn, or the damaging of the government utilities, or the guarding of the frontiers without following the law or the employing of the dismissed officials again, could all be punished by "Zi" (atoning for the punishment) instead. The people who could not afford the alternative punishment of "Zi" (atoning for the punishment) or could not repay the debts to the government were allowed to compensate by providing labor service. In *Si Kong Lv* (*Statutes on National Projects*), there are the following records: "The offenders who compensate for their punishment by 'Zi' (atoning for the punishment) or who owe debts to the government will be asked to repay the money on the fixed day and those who cannot afford the money will be required to serve corvée, which account for eight *qian* per day." In "Zhang Lu" (The Office of Execution) in *Zhou Li* (*Rites of the Zhou*), Zheng made the following annotation: "serving penal servitude for three years without doing harm to their bodies." Moreover, about one hundred skeletons and eighteen pieces of file inscriptions were unearthed in Zhaobeihu County in Xi'an, half of which bore the penalty called "Ju Zi," which meant atoning for the crimes or debts by corvée.

From "Wa Wen" (the inscriptions on tiles) in Qin Dynasty, we can also find that the people who served corvée were not just been sent to "Xian" (county) prescribed in *Qin Lv* (*Qin Code*), but to "Jun" (shire) thousands of miles away without the restriction of mileage. For example, the criminals who served corvée in Lishan were all sent from Shandong and "Liu Guo" (six states). As to the age of the offenders of "Ju Zi" (atoning for the crimes or debts by corvée), according to law, the people who should take criminal liability should be six *chi* and five *cun* (male) or six *chi* and two

---

[66]"Qi Yu" (The Historical Records of Qi State) in *Guo Yu* (*The Historical Records of Various States*).

cun (female) tall, or around sixteen years old in other words. But among the one hundred skeletons unearthed in Zhaobeihu County in Xi'an, there were the skeletons of two children between two and six years old and three women between twenty-five and thirty years old, while others were men between twenty and thirty years old. This shows that the rules about the age of criminal liability in *Qin Lv* (*Qin Code*) do not have a binding force in practice.

As is stated above, although the punishment of "Ju Zi" (atoning for the crimes or debts by corvée) and "Cheng Dan Chong" (the punishment of men building cities and women thrashing rice for lifetime) were linked together under certain conditions, for "Cheng Dan Chong" (the punishment of men building cities and women thrashing rice for lifetime) there was not a fixed sentence term, while for the offenders of "Ju Zi" (atoning for the crimes or debts by corvée), except for the time of "going back home to plant, to cultivate and to harvest the crops," they could make "eight *qian* per day or six *qian* per day with meals provided" if they were atoning for their penalty or repaying debts to government by corvée. The term ended when the amount of money earned by them was enough to offset the debt.[67] Therefore, it was evident that there was a fixed sentence term for "Ju Zi" (atoning for the crimes or debts by corvée).

"Shu Xing" (atonement). The system of "Shu Xing" (atonement) was set up in Qin Dynasty by imitating that of Western Zhou Dynasty and it was classified into different levels and divided into different categories, including the atonement for "Nai" (having the criminal's beard shaven for two years), "Qian" (the penalty of banishing the criminals to do forced labor in remote areas), "Qing" (to tattoo on the face), "Gong" (castration) and the atonement for death penalty. According to *Yu Pian* (*The Chapter on Jade*), "Shu" was interpreted as "Zhi," and it refers to paying for atonement."[68] In *Fa Lv Da Wen* (*Legal Questions and Answers*), the following three examples were recorded: first, "those who secretly change the land boundary shall be punished by 'Shu Nai' (to use money to atone for the crime of having the criminal's beard shaven for two years)." Second, "A planned and asked B to steal things. One day, B did go to steal something but before he arrived at the place, he was arrested. So both of them were punished by 'Shu Qing' (to use money to atone for the crime of branding on the face)"; third, "for the leader of a subjugated state, preferential treatments were prescribed for the atonement. If his rank is above 'Shang Zao' (title of nobility) and he has committed the crime of theft together with others, he can atone for the crime of 'Gui Xin' (The male criminal was sentenced go up the mountain to cut firewood for sacrificial ceremony) and 'Wu Zu' (cutting off the criminal's feet); if he is punished by 'Gong' (castration), he is also allowed to atone for it." It was recorded in *Si Kong Lv* (*Statutes on National Projects*) that "if the

---

[67]"Si Kong Lv" (Statutes on National Projects) in "Qin Lv Shi Ba Zhong" (Eighteen Kinds of Laws of Qin Dynasty) in *Qin Jian* (*The Bamboo Writing Slips in Qin Dynasty*).
[68]Zhu Xi (Song Dynasty), "Shun Dian Xiang Xing Shuo" (Comment on Shun Code and Xiang Penalty) in *Zhu Zi Da Quan* (*The Collected Works of Master Zhu*), Vol. 67.

criminal wants to atone for his crime by 'Shu Qing' (to use money to atone for the crime of branding on the face), he should pay eight *qian* per day."

For the punishment of "Shu Xing" (atonement), it was divided into "Jin Shu" (atone for the punishment with money), "Zi Shu" (atone for the punishment with property) and "Yao Shu" (atone for the punishment with corvée). "Jin Shu" (atone for the punishment with money) was applied to people with titles, the members of the royal family or the upper class of minority groups. "Zi Shu" (atone for the punishment with property) and "Yao Shu" (atone for the punishment with corvée) were more widely applied. Since "Jin Shu" (atone for the punishment with money) and "Zi Shu" (atone for the punishment with property) were meaningful only to the wealthy people, the practice had led to the phenomenon that "the rich people can live while the poor people must only die, because penalties are different for the rich and poor and law is not enforced uniformly."[69] One case in point could be found in *Qin Jian* (*The Bamboo Writing Slips in Qin Dynasty*): "'Nei Gong Sun' (members of the royal family) who do not have titles should be sentenced to 'Shu Xing' (atonement). So should they be sentenced to 'Shu Nai' (to use money to atone for the crime of having the criminal's beard shaven for two years) as "Gong Shi" (the lowest rank of nobility)? The answer is yes."[70] In other words, if the members of the royal family without titles should be sentenced to "Shu Xing" (atonement), the sentence could be reduced to "Shu Nai" (to use money to atone for the crime of having the criminal's beard shaven for two years) by referring to the punishment for "Gong Shi" (the lowest rank of nobility). Therefore, we can conclude that whether in slavery or in feudal society, the system of "Shu Xing" (atonement) was set up for the penalty reduction of a small group of people.

"Fei" (deposition), "Sui" (condemn) and "Mian" (removal from office) were the various compensatory penalties applied to officials who had committed minor offenses. "Fei" (deposition) meant exempting one from punishment by depriving him of his post or his royal identity and it was only applied to the officials above a certain rank and the people in the royal family. It was stated in *Qin Lv Za Chao* (*Miscellaneous Copies of Decrees of the State of Qin*) that "if the official has pretended to listen to the court's order,... or has not stood attentively beside the table when listening, he shall be imposed with a fine of two *jia*, be dismissed and never be reemployed." It was also stated in *Fa Lv Da Wen* (*Legal Questions and Answers*) that "if the officials have committed fraud or resorted to deceit, they will be punished by the penalties severer than 'Zi Dun' (the fine of paying shield) and they will never be reemployed." According to *Qin Lv* (*Qin Code*), as long as an official was deposed, he would never be employed again, so "anyone who has employed the

---

[69]"Xiao Wang Zhi Zhuan" (The Biography of Xiao Wangzi) in *Han Shu* (*The History of Han Dynasty*).
[70]"Fa Lv Da Wen" (Legal Questions and Answers) in *Qin Jian* (*The Bamboo Writing Slips in Qin Dynasty*).

deposed officials shall be punished by the fine of two *jia*."[71] So the punishment of "Fei" (deposition) is much severer than "Zi" (atone for the punishment with property) but more lenient than the punishment of "Zuo" (imprisonment and labor service).

According to *Shuo Wen Jie Zi* (*The Origin of Chinese Characters*), "Sui" (condemn) meant "Rang," namely, scolding or reprimanding the officials, which was the most lenient punishment to officials who had committed the offenses lighter than "Zi" (atone for the punishment). Thus, it is equivalent to the punishment of "reprimand" in modern criminal law. According to *Yao Lv* (*Statutes on Corvée and Tax*), "for corvée demanded by the imperial government, if the local officials did not take actions, they would be imposed with a fine of two *jia*; if it is delayed for three to five days, they would be rebuked."

"Mian" meant removal from office. For instance, "if the county officials dare to take those who should join the army as disciples (to help them to escape military service), they shall be imposed with a fine of two *jia* and be dismissed."[72] However, it was allowed for the officials who were punished by "Mian" (the removal from the offices) to be reemployed later and some other similar penalties included "Duo Jue" (the removal of titles of nobility) and "Qi Lao" (to write off the given titles of nobility, merits and accomplishments).

"Shou," also called "Shou Lu" or "Ji Mo," meant having the offenders and their families punished, as was said by Sima Zhen: "His wife and children were taken as 'Shou Lu' to serve as official slaves."[73] It was also recorded in "Shang Jun Lie Zhuan" (The Collected Biographies of Shang Yang) in *Shi Ji* (*The Records of the Grand Historian*) that "according to the laws of Shang Yang, those who fail in trade because of their laziness shall become slaves, so shall their wives and children." It was recorded in "Lv Bu Wei Lie Zhuan" (The Collected Biographies of Lv Buwei) in *Shi Ji* (*The Records of the Grand Historian*) that "all the followers of Lao Ai were punished with their families confiscated by the government," so the method of "taken" in *Qin Lv* (*Qin Code*) had shown the implicated nature of the penalties in Qin Dynasty. In the meanwhile, "those who fail in trade because of their laziness" were "taken" as slaves, which had shown that the policy of "Zhong Nong Yi Shang" (encouraging agriculture and restraining commerce) was promoted forcefully by the government to develop the agriculture-based feudal economy.

In conclusion, from the summarization of the practical experience, the criminal penalty of Qin Dynasty became more systematic and it had reflected the characteristics of the times. As to the implementation of punishment, it had developed from the single kind of penalty to a comprehensive application of different kinds of

---

[71]"Chu Li Lv" (Statutes on the Removal of Officials) in "Qin Lv Za Chao" (Miscellaneous Copies of Decrees of the State of Qin) in *Qin Jian* (*The Bamboo Writing Slips in Qin Dynasty*).

[72]"Chu Li Lv" (Statutes on the Removal of Officials) in "Qin Lv Za Chao" (Miscellaneous Copies of Decrees of the State of Qin) in *Qin Jian* (*The Bamboo Writing Slips in Qin Dynasty*).

[73]"Shang Jun Lie Zhuan" (The Collected Biographies of Shang Yang) in *Shi Ji* (*The Record of the Grand Historian*).

penalties, which had fully shown the development of criminal law and the impact of the doctrine of severe punishment. As to the extensive replacement of corporal punishment which had done great harm to the offenders' bodies by a great varieties of the punishment of "Zuo" (imprisonment and labor service), it had fully shown the emphasis on the value of labor and the progress of legal culture. But sometimes, the punishment of "Zuo" (imprisonment and labor service) was also supplemented by corporal punishments or the penalty of humiliation, which had shown that it was still in its early stage for the enforcement of "Zuo" (imprisonment and labor service). Anyway, the criminal penalty system recorded in *Qin Jian* (*The Bamboo Writing Slips in Qin Dynasty*) not only inherited the basic methods of punishment from slavery society, but also initiated the feudal legal penalty of "Wu Xing" (the five penalties).

4.1.2.2.4 Under the guidance of the legalist ideology, rich experience was accumulated and a set of basic principles about the enforcement of criminal law were formed in Qin Dynasty by the practice of regulating the society and ruling the country through extensive enforcement of the law, which had exerted a great influence on later generations.

In Qin Dynasty, the age for criminal liability was decided by the height of a person. Therefore, when it came to the decision of punishment, there were often such rules in *Qin Lv* (*Qin Code*) as "six *chi*" or "less than six *chi*," so the people "less than six *chi*" did not have criminal liability. According to the annotations of *Zhou Li* (*The Rites of Zhou Dynasty*) by Jia Gongyan, "seven *chi* means twenty years old and six *chi* means fifteen years old." Therefore, if a person's height was six *chi* and five *cun*, he might be sixteen or seventeen years old. One thing needed to be pointed out is that the age for criminal liability refers to the ages of the offenders themselves, and it is not applied to the family members involved in the punishment, which could be proven by a statement of *Qin Jian* (*The Bamboo Writing Slips in Qin Dynasty*): "The child is too young to be separated from his/her mother, so is required to be taken away with her together." When the offender was older than the legal age of criminal liability but shorter than the legal height of six *chi* and seven *cun*, the penalty would be reduced.

"Lian Zuo" (being punished for being related to somebody who committed an offense), also called "Yuan Zuo," "Cong Zuo" and "Sui Zuo," meant that the innocent people in connection with the offender were punished for the offender's crimes. "Nu Lu" in slavery age was the early form of "Lian Zuo" (being punished for being related to somebody who committed an offense). At the time of Shang Yang's reform, to tightly control the residents of Qin state and to crack down on crimes, the punishment of "Lian Zuo" (being punished for being related to somebody who committed an offense) was so widely applied that it became one of the most significant principles of criminal law of Qin state. The punishment was used throughout the whole period without any changes. According to *Han Jian* (*The Bamboo Slips of Han Dynasty*) unearthed in Yin Que Shan in 1972, "Lian Zuo" (being punished for being related to somebody who committed an offense) was also adopted by some states in Warring Period, such as the State of Qi, so it was inherited

4.1 The Legal System of Qin Dynasty Recorded in *Yun Meng Qin Jian* (Amounts...

by later feudal imperial courts and finally became a distinctive symbol of the cruelty of feudal penalty.

In Qin Dynasty, "Lian Zuo" (being punished for being related to somebody who committed an offense) was applied not only to the people who lived together, but also to "Shi Wu" (a basic level organization grouped by five or ten households), to the senior and inferior civil officials, to the military officers and the soldiers, to the recommenders and the recommended, etc.

"Tong Ju Lian Zuo" (the people living together being punished for being related to somebody who committed an offense). "According to *Qin Lv (Qin Code)*, if a person commits a crime, his family members shall also be punished."[74] In was stated in Zhang Yan's collective annotations of "Gao Zu Ben Ji" (Biographic Sketches of Emperor Gaozu) in *Shi Ji* (*The Records of the Grand Historian*) that "according to *Qin Lv (Qin Code)*, if a person commits a crime, his whole family and his neighbors in the same "Wu" (a grassroot unit of five families) shall also be punished." There were many such terms in *Qin Lv (Qin Code)*. For example, "for theft and for some other crimes, the people who live together with the offender shall be punished as well. What is 'Tong Ju' (living together)? A house is considered as a unit of 'Tong Ju', so even the slaves living in this house should also be punished together, but if the slave is the offender, the family would not be punished together with him."[75] This showed that not only the family members but also the slaves would be punished in "Lian Zuo" (being punished for being related to somebody who committed an offense). However, if a slave had committed a crime, his master would not be implicated. The difference of the concept of "Tong Ju" and "Shi Ren" was explained in *Qin Lv (Qin Code)*: "What is 'Tong Ju' and 'Shi Ren'? 'Tong Ju' refers to people with the same mother while 'Shi Ren' refers to the people living in the same family, they shall all be punished together with the offender."[76] However "if a husband commits a crime and his wife reports his offense to the authority, she shall be exempted from punishment." In "Shou Fa" (Observance of the Law) in *Han Jian* (*The Bamboo Slips of Han Dynasty*) unearthed in Yin Que Shan, the criminal provisions concerning "Lian Zuo" (being punished for being related to somebody who committed an offense) for "Tong Ju" (living together) was recorded: "...the soldiers who are absent from duty shall be killed and their parents and wives shall also be punished by the same penalty."[77]

"Lin Wu Lian Zuo" (the neighbors being punished for being related to somebody who committed an offense). In Shang Yang's reform, the residents "were divided

---

[74]"Xiao Wen Ben Ji" (The Biographic Sketches of Emperor Xiaowen) in *Shi Ji* (*The Record of the Grand Historian*), annotated by Ying Shao.

[75]"Fa Lv Da Wen" (Legal Questions and Answers) in *Qin Jian* (*The Bamboo Writing Slips in Qin Dynasty*).

[76]"Fa Lv Da Wen" (Legal Questions and Answers) in *Qin Jian* (*The Bamboo Writing Slips in Qin Dynasty*).

[77]"Yin Que Shan Shu Shu Shou Fa Shou Ling Deng Shi San Pian" (Thirteen Chapters from Yin Que Mountain's Bamboo slips of the Han Dynasty, including Observance of the Law and Personal Order) in *Wen Wu* (*Cultural Relic*), No. 4, 1985.

into 'Shi' (a grassroot unit of ten families) and 'Wu' (a grassroot unit of five families) so that the neighbors shall watch and supervise each other, and if there is any offender living in the same 'Shi' (a grassroot unit of ten families) or 'Wu' (a grassroot unit of five families), everyone will be punished together."[78] According to *Suo Yin* (*Index*) in the annotation of "Shang Jun Lie Zhuan" (The Collected Biographies of Shang Yang) in *Shi Ji* (*The Records of the Grand Historian*), "the people living in the same neighborhood are expected to report each other's offenses to the officials and if one family commit a crime, other nine families are obliged to report; otherwise, they shall all be punished together. For fear of non-compliance, strict restrictions and punishments are stipulated in the law." For the most cases of "Lian Zuo" (being punished for being related to somebody who committed an offense) in *Qin Lv* (*Qin Code*), those involved were mostly "Li Dian" (local village officials) and the neighbors living in the same "Wu" (a grassroot unit of five families). According to the *Fa Lv Da Wen* (*Legal Questions and Answers*), "it is prescribed in the law that (they) shall be dealt with in the same way as the thieves, while according to another provision, the same conviction should be made, all of which means that the people living together with the offender and the 'Dian' (the people in charge) shall all be punished." However, not all neighbors involved were punished by the same penalty as the offenders, which were proved by *Qin Jian* (*The Bamboo Writing Slips in Qin Dynasty*). For example, "if people are too old or too young, they can be exempted from military service responsibility; but if they tell lies about their age, they shall be imposed with a fine of two *jia*; if 'Dian' (the people in charge) and 'Lao' (elder) do not report, they shall be imposed with a fine of one *jia*, while the neighbors in the same 'Wu' (a grassroot unit of five families) and the family shall all be imposed with a fine of one *dun*. Besides, all these people shall be forced to move to other remote areas."[79] Nevertheless, the officials in the government or the people of higher ranks of nobility above "Da Fu" (senior officials in ancient China) were usually not punished for their neighbors' offenses in the same "Wu" (a grassroot unit of five families). According to *Fa Lv Da Wen* (*Legal Questions and Answers*), "are the officials that work in the government going to be punished together with their criminal neighbors in the same 'Wu' (a grassroot unit of five families)? The answer is no."

"Guan Li Zhi Wu Lian Zuo" (being punished for duty-related crimes). Because the legalist idea that "wise rulers administering their officials, rather than their people" was carried out, it was strictly required that officials must be devoted to their duties. According to law, the officials might be punished by "Lian Zuo" (being punished for being related to somebody who committed an offense) for their duty-related crimes. It was stated in *Xiao Lv* (*Statutes on the Inspection of the Supplies and Property of State Offices*) that "if 'Wei Ji' (an accountant just below the head of

---

[78]"Shang Yang Lie Zhuan" (The Collected Biographies of Shang Yang) in *Shi Ji* (*The Record of the Grand Historian*).
[79]"Fu Lv" (Statutes on the Household Registration) in "Qin Lv Za Chao" (Miscellaneous Copies of Laws of Qin) in *Qin Jian* (*The Bamboo Writing Slips in Qin Dynasty*).

4.1 The Legal System of Qin Dynasty Recorded in *Yun Meng Qin Jian* (Amounts...

a county) or any of his colleagues in the county government commits a crime, 'Ling' (magistrate) and 'Cheng' (the assistant of county magistrate) shall also be punished together with the offender." The officials who recommended other incompetent people to official posts would also be punished by "Lian Zuo" (being punished for being related to somebody who committed an offense). It was stated in *Fa Lv Da Wen* (*Legal Questions and Answers*) that "someone recommends a 'Cheng' (the assistant of county magistrate), who later is removed from the office; then he is appointed 'Ling' (magistrate), but later on his predecessor is found guilty. Should 'Ling' (magistrate) be dismissed? The answer is no." All these records corroborate with the relevant contents in *Qin Jian* (*The Bamboo Writing Slips in Qin Dynasty*), but for some duty-related crimes, the offenders' families were not punished by "Lian Zuo" (being punished for being related to somebody who committed an offense). For example, "if a minor official does not perform his duties and just plays some mean tricks instead...he shall be punished with 'Qian' (the penalty of banishing the criminals to do forced labor in remote areas). Is his wife going to be forced to move, too? The answer is no."[80]

The principle of "Lian Zuo" (being punished for being related to somebody who committed an offense) was also applied in the army. According to "Jing Nei" (Within the Territory) in *Shang Jun Shu* (*The Book of Lord Shang*), during wartime, "if one soldier is killed, the other four in the same 'Jun Wu' (a military unit of five soldiers) shall also be killed"; "if the general...fights and dies, the soldiers will be killed."

Even when the criminal himself has died or escaped, those who are involved with him shall still be punished. For example, "a criminal should be punished by 'Qian' (the penalty of banishing the criminals to do forced labor in remote areas)...but he died before starting, so those involved shall still be moved to the designated place."[81] There were also rules according to which the people should be exempted from the punishment of "Lian Zuo" (being punished for being related to somebody who committed an offense). For example, if the neighbors belonging to the same "Wu" (a grassroot unit of five families) were indeed not home when robbery or theft occurred, they could be exempted from the punishment of "Lian Zuo" (being punished for being related to somebody who committed an offense): "A thief broke into A's home and hurt A. A called out for help, but all his neighbors were not home and could not hear him, which had been investigated and proved to be true, then the neighbors would be exempted from punishment."[82] However, if a crime

---

[80]"Fa Lv Da Wen" (Legal Questions and Answers) in *Qin Jian* (*The Bamboo Writing Slips in Qin Dynasty*).

[81]"Fa Lv Da Wen" (Legal Questions and Answers) in *Qin Jian* (*The Bamboo Writing Slips in Qin Dynasty*).

[82]"Fa Lv Da Wen" (Legal Questions and Answers) in *Qin Jian* (*The Bamboo Writing Slips in Qin Dynasty*).

were not discovered until after the criminal's death, his family members would not be punished.[83]

To restrict the privileges of the aristocratic slave owners, the legalists suggested that "penalties should be enforced equally for everyone and the law shows no partiality even to the noble and the powerful," but at the same time, they tried to maintain a new hierarchy of privilege with the king as the supreme authority. In consequence, the criminal principle of "executing different punishments for the same crime" was put forward, which was clearly against the notion that everything should be uniformly settled in accordance with law. The principle referred to making convictions according to the identities of offenders, so the people with noble titles or the officials enjoyed privileges could have their penalties reduced or cancelled. According to *Han Jiu Yi* (*Traditional Rituals of Han Dynasty*), it was stipulated in *Qin Lv* (*Qin Code*) that "if the people with the lowest noble titles have committed crimes, their punishment could be mitigated." According to *Qin Jian* (*The Bamboo Writing Slips in Qin Dynasty*), if people with higher ranks above 'Bao Zi' (title of nobility) were punishable by corporal punishment, it can be changed to 'Zuo' (imprisonment and labor service). Besides, officials and nobilities of different ranks would serve different kinds of 'Zuo' (imprisonment and labor service). For example, "if people whose titles are above 'Shang Zao' (title of nobility) help the inhabitants of Qin state to move out of the country or cancel their household registration, they will be punished by 'Gui Xin' (The male criminal was sentenced go up the mountain to cut firewood for sacrificial ceremony), while those below "Gong Shi" (the lowest rank of nobility) will be punished by 'Cheng Dan' (the punishment of men building cities)." Although there was just one level of difference between "Shang Zao" (title of nobility) and "Gong Shi" (the lowest rank of nobility), if they had committed the same crime, there was a two-year difference for their punishment.

In addition, the people who atoned for the crimes or debts by corvée were also treated discriminately according to their different social status. For example, the people who atoned for crimes by "Cheng Dan" (the punishment of men building cities) had to wear red prison uniforms, wooden instruments of torture, black ropes and shin clamps during the labor service, but the common people below "Gong Shi" (the lowest rank of nobility) were not required to wear the red prison uniforms or instruments of torture. The descendants of officials above "Bao Zi" could serve penal servitude in the government. Moreover, it was forbidden for them to be detained for long or the settlement of their cases to be delayed; otherwise, "'Da Se Fu' (local officials), "Cheng" (the assistant of county magistrate), and "Guan Se Fu" (a minor official in the county) shall all be punished."[84]

---

[83]"Fa Lv Da Wen" (Legal Questions and Answers) in *Qin Jian* (*The Bamboo Writing Slips in Qin Dynasty*).

[84]"Si Kong Lv" (Statutes on National Projects) in "Qin Lv Shi Ba Zhong" (Eighteen Kinds of Laws of Qin Dynasty) in *Qin Jian* (*The Bamboo Writing Slips in Qin Dynasty*).

To distinguish intentional and negligent crimes, "Duan" or "Duan Wei" for intentional was used in *Qin Lv* (*Qin Code*). It was stated in "Hao Ling" (Orders) in *Mo Zi* (*Mo Zi*) that "the people who deliberately set fire shall be punished by 'Che Lie' (tearing a person asunder with carts)." Bi Yuan made an annotation by saying that "it means hurting others deliberately to hurt others by 'Duan' in *Qin Lv* (*Qin Code*)."[85] In *Fa Lv Da Wen* (*Legal Questions and Answers*), it was recorded that "A sues B claiming that B has stolen his cow and hurt A. Now if B does not steal the cow, or hurt A, how to punish A? If A is intentional, he shall be convicted of 'Wu Ren' (lodging a false accusation intentionally); if not, he shall be convicted of 'Gao Bu Shen' (lodging a false accusation unintentionally)." When settling cases, if any official intentionally gave false judgments by bending the law, he would be convicted of "Bu Zhi" (lack of integrity) or "Zong Qiu" (indulgence of offenders). It was stated in *Fa Lv Da Wen* (*Legal Questions and Answers*) that "'Bu Zhi' refers to the circumstance where the judge executes a lenient penalty for a serious crime or executes a severe penalty for a minor offense intentionally. If an offender should be punished but the official lets him off or tries to reduce his penalty by making up facts, it is called 'Zong Qiu' (indulgence of offenders)." Intentional offenders should be punished severely according to the law. For example, the officials who were "not honest in making sentences of 'Zi Dun' (the fine of paying shield)" would be punished by paying a certain amount of fine.

In *Qin Lv* (*Qin Code*), the cases concerning stealing money, cows and clothes, or escaping, avoiding corvée, killing others and fighting with each other were all regarded as intentional crimes, so all of those involved would be held criminally liable. As for negligence, it was termed as "Shi" or "Shi Xing" in *Qin Lv* (*Qin Code*). It was stated in *Fa Lv Da Wen* (*Legal Questions and Answers*) that "solider A stole something which was worth more than 660 at the time of his capture, but the judge had underestimated the stolen goods, and the value of stolen goods was estimated to be 110, and the thief was sentenced to 'Nai' (having the criminal's beard shaven for two years). How should A and the official be punished? A should be punished by 'Qing' (to tattoo on the face) and "Cheng Dan" (the punishment of men building cities), while the official shall be charged with 'Shi Xing' (wrong judgment of a case)." Namely, it referred to the circumstance where the official underestimated the stolen goods so that wrong judgment was made. This was an offense of negligence and the punishment was relatively lenient. For people who should be imposed with a fine of one *dun*, mostly it could be settled by the penalty of "Sui" (condemn). Another example is "She Gong Guan," if a public house was on fire because of negligence, although the public house was burnt down, the person causing the fire would not be asked to pay for the damages of the public property.

The principle of severer punishment. Some cases in point are as follows.

Instigators Should Be Severely Punished In *Fa Lv Da Wen* (*Legal Questions and Answers*) it was recorded that, "A planned and asked B to steal things. One day, B

---

[85] *Shui Hu Di Qin Mu Zhu Jian* (*The Bamboo Slips from the Tombs of Qin in Shui Hudi*), p. 166, Cultural Relics Press, 1978.

did go to steal something but before he arrived at the place, he was arrested. Both of them were punished with 'Shu Qing' (to use money to atone for the punishment of branding on the face)." Because A abetted B, so he was sentenced to the same penalty as that enforced for B. For abetting adolescents, the punishment would be much severer." "A paid B 10 *qian* and asked him to kill someone. If B was not less than six *chi* tall (not coming of age), how should A be punished? A should be punished by 'Zhe' (to open and split, breaking apart the criminal's body)."

Organized Crimes Should Be Severely Punished It was recorded in *Fa Lv Da Wen* (*Legal Questions and Answers*) that, "five people have stolen together and the value is more than one *qian*, they should be punished with their left feet cut off and should be punished by 'Qing' (to tattoo on the face) and 'Cheng Dan' (the punishment of men building cities); if there are fewer than five people and the value of the booty is more than 660 *qian*, they should be punished by 'Qing' (to tattoo on the face) and 'Yi' (to cut down the nose) in addition to 'Cheng Dan' (the punishment of men building cities); if the value of the booty is less than 660 *qian* and more than 220 *qian*, they shall be punished by 'Qing' (to tattoo on the face) and 'Cheng Dan' (the punishment of men building cities)." It can be inferred that if more than five people committed a crime together, although the value of the booty might be as little as one *qian*, their punishment was severer than that for the crime committed by fewer than five people with the booty valued 660 *qian*. This was called "Jia Zui" (aggravated punishment) in *Qin Lv* (*Qin Code*).

Recidivists Should Be Severely Punished It was recorded in *Fa Lv Da Wen* (*Legal Questions and Answers*) that, "A falsely accused someone of stealing things valued 20 *qian*. Before the case settled, A himself stole things worth 100 *qian*, which was discovered later. A should be punished for committing two crimes and fined two *jia* one *dun*." According to the documents of "Yuan Shu" (The Confession) in *Feng Zhen Shi* (*Judicial Principles, Methods and Cases*), relevant records should be noted concerning whether the offender had violated the law before, and those who had would be sentenced to severer punishment.

The Premeditated Crime Should Be Severely Punished It was recorded in *Fa Lv Da Wen* (*Legal Questions and Answers*) that "A and B did not know each other. A went to steal something from C, but just after his arrival, B also came to steal from C. B agreed with A to steal separately without interfering with each other, and finally each of them stole things valued about 400 *qian* and left. However, both of them were caught later. Since they had conspiracy before committing theft, their amount of the booty should be 800 *qian*." Namely, if A and B had planned beforehand, the value of the stolen goods would be the total value of the booty. "If they had not planned in advance, they would have been punished separately according to the amount each of them had stolen." So without premeditation, the offenders would be punished respectively.

The Behaviors That Violated Sacrificial Ceremonies or Ethical Rules Should Be Severely Punished It was recorded in *Fa Lv Da Wen* (*Legal Questions and Answers*) that, "if someone steals the tribute offerings in public rooms before the sacrificial ceremonies are over, he shall be sentenced to 'Nai' (having the criminal's beard shaven for two years) in addition to serving as a 'Li Chen' (male servants) even if the penalty for theft is lighter than 'Zi' (atoning for the punishment)." That was to say, he received a severer penalty for being blasphemous. Another example: "if a person beats his or her grandparents, he or she shall be punished by 'Qing' (to tattoo on the face) and 'Cheng Dan' (the punishment of men building cities)." However, if a person beat other people even with weapons such as sticks and had caused injuries, the usual punishment would be "Zi" (atoning for the punishment) or "Wan Cheng Dan" (the punishment of men building cities without other corporal punishments).

The Voluntary Surrenderor Should Be Punished Leniently Voluntary surrender was called "Zi Chu" or "Zi Gao" in *Qin Lv* (*Qin Code*). It was recorded in *Fa Lv Da Wen* (*Legal Questions and Answers*) that "if a 'Si Kou' (the minister of justice) stole money valued 110 *qian*, but he voluntarily surrendered himself, then how should he be punished? He should be sentenced to 'Nai' (having the criminal's beard shaven for two years) and serving as a 'Li Chen' (male servants) or being imposed with a fine of two *jia*." "If 'Li Chen Qie' ('Li Chen': male servants and 'Li Qie': female servants) ran away while serving penal servitude and surrendered himself before being caught, he would be subject to the punishment by 'Chi' (flogging with light sticks) for fifty strokes and would still be kept in custody until the expiration of term." These two examples both belonged to abated punishments. If the wrongdoers had not surrendered themselves but were arrested by the officials instead, they would have got much severer punishment. According to the legal regulations of Qin Dynasty, the common people who stole 110 *qian* would be punished by 'Nai' (having the criminal's beard shaven for two years) and serving as a 'Li Chen' (male servants). As a criminal, "Si Kou" (the minister of justice) ought to be punished more severely for the same amount of stolen goods, but he got the same penalty as common people just because he had voluntarily surrendered himself.

If the Offender Undertook the Due Consequence of Crime by His Own Effort, He Should Be Punished Leniently For example, if the prisoner escaped, as long as the warden who was in charge of the prison or his relatives and friends had helped to capture the prisoner again, the official could be exempted from punishment.

"Wu Gao Fan Zuo" (Punishments for Those Lodging Wrong Accusations) In *Qin Lv* (*Qin Code*), "Wu Gao" (false accusation) was also called "Wu," "Wu Ren" (lodging a false accusation intentionally), "Gao Bu Shen" (lodging a false accusation unintentionally), and "Gao Dao Jia Zang" (bringing a false charge of theft with exaggerated amount of stolen goods). Although there were differences between these accusations, they should all be criminally liable for lodging malicious or false accusations. "Wu" and "Wu Ren" (lodging a false accusation intentionally) referred to frame others out of thin air, as was recorded in *Fa Lv Da Wen* (*Legal Questions and Answers*), "A sues B claiming that B has stolen his cow and hurt A. Now if B does not steal the cow, nor hurt A, how should A be punished? If A is intentional, he shall be convicted of 'Wu Ren' (lodging a false accusation intentionally); if not, he shall be convicted of 'Gao Bu Shen' (lodging a false accusation unintentionally)." Therefore, "Duan" meant intentional and "Gao Bu Shen" (lodging a false accusation unintentionally) referred to lodging a false accusation without malicious intention, which showed that malicious accusation was clearly distinguished from the unintentional one in *Qin Lv* (*Qin Code*). However, if a false accusation was about the charge of murder, even when there was no malicious intention, the accuser should still be punished for the crime of "Wu Gao" (false accusation). In *Fa Lv Da Wen* (*Legal Questions and Answers*), there were records of some cases in which criminals were punished for the combination of the crimes of "Wu Gao" (false accusation) and other crimes. "A had stolen a sheep but he was not convicted yet, and then he falsely accused another person of stealing a pig." Thus, A was convicted for the two crimes and was punished by "Wan Cheng Dan" (the punishment of men building cities without other corporal punishments). In addition, the behavior of intentionally exaggerated account of theft did not belong to "Gao Bu Shen" (lodging a false accusation unintentionally), but the charge of theft with exaggerated amount of stolen goods, such as "A stole a sheep and B knew about it. But B charged A of stealing a cow intentionally...then this should be a false charge of theft with exaggerated amount of stolen goods."

With regard to "Wu Gao Fan Zuo" (Punishments for Those Lodging Wrong Accusations), there were specific regulations in *Qin Lv* (*Qin Code*): "if a person brings up a false accusation punishable by 'Bi' (death penalty) against someone from the same 'Wu' (a grassroot unit of five families) without solid evidence, then the accuser shall be sentenced to the penalty of 'Bi' (death penalty)." In *Fa Lv Da Wen* (*Legal Questions and Answers*), there were also records about someone falsely accusing other people of "a crime punishable by 'Nai' (having the criminal's beard shaven for two years) and 'Li Chen' (male servants)," for which he himself was sentenced to the same punishment.

The strict implementation of the principle of "Wu Gao Fan Zuo" (Punishments for Those Lodging Wrong Accusations) in Qin Dynasty was closely connected with the historical conditions at the time. Back in the period of Shang Yang's reform, the people who informed against others' crimes could be awarded with the same price as was awarded to the soldiers who had killed the enemies in battles, which had led to the prevalence of indictment. To prevent malicious accusation to avoid causing disorder in society, severe punishments were prescribed for false accusation. Moreover, according to legalism which was held as the ruling ideology, it had always been proposed that "punishments should be enforced according to crimes," and the principle of "Wu Gao Fan Zuo" (Punishments for Those Lodging Wrong Accusations) was an exact reflection of the thought, so it had exerted a far-reaching influence on later generations.

For a defendant with two or more crimes, although charges should be separately lodged, the judgment would be made according to the principle of enforcing punishment according to the severer one. It was stated in *Fa Lv Da Wen* (*Legal Questions and Answers*) that, "if a person fled with the public property and then got arrested, according to the amount of stolen goods, the person should be sentenced for the crime of theft, but the punishment for the crime of theft was lighter than that for escaping, therefore, in light of the principle of making judgment according to the severest crimes, he should be punished for the crime of escaping." In the feudal criminal laws after Tang Dynasty, the rule that "a person with several offenses should be punished in accordance with the severer one" was also inherited from *Qin Lv* (*Qin Code*).

As for the attempted offenses that had been embarked on but did not succeed, they should also be punished, but their punishments were certainly more lenient than those for the accomplished ones.

In *Qin Lv* (*Qin Code*), statutory period of validity for the prosecution of offenders' criminal liability, namely the so-called time limitation, was stipulated. The specific provisions are as follows. It was recorded in *Fa Lv Da Wen* (*Legal Questions and Answers*) that, "A killed a person and it was not discovered until A died of disease and was buried, then A's behavior was reported. Since A indeed killed a person, should A be tried and his families be punished? The case should not be accepted." For another example, the crimes committed before the issuing of amnesty should not be punished: "A stole several hundred *qian* before the general amnesty and had spent them all. He was arrested later...and should not be punished." However, to force officials to remain dedicated to their duties and strictly abide by disciplines and rules, any "Fei Ling" (Failure to Obey Orders) or "Fan Ling" (The Breach of Orders) committed during their services would have to be investigated, even after they were dismissed or transferred to other positions, "should a dismissed or transferred official be prosecuted for "Fei Ling" (Failure to Obey Order) or "Fan Ling" (The Breach of Orders) which they committed while in service or in former positions? Yes." "Ta Zhi" meant holding accountable for criminal liabilities.

The guilty consciences of the criminal should also be investigated. It was stipulated in *Qin Lv* (*Qin Code*) that the presence or absence of a clear criminal knowledge was an important factor in deciding whether to have the accused convicted. It was recorded in *Fa Lv Da Wen* (*Legal Questions and Answers*) that "A stole something valued about 1000 *qian*. B knew this and obtained less than one *qian* from the stolen money. How should B be punished? B should receive the same penalty as A." On the contrary, in another case, "A stole money to buy silk and sent it to B; B then accepted it without knowing A's crime of theft. What should be the penalty for B? B should not be punished." One more relevant case: "One husband stole 1000 *qian* and his wife hid 300 of them. What should be done about the wife? If the wife knew about her husband's crime of theft, she should be punished for the theft of 300 *qian*; if she did not know about this, she would be taken as an official slave for her husband's crime." As the wife was a close family member, if she knew about her husband's crime of theft, she should receive the same penalty as her husband. Although she knew nothing about the theft, she would still be implicated, but her sentence would be more lenient.

To sum up, although still immature and not finalized, the basic principles of the criminal law of Qin Dynasty were not only a product of the new historical conditions, but also a summary of the experience of legal practice of the criminal laws after China's entry into the class society. It had reflected the legal wisdom of the Chinese nation and the achievement in China's legal civilization, so it had not only provided a guidance to the application of the criminal law of Qin Dynasty, but also provided valuable experience for the development of criminal law after the Qin Dynasty.

4.1.2.3 The Civil Laws Beginning to Taking Shape

In "Qin Lv Shi Ba Zhong" (Eighteen Kinds of Laws of Qin Dynasty) in *Shui Hu Di Qin Mu Qin Jian* (*The Bamboo Slips of Qin Dynasty Unearthed in the Tomes of Qin in Shuihudi*), there were many records concerning civil law, and some provisions could also be found in "Fa Lv Da Wen" (Legal Questions and Answers) in *Qin Lv Za Chao* (*Miscellaneous Copies of Decrees of the State of Qin*), which will be illustrated in the following passages:

4.1.2.3.1 The people from the officials of various levels to the land-holding farmers were all statutory subjects of civil rights. According to the records of "Jing Nei" (Within the Territory) in *Shang Jun Shu* (*The Book of Lord Shang*), "the people within the state, whether men or women, all have their registration in the government since their birth and their registration will be cancelled after they died." It meant that all the people who were born in the state of Qin and who had gotten the registration had the legal capacity. The chapter of *Fu Lv* (*Statutes on the Household Registration*) in *Qin Jian* (*The Bamboo Writing Slips in Qin Dynasty*) was about household registration. With the success of Qin state in the war of annexation, the words like "Xin Qin Ren" (New Residents of Qin) began to appear in *Qin Jian* (*The Bamboo Writing Slips in Qin Dynasty*), and they lived in the same "Wu" (a grassroot unit of five families) with the original civil residents of the state of Qin, so were also entitled with legal capacity. However, the criminals and fugitives would be eliminated from the book of registration.

The businessmen, servants, sons-in-law who lived in the homes of the parents of their wives and stepfathers were subjects with limited legal civil capacities. Although they might become rich, their social status would remain very low and their children or they themselves would not be admitted into political circle, as was stated in a saying that, "a person can be rich without enjoying due respect."[86] The person here referred to such people.

The foreigners living in Qin Dynasty and "You Shi" (lobbyists) were subjects to special legal civil capacities. Because of the respect shown to these people in Qin Dynasty, they not only had the same status and rights as the local residents in the aspect of person, property, marriage, and family, but also had the rights to be granted the rank of nobility and official posts because they were protected by law. Shang

---

[86]"Shang Jun Lie Zhuan" (The Collected Biographies of Shang Yang) in *Shi Ji* (*The Record of the Grand Historian*).

Yang, Lv Buwei, Li Si, and some other people all helped to rule the state as foreign guests.

"Li Chen Qie" ('Li Chen': male servants and 'Li Qie': female servants) was transformed from "Guan Nu Bi" (the slave girls and maidservants working in government offices), so it was essentially a kind of "Tu Xing" (penal servitude). People who were sentenced to be "Li Chen Qie" ('Li Chen': male servants and 'Li Qie': female servants) had the obligation to serve military service, and they also had certain rights of property and the freedom of marriage. Moreover, they are not allowed to be killed randomly; therefore, they were subjects with incomplete legal civil capacities.

In addition, there were many household and official servants. They had no personal freedom, no political or property rights nor complete marriage rights, because they existed only as objects for trade or as gifts for people to bequeath, thus they were objects of civil rights.

As for the behavioral competence, according to *Qin Lv* (*Qin Code*), anyone who had reached to fifteen years old and who had been registered had the obligation to serve military service; therefore, he was redeemed as fully capable of civil actions, or with complete behavioral competence. In "Cang Lv" (Statutes on Storage of Forage) and "Fa Lv Da Wen" (Legal Questions and Answers) in *Qin Jian* (*The Bamboo Writing Slips in Qin Dynasty*), proper height of a person was stipulated as the standard for behavior competence. According to *Cang Lv* (*Statutes on Storage of Forage*), "Li Chen (male servants) who were not as tall as six *chi* and five *cun*, and "Li Qie" (female servants) who were not as tall as six *chi* and two *cun*, were all considered as 'Xiao' (youth)." It was stated in *Fa Lv Da Wen* (*Legal Questions and Answers*) that "A was the wife of a man and she ran away from home but later surrendered herself. She had not attained the height of six *chi*, therefore, she was not considered as an adult yet. Should she be punished? If her marriage had been registered by the government, then she should be punished; if not, she should not be punished." Here, the standard for civil behavioral competence and criminal liability is the same: the height. According to Jia Gongyan's annotation of *Zhou Li* (*The Rites of Zhou Dynasty*), "the height of seven *chi* refers to the age of twenty, while six *chi* refers to the age of fifteen." It showed that the height of six *chi* was in fit with the age of "Fu Ji" (registration for men liable for military service). But it needs to be pointed out that a person who was tall enough did meant that he had the full civil legal capacity until after the ceremony of "Guan Li" (a Chinese traditional ceremony for adolescents as a symbol of becoming adults) was held. For those without civil capacity, their legal behaviors were not deemed as valid unless permitted by their guardians and recorded in the government. For the illegal behaviors conducted by people without legal civil capacity, no legal sanctions would be imposed. For example, it was recorded in *Fa Lv Da Wen* (*Legal Questions and Answers*) that, "A is shorter than 6 *chi* and has a horse of his own. If the horse eats one *dan* of someone else's grain and is caught, should A be punished? No, A shall not be punished and does not need to compensate for the loss of the grain."

4.1.2.3.2 The acquisition, change and cancelling of ownership were the core contents of the civil law in Qin Dynasty. An analogy was once made by Shang Yang: "If a rabbit is running, there will be one hundred people running after it. It is not because the rabbit can be divided into one hundred parts, but because the rabbit is not owned by anyone. However, even if there are hundreds of rabbits in the market, nobody dare to take any one of them except the thieves because the ownership was confirmed." This had reflected the importance of deciding the ownership according to law. In Qin Dynasty, the main object of ownership was land, and the state-owned land, which was mainly obtained from political deprivation and war plundering, still accounted for a large proportion. The state-owned land was operated through land tenancy and granting, so the peasants only had the rights to cultivate the land but not its ownership. In *Fa Lv Da Wen* (*Legal Questions and Answers*) it was recorded that, "if the officials who have rented land to farmers secretly without reporting to the state, it is called 'Ni Tian' (concealing the field); but if the land is not rented to the farmers, then the officials would not be charged with the crime."

Besides state-ownership, "the imperial system was changed and "Jing Tian Zhi" (the nine-square system of land ownership) was abolished in Shang Yang's reform so that the land could be traded freely by the people," which had symbolized the establishment of the feudal landlord ownership by which the farmers also got a small amount of land. According to *Fa Lv Da Wen* (*Legal Questions and Answers*), "anyone who secretly moves the boundary label of fields shall be punished by 'Shu Nai' (to use money to atone for the crime of having the criminal's beard shaven for two years)." It was similarly recorded in "Feng Ren" (Official in charge of City Wall and the Border) in "Di Guan" (Land Official) in *Zhou Li* (*The Rites of Zhou Dynasty*) that "the 'Feng' on the land around the capital equals to the land boundary label today." Those who moved the land boundary label without authorization would be sentenced to "Shu Nai" (to use money to atone for the crime of having the criminal's beard shaven for two years), which showed that the private land ownership was legally protected.

In the spring of 1979, two pieces of wood slips containing one hundred and twenty-one Chinese characters were found in an ancient tomb of the Warring States Period in Qingchuan county in Sichuan province, which could serve as an important supplement to *Tian Lv* (*Statutes on Farming and Forest Protection*) in Qin Dynasty. It was recorded in these wood slips that in the 2nd year of Qin Wu Emperor, the prime minister Gan Mao and "Nei Shi" (official in charge of passing and reading the orders from the king) Yan had revised *Tian Lv* (*Statutes on Farming and Forest Protection*) for the state of Shu (now Sichuan province) according to the land system of Qin state to manage and open up the waste land, and it was stipulated that every field with one *bu* (a unit of length, one *bu* is about five *chi*) width and eight *ze* (two hundred and forty *bu*) length would be one *zhen* (land boundary); one *mu* (a unit of area, one *mu* is about 0.0667 hectares) consisted of two *zhen* and one *mo* (footpath) and one hundred *mu* of land consisted of one *qian* (footpath). Both *qian* and *mo* were three *bu* wide. "Feng," as the boundary of land, was four *chi* high. "Lie" was one *chi* high and its base was two *chi* wide. In August, "Feng" and "Lie" were set up to clarify the boundary of different fields and the weeds on *qian* and *mo* were cleaned up; in October, bridges, slope dikes, and roads were repaired, etc.

The evidence of the private ownership of land in Qingchuan wood slips was consistent with the provisions in *Fa Lv Da Wen* (*Legal Questions and Answers*), in which it was recorded that "anyone who secretly moves the land boundary label shall be punished by 'Shu Nai' (to use money to atone for the crime of having the criminal's beard shaven for two years)." The regular maintenance of land boundaries also reflected the protection of feudal land ownership.

In Qin Dynasty, the "pre-empt" principle for personal property was adopted. In "Tian Lv" (Statutes on Farming and Forest Protection) in *Qin Jian* (*The Bamboo Writing Slips in Qin Dynasty*) the people's ownership of the preemptive rights for trees, fish and preys which they had obtained within due time and space was recognized by the government, at the same time, the ownership of derivatives and the rewarded property were also recognized. As land, slaves, gold, and so on were often rewarded by the state and the empire of Qin to those who had devoted themselves to farming, military feat, and reporting of crimes, the people who were rewarded thereby had obtained the legal ownership of the awarded prize and property. The ownership obtained through trade was the most common and most basic, so it was under the protection of law. According to *Qin Lv Za Chao* (*Miscellaneous Copies of Decrees of the State of Qin*), "if a soldier with military merits dies, his title and rewards can be passed onto his sons."

As to the cancelling of ownership, besides the transferring of ownership, the owners' voluntary abandonment and the confiscation of ownership because of crimes, the slave's escaping, the subsistence consumption and the losses caused by fire also meant the loss of ownership.

4.1.2.3.3 During Shang Yang's reform, the private ownership of land was established and the policies of encouraging farming and war were carried out, which had not only rapidly fostered the economic development but also promoted the development of contractual relationship. It was recorded in "Jun Dao" (On the Way of a Lord) in *Xun Zi* (*Xun Zi*) that "when 'Fu Jie' (the two wood slips with the same agreement content on them) of the contractual parties match each other, the people who possess them can be trusted." In "Zhu Dao" (The Way of Ruling the State) in *Han Fei Zi* (*Han Feizi*), it was also stipulated that "'Qi' (contract) should be made after an official has put forward his proposal and 'Fu' (symbol-assumpsit, an authoritative piece of paper to give orders in ancient China) should be made after the transaction has been completed. The matter of reward or punishment would be decided according to whether 'Fu' (symbol-assumpsit, an authoritative piece of paper to give orders in ancient China) and 'Qi' (contract) are consistent or not." It was stated in "Ping Yuan Jun Lie Zhuan" (The Collected Biographies of King Pingyuan) in *Shi Ji* (*The Records of the Grand Historian*) that "if the matter is handled successfully, the person would ask for rewards with the right half of 'Quan' (the bamboo slip of agreement)." It was recorded in *Suo Yin* (*Index*) that "it was said that when Yu Qing successfully obtained fiefdom for king Pingyuan, he came with the right half of 'Quan' (the bamboo slip of agreement) for rewards." All these have fully reflected contractual relationship in the Warring States Period.

In *Qin Jian* (*The Bamboo Writing Slips in Qin Dynasty*), it was quite common to see the debt relationship concerning the contract between the government and the people. The debts caused by tax, fine, damage, loss of public property and the illegal benefit obtained from public offices were called creditor's rights of the nation, which were often forced to be fulfilled by the debtors by coercive means.

The debt caused by contracts between individuals was also a very common form. In *Fa Lv Da Wen* (*Legal Questions and Answers*), it was noted that, "what is 'the harmfulness of a lost 'Quan' (the bamboo slip of agreement)? The loss of the right half of 'Quan' (the bamboo slip of agreement) will render the contract invalid." This not only showed that "Quan" (the bamboo slip of agreement) was a form of debt, but also showed that if the creditor lost his right half "Quan" (the bamboo slip of agreement), namely, the right half of the agreement, the contract would become invalid.

In Qin Dynasty, contracts were required in the transaction of land, slaves, cows, and horses. In "Gao Chen" (Warnings to Officials) in "Feng Zhen Shi" (Judicial Principles, Methods and Cases) in *Qin Jian* (*The Bamboo Writing Slips in Qin Dynasty*), a complete contract for a slave trade was recorded: "A from a 'Wu' (a grassroot unit of five families) tied a male slave and took him to the government, hoping to sell him to the government and to know the official offer for that. After conducting an examination of the slave's identity and health, the government offered according to the market price. A agreed to the offer, so both parties made the deal before the county magistrate. Because there was a market price for slaves, then slave trade must be quite common. Moreover, according to *Fa Lv Da Wen* (*Legal Questions and Answers*), "male slave A asked female slave B to steal her master's cow and then they sold it. Afterwards, they ran away with the money but quickly got caught. How should they be punished? They should be punished by 'Qing' (shameful tattoos on the face) and 'Cheng Dan' (the punishment of men building cities) before being returned to their masters." From this record, we can see a historical fact of cow and horse-trading. The Wu Shiluo who was highly regarded and relied on by Qin Shi Huang (the first emperor of China) was in fact a merchant doing cow and horse business.

In addition to trade contracts, debt contracts were also popular in Qin Dynasty. According to *Qin Jian* (*The Bamboo Writing Slips in Qin Dynasty*), public utilities could be lent to people according to law, including public carts, weapons, farming appliances, etc. To borrow a public instrument, "Qi" (contract) was needed and "Jiu Ke" (a mark) should be made on the instrument. When the instrument was returned, the sign must fit in with the record on the "Qi" (contract); otherwise, the borrower had to compensate for it with money. According to *Jiu Yuan Lv* (*Statutes on Livestock Breeding and Gardening*), "if a person borrowed an old iron instrument from the government and the instrument broke because of the lack of maintenance, he did not need to compensate for the loss." It proved that if the old iron instrument borrowed from the government was broken because of poor quality, the borrower

4.1 The Legal System of Qin Dynasty Recorded in *Yun Meng Qin Jian* (Amounts...

did not need to compensate for it. In civil debt relationship, no hostages could be used as mortgages; otherwise, the parties would be punished. It was stated in *Fa Lv Da Wen* (*Legal Questions and Answers*) that "if a person owes debt, no hostages should be held as mortgages and the parties reaching an agreement on hostages shall be imposed with a fine of two *jia*.' According to the cases settled in the past, a person who forces the other party to agree on hostages shall be punished, while the other party shall not; if the other party agrees to compensate for it by hostages out of his own will, both shall be punished."

As for the debt relationships resulted from torts, if anything was damaged by a tort, the infringer should be required to restore it to the original state; for things that could not be restored to the original state, the infringer should compensate for the loss with something similar or with money. A person who stole money or other property should not only have the stolen goods returned, but also should compensate for the relevant losses. According to *Qin Lv* (*Qin Code*), "anyone who buys other things by selling the stolen goods should have both the booty and the newly-bought goods returned"; if public property was damaged, the loss should be compensated for by the official in charge. In *Xiao Lv* (*Statutes on the Inspection of the Supplies and Property of State Offices*), a rule was made: when the grain in the granary got rotten, "Guan Se Fu (a minor official in the county) and "Rong Li" (official in charge) should be required to compensate for the losses."

As for the fulfillment of debt, if the debtor owed money to the government and could not repay it, he could make compensation for it by serving "Ju Zuo" (labor service). According to *Si Kong Lv* (*Statutes on National Projects*), "the offenders can compensate by 'Zi Shu' (atone for the punishment with property) or will be asked to repay the money on the fixed day. Those who cannot repay the money will be required to serve labor service beginning from the due date, which accounts for eight *qian* per day and which accounts for six *qian* if the person needs food from the government." If the debtor owed money to the government but moved to another county, the original government could transfer the rights to the county government where the debtor moved in and continued to ask him to repay the debt. If the creditor moved to a new county, the government would continue to perform the obligation of urging the debtor to repay the debt.

When an official who was still in office could not repay his debt, part of his salary would be deducted to pay his debt and he did not need to serve "Ju Zuo" (labor service). For example, it was stated in *Jin Bu Lv* (*Statutes on Currency and Property*) that "a little money was deducted from his salary every month to repay the debt instead of making him serve 'Zuo' (imprisonment and labor service)." For those officials who had been removed from office, if they could not repay the debt, they had to be punished by "Zuo" (imprisonment and labor service).

When "Li Chen Qie" ('Li Chen': male servants and 'Li Qie': female servants) could not repay the debt, "their monthly supply of cloth and food will be deducted," but "the amount of deduction should not be more than one third of the whole supply."

As for the termination of debt, it could be exempted by the change or fulfillment of debt, or the agreement of bilateral parties or the death of the debtor.

In *Qin Lv* (*Qin Code*), provisions were also made about debt guaranty. There was property guaranty, which meant that the debtor or the third party provided property to guarantee the performance of debt, or transferred personal property to the creditor or offered real entity as a guarantee. However, in the state of Qin, the most common guarantee was the guaranty by people, namely, a guaranty provided by the person handling the debt or the third party. It was recorded in *Jin Bu Lv* (*Statutes on Currency and Property*) that "if a person borrows a public instrument from the government or has debt unpaid, when the debt is due and when officials go to collect the debt they only find the debtor has died...then 'Guan Se Fu' (a minor official in the county) of the debtor and the official in charge should repay the debt for him." This was clearly a personal guaranty by the official who was in charge of handling the case. In addition, there was joint guarantee, as was illustrated in *Gong Lv* (*Statutes on Handicraft Industry*) that "if a person borrows something from the government, but if he dies when serving labor service in the capital or living in official residence on business, his colleagues or the owner of the place where he stays should serve labor service, or guard the frontier for him."

It can be inferred that according to what was reflected in *Qin Jian* (*The Bamboo Writing Slips in Qin Dynasty*), compared with Western Zhou Dynasty, a much great progress had been made for the law of obligation, and it was more widely applied in social life.

4.1.2.3.4 Qin state was originally a small state in the remote northwest area and its culture was backward compared to that of Central Plain areas, therefore, its marriage system was less influenced by the Confucian ethical doctrines. According to *Qin Jian* (*The Bamboo Writing Slips in Qin Dynasty*), the height of a person was the standard for marriage age and a girl could get married when she was six *chi* and two *cun* tall. Besides, a marriage was not legal unless registered in the government. In *Fa Lv Da Wen* (*Legal Questions and Answers*) it was recorded that, "A was the wife of a man and she ran away from home but later surrendered herself. She had not attained the height of six *chi*, therefore, she was not considered as an adult yet. Should she be punished? If her marriage had been registered by the government, then she should be punished; if not, she should not be punished." Namely, if a girl under age ran away from her husband and their marriage had been registered in the government, she should be punished; if their marriage was not registered, it was invalid, and she would not be punished.

To consolidate the family system based on small-scale peasant economy, in Qin Dynasty, legal marriages were protected and illegal ones were punished. According to *Qin Lv* (*Qin Code*), both the establishment and termination of legal marriage relationship were under the protection of law if it was registered in the government. In *Fa Lv Da Wen* (*Legal Questions and Answers*), it was recorded that, "A was the wife of a man and she ran away from home but later surrendered herself. She had not attained the height of six *chi*, therefore, she was not considered as an adult yet. Should she be punished? If her marriage had been registered by the government, then she should be punished; if not, she should not be punished." Here, "registered by the government" meant that it was once acknowledged by the government, so although the girl was not an adult yet, she should be punished according to the law. However, without the acknowledgement of the marriage by the government, she would not be punished. Another example was that a woman left her husband and ran away, and later she married another man who was also a fugitive. Although two years had passed and she had given birth to a son, she was punished after being caught by the government. The man was sentenced to "Qing" (to tattoo on the face) and "Cheng Dan" (the punishment of men building cities), while the woman was sentenced to "Dan Chong" (the punishment of women thrashing rice for lifetime) to punish the illegal marriage between fugitives.

Marriage relationship was also regulated by "Lian Zuo" (being punished for being related to somebody who committed an offense). Both parties had the rights and obligations to report each other's illegal actions to the government; otherwise, the wife would be punished as well when the husband committed a crime.

The wife's property was generally dominated by the husband, but if the husband was guilty, and his wife had reported it to the government, the wife could keep the slaves, clothes and appliances, and they would not be confiscated by the government. Because of the relatively weak influence of Confucianism, the authority of husband was not so prominent in the family. For example, according to a prescription in *Qin Lv* (*Qin Code*), it was forbidden for the husband to beat his wife, even though his wife was a hellcat, so "if the husband beats his wife with a bamboo strip," he would be punished by "Nai" (having the criminal's beard shaven for two years).

As for the dissolution of marriage, it was required that the husband should go to the government to have it recorded, "if a husband abandoned his wife but did not record it in the government, he should be imposed with a fine of two *jia*." Moreover, the divorced wives "should also register the divorce in the government; otherwise, she would also be imposed with a fine of two *jia*."[87]

During Shang Yang's reform, big families were forced to be divided into smaller ones by law so that a system with a head in each household was initiated. The patriarchal and parental power were integrated, however, in Qin Dynasty, the father still had not the power to "kill the children" or "drive the children away" arbitrarily. If a father killed his child, he would be punished by "Cheng Dan Chong" (the punishment of men building cities and women thrashing rice for lifetime). At the same time, it was also stipulated in *Qin Lv* (Qin Code) that if the parents killed their children, it belonged to the "litigation related to the relationships within the family, so the case would not be accepted by the government." This was clearly a contradiction but it had predicted the development tendency of the patriarchal power. If the children did not show filial obedience, they would be severely punished. In *Fa Lv Da Wen* (*Legal Questions and Answers*) it was stated that, "an old man over sixty years old had accused his son because he did not show filial obedience, so the father required his son to be punished by death penalty." If a son stole his father's property,

---

[87]"Fa Lv Da Wen" (Legal Questions and Answers) in *Qin Jian* (*The Bamboo Writing Slips in Qin Dynasty*).

he would be punished severely, but "if a father stole his son's property, it was not considered as theft."

However, in Qin Dynasty the penalty for the offense of distinguished people by those in a lower social position was more lenient than that after Han Dynasty. For example, the people who beat their grandparents would only be punished by "Qing" (to tattoo on the face) and "Cheng Dan Chong" (the punishment of men building cities and women thrashing rice for lifetime) in the state of Qin, while in later generations this kind of crime was often punished by death penalty, which had reflected the characteristics of the feudal family relationship in the earlier period.

Inheritance included two parts: the inheritance of official positions or titles and the inheritance of property. Since the abolishment of hereditary titles and property in Shang Yang's reform, the system of election and appointment was widely used except for the positions that required special knowledge, such as historians and diviners. In the Warring States Period when fierce wars of annexation continued, to guarantee the victory of wars, the titles of military merits could also be inherited under certain conditions. According to *Jun Jue Lv* (*Statutes on Military Exploit and Official Titles*), if a person fought in wars with military merits but died before he was honored with the award, the title of the dead could be inherited by his prescribed successors, as long as they did not commit crimes more serious than those punishable by "Fei" (cutting off the left or right foot or both feet), "Nai" (having the criminal's beard shaven for two years) and "Qian" (the penalty of banishing the criminals to do forced labor in remote areas).

The inheritance of property included houses, trees, cloth and appliances, livestock, slaves, etc. However, according to *Fen Hu Ling* (*Order to Separate the Family*), "if there are more than two men in a family but they have not lived separately, the tax levied would be doubled."[88] Therefore, the person who was entitled to inherit the property could only be the only son or the youngest son, because the older sons had already been separated to form their own households. Jia Yi in Han Dynasty said, "In Qin Dynasty, if a family was wealthy and the son was strong, the son would usually have his own independent household, while the healthy son from a poor family would get married and live with the bride's family."[89] In addition, credit and debt were inherited by the sons of creditors and debtors respectively. According to *Jin Bu Lv* (*Statutes on Currency and Property*), except the debt borrowed from government in specific situations or the debt concerning the labor service of slaves, the common debt between ordinary people were usually paid by the sons when the father died.

---

[88]"Jian Jun Lie Zhuan" (The Biography of Jian Jun) in *Shi Ji* (*The Record of the Grand Historian*).
[89]"Jia Yi Zhuan" (The Biography of Jia Yi) in *Han Shu* (*The History of Han Dynasty*).

4.1.2.4 The Economic Laws Adjusted According to Different Categories

According to *Qin Jian* (*The Bamboo Writing Slips in Qin Dynasty*), dozens of specific economic regulations were made, such as *Tian Lv* (*Statutes on Farming and Forest Protection*), *Jiu Yuan Lv* (*Statutes on Livestock Breeding and Gardening*), *Niu Yang Ke Lv* (*Statutes on Cows and Sheep Management*), and *Cang Lv* (*Statutes on Storage of Forage*), which were about agriculture, animal husbandry, and grain storage; *Gong Lv* (*Statutes on Handicraft Industry*), *Gong Ren Cheng Lv* (*Statutes on Handicraft Production*), and *Jun Gong Lv* (*Statutes on Controlling Handicraftsmen*), which were about the product specifications, product quality, production quota, and allocation of labor force of the government-run handicrafts; *Guan Shi Lv* (*Statutes on Border Market*), *Shi Jing Lv* (*Market Law*), and *Jin Guan Lv* (*Port Law*), which were about market management, commercial trade, and the operation of salt and iron industries; *Jin Bu Lv* (*Statutes on Currency and Property*), *Xiao Lv* (*Statutes on the Inspection of the Supplies and Property of State Offices*), *Qian Lv* (*Statutes on Currency*), which were about jurisdiction of currency circulation and finance; *Tian Lv* (*Statutes on Farming and Forest Protection*), *Cang Lv* (*Statutes on Storage of Forage*), *Yao Lv* (*Statutes on Corvée and Tax*), *Jun Shu Lv* (*Statutes on Goods Supply*), and *Za Lv* (*Miscellaneous Laws*), which were about tax and corvée.

Economic laws mentioned above covered land, tax, commerce, finance, government finance and the system of weight and measure, which had shown that the rulers of Qin Dynasty had attached great importance to the regulation of economic relations by law. No doubt, it had played a positive role in guaranteeing the public and private production, in managing national fiscal finance and in maintaining the new economic relationship, and it had become an important part of the legal system of Qin Dynasty.

4.1.2.4.1 In Qin Dynasty, the policy of encouraging farming and preparing for war was adopted, so it was emphasized that "the fundamental element for the prosperity of a state is farming and war.[90]" To enhance the state's administration of agriculture, the position of "Da Si Nong" (Minister of National Treasury) was set up in the central government and the official in this department was a member of "Jiu Qing" (the nine high-rank officials in ancient times) with "Da Tian" (official in charge of agriculture) under him to be responsible for specific affairs. "Tian Se Fu" (a minor official in the county in charge of agriculture) was established in regional areas to manage the agricultural affairs, while "Cang Se Fu" (a minor official in the county in charge of grain granary) was responsible for grain granaries, and "Jiu Se Fu" (a minor official in the county in charge of stable) was responsible for managing husbandry. One thing needs to be pointed out is that the laws about the management of agricultural production are quite detailed and elaborated.

---

[90]"Nong Zhan" (On Farming and Warring) in *Shang Jun Shu* (*The Book of Lord Shang*).

Anyone who had been allotted land ("Shou Tian" or obtaining the ownership thereby from the state), whether it was because "he had not cultivated the land or the land just could not be cultivated," he must pay tax to the state according to the area of his fields, and the standard was "three *dan* of 'Chu' and two *dan* of 'Gao' (hay) for every *qing*."[91] The county officials were required to report to the superior officials when natural disasters affected the growth and production of crops; even if the weather was good, the acreage of the flooded land, the condition of the growth of the crops and the quantity of land reclamation should all be reported to the government in time.

A peasant who "had not cultivated his fields" would be punished to be slave as a warning for other people. As for the slaves "who did not do farm work," they would be arrested and sent to the government to be punished.

"Cang Se Fu" was in charge of grain granary, and if there occurred rain leaking, rotten grain or theft because of his neglect of duty, the official in charge would be reprimanded when the loss was not very serious; but if the loss was heavy, he would be imposed with a fine of one to two *jia* or even receive criminal penalty for serious damages. In addition, if the barn door was not well kept or there were three or more mouse holes, the official in charge would also be punished.

To protect the state-owned water and forest resources, "during February in the spring, people should not cut down trees or clean up forests so that rivers won't get clogged. In summer, people should clean up the grass and set fire to burn down the weeds, pick the sprouting plants, or capture little deer, young birds... people are not allowed to kill turtles or fish, or set traps to capture animals. The ban will not be lifted until July. It can only be an exception for seasonal restrictions to make coffins for the unfortunate dead to cut down trees. If houses are near animal habitats, cattle sheds or other forbidden gardens, it is forbidden for people to go hunting by taking the dogs during the season of breeding cubs. Besides, it is forbidden to capture or kill the neighbors' dogs when they enter into the forbidden gardens as long as they do not run after animals, but if they do, they might be killed. In the specially established area, the dogs killed should be turned over to the government and the dogs killed in other forbidden gardens could be eaten by people but the dog skin should be turned over to the government."[92]

A cattle rearing rating system was established to promote livestock production. According to *Jiu Yuan Lv* (*Statutes on Livestock Breeding and Gardening*), cattle rearing competitions were held in January, April, July and October of lunar year; in January, a large-scale assessment would be conducted. For cattle with outstanding performance, "Tian Se Fu" (a minor official in the county in charge of agriculture) would be awarded a jug of wine and ten stripes of dried meat, and the cattle raiser would be exempted from "Geng Yi" (monthly shift labor service). For cattle with

---

[91]"Tian Lv" (Statutes on Farming and Forest Protection) in *Qin Jian* (*The Bamboo Writing Slips in Qin Dynasty*).

[92]"Tian Lv" (Statutes on Farming and Forest Protection) in *Qin Jian* (*The Bamboo Writing Slips in Qin Dynasty*).

poor scores, "Tian Se Fu" (a minor official in the county in charge of agriculture) would be rebuked and the cattle raiser would be punished by serving labor service for more than two months. If the cow was not taken good care of, or the waist of the cow became one *cun* thinner, the person in charge would be punished by "Chi" (flogging with light sticks) for ten strokes; if certain number of cows and horses owned by the government died, then the official in charge would be punished by criminal penalty. In *Niu Yang Ke* (*Statutes on Cows and Sheep Management*), it was stipulated that if six out of ten adult cows did not give birth to calves, "Se Fu" (a minor official in the county) and "Zuo" (assistant) would both be imposed with a fine of one *dun*; if four out of ten ewes did not give birth, "Se Fu" (a minor official in the county) and "Zuo" (assistant) would both be imposed with a fine of one *dun*.

4.1.2.4.2 In Qin Dynasty, the state-owned handicraft workshops provided weapons, household utensils and handicraft products for the daily use of the state and the royal families, therefore, they were subjected to legislative adjustment, including the legitimacy of production, the product specification and quota, the labor distribution, the marketing and currency management, and many other aspects.

As for the production of handicraft products, an imperial order had to be obtained beforehand so that the production was legitimate. For the handicrafts manufactured without authorization, the craftsman and "Cheng" (the assistant of county magistrate) would both be imposed with a fine of two *jia*. As for the construction of government buildings, the official permission should also be obtained, and it was forbidden to be built without authorization. Besides, the process of the project needed to be strictly conducted in accordance with the original plan, and if it were completed ahead of schedule or two days overdue, the officials in charge would be punished according to law.

Moreover, specific production quotas and product specifications were made for the official handicraft workshops. According to *Gong Lv* (*Statutes on Handicraft Industry*), "the size, length and width of the same category of products must be the same" so that the production could be standardized. To ensure the quality of products, a responsibility system for the production and a product inspection and assessment system were established. For example, the names of the relevant government offices and artisans should be engraved on the products so that responsibilities could be undertaken by the producers later, namely, "the items should be engraved with the names of the producers to guarantee the quality." Besides, product rating competition was held annually, and for the products of "Sheng Dian" or the inferior-quality products, the artisans, "Cheng" (the assistant of county magistrate) and "Cao Zhang" (namely: Shang Shu: the minister and "Lang Zhong": head of a subministry department) would be imposed with a fine of one *jia* and one *dun*. According to the examples recorded in *Yun Meng Qin Jian* (*Amounts of Bamboo Writing Slips in Qin Dynasty Excavated in Yunmeng*), for the silk braids that were rated as inferior in three consecutive years, the punishment for the producers would be doubled. In the competition of paint products, if the product was assessed as "Dian" (inferior quality), then "'Se Fu' (a minor official in the county) would be imposed with a fine of one *jia*, and 'Ling' (magistrate), 'Cheng' (the assistant of county magistrate) and 'Zuo' (assistant) would be each be imposed with a fine of one *dun*." "If the paint product was assessed as inferior, 'Se Fu' (a minor official in the county) would be imposed with a fine of two *jia* and dismissed, while 'Ling' (magistrate) and 'Cheng' (the assistant of county magistrate) would be imposed with a fine of one *jia*."[93] Besides, the accuracy of measuring instruments that could affect product specifications was also regulated in details, for example, the error for *dan* should not exceed four thousandths.

According to *Gong Ren Cheng* (*Statutes on Public-owned Handicraft Production*), "for those who were punished by 'Li Chen' (male servants), 'Xia Li' (slaves), 'Cheng Dan' (the punishment of men building cities) who had worked together with 'Gong' (craftsmen) in winter, their work quota was fewer than that in summer, so it was allowed that work quota for two days in summer could be completed in three days in winter. Such regulation of the work quota, which was made in accordance with the different length of days, was undoubtedly reasonable. In addition, it was stipulated that the work quota for two women who did odd jobs was equal to that for one man, and that the work quota for five children above the age of seven was equal to that for a male craftsman. However, for embroidery work, the quota for one woman was equal to that for a male craftsman." According to *Jun Gong Lv* (*Statutes on Controlling Handicraftsmen*), new craftsmen were asked to complete half of the work quota for the skilled craftsmen in the first year, "At the beginning, the new workers shall complete half of the work quota," but in the second year, they "shall complete the same work quotas as the veteran craftsmen."

Except the craftsmen, numerous people working in the state-owned handcraft workshops, including "Xing Tu" (criminals forced to do labor service) and official handmaiden, were deprived of their freedom. Therefore, the laws about the allocation of handicraft labor force were often clearly targeted. For example, according to *Jun Gong Lv* (*Statutes on Controlling Handicraftsmen*), "'Li Chen' (male servants) who is skilled and who can do the work of craftsmen shall not be made to drive a cart or to cook." Therefore, ordinary work was differentiated from the technical one by the law of labor allocation, which had played a positive role in the development of the state-owned handicraft trade in Qin Dynasty.

In Qin Dynasty, despite the policy of "Zhong Nong Yi Shang" (encouraging agriculture and restraining commerce), great progress was evidently made in commodity economy. To protect legitimate commodity exchange and to prohibit illegal trade, a relatively detailed market management law was made. According to *Qin Lv* (*Qin Code*), the heads of "Wu" (a grassroot unit of five families) also acted as town officials, so they were responsible for the inspection and management of the markets. The merchants who were specialized in trade and who wanted to get the rights to live and do business in the cities had to be registered in the government to get city membership. Besides, the price of goods at the market should be clearly marked and according to *Jin Bu Lv* (*Statutes on Currency and Property*), "for trade, the price

---

[93]"Qin Lv Za Chao" (Miscellaneous Copies of Decrees of the State of Qin) in *Qin Jian* (*The Bamboo Slips of the Qin Dynasty*).

must be marked on the goods, but the small items whose price was less than one *qian* did not need to be marked." To prevent the salespersons from obtaining personal gains, it was also stipulated in *Guan Shi Lv* (*Statutes on Border Market*) that people who sold handicrafts for the government should toss the money into "Xiang" (or Pu Man: money box) in the presence of the buyer; otherwise, they would be imposed with a fine of one *jia*.

It was forbidden for the officials and their assistants to sell public properties, to use the public horses and to employ errand boys to engage in commercial activities; otherwise, the offenders would be punished by the penalty of "Qian" (the penalty of banishing the criminals to do forced labor in remote areas).

To ensure the accuracy of the measuring instruments at the market, the instruments must be checked and calibrated at least once a year by the county officials and the officials in charge of the handicraft industry; meanwhile, the error occurrence rate was clearly defined, which had helped to maintain the market credit and order and guaranteed the fair deal. If the measuring standard of *heng shi,* y*ong* (barrel), *dou, ban dan, jun, jin, bandou, can sheng,* and *huang jin heng ying* (*lei*) (all are Chinese ancient weights and measures) was different, the officials in charge of the market would be imposed with a fine of one *jia* or one *dun*.

From the perspective of protecting the national interests of the centralized country, strict policy was adopted in foreign trade by Qin Dynasty, and it was stipulated that foreign trade could only be conducted after certificates were obtained and examined by the government; otherwise, the offenders would be imposed with a fine of one *jia*. At the same time, rewards would be granted to anyone who "has reported the illegal acts" of smuggling pearls and jades to the government. According to *Fa Lv Da Wen* (*Legal Questions and Answers*), anyone who smuggled pearls or jade out of the country and sold them to foreigners should hand them to the government officials if discovered, and the informers should be rewarded accordingly." However, as to how to punish the smugglers, no rules were found.

In addition, currency circulation, which was closely connected with the development of the market, was also regulated by the law. There were three kinds of legitimate currency in the Qin Dynasty: *qian* (copper coins), *jin* (gold), and *bu* (cloth). Gold was valuable, so it was called "Shang Bi" (the superior currency), and the copper coin was called "Xia Bi" (the inferior currency). Cloth, which was used as the things of universal equivalent, must meet the legal specification: "the length of cloth should be 8 *chi* and the width should be two *chi* and five *cun*." The cloth that failed to meet the standard was called "Bu Ru Shi" (not up to the standard), so was not allowed to circulate. Because *qian* and *bu* were legitimate currency, they were not allowed to be rejected by the traders. According to *Jin Bu Lv* (*Statutes on Currency and Property*), the traders at the market were not allowed to "favor *qian* over *bu*, or vice versa," otherwise, they would be punished and the head of "'Lie Wu' (organization of businessman in Qin) who didn't make report to the government" would be punished. To facilitate the circulation of the three legitimate currencies, their exchange rates were also elaborated in *Jin Bu Lv* (*Statutes on Currency and Property*): "eleven *qian* was equal to one *bu*." "The exchange of *qian, jin* or *bu* must be conducted in accordance with the law" and after the government had received the money, "it should be put in 'Ben' (container made of bamboo) for every 1000 *qian* and be stamped with the official seal of 'Cheng' (the assistant of county magistrate); if less than 1000 *qian*, it should also be sealed" to clarify the responsibilities of keeping the money.

In addition, from the regular inspection of the accounts and inventory recorded in *Xiao Lv* (*Statutes on the Inspection of the Supplies and Property of State Offices*), it was easy to infer that preliminary financial auditing already appeared in Qin Dynasty.

In conclusion, the contents of the economic law were quite detailed and the scope of adjustment was very extensive, which showed that the rulers of Qin Dynasty had begun to adjust the economic relationship, to expand the country's fiscal revenue, and to coordinate the economic conflict between the people and the state by employing legal methods. This had helped to boost the development of social economy, as was recorded in history that "the land of Guan Zhong (middle of Shaanxi province) constitutes only one third of the land of the world… but its wealth accounts for as much as six tenths of it."[94]

In the economic law of Qin Dynasty, the guiding principle of the unitary and centralized authoritarianism was reflected, as was illustrated in the fact that there was even a standard for seeds to be sown in each *mu* of land. Thus, the amount of wheat and millet seeds per *mu* should be one *dou* and that for bean seeds should be half a *dou* per *mu*. Moreover, the legalist principle of granting ample rewards and enforcing severe punishments was clearly reflected in the economic law, which had constituted an important means to promote the economy.

In the past, it was thought that the laws of "Hu" (Household), "Xing" (Recruitment), and "Jiu" (Stable) were formulated by the minister Xiao He in Han Dynasty. According to "Xing Fa Zhi" (The Record of the Criminal Law) in *Jin Shu* (*The History of Jin Dynasty*), "the systems of Qin were inherited in Han Dynasty, and the law was made by Xiao He…with three chapters of 'Hu' (Household), 'Xing'(Recruitment) and 'Jiu' (Stable) improved and added (Yi Shi)." However, the discovery of *Yun Meng Qin Jian* (*Amounts of Bamboo Writing Slips in Qin Dynasty Excavated in Yunmeng*) proved that the basic contents of laws concerning "Hu" (Household), "Xing"(Recruitment) and "Jiu" (Stable)" were already mentioned in Qin Dynasty. Xiao He merely improved the contents and made them more systematic. Therefore, it can be seen that the inheritance relationship of the economic laws between Qin and Han Dynasties was accurately summarized by the two words "Yi Shi" (further enrichment and development).

---

[94]"Huo Zhi Lie Zhuan" (The Collected Biographies of Businessmen) in *Shi Ji* (*The Record of the Grand Historian*).

4.1.3 The Judicial System Stressing the Responsibility of Officials

The judiciary institution of Qin state was already quite systematic to some extent in the Warring States Period.

"Ting Wei" (the supreme official in charge of judicature) was the central judicial authority in the Qin Dynasty with its chief official ranked among "Jiu Qing" (the nine high-rank officials in ancient times). "Ting Wei" was responsible for settling the cases of imperial families as well as the difficult and complicated cases transferred from the local authorities. Below "Ting Wei" (the supreme official in charge of judicature), there were the subordinate officials like "Zheng" (director) and "Zuo You Jian" (the chief and deputy officials in charge of supervision), etc., who were responsible for assisting "Ting Wei" (the supreme official in charge of judicature) to handle the specific affairs.

The local judicial organs performed the judicial and administrative functions, with the leader of "Jun" (shire) or "Xian" (county) as the judicial sheriff. In each "Jun" (shire), there was a "Jue Cao Chuan" who acted as the full-time sheriff and "Cheng" was the director of judicial affairs in the county. The leaders of "Jun" (shire) and "Xian" (county) had the rights to hear the common cases in their own areas, while the difficult and important cases had to be transferred to "Ting Wei" (the supreme official in charge of judicature) for settlement. As for the grassroots organization of township, which was under "Xian" (county), "Se Fu" (a minor official in the county) and "You Zhi" (local official) were set up to deal with the private civil disputes, to assist the county sheriff to arrest criminals, and sometimes to accept the cases directly. It was recorded in "Bai Guan Gong Qing Biao" (the Table of Officials of Higher Ranks) in *Han Shu* (*The History of Han Dynasty*) that in the Qin Dynasty, "it is the duties of 'Se Fu' (a minor official in the county) to hear cases and collect tax." Besides, the cases that the township official could not settle should be submitted to "Xian" (county) in time; if they could not be settled by "Xian" (county), they should be submitted to "Jun" (shire); if they could not be settled by "Jun" (shire), they should be submitted to "Ting Wei" (the supreme official in charge of judicature); if they still could not be decided, then they should be submitted to the emperor. Thus, it could be seen that the centralized autocracy of the judicial system was already formed in the state of Qin.

As for the ways of litigation in the state of Qin, first, the litigant or his relatives could file the lawsuit to the county official, which was the so-called "litigant's complaint to the court." This belonged to private prosecution, and it was called "He" (impeachment) in *Qin Jian* (*The Bamboo Writing Slips in Qin Dynasty*). Second, an official could file the lawsuit by himself, which belonged to indictment. In many cases, the grassroots officials were in charge of filing the lawsuits to the county executives.

Since Qin Dynasty, "Gao Jian" (informing the evil-doing) was awarded and the system of "Lian Zuo" (being punished for being related to somebody who committed an offense) was carried out, all the neighbors had the duty to report the crimes to the government, so if they knew the crime but did not report to the government, they would be punished. In "Tun Biao Lv" (Statutes on Guarding the Frontiers) in *Qin Lv Za Chao* (*Miscellaneous Copies of Decrees of the State of Qin*), it was stipulated that if anyone of "Wu" (a grassroot unit of five families) had exaggerated their own military achievements, but if the neighbors did not make report to the government, they would be imposed with "a fine of one *jia*." In "Jian Yuan Shu" (Book of Jian Yuan) in *Feng Zhen Shi* (*Judicial Principles, Methods and Cases*), a case of accusation in the neighborhood was documented, "in a certain 'Li' (basic resident organization consisting of five neighborhoods) of 'Shi Wu' (a basic level organization grouped by five or ten households), A accused a man B and a woman C of adultery. He said that he saw them meet in the day, so he took them to the government." In the state of Qin, the informant was not only rewarded for reporting the crime, he was also permitted to "seize" the criminals and send them to the government.

According to the nature of the crimes and the identities of the litigants, the cases were divided into "official litigation" and "non-official litigation." The cases concerning "murder, injury or theft belonged to official litigation," but "if a master killed his sons or servants or executed the penalty of 'Xing' (punishment) and 'Kun' (having the criminal's long hair cut short), it was non-official litigation"; "if the children had stolen from their parents, or parents killed, hurt or tortured their children, slaves and concubines, it was non-official litigation."[95] Because official litigation was concerned with public offense, it would be accepted; but non-official litigation was concerned with domestic crime, it would not be accepted (Wu Ting). The goal of the division of official and non-official litigation was to crack down on major crimes timely and to maintain the hierarchical relationship of feudal ethics and of the master and slave. However, it was recorded in *Qin Lv* (*Qin Code*) that "the cases of children prosecuting their parents, and male or female servants prosecuting the masters" would not be accepted. Since Han Dynasty, with the establishment of the dominance of Confucianism, it would be considered being "unfilial" for children to sue their parents and it would be considered as "Gan Ming Fan Yi" (violating the feudal ethics) for slaves to sue their masters or wives to sue their husbands, so if the rules were violated, those involved would be punished in accordance with the law.

However, it was allowed for parents to sue their children and for masters to sue their male and female servants. In the four books of "Gao Chen" (Warnings to Officials), "Qing Qie" (Punishing Concubines by "Qing"), "Gao Zi" (Suing Children), "Qian Zi" (Expelling Children) in *Feng Zhen Shi* (*Judicial Principles, Methods and Cases*), it showed that masters could request the government to have his male slaves punished by "Cheng Dan" (the punishment of men building cities) and female slaves by "Qing" (to tattoo on the face) and "Yi" (to cut down the nose) with the excuse that "they were proud and fierce." Fathers could also ask the government to have their sons killed or punished by "Wu Zu" (cutting off the

---

[95]"Fa Lv Da Wen" (Legal Questions and Answers) in *Qin Jian* (*The Bamboo Slips of the Qin Dynasty*).

4.1 The Legal System of Qin Dynasty Recorded in *Yun Meng Qin Jian* (Amounts...

criminal's feet), or have them expelled to the remote areas in Sichuan on the pretext that they were unfilial.

If the accusation were not true, the accuser would be punished severely as a kind of warning for others.

To split the criminal group and crack down on the stubborn criminals, the criminals who turned themselves in could get penalty reduction, as was recorded that "it could help to reduce his penalty if he turned himself in."

For cases which the judicial authorities decided to accept, the local "Li Dian" (local village officials) should not only examine the defendant's name, identity, birthplace, primary crime records and punishments, but also check whether he had been pardoned before or whether he had ever escaped, then he should include them into written reports and submit them to the county judicial authority. After that a "Ling Shi" (assistant officials to the magistrate) sent by "Xian Cheng" (county magistrate) should go to investigate or inquest the parties and make a record of investigation or examination, which was called "Yuan Shu." If it was necessary to implement "Feng Shou" ("Feng" refers to the sealing up of property, while "Shou" refers to the guarding of the family), detailed records should be prepared to be reported to the county.

For the case that had been accepted by the judicial authority, after evidence was collected from the crime scene with investigation, trials would follow, which was also called "Xun Yu" (interrogating the accused).

In a trial, the testimony of the parties was the most important evidence, so in all the trials "the testimony of the parties had to be first listened to and recorded." If the confessions were mutually contradicted, or the crime circumstances were not clearly stated, then the suspect could be repeatedly interrogated and if the suspect changed his confession many times and refused to plead guilty, the torture of "Chi Lue" (beating with bamboo strips) could be applied. However, in Qin Dynasty, torture was not encouraged, and according to "Zhi Yu" (trial of cases) in *Feng Zhen Shi* (*Judicial Principles, Methods and Cases*), "when hearing a case, what was recorded should be based on the defendant's confessions, so it was the best strategy to obtain truthful confession without applying 'Chi Lue' (beating with bamboo strips), it was worst to do so, and it was a failure to intimidate the suspect."

As oral confession was considered as the basis of a trial and torture was not encouraged, more attention was paid to the adjudication methods, so the judges were requested to listen to all parties' presentation patiently, and they were forbidden to conduct interrogations anxiously. The whole process would be recorded in the form of "Yuan Shu" and "whenever a trial or interrogation took place, it should be guaranteed that each party had the opportunity to make statements to fully express themselves. Besides, what they said should be recorded in the books. Even though there might be fraud, the speaker should not immediately scolded. If the situation was still not clarified after the speech, the judge was allowed to question about some doubtful issues." "The cross-examination process should also be recorded if there were still doubtful points, and the interrogation should be continued until the parties had nothing more to confess. Torture could be applied only when the suspect changed his confession repeatedly and refused to plead guilty." "Torture can be conducted according to law if needed, but the following words had to be recorded in 'Yuan Shu': the person changed his confessions many times and did not plead guilty, so he was tortured.[96]

These regulations had reflected the spirit of ruling the country by law in Qin Dynasty, but the principle of "finding traces from what the criminal says" which was formed based on the officials' subjective judgment was stressed first, which was followed by the torture of "Chi Lue" (beating with bamboo strips), so it would inevitably to lead to the malpractice of arbitrary judgment, because it was determined by the nature of feudal trial system.

According to the cases recorded in *Qin Jian* (*The Bamboo Writing Slips in Qin Dynasty*), the judges also paid great attention to the collection of testimonies from witnesses, so the physical evidence in the trial, such as the examination and inspection of the relatives and neighbors of the dead and the examination of the tools used by criminals when committing the crime. They especially attached great importance to on-site inspection and judicial authentication, because a number of cases about "murder," "suicide," "burglary" and "Chu Zi" (the son of a divorced concubine) were recorded in great detail in the form of "Yuan Shu" (The Confession) in *Feng Zhen Shi* (*Judicial Principles, Methods and Cases*). Not only the details about the victims' clothes, injured parts and remains of the perpetrators, etc., but also the surrounding and evidence materials provided by the insiders were all recorded. Besides, a medical appraisal was also conducted on whether the party concerned was suffering from leprosy, which not only showed the law executor's emphasis on evidence, but also his rich experience in judicial practice and the high level reached in physiology and forensic science.

If the defendant lived in another county, the case would be transferred by the local officials in charge of the case to the county to assist in finding out the fact. If someone defaulted on the government's debt and was sentenced to "Zi" (atone for the punishment) or "Shu" (ransom), the documents of the case should also be transferred to that county to have the person arrested: "if a person who owed money to the government, or who was sentenced to 'Zi' (atone for the punishment) or 'Shu' (ransom) had moved to another county, he should continue to pay the debt and to be punished by the county where he moved to."[97] Moreover, the prisoners' property should be sealed up and registered by the government with the assistance of "Li Dian" (local village officials) and the neighbors of the criminal. If the criminal's family needed to be supervised, "Li Dian" (local village officials) and the people in the same "Li" (a basic resident organization consisting of five neighborhoods) were responsible to take turns to have them supervised for later investigation and punishment.

---

[96]"Feng Zhen Shi" (Judicial Principles, Methods and Cases) in *Qin Jian* (*The Bamboo Writing Slips in Qin Dynasty*).

[97]"Jin Bu Lv" (Statutes on Currency and Property) in "Qin Lv Shi Ba Zhong" (Eighteen Kinds of Laws of Qin Dynasty) in *Qin Jian* (*The Bamboo Writing Slips in Qin Dynasty*).

4.1 The Legal System of Qin Dynasty Recorded in *Yun Meng Qin Jian* (Amounts...)

After a sentence was made by a judge, it should be read to the defendant, which was known as "Du Ju" (reading the judgment); if the party disagreed with the sentence, he could request a review, which was called "Qi Ju" (requesting a review). "Qi Ju" (requesting a review) was not limited to the litigant himself, if a defendant was sentenced to more than two years of imprisonment, the family could request "Qi Ju" (requesting a review) on his behalf. It was recorded in *Fa Lv Da Wen* (*Legal Questions and Answers*) that "it could only be accepted after the judgment whether 'Qi Ju' (requesting a review) was required by the litigant himself or his family." Moreover, "Qi Ju" (requesting a review) could only be put forward after the first-instance judgment, but it was an exception "for the old people over seventy years old to accuse their unfilial children": "it is allowed for the old people over seventy years old to accuse their unfilial children to be punished by death penalty. Should the case be settled by 'San Huan' (being accused for three times)? The answer was no, so the defendant was supposed to be arrested instantly for the punishment." Here "San Huan" was similar to "San You" (the three kinds of circumstances for lenient treatment).

The rulers of the state of Qin attached great importance to law enforcement, so the responsibilities of officials in juridical practice were especially emphasized.

First, the government officials were required to be well acquainted with the law. Usually, they were required to copy the laws repeatedly and to be familiar with the laws within the scope of their duties. Moreover, they were also required to check with the judicial officials in the central government every year, which was called "Sui Chou Bi Lv Yu Yu Shi." If the laws and decrees had been abolished, they should not be applied anymore. Thus, "if the officials still applied the laws which were abolished, they should be found guilty." *Qin Lv* (*Qin Code*) should be mainly followed in making verdicts, but "Ting Xing Shi" (judicial precedents) could also be used, namely, the precedents could also be used as the basis of trial. In reality, the practice of settling lawsuits according to judicial precedents increased gradually, so in most cases its efficacy was equaled to *Qin Lv* (*Qin Code*). According to *Fa Lv Da Wen* (*Legal Questions and Answers*), "A accused B of stealing one hundred and ten *qian*, but the court found out that the accused only stole one hundred *qian*. How should the accuser be punished? He should be imposed with a fine of two *jia*. While in line with *Qin Lv* (*Qin Code*), if the accuser had intentionally added extra ten *qian*, he would be imposed with a fine of one *dun*. However, according to judicial precedents, the accuser would be convicted of 'Wu Gao' (false accusation), and he should be imposed with a fine of two *jia*." Under the circumstances of incompleteness of laws, it could not only make up for the deficiency of laws or the limitation of articles, but also improve the efficiency of settling cases by judiciaries to settle the lawsuits according to judicial precedents.

Second, if government officials failed to discover the crimes in his jurisdiction timely, he would be accused of "incompetence"; if he knew the crime but dared not enforce the punishment, he would be considered "corruptive"; if the sentence he made was too lenient or too severe, he would be accused of "Shi Xing" (wrong judgment of a case); if he had intentionally enforced lenient punishments for serious crimes, or vice versa, he would be blamed for "Bu Zhi"(lack of integrity); if he failed to punish those who were guilty, or mitigated the criminal circumstances to deliberately exempt the convicts from punishment, he would be charged with "Zong Qiu" (indulgence of offenders). "Shi Xing" (wrong judgment of a case), "Bu Zhi" (lack of integrity), and "Zong Qiu" (indulgence of offenders) were all regarded as felonies, so the official involved would be punished according to law. It was recorded In *Fa Lv Da Wen* (*Legal Questions and Answers*) that "soldier A committed theft. If the value of the stolen goods were assessed at the time they were found, it would be 110 *qian*, but the official did not have timely assessment. When the stolen goods were assessed at the trial, the value increased to 660 *qian*. Thus, the thief was punished by 'Qing' (to tattoo on the face) and 'Cheng Dan' (the punishment of men building cities). How would A and the official be punished respectively? A should be leniently punished by 'Cheng Li Chen' (to serve penal servitude) after the punishment of 'Nai' (having the criminal's beard shaven for two years), and the official would be punished by 'Shi Xing' (wrong judgment of a case)."

If the local officials could not enforce law effectively or neglected their duties, they would be held accountable by law. For example, if the official "did not know that he had issued false documents," even if he did not committed crime intentionally, he should be imposed with a fine of two *jia*. As for those "Ting Zhang" (police inspector) and warden who were exclusively responsible for arresting robbers and the management of prisons, a severe sentence would be imposed on them if they had violated the law.

Finally, the situation of law enforcement served as an important standard for the assessment of officials. According to *Qin Jian* (*The Bamboo Writing Slips in Qin Dynasty*), it was announced by "Jun Shou" (governor) of Nanjun named Teng in *Yu Shu* (*Official Notice*) that, "all good officials know very well of laws and decrees," but "the bad officials are ignorant of them."

In the state of Qin, prisons were also called "Ling Yu." Because the policy of imposing severe penalties on minor offenses was carried out in Qin Dynasty, "the criminals in prison uniforms crowded the street, and prisons were as busy as markets."[98] Xianyang Prison subordinated to "Ting Wei" (the supreme official in charge of judicature) was built in the capital of the country, and prisons were built in each "Xian" (county). For example, the general Meng Tian "was imprisoned in Yangzhou."[99] Moreover, according to historical records, "Cheng Miao, the prison guard of Qin Dynasty was put in Yunyang prison because he had offended Emperor Qin Shi Huang (the first emperor of Qin)."[100] The occupant of the tomb where *Yun Meng Qin Jian* (*Amounts of Bamboo Writing Slips in Qin Dynasty Excavated in Yunmeng*) was discovered had once served as the guard of Yan prison. Besides, "Du Yu" and "Yu Chuan" were in charge of prisons in "Jun" (shire) and "Xian" (county) respectively.

---

[98]"Xing Fa Zhi" (The Record of the Criminal Law) in *Han Shu* (*The History of Han Dynasty*).
[99]"Li Si Lie Zhuan" (The Biography of Li Si) in *Shi Ji* (*The Record of the Grand Historians*).
[100]Zhang Huaijin (Tang Dynasty), *Shu Duan Lie Zhuan* (*The Collected Biographies of Shu Duan*).

According to the records in *Qin Jian* (*The Bamboo Writing Slips in Qin Dynasty*), the prisoners were closely guarded. "Shu Ren" and "Geng Ren" were responsible for watching and monitoring prisoners. If criminals in prison went out for service, they were forbidden to go to the market or to rest at the market entrance. When walking by markets, the prisoners should pass round it rather than walk straight through it. It was stipulated in *Si Kong Lv* (*Statutes on National Projects*) that "if the criminals punished by 'Cheng Dan Chong' (the punishment of men building cities and women thrashing rice for lifetime) went out to serve the penal servitude, they were forbidden to go to the market or live outside; if the criminal was walking in the market, he should be stopped and turned back. But if the ranks of the criminals were above 'Bao Zi' (title of nobility) or 'Shang Zao' (title of nobility), or if they had been sentenced to atoning for the penalty or atoning for the death penalty by penal labor, or they had served the penal servitude in government offices, they were not supervised. The prisoners should wear red clothes and the torture instruments like shackles and iron chains. If a "Gong Shi" (the lowest rank of nobility) who was at the lowest level of noble ranks was sentenced to penal labor to atone for death penalty or other penalties, he did not have to wear the torture instruments during his labor service.

The prisoners were not allowed to submit a written statement to a higher authority or to lodge a false accusation against others; otherwise, they would be more severely punished. "If the prisoner falsely accused someone of the crime punishable by 'Nai Li Chen' (having the criminal's beard shaven for two years to be a servant), who actually committed the crime punishable by 'Nai Si Kou' (having the criminal's beard shaven for two years to be forced to serve penal servitude), he should be sentenced to 'Nai Li Chen'",[101] namely, he should get the same punishment of which he had falsely accused others.

"Li Chen" (male servants) who served in the government could get two *dan* of grain monthly and "Li Qie" (female servants) could get one *dan* and a half. The amount of grain could be increased according to the labor intensity. For example, the prisoners who served "Cheng Dan" (the punishment of men building cities) to build the walls could get half a *dou* more for breakfast, and one-third *dan* for dinner. The prisoners who were sick could also get some extra food according to his condition, but those who served less than a month would have their food supply reduced.

If the warders broke the law, they would also be punished by law.

4.2 The Legal System of Qin Dynasty After Its Unification

Before its unification, Zheng, the king of Qin Dynasty, adopted the theory of legalism and carried out the policy of ruling the state by law throughout the country to try to develop the feudal economy, to strengthen centralization and to annex the

---

[101]"Fa Lv Da Wen" (Legal Questions and Answers of Law) in *Qin Jian* (*The Bamboo Slips of the Qin Dynasty*).

other six states finally by making use of the authority of law. In this process, he deeply felt the positive effects of promoting "Fa Zhi" (the ruling of law). Therefore, after the unification, he continued to build and consolidate the newly born state with despotism and centralization of authority by implementing this policy. To deal with the new situation that "all other states had become 'Jun' (shire) and 'Xian' (county) after the unification of the whole country," the laws of the other six states were abolished by Emperor Qin Shi Huang (the first emperor of Qin) to "combine the other laws into one." In the meanwhile, he accepted the advice of Li Si and made strict rules on the official interpretation of law. If the civilians wanted to study law, they must learn from the officials. However, being carried away with victory, Emperor Qin Shi Huang (the first emperor of Qin) ceaselessly expanded his autocratic power by breaking the law, made extremely complicated laws, executed harsh penalties, and extorted excessive tax, so he was opposed by the people nationwide, which had led to the perish of regime after his son succeeded the throne. It was eloquently proved by history that although the rulers of Qin had gone with the tide of the times and realized the unification of the country, which was a great event even in world history, however, when "the civilians were endlessly tormented by the military and bureaucratic systems of the rulers led by Qin Shi Huang (the first emperor of Qin),"[102] the regime ended up crumbling like a colossus with clay feet. Although he was with huge military forces and various bureaucratic systems, he were powerless in saving Qin Dynasty.

4.2.1 The State System Reflecting Despotism and the Centralization of State Power

4.2.1.1 The Initiation of the Imperial System

After the unification of Qin Dynasty, Zheng, the emperor of Qin believed that his virtue had encompassed that of "San Huang" (three emperors), and that his contribution had exceeded that of "Wu Di" (five kings), therefore he named himself "The First Emperor." Since then, the title of emperor became a common honorific title to the sovereigns of feudal times. Qin Shi Huang (the first emperor of Qin) had the supreme power, so the state affairs such as administration, legislation, judiciary, the appointment and dismissal of officials, military affairs, tax collection, and significant engineering projects, etc. were all decided by the emperor himself. It was recorded in history book that "all the things in the world, regardless of the important or the trivial matters, were all decided by the emperor himself. Every day the emperor had to read as many as one *dan* of documents, and he could not even get rest because documents

---

[102]"Qin Shi Huang Ben Ji" (The Biography of Qin Shi Huang) in *Shi Ji* (*The Record of the Grand Historian*).

were submitted to him day and night."[103] So imperial power was exclusively dominated by him and the will of the emperor had become the law. Consequently, the emperor's orders were called "Zhi," and his commands were "Zhao," among which "Ri Zhao" (imperial edicts daily issued) issued by Qin Shi Huang (the first emperor of Qin) had the greatest legal effect. Through issuing decrees to "Jun" (shire) and "Xian" (county), the emperor divided the whole nation into thirty-six "Jun" (shire), and "Jun Shou" (governor) and "Xian Ling" (county magistrate) were appointed by the emperor to be in charge of the local business on behalf of the emperor to ensure the centralization of power through the system. Qin Shi Huang (the first emperor of Qin) called himself "Zhen" (meaning I), and his subjects called him "Bi Xia" (Your Majesty). The visiting and presence of the emperor was respectively referred as "Xing" and "Xing Zai Suo," and his residence was called "Jin Zhong" (forbidden place), while his death was called "Beng." In official documents, the systems such as address and naming taboo were recorded, which meant that if "Emperor," "First Emperor" or "declared by the emperor" happened to be used, they needed to be written in the way of "Ding Ge" (without leaving spaces), and the name of the emperor had to be avoided to be mentioned.

The systems of "Chao Yi" (imperial court consultation) and "Chao Hui" (Imperial Court Convention) were set up to for the bureaucrats to help the emperor to exercise power and to play a better role in assisting the emperor. The system of "Chao Yi" (imperial court consultation) could be dated back to the meeting system in clan society and it was developed after some changes in Shang and Zhou Dynasties. Although Qin Shi Huang (the first emperor of Qin) had the supreme power, the things regarding the affairs of national defense and administration, such as change of the emperor's titles of the year, the implementation of county system, the banning on private school, and the expropriation of private books, were usually discussed by the officials at court. Sometimes the disciples of "Bo Shi" (learned scholars) also joined in the discussion and debates, but it was still decided by the emperor finally. The system of "Chao Yi" (imperial court consultation) helped the emperor to make decisions after listening to different opinions, but it had acted as a restrictive function to the emperor's power in dealing with significant military and national affairs.

The system of "Chao Hui" (imperial court convention) referred to the system by which the emperor regularly listened to reports from officials, and the dates of "Chao Hui" (imperial court convention) were usually legally fixed.

The emperor exercised his power by using the certificate of "Xi" (Seal), "Fu" (tally), and "Jie" (documentary evidence). The "Seal" owned by the emperor was called "Yu Xi." "Yu Xi" used by Qin Shi Huang (the first emperor of Qin) was engraved with the words like "ruling on behalf of 'Tian' (Heaven), and being long-living and prosperous forever,"[104] which meant that the power was granted by

---

[103]"Qin Shi Huang Ben Ji" (The Biography of Qin Shi Huang) in *Shi Ji* (*The Record of the Grand Historian*).

[104]"Qin Shi Huang Ben Ji" (The Biography of Qin Shi Huang) in *Shi Ji* (*The Record of the Grand Historian*).

"Tian" (Heaven) and it would be passed down to eternity. "Fu" (tally) was the certificate of the emperor's power to mobilize the army and "Jie" (documentary evidence) was the credential given to the envoy to be sent on a diplomatic mission.

Besides, the harem system, succession system, temple and mausoleum system, which were related to the imperial system, were also set up, among which, the succession system was concerned with the continuation of despotism, so it was regarded as "the foundation of the country."

The imperial system set up by Qin Shi Huang (the first emperor of Qin) was theoretically based on the theories of legalism. Han Fei, one of the representatives of legalists emphasized that the emperor's power "could never be given to anyone else because if he had lost one percent of his power, his subjects would think he had lost one hundred percent of the power altogether."[105] Han Fei also thought that "not even one in one thousand could still rule his country if he had lost his power."[106] Qin Shi Huang (the first emperor of Qin) applauded Han Fei's thoughts on the integrated application of "Fa" (law), "Shu" (tactics) and "Shi" (power) and had even regretted for not being able to make friends with him.

The establishment of the imperial system realized the centralization of state power, so the power of the emperor was strengthened. For every single detail, the imperial system had reflected the ruling of despotism and the absolute power of the emperor. However, as Lu Sheng and Hou Sheng said, "Although there were seventy learned scholars, they had no real power; 'Cheng Xiang' (the prime minister) and other officials just waited for the orders and decisions of the emperor"[107] so all they were allowed to do was to obey the orders. To expand the emperor's power, Qin Shi Huang (the first emperor of Qin) even challenged the divine power. In 219 B.C., "when he traveled to Xiang Shan Temple by boat, the wind was so strong that the boat could not move. He asked a 'Bo Shi' (learned scholars): 'what god is Xiang Jun?' The 'Bo Shi' (learned scholars) answered that 'she is the daughter of Yao and the wife of Shun, so is buried here'. Qin Shi Huang (the first emperor of Qin) raged and ordered 3000 prisoners to cut down all the trees on Xiang Shan Mountain."[108]

As the emperor lived in the palace far away from ordinary people and was wary of the officials, eunuchs seized the chance to intervene in politics. Eunuch Zhao Gao and Prince Hu Hai had faked the posthumous edict and usurped the emperor's power, so it was the first example of bringing ruin to the country by eunuchs' intervening in politics. It was the inherent evil of despotism for eunuch to intervene in the state affairs, and the perishing of Han, Tang, and Ming Dynasties were closely related to it.

From the burning books and burying scholars by Qin Shi Huang (the first emperor of Qin) to "Wen Zi Yu" (literary inquisition) in Ming and Qing Dynasties, we can

---

[105]"Nei Chu Shuo" (The Inner Categories of Saying) (Part 2) in *Han Fei Zi* (*Han Feizi*).

[106]"Ren Zhu" (The Monarch) in *Han Fei Zi* (*Han Feizi*).

[107]"Ren Zhu" (The Monarch) in *Han Fei Zi* (*Han Feizi*).

[108]"Qin Shi Huang Ben Ji" (The Biography of Qin Shi Huang) in *Shi Ji* (*The Record of the Grand Historian*).

see that despotism in politics is always closely related to the despotism in culture. The supreme despotism requires people to stay stupid and ignorant, however, in such a special historical period like Qin Dynasty, despotism and centralization had played an active role in the unification of the country, the formation of the nation, the development of economy and culture and the defense against foreign invasions, but at the same time, the disadvantages of a dictatorial system also began to appear in the reign of Qin Shi Huang (the first emperor of Qin).

4.2.1.2 The Establishment of Bureaucratic System of "San Gong," "Jiu Qing" and the Administrative System of "Jun Xian"

Below the emperor, "Cheng Xiang" (the Prime Minister) was appointed, who was the highest executive official responsible for state administration. "Tai Wei" (the minister of defense) was the highest military officer. "Yu Shi Da Fu" (Grand Censor) was the vice prime minister who was responsible for submitting memorials and edicts to the throne as well as the surveillance commission. "Cheng Xiang" (the prime minister), 'Tai Wei' (the minister of defense), and "Yu Shi Da Fu" (Grand Censor) consisted of "San Gong" of the state, and they were the center for issuing orders. However, during the reign of Qin Shi Huang (the first emperor of Qin), as dictatorship was implemented throughout the country, "Cheng Xiang" (the prime minister) was deprived of the rights to make decisions, so he just carried out the emperor's orders.

Below "San Gong" (the three councilors) [it was initiated in the Qin Dynasty consisted of "Cheng Xiang" (the prime minister), "Tai Wei" (the minister of defense) and "Yu Shi Da Fu" (Grand Censor), which was replaced by "Da Si Tu" (the senior minister of civil affairs), "Da Si Ma" (the minister of military affairs) and "Da Si Kong" (the minister of public works) later], "Jiu Qing" (the nine high-rank officials in ancient times) was appointed, and they were responsible for different affairs: "Feng Chang" was responsible for temple ritual; "Lang Zhong Ling" (official commanding the bodyguards of the emperor) for guarding the main portals of the palaces and commanding the bodyguards of the emperor; "Wei Wei" (official in charge of emperor's personal safety) for the guards of the palace; "Tai Pu" (official in charge of emperor's carriages and horses) for the royal horses and horse policy; "Ting Wei" (the supreme official in charge of judicature) for the highest central judicial offices and the criminal affairs; "Dian Ke" (official in charge of foreign affairs) for foreign affairs and minority groups; "Zong Zheng" (official in charge of the royal affairs) for the royal affairs; "Zhi Su Nei Shi" (official in charge of financial revenue) for the tax, financial revenue and expenditure; "Shao Fu" (official in charge of emperor's income and royal affairs) for the "taxation of mountains, seas, ponds and lakes used for royal affairs." Among "Jiu Qing" (the nine high-rank officials in ancient times), besides "Ting Wei" (the supreme official in charge of judicature), "Zhi Su Nei Shi" (official in charge of financial revenue) and "Dian Ke" (official in charge of foreign affairs), the other six ministers were not royal officials, but they also had the function of serving the royal households, which had reflected the influence of autocratic politics on state organs.

The system of "San Gong" (the three councilors) and "Jiu Qing" (the nine high-rank officials in ancient times) was not only recorded in the history books of Qin Dynasty, but also confirmed by the system of "Zhong Shu Guan Zhi" (national central organization) in Han Dynasty.

After the unification of Qin Dynasty, the system of "Jun" (shire) and "Xian" (county) was implemented in the country. It was recorded in "Di Li Zhi" (The Record of Geography) in *Han Shu (The History of Han Dynasty)* that "the rulers of Qin Dynasty realized that Zhou Dynasty perished because its vassal system had undermined the power of central government, so fiefdom was abolished and a two-level system of 'Jun' (shire) and 'Xian' (county) was established instead." In the 26th year of Qin Shi Huang's reign (21 B.C.), the country was divided into thirty-six "Jun" (shire), the fiefdom system of "ruling by dividing the states and living by dividing the land" was completely abolished, and a set of local administrative authorities was established instead "within the four seas (nationwide)." Afterwards, five new "Jun" (shire), namely, Jiuyuan, Nanhai, Guilin, Xiangjun, and Minzhong were established successively.

"Jun" (shire) was the highest level of local administrative authority, with "Jun Shou" (governor) as the head. Under "Jun Shou" (governor), "Jun Wei" (assistant of governor in charge of military affairs) was established to be responsible for the army and "Jun Jian" (judicial supervisor) for judicial supervision.

Under "Jun" (shire) was "Xian" (county). According to research, about 1000 "Xian" (county) were established after the unification of the country. "Xian Ling" (county magistrate), also called "Xian Se Fu" in *Qin Jian (The Bamboo Writing Slips in Qin Dynasty)*, was in charge of the administration as well as judicature within "Xian" (county). Under "Xian Ling" (county magistrate) was "Cheng" (the assistant of county magistrate), the assistant of county magistrate, whose duty was to assist "Xian Ling" (county magistrate) to manage the county government affairs. "Xian Wei" (commandant of county) was responsible for the recruitment and the training of soldiers in "Xian" (county).

Under "Xian" (county), "Xiang" (townships) and "Li" (a basic resident organization consisting of five neighborhoods) were set up as the basic-level administrative organizations according to population and residential zones. In "Xiang" (townships), "You Zhi" (local official) was in charge of township administration; "San Lao" (local officials in charge of education) was in charge of education; "Se Fu" (a minor official in the county) was in charge of hearing lawsuits and collecting tax, and "You Jiao" (village official in charge of patrolling) was in charge of "patrolling and preventing theft." "Li Zheng" was the head of "Li" (a basic resident organization consisting of five neighborhoods), and under "Li," the residents were organized by "Shi Wu" (a basic level organization grouped by five or ten households). Seen from the administration system in general, "'Xian' (county) was set up to govern 'Xiang' (townships), and 'Xiang' (townships) was set up in turn to govern 'Li' (a basic resident organization consisting of five neighborhoods)." "Ting" belonged to defense system, which was not under the jurisdiction of the officials of "Xiang" (townships).

All the officials ranging from central officials of "San Gong" (the three councilors) to the local officials of "Xian Ling" (county magistrate), were all appointed by the emperor. These officials only earned salary and were not granted fiefdom, so they were a large group of professional officials in charge of managing national affairs concerning military, law, finance, agriculture, and so on.

The emperor-dominated centralized feudal administrative system established in Qin Dynasty had exerted a profound influence on later generations, so the systems set up after Han Dynasty were basically an evolution and development of those of Qin Dynasty.

4.2.2 "Ming Fa Du" (Make Law Known to the People) and "Ding Lv Ling" (Making Laws and Decrees)

To "settle all things according to law," a lot of work was done based on the existing laws to achieve the goal of "Ming Fa Du" (Make Law Known to the People) and "Ding Lv Ling" (Making Laws and Decrees). On the one hand, the measures taken were recorded in the stone inscriptions praising Qin Shi Huang's achievements in patrolling around the country. For example, in the 28th year of the reign of Qin Shi Huang (the first emperor of Qin) (219 B.C.), it was recorded on the stone inscription on Mount Tai that, "when the emperor took his reign, he wisely made the laws, and his ministers were all well administered....His method of administration was successful, so the country was prosperous and everything was settled in accordance with law." The stone inscription of the same year on Mount Lang Ya read: "The justice of law is the discipline for all things....The law is made to eliminate the uncertainties so that everyone knows what to do and the law is obeyed by everyone." The stone inscription on Mount Zhifu, which was written in the 29th year (218 B.C.), read: "The sage emperor made the law and maintained social order by making the law known to the people and... ruling in the country by law. The law will be the eternal code of behavior." The stone inscription on Kuaiji Mountain, which was written in the 37th year (210 B.C.), read: "Not until the sage emperor ascended the throne, the names of criminal penalties were defined, the outdated constitutions were abolished and the types of punishments were renewed. Moreover, the duties of officials were clarified and a statute code was established." The stone inscriptions mentioned above were the specific manifestation of the legislative guiding principles of Qin Shi Huang, which had clarified the purpose of strict law implementation, namely, to regulate the officials' behaviors and to let them know about their duties, meanwhile, to make the people all over the country to know the law and know what to do. What is the most important is that the law is widely publicized to be used as the guiding line of ruling the country by law. Therefore, according to the legal provisions in *Yun Meng Qin Jian (Amounts of Bamboo Writing Slips in Qin Dynasty*

Excavated in Yunmeng) and the establishment of legislative organizations after the unification of Qin Dynasty, it was eloquently proved that everything was settled according to law in Qin Dynasty from society to the nation, from economy to politics, from manufacture to livelihood and from family to individuals. The people in Han Dynasty had criticized that "the laws in Qin Dynasty were as many as the autumn flowers called 'Qiu Tu' and its coverage was as dense as the congealed fat."[109]

On the other side, a series of single laws were made to promote the centralization of political and cultural authority, such as *Fen Shu Ling* (*Decree for Burning Books*), *Li Jian Zhi Bu Ju Ling* (*Decree on the Officials Failing to Report What They Know*) and *Yi Gu Fei Jin Ou Yu Shi Shu Ling* (*Decree on Satirizing the Present by Discussing Ancient Classical Books*).

4.2.2.1 The Felony of Offending the Emperor

Under dictatorship, the emperor was the center of the state. Thus, the main task of the law in the Qin Dynasty was to safeguard the dignity and the absolute authority of the emperor. In the 29th year of Qin Shi Huang (the first emperor of Qin) (218 B.C.), he traveled eastward to Bolangsha in Yangwu (now Yuanyang in Henan) and was attacked by Zhang Liang and other people, which was referred to as "being robbed by the bandits." For this serious crime, it was ordered by Qin Shi Huang (the first emperor of Qin) "to search for the criminals all around the country for ten days"[110] to have the criminal arrested and severely punished. Thus, Zhang Liang had to change his name and ran away to other states for life.

To safeguard the dignity of Qin Shi Huang (the first emperor of Qin) and to protect his personal safety, his whereabouts must be kept a secret, and anyone who leaked the information would be sentenced to death. In "Qin Shi Huang Ben Ji" (The Biography of Qin Shi Huang) in *Shi Ji* (*The Records of the Grand Historian*), it was recorded that "as for the whereabouts of the emperor, anyone who leaks it to others will be punished by death penalty." If the ministers and attendants by his side had leaked out what Qin Shi Huang (the first emperor of Qin) said to the officials outside court, they would be convicted with felony. When he once traveled to Liangshan Palace, "he saw a splendid show of horses and coaches by 'Cheng Xiang' (the prime minister), so he said it was not good. Maybe somebody passed these words to 'Cheng Xiang' (the prime minister), so he then destroyed his carts. The emperor got furious because he believed that somebody had passed his words to 'Cheng Xiang' (the prime minister). When he asked about this, nobody claimed responsibility for it, so he ordered to kill all the people who were present when he said those words."[111]

---

[109]"Xing De" (The Penal Morality) in *Yan Tie Lun* (*Debates on Salt and Iron*).
[110]"Xing De" (The Penal Morality) in *Yan Tie Lun* (*Debates on Salt and Iron*).
[111]"Xing De" (The Penal Morality) in *Yan Tie Lun* (*Debates on Salt and Iron*).

4.2 The Legal System of Qin Dynasty After Its Unification

When the second emperor of Qin Dynasty was in reign, he often killed his kinsmen and officials on the excuse of their disloyalty. He stated in the imperial edict on the death penalty for Meng Tian that "You (Meng Tian) have tried to prevent the late emperor from appointing me as the crown prince. Now 'Cheng Xiang' (the prime minister) has charged you with disloyalty, for which your family would be implicated. I am sympathetic with you, so only order you yourself to die, which is fortunate enough for you. Please do it."[112]

Against the background of strengthening the cultural absolutism, the crimes of slander and heresy were enacted. After the unification of Qin Dynasty, to formulate a unified ideology, the Chinese characters were unified based on "Xiao Zhuan" (a kind of calligraphy) and then severe punishments were imposed upon the ideas and speeches that might do harm to the centralization of power.

According to "Gao Zu Ben Ji" (Biographic Sketches of Emperor Gaozu) in *Shi Ji* (*The Records of the Grand Historian*), after occupied Xianyang, when Liu Bang (the First Emperor of Han) complained the violent and bloody crimes of the regime of Qin Dynasty to the countrymen, he said, "All the people have been suffering from the harsh laws of Qin Dynasty for a long time. The detractors are sentenced to death penalty (together with all his clan people), and those who whisper to each other are sentenced to 'Qi Shi' (exposing the executed body publicly at markets)." Besides, it was quoted from Ying Shao in *Ji Jie* (*Collected Interpretations*) that "public gathering and talking were banned in Qin Dynasty" to prevent people from slandering the emperor. According to the law of Qin, those convicted of slandering would be sentenced to "Zu Zhu" (killing of the whole clan of a criminal). In the 35th year of Qin Shi Huang (the first emperor of Qin), Hou and Lu talked about the dictatorship of Qin Shi Huang (the first emperor of Qin) and said, "he likes to demonstrate his authority by using penalty." Qin Shi Huang (the first emperor of Qin) said: "These people are defaming me and have exaggerated my violence and immorality," so "they are confusing the public by spreading rumors." Consequently, "more than 460 people were arrested and killed in Xianyang."[113]

In the 36th year of Qin Shi Huang (the first emperor of Qin), when a meteor landed in the east of the country, some people engraved words on it, which read: "When Qin Shi Huang (the first emperor of Qin) died, the land would be divided." When the emperor heard about it, he asked "Yu Shi" (the censor) to have an investigation, but nobody claimed responsibility for it. Then in the name of heresy, the emperor "ordered to kill all the people living near the place where the meteor landed."[114]

---

[112]"Meng Tian Lie Zhuan" (The Biography of Meng Tian) in *Shi Ji* (The Record *of the Grand Historian*).

[113]"Qin Shi Huang Ben Ji" (The Biography of Qin Shi Huang) in *Shi Ji* (*The Record of the Grand Historian*).

[114]"Qin Shi Huang Ben Ji" (The Biography of Qin Shi Huang) in *Shi Ji* (*The Record of the Grand Historian*).

Apart from the crime of slandering and heresy, "Wang Yan" (instigation) and "Fei Suo Yi Yan" (speaking inappropriate words) were also felonies. The so-called "Wang Yan" (instigation) referred to speeches against the regime of Qin Dynasty. According to "Xiang Yu Ben Ji" (The Biographic sketches of Xiang Yu) in *Shi Ji* (*The Records of the Grand Historian*), "when Qin Shi Huang (the first emperor of Qin) traveled to Kuaiji, crossing Zhejiang, Xiang Ji said to Xiang Liang that 'you could replace him'. Xiang Liang quickly hushed him and told him not to say things like that, because it could lead to the punishment of 'Zu' (killing of the whole clan of a criminal)!" At the end of the Qin Dynasty, Li Shiqi visited "Xian Ling" (county magistrate) of Chenliu county at night and said to him: "'Because of Qin Shi Huang's cruelty, the public rebel against it. If you could follow the tide of the public, you will succeed'. "Xian Ling" (county magistrate) of Chenliu county told him that 'under the harsh laws of Qin Dynasty, they shouldn't say things like that because anyone who commits the crime of 'Wang Yan' (instigation) would be killed, with all the members of his clan implicated'."[115] Thus, it can be seen that "Wang Yan" (instigation) was a felony and anyone being convicted of this crime would be sentenced to the punishment of "Zu" (killing of the whole clan of a criminal).

During the reign of the second emperor of Qin Dynasty, upon the revolt of Chen Sheng and Wu Guang, the second emperor gathered the Confucian scholars and inquired about it. Some people answered, "they are rebels, but some say they are robbers." Those who said they were rebels were sentenced to death for the crime of "Fei Suo Yi Yan" (speaking inappropriate words).[116] As for the so-called "Fei Suo Yi Yan" (speaking inappropriate words), there were no fixed contents, so it could be interpreted arbitrarily. This accusation was enacted at the end of the Qin Dynasty and it became very popular in Han Dynasty.

To unify the ideology and tighten the control over people's speeches, anyone who satirized the current situation by using the past or owned the banned books would be punished. In the 34th year of Qin Shi Huang (the first emperor of Qin), *Fen Shu Ling* (*Decree for Burning Books*) was issued and it was stipulated that "anyone who satirized the present situation by using the past be punished by 'Zu' (killing of the whole clan of a criminal)."[117] Therefore, if a person satirized the current affairs by using the past, he would be sentenced to severe penalties, and the officials who were well aware of it but did not make reports would be sentenced to the same penalty. The brutal law was well targeted, just as Li Si said:

> Now that the emperor has unified the country, he should decide what is right and what is wrong. Previously people have established different schools to study ancient classics. When they hear about a new policy, they began to discuss about it. At court, they would praise the policy regardless of their real intentions, but when outside the court, they would discuss its

---

[115]"Li Sheng Lu Jia Lie Zhuan" (The Biography of Li Sheng and Lu Jia, et al) in *Shi Ji* (*The Record of the Grand Historian*).

[116]"Liu Jing Shu Sun Shu Tong Lie Zhuan" (The Collected Biographies of Liu Jingshu and Sun Tong) in *Shi Ji* (*The Record of the Grand Historian*).

[117]"Qin Shi Huang Ben Ji" (The Biography of Qin Shi Huang) in *Shi Ji* (*The Record of the Grand Historian*).

4.2 The Legal System of Qin Dynasty After Its Unification

shortcomings. So they praise the emperor just to obtain personal fame, but their real intention is to show their cleverness by unconventional methods, and to instigate his followers to criticize and slander others.[118]

To control the opinion of the public, to maintain the dignity of the emperor and to support then current policy, the crime of "Yi Gu Fei Jin" (to satirize the current affairs by using the past) was formulated, and those violators were severely punished.

For the same purpose, *Xie Shu Lv* (*Statutes Forbidding the Possession of Books*) was made, and it was stipulated that "for the people who were not 'Bo Shi' (learned scholars) but who had ancient classical books of other schools, 'Shou' and 'Wei' (both were county officials) would be asked to have all these books burned completely." "If they didn't have the books burned within thirty days, they would be punished by 'Qing' (to tattoo on the face) and 'Cheng Dan' (the punishment of men building cities)."[119] In the period of "San Guo" (Three Kingdoms), Zhang Yan made an annotation in "Hui Di Ji" (The Record of the Emperor Hui) in *Han Shu* (*The History of Han Dynasty*) that according to the laws of Qin Dynasty, "if people dared to carry books, they and their families would be killed." Following *Xie Shu Lv* (*Statutes Forbidding the Possession of Books*), "the gathering and talking about ancient classical books" was prohibited; "if anyone had violated the rule, he or she would be punished by 'Qi Shi' (exposing the executed body publicly at markets),"[120] so the scale of punishment was further expanded.

During the reign of the second emperor of Qin Dynasty, Li Si and Zhao Gao competed fiercely for power, so Li Si reported Zhao Gao's conspiracy to the emperor. However, the second emperor of Qin believed in Zhao Gao and Li Si was severely punished by "Ju Wu Xing" (a brutal punishment in ancient China) and "Yi San Zu" (the law of killing the three generations of a family) for the crime of treason. It was recorded in "Li Si Lie Zhuan" (The Biography of Li Si) in *Shi Ji* (*The Records of the Grand Historian*) that "so the Second Emperor of Qin sent Zhao Gao to try Li Si's case and had him punished. Zhao Gao charged Li Si and his son with treason and arrested all their friends and family members. Li Si was tortured and beaten by Zhao Gao for more than 1000 strokes, and it was too painful for Li Si to bear so he fabricated his own crimes and pleaded guilty." In September of 208 B.C., Li Si was executed by "Ju Wu Xing" (a brutal punishment in ancient China) and "Yao Zhan" (cutting at waist) at the market of Xianyang,...with all his family members punished by 'Yi San Zu' (the law of killing the three generations of a family)."

---

[118]"Qin Shi Huang Ben Ji" (The Biography of Qin Shi Huang) in *Shi Ji* (*The Record of the Grand Historian*).

[119]"Qin Shi Huang Ben Ji" (The Biography of Qin Shi Huang) in *Shi Ji* (*The Record of the Grand Historian*).

[120]"Qin Shi Huang Ben Ji" (The Biography of Qin Shi Huang) in *Shi Ji* (*The Record of the Grand Historian*).

After the rebellion of Chen Sheng and Wu Guang, more brutal suppression was conducted by the second emperor of Qin. According to historical records, "there were many gang robberies in the east, but they were ruthlessly suppressed, which had resulted in the death of many people, but the rebellions were not stopped."[121]

In the ancient books and records of Qin Dynasty, the gang robbery referred to the farmers' rebellion against the regime of Qin Dynasty. In "Qing Bu Lie Zhuan" (The Collected Biography of Qing Bu) and "Shu Sun Tong Lie Zhuan" (The Collected Biography of Shu Suntong) in *Shi Ji* (*The Records of the Grand Historian*), there were similar accounts: "Qing Bu made acquaintance with those leaders of criminals and bandits and finally became rebels in the Jiangzhong area"; "when Chen Sheng revolted in Shandong province, the emperor heard about that and gathered all 'Bo Shi' (learned scholars) to consult..., Shu Suntong answered that 'your majesty don't need to worry too much about these people, because they are just roving bandits stealing and robbing on a small scale, and it is no big deal'." The punishment for the crime of conspiring against the emperor was one of the key targets of the making of criminal law from the beginning of Qin Dynasty to the period of second emperor of Qin.

Besides, strict laws and severe punishments were also adopted by Qin Shi Huang (the first emperor of Qin), because he "liked to demonstrate his authority by using penalties."[122] Moreover, he emphasized that everything should be decided according to law and that the rules for awards and punishments should be strictly kept, so "no amnesty was offered for a long time."[123] In the history of Qin Dynasty, before Qin Shi Huang (the first emperor of Qin), general amnesties had been proclaimed by King Zhao Xiang, Xiao Wen and Zhuang Xiang. After Qin Shi Huang's death, the criminals were pardoned by the second emperor of the Qin Dynasty, Hu Hai. Hence, in the second year of his reign, he "issued an order to have the prisoners in Li Shan pardoned and to teach them to fight against the rebels." But in the reign of Qin Shi Huang (the first emperor of Qin), severe punishments were adopted and general amnesties were never declared, so the number of prisoners increased dramatically, which had led to the serious social problem that "the streets were crowded with people wearing prison uniforms and all the prisons were as busy as markets."[124] To build E-Fang Palace and Li Shan mausoleum, more than 700,000 people were punished by castration together with labor service, from which we can see the prevalence of the penalty of castration.

As far as "Xing Fa" (The Criminal Law) was concerned, the penalties recorded in *Qin Jian* (*The Bamboo Writing Slips in Qin Dynasty*) were continued to be used in

---

[121]"Qin Shi Huang Ben Ji" (The Biography of Qin Shi Huang) in *Shi Ji* (*The Record of the Grand Historian*).

[122]"Qin Shi Huang Ben Ji" (The Biography of Qin Shi Huang) in *Shi Ji* (*The Record of the Grand Historian*).

[123]"Qin Shi Huang Ben Ji" (The Biography of Qin Shi Huang) in *Shi Ji* (*The Record of the Grand Historian*).

[124]"Xing Fa Zhi" (The Record of the Criminal Law) in *Han Shu* (*The History of Han Dynasty*).

the Qin Dynasty. However, after the unification, cruel punishments were used and brutal officials were everywhere, so people were frequently punished for trifle matters, and "Tu Xing" (penal servitude) was often applied, which had resulted in the phenomenon that "the streets were crowded with people wearing prison uniforms and all the prisons were as busy as markets."[125] In the end, many criminals did labor service for the government. Especially during the reign of the second emperor of Qin Dynasty, Zhao Gao was favored by the emperor, so severe punishments were more frequently used. Moreover, the method for the execution of death penalty was also very brutal, and even the nobilities was often punished. For example, the twelve sons from noble families were executed in Xianyang, and "the tenth princess was punished by 'Zhai' at a sacrifice ceremony." According to the index of Sima Zhen, "'Zhai,' and 'Zhe' (to open and split, breaking apart the criminal's body) have the same meaning, but they are just written differently in different dynasties. 'Zhe' means to kill people by tearing their bodies apart."[126]

4.2.2.2 The Supplement of National Civil and Economic Laws

After the unification of Qin Dynasty, all the land in the country became the property of the emperor, as was described in the saying that "all the land in the state belonged to the emperor. The west boundary was Liu Sha, the south was to Bei Hu, the east was to the Sea and the north was beyond Bei Xia, so all people within the boundary were the subjects of the emperor."[127] In the year when Qin Shi Huang (the first emperor of Qin) united the six states, a decree was issued to "change the reference to the people from 'Min' to 'Qian Shou'," by which most of the slaves were turned into farmers to be engaged in farming. This decree confirmed the great changes of the relationships of production and class, so it was warmly welcomed by the public and "was greatly celebrated throughout the country."[128] In the 31st year of Qin Shi Huang's reign, the law of "privatizing the land to the peasants" was issued, according to which, the land owners who had obtained the ownership of the land should report the acres of land which they owned to the government and pay tax in accordance with the law, so that the feudal land system was established nationwide. After the enforcement of the law, the private ownership of the land by feudal landlords was developed quickly, which had predicted its dominant position in the later times.

With the establishment of the feudal private ownership of land, it was allowed for the landlord class to merge the land of the peasants legitimately, and "the people

---

[125]"Xing Fa Zhi" (The Record of the Criminal Law) in *Han Shu* (*The History of Han Dynasty*).

[126]"Li Si Lie Zhuan" (The Biography of Li Si) in *Shi Ji* (*The Record of the Grand Historian*).

[127]"Qin Shi Huang Ben Ji" (The Biography of Qin Shi Huang) in *Shi Ji* (*The Record of the Grand Historian*).

[128]"Qin Shi Huang Ben Ji" (The Biography of Qin Shi Huang) in *Shi Ji* (*The Record of the Grand Historian*).

could have a large amount of land as much as 1000 *mu* with no limitations."[129] Therefore, the feudal tenant system gradually became the basic mode of management of the landlords. Farmers rented land from the landlords but the rent could be as much as half of the harvest, as was recorded in "Shi Huo Zhi" (The Records of National Finance and Economy) in *Han Shu* (*The History of Han Dynasty*) that, "some people rented land from the wealthy landlords, but they had to pay five out of ten of the harvest as rent."

Except for the feudal rent exploitation, the super-economic exploitation represented by corvée still accounted for a large proportion. According to "Shi Huo Zhi" (The Records of National Finance and Economy) in *Han Shu* (*The History of Han Dynasty*), "the brutal corvée in Qin Dynasty was thirty times more than that of the previous times."

After the unification of Qin Dynasty, to maintain a stable marriage relationship, to eradicate the outdated convention, and to form good social atmosphere, laws were issued to "take strict precautions against adultery." According to the inscriptions on *Kuai Ji Ke Shi* (*Kuaiji Stone Inscription*), it was proclaimed by Qin Shi Huang (the first emperor of Qin) that "if the husband was like 'Ji Xia' (a boar, or being licentious with other women), the wife can kill him without having any legal liability." According to the annotation of "Qin Shi Huang Ben Ji" (The Biography of Qin Shi Huang) in *Shi Ji* (*The Records of the Grand Historian*), "'Xia' means a boar. So the husband messing around with other women is just like a boar having sexual intercourse with other swines." At the same time, a woman having an affair with other men would also be punished. If a woman married again after her husband died, she would "be punished by 'Qing' (to tattoo on the face) and 'Cheng Dan' (the punishment of men building cities)." According to some other records in *Kuai Ji Ke Shi* (*Kuaiji Stone Inscription*), "even if the woman had escaped from the wedlock and made the children motherless, or if the woman with children had remarried, she would also be punished."

As for the system of inheritance, the system of primogeniture practiced since Shang and Zhou Dynasties was applicable both to the royal family and to the public. Fu Su, the first son of Qin Shi Huang (the first emperor of Qin) should have succeeded to the throne, but because he was against the policy of "Fen Shu Keng Ru" (burning books and burying Confucian scholars), he had advised that, "now the country has just come to peace and the people in remote areas have not submitted themselves to the ruling yet. Besides, Confucianism is accepted by all the scholars, so if your majesty have them punished severely, the country would be in turmoil. Please be cautious on this matter."[130] However, he was driven away by Qin Shi Huang (the first emperor of Qin) and was forced to supervise the army of Meng Tian in Shangjun. Because of the failure of establishing of Fu Su as the crown prince after

---

[129]"Tian Fu Kao" (A Textual Research on Land Tax) in *Wen Xian Tong Kao* (*A General Examination of Documents*) (Book 1).

[130]"Qin Shi Huang Ben Ji" (The Biography of Qin Shi Huang) in *Shi Ji* (*The Record of the Grand Historian*).

4.2 The Legal System of Qin Dynasty After Its Unification

the death of Qin Shi Huang (the first emperor of Qin), the eunuch Zhao Gao and the second emperor of Qin Dynasty conspired to fake the emperor's will, ordered Fu Su and Meng Tian to kill themselves and usurped the throne, which had caused the rapid decline of the Qin Dynasty. Some thinkers and statesmen in early Han Dynasty regarded this as a lesson to learn from. When Han Gao Zu (the first emperor of Han) was prepared to establish the crown prince by replacing the elder with the younger son, Shu Suntong admonished him that "Qin Dynasty perished just because Qin Shi Huang (the first emperor of Qin) didn't adopt Fu Su as the crown prince early, which had caused the falsification of emperor's will and the disastrous consequence which you have seen."[131]

As for the supplement of economic laws, first, the tax system centering on "Hu Fu" (household tax) and "Kou Fu" (poll tax) was legalized to support the function of the mechanism of the state and large-scale construction work. According to "Si Lun Xun" (Instructions of Si Lun) in *Huai Nan Zi* (*Masters from Huainan*), "in the Qin Dynasty...the tax levied according to the population (Tou Kuai Ji Fu) was all transported to the royal court." Gao You made an annotation that "'Tou Kuai' refers to the number of people and it is the basis of tax. 'Ji Lian' means that the tax is collected with dustpan, which shows the taxis heavy." The policies like registering separately if there were more than two men in one household and forbidding people to emigrate which was carried out since Shang Yang's reform were undoubtedly continued to be applied.

Second, the various weights and measurements and currency, which were used in Warring States Period, were unified. In 226 B.C., an imperial edict was issued and it was stipulated that "if there was no standards for weight, people would be confused, so a standard for weights and measurements and the currency should be made clear.[132]" Therefore, according to the decree issued, it was required that a general standard should be set up to ensure that "all the weights and measurements such as *dan, zhang, chi* should have the same standard; all carts shall have the same size of wheels and the same characters shall be used in all books."[133] As for the currency, except for the conventional laws for currency management, in the 37th year of Qin Shi Huang's reign (210 B.C.), "Fu Xing Qian" (Fu Xing Money) was released to have the copper coins standardized. According to "Ping Zhun Shu" (On Fair Trade) in *Shi Ji* (*The Records of the Grand Historian*), quoted from *Suo Yin* (*Index*) in *Gu Jin Zhu* (*Annotations of Modern and Ancient Times*), "the coin in the Qin Dynasty weighed half *liang*, with the diameter of one *cun* and two *fen* (a unit of length, one *fen* is about 1/3 centimeter)."

---

[131]"Shu Sun Tong Zhuan" (The Biography of Shu Suntong) in *Han Shu* (*The History of Han Dynasty*).

[132]*Qin Shi Huang Er Shi Liu Nian Zhao Shu Ming Wen* (*Inscriptions of Imperial Edict Issued in the 26th Year of Qin Shi Huang's Reign*).

[133]"Qin Shi Huang Ben Ji" (The Biography of Qin Shi Huang) in *Shi Ji* (*The Record of the Grand Historian*).

4.2.2.3 The Highly Centralized Judicial Trials

After the unification of Qin Dynasty, "Ting Wei" (the supreme official in charge of judicature) was still the supreme official in charge of judicature and the officials of "Jun" (shire) and "Xian" (county) continued to be in charge of jurisdiction. But because strict autocracy was implemented by Qin Shi Huang (the first emperor of Qin), and the legalist idea of "ruling by law" was stressed, much attention was paid to judicial affairs, so some of the important cases were tried and adjudicated by the emperor himself in person. History records showed that Qin Shi Huang (the first emperor of Qin) "often read and wrote in person, and he judged the cases in the day, read the reports of the officials at night and settled all the cases by himself. The documents he read every day even weighed one *dan*."[134] Therefore, it can be seen that it was not Qin Shi Huang's occasional behavior to try the cases by himself but rather an important activity to exercise the supreme judicial power. To assist the emperor to exercise the supreme judicial authority, it was not surprising that "the judicial officials were usually appointed from the royal family members or the people closer to the emperor." It was stated in history records that "officials...especially professional judicial officials were appointed by Shi Huang (the first emperor of Qin),"[135] and that "penalties were imposed by him at his will."[136] However, that was only part of the story, because the misconducts of the judicial officials were also punished Qin Shi Huang (the first emperor of Qin). For example, in the 34th year of Qin Shi Huang's reign (213 B.C.), "the officials who were convicted of 'Bu Zhi' (dishonest) were forced to serve labor service to build the Great Wall in Nanyue area."[137]

During the reign of the second emperor of the Qin Dynasty, with the intensification of class struggle, the emperor became more and more brutal, which had led to the destruction of the entire legal system, consequently, law and penalty became the means of struggle. For example, it was stipulated that the criminals in prison were deprived of their rights to appeal. While detained at the jail in Xianyang, Li Si had once written to the emperor, but he was rejected because Zhao Gao had used the provision as an excuse. Zhao Gao asked, "How could a prisoner write to the emperor?"[138] Thus, he sent the messenger away without reporting to the emperor. Worse, "Li Si was tortured and beaten by Zhao Gao for more than 1000 strokes, and

---

[134]"Qin Shi Huang Ben Ji" (The Biography of Qin Shi Huang) in *Shi Ji* (*The Record of the Grand Historian*).

[135]"Qin Shi Huang Ben Ji" (The Biography of Qin Shi Huang) in *Shi Ji* (*The Record of the Grand Historian*).

[136]"Shi Huo Zhi" (The Records of National Finance and Economy) (Part 1) in *Han Shu* (*The History of Han Dynasty*).

[137]"Qin Shi Huang Ben Ji" (The Biography of the First Emperor of Qin) in *Shi Ji* (*The Record of the Grand Historian*).

[138]"Li Si Lie Zhuan" (The Biography of Li Si) in *Shi Ji* (*The Record of the Grand Historian*).

it was too painful for Li Si to bear so he fabricated his own crimes and pleaded guilty".[139]

Overall, it can be seen clearly that the unification of the legal system of Qin Dynasty had played a very important role in the protection of the feudal economic system centered on agriculture, in the establishment of a centralized system of despotism, and in the implementation of unified economic, political, cultural, and ethnic policies, etc. However, people's minds were imprisoned by the autocratic politics and their behaviors were fettered by the ruling of cultural ideology. Besides, the heavy tax, labor service, and brutal punishments had ultimately triggered the large-scale rebellion of the peasants, which had led to the downfall of second emperor of Qin Dynasty.

---

[139]"Li Si Lie Zhuan" (The Biography of Li Si) in *Shi Ji* (*The Record of the Grand Historian*).

Chapter 5
The Confucianization of the Legal Systems in Western and Eastern Han Dynasties

(206 B.C.–220 A.D.)

In Han Dynasty, the system of Qin Dynasty was inherited and under the new historical circumstances, a stable feudal country with unified politics, economy, and culture was developed. However, with the stabilization and expansion of the country, especially with the need of the development of the society, the governing strategy of the rulers changed from the ideology of "Huang Lao" (a branch of Taoism represented by Huang Di and Lao Zi) in earlier times to that of Confucianism, which was in support of great unity. Since Emperor Wu, the policy of "rejecting the other schools of thoughts and respecting only Confucianism" was carried out in the Western Han Dynasty. Hence then, "Lun Li" (ethics) and "Gang Chang" (the Chinese ethical tradition) of Confucianism centered by "San Gang" (three cardinal guides) became the dominant ideology. Emperor Wu also approved of the proposal of making judicial judgment in accordance with *Chun Qiu* (*Spring and Autumn Annals*) put forward by the Confucianism expert, Dong Zhongshu, by which Confucianist ideology was introduced into the judicial field. Thus, from Qin Dynasty to early Han Dynasty, a transformation from the domination of legalism to that of Confucianism was undertaken. Just as Emperor Xuan had said, "Han Dynasty has established its own systems on the basis of legalism. How can we just use Confucianism? Are you prepared to adopt the system of Zhou Dynasty?"[1] It can be inferred that the sole respection of Confucianism just meant that Confucianism was only used as the outerwear, but in the practice of ruling the country, it was unavoidable that the law of Shen Buhai and Shang Yang would be used, which was the so-called "Confucianism outside with legalism inside." But the feudal ethics of "Lun Li" (ethics) and "Gang Chang" (the Chinese ethical tradition) were more compatible with the moral codes and mental state of the Chinese people, so they were gradually accepted by the society, and were used in every aspect of social life, by which the status of Confucianism was consolidated.

---

[1] "Han Ji Shi Jiu" (The 19th Record of Han Dynasty) in *Zi Zhi Tong Jian* (*History as a Mirror*), Vol. 27, the 1st year of Gan Lu during the Reign of Emperor of Xuan.

A series of principles of "Da De Xiao Xing" (highlighting morality while lightening penalty) were advocated by Dong Zhongshu. For example, he proposed that "it is as sweet as the honey and as solid as varnish gums to rule the country with 'De' (virtue). It is even applauded by many sages who dare not have it abandoned."[2] Therefore, the principle of "De Zhu Xing Fu" (employing moral teaching as the primary means, punishment as the supplement) became the basic strategy of managing the state affairs in Han Dynasty.

After Dong Zhongshu, the experts of Confucian classics started to explain the then current law with Confucian canons, so there emerged the co-existence of a dozen schools represented by Shu Sunxuan, Guo Lingqing, Ma Rong, Zheng Xuan, and so on, which had not only consolidated the dominant status of Confucianism, but also pioneered in the interpretation of law by individuals. Thus, "Lv Xue" (the study of statutory laws) became the accessory study of Confucian classics, which was the main feature of legal study in the Western and Eastern Han Dynasties.

During the Eastern and Western Han Dynasties, the introduction of "San Gang" (three cardinal guides) into law had laid the ethical foundation of the feudal law. The principle of sole application of punishment was replaced by that of "De Zhu Xing Fu" (employing moral teaching as the primary means, punishment as the supplement), which was more suitable to the new situation of the country, the new social reality and "Ren Qing" (human feeling). Thus, the basic principles of Confucianism were constantly institutionalized and legalized, which not only constituted the main characteristics of the laws of the Western and Eastern Han Dynasties, but also symbolized that the Chinese legal civilization had developed into a new stage, namely, the stage of Confucianization.

5.1 The Establishment of Western Han Dynasty and the Change of the Legislative Policy

The peasant rebellion at the end of Qin Dynasty toppled the arrogant government of Qin Empire. In 206 B.C., Liu Bang and his followers unified and established the new feudal empire, Han Dynasty, and made Chang'an its capital. This dynasty was called Western Han in history.

At the beginning of Han Dynasty, the urgent problem was to ease up the class conflicts, to restore the seriously damaged economy, to pull the country out of extreme poverty, to stop the decrease of population and to establish the stabilized rule of the state. Under such harsh circumstances, the regime headed by Liu Bang carefully examined the reasons for the perishing of Qin Dynasty, accepted the idea of the rehabilitation put forward by "Huang Lao" (a branch of Taoism represented by

---

[2]"Li Yuan Shen" (The Establishment of the First God) in *Chun Qiu Fan Lu* (*The Luxuriant Dew of Spring and Autumn Annals*).

5.1 The Establishment of Western Han Dynasty and the Change of the Legislative...

Huang Di and Lao Zi) and used it as the strategy of ruling the country. No doubt, the thinkers like Lu Jia and Jia Yi had played a very important role in this process.

Lu Jia inherited the ideas of "Huang Lao" (a branch of Taoism represented by Huang Di and Lao Zi) from the pre-Qin period and put forward the theory of "Wu Wei" (letting things take their own course) in the management of state by combining it with the idea of "Ren" (benevolence) and "Yi" (justice) in Confucianism. Jia Yi made a comprehensive investigation of the reasons for the perishing of Qin Dynasty and he discovered that Qin Shi Huang (the first emperor of Qin) "was not only greedy, self-assertive and distrustful of the meritorious officials, but also separated himself from the people of the lower classes. He also abandoned the kingly way of benevolence and showed favor to the people he liked; he banned books and implemented severe penalties; he stressed the use of force while neglected the use of benevolence, so he had initiated the rule of brutality." The second emperor of Qin Dynasty "was simply ruthless...with numerous brutal penalties, cruel officials, and excessive tax. Thus, neither the rules of rewarding nor punishment were implemented appropriately. Besides, the state was so troublesome that it was difficult for the officials to handle; the people suffered miserably but they were not sympathized nor helped by their masters."[3] Thus, it was inevitable for the perishing of Qin Dynasty after the second reigning. He emphasized that "Li" (rites) was the foundation of "a stable state because it could help the emperor to win the support of his people",[4] while "Fa" (Law) was just the means to force people to obey certain behavioral codes, as was illustrated in the statement that "'Gui' (on the right track) means to act in accordance with law."[5] So only "Li" (rites) could "nip the evil in the bud."[6] He also differentiated the roles that "Li" (rites) and "Fa" (law) played: "'Li' (rites) prevented the evilness beforehand, while 'Fa' (law) punishes that afterward. So it is easy to see the effect of 'Fa' (law), but it is difficult to understand how 'Li' (rites) works."[7] He warned the rulers of early Han Dynasty that it could keep the regime "lasting scores of generations" to govern the state with 'Li' (rites) and 'Yi' (justice) because those who ruled only by 'Fa' (law) would incur misfortune with all of his offsprings killed."[8] So only by combining "Ren" (benevolence) and "Yi" (justice) (which were compared to the blade of knife of a monarch) with power and legal system (which were compared to weapons) could long-lasting peace and prosperity be maintained in Han Dynasty.

After the conclusive reasoning made by Lu Gu and Jia Yi, the ideology concerning the relationship between "De" (virtue) and "Xing" (punishment) and that between "Li" (rites) and "Fa" (law) from pre-Qin Dynasties were combined with the thought of "Huang Lao" (a branch of Taoism represented by Huang Di and Lao

---

[3] Jia Yi (Han Dynasty), "Guo Qin Lun" (On the Errors of Qin) in *Xin Shu* (*New Writings*) (Book 2).
[4] Jia Yi (Han Dynasty), "Li" (Rites) in *Xin Shu* (*New Writings*).
[5] Jia Yi (Han Dynasty), "Dao Shu" (The Practice of Daoist Rules) in *Xin Shu* (*New Writings*).
[6] "Jia Yi Zhuan" (The Biography of Jia Yi) in *Han Shu* (*The History of Han Dynasty*).
[7] "Jia Yi Zhuan" (The Biography of Jia Yi) in *Han Shu* (*The History of Han Dynasty*).
[8] "Jia Yi Zhuan" (The Biography of Jia Yi) in *Han Shu* (*The History of Han Dynasty*).

Zi), which not only influenced several generations of rulers in early Han Dynasty, but also became the guiding principle of the ruling regime, and which had fostered the formation of the rehabilitating policy of levying less tax, imposing lighter corvée and enforcing lenient punishments in the early Han Dynasty.

Tax and Corvée Reduction During the period of Emperor Gao, the tax rate was one fifteenth, but during the reign of Emperor Jing, it was changed into one thirtieth. This policy benefited mainly the landlords, but it did reduce the farmers' burden as well. Learning the lesson from the destruction of Qin Dynasty, which was caused by the increasing unbearable burden of heavy tax and public corvée, Emperor Wen told the officials of "Jun" (shire) and "Xian" (county) to "reduce corvée and tax to benefit the people"[9] so that they could live a relatively stable life to restore and develop agriculture. During the first sixty years of Han Dynasty, there were almost no large-scale construction project and expedition.

Releasing "Nu Bi" (The Slave Girls and Maidservants) After emperor Gao took the crown, to ease class tension and increase labor force, he issued an order to set free "those who have sold themselves as 'Nu Bi' (the slave girls and maidservants) out of hunger and to treat them as common people."[10] In Qin Dynasty, it was once stipulated that the relatives of the criminals should be condemned to be 'Nu Bi' (the slave girls and maidservants), but during the period of the reign of emperor Wen, the law was abolished, and at the same time those "who served labor service for the government were changed into common people."[11]

"Zhong Nong Yi Shang" (Encouraging Agriculture and Restraining Commerce) To foster agriculture, the policy of obtaining noble titles by handing in agricultural products was adopted, namely, one's ranks was decided according to the amount of agricultural products one handed in. Meanwhile, measures were taken to restrict the development of business. For example, the descendants of the businessmen were "not allowed to be officials,"[12] and they were "not even allowed to wear silk clothes or to take wagons."[13] However, the giant businessmen still possessed great fortune and political power.

Abolishing the Harsh Laws and Severe Punishments Cruel punishment was the main cause of the peasant rebellion at the end of Qin Dynasty. Thus, in the early Han Dynasty, as an important part of the rehabilitating policy, severe penalties were abolished. When Emperor Gao came to Xianyang, with regard to the numerous laws and severe penalties of Qin Dynasty, he announced at Bashang that "(I now) make a

---

[9]"Xiao Wen Ben Ji" (The Biographic Sketches of Emperor Xiaowen) in *Shi Ji* (*The Record of the Grand Historian*).

[10]"Gao Di Ji" (The Record of the First Emperor of Han Dynasty) in *Han Shu* (*The History of Han Dynasty*).

[11]"Wen Di Ji" (The Record of Emperor Wen) in *Han Shu* (*The History of Han Dynasty*).

[12]"Ping Zhun Shu" (On Fair Trade) in *Shi Ji* (*The Record of the Grand Historian*).

[13]"Ping Zhun Shu" (On Fair Trade) in *Shi Ji* (*The Record of the Grand Historian*).

treaty of 'Yue Fa San Zhang' (three-point covenant) with you, my folks: those who kill shall be sentenced to death; those who hurt others or commit robbery shall be punished but the rest of the laws of Qin Dynasty will be abolished."[14] The spirit of "Yue Fa San Zhang" (three-point covenant) was to simplify the laws to their essentials, to be lenient in the enforcement of law and to protect the people and private property, so it undoubtedly was in line with the expectation of the people under the new historical conditions, so it was called "an agreement to meet the need of the people"[15] by historians. Later on, the policy of enforcing lenient punishment was also adopted by Emperor Hui, Queen Gao, Emperor Wen, and Jing. For example, in the 4th year of emperor Hui (191 B.C.), *Xie Shu Lv* (*Statutes Forbidding the Possession of Books*) was abolished; in January of the first year of Queen Gao (187 B.C.), the punishment of "Yi San Zu" (the law of killing the three generations of a family) and "Yao Yan Ling" (Decree for Heresy) were abolished. When Emperor Wen came to power, he abolished the collective punishment system and announced that "the law if applied properly was to stop the evil and to guide the good. I can't accept the so-called collective punishment system, according to which if the criminal has been condemned, his innocent parents, wife, children and siblings will also be punished and taken away as slaves." He insisted that "if the law is proper, then the public will behave well; if the judgment is fair, then people will follow."[16] In the 2nd year of emperor Wen (178 B.C.), the crimes of slander and heresy were abolished and it was stated in the imperial edict that "the crime of slander and heresy has prevented the officials from expressing themselves freely. If the emperor can't learn about his own mistakes from his officials, then how to attract the sages afar? So the law must be abolished." "From now on, the people who commit these crimes will be exempted from punishment."[17] In the meanwhile, for the measurement of punishment, the principle of "regarding the suspects as innocent people" was adopted,[18] which had obviously reduced the number of crimes.

In early Han Dynasty, guided by the principle of eliminating redundancy and harshness, simplifying laws and reducing penalties, the social conflicts were eased and the society became stable. According to "Xing Fa Zhi" (The Record of the Criminal Law) in *Han Shu* (*The History of Han Dynasty*), during the reign of Emperor Wen, "the people were tolerant of different opinions and ashamed of finding fault with others. Besides, it was prevalent to moralize people by teaching and the evilness of informing against other people was eradicated. So the officials were devoted to their duties and the people enjoyed their work." "There were only

---

[14]"Gao Di Ji" (The Record of the First Emperor of Han Dynasty) in *Han Shu* (*The History of Han Dynasty*).

[15]"Gao Di Ji" (The Record of the First Emperor of Han Dynasty) in *Han Shu* (*The History of Han Dynasty*).

[16]"Xiao Wen Ben Ji" (The Biographic Sketches of Emperor Xiaowen) in *Shi Ji* (*The Record of the Grand Historian*).

[17]"Wen Di Ji" (The Record of Emperor Wen) in *Han Shu* (*The History of Han Dynasty*).

[18]"Xing Fa Zhi" (The Record of the Criminal Law) in *Han Shu* (*The History of Han Dynasty*).

several hundred cases in a year, and criminal punishments were almost not applied."[19] It was also recorded in "Jing Di Ji" (The Biography of Emperor Jing) that "after the founding of Han Dynasty, the redundant and harsh laws were abolished and the people were rehabilitated. Moreover, during the reign of Emperor Xiaowen, the custom of being respectful and frugal was formed, while during the reign of Xiao Jing the spirit of dedication to one's work was encouraged. So during the fifty to sixty years, the obsolete customs were removed and the people were honest and kindhearted." As to these official records, undoubtedly, there were some compliments by the historians, but it was true that there was a transformation in social spirit caused by the policy of simplifying laws and reducing penalties in early Han Dynasty. However, it did not mean that there were no crimes and that the law was useless. On the contrary, in September of the 5th year of Emperor Jing, an imperial order was issued and it was clearly stated that "the purpose of law is to curb violence and prevent evilness in the society,"[20] which had clearly demonstrated the value and goal of law.

The rulers in early Han Dynasty tried hard to restore and reestablish the order of legal systems at the time of rectifying the malpractice of Qin Dynasty. During the reign of Emperor Wen, Zhang Shizhi was "Gong Che Ling" (official in charge of guards and receptions). When the prince came through Si Ma Gate (the outer gate of the palace) and did not get off from the wagon, Zhang Shizhi ran after the wagon, stopped it from entering the gate of the palace, and charged the prince with "Bu Jing" (being irreverent). Emperor Wen apologized to his queen mother Bo for this, and admitted that "he has not taught his son good manners."[21] Afterwards, Zhang Shizhi became "Ting Wei" (the supreme official in charge of judicature) and Emperor Wen was very much impressed by Zhang Shizhi's settlement of legal cases for many times. Example one: one day, Emperor Wen was crossing the Zhong Wei Bridge when someone stepped out from under the bridge and frightened his horses. Zhang Shizhi "charged him with 'Bi' (clearing way for the emperor to pass by prohibiting others to go nearer) and ruled that he was to be imposed with a fine." Emperor Wen demanded a much severer penalty, but Zhang Shizhi suggested that "the law is agreed on by the emperor and the public. According to the law, the accused should be imposed with a fine, so if I impose a severer penalty on him, the public will lose their faith in law." Zhang Shizhi added, "If your majesty order to have him killed on the spot, the public won't make any comment. But now the case is decided by me, I need to make fair judgment, because if not, the law will be enforced in the country without a fixed standard. Then the people won't know what to do. So please think it over." Emperor Wen finally agreed and said, "'Ting Wei' (the supreme official in

---

[19]"Wen Di Ji" (The Record of Emperor Wen) in *Han Shu* (*The History of Han Dynasty*).
[20]"Jing Di Ji" (The Record of Emperor Jing) in *Han Shu* (*The History of Han Dynasty*).
[21]"Zhang Shi Zhi Zhuan" (The Biography of Zhang Shizhi) in *Han Shu* (*The History of Han Dynasty*).

charge of judicature) is right."[22] Example two: someone stole the jade ring in front of the seat in the imperial temple. Zhang Shizhi made the judgment and punished him by "Qi Shi" (exposing the executed body publicly at markets) for the crime of stealing the decoration of ancestral temples. Emperor Wen wanted to have the criminal punished by "Zu Zhu" (killing of the whole clan of a criminal) for his infringement on the authority of the emperor. Zhang Shizhi took off his hat and knelt down, insisting that the judgment was in accordance with the law. Emperor Wen was convinced again, and said, "'Ting Wei' is right."[23] In the feudal society where the law was made by the emperor, Emperor Wen not only obeyed the law, but also did not change the law at his own will, which had exerted a great influence on the maintenance of the authority of law as well as the legal order. Emperor Wen did so because he realized the importance of obeying law and that the peace and order of the country relied on the emperor. He once said, "In spite of my humbleness, I was granted the position by my ancestors and became the emperor of the people. So it depends on me alone to restore the stability and order of the country."[24]

To the reign of Emperor Wu, the feudal economy was prosperous, the centralized power was consolidated, the treasury was rich and military was strong. Thus, Emperor Wu gradually cast off the restriction of the politics of "Wu Wei" (letting things take their own course) and "began to take aggressive policies towards neighboring countries and live an extravagant life at home. So wars with bordering countries were frequently waged, which had cost much of the public fund. Consequently, many people committed crimes out of poverty and the brutal officials made verdicts arbitrarily."[25] Against such background, the ideas of "Huang Lao" (a branch of Taoism represented by Huang Di and Lao Zi) became obsolete and a new theoretical system was needed to support Emperor Wu's political and economic policies to achieve feudal unification. Thus, a new school named new Confucianism was formed by Dong Zhongshu with the combination of *Gong Yang Chun Qiu* (the theory put forward by "Gong Yang" Scholars during "Chun Qiu" or the Spring and Autumn period, the theory holds that society develops in three stages) and the other different schools of thoughts of "Yin Yang"(the two opposing principles in nature, the former feminine and negative, the latter masculine and positive), "Fa" (Legalist), "Dao" (Taoist) and "Ming" (the Logicians), etc. This new Confucianism had become the orthodox legal thought and had dominated China for more than 2000 years.

Dong Zhongshu, who lived in Western Han Dynasty, was born in Guangchuan, He Bei Province in the 5th or 6th year of the reign of Queen Lv and died in the 2nd year of Yuan Ding in the reign of Emperor Wu. He studied *Chun Qiu* (*Spring and Autumn Annals*) at a very young age and had special talent for "Gong Yang Xue"

---

[22]"Zhang Shi Zhi Zhuan" (The Biography of Zhang Shizhi) in *Han Shu* (*The History of Han Dynasty*).

[23]"Zhang Shi Zhi Zhuan" (The Biography of Zhang Shizhi) in *Han Shu* (*The History of Han Dynasty*).

[24]"Wen Di Ji" (The Record of Emperor Wen) in *Han Shu* (*The History of Han Dynasty*).

[25]"Xing Fa Zhi" (The Record of the Criminal Law) in *Han Shu* (*The History of Han Dynasty*).

(the study of *Gong Yang Zhuan* and the interpretation of *Chun Qiu* by "Gong Yang" scholars), which won him great honor in the study of Confucianism in Han Dynasty. He was a "Bo Shi" (learned scholars) during the reign of Emperor Jing. After Emperor Wu ascended the throne, he stated the importance and necessity of "rejecting the other schools of thoughts and respecting only Confucianism" from the perspective of the "grand unity of Chun Qiu" when asked about his ideas of policy making by the emperor. He said, "the grand unity of Chun Qiu is the natural and universal law for the past and the present. But now different theories are taught by teachers and people hold different opinions, so various schools of thoughts differ from each other, each aiming at different goals. Therefore, there are no consistent guidelines for the emperor and the laws are often changed so that the public don't know what to do. My humble opinion is that the ideologies and schools which are not included in 'Liu Yi' (six skills) or Confucianism shall be abandoned, rather than be treated equally with Confucianism."[26] Considering the grand unity of Chun Qiu, he suggested, "retaining the trunk while at the same time cutting off the branches and prioritizing the key parts over the less important ones."[27] Moreover, "the emperor is endowed with the mission by 'Tian' (Heaven) and the public are subjected to the emperor."[28] He also advised that "it is the ruler's responsibility to reform the systems."[29] Because Dong Zhongshu's ideas could be used as the theoretical foundation for the centralized autocratic system and they catered to the need of Emperor Wu for his military achievements, they were applauded and adopted by the emperor, so that Confucianism was made the official school of thoughts and Confucianist theory the orthodox ideology. The change from the thoughts of "Huang Lao" (a branch of Taoism represented by Huang Di and Lao Zi) to Confucianism proved that besides the requirement of historical circumstances, the rulers of Han Dynasty realized through experience that compared with the application of severe penalties and the thoughts of "Huang Lao" (a branch of Taoism represented by Huang Di and Lao Zi) in Qin Dynasty, it was more effective in maintaining the stability of the country, in fostering the economy and in consolidating the regime to apply the theories of Confucianism.

It was not accidental that the ideas of "Huang Lao" (a branch of Taoism represented by Huang Di and Lao Zi) were replaced by Confucianism. Besides the needs of political development, the possibility was also contained in the component of the ideology of "Huang Lao" (a branch of Taoism represented by Huang Di and Lao Zi) itself.

---

[26]"Dong Zhong Shu Zhuan" (The Biography of Dong Zhongshu) in *Han Shu* (*The History of Han Dynasty*).

[27]Dong Zhongshu (Han Dynasty), "Shi Zhi" (Ten Important Issues) in *Chun Qiu Fan Lu* (*The Luxuriant Dew of Spring and Autumn Annals*).

[28]Dong Zhongshu (Han Dynasty), "Wei Ren Zhe Tian" (The Destiny of Man being Determined by Heaven) in *Chun Qiu Fan Lu* (*The Luxuriant Dew of Spring and Autumn Annals*).

[29]Dong Zhongshu (Han Dynasty), "Chu Zhuang Wang" (King Zhuang of the State of Chu) in *Chun Qiu Fan Lu* (*The Luxuriant Dew of Spring and Autumn Annals*).

5.1 The Establishment of Western Han Dynasty and the Change of the Legislative... 257

Actually, the thought of "Huang Lao" (a branch of Taoism represented by Huang Di and Lao Zi) advocated by the rulers of early Han Dynasty was different from that in pre-Qin period. They advocated the theory of "Yue Fa Sheng Jin" (to make simple laws and to enforce lenient penalties), "Wu Zai An Min"(to ensure people's safety and livelihood), "Wu Wei Er Zhi" (to govern by doing nothing that goes against nature), at same time, they also supported "Ren" (benevolence) and "Yi" (justice) advocated by Confucianism and the criminal laws of legalist school, so finally the theories of "Huang Lao" was formed by integrating and absorbing part of Confucianism and legalism, by which it had possessed the inner possibility to be transformed to Confucianism.

The characteristic of the times of the thoughts of "Huang Lao" (a branch of Taoism represented by Huang Di and Lao Zi) in early Han Dynasty could be seen from the book *Huai Nan Zi* (*Masters from Huainan*) written by the guests and staff of Duke of Huainan, Liu An, which was a collection of the ideology of Confucianism, legalism, Mohism, and the ideas of "Yin" and "Yang" based on Taoism. It advocated the theory of "Wu Wei" (letting things take their own course), suggesting that action be achieved through non-action. But at the same time, the value of the law was affirmed in the book, and it was pointed out that laws should be applied to prevent the emperor from making decisions arbitrarily, because "the law is the code of behavior for the public and the standard for the ruler....When the law is made, those who obey the law shall be awarded and those who failed to do so shall be punished. Besides, the punishment for the noble should not be mitigated and the punishment for the humble should not be aggravated; even the virtuous shall be punished if he violates the law, the common people should not be punished just because they are not talented enough,...so legal documents and 'Li' (rites) are applied to prevent the rulers from making arbitrary judgments."[30] This passage served as a footnote for the legalist idea that "everything should be settled by law," but its concept of restricting the emperor by law was much advanced than the legalist theory of the combination of "Fa" (law), "Shu" (tactics) and "Shi" (power).

The book also advocated that "Ren" (benevolence) and "Yi" (justice) should be the guiding principle of administration, boasting that it was "the everlasting and unchangeable law,"[31] which implied that Confucianism had already become an important part of the thoughts of "Huang Lao" (a branch of Taoism represented by Huang Di and Lao Zi) in early Han Dynasty.

During the early years of the reign of Emperor Wu, his grandmother Madame Dou held the power. Because "she preferred the ideas of 'Huang Lao' (a branch of Taoism represented by Huang Di and Lao Zi), the emperor, the crown prince and all those named Dou had to read *Huang Di* and *Lao Zi* to study the ideas therein."[32] At that time, the officials such as Dou Ying, Tian Fen, and Zhao Guan had all insisted

---

[30]"Zhu Shu Xun" (Tactics for the Monarch) in *Huai Nan Zi* (*Masters from Huainan*).

[31]"Fan Lun Xun" (General Remarks) in *Huai Nan Zi* (*Masters from Huainan*).

[32]"Wai Qi Shi Jia" (The Saga of Maternal Relatives) in *Shi Ji* (*The Record of the Grand Historian*).

upon the upholding of Confucianism, but they were rejected and dismissed from their positions. After the death of Queen grandmother Dou, Emperor Wu began to deal with state affairs by himself, so he appointed Tian Fen as "Cheng Xiang" (the prime minister), which had provided the authoritative guarantee for abolishing the thoughts of "Huang Lao" (a branch of Taoism represented by Huang Di and Lao Zi) and showing only respect to Confucianism.

The Confucianization of legislation is mainly expressed in the following ways:

First, "De Zhu Xing Fu" (employing moral teaching as the primary means, punishment as the supplement) and applying morality instead of punishment. In the early years of Western Zhou Dynasty, Zhou Gong Dan (Dan, Duke of Zhou) put forward the principle of "Ming De Shen Fa" (promoting virtue and being prudent in the enforcement of punishment) which had provided the guidance for the legal construction of Zhou Dynasty. In Han Dynasty, Dong Zhongshu established a complete legal system of "De Zhu Xing Fu" (employing moral teaching as the primary means, punishment as the supplement) and used the theory of "Tian Ren Gan Ying" (interactions between Heaven and Mankind) as the philosophical and complementary basis of "Yin Yang" (the two opposing principles in nature, the former feminine and negative, the latter masculine and positive) and "Wu Xing" (the five elements, including metal, wood, water, fire and earth, held by the ancients to compose the physical universe) to prove that "De Zhu Xing Fu" (employing moral teaching as the primary means, punishment as the supplement) was compatible with "Tian Li" (heavenly principle). He said:

> One of the most important heavenly principles is 'Yin' and 'Yang'. 'Yang' is 'De' (morality) and 'Yin' is 'Xing' (punishment); 'Xing' (punishment) mainly refers to killing and 'De' (morality) mainly refers to birth, therefore 'Yang' lies in summer and brings about life and growth; 'Yin' lies in winter and in useless and void places. Because 'Tian' (Heaven) favors 'De' (morality) over 'Xing' (punishment)...,the monarch should obey the heaven's will and promote 'De' (morality) rather than 'Xing' (punishment). 'Xing' (punishment) can't be used to rule just as 'Yin' can't bring about harvest. It is incompatible with 'Tian Li' (heavenly principles) to rule by 'Xing' (punishment), therefore it is not adopted by the reverend ancestors.[33]

He also said that "the sages have made the principles by following 'Tian' (Heaven),"[34] and "they have increased love, reduced harshness, promoted morality, and simplified the law."[35] Dong Zhongshu expounded the theory of "applying 'De' (morality) rather than 'Xing' (punishment)"[36]; "stressing 'De' (morality) rather than 'Xing' (punishment)" and "promoting 'De' (morality) rather than 'Xing'

---

[33] "Dong Zhong Shu Zhuan" (The Biography of Dong Zhongshu) in *Han Shu* (*The History of Han Dynasty*).

[34] "Dong Zhong Shu Zhuan" (The Biography of Dong Zhongshu) in *Han Shu* (*The History of Han Dynasty*).

[35] Dong Zhongshu (Han Dynasty), "Ji Yi" (Basic Morals) in *Chun Qiu Fan Lu* (*The Luxuriant Dew of Spring and Autumn Annals*).

[36] Dong Zhongshu (Han Dynasty), "Ji Yi" (Basic Morals) in *Chun Qiu Fan Lu* (*The Luxuriant Dew of Spring and Autumn Annals*).

(punishment)",[37] at the same time, elaborated on the role played by 'Xing' (punishment), and said that 'Yang' was dominant while 'Yin' was supplementary, so "'Xing' (punishment) is supplementary to 'De' (morality) just as 'Yin' is supplementary to 'Yang'."[38]

Apart from Dong Zhongshu, Liu Xiang also discussed the relationship between "De" (morality) and "Xing" (punishment) and their different functions in *Shuo Yuan* (*Collection of Stories*): "two important things are needed in governing a country: 'De' (morality) and 'Xing' (punishment). The wise rulers pay more attention to 'De' (morality) rather than 'Xing' (punishment); the despots use both 'De' (morality) and 'Xing' (punishment); the powerful state prioritizes 'Xing' (punishment) over 'De' (morality). 'Xing' (punishment) and 'De' (morality) are where education starts; 'De' (morality) boosts the good and improves the imperfect; 'Xing' (punishment) punishes the bad and warns against evils, so those who support the application of 'De' (morality) give rewards generously, while those who support the application of 'Xing' (punishment) enforce punishment severely."[39]

After various argumentation by the Confucian scholars from different perspectives, "De Zhu Xing Fu" (employing moral teaching as the primary means, punishment as the supplement) gradually became the guiding legislative and administrative principle. Just as Emperor Xuan said, "Han Dynasty has established its own systems on the basis of legalism. How can we just use Confucianism? Are you prepared to adopt the system of Zhou Dynasty?"[40] The so-called "Ba Wang Dao Za Zhi" simply meant the combination of "Li" (rites) and "Fa" (law), and "De Zhu Xing Fu" (employing moral teaching as the primary means, punishment as the supplement). Because it met the need of the ruling of feudal countries, it became a very influential and long-lasting guiding principle for the legal construction of feudal countries after Han Dynasty.

The disputes between Confucianism and legalism originated from pre-Qin period and it was finally settled and integrated by Dong Zhongshu in Western Han Dynasty. The academic development is always achieved through debates and absorption between different schools of thoughts, so this rule is also applicable to the process of the practical development from "Bai Jia Zheng Ming" (the contention of a hundred schools of thoughts) which was started from Spring and Autumn Periods through Warring States Period to the sole respection of Confucianism. Of course, Confucianism initiated by Confucius did not reject the existence of law, nor negate the value of law, instead it just insisted that law should be guided and dominated by "Li" (rites). Just because of this, to the time of "Ji Xia" school of thought (scholars in

---

[37]Dong Zhongshu (Han Dynasty), "Yang Zun Yin Bei" (Yang Noble and Yin Humble) in *Chun Qiu Fan Lu* (*The Luxuriant Dew of Spring and Autumn Annals*).

[38]Dong Zhongshu (Han Dynasty), "Tian Bian Zai Ren" (The Interaction between Man and Heaven) in *Chun Qiu Fan Lu* (*The Luxuriant Dew of Spring and Autumn Annals*).

[39]Liu Xiang (Han Dynasty), "Zheng Li" (The Principles of Government) in *Shuo Yuan* (*Collection of Stories*).

[40]"Yuan Di Ji" (The Biography of Emperor Yuan) in *Han Shu* (*The History of Han Dynasty*).

the state of Qi) represented by Xunzi, some element of legalism was already absorbed in Confucianism, so both "Li" (rites) and "Fa" (law) were stressed. As a master of legalism, when criticizing the discrimination of "Li" (rites) held by Confucianism, Han Fei accepted the regulations of "Li" (rites) about the superior and inferior, the noble and the humble, the emperor and the minister, and the father and son. He said, "If the official serves the emperor, the son serves the father and the wife serves the husband, the society will be in good order; if not, the world will be in chaos, which is the natural law of the world."[41] He also insisted on replacing the slavery hierarchal system with the feudal one, which had determined the possibility of the integration of Confucianism and legalism.

Han Fei's combination of "Fa" (law), "Shu" (tactics), and "Shi" (power) had laid the theoretical foundation for the autocratic political system. The so-called principle that "everything should be settled by law" was only a tool of government by monarchs and the derivative of the emperor's power. It was in fact a kind of "Fa Zhi" (the ruling of law) based on "Ren Zhi" (the ruling of man) and "Jun Zhi" (the ruling of emperor), which was similar to the principle of "Ren Zhi" (the ruling of man) advocated by Confucianism. Especially in early Han Dynasty, the Confucian scholars advocated that the emperor's power was granted by "Tian" (Heaven) by applying the theory of "Tian Ren Gan Ying" (interactions between Heaven and Mankind), claimed that "the emperor is the son of 'Tian' (Heaven) and the parent of the public and tried to strengthen the power of the emperor by making use of the ethical patriarchal system."[42] They rejected the theory of the superiority of the common people and the inferiority of the rulers and denied Meng Zi's theory that "the people is the most important, next comes the state and finally comes the emperor"[43] and Xun Zi's theory of "following the way of nature rather than that of the emperor".[44] Instead, they advocated that the emperor was respectable and the subjects were humble, which was coherent with the legalist idea of emperor's divine rights.

Although the rulers of the early Han Dynasty criticized the cruelty of Qin Shi Huang (the first emperor of Qin), they had inherited the autocratic regime with the superior authority of the emperor, which was the so-called "Han Cheng Qin Zhi" (inheriting the system of Qin Dynasty). They examined the lessons that could be learned from the downfall of Qin Dynasty to strengthen the rule of despotism, which was also demanded by the dual combination of Confucian and legalist ideas characterized by the alternative application of kindness and severity. The Chinese feudal political history has testified repeatedly that where there exits despotism, the neo-Confucianism established by Confucian scholars in Han Dynasty, which is characterized by the combination of Confucianism with legalism, will never lose its dominant position.

---

[41]"Zhong Xiao" (Loyalty and Filial Piety) in *Han Fei Zi* (*Han Feizi*).

[42]"Bao Xuan Zhuan" (The Biography of Bao Xuan) in *Han Shu* (*The History of Han Dynasty*).

[43]"Jin Xin" (With all One's Heart) in *Meng Zi* (*Mencius*).

[44]"Chen Dao" (The Way of Being a Subject) in *Xun Zi* (*Xun Zi*).

Since the founding of Han Dynasty, the function of law in state affairs was widely accepted and the guiding rules of legislation were gradually changed to the Confucian principle of "Gang Chang Ming Jiao" (feudal cardinal guides and constant virtues). Thus, "De Zhu Xing Fu" (employing moral teaching as the primary means, punishment as the supplement) advocated by Dong Zhongshu was taken as the guideline of ruling the country, which had initiated the confucianization of the legal system. "De Zhu Xing Fu" (employing moral teaching as the primary means, punishment as the supplement) was not only the product and manifestation of the integration of legalism and Confucianism, but also the main contents of the feudal legal culture, and its influence had lasted until the end of the feudal society.

Under the guidance of "De Zhu Xing Fu" (employing moral teaching as the primary means, punishment as the supplement), "Lun Li" (the rites and rituals of Confucianism) and "Dao De" (virtue) of Confucianism not only were adopted in the form of law but also was applied in judicial practice, which had brought about the popularity of "Chun Qiu Jue Yu" (Settling Lawsuits by Chun Qiu or Confucianism Classics).

Second, "San Gang" (three cardinal guides) was the highest principle of legislation, which was closely related to the dominant position of Confucianism. In early Han Dynasty, Gaozu (the first emperor of Han Dynasty) showed contempt for Confucianism, criticized Lu Jia for his advocation of *Shi* (*Shi Jing*: *Book of Songs*) and *Shu* (Confucian classics) and said: "I win the war on horseback rather than by reading *Shi* (*Shi Jing*: *Book of Songs*) and *Shu* (Confucian classics)." Lu Jia retorted, "You do win the war on horseback, but can you rule on horseback? Tang of the Shang dynasty and Wu of the Zhou Dynasty have all won by force but ruled by law, because the combination of civil and military methods is the secret to everlasting ruling",[45] which had played a positive role in changing Emperor Gaozu's attitude towards Confucianism. Afterwards, Confucian scholar Shu Suntong made court etiquette and the behavioral codes for the emperor and his officials. Emperor Gaozu sighed: "Today I realized the dignity of an emperor."[46] Therefore, in the 11th year of Gaozu (196 B.C.), on his way back from the conquest of Ying Bu, Gaozu passed by Lu and paid tribute to Confucius with the ceremony of "Tai Lao" (the sacrificial ceremony for the god of land and the god of grain), which had initiated the imperial custom of offering sacrifice to Confucius. With the policy of "rejecting the other schools of thoughts and respecting only Confucianism" initiated in the reign of Emperor Wu, Confucianism represented by Dong Zhongshu started to be respected by the rulers. Hence, Dong Zhongshu's thought, with "San Gang" (three cardinal guides) at the core, became not only the national law, but also the highest principle of legislation.

---

[45]"Li Sheng Lu Jia Lie Zhuan" (The Biography of Li Sheng and Lu Jia, et al) in *Shi Ji* (*The Record of the Grand Historian*).

[46]"Shu Sun Tong Zhuan" (The Biography of Shu Suntong) in *Shi Ji* (*The Record of the Grand Historian*).

The so-called "San Gang" (three cardinal guides) mainly refers to the three guides, namely, the ruler guides the subject, the father guides the son, and the husband guides the wife, which has manifested the monarchical power, the patriarchal authority of the husband based on the strict feudal hierarchy. It highlighted the etiquette of superiority and inferiority, which should be obeyed by both the monarch and the minister, the father and the son, and the husband and the wife. "So there is not only the difference between the noble and the humble, but also the distinction of clothes, the difference of positions at court and among villagers so that the public won't fight for what doesn't belong to them."[47] To expand the authority of "San Gang" (three cardinal guides), Dong Zhongshu boasted that "'San Gang' (three cardinal guides) of the way of kings can be obtained from 'Tian' (Heaven),"[48] which had given the theory a touch of mystery.

In Han Dynasty, "San Gang" (three cardinal guides) was not only the highest moral standard of the society, but also the fundamental principle for legislation. Therefore, it had not only guided the ratification of law, but also was represented by law. For example, the enacting of the crimes of "Da Bu Jing" (being greatly irreverent), "Bu Xiao" (being unfilial), "Bu Dao" (Depravity), and "Qin Shou Xing (Beastly Conducts), etc., and the principles of "Qin De Xiang Shou Ni" (a law in Han Dynasty which ruled that crimes committed among the kinsfolks should be concealed and should not be reported to the government), "Yuan Xing Ding Zui" (punishment given in accordance with the convict's motive for the crime), "Yi" (cases involving eight privileged groups were not to be tried directly by judicial organs, but to be reported to and decided by the emperor, thus the accused would usually be pardoned or remitted), "Qing" (cases involving officials above "Wu Pin" [the fifth rank] shall be reported to and decided by the emperor, the punishment other than death penalty would be remitted by one degree) and so forth, were all the embodiments of "San Gang" (three cardinal guides) in law. The legalization of "San Gang" (three cardinal guides), which had combined the spiritual power of morality and the material power of legal force, had woven a tight net for protecting the society against crimes and for stabilizing the regime of Han Dynasty.

Third, enforcing punishments in autumn and winter and offering amnesties in accordance with 'Tian' (Heaven). Under the guidance of the principle of "Yin Yang" (the two opposing principles in nature, the former feminine and negative, the latter masculine and positive) and "Wu Xing" (the five elements, including metal, wood, water, fire and earth, held by the ancients to compose the physical universe), the important state affairs such as the making of policies, the expedition and punishment of criminals which were recorded in the book *Lv Shi Chun Qiu* (*Spring and Autumn Annals of Master Lv*) written by the end of Warring States Period and *Huai Nan Zi* (*Masters from Huainan*) written in early Han Dynasty were all closely related with

---

[47] Dong Zhongshu (Han Dynasty), "Du Zhi" (On the Systems) in *Chun Qiu Fan Lu* (*The Luxuriant Dew of Spring and Autumn Annals*).

[48] Dong Zhongshu (Han Dynasty), "Ji Yi" (Basic Morals) in *Chun Qiu Fan Lu* (*The Luxuriant Dew of Spring and Autumn Annals*).

5.1 The Establishment of Western Han Dynasty and the Change of the Legislative...

nature. Dong Zhongshu further testified the importance of "enforcing punishments by following the season" by making use of the concept of "Tian Ren Gan Ying" (interactions between Heaven and Mankind). He said, "There are four seasons in nature, so there are four administrative tasks for the emperor...there are similarities between nature and mankind. In spring we celebrate, in summer we appreciate, in autumn we impose fines, and in winter we enforce penalties."[49] "In spring, 'Tian' (Heaven) gives birth to everything, so the emperor shows love to the people; in summer, 'Tian' fosters growth, so the emperor promotes morality; frost is the way by which 'Tian' kills, so the emperor punishes crimes by penalty. Therefore, the interaction between man and 'Tian' is universal."[50] The statement of Dong Zhongshu had prepared the public opinion for the execution of penalty in autumn and winter, which was institutionalized and legalized with the establishment of the orthodox position of Confucianism.

There were also some discussion about the punishment in autumn and winter in "Yan Tie Lun" (Debates on Salt and Iron) and "Yue Ling" (Monthly Orders) in *Li Ji* (*The Book of Rites*). It was recorded in the former that "spring and summer are seasons for growing, so it is time for benevolence; autumn and winter are seasons that kill and restore, so it is time for punishment. It was recorded in "Yue Ling" (Monthly Orders) in *Li Ji* (*The Book of Rites*) that "in middle of spring... it is time for new lives to take roots, to raise the young and to keep orphans...so it is better to ask 'You Si' (official) in charge to reduce the number of prisoners, to get rid of shackles, to stop the plundering and to cancel the lawsuits"; "in the first month of summer... it is better to try minor crimes, to enforce lenient penalties and to release minor offenders"; "in the first month of autumn...it is time to order the officials in charge to review the laws, to repair prisons, to prepare shackles, to prohibit evil-doing, to keep watch on crimes, to arrest the accused, to ask jailors to look at the wound of the jailed, to hear the cases, to make judgments, to guarantee fairness, to kill the criminals, and to impose severe punishments. The weather turns cold and the punishment should be more strict"; "in the 2nd month of autumn...order 'You Si' (official) in charge to reexamine the cases and make appropriate judgments; if there are any inappropriateness or unjust judgments, the officials in charge will be punished"; "in the 3rd month of autumn...making haste to try the cases to have all those guilty punished"; "in the 1st month of winter...finding out those who have flattered the emperor and those who have formed cliques for personal gains, and they should be all punished without being sheltered."

According to the Confucian theory of "showing respect to and following natural order" and "enforcing penalties by following the seasons," it was regarded as following "Yin Yang" (the two opposing principles in nature, the former feminine and negative, the latter masculine and positive) and "Wu Xing" (the five elements,

---

[49]Dong Zhongshu (Han Dynasty), "Si Shi Zhi Fu" (The Equivalents of Four Seasons) in *Chun Qiu Fan Lu* (*The Luxuriant Dew of Spring and Autumn Annals*).
[50]"Dong Zhong Shu Zhuan" (The Biography of Dong Zhong Shu) in *Han Shu* (*The History of Han Dynasty*).

including metal, wood, water, fire and earth, held by the ancients to compose the physical universe) as well as natural order to enforce punishments in autumn and winter, so the cruel judicial suppression in reality was connected with "Tian Dao" (The Way of Heaven) which dominated the operation of four seasons. The dignity of "Tian" (Heaven) had helped to strengthen the seriousness and deceptiveness of the law; therefore, it was supported, institutionalized, and legalized by the rulers. In Han Dynasty, the execution of death penalty was started in autumn and winter (October, November, and December of the lunar year) and stopped at the beginning of spring (Li Chun). Emperor Wu "killed Wei Qi in December of the 4th year of Yuan Guang in the city of Wei." Hu Sansheng noted that "in Han Dynasty, severe punishment was executed in winter, but in spring, the criminals would be freed. So he killed Wei Qi at the end of December."[51]

In Eastern Han Dynasty, in light of the intensification of contradiction in the society, Emperor Zhang ordered to execute death penalty in October of lunar year rather than in October, November and December in the 2nd year of Yuan He (85 A. D.), and he said: "I consulted many Confucian experts and books and learned that it is appropriate to live and kill in accordance with the seasons. So do not pass sentences in November and December."[52] As for the exact date of punishment, it should be "some day after the full moon,"[53] that is after the 15th or 16th day of lunar month. Because at that time the weather became colder and dreary, it was the exact time to enforce punishments on behalf of "Tian" (Heaven). However, the punishment for felonies that threatened the safety of the country was not limited by this rule. In the 1st year of Jian Chu (76 A.D.), Emperor Zhang stated clearly that "if the crime does not involve death penalty, then investigations should be postponed....In the beginning of autumn, it should be done the same."[54] Nevertheless, if the criminal had committed felonies deserving to be punished by death penalty, then there was no need to wait for the right time. During the reign of Emperor Gao, Han Xin and Peng Yue were sentenced to "Yi San Zu" (the law of killing the three generations of a family), so they were killed together with their families in January and March of spring, though the rule of the execution of death penalty in autumn and winter was not institutionalized at the time.

With the establishment of the rule of executing death penalties in autumn and winter, if death penalty for ordinary cases were carried out in spring and summer, it would be treated as atrocity. It was recorded in "Zhuge Feng Zhuan" (The Biography of Zhuge Feng) in *Han Shu* (*The History of Han Dynasty*) that "Feng used to punish people in spring and summer," so the emperor criticized him for "enforcing punishments without following seasons and gaining intangible authority by imposing violence and changing the laws." However, the theory of executing death penalties

---

[51]*Zi Zhi Tong Jian* (*History as a Mirror*), Vol. 18.
[52]"Zhang Di Ji" (The Record of Emperor Zhang) in *Latter Han Shu* (*The History of Latter Han Dynasty*).
[53]"Qiu Guan" (Ministry of Penalty) in *Zhou Li Zhu Shu* (*Interpretation of Zhou Li*).
[54]"Qiu Guan" (Ministry of Penalty) in *Zhou Li Zhu Shu* (*Interpretation of Zhou Li*).

in autumn and winter was criticized by Wang Chong in Han Dynasty, and it was more violently attacked by Liu Zongyuan in Tang Dynasty, who pointed out that it was better to follow humanity and "Dao" (virtue) instead of seasons. It is one of the reasons for the so-called "cancelling of criminal punishment" to enforce punishment in autumn and winter.[55]

Because of its deceptive effect, the principle of enforcing punishment in autumn and winter was carried out through to the later feudal dynasties. "Qiu Shen" (Autumn Trial) in Ming and Qing Dynasties originated from this policy.

Since the beginning of Han Dynasty, the tradition of enforcing severe punishments according to law without offering amenities which was carried out in Qin Dynasty was abandoned by the rulers. Starting from Emperor Gaozu, amenities were offered frequently. Later on, under the influence of "Tian Ren Gan Ying" (interactions between Heaven and Mankind), the emperors claimed to offer amenities in accordance with heavenly will, so amenities were often offered at the time of the emperor's ascending of the throne, funerals, disasters and the celebrity of birthday, etc. During the twelve years of reigning, Emperor Gaozu offered amnesties for nine times; during the twenty-three years of reigning, Emperor Wen offered amnesties for four times; during the sixteen years of reigning, Emperor Jing offered amnesties for five times; during the fifty-five years of reigning, Emperor Wu offered amnesties for eighteen times; during the thirteen years of reigning, Emperor Zhao offered amnesties for seven times; during the twenty-five years of reigning, Emperor Xuan offered amnesties for ten times; during the sixteen years of reigning, Emperor Yuan offered amnesties for ten times; during the twenty-six years of reigning, Emperor Cheng offered amnesties for nine times; during the six years of reigning, Emperor Ai offered amnesties for four times. From the perspective of the rulers, it was the best way to warn the public under the disguise of benevolent policy to apply law and punishment in the first place and to conduct pardoning in the second. Thus, it can be seen that amnesties in Han Dynasty had lost their original meaning in "Lv Xing" (The Penal Code of Lv) in *Shang Shu* (*The Book of Historical Document*), according to which, "pardoning should be conducted when there are doubts about 'Wu Xing' (Five Penalties) and 'Wu Fa' (Five Fines)."

Consequently, the abusing of pardoning had led to more and more crimes, so the society became more and more turbulent. The famous thinkers such as Wang Fu and Cui Shi had commented on the disadvantages of the abuse of pardoning. Wang Fu said:

"The reason why there are so many criminals today is that amnesties are frequently offered, because frequent amnesties have made bad people prosperous and good people suffering…, the frivolous man, even if not an evil person, would think about doing evil things and committing crimes, such as killing other people's parents for fortune and beauty, killing other's children, killing the whole family, taking bribes, obtaining money by violating the law; the cruel official would kill the innocent and treat the ordinary people unjustly. All these crimes should be punished by the wise rulers to redress the grievance, but they are all

---

[55](Tang) Liu Zongyuan, "Duan Xing Lun" (On Sentence) in *Liu He Dong Ji* (*The Collected Works of Liu Zongyuan*), Vol. 3.

pardoned instead. Thus, the evil person will show off and become more arrogant; a veteran thief will take the booty and leave brazenly; a filial son can't revenge for the crimes committed to his parents; the owner of the lost property can't take it back by his own; so there is nothing more painful than this. ...a man born evil...if committing crimes repeatedly, is truly a villain and is an extremely evil person, so even if he is set free from prison, it is almost impossible for him or her to repent...; those who come out of prison in a respectful way will still commit crime again..., because they are born evil and their evil nature can't be changed. So it is like encouraging people to do evil things to have these people pardoned."[56] "No doubt, offering amenities may lead to evil doing, while evil doing may in turn lead to the offering of amenities, which is like a vicious circle, so neither can be stopped in the end. Even if amnesty is announced every day, there will still be many crimes."[57]

Although Cui Shi exposed the evil consequence of "offering amenities for four times within one term," he did not argue against the general amnesty because he was only against offering frequent amenities. Thus, he proposed "amenities being offered once in every ten years."[58] Wang Fu criticized the abuse of amnesties, at the same time, he highlighted the importance of law. He said, "the ruler who can unite the country with law is like 'San Wang' (the three kings, namely, the three rulers of Xia, Shang, and Zhou Dynasties);... if the ruler makes the law but does not have it enforced, the country will be in chaos...so the officials who violate law or forged imperial orders must be punished by death penalty;.... if the ruler makes the law and offers amnesties sometimes, or issues orders and has it enforced, then it will be obeyed by the officials and the public because they dare not violate them. So the law made must be enforced. Therefore, all the countries can be well governed if the administrative laws and prohibitions are duly obeyed."[59] Although the criticism made by the thinkers in Han Dynasty did not help to rectify the malpractice of the Western and Eastern Han Dynasties, it had indeed added new contents to the treasure house of Chinese legal culture and had exerted a positive influence on later generations.

5.2 The Legislative Activities and the Forms of Law

In 206 B.C., Liu Bang, Gaozu of Han Dynasty, entered Xianyang. To expand the political influence and win the support of the public, he reached an agreement with the locals, saying that "(I now) make a three-item agreement with you, my folks: those who kill shall be sentenced to death; those who hurt others or commit robbery shall be punished and the rest of the laws of Qin Dynasty will be abolished."[60]

---

[56]Wang Fu (Han Dynasty), "Shu She" (On Remission) in *Qian Fu Lun* (*On Hermits*).
[57]Cui Shi (Han Dynasty), *Zheng Lun* (*On Politics*).
[58]Cui Shi (Han Dynasty), *Zheng Lun* (*On Politics*).
[59]Wang Fu (Han Dynasty), "Shuai Zhi" (The System of a Declining Society) in *Qian Fu Lun* (*On Hermits*).
[60]"Gao Di Ji" (The Record of the First Emperor of Han Dynasty) in *Han Shu* (*The History of Han Dynasty*).

5.2 The Legislative Activities and the Forms of Law

Though "Yue Fa San Zhang" (three-point covenant) was just a matter of political strategy, it had reflected the public will, so "the people were greatly delighted."[61] Surely, it had exerted a positive influence on Gaozu's unification of the whole country.

After the establishment of Han Dynasty, confronted with various complicated issues, it was not easy to handle all the matters with the temporary measures like the signing agreements. Therefore, in the 5th year of Gaozu in Han Dynasty (202 B.C.) Xiao He was ordered to "make *Jiu Zhang Lv* (*The Code in Nine Chapters*) by adopting the useful parts of the laws of Qin Dynasty",[62] because "the savage tribes in the bordering areas have not been conquered, the war is still on and the crimes cannot be prevented just by 'Yue Fa San Zhang' (three-point covenant)." As Xiao He used to be "Dao Bi Li" (petty officials who draws up indictments) in Qin Dynasty, and after entering Xianyang, he had collected some laws, decrees and legal codes of Qin Dynasty, it was natural that the laws he made were mainly based on those of Qin Dynasty with some new provisions added. In Chinese legal history, it is a common rule for the newly founded dynasty to adopt the laws which were suitable for the new situation from the previous ones with some necessary reforms and creations. Thus, it is just because of this that it is possible to have such a clear line of the inheritance relationship of the long history of Chinese legal system and that it is possible for us to easily find out what is newly added and what is deleted.

Jiu Zhang Lv (*The Code in Nine Chapters*) was the earliest and most important law of Han Dynasty. According to some records, *Jiu Zhang Lv* (*The Code in Nine Chapters*) had its origin as far back as in *Fa Jing* (*Canon of Laws*) made by Li Kui, and as near as in *Qin Lv* (*Qin Code*). Therefore, another three chapters of "Hu Lv" (Statutes on Households), "Xing Lv" (Statutes on Corvée), and "Jiu Lv" (Statutes on Livestock Breeding) were added to the six statutes of "Dao" (Robbery), "Zei" (Banditry), "Qiu" (Imprisonment), "Bu" (Arresting), "Za" (Miscellaneous Laws), and "Ju" (Specific Laws)." Except for the record about the origins of *Jiu Zhang Lv* (*The Code in Nine Chapters*) in "Xing Fa Zhi" (The Record of the Criminal Law) in *Han Shu* (*The History of Han Dynasty*), there were similar records in "Xing Fa Zhi" (The Record of the Criminal Law) in in *Jin Shu* (*The History of Jin Dynasty*) and *Tang Lv Shu Yi* (*The Comments on Tang Code*):

> As for the laws made by Xiao He, besides inheriting the laws on the crimes of 'San Yi Lian Zuo' (being punished for being related to somebody who committed an offense) from Qin Dynasty, the provision of 'Bu Zhu Jian Zhi' (the reporting of the subordinates' crimes by department heads) and the three chapters of "Xing" (Statutes on Corvée) and "Jiu" (Statutes on Livestock Breeding) and "Hu" (Statutes on Households) were added, so it consisted of totally nine chapters.

Therefore, *Jiu Zhang Lv* (*The Code in Nine Chapters*) was based on *Fa Jing* (*Canon of Laws*) with three other chapters added, which were mainly about civil and economic laws.

---

[61] "Xing Fa Zhi" (The Record of the Criminal Law) in *Han Shu* (*The History of Han Dynasty*).

[62] "Xing Fa Zhi" (The Record of the Criminal Law) in *Han Shu* (*The History of Han Dynasty*).

However, *Jiu Zhang Lv* (*The Code in Nine Chapters*) was lost long ago. According to "Xing Fa Zhi" (The Record of the Criminal Law) in *Jin Shu* (*The History of Jin Dynasty*), there were altogether forty-six articles: there were nine articles in *Dao Lv* (*Statutes on Theft*), including robbery, intimidation, human trafficking, kidnaping, taking bribes from one's juniors, taking bribes by bending the law, humiliating and hurting the arrested criminal, returning the booty to the owner, murder; there were ten articles in *Zei Lv* (*Statutes on Banditry*): great sedition, deception, fraud, "Yu Feng" (going beyond the limits), acting in the name of monarchs, cutting down trees without being authorized, hurting people or farm animals, losing seals, delaying doing things and stealing seals; there were seven articles in *Qiu Lv* (*Statutes on Imprisonment*): pretending to be alive or dead, evading tax and corvée, prosecution, reexamination, imprisonment, trial, and judgment; there were four articles in *Za Lv* (*Miscellaneous Laws*): using excuses, being dishonest, obtaining bribes by threatening the suspects, obtaining bribes when checking goods; there were two articles in *Ju Lv* (*Specific Laws*): selling official documents and refurbishing houses without authorization; there were six articles in *Xing Lv* (*Statutes on Corvée and Garrisoning the Frontier*): sending criminals to higher level offices, reporting judgments to higher level offices, recruiting corvée without authorization, evading corvée, delaying in recruiting soldiers and craftsmen and signal fire; there were nine articles in *Jiu Lv* (*Statutes on Livestock Breeding*): arresting, being punished for false accusation, being arrested and punished, notifying the emperor of something urgent by beating a drum to give account of the matter, delaying in military action, being negligent in carrying out decrees, failing to carry out decrees, presenting a false account to the emperor and reporting to the emperor of something urgent. Besides, no articles were added in *Bu Lv* (*Statutes on Arrest*) and *Hu Lv* (*Statutes on Households*). *Jiu Zhang Lv* (*The Code in Nine Chapters*) was made hastily so that there were a lot of repetitions and overlapping parts in its contents. It was criticized in "Xing Fa Zhi" (The Record of the Criminal Law) in *Jin Shu* (*The History of Jin Dynasty*) because "the provision of 'Zei Shang' (murder) was included in *Dao Lv* (*Statutes on Theft*), while the provision of 'Dao' (robbery) was included in *Zei Lv* (*Statutes on Banditry*); the provision of 'Shang Yu' (sending criminals to higher level offices) was included in *Xing Lv* (*Statutes on Corvée and Garrisoning the Frontier*), while the matters about arresting were included in *Jiu Lv* (*Statutes on Livestock Breeding*). So such provisions were complicated, chaotic, and misleading so that people of later generations can only understand their meaning according to their own interpretations."

Because of the discovery of *Yun Meng Qin Jian* (*Amounts of Bamboo Writing Slips in Qin Dynasty Excavated in Yunmeng*), it was newly verified whether *Hu Lv* (*Statutes on Households*), *Xing Lv* (*Statutes on Corvée and Garrisoning the Frontier*) and *Jiu Lv* (*Statutes on Livestock Breeding*) were created by Xiao He. According to its record, in the 25th year of Wei An Xi Wang (King Anxi in Wei Dynasty), *Hu Lv* (*Statutes on Households*) was issued. Further, the existing provisions proved that strict registration system was already established in the State of Wei. For example, the merchants, inn owners, and "Zhui Xu" (a son-in-law who lives in the home of his parents-in-law) were not allowed to be registered, nor were they allotted land and houses.[63] The existing laws showed that some strict laws about registration were already made based on "Shi Wu" (a basic level organization grouped by five or ten households) at the time of Shang Yang's reform in Qin Dynasty. For example, businessmen, the owners of the hotel and "Zhui Xu" (a son-in-law who lives in the home of his parents-in-law) were not allowed to establish a family, so they were not given the land and the houses. Records like "Ni Hu" (to evade the levying of tax and corvée by concealing the households), "Tu Ju" (recuperating), and "Fu Ji Fu Yi" (the system of men registered serving military service) had proved that *Hu Lv* (*Statutes on Households*) was already made in Qin and Wei states before Xiao He.

Xing Lv (*Statutes on Corvée and Garrisoning the Frontier*) included two parts, namely, "Gong Xing" (projects) and "Jun Xing" (military). *Yao Lv* (*Statutes on Corvée and Tax*), *Shu Lv* (*Statutes on Guarding the Borders*), *Dun Biao Lv* (*Statutes on Military Stationing*), *Gong Lv* (*Statutes on Handicraft Industry*) and *Si Kong Lv* (*Statutes on National Projects*) which were recorded in *Qin Jian* (*The Bamboo Writing Slips in Qin Dynasty*) all belonged to this category. In Han Dynasty, the government offices in charge of civil engineering were also the places where the prisoners were imprisoned to serve forced labor. As criminals were also sent to guard borders, the provisions like "Shang Yu"(sending criminals to higher level offices), "Kao Shi Bao Yan" (reporting judgments to higher level offices), "Feng Sui" (signal fire), "Ji Liu" (delaying in recruiting soldiers and craftsmen), and "Fa Yao" (evading corvée), etc. were included in *Xing Lv* (*Statutes on Corvée and Garrisoning the Frontier*). Thus, it can be seen that the contents of *Xing Lv* also existed earlier than the laws made by Xiao He.

Besides, the historical prototype of the nine articles of *Jiu Lv* (*Statutes on Livestock Breeding*) recorded in "Xing Fa Zhi" (The Record of the Criminal Law) in *Jin Shu* (*The History of Jin Dynasty*) could also be found in "Jiu Yuan Lv" (Statutes on Livestock Breeding and Gardening), "Qin Lv Shi Ba Zhong" (Eighteen Kinds of Laws of Qin Dynasty) and "Jiu Lv" (Statutes on Livestock Breeding) which were included in *Nei Shi Za* (*Statutes on State Offices in the Capital*).

Overall, there were obvious connections between *Qin Lv* (*Qin Code*) and the three chapters of *Hu Lv* (*Statutes on Households*), *Xing Lv* (*Statutes on Corvée and Garrisoning the Frontier*) and *Jiu Lv* (*Statutes on Livestock Breeding*) which were added by Xiao He. From *Hu Lv* (*Statutes on Households*), *Xing Lv* (*Statutes on Corvée and Garrisoning the Frontier*), and *Jiu Lv* (*Statutes on Livestock Breeding*), which were recorded in *Qin Jian* (*The Bamboo Writing Slips in Qin Dynasty*), revisions were made by Xiao He to make it more complete and systematic. The laws of Han Dynasty represented by *Jiu Zhang Lv* (*The Code in Nine Chapters*) had mainly focused on criminal laws, but it also included the contents of many aspects such as making judgments, economy, and household registration. Thus, it was an

---

[63]"Wei Li Zhi Dao" (The Way of Being an Official) in *Shui Hu Di Qin Mu Zhu Jian* (*The Bamboo Slips from the Tombs of Qin in Shuihudi*).

important tool to punish crimes, to maintain social order, and to strengthen the rule of the state in early Han Dynasty.

In addition to *Jiu Zhang Lv* (*The Code in Nine Chapters*), Emperor Gaozu had ordered the Confucian scholar Shu Suntong to revise the laws for etiquettes by writing *Yi Pin* (*Etiquette and Official Ranks*) and *Yi Li* (*Etiquette and Ceremony*) successively to uphold the authority of the emperor and to make the officials show respect to him, so Shu Suntong was promoted to be "Feng Chang" (one of the nine ministers). During the reign of Emperor Hui, he ordered Shu Suntong to carry out further revision of the law and add the etiquettes which were left out to the law of etiquettes, so *Bang Zhang Lv* (*Law of Rites*) consisting of eighteen articles was completed. It was recorded in "Xing Fa Zhi" (The Record of the Criminal Law) in *Jin Shu* (*The History of Jin Dynasty*) that "Shu Suntong added what was left out to the law and made *Bang Zhang Lv* (*Law of Rites*) consisting of eighteen articles." "Bang Zhang" meant "Han Yi" (the laws of etiquette for Han Dynasty). There were similar records in "Li Yue Zhi" (The Record of Rites and Music) in *Han Shu* (*The History of Han Dynasty*): "'Li Yi' (*Etiquette and Ceremony*) written by Shu Suntong was recorded together with imperial statutes and decrees and was kept by judicial officials."

During the reign of Emperor Wu, he ordered Zhang Tang, "Ting Wei" (the supreme official in charge of judicature), to make *Yue Gong Lv* (*Statutes on the Security within the Imperial Palace*) which was about the palace guards in the imperial court and which consisted of twenty-seven articles. He also ordered "Yu Shi" (the censor) Zhao Yu to make *Chao Lv* (*Statutes on the Etiquettes in the Imperial Court*) which was about paying tributes and which consisted of six articles. Together with *Jiu Zhang Lv* (*The Code in Nine Chapters*) and *Bang Zhang Lv* (*Law of Rites*), there were sixty passages and three hundred and fifty-nine chapters, which were generally called *Han Lv* (*Han Code*). Some traditional expressions in this document were supplemented by *Han Jian* (*The Bamboo Slip of Han Dynasty*) unearthed in Zhangjiashan. From December 1983 to January 1984, more than five hundred bamboo slips were unearthed in Zhangjiashan in Jiangling, Hu Bei province. Among the twenty-seven kinds of laws, some were similar to *Qin Lv* (*Qin Code*) unearthed from Shuihudi, such as *Jin Bu Lv* (*Statutes on Currency and Property*), *Yao Lv* (*Statutes on Corvée and Tax*), *Zhi Li Lv* (*Statutes on the Regulation of Officials*), *Xiao Lv* (*Statutes on the Inspection of the Supplies and Property of State Offices*), *Chuan Shi Lv* (*Statutes on the Accommodation of Officials in Courier Stations*), *Xing Shu Lv* (*Statutes on the Delivery of Documents*) and *Tian Lv* (*Statutes on Farming and Forest Protection*); some were different, such as *Za Lv* (*Miscellaneous Laws*), *Shi Lv* (*Statutes on Market*), *Jun Shu Lv* (*Statutes on Goods Supply*), *Shi Lv* (*Statutes on Historical Documents*), *Gao Lv* (*Statutes on Prosecution*), *Qian Lv* (*Statutes on Currency*) and *Ci Lv* (*Statutes on Granting a Reward*), etc. The main contents of *Lv Ling Er Shi Ba Zhong* (*Twenty-Eight Kinds of Laws and Decrees*) included *Yao Lv* (*Statutes on Corvée and Tax*), *Jue Lv* (*Statutes on Official Titles*), *Hu Lv* (*Statutes on Households*), *Jin Bu Lv* (*Statutes on Currency and Property*), *Jin Guan Ling* (*Decree on Strategic Passes*), *Zei Lv* (*Statutes on Banditry*), *Dao Lv* (*Statutes on Theft*), *Bu Lv* (*Statutes on Arrest*), *Gao Lv* (*Statutes on*

Prosecution), *Wang Lv* (*Statutes on Fugitives*), *Chuan Shi Lv* (*Statutes on the Accommodation of Officials in Courier Stations*), *Ci Lv* (*Statutes on Granting a Reward*), *Xing Shu Lv* (*Statutes on the Delivery of Documents*), *Qian Lv* (*Statutes on Currency*), *Zhi Li Lv* (*Statutes on the Regulation of Officials*), *Shi Lv* (*Statutes on Historical Documents*), *Jun Shu Lv* (*Statutes on Goods Supply*), *Ju Lv* (*Specific Laws*), *Xiao Lv* (*Statutes on the Inspection of the Supplies and Property of State Offices*), etc.[64]

The title "Er Nian Lv Ling" (the law of the second year) is written at the back of the first bamboo slip discovered in Zhangjiashan and research shows that it is the law made in the 2nd year of Queen Lv (186 B.C.), which was enforced from the 5th year of Gaozu to the 2nd year of Queen Lv. It has testified the inheritance relationship between the law of Qin and Han Dynasties and its complicated and rich contents have mirrored the state of the legal system in early Han Dynasty.

The activities of lawmaking in Western Han Dynasty were mainly carried out in two periods: the period of the reigning of Gaozu and Emperor Hui and the period of the reigning of Emperor Wu. After half a century of rehabilitation, during the reigning of Emperor Wu, the economy boomed and the national power was strong, which had made it possible for Emperor Wu "to make military achievements on the borders." He fought "Xiong Nu" (an ancient nationality in China) in the north, conquered "Bai Yue" (an ancient nationality in China) in the south, "made merry in the court and launched numerous expeditions," which had led to very dangerous situations where "the common people were poverty-stricken, the poor people frequently committed crimes, the cruel officials acted arbitrarily and law breakers acted outrageously."[65] Within the ruling party, the rebellion of Duke Hengshan and Duke Huainan took place after the riot of seven states, which had led to turmoil in the country. Thus, Emperor Wu "called in Zhang Tang, Zhao Yu and others to make laws and regulations for the punishment of the crimes such as 'Jian Zhi Gu Zong' (failing to report the crime which one knows about intentionally) and 'Jian Lin Bu Zhu' (deliberately releasing the criminals by the officials in charge) and to mitigate the punishment for the crime of 'Shen Gu' (to intentionally sentence an innocent person guilty or a misdemeanor felony) and to aggravate the punishment for the crime of 'Zong Chu' (to intentionally sentence a guilty person innocent or a felony misdemeanor)." According to the notes by Yan Shigu, "if a person saw someone committing crimes but did not report, it is 'Gu Zong' (intentional connivance without intervention), so if somebody committed crime, his supervisors would be punished as well."[66] In "Wei Lv Xu" (Preface to Wei Code) in "Xing Fa Zhi" (The Record of the Criminal Law) in *Jin Shi* (*The History of Jin Dynasty*), further annotation was made: "when the law was first made, no articles were made about

---

[64]Chen Yaojun, Yan Pin, "Jiang Ling Zhang Jia Shan Han Mu De Nian Dai Ji Xiang Guan Wen Ti" (Some Questions Concerning the Time of the Han Tomb in Zhangjiashan in Jiangling) in *Kao Gu* (*Archaeology*), Vol. 12, 1985.

[65]"Xing Fa Zhi" (The Record of the Criminal Law) in *Han Shu* (*The History of Han Dynasty*).

[66]"Xing Fa Zhi" (The Record of the Criminal Law) in *Han Shu* (*The History of Han Dynasty*).

'Mian Zuo' (being exempted from punishment), so Zhang Tang and Zhao Yu made laws about 'Jian Zhi Gu Zong' (failing to report the crime which one knows about intentionally) and 'Jian Lin Bu Zhu' (deliberately releasing the criminals by the officials in charge). Those who witness people committing crimes without reporting intentionally will be sentenced to the same penalty with the criminal; those who witness people committing crimes without reporting will be sentenced to the punishment of 'Shu' (atonement), while those who do not see nor know about it shall not be implicated." Therefore, the purpose of making the law was to strengthen the sense of responsibility of the supervisors and to improve the efficiency of the whole bureaucratic system. The following comments were made on the laws by Zhang Tang and Zhao Yu in history books: "When Zhang Tang and Zhao Yu made laws, strict and severe legal provisions were applied",[67] which not only reflected the brutality and cruelty of Zhang Tang and Zhao Yu, but also mirrored characteristics of times of the transition from "Wu Wei Er Zhi" (to govern by doing nothing that goes against nature) in early Han Dynasty to the foreign military expeditions and domestic construction in the reign of Emperor Wu.

More than that, a law called *Shen Ming Fa* (*Laws on the Misconduct of Officials*) was made to urge the officials in charge to have the thieves and robbers arrested. "If revolts were not discovered or if they were discovered but not all those involved were arrested, everyone, from those whose salary was below 'Er Qian Dan' (the ancient official with a monthly salary of 2,000 *dan*) to 'Xiao Li' (junior official), would all be sentenced to death."[68] So the law was made to supervise and punish those officials who were inefficient in arresting the thieves and robbers. However, after *Shen Ming Fa* (*Laws on the Misconduct of Officials*) was issued, the officials in charge were afraid of being killed for failing to arrest the criminals, so they concealed the facts and lied to each other, even the supervisor also lied to his subordinates.

To strengthen the centralized power, Emperor Wu carried on the policy of "Qiang Gan Ruo Zhi" (strengthen the central forces and weaken the local ones), so a series of specific laws were made, such as *Zuo Guan Lv* (*Law on the Officials in Violation of the Provisions of Privately Working in the Vassal State Office*) and *Fu Yi Fa* (*The Law to Solve the Issue of Vassal State*) to weaken the power of vassal states. Moreover, *Shang Ji Lv* (*The Law for Officials to Report Statistical Books*) was made to specify the duties of local officials.

In conclusion, Emperor Wu, based on *Jiu Zhang Lv* (*The Code in Nine Chapters*) and *Bang Zhang Lv* (*Law of Rites*), made a series of special laws that were known to be more strict and severe. According to the history book, totally about "359 chapters of laws and orders, 409 articles of 'Da Bi' (capital punishment), 1882 cases, and 3472 'Jue Shi Bi' (the precedents in lawsuit settlements) about death penalty were made."[69] It was so complicated that during the reign of Emperor Xuan he had to

---

[67]"Zhang Tang Zhuan" (The Biography of Zhang Tang) in *Han Shu* (*The History of Han Dynasty*).
[68]"Ku Li Zhuan" (The Biographies of Brutal Officials) in *Han Shu* (*The History of Han Dynasty*).
[69]"Xing Fa Zhi" (The Record of the Criminal Law) in *Han Shu* (*The History of Han Dynasty*).

5.2 The Legislative Activities and the Forms of Law

rearrange the laws and categorize them into "Decree A," "Decree B" and "Decree C." Under "Decree A," there were more than 300 passages.[70] However, the phenomenon of "Xian Ling Shao Zeng, Ke Tiao Wu Xian" (laws and decrees were slightly increased, but countless rules were added) was not fundamentally changed.[71] In the reign of Emperor Cheng, "more than 1,000 articles of laws relating to death penalty were made, and there were numerous laws with a total of more than one million words."[72] Thus, even legal experts could not understand all of them, let alone the ordinary officials and the public.

Han Lv (*Han Code*) was lost in Tang Dynasty, with only titles of passages, the names of laws and fragmented records remained. *Han Lv Ji Zheng* (*Annotation of the Law of Han Dynasty*) written by Du Guixi in the Qing Dynasty and *Han Lv Zhi Yi* (*Collections of Laws in Han Dynasty*) written by Shen Jiaben had provided materials for the study of the laws in Han Dynasty.

The law of Han Dynasty was based on *Zheng Lv* (*Official Law*) and was supplemented by special laws. During the reign of Emperor Wu, with the increase of domestic and foreign activities, along with the sole respection of Confucianism, great emphasis was put on law. Moreover, the development of the dictatorial power of the emperor had made "Ling" (decree) a form of law with more authority and flexibility.

"Ling" (decree) was an important form of law in Han Dynasty. Wen Ying noted in "Xuan Di Ji" (The Biography of Emperor Xuan) in *Han Shu* (*The History of Han Dynasty*) that "if not listed within the law, the rules made by the emperor are called 'Ling' (decree)." As "Ling" (decree) was made by the emperor, they could be used to modify, supplement, and even replace some current laws. It was recorded in "Du Zhou Zhuan" (The Biography of Du Zhou) in *Han Shu* (*The History of Han Dynasty*) that in face of the criticism of his dealing with things according to the emperor's "Ling" (decree), Du Zhou said: "where does the law come from? It comes from the previous emperors, while 'Ling' (decree) was from the current emperor. The current law should be used rather than the law in the past." The range of application of "Ling" (decree) was very extensive: "Ting Wei Qie Ling" was made to provide guidance to the judicial process; "Yu Ling" was made to strengthen judicial management; "Gong Wei Ling" was made to protect the safety of the emperor; "Tian Ling" was made to collect tax and administer agriculture; "Jin Bu Ling" (Decree on Treasury) was made to manage treasury; "Si Ling" and "Zhai Ling" were made for sacrificial ceremony in ancestral temples; "Ren Zi Ling" was made for inheritance of titles; "Gong Ling" was made for the selection and assessment of officials and "Min Qian Ling" was made to control the merchants. Besides, the following "Ling" (decree) are also made: "Wu Shi Ling" (Decree on Seasonal Changes), "Yao Yan Ling" (Decree on Heresy), "Pin Ling" (Decree on Official

---

[70]"Xing Fa Zhi" (The Record of the Criminal Law) in *Jin Shu* (*The History of Jin Dynasty*).

[71]"Chen Chong Zhuan" (The Biography of Chen Chong) in *Latter Han Shu* (*The History of Latter Han Dynasty*).

[72]"Xing Fa Zhi" (The Record of the Criminal Law) in *Han Shu* (*The History of Han Dynasty*).

Appointment), "Yu Gao Ling" (Decree on Taking Vocations), "Zhi Lu Ling" (Decree on Official Salaries), "Shu Xing Ling" (Decree on Atonement), "Zu Qie Ling" (Decree on Land Contract), "Ma Fu Ling" (Decree on Horse Raising), "Mai Jue Ling" (Decree on Selling of Titles of Nobility), "Shu Zu Ling" (Decree on Guarding Borders), "Bu Sha Chan Yu Ling" (Decree on Killing the Head of Huns), "Shui Ling" (Decrees on Irrigation), "Gong Ling" (Decree on Publics), "Yang Lao Ling" (Decrees on the Provision of the Aged), etc. "Jin Guan Ling" (Decree on Strategic Passes) which was recently unearthed in Zhangjiashan and "Shou Fa Shou Ling Shi San Pian" (13 Chapters of Decrees to be Abided by) which was unearthed in Yinqueshan, in Shandong province were bamboo slip recording of the laws of Han Dynasty, concerning land, tax, market, treasury, defense and obedience to "Ling" (decree), etc.

"Ling" (decree) was made to solve some specific problems, so it was numerous and complicated. Besides, some procedures were needed to change "Ling" (decree) into law. The imperial orders ended with the letters like "Ju Wei Ling," "Zhu Wei Ling," "Yi Wei Ling" and "Yi Zhu Wei Ling" could achieve legal effect only after they were approved by the emperor.

"Ke"(rule), also known as "Ke Tiao," was the general name for the articles of law, so there was the saying like "Xian Ling Shao Zeng, Ke Tiao Wu Xian" (laws and decrees were slightly increased, but countless rules were added).[73] "Ke"(rule) had the legal function of legal precedents, as was defined by *Shi Ming (The Origin of the Word Meaning)* written by Liu Xi that "'Ke' is used to punish those whose behavior is against the law." Therefore, there often appeared the phenomenon of "one law and two 'Ke' (rule)" in judicial practice. In "Han Ke" (The Rules of Han Dynasty) in "Xing Fa Zhi" in *Jin Shu (The History of Jin Dynasty)*, there were the following provisions like "Deng Wen Dao Ci" (notifying the emperor of something urgent by beating a drum to give account of the matter), "Kao Shi Bao Yan" (reporting judgments to higher level offices), "Shi Zhe Yan Lu" (obtaining bribes when checking goods), "Shan Zuo Xiu She (repairing houses without authorization)," "Ping Yong Zuo Zang" (incompetent), "Tou Shu Qi Shi" (writing anonymous letters), etc., which proved that "Ke" (rule) had developed into an independent form of law, but it must be approved by the emperor to achieve legal effect.

"Bi" (analogy) referred to a collection of precedents. The application of precedents in judicial practice originated from Spring and Autumn and Warring States Period. After the founding of Han Dynasty, in the 7th year of Gaozu (200 B.C.), the emperor announced that "if there are cases which 'Ting Wei' (the supreme official in charge of judicature) can't decide, they should be reported to the emperor and be judged according to 'Bi' (analogy)." Yan Shigu noted that "it means making judgments by using 'Li' (precedent) for reference."[74] During Han Dynasty, all the judgments made by referring to "Li" (precedent) were called "Jue Shi Bi," which had

---

[73]"Chen Chong Zhuan" (The Biography of Chen Chong) in *Latter Han Shu (The History of Latter Han Dynasty)*.

[74]"Xing Fa Zhi" (The Record of the Criminal Law) in *Han Shu (The History of Han Dynasty)*.

the features of the common law. During the reign of Emperor Wu, because of the incompleteness of the law and the large number of cases, all the offenses which were not listed in the law were judged by "Bi Fu" (legal analogy), which included three categories: "Jue Shi Bi" (the precedents in lawsuit settlements), "Si Zui Jue Shi Bi"(the precedents for capital crimes) and "Ci Song Bi"(the precedents compiled according to judicial experiences), and they were used as important supplements of law. For "Si ZuiJue Shi Bi" (the precedents for capital crimes) alone, there were as many as 13,472 cases. In *Han Jian* (*The Bamboo Slips of Han Dynasty*) unearthed in Zhangjiashan, there were more than 200 slips of *Zou Yan Shu* (*Collections of Legal Precedents*). According to *Shuo Wen Jie Zi* (*The Origin of Chinese Characters*), "'Yan' means discussing the crimes." The cases recorded in *Zou Yan Shu* (*Collections of Legal Precedents*) were similar to those in "Xing Fa Zhi" (The Record of the Criminal Law) in *Han Shu* (*The History of Han Dynasty*) in terms of procedures, and they concerned with extensive contents, from those of the nobles to the public, which were of great significance in guiding the judicial practices. Besides, the legislation that was made in Han Dynasty included *Jue Shi Bi* (*The Precedents in Lawsuit Settlements*) submitted by Chen Chong and his son, *Ci Song Bi* (*The Precedents Compiled according to Judicial Experiences*) by Chen Chong, *Fa Bi Du Mu* (*Outline of Legal Precedents*) and *Jia Qu Ci Song Jue* (*Legal Cases on Marriages*) by Bao Yu, *Si Tu Du Mu* (*Outline of Si Tu*) and *Jue Shi Bi Li* (*The Precedents and Cases in Lawsuit Settlements*) by Ying Shao, etc.

In conclusion, there are more forms of laws in Han Dynasty than in Qin Dynasty, and the contents are much enriched, so it is a great milestone in the history of Chinese legal civilization. Because of the extensive application of "Bi" (analogy) as a supplement of the law, it can be said that Han Dynasty is an age when the common law is very popular. Moreover, the accumulation of the experience of mutual complementation of precedents, case law, and statutory law had exerted a great influence on later generations. Because of the mutual complementation of different forms of laws, a tight net of law was formed so that "documents were piled up high on the tables in the room but it was difficult for people to read all of them." Consequently, some laws were deceitfully used for cunning purpose and analogies were illegally applied. Besides, "for the same crime, there might be different sentences and the judges often took bribery by perverting the law; if they want to exempt someone from punishment, they would find excuses to let him live; if they want to let someone die, they would kill him by referring to the precedents of death penalty."[75] All these had broken the proper legal order and predicted the decline of the Western Han Dynasty.

---

[75]"Xing Fa Zhi" (The Record of the Criminal Law) in *Han Shu* (*The History of Han Dynasty*).

5.3 The Enriching and Development of Administrative Law

5.3.1 The Establishment of the Operation Mechanism of State Institutions Headed by the Emperor

The imperial system created by Qin Shi Huang (the first emperor of Qin) was further consolidated and developed, which was reflected in the legalization of the sovereign status of the emperor.

According to the first volume of *Du Duan* (*Dictatorial*) by Cai Yong, "'Tian Zi' (the son of Heaven) in the Han Dynasty was named 'Huang Di' (emperor). He called himself 'Zhen' (meaning I). The subjects called him 'Bi Xia' (Your Majesty); the words of the emperor were called 'Zhi Zhao'; the official who was in charge of recording history called him 'Shang'; the wagon, the clothes and utilities were called 'Cheng Yu'; the presence of the emperor was referred as "Xing Zai Suo" and his residence was called "Jin Zhong" (forbidden place), which was later called 'Sheng Zhong'; the seal of the emperor was called 'Xi'; the visiting of the emperor was called 'Xing' and after his presence, it was called 'Yu'; his order was called 'Ce Shu', 'Zhi Shu', 'Zhao Shu' and 'Jie Shu' respectively." Thus, the power of the emperor was mystified by the Confucian scholars' theory of "Tian Ren Gan Ying" (interactions between Heaven and Mankind).

According to Dong Zhongshu's theory of "Tian Ren Gan Ying" (interactions between Heaven and Mankind), the emperor was respected as "Tian Zi" (the son of Heaven), with "'Tian' (Heaven) as father and 'Di' (earth) as mother."[76] Thus, the emperor's rule of the country was said to be "following the will of 'Tian' (Heaven)"[77] and "was granted by 'Tian' (Heaven)."[78] Therefore, it was following the will of 'Tian' (Heaven) to follow the rule of the emperor. Some experts of Confucianism even connected theocracy with the ethical patriarchal power and preached that "the emperor was 'Tian Zi' (the son of Heaven) high above and the parent of the common people down below"[79] to further expand the imperial power.

To establish the etiquette system of "showing respect to the emperor and taking control of the officials," Shu Suntong formulated a series of behavioral rules. "If this system is applied within the court, then the hierarchal status will be maintained between the emperor and the officials; if this system is applied in the whole country, then the vassal states will submit themselves and obey the rules."[80] Duke of Jiang named Zhou Bo had made great contribution to the founding of Han Dynasty and the enthroning of Emperor Wen, so when he went to the court, he was always

---

[76]"Jue" (Nobility) in *Bai Hu Tong Yi* (*The Virtuous Discussions in White Tiger Hall*).

[77]"Dong Zhong Shu Zhuan" (The Biography of Dong Zhongshu) in *Han Shu* (*The History of Han Dynasty*).

[78]Dong Zhongshu (Han Dynasty), "Shen Cha Ming Hao" (A Thorough Investigation of the Names and Titles) in *Chun Qiu Fan Lu* (*The Luxuriant Dew of Spring and Autumn Annals*).

[79]"Bao Xuan Zhuan" (The Biography of Bao Xuan) in *Han Shu* (*The History of Han Dynasty*).

[80]*Zi Zhi Tong Jian* (*History as a Mirror*), Vol. 11.

self-conceited and even the emperor showed great respect to him. For this, Yuan Ang admonished that "if 'Cheng Xiang' (the prime minister) is arrogant toward your majesty and your majesty is modest, it is against the etiquette. So according to my opinion, it is improper." Thereafter, whenever at court "the emperor became so solemn that 'Cheng Xiang' (the prime minister) was very respectful to the emperor."[81]

The practice of "showing respect to the emperor and taking control of the officials" led to the weakening the power of "Cheng Xiang" (the prime minister) and the establishment of the inner court. In early Han Dynasty, "Cheng Xiang" (the prime minister) held the real power and was in charge of all of the government affairs. During the 54th years of reign of Emperor Wu, to expand the power of the emperor and to weaken the power of "Cheng Xiang" (the prime minister), he appointed thirteen "Cheng Xiang" (the prime minister), among whom two committed suicide for fear of punishment, three were killed, four were found guilty and dismissed and one was sentenced to "Qi Shi" (exposing the executed body publicly at markets). Thus, when Emperor Wu asked Gongsun He to hold the post of "Cheng Xiang" (the prime minister), he even wept and dared not accept the seal.

Along with the weakening power of "Cheng Xiang" (the prime minister), the courtiers were favored by emperor, which had enabled it to hold the real power by gradually expanding the court organization. This evolution was the natural result of autocratic politics. In feudal times, besides through governmental agencies, the emperor who had the supreme power of the state and who had stayed back in the court usually got to know about state affairs through the court organizations, so the real power of managing the state affairs was transformed from the imperial court to the inner court. During the reign of Emperor Wu, he had selected many talented people and "Shi Da Fu" (literati and officials) and appointed them as "Shi Zhong" (the assistant official), "Ji Shi Zhong" (the senior assistant of the emperor and the supervisor of officials), "Shang Shu" (the minister), and some other affiliated officials. They had the advantage of entering the forbidden door and discussing policies with the emperor. Meanwhile, they were also asked by the emperor to attend the meeting of the ministers, by which the "intermediate court" and "outer court" were gradually formed. The palace agencies waiting on the emperor formed the intermediate court and began to participate in policymaking, but the "outer court" headed by "Cheng Xiang" (the prime minister) was reduced to the position of carrying out the state affairs.

The distinction of "intermediate court" and the "inner court" in the Western Han Dynasty was an important change in feudal administrative system, which had not only reflected the power conflict between the emperor and "Cheng Xiang" (the prime minister), but also the strengthening of the power of the emperor. The most important position in the "intermediate court" was "Xiao Guan Shang Shu," which used to be in charge of books, esoterica, and memorials submitted to the emperor in "Shao Fu" (in charge of emperor's income and royal affairs). Because they were granted

---

[81]"Yuan Ang Zhuan" (The Biography of Yuan Ang) in *Han Shu* (*The History of Han Dynasty*).

the right to handle state affairs by the emperor, they became the most significant court organizations directly under the control of the emperor. Besides, "Shang Shu Tai" (Imperial Secretariat) was built up and different official positions and duties were established. In the Eastern Han Dynasty, the organization of "Shang Shu Tai" (Imperial Secretariat) was just like a mini-court within the imperial court, with its power overriding that of "outer court," as was described in the saying that "although there was 'San Gong' (the three councilors), all things were decided by 'Shang Shu Tai' (Imperial Secretariat)."[82]

In the feudal times, the power and authority of the emperor lay in the people whom he trusted, which was an important feature of autocratic politics. To prevent power from falling into the hands of others who were not from the royal family, the emperor would rather hand over the power to the inner court deliberately. Consequently, the power of the officials were greatly restricted, which had made it convenient for the eunuchs and "Wai Qi" (relatives of an emperor on the side of his mother or wife) to usurp power. All this had intensified the conflict within the governing regime and deepened political corruption, which was the natural result and inevitable trend of despotism.

During the reign of emperor Wu, he ordered "Ting Wei" (the supreme official in charge of judicature) Zhang Tang to make *Yue Gong Lv* (*Statutes on the Security within the Imperial Palace*) which was about palace guards consisting of twenty-seven articles to "ensure the emperor's safety."

The system of "Chao Yi" (imperial court consultation) carried out in Qin Dynasty became institutionalized in Han Dynasty to ensure the functioning of the state machines and to strengthen the ruling efficacy. In Western Han Dynasty, "Chao Yi" (imperial court consultation) would be held by the emperor when something important happened. For example, Gaozu called for a meeting of vassals to "discuss who could be appointed 'Yan Wang' (the king of Yan state)."[83] In the first year of Yuan Ping (74 B.C.), "Emperor died without a successor....So the ministers gathered to discuss who would be the candidate."[84] During the reign of Emperor Cheng, "Zhong Er Qian Dan" (the ancient official with a monthly salary of full 2000 *dan*), "Er Qian Dan" (2000 *dan*: ancient officials or head of prefecture), "Bo Shi" (learned scholars) and other legal experts had discussed the abolishment of death penalty and other punishments that should be abolished or simplified."[85] However, except the emperor, no one was allowed to call for the convention of "Chao Yi" (imperial court consultation). Sometimes "Cheng Xiang" (the prime minister) or the general was asked to preside over the meeting and the ministers and officials attending the discussion could express their opinions freely, but the final decision

---

[82]"Zhi Guan" (State Officials) (Part 10) in *Xi Han Hui Yao* (*Collections of Historical Records in Western Han Dynasty*), Vol. 40.

[83]"Gao Di Ji" (The Record of the First Emperor of Han Dynasty) in *Han Shu* (*The History of Han Dynasty*).

[84]"Huo Guang Zhuan" (The Biography of Huo Guang) in *Han Shu* (*The History of Han Dynasty*).

[85]"Xing Fa Zhi" (The Record of the Criminal Law) in *Han Shu* (*The History of Han Dynasty*).

5.3 The Enriching and Development of Administrative Law

was made by the emperor, as was stated by Liu Xiang that "(the emperor) listened to all but made decisions by himself."[86] As to the system of "Chao Yi" (imperial court consultation), there were some routines. Emperor Xuan attended "Chao Yi" (imperial court consultation) once in every five days and on the first day of October of the lunar calendar and the first day of a new year, a grand "Chao Yi" (imperial court consultation) would be held and the emperor would listen to the proposals about state affairs made by hundreds of officials, for which an act called *Shang Ji Lv* (*The Law for Officials to Report Statistical Books*) was made. During the reign of Emperor Wu, Zhao Yu was ordered to make *Chao Lv* (*Statutes on the Etiquettes in the Imperial Court*) consisting of six articles.

The development of the imperial system was an important process of strengthening the central authority and it was a reflection of the increasing power of the emperor.

Beneath the emperor was the system of central administration, including "Cheng Xiang" (the prime minister) and "San Gong" (the three councilors). In early Han Dynasty, the power of "Cheng Xiang" (the prime minister) was great, who had the right to "assist 'Tian Zi' (the son of Heaven) to deal with thousands of issues."[87] In the Western Han Dynasty, there were altogether fifty-six "Cheng Xiang" (the prime minister), and thirty-three of them were from humble background, such as Xiao He, Chen Ping, Zhang Cang, Gong Sunhe, and Che Qianqiu, all of whom had served in the post for more than ten years. During the reign of Emperor Wu, with increasing economic and political power and the military victories, the emperor's status was improved greatly, while although the position of "Cheng Xiang" (the prime minister) was still very high, his power was weakened gradually. The emperor often dealt with the problems by himself through "Shang Shu Chu" (The Department of Secretary) of the inner court. Sometimes he appointed the eunuchs as "Zhong Shu Ling" (head of the secretariat) and allowed them to discuss state affairs. The system of "San Gong" (the three councilors) which was initiated in the Qin Dynasty and which consisted of "Cheng Xiang" (the prime minister), "Tai Wei" (the minister of defense) and "Yu Shi Da Fu" (Grand Censor) was replaced by "Da Si Tu" (the senior minister of civil affairs), "Da Si Ma" (the minister of military affairs) and "Da Si Kong" (the minister of public works).

The position of "Jiu Qing" (the nine high-rank officials in ancient times) was the same as that of the Qin Dynasty, with just a little change of the names. For example, "Feng Chang" (official responsible for temple ritual) was changed into "Tai Chang" (the Minister of Sacrificial Worship), "Lang Zhong Ling" (official commanding the bodyguards of the emperor) into "Guang Lu Xun"(official in charge of banqueting department), "Dian Ke" (Reception Office) into "Da Hong Lu" (the court of state ceremonial), "Zhi Su Nei Shi" (official in charge of the tax and financial revenue and expenditure) into "Da Si Nong" (Minister of National Treasury). All the nine

---

[86] Liu Xiang (Han Dynasty), "Quan Mou" (Tactics) in *Shuo Yuan* (*Collection of Stories*), Vol. 13.
[87] "Bai Guan Gong Qing Biao" (The Table of Officials of Higher Ranks) in *Han Shu* (*The History of Han Dynasty*) (Book 1).

ministers were under the supervision of "Cheng Xiang" (the prime minister). To make laws for different organizations to follow, the laws such as *Da Hong Lu Qie Ling* (*Decree on State Ceremonial*), *Ting Wei Qie Ling* (*Decree on Judicial Process*), *Guang Lu Qie Ling* (*Decree on Banqueting*) and *Han Guan Yi* (*The Etiquette for the Officials of Han Dynasty*) were made, and the last one was made to confirm the official system and the division of departmental functions of the administrative organs.

As for local governments, those of Qin Dynasty were followed in the Western Han Dynasty, which was made up of two levels, namely, "Jun" (shire) and "Xian" (county). However, Emperor Gaozu learned a lesson from "the downfall of Qin Dynasty caused by the emperor's isolation from other people,"[88] so he appointed his children to be vassals to control the local areas. Thus, a political system centered on the clan of "Liu" was set up and extended to the whole country. He also swore that "if the government was set up by those who were not from the family of 'Liu', they would be attacked by the people of the entire country."[89] Therefore, an administrative system with the coexistence of kingdom, vassal states, "Jun" (shire) and "Xian" (county) was set up. However, contrary to Gaozu's will, the vassals had occupied vast areas of land and "combined dozens of towns, and annexed many 'Zhou' (subprefecture) and 'Jun'".[90] Besides, they had all the power within their states, including the collection of rents and tax, the appointment of officials, so in fact they had formed their own separate regimes.

To strengthen its control, the imperial court retained the power of appointing "Cheng Xiang" (the prime minister) to the different vassal states by the central government. According to *Han Shu* (*The History of Han Dynasty*), the local kings "tried to find fault with 'Cheng Xiang' (the prime minister) by making reports to the emperor; if they couldn't find him guilty, they would rather kill him with poison"[91]; or plot to have him trapped so that "no one can stay in his position for more than two years. So in the end, 'Cheng Xiang' (the prime minister) would either be dismissed on the excuse of crimes; or punished for minor crimes; or sentenced to death for serious ones."[92] Some vassal states even openly rejected "'Cheng Xiang' (the prime minister) appointed by the central government of the Han Dynasty."[93] During the reign of Emperor Wen, the vassal states were too powerful to be obedient to the emperor, with each of them having his own regime independently. During the reign of Emperor Jing, there occurred "Qi Guo Zhi Luan" (the Revolt of Seven States)

---

[88]"Zhu Hou Wang Biao" (A List of the Vassals) in *Han Shu* (*The History of Han Dynasty*).

[89]"Lv Tai Hou Ben Ji" (The Record of Queen Lv) in *Shi Ji* (*The Record of the Grand Historian*).

[90]"Zhu Hou Wang Biao" (A List of the Vassals) in *Han Shu* (*The History of Han Dynasty*).

[91]"Jiao Xi Wang Duan Zhuan" (The Biography of Liu Duan, the Vassal of Jiaoxi) in *Han Shu* (*The History of Han Dynasty*).

[92]"Zhao Jing Su Wang Peng Zu Zhuan" (The Biography of Liu Pengzu, the Vassal of Zhao) in *Han Shu* (*The History of Han Dynasty*).

[93]"Huai Nan Li Wang Zhuan" (The Biography of the Vassal of Huainan) in *Han Shu* (*The History of Han Dynasty*).

5.3 The Enriching and Development of Administrative Law

launched by the local kings against the central government, which was not only harmful to the recovery of the economy but also against people's will to live a peaceful and happy life. Hence, within three months it was suppressed by the imperial court. Afterwards, the vassals were deprived of their military and financial power and they were returned to the central government. Thus, the number of organizations and officials of the vassal states were greatly reduced. Besides, the vassals were not allowed to govern their fiefdoms directly and they could only take rents and tax in "Jing Shi" (the capital city). This measure of "receiving land without the right of governing of the people" greatly weakened the power of the vassal states and strengthened the rule of the central government.

The vassal states set up in early Han Dynasty was small in territory. As to the population, the bigger ones had at most 30,000 or 40,000 households and the smaller ones only about 1000 households. The vassals used to have independent administrative and financial power, but with the reform of the vassal states, they lost the independent rights.

During the period of Emperor Wu, the policy of "Qiang Gan Ruo Zhi" (strengthen the central forces and weaken the local ones) and "Tui En Xiao Fan" (showing kindness and weakening the vassal states) was adopted, which had further reduced the amount of land and weakened the power of vassal states. Besides, *Fu Yi Lv* (*The Statute on the Punishment of the Collusion of Officials and Princes*) was made to impose punishment upon vassals and *Shang Fang Lv* (*The Statutes on Preventing Officials from being Randomly Promoted*) was made to control the promotion and the number of officials, which had made the administrative power of the area of a vassal state similar to that of "Jun" (shire). Meanwhile, the power of principality was also weakened and its power was similar to that of "Xian" (county). At the end of Han Dynasty, although "fiefdom" still existed, the local government system was mainly in the form of "Jun" (shire) and "Xian" (county). It was only after the power of the separatist vassal states were greatly weakened that the policies of the central government could be timely carried out nationwide.

"Jun" (shire) in Han Dynasty was granted the highest local political power, with "Jun Shou" (governor, later called "Tai Shou": governor of a prefecture) as the head official. Because his salary was about 2000 *dan*, he was generally called "Er Qian Dan" (the ancient official with a monthly salary of 2000 *dan*). "Jun Shou" (governor) had the power to deal with the military, judicial, financial, and agricultural affairs of the "Jun" (shire), as well as the power to nominate the junior officials in "Jun" (shire) and "Xian" (county). "'Tai Shou' (governor of a prefecture) was in charge of handling all kinds of affairs in "Jun" (shire), including promoting the development of agriculture, relieving the poor, making legal judgments, bringing benefits to the people, preventing crimes, supervising criminal acts, promoting the good and wiping out the evil, and condemning and punishing the savage and vicious."[94] Emperor Xuan said, "The people are contented with working in fields without worrying or complaining bitterly about others because good policies and fair judgments are

---

[94] *Han Guan Jie Gu* (*Explanation of the Officials in Han Dynasty*).

implemented. So only those competent officials of 'Er Qian Dan' (the ancient official with a monthly salary of 2,000 *dan*) can fulfill the mission with me."[95]

Below "Jun" (shire), "Xian" (county) was the basic local administrative unit, headed by "Xian Ling" (county magistrate) who was nominated directly by the central court. In Han Dynasty, both "Xian Ling" (county magistrate) and "Jun Shou" (governor) held their office for a long term so that they could make achievements to eliminate their thoughts of "Wu Ri Jing Zhao" (for a short term in office).[96]

Below "Xian" (county), "Xiang" (townships) and "Li" (a basic resident organization consisting of five neighborhoods) were established. The head official of "Xiang" (townships) was called "Se Fu," and the head of "Li" (a basic resident organization consisting of five neighborhoods) was called "Li Kui." Below "Li," the residents were organized into "Shi Wu" (a basic level organization grouped by five or ten households), "'Shi' (a grassroot unit of ten families) is with ten families, and 'Wu' (a grassroot unit of five families) is with five families. They keep an eye on each other and report the good and bad deeds to the supervisors."[97] Besides, strict registration system was set up, and the information about people's age, gender, social relationship, land and property, height, and complexion, etc., were all recorded in great detail as a reference for levying tax, labor service or arresting fugitives. Because the farmers organized by households were the objects of exploitation of tax, corvée, and military service, the rulers paid much attention to the management of registration. When Liu Bang just entered the pass, what Xiao He paid attention to first was the household registration of the Qin Dynasty. After the founding of Han Dynasty, household registration was checked in every August and it was forbidden to conceal the registration, let alone migration of the people. The management of household registration was one of the most important criteria for the assessment of local officials. The so-called "Xun Li" (Excellent Officials) in Han Dynasty referred to those officials who were praised because "the registered households increased annually"[98] when they were in office.

As the basic-level administrative units, besides "Xiang" (townships) and "Li" (a basic resident organization consisting of five neighborhoods), "Ting" (local administrative units) was set up for every ten *li*. At the beginning, "Ting" was set up near the boundaries to prevent foreigners from entering the country, which could be found the records in *Ju Yan Han Jian* (*Ju Yan Bamboo Slips of Han Dynasty*) and some other historian books. Later it was developed into an institution in charge of

---

[95]"Xun Li Zhuan" (The Biography of Excellent Officials) in *Han Shu* (*The History of Han Dynasty*).

[96]"Zhang Chang Zhuan" (The Biography of Zhang Chang) in *Han Shu* (*The History of Han Dynasty*).

[97]"Bai Guan Zhi" (The Record of the Officials of all Ranks) in *Latter Han Shu* (Book 5).

[98]"Xun Li Zhuan" (The Biography of Excellent Officials) in *Han Shu* (*The History of Han Dynasty*).

arresting thieves and robbers, with the function of police station.[99] Therefore, a tight net of supervision was formed by the extensive establishment of "Ting."

In the Eastern Han Dynasty, the system of "Jun" (shire) and "Xian" (county) was continued to be followed. "Zhou" (subprefecture) was a supervised area rather than a level of local administration. During the reign of Emperor Ling at the end of the Eastern Han Dynasty, out of the need of suppressing the riots of "Huang Jin Jun" (The Yellow Scarves Army), "Zhou" (subprefecture) was established as the highest level of local government, by which the three-level system of "Zhou" (subprefecture), "Jun" (shire) and "Xian" (county) was formed.

5.3.2 The Strengthening of Official Management

The bureaucratic system of the feudal China developed into a new stage through Warring States Period, Qin, and Han Dynasty. Because the feudal bureaucracy was an important tool to maintain and carry out the ruling of the country, it was a very important event to select the officials to fill up the bureaucratic organizations for the consolidation of feudal ruling. Emperor Gaozu, when summarizing the experience of defeating Xiang Yu, claimed that it was decisive to appoint Zhang Liang, Xiao He, and Han Xin in very important positions. In the 11th year of Gaozu (196 B.C.), *Qiu Xian Zhao* (*Decree for Recruiting Talented People*) was issued, in which the selection of talents was connected with "making sacrifice to the ancestors." Thus, it was required that talented people be recommended and recruited by the central and the local government.[100]

With the demand of the expansion of the bureaucratic system, a set of rules for the appointment and dismissal of officials were established. *Gong Ling* (*Decrees for Achievements*) unearthed was a law about the official selection and assessment. The ways of selecting officials in Western Han Dynasty included "Lang Xuan" (selection of candidate officials), "Cha Ju" (election system of Han Dynasty: the talents are recommended by the dukes, heads of different ministry, provincial governors and appointed by the court), "Zheng Bi" (recommended by the emperor is called "Zheng" and recommended by the government is called "Bi"), "Gong Ju"(the civil examinations for government degrees), "Te Zhao"(special recruit), "She Ce"(explaining the relevant issues by choosing a topic), and "Dui Ce" (answering questions about the political issues or classics), among which "Cha Ju" and "Zheng Bi" were used most often. During the period of Emperor Wen, it was made clear by the emperor that every year "talented, righteous, and free-speaking people" should be recommend by ministers and local officials and "be examined by the emperor in

---

[99]"Bai Guan Zhi" (The Record of the Officials of all Ranks) in *Latter Han Shu* (*The History of Latter Han Dynasty*) (Book 5).
[100]"Gao Di Ji" (The Record of the First Emperor of Han Dynasty) in *Han Shu* (*The History of Han Dynasty*) (Book 2).

person."[101] However, there was a strict restriction for those who could be recommended. They should the officials above "Er Qian Dan" (the ancient official with a monthly salary of 2000 *dan*) or the children of the wealthy people, so it was impossible to select the talented people who were needed by the country extensively and to satisfy the desire of the middle or small landowners to enter the official circle. Thus, Emperor Wu adopted Dong Zhongshu's proposal, according to which one out of 200,000 people who were filial and frugal should be recommended to be appointed as officials. It was recorded in "Dong Zhong Shu Zhuan" (The Biography of Dong Zhongshu) in *Han Shu* (*The History of Han Dynasty*) that "...Zhongshu consulted classics, upheld Confucianism, rejected all the other schools of thoughts, and appointed the officials to run the schools. The system of recommending "Xiao Lian" (one of the subjects of selecting officials: being filial to parents and impartial in dealing with things) and "Mao Cai" (or "Xiu Cai": one of the subjects of selecting officials in ancient China) by 'Zhou' (subprefecture) and 'Jun' (shire) was initiated by Zhongshu'."

The subjects for selecting officials were divided into "Xian Liang Fang Zheng" (one of the imperial examinations to select talented scholars of moral excellence), "Xiao Ti Li Tian" (being filial and industrious), "Mao Cai" (or "Xiu Cai": one of the subjects of selecting officials in ancient China) and "Xiao Lian" (one of the subjects of selecting officials: being filial to parents and impartial in dealing with things). Besides, frankness was taken as the sign of integrity, and those who were recommended would be examined by the emperor in person to show the importance of the event. One thing needs to be pointed out is that whenever there were changes in astronomical phenomena, such as earthquake, solar eclipse, flood and draught, talented people would be ordered to be recommended by the officials, because in the eyes of the rulers, one of the reasons for the warning of astronomical phenomena was the neglect and loss of talents. In Han Dynasty, the importance of talents was connected to celestial phenomena, which was unprecedented in the previous dynasties. In the imperial edict "On the Crime of Failing to Recommend 'Xiao Lian' (one of the subjects of selecting officials: being filial to parents and impartial in dealing with things)" issued by Emperor Wu, it was clearly stated that "those who have recommended the virtuous people will be awarded, while those who have concealed the virtuous people will be punished."[102] Thus, the Western and Eastern Han Dynasties were famous for their having gotten large number of talented people, such as Chao Cuo, Dong Zhongshu, Gong Sunhong, Huang Ba, Lu Pi, Shen Tugang, Lu Wenshu, Bao Xuan, Zhao Guanghan, Xiao Wangzhi, Zhang Heng, Li Gu, Chen Fan, and Li Ying, etc., all of whom were selected as officials through examination and recommendation. The local officials had many opportunities to be recommended, so most of them were quite self-disciplined, which was why the official administration was honest and clear for some time in Han Dynasty.

---

[101]"Wen Di Ji" (The Record of Emperor Wen) in *Han Shu* (*The History of Han Dynasty*).
[102]"Wu Di Ji" (The Record of Emperor Wu) in *Han Shu* (*The History of Han Dynasty*).

5.3 The Enriching and Development of Administrative Law

In Eastern Han Dynasty, more subjects were included in "Cha Ju" (election system of Han Dynasty: the talents are recommended by the dukes, heads of different ministry, provincial governors and appointed by the court) compared with Western Han Dynasty, such as "Xian Liang Fang Zheng" (one of the imperial examinations to select talented scholars of moral excellence), "Xiao Lian" (one of the subjects of selecting officials: being filial to parents and impartial in dealing with things), "Xiu Cai" (one of the subjects of selecting officials in ancient China), "Ming Jing" (master of classics), etc. During the reign of Emperor He, he ordered that the quota of "Xiao Lian" (one of the subjects of selecting officials: being filial to parents and impartial in dealing with things) be allocated in proportion to the number of registration in border areas. For a population of more than 100,000 people, one person should be recommended annually; for a population fewer than 100,000 people, one person should be recommended for every two years; for a population fewer than 50,000 people, one person should be recommended for every three years.[103] During the reign of Emperor Shun, the restriction of age, talents, and learning was added, and generally, the age limitation was over forty years old, but there was no restriction for people with special gifts.[104] In Eastern Han Dynasty, the system of "Cha Ju" (election system of Han Dynasty: the talents are recommended by the dukes, heads of different ministry, provincial governors and appointed by the court) became a method of the bureaucrats to take control of the political issues by colluding with local powerful families. Thus, upon succession to the throne, an imperial edit was specially issued by Emperor Ming in which it was announced that "now there are deceptive behaviors in the selection of officials, so the bad officials are not removed and the people with power seek for special favor and vicious officials are at large. Consequently, it had led to the hatred of the ordinary people, but they have nowhere to complain about. So 'You Si' (official) in charge should submit memorials to me about their accusation to have the recommenders punished."[105] In the 1st year of Jian Chu in the reign of Emperor Zhang, the emperor condemned in an imperial order that "the official selection is not fair, which is harmful to the people."[106] Emperor He tried to rectify the situation and ordered that if there was fraud in the selection, "those in charge shall be punished."[107] However, the tendency of the increasing of political corruption in the Eastern Han Dynasty had rendered it impossible to change the phenomenon so that "the talented officials have not been recommended because of the fraud in the selection." This phenomenon was described vividly by Ge Hong in his work "Bao Pu Zi" in *Shen Ju Pian* (*On*

---

[103]"He Di Ji" (The Record of Emperor He) in *Latter Han Shu* (*The History of Latter Han Dynasty*).

[104]"Shun Di Ji" (The Record of Emperor Shun) in *Latter Han Shu* (*The History of Latter Han Dynasty*).

[105]"Ming Di Ji" (The Record of Emperor Ming) in *Latter Han Shu* (*The History of Latter Han Dynasty*).

[106]"Zhang Di Ji" (The Record of Emperor Zhang) in *Latter Han Shu* (*The History of Latter Han Dynasty*).

[107]"He Di Ji" (The Record of Emperor He) in *Latter Han Shu* (*The History of Latter Han Dynasty*).

Selection): "'Xiu Cai' recommended knows nothing about the classic books; the so-called "Xiao Lian" does not live together with their parents; the recommended people who are so-called frugal and clean take dirty money and the general is as timid as a hare."

Besides "Cha Ju" (election system of Han Dynasty: the talents are recommended by the dukes, heads of different ministry, provincial governors and appointed by the court), the system of "Zheng Bi" (recommended by the emperor is called "Zheng" and recommended by the government is called "Bi") was established, which meant that scholars were appointed as officials by the emperor, ministers or the head officials of "Zhou" (subprefecture) and "Jun" (shire). At the time of Queen Lv, she had recruited "Shang Shan Si Hao" (four learned and virtuous hermits living in Mount Shang) for the crown prince, which had started the precedent of "Zheng Bi" (recommended by the emperor is called "Zheng" and recommended by the government is called "Bi"). As for the recruiting of local officials, if the position was above one hundred *dan*, the recruited had to be approved by the emperor. Actually, "Zheng Bi" (recommended by the emperor is called "Zheng" and recommended by the government is called "Bi") was often used as a pretentious decoration of the country's respect for the virtuous people. As the opinions of "Xiang Dang" (fellow villagers), which was made up of retired bureaucrats and local bullies, were of primary importance for recommendation and recruitment, the system became a bridge between the feudal government and local powers, but its limitation was quite evident.

In the period of Emperor Wu, the standard of "Si Ke" and "Si Xing" was set up for emperors to select officials. The so-called "Si Ke" included: first, "De Xing Gao Miao, Zhi Jie Qing Bai" (being morally superior, innocent and with high aspiration); second, "Xue Tong Xing Xiu, Jing zhong Bo Shi" (being knowledgeable in classics and engaging oneself in social activities good for the people); third, "Ming Xiao Fa Ling, Zu Yi Jue Ce" (being well acquainted with the law and able to make judgment);...fourth, "Gang Yi Duo Lue, Yu Shi Bu Huo" (being persevered and resourceful without being puzzled in handling matters."[108] "Si Xing" included "honesty, unaffectedness, modesty, and benevolence."[109] Anyone chosen by the emperor would be promoted by bypassing the immediate leadership regardless of the required qualities to show the emperor's high regard for the talented and virtuous.

To cultivate reserve forces for bureaucrats, "Tai Xue" (The Imperial College) and "Bo Shi Di Zi Yuan" (students prepared to be "Bo Shi") were set up in the capital by Emperor Wu to study the Confucian classics. Exams were taken once a year and the qualified would be appointed as officials. "Tai Xue" (The Imperial College) in the Western Han Dynasty not only set an example for the construction of the feudal schools but also promoted the Confucianization of the bureaucrats, and it had made

---

[108] *Han Jiu Yi* (*Traditional Rituals of Han Dynasty*).
[109] *Han Guan Yi* (*The Etiquette for the Officials of Han Dynasty*).

5.3 The Enriching and Development of Administrative Law

"the officials more gentleman-like and knowledgeable about Confucianism."[110] Some scholars were promoted because they had put forward suggestions beneficial to the ruling of the country. For example, the poverty-stricken Zhu Fuyan was promoted because his proposal was applauded by the emperor and was appointed as "Lang Zhong" (head of a subministry department). He then was promoted four times within one year. Since then, it became an important method for the scholars to enter the bureaucratic system "to put forward proposals by submitting memorials to the emperor."

"She Ce" and "Dui Ce" were two types of exams for the selection of officials. "She Ce" referred to explaining the relevant issues by choosing a topic; "Dui Ce" referred to answering questions about the political issues or classics. The emperor decided who were more excellent according to the performance of the candidates in these exams. If a person passed "Dui Ce" (answering questions about the political issues or classics), then he would possibly become officials responsible for giving advice to the emperor; if a person passed "She Ce" (explaining the relevant issues by choosing a topic), he would possibly be appointed "Lang Guan" (directors of bureaus).

The nobles, bureaucrats and people from rich families were not only candidates for "Cha Ju" (election system of Han Dynasty: the talents are recommended by the dukes, heads of different departments, provincial governors and appointed by the court) and "Zheng Bi" (recommended by the emperor is called "Zheng" and recommended by the government is called "Bi"), but also had the rights to inherit the official positions of their parents. For example, an official above "Er Qian Dan" (the ancient official with a monthly salary of 2000 *dan*), after three years in office, could recommend a young man from his family to be "Lang" (a general official title of departmental officials). In the reign of Emperor Wu, to solve the financial problem resulted from wars, the custom of forbidding merchants to become officials was given up, and "Mai Guan Yu Jue" (selling the official ranks and titles) was allowed, which had made it convenient for merchants and wealthy people to "buy official positions." However, it was often looked down upon by the people to inherit or buy official positions rather than select or recommend officials according to one's merits and virtue. This phenomenon was openly criticized by Dong Zhongshu who said that "not all the sons of the officials whose ranks are above 'Er Qian Dan' (the ancient official with a monthly salary of 2,000 *dan*) or those of the wealthy family are virtuous."[111]

Besides, it was also an important ways to gain official positions by military achievements, which was proved by *Han Jian (The Bamboo Slips of Han Dynasty)* unearthed from Shangsunjiazhai in Datong, Qinghai province: "Those who kill two enemies shall be awarded the official titles of the first rank; those who kill five

---

[110]"Ru Lin Zhuan" (The Biography of the Confucian Scholars) in *Han Shu (The History of Han Dynasty)*.

[111]"Dong Zhong Shu Zhuan" (The Biography of Dong Zhongshu) in *Han Shu (The History of Han Dynasty)*.

enemies shall be awarded the official titles of the second rank; those who kill eight enemies shall be awarded official titles of the third rank; those who kill fewer than two enemies will be awarded 1,000 *qian*." This was consistent with what was recorded in "Ding Fa" (Law Making) in *Han Fei Zi* (*Han Feizi*): "According to Lord Shang, those who beheaded one enemy shall be awarded the official titles of the first rank, if they want to become officials, they shall be appointed as officials with a salary of 50 *dan*; those who beheaded two enemies shall be awarded the official titles of the second rank, if they want to become officials, they shall be appointed as officials with a salary of 100 *dan*." It was evident that in the Han Dynasty the system of awarding titles and official positions according to military achievements was inherited.

In Han Dynasty, there are the following ways of recruiting officials: "Bai" (be an official for the first time or reassigned), "Zheng" (the special call from the emperor), "Shou" (temporary employment), "Jia" (representing), "Jian" (remaining on one's post to be responsible for other duties), "Ling" (holding concurrent posts), "Xing" (doing duties on behalf of others), "Qian" (being transferred), etc.

As for the employment system in early Han Dynasty, on the one hand, the class bases of the regime was expanded, a large number of talents were recruited, and the power of the state was strengthened; on the other hand, because family background and social relationship were considered in official selection, and it was often under the control of local officials and despots, so that it was changed from a measure of consolidating the power of central government to that of fostering of the development of local powers.

As for the removal of officials from their posts, there were mainly three ways: the voluntary resignation, the dismissal as a punishment and the dismissal because of "Lian Zuo" (being punished for being related to somebody who committed an offense).

The development of the bureaucratic system promoted the legalization and specialization of the performance assessment system. The unearthed *Shi Lv* (*The Law on History*) was a special law used to assess the work of "Shi Guan" (official in charge of recording and compiling history). The assessment in Han Dynasty was conducted from the bottom up, so the head officials of counties and the ministers of vassal states submitted "Ji Bu" (book recording information about household registration, tax, and personnel) to "Jun" (shire) at the end of the year, which was then examined by the head of "Jun" (shire). Those who were considered excellent might be transferred to a better place or be promoted. Zhao Guanghan did very well as the magistrate of Yangzhai, for which he "was transferred to the position of 'Du Wei' (a military officer below the general) in the capital area."[112]

The head officials of "Jun Guo" (vassal state) needed to report to "Cheng Xiang Fu" [(the prime minister's office) or "Shang Shu Tai" (Imperial Secretariat) in Eastern Han Dynasty] and "Yu Shi Fu" (an office responsible for the supervision

---

[112]"Zhao Guang Han Zhuan" (The Biography of Zhao Guanghan) in *Han Shu* (*The History of Han Dynasty*).

5.3 The Enriching and Development of Administrative Law

of officials), as was illustrated in the statement that "the assessment of the officials' performance was made by 'Liang Fu' (two government offices)." Yan Shigu noted that "'Liang Fu' (two government offices) referred to 'Cheng Xiang Fu' (the prime minister's office) and 'Yu Shi Fu' (an office responsible for the supervision of officials)."[113] According to law, the report made must include household registration, agriculture, canal, money and grain transportation, crime, lawsuit, education, selection, epidemic disease and natural disaster, etc.[114] Those with better achievements would be reported to the emperor, to be transferred to a better place or to be promoted. Huang Bo, "Tai Shou" (governor of a prefecture) in Yingchuan "ranked the first in terms of household registration and tax, so he was promoted" to be "Jing Zhao Yin" (an official position equivalent to the mayor of the capital city in modern time), which was equivalent to "Jiu Qing" (the nine high-rank officials in ancient times).[115] Besides "Jun Guo" (vassal state), "Shi San Ci Shi" (feudal provincial or prefectural governor) which was set up during the reign of Emperor Wu, was also required to report to the emperor at the end of year according to the requirement for the head officials of "Jun Guo," which was helpful to have a check of the reports made by the officials of "Jun Guo" (vassal state).

In the various departments of the imperial court, the head officials were in charge of evaluating the performance of their subordinates, "the officials below 'Cheng Xiang' (the prime minister) should do their duties and report what they want to say, according to which they would be assessed. 'Shi Zhong' (the assistant official), and 'Shang Shu' (the minister) who have made achievements shall be promoted, and if they have done something outstanding, they would be rewarded generously."[116]

In general, an assessment was held every year, which was called "Chang Ke" and a larger-scale assessment was held once every three years, which was called "Da Ke." The result of the assessment was decided by "Cheng Xiang Fu" (the prime minister's office) and "Yu Shi Fu" (an office responsible for the supervision of officials), with the excellent graded "Zui" and the poor graded "Dian," which was called "Hui Ke." To avoid unfairness, the assessment was conducted openly, and the examiners would ask various questions and the examinees would answer them truthfully in accordance with their performance. Afterwards, the result was collected and submitted from bottom up, namely, from "Xian" (county) to "Jun" (shire), then to the imperial court, and finally to "Cheng Xiang" (the prime minister) ("Shang Shu Ling" or 'Lu Shang Shu Shi': ancient official in charge of assisting emperors in Eastern Han Dynasty), who was responsible to summarize what he had collected and submitted it to the Emperor. In Han Dynasty, the assessment of the officials was regarded as a very important measure to improve official administration, so it was a

---

[113]"Xue Xuan Zhuan" (The Biography of Xue Xuan) in *Han Shu* (*The History of Han Dynasty*).

[114]"Bai Guan Zhi" (The Record of the Officials of all Ranks) in *Latter Han Shu* (*The History of Latter Han Dynasty*) (Book 5).

[115]"Xun Li Zhuan" (The Biography of Excellent Officials) in *Han Shu* (*The History of Han Dynasty*).

[116]"Xuan Di Ji" (The Record of Emperor Xuan) in *Han Shu* (*The History of Han Dynasty*).

very important event in the country, just as was recorded in "Kao Ji" (performance evaluation) in *Qian Fu Lun* (*On Hermits*) (Book 7) that "if the officials are not examined, they will become sluggish and arrogant, with evil ones gaining the upper hand; if the rulers are not examined, the righteous and talented will be suppressed, with the dishonest ones gaining the upper hand." Thus, the emperor usually collected the report on the first day of lunar year when the officials gathered for celebration at imperial court, or at the sacrificial ceremony on Mount Tai or in "Ming Tang" (the grandest buildings built for the emperor to meet heads of the kingdoms, issue orders, worship heaven and pay tribute to ancestors).

Special laws like *Shang Ji Lv* (*The Law for Officials to Report Statistical Books*) were made about the performance evaluation in Han Dynasty, so specific regulations about the contents of examinations were laid down for officials of different ranks and different posts. For example, Xue Fan was promoted to the post of "Yu Shi Zhong Cheng" (Grand Censor) because he was expert at law.[117] So, because laws were made for the evaluation and evidence was recorded for the excellent and poor performance, the implementation of the evaluation system was fully guaranteed. The officials who made achievements would be promoted, those who did not would be degraded, and those who took bribes by bending the law or those who were incompetent would be punished. Moreover, the officials who were dismissed were not allowed to come to the capital without authorization. It was stipulated in the law of Han Dynasty that "those 'Shou Ling' (prefects or magistrates) who have been dismissed are not allowed to enter the capital without the imperial order."[118] According to the assessment system in Han Dynasty, it was not allowed "to be promoted for having served in the government office for a long time, or to be appointed as officials for the same reason."[119] Moreover, it was not allowed for an official to stay in the same position for his lifetime, which had made it possible to recruit new forces in the government and to keep its vitality.

The officials working in the central and local government were paid by the government in accordance with their ranks. According to the law of the Han Dynasty, there were altogether fifteen official ranks and *Dan* was used to differentiate the order and *hu* to decide the amount of the salary. The amount of salary was the label to distinguish the official ranks. In early Han Dynasty, economy was in such recession that "it was difficult for the emperor to have a carriage drawn by four horses of the same color, and the generals and ministers had to take cow-drawn carriages." Therefore, Gaozu had to "cut down the officials' salary and the expenditures of the government."[120] Because of the humble salary of the officials, a special

---

[117]"Xue Xuan Zhuan" (The Biography of Xue Xuan) in *Han Shu* (*The History of Han Dynasty*).

[118]"Su Bu Wei Zhuan" (The Biography of Su Buwei) in *Latter Han Shu* (*The History of Latter Han Dynasty*).

[119]"Dong Zhong Shu Zhuan" (The Biography of Dong Zhongshu) in *Han Shu* (*The History of Han Dynasty*).

[120]"Shi Huo Zhi" (The Records of National Finance and Economy) in *Han Shu* (*The History of Han Dynasty*).

5.3 The Enriching and Development of Administrative Law

order was issued by Emperor Hui, in which it was stated that "the officials are to rule the people, and they will be trusted if they do their best, therefore, they should be paid a high salary because it is in the people's interest."[121] During the reign of Emperor Xuan, with the recovery and development of economy, the payment for the officials of 100 *dan* was increased.

The salary was mainly paid with agricultural product but sometimes it was also paid with money. Besides the salaries paid by government, the officials were also exempted from tax and corvée service. According to law, the officials above 600 *dan* were exempted from all corvée except military service, so were their families. Moreover, the junior officials and the children of "Bo Shi" (learned scholars) were also exempted from corvée.

The officials aged seventy years old who had poor hearing or eyesight, or who could not walk steadily could retire also retire for illness. After retirement, the officials above "Er Qian Dan" (the ancient official with a monthly salary of 2000 *dan*) could have one third of the original payment. It was stipulated in the 1st year of Yuan Shi during the reign of Emperor Ping (1 A.D.) that "the officials above 'Er Qian Dan' (the ancient official with a monthly salary of 2,000 *dan*) can earn one third of the original payment after retirement and they will be so paid until death."[122] However, the officials below "Yi Qian Dan" (the ancient official with a monthly salary of 1000 *dan*) would not be paid after retirement. The reason why the officials above "Er Qian Dan" (2000 *dan*: ancient officials or head of prefecture) were well treated was that they had not only shouldered heavy responsibility but also had made greater contribution to the country. Moreover, because of the strict official management, it was rare that an official did not make mistakes after a long time of service. Considering the officials' long-standing service to the country, those who retired at the age of 70 were granted gold and salary by the government.

Because of the institutionalization of retirement of the officials, the officials should resign if they were old to give rooms to other gifted men. For example, Zhou Bo, "Cheng Xiang" (the prime minister), knew that he was not as capable as Chen Ping, so he claimed that he was ill and retired home to make room for Chen Ping to take office. When high-rank officials retired, they were favorably treated by the emperor. "Cheng Xiang" (the prime minister) Wei Xian and "Yu Shi Da Fu" (Grand Censor) Du Yannian retired at an old age and they were rewarded generously by the emperor, each of them was granted one hundred *jin* of gold, a luxurious carriage drawn by four horses, beef, and wine. This practice contributed to the implementation of the retirement system, which had not only updated the officials at all levels, reduced lethargy and improved efficacy, but also played a positive role in the development of politics, economy, science and culture.

To effectively supervise the officials, the political system of the Qin Dynasty was inherited in Han Dynasty and "Yu Shi Da Fu" (Grand Censor) was appointed to exercise the power of central supervision. As one of the three councilors, "Yu Shi Da

---

[121]"Hui Di Ji" (The Record of Emperor Hui) in *Han Shu* (*The History of Han Dynasty*).

[122]"Ping Di Ji" (The Record of Emperor Ping) in *Han Shu* (*The History of Han Dynasty*).

Fu" (Grand Censor) had the right to impeach "Cheng Xiang" (the prime minister), by which the power of the balance mechanism was constituted. During the reign of Emperor Cheng, in line with the changes of the central administrative system, "Yu Shi Tai" (The Censorate) was established as a supervisory organ to exercise the supervisory power, with "Yu Shi Zhong Cheng" (Grand Censor) as the head official, which was a landmark in the development of supervision system in ancient China, so although nominally under the control of "Shao Fu" (in charge of emperor's income and royal affairs), it was independent and was in charge of many different affairs, such as monitoring etiquette, treasury and military affairs, supervising officials, informing against crimes, participating in legislation making, conducting official assessment, recommending talents, managing the books kept in central archive, supervising "Bu Ci Shi" (a supervisor assigned by the central government to a local area), etc. The emperor also selected "Xiu Yi Zhi Yu Shi" (a censor sent by the emperor to settle specific cases) from among "Shi Yu Shi" (subordinate of Grand Censor) to punish the treacherous people in local places, to help the officials of "Zhou" (subprefecture) and "Jun" (shire) to settle major cases, or to be responsible for the suppression of the rebels.

During the reign of Emperor Wu, the post of "Si Li Xiao Wei" (local censor) was set up to supervise the officials in the capital and the seven "Jun" (shire) close to the capital, including, "San Fu" ("Jing Zhao," "You Fu Feng," "Zuo Feng Yi") (all official titles who in charge of the three places near the capital), "San He" (Henan, Henei, Hedong) and Hongnong. "Si Li Xiao Wei" (local censor) had the power to supervise the officials below "the crown prince, and to handle all matters from travelling to domestic affairs."[123] Moreover, he was in charge of "informing against the officials below the crown prince and 'San Gong' (the three councilors), including those in 'Zhou' (subprefecture) and 'Jun Guo' (vassal state) with no exception."[124] In court assembly, "Si Li Xiao Wei" (local censor) occupied one special seat and was called "San Du Zuo" (three detached seats) together with "Shang Shu Ling" (ancient official equivalent to prime minister) and "Yu Shi Zhong Cheng" (Grand Censor), enjoying special attention from the emperor. With many subordinates, "Si Li Xiao Wei" (local censor) also had the power to arrest the criminals directly. However, with the opposition of "Cheng Xiang" (the prime minister), the power of "Si Li Xiao Wei" (local censor) was constantly undermined after Emperor Wu. In the 4th year of Chu Yuan in the reign of Emperor Yuan, "Si Li Xiao Wei" (local censor) was deprived of the title of "Chi Jie" (official title). Towards the end of the Western Han Dynasty, this post was affiliated to "Da Si Kong" (the minister of public works), and to the time of Eastern Han Dynasty, "Si Li Xiao Wei" (local censor) became a procurator in charge of seven "Jun" (shire).

At the beginning of Han Dynasty, "Jian Yu Shi" (inspector of the royal division) which was set up in "Jun" (shire) in the Qin Dynasty was abolished and "Cheng Xiang Shi" (senior assistant of the prime minister) was dispatched by "Cheng

---

[123]"Zhi Guan" (State Officials) in *Tong Dian* (*The General Codes*) (Book 14).

[124]"Zhi Guan" (State Officials) in *Tai Ping Yu Lan* (*Imperial Readings of the Taiping Era*), Vol. 48.

5.3 The Enriching and Development of Administrative Law

Xiang" (the prime minister) to inspect "Jun" (shire) whenever it was necessary. To strengthen the central government's control over local officials, one "Jian Yu Shi" (inspector of the royal division) was stationed in every "Jun" (shire) to be responsible for supervising its work. Emperor Wu devoted himself to the consolidation of centralized government, so he divided the whole country into thirteen supervision areas called "Bu Zhou," with "Ci Shi" (a supervisor assigned by the central government to a local area) as the regular supervisor for each area. The establishment of the thirteen "Bu Zhou" is a very important development of the supervision system of Han Dynasty.

It is worth mentioning that the jurisdiction of local supervisors in Han Dynasty was gradually legalized. "In the 3rd year of Emperor Hui, Xiang Guo asked the emperor to send "Yu Shi" (the censor) to supervise the illegal affairs in "San Fu" ("Jing Zhao," "You Fu Feng," "Zuo Feng Yi") (all official titles who in charge of the three places near the capital) including nine items in total, such as litigation, robbery and theft, casting of fake money, unfair judgments, improper corvée and tax, corrupted and brutal officials, addiction to luxury, those whose pull of crossbow was above ten dan and those engaging in what one was not supposed to do."[125] The previously mentioned nine items concerned with many important aspects such as administration, jurisdiction, finance, and official management. Though applicable only to "San Fu" ("Jing Zhao," "You Fu Feng," "Zuo Feng Yi") (all official titles who in charge of the three places near the capital), they were the most important achievements of the local supervision law in feudal China. After Emperor Hui, the expansion of local powers restricted the censor's function of supervising "Jun" (shire), so that in the 13th year of Emperor Wen (67 B.C.), the emperor had to issue an order and it was stated that "since 'Yu Shi' (the censor) failed to obey the law and was incompetent, "Cheng Xiang Shi" (senior assistant of the prime minister) is now sent to act as "Ci Shi" (a supervisor assigned by the central government to a local area) to supervise "Yu Shi" (the censor) as well."[126] Though the appointment of "Cheng Xiang Shi" (senior assistant of the prime minister) as "Ci Shi" (a supervisor assigned by the central government to a local area) was a temporary measure, it had increased the power of "Cheng Xiang" (the prime minister), which was equally upsetting to the emperor. Therefore, Emperor Wu readjusted the responsibilities and power of supervising organs by making "Liu Tiao" (six articles) and demanded "Bu Ci Shi" (a supervisor assigned by the central government to a local area) to supervise "Jun Guo" (vassal state) in their charge in accordance with "Liu Tiao" (six articles). "Liu Tiao" (six articles) which were recorded in *Han Guan Dian Zhi Yi* (*The Etiquette for the Officials to Handle Affairs in Han Dynasty*) are as follows:

> It is stipulated in the imperial edict to 'Ci Shi' (a supervisor assigned by the central government to a local area) that he should travel around 'Jun Guo' (vassal state) to examine the situation of administration, to dismiss the incompetent, to award the competent, to rectify

---

[125]"Yu Shi Tai" (The Censorate) in *Tang Liu Dian* (*The Six Statutes of Tang Dynasty*), Vol. 13.
[126]"Zhi Guan" (State Officials) in *Tong Dian* (*The General Codes*) (Book 14).

the unjust verdicts and to punish the offenders. Besides, the affairs should be handled according to 'Liu Tiao' (six articles), beyond which nothing will be inquired about.

First, whether the land and houses owned by rich and powerful families have exceeded the standards, or whether the people from these powerful families have oppressed the poor, and bully the weak.

Second, whether the officials with the rank of "Er Qian Dan" (the ancient official with a monthly salary of 2000 *dan*) have disobeyed imperial orders, decrees and regulations, or worked for private interests against public good, or taken the advantage of the imperial edicts for private purpose, or infringed upon the ordinary people's interests and conspire to do evil things.

Third, whether the officials with the rank of "Er Qian Dan" (the ancient official with a monthly salary of 2000 *dan*) have failed to investigate the cases involving the suspect who might be innocent, or have killed people randomly, or imposed penalties at their own will when they are angry or granted award abundantly when they are happy; whether they are hated by the ordinary folks because they have been cruel to or have been exploitive of them; whether they have taken the landslides and the collapse of mountains as ill omens.

Forth, whether the officials with the rank of "Er Qian Dan" (the ancient official with a monthly salary of 2000 *dan*) are unfair in selecting subordinates to show favor to their loved ones who are stubborn and disobedient; whether they have refused to get alone with the virtuous people.

Fifth, whether the officials with the rank of "Er Qian Dan" (the ancient official with a monthly salary of 2000 *dan*) are snobbish or have conducted illegal backstage deals.

Sixth, whether the officials with the rank of "Er Qian Dan" (the ancient official with a monthly salary of 2000 *dan*) have associated with the powerful local families or have taken bribes by violating the imperial orders."[127]

"Ci Cha Liu Tiao" (the six articles for supervision) was different from the nine articles of "Ci Sha San Fu" (The supervision of "Jing Zhao," "You Fu Feng," "Zuo Feng Yi") in that it was a national law made to supervise the local areas with the rich and powerful families as the main targets, to strictly guard against the collusion between "Jun Shou" (governor) and the local powers which might lead to the establishment of independent regimes harmful to the centralized government. This was surely a mark left by the special historical background. At the end of Ming Dynasty, Gu Yanwu wrote that "in Han Dynasty, 'Bu Ci Shi' (a supervisor assigned by the central government to a local area) was just responsible for the supervision of the counties according to 'Liu Tiao' (six articles) without sharing the duty of 'Shou Ling' (prefects or magistrates)...so when Huang Bo was appointed 'Ci Shi' (feudal provincial or prefectural governor) in Jizhou, he told the officials and the public that 'Ci Shi' (feudal provincial or prefectural governor) was not responsible for the

---

[127]"Bai Guan Gong Qing Biao" (The Table of Officials of Higher Ranks) in *Han Shu* (*The History of Han Dynasty*), quoted from *Han Guan Dian Zhi Yi* (*The Etiquette for the Officials to Handle Affairs in Han Dynasty*).

5.3 The Enriching and Development of Administrative Law

supervision of the work of 'Huang Shou' (low-rank officials, such as Cheng: the assistant of county magistrate and Wei) who should obey the orders of 'Jun' (prefecture). Bao Xuan, when working as 'Yu Zhou Mu' (the governor of Yu), was impeached for interfering with matters beyond the regulation of 'Liu Tiao' (six articles). Xue Xuan once presented a memorial to the emperor and said that many officials were cruel and made a great fuss about trifles, because 'Bu Ci Shi' (a supervisor assigned by the central government to a local area) had made decisions at their own will and interfered with the affairs of 'Jun' (prefecture) and 'Xian' (county) without following 'Liu Tiao' (six articles)."[128]

In Han Dynasty, the political regime was based on landlords, the rich, and the powerful. However, there was a constant struggle for power and interest between the ruling group headed by the emperor and the local powers. Especially when the influence of local powers went beyond the control of "Jun" (shire) and "Xian" (county), they began to oppose the imperial orders openly. Therefore, the local powers must be suppressed to protect the overall benefit of the country and to maintain the central government's control over the local areas. This contradiction within the ruling class continued to exist, which sometimes might develop into much sharper conflicts. Although it was not the fundamental conflict of the society, the solution of which concerned the future of the country, so it was one of the most important issues which the feudal rulers had always paid close attention to.

Besides the aforesaid "Jiu Tiao" (nine articles) and "Liu Tiao" (six articles), there was an unwritten rule: if "Ci Shi" (a supervisor assigned by the central government to a local area) had discovered crimes when he was inspecting the vassal states, he must report them to the emperor to fulfill his responsibility as his local spy. In this way, the real power of "Ci Shi" (a supervisor assigned by the central government to a local area) continued to be expanded. At the end of the Han Dynasty, the power and responsibility of "Ci Shi" (a supervisor assigned by the central government to a local area) was so great that he even had the right to "select and remove officials and to recommend the senior officials like 'Jiu Qing' (nine high-rank officials in ancient times)."[129] At the time of the Han Dynasty, the area under administration (generally called "Zhou": subprefecture) was not a level of political organization, but a zone of supervision, so "Bu Ci Shi" (a supervisor assigned by the central government to a local area) was only a supervisor dispatched by the imperial court, so he was not a local official above "Jun Shou" (governor). If "Jun Shou" (governor) failed to perform his duty, "Ci Shi" (a supervisor assigned by the central government to a local area) could report it to the emperor but he had no right to handle it directly by himself. If "Ci Shi" (a supervisor assigned by the central government to a local area) transgressed his power which was limited by "Liu Tiao" (six articles), he would be impeached by "Cheng Xiang" (the prime minister). In fact, at the end of the Western Han Dynasty, "Ci Shi" (a supervisor assigned by the central government to a local

---

[128] Gu Yanwu (Ming Dynasty), "Liu Tiao Zhi Wai Bu Cha" (No Examination of Other Than the Six Articles) in *Ri Zhi Lu* (*The Record of Daily Reading*).

[129] "Zhu Bo Zhuan" (The Biography of Zhu Bo) in *Han Shu* (*The History of Han Dynasty*).

area) had interfered with the local administrative affairs by exercising power beyond "Liu Tiao" (six articles). Finally, the emperor had to acknowledge the established fact and asked "Ci Shi" (a supervisor assigned by the central government to a local area) to deal with local issues on behalf of "Jun Shou" (governor), which had legalized his infringement of power to some extent, which was because the increasingly violent rebellion of farmers had compelled the emperor to grant local officials more power to deal with the urgent situation.

The establishment of central supervision institution of "Yu Shi Tai" (The Censorate) and the local stationary procurator not only reflected the development of the feudal supervision system, it was also the result of the further strengthening of the centralized power system, so it had indeed played an effective role in strengthening the disciplines of official administration and rectifying the illegal activities. For example, in the reign of Emperor Cheng, "Cheng Xiang" (the prime minister) Kuang Heng was accused of "disobeying the law, usurping land for private good…changing the boundaries of the county randomly, colluding the subordinates, cheating the emperor and bribing ministers with land," so he was dismissed and changed to "Shu Ren" (the common people).[130] In the reign of Emperor Shun, the great general Liang Ji was impeached by "Shi Yu Shi" (subordinate of Grand Censor) Zhang Gang, which had "shocked the whole capital."[131] The supervision system in Han Dynasty had offered valuable historical experience. For example, the official supervision was carried out according to the law without being interfered by administrative organs. In addition, although the supervisor was low in ranking, he had great power and he could even prosecute the high-ranking officials such as "Zai Xiang" (the prime minister), so he was very authoritative and at the same time, it was much easier for him to be controlled by the emperor. Moreover, there was a time limit for the term of office for "Bu Ci Shi" (a supervisor assigned by the central government to a local area) and they must not be a native of the area under their jurisdiction to avoid colluding with local powers and officials. As for the post of "Zhi Shu Shi Yu Shi" (official in charge of impeaching the other officials in central government) which was in charge of doubtful cases, it should be held by those with legal knowledge so that the "cases under the suspicion of the emperor can be settled in accordance with law."[132] Moreover, the remonstrance system was established and "Yan Guan" (official responsible for giving advice to the emperor) could even admonish the emperor face to face and pointed out the mistakes of the emperor in imperial edicts. The coexistence of "Yan Guan" (official responsible for giving advice to the emperor) and "Cha Guan" (supervisor) had greatly expanded the contents of supervision in the Han Dynasty. However, to prevent "Jian Cha Yu Shi" (the supervisory censor) from abusing his power, on the one hand, a strict

---

[130]"Kuang Heng Zhuan" (The Biography of Kuang Heng) in *Han Shu* (*The History of Han Dynasty*).

[131]"Zhang Gang Zhuan" (The Biography of Zhang Gang) in *Latter Han Shu* (*The History of Latter Han Dynasty*).

[132]"Zhi Guan" (State Officials) in *Tai Ping Yu Lan* (*Imperial Readings of the Taiping Era*), Vol. 24.

5.3 The Enriching and Development of Administrative Law

procedure of selecting "Yu Shi" (the censor) was set up and it was greatly emphasized to improve their quality; on the other hand, the post of "Si Zhi" (official in charge of supervising the officials in capital) was set up under "Cheng Xiang" (the prime minister) to be in charge of rectifying and impeaching the misbehaviors of "Yu Shi" (the censor).

In the supervision work of Han Dynasty, judicial supervision was greatly stressed by the emperor, so various supervisory measures were taken by him. For example, the supervision work was conducted by the emperor either by issuing orders or by hearing the cases by himself, or by sending officials to inspect the local affairs. In the 7th year of Gaozu (198 B.C.), it was announced that "as for the cases which are uncertain and ambiguous, which the officials do not dare to settle, which involved situation that the guilty were not punished and the innocent were not released, if they can't be settled by the county magistrate, from now on, they must be reported to the officials of 'Er Qian Dan' (the ancient official with a monthly salary of 2,000 *dan*); if they can be settled, they should be reported to the superior, but if they cannot be settled by the officials of 'Er Qian Dan' (the ancient official with a monthly salary of 2,000 *dan*), they should be reported to and settled by 'Ting Wei' (the supreme official in charge of judicature), who should report them to the emperor; if they can be settled by 'Ting Wei' (the supreme official in charge of judicature), they should be recorded in memorial and be reported to the emperor with relevant supplementary laws."[133]

To effectively supervise the local jurisdiction, in the 6th year of Yuanshou in the reign of Emperor Wu, "six 'Bo Shi' (learned scholar) were sent to inspect different areas to inquire about and to give relief to the people who were widowed, disabled, ill, and those who can't make a living by themselves....They were asked to find out those who were talented and unemployed, those who were wronged, those who were unable to live a normal life, those who were cunning and evil, those who had laid the land wasted and who were cruel to the people and reported them to the emperor. If there were people who had worked for their private interests in 'Jun Guo' (vassal state), they should be reported to 'Cheng Xiang' (the prime minister) and 'Yu Shi' (censor) to be settled."[134]

In the 4th year of Wu Feng during the reign of Emperor Xuan (54 B.C.), "altogether twenty-four people headed by 'Cheng Xiang' (the prime minister) and "Yu Shi" (the censor) were sent to have an inspection tour of the country to have an investigation of the unjust verdicts and to punish the cruel officials who did not repent or mend them ways."[135]

In the 5th year of Jianchu in the reign of Emperor Zhang (80 B.C.), a special order was issued: "Confucius says, 'inappropriate punishments will render people puzzled as to how to behave.' But now there are many vicious officials who make judgments arbitrarily, or who do not settle cases according to law, or who just intimidate the

---

[133]"Xing Fa Zhi" (The Record of the Criminal Law) in *Han Shu* (*The History of Han Dynasty*).
[134]"Wu Di Ji" (The Record of Emperor Wu) in *Han Shu* (*The History of Han Dynasty*).
[135]"Xuan Di Ji" (The Record of Emperor Xuan) in *Han Shu* (*The History of Han Dynasty*).

innocent people so that more people have committed suicide than those who have been brought to trial in a year, which are not be the intention of parents. So, this kind of misbehavior should be reported and impeached by 'You Si' (official) in charge."[136]

The judicial practice of the Western and Eastern Han Dynasties was barely satisfactory for a long time, which was largely because of judicial supervision regularly conducted.

The rise and fall of the supervising system of the Han Dynasty had fully reflected the great influence of the imperial power. When great efforts were made by the emperor to build a prosperous county and great attention was paid to the function of supervisory institutions, then it was possible for the supervisory institutions to play the role of eliminating political corruption, redressing the wrongdoing and maintaining the legal order; nevertheless, when the emperor was fatuous and lacking the imperial authority, then they would lose their due mechanism of check and balance.

5.4 The Criminal Law in Documents and *Han Jian* (*The Bamboo Slip of Han Dynasty*)

The criminal law was the main body of the legal system of Han Dynasty, so there were collections of criminal legislations such as *Jiu Zhang Lv* (*The Code in Nine Chapters*), which included laws of theft, robbery, jail and arrest; at the same time, there were independent criminal laws such as *Shen Ming Fa* (*Laws on the Misconduct of Officials*), which included the laws like *Ting Wei Qie Ling* (*Decree on Judicial Process*), *Yu Ling* (*Decree on Judicial Management*), *Chui Ling* (*Decree on the Punishment of Flogging*) and *Gong Wei Ling* (*Decree on the Safeguarding of the Palace*). As for "Bi" (analogy), it was a collection of criminal precedents. In Western Han Dynasty, the main purpose of the law was to crack down on the crimes that endangering the government of centralized authority and to maintain the stability of the newly established feudal state, just as was stated in "Xing Fa Zhi" (The Record of the Criminal Law) in *Han Shu* (*The History of Han Dynasty*) that "a country can't do without criminal penalties."

The criminal law in the Western Han Dynasty clearly reflected the influence of the Confucian theory of "absorbing 'Li' (rites) into 'Fa' (law)" and "combination of 'Xing' (criminal law) with 'De' (virtue)," which was the brand of times of "rejecting the other schools of thoughts and respecting only Confucianism." Thereafter, a series of criminal principles and charges with long-lasting influence were made. It was stated in "Xing Fa Zhi" (The Record of the Criminal Law) in *Ming Shi* (*History of Ming Dynasty*) that "as for the laws made in each dynasty, their origins could be

---

[136]"Zhang Di Ji" (The Record of Emperor Zhang) in *Latter Han Shu* (*The History of Latter Han Dynasty*).

traced in *Jiu Zhang Lv* (*The Code in Nine Chapters*) made in Han Dynasty," which had indicated that the criminal law of the Han Dynasty had played a fundamental role in Chinese legal history.

During the reign of Emperor Wen and Emperor Jing, under the influence of the historical tide of abolishing the cruel laws and brutal punishments of the Qin Dynasty, reforms aiming at abolishing corporal punishments were carried out. Emperor Wen learned the lessons from the downfall of Qin Dynasty and the experience of the establishment of Han Dynasty and realized that the criminal law should not just include punishment, so it should be combined with education to show people the way to live rather than drive them to the road of ruin, which had played a positive role in the maintenance of social order. The abolishment of corporal punishment was an important reform in the history of Chinese criminal law, which had reflected the progress of legal civilization and which had served as the historical origin of the statutory law of "Wu Xing" (five penalties), namely, "Chi" (flogging with light sticks), "Zhang" (flogging with heavy sticks), "Tu" (imprisonment), "Liu" (exile), and "Si" (death penalty) which were implemented after Sui and Tang Dynasties.

5.4.1 The Main Accusation in the Laws of Han Dynasty

In Western Han Dynasty, the economic and political development as well as the sharpening of social conflicts resulted in the increase of the varieties of crimes and the formulation of new accusation.

5.4.1.1 The Crime of Endangering the Political Power

"Fan Ni" (treachery) referred to "Mou Fan" (plotting rebellion or plotting to endanger the country) and "Da Ni" (great sedition). "Mou Fan" (plotting rebellion or plotting to endanger the country) referred to the most serious crime endangering the government by violence and was therefore considered a felony, so it was the key target of the criminal law and the offenders would be severely punished. In the 11th year of Gaozu (195 B.C.), "Han Xin, the vassal of Huaiyin had conspired against the state in Changan, so he was punished by 'Yi San Zu' (the law of killing the three generations of a family)."[137] In the same year, Peng Yue, the king of Liang state had conspired to rebel, so he received the same punishment.[138] Emperor Wen said, "the

---

[137]"Gao Zu Ji" (The Record of Emperor Gaozu) in *Han Shu* (*The History of Han Dynasty*) (Book 2).
[138]"Gao Zu Ji" (The Record of Emperor Gaozu) in *Han Shu* (*The History of Han Dynasty*) (Book 2).

law is applied to safeguard justice, to curb violence and to protect the good,"[139] which had reflected the goal of the punishment of criminal law.

"Da Ni" (great sedition), also known as "Da Ni Bu Dao" (against all the heavenly laws of morality and filial love) was also a felony, so the offenders would be severely punished with many people implicated. In "Jing Di Ji" (The Biography of Emperor Jing) in *Han Shu (The History of Han Dynasty)*, Ru Chun quoted from the laws of Han Dynasty and noted that "those who committed 'Da Ni Bu Dao' (against all the heavenly laws of morality and filial love) would be sentenced to 'Qi Shi' (exposing the executed body publicly at markets) with their parents, wives, children and siblings implicated," so even their grandparents would not be pardoned. If the criminal had escaped, arrest warrants would be sent throughout the country to have him arrested and those who had contributed to his capture would be reward. As "Fan Ni" (treachery) endangered the rule of the government, pardoning was not allowed.

"Shou Ni." It meant, "the ringleader has harbored the criminals."[140] In the reign of Emperor Wu, "the offenders who committed the crime were severely punished."[141] Those who had harbored the criminals who had committed "Mou Fan" (plotting rebellion or plotting to endanger the country) and "Da Ni Bu Dao" (against all the heavenly laws of morality and filial love) would be sentenced to "Qi Shi" (exposing the executed body publicly at markets); if the cases were serious, they would be sentenced to "Yi San Zu" (the law of killing the three generations of a family). Even the nobles and vassals would not be exempted. For example, in the 1st year of Yuan Kang, Emperor Xuan (5 A.D.), Hou Fu, the vassal of Xiu Gu, "was sentenced to 'Qi Shi' (exposing the executed body publicly at markets) for harboring the gangsters."[142]

"Tong Xing Yin Shi." It referred to helping the rebels such as sending information to them, acting as guides or providing foods. According to the law, this crime should be punished by "Da Bi" (capital punishment) to cut off the connection between the rebels and the public and to disintegrate the rebel forces. Emperor Wu once killed more than 10,000 revolting farmers with "thousands of them executed for offering help to the rebels in the neighboring 'Jun' (shire)."[143]

"Qun Dao" (gang robbery). It was a crime inherited from Qin Dynasty. During the reign of Emperor Wu, excessive exploitation led to numerous uprisings, so "people gathered together, blocked the way in the mountains and on the rivers and

---

[139]"Xing Fa Zhi" (The Record of the Criminal Law) in *Han Shu (The History of Han Dynasty)*.

[140]"Xuan Di Ji" (The Record of Emperor Xuan) in *Han Shu (The History of Han Dynasty)*, annotated by Yan Shigu.

[141]"Liang Tong Lie Zhuan" (The Biography of Liang Tong) in *Latter Han Shu (The History of Latter Han Dynasty)*.

[142]"Wang Zi Hou Biao" (The Table of Princes and Marquises) in *Han Shu (The History of Han Dynasty)*.

[143]"Ku Li Zhuan" (The Biographies of Brutal Officials) in *Han Shu (The History of Han Dynasty)*.

organized secret groups."[144] To intensify the suppression, *Shen Ming Fa* (*Laws on the Misconduct of Officials*) was made by Emperor Wu to punish the officials who were not efficient in catching the rebellious people. According to Ying Shao, "'Shen' means to kill, so 'Shen Ming' means 'killing anyone who harbor the robbers'." "If gang robbery was not discovered or if it was discovered but not all those involved were arrested, the relevant officials in charge from 'Er Qian Dan' (the ancient official with a monthly salary of 2,000 *dan*) to 'Xiao Li Zhu' (junior official) would be sentenced to death."[145]

"Jian Zhi Gu Zong" (failing to report the crime one knows about intentionally). To strengthen the reporting of the crimes, the rules like "Jian Zhi Gu Zong" (failing to report the crime which one knows about intentionally) and "Jian Lin Bu Zhu" (deliberately releasing the criminals by the officials) were made by Emperor Wu to force officials to conduct mutual supervision; those who failed to do so would be punished in accordance with law. According to the notes by Yan Shigu, "if somebody sees someone committing crimes but does not report it to the government, he has committed the crime of intentional indulgence; meanwhile if somebody has committed a crime, his supervisor will also be punished by 'Lian Zuo' (being punished for being related to somebody who committed an offense)."[146] However, these laws failed to achieve the expected effect, because "the junior officials were afraid of being killed for not being able to catch the rioters, they dared not make reports. Moreover, because the officials of relevant 'Fu' (ancient administrative district between province and county) would also be implicated for their offenses, the junior officials were also asked to keep secret. As a result, the cases of theft occurred frequently, but the senior and junior officials had concealed the facts to avoid punishment."[147] For this reason, in early Eastern Han Dynasty, the regulation had to be changed: "The junior officials are not to be punished for their delaying or failure to inform about the gang robbery timely, and their performance should be assessed by the numbers of the rioters they have arrested."[148]

5.4.1.2 The Crime of Profaning Royal Power and Endangering the Personal Safety of the Emperor

"Bu Jing" (being irreverent) and "Da Bu Jing" (being greatly irreverent). It was stated in *Tang Lv Shu Yi* (*The Comments on Tang Code*) that "*Jiu Zhang Lv* (*The Code in Nine Chapters*) made in Han Dynasty had gotten lost, but the articles about 'Bu Dao' (depravity) and 'Bu Jing' (being irreverent) were inherited, so these

---

[144]"Ku Li Zhuan" (The Biographies of Brutal Officials) in *Han Shu* (*The History of Han Dynasty*).
[145]"Ku Li Zhuan" (The Biographies of Brutal Officials) in *Han Shu* (*The History of Han Dynasty*).
[146]"Xing Fa Zhi" (The Record of the Criminal Law) in *Han Shu* (*The History of Han Dynasty*).
[147]"Ku Li Zhuan" (The Biographies of Brutal Officials) in *Han Shu* (*The History of Han Dynasty*).
[148]"Guang Wu Di Ji" (The Record of Emperor Guangwu) in *Latter Han Shu* (*The History of Latter Han Dynasty*) (Book 2).

charges of crimes possibly originated from Han Dynasty." The so-called "Bu Jing" (being irreverent) meant "lack of etiquette and rites" and it covered a wide scope, such as being frank in writing the memorial, using impolite expressions, inappropriate allusions and styles, failing to show respect when receiving imperial orders and being dispatched as diplomats, or failing to getting down from horses or getting off from one's cart when arriving at Sima Gate. In the 1st year of Gan Lu, in the reign of Emperor Xuan (53 B.C.), Wei Hong, the successor to "Gao Ping Xian Hou" (marquis of Gaoping, namely Wei Xiang) "arrived at Sima Gate on horseback to pay tribute to the sacrifice at the temple and was demoted one rank lower to 'Guan Nei Hou' (title of nobility, ranked 19th among the twenty ranks of the titles of nobility) for being 'Bu Jing' (being irreverent)."[149] Moreover, it was also an offense of "Da Bu Jing" (being greatly irreverent) to handle the utilities which had been used by the emperor inappropriately, for example, it was considered "Da Bu Jing" (being greatly irreverent) to put the emperor's bow on the ground. It was recorded in *Tai Ping Yu Lan (Imperial Readings of the Taiping Era)* that a guard was charged with the crime of "'Da Bu Jing' (being greatly irreverent) and was put on trial because he had put the emperor's bow on the ground at court assembly. How dare he put the bow of 'Tian Zi' (the son of Heaven) on the ground?"[150] Besides, it also belonged to the category of "Da Bu Jing" (being greatly irreverent) to call the emperor's name and to talk about the past emperors, so those who violated the rule would be punished by "Qi Shi" (exposing the executed body publicly at markets).[151] Indeed, there were no clear regulations about the crime of "Bu Jing" (being irreverent) or "Da Bu Jing" (being greatly irreverent), so its implementation had fully reflected the consolidation of autocratic system in the Han Dynasty, meanwhile, it also reflected the influence of the theory of "Jun Wei Chen Gang" (monarchs being the guide of his subjects).

Disobeying imperial decrees and orders. Imperial decrees and orders were the embodiment of the emperor's will and the important guidelines of state activities, so they must be strictly obeyed. It was stated in the imperial edict issued in the 5th year of Emperor Gaozu (202 B.C.) that "the people who disobey my orders shall be severely punished."[152] An order was issued by Emperor Jing when he was attacking Bi, the vassal of Wu, and it was stated that "those who criticize me or disobey my order shall be killed."[153] There were many records to the effect that "it shall be charged with 'Bu Jing' (being irreverent) to disobey imperial orders" in *Ju Yan Han Jian (Ju Yan Bamboo Slips of Han Dynasty)*. In Han Dynasty, it was called "Fei Ge" to refuse to carry out imperial orders. Because it was a felony to infringe upon

---

[149]"Wai Qi En Ze Hou Biao" (The Table of Maternal Relatives of the Emperor with the Title of Marquis) in *Han Shu (The History of Han Dynasty)*.

[150]"Bing Bu" (Military Department) in *Tai Ping Yu Lan (Imperial Readings of the Taiping Era)*, Vol. 347.

[151]"Wei Xian Zhuan" (The Biography of Wei Xian) in *Han Shu (The History of Han Dynasty)*.

[152]"Gao Di Ji" (The Record of the First Emperor of Han Dynasty) in *Han Shu (The History of Han Dynasty)*.

[153]"Jing Yan Wu Zhuan" (The Biography of King Jing, Yan and Wu) in *Han Shu (The History of Han Dynasty)*.

5.4 The Criminal Law in Documents and *Han Jian* (*The Bamboo Slip of Han Dynasty*)

imperial power, the violators would be severely punished. During the reign of Emperor Wu, "An, the vassal of Huainan committed 'Fei Ge', so he was sentenced to 'Qi Shi' (exposing the executed body publicly at markets)."[154] Besides, those who told lies, fabricated and distorted imperial orders would be charged with the crime of "Jiao Zhao" or "Jiao Zhi" (acting in the name of monarchs) which was divided into three categories according to seriousness: "Da Hai" (extremely harmful), "Hai" (harmful) and "Bu Hai" (harmless) and they would be punished accordingly. According to law, "'Jiao Zhao' was 'Da Hai' (extremely harmful), so it should be punished by death penalty,"[155] so was "Jiao Zhi" (acting in the name of monarchs). During the reign of Emperor Wu, "Xu Yan, 'Bo Shi' (learned scholar), was sent to inspect local conditions, but he had arbitrarily fabricated an imperial order and ordered Jiaodong and the state of Lu to produce salt and cast iron," so he was charged of the crime of "'Da Hai' (extremely harmful) in 'Jiao Zhi' (acting in the name of monarchs) by Zhang Tang and was sentenced to death."[156] Although "Hai" (harmful) in "Jiao Zhi" (acting in the name of monarchs) should be punished by "Qi Shi" (exposing the executed body publicly at markets), it could be still be exempted. For example, it was recorded in "Wu Di Gong Chen Biao" (Table of Meritorious Statesman in the Reign of Wu Di) in *Han Shu* (*The History of Han Dynasty*) that Wang Hui, the vassal of Hao "was sent to Jiuquan but he had committed crime of 'Jiao Zhi' (acting in the name of monarchs), so he should be sentenced to death, but he was exempted by paying ransom." For the category of "Bu Hai" (harmless) in "Jiao Zhi," the offender should be dismissed from his office. It was recorded in "Wai Qi En Ze Hou Biao" (Table of Maternal Relatives of an Emperor who are Conferred the Title of Marquis) in *Han Shu* (*The History of Han Dynasty*) that Kang, the vassal of Yichun "was dismissed because he was considered "Bu Hai" (harmless) although he has committed the crime of 'Jiao Zhi' (acting in the name of monarchs)."

"Qi Man" (being dishonest), "Wu Wang" (to accuse an innocent person) and "Zhu Zu" (cursing the emperor). "'Man' referred to being dishonest and lying to the emperor."[157] During the reign of Emperor Xuan, Yan, the vassal of Xinli "was dismissed for lying in his memorial to the emperor."[158] "Wu Wang" (to accuse an innocent person) referred to being immoral for "the violation of rituals and reason," so it should be punished with death penalty. During the reign of Emperor Wu, Luan Da, the vassal of Letong "was killed for 'Wang Shang'."[159] "Zhu Zu" (cursing the

---

[154]"Huai Nan Heng Shan Lie Zhuan" (The Biography of King Huainan and King Hengshan) in *Shi Ji* (*The Record of the Grand Historian*).

[155]"Jing Wu Zhao Xuan Yuan Cheng Gong Chen Biao" (Table of Meritorious Statesman in the Times of Jing Wu, Zhao Xuan and Yuan Cheng) in *Han Shu* (*The History of Han Dynasty*), annotated by Ru Chun.

[156]"Zhong Jun Zhuan" (The Biography of Zhong Jun) in *Han Shu* (*The History of Han Dynasty*).

[157]"Xing Fa Zhi" (The Record of the Criminal Law) in *Jin Shu* (*The History of Jin Dynasty*).

[158]"Wang Zi Hou Biao" (The Table of Princes and Marquises) in *Han Shu* (*The History of Han Dynasty*) (Book 2).

[159]"Wai Qi En Ze Hou Biao" (The Table of Maternal Relatives of the Emperor with the Title of Marquis) in *Han Shu* (*The History of Han Dynasty*).

emperor) referred to cursing the emperor in the form of prayer, so it would be punished in line with 'Da Ni' (great sedition). In Han Dynasty, dozens of vassals were killed for speaking ill of the emperor.

Damaging mausoleums or palaces and stealing imperial utensils. Royal ancestral temples, mausoleums, palaces, and imperial utensils were the symbols of imperial power, so if they were destroyed or stolen, the offenders would be severely punished. For example, during the reign of Emperor Wen, a man stole the jade rings in front of the royal temple, so he should be sentenced to "Qi Shi" (exposing the executed body publicly at markets) according to the law, but Emperor Wen regarded it as "stealing the late emperor's utensils…so he thought the man should be sentenced to the punishment of 'Zu Zhu' (killing of the whole clan of a criminal)." After Zhang Shizhi argued based on law, the man was finally exempted from the punishment of "Zu Zhu" (killing of the whole clan of a criminal).[160] It was quoted from *San Fu Jiu Shi* (*Reminiscence of San Pu*) in *Tai Ping Yu Lan* (*Imperial Readings of the Taiping Era*) (Vol. 954) that during the Han Dynasty, a man was sentenced to "Qi Shi" (exposing the executed body publicly at markets) because he had stolen cypress trees from a mausoleum, from which we can see how strict the law is at that time.

Trespassing palaces, palace gates or royal gardens or parks without permission. "Lan Ru," according to the notes of Ying Shao, means, "trespassing the palace without talisman or registration."[161] Because it was a threat to the safety of the emperor, the people who committed the crime of "Lan Ru" (trespassing the palace without talisman or register) must be severely punished and those who entered the palace gate without permission would be sentenced to "Cheng Dan" (the punishment of men building cities), while those who broke into the palace hall would be sentenced to "Qi Shi" (exposing the executed body publicly at markets). According to "Wai Qi Zhuan" (The Biography of Maternal Relatives of the Emperor) in *Han Shu* (*The History of Han Dynasty*), "Chong Guo, who was the supervisor of the royal doctor, had entered the palace hall without permission, so he should be put into prison and be sentenced to death," but he was redeemed by paying a ransom of twenty horses. If the officials who guarded the palace and the hall had failed to notice and stop people from entering the hall without permission, they would be dismissed; even if the marquis himself had entered the royal garden or park without permission, he would be deprived of his title. For example, Marquis Zhen of Shandu "was dismissed from his position for entering Shanglin Park in Mount Ganquan."[162]

"Fan Bi." According to Yan Shigu's interpretation, "Bi" meant "when the imperial carriage started out from his palace, the escorting personnel give warning

---

[160]"Zhang Shi Zhi Zhuan" (The Biography of Zhang Shizhi) in *Han Shu* (*The History of Han Dynasty*).

[161]"Cheng Di Ji" (The Record of Emperor Cheng) in *Han Shu* (*The History of Han Dynasty*).

[162]"Wen Di Gong Chen Biao" (The Table of Meritorious Statesman in the Reign of Emperor Wu) in *Han Shu* (*The History of Han Dynasty*).

in advance and clear the way for the emperor."[163] "Fan Bi" referred to offending the guard of honor when the emperor showed up, so those violators would be imposed with a fine. It was recorded in "Zhang Shi Zhi Zhuan" (The Biography of Zhang Shizhi) in *Han Shu* (*The History of Han Dynasty*) that once when Emperor Wen was travelling to Zhongwei Bridge, suddenly someone came out from under the bridge and startled the horses of his majesty's carriage. Emperor Wen had intended to have the man severely punished, but he was persuaded by Zhang Shi, who was "Ting Wei" (the supreme official in charge of judicature) at the time, because it was stipulated that "those who defy the order of 'Bi' will be imposed with a fine of four *liang* of silver money," finally the violator was sentenced to pay a sum of a fine in accordance with the law.

5.4.1.3 The Crime of Endangering the Centralization of Authority

At the beginning of Han Dynasty, the conflict between the central government and separatist princes and marquises was the main conflict inside the ruling regime, which was prominently expressed by "Qi Guo Zhi Luan" (the Revolt of Seven States). Because the unity of the country was in line with the social development and the demand of the people, the rebellion failed. Since Emperor Wu, the policy of strengthening the centralization of authority and fighting against the separatist regimes set up by princes and marquises was strictly enforced, so a series of new charges were formulated.

"A Dang" and "Wai Fu Zhu Hou." "If a vassal is guilty but the ministers fail to report the crime to the emperor, it is the crime of 'A Dang' (A Dang: to be flattery, to get benefit for relatives or friends by bending the law, to pursue selfish interest by forming cliques),"[164] which was regarded as a felony. For example, in the reign of Emperor Wu, the vassals of Huainan and Hengshan revolted, which led to thousands of death among the partisans[165]; during the Eastern Han Dynasty, the great general Liang Yi was killed and Han Yan was "discharged to his native town instead of being sentenced to death for the crime of 'A Dang'."[166]

To prevent the vassals from colluding with the officials in court, the crime of "Wai Fu Zhu Hou" (attachment to vassals away from court) was established. Thus, "anyone who has been found to be connected with the vassals"[167] would be severely punished. It was recorded in "Yan Zhu Zhuan" (The Biography of Yan Zhu) in *Han*

---

[163]"Liang Xiao Wang Zhuan" (The Biography of the King of Liang State) in *Han Shu* (*The History of Han Dynasty)*, annotated by Yan Shigu.

[164]"Qi Dao Hui Wang Zhuan" (The Biography of King Dao Hui of Qi) in *Han Shu* (*The History of Han Dynasty*), annotated by Zhang Yan.

[165]"Wu Di Ji" (The Record of Emperor Wu) in *Han Shu* (*The History of Han Dynasty*).

[166]"Han Leng Zhuan" (The Biography of Han Leng) in *Latter Han Shu* (*The History of Latter Han Dynasty*).

[167]"Huo Guang Zhuan" (The Biography of Huo Guang) in *Han Shu* (*The History of Han Dynasty*).

Shu (*The History of Han Dynasty*) that "the vassal of latter Huainan came to court, made friends with Yan Zhu and discussed state affairs by bribery. When the vassal of Huainan revolted, Yan Zhu was involved, but the emperor made light of his crime and did not want to sentence him to death. However, Zhang Tangzheng, "Ting Wei" (the supreme official in charge of judicature) at the time insisted that as a trusted subordinate, Yan Zhu had the right to enter and go out of the forbidden gate freely, but at the same time he had kept so close a relationship with a vassal outside the capital, so he must be punished by death penalty; otherwise, there would be no way to deal with similar cases in the future. Finally Yan Zhu was sentenced to 'Qi Shi' (exposing the executed body publicly at markets)."[168]

In Eastern Han Dynasty, "the old law which prohibits court officials from attaching to vassals" was reiterated by Emperor Guangwu,[169] which proved that this relationship had always been a threat to the central government, so it was always considered a felony. The charge of "Jian Dang" (treacherous cliques) made in later criminal law originated from this law.

The princes and marquises crossing the border illegally. To prevent the princes and marquises from forming cliques with local forces for their selfish gains and bringing harm to the central government, the princes and marquises were forbidden to leave their territories; otherwise, they would be dismissed, or be reduced to a lower position of "Si Kou" (the minister of justice), or be heavily fined. During the reign of Emperor Jing, marquise Yan of Yangqiugong "was removed from his position and appointed "Si Kou" (the minister of justice) for "leaving his principalities."[170] During the reign of Emperor Wu, marquise Li Shou of Han "was put to death, because as an official who was in charge of defending the capital, he had left Chang'an to see the marquise of Haixi off at Gaoqiao and had ordered his men to kill the alchemists."[171]

The princes and marquises transgressing the system. To prevent the princes and marquises from break through the restriction, *Shang Fang Lv* (*The Statutes on Preventing Officials from being Randomly Promoted*) was promulgated by Emperor Wu. Thus, *Han Lv* (*Han Code*) was quoted in "Wu San Wang Zhuan" (The Biography of Wu Sanwang) in *Song Shu* (*The History of Song Dynasty*):

> Carriages and clothes should remain plain, as is required in *Yu Shu* (*The Book of Yu*); 'Ming Qi' (titles and the system of cars, clothes, and rituals) should be true, as is warned in *Chun Qiu* (*Spring and Autumn Annals*). Therefore, 'Shang Fang' responsible for making imperial utensils was strictly controlled, and the princes and marquises would be severely punished, if they have transgressed the system, no matter how intimate they are to the emperor.

---

[168] "Wai Qi En Ze Hou Biao" (The Table of Maternal Relatives of the Emperor with the Title of Marquis) in *Han Shu* (*The History of Han Dynasty*).

[169] "Guang Wu Di Ji" (The Record of Emperor Guangwu) in *Latter Han Shu* (*The History of Latter Han Dynasty*) (Book 2).

[170] "Wang Zi Hou Nian Biao" (The Table of Princes and Marquises) in *Han Shu* (*The History of Han Dynasty*).

[171] "Wu Di Gong Chen Biao" (The Table of Meritorious Statesman in the Reign of Emperor Wu) in *Han Shu* (*The History of Han Dynasty*).

5.4 The Criminal Law in Documents and *Han Jian* (*The Bamboo Slip of Han Dynasty*)

In Han Dynasty, "besides utensils, clothes, decorations, music, dancing, speaking voices and appearances," it was especially forbidden for princes and marquises to violate the rituals of the emperor. For example, the princes and marquises should never "face the south while listening to reports"; they were forbidden to give warning in the name of "Bi" (when the imperial carriage started out from his palace, the escorting personnel give warning in advance and clear the way for the emperor) when travelling. The king of Huainan was convicted as a traitor because "he had violated the laws of Han Dynasty by giving warning in the name of 'Bi' whenever he showed up. Moreover, he also made laws and behaved like 'Tian Zi' (the son of Heaven)."[172]

Besides, the number of officials in a principality was limited. If outnumbered, the vassal would be punished for the crime of "Shi Guo Ren Guo Lv" (having too many subordinate officials). According to Yan Shigu, "Shi" means "using" and "Yuan" means "number." During the reign of Emperor Wen, Liu Gao, the marquise of Dongmaojing principality was dismissed for "employing too many subordinates."

"Zhou Jin Bu Ru Fa" (violating the law about paying tribute to the memorial ceremony). In the reign of Emperor Wen, *Zhou Jin Lv* (*Statutes on Gold or Tribute Paid to the Memorial Ceremony*) was made. According to Zhang Yan, "the word 'Zhou' means 'purity'," and "'Zhou' refers to the wine made after eight months of fermentation started from 'Zheng Yue' (the first month of the lunar year)."[173] According to the law of Han Dynasty, the vassals should help 'Zhou' by giving gold to him, so it is called "Zhou Jin." During the reign of Emperor Wu, the amount and purity of gold were increased for "Zhou Jin" to weaken the power of vassals. Thus, if (the gold) "didn't meet the standard of weight or purity," the princes would be deprived of their territories and the marquises would be deprived of their titles.[174] In the 5th year of Yuanding (112 B.C.), "one hundred and six marquises were deprived of their titles for failing to meet the standard for 'Zhou Jin'."[175]

"Lu Xie Sheng Zhong Yu" (leaking imperial secrets). This was an accusation in Qin Dynasty, but in Han Dynasty, to maintain imperial authority and to prevent the leakage of important information, it was continued to be enforced. Since the reign of Emperor Zhao, the number of people who were convicted of this crime greatly increased. The following case was recorded in the second volume of *Rong Zhai Sui Bi* (*Notes Written in the Room of Rong Zhai*) by Hong Mai: "Probably it was a felony to leak imperial secrets..., after (Jing) Fang met the emperor (Yuan of Han Dynasty), he told it to "Yu Shi Da Fu" (Grand Censor) Zheng Jun, then he told it to Zhang Bo, who secretly memorized what had been told to him. Later, Fang was put in prison and sentenced to 'Qi Shi' (exposing the executed body publicly at

---

[172]"Huai Nan Heng Shan Lie Zhuan" (The Biography of King Huainan and King Heng Shan) in *Shi Ji* (*The Record of the Grand Historian*).

[173]"Jing Di Ji" (The Record of Emperor Jing) in *Han Shu* (*The History of Han Dynasty*), annotated by Zhang Yan.

[174]"Ping Zhun Shu" (On Fair Trade) in *Shi Ji* (*The Record of the Grand Historian*).

[175]"Wu Di Ji" (The Record of Emperor Wu) in *Han Shu* (*The History of Han Dynasty*).

markets) for this reason." Qi Songdeng, 'Du Wei' (a military officer below the general) in Donglai was "put in prison for leaking imperial secrets, so he committed suicide."[176]

5.4.1.4 The Crime of Endangering the Social Order

Misleading the public by heresy. Anyone who misled the public with heretic ideas would be sentenced to death. According to "Du Zhou Zhuan" (The Biography of Du Zhou) in *Han Shu* (*The History of Han Dynasty*), Du Ye informed against Shi Dan for "his violating the classics and being preoccupied with heresy" by submitting a statement to Emperor Cheng and suggested he should be punished by "Da Bi" (capital punishment). It was recorded in "Wang Shang Zhuan" (The Biography of Wang Shang) in *Han Shu* (*The History of Han Dynasty*) that "Zuo Jiang Jun" (the left general) Shi Dan presented a memorial to the emperor and accused the minister Wang Shang of "disrupting social order with heresy, being disloyal to and deceiving the emperor. Thus, in accordance with *Fu Xing* (refer to the penalties in Zhou Dynasty) he should be punished by 'Shang Lu'," which referred to such severe punishment as "Qi Shi" (exposing the executed body publicly at markets) and "Yao Zhan" (cutting in two at the waist).

Witchcraft. The act of doing harm to other people with witchcraft is called "Wu Gu." In ancient China, because of underdevelopment of science, superstition was prevalent and the phenomenon of harming people with witchcraft was quite common. Because the behavior of "Wu Gu" misled people and endangered the public social order, it had been listed in the criminal law from Han Dynasty down to Qin Dynasty, and whoever committed this crime would be severely punished. During the reign of Emperor Wu, crown prince Liu Ju was accused by Jiang Chong because he was found to have buried a wooden figure of Emperor Wu in his palace, so the crown prince committed suicide, and many princess, queens, and ministers were involved. "Consequently, thousands of people were implicated and killed."[177]

5.4.1.5 The Crime of Disrupting Economic Order

Casting iron and making salt without permission. To consolidate the economic foundation of the central government, during the reign of Emperor Wu, the policy of "the state-running of salt and iron" was implemented, so the managements of iron and salt was taken back from despotic landlords and wealthy merchants, and those who cast iron and made salt in private were severely punished. Accordingly, "those

---

[176]"Bai Guan Gong Qing Biao" (The Table of Officials of Higher Ranks) in *Han Shu* (*The History of Han Dynasty*) (Book 2).
[177]"Jiang Chong Zhuan" (The Biography of Jiang Chong) in *Han Shu* (*The History of Han Dynasty*).

5.4 The Criminal Law in Documents and *Han Jian* (*The Bamboo Slip of Han Dynasty*)

who dare to cast iron and make salt in private would be punished by having their left foot cut off and their equipment confiscated."[178]

Casting coins in private. According to the law of Qin Dynasty, those who minted money in private would be sentenced to death, and the law remained in effect until the beginning of Han Dynasty. During the reign of Emperor Wen, the law was abolished and the people were allowed to mint money. Consequently, the nobility Wu Wang named Bi and the emperor's favorite official named Deng Tong became extremely rich, as was recorded in the saying that "money minted by Wu and Deng is everywhere under the sun,"[179] which had led to the disorder of the monetary system at the beginning of Han Dynasty. During the reign of Emperor Jing, the prohibition was restored and it was decreed that "those who mint money illegally will be sentenced to 'Qi Shi' (exposing the executed body publicly at markets)."[180] However, because private mintage had been in existence for long, it could not be eradicated overnight. Emperor Wu reinforced the state's control of treasury and took the right of mintage back to the central government by issuing the currency of 'Wu Zhu' and by prohibiting 'Jun Guo' (vassal state) from coining money, so "anyone who has coined money illegally is to be sentenced to death." However, there were so many offenders that it was impossible to have them all punished. Five years after the use of the money of "Wu Zhu" (Wu Zhu Coin), "thousands of people who were sentenced to death for minting money were pardoned...and millions surrendered themselves."[181]

Encroaching upon public or private property. The "crime of theft" was included in "Yue Fa San Zhang" (three-point covenant) which was put forward by Liu Bang, Gaozu of Han Dynasty, when he entered the pass; "*Dao Lv*" (*Statutes on Theft*) was also put at the beginning of *Jiu Zhang Lv* (*The Code in Nine Chapters*). According to "Xiao Wang Zhi Zhuan" (The Biography of Xiao Wangzi) in *Han Shu* (*The History of Han Dynasty*), theft, taking bribery and murder were all unpardonable crimes and the punishment for theft was in proportion to the amount of booty, as was described in the records that "there is a quantitative difference for the amount of booty, so it has made it impossible to decide on the charge in advance. Therefore, when talking of punishment, I don't know what the punishment should be."[182] It was permitted in the law that those who broke into others' houses or vehicles or those being suspected of theft could be killed on the spot.[183]

---

[178]"Shi Huo Zhi" (The Records of National Finance and Economy) in *Han Shu* (*The History of Han Dynasty*).

[179]"Cuo Bi" (Wrong Currency) in *Yan Tie Lun* (*Debates on Salt and Iron*).

[180]"Jing Di Ji" (The Record of Emperor Jing) in *Han Shu* (*The History of Han Dynasty*).

[181]"Shi Huo Zhi" (The Records of National Finance and Economy) in *Han Shu* (*The History of Han Dynasty*) (Book 2).

[182]"Gao Zu Ji" (The Record of Emperor Gaozu) in *Han Shu* (*The History of Han Dynasty*) (Book 1), annotated by Li Qi.

[183]"Chao Shi" (Official in Charge of Official Assessment and Justice) in "Qiu Guan" (Ministry of Penalty) in *Zhou Li* (*The Rites of Zhou Dynasty*), annotated by Zheng Xuan.

In addition, the punishment for stealing goods and utensils from local authorities is especially severe. According to records, "the brother of the crown prince's wife was an official in Quzhou county, and because he had stolen the official cloth, he was sentenced to 'Qi Shi' (exposing the executed body publicly at markets)."[184] The marquise of Yangcheng named Tian Yanping "had worked as "Da Si Nong" (Minister of National Treasury), but after stealing 30,000,000 from the national treasury (Du Nei Qian), he committed suicide."[185] If an official in the position of "Zhu Shou" (the person in charge of guarding) had committed theft with the booty worth ten *jin*, he would be sentenced to "Qi Shi" (exposing the executed body publicly at markets), because he had knowingly broken the law. The punishment for "stealing royal carriages and clothes" was severer than that for other crimes.

5.4.1.6 The Malpractice of the Officials

In Han Dynasty, the traditional concept of Qin Dynasty that "the wise monarchs rule the officials rather than the people" was inherited,[186] so much emphasis was put on the role played by officials in placating the people and running the state. Emperor Jing in his imperial edict demanded that "those who are not devoted to their official duties will be reported by 'Cheng Xiang' (the prime minister) and be punished." Moreover, the official evaluation system was established, in which it was required that "the officials' performance should be checked at the end of the year by 'Cheng Xiang' (the prime minister), who should present memorials to the emperor about the awards and punishments." Under the guidance of the rulers' ideology of emphasizing the rule of the officials, more articles were added about the crime of malpractice committed by officials in the law of Han Dynasty. The main charges are as follows:

Corruption. There are many charges of corruption in the law of Han Dynasty, such as taking what one is in charge of, taking property, being treated to a feast, taking property by perverting the law, etc. "Qiu" (賕) is interpreted in *Shuo Wen Jie Zi (The Origin of Chinese Characters)* "as giving property in return by perverting law." According to Yan Shigu's annotation in *Ji Jiu Pian (Reading Primer Compiled Imperatively)*, "'Qiu' means asking for help with money." In the law of Han Dynasty, the officials were severely punished for corruption. For example, those who took drinks, food, and money from their subordinates would be removed from their positions or fined two *jin* of gold and those who took bribes by perverting the law would be severely punished. In the 13th year of Emperor Wen (191 B.C.), it was stipulated by the emperor in the imperial decree that "any official who took bribes by

---

[184]"Bao Xun Zhuan" (The Biography of Bao Xun) in "Wei Shu" (The History of Northern Wei Dynasty) in *San Guo Zhi (The Record of the Three Kingdoms)*.

[185]"Wai Qi En Ze Hou Biao" (The Table of Maternal Relatives of the Emperor with the Title of Marquis) in *Han Shu (The History of Han Dynasty)*.

[186]"Wai Chu Shuo You" (The Outer Categories of Sayings) (Part 2) in *Han Fei Zi (Han Feizi)* (Book 2).

perverting the law...would be sentenced to 'Qi Shi' (exposing the executed body publicly at markets)."[187] As for "Ting Qing," penalties were enforced according to whether money was taken, and those who committed the crime of "Ting Qing" by taking the money would be more severely punished. Wang Qian, the marquise of Pingqiu had accepted the booty that was worth six million *qian*, so he should be sentenced to death for "Bu Dao" (depravity), but he committed suicide to evade punishment. Besides those who took bribes, those who offered bribes were also punished, "Guan Xian, the marquise of Linru was deprived of the title of nobility for offering bribes"[188] and Yi, the marquise of Fenyindaosi "was sentenced to 'Cheng Dan' (the punishment of men building cities) for the same crime."[189] Although severe penalties were imposed on corruption according to the law of Han Dynasty, because corruption was determined by the nature of feudal state, it was naturally unavoidable. Especially, during the reign of Emperor Wu, official positions were sold to make up for the financial deficit, which had further led to corruption of officials.

"Ju Yu Bu Zhi" and "Gu Zong." "Bu Zhi" (making unfair convictions) and "Gu Zong" (intentional connivance without intervention) were two crimes included in the laws of Qin Dynasty and they referred to the crimes committed by officials in the judgment. Generally speaking, according to the laws of Han Dynasty, the crime of "Ju Yu Bu Zhi" (making unfair convictions) should be punished by "Qi Shi" (exposing the executed body publicly at markets), but because "Bu Zhi" (making unfair convictions) meant making conviction without following fact, although it was punishable by death, it could still be exempted by paying a certain amount of money, just as was noted by Jin Zhuo that "'Chu Zui' (to intentionally sentence a guilty person innocent or a felony misdemeanor) is called 'Gu Zong' (intentional connivance without intervention) in law while 'Ru Zui' (to intentionally sentence an innocent person guilty or a misdemeanor felony) is called 'Bu Zhi' (making unfair convictions)."[190] Zhao Di, the marquise of Xinchou and "Tai Chang" (the Minister of Sacrificial Worship) at the time, had committed the crime of "Ju Yu Bu Shi," but he redeemed himself by paying one million, so was sentenced to 'Cheng Dan' (the punishment of men building cities) in the end."[191]

"Gu Zong" belonged to "Chu Zui" (to intentionally sentence a guilty person innocent or a felony misdemeanor), so it meant conniving with the criminals. The penalty for "Chu Zui" (to intentionally sentence a guilty person innocent or a felony misdemeanor) was extremely severe and no redemption was allowed since Emperor Wu. During the reign of Emperor Zhao, "Li Zhong in the position of 'Ting Wei' (the

---

[187]"Jing Di Ji" (The Record of Emperor Jing) in *Han Shu* (*The History of Han Dynasty*).

[188]"Bing Ji Zhuan" (The Biography of Bing Ji) in *Han Shu* (*The History of Han Dynasty*).

[189]"Xing Fa Zhi" (The Record of the Criminal Law) in *Han Shu* (*The History of Han Dynasty*).

[190]"Gao Zu Gong Chen Hou Zhe Nian Biao" (Table of Meritorious Ministers and Marquises During Gaozu's Reign) in *Shi Ji* (*The Records of the Grand Historian*).

[191]"Gao Di Gong Chen Biao" (The Table of Meritorious Ministers in the Reign of Emperor Gao) in *Han Shu* (*The History of Han Dynasty*).

supreme official in charge of judicature) was sentenced to death and executed by 'Qi Shi' (exposing the executed body publicly at markets)."[192] But "imposing severe punishment on the crime of 'Shen Gu' (to intentionally sentence an innocent person guilty or a misdemeanor felony) while imposing lenient punishment on the crime of 'Zong Chu' (to intentionally sentence a guilty person innocent or a felony misdemeanor)"[193] had caused such serious consequences that the officials "competed with each other to enforce severe punishments in hearing cases because they regarded harshness as justice. In addition, the officials who imposed severe punishment on crimes were often promoted, while the officials who adhered to principles and upheld justice were often persecuted. Consequently, all officials who were in charge of hearing cases actually wanted the criminals to be punished by death penalty, this was not because they hated them, but because they wanted to protect themselves by sentencing others to death."[194]

Dishonesty in election. "Cha Ju" (election system of Han Dynasty: the talents are recommended by the dukes, heads of different ministry, provincial governors and appointed by the court) was the basic system for electing talented people in Han Dynasty, so if the officials failed to recommend talents, or if they cheated in recommendation, they would all be punished. The provision on the crime of cheating in election stipulated in the criminal law of Han Dynasty was a development of that of Qin Dynasty under the new historical conditions, according to which "those who had appointed incompetent people would be punished the same as the latter."[195] During the reign of Emperor Wu, "Zhang Dangju, the marquise of Shanyang and 'Tai Chang' (the Minister of Sacrificial Worship) of the government, was dismissed for cheating in the appointment of his disciples."[196] Therefore, it was not rare that those who were dishonest in election were either dismissed, or imprisoned or deprived of their fiefdom.

Disobeying military laws. This crime covered a much wider scope. For example, those who dispatched troops without obtaining a commander's seal would be convicted of "Shan Fa Bing" and would be sentenced to death; those who had deliberately retreated or delayed actions accidentally in war would be convicted of "Dou Liu" (tardiness) and "Shi Qi" (delaying); the former crime would be punished by death penalty, as to the latter crime, although it should be punished by death penalty, it could be ransomed. If the generals had failed to command competently and led to injury and death, they would be convicted of "Shi Wang" (loss and death) and punished by death penalty, but it could be ransomed as well. The soldiers who

---

[192]"Cheng Di Gong Chen Biao" (The Table of Meritorious Ministers in the Reign of Emperor Cheng) in *Han Shu* (*The History of Han Dynasty*).

[193]"Cheng Di Gong Chen Biao" (The Table of Meritorious Ministers in the Reign of Emperor Cheng) in *Han Shu* (*The History of Han Dynasty*).

[194]"Zhao Di Ji" (The Record of Emperor Zhao) in *Han Shu* (*The History of Han Dynasty*).

[195]"Xing Fa Zhi" (The Record of the Criminal Law) in *Han Shu* (*The History of Han Dynasty*).

[196]"Lu Wen Shu Zhuan" (The Biography of Lu Wen Shu) in *Han Shu* (*The History of Han Dynasty*).

fled from the battlefield would be convicted of "deserting the army" and would be sentenced to death with his wife and children implicated. Besides, other military crimes were also stipulated, such as "Fa Jun Xing" (delay in the allocation of provisions), abandoning cities during enemy's attack, failing to suppress the rebels, deserting the towns and cities, failing to capture the traitors, deserting army, cheating in counting up the number of captives, and fighting for feat and falsely claiming the award, etc.

5.4.1.7 Speeches and Thoughts

With the development of autocratic system, the crimes related to speeches and thoughts in Qin Dynasty were inherited in Han Dynasty with new articles added. Besides the crime of defamation, praying for other's doom, false accusation and slandering, the other crimes such as the crime of detraction and heresy, the crime of inappropriate speeches, and the crime of "Fu Fei" (complaining secretly) were also included.

The crime of detraction and heresy. In Qin Dynasty, the provision that "the detractors would be punished by 'Zu Zhu' (killing of the whole clan of a criminal)" was one of the harsh laws that had incurred revolt, so it was abolished by Liu Bang immediately after his army entered Guanzhong. This crime was officially repealed in an imperial edict issued in May of the 2nd year of Emperor Wen (178 B.C.):

> Now the crime of detraction and heresy is stipulated in law, for which the officials are afraid of fully expressing themselves and the emperor is unable to get to know their misconducts, how can we attract men of ability from afar to come here? So it should be abolished.... From now on, no one will be punished for this crime.[197]

To the time of Emperor Wu, Zhang Tang, who was famous for his cruelty, was appointed in an important position, so the punishment for the crime of detraction and heresy was restored. During the reign of Emperor Xuan, Lu Wenshu proposed that "the crime of detraction should be abolished so that people can put forward their sincere advice and express their thoughts freely to broaden the channel of taking advice and admonishment."[198] Although he was praised by Emperor Xuan, the law was not abolished. On the contrary, Yan Yannian, "Tai Shou" (governor of a prefecture) of Henan, "was sentenced to death penalty by 'Qi Shi' (exposing the executed body publicly at markets) because he had shown his resentment and defamed the imperial court."[199] During the reign of Emperor Ai, "the crime of detraction and heresy was abolished again."[200] However, until the Eastern Han Dynasty, many people were still punished for the crime of detraction, which has shown that under the autocratic system, it is even impossible to completely eradicate

---

[197] "Wen Di Ji" (The Record of Emperor Wen) in *Han Shu* (*The History of Han Dynasty*).
[198] "Lu Wen Shu Zhuan" (The Biography of Lu Wenshu) in *Han Shu* (*The History of Han Dynasty*).
[199] "Ku Li Zhuan" (The Biographies of Brutal Officials) in *Han Shu* (*The History of Han Dynasty*).
[200] "Ai Di Ji" (The Record of Emperor Ai) in *Han Shu* (*The History of Han Dynasty*).

the atrocities of persecuting people for their speeches and thoughts, let alone thoroughly abolish the accusation of detraction and heresy.

The heresy in criminal law of Han Dynasty was different from that in *Tang Lv* (*Tang Code*), because in *Tang Lv* (*Tang Code*) it meant, "falsely claiming as the words of ghosts or gods." According to Yan Shigu's annotation of "Gao Hou Ji" (The Records of Queen Gao) which was recorded in *Han Shu* (*The History of Han Dynasty*), "false speeches were taken as heresies." It was thus clear that the so-called heresy was nothing more than careless usage of words or inappropriate remarks. The people who were convicted of such misconducts would either be exiled to bordering areas, or be reduced to official slaves or be removed from their positions to be common people, and some even were punished by "Qi Shi" (exposing the executed body publicly at markets) because they were considered "high treason" according to "Bi Fu" (legal analogy).

Inappropriate speeches. During the reign of the second Emperor of Qin Dynasty, Confucian scholars were suppressed in the name of the crime of inappropriate speeches. In Han Dynasty, the ministers, officials, and common people were punished on the pretext of "inappropriate speech" by referring to the laws of *Qin Lv* (*Qin Code*). For example, it was recorded in "Chen Tang Zhuan" (The Biography of Chen Tang) in *Han Shu* (*The History of Han Dynasty*) that "it was reported to the emperor by 'Cheng Xiang' (the prime minister) and 'Yu Shi' (the censor) that Chen Tang had confused people by falsely claiming and attributing the anomaly to the emperor, by which he had shown great disrespect to the emperor, so what he said was regarded as inappropriate speeches." It was noted in "Wang Zun Zhuan" (The Biography of Wang Zun) in *Han Shu* (*The History of Han Dynasty*) that "Wang Zun had reported to the emperor that the people like 'Cheng Xiang' (the prime minister) and 'Yu Shi' (the censor) had shown contempt to the emperor by elevating themselves, which was inappropriate because they had violated the officials' manners.... So they were disrespectful to the emperor." Thus, it can be seen that the same crime of inappropriate speeches was punished differently, either by "Bu Jing" (being irreverent), or by "Da Bu Dao" (great depravity) or by "Da Bu Jing" (being greatly irreverent), which had fully shown that there were no specific criminal elements nor any statute laws for such crimes, and they were just arbitrarily interpreted according to the need of the emperor; which had also reflected the characteristics of criminal law that under autocratic system speeches would incur crimes that would be punished at will.

"Fu Fei" (complaining secretly). In Qin Dynasty, the people who committed the crime of "Fu Fei" (complaining secretly) would be executed. During the reign of Emperor Wu, "Ting Wei" (the supreme official in charge of judicature) Zhang Tang killed Yan Yi, his personal enemy, who was "Da Nong Ling" (official in charge of finance) in charge of "Fu Fei" (complaining secretly) at the time. "When Yan Yi was talking about the new imperial edict with his guest, the guest said that there was something wrong in the edict. Yan Yi did not care about it but just flipped his lips slightly to express his contempt. Zhang Tang reported to the emperor that Yan Yi, as one of "Jiu Qing" (the nine high-rank officials in ancient times), did not give any advice to the emperor but instead criticized it in the way of "Fu Fei" (complaining secretly) when he knew that it was illegal for him to make comments on the edict, so he deserved to be punished by death penalty. From then on, the legal regulation of "Fu Fei" (complaining secretly) was applied, so the aristocracies and officials mostly tried their best to please the emperor and their superiors."[201] In fact, Yan Yi did not make any improper comments on Emperor Wu's edict on minting "Bai Lu Pi Bi" (white deer skin currency), but he was executed for the crime of "Fu Fei" (complaining secretly), which had exceeded the limit of convicting according to speeches. However, the charge was approved by Emperor Wu to strengthen the policy of the centralization of autocracy.

5.4.1.8 The Violation of Ethics and Morality

After the hundreds of schools of thoughts were banned by Emperor Wu, the influence of Confucian ethical concepts was further strengthened, so all behaviors against ethics and morality were the targets to be suppressed.

"Bu Xiao" (being unfilial). Since Xia and Shang Dynasties, the crime of "Bu Xiao" (being unfilial) had been a felony, so in Han Dynasty this tradition was followed with some specific provisions added. For example, He Xiu emphasized in his annotation of "Wen Gong Shi Liu Nian" (the 16th Year of the Duke of Wen) in *Chun Qiu Gong Yang Zhuan* (*Annotation to Chun Qiu by Master Gong Yang*) that "those who did not show respect to their superiors or defamed sages and those who were unfilial would be beheaded with his cut-off head exposed to the public." Emperor Wu put King of Hengshan, the crown prince to death on the charge of "Bu Xiao" (being unfilial).[202] Emperor Xuan even called on his people in the name of filial piety and he stated in the imperial edict issued in the 4th year of Dijie (66 B.C.) that "it would make all people obedient to guide people with filial piety."[203] According to the laws of Han Dynasty, "Bu Xiao" (being unfilial) was convicted as a felony, so it was also stipulated that those who killed others to avenge their own parents would be punished leniently; those who beat up their parents would be beheaded with their cut-off heads exposed to the public; those who killed their parents would be convicted of "Da Ni" (great sedition) and be punished by "Yao Zhan" (cutting at waist) with their wives punished by "Qi Shi" (exposing the executed body publicly at markets).

Beastly conducts. It referred to adultery between the inferior and the young and the concubines of their superior and elder. According to the laws of Han Dynasty, the common people who committed adultery would be sentenced to three years in prison. If the inferiors had raped the superior, they had violated the ethics and

---

[201]"Shi Huo Zhi" (The Records of National Finance and Economy) (Part 2) in *Han Shu* (*The History of Han Dynasty*).

[202]"Heng Shan Wang Zhuan" (The Biography of the King of Hengshan) in *Han Shu* (*The History of Han Dynasty*).

[203]"Xuan Di Ji" (The Record of Emperor Xuan) in *Han Shu* (*The History of Han Dynasty*).

morality, so their behaviors belonged to beastly conducts, which was supposed to be severely punished. It was recorded in "Yan Wang Zhuan" (The Biography of King of Yan) in *Han Shu* (*The History of Han Dynasty*) that "Ding Guo committed adultery with his father's, namely, King of Kang's concubine and gave birth to a son. What's more, he took his younger brother's wife as his own concubine and even committed adultery with his own three daughters.... So other dukes and princes said, 'Ding Guo has conducted beastly, violated human relationship and treaded on the natural law, so he should be killed.' The emperor agreed, so Ding Guo committed suicide."

5.4.1.9 The Infringement of Human Body

"Sha Ren" (killing a person). It was the primary content of "Yue Fa San Zhang" (three-point covenant) that the killers should be killed. In the criminal law of Han Dynasty, "Sha Ren" (killing a person) included "Mou Sha" (murder), "Zei Sha" (premeditated murder), "Dou Sha" (killing during fighting), "Xi Sha" (killing during playing), "Wu Sha" (manslaughter), "Shi Ren Sha Ren" (instigating to kill, i.e. abetting or inciting other people to kill), "Qing Wu Sha Ren" (killing for insulting), "Fu Chou Sha Ren" (killing for revenge), and "Kuang Yi Sha Ren" (killing for madness), etc.

"Mou Sha" (murder). "'Mou' means the discussion held by two people."[204] The so-called "Sha Ren" (killing a person) in the laws of Han Dynasty usually referred to "Mou Sha" (murder). People who committed the crime of "Mou Sha" (murder) would be sentenced to "Qi Shi" (exposing the executed body publicly at markets), however, if the attempt of murder failed, the penalty could be reduced. According to "En Ze Hou Biao" (Table of People who are Conferred the Title of Marquis) in *Han Shu* (*The History of Han Dynasty*), Dou Changsheng, Marquis of Zhangwusi, "was exempted from punishment because he did not accomplish the murdering."

"Zei Sha" (premeditated murder). It meant "Gu Sha" (intentional killing) in the legal provisions of later dynasties. The crime of "Zei Sha" (premeditated murder) would be severely punished and the crime of "Zei Dou Sha Ren" (killing in wrestling) was included in the laws of Han Dynasty.

"Dou Sha" (killing during fighting). "'Dou' (fighting) refers to two parties fighting in argument."[205] In Han Dynasty, the system of Qin Dynasty was inherited, so fighting for the country was encouraged and private fighting was strictly prohibited. The people who killed others in private fighting would be "put in prison

---

[204]"Xing Fa Zhi" (The Record of the Criminal Law) in *Han Shu* (*The History of Han Dynasty*), quoted from *Zhu Lv Biao* (*Table of Annotations for Codes*) by Zhang Fei.
[205]"Xing Fa Zhi" (The Record of the Criminal Law) in *Han Shu* (*The History of Han Dynasty*), quoted from *Zhu Lv Biao* (*Table of Annotations for Codes*) by Zhang Fei.

together with his companions and neighbors in the same 'Wu' (a grassroot unit of five families)."[206]

"Xi Sha" (killing during playing). "'Xi' refers to that the two people kill each other in playing." The crime of "Xi Sha" (killing during playing) could be mitigated and according to the citation of *Han Lv* (*Han Code*) in "Li Yi" (Different Rites) in *You Yang Za Zu* (*Miscellaneous Notes of Youyang*), "it was recorded in law that: when celebrating Mr. A's wedding, Mr. B and Mr. C played a trick on A, so they took a cabinet as a jail and put A into it. When getting A out, they found A had stopped breathing. So B and C were sentenced to 'Gui Xin' (The male criminal was sentenced go up the mountain to cut firewood for sacrificial ceremony)." In other words, they were just sentenced to three years in prison.

"Wu Sha" (manslaughter). According to "Guo Gong Zhuan" (The Biography of Guo Gong) in *Latter Han Shu* (*The History of Latter Han Dynasty*), there was a differentiation between "intentional and accidental homicide," so "Wu Sha" (manslaughter) referred to accidental homicide and the killer be exempted from death penalty.

"Shi Ren Sha Ren" (instigating to kill, i.e., abetting or inciting other people to kill). The criminal would be given a severer punishment as the principal criminal among accomplices. Some nobles and high officials with titles of nobility were also punished by "Qi Shi" (exposing the executed body publicly at markets) for the crime of asking other people to kill.

"Fu Chou Sha Ren" (killing for revenge). In Western Zhou Dynasty, under the influence of patriarchal system, it was allowed in law for the descendants to revenge for their family members, and the revenger would be exempted from punishment. In early Han Dynasty, it was prohibited in criminal law to revenge for personal reasons. However, this law was effectively implemented, so there were many cases of killing or injuring for personal revenge. Therefore, Huan Tan in Latter Han Dynasty proposed that "now the old law should be issued again, so the people who personally killed or injured the criminal who was supposed to be executed officially would be punished two levels severer, and it was forbidden for them to hire other people to cut firewood in place of them for atonement. Even if he escaped, all of his family members would be exiled to bordering areas."[207]

"Kuang Yi Sha Ren" (killing for madness). It meant that people killed others because his personal nature was changed due to mental disease. In Latter Han Dynasty, Chen Zhong's proposal that "the punishment for 'Kuang Yi Sha Ren' (killing for madness) should be mitigated" was adopted by the emperor and was thus put into practice.[208]

---

[206] *Ji Jiu Pian* (*Reading Primer Compiled Imperatively*), annotated by Yan Shigu.

[207] "Huan Tan Zhuan" (The Biography of Huan Tan) in *Latter Han Shu* (*The History of Latter Han Dynasty*).

[208] "Chen Zhong Zhuan" (The Biography of Chen Zhong) in *Latter Han Shu* (*The History of Latter Han Dynasty*).

In Han Dynasty, the crime of killing both uncles and brothers was punished by "Qi Shi" (exposing the executed body publicly at markets) and there were no differences in the measurement of penalty. As for the crime of parents' killing their children, the punishment was not to be mitigated and the criminals should be punished the same as murders. It was recorded in "Dang Gu Lie Zhuan" (The Record of the Prohibitions of Participating Politics by Cliques) in *Latter Han Shu* (*History of the Latter Han Dynasty*) that "the ordinary people were so poor that many of them could not afford to bring up their children. So the law was strictly implemented by (Jia) Biao, and many of them were convicted of the crime of murder." Besides, because private killing was forbidden, it should also be reported to the officials to kill "Nu Bi" (the slave girls and maidservants); otherwise, the killers would be punished.

"Shang Ren" (injuring people). It was also stipulated in "Yue Fa San Zhang" (three-point covenant) that those who had committed the crime of "Shang Ren" (injuring people) would be punished. In the laws of Han Dynasty, the crime of "Shang Ren" (injuring people) included "Dou Shang" (injuring during fighting), "Zei Shang" (premeditated injuring), and "Dao Shang" (injuring during robbing).

"Dou Shang" (injuring during fighting). The crime referred to injuring in a fighting, and it occupied the largest proportion among the three kinds of crimes of injuring. "Dou Shang" (injuring during fighting) could be divided into injuring with or without using knives, and the punishment for the former was much severer than that for the latter. Those who "injured people with knives during fighting would be punished by 'Cheng Dan' (the punishment of men building cities). If the crime was premeditated, the criminal would be punished two levels severer, and the accessories would get the same punishment."[209]

"Zei Shang" (premeditated injuring). The crime referred to the crime of infringing other people's body in various ways intentionally.

"Dao Shang" (injuring during robbing). The crime included injuring in robbery and injuring in stealing. As for the punishment of the crime of "Dao Shang" (injuring during robbing), "the same rules for the crime of murder should be applied," so it was stipulated that "the criminal should be made humiliated with his intentions condemned."[210] If the thief resisted arresting and harmed other people, he would be found guilty of robbing, as was stipulated that "the thief who has injured other people and wounded the guards will get the same punishment as that for robbers."[211]

In the criminal law of Han Dynasty, the system of "Bao Gu" (the system whereby an offender was ordered by law to help the victim recover within a prescribed period, and the punishment for the crime committed by the offender was determined according to the means of injury and the degree of recovery) was also established. The so-called "Bao Gu" meant that in the case of injuring people during fighting, the defendant was supposed to be responsible for the victim's condition of injury within a certain period, that was called "Gu Qi" (protection period). If the victim died of

---

[209]"Xue Xuan Zhuan" (The Biography of Xue Xuan) in *Han Shu* (*The History of Han Dynasty*).
[210]"Xing De" (The Penal Morality) in *Yan Tie Lun* (*Debates on Salt and Iron*).
[211]"Xing Fa Zhi" (The Record of the Criminal Law) in *Jin Shu* (*The History of Jin Dynasty*).

5.4 The Criminal Law in Documents and *Han Jian* (*The Bamboo Slip of Han Dynasty*)

worsening injury during the period, the defendant would be punished for the crime of murder. It was noted in *Ji Jiu Pian* (*Reading Primer Compiled Imperatively*) that "'Bao Gu' meant that according to the victim's condition of injury, the defendant would be given several days to have the victim's injury treated, but the defendant would be convicted of felony if the victim died during the period." It was explained in *Da Qing Lv Li* (*Code of the Qing Dynasty*) that, "'Bao' means 'attending'; 'Gu' means 'crimes', so it meant that if the victim did not die of injury, the official would set a time limit for the defendant to have him treated. Because it was exactly the way to protect the defendant from being more severely punished to treat the victim's wound," "Bao Gu" was considered as a system of protecting the victims. The system of "Bao Gu" had a long history in China's ancient criminal law, because in fact it had existed in the Spring and Autumn Period. For example, in the 7th year of Duke Xiang of Lu, Kun, the Earl of Zheng, was injured by a senior official on the way to attend the meeting of marquis and then died before he arrived home. In the annotation of *Gong Yang Zhuan* (*The Biography of Gongyang*), He Xiu adopted the view of "Bao Gu": "In ancient times, in terms of the protection of victims… if the monarch died during the victim period, it would be considered as crime of regicide; if the monarch died beyond the time of "Gu Qi" (protection period), it would be considered as a crime of injuring the monarch." It was further explained by Xu Yan's commentary that, "the criminal who was convicted of regicide would be punished by 'Xiao Shou' (the penalty of hanging the head of the criminal on top of a pole for public display), and his families would also be arrested; while for the criminal who was convicted of injuring the monarch, he be punished by 'Xiao Shou' (the penalty of hanging the head of the criminal on top of a pole for public display), but his families would not be incriminated."[212] In the laws of Han Dynasty, the system of "Bao Gu" (the system whereby an offender was ordered by law to help the victim recover within a prescribed period, and the punishment for the crime committed by the offender was determined according to the means of injury and the degree of recovery) had been widely used. For example, Shan De, the marquis of Wujingxin in Sichang, "had injured a person in the 3rd year of Yuanshuo, but the victim then died in twenty days, so Shan De was sentenced to 'Qi Shi' (exposing the executed body publicly at markets)."[213]

"Jian Qing" (Adultery). In the laws of Han Dynasty, the crime of adultery included raping and adultery. Raping referred to a criminal act of infringing upon women's body by violence or other means of intimidation. Zhang Fei's explanation of raping proposed in his book *Zhu Lv Biao* (*Table of Annotations for Codes*) was quoted in "Xing Fa Zhi" (The Records of Criminal Law) in *Jin Shu* (*The History of Jin Dynasty*): "Raping means inharmonious intercourse by violence." The punishment for the crime of raping was very severe. For example, Marquis Duan in Yongli

---

[212]"Xiang Gong Qi Nian" (The 7th Year of Duke Xiang) in *Chun Qiu Gong Yang Zhuan Zhu Shu* (*Annotation and Commentary on Annotation to Chun Qiu by Master Gong Yang*).

[213]"Gao Di Gong Chen Biao" (The Table of Meritorious Ministers in the Reign of Emperor Gao) in *Han Shu* (*The History of Han Dynasty*).

was sentenced to death for raping the wife of other people, but he was then exempted from death penalty because of amnesty.[214] Although the crime of adultery was not so serious as to be punished by death penalty, it was also a felony. Xuan Sheng, marquis of Tujun, "had committed adultery with other people's wife, so he was dismissed from his post."[215]

5.4.2 The Penalty System Reform of Abolishing Corporal Punishment

5.4.2.1 The Process of Abolishing Corporal Punishment

In the 13th year of Emperor Wen (67 B.C.), "Chunyu Gong, "Tai Cang Ling" (official in charge of granary) of Qi state, was supposed to be punished for a crime, so he was arrested and sent to Chang'an. Chunyu Gong had no sons but five daughters. Before being arrested, he scolded his daughters: "I don't have any son, and all of you are good-for-nothing!" Ti Ying, his youngest daughter sobbed alone with sorrow and then went to Chang'an with his father. She wrote to the emperor:

> My father, as an official, has been praised for his honesty and justice by all in Qi state, but now he is to be punished for committing a crime. I feel sorry for those dead men because they cannot become alive again, and I also feel sorry for those executed because they cannot recover. Even though they want to turn over a new leaf, there is no way. I am willing to be degraded to be an official slave to atone for my father's crime so that he can correct his mistakes.

When the emperor read her letter, he felt sympathetic for her, so issued an order:

> ... Now although there are three kinds of corporal punishment, yet evildoing has not been eliminated, then what is wrong?...There is a man of guilty, who has been punished before being educated. I have mercy on those people who want to repent and start anew but who have no ways to do so. The penalty is so severe that the limbs of the criminal are amputated and his skin is tattooed, which has brought suffering to all his life. How torturing and immoral the penalty is! Can it be said that it is the intention of the people's parents (referring to the officials)? Now I command the corporal punishment be abolished and changed.[216]

According to Emperor Wen's imperial decree, "Cheng Xiang" (the prime minister) Zhang Cang and "Yu Shi Da Fu" (Grand Censor) Feng Jing reached an agreement: "Changing the penalty of 'Qing' (to tattoo on the face) into that of 'Kun Qian Cheng Dan Chong' (the punishment of men building cities and women

---

[214]"Wang Zi Hou Biao" (The Table of Princes and Marquises) (Part 2) in *Han Shu* (*The History of Han Dynasty*).

[215]"Gao Hui Gao Hou Wen Gong Chen Biao" (The Table of Meritorious Ministers during the Reign of Emperor Gao, Emperor Hui, Queen Gao and Emperor Wen) in *Han Shu* (*The History of Han Dynasty*).

[216]"Xing Fa Zhi" (The Record of the Criminal Law) in *Han Shu* (*The History of Han Dynasty*).

thrashing rice for lifetime with their hair cut and with an iron rings tied on their neck); changing the penalty of 'Yi' (to cut down the nose) into that of 'Chi' (flogging with light sticks) for 300 strokes; changing the penalty of cutting off the left foot into that of 'Chi' (flogging with light sticks) for 500 strokes; changing the penalty of cutting off the right foot .... All should be sentenced to 'Qi Shi' (exposing the executed body publicly at markets)."[217]

The corporal punishment, which mainly consisted of "Qing" (to tattoo on the face), "Yi" (to cut down the nose) and cutting off the left or right foot, had a history of more than 2000 years from the three dynasties of Xia, Shang, and Zhou to the time of Emperor Wen. The abolishment of this penalty in the 13th year of Emperor Wen (167 B.C.) was not simply out of the emperor's sympathy to the filial daughter, but was closely related to the overall situation in the early Han Dynasty and the emperor's policy of prudent punishment. On the one hand, after rehabilitation, the economy was gradually recovered and developed and the social order was relatively stable, which had brought about a favorable situation where "everyone is self-respected and criminal activities are taken seriously."[218] Moreover, "ethical education is conducted in the whole country so that the common practice of 'Gao Jian' (informing the evil-doing) is completely changed, so that officials are all devoted to their duties, common people are all working hard, livestock and grain production increase annually and population grow rapidly".[219] All of these had prepared the necessary social condition for Emperor Wen's reformation of penalty system and punishment reduction. On the other hand, during the first two decades of Han Dynasty, a series of wars took place. For example, the war against "Xiong Nu" (an ancient nationality in China) occurred in 200 B.C.; the interim prime minister Chen Xi colluded with "Xiong Nu" (an ancient nationality in China), made himself the emperor and waged a reactionary war against Han Dynasty in 197 B.C.; Ying Bu revolted after Han Xin and Peng Yue were killed in 196 B.C.; Han Dynasty was invaded by "Xiong Nu" (an ancient nationality in China) in 182 to 181 B.C.; all the gang of Lv family was suppressed by Han Dynasty in 180 B.C.. Therefore, Emperor Wen tried to use this policy to further win over people's support, to expand the mass bases of his ruling and to establish a stable order of government.

Besides, the abolishment of corporal punishment was also the result of the further development of a series of measures like penalty reduction taken since the establishment of the Han Dynasty.

As for Emperor Wen's abolishment of corporal punishment, some severe punishments were mitigated, but accordingly, some other lenient punishments were aggravated. For example, formerly the crimes punishable by cutting off the right foot were not supposed to be punished by death penalty, but it was later changed into death penalty. In addition, as for the crimes punishable by "Chi" (flogging with light

---

[217]"Xing Fa Zhi" (The Record of the Criminal Law) in *Han Shu* (*The History of Han Dynasty*).
[218]"Shi Huo Zhi" (The Records of National Finance and Economy) (Part 1) in *Han Shu* (*The History of Han Dynasty*).
[219]"Xing Fa Zhi" (The Record of the Criminal Law) in *Han Shu* (*The History of Han Dynasty*).

sticks) for over three hundred strokes, the criminals suffered so much that they often died before the flogging was completed. Therefore, "it was actually killing people in the name of penalty reduction. The criminals who were punishable by death penalty would have their right foot cut off, the criminals who were punishable by cutting off their left foot would be punished by "Chi" (flogging with light sticks) for over five hundred strokes; the criminals who were punishable by "Yi" (to cut down the nose) would be punished by "Chi" (flogging with light sticks) for over three hundred strokes, but most of them died because of those punishments."[220] For this reason, immediately after enthronement, Emperor Jing issued an imperial decree and it was stipulated that "there is no distinction between enforcing severe punishments and increasing the strokes of flogging. Even though the criminal is lucky to survive, he cannot live like a normal person. So it is ruled that 'the five hundred strokes of flogging should be changed into three hundred strokes, and the three hundred strokes should be changed into two hundred strokes.'" Soon another decree was issued: "I feel great pity for the flogged criminal who may die before the flogging was completed. So the three hundred strokes of flogging should be changed to two hundred, and two hundred to one hundred." He then said: "The purpose of flogging is to have the criminals educated, so the rule of flogging should be made." In accordance with the emperor's order, the rule about "Chi" (flogging with light sticks) was made by "Cheng Xiang" (the prime minister) Liu She and "Yu Shi Da Fu" (the Grand Censor) Wei Guan, according to which "the flogging bamboo board should be five *chi* long, with its main part one *cun* in thickness and the end part half a *cun*. Moreover, all the bamboo joints should be removed and the buttocks should be flogged instead of other parts of human body. It is forbidden for the person in charge of flogging to be replaced by others during the process of flogging, so he should not be replaced until after the punishment. From now on, the safety of the flogged criminal can be guaranteed, at the same time, it can serve as a warning for the cruel officials."[221]

Thus, it can be seen that the abolishment of corporal punishment was initiated by Emperor Wen, continued by Emperor Jing, and completed by the efforts of two generations. This important reform of penalty system was generally highly praised as a policy of benevolence by the historians. For example, Qiu Rui in the Ming Dynasty wrote in *Da Xue Yan Yi Bu* (*Supplement to the Deductive Meaning of the Great Learning*) that "the penalty of 'Chi' (flogging with light sticks) in later ages starts from this.... From then on, the criminals across the country are exempted from having their body amputated and skin tattooed. So it was because of Emperor Wen's great virtue that for hundreds of years the guilty men could be protected from being cruelly killed and their families avoided to be exterminated." In the historical perspective of the criminal system, the abolishment of corporal punishment indeed reflected a progress of legal civilization, so it had laid an important foundation for the establishment of the five kinds penalty systems of "Chi" (flogging with light sticks),

---

[220]"Xing Fa Zhi" (The Record of the Criminal Law) in *Han Shu* (*The History of Han Dynasty*).
[221]"Xing Fa Zhi" (The Record of the Criminal Law) in *Han Shu* (*The History of Han Dynasty*).

5.4 The Criminal Law in Documents and *Han Jian* (*The Bamboo Slip of Han Dynasty*)

"Zhang" (flogging with heavy sticks), "Tu" (imprisonment), "Liu" (exile) and "Si" (death penalty) in feudal times.

However, although Emperor Jing redressed the malpractice of penalty aggravation in the process of the abolishment of corporal punishment, a new problem arose. Thus, "the people are more liable to commit crimes because the death penalty is too severe, while the other penalties are much too lenient."[222] Ban Gu said that, "the original purpose of abolishing the corporal punishment is to ensure the safety of the people, but now the punishment of "Kun Qian" (the punishment of having the criminal's hair cut with an iron ring tied on his neck) is replaced by 'Da Bi' (capital punishment), which is not only deceiving but also against the emperor's original good intention. Therefore, it is because of harsh punishment that tens of thousands of people are killed every year. As for the crimes of burglary, injury, adultery, and corruption of officials, the penalties like "Kun Qian" (the punishment of having the criminal's hair cut with an iron ring tied on his neck) are too lenient to have punished. Therefore, although hundreds of thousands of people are punished every year, the people are neither afraid nor ashamed of themselves, which is caused by lenient punishment."[223] In fact, early before Ban Gu, it was already pointed out by "Guang Lu Xun" (official in charge of banqueting department) Du Lin that "in ancient times, corporal punishment is very severe, so people are scared by law, but nowadays penalties are too lenient, so evil doings can never be prevented...."[224]

It needs to be pointed out that after the abolishment of corporal punishment, as a corporal punishment next only to death penalty, the penalty of "Gong" (castration) was supposed to be abolished. Chao Cuo said in the 15th year of Emperor Wen (169 B.C.): "Now that corporal punishment has been abandoned ...the penalty of 'Yin' (castration) should be abolished, too." According to Zhang Yan's annotation, "the penalty of 'Yin' meant the penalty of 'Gong' (castration)."[225] It was stipulated in the decree issued in the 1st year of Emperor Jing (156 B.C.) that "Emperor Xiaowen ... abolished corporal punishment, set free the aged untitled beautiful maids in the imperial palace, and paid much attention to the custom of castration."[226] However, according to Cui Hao's preface to *Han Lv* (*Han Code*) which was quoted in the index of "Xiao Wen Ben Ji" (The Biographic Sketches of Xiao Wen) in *Shi Ji* (*The Records of the Grand Historian*), "although Emperor Wen abolished corporal punishment, the punishment of castration was retained." Moreover, according to Zhang Fei's annotation, "castration is not abolished because adultery has disturbed people's family order." It showed that the penalty of castration was still applied to certain crimes, and it was in the 4th year of Zhongyuan in the reign of Emperor Jing (148 B.C.) that it was officially permitted for death penalty to be replaced by the

---

[222]"Xing Fa Zhi" (The Record of the Criminal Law) in *Han Shu* (*The History of Han Dynasty*).

[223]"Xing Fa Zhi" (The Record of the Criminal Law) in *Han Shu* (*The History of Han Dynasty*).

[224]"Du Lin Zhuan" (The Biography of Du Lin) in *Latter Han Shu* (*The History of the Latter Han Dynasty*).

[225]"Chao Cuo Zhuan" (The Biography of Chao Cuo) in *Han Shu* (*The History of Han Dynasty*).

[226]"Jing Di Ji" (The Record of Emperor Jing) in *Han Shu* (*The History of Han Dynasty*).

penalty of "Gong" (castration), as was declared that "it is allowed if a criminal who is convicted of death penalty wants to be punished by 'Fu' (rotten, or being castrated) instead." According to Su Lin's annotation, "after the punishment of 'Gong' (castration) the wound will give off a rotten smell, so 'Fu' (rotten) is used here."[227] So it might be a "medium penalty" adopted to overcome the contradiction of "the over-severity of the death penalty and the over-leniency of other penalties" to replace death penalty by the punishment of "Gong" (castration).

In the reign of Emperor Ming of the Eastern Han Dynasty, the penalty of cutting off the criminal's right foot was restored to replace death penalty as a response to Emperor Guangwu's policy of penalty reduction. Emperor Guangwu had said: "I would like to govern the country through conciliation."[228] In late Eastern Han Dynasty, with the intensification of class struggle, there was a great call for resuming corporal punishment, so according to the records in "Xing Fa Zhi" (The Records of Criminal Law) in *Jin Shu* (*The History of Jin Dynasty*), "in the 1st year of Jian'an ...Cui Shi, 'Tai Shou' (governor of a prefecture) of Eastern Liao, Zheng Xuan, 'Da Si Nong' (Minister of National Treasury) and Chen Ji, 'Da Hong Lu' (the court of state ceremonial) all proposed that it is the time to restore corporal punishment." Among these supporters of restoring corporal punishment, Zhong Changtong's view was the most representative. He said:

> After the abolishment of corporal punishment, there are not fixed standards anymore for the measurement of punishment. The crimes which are not punishable by death penalty will be replaced by 'Kun Qian' (the punishment of having the criminal's hair cut with an iron ring tied on his neck), and the crimes which are not punishable by 'Kun Qian' (the punishment of having the criminal's hair cut with an iron ring tied on his neck) will be replaced by 'Chi' (flogging with light sticks). Indeed the dead cannot come back to life, but no harm is really done to the criminals by the punishment of 'Kun Qian' (the punishment of having the criminal's hair cut with an iron ring tied on his neck). Moreover, the punishments like 'Kun Qian' (the punishment of having the criminal's hair cut with an iron ring tied on his neck) and 'Chi' (flogging with light sticks) are not severe enough to punish the less serious crimes so that the guilty people can often escape death, while the crimes like theft, adultery, bribery and accidental injury are not serious enough to be punished by death penalty, so it is too harsh to put the criminals to death and too lenient to have them punished by 'Kun Qian' (the punishment of having the criminal's hair cut with an iron ring tied on his neck). If we do not make a medium penalty to match such crimes, how can it be that there will not be unfairness in the enforcement of law? How can it be that the criminals are not punished too severely? Nowadays, people are worried that the penalty is not harsh enough to punish the evil doing, so they try to increase the charges by bribing with expensive gifts, or to avoid death by pleading illness, because there are no standards for the legal provisions and the practices are not correspondent to the charges. I am afraid that it is not what the general law of the emperors or the good systems of the sages should be. Someone will say that 'it is acceptable to enforce severe punishment on evil people, but how can the severe punishment be restored for the good people?' My answer is: 'if no decent person has been wrongly sentenced since the reign of previous emperor, it is because although the rulers have the intention to kill, they cannot bear to enforce the punishment so that the criminals have not been sentenced to death

---

[227]"Jing Di Ji" (The Record of Emperor Jing) in *Han Shu* (*The History of Han Dynasty*).
[228]"Guang Wu Di Ji" (The Record of Emperor Guangwu) (Part 2) in *Latter Han Shu* (*The History of Latter Han Dynasty*).

penalty for their crimes. Therefore, now the standard for 'Wu Xing' (Five Penalties) should be set up, the scope of punishment should be clarified, legal provisions should be listed in good order and practices should be made correspondent to the charges. Besides, people should not be sentenced to death unless they have committed the crime of murder, rebellion or fornication and the secret codes of Zhou Gong (Duke of Zhou) should be followed and Master Lv's excellent penalties should be adopted. So it is the time to have the good policies restored.[229]

At the same time, many people were against restoring the corporal punishment, among whom Kong Rong was a representative. He said:

...Therefore, it has been a long time since the emperor does not rule according to 'Dao' (way, or the great universal truth), which has made the people disunited, but he still intends to apply ancient penalties to have the people punished and their bodies harmed, so it cannot be said that he is keeping pace with the times. King Zhou in Shang dynasty had punished people who waded across rivers in the morning by cutting off their feet, which was regarded as a brutal punishment by all the people. At that time, there were 1,800 kings on Chinese land, so if each king cut off a person's feet, then there would have 1800 'Kings of Zhou' all over the land. In this case, it would be impossible to maintain the peace and harmony of the society. Furthermore, the people punished would not like to live anymore, but only would like to die. So most of them continued to do evil things and could never go back to the right track. 'Su Sha' (ancient Chinese tribe) disturbed the state of Qi; Yi Li brought misfortune to the state of Song; Zhao Gao and Ying Bu became great trouble makers for the society, so it is wrong if we cannot eliminate these evil doings; if we enforce wrong penalties, it is just preventing people from starting anew. Even for the people who are as loyal as Yu Quan, as honest as Bian He, as intelligent as Sun Bin, as innocent as Xiang Bo, as talented as Shi Qian or as successful as Zi Zheng, if they are punished by corporal punishment, the executioners would be despised by later generations.... The policies of encouraging people to correct their misconducts in Han Dynasty are made in view of all these cases. So a wise and virtuous emperor must look far ahead, think in the long run and be very careful with the reform of political policies.

Kong Rong's proposal was "approved by the imperial court," so the penalty system established "remains changed finally."[230]

There were still discussions on the enforcement of corporal punishment until Wei and Jin Dynasties after Han Dynasty. Basing on the basic thoughts of Ban Gu, the supporters of corporal punishment represented by Chen Qun from Cao Wei and Liu Song from Western Jin Dynasty tried to fill the void caused by the situation of "the over-severity of the death penalty and the over-leniency of other penalties" by applying corporal punishment. However, the corporal system had never been officially restored or included in the legal system, just as Wang Dun, the great general of Eastern Jin Dynasty had said that "now that the common people had been accustomed to the practice for a long time, it would be shocking to restore the corporal punishment suddenly.... So there should be no miserable cries to be heard by all the

---

[229] "Zhong Chang Tong Zhuan" (The Biography of Zhong Changtong) in *Latter Han Shu* (*The History of Latter Han Dynasty*).

[230] "Kong Rong Zhuan" (The Biography of Kong Rong) in *Latter Han Shu* (*The History of Latter Han Dynasty*).

people."²³¹ However, the application of the penalty of "Qing" (to tattoo on the face) in judicatory practice had never been stopped from Han to Qing Dynasties and it had even become much severer in certain periods. It belonged to the cruel penalty beyond the statutory punishment of "Wu Xing" (the five penalties).

In conclusion, the abolishment of corporal punishment by Emperor Wen and Emperor Jing of Western Han Dynasty is an important reform of Chinese penalty system, which is of great progressive significance because it has not only fostered the transformation of the penalty system from barbarism to civilization, but also changed part of the superstructure that does not fit in with the economic foundation by following the trend of the historical development. This is also the very reason why the corporal punishment is never restored again, although there are so many supporters in the periods after Emperor Wen and Emperor Jing.

5.4.2.2 The Death Penalty

There are six hundred and ten articles on the death penalties in the laws and decrees of Han Dynasty. As to the execution methods of death penalty, there are following categories.

"Zan Shou" (decapitation). It is also called "Shu Si." According to "Gao Di Ji" (The Record of the First Emperor of Han Dynasty) in *Han Shu* (*The History of Han Dynasty*), in the 6th year of Emperor Gao (199 B.C.), a decree was issued: "The troops have not rested for eight years and all my people are living miserably, now that the great event has been completed, all criminals whose punishments are below the penalties of 'Shu Si' (decapitation) shall be pardoned." According to Wei Zhao's annotation, "'Shu Si' (decapitation) means the penalty of decapitation." Yan Shigu said: "'Shu' means 'disconnection and difference', which indicates that the body and the head are disconnected and are in different places." In the period of Emperor Jing, seven states had plotted a rebellion, so "'Yu Shi Da Fu' (Grand Censor) Chao Cuo was decapitated in order to apologize to them."²³²

"Xiao Shou" (the penalty of hanging the head of the criminal on top of a pole for public display). "'Xiao' means 'cutting off the head and then hanging it on the wall'."²³³ "All people who do not show respect to their superiors or who defame the sages or who are not filial will be beheaded with their cut-off heads exposed to the public."²³⁴ In early Han Dynasty, Peng Yue was executed by "Xiao Shou" (the penalty of hanging the head of the criminal on top of a pole for public display) for the crime of "Mou Fan" (plotting rebellion or plotting to endanger the country) in

---

²³¹"Xing Fa Zhi" (The Record of the Criminal Law) in *Jin Shu* (*The History of Jin Dynasty*).

²³²"Jing Di Ji" (The Record of Emperor Jing) in *Han Shu* (*The History of Han Dynasty*).

²³³"Chen Tang Zhuan" (The Biography of Chen Tang) in *Han Shu* (*The History of Han Dynasty*), annotated by Yan Shigu.

²³⁴"Wen Gong Shi Liu Nian" (The 16th Year of the Duke of Wen) in *Chun Qiu Gong Yang Zhuan Zhu Shu* (*Annotation and Commentary on Annotation to Chun Qiu by Master Gong Yang*).

Luoyang. It was written in "Wai Qi Zhuan" (The Biography of Maternal Relatives of the Emperor) in *Han Shu* (*The History of Han Dynasty*) that, "a woman named Chu Fu had conducted witchcraft, sacrificing and praying for the Queen, which was a monstrous crime.... So she was beheaded and her head was exposed in the market." It shows that women in Han Dynasty were also sentenced to "Xiao Shou" (the penalty of hanging the head of the criminal on top of a pole for public display) if they had committed felonies.

"Yao Zhan" (cutting in two at the waist). According to "Shi Sang Zhi" (Explanation of Funeral System) in *Shi Ming* (*The Origin of the Word Meaning*), "it is called 'Zhan' to cut the head off, and it is called 'Yao Zhan' to cut the waist into two." In Zheng Xuan's annotation for "Zhang Lu" (The Office of Execution) in "Qiu Guan" (Ministry of Penalty) in *Zhou Li* (*The Rites of Zhou Dynasty*), it was explained that "the beheading is executed with an axe, so it is like the punishment of 'Yao Zhan' today; the killing is done with a knife and it is like the punishment of 'Qi Shi' (exposing the executed body publicly at markets) today." It is thus clear that "Yao Zhan" (cutting in two at the waist) and "Qi Shi" (exposing the executed body publicly at markets) are different not only in the punished parts of body but also in the way of punishment, and "Yao Zhan" (cutting in to two at the waist) is often applied for the felonies like "Da Ni" (great sedition). According to "Wu Di Ji" (The Records of Emperor Wu) in *Han Shu* (*The History of Han Dynasty*), "Cheng Xiang" (the prime minister) Liu Qumao's wife was sentenced to the penalty of "Xiao Shou" (the penalty of hanging the head of the criminal on top of a pole for public display), so he was implicated to be sentenced to "Yao Zhan." In the military law of Han Dynasty, the crimes like "delaying military action" or other felonies were all punished by "Yao Zhan."

"Qi Shi" (exposing the executed body publicly at markets). According to Yan Shigu's annotation, "it means killing the criminal at the market. Thus, "Qi Shi" means killing the criminal at the market and abandoning his body to the public."[235] "Qi Shi" was a common death penalty in Han Dynasty and was often applied to the crimes of "Fan Ni" (treachery), "Sha Ren" (killing a person), and "Qi Wang" (deceiving).

"Zu Xing" (killing of the whole clan of a criminal). The criminals of "Da Ni" (great sedition) would be sentenced to the penalty of "Yao Zhan" (cutting in two at the waist), with his parents, wife and other family members sentenced to "Qi Shi" (exposing the executed body publicly at markets) regardless of their age, which was also called "Zu Xing" (killing of the whole clan of a criminal). Gongsun Ao, Zhufu Yan, and Guo Xie and so on were all punished by "Zu Xing" (killing of the whole clan of a criminal) for the crime of "Da Ni" (great sedition) or for just being implicated in other crimes. In early Han Dynasty, the penalty of "Yi San Zu" (the law of killing the three generations of a family) was retained. The three clans referred

---

[235]"Jing Di Ji" (The Record of Emperor Jing) in *Han Shu* (*The History of Han Dynasty*).

to "the father's clan, the mother's clan and the wife's clan."[236] Peng Yue and Han Xin both were both punished by "Yi San Zu" (the law of killing the three generations of a family). In the 1st year of Queen Lv, this penalty was abolished, however, after that, Xin Yuanping was sentenced to penalty of "Yi San Zu" (the law of killing the three generations of a family) for rebellion, and the cruel official Wang Wenshu was even punished by "Yi Wu Zu" (the law of killing the five generations of a family).

"Zhe Xing" (to open and split, breaking apart the criminal's body). Yan Shigu said that "'Zhe' referred to dismembering the body."[237] "Zhe Xing" (to open and split, breaking apart the criminal's body) was often applied to the felony of "Fan Ni" (treachery). In the 2nd year of Zhongyuan during the reign of Emperor Jing (148 B. C.), "Zhe Xing" (to open and split, breaking apart the criminal's body) was changed into "Qi Shi" (exposing the executed body publicly at markets).

5.4.2.3 Corporal Punishment

In early Han Dynasty, there were four kinds of corporal punishments including "Qing" (to tattoo on the face), "Yi" (to cut down the nose), cutting off the right and the left foot, and "Gong" (castration).

"Gong" (castration) was also called "Fu Xing" (rotten, or being castrated) or "Can Xing" (Can penalty). In Han Dynasty, the punishment of "Gong" (castration) was not only applied to criminals conducting adultery, but also to people for political reasons. For example, Sima Qian was sentenced to the punishment of "Gong" (castration) for defending for Li Ling's surrendering to "Xiong Nu" (an ancient nationality in China). There were two reasons for Emperor Wen to abolish corporal punishments "without changing the penalty of 'Gong'": the first was that "it was not abolished because adultery had disturbed people's family order"[238]; the second was that it was retained to fill the void left by the great imbalance of the severity of death penalty and leniency of "Chi" (flogging with light sticks).

Cutting off the right foot. When Emperor Wen abolished corporal punishment, he "replaced the penalty of cutting off the right foot ... by 'Qi Shi' (exposing the executed body publicly at markets)"[239] so that some criminals who were not punishable by death penalty were executed; therefore, it was widely criticized. After enthronement, Emperor Jing changed the punishment for some criminals who were not punishable by "Qi Shi" (exposing the executed body publicly at markets) back into the punishment of cutting off the right foot, which was the so-called "Yi Sheng Yi Si" (exchanging death with life), which had not only made

---

[236]"Gao Zu Ji" (The Record of Emperor Gaozu) in *Han Shu* (*The History of Han Dynasty*), annotated by Ru Chun.

[237]"Jing Di Ji" (The Record of Emperor Jing) in *Han Shu* (*The History of Han Dynasty*).

[238]"Xiao Wen Ben Ji" (The Biographic Sketches of Emperor Xiaowen) in *Shi Ji* (*The Record of the Grand Historian*), annotated by Zhang Fei.

[239]"Xing Fa Zhi" (The Record of the Criminal Law) in *Han Shu* (*The History of Han Dynasty*).

penalties in agreement with the crimes, but also given the criminals a warning and overcome the malpractice of Emperor Wen's abolishment of corporal punishment.

5.4.2.4 The Punishment of "Chi" (Flogging with Light Sticks)

After Emperor Wen replaced the punishment of "Qing" (to tattoo on the face), "Yi" (to cut down the nose) and cutting off the left foot with the punishment of "Chi" (flogging with light sticks), the punishment of "Chi" (flogging with light sticks) became an important penalty in Han Dynasty. According to "Ming Li" (The Categories of Penalties and General Principles) in *Tang Lv Shu Yi* (*The Comments on Tang Code*), "the punishment of 'Chi' (flogging with light sticks) was executed with bamboo sticks in Han Dynasty but now it is executed with twigs." Although the punishment of "Chi" (flogging with light sticks) was not a corporal punishment that could damage the body, it could still hurt the skin and flesh and make the criminal injured even if not dead. Thus, during the reign of Emperor Jing, not only the relevant rules of the punishment of "Chi" (flogging with light sticks) were made and the forms were regulated, but also the specific parts of the body to be flogged were stipulated. The punishment of "Chi" (flogging with light sticks) was followed by the later generations, and it was regarded as one of the statutory penalties of "Wu Xing" (the five penalties).

5.4.2.5 The Punishment of "Tu" (Imprisonment)

In Han Dynasty, the punishment of "Tu" (imprisonment) of Qin Dynasty was followed. During Emperor Wen's reform, the unscheduled imprisonment was changed into fix-term imprisonment, as was stated in his decree that "corporal punishment should be abolished and replaced by other punishments. Now according to the severity of the criminals' crimes, those who do not escape can be released after the completion of imprisonment. This is my command."[240] Hereby, Zhang Cang, "Cheng Xiang" (the prime minister) and Feng Jing, "Yu Shi Da Fu" (Grand Censor) had made specific rules for the term of imprisonment: "the criminals who have been sentenced will be punished by 'Cheng Dan Chong' (the punishment of men building cities and women thrashing rice for lifetime); three years later, their punishment can be reduced to 'Gui Xin Bai Can' (The male criminal went up the mountain to cut firewood, and the woman criminal was sentenced to choose grains of rice); one year later, their punishment can be reduced to 'Li Chen Qie' ('Li Chen': male servants and 'Li Qie': female servants); after one year of labor, they can be exempted from punishment and become common people."[241] During the reign of Emperor Jing, the term of imprisonment was further specified: "All criminals should serve their

---

[240]Xing Fa Zhi" (The Record of the Criminal Law) in *Han Shu* (*The History of Han Dynasty*).
[241]Xing Fa Zhi" (The Record of the Criminal Law) in *Han Shu* (*The History of Han Dynasty*).

sentences respectively: if people have committed crimes, the male punishable by 'Kun Qian Cheng Dan Chong' (the punishment of men building cities and women thrashing rice for lifetime with their hair cut and with an iron ring tied on the neck) will serve for five years; the male punishable by 'Wan Cheng Dan' (the punishment of men building cities without other corporal punishments) will serve for four years; the male punishable by 'Si Kou' (forcing criminals to serve penal servitude) will serve as guards and the female will serve 'Zuo Ru Si Kou'(punishment like serve penal servitude), both for two years; the male punishable by 'Fa Zuo' (the penalties of garrison frontiers by men) and the female punishable by 'Fu Zuo' (compulsory servitude in the government by women) will serve for both three months to one year."[242] The detailed explanations are as follows:

"Si Kou" (forcing criminals to serve penal servitude). According to *Han Jiu Yi* (*Traditional Rituals of Han Dynasty*), "as to the punishment of 'Si Kou' (forcing criminals to serve penal servitude), the male will serve as guards and the female will serve 'Zuo Ru Si Kou' (punishment like serve penal servitude), both for two years. In the reign of Emperor Huan, Duan Jiong "had forged an imperial edict, so he was supposed to be severely punished, but he was sentenced to 'Si Kou' (forcing criminals to serve penal servitude) for his achievements made in the war."[243] Besides, it was recorded that six people were punished by "Nai" (having the criminal's beard shaven for two years) and "Si Kou" (forcing criminals to serve penal servitude) in "Wang Zi Hou Gong Chen Biao" (Table of Meritorious Statesman of Dukes and Princes) in *Han Shu* (*The History of Han Dynasty*). When serving the sentence, these people could undertake the task of "spying upon enemies" and monitoring other criminals.

"Fa Zuo" (the penalties of garrison frontiers by men) and "Fu Zuo" (compulsory servitude in the government by women) were both one-year penalties. "Fa Zuo" (the penalties of garrison frontiers by men) was applied to male criminals, while "Fu Zuo" (compulsory servitude in the government by women) was applied to female criminals, both referring to official compulsory servitude. It was written in "Xuan Di Ji" (The Biography of Emperor Xuan) in *Han Shu* (*The History of Han Dynasty*) that: "female criminals were made to serve 'Fa Zuo' (the penalties of garrison frontiers by men)." According to the annotation of Li Qi, "female criminals were punished by 'Fu Zuo' (compulsory servitude in the government by women), and it was a much lenient punishment. Generally, men were sentenced to garrison frontiers for one year, but because women were too weak to do that, they were required to do servitude in the government for one year as well. So it was called the penalty of 'Fu Zuo' (compulsory servitude in the government by women)." Meng Kang said: "'Fu' has the same pronunciation with 'Fu' (clothes) and it referred to penalty reduction. Sometimes, imperial edicts were issued to free the criminals from wearing torture

---

[242]"Han Jiu Yi" (Traditional Rituals of Han Dynasty) (Part 2) in *Han Gong Liu Zhong* (*Six Categories of Imperial Court of Han*).
[243]"Duan Jiong Zhuan" (The Biography of Duan Jiong) in *Latter Han Shu* (*The History of the Latter Han Dynasty*).

equipment and prison uniforms and to reduce their punishments. After a woman committed crime, she would not be imprisoned, instead, she would be sentenced to labor service in the government, and she must serve her term in full, which was called 'Fu Zuo' (compulsory servitude in the government by women)." Yan Shigu thought that Meng Kang was right. During the reign of Emperor Wen, Wei Shang, "Tai Shou" (governor of a prefecture) of Yunzhong, was "punished by depriving of his titles and garrisoning frontiers"[244] because he had left out six people when he recorded the number of enemies he had killed.

"Li Chen Qie" ('Li Chen': male servants and 'Li Qie': female servants) was also a one-year penalty. According to Yan Shigu's annotation, "male slaves are 'Li Chen' (male servants) and female slaves are 'Li Qie' (female servants). After serving the penalty of 'Gui Xin Bai Can' (The male criminal went up the mountain to cut firewood, and the woman criminal was sentenced to choose grains of rice) for one year, the criminal would become 'Li Chen' (male servants), and then be exempted from punishment to become common people after another one year, so was 'Li Qie' (female servants)."[245] In Qin Dynasty, "Li Chen Qie" had the property of the combination of prisoners and officials slaves. After the penal reform in Han Dynasty, "Li Chen Qie" became a penal servitude in the full sense. However, after the reign of Emperor Wu, "Li Chen Qie" ('Li Chen': male servants and 'Li Qie': female servants) was replaced by "Fa Zuo" (the penalties of garrison frontiers by men) and "Fu Zuo" (compulsory servitude in the government by women), so the penalty of "Li Chen Qie" has not been seen in historical records anymore.

The prisoners in Han Dynasty led a miserable life, because they were often forced to do all kinds of heavy labor. Therefore, in the reign of Emperor Cheng, several riots happened successively among the prisoners, which had forced the rulers to reduce punishment and to pardon the prisoners.

5.4.2.6 "Qian Xi" (The Penalty of Banishing the Criminals To Do Forced Labor in Remote Areas)

In Han Dynasty, the punishment of "Liu" (exile) was not established, but the punishment of "Xi" was enacted instead, which was also called "Qian" (the penalty of banishing the criminals to do forced labor in remote areas) or "Liu Xi." It was recorded in "Peng Yue Zhuan" (The Biography of Peng Yue) in *Han Shu* (*The History of Han Dynasty*) that Emperor Gao once pardoned the criminals implicated in criminal cases and ordered them to be moved to Shu, which was the earliest case of the penalty of "Qian Xi" (the penalty of banishing the criminals to do forced labor in remote areas). After that, this penalty was mostly applied to guilty marquises. The punishment of "Zhe Shu" (relegating to garrison frontiers) was included in "Qian

---

[244]"Feng Tang Lie Zhuan" (The Biography of Feng Tang) in *Shi Ji* (*The Record of the Grand Historian*).
[245]"Xing Fa Zhi" (The Record of the Criminal Law) in *Han Shu* (*The History of Han Dynasty*).

Xi," which referred to being exiled to the bordering areas. In the 5th year of Yuanshou in the reign of Emperor Wu (118 B.C.), "all treacherous officials were exiled to borders."[246] In the 1st year of Tianhan (100 B.C.), "the suspects of the doubtful cases in the four 'Jun' (shire) to the right bank of Qi River started to be exiled to other places."[247] In Eastern Han Dynasty, "Qian Xi" (the penalty of banishing the criminals to do forced labor in remote areas) was commonly used as a way of reducing the death penalty, which had gradually become a need for border defense and lost its original function of punishment. The criminals exiled to border regions could be released in amnesty. For example, Ma Rong, a celebrated scholar, who had been exiled to the north border for offending the great general Liang Yi, "was able to go back for amnesty and was selected to be 'Yi Lang' (ancient official title in China) again."[248] In later Eastern Han Dynasty, "Qian Xi" became an implicated penalty of death penalty. In the cases of felony, the criminal would be sentenced to death while his wife would be exiled to frontier regions.

5.4.2.7 "Jin Gu"

According to Yan Shigu's annotation, "Jin Gu" referred to "forbidding to hold office for all one's life."[249] It was regulated in the period of Emperor Wen that "merchants, 'Zhui Xu' (a son-in-law who lives in the home of his parents-in-law) and the officials who have taken bribes are not allowed to hold official posts."[250] However, in the history of Han Dynasty, this penalty was applied to officials who had violated the law more frequently. In Eastern Han Dynasty, the scope of prohibition was continuously extended, so even the descendants and relatives were implicated.

5.4.2.8 "Shu Xing" (Atonement)

"Shu Xing" (atonement) was widely applied and specific regulations were stipulated at different times. For example, in the reign of Emperor Hui, if a guilty man wanted to be exempted from death penalty, he had to buy thirty ranks of the titles of nobility." According to Ying Shao's annotation, "every rank was worth 2,000 *qian*, so the total was 60,000,"[251] which was the beginning of redeeming penalty with money. To the reign of Emperor Wu, to eliminate fiscal deficit, "Shu Xing"

---

[246]"Wu Di Ji" (The Record of Emperor Wu) in *Han Shu* (*The History of Han Dynasty*).
[247]"Xing Fa Zhi" (The Record of the Criminal Law) in *Wei Shu* (*The History of Northern Wei Dynasty*).
[248]"Ma Rong Zhuan" (The Biography of Ma Rong) in *Latter Han Shu* (*The History of the Latter Han Dynasty*).
[249]"Xi Fu Gong Zhuan" (The Biography of Xi Fugong) in *Han Shu* (*The History of Han Dynasty*).
[250]"Gong Yu Zhuan" (The Biography of Gong Yu) in *Han Shu* (*The History of Han Dynasty*).
[251]"Hui Di Ji" (The Record of Emperor Hui) in *Han Shu* (*The History of Han Dynasty*).

5.4 The Criminal Law in Documents and *Han Jian* (*The Bamboo Slip of Han Dynasty*)

(atonement) was widely carried out. In the 4th year of Tianhan (97 B.C.), "it was ruled in an imperial edict that "the criminals who are punishable below the sentence of death penalty could get their penalties reduced by one level by paying 500,000 *qian*."[252] Further, it was also stipulated in the 2nd year of Taishi (96 B.C.) that "the criminals who are punishable below the sentence of death penalty could get the penalty reduced by one level by paying 500,000 *qian*."[253] Zhang Chang, "Jing Zhao Yin" (an official position equivalent to the mayor of the capital city in modern time) even proposed that "except those who have committed the crime of robbing money, murdering and other crimes unpardonable by law, all criminals should be allowed to redeem their penalties by sending grain to the eight 'Jun' (shire)." However, he was refuted by Xiao Wangzhi: "If so, rich men can survive, while poor men can only die, so that the rich and the poor are punished differently, which has made the law discriminated."[254] From Zhang Chang and Xiao Wangzhi's argumentation, it can be seen that penalty redeeming was just a temporarily measure but not a fixed law at that time. However, it was gradually developing to be systematized, which can be proved by Sima Qian's words in *Bao Ren Shao Qing Shu* (*The Letter in Reply to Shao Qing*): "I am too poor to redeem myself." The systematization and legalization of "Shu Xing" (atonement) occurred after Emperor Ming in Eastern Han Dynasty.

"Nv Tu Gu Shan" (punishment redemption set up specifically for female prisoners in Han Dynasty), which was carried out from late Western Han Dynasty to early Eastern Han Dynasty, was a kind of atonement penalty. In the 1st year of Yuan Shi during the reign of Emperor Ping (86 B.C.), an imperial edict was issued and it was stipulated that "female criminals could be atoned by paying three hundred silver money in cash monthly to the government to employ someone else to chop wood." Yan Shigu further explained that "the female criminal, after being convicted, can be released and go home by paying three hundred silver money in cash monthly to the government to hire someone to chop wood so that she did not need to do this by herself."[255] In the 29th year of Jian Wu during the reign of Emperor Guangwu (53 A.D.), an imperial edict was issued and it was stipulated that "all the prisoners who have committed the crimes punishable below the death penalty and those who are condemned by penal servitude shall receive a reduced penalty. Besides, the criminals liable for other atonement penalties and penal servitude shall all receive some sort of penalty reduction."[256] In the 2nd year of Jianwuzhongyuan during the reign of Emperor Ming (57 A.D.), an imperial edict was issued and it was stipulated that "all the prisoners on the run who have committed crimes punishable below death penalty can atone for their crimes by delivering certain amount of silk to the

---

[252]"Wu Di Ji" (The Record of Emperor Wu) in *Han Shu* (*The History of Han Dynasty*).

[253]"Wu Di Ji" (The Record of Emperor Wu) in *Han Shu* (*The History of Han Dynasty*).

[254]"Xiao Wang Zhi Zhuan" (The Biography of Xiao Wangzhi) in *Han Shu* (*The History of Han Dynasty*).

[255]"Ping Di Ji" (The Record of Emperor Ping) in *Han Shu* (*The History of Han Dynasty*).

[256]"Guang Wu Di Ji" (The Record of Emperor Guangwu) in *Latter Han Shu* (*The History of Latter Han Dynasty*) (Book 2).

government. The penalties below death penalty can be atoned with twenty *pi* of silk (*pi*: a unit of measurement for cloth, it means a bolt of cloth); the penalties from cutting off the right foot to 'Kun Qian Cheng Dan Chong' (the punishment of men building cities and women thrashing rice for lifetime with their hair cut and with an iron ring tied on the neck) can be atoned with ten *pi* of silk; the penalties from 'Cheng Dan Chong' (the punishment of men building cities and women thrashing rice for lifetime) to 'Si Kou' (forcing criminals to serve penal servitude) can be atoned with three *pi* of silk; those who surrender themselves before the crime is discovered can atone for their crimes by paying only half of what is needed by their crimes." After Emperor He, imperial edicts were issued by almost all the emperors for penalty atonement, which had led to the prevalence of penalty atonement in the Eastern Han Dynasty. It was recorded in "Chen Chong Zhuan" (The Biography of Chenchong) in *Latter Han Shu* (*The History of Latter Han Dynasty*) that "there were about 2,681 crimes under the category of penalty atonement in this law."

5.4.2.9 "Fa Jin" (Fines)

"Fa Jin" (fines), the most lenient punishment, was applied to minor crimes. For instance, "it shall be imposed with a fine of four *liang* of gold to drink together with more than three people for celebration for no reason"[257]; "article B: it shall be imposed with a fine of four *liang* of gold to walk before the king to be disrespectful of him"[258]; "article A: 'Zhu Hou' (Dukes or Princes) who have owned land in other counties will be imposed with a fine of two *liang* of gold."[259]

5.4.3 The Criminal Principle Under the Influence of Confucianism

The criminal principle in Han Dynasty was based on the legal practice since the Warring States Period, and they could be summarized as the following after textual research:

Petition and Atonement. Petition is a legal privilege granted to royal families, aristocrats, and bureaucrats according to the law of Han Dynasty. The judges did not have the right to hear the cases involving the royal family members and officials above 600 *dan*, so they had to file petitions to the emperor to make judgments. In the

---

[257]"Wen Di Ji" (The Record of Emperor Wen) in *Han Shu* (*The History of Han Dynasty*), annotated by Wen Ying.
[258]"Zhang Shi Zhi Zhuan" (The Biography of Zhang Shizhi) in *Han Shu* (*The History of Han Dynasty*), annotated by Ru Chun.
[259]"Ai Di Ji" (The Record of Emperor Ai) in *Han Shu* (*The History of Han Dynasty*), annotated by Ru Chun.

5.4 The Criminal Law in Documents and *Han Jian* (*The Bamboo Slip of Han Dynasty*)

7th year of Emperor Gaozu (200 B.C.), an imperial edict was issued and it was stipulated that "if the official who holds the position of 'Lang Zhong' (head of a subministry department) has committed crimes which were more serious than those punishable by 'Nai' (having the criminal's beard shaven for two years), the case shall be reported to the emperor." Ying Shao further explained that "the crimes which are more serious than those punishable by 'Nai' (having the criminal's beard shaven for two years) shall first be reported to the emperor,"[260] which had fully shown the establishment of "petition system." Zheng Xuan gave an elaborate account of the scope of application of the petition system in "Ba Bi" (the eight conditions for mitigating punishments) in *Zhou Li* (*The Rites of Zhou Dynasty*). For example, it was explained in the notes about the cases related to the royal family that "when anyone from the royal family has committed crimes, it shall be reported by the judges to the emperor first"; it was explained in the notes about the cases related to virtuous officials that "if the honest officials have committed crimes, they shall be first reported to the emperor by the judges"; it was explained in the notes about the cases related to senior officials that "if the officials whose ranks are above 600 *dan* have committed crimes, they shall be reported first to the emperor by the judges."

The age-old principle of "Shu Xing" (atonement) was affirmed in Han Dynasty, so money, property, and peerage could be used to atone for the crimes. Moreover, crime-redemption was also applied to death penalty. During the reign of Emperor Hui, "a criminal condemned to death penalty can be atoned by buying thirty ranks of the titles of nobility." Ying Shao further explained that "each rank of the titles of nobility cost about 2,000 *qian*." It was further explained by Yan Shigu that "the convicted can be exempted from punishment by buying the titles of nobility."[261] During the reign of Emperor Jing, Chao Cuo's proposal was approved, according to which "those who pay the tribute of grain should be exempted from penalties."[262] It was stipulated by Emperor Wu that death penalty could be mitigated by one level if the condemned paid 500,000 *qian*. The crime-redemption system had made it convenient for the rich to escape from penalty, but the poor had no choice but to sacrifice their lives. The most famous example was Sima Qian, the historian who was punished by castration because he had no money to atone for his crime. This system of "enforcing different punishment for the same crimes committed by the rich and the poor"[263] was widely criticized by some enlightened officials, however, because it was determined by the nature of the law of feudal hierarchy system, it was not abolished, instead, its scope of application was constantly extended.

---

[260]"Gao Zu Ji" (The Record of Emperor Gaozu) in *Han Shu* (*The History of Han Dynasty*) (Book 2).

[261]"Hui Di Ji" (The Record of Emperor Hui) in *Han Shu* (*The History of Han Dynasty*).

[262]"Shi Huo Zhi" (The Records of National Finance and Economy) in *Han Shu* (*The History of Han Dynasty*) (Book 1).

[263]"Xiao Wang Zhi Zhuan" (The Biography of Xiao Wangzhi) in *Han Shu* (*The History of Han Dynasty*).

"Zi Shou Yu Guo Shi Jian Xing" (reducing penalties for those who have surrendered themselves and those who have committed crimes out of negligence) and "Gu Yi Yu Shou E Cong Zhong" (enforcing severer punishment for those who have committed crimes intentionally and for the principal criminal). It was explicitly stipulated in the law of Han Dynasty that "those who have confessed voluntarily (Zi Gao) can be pardoned."[264] Therefore, "Zi Gao" means "surrender." However, penalty reduction was only limited to what was confessed, and the murderer would still be sentenced to "Qi Shi" (exposing the executed body publicly at markets) even after his voluntary confession.

According to the law of Han Dynasty, severe punishments were imposed on the principal criminal. It was stated in "Zhu Fu Yan Zhuan" (The Biography of Zhu Fuyan) in *Han Shu* (*The History of Han Dynasty*) that "as the principal criminal, Yan must be executed to make an apology to the nation, thus Yan was sentenced to the punishment of 'Zu' (extermination of the entire family)." It was recorded in "Wu Bei Zhuan" (The Biography of Wu Bei) in *Han Shu* (*The History of Han Dynasty*) that "Zhang Tang advised the Emperor that Bei, the leader of the mutinous plot shall not be forgiven, so Bei was executed." Moreover, the principle of "Gu Yi Yu Shou E Cong Zhong" (enforcing severer punishment for those who have committed crimes intentionally and for the principal criminal) which was commonly adopted in the reign of the Western Zhou Dynasty was specified in Han Dynasty. For example, as for the case of murder, it was stipulated in the law of Han Dynasty that those who had committed intentional killing should be sentenced to death, but as for the negligent homicide, death penalty should not be enforced. The age-old judicial practice had proved that "Zi Shou Yu Guo Shi Jian Xing" (reducing penalties for those who have surrendered themselves and those who have committed crimes out of negligence) was not only helpful to cracking down on the intentional and principal criminals, but also helpful to disintegrating the criminal groups. Moreover, it had also taken into consideration the motives of the criminals and the social effect of enforcing different penalties under different circumstances.

"Qin Qin De Xiang Shou Ni" (a law in Han Dynasty which ruled that crimes committed among the kinsfolks should be concealed and should not be reported to the government). Under the influence of Confucian theory of "benevolence and filial piety" which was illustrated by the statement that "justice is shown in parents' harboring of their children and children's harboring of their parents,"[265] since Emperor Xuan, the law which was made during the reign of Emperor Wu concerning the mutual concealment of the crimes committed by father and son and husband and wife was changed. In the 4th year of Di Jie (66 B.C.), an imperial edict was issued and it was ruled that "the love between father and son and between husband and wife is the nature of human beings, so people should help their relatives survive even if it might endanger themselves. Therefore, it is out of love of their hearts to harbor their

---

[264]"Heng Shan Wang Zhuan" (The Biography of the King of Hengshan) in *Han Shu* (*The History of Han Dynasty*).
[265]"Zi Lu" (Zi Lu, one of Confucius' disciples) in *Lun Yu* (*The Analects*).

relatives, which is the best form of benevolence. How can we go against human nature? From now on, it shall not be punished for parents to harbor their children, for wife to harbor her husband and for grandchildren to harbor their grandparents. However, if parents conceal the crimes of their children, husband conceals the crimes of his wife, and grandparents conceal the crimes of their grandchildren, they should be punished by death penalty, but the case shall be first reported to 'Ting Wei' (the supreme official in charge of judicature) by the judges."[266] This criminal principle, according to which the concealment of the crimes between relatives was allowed within certain limits of blood relationship without punishment or with mitigated punishment, was an important reflection of the principle of introducing "Li" (rites) into "Fa" (law) and integrating "Fa" (law) with "Ren Qing" (human feeling). Even during the reign of Emperor Wu when concealment of crimes might involve the punishment of "Lian Zuo" (being punished for being related to somebody who committed an offense), Dong Zhongshu, based on the cardinal principle of "Yi" (justice) which was advocated in *Chun Qiu* (*Spring and Autumn Annals*), suggested that if a father had harbored his adopted son who had committed murder, he should be exempted from the punishment of "Lian Zuo" (being punished for being related to somebody who committed an offense). Emperor Xuan even legalized the Confucian ideology of the concealment of crimes between relatives and boasted of ruling the country with "Ren" (benevolence) and "Xiao" (the filial piety), which had reflected the consolidation of the legitimate position of Confucianism.

Seen from the essence, the "righteous" of the concealment of crimes between father and son which was preached by Confucius was in fact to compel the inferior and the young to "conceal the crimes for the venerable" and "the kindred,"[267] which was certainly applauded by the feudal rulers. The principle of mutual concealment of crimes between family members was adopted in the criminal law after the Han Dynasty with the exception of the crime of "Fan Ni" (treachery).

Showing Mercy to the Aged, the Young, Women, and the Disabled Because the aged, the young, women and the disabled were less dangerous to the society, according to the law of Han Dynasty, their criminal responsibilities could be mitigated. During the reign of Emperor Hui, an imperial edict was issued and it was stipulated that "as to those over the age of seventy or under ten, if they have committed crime, they shall be sentenced to 'Wan' (lenient punishments of cutting off criminal's hair or beard)."[268] During the reign of Emperor Hui, "as to those over eighty or under eight years old, the pregnant women, the teachers and the dwarfs, if they should be punished by imprisonment, they can serve the sentence without shackles."[269] "Given that the old, with few teeth and thinning hair, were too senile

---

[266]"Xuan Di Ji" (The Record of Emperor Xuan) in *Han Shu* (*The History of Han Dynasty*).

[267]"Min Gong Yuan Nian" (The 1st year of the Duke of Min) in *Chun Qiu Gong Yang Zhuan* (*Annotation to Chun Qiu by Master Gong Yang*).

[268]"Hui Di Ji" (The Record of Emperor Hui) in *Han Shu* (*The History of Han Dynasty*).

[269]"Xing Fa Zhi" (The Record of the Criminal Law) in *Han Shu* (*The History of Han Dynasty*).

to committed monstrous crime," Emperor Xuan issued an edict in which it was stipulated that "from now on, if those over eighty have committed crimes, they shall be exempted from punishment unless for the crime of false accusation or murder."[270] During the reign of emperor Cheng, it was stipulated that "if those under seven have killed someone in fighting or committed crimes punishable by death penalty, it shall be reported to 'Ting Wei' (the supreme official in charge of judicature) and they shall be exempted from death penalty."[271] Towards the end of Western Han Dynasty, in the 4th year of Yuanshi during the reign of Emperor Ping (4 A.D.), because "a lot of relatives of offenders, the women, the old people or the weak have been detained by the cruel officials, which has not only brought great suffering to the people and caused great discontents among them, but also done great harm to social atmosphere in general," the emperor issued a special edict to make it clear to the officials that "penalties shall not be imposed on the elderly over seventy and the young under seven, because it is the governing principle of the virtuous rulers.... The female, if not committing crimes by herself or the male over eighty or under seven years old, shall not be put into prison except for the cases of 'Bu Dao' (depravity) or for the cases particularly mentioned by the emperor in the imperial orders."[272] In the 3rd year of Jianwu in the reign of Emperor Guangwu in the Eastern Han Dynasty (27 A. D.), an imperial edict was issued to reaffirm this stipulation by changing the age from seven to ten years old: "The people over seventy years old should be respected by others, so if they are not the principal criminal of murder, they shall not be charged and punished. As for those over eighty, can they live in this world for long?"[273] In *Han Jian (The Bamboo Slips of Han Dynasty)* entitled *Wang Zhang Zhao Shu Ling (Edict Concerning Walking Sticks Granted by the Emperor)* unearthed in Wuwei in 1981, an imperial edict was recorded in detail:

> To 'Yu Shi' (the censor) responsible for drafting the edict: those over seventy years old are given walking sticks by the emperor, so they should get the same treatment as the officials of 600 *dan*. When entering the government, they should not be urged to go fast; whoever dares to assault them or to show disrespect to them shall be convicted of 'Da Ni Bu Dao' (against all the heavenly laws of morality and filial love) and be sentenced to 'Qi Shi' (exposing the executed body publicly at markets). This order was recorded in the 23rd of 'Lan Tai' (archive). Wang Anshi, a man from Runan county was sentenced to 'Qi Shi' (exposing the executed body publicly at markets) and executed in public for assaulting an old man who had an imperial walking stick. Tian Xuan, 'Se Fu' (a minor official in the county) of Dongxiang, Chang'An, was sentenced to 'Qi Shi' (exposing the executed body publicly at markets) for attacking an old man who had an imperial walking stick after being prosecuted by a man named Jin Li. Zhang Tang, a man from Longxi, assaulted an old man who had an

---

[270]"Xing Fa Zhi" (The Record of the Criminal Law) in *Han Shu (The History of Han Dynasty)*.
[271]"Xing Fa Zhi" (The Record of the Criminal Law) in *Han Shu (The History of Han Dynasty)*.
[272]"Ping Di Ji" (The Record of Emperor Ping) in *Han Shu (The History of Han Dynasty)*.
[273]Li Junming, He Shuangquan, *San Jian Jian Du He Ji (Collection of Scattered Bamboo Texts)*, Cultural Relics Press, 1990.

imperial walking stick and broke the walking stick, for which he was also sentenced to 'Qi Shi' (exposing the executed body publicly at markets).[274]

The principle of "Xu Xing" (penalty reduction) was adopted by the rulers of the Han Dynasty because they had learned from long-standing judicial experience that the aged, the young, the women and the disabled had little chances of committing crimes, which had helped to whitewash their ruling as "Ren Dao" (the Way of Human) and "Ai Min" (loving the people) without affecting the stability of their regime. The criminal principle of "Xu Xing" (penalty reduction) reflected the development of legal civilization in ancient times. Besides, only in case of treason would the aged and the young be subject to severe punishments like "Lian Zuo" (being punished for being related to somebody who committed an offense) and "Zu" (killing of the whole clan of a criminal) with no one exempted.

"Wu Gao Fan Zuo" (Punishments for Those Lodging Wrong Accusations) The principle "Wu Gao Fan Zuo" (Punishments for Those Lodging Wrong Accusations) was a traditional criminal principle. "Wu Gao" (false charge) meant that the accuser fabricated facts and reported them to the judicial officials to incriminate the accused, which not only did great harm to the accused, but also endangered the stability of social order and disturbed judicial work. Thus, the crimes such as "Wu Wang" (to accuse an innocent person) and "Jiao Ren Wu Xian" (Inciting False Accusation) were included in the criminal law of Han Dynasty and the violators were severely punished. The purpose of applying "Wu Gao Fan Zuo" (Punishments for Those Lodging Wrong Accusations) was recorded in "Xu Lue" (Outline of the Preface) in "Wei Lv" (Wei Code) which was included in "Xing Fa Zhi" (The Record of the Criminal Law) in *Jin Shu* (*The History of Jin Dynasty*): It was made to "reduce false accusation by severe punishment." In the 4th year of Yuankang during the reign of Emperor Xuan (62 B.C.), it was proclaimed in a special imperial edict that "from now on, as to those over eighty years old, if they have committed crimes, they shall be exempted from punishment except for case of false accusation or murder." Shigu further explained that "the accuser of false charge or the murderer shall be punished without exception."[275] Thus, it can be seen that in the criminal law of Han Dynasty, "Wu Gao" (false charge) was a serious crime like murder, for which even those aged who were over eighty could not be pardoned. In the false accusation of rebellion, the accuser would be sentenced to death even if the accused was innocent. The aggravated punishment was also applied to the crime of instigating others to lodge false accusation. In the reign of Emperor Xuan, Liu Jiande was sentenced to "Qi Shi" (exposing the executed body publicly at markets) and was dismissed from the office of "Zhong Wei" (an officer in charge of defending the capital) which was in charge of eight counties for abetting a false accusation against "Nei Shi" (the official in charge of revenue) who had grudges with him. It was recorded in "Yang Xuan Zhuan" (The

---

[274]Li Junming, He Shuangquan, *San Jian Jian Du He Ji* (*Collection of Scattered Bamboo Texts*), Cultural Relics Press, 1990.

[275]"Xuan Di Ji" (The Record of Emperor Xuan) in *Han Shu* (*The History of Han Dynasty*).

Biography of Yang Xuan) in *Latter Han Shu* (*The History of Latter Han Dynasty*) that Zhao Kai, "Ci Shi" (a supervisor assigned by the central government to a local area) of Jingzhou, received severe punishment for falsely accusing Yang of faking merits and achievements. In *Ju Yan Han Jian* (*Ju Yan Bamboo Slips of Han Dynasty*) unearthed in recent years, there recorded "a lawsuit filed by Sujun against Kou En in the 3rd year of Jian Wu." It not only recorded the legal provision that "those who intentionally deliver false information and cause wrongful judgment shall receive the punishment he falsely accused," but also fully demonstrated that the criminal principle for the punishment of "Wu Gao" (false charge) was already carried out in Han Dynasty.

"Shu Zui Yi Zhong Zhe Lun" (Enforcing Punishment on the Most Serious One in the Case of Plural Crimes) Zheng Xuan had once interpreted "Duo Fang" (In Many Ways) in *Shang Shu Da Zhuan* (*Interpretations of Shang Shu*) according to *Han Lv* (*Han Code*) and he pointed out that "a criminal who committed five crimes" meant "plural crimes.... And the punishment was measured only according to the most serious crime." He Xiu quoted *Han Lv* (*Han Code*) in the explanatory note to "Qi Bo Yi Gu Zu" (The Death of Qi Wen Gong) recorded in the 6th year of Zhaogong in *Gong Yang Zhuan* (*The Biography of Gongyang*): "If a man committed plural crimes, he should be punished according to the most serious one without additional punishment." It proved that punishment was decided by the most serious one in plural crimes rather than by combined punishment. This criminal principle was made not only to avoid inflicting repeated torture on the criminal, but also to avoid being too indulgent to felonies, which had manifested the progress of ancient criminal law towards civilization.

Punishment Imposed Only on the Perpetrator Based on the ideology that "the punishment for evil doing shall only befall on the perpetrator, while the awarding of good deeds shall benefit the offspring" which was recorded in "Zhao Gong Er Shi Nian" (The 20th Year of Zhao Gong) in *Chun Qiu Gong Yang Zhuan* (*Annotation to Chun Qiu by Master Gong Yang*), the Confucian scholars in Han Dynasty proved that only the criminal himself should be punished for the crime he committed, which was applauded by the rulers of Han Dynasty and adopted in the judicial practice. During the reign of Emperor An, Fan Bin, "Du Wei" (a military officer below the general) of Juyan, was accused of corruption, so he was supposed to be punished together with his son. However, Liu Kai, who was "Tai Wei" (the minister of defense) at the time, said that "in my humble opinion, the doctrine that 'the punishment for evil doing shall only befall on the perpetrator, while the awarding of good deeds shall benefit the offspring' which are included in *Chunqiu* (*Spring and Autumn Annals*) are made to cultivate goodness.... But if the sons of the corrupt officials are imprisoned for their father's offenses..., it is against the late emperors' wish for showing prudence in jurisdiction. The Emperor then issued an order: "'Tai Wei' (the minister of defense) is right.'"[276] During the period of Eastern Han

---

[276]"Liu Kai Zhuan" (The Biography of Liu Kai) in *Latter Han Shu* (*The History of Latter Han Dynasty*).

Dynasty, there were many thieves on the central plains. Zhao Xi killed the principal and took thousands of those who should have been put to death into custody in the areas near the capital by following the principle of enforcing punishment only on the perpetrator, so it had eased the tension in the area and was approved by the Emperor.[277]

"Jun Qin Wu Jiang, Jiang Er Zu Yan" (No Offending of the Monarchs and Parents, or the Offender Shall Be Put to Death) The principle of "Jun Qin Wu Jiang, Jiang Er Zu Yan" (No offending of the monarchs and parents, or the offender shall be put to death) was recorded in "Zhuang Gong San Shi Er Nian" (The 32nd year of Zhuanggong) in *Chun Qiu Gong Yang Zhuan (Annotation to Chun Qiu by Master Gong Yang)*. According to Shigu's note to this statement, "the word 'Jiang' means 'having the intention of offending'." That is to say, the monarchs and parents are the supreme authority, so the inferior and youth should not harbor ill intention toward them; otherwise, they would be sentenced to death. This was a manifestation of the Confucian ethical thought, therefore, was accepted in Han Dynasty as a criminal principle. For instance, in the discussion of the punishment for An, who was the vassal of Huainan, Duan, the vassal of Jiaoxi had pointed out that "it is stated in *Chun Qiu (Spring and Autumn Annals)* that the subjects must not offend the sovereign, or they shall be put to death. The crime of An is much severer than that which is mentioned above, because it is definitely a conspiracy against the sovereign…so An should be executed."[278] The condemnation and penalty measurement of this criminal principle was based on the motive of the criminal, which in effect was to maintain the supremacy of the monarchs and parents through the punishment of the ill intention against the monarchs and parents.

Non-retroactivity It was stipulated in *Han Lv (Han Code)* that "those who break laws shall be judged according to the law which is in force when the crime is committed, which has made it clear that some laws might be invalid."[279] Therefore, it meant that judgments should be made according to the law which was effective when the crime was committed instead of the law and legal relationship which had become invalid to maintain the stability of legal order. For example, in the years of Suihe during the reign of Emperor Cheng in the Western Han Dynasty, Chun Yuchang, the marquis of Dingling, was executed for the crime of "Da Ni" (great sedition). Some officials, such as "Cheng Xiang" (the prime minister) Zhuo Fangjin and "Si Kong" (the minister of public works) He Wu, suggested that the six concubines of Chun who had been divorced before the committing of the crime should be executed for Chun's crime. However, Kong Guang, "Ting Wei" (the

---

[277]"Zhao Xi Zhuan" (The Biography of Zhao Xi) in *Latter Han Shu (The History of Latter Han Dynasty)*.

[278]"Huai Nan Wang An Zhuan" (The Biography of An, the Vassal of Huainan) in *Han Shu (The History of Han Dynasty)*.

[279]"Kong Guang Zhuan" (The Biography of Kong Guang) in *Han Shu (The History of Han Dynasty)*.

supreme official in charge of judicature), suggested that the concubines who had been divorced should not be charged. He said that "the parents, wife, children and siblings of whoever committed the crime of 'Da Ni' (great sedition) shall be sentenced to 'Qi Shi' (exposing the executed body publicly at markets), no matter how old they are, which is to warn other people against committing similar crimes in the future. The marriage of husband and wife is decided by their own will, so they are bonded together with affection for each other; otherwise, they have been divorced. Chun has divorced his six concubines, some of them are remarried before he realizes he is going to be punished for the crime of 'Da Ni' (great sedition). The marriage relationship between them has been ended, thus, it is unreasonable to punish them as Chun's wives."[280] This discussion ended up with Emperor Cheng's support for Kong Guang, so the six concubines were exempted from criminal penalty.

As crimes committed before the amnesty was offered were still investigated after the amnesty was proclaimed, Emperor Ai issued a special imperial edict: "The officials shall not report the cases which have occurred before the proclamation of amnesty to the imperial court."[281] After enthronement, Emperor Ping thought that "in the past, officials often report the cases that have occurred before the announcement of amnesty to the imperial court, which not only has increased the number of crimes and cost countless innocent lives, but also is contrary to the principle of prudent penalty and the spirit of reform." Thus, he emphasized in an imperial edict that "from now on, the cases that have occurred before the amnesty is offered shall not be reported by the officials. Whoever disobeys the order is to be considered as 'Kui En' (ungrateful) and will be charged with the crime of 'Bu Dao' (depravity). This is an order and shall be proclaimed to the public so that the people are fully aware of it."[282]

In conclusion, as far as the criminal principle of Han Dynasty is concerned, some achievements have been made compared with those of Qin Dynasty, at the same time, it has fully manifested the influence of Confucianism. Therefore, it had played an important role in the stabilization of the judicial order and the realization of the purpose of criminal law; indeed, it had also exerted a great influence on the later periods after Han Dynasty.

---

[280]"Kong Guang Zhuan" (The Biography of Kong Guang) in *Han Shu* (*The History of Han Dynasty*).
[281]"Ai Di Ji" (The Record of Emperor Ai) in *Han Shu* (*The History of Han Dynasty*).
[282]"Ping Di Ji" (The Record of Emperor Ping) in *Han Shu* (*The History of Han Dynasty*).

5.5 The Development of Civil Legal Relationship and Civil Legislation

The economic recovery and development in Western Han Dynasty greatly promoted the circulation of property relationships and the formation of personal relationships under the feudal hierarchy, which had given impetus to the development of civil law.

Hu Lv (*Statutes on Households*), *Zhi Hou Lv* (*Statutes on Young Successor Placement*), and *Fu Lv* (*Statutes on the Household Registration*) in *Er Nian Lv Ling* (*Second-year Decree*) were mainly civil laws, with *Hu Ling* (*Household Decrees*) as a supplement to *Hu Lv* (*Statutes on Households*). Imperial edicts on some special civil legal relationships, which were issued through ministers' petitions, could also be seen as a source of civil law. In the chapter of "Jin Guan Ling" (Decree on Strategetic Passes) in *Er Nian Lv Ling* (*Second-year Decree*), there were both records of orders issued by the emperors to make laws and the records of petitions for legislation submitted by the common people; there were both complete civil stipulations and civil stipulations attached with criminal laws. In a word, *Er Nian Lv Ling* (*Second-year Decree*) is a valuable document for the analysis of the civil laws of the Han Dynasty.

It is inevitable that with the development of civil legal relationship, corresponding laws should be made to provide standards and protection. The civil law of Western Han Dynasty were scattered in different decrees. For example, *Hu Lv* (*Statutes on Households*) was made to define the household registration and identity; *Jin Bu Lv* (*Statutes on Currency and Property*) was made to regulate market and currency and *Bang Zhang Lv* (*Law of Rites*) was made to regulate many of the civil legal relationships. Through the adjustment of specific property and personal relationships, these scattered laws had helped to maintain the feudal economic system and the stability of social order, to clarify the relationship of rights and obligations between the two parties in civil legal relationship, so it had played an important role in regulating social order.

5.5.1 Identity and Civil Rights

The people in different classes had different legal status in Han Dynasty, so the rights and obligations in civil legal relationships for different classes were also different.

The vassals, dukes, princes, feudal bureaucrats, landlords, and wealthy merchants had complete civil rights.

The free peasants were also the subjects of civil rights. However, the peasants who were hired for their labor and tied with the land were often transferred to new landlords when the land ownership was transferred. Because they had suffered extra-economic exploitation, they did not have complete personal liberty, consequently their civil rights were limited and incomplete. Similarly, under the complete control of the government, the peasant who worked on the state-owned land did not have complete personal liberty nor complete civil rights.

As the subjects in commodity circulation, merchants did have civil competence; however, because of the policy of "Zhong Nong Yi Shang" (encouraging agriculture and restraining commerce), it was stipulated by Emperor Gaozu that the merchant must not wear silk clothes or ride horses, nor were their offspring allowed to take public office or possess land. Emperor Hui even issued orders to impose double tax on merchants. Thus, it can be seen that the civil rights of merchants were also limited.

Although "Zhui Xu" (a son-in-law who lives in the home of his parents-in-law) and women had personal liberty, their civil rights were limited in many ways. Even worse, a great number of state-owned and private slaves who were treated as flocks, herds, land and houses and who could be given away as presents or be traded, did not have any rights, as was recorded in "Dong Zhong Shu Zhuan" (The Biography of Dong Zhongshu) in *Han Shu* (*The History of Han Dynasty*) that "(the landlords and bureaucrats) have numerous slaves, many flocks and herds, a lot of land and houses and a great amount of property." Because there were a large number of official and private slaves, they became a great working class. In Western and Eastern Han Dynasties, many imperial edicts had been issued to set them free, so that they were given the same civil rights as common people.

As for civil competence, no clear definition and specific stipulation were given in the laws of the Han Dynasty. Normally it was subjected to the age when a person was able to serve corvée, which was so-called "Ding Nian." In the early years of Han Dynasty, males "at the age of twenty-three shall be registered at 'Chou Guan' (a special official position)." According to the explanatory note of Yan Shigu, the above sentence meant, "getting registered in the registration book so that they can serve corvée."[283] In the 2nd year of Emperor Jing (155 B.C.), the age was changed to twenty.[284] When a male was registered, he was considered as having civil competence. The age when a male was to be enlisted for labor service was normally from twenty to fifty-six, except for the time when it was changed to twenty-three during the reign of Emperor Wu. Those under twenty and over fifteen should pay "Suan Fu" (capitation tax), though they did not need to serve labor service. Those under fifteen and over seven also needed to pay "Kou Qian" (child poll tax).

In Han Dynasty, the government would loan state-owned seeds and grain to people in the famine years or rent state-owned land to peasants who owned no land or owned little land, which had not only promoted the appearance of debtor-creditor relationship, but also made government a special subject of civil legal relationship. As the basic unit to pay tax, the common people were also the subjects of the rights.

---

[283]"Gao Di Ji" (The Record of the First Emperor of Han Dynasty) in *Han Shu* (*The History of Han Dynasty*) (Book 1).
[284]"Jing Di Ji" (The Record of Emperor Jing) in *Han Shu* (*The History of Han Dynasty*).

5.5 The Development of Civil Legal Relationship and Civil Legislation 345

Most of the objects of civil rights were land, houses, flocks, herds, slaves, other handicraft products, and the agricultural products that were allowed to be traded in the market.

5.5.2 The Ownership and Legal Protection

The essence of ownership is land property. In Han Dynasty, the mountains, forests, rivers, gardens, ponds, uncultivated land and the arable land were called "Guan Tian" (state-owned land) or "Gong Tian" (public land), which the government had the right to manage, to make profit and to dispose. The government could also obtain the land freely through the system of "Tun Tian" (wasteland opened up by garrison troops or peasants).

The land owned by the Emperor, the nobilities, the bureaucrats, landlords, wealthy merchants, and free peasants was called "Si Tian" (private land). Emperor Cheng "had his own land in the country."[285] As early as the 5th year of Gaozu (202 B.C.), it was stipulated in the imperial edict that for one rank of promotion, the officials above "Da Fu" (senior officials in ancient China) "would be granted land and houses first," by which the bureaucrats were turned into landlords.[286] Emperor Ai did declare that no one should occupy over thirty *qing* of land; otherwise, "they shall be punished in accordance with law," however he had granted Dong Xian, one of his favorites, 2000 *qing* of land.[287]

Tian Lv (*Statutes on Farming and Forest Protection*), *Tian Ling* (*Decrees on Farmland*) and *Tian Zu Shui Lv* (*Statutes on Land Tax*) which were promulgated in the early years of Han Dynasty focused on the protection of the ownership of state-owned and private land, so the land tax for both state-owned and private land was stipulated. According to "Gou Xu Zhi" (The Records of Irrigation and Water Conservancy) in *Han Shu* (*The History of Han Dynasty*), an order was once issued by Emperor Wu: "Now the rent of the rice land stipulated in 'Zu Qie' at 'Nei Shi' (a name of ancient place) was very high, and it was different from that of the local 'Jun' (shire), so I suggest that it should be reduced." Shigu explained that "'Zu Qie' referred to the agreement of farm rent, and 'Jun' referred to local areas." This edict showed that the government of Han Dynasty had collected rents from peasants by renting land to them, which was called "Jia Min Gong Tian" or "Ci Min Gong Tian." What needs to be pointed out is that most of the peasants rented land from landlords

---

[285]"Wu Xing Zhi" (The Record of Five Elements) in *Han Shu* (*The History of Han Dynasty*) (Book 2).

[286]"Gao Di Ji" (The Record of the First Emperor of Han Dynasty) in *Han Shu* (*The History of Han Dynasty*) (Book 3).

[287]"Ai Di Ji" (The Record of Emperor Ai) in *Han Shu* (*The History of Han Dynasty*).

instead of from the government, namely, "tilling the land of the wealthy and paying them half of the harvest."[288]

To force peasants to pay rents according to law, in July of the 6th year of Shiyuan in the reign of Emperor Zhao (81 B.C.), an imperial order was issued and it was demanded that "peasants should report their rent in accordance with the law." Ru Chun explained that "according to law, the tenant peasants shall report their rent to the government by themselves and those who falsely report or ask other people to report for them shall be imposed with a fine of two *jin* of copper. The harvested grain that has not been reported shall be confiscated by the county magistrates,"[289] while those who refused to pay rent would be punished by law.

Besides, the state-owned land was forbidden to be traded to protect the ownership, and those who secretly sold the state-owned land would be punished by death penalty. Moreover, the sale, bequest, leasing, and inheritance of land must be dealt with according to contracts which were used as the legal documents of the change of ownership. The certificate of land sale discovered in *Han Jian* (*The Bamboo Slips of Han Dynasty*) unearthed in Yuyan and the inscribed stones for selling the hills were two kinds of legal documents at the time. When the property was illegally occupied or damaged by others, the owner could sue to the government to demand the return of the original property or compensation for the damage or penalty of the infringer in serious cases.

The legal approval of free transaction and inheritance of land had caused widespread land annexation. During the reign of Emperor Wu, "the rich had vast area of land with numerous footpaths, while the poor could not find a place to shelter themselves."[290] The ruthless land annexation of the landlords deprived the free peasants of their land, intensified the conflicts between different classes, and did great harm to the consolidation of the basis of the centralized government. Dong Zhongshu, the famous politician who had supported the centralization of the authority at that time put forward the proposal of "restricting the occupation of land to make up the insufficiency."[291] In addition, decrees were frequently issued by the government of Han Dynasty to restrict the occupation and annexation of land, which, however, were rejected by the noble, the rich, and the great landlords, so they could not be carried out. In addition, the nature of the feudal state had also decided that they could not be seriously put into practice. In fact, the Emperors themselves also bought private land. For example, Emperor Cheng had "his own land in the country."[292] Besides the private land, the government also occupied large

---

[288]"Shi Huo Zhi" (The Records of National Finance and Economy) in *Han Shu* (*The History of Han Dynasty*) (Book 1).

[289]"Zhao Di Ji" (The Record of Emperor Zhao) in *Han Shu* (*The History of Han Dynasty*).

[290]"Shi Huo Zhi" (The Records of National Finance and Economy) in *Han Shu* (*The History of Han Dynasty*) (Book 1).

[291]"Shi Huo Zhi" (The Records of National Finance and Economy) in *Han Shu* (*The History of Han Dynasty*) (Book 1).

[292]"Wu Xing Zhi" (The Record of Five Elements) in *Han Shu* (*The History of Han Dynasty*) (Book 2).

areas of land which was forbidden to be traded, so those who secretly sold state-owned land would be executed. The establishment of the system of "Tun Tian" (wasteland opened up by garrison troops or peasants) had enabled the government to occupy land without restrictions. During the reign of Wang Mang, the large-scale land annexation had led to the ruling crisis of the Han Dynasty.

5.5.3 The Legal Adjustment and Protection of Debt

In Han Dynasty, the debt resulting from contract had become a common social phenomenon, which was closely related to the development of commodity economy. The bamboo slips and cultural relics of the Han Dynasty discovered in recent years provided physical evidence for the legal relationship and legal disputes arising from debts. Just as what was annotated on *Zhou Li* (*The Rites of Zhou Dynasty*) by Zheng Xuan: "Contracts are signed in business transaction, so each party keeps half of the contract and both parties should produce their half when a lawsuit is filed." "The judge shall make judgment in accordance with the contract," so sale contract was the most common among the debt of contract.

Sale contract was called "Quan" or "Quan Shu" in Han Dynasty and it was one of the most common forms of contract. "Quan" or "Quan Shu" was the legal document for the establishment of sale relationship, which was used as evidence in case of litigation. As the owners of private land in the Han Dynasty "could trade their land at their own will,"[293] many land contracts made of stone, brick, lead, wood, and jade were found in the tombs of Han Dynasty, in which the time, the parties, the size of land and the boundaries, price, witnesses and articles against violation, etc. were included. For example, it was recorded in the jade contract concerning the land transaction of Mi Ying in Mengwu in the 6th year of Jianchu (81 A.D.) that "at the time of 'Yi You' on the 16th day of the November of the 6th lunar year of Jianchu, Mi and Ying, the sons of Wu Meng, bought the land from Ma Qibo and Zhu Dadi to be used as graveyards, which was 94 *bu* in the south, 68 *bu* in the west, 65 *bu* in the north, 79 *bu* in the east with totally 23 *mu* and 64 *bu*. The east boundary was measured by Chen Tian; the north, west and south, by Zhu Shao. The price was 102,000 *qian*. Zhao Man and He Fei were witnesses, each of them were given wine worth 2,000 *qian*."[294] In the 2nd year of Jianning (169 A.D.), it was recorded in the

---

[293]Xun Yue (Han Dynasty), "Shi Shi" (Current Affairs) in *Shen Jian* (*Learning from the Historical Experience*).

[294]Zhang Chuanxi, *Zhong GuoLi Dai Qi Yue Hui Bian Kao Shi* (*A Textual Research and Interpretation of the Collected Contracts of the Past Dynasties of China*), Peking University Press, 1995, p. 45.

"Qian Quan" (land contract) of buying land by Wang Weiqing that "the license granted by the emperor could be used as contract."[295]

Among the sale contracts, land sale contract was the most common. In *The Land Sale Contract of Yue Nuin Chang Dong Li* from Changdongli discovered in *Han Jian* (*The Bamboo Slips of Han Dynasty*), the seller, the size of the land, the price, the transaction, the responsibilities of the seller, the witnesses and so on were recorded in detail.

Not only in land deal, the contract and witnesses were also required in the sale of cloth robes and trousers. For example, the contract of "Shi Mai" was discovered among *Ju Yan Han Jian* (*Ju Yan Bamboo Slips of Han Dynasty*). According to *Shuo Wen* (*The Origin of Chinese Characters*), "'Shi' means loaning out"; while according to *Guang Ya* (the first encyclopedia in ancient China), "'Shi' means 'She' (on credit)," so it meant getting the goods first and paying afterwards. For example, "in the month of Bingxu of the leap month of the 2nd year of Jianzhao, Dong Zifang, "Ling Shi" (assistant officials to the magistrate) of Jiaqu, bought a fur coat from Zhang Cuiwei, which cost 750. They agreed on full payment before Spring came, with the testimony of Du Junxue."[296] From a large number of bamboo slips unearthed in Juyan, it can be inferred that all personal property could be traded, and after the transaction, contracts should be signed with the witness of intermediary agents.

As slaves were primary objects of trade, there were many contracts regarding slave trade among the sale contracts of the Han Dynasty. In the 598th chapter of *Tai Ping Yu Lan* (*Imperial Readings of the Taiping Era*) and the 20th chapter of *Du Gu Wen Yuan* (*Reading the Ancient Literature*) by Sun Xingyan, a contract of slave trade entitled *Tong Yue* was included, in which the process of slaves trade in Han Dynasty was recorded. For example, it was recorded in the contract that on "the 15th day of the January of the lunar year in the 3rd year of Shenjue, Wang Ziyuan, a man from Zizhong, had bought from Yang Hui, a woman from Anzhi in Chengdu, a slave called Bianliao who used to serve Yang Hui's late husband at the price of 15,000. The slave should follow the master's order without any complaint. . . .or he would be punished by 'Chi' (flogging with light sticks) for one hundred strokes." With the prevalence of slave trade, special slave trading markets were also set up. For example, it was recorded in "Wang Mang Zhuan" (The Biography of Wang Mang) in *Han Shu* (*The History of Han Dynasty*) that in Western Han Dynasty, "slaves were placed at markets, together with cattle and horses, so the life of slaves and civilians was controlled in the hands of local bigwigs and the treacherous and ferocious masters even sold the wives and children of the poor by force in order to make profit."

---

[295]Zhang Chuanxi, *Zhong GuoLi Dai Qi Yue Hui Bian Kao Shi* (*A Textual Research and Interpretation of the Collected Contracts of the Past Dynasties of China*), Peking University Press, 1995, p. 45.
[296]Xie Guihua, et al., *Ju Yan Han Jian Shi Wen He Jiao* (*Proofreading of the Interpretation of the Bamboo Slips of Han Dynasty Unearthed in Juyan*), Cultural Relics Press, 1987.

5.5 The Development of Civil Legal Relationship and Civil Legislation

As for those who jacked up the price to conduct unfair transactions, they would all be punished, so even the royals and high officials would not be exempted. In the 4th year of Taishi during the reign of Emperor Wu (92 B.C.), Ren Dangqian, successor vassal of Liangqi, had sold his horse at the price of 150,000 *qian*, which was 500 more than the normal price, so he was dismissed from office."[297] Although this case reflected the political intention of Emperor Wu to reduce the number of vassal states and to undermine the power of the vassals by carrying out the policy of "Qiang Gan Ruo Zhi" (strengthen the central forces and weaken the local ones), yet it also reflected the requirement for fair trade at the time. Besides, it was especially required to abide by law in the trade with foreigners. For example, anyone buying prohibited materials from beyond the frontier or selling horses and weapons to the foreign countries would be punished. In the 2nd year of Emperor Jing (155 B.C.), Song Jiu, an inherited vassal, was "dismissed from his post for sending messengers to 'Xiong Nu' (an ancient nationality in China) and buying prohibited materials from them."[298]

In Han Dynasty, the transaction of loaning and borrowing were numerous, and "many people have made loans and shared the benefits."[299] Moreover, contracts must be used in transactions, laws were formulated to protect the benefits of creditors, and the overdue debtors should be held liabilities. During the reign of Emperor Wendi, Chen Xin, who had inherited the vassal title of Heyang, was "dismissed from his post for owing debts which was six months overdue."[300]

In Han Dynasty, the nobility, bureaucrats, and merchants were all keen on engaging in loaning activities to obtain higher benefits. It was recorded in the explanatory note of Yan Shigu that "some rich merchants had made loans in their own name for other people so that they could share the interests or receive some goods in return."[301] The interest rate was so high at that time that it became a very important method to make a fortune. For example, it was recorded in "Huo Zhi Lie Zhuan" (The Collected Biographies of Businessmen) in *Shi Ji* (*The Records of the Grand Historian*) that a man with the family name of Wuyan became extremely rich by earning interests which was as much as ten times within a year. On the other hand, the debtors often fled or engaged in theft because they were unable to pay the due debts, which had caused the instability of society. Under this circumstance, laws were made in the Han Dynasty to restrict the usurious exploitation by setting the interest rate. According to "Shi Huo Zhi" (The Records of National Finance and Economy) in *Han Shu* (*The History of Han Dynasty*), "the law should be abided by

---

[297]"Wu Di Gong Chen Biao" (The Table of Meritorious Statesman in the Reign of Emperor Wu) in *Han Shu* (*The History of Han Dynasty*).

[298]"Gao Di Gong Chen Biao" (The Table of Meritorious Ministers in the Reign of Emperor Gao) in *Han Shu* (*The History of Han Dynasty*).

[299]"Gu Yong Zhuan" (The Biography of Gu Yong) in *Han Shu* (*The History of Han Dynasty*).

[300]"Gao Di Gong Chen Biao" (The Table of Meritorious Ministers in the Reign of Emperor Gao) in *Han Shu* (*The History of Han Dynasty*).

[301]"Gu Yong Zhuan" (The Biography of Gu Yong) in *Han Shu* (*The History of Han Dynasty*).

all creditors and the interest rate should be no more than ten percent except the cost," so those who received interest higher than this rate should be punished in accordance with law. In the 1st year of Yuanding during the reign Emperor Wu (116 B.C.), Liu Yin, the marquis of Pangguang, was dismissed from his post for making monetary loans to get interest which was higher than that which was stipulated in the law without paying tax."[302] In the 2nd year of Emperor Cheng (31 B.C.), Liu Xin, marquis of Lingxiang, was "dismissed from his post due to receiving interest of grain loans higher than that stipulated in the law."[303] Besides, one could be "disentitled or dismissed" for charging interest higher than that of the legal rate. Although to some extent such severe punishments had obvious political motives, it did reflect the fact that usury had seriously endangered the social order. In Han Dynasty, some people even became slaves for failing to pay debts. For example, Liu Xiang's *Xiao Zi Tu* (*A Picture of Dutiful Son*) was quoted in Vol. 411 of *Tai Ping Yu Lan* (*Imperial Readings of the Taiping Era*) and it was described that "a man named Dong Yong was from Qiansheng, and his mother died when he was a child, so he lived with his father. When his father died, he had no money to bury him, so he borrowed 10,000 *qian* from other people and told the creditor that if he had no money to pay the debt, he was willing to become the creditor's slave."

To guarantee the payment of debt, guarantors called "Ren Zhe" and witnesses called "Pang Ren" were usually appointed. The debt guarantee, either secured by goods or man, was used to guarantee the payment of debts, so when the debt was paid off, it should be marked out in the original contract. For example, there was a contract of loaning on the front of No 170 bamboo slip in *The Bamboo Slips of Han Dynasty Unearthed in the River Valley of Shule in Dunhuang*, and there was a note indicating that the debt had been paid off in January of the lunar year on the back.

Besides the contracts mentioned above, there were also lease and employment contracts.

In addition to debts resulting from contracts, there were also debts concerning the compensation for personal and property damages. In "Liang Hong" (The Biography of Liang Hong) in "Yi Min Zhuan" (Biographies of Recluses) in *Latter Han Shu* (*The History of Latter Han Dynasty*), the following story was recorded:

> Later (Liang Hong) had studied in 'Tai Xue' (The Imperial College). Though poor, he had high moral integrity and had read widely, but he refused to put down his thoughts in books. After school, he fed pigs in Shang Lin Yuan. During that time, a fire broke out and spread to the neighbor's house. Liang Hong visited his neighbor and promised he would compensate for the loss with all his pigs. Even so, it did not satisfy his neighbor. Liang Hong said, "I do not have any other property, but I'd like to work for you to make up for your loss." The neighbor agreed, so Liang Hong worked for him day and night.

---

[302]"Wang Zi Hou Biao" (The Table of Princes and Marquises) in *Han Shu* (*The History of Han Dynasty*).
[303]"Wang Zi Hou Biao" (The Table of Princes and Marquises) in *Han Shu* (*The History of Han Dynasty*).

5.5.4 Marriage, Family and Inheritance

After the policy of "rejecting the other schools of thoughts and respecting only Confucianism" was adopted by Emperor Wu, the theory of "San Gang" (three cardinal guides) and "Wu Chang" (five constant virtues, namely, benevolence, righteousness, propriety, knowledge and sincerity) became the basic legal principles of Han Dynasty, which was especially obvious in marriage and family systems. The orders of parents and the help of matchmakers were of primary importance in the marriage relationship. With the development of merchandise economy, the bride price of "Liu Li" (six kinds of etiquette in feudal marriage) was prevalent. Because of the sharp decrease of population in early Han Dynasty, it was encouraged to get married at an early age to increase population. Thus, an imperial order was issued and it was stipulated that "females between fifteen and thirty shall pay tax five times more than that paid by the normal people," which had aroused great resentment among people in the Han Dynasty. It was stated in "Wang Ji Zhuan" (The Biography of Wang Ji) in *Han Shu* (*The History of Han Dynasty*) that "the people get married so young that they have children before really knowing what parents mean, which has not only led to great trouble in moral education, but also high mortality rate." It was stated in "Nei Ze" (The Pattern of the Family) in *Li Ji* (*The Book of Rites*) that "man shall have family at the age of thirty and women at the age of twenty." However, it was not the case in reality. As for the marriage taboo, it was recorded in *Xing Ming* (*Law*) in *Bai Hu Tong* (*The Virtuous Discussions in White Tiger Hall*) that "for ethic reason, the people with the same surnames shall not get married." Besides, the consanguineous marriage or marriages between people of different hierarchy were forbidden and no one should marry the wife of fugitives; otherwise, he shall be punished.

According to the law and rites in the Han Dynasty, the purpose of marriage was to "serve ancestors and give birth to offsprings."[304] Therefore, patriarchy was emphasized, which was demonstrated by the statement that "husband is the heaven of wife"[305]; at the same time, reproduction was also very important, because it was the demand of patriarchal clan system. Therefore, to encourage procreation, an order was issued in the 7th year of Gaozu and it was stipulated that if a child was born, the family could be exempted from two years of corvée. As the purpose of marriage was to produce offspring, those without sons were allowed to have concubines, although monogamy was clearly stipulated in the law of Han Dynasty. For emperors, royalties and bureaucrats, polygamy was practiced. Starting from Emperor Wu, there were fourteen ranks of wives for the emperor under the empress, which was generally called "Hou Gong San Qian" (Harem with 3000 beauties). Zhang Chang, "Cheng Xiang" (the prime minister), "had hundreds of wives."[306] However, the status of

---

[304]"Hun Yi" (The Significance of Marriage) in *Li Ji* (*Book of Rites*).

[305]"Sang Fu" (Mourning Apparel) in *Li Yi Shu Zhu* (*Interpretation of Etiquette and Ceremonials*).

[306]"Zhang Cheng Xiang Lie Zhuan" (The Collected Biographies of Prime Minister Zhang) in *Shi Ji* (*The Record of the Grand Historian*).

concubine was inferior to that of the legal wife and the hierarchies between wife and concubines must be observed in accordance with patriarchal principle and the law. Fu Yan, the marquis of Kongxiang, was "dismissed and imprisoned for violating the hierarchies between wife and concubines."[307]

According to the laws of Han Dynasty, it was allowed for a man to marry into or live with his wife's family, as was described in the saying that "if there are several sons in a poor family, some of them can marry into or live with their wives' family."[308] Being too poor to get a bride or having no rights to succeed their own ancestry, these men were discriminated and unfairly treated in the law. For example, it was stipulated during the reign of Emperor Wen that "businessmen, 'Zhui Xu' (a son-in-law who lives in the home of his parents-in-law) and those who bring false charges against others shall be banned from being officials."[309]

The dissolution of marriage was decided by the husband, which was exemplified in the provision of "Qi Qu" (the seven possible reasons for divorcing one's wife), which included "being unfilial to the parents-in-law," "failing to bear a male offspring," "being lascivious," "being jealous," "having severe illness," "gossiping" and "committing theft." It was explained in "Ben Ming" (Sexagenary Cycle of one's Birth) in *Da Dai Li Ji* (*The Rites of Da Dai*) that "the wife who is not filial to the parents-in-law shall be divorced for her immorality; the wife who does not give birth to sons shall be divorced for giving the family no offspring; the wife who commits adultery shall be divorced for disrupting the kinship relationship; the wife who is jealous shall be divorced for disrupting the harmony of the family; the wife who has severe illness shall be divorced for not being able to attend the sacrificial ceremony; the wife who loves gossiping shall be divorced for sowing the seed of discord among relatives; the wife who steals shall be divorced for unrighteousness." In addition, the reasons for "San Bu Qu" (the three conditions under which women should not be divorced) were also listed: "The circumstance under which there is none alive in her parents' home when her husband wants to divorce her, while when he marries her, they are still alive; the circumstance under which the wife has mourned for three years for her deceased father-in-law and mother-in-law together with her husband; the circumstance under which the husband is poor when he marries her while rich when trying to divorce her."[310] In a word, a husband could divorce his good and virtuous wife under any pretext, but a wife had no rights even to divorce an immoral husband. According to Confucian doctrines, "the wife shall not divorce her husband even though he is very bad, just as the earth never departs from the heaven."[311]

As for the division of marital property, rules were unprecedentedly made in the law of Han Dynasty: according to Zheng Xuan's explanatory note of "Za Ji"

---

[307] "Wai Qi En Ze Hou Biao" (The Table of Maternal Relatives of the Emperor with the Title of Marquis) in *Han Shu* (*The History of Han Dynasty*).
[308] "Jia Yi Zhuan" (The Biography of Jia Yi) in *Han Shu* (*The History of Han Dynasty*).
[309] "Gong Yu Zhuan" (The Biography of Gong Yu) in *Han Shu* (*The History of Han Dynasty*).
[310] "Ben Ming" (The Sexagenary Cycle of one's Birth) in *Da Dai Li Ji* (*The Rites of Da Dai*).
[311] "Jia Qu" (Marriage) in *Bai Hu Tong Yi* (*The Virtuous Discussions in White Tiger Hall*).

5.5 The Development of Civil Legal Relationship and Civil Legislation

(Manuscript of Miscellaneous Notes) in *Li Ji* (*The Book of Rites*), if the husband wanted a divorce, the wife could take away the property that they had when they were newly married.

The marriage relationship featured by the ideology that women were inferior to men was confirmed by *Han Lv* (*Han Code*), which was also reflected in the provision that if the woman had remarried without permission or had remarried before the burial of her deceased husband, she would be punished by "Qi Shi" (exposing the executed body publicly at markets); nevertheless, if the husband had committed adultery, he would only be sentenced to imprisonment, while the adulteress would be put to death.

Regarding inheritance, under the influence of patriarchal clan system, the most important was the inheritance of ancestral titles, and next came the inheritance of property, whether for the Emperor, royalty, bureaucracy or common people. Therefore, the most important thing in inheritance was to determine the heir, which was called "Zhi Hou" or "Dai Fu Hou." The right of succession was passed on to "Di Zhang Zi" (the eldest son born of the legal wife), whether it was the throne or the title of nobility, as was illustrated in the saying that "it is the covenant of the Han Dynasty to hand down the right of succession from father to son."[312] It was recorded in "Xiao Wen Ben Ji" (The Biographic Sketches of Xiao Wen) in *Shi Ji* (*The Records of the Grand Historian*) that "the heir shall be male, which has had a long history.... Sons and grandsons are the heirs, so that the family will last for generations without extinction. This is the great justice of the country." When Emperor Jing intended to pass the throne to his brother, Prince Liang Xiao, the minister Dou Ying admonished that "it is the tradition of the Han Dynasty to pass the throne down to son or grandson. Today why shall you pass the throne down to your brother, it will violate the tradition of our ancestor?" Another minister Yuan Ang said, "In Han Dynasty, the tradition of the Zhou Dynasty was followed. So it was the son but not the brother who should inherit the throne according to the rule of Zhou Dynasty."[313]

In addition, the order of inheritance and the restrictions for families without male heirs were stipulated in "Zhi Hou Lv" (Statutes on Young Successor Placement) in *Er Nian Lv Ling* (*Second-year Decree*). The main contents are as follows:

> If a person dies without a son, his parents should get the inheritance; if they have predeceased, his widowed wife should get the inheritance; if she has predeceased, his daughters should get the inheritance; if they have predeceased, his grandsons should get the inheritance; if they have predeceased, his great-grandsons should get the inheritance; if they have predeceased, his grandparents should get the inheritance; if they have predeceased, the sons of his brothers' should get the inheritance by law, but they must have lived together. The son of the divorced wife should not compete with the son of the second legal wife in the matter of inheritance.[314]

---

[312]"Dou Ying Zhuan" (The Biography of Dou Ying) in *Han Shu* (*The History of Han Dynasty*).

[313]"Liang Xiao Wang Shi Jia" (The Saga of King Xiao of Liang) in *Shi Ji* (*The Record of the Grand Historian*).

[314]"Zhi Hou Lv" (Statutes on Young Successor Placement) in *Er Nian Lv Ling* (*The Decree Issued in the Second Year*), pp. 279-380.

The lineal primogeniture system of "Di Zhang Zi" (the eldest son born of the legal wife) was particularly important in the succession of the titles of nobility, and in Han Dynasty, the crime of "Fei Zheng" (non-direct line of descent) and "Fei Zi" (non-biological son) was especially established. If the heir inheriting the title of nobility was not from the direct line of descent, he had committed the crime of "Fei Zheng," so he would be degraded to common people according to the law. During the reign of Emperor Ping, "Ding Man, the inherited marquis of Ping Zhou was dismissed for 'Fei Zheng'."[315] If the heir inheriting the title of nobility was not the natural son, he would be convicted of the crime of "Fei Zi." During the reign of Emperor Xuan, after the death of Zhao Qin, the marquis of Yingping, had adopted Zhao Chen, the son of Wang Junxia in Chang'An to succeed to the title, but he was reported and "punished for the crime of 'Fei Zi' with his fiefdom confiscated."[316] The lineal primogeniture system of "Di Zhang Zi" (the eldest son born of the legal wife) was stressed in the succession of the title of nobility, because the rulers wanted to keep the prerogatives of ruling in the same family lineage from generation to generation and to avoid the loss of hereditary power. However, "if the heir is found guilty, he shall not inherit the titles."[317] Therefore, the purpose of forbidding someone else from other families to inherit the title was to ensure the purity of the patriarchal blood and to avoid the patriarchal clan being contaminated.

As for the inheritance of property, all sons had the equal rights of inheritance. For example, a man named Lu Jia had 1000 *jin* of gold, which he distributed to his five sons, with 200 for each "of them to make a living."[318] This was a typical example of the legal property inheritance in the Han Dynasty.

There had appeared testamentary inheritance in the Han Dynasty, which was called "Xian Ling." According to the explanatory note of Shigu, "'Xian Ling' means testament."[319] The bamboo slips entitled *Xian Ling Quan Shu* (*The Book Voucher of Testamentary Inheritance*) unearthed in No. 101 tomb of the Han Dynasty in Yuzhengxupu, in Yang Zhou, Jiangsu province was the earliest known evidence of testamentary inheritance:

> At the time of Renchen of Xinchou on the 29th day of September of the 5th year of Yuanshi, Zhu Ling from Gaoduli, who lived in Xin'anli, made his will in the form of 'Xian Ling' before death in the presence of 'San Lao' (local officials in charge of education) from 'Xian' (county) and 'Xiang' (townships), You Zhi from Duxiang, Zuo Li and Tian Tan, etc.

---

[315]"Wai Qi En Ze Hou Biao" (The Table of Maternal Relatives of the Emperor with the Title of Marquis) in *Han Shu* (*The History of Han Dynasty*).

[316]"Zhao Chong Guo Zhuan" (The Biography of Zhao Chongguo) in *Han Shu* (*The History of Han Dynasty*).

[317]"Gao Hui Gao Hou Wen Gong Chen Biao" (The Table of Meritorious Ministers during the Reign of Emperor Gao, Emperor Hui, Queen Gao and Emperor Wen) in *Han Shu* (*The History of Han Dynasty*).

[318]"Lu Jia Zhuan" (The Biography of Lu Jia) in *Han Shu* (*The History of Han Dynasty*).

[319]"Jing Shi San Wang Zhuan" (The Biographies of Emperor Jing's Thirteen Sons) in *Han Shu* (*The History of Han Dynasty*).

Ling said by himself that his six children were begotten by three different fathers and that he wanted them to know their biological fathers. The names of the six brothers and sisters were Yi Jun, Zi Zhen, Zi Fang, Xian Jun, whose father was Zhu Sun; his brother Gong Wen, whose father was Wu Shuai Jin; and Ruo Jun, whose father was Quabingchangbin. Their mother said that Gong Wen left home at the age of fifteen, with his own surname changed, and never returned home or brought back a penny. So their mother gave the estate to Zi Zhen and Zi Fang separately. But Xian Jun and Ruo Jun were poor and had no properties. On the 10th day of April, the mother gave Xian Jun a paddy field and two mulberry fields and Ruo Jun a hillside plot. The term ended in December of the year. Gong Wen was sentenced to the punishment of 'Tu' (imprisonment) for harming other people and he was poor when he came back. So on the 11th day of December, Xian Jun and Ruo Jun returned the land to the mother, who gave them to Gong Wen. There were two paddy fields and two mulberry fields, with clear borders, and Gong Wen shall not sell or give the land to other people. The witnesses include Tan, who belongs to the same 'Li' (a basic resident organization consisting of five neighborhoods) and 'Wu' (a grassroot unit of five families), and some relatives, namely, Kong Ju, Tian Wen and Man Zhen. This will is clearly made and shall be followed.[320]

In conclusion, the theory about marriage and family in Han Dynasty was already systematic. As family was the foundation of the feudal social structure, the relationship between husband and wife and between parents and children were defined as that of legal subordination in Han Dynasty to maintain the dominance of father or husband in a family. In the two thousand years of feudal society, the patriarchal system was always stable and it had acted as an important pillar of the autocratic political system, because it was protected by law.

5.6 The Economic Laws of "Zhong Nong Yi Shang" (Encouraging Agriculture and Restraining Commerce)

The complicated economic relationship and the despotic economic policy had contributed to the development of economic laws in the Han Dynasty, which was mostly reflected in *Jiu Zhang Lv* (*The Code in Nine Chapters*), *Bang Zhang Lv* (*Law of Rites*) and other separate editions of laws and decrees like *Tian Lv* (*Statutes on Farming and Forest Protection*), which was about farmland management and farm tax; *Jiu Lv* (*Statutes on Livestock Breeding*), which was about animal husbandry; *Xing Lv* (*Statutes on Corvée and Garrisoning the Frontier*) and *Yao Lv* (*Statutes on Corvée and Tax*) and *Jun Shu Lv* (*Statutes on Goods Supply*), which were about civil engineering and corvée; *Jin Bu Lv* (*Statutes on Currency and Property*), *Jin Bu Ling* (*Decree on Treasury*) and *Qian Lv* (*Statutes on Currency*), which were about financial management. In addition, the laws about the monopoly of salt and iron and the banning of forging money were also made.

---

[320]Yangzhou Museum, "Jiang Shu Yi Zheng Xu Pu Yi Bai Ling Yi Hao Xi Han Mu" (No. 101 Tomb of the Western Han Dynasty Unearthed in Xupu, Yizheng, Jiangsu), *Cultural Relics*, No. 1, 1987.

To prohibit land annexation, laws were issued by Emperor Wu in Han Dynasty to restrict landlords from annexing land, so it was announced that "the vassals who own land in other counties shall be imposed with a fine of two *liang* of gold."[321] Meanwhile, merchants were prevented from owning land, so "in order to protect agriculture, the merchants registered in the city and their families are not allowed to own land; otherwise, their agricultural products would be confiscated."[322] Another edict was issued by Emperor Ai to ban land annexation, and it was regulated that "the vassals can only own land in their own states and the standard of owning land for vassals and princesses who live in the capital is the same as that for county officials; the amount of land owned by "Guan Nei Hou" (title of nobility, ranked 19th among the twenty ranks of the titles of nobility), "Li" (official) and the common people should not exceed thirty *qing*."[323] During the reign of Wang Mang, to solve the conflicts caused by land annexation, it was ordered that "all the land belongs to the Emperor… so it is forbidden to be traded."[324] However, Wang Mang's reform was against the trend of history, so it only accelerated the downfall of his rule.

To ensure the implementation of the basic national policy of "Zhong Nong" (encouraging agriculture), Emperor Jing stated in one of the edicts: "I have cultivated farmland and planted mulberry trees myself so that I have grain and silk to worship my ancestors, which is unprecedented for an emperor."[325] The policy of "granting official position to those who hand in grains, who are obedient and respectful to their elders and who are working hard at farm work," which was made in early Han Dynasty was aimed to encourage agriculture. In addition to *Tian Lv* (*Statutes on Farming and Forest Protection*), the temporary orders concerning agriculture were collected and compiled into *Tian Ling* (*Decrees on Farmland*). To build irrigation works to make best use of water resources, *Shui Ling* (*Decrees on Irrigation*) was specially made, and farmland irrigation management was taken as most important criteria for the evaluation of officials' performance. The punishments on lazy peasants and especially those who did not participate in farm work were documented in *Zou Yan Shu* (*Collections of Legal Precedents*).

Because cattle were the main productive force of agriculture, they were strictly protected by the law of Han Dynasty. Thus, indiscriminate killing and private killing of cattle were forbidden and stealing farm cattle would be severely punished. It was recorded in *Dao Lv* (*Statutes on Theft*) that "those who steal horses shall be sentenced to death, while those who steal cattle shall be severely punished."[326]

---

[321]"Ai Di Ji" (The Record of Emperor Ai) in *Han Shu* (*The History of Han Dynasty*), annotated by Ru Chun.
[322]"Shi Huo Zhi" (The Records of National Finance and Economy) in *Han Shu* (*The History of Han Dynasty*).
[323]"Ai Di Ji" (The Record of Emperor Ai) in *Han Shu* (*The History of Han Dynasty*) (Book 2).
[324]"Wang Mang Zhuan" (The Biography of Wang Mang) in *Han Shu* (*The History of Han Dynasty*).
[325]"Jing Di Ji" (The Record of Emperor Jing) in *Han Shu* (*The History of Han Dynasty*).
[326]*Yan Tie Lun* (*Debates on Salt and Iron*).

5.6 The Economic Laws of "Zhong Nong Yi Shang" (Encouraging Agriculture...

Besides, selling cattle to foreign countries was banned *Jin Guan Ling* (*Decree on Strategic Passes*) and the offenders would be punished by law.

In Han Dynasty, salt and iron were owned by the state to strengthen the nation's economy. The production of salt and iron were primary manufacturing industries in Han Dynasty, but in early Han Dynasty they were controlled by rich people who "were wealthy but do not donate a penny to the nation",[327] which could not be tolerated by Emperor Wu, because "his successive wars with foreign countries" "had led to serious deficit in the counties."[328] Therefore, he carried out the policy of the state-ownership of salt and iron business management, seized its right from despotic landlords, big businessmen, and rich people, and prohibited people's private production of salt and iron. Therefore, anyone who had violated the law would have "their left feet cut off and their equipment confiscated."[329] Since then, it became an established system for the stated-ownership of the salt and iron business. Indeed, it had strengthened the material basis of centralization system to transfer the rights of running the business of salt and iron from the rich merchants to the ruling class.

Considering that the low efficiency of stated-owned salt and iron business was not only adverse to taxation but also a waste of labor, in the 2nd year of Zhanghe (88 A. D.) in the Eastern Han Dynasty, it was ordered by Emperor He to "lift the ban on the private production of salt and iron to allow people to run the business and pay tax to the county as usual."[330] Since then, the policy was changed again to private-owned business of salt and iron, but actually, the state-ownership of salt and iron businesses was the primary policy of most of the feudal dynasties.

In addition to the state-owned handicraft industry, the private handicraft business such as silkworm breeding, textile, architecture, bamboo, and wood utensils were also regulated by law.

The special laws about handicraft made in the Qin Dynasty were adopted in Han Dynasty, such as *Gong Lv* (*Statutes on Handicraft Industry*), *Gong Ren Cheng Lv* (*Statutes on Public-owned Handicraft Production*), *Jun Gong Lv* (*Statutes on Controlling Handicraftsmen*), and *Xiao Lv* (*Statutes on the Inspection of the Supplies and Property of State Offices*).

In early Han Dynasty, in the 2nd year of Houyuan (144 B.C.) during the reign of Emperor Jing, "Suan Zi Qian Fa" (the law about property tax) was issued, according to which people who owned 10,000 *qian* must pay 127 *qian* of tax, which meant that the tax rate was about 1.3%. In the 4th year of Yuanshou (119 B.C.), Emperor Wu tried every way to extort wealth from the merchants to make up for the fiscal revenue, so "Suan Min Ling" (the decree on assessing wealth) and "Gao Min

---

[327]"Shi Huo Zhi" (The Records of National Finance and Economy) in *Han Shu* (*The History of Han Dynasty*) (Book 2).

[328]"Shi Huo Zhi" (The Records of National Finance and Economy) in *Han Shu* (*The History of Han Dynasty*) (Book 2).

[329]"Shi Huo Zhi" (The Records of National Finance and Economy) in *Han Shu* (*The History of Han Dynasty*) (Book 2).

[330]"He Di Ji" (The Record of Emperor He) in *Han Shu* (*The History of Han Dynasty*).

Ling" (the decree on reporting wealth) were issued to collect heavy property tax from merchants, and it was ordered that 120 *qian* should be paid for tax for every 2000 *qian* of property; for the goods of handicraftsmen, 120 *qian* should be paid for tax for every 4000 *qian* of profit, so if anyone had failed to report his property or falsely reported his property to the government, they would be convicted of the crime of tax evasion and be sentenced to guarding the border for one year with his property confiscated. Moreover, the informant of the crime would be rewarded with half of the confiscated property, so many merchants who owned middle-sized or bigger businesses were impeached and went broke at that time. However, the government of the Western Han Dynasty had seized the opportunity to "plunder billions of property, thousands of servants, hundreds of *qing* of land and many houses from the people."[331]

In addition, Emperor Wu also adopted Sang Hongyang's proposal and set up the post of "Jun Shun Ping Zhun" in "Jun Guo" (vassal state) to be in charge of the transportation of the tributes from counties and vassal states to the capital as well as some state-owned businesses, which was called "Jun Shu Ping Zhun" at the time. According to Huan Kuan's explanation in "Ben Yi" (Original Meaning) in *Yan Tie Lun* (*Debates on Salt and Iron*), "previously the vassal states paid tributes to emperors by themselves, which had caused many troubles or had even damaged the tributes sometimes. Therefore, officials were appointed to be in charge of the transportation of tributes, which was called 'Jun Shu'. Moreover, the government office (called 'Wei Fu') was set in the capital to store the tributes. The central government adjusted the price of goods by buying goods when the price was below the average and selling goods when the price was above the average to prevent county official from making false reports and to prevent the merchant from making extra profits, which was called 'Ping Zhun'." From this account, it can be inferred that the purpose of implementing "Jun Shu Ping Zhun" was to adjust transportation and price, so that the government could control the market to obtain new sources of wealth. In this way, the government could not only prevent the merchants from speculating and doing harm to the nation, but also maintain necessary economic order. However, the high commercial tax rate and the policy of "Ping Zhun Jun Shu" (the measures to solve the problems of tribute transportation and price management) had deterred the development of commodity economy, so its negative influence was non-negligible in the end, although they were temporarily beneficial for the nation.

Because of the exploration of "Xi Yu" (the Western Regions), the foreign trade in Han Dynasty was far more developed than that in the Qin Dynasty, so laws were accordingly made to regulate the trade transaction. For example, "Chuan" (passport) was required for passing the customs, and it was recorded in "Wen Di Ji" (The Records of Emperor Wen) in *Han Shu* (*The History of Han Dynasty*) (interpreted by Ru Chun) that "only with the passport (called 'Chuan') issued by the government

---

[331]"Shi Huo Zhi" (The Records of National Finance and Economy) in *Han Shu* (*The History of Han Dynasty*) (Book 2).

5.6 The Economic Laws of "Zhong Nong Yi Shang" (Encouraging Agriculture...

could one pass the customs. 'Chuan' was divided into two parts, one for exit, and one for entrance. So only when two of them matched each other could the holder pass the customs"; otherwise, they would be accused of "transgression" and be sentenced to death. At the same time, the government also prohibited the export of horses and weapons and the import of "banned goods," so all these regulations were made to control foreign trade and protect the security of the nation.

At the beginning of Han Dynasty, the currency system was in disorder, because the central government had allowed the nobles, officials and landlords to mint money, which had led to the serious result that "the wealth of king Bi of Wu state had surpassed that of the emperor by minting money by himself, which had led to his ultimate betrayal."[332] Thus, Emperor Jing had banned the private minting of money by taking back the rights of minting money. To strengthen the government's control of finance, "Wu Zhu Qian" (Wu Zhu Coin) was issued by Emperor Wu as the standard of nationwide currency circulation to prohibit "Jun Guo" (vassal state) from minting money randomly and the old currency of the vassal states were thus destroyed. Besides, anyone who minted money secretly would be "sentenced to death,"[333] consequently, thousands of people were killed. No doubt, the currency system reform had stabilized the nation's finance, undermined the power of separatists, and strengthened the central government.

Because of grim economic situation after the peasant uprising, in Han Dynasty the policy of "land taxation reduction," namely, the policy of collecting one for every fifteen copper money was carried out.[334] Emperor Wen had once ordered, "to reduce half of the land tax"[335] because of natural disaster; while Emperor Jing reduced the tax to one for every thirty copper money, which became the established standard ever since. Meanwhile, it was required that the peasants should honestly report the amount of land and tax to government, which was called "Zhan Zu Lv" (the rate of rent). In addition, it was stipulated that "the people who made false report of the amount of land and tax to the government would be imposed with a fine of two *jin* of copper with their property confiscated."[336]

Besides the land taxation, the people from seven to fourteen years old needed to hand in twenty *qian* as "Kou Fu" (poll tax). Emperor Wu added three more *qian* to compensate for the military cost of battle horses.[337] During the reign of Emperor

---

[332]"Shi Huo Zhi" (The Records of National Finance and Economy) in *Han Shu* (*The History of Han Dynasty*) (Book 2).

[333]"Shi Huo Zhi" (The Records of National Finance and Economy) in *Han Shu* (*The History of Han Dynasty*) (Book 2).

[334]"Shi Huo Zhi" (The Records of National Finance and Economy) in *Han Shu* (*The History of Han Dynasty*) (Book 2).

[335]"Shi Huo Zhi" (The Records of National Finance and Economy) in *Han Shu* (*The History of Han Dynasty*) (Book 2).

[336]"Zhao Di Ji" (The Record of Emperor Zhao) in *Han Shu* (*The History of Han Dynasty*), annotated by Ru Chun.

[337]"Zhao Di Ji" (The Record of Emperor Zhao) in *Han Shu* (*The History of Han Dynasty*), annotated by Ru Chun.

Zhao, because of "the poverty of people," "the officials pleaded for tax reduction, which was approved by the Emperor."[338]

It was called "Suan Fu" to collect tax from the adults of various status. In August of the 4th year of Gaozu (203 B.C.), "'Suan Fu' was begun to be collected."[339] In general, the adults aging from fifteen to fifty-six years old were collected one hundred and twenty *qian*"[340]; but merchants and maid-servants were doubly collected, namely, two hundred and forty *qian* was collected, to restrict people from doing business and keeping maid-servants. To encourage population growth, the single females aging from fifteen to thirty years old were divided into five levels, and an extra of one hundred and twenty *qian* would be collected for each level. It was regulated by Emperor Wu that if people was over eighty years old, they did not need to pay tax for two years.

Moreover, every family needed to hand in two hundred *qian* as "Hu Shui" (the household taxation) every year. For male, from the time he grew into adulthood to the time when he was fifty-six years old, he needed to serve corvée or hand in money instead, which was called "Geng Fu."

From the taxation system in Western Han Dynasty, it can be seen that the poll tax is higher than the land tax, which had surely aggravated the burden of peasants.

5.7 The Judicial System Under the Influence of Confucianism

Although the judicial system in Han Dynasty was based on that of the Qin Dynasty, prominent achievements had also been made in the aspect, with both central and local judicial system established. Moreover, measures were taken to regulate the system of procedural law and there began to appear typical cases of civil lawsuits. Especially, under the influence of Confucianism, "Chun Qiu Jue Yu" (Settling Lawsuits by Chun Qiu or Confucianism Classics) had become the main feature of the time, which not only reflected the characteristics of ancient Chinese legal culture, but also exerted profound influence.

---

[338]"Zhao Di Ji" (The Record of Emperor Zhao) in *Han Shu* (*The History of Han Dynasty*), annotated by Ru Chun.
[339]"Zhao Di Ji" (The Record of Emperor Zhao) in *Han Shu* (*The History of Han Dynasty*), annotated by Ru Chun.
[340]"Zhao Di Ji" (The Record of Emperor Zhao) in *Han Shu* (*The History of Han Dynasty*), annotated by Ru Chun.

5.7 The Judicial System Under the Influence of Confucianism 361

5.7.1 The Judicial System

In Western Han Dynasty, "Ting Wei" (the supreme official in charge of judicature) (Emperor Jing and Ai changed the official title into "Da Li") was the highest judicial official, who was in charge of handling the "cases ordered to be settled by Emperor" as well as "the wrong or doubtful cases." Below "Ting Wei" (the supreme official in charge of judicature), the subordinate officials such as "Zuo You Zheng" (the chief and deputy prime minister), 'Zuo You Jian" (the chief and deputy officials in charge of supervision), "Zuo you Ping" (the chief and deputy officials in charge of judicial work) and so on were appointed, who were in charge of specific judicial work. When hearing important cases, "Cheng Xiang" (the prime minister), "Yu Shi Da Fu" (Grand Censor) also participated in the trial process, which were called "Za Zhi" (joint trial). During Emperor Cheng's time, "San Gong Cao" (the office of the three councilors) was set up in "Shang Shu Tai" (Imperial Secretariat) to be in charge of lawsuit settlement,"[341] meanwhile, it also was granted certain judicial power.

Similar to the judicial system of Qin Dynasty, the Emperor of Han Dynasty also had the highest judicial power. In the 7th year of Gaozu (200 B.C.), the Emperor told "Yu Shi" (Censor) that "from now on, if the case cannot be handled by the county officials, it should be reported to higher-level officials to be handled; if it cannot be handled by the higher-level officials, it should be reported to 'Ting Wei' (the supreme official in charge of judicature) to be handled; if it still cannot be handled by 'Ting Wei' (the supreme official in charge of judicature), it should be reported to the Emperor who should made final judgments according to relevant laws and judicial precedents."[342] For those officials who had committed crimes, they should be tried only with the permission of Emperor. In the recently discovered *Zou Yan Shu (Collections of Legal Precedents)*, there recorded many cases needed to be reported to Emperor. In Eastern Han Dynasty, the category of cases that needed to be reported to the Emperor increased. In the 3rd year of Jianwu (27.A.D.), it was stated by Emperor Guangwu that "the scope of the cases which are needed to be reported is extended: from the officials whose income is less than 600 *dan* to the officials of 'Mo Shou Chang Xiang' (lower-level official), if they have committed crimes, their cases should be reported to the emperor,"[343] but if the judicial officials failed to report the cases to the Emperor, they would be punished for their crimes. For example, Qiao Xuan once was sentenced to "Cheng Dan" (the punishment of men building cities) because of his failure to make reports. Another example, "Zhong Lang" (department director) named Zhang You had killed the criminal without the permission of the emperor, so he was sent to prison and was tried and sentenced to death by "Ting

---

[341]"Bai Guan Zhi" (The Record of the Officials of all Ranks) in *Han Shu (The History of Han Dynasty)*.
[342]"Xing Fa Zhi" (The Record of the Criminal Law) in *Han Shu (The History of Han Dynasty)*.
[343]"Guang Wu Di" (Emperor Guangwu) in *Latter Han Shu (The History of Latter Han Dynasty)*.

Wei" (the supreme official in charge of judicature).[344] Sometimes, the Emperor also tried the cases by himself. For example, Emperor Xuan "had often heard the cases in court."[345] In the Eastern Han Dynasty, Emperor Guangwu often "went to court to hear cases and he also handled the difficult cases by himself."[346]

In local counties, the judicial and administrative systems were closely integrated, so the judicial power was controlled by "Shou Ling" (prefects or magistrates) of "Jun" (shire) and "Xian" (county). In "Jun" (shire), a special judicial position of "Jue Cao Yuan" (a judiciary official position) was established to be in charge of judicial work. In Han Dynasty, the judicial power of local officials were so great that they could settle all the ordinary cases by themselves, moreover, they even had the power to sentence criminals to death penalty. According to *Gai Yu Cong Kao* (*Investigation Made by Gai Yu*), "in Han Dynasty, all 'Shou Ling' (prefects or magistrates) of 'Jun' (shire) and 'Xian' (county) had the power to sentence criminals to death." When Wang Wenshu was "Tai Shou" (governor of a prefecture) in Henan, he "arrested the powerful landlords, so thousands of families were punished by 'Lian Zuo' (being punished for being related to somebody who committed an offense)."[347] As to serious and doubtful cases, they should be sent to "Ting Wei" (the supreme official in charge of judicature), "Cheng Xiang" (the prime minister), or other administrative officials to be discussed so that the Emperor could make the final decision. In "Jing Shi" (the capital city), the cases were jointly heard by "San Fu" ("Jing Zhao," "You Fu Feng," "Zuo Feng Yi") (all official titles who in charge of the three places near the capital) without necessarily being sent to "Ting Wei" (the supreme official in charge of judicature) for settlement.

In early Han Dynasty, the vassal states also had relevant independent judicial power, which was owned by "Nei Shi" (the official in charge of revenue). Since the time of Emperor Jing, this power was owned by "Cheng Xiang" (the prime minister) of the vassal states. In the reign of Emperor Ling of the Eastern Han Dynasty, "Zhou" (subprefecture) became the most powerful local authority and it was the authority for appeal by "Jun" (shire) and "Xian" (county).

To guarantee the function of judicial authority, the superior judicial authority often sent officials to supervise the work of judicial officials, which was called "Lu Qiu Tu."

---

[344]"Qiao Xuan Zhuan" (The Biography of Qiao Xuan) in *Latter Han Shu* (*The History of Latter Han Dynasty*).
[345]"Nan Xiong Zhuan" (The Biography of Nan Xiong) in *Latter Han Shu* (*The History of Latter Han Dynasty*).
[346]"Xing Fa Zhi" (The Record of the Criminal Law) in *Jin Shu* (*The History of Jin Dynasty*).
[347]"Xing Fa Zhi" (The Record of the Criminal Law) in *Jin Shu* (*The History of Jin Dynasty*).

5.7.2 The Litigation and Jurisdiction

According to *Xin Lv Xu Lue* (*Outline of the Preface to the New Law*) quoted in "Xing Fa Zhi" (The Record of the Criminal Law) in *Jin Shu* (*The History of Jin Dynasty*), special laws were made for litigation and jurisdiction. "As for *Qiu Lv* (*Statutes on Imprisonment*), it consisted of 'Gao He' (prosecution) and 'Chuan Fu' (review of a case)....Besides, the laws on 'Xi Qiu' (prisoners), 'Ju Yu' (trial and judgment) and 'Duan Yu' (Trials and Punishments) were also made."

In Han Dynasty, lawsuits could be filed to the government by the parties involved or by other people, which was called "Gao He" (prosecution), and it is similar to the private prosecution of today. It was stipulated in *Er Nian Lv Ling* (*Second-year Decree*) that if one wanted to prosecute the criminals or to surrender himself to the government, he could do so to the authority in the township government on condition that he was far away from the county government. The officials should carefully listen to the indicter, make records, and submit the records to the county officials; the county officials should also carefully listen to the indicter." The documents recording the indicter's words or the complaint were called "Yuan Shu." Besides, in *Ju Yan Han Jian* (*Ju Yan Bamboo Slips of Han Dynasty*), there were following records: "a man named Fang Changshi had written 'Yuan Shu'"; "the prosecutors objected to 'Yuan Shu', so they wrote the documents themselves according to law," and so on.

Another form of lawsuit referred to the lawsuits filed by the government, mainly the judicial departments ["Jian Cha Yu Shi" (supervisory censor) and "Si Li Xiao Wei" (local censor)], which is similar to the public prosecution of today. Besides, the officials could also charge against each other. During the reign of Emperor Wu, to strengthen the official's responsibility to initiate public prosecution, it was ruled in law by Zhao Tang and Zhao Yu that the official must make reports once they had discovered the crimes; otherwise, they would be punished by the crime of "Gu Zong' (intentional connivance without intervention). According to Shigu's annotation, "if officials did not report the crimes to the government, they had committed the crime of 'Gu Zong" (intentional connivance without intervention), so even the supervisors also were guilty and they should be punished by 'Lian Zuo' (being punished for being related to somebody who committed an offense)."[348] In addition, laws were also formulated by Emperor Wu about awarding officials and common people who reported crimes to the government. For example, in November of the 3rd year of Yuanding (116 B.C.), it was stipulated that "the people who inform against the merchants' tax evasion can be awarded half of the tax." Meng Kang commented that "the people who inform against someone who do not pay land tax could be awarded half of the tax."[349]

---

[348]"Bai Guan Zhi" (The Record of the Officials of all Ranks) in *Han Shu* (*The History of Han Dynasty*).

[349]"Xing Fa Zhi" (The Record of the Criminal Law) in *Han Shu* (*The History of Han Dynasty*).

In general, people must report the crimes to the governments level by level, but if they received unjust verdicts, they could directly report to the Emperor by bypassing the immediate level, which is called "Zhi Que Gao Su." Some people who were wrongly sentenced had spared no effort to travel long distance to visit the Emperor to report the unjust verdicts by "cutting their hair and piercing their skin." However, in the end, they usually could hardly see the Emperor, let alone report their unjust verdicts.[350]

Because of the establishment of the principle of "Qin Qin De Xiang Shou Ni" (a law in Han Dynasty which ruled that crimes committed among the kinsfolks should be concealed and should not be reported to the government), according to law, generally it was forbidden for the junior to inform against their senior relatives or for "Nu Bi" (the slave girls and maidservants) to inform against their master, except for the crime of "Mou Fan" (plotting rebellion or plotting to endanger the country). Besides, the children under ten years old had no rights to make report, neither did the criminals in prison. The criminals who inform against the crime of "Mou Fan" (plotting rebellion or plotting to endanger the country) could be exempted from punishment, but if the report constituted intentional false accusation and wrong accusation, they should take legal liability.

After accepting the complaints of the prosecutor, the government could have the defendants arrested if necessary. As for the felonies like "Mou Fan" (plotting rebellion or plotting to endanger the country), the criminals and "all those involved" would be arrested together, but for the nobilities and officials, the procedure of "You Zui Xian Qing" (if the nobilities have committed crimes, they should not be arrested without permission) should be followed, namely, only with the permission of the Emperor could the nobles be arrested, which was called "Zhao Bu." The arrested generally must wear shackles and chains except the officials, the old, the young, the disabled and the pregnant.

5.7.3 Trial

In Han Dynasty, it was called "Ju Yu" to try the defendants. It was documented in "Lv Xing" (The Penal Code of Lv) in *Shang Shu* (*The Book of Historical Document*) that "in Han Dynasty it was called 'Gou' to try the defendants" and the method of "Wu Ting" (listening to what the defendant says and observing facial emotions, breathing, hearing and eye contacting) was followed at the time. During the trial, what the defendant said, which was called "Ci Fu," was the main basis of making convictions and passing sentences. Therefore, the judge believed that "the defendant could be made to admit his crime by torture,"[351] so the innocent defendants were

---

[350]"Wu Di Ji" (The Record of Emperor Wu) in *Han Shu* (*The History of Han Dynasty*).
[351]"Yu Yu Zhuan" (The Biography of Yu Yu) in *Latter Han Shu* (*The History of Latter Han Dynasty*).

5.7 The Judicial System Under the Influence of Confucianism

often forced to acknowledge the crimes that were not committed by them because of torture.

After obtaining oral confession, the judges tried the defendants again after three days to see whether the oral confession was the same, and the rules for judgment were documented in "Zhang Tang Zhuan" (The Biography of Zhang Tang) in *Han Shu* (*The History of Han Dynasty*).

Besides oral confession, the evidence system of Qin Dynasty, such as documentary evidence, physical evidence, the testimony evidence and so on was also followed in Han Dynasty.

The judges needed to read the judgment to the defendant before making the verdict. If the defendant thought the judgment was unjust, he could appeal for retrial; if the defendant was sentenced to over two years of imprisonment, his family could appeal too. But the appealing for retrial must be made within a designated date, just as Zheng Xuan said in "Chao Shi" (an ancient official position in charge of the ranking of officials in the outer court and justice) in "Qiu Guan" (Ministry of Penalty) in *Zhou Li* (*The Rites of Zhou Dynasty*) that, "appealing for retrial would be rejected after the designated date; if it was over three months, the defendant was prohibited to make the appeal for retrial any longer." Thus, it can be concluded that the period of appealing was three months in the Han Dynasty. Anyway, it was a reflection of prudent punishment in trial procedure at the beginning of Han Dynasty to allow people to appeal for retrial. But the officials who accepted the appeal seldom retried the case immediately, so they always delayed the trial instead, which had often led to the phenomenon that "for a long time the guilty was not punished while the innocent was not released".[352] Because the law was often ignored by the judges, "if he wanted to have the defendant released, he could surely find the reasons; but he could also find the reasons if he wanted to sentence the defendant to death."[353] "Because bribes were often offered by the rich and the laws were ignored by the officials, the guilty were often released while the innocent were sentenced."[354] Because Emperor Wu upheld the guiding principle that "the judges aggravating the punishment of the criminals should be pardoned; while the judges releasing the defendants in a hurry should be punished," the cruel judicial officials like Zhang Tang and Zhao Yu were appointed as "Ting Wei" (the supreme official in charge of judicature) and "Yu Shi Zhong Cheng" (Grand Censor), so laws were randomly applied just for repression. In the end, "the judges who enforced severe punishments were promoted, while those who enforced fair and just punishments were punished," "therefore, defendants were tended to be punished by death penalties by the judicial officials,"[355] which had made the appeal for retrial a mere formality.

---

[352]"Lu Wen Shu Zhuan" (The Biography of Lu Wenshu) in *Han Shu* (*The History of Han Dynasty*).
[353]"Xing Fa Zhi" (The Criminal Law) in *Han Shu* (*The History of Han Dynasty*).
[354]"Xing Fa Zhi" (The Record of the Criminal Law) in *Han Shu* (*The History of Han Dynasty*).
[355]"Lu Meng Shu Zhuan" (The Biography of Lu Meng Shu) in *Han Shu* (*The History of Han Dynasty*).

To supervise the judiciary and to rectify the unjust verdicts, the Emperor, the senior judicial officials, the supervision authorities and the special officials often interrogated the criminals by themselves in prison, which was called "Lu Qiu" and which was started in the reign of Emperor Wu. In the 5th year of Yuanfeng (106 B. C.), it was regulated that "Ci Shi" (a supervisor assigned by the central government to a local area) "shall inspect their jurisdiction and interrogate the criminals by themselves."[356] Juan Buyi, "Ci Shi" (a supervisor assigned by the central government to a local area) of Qingzhou, "would be asked by his mother if he had rectified the wrong cases and how many people had been released every time after inspecting and interrogating criminals."[357] In Eastern Han Dynasty, Xie Yiwu, "Ci Shi" (a supervisor assigned by the central government to a local area) of Jingzhou often rectified the wrong cases through the system of "Lu Qiu" (the inquisition of criminals) and Emperor Guangwu had questioned criminals in person. The system of "Lu Qiu" (the inquisition of criminals) was combined with the supervision system, which had had a positive effect on the improvement of prison management, the correction of wrong cases, the supervision of judicial activities and the uniformity of the application of laws. That was one of the reasons for the system of "Lu Qiu" (the inquisition of criminals) to have lasted for over 1000 years after the Han Dynasty.

In Han Dynasty, it was imperative that the disputed cases be reported to the government level by level. "Xian" (county) could only report the disputed cases to "Jun" (shire); "Jun" (shire) could only report the disputed cases to the central authority called "Ting Wei" (the supreme official in charge of judicature); "Ting Wei" then reported the disputed cases to the Emperor. According to *Er Nian Lv Ling* (*Second-year Decree*), judges "should not make judgments based on anonymous reports, or they would be regarded as misconducting in the trials"; "the officials who ignored the report of 'Qun Dao' (gang robbery) and 'Dao Zei' (theft) or failed to report to the county officials or reported one day later would all be regarded as 'Gu Zong' (intentional connivance without intervention) in making sentences." This legal obligation of judicial officials was obviously a development of the laws of the Qin Dynasty.

After Confucianism became the dominant political ideology, the Confucian ideology influenced both legislation and judiciary in many ways. The most obvious example was *Chun Qiu Jue Yu* (*Settling Lawsuits by Chun Qiu or Confucianism Classics*), which meant that lawsuits should be settled according to the doctrines of *Chun Qiu* (*Spring and Autumn Annals*) rather than legal provisions. In the legal practice of the Han Dynasty, the basis of trial was the legal provisions, however, since the reign of Emperor Wu, Gongsun Hong, Dong Zhongshu, and other officials

---

[356]"Bai Guan Zhi" (The Record of the Officials of all Ranks) in *Latter Han Shu* (*The History of Latter Han Dynasty*).

[357]"Juan Bu Yi Zhuan" (The Biography of Juan Buyi) in *Han Shu* (*The History of Han Dynasty*), Vol. 5.

5.7 The Judicial System Under the Influence of Confucianism

had advocated settling cases according to *Chun Qiu* (*Spring and Autumn Annals*), and so Confucianism was introduced to judiciary.

Chun Qiu (*Spring and Autumn Annals*) was the product of social instability and its goal was to stabilize the feudal order represented by the monarch, the father, the official, the son, the husband and the wife, to rescue the society of "Li Beng Yue Huai" (the disintegration of rites and the collapse of rituals), to maintain the hierarchical system of "Zun Zun" (showing respect to nobility represented by the emperor), "Qin Qin"(showing respect to relatives represented by parents), "Zhang Zhang" (showing respect to the seniors) and "Nan Nv You Bie" (giving different treatments to males and females). As Dong Zhongshu said, "The basic thought of *Chun Qiu* (*Spring and Autumn Annals*) is to comply with Heaven's will and to follow the examples of ancient sages."[358] The main thought of *Chun Qiu* (*Spring and Autumn Annals*) was the so-called Great Unification, which was perfectly in agreement with the political need of Han Dynasty to establish a united centralized feudal state by "Qiang Gan Ruo Zhi" (strengthen the central forces and weaken the local ones), therefore, it became the basis of the interpretation of the law, so was directly adopted in making judgments.

In Confucianism, benevolent politics and feudal ethical codes were advocated, so the monarch was taken as the main object of "Zun Zun" (showing respect to nobility represented by the emperor) and father was taken as the main object of "Qin Qin"(showing respect to relatives represented by parents). Moreover, the respect for the monarch was regarded as loyalty and the love for father was regarded as filial piety, so loyalty was regarded as the basis of the filial piety and filial piety was regarded as the source of loyalty, which were all reflected in *Chun Qiu* (*Spring and Autumn Annals*). Obviously, *Chun Qiu Jue Yu* (*Settling Lawsuits by Chun Qiu or Confucianism Classics*) not only was in accordance with the essential legal spirit, but also expressed the ruler's consciousness of stressing ethical codes, therefore, it was naturally accepted by Emperor Wu.

As legislation always falls behind realistic life, the social relationship formed by "rejecting the other schools of thoughts and respecting only Confucianism" could not be totally legalized within such short time, let alone the establishment of a legal system based on Confucianism. Under such circumstances, *Chun Qiu Jue Yu* (*Settling Lawsuits by Chun Qiuor Confucianism Classics*) not only provided a supplement for the insufficiency of law but also reflected the will of the state. That is why *Chun Qiu Jue Yu* (*Settling Lawsuits by Chun Qiuor Confucianism Classics*) did not retreat from the historical stage until after the totally Confucianized laws of *Tang Lv Shu Yi* (*The Comments on Tang Code*) was made.

Under the influence of *Chun Qiu Jue Yu* (*Settling Lawsuits by Chun Qiuor Confucianism Classics*), a series of judicial principles that had reflected Confucian ethical codes were made.

---

[358]Dong Zhongshu (Han Dynasty), "Chu Zhuang Wang" (King Zhuang of the State of Chu) in *Chun Qiu Fan Lu* (*The Luxuriant Dew of Spring and Autumn Annals*).

"Yuan Xin Ding Zui" (executing convictions according to criminal's motives). Dong Zhongshu said, "When settling lawsuits with *Chun Qiu* (*Spring and Autumn Annals*), one must investigate both the truth and criminal motives. The attempted crimes shall be regarded as accomplished if the criminal motive is evil, so the chief criminal shall be punished severely, but the criminal with venial motives shall be punished leniently."[359] Namely, one should make judgments according to the criminals' motives by following the spirit of *Chun Qiu* (*Spring and Autumn Annals*). In volume 640 of *Tai Ping Yu Lan* (*Imperial Readings of the Taiping Era*), a case was cited from the judgment made by Dong Zhongshu according to *Chun Qiu* (*Spring and Autumn Annals*):

> B, A's father argued and fought with C, so C stabbed B with a knife and A attempted to hit B with a stick but accidently hit B. How to sentence A? Someone said A should be sentenced to death because he hit his father. The official said, 'I think father and son are close relatives, so when A heard about the fighting, he wanted to save his father rather than hit his father. According to *Chun Qiu* (*Spring and Autumn Annals*), Xu Zhi's father was sick and Xu Zhi prepared medicine to him, who died unexpectedly. So Xu Zhi was released in terms of his good motives. A's behavior was not 'hitting his father' as was stated in the law, therefore, he should not be punished.

This case demonstrated that although A caused serious consequences, he was released because of his good motives. Another example could be seen in "Huo Xu Zhuan" (The Biography of Huo Xu) in *Latter Han Shu* (*The History of Latter Han Dynasty*):

> Someone falsely accused Huo Xu's uncle Song Guang to General Liang Shang, saying that he wrote many illegal articles, so Song Guang was put in prison in Luoyang and was tortured severely. Huo Xu was fifteen years old. He wrote to Liang Shang.... Huo Xu learned that according to the spirit of *Chun Qiu* (*Spring and Autumn Annals*) the criminals should be convicted according to their motives, so the guilty with good motives should be released but those with evil motives should be punished. Therefore, Xu Zhi was not guilty though he killed his father. So Zhao Dun's pardoning of criminals was recorded in history book. This is the reason why the law was passed down by Confucius and the laws of preceding dynasties also were also followed in Han Dynasty....There were reasonable motives for Guang's punishment, but although he had waited for many years at the palace gate to file his lawsuits, his case was not accepted by the Emperor any way. ... is this impartiality? Liang Shang spoke highly of Huo Xu's talent and appealed to the Emperor that Song Guang should be forgiven.

"She Shi Zhu Yi" (to infer their intentions to determine culpability without regarding to their actual actions) mentioned above also meant that criminals should be punished according to their motives. Even if people had made great achievements, if their intentions were evil, they should also be punished.

Thus, "Yuan Xin Ding Zui" (executing convictions according to criminal's motives) is reasonable, because it has considered both motives and facts. However, it was wrong to partially investigate the motives, to take motives as the only evidence for making conviction and to take Confucian ethics as the only measurement of

---

[359]Dong Zhongshu (Han Dynasty), "Jing Hua" (Quintessence) in *Chun Qiu Fan Lu* (*The Elite of the Political Philosophy of Chun Qiu*).

motives. Consequently, there appeared the phenomenon of enforcing different punishments for the same crime and drawing far-fetched conclusions, which had made it easier for the officials to make arbitrary judgment and engage in malpractices for selfish ends. Some thinkers commented that "'Yuan Xin Ding Zui' (executing convictions according to criminal's motives) means that the person who has violated the law but who is with good motives should be released, while the person who has not violated the law but who is with evil motives should be punished."[360] So it had violated the basic requirement of making convictions according to law.

"Wei Qin Zhe Hui" (to avoid referring to the shortcomings and the privacy of relatives) and "Wei Zun Zhe Hui" (to avoid referring to the shortcomings and the privacy of the senior). "Wei Qin Zhe Hui" (to avoid referring to the shortcomings and the privacy of relatives) was reflected in "Qin Shu Xiang Rong Yin" (concealment of crimes among relatives, or, refusing to testify among relatives in court) and "Qin Qin De Xiang Shou Ni" (a law in Han Dynasty which ruled that crimes committed among the kinsfolks should be concealed and not reported to the government). As for "Wei Zun Zhe Hui" (to avoid referring to the shortcomings and the privacy the senior), it covered a relatively more extensive scope, including royal family and aristocrats. The following case was recorded in "Liang Xiao Wang Zhuan" (The Biography of the King of Liang State) in *Han Shu* (*The History of Han Dynasty*):

> When the officials investigated the cases, they found that the king of Liang state had done many promiscuous things, so they reported the beastly conducts to the Emperor to require that the king of Liang state should be killed. An official of 'Tai Zhong Da Fu' (vice minister) named Gu Yong stated that '... the rule of 'Wei Qin Zhe Hui' (to avoid referring to the shortcomings and the privacy of relatives) is stipulated in *Chun Qiu* (*Spring and Autumn Annals*),... Now being young, the king of Liang state is arrogant and insane. He is first charged with saying abusive languages and we have investigated the reported crime but have not found any evidence. Now disclosing the privacy of the king of Liang state..., so it is not an act of concealing for the aristocrats'....Therefore, the Emperor put it aside and did not punish him.

The principle of "Wei Qin Zhe Hui" (to avoid referring to the shortcomings and the privacy of relatives) and "Wei Zun Zhe Hui" (to avoid referring to the shortcomings and privacy the senior) which was based on Confucian principle of "Gang Chang" (the Chinese ethical tradition) and "Lun Li" (ethics) had had significant influence on the legal practice. This principle had in turn contributed to the formation of the legal principle of "Jun Qin Wu Jiang, Jiang Er Zu Yan" (No offending of the monarchs and parents, or the offender shall be put to death), which had further legalized the ethics and morality.

Based on his experience of settling cases according to Confucian classics, Dong Zhongshu wrote a book called *Chun Qiu Jue Yu* (*Settling Lawsuits by Chun Qiuor Confucianism Classics*), which was greatly praised by the Emperor and was widely applied in handling cases because it was of guiding significance to judicial trials. Dong Zhongshu retired home because of illness, but every time the Emperor had

---

[360]"Xing De" (The Penal Morality) in *Yan Tie Lun* (*Debates on Salt and Iron*).

troublesome cases, "he would sent Zhang Tang, 'Ting Wei' (the supreme official in charge of judicature) at the time, to Dong Zhongshu's home to consult with him. Dong Zhongshu wrote two hundred and thirty-two articles about how to settle cases according to *Chun Qiu* (*Spring and Autumn Annals*) and had made specific suggestions."[361] His disciple Lv Bushu was also appointed by the Emperor to "try the case of Huai Nan Wang (Vassal of Huainan) and Lv Bushu was allowed to directly handle the case according to *Chun Qiu* (*Spring and Autumn Annals*)."[362] In addition, an official named Er Kuan at the time "was appreciated by Zhang Tang because he had settled cases according to *Chun Qiu* (*Spring and Autumn Annals*)."[363] During the reign of Emperor Zhao, Juan Buyi settled an important case according to *Chun Qiu* (*Spring and Autumn Annals*) and was praised by the emperor: "Confucian classics should be applied by the high-ranking officials to show the general principles."[364]

Chun Qiu Jue Yu (*Settling Lawsuits by Chun Qiuor Confucianism Classics*) included altogether two hundred and thirty-two settled cases. Although the book was lost, its spirit and value could be seen from the sporadically discovered cases scattered in other books.

In conclusion, *Chun Qiu Jue Yu* (*Settling Lawsuits by Chun Qiuor Confucianism Classics*) was a special trial principle made under the specific circumstances of the early Western Han Dynasty. By explaining the profound meaning of Confucian classic works, Dong Zhongshu propagated Confucian legal values, which met the Emperor's need to establish an autocratic and unified country with centralized authority. Meanwhile, it had also decorated the harsh legal practices with a touch of color of "Ren Zheng" (benevolent administration). During this process, the codified Confucian classics and the legalized morality and ethics became the mandatory norm to regulate citizens' activities and provided a new way to absorb "Li" (rites) into "Fa" (law).

As for *Chun Qiu Jue Yu* (*Settling Lawsuits by Chun Qiuor Confucianism Classics*), seen from the perspective of historical development, it had its inevitability. To some extent, it not only restricted the malpractice of the Emperor, but also made some special contribution to the integration of "De Zhi" (the ruling of virtue) and "Fa Zhi" (the ruling of law) and to the realization of applying Confucian classics as the "Ti" (system) and applying "Fa" (law) as the "Yong" (application). Wang Chong said, "It was reasonable that Dong Zhongshu has integrated the spirit of *Chun Qiu* (*Spring and Autumn Annals*) with law. ...those who admire legalists but do not attach importance to *Chun Qiu* (*Spring and Autumn Annals*) are foolish because the

---

[361]"Ying Shao Zhuan" (The Biography of Ying Shao) in *Latter Han Shu* (*The History of Latter Han Dynasty*).

[362]"Wu Xing Zhi" (The Record of Five Elements) in *Han Shu* (*The History of Han Dynasty*) (Book 1).

[363]"Er Kuan Zhuan" (The Biography of Er Kuan) in *Han Shu* (*The History of Han Dynasty*).

[364]"Juan Bu Yi Zhuan" (The Biography of Juan Buyi) in *Han Shu* (*The History of Han Dynasty*).

5.7 The Judicial System Under the Influence of Confucianism

spirit of legalism has been absorbed in *Chun Qiu* (*Spring and Autumn Annals*)."[365] Shen Jiaben also said, "if all the judicial officials during the reign of Emperor Wu could work this way, it would have been unnecessary to write *Ku Li Zhuan* (*The Biographies of Brutal Officials*)."[366] However, the development of "Chun Qiu Jue Yu" (Settling Lawsuits by Chun Qiu or Confucianism Classics), with its arbitrary analogy, had destroyed the certainty of law, weakened the seriousness of the principle of settling cases by law and narrowed the space of legal application. Especially, the cases were frequently unfairly settled because of the different qualities of judges, which had further caused the corruption of judiciary. The modern scholars Zhang Binglin and Liu Shipei criticized the system of "Chun Qiu Jue Yu" (Settling Lawsuits by Chun Qiu or Confucianism Classics). Zhang Binglin said:

> Dong Zhongshu's proposal of 'Chun Qiu Jue Yu' (Settling Lawsuits by Chun Qiu or Confucianism Classics) and the integration of 'De Zhi' (the ruling of virtue) and 'Fa Zhi' (the ruling of law) is against the spirit of Confucianism. Therefore, this is not what a Confucianist should do, so Dong Zhongshu is not the real Confucian. ...Dong Zhongshu has included two hundred and thirty two cases.... The senior officials have made those cases complicated to prevent citizens from understanding them; while in implementation, they have made arbitrary judgments, and torn away the pretense of justice. How pathetic it is! The Confucian classics have become 'Ji Shi" (the spawn of louses: meaning unimportant things) and the law had become 'Bi Bai' (the imperfect grain and rice seedling like weeds: meaning trivial things).[367]

Liu Shipei said that "in his book (referring to *Chun Qiu Jue Shi* (*The Records of Convictions during Spring and Autumn Period*), Dong Zhongshu has interpreted the current law by quoting Gong Yang's theories, and has superficially meant to settle the cases according to Confucian classics; however, this book has in fact made it easier for cruel officials to act at their own will. At that time, Gongsun Hong also ruled by adopting the rules of *Chun Qiu*..., and on the surface, he had adopted the values of Confucianism..., but in fact, the law was much severer than before. ...Only similar words were chosen, and accorded just in form. However, the judge could deal with things at his own will, so it was easier for him to play with literary skills and take the benefits. Moreover, the law was made ambiguous and the cruel officials made judgments according to their own preference by making use of the laws for their own private purposes."[368]

Hou Su Jun Suo Ze Kou En Shi (*The Case of Marquis Su Jun Suing Kou En for Debts*) which was discovered in *Ju Yan Han Jian* (*Ju Yan Bamboo Slips of Han Dynasty*) was a civil lawsuit filed at the beginning of Eastern Han Dynasty, among which there were two pieces of the contract. One piece was about the report of this

---

[365] Wang Chong (Han Dynasty), "Cheng Cai" (The Analysis of Employment System) in *Lun Heng* (*On Balance*).

[366] Shen Jiaben (Qing Dynasty), "Chun Qiu Duan Yu" (Settling Lawsuits in Chun Qiu) in *Han Lv Zhi Yi* (*Collections of Laws in Han Dynasty*), vol. 12.

[367] Zhang Taiyan, "Yuan Fa" (On Law) in *Jian Lun* (*Essential Discussions*).

[368] Liu Shipei (Qing Dynasty), *Ru Jia Fa Xue Fen Qi Lun* (*On the Difference between Confucianism and Legalism*).

case by Gong, "Se Fu" (a minor official in the county) from Duxiang and the other piece was about the settlement of this case which was reported to the senior authority by the magistrate of Juyan county. The bamboo slips provided solid evidence for the real condition of civil lawsuits in Han Dynasty, therefore they were of great historical significance. The content of the case is as follows:

On the 1st day of Yimao of Guichou in December of the 3rd year of the reign of Emperor Jianwu (27 A.D.), Gong, "Se Fu" (a minor official in the county) from Duxiang sent the indictment of the duke of Jiaqu to Kou En (the defendant) and asked Kou En to go back. Before interrogating Kou En, Gong, "Se Fu" (a minor official in the county) from Duxiang announced that if Kou En's confession was not true, Kou En would be charged with "hiding property worth above five hundred"; if Kou En did not change his testimony within three days, he would be convicted of the same crime as that for the plaintiff because of his false testimony." Then Gong, "Se Fu" (a minor official in the county) from Duxiang interrogated Kou En, who confessed that he was sixty-six years old and was from Nanli county, Kunyang city. In mid-December of last year, "Ling Shi" (assistant officials to the magistrate) named Hua Shang in Jiaqu and "Wei Shi" (local official in charge of patrolling) named Zhou Yu should have helped marquis Su Jun (the plaintiff) to transport fish to Hude (the name of a place) for sale. However, Hua Shang and Zhou Yu were not able to transport the fish. Therefore, Hua Shang gave an eight-year-old yellow cow which was worthy of sixty *dan* of cereals and fifteen *dan* of cereals, which was altogether about seventy-five *dan* of cereals, to Su Jun as the salary to employ people to transport fish. Zhou Yu gave a five-year-old black cow which was worthy of sixty *dan* of cereals and forty *dan* of cereals to Su Jun, which was altogether about one hundred *dan* of cereals as the salary of employing people to transport fish. Su Jun employed Kou En to transport five thousand fish to sell at Hude. The employment cost was a cow and twenty-seven *dan* of cereals. In addition, they agreed the price of fish was in total 400,000 *qian*. At that time, Su Jun gave the eight-year-old yellow cattle and twenty-seven *dan* cereals to Kou En as the fee. After two or three days, when Kou En was about to set off, Su Jun told Kou En that "the yellow cattle is thinner and the black cattle is fatter though small, so the value of two cattle was same. You can choose one of them." Therefore, Kou En chose the black cattle and gave up the yellow one, without borrowing cattle from Su Jun. Kou En sold fish at Hude but the total earning was not too much. Therefore, Kou En sold the black cattle and gave 320,000 *qian* to Su Jun's wife named Ye, which was 80,000 *qian* less than the agreed amount. Kou En loaded a big wheel worthy of 10,000 *qian*, a bag made of sheepskin worthy of 3000 *qian*, a container made of bamboo worthy of 1000 *qian*, a container worthy of 600 *qian*, two ropes worthy of 1000 yuan on Ye's carriage. Kou En went back with Ye. Then they went shopping for the third time, Kou En bought two *dan* of cereals for Ye, which was worth 6000 *qian*. When they arrived in the north, Kou En sold ten *jin* of meat for Ye, which was one *dan* and 3000 *sheng*. The total value was 24,600 *qian*, which were all kept at Su Jun's house. Because Kou En owed Su Jun money, he did not get his utensils back. Kou En's son named Qin had been employed to go fishing by Su Jun since the 20th of December of the year before. Until now, it had been three months and ten days. However, Qin did not get

5.7 The Judicial System Under the Influence of Confucianism 373

the payment. The market price of employing adult is two *dou* cereals every day. The salary for an adult man as was stipulated by the government was twenty *dan* of cereals a day. When Kou En gave money to Ye at Hude, the market price was 4000 *qian* for every *dan* of cereals. Therefore, Qin's salary should be 55,400 *qian*. A sum of 80,000 *qian* had been paid to Su Jun. Besides, Kou En should get the rest of Qin's salary, which was six *dan*, one *dou*, and five *sheng* from Su Jun. It took over twenty days for Kou En to drive the carriage to Juyan for Ye at his own cost, but his salary was not paid. The price of the cow was sixty *dan* of cereals when Hua Shang and Zhou Yu gave it to Su Jun who gave it to Kou En at the same price. Therefore, Kou En did not owe a cow to Su Jun, so Kou En need not pay twenty *dan* of cereals to Su Jun. Kou En swore that the statement made above was true.

On the 1st day of Wuchen of Guichou in December of the 3rd year of the reign of Emperor Jianwu (27 A.D.), Gong, "Se Fu" (a minor official in the county) from Duxiang sent the indictment of the duke of Jiaqu to Kou En (the defendant) and asked Kou En to go back. Before interrogating Kou En, "Se Fu" (a minor official in the county) from Duxiang announced that if Kou En's confession was not true, Kou En would be charged with "hiding property worth above five hundred"; if Kou En did not change his testimony within three days, he would be convicted of the same crime as that for the plaintiff because of his false testimony." Then Gong, "Se Fu" (a minor official in the county) from Duxiang interrogated Kou En who confessed that he was sixty-six years old and was from Nanli county, Kunyang city. In mid-December of last year, "Ling Shi" (assistant officials to the magistrate) named Hua Shang in Jiaqu and "Wei Shi" (local official in charge of patrolling) named Zhou Yu should have helped marquis Su Jun (the plaintiff) to transport fish to Hude (the name of a place) for sale. But Hua Shang and Zhou Yu were not able to transport the fish, therefore, Hua Shang gave an eight-year-old yellow cow which was worthy of sixty *dan* of cereals and fifteen *dan* of cereals, which was altogether about seventy-five *dan* of cereals, to Su Jun, as the salary to employ people to transport fish. Zhou Yu gave a five-year-old black cow which was worthy of sixty *dan* of cereals and forty *dan* of cereals to Su Jun, which was altogether about one hundred *dan* of cereals as the salary of employing people to transport fish. Su Jun employed Kou En to transport 5000 fish to sell at Hude. The employment cost was a cow and 27 *dan* of cereals. Further, they agreed the price of fish was in total 400,000 *qian*. At that time, Su Jun gave the 8-year-old yellow cattle and 27 *dan* cereals to Kou En as the fee. After two or three days, when Kou En was about to set off, Su Jun said to Kou En, "The yellow cattle is thinner and the black cattle is fatter though small, so the value of two cattle was same. You can choose one of them." Therefore, Kou En chose the black cattle and gave up the yellow one, without borrowing cattle from Su Jun. Kou En sold fish at Hude but the total earning was not too much. Therefore, Kou En sold the black cattle and gave 320,000 *qian* to Su Jun's wife named Ye, which was 80,000 *qian* less than the agreed amount. Kou En loaded a big wheel worthy of 10,000 *qian*, a bag made of sheepskin worthy of 3000 *qian*, a container made of bamboo worthy of 1000 *qian*, a container worthy of 600 *qian*, two ropes worthy of 1000 *qian* on Ye's carriage. Kou En went back with Ye. When they arrived in the north, Kou En sold ten *jin* (a unit of weight, one *jin* is about 500 g) of meat for Ye, which was one *dan*. Then they went shopping for the third time, Kou En bought two *dan* of wheat for Ye, three *dan* of grain and 15,600 *qian* in total, all kept in Ye's place. When they arrived at Juyan, Kou En wanted to get his wheels and other property back. Su Jun said to Kou En angrily: "You owe me 80,000 *qian*. How can you take away the equipment?" Kou En did not dare to take away the equipment. Kou En's son named Qin had been fishing for Su Jun since the 20th of December if the year before. Until then, it had been three months and ten days. However, Qin did not get the salary. The salary stipulated by the government for an adult man was two *dou*, which was twenty *dan* of cereals for a day. When Kou En gave money to Ye at Hude, the market price was 4000 *qian* for every dan of cereals. The salary Qin should have got from Su Jun could have paid off the debt. Besides, it took over twenty days for Kou En to drive the carriage to Juyan for Ye at his own cost and his wages were not paid. The price of the cattle was sixty *dan* of cereals when Hua Shang and Zhou Yu gave it to Su Jun, who gave the cattle to Kou En at the same price. Therefore, the sentence was made: Kou En did not owe a cow to Su Jun and Kou En need not pay twenty *dan* of cereals to Su Jun. Kou En swore that the statement made above was true.

On the 1st day of Xinmo of Guichou in December of the 3rd year of the reign of Emperor Jianwu (27 A.D.), Gong, "Se Fu" (a minor official in the county) from Duxiang sent the indictment of the duke of Jiaqu and said: "In December last year, I employed Kou En, a migrant to transport 5,000 fish to Hude for sale. The salary of employment was a cow and twenty-seven *dan* of cereals. Kou En agreed the yield was to be estimated 400,000 *qian*, but the actual yield was 320,000 *qian*. Kou En sold the cow, which I had lent him for transportation and returned me the cow which I gave him as the payment of his salary. But there was a difference of twenty *dan* of cereals between the two cows." Gong, "Se Fu" (a minor official in the county) from Du Xiang interrogated Su Jun and Kou En to make judgment. He sent the verdict and records of inquisition to the county court. It was stated that "Kou En's confession was different from Su Jun's indictment, so Su Jun doubted the validity of Kou En's confession and appealed to the court of the prefecture, saying that he was willing to present the records made by Gong, 'Se Fu' (a minor official in the county) from Duxiang. The court of the prefecture demanded Gong, 'Se Fu' (a minor official in the county) to conduct further investigation and make a second verdict." Thus, Gong, "Se Fu" (a minor official in the county) from Duxiang interrogated them again and Kou En confessed: "I needn't return the cow and the twenty *dan* of cereals to Su Jun. The property detained by Su Jun is worth 15,600 *qian* and the cereals and meat I have bought for Su Jun is worth three *dan* of cereals. Su Jun should pay my son, who is named Qin, the salary worth twenty *dan*, which is enough to pay the debt. Su Jun wants to return the detained property to Kou En, but Kou En does not accept them because they have been used by Su Jun and are broken." Kou En's confession was in accordance with the evidence and the fact, so the criminal should be punished by death penalty. Therefore, "Se Fu" (a minor official in the county) sent the record and the decision to Juyan government.

In December of the year of Yimao in the 3rd year of the reign of Emperor Jianwu (27 A.D.), "Shou Cheng" (assistant official) of Juyan county government received

5.7 The Judicial System Under the Influence of Confucianism

the report from the marquis of Jiaqu and made the final judgment. ...about the matter...of Kou En...[369] Kou En's confession was in accordance with the evidence and the fact. The record and the decision was submitted to Juyan government. It was wrong for Su Jun to require Kou En to pay debt, so according to the law, Su Jun should be severely punished, which was approved by the assistant and "Shou Ling" (prefects or magistrates) named Shi.[370]

It can be inferred from the above statement that in Han Dynasty, the civil case was prosecuted by the plaintiff. According to the principle of "the plaintiff accommodated to the defendant," the civil case was heard by the county government where the defendant lived. The county government appointed Gong, "Se Fu" (a minor official in the county) from Duxiang to be in charge of investigation and trial, so he must report the proceedings of the case to the county government in time to get new instructions. The case mentioned above was investigated and settled according to the instructions of the county government.

After hearing the case, Gong, "Se Fu" (a minor official in the county) from Duxiang began to try the case and the defendant made the confession. To investigate the facts and determine the credibility of the defendant's confession, Gong, "Se Fu" (a minor official in the county) from Duxiang should interrogate the defendant at least twice at different times to make the sentence, which would be sent to the court at the county level for approval. The case mentioned above demonstrated that in Han Dynasty, there already formed a series of established judicial proceedings, so it was an important step in the development of the system of Chinese civil lawsuit.

It needs to be pointed out that in civil lawsuits, besides making judgment by the government of the Han Dynasty, there also began to have the practice of settling the lawsuits by the mediation. It was recorded in "Di Li Zhi" (The Record of Geography) in *Han Shu* (*The History of Han Dynasty*) that the citizens of Yingchuan city liked to argue and bring lawsuits to courts, but the officials named Huang and Han persuaded them to solve disputes by mediation. It was recorded in "Huan Rong Zhuan" (The Biography of Huan Rong) in *Latter Han Shu* (*The History of Latter Han Dynasty*) that because Huan Ye crossed the sea and lived in Jiaozhi (Cochin), the citizens there solved their own disputes and did not go to court anymore. The famous and excellent official named Liu Ju often solved disputes by adopting the method of mediation. It was recorded in "Liu Ju" in "Xun Li Zhuan" (The Biography of Excellent Officials) in *Han Shu* (*The History of Han Dynasty*) that Liu Ju often told citizens who filed the civil lawsuits that their disputes were not serious enough, so the county government would not get involved. Thereafter, the plaintiffs would go back and thought about it, finally they would withdraw the lawsuits and find other ways to solve the disputes. During the reign of Emperor Zhao, when Han Yanshou was appointed to govern Zuofengyi, "two brothers filed lawsuit to the government because of field disputes." Han Yanshou thought that he had not done a good job in educating and governing

---

[369] The words of the original text are missing.

[370] "Jian Wu San Nian Hou Su Jun Suo Ze Kou En Shi Shi Wen" (*The Explanation of the case of Su Jun Suing Kou En for the Debts*) in *Wen Wu* (*Culture Relic*), vol. 1, 1978.

the citizens, therefore, he reflected on himself at home. The two brothers also had a deep reflection by themselves and swore that they would not argue anymore. Because of this case, Han Yanshou "became well-known around the nearby twenty-four counties and no civil lawsuits were filed anymore."

The settlement of cases by mediation in Han Dynasty was closely connected with the social circumstance under which Confucianism was established as the dominant thought. Confucius had said: "The purpose of hearing cases is to eradicate the root of disputes," which was very influential. Besides, mediation was one of the most important criteria for awarding excellent officials and it was the standard of good governance. In Western Han Dynasty, Zhao Xinchen (an official) was appointed as "Tai Shou" (governor of a prefecture) of Nanyang city, so since then "there was a two-fold increase of population and thefts and lawsuits were eliminated"[371]; in Eastern Han Dynasty, Wang Tang (an official) was appointed as the minister of Lu state, thereafter, "the administration was effective and no lawsuits were filed for many years."[372]

5.8 The Rising of the Private Law Annotation

In Eastern Han Dynasty, most of the laws were enacted to solve the specific social problems, therefore, there lacked a comprehensive planning, which had often led to different and contradictory application. Especially, with the complexity and diversity of the sources of laws, it was difficult for the laws to be understood by both officials and citizens. During the reign of Emperor He, "Ting Wei" (the supreme official in charge of judicature) who was named Chen Chong thought that during the three hundred and two years after the establishment of Han Dynasty, "although the number of 'Xian Ling' (constitution) has slightly increased, yet too many 'Ke Tiao' (legal provisions) has been made," so the redundant legal provisions should be reduced. Although there was sufficient historical foundation for this suggestion, it was not adopted. In late Eastern Han Dynasty, more laws were made, so they became more complicated.

To interpret the relationship between the legal sources, to reduce the conflicts and to unify the application of law, private law annotation began to arise.

In the period of the government of Qin Dynasty, the right of interpreting law was exclusively controlled by officials, so individuals were forbidden to interpret law. Therefore, anyone who wanted to study law should learn from the government officials. However, at the beginning of Western Han Dynasty, the individuals were allowed to annotate law, which not only indicated that the united country had already

---

[371]"Zhao Xin Chen" (Zhao Xinchen) in "Xun Li Zhuan" (The Biography of Excellent Officials) in *Han Shu* (*The History of Han Dynasty*).
[372]"Wang Tang Zhuan" (The Biography of Wang Tang) in *Latter Han Shu* (*The History of Latter Han Dynasty*).

been consolidated, but also indicated that although the private law annotation by different schools were different and each of them had sticked to their own arguments, they were in accordance with the interests and needs of the state, so they had reflected the ruler's legal consciousness. Because the Confucian scholars in Han Dynasty had advocated interpreting law with Confucian classics, the scholars who were expert at Confucian classics were often great interpreters of law. Thus, they usually took in disciples to teach them their thoughts and they had engaged in this profession for many generations. According to historical records, Guo Gong and Ma Rong each had hundreds of disciples and Zheng Xuan had even thousands of disciples. Besides, the father and son in Nanchang city whose family name was Du and the brothers in Shandong province whose family name was Zheng were all "expert at Confucian classics and were familiar with the law and politics."[373] The government's approval of private law annotation by different schools and the application of legal interpretation in lawsuit settlement had demonstrated the rising of "Lv Xue" (the study of statutory laws) and the non-negligible role it had played in legislation and judiciary. However, the co-existence of different legal annotation was harmful to its unified application, so in Eastern Han Dynasty, Zheng Xuan's annotation was regarded as the mandatory standard.

In Eastern Han Dynasty, the famous annotators such as the three generations of Guo family in Yingchuan city, the Chen family in Pei State, the Wu family in Henan province had all studied law by generations, so were all very familiar with legal provisions. Moreover, they had all become high-ranking officials and performed well in governance. According to "Guo Gong Zhuan" (The Biography of Guo Gong) in *Latter Han Shu* (*The History of Latter Han Dynasty*), "Guo Hong's descendants had all studied law. Among those descendants, one held the position of 'Gong Fu' (the central official), seven held the position of 'Ting Wei' (the supreme official in charge of judicature), three held the position of 'Hou' (marquis), over twenty held the position of 'Ci Shi' (a supervisor assigned by the central government to a local area), 'Er Qian Dan' (the ancient official with a monthly salary of 2,000 *dan*), 'Shi Zhong' (assistant officers), 'Zhong Lang Jiang' (ancient official title), and many held the position of 'Shi Yu Shi' (subordinate of Grand Censor), and 'Zheng' (Director), 'Jian' (ancient supervisory official), 'Ping' (ancient official titles)." "So many law annotators like these mentioned above had been prosperous for generations." It is noteworthy that the scholars of Confucian classics named Ma Rong and Zheng Xuan also annotated and interpreted laws by themselves. *Han Lv Zhang Ju* (*The Interpretation of Law in Han Dynasty*) written by Zheng Xuan was a complete works of legal study in the Han Dynasty and was as famous as his other annotation works. It was recorded in "Xing Fa Zhi" (The Record of the Criminal Law) in *Jin Shu* (*The History of Jin Dynasty*) that "Shu Sunxuan, Guo Lingqing, Ma Rong, Zheng Xuan, and other Confucian scholars had all interpreted laws with more than 100,000 words. So totally, more than 26,272 legal articles were applied in legal practice, with altogether

---

[373]"Zheng Hong Zhuan" (The Biography of Zheng Hong) in *Han Shu* (*The History of Han Dynasty*).

7,732,200 words." It was also recorded in volume six of *Tang Liu Dian* (*The Six Statutes of Tang Dynasty*) that "in Latter Han Dynasty, ten annotators like Ma Rong, Zheng Xuan and others had made law annotations with tens of thousands of words, with over 26,000 legal articles applied in legal practice." Thus, it can be seen that the interpretation of law was flourishing in the Eastern Han Dynasty. However, the large number of annotation made to complement the provisions of *Han Lv* (*Han Code*) had become "too complex to be understood by the common people," so it was stipulated that "Zheng Xuan's annotation should be regarded as the official standard and it is forbidden for the annotation made by other schools to be applied in settling cases."[374] Since then, Zheng Xuan's annotation became one of the most important sources of law. The following passages taken from Zheng Xuan's annotation can be used as examples to demonstrate its value in the history of "Lv Xue" (the study of statutory laws) in China. About private prosecution, Zheng Xuan said that "the party can file lawsuit to the government if he has 'Quan Shu' (contract)," namely, if the litigant had contract, he could file the lawsuit to the government. About "Du Ju" (reading the judgment to the defendant), Zheng Xuan explained that "it refers to the fact laws are applied in 'Du Shu' (reading the judgment to the defendant) so that the criminals are punished according to law." "'Ju' refers to the words used in the judgment, and 'Du Ju' refers to the reading of the final judgment." It meant that "the judge made the final judgment in the trial after reading the indictment." About "Qi Ju" (the petition for retrial), it was annotated by Zheng Xuan that "the petition for retrial will be heard within the period of validity, if not, it will not be heard; if the sentence is beyond three months, the petition for retrial will not be accepted",[375] which means that if either parties are dissatisfied with the judgment, they could request a retrial within three months.

Zheng Xuan was also good at using historical comparative approaches, namely, comparing the laws and regulations of Han Dynasty with those of Confucian classics to elaborate the development and the inner relationship of ancient Chinese legal system. It was stated in "Zheng Xuan Zhuan" (The Biography of Zheng Xuan) in *Latter Han Shu* (*The History of Latter Han Dynasty*) that "in Zheng Xuan's interpretation, many important codes and the opinions of other scholars are included, the redundant ones are deleted, the wrong ones are corrected and the omitted ones are added so that generally the scholars can know their sources and origins." Zheng Xuan's law annotation had a profound influence on "Lv Xue" (the study of statutory laws) of later generations.

Because the law annotators were well aware that it was related to the ups and downs of a country to maintain the dignity of law, they were brave enough to make suggestions according to law, to criticize the society and to point out the current malpractice. For example, in Eastern Han Dynasty, two brothers killed a person together. Emperor Ming thought that the elder brother did not discipline his younger

---

[374]"Xing Fa Zhi" (The Record of the Criminal Law) in *Jin Shu* (*The History of Jin Dynasty*).
[375]"Si Kou" (The Minister of Justice) in "Qiu Guan" (Ministry of Penalty) in *Zhou Li* (*The Rites of Zhou*), annotated by Zheng Xuan.

5.8 The Rising of the Private Law Annotation

brother, so he should be sentenced to death while the younger brother should not. However, "Zhong Chang Shi" (an official position of counselor) named Sun Zhang made a mistake in delivering this decree and announced that both brothers should be sentenced to death. "Shang Shu" (the minister) thought that Sun Zhang should be sentenced to death because of his mistake. Emperor Ming then asked the law annotator named Guo Gong for his opinion, Guo Gong suggested that Sun Zhang "should be imposed with a fine." Emperor Ming asked the reason, and then Guo Gong replied: "The law discriminates between intentional and accidental crimes. Sun Zhang's action was accidental, so Sun Zhang should be punished leniently according to law. Since the law is made by the Emperor by following the orders of 'Tian' (Heaven), it shall not be misinterpreted."[376]

To make the severe punishment lenient, an expert of "Lv Xue" (the study of statutory laws) named Chen Zhong had suggested to Emperor An that the twenty-three articles of "Jue Shi Bi" (the precedents in lawsuit settlements), such as the article of castration and imprisonment of the three generations of the families of the corrupted officials should be abolished, the negligent murders should be punished leniently, and the implicated death penalty of mothers, sons and brothers should be exempted,[377] which were all adopted by Emperor An.

Therefore, the study of law annotation was developed from being exclusively monopolized by government in the Qin Dynasty to the opening to individuals in the Eastern Han Dynasty, which had demonstrated the transformation from authoritarian politics to liberal government. The upsurge of the private annotation of law is not only beneficial to eliminating the perplexity in legal practice, it also opened a new way for Confucianism to be introduced into the existing law at the time. Indeed, the private law annotation has also enriched the ancient criminal jurisprudence and procedural law, so both the abstract conception and law annotation have reflected the progress of legal civilization and the brilliance of ancient law, which has provided an important basis for the public and private law annotation.

In conclusion, the legal system in Han Dynasty is an important stage of the development of Chinese legal history, so great progress has been made in both legislation and judiciary. In the preface of *Han Lv Zhi Yi* (*Collections of Laws in Han Dynasty*), Shen Jiaben wrote: "As for the laws of Tang Dynasty, those which are inherited from Han Dynasty are too numerous to mention, among which, some are slightly similar to those in Han Dynasty and some are totally different. By comparison, the rights and wrongs can be proven by the gains and losses. So it is necessary to study *Han Lv* (*Han Code*) to seek the origins of *Tang Lv* (*Tang Code*)." Especially, the permeation of Confucianism had further demonstrated its color of "civilization." In Western Han Dynasty, the famous Confucian expert Dong Zhongshu had held high the banner of "De Zhu Xing Fu" (employing moral teaching

---

[376]"Guo Gong Zhuan" (The Biography of Guo Gong) in *Latter Han Shu* (*The History of Latter Han Dynasty*).

[377]"Chen Zhong Zhuan" (The Biography of Chen Zhong) in *Latter Han Shu* (*The History of Latter Han Dynasty*).

as the primary means, punishment as the supplement) and made Confucianism the dominant ideology, then in Eastern Han Dynasty, many famous Confucian scholars had appeared in succession and they were like shining stars. They advocated that "it is the universal principle of legal practice to integrate 'De' (virtue) with 'Xing' (punishment)."[378] Moreover, they proposed that "the deeds beyond the regulation of 'Li' (rites) should be regulated and included in the scope of 'Fa' (law)."[379] Meanwhile, "'Li' (rites) prevents people from doing bad deeds beforehand, while 'Fa' (law) punishes the violators afterwards,"[380] both of which had their own functions. These scholars had made great contribution to the establishment of orthodox legal thoughts in feudal society.

Moreover, Emperor Wen and Jing in Western Han Dynasty and Emperor Guangwu in the Eastern Han Dynasty had strictly disciplined themselves by law and shown great respect to and carried out the laws in administration, which not only fostered the establishment of legal order, but also provided important conditions for the emergence of prosperous societies. The prosperity of a society is closely connected with "Fa Zhi" (the rule of law), and it is worth learning from that "the law will be thoroughly carried out if it is respected by the rulers, while the law will not effectively enforced if it is violated by the rulers."[381]

---

[378]Xun Yue, "Shi Shi" (Current Affairs) in *Shen Jian* (*Learning from the Historical Experience*).
[379]Wang Chong (Han Dynasty), "Xie Duan" (The Analysis of Employment System) in *Lun Heng* (*On Balance*).
[380]Wang Chong (Han Dynasty), "Shuai Xing" (Frankness) in *Lun Heng* (*On Balance*).
[381]Wang Fu (Han Dynasty), "Shu She" (On Remission) in *Qian Fu Lun* (*On Hermits*).

Chapter 6
The Legal Systems of Wei, Jin, Southern and Northern Dynasty: The Legislative Progress and Cultural Amalgamation

(220 A.D.–581 A.D.)

During the period of Wei, Jin, Southern and Northern Dynasty, the country was in a state of separation and military confrontation, so the society was in turmoil, the class and national conflict was intense and complicated. As a consequence, the rulers in each dynasty had tried to maintain their dominance by using the method of legislation, so the legislative actions were very active. *Tai Shi Lv* (*Tai Shi Code*) made in Jin Dynasty, was a major achievement of West Jin and Southern Dynasty, so it was not only a comprehensive summary of *Han Lv* (*Han Code*), but also the crystallization of the age which reflected the historical trend of "the Confucianization of law," so it had a far-reaching influence.

Besides, "Lv Xue" (the study of statutory laws), which aimed at providing a service for legislation and judicature, also sprang up at that time, and it gradually separated and freed itself from the subordinate position of Confucian classics in Wei and Jin dynasties. Focusing on the research of legislative techniques, the statute structure, the theories of law, the principles on making convictions and passing sentences and regarding interpreting the current law for a uniform application as its major task, "Lv Xue" (the study of statutory laws) gradually became more scientific, so it finally became a very important scale for the measurement of the level of legal civilization with both theoretical values and practical guiding significance. However, in the wake of "Ba Wang Zhi Luan" (The Rebellion of Eight Princes) and "Yong Jia Zhi Luan" (The Rebellion of Yongjia) during the Western Jin Dynasty, the center of legal civilization was transferred from the central plains to Jiangsu and Zhejiang regions.

After the small minorities from North China entered the central plains, they took the policy of actively adapting and absorbing Han culture to establish their ruling in the area inhabited by Han nationality, so they consequently established an institution featured by the culture of Han people. In this process, the representatives of the aristocrats of the of Northern Dynasty, such as Cui Hao and Gao Yun, who were familiar with "Lv Xue" (the study of statutory laws) of Han nationality, had played the role of intermediary agents in introducing the civilized culture of Han nation to the rulers of Northern Wei Dynasty, so they had exerted a great influence on the lawmaking in Northern Dynasty.

During the period of Taihe in Northern Wei Dynasty, Emperor Xiaowen actively carried out political reform, made *Bei Wei Lv* (*Bei Wei Code*), which was mainly based on Confucian "Gang Chang" (feudal cardinal guides) and "Lun Li" (the rites and rituals of Confucianism), realized the large scale cultural amalgamation centered around the culture of Han Dynasty and the great renaissance of Chinese legal civilization.

Following Northern Wei Dynasty, Northern Qi, and Northern Zhou also formulated a series of statutes according to the laws of Han and Wei nationalities and their own customs, which was unprecedented for small minorities in Chinese legal history.

Based on the cultural amalgamation of various nationalities, Chinese legal civilization, which surpassed that of Qin and Han dynasties, was created, with the rise of "Wei Jin Lv Xue" (the study of statutory laws in Wei and Jin dynasties) and the legislative achievements of each dynasty during this period as its major symbols.

6.1 The Legislative Achievements in Wei, Jin, Southern and Northern Dynasty

Since the end of Eastern Han Dynasty, in the annexing war of suppressing "Huang Jin Qi Yi"(The Yellow Scarves Army Rebellion), three feudal regimes, namely, Wei, Shu and Wu, respectively led by Cao Cao, Sun Quan, and Liu Bei, were established, which was called "San Guo" (Three Kingdoms) (220 A.D.–265A.D.) in history. The setting up of these three regimes was an inevitable result of the development of the merging and separation of the prominent families, meanwhile, it also reflected the regional unity, which was formed under the condition that it was impossible to achieve national unity.

Among the three regimes, the state of Wei was the strongest, whose dominator Cao Cao, a renowned statesman and militarist, adopted a farming system called "Tun Tian Zhi" (the farmland system of opening up wasteland by garrison troops or peasants). Moreover, he was against the tyrannical local despots for their concealing the fact that they were actually depending on the local farmers; he was also against recruiting some so-called "unfilial and merciless people who were talented in ruling the state and in commanding troops."[1] With these measures, the economy in the north was gradually recovered, so Cao Cao's regime was thus consolidated. Because Cao Cao's regime was established and developed by depending on the prominent families at that time, in the reign of Emperor Wen, the policy of "Jiu Pin Zhong Zheng Zhi" (The Nine Rank System, an important election system in Wei, Jin,

---

[1]"Wu Di Ji" (The Record of Emperor Wu) (Part 1) in "Wei Shu" (The History of Northern Wei Dynasty) in *San Guo Zhi* (*The Record of the Three Kingdoms*).

Southern and Northern Dynasty) was taken to confirm the privileges of these noble families to be appointed as officials in system. Consequently, the regime of Wei eventually fell into the hands of the powerful aristocratic Sima family.

The establishment and development of the state of Wu and Shu, though unlike the state of Wei, were in fact similar to it in terms of the dependence on the prominent noble families at that time, with the former depending on immigrants and the prominent noble families and the latter on the intelligentsia of Jingzhou and prominent noble families of Yizhou. In this relatively stable environment of the three kingdoms, the economy of both north and south was revived and developed, which had provided a significant condition for the reestablishment of a unified country. In 280 A.D., Emperor Wu of Western Jin, Sima Yan unified China and established Jin Dynasty, which was also called Western Jin in history.

At the very beginning, the rulers of Western Jin Dynasty laid great emphasis on land annexation, so a farming system of occupying land was adopted, by which the government officials were allowed to seize land, to plunder tenants by force and to confer privileges on their own relatives according to their ranks, which had legalized the officials' privileges of occupying farm land and consolidated the economic foundation of the prominent noble families. Besides, a number of official positions were offered to the members of prominent families according to the system of enfeoffment. However, consequently, it had increased the burden of the common people and intensified the power conflicts inside the ruling class, which had finally led to the occurrence of "Ba Wang Zhi Luan" (The Rebellion of Eight Princes). Meanwhile, many rulers of the minority groups who had migrated into central plains and who were hostile to the Western Jin regime, such as "Xiong Nu", "Xian Bei," "Jie," "Di," and "Qiang" (all were ancient Chinese small nationalities) also actively strived for power and established numerous small separatist regimes in the north one after another. These small states were fighting with each other in the wars of annexation, which had led to the chaotic situation of "Sixteen Kingdoms." The country's economy was seriously damaged, as was illustrated in the statement that "the country was in chaos and nobody was engaged in farming."[2]

In 316 A.D., Western Jin was replaced by Han state, a kingdom established by the aristocrats of "Xiong Nu" (an ancient nationality in China). In 317 A.D., Sima Rui, a member of the royal clan in Western Jin Dynasty, established the Eastern Jin Dynasty with the support of aristocrats in Jiangnan (in the areas of today's Jiangsu and Zhejiang).

In 420 A.D., Eastern Jin was overthrown by Song Dynasty headed by Liu and Song families. In the next one hundred and sixty years, four dynasties, namely, Song, Qi, Liang and Chen dynasties ruled the country successively, which were collectively called "Southern Dynasty" in history. Although the emperors of Southern Dynasty came from "Shu Zu" (humble background) themselves, and had selected talents from "Han Men" (humble and ordinary families) to help them to govern the country, they failed to change the privileged position of prominent noble

---

[2]"Shi Ji Long Zai Ji" (The Record of Shi Jilong) in *Jin Shu* (*The History of Jin Dynasty*) (Book 2).

families at that time. Therefore, it was not until late in Liang Dynasty that these prominent noble families were heavily hit by "Latter Jing Zhi Luan" (The Rebellion of Hou and Jing) and began to decline gradually. Thereafter, the newly arising ordinary landlords and powerful despotic gentry came into power. At the same time, Tuoba Family from Xian Bei nationality changed the chaotic situation in the north and established a unified Northern Wei Dynasty, which was split into East Wei and West Wei dynasties towards the end of the dynasty, with the former being replaced by Northern Qi Dynasty, while the latter Northern Zhou Dynasty. The period from Northern Wei Dynasty to Northern Zhou Dynasty was known as "Northern Dynasty" in history and most emperors at that time had endeavored to maintain the power and influence of prominent noble families so as to win their support. When Emperor Xiaowen of Northern Wei was in power, priority was given to members of such families in selecting officials; moreover, the members of the royal families of Xian Bei were ordered to marry Han people of the prominent noble families to strengthen the cooperation between the two nationalities with blood ties. It was not until late in the sixth century that this South-North confrontation came to an end, and a minister from Northern Zhou Dynasty, Yang Jian usurped the throne by establishing Sui Dynasty in 581 A.D.. In 589 A.D., Yang Jian defeated South Chen and unified China, which had remained divided for hundreds of years.

During the period of South-North confrontation, economy was revived and developed. In particular, during the reign of emperor Xiaowen in Northern Wei Dynasty, "Jun Tian Zhi" (The System of Land Equalization) was established, and the state-owned wasted land was allocated to landless farmers to cultivate so that tax would be collected by the state. Besides, it was stipulated that a portion of land was owned by the farmers themselves. Therefore, all these measures had played a significant role in promoting the economic development of the north and had also provided the historical condition for the unification of China by Sui Dynasty.

During the hundreds of years of ruling of "San Guo" (Three Kingdoms), Western and Eastern Jin, and Southern and Northern Dynasty, there were endless wars and the regimes were changed frequently. To ensure the survival and development of the state in the turmoil, the rulers of each dynasty had paid great attention to the application and function of law. Consequently, legislation was emphasized and the development of legal system was promoted. In each dynasty, based on inheriting the legal systems of Eastern and Western Han dynasties, reform and innovation were carried out either in legislation and judicature or "Lv Xue" (the study of statutory laws). Especially, *Jin Lv* (*Jin Code*) was made, which was the product of the comprehensive summary of the laws of Western and Eastern Han dynasties. Besides, "Lv Xue" (the study of statutory laws) in Jin Dynasty also marked the climax in the history of the study of statutory laws in China.

After the rulers of the Northern minority groups entered the vast areas lived by Han nationality, they began to adapt to its advanced culture actively. In Northern Dynasty, the legal systems of Western and Eastern Han and Jin dynasties were adopted. Moreover, bold reforms and innovations were carried out, which had reflected the positive contribution of the small minorities to the Chinese legal system and the integration of the legal cultures of different nationalities.

In conclusion, the legal systems of Wei, Jin, Southern and Northern Dynasty were established in an important stage of development, so it had served as a key link between the past and the future. Besides, they were the products of the maturity of the feudal legal system of our country, so they had laid a solid foundation for the development of legal system in Sui and Tang dynasties.

6.1.1 The Legislative Achievement of "San Guo" (Three Kingdoms) Represented by Wei Lv (Wei Code)

Cao Cao, the founding father of the state of Wei, was an advocator of "Fa Zhi" (the ruling of law) under feudal system. Besides, he was "very familiar with the principles of legalists such as Shen Buhai and Shang Yang,"[3] and emphasized that "'Li' (rites) should be taken as the priority in the ruling of the country and 'Xing' (punishment) should be stressed in ending the turmoil."[4] When he was a "Du Wei" (a military officer below the general) in Luoyang, he made a stick with five colors and hang it over the gate. He said: "Anyone, whether rich or poor, is to be beaten to death once with this stick if he has violated the law."[5] After unifying Central China, Cao Cao issued *Jia Zi Ke* (*The Law Issued in the Year of Jiazi*) to win over people's support by reducing the old punishments. For example, "the punishment of having the criminal's right and left feet clamped by iron pliers was changed to having their feet clamped by wooden pliers.... He also thought that the penalty of Han Dynasty was too severe, so he reduced the levels of penalty by half."[6] The most important law ever made during the period of Wei Dynasty was *Xin Lv* (*New Code*) issued by Emperor Ming.

Because since Eastern Han Dynasty "although various rules and regulations had been made, yet more and more people had committed crimes; although various severe penalties had been enforced, yet the evil doings had not been stopped,"[7] an imperial edict was issued by Emperor Ming of Wei state in the 3rd year of Taihe (229 A.D.) to order "Si Kong" (the minister of public works) Chen Qun, "San Qi Chang Shi" (ancient official helping emperor to deal with court affairs) Liu Shao, "Ji Shi Huang Men Shi Lang" (ancient official, attendants inside palace door) Han Xun, "Yi Lang" (ancient official) Yu Yi, "Zhong Lang" (department director) Huang Xiu

---

[3] "Wu Di Ji" (The Record of Emperor Wu) in "Wei Shu" (The History of Northern Wei Dynasty) in *San Guo Zhi* (*The Record of the Three Kingdoms*) (Book 1).

[4] "Han Cui Gao Sun Wang Zhuan" (The Biography of Han Ji, Cui Lin, Gao Rou, Sun Li and Wang Guan) in "Wei Shu" (The History of Northern Wei Dynasty) in *San Guo Zhi* (*The Record of the Three Kingdoms*).

[5] "Wu Di Ji" (The Record of Emperor Wu) in "Wei Shu" (The History of Northern Wei Dynast) in *San Guo Zhi* (*The Record of the Three Kingdoms*) (Book 1).

[6] "Xing Fa Zhi" (The Record of the Criminal Law) in *Jin Shu* (*The History of Jin Dynasty*).

[7] "Ming Di Ji" (The Record of Emperor Ming) in "Wei Shu" (The History of Northern Wei Dynast) in *San Guo Zhi* (*The Record of Three Kingdoms*).

and Xun Xian to make *Wei Lv* (*Wei Code*) by deleting the old rules and regulations according to *Han Lv* (*Han Code*). *Wei Lv* (*Wei Code*) consisted of eighteen new chapters. Chen Qun, the major drafter of *Xin Lv* (*New Code*), was an outstanding scholar during the time of "San Guo" (Three Kingdoms) and his grandfather Chen Shi and father Chen Ji were both virtuous and knowledgeable people; another drafter Liu Shao was also a prominent scholar in "Lv Xue" (the study of statutory laws), all of which had decided that *Xin Lv* (*New Code*) was a work of creativity.

First, the stylistic rules and layout were reformed. Owing to the limited chapters of formal contents, in *Han Lv* (*Han Code*), there were many supplementary laws like "Bang Zhang" (law of rites, here it refers to supplementary regulations), "Ke" (rule), "Ling" (decree) and "Shi Bi" (the precedents), which had caused inconsistent categories and inappropriate titles, with the contents of different rules and regulations overlapping one another. For example, "the articles of 'Zei Shang' (premeditated hurting) were included in *Dao Lv* (*Statutes on Theft*), but the articles of 'Dao Zhang' (The Chapter on Theft) were included in *Zei Lv* (*Statutes on Banditry*); the articles of "Shang Yu" (imprisonment) were included in *Xing Lv* (*Statutes on Corvée and Garrisoning the Frontier*), but the articles of 'Dai Bu' (arresting) were included in *Jiu Lv* (*Statutes on Livestock Breeding*)."[8] For this reason, the chapters of *Wei Lv* (*Wei Code*) were increased to totally eighteen chapters. According to *Wei Lv Xu Lue* (*Outline of the Preface to Wei Code*), which was quoted in "Xing Fa Zhi" (The Record of the Criminal Law) in *Jin Shu* (*The History of Jin Dynasty*), "The new law has been made with the main categories revised and chapters and articles added." Therefore, the new law consisted of eighteen chapters. The original six chapters remained unchanged, such as "Dao Fa" (Laws on Theft), "Zei Fa" (Laws on Banditry), "Qiu Fa" (Laws on Imprisonment), "Bu Fa" (Laws on Arresting), "Za Fa" (Miscellaneous Laws), and "Hu Fa" (Laws on Households), while *Xing Lv* (*Statutes on Corvée and Garrisoning the Frontier*) was changed to *Shan Xing Lv* (*Statutes on Sending Troops without Authorization*); *Ju Lv* (*Specific Laws*) was changed to *Xing Ming* (*Law*); *Jiu Lv* (*Statutes on Livestock Breeding*) was deleted and the ten chapters of *Jie Lue* (*Statutes on Robbery*), *Zha Wei* (*Statutes on Fraud and Forgery*), *Hui Wang* (*Statutes on Damages and Death*), *Gao He* (*Statutes on Prosecution*), *Xi Xun* (*Statutes on Interrogation*), *Duan Yu* (*Statutes on Trials and Punishments*), *Qing Qiu* (*Statutes on Asking for Bribery*), *Jing Shi* (*Statutes on Dangerous and Emergent Matters*), *Chang Zang* (*Statutes on Accepting Bribes*) and *Mian Zuo* (*Statutes on Exemption from Punishment*) were added.

Xing Ming (*Law*), a substitute for *Ju Lv* (*Specific Laws*), was put at the beginning of the whole statute, which was a great reform for the newly made *Wei Lv* (*Wei Code*). In *Fa Jing* (*Canon of Laws*), a statute composed by Li Kui in Warring States Period, *Ju Fa* (*Specific Laws*) was placed after "Wu Fa" (Five Punishments), namely, "Dao Fa" (Laws on Theft), "Zei Fa" (Laws on Banditry), "Qiu Fa" (Laws on Imprisonment), "Bu Fa" (Laws on Arresting) and "Za Fa" (Miscellaneous Laws), so as to summarize the cases of the aggravation and mitigation of penalties listed in

---

[8]"Xing Fa Zhi" (The Record of the Criminal Law) in *Jin Shu* (*The History of Jin Dynasty*).

6.1 The Legislative Achievements in Wei, Jin, Southern and Northern Dynasty

each chapters. In *Han Lv* (*Han Code*), however, *Ju Lv* (*Specific Laws*) was put between *Za Lv* (*Miscellaneous Laws*) and *Hu Lv* (*Statutes on Households*), which had led to the chaotic layout of the laws. Chen Qun and Liu Zhao, after drawing lessons from the past, collected the various regulations separated in the chapters in the old laws and included them into *Ju Lv* (*Specific Laws*), then combined the revised criminal system with *Ju Lv* (*Specific Laws*), renamed it *Xing Ming* (*Law*) and put it at the beginning of *Wei Lv* (*Wei Code*). This reform was highly praised by most of the later generations. According to *Wei Lv Xu Lue* (*Outline of the Preface to Wei Code*), which was quoted in "Xing Fa Zhi" (The Record of the Criminal Law) in *Jin Shu* (*The History of Jin Dynasty*), "as for the old laws, those of the Qin Dynasty were copied and three more chapters were added; *Ju Lv* (*Specific Laws*) remained unchanged because it was put in chapter six. The legal provisions were listed neither at the beginning nor the end, because its meaning was not in accordance with the chapter. So, the criminal cases were collected in the chapter of *Xing Ming* (*Law*) and was put at the beginning of the code." It was also stated in the preface of *Tang Lv Shu Yi* (*The Comments on Tang Code*) that "because *Jiu Zhang Lv* (*The Code in Nine Chapters*) made in Han Dynasty was fragmentary and was not systematic, in Wei Dynasty the criminal cases were collected together in *Xing Ming* (*Law*) and were put at the very beginning of the code." The stylistic rules and layout of the new law was made based on the summary of *Qin Lv* (*Qin Code*) and *Han Lv* (*Han Code*), so it not only exerted a direct influence on the development of *Jin Lv* (*Jin Code*), but also became a universal standard for the making of feudal codes in the later generations.

Second, the chapters of the new statutes were restructured. According to *Wei Lv Xu Lue* (*Outline of the Preface to Wei Code*), the following adjustments are made:

> Robbery, threatening and human trafficking are included in *Dao Lv* (*Statutes on Theft*), while 'Chi Zhi' (hostage-taking) is included in 'Ke' (rule), both of which do not belong to the category of 'Dao' (theft), so they are re-categorized in *Jie Lue Lv* (*Statutes on Robbery*). In *Zei Lv* (*Statutes on Banditry*), 'Qi Man' (being dishonest), 'Zha Wei' (fraud and forgery), 'Yu Feng' (going beyond the limits), and 'Jiao Zhi' (acting in the name of monarchs) are included, but none of them belong to 'Zei' (banditry); in *Qiu Lv* (*Statutes on Imprisonment*), 'Zha Wei' (Fraud and Forgery) is also included, but there are many other affairs such as self-deception and tax and corvée exemption, so consequently these crimes are included into a new category named *Zha Lv* (*Statutes on Cheating*). Besides, in *Zei Lv* (*Statutes on Banditry*) the prohibition of cutting down trees, killing and wounding people and animals and losing official stamps were included, while in *Jin Bu Lv* (*Statutes on Currency and Property*), the prohibition of killing and wounding people and animals and destroying public property are also included; so they are rearranged into *Hui Wang Lv* (*Statutes on Damages and Death*); in *Qiu Lv* (*Statutes on Imprisonment*), the provisions on impeachment and reexamination are included, while in *Jiu Lv* (*Statutes on Livestock Breeding*) those on false accusation and arresting and on reporting the things urgent to the emperor are also included, so they are separately edited and included in *Gao He Lv* (*Statutes on Prosecution*); in *Qiu Lv* (*Statutes on Imprisonment*), the provisions on imprisonment, interrogation and trial are included, while in *Xing Lv* (*Statutes on Corvée and Garrisoning the Frontier*), those on prisoners and on sending officials to local areas to hear cases are included, so they are separately edited and included in *Xi Xun* (*Statutes on Interrogation*) and *Duan Yu Lv* (*Statutes on Trials and Punishments*); in *Dao Lv* (*Statutes on Theft*), the provisions on officials' taking bribes from suspects are included, while in *Za Lv* (*Miscellaneous Laws*), the provisions on dishonest officials' getting bribes by threatening the suspects and officials' taking bribes when

checking goods are included, because all these articles are similar, a new chapter called *Qing Qiu Lv* (*Statutes on Asking for Bribery*) is added; in *Dao Lv* (*Statutes on Theft*), the provisions on humiliating criminals are included, while in *Xing Lv* (*Statutes on corvée and Garrisoning the Frontier*), the provisions on assigning corvée service without authorization are included, in *Ju Lv* (*Specific Laws*), the provisions on trade and repairing houses without authorization are included, so they are recategorized and included in *Shan Xing Lv* (*Statutes on Sending Troops without Authorization*). Furthermore, in *Xing Lv* (*Statutes on Corvée and Garrisoning the Frontier*), the provisions on evading and delaying corvée service are included, in *Zei Lv* (*Statutes on Banditry*), the provisions on failing to handle stored goods properly are included, in *Jiu Lv* (*Statutes on Livestock Breeding*), the provisions on delaying military affairs and failing to carefully carry out imperial decrees or failing to follow imperial decrees are included. In Han Dynasty, those who violate imperial order will be sentenced to death for the crime of failing to carry out the imperial decree, so the punishment is mitigated according to 'Ding You Zhao Shu' (an imperial decree made in the year of Dingyou) which was made during the reign of Emperor Wen. So separate laws are not made, because it is not suitable to include it in law at the moment. In Qin Dynasty, rules were made about courier stations, stagecoaches, royal carriages and restaurants, and they were continued to be applied in early Han Dynasty. But later on, because of the heavy cost, stagecoaches and carriages were not used any more in Eastern Han Dynasty with only horses remained, but these articles mentioned above are still retained in the law, which is useless, so *Jiu Lv* (*Statutes on Livestock Breeding*) is abolished and the relevant provisions are combined into *You Yi Ling* (*Decrees for Postal Service and Courier Station*). The provisions on false accusation and arrest are categorized into *Gao He Lv* (*Statutes on Prosecution*) and those on reporting things urgent to the emperor and defense affairs are categorized into *Jing Shi Lv* (*Statutes on Dangerous and Emergent Matters*); in *Dao Lv* (*Statutes on Theft*), the provisions on returning the booty to the owner is included, while *Jin Bu Lv* (*Statutes on Currency and Property*), the provisions on the penalty of fine and the estimation of booty and the amount of fine are included, so all these are categorized into *Chang Zang Lv* (*Statutes on Accepting Bribes*).[9]

All these had shown that the provisions were classified in great detail in *Wei Lv* (*Wei Code*) from adopting "Bang Zhang" (law of rites, here it refers to supplementary regulations), "Ke" (rule), "Ling" (decree) and summarizing and restructuring the contents of each chapter. Thus, "redundancy was avoided with fewer chapters, narrower coverage and deletion of the names of crimes."[10] At the same time, the confusion of laws and decrees and the overlapping of rules and analogies in the laws of Eastern Han Dynasty were also avoided, so the contents were basically authentic and cases were basically coherent, which was not only a great improvement in legislative technique but also of great value in Chinese legislative history. However, for all its value, *Wei Lv* (*Wei Code*) also received criticism from jurists like Shen Jiaben at the end of Qing Dynasty. In his *Han LvZh Yi* (*Collections of Laws in Han Dynasty*), Shen Jiaben made the following remarks:

> 'Chuan' means 'Dai' (arresting), while 'Fu' means 'Fu An' (reviewing); they are different things, so if these two are combined together it refers to having the criminal arrested and the case retried. Therefore, this is a matter of 'Ju Qiu' (investigation and trial) rather than 'Gao He' (prosecution), so it is wrong to categorize it into *Gao He Lv* (*Statutes on Prosecution*) in *Wei Lv* (*Wei Code*). Regarding prisoners, the chapter of 'Xi Xun Lv' (Statutes on

---

[9]"The Record of the Criminal Law" in *Jin Shu* (*The History of Jin Dynasty*).
[10]"The Record of the Criminal Law" in *Jin Shu* (*The History of Jin Dynasty*).

Interrogation) is added in *Wei Lv* (*Wei Code*), while trials and punishments are included in the category of *Duan Yu Lv* (*Statutes on Trials and Punishments*), with the former referring to interrogation while the latter referring to judgment. It is very hard to separate *Xi Xun* (*Statutes on Interrogation*) from *Duan Yu* (*Statutes on Trials and Punishments*), therefore, it is more reasonable to collect them into *Qiu Lv* (*Statutes on Imprisonment*) in Han Dynasty.

So it can be seen that there are still some shortcomings in *Wei Lv* (*Wei Code*) owing to various reasons at that time.

Finally, some of the criminal principles and crimes and punishments were reformed. Faced with the increasing serious phenomenon of malicious accusation against other people, an order was issued by Emperor Wen in January of the 5th year of Huangchu (224 A.D.) and it was stipulated that "except for 'Mou Fan' (plotting rebellion or plotting to endanger the country) and 'Da Ni' (Great Sedition), no cases of informing against others will be accepted, so anyone who has made an attempt to accuse others will be charged with the same crime accused."[11] Besides, malicious accusation against others was also prohibited in the new law, so "if a prisoner falsely accuses someone of rebellion, his family members will be implicated; if the decent people is falsely accused, those involved will be severely punished to prevent the crime of slandering."[12] In the meantime, with the view of protecting labor force and recovering agricultural production, it was also prohibited to revenge by killing each other. In January of the 4th year of Huangchu (223 A.D.), an order was issued by Emperor Wen of Wei Dynasty to forbid people to revenge by slaughter each other: "Since the beginning of the riot, wars have never been stopped and people have been killing each other, now that peace has just been restored in the country, anyone who revenges for private purpose will have his whole family executed." Besides, according to *Wei Lv Xu Lue* (*Outline of the Preface to Wei Code*) quoted in "Xing Fa Zhi" (The Record of the Criminal Law) in *Jin Shu* (*The History of Jin Dynasty*), "if someone is killed in a fighting or if the murderer escapes, it is allowed for the victim's sons to arrest him or have him killed. In case of accidental killing, no revenge is allowed to prevent further killing." Here on the one hand, the precondition for vengeance and the specific identity of a revenger were stipulated; on the other hand, it was stressed that "no revenge is allowed for the cases caused by accidental killing," which had reflected the basic spirit of prohibiting revenge.

In the new law, an accusation called "Bu Dao" (depravity) was abolished because "it was often used as an excuse to punish the officials and ministers randomly since Han Dynasty." Moreover, the scope of "Lian Zuo" (being punished for being related to somebody who committed an offence) was narrowed, so grandparents were no longer punished for the crimes committed by their grandchildren, and vice versa. In addition, the provision that "those who make anonymous reports shall be punished by 'Qi Shi' (exposing the executed body publicly at markets)" was also revised to show lenient punishment. At the same time, the punishments for corruption were

---

[11]"Wen Di Ji" (The Record of Emperor Wen) in "Wei Shu" (The History of Northern Wei Dynasty) in *San Guo Zhi* (*The Record of the Three Kingdoms*).

[12]"Xing Fa Zhi" (The Record of the Criminal Law) in *Jin Shu* (*The History of Jin Dynasty*).

aggravated, so *Qing Qiu Lv* (*Statutes on Asking for Bribery*) was specially made to punish the crime.

With the further introduction of ethics and moral principles into law and legislation, it was made clear in the new law that it would be regarded as a killing one's biological mother to kill one's stepmother. The law of "Yi Zi Zhi Ke" (if any one of the two sons has reached the age of registering for household, but they do not live separately, and the collection of household registration tax will be doubled) was abolished and the stepson and adopted son were equal in inheriting the father's property. Besides, harsher punishment was enforced to punish those who had assaulted their brothers and sisters. Therefore, the law was applied as a tool to maintain social ethical order and to consolidate the rule of the regime.

In Wei Dynasty, the criminal legal system of Han Dynasty was inherited. For example, death penalty was classified into three levels: "Xiao Shou" (the penalty of hanging the head of the criminal on top of a pole for public display), "Yao Zhan" (cutting people in two at the waist) and "Qi Shi" (exposing the executed body publicly at markets), as was recorded in "Xing Fa Zhi" in *Jin Shu* (*The History of Jin Dynasty*) and *Tang Liu Dian* (*The Six Statutes of Tang Dynasty*) that "there are three punishments for 'Da Bi' (the capital punishment): 'Xiao Shou' (the penalty of hanging the head of the criminal on top of a pole for public display), 'Yao Zhan' (cutting people in two at the waist) and 'Qi Shi' (exposing the executed body publicly at markets), but for "the crime of 'Mou Fan' (plotting rebellion or plotting to endanger the country) and 'Da Ni' (Great Sedition), those involved will be arrested immediately and be punished by 'Zhu' (being drowned), 'Xiao Zu' (cutting off and hanging up the head, and then chopping it into meat before a large crowd) or 'Yi San Zu' (the law of killing the three generations of a family)" without necessarily following the provisions in the law. Although those uncivilized penalties, which were originally used by small minorities, were not abolished in *Wei Lv* (*Wei Code*), the cruel penalties like "Gong" (castration) were not included in the law, so they were seldom applied, which was surely a great progress compared with Han Dynasty. In addition, the corporal punishment reform undertaken by emperor Wen in Han Dynasty was continued and some cruel penalties such as "Qing" (to tattoo on the face), "Yi" (to cut down the nose) and "Yue" (to amputate the feet) were abolished. The notorious "Wu Xing" (the five Penalties), which were applied during the period of Cao Wei, including "Si" (death penalty), "Kun" (having the criminal's long hair cut short), "Wan" (forced labor), "Zuo" (imprisonment and forced labor), and "Shu" (atonement) were just transitional penalties used in the period from Han to Tang dynasties.

As to the criminal legal principles, "Ba Yi" (The Eight Deliberations) was adopted in *Wei Lv* (*Wei Code*) for the first time. "Ba Yi" (The Eight Deliberations) originated from "Ba Bi" (the eight conditions for mitigating punishments) in *Zhou Li* (*The Rites of Zhou Dynasty*), which referred to eight categories of people, namely, "Yi Qin" (the cases that involved "Huang Qin": the relatives of the Emperor), "Yi Gu" (the old retainers of the Emperor: including those who had been in the emperor's service for a long time), "Yi Xian" (the morally worthy: including worthy men or superior men whose speech and conduct were greatly virtuous and may be taken as a model for the country), "Yi Neng" (the great ability: including people of great talent), "Yi Gong" (great achievement: including those of great achievement and glory), "Yi Gui" (the high status: including all active duty officials of the third rank and above), "Yi Qin" (diligent: including military and civil officials who have displayed great diligence in their work through thorough occupation of public affairs), and "Yi Bin" (the guests of the state: to treat the descendants of previous dynasties as guests of the state who could enjoy a legal privilege). Therefore, these people could enjoy the privilege of penalty reduction if they had committed crimes. In pre-Wei times, this was just a special institution which was not included as a part of law. However, it was incorporated into law by Chen Qun and Liu Zhao to win the political support of the prominent families who were gaining momentum at that time. Since then, "Ba Yi" (The Eight Deliberations) had become a very important part of law. It was recorded in *Tang Liu Dian* (*The Six Statutes of Tang Dynasty*) that "Ba Yi" (The Eight Deliberations) was contained in all of the laws of Wei, Jin, Song, Qi, Liang, Chen, Hou Wei, Bei Qi, Latter Zhou and Sui dynasties."

To conclude, it can be seen that the new law of Wei Dynasty was a conclusive legal code made from reorganizing the laws of in Qin and Han dynasties. As some Confucian ideology was incorporated in *Wei Lv* (*Wei Code*), it also promoted the process of the Confucianization of law. For example, "Qin Qin" (showing respect to relatives represented by parents) was advocated in Confucianism, so accordingly, it was also advocated in the new law; the provision of "Yi Zi Zhi Ke" (if any one of the two sons has reached the age of registering for household, but they do not live separately, and the collection of household registration tax will be doubled) was abolished so that "sons can share the same family property with the father; what's more, the people who assault their brothers and sisters shall be sentenced to an additional five-year imprisonment."[13] Moreover, under the influence of the guiding principle of "Jun Wei Chen Gang" (monarchs being the guide of his subjects), the cruel penalties, such as "Xiao Zu" (cutting off and hanging up the head, and then chopping it into meat before a large crowd), "Zhu" (being drowned) and "Yi Qi San Zu" (the law of killing the three generations of a family) were imposed upon the crime of "Mou Fan" (plotting rebellion or plotting to endanger the country) and "Da Ni" (great sedition) to "eradicate the root of evils." Thus, the incorporation of "Ba Yi" (The Eight Deliberations) into *Wei Lv* (*Wei Code*) further reflected the legalization and institutionalization of Confucianism.

During the time of Wei, "Ling" (decree) was used as supplement to law, which mainly consisted of forty five chapters of "Ling" (decree) issued by "Zhou" (subprefecture) and "Jun" (shire) and over one hundred and eighty chapters of "Shang Shu Guan Ling" (orders from the minister) and "Jun Zhong Ling" (military orders).

---

[13] "Xing Fa Zhi" (The Record of the Criminal Law) in *Jin Shu* (*The History of Jin Dynasty*), quoted in *Wei Lv Xu Lue* (*Outline of the Preface to Wei Code*).

During the time of "San Guo" (Three Kingdoms), except the legal achievements represented by *Wei Lv* (*Wei Code*), necessary legislation was also enacted by the state of Shu and Wu.

After capital was founded in Chengdu, Zhuge Liang, the very famous statesman of the state of Shu, strongly supported making laws and regulations to rule the kingdom by law. He said, "We should only speak of law and act in accordance with moral principles,"[14] "because only by enforcing law is it possible for people to know that they should be grateful"[15]; "those who are loyal to the country should be awarded even though they are our personal enemies, while those who disobey the law shall be punished even though they are our relatives."[16] Therefore, "even thought the law is strict, nobody will complain about; this is because the law is just and the admonition is clear."[17] At the same time, Zhuge Liang also insisted that "education should be put before punishment," and he said that "an emperor himself should be upright and impartial, because only in this way can his orders be thoroughly carried out."[18] *Shu Ke* (*Shu Code*), which was drafted together by Zhuge Liang and Fa Zheng, was the most important law of Shu state. Besides, the chapters like "Fa Jian" (collections of law), "Ke Ling" (rules and decrees) and "Jun Ling" (military orders) were included in the appendix of *Jin Zhuge Liang Ji Biao* (*Collected Tables of Zhuge Liang*) written by Chen Shou, but only a few chapters of "Jiao" (instructions) and "Jun Ling" (military orders) remained, while the rest was all lost.

The kingdom of Sun Wu was best known for its severe penalties, some of which had already been abolished in Han Dynasty, such as "Yi San Zu" (the law of killing the three generations of a family) and "Zu Zhu" (killing of the whole clan of a criminal), but they were frequently used in Wu state. Sun Quan once tried to justify the application of severe penalties in Wu state and said that they had to do so because there were no other alternatives.[19] In the spring of the 5th year of Huangwu (226 A. D.), Lu Xun tried to persuade Sun Quan to give up such severe punishments and to reduce the penalty by implementing "De Zhi" (the ruling of virtue). Thus, Sun Quan "accordingly ordered the relevant officials to have laws and regulations drafted, and he then ordered Chu Fengji, "Lang Zhong" (head of a subministry department) at the time to rectify the inappropriate provisions after consulting Jiu Xun and Zhuge

---

[14]"Jiao Ling" (Doctrines and Instructions) in *Zhuge Liang Ji* (*The Collected Works of Zhuge Liang*).

[15]"Da Fa Zheng Shu" (Reply to Fa Zheng) in *Zhuge Liang Ji* (*The Collected Works of Zhuge Liang*).

[16]"Zhuge Liang Zhuan" (The Biography of Zhuge Liang) in "Shu Shu" (The History of Shu State) in *San Guo Zhi* (*The Record of the Three Kingdoms*).

[17]"Zhuge Liang Zhuan" (The Biography of Zhuge Liang) in "Shu Shu" (The History of Shu State) in *San Guo Zhi* (*The Record of the Three Kingdoms*).

[18]"Jiao Ling" (Doctrines and Instructions) in *Zhuge Liang Ji* (*The Collected Works of Zhuge Liang*).

[19]"Wu Zhu Zhuan" (The Biography of the Kings of Wu) in "Wu Shu" (The History of Wu State) in *San Guo Zhi* (*The Record of the Three Kingdoms*).

Jin."[20] "In the 3rd year of Jia He... 'Ke Ling' (rules and decrees) was finally made." According to *Wen Xian Tong Kao* (*A General Textual Research of the Documents*), "most of the laws of Han Dynasty were followed by Wu state," but unfortunately they were all lost.

6.1.2 The Legislative Achievements of Western and Eastern Jin and Southern Dynasty Represented by **Jin Lv** (**Jin Code**)

Even before Wei Dynasty was replaced by the Sima families of Western Jin Dynasty, Sima Zhao, the king of Jin state, "was afraid that the laws in the past were too complicated with miscellaneous trifles," so in the 1st year of Xianxi of Wei state (264 A.D.), he ordered Jia Chong, Zheng Chong, Yang Gu, Du Yu and some other officials to draft *Jin Lv* (*Jin Code*) based on the *Han Lv* (*Han Code*) and *Wei Lv* (*Wei Code*) by following the principle of "deleting what is the cruel and abominable and retaining what is the clear and simple by making reference to the Confucian classics to serve for the timely politics."[21] This law was enacted nationwide in the 4th year of Taishi during the reign of Emperor Wu of Jin (268 A.D.), so it was also called *Tai Shi Lv* (*Tai Shi Code*). Because *Jin Lv* (*Jin Code*) was annotated by Zhang Fei and Du Yu, it was also called "Zhang Du Lv."

Jin Lv (*Jin Code*) consisted of 20 chapters, 620 articles and 27,657 provisions. The twenty chapters include: *Xing Ming* (*Law*), *Fa Li* (*Precedents*), *Dao Lv* (*Statutes on Theft*), *Zei Lv* (*Statutes on Banditry*), *Zha Wei* (*Statutes on Fraud and Forgery*), *Qing Qiu* (*Statutes on Asking for Bribery*), *Gao He Lv* (*Statutes on Prosecution*), *Bu Lv* (*Statutes on Arrest*), *Xi Xun Lv* (*Statutes on Interrogation*), *Duan Yu Lv* (*Statutes on Trials and Punishments*), *Za Lv* (*Miscellaneous Laws*), *Hu Lv* (*Statutes on Households*), *Shan Xing Lv* (*Statutes on Sending Troops without Authorization*), *Hui Wang Lv* (*Statutes on Damages and Death*), *Wei Gong Lv* (*Statutes on the Protection of the Emperor's Personal Safety and National Sovereignty*), *Shui Huo Lv* (*Statutes on on Water and Fire*), *Jiu Lv* (*Statutes on Livestock Breeding*), *Guan Shi Lv* (*Statutes on Border Market*), *Wei Zhi Lv* (*Statutes on Punishing Officials' Dereliction of Duty*) and *Zhu Hou Lv* (*Statutes on Dukes and Princes*). In spite of the fact that there were only two more chapters in *Jin Lv* (*Jin Code*), compared to *Wei Lv* (*Wei Code*), its structure was much more reasonable and substantial than that of the former and the annotation of *Jin Lv* (*Jin Code*) also reached the standardized criterion.

---

[20] "Wu Zhu Zhuan" (The Biography of the Kings of Wu) in "Wu Shu" (The History of Wu State) in *San Guo Zhi* (*The Record of the Three Kingdoms*).

[21] "Xing Fa Zhi" (The Record of the Criminal Law) in *Jin Shu* (*The History of Jin Dynasty*).

6.1.2.1 *Jin Lv* (*Jin Code*) was completed based on the "Lv Xue" (the study of statutory laws) (mainly criminal law), which was much well developed at the time, so it is as a code with a strong color of Confucianism in Chinese feudal society. Mr. Chen Yinque also pointed out this prominent characteristic of *Jin Lv* (*Jin Code*): "Sima Family set up Jin Dynasty and unified China by depending on the distinguished Confucian scholars of the Eastern Han Dynasty, so the criminal law which he made was specially Confucianized."[22]

The Confucianization of *Jin Lv* (*Jin Code*) was realized by appointing Confucian scholars to be in charge of drafting and interpreting laws. In *Lv Biao* (*Standards of Law*), which he submitted to the emperor, Du Yu stated that the basic principle of *Jin Lv* (*Jin Code*) was "ruling according to people's social status," because it was emphasized by "Li" (rites)[23]; therefore, in compiling *Lv Biao* (*Standards of Law*), the principle of "showing respect to the ancients rites by adopting the current etiquette"[24] was accepted, so "Fa" (law) and "Li" (rites) were further integrated through the annotation of law.

The Confucianization of *Jin Lv* (*Jin Code*) is well illustrated in the following aspects:

First, "preventing crimes by applying 'Li Jiao' (feudal ethical code) and enforcing punishment according to 'Wu Fu' (relatives within the five degrees of mourning)."[25] So anyone who had violated the etiquette at that time would be sentenced to severe punishments. For example, "those who raped their aunts would be sentenced to 'Qi Shi' (exposing the executed body publicly at markets), while those who raped a widow would be sentenced to three years of imprisonment."[26] Meanwhile, the social position of the convicted should be taken into consideration when specific punishment was enforced to "have the gentlemen awarded and the scoundrels punished."[27] The legal principle of "enforcing punishment according to 'Wu Fu' (relatives within the five degrees of mourning)" was established during Jin Dynasty and it had been used until the late Qing Dynasty.

Second, both "Li" (rites) and "Fa" (law) were stressed, and "Li" (rites) could also be used as the evidence in criminal punishment. It was recorded in "Yin Zhong Kan Zhuan" (The Biography of Yin Zhongkan) in *Jin Shu* (*The History of Jin Dynasty*) that "it is forbidden in 'Li' (rites) and 'Lv' (criminal law) for people to adopt those with different family names." It was stated in "Yu Chun Zhuan" (The Biography of Yu Chun) in *Jin Shu* (*The History of Jin Dynasty*) that "'Li' (rites) should be taken as the priority when making judgments."

---

[22]Chen Yinque, "Xing Lv" (Criminal Law) in *Sui Tang Zhi Du Yuan Yuan Lve Lun Gao* (*The Origin of the Systems of Sui and Tang Dynasties*), SDX Joint Publishing Company, 2001. p. 111.

[23]"Yang Gu Du Yu Lie Zhuan" (The Collected Biographies of Yang Gu and Du Yu) in *Jin Shu* (*The History of Jin Dynasty*).

[24]"Li Zhi" (The Record of Rites) in *Jin Shu* (*The History of Jin Dynasty*) (Book 2).

[25]"Xing Fa Zhi" (The Record of the Criminal Law) in *Jin Shu* (*The History of Jin Dynasty*).

[26]"Xing Fa Zhi" (The Record of the Criminal Law) in *Jin Shu* (*The History of Jin Dynasty*).

[27]"Xing Fa Zhi" (The Record of the Criminal Law) in *Jin Shu* (*The History of Jin Dynasty*).

Third, "Li" (rites) was not only incorporated into law, but also was legalized. For example, "Ba Yi" (The Eight Deliberations), which had been discussed previously, became legal rules. Thus, accordingly, "if the vassals have committed crimes, they should handled according to the procedure of 'Ba Yi' (The Eight Deliberations) and be granted the privilege of 'Jian Shou Liu Su' (reducing penalty by paying ransom), so they should be exempted from the punishment of 'Kun' (having the criminal's long hair cut short), 'Qian' (the penalty of banishing the criminals to do forced labor in remote areas) and 'Chi' (flogging with light sticks)."[28] Another example: "Bu Jing" (being irreverent), "Bu Dao" (depravity), "E Ni" (abusing or murdering the elders), "Wu Wang Fu Mu" (slandering parents) and "Fan Ni" (treachery) were all included in law for their violation of "Li" (rites).

Since *Jin Lv* (*Jin Code*) was made by introducing "Li" (rites) into "Fa' (law) and combining "Li" (rites) with "Fa' (law), its stylistic rules and layout were much stricter and interpretation more standardized, so it was not only more suitable to Chinese national conditions, it also exerted a far-reaching influence on Northern and Southern Dynasty.

6.1.2.2 Another feature of *Jin Lv* (*Jin Code*) was that its layout and structure were improved and the codes, decrees and interpretations were all simplified.

First, the chapter of *Xing Ming* (*Law*) was divided into two parts: *Xing Ming* (*Law*) and *Fa Li* (*Precedents*), both of which were placed at the beginning of *Jin Lv* (*Jin Code*). The categories of specific severe and lenient penalties, the methods of passing sentences properly, the examples of legal sections and provisions were all explained in detail in these two chapters. *Xing Ming* (*Law*) and *Fa Li* (*Precedents*) acted as the pandect of *Jin Lv* (*Jin Code*). Zhang Fei said that "*Xing Ming* (*Law*) is made to explain the seriousness of a crime, to justify the proper enforcement of punishment, to clarify the meaning of the provisions, to make up the inefficiency of articles, and to summarize the essentials of the law,.... 'Ming' and 'Li' are used to make the legal system perfect."[29]

Second, new laws were made and the old ones were amended. For example, *Wei Gong Lv* (*Statutes on the Protection of the Emperor's Personal Safety and National Sovereignty*) was made to strengthen palace security; *Guan Shi Lv* (*Statutes on Border Market*) was made to regulate the increasingly frequent commercial intercourses along ferries and fortresses; *Shui Huo Lv* was made to prevent the disasters of flood and the fire; *Wei Zhi Lv* (*Statutes on Punishing Officials' Dereliction of Duty*) was made to maintain the centralized authority and *Zhu Hou Lv* (*Statutes on Dukes and Princes*) was made to adjust the system of enfeoffment. Besides, *Qiu Lv* (*Statutes on Imprisonment*) was combined with *Xi Xun Lv* (*Statutes on Interrogation*); *Jiu Lv* (*Statutes on Livestock Breeding*), which was abolished in *Wei Lv* (*Wei Code*), was restored; the other four laws, namely, *Jie Lue Lv* (*Statutes on Robbery*),

---

[28]"Xing Fa Bu" (The Section of Penal Law) (Part 2) in *Bei Tang Shu Chao* (*Excerpts Written in North Hall*), Vol. 44, quoted from *Jin Lv* (*Jin Code*).

[29]"Xing Fa Zhi" (The Record of the Criminal Law) in *Jin Shu* (*The History of Jin Dynasty*).

Jing Shi Lv (*Statutes on Dangerous and Emergent Matters*), *Chang Zang Lv* (*Statutes on Accepting Bribes*) and *Mian Zuo Lv* (*Statutes on Exemption from Punishment*) were abolished. These revisions not only reflected the natural law of changing with times, but also showed the demand of the development of social economy and the strengthening of the autocratic system.

Third, the status of "Zheng Lv" (Official Law) was improved and the dividing line between "Lv" (criminal law) and "Ling" (decree) was clarified. "Lv" referred to relatively stable norms and rules while "Ling" (decree) referred to the temporary ones. According to *Lv Xu* (*Preface to Law*) written by Du Yu, which was quoted in *Tai Ping Yu Lan* (*Imperial Readings of the Taiping Era*), "'Lv' (criminal law) is to give names to crimes, while 'Ling' (decree) is to provide standards for doing things." "The other regulations, such as the regulations on military affairs, farm and agriculture and liquor trade are just made temporarily according to people's suggestions, so they are all included in 'Ling' (decree) without being contained in law. They are carried out to educate people, so if people are guilty for violating 'Ling' (decree), then they will be punished by 'Lv' (criminal law); if not, they will be educated by relevant offices."[30] Therefore, it can be seen that "Lv" (criminal law) is the established standard, while "Ling" (decree) is just a temporary system; if people are guilty for violating 'Ling' (decree), then they belong to the category of "Lv"; so people should not be punished if they have not violated 'Lv' (criminal law), which has thoroughly eliminated the misconduct caused by the confusion of "Lv" (criminal law) and "Ling" (decree) in Qin Dynasty and which has further clarified the boundary of "Lv" (criminal law) by differentiating it from "Ling" (decree). According to the definition in Han Dynasty, "the laws promulgated by the previous emperors are 'Lv', while those by the current emperor are 'Ling' (decree)," which is very misleading.[31]

Lastly, the number of laws and orders were greatly reduced in *Jin Lv* (*Jin Code*) and the over 7,730,000 words in the laws and interpretations of *Han Lv* (*Han Code*) were simplified and were reduced to about 126,300 in *Jin Lv* (*Jin Code*), which could be described as "eliminating what is redundant and retaining what is necessary." This was highly spoken of by Du Yu, who commented that "the law is not about interpreting the reasons, but about setting up standards for making judgments. So it should be direct, concise, easy to be understood and carried out. Besides, the prohibition should be clear and simple, because if it is clear, people will know what they should not do, then there is no need to enforce penalties."[32] To prevent evil people from committing crimes, Emperor Wu of Jin, at the invitation of "Shi Zhong" (the assistant official) Lu and others, had copied the provisions on death

---

[30]"Xing Fa Zhi" (The Record of the Criminal Law) in *Jin Shu* (*The History of Jin Dynasty*).
[31]"Du Zhou Zhuan" (The Biography of Du Zhou) in *Han Shu* (*The History of Han Dynasty*).
[32]"Yang Gu Du Yu Lie Zhuan" (The Collected Biographies of Yang Gu and Du Yu) in *Jin Shu* (*The History of Jin Dynasty*).

penalty and posted them on pavilions so as "to make them known to the ordinary people."[33]

6.1.2.3 Much progress had been made in "Lv Xue" (the study of statutory laws) in Jin Dynasty based on that of Han Dynasty. Because *Han Lv* (*Han Code*) was compiled by more than ten schools of Confucian scholars with about 100,000 words for each of them, and altogether 26,272 articles and 7,732,200 words were used in trial, it was very complicated, redundant, and dull. Moreover, it was very difficult for judicial officials to make sentences under these legal provisions, an order was once issued by Emperor Wen and it was stipulated that "it is forbidden to use other annotation except the one written by Zheng,"[34] which had undoubted promoted the unification of "Lv Xue" (the study of statutory laws).

Besides, the position of "Lv Xue Bo Shi" (Scholar of Law) was set up in government offices since Western Jin Dynasty to be in charge of teaching the knowledge of "Lv Xue" (the study of statutory laws), so this institution was retained in many dynasties ever since. In Jin Dynasty, Du Yu and Zhang Fei were two representatives of the scholars of law. Zhang Fei wrote *Lv Jie* (*Annotations of Laws*) consisting of twenty-one volumes and *Han Jin Lv Xu Zhu* (*Comments on Han Lv and Jin Lv*) consisting of one volume; Du Yu wrote *Lv Ben* (*Law*) consisting of twenty-one volumes and *Za Lv* (*Miscellaneous Laws*) consisting of seven volumes. Although these works were lost, it can be seen through the fragmentary records that in Jin Dynasty "Lv Xue" was already separated from Confucian classics and the former was no longer a accessory of the latter. In "Lv" (criminal law), great emphasis was laid on the legislative techniques, the legal practices, the principles of making sentences and the implementation of corresponding punishments, which was the main feature of "Lv Xue" (the study of statutory laws) at its new stage of development. Apart from Zhang Fei and Du Yu, other famous scholars included Liu Song, Zhong You, Zhong Hui, Fu Gan, Cao Xi, Ding Yi and Liu Shao, etc.

During the reign of Emperor Wen in Jin Dynasty, laws were made by Jia Chong and Du Yu. After that, annotations were added by Du Yu. Du Yu was not only an expert in "Lv Xue" (the study of statutory laws), but also an expert in Confucian classics. In his *Chun Qiu Zuo Shi Jing Zhuan Ji Jie* (*Collected Commentaries on the Spring and Autumn Annals and the Chronicle of Zuo*), an elaborate analysis of political and legal institutions of the pre-Qin period was conducted, which had no doubt influenced his annotation to law. For example, from the basic Confucian ideology of stressing etiquettes and social status, he pointed out that "the essence of law lies in its conciseness and clarity, so a person's social status should be considered.....in this annotation, the meaning of the law is outlined and a person's social status is studied. The users should make their choices according to "Ming Li" (The Categories of Penalties and General Principles) and make fair judgments

---

[33]"Xing Fa Zhi" (The Record of the Criminal Law) in *Jin Shu* (*The History of Jin Dynasty*).

[34]"Xing Fa Zhi" (The Record of the Criminal Law) in *Jin Shu* (*The History of Jin Dynasty*).

according to law to eliminate the contents of 'Xi Xin' (chop firewood, the trifles)."[35] So obviously law annotation also further promoted the Confucianization of *Jin Lv* (*Jin Code*). From the fragmentary records of *Lv Ben* (*Law*), it can be seen that through Du Yu's annotation not only the legislative principles of *Jin Lv* (*Jin Code*) were set up, a clear requirement was also expressed to regard law enforcement as a set of universal rules of behavior, which had provided the law executors with a unified standard to follow in law enforcement.

Zhang Fei, in his *Lv Jie* (*Annotations of Laws*) and *Zhu Lv Biao* (*Table of Annotations for Codes*), made a concise and exact interpretation of twenty kinds of crimes. He said, "It is 'Gu' (an intentional act) to deliberately break the law; it is 'Shi' (a negligent act) to always think oneself correct; it is 'Man' (deception) to rebel against and deceive the superiors; it is 'Zha' (fraud) to break promise and to conceal hypocrisy; it is 'Bu Jing' (being irreverent) to abandon etiquettes; it is 'Dou' (fighting) for two litigators to contend with each other; it is 'Xi' (harming each other) for two friends to harm each other; it is 'Zei' (banditry) to assault another people for no reason; it is 'Guo Shi' (negligence) to unconsciously commit an offence; it is 'Bu Dao' (depravity) to violate moral integrity and principles; it is 'E Ni' (abusing or murdering the elders) to humiliate one's superiors or to infringe upon the reputation of the noble; it is 'Qiang' (intention to harm) to attempt to harm another person without being accomplished; it is 'Zao Yi' (putting forward a suggestion) to put forward a suggestion untimely; it is 'Mou' (conspiracy) for two people to plot an unlawful act; it is 'Shuai' (leading a rebellion) to instigate others to take illegal actions; it is 'Qiang' (conflict) to be on bad terms; it is 'Lue' (plundering) to attack people; it is 'Qun' (mobbing) to conduct an unlawful act by three people; it is 'Dao' (theft) to take away the property which do not belong to oneself and it is 'Zang' (booty) to make profits from goods or other property. In a word, all these twenty definitions are provided so as to rectify the general legal terms."[36] He clarified the boundary between intentional crime and criminal negligence and put forward the basic constituents of crimes such as "Zao Yi" (putting forward a suggestion), "He Mou" (conspiracy) and "Qun" (mobbing). Moreover, he also drew a dividing line between malpractice and criminal negligence and explained the meaning of "Zang" (booty), "Xi" (harming each other), "Dou" (fighting), "Zha" (killing), "Qiang" (intention to harm), "Lue" (plundering), "Qiang" (conflict) and "Shuai" (leading a rebellion) in detail. Thus, Zhang Fei's normative explanation reflected the new level reached by ancient Chinese "Lv Xue" (the study of statutory laws), meanwhile, he had made groundbreaking contribution not only to eliminating the farfetched way of interpreting laws by making use of Confucian classics but also to making "Lv Xue" (the study of statutory laws) develop more scientifically.

Zhang Fei not only explained the literal meaning of law, but also clarified the similar crimes which were easy to be confused in *Jin Lv* (*Jin Code*). For example, "it

---

[35]"Yang Gu Du Yu Lie Zhuan" (The Collected Biographies of Yang Gu and Du Yu) in *Jin Shu* (*The History of Jin Dynasty*).

[36]"Xing Fa Zhi" (The Record of the Criminal Law) in *Jin Shu* (*The History of Jin Dynasty*).

is 'Zei (banditry) for people to fight with their superiors', but it is more serious than 'Xi' (harming each other) to fight with weapons." "So 'Xi' (harming each other) is similar to 'Dou' (fighting), while it is similar to 'Wu' (unintentional harming others) to injury others in 'Dou' (fighting)"; "it is not 'Guo' (going beyond the limit) but 'Shi' (violation) to shoot at people's houses and roads; it is 'Zei' (banditry) to ride a horse among the crowds in the city"; "it is 'Qiang Dao' (robber) to take property from others by threatening."[37] But the crimes such as "Fu Shou," "Kong," "He Ren," "Shou Qiu," "Chi Zhi," "Dao Zang," "Liu Nan," "Shan Fu," "Chuo Ru," etc. all referred to robbing property by force. They were either different from the crime of "Qiang Dao" (robber) in name or similar to it in the crimes committed.

Zhang Fei also explained concisely the category of *Xing Ming* (*Law*) and the methods of aggravating and mitigating the punishment in *Jin Lv* (*Jin Code*): "If one means well but causes bad results, he can atone for his crime with money. So there are altogether fourteen levels of ordinary penalties; there are no more than three kinds of death penalties; there are no more than six years of the term of imprisonment for 'Tu' (imprisonment); there are no more than five years for the term of 'Qiu' (putting under arrest); there are no more than eleven years for the accumulated term of 'Zuo' (imprisonment and labor service); there are no more than 1200 strokes for the accumulated punishment of 'Chi' (flogging with light sticks); there is no more than one year of difference between different levels of punishment and the difference between different levels of punishment is no more than four *liang* of gold." "The most severe penalty for all crimes is death, so if a person has been sentenced to death penalty, no other penalties should be added. But if a person has committed plural crimes, cumulative penalties should be adopted; if cumulative penalties cannot be adopted, combined penalties should be adopted, and vice versa. If a penalty needs to be added to the original one but the crimes are the same, these penalties shall be accumulated and enforced together; if the penalties are not within the range of the cases discussed, such practice won't be carried out."[38]

It is noteworthy that Zhang Fei and Du Yu's interpretation of *Jin Lv* (*Jin Code*) was not only of great theoretical value, but also was of great significance in providing practical guidance.

In addition to Zhang Fei and Du Yu who had made great contribution to the development of ancient "Lv Xue" (the study of statutory laws) by their annotation of *Jin Lv* (*Jin Code*), Liu Song also proposed some epoch-making ideas on legal reforms, which were directed at the malpractice of "redundant laws and inconsistent decrees." First, he demonstrated that "because there is the difference between the monarch and the ministers, they should perform their own duties." He also explained by citing examples that, "the supervisor prosecutes according to law, the warder makes judgment according to facts and the judicial official settles the cases according to the confession of criminals," so the major task of the emperor was to make the judicial agencies fulfill their duties without interfering with their work.

---

[37]"Xing Fa Zhi" (The Record of the Criminal Law) in *Jin Shu* (*The History of Jin Dynasty*).
[38]"Xing Fa Zhi" (The Record of the Criminal Law) in *Jin Shu* (*The History of Jin Dynasty*).

Second, he stressed that after a law was enacted, the emperor should keep his promise and make no random changes. Because "law is the only thing which is shared by the emperor and his people in the country, it must be taken seriously. People cannot be governed by laws which are always changeable."[39] Third, for the sake of impartiality, Liu Song insisted that "cases should only be settled according to main text of the law; if there are no main texts, the accessory 'Ming Li' (Categories of Penalties and General Principles) should be used; if there are no main texts nor accessory 'Ming Li' (Categories of Penalties and General Principles), the sentences should not be made."[40] He suggested at the same time that "when there is a controversy among the judicial officials like 'Fa Cao' (judicial officials), 'Lang'(a general official title of departmental officials), 'Ling' (magistrate) and 'Shi' (official in charge of the measurement of penalty), they should resort to the law rather than anything else. This is to show that judges should exercise their power according to law."[41]

Liu Song's idea about independent judicature and "nulla poena sine lege" is not only a summary of his many years of experience as a supervisor and practitioner of law, but also a inheritance and development of feudal legal system. Indeed there are considerable similarities between Liu Song's ideas and the theory of independent judicature, as well as the principle of "nulla poena sine lege," which was put forward in the seventeenth and eighteenth centuries by western bourgeoisie. Nevertheless, Liu Song had already shown his concern over these principles in the third century, which was 1000 years earlier than the west. After his proposals were put forward, they were applauded by many people. For example, "Shi Zhong Tai Zai" (ancient officials in charge of state codes), Duke of Runan agreed with Liu Song and said that "what Liu Song suggested could be used as a permanent system,"[42] while at the same time his theory was criticized by some people. For example, Xiong Yuan, who was "Zhu Bu" (assistant official in charge of clerical work) at the time, spoke in defense of the monarch's random interference with law and said in a memorial that "so it is not the exclusive rights of the ministers, but the rights of the emperor to reform and change the law and to use provisional measures to deal with the urgent affairs."[43] Unfortunately, most emperors of West Jin Dynasty were fatuous, which had inevitably led to the formation of corrupted political circles, so in fact it was impossible for Liu Song's proposals to be carried out.

Apart from *Jin Lv* (*Jin Code*), orders and decrees consisting of 40 chapters and 2306 articles were also made. According to "Shang Shu Xing Bu" (The Minister of the Department of Punishment) in *Tang Liu Dian* (*The Six Statutes of Tang Dynasty*) (Vol.6), these forty chapters include "Hu" (Household), "Xue" (Learning), "Gong Shi" (the lowest rank of nobility), "Guan Pin" (Official Ranks), "Li Yuan" (Petty

---

[39]"Xing Fa Zhi" (The Record of the Criminal Law) in *Jin Shu* (*The History of Jin Dynasty*).
[40]"Xing Fa Zhi" (The Record of the Criminal Law) in *Jin Shu* (*The History of Jin Dynasty*).
[41]"Xing Fa Zhi" (The Record of the Criminal Law) in *Jin Shu* (*The History of Jin Dynasty*).
[42]"Xing Fa Zhi" (The Record of the Criminal Law) in *Jin Shu* (*The History of Jin Dynasty*).
[43]"Xing Fa Zhi" (The Record of the Criminal Law) in *Jin Shu* (*The History of Jin Dynasty*).

Officials), "Feng Lin" (Salary), "Fu Zhi" (mourning apparel system), "Ci" (Ancestral Temple), "Hu Diao" (Household Tax), "Dian" (Tenant), "Fu Chu" (Absolution of Tax and Corvée), "Guan Shi" (Border Market), "Bu Wang" (Arresting), "Yu Guan" (Warden), "Bian Zhang" (Flogging), "Yi Yao Ji Bing" (Medicine and Disease), "Sang Zang"(Funeral), "Za Shang" (The Miscellaneous: Part One), "Za Zhong" (The Miscellaneous: Part Two), "Za Xia" (The Miscellaneous: Part Three), "Men Xia San Qi Zhong Shu" (ancient official in charge of emperor's attendants), "Shang Shu" (the minister), "San Tai Mi Shu" (ancient official of three offices of 'Shang Shu', 'Yu Shi' and 'He Zhe'), "Wang Gong Hou" (Prince, Duke and Marquis), "Jun Li Yuan" (Military Officials), "Xuan Li" (Selecting Able and Virtues People as Officials), "Xuan Jiang" (Selecting Able and Virtuous People as Generals), "Xuan Za Shi"(Selecting other Professionals), "Gong Wei" (Palace Guards), "Shu" (Atonement), "Jun Zhan'(Battles), "Jun Shui Zhan" (Water Battle), "Jun Fa" (Military Law), "Za Fa" (Miscellaneous Laws). *Jin Ling* (*Orders and Decrees in Jin Dynasty*) was said to be famous for its detailed contents in history books.

Besides, *Gu Shi* (*Old Rules for Handling Things*) consisting of thirty volumes was also made by Jia Chong by referring to "Zhi Zhao Zhi Tiao" (Articles of Emperor's Decrees). *Gu Shi* (*Old Rules for Handling Things*) consisted of administrative regulations governing government officials, which was enforced concurrently with "Lv" (criminal law) and "Ling" (decree). "Lv" (criminal law) referred to the great law of the country, so if "Ling" (decree) was violated, those violators would be punished according to "Lv" (criminal law). "Ling" (decree) referred to the system ensuring the implementation of political education, while *Gu Shi* (*Old Rules for Handling Things*) referred to the detailed rules and regulations of government institutions. No doubt, this division had reflected the progress of legal thoughts and techniques.

Although "Ke" (rule) was already used as a form of law in Jin Dynasty, to avoid the phenomenon of "Yi Lv Liang Ke" (one law and two rules), it had no independent status. Besides, according to "Shi Huo Zhi" (The Records of National Finance and Economy) in *Jin Shu* (*The History of Jin Dynasty*), after Jin state defeated Wu state, "'Hu Tiao Shi' (the standard to adjust households) was made, which included contents like the adjustment of households, land occupation, land tax, "Yin Zu" (sheltering the clan members) and "Yin Ke" (sheltering the guests). Thus, it can be inferred that "Shi" (standard) was also a form of law at that time.

After the disintegration of Jin Dynasty, a unified China was suddenly split into two parts, namely, the south and the north. In the south, in the four dynasties, namely, Song, Qi, Liang and Chen, *Jin Lv* (*Jin Code*) was adopted. Song Dynasty in the south once had its laws and decrees revised in the 4th year of Daming during the reign of Emperor Xiaowu (460 A.D.), yet according to the 6th volume of *Tang Liu Dian* (*The Six Statutes of Tang Dynasty*), its chapter, basic structure and "Xing Ming" (law) were not changed.

In the early years of Qi Dynasty, *Jin Lv* (*Jin Code*) was still used, and it was stated in "Kong Zhi Gui Zhuan" (The Biography of Kong Zhigui) in *Nan Qi Shu* (*The History of Southern Qi Dynasty*) that in (Southern Qi) the system which was established in the east of Yangtz River was continued, so the twenty volumes of

'Lv' (criminal law) made by Zhang and Du in the Jin Dynasty were applied." In the 7th year of Yongming during the reign of Emperor Wu (489 A.D.), *Yong Ming Lv* (*Yong Ming Code*) consisting of 1532 articles was made based on the *Jin Lv* (*Jin Code*), but the new code was not implemented.

Emperor Wu of Liang Dynasty once ordered Cai Fadu and Shen Yue to draft *Liang Lv* (*Liang Code*) based on the *Jin Lv* (*Jin Code*). *Liang Lv* (*Liang Code*) was made up of 20 chapters and 2529 articles and the difference between the two codes includes the following: *Zei Lv* (*Statutes on Banditry*) was replaced by *Zei Pan* (*Statutes on Banditry and Rebelling*); *Dao Lv* (*Statutes on Theft*) was replaced by *Dao Jie* (*The Statute on Theft and Robbery*); *Qing Qiu* (*Statutes on Asking for Bribery*) was replaced by *Shou Qiu* (*Statutes on Accepting Bribery*); *Bu Lv* (*Statutes on Arrest*) was replaced by *Tao Bu* (*Statutes on Tracking and Arresting*). Besides, *Zhu Hou* (*Statutes on Dukes and Princes*) was deleted and *Cang Ku* (*Warehouse*) was added.

In addition to these modifications, Cai Fadu also made *Liang Ling* (*Orders in Liang Dynasty*) and *Liang Ke* (*Rules in Liang Dynasty*), each consisting of 30 volumes. In *Liang Lv* (*Liang Code*) the punishments were more strictly enforced. For example, death penalty was divided into "Qi Shi" (exposing the executed body publicly at markets) and "Xiao Shou" (the penalty of hanging the head of the criminal on top of a pole for public display); the term for the punishment of "Nai" (having the criminal's beard shaven for two years) was increased from two to five years; the punishment of "Bian" (whipping) was classified into "Zhi Bian" (the crude ribbed lashes), "Fa Bian" (the crude unribbed lashes) and "Chang Bian" (the processed unribbed lashes); "Zhang" (flogging with heavy sticks) was classified into "Da Zhang" (flogging with big sticks), "Zhong Zhang" (flogging with medium sticks) and "Xiao Zhang" (flogging with small sticks). Besides, "Shu Xing" (atonement) was also established. Thus, the penalty system of Southern Liang had exerted a great influence on Northern Dynasty.

In Southern Chen Dynasty, laws and decrees were also made. According to *Tang Liu Dian* (*The Six Statutes of Tang Dynasty*), "Fan Quan and Xu Ling were ordered to participate in making "Lv Ling" (*The Laws and Decrees*), which consisted of thirty volumes of "Lv" (criminal law), "Ling" (decree) and "Ke" (rule) respectively. As to "Lv" (criminal law), it was almost a copy of *Liang Fa* (*Liang Code*) either in contents or in the degree of severity. Yet according to "Xing Fa Zhi"(The Record of the Criminal Law) in *Sui Shu* (*The History of Sui Dynasty*), *Chen Lv* (*Chen Code*) was extensively criticized because its articles were redundant, its outline was cumbersome and its scope was wide but without focusing points. It is noteworthy that the provision of "Guan Dang" (giving up one's official position for the atonement for a crime), which meant that the officials could stone for their crimes by giving up their positions, was first included in law, so it was continuously applied by generations of people ever since and became a very important part of feudal statutes in China.

In conclusion, *Jin Lv* (*Jin Code*) was basically applied by the four Southern Dynasty of Sun, Qi, Liang, and Chen with few modifications. As the rulers of Southern Dynasty liked empty talk and advocated metaphysics and Buddhism,

"Lv Xue" (the study of statutory laws) increasingly declined. The people like Wang Zhizhi, Cai Fadu had no choices but to use *Jin Lv* (*Jin Code*) as the basis of law revision. Relatively speaking, "Lv Xue" (the study of statutory laws) in Northern Dynasty was more advanced than that in Southern Dynasty and the people like Cui Hao and Gao Yun were renowned for their proficiency in *Han Lv* (*Han Code*), so that after Chen state was annexed by Sui state, the laws in Northern Dynasty were regarded as the model in drafting *Sui Lv* (*Sui Code*). Thus, the laws in Southern Dynasty that came down in a continuous line from Wei and Jing dynasties had come to an end.

6.1.3 The Legislative Achievements in Northern Dynasty Represented by Bei Wei Lv *(Bei Wei Code)* and Bei Qi Lv *(Bei Qi Code)*

6.1.3.1 Northern Wei Dynasty (also called Hou Wei and Yuan Wei) was established by the Tuoba family of Xian Bei nationality in 386 A.D., which marked the beginning of Northern Dynasty. Before their entry to central China, there were neither written languages nor laws for the North Wei Dynasty. It was recorded that "at first, the 'Li' (rites) of Wei Dynasty was unsophisticated and penalties were simple.... So disputes were resolved orally and people were restricted by verbal speech. Moreover, events were recorded by inscribing on the stone or somewhere else, and there were no laws about imprisonment or interrogation, so the criminals were punished on the spot."[44] As they settled down in central China, the concept of the relevant advanced legal ideology began to be absorbed, so law was used as a method of their governance to adapt to the need of ruling the extensive areas of central China. For example, Emperor Taizu of North Wei ordered "'Wang De', 'San Gong Lang Zhong' (an official helping to deal with state affairs) at the time, to make laws and decrees and to have an review of the rules; . . .then he ordered Cui Xuanbo, 'Li Bu Shang Shu' (the minister of the department of personnel), to make a summary and to give a final touch."[45] To absorb the advanced legal culture of Han nationality, Emperor Shizu ordered Cui Hong and Cui Hao who were specialized in law "to be in charge of law revision."[46] Moreover, he also ordered Gao Yun, who was "expert at philosophy, literature, astronomy and arithmetic and who was especially fond of the theory of "Chun Qiu Gong Yang" (Chun Qiu by Master Gong Yang)"[47] to participate in the reformation of the country's legal system. The practice of "Chun Qiu Jue

---

[44]"Xing Fa Zhi" (The Record of the Criminal Law) in *Wei Shu* (*The History of Northern Wei Dynasty*).
[45]"Tai Zu Ji" (The Record of Emperor Taizu) in *Wei Shu* (*The History of Northern Wei Dynasty*).
[46]"Shi Zu Ji" (The Record of Emperor Shizu) in *Wei Shu* (*The History of Northern Wei Dynasty*).
[47]"Gao Yun Zhuan" (The Biography of Gao Yun) in *Wei Shu* (*The History of Northern Wei Dynasty*).

Yu" (Settling Lawsuits by Chun Qiu or Confucianism Classics) also gained momentum in the legal practice of Northern Wei Dynasty. It was recorded in "Shi Zu Ji" (The Record of Emperor Shizu) in *Wei Shu* (*The History of Northern Wei Dynasty*) that "if there are any doubtful cases, they would be settled by 'Zhong Shu' (the prime minister) according to Confucian classics." Especially after the new capital of Wei was established in Luoyang, with the carrying out of a series of very important reforms such as the reform of "Jun Tian Zhi" (The System of Land Equalization), the system for tax and corvée, and "San Zhang Zhi" (a system of household registration), the feudal agriculture economic went on the right track, and the unification of the state and centralization of authority in the north were consolidated. Consequently, it was possible to begin a large-scale legislation and legal system construction. Because "the evil officials might make unfair judgments by abusing the laws and decrees because of the insufficiency of legal provisions,"[48] laws were revised for many times, and Emperor Xiaowen even made revisions by himself. It was recorded in history books that "Xiaowen adopted the system of Xia and changed the customs of Wei by making laws. Moreover, he often made notes by himself and settled the lawsuits in person whenever there were disputes. So he was highly praised by the later generations."[49] Thus, we can see that obviously great attention was paid to law enactment by the Tuoba family.

Emperor Xiaowen had actively absorbed the advanced legal culture of Han nationality and put forward the strategies of ruling the state by applying both "Li" (rites) and "Fa" (law), which mainly focused on the principle of "regarding 'Li Jiao' (feudal ethical code) as the essence of governing the country"[50] and "regarding 'Fa' (law) as the priority of politics."[51] The policy of regarding "Li Jiao" (feudal ethical code) as the essence was also reflected in law and it mainly includes the following aspects. First, "Bu Xiao" (being unfilial) was more severely punished. It was stated in an imperial edict issued in the 1st year of Taihe (477 A.D.) that "among the 3000 crimes, "Bu Xiao" (being unfilial) is the most serious, but according to law, the maximum penalty for showing no respect to one's parents is "Kun" (having the criminal's long hair cut short). So it is not suitable and should be modified."[52] Second, the law of "Cun Liu Yang Qin" (the criminal can be pardoned to take care of their parents if their parents are old and have nobody to depend on) was made: the criminals who still had filial duties to do could be exempted from death

---

[48]"Xing Fa Zhi" (The Record of the Criminal Law) in *Wei Shu* (*The History of Northern Wei Dynasty*).

[49]Cheng Shude, "Hou Wei Lv Kao Xu" (Preface to the Textual Research of the Laws of Latter Wei Dynasty) in *Jiu Chao Lv Kao* (*A Textual Research of the Laws of the Nine Dynasties from Han to Sui*).

[50]"Ren Cheng Wang Yun Zhuan" (The Biography of Wang Yun in Ren Cheng) in *Wei Shu* (*The History of Northern Wei Dynasty*).

[51]"Gao Zu Ji" (The Record of Emperor Gaozu) in *Wei Shu* (*The History of Northern Wei Dynasty*).

[52]"Xing Fa Zhi" (The Record of the Criminal Punishment) in *Wei Shu* (*The History of Northern Wei Dynasty*).

penalty or temporarily exempted from exile (until their parents passed away) if their parents or grandparents were old with no other children or relatives to take care of them.[53] In the 18th year of Taihe (494 A.D.), an amendment was made for the returned criminals who had been exiled and it was stipulated that "those who are sentenced to guard the border in the north can go back to their hometown if they have reached the age of seventy and got disabled. One of their sons can go together with them to take care of them. After they have died, their sons should return to the border to continue their services. All those exiled who have reached the age of eighty shall return to their hometown."[54] Thus, "Cun Liu Yang Qin" (the criminal can be pardoned to take care of their parents if their parents are old and have nobody to depend on) had been applied in China for a long time and it was not abolished until Qing Dynasty. Third, the children, grandchildren, great-grandchildren or great great-grandchildren could conceal the crimes committed by their parents, grandparents, great-grandparents or great great-grandparents; otherwise, "they would be sentenced to death."[55] Dou Yuan explained that "if parents or grandparents have stolen something or even killed someone, the children should keep it as a secret and make no report. The law is so made, so we can see its justice."[56] Fourth, those who committed the crime of "Qin Shu Xiang Fan" (infringement among relatives) should be severely punished according to "Lun Chang" (feudal order of importance). Fifth, according to the principle of "Xu Xing" (penalty reduction), the rule of "Men Fang Zhi Zhu" (a penalty to punish those related to a criminal, including his grandparents, grandchildren, parents, wife, children, brothers and sisters born of the same mother) was abolished. It was stated in an imperial edict issued in the 11th year of Taihe (487 A.D.) that "it is against the principle of *Zhou Shu* (*The History of Zhou Dynasty*) that father and son should be punished differently for the same crime committed. But the rule of "Men Fang Zhi Zhu" (a penalty to punish those related to a criminal, including his grandparents, grandchildren, parents, wife, children, brothers, and sisters born of the same mother) is still applied. Seen from the ancient customs and human sentiment, it is really absurd, so it should be carefully discussed and modified with the complicated and cruel provisions deleted."[57]

The principle of "Fa Wei Zhi Yao" (law being the most important element in ruling a country) was also reflected in legislation. For example, in the law revision carried out in the periods from the 1st year (477 A.D.) to the 5th year (481 A.D.) and from the 15th year (491 A.D.) to the 18th year of Taihe (494 A.D.), Emperor Xiaowen participated in lawmaking by himself to think over every word of the

---

[53]"Gao Zu Ji" (The Record of Emperor Gaozu) in *Wei Shu* (*The History of Northern Wei Dynasty*).
[54]"Gao Zu Ji" (The Record of Emperor Gaozu) in *Wei Shu* (*The History of Northern Wei Dynasty*).
[55]"Liang Li Zhuan" (The Biographies of Good Officials) in *Wei Shu* (*The History of Northern Wei Dynasty*).
[56]"Liang Li Zhuan" (The Biographies of Good Officials) in *Wei Shu* (*The History of Northern Wei Dynasty*).
[57]"Xing Fa Zhi" (The Record of the Criminal Law) in *Wei Shu* (*The History of Northern Wei Dynasty*).

text or to deliberate on the restrictions on the punishment of "Liu" (exile) and "Tu" (imprisonment).[58]

In terms of judiciary, Emperor Xiaowen often participated in the settlement of criminal cases in person, and he stressed that if laws were violated by the law-executors themselves, the laws would be useless. Therefore, the officials were strictly prohibited from perverting law or abusing power, or enforcing punishment without applying law, so jurisdiction supervision was strictly implemented. During the period of Taihe, a post called "Si Zhi" (official in charge of supervising the officials in capital) was established under "Ting Wei" (the supreme official in charge of judicature) to determine whether the criminal law and judicial procedure was appropriate. At the end of Northern Wei Dynasty, "Si Zhi" (official in charge of supervising the officials in capital) was in charge of "inspecting the supervisory work of 'Yu Shi' (the censor)"[59] to prevent him from abusing his impeachment power.

During the period of Northern Wei Dynasty, because judicature was frequently disturbed by administrative organs, which had led to a lot of misjudged cases, some insightful people at that time were devoted themselves to making "Fu Zhi Zhi Lv" (laws and regulations about rehearing the cases) more perfect to change the passive situation of struggling to deal with the appealing to find out the truth of the cases and to rectify the wrong ones. Xinxiong, who was "Lang Zhong" (head of a subministry department) at the time, put forward many suggestions systematically from his rich judicial experience: "first, if 'Yu Shi' (censor) has accused the criminal of trying to escape, but if the latter can prove that he has been away on business by the testimony of the department directors he is working with and that the evidence is certain, there is no need for reexamination and the wronged must be rehabilitated. Second, before amnesty is offered, if "Yu Shi" (the censor) knows that the bribery has been discovered but he does not make clear who offer the bribes, yet if investigation proves that the briber does not offer bribes to win the case or to be pardoned, he should also be rehabilitated. Third, if sometimes the suspect doesn't admit his offense or if there is not the third witness, but if the suspect is still sentenced to have committed the crime of bribery, those involved should also be rehabilitated; if some of the reviewed cases are inconsistent with facts or are not judged according to general rules, there must be a standard for the required number of witnesses. It is too lenient to require three witnesses as the evidence of bribery in the sentence, while it is too harsh to make convictions according to gossip. If three people have witnessed the bribes and the evidence for bribery is obvious, it is enough for conviction. Fourth, if there is misuse of law, which has led to wrong judgments before an amnesty, the case should be redressed although it has been settled or the convict has been pardoned. Fifth, if someone has been removed from his position because of a felony after the amnesty or has stopped the emperor's carriage to complain that he

---

[58]"Xing Fa Zhi" (The Record of the Criminal Law) in *Wei Shu* (*The History of Northern Wei Dynasty*).
[59]"Guan Shi Zhi" (The Record of Mr. Guan) in *Wei Shu* (*The History of Northern Wei Dynasty*).

has been wronged, if a reexamination has been approved by the emperor or if someone has appealed to the provincial government or has been approved to have the case reviewed, but if another amnesty has been issued before the judicial authority decides to reject the original judgment, the case should not be tried again and the original judgment should be adopted. However, for people who have regained their original official posts and who are not suitable for retrial, no more investigation should be made. Sixth, if a case has been reexamined and it proves that it should be reheard, but an amnesty is offered before a judgment is made, it is unconventional to declare the convict innocent; if the sentence is changed according to evidence, then it is against the formal rules; if the person involved is removed from his official position, then a decent man may be wronged. So in my opinion, conviction should be based on the final judgment, while the redressing of the cases should be based on evidence; if the interrogation procedure is not completed or important witnesses are not present, conviction should not be made."[60] These proposals not merely provided a unified basis and a clear, brief and reasonable method for the previous ambiguous and messy procedure of judicial review, but also developed the theories of evidence, inquisition and absolution, so they are of great value. To let the emperor to accept his proposals mentioned above, Xin Xiong presented his statement excitingly: "Although the ancient people are not so accurate in making judgments, they would not ignore the mishandled cases once they have discovered them. What I talk about today is what the legal officials have concerned about, so it is quite urgent. I hope your majesty can conduct a thorough investigation."[61] Because what he said in his memorial was reasonable and true and had cut into the then current evils, they were accepted by the emperor, so an imperial edict was issued: "Please do as what Xin Xiong has suggested." Thus, "Fu Zhi Zhi Lv" (laws and regulations about rehearing the cases) was made. It was recorded in "Xing Fa Zhi" (The Record of the Criminal Law) in *Wei Shu* (*The History of Northern Wei Dynasty*) that "if the judgment has been made, but if it is found out or suspected that the case is wrongly settled, or if the accused has complained that the case is unjustly handled, the case shall be retried." Thus, the making of "Fu Zhi Zhi Lv" (laws and regulations about rehearing the cases) showed the rulers of Northern Wei Dynasty had tried to make themselves perfect by continuously improving the judicial effect.

As government officials are the law executors, and the law is enforced by their activities, at the time of advocating "Fa Wei Zhi Yao" (law being the most important element in ruling a country), Emperor Xiaowen also paid great attention to the legislation on official administration. In the 8th year of Taihe (484 A.D.), the standard of death penalty for bribery was changed: previously it was stipulated that "officials who took bribes amounting to ten *pi* by bending the law, or had accepted a gift valued two hundred *pi* would be sentenced to death," so this provision

---

[60]"Xin Xiong Zhuan" (The Biography of Xin Xiong) in *Wei Shu* (*The History of Northern Wei Dynasty*).

[61]"Xin Xiong Zhuan" (The Biography of Xin Xiong) in *Wei Shu* (*The History of Northern Wei Dynasty*).

was changed, and it was stipulated that "the officials who took bribes amounting to one *pi* would be sentenced to death no matter whether they had bent the law or not."[62] In that year alone, more than forty local officials were executed for the crime of taking bribes. Even the members of royal family who had committed such crime were deprived of their titles of nobility, or being exiled or executed.[63]

To make all officials perform their duties and have an effective management of their subordinates, *Zhi Yuan Ling* (*Regulations on Government Officials*) was issued twice: in the 17th year (493 A.D.) and the 23rd year (499 A.D.) of Taihe respectively, according to which the power and duties of officials, the rules they should abide by and the criteria for a qualified official was stipulated.

Emperor Xuanwu, who came to power after Emperor Xiaowen, ordered Wang Xie, "Tai Shi" (ancient senior official in charge of state affairs), to be in charge of the law revision based on *Tai He Lv* (*Tai He Code*) according to the principle of "making unified laws in line with the changing of times." Wang Xie gathered all scholars and men of knowledge to discuss the measures taken in law revision by meeting once every five days to have *Zheng Shi Lv* (*Zheng Shi Code*) finally completed. The law was made up of twenty chapters and it was a collection of achievements of law revision that was made within the century in Northern Wei Dynasty, so it was the representative of the laws in the period. Among these twenty chapters, eighteen had the same titles with those of the laws of Han, Wei, and Jin dynasties with the exception of *Dou Lv* (*Statutes on Fighting*), which was separated from *Xi Xun Lv* (*Statutes on Interrogation*) in Taihe Period. In addition, *Hun Yin Lv* (*Marriage Law*) was made for the first time by the legislators of Northern Wei dynasty.

As for *Zheng Shi Lv* (*Zheng Shi Code*), the depth and scope of the integration of "Li" (rites) and "Fa" (law) were expanded, which had made it more practical and operable, so *Zheng Shi Lv* (*Zheng Shi Code*) was taken as the final text of the law of Northern Wei Dynasty in "Jing Ji Zhi" (The Record of Classic Books) in *Sui Shu* (*The History of Sui Dynasty*).

According to *Tai Ping Yu Lan* (*Imperial Readings of the Taiping Era*), during the reign of Xiaowen, besides the laws mentioned above, *Tai He Zhi Yuan Ling* (*Decrees on Government Officials in Tai He Period*) consisting of twenty-one volumes were also made.

In conclusion, during the more than one and a half centuries of ruling by Northern Wei Dynasty, after absorbing the advanced legal culture of the Han nationality, the concept of statutory law was gradually formed based on the common law that had reflected the customs of the nomad tribes. Beginning with "Tian Xing Ding Lv" (Laws Made in the Period of Tianxing), laws were revised repeatedly, so

---

[62]"Xing Fa Zhi" (The Record of the Criminal Law) in *Wei Shu* (*The History of Northern Wei Dynasty*).

[63]Yuanti, the vassal of Linhuai and prefectural governor of Liangzhou; Yuan Bin, the Vassal of Zhangwu and prefectural governor of Xiazhou; Yuan Tian Ci, the vassal of Ruyin and the officer of Huaishuo; Yuan Zhen, the vassal of Nanan and the officer of Changan; Yuan Tai Xing, the vassal of Jing Zhao; Yuan Yu, the vassal of Jiyin and prefectural governor of Xuzhou. See "Zhu Wang Ben Zhuan" (The Biographies of all the Vassals) in *Wei Shu* (*The History of Northern Wei Dynasty*).

6.1 The Legislative Achievements in Wei, Jin, Southern and Northern Dynasty

considerable progress had been made in legislation, judiciary and penalty system in the Northern Wei Dynasty. Especially during the reign of Emperor Xiaowen, the policy of overall Chinesization was introduced, and during the law revision he had revised the laws in person and had even frequently consulted the scholars. During the reign of Emperor Xiaowen, the law was revised mainly based on the laws of Han and Wei dynasties, with the adoption of some of the contents of the laws of Jin and Southern Dynasty, so "Ba Yi" (The Eight Deliberations), "Bu Jing" (being irreverent) and "Bu Xiao" (being unfilial) were all included in the revised law. Moreover, more severe punishments were enforced for the crime of "Bu Dao" (depravity) and "Wu Wang" (to accuse an innocent person) and all doubtful cases were judged according to Confucian classics, which not only sped up the process of the feudalization and confucianization of laws, but also indicated the direction of the development of the legal system of the Northern Dynasty and fostered the progress of the entire society. At the same time, the essence of the laws of the various ethnic groups since Han Dynasty was integrated, so they were more creative compared with the laws of Southern Dynasty. Modern scholar Chen Yinque had discussed the origins as well as the reasons of the development of the laws in Northern Wei Dynasty in his book *Sui Tang Zhi Du Yuan Yuan Lue Lun Gao* (*Study on the Origins of Sui and Tang Systems*):

> The criminal law of the Northern Wei Dynasty is an epitome of the greatest works of that time, because it had in fact comprehensively assimilated not only the classics of Han Dynasty which were only passed down to the noble families in the central plains, but also the laws of Han, Wei and Jin dynasties which were preserved and developed by the Confucian scholars in the west of the river basin after "Yong Jia Zhi Luan" (The Rebellion of Yongjia), as well as the study of criminal laws since the Western Jin Dynasty conducted by the scholars in the lower reaches of the Yangtze River. If it had been formulated only according to *Jin Lv* (*Jin Code*) which had been followed by the Southern Dynasty, then it would have been relatively well-developed than *Han Lv* (*Han Code*); however, the officials in the lower reaches of the Yangtze River thought it unworthy to do the research on criminal laws, so the study of criminal law had witnessed no evident development. In addition, the exquisite principle of 'Lv Xue' (the study of statutory laws) in Han Dynasty were actually abandoned by the scholars in the east of the river basin. Nevertheless, 'Lv Xue' (the study of statutory laws) since Han dynasties in the west of the river basin had developed independently, which was slightly different from what was remained in the central plains at the beginning of the Northern Wei Dynasty. Consequently, it was possible for the legislators in Northern Wei Dynasty to make comprehensive comparisons by absorbing the quintessence. Therefore, such marvelous achievements were not made accidentally, but by extensive adoption and collection.

6.1.3.2 In late Northern Wei Dynasty, the generals of border areas began to rise to power. In 534 AD, the Northern Wei Dynasty was split into the Eastern and Western Wei dynasties. In October of the 3rd year of Xinghe (541 A.D.), Emperor Xiaojing of the Eastern Wei Dynasty "gathered king Wenxiang and other officials in Lin Zhi Ge (Lin Zhi Palace) to have a discussion of the new system, so it was made and promulgated nationwide in the year of Jiayin."[64] According to the notes in *Tang Liu Dian* (*The Six Statutes of Tang Dynasty*), "in late Wei Dynasty, 'Ke' (rule, a form of criminal law) was replaced by 'Ge' (injunction). Because it was decided in Lin Zhi Ge (Lin Zhi Palace), the law was called *Lin Zhi Ge*." *Lin Zhi Ge* (*Lin Zhi Injunction*) was the most important code in the Eastern Wei Dynasty and it was a significant change in the form of law since Han Dynasty to replace "Ke" (rule) with "Ge" (injunction).

In Western Wei Dynasty, *Da Tong Shi* (*Da Tong Standard*) was made. According to "Wen Di Ji" (The Records of Emperor Wen) in *Zhou Shu* (*The History of Zhou Dynasty*), in March of the 1st year of Datong (535 A.D.), "on account of the fact that excessive military and corvée service had exhausted both the people and the officials, Taizu (Yu Wentai) ordered the relevant departments to make new laws by deliberating on the laws in both ancient and current times and by making reference to and changing the laws to adapt to the times. So twenty-four new provisions were drafted and presented to the emperor for approval." In November of the 7th year (541 A.D.), "another twelve provisions were submitted to the emperor. Because Taizu worried that the officials may not fulfill their duties, they were declared once again." In July of the 10th year (544 A.D.), "the twenty-four provisions and the twelve new provisions which were made by Taizu were adopted by Emperor Wei, which was called "Zhong Xing Yong Shi." So Su Chuo, 'Shang Shu' (minister) was ordered to have them revised. Finally they were collected in five volumes (called *Da Tong Shi*) and implemented throughout the country." It was another change in the history of feudal legislation to regard "Shi"(standard) as the most important form of code.

In the 1st year of Tianbao (550 A.D.), Gao Yang from Eastern Wei Dynasty took office and proclaimed himself emperor. He changed the title of the country from Eastern Wei to Qi, which was called Northern Qi in history. In the early years of Northern Qi, *Lin Zhi Ge* (*Lin Zhi Injunction*) of the Eastern Wei Dynasty was adopted, but "because it was troublesome in the country, political orders and punishments were disunified, judgments were made randomly without following the law."[65] *Bei Qi Lv* (*The Penal Code of the Northern Qi Dynasty*) consisting of twelve chapters and 949 provisions were made in the 3rd year of Heqing during the reign of Emperor Wucheng (564 A.D.) according to the laws of the Northern Wei Dynasty. *Bei Qi Lv* (*The Penal Code of the Northern Qi Dynasty*) was completed by many scholars who were expert at "Lv Xue" (the study of statutory laws), such as Feng from Bohai and the Confucian scholars like Cui Xian, Li Yang and Wei Shou after fifteen years of research by absorbing the experience of the early dynasties, as was described in the saying that "the law was modified according to those of the

---

[64]"Xiao Jing Di Ji" (The Biography of Emperor Xiaojing) in *Wei Shu* (*The History of Northern Wei Dynasty*).

[65]"Xing Fa Zhi" (The Record of the Criminal Law) in *Sui Shu* (*The History of Sui Dynasty*).

ancient and modern times with seven to eight provisions added or deleted."[66] Although originating from the laws of Northern Wei Dynasty, *Bei Qi Lv* (*The Penal Code of the Northern Qi Dynasty*) was only made up of the following twelve chapters: "Ming Li" (The Categories of Penalties and General Principles), "Jin Wei"(Palace Guards), "Hu Hun" (Marriage, Tax and Household Registration), "Shan Xing" (Sending Troops without Authorization), "Wei Zhi" (Punishing Officials' Dereliction of Duty), "Zha Wei" (Fraud and Forgery), "Dou Song" (Litigation) "Dao Zei" (Theft), "Bu Duan" (Arresting), "Hui Sun" (Damaging), "Jiu Mu" (Farming and Husbandry) and "Za Lv" (Miscellaneous Laws). So *Bei Qi Lv* (*The Penal Code of the Northern Qi Dynasty*) was much simpler in content, and it was renowned for its "explicitness and terseness."

In *Bei Qi Lv* (*The Penal Code of the Northern Qi Dynasty*), "Zhong Zui Shi Tiao" (Ten Felonies) was created for the first time, which was the most important content of feudal law and which had become the predecessor of 'Shi E' (The Ten Abominations) of the Sui and Tang dynasties. It was recorded in "Xing Fa Zhi" (The Record of the Criminal Law) in *Sui Shu* (*The History of Sui Dynasty*) that "in the 3rd year of Heqing in Northern Qi (564 A.D.), Rui, 'Shang Shu Ling' (ancient official equivalent to prime minister) and the vassal of Zhaojun (a prefecture called Zhao) presented *Qi Lv* (*Qi Code*) consisting of twelve chapters to the emperor;...he also listed another ten felonies: "Fan Ni" (treachery), "Da Ni" (great sedition), "Pan" (treason), "Xiang" (surrender), "E Ni" (abusing or murdering the elders), "Bu Dao" (depravity), "Bu Jing" (being irreverent), "Bu Xiao" (being unfilial), "Bu Yi" (injustice), and "Nei Luan" (committing incest). Therefore, "no one who has committed these ten crimes will be exempted from punishment for 'Ba Yi' (The Eight Deliberations) or 'Lun Shu' (ransom)."

Bei Qi Lv (*The Penal Code of the Northern Qi Dynasty*) had a direct influence on the legislation in Sui and Tang dynasties either in terms of system and content. Cheng Shude put it in *Jiu Chao Lv Kao* (*A Textual Research of the Laws of the Nine Dynasties form Han to Sui*) that "among all the laws made in the Northern and Southern dynasties, those of the Northern Dynasty are better than those of the Southern Dynasty. And the laws of the Qi Dynasty are the best among the laws of the Northern Dynasty... on which the laws of both Sui and Tang dynasties are based...despite all the revisions. The twelve chapters of *Bei Qi Lv* (*The Penal Code of the Northern Qi Dynasty*) were all adopted in *Tang Lv* (*Tang Code*), although there were changes of titles of the passages; the five categories of criminal punishment were followed, although there were changes of the names of the punishment; "Zhong Zui Shi Tiao" (Ten Felonies) was inherited, although there were changes of the names of 'Shi E'' (The Ten Abominations),.... So anyone reading *Tang Lv* (*Tang Code*) can notice the traces of *Bei Qi Lv* (*The Penal Code of the Northern Qi Dynasty*)."

---

[66]"Cui Ang Zhuan" (The Biography of Cui Ang) in *Bei Qi Shu* (*The History of Northern Qi Dynasty*).

Besides laws, forty chapters of "Ling" (decree) were also made in Northern Qi Dynasty, so "those that cannot be included into laws are especially collected in two volumes of 'Qiang Quan Ling' (enforced orders or ordinances) and were implemented together with *Bei Qi Lv* (*The Penal Code of the Northern Qi Dynasty*)."[67]

The rulers of Northern Qi Dynasty also attached great importance to legal study and propaganda, so "the children of officials were ordered by the emperor to study law. That was why many of the people of Qi Dynasty were familiar with law."[68]

The regime of the Northern Qi Dynasty lasted for twenty-seven years and then it was replaced by Northern Zhou Dynasty in 557 A.D.. Northern Zhou Dynasty was founded by Yu Wenjue in 557 A.D. after overthrowing Emperor Gong of Western Wei Dynasty. Therefore, north China was finally unified with the extinction of Northern Qi Dynasty. In 581 A.D., Northern Zhou was overthrown by Yang Jian, so Sui Dynasty was established.

After Northern Qi Dynasty was overthrown by Northern Zhou Dynasty, *Bei Qi Lv* (*The Penal Code of the Northern Qi Dynasty*) was abolished and *Xing Shu Yao Zhi* (*Penal Codes and Important Systems*) was made specially to govern the original land of Northern Qi Dynasty. It was recorded in "Xing Fa Zhi" (The Record of the Criminal Law) in *Sui Shu* (*The History of Sui Dynasty*) that Emperor Wu of Zhou "thought that the fatuous governance was not changed by the old laws of Qi Dynasty, on the contrary, banditry and theft were still prevalent in these areas and laws were often violated. Thus, *Xing Shu Yao Zhi* (*Penal Codes and Important Systems*) was laid down to conduct supervision in the following year. Accordingly, the following criminals would all be punished by death penalty: those gang robbers who had robbed property amounting to one *pi* with weapons or who had robbed property amounting to five *pi* without weapons; those who had stolen the property amounting to twenty *pi* which was in his charge; those who had borrowed public utilities amounting to thirty *pi* by fraud; those head officials concealing information about five households, ten *ding* (adult man), or one *qing* of land or above. From now on, all crimes should be dealt with in accordance with law to eliminate the fraud and bring order to society."

The representative code made during the period of Northern Zhou Dynasty was *Bei Zhou Da Lv* (*Great Code of Bei Zhou*), which was made based on the *Bei Wei Lv* (*The Code of the Northern Wei Dynasty*). However, it was different from *Bei Qi Lv* (*The Penal Code of the Northern Qi Dynasty*) in the category of contents, because the original twenty chapters of *Bei Wei Lv* (*The Penal Code of the Northern Qi Dynasty*) were expanded to twenty five chapters, including "Xing Ming" (Law), "Fa Li" (Precedents), "Si Xiang" (Sacrificial Offering), "Chao Hui" (Imperial Court Convention), "Hun Yin" (Marriage), "Hu Jin" (Household Restriction), "Shui Huo" (Water and Fire), "Xing Shan" (Construction), "Wei Gong" (Protection of the Emperor's Personal Safety and National Sovereignty), "Shi Chan" (Markets),

---

[67]"Xing Fa Zhi" (The Record of the Criminal Law) in *Sui Shu* (*The History of Sui Dynasty*).
[68]"Xing Fa Zhi" (The Record of the Criminal Law) in *Sui Shu* (*The History of Sui Dynasty*).

"Dou Jing" (Fighting), "Qie Dao" (Robbing and Theft), "Pan Zei" (Rebellion), "Hui Wang" (Damages), "Wei Zhi" (Punishing Officials' Dereliction of Duty), "Guan Jin" (Strategic Pass and Ferry), "Zhu Hou" (Dukes or Princes), "Jiu Mu" (Farming and Husbandry), "Za Fan" (Miscellaneous Crimes), "Zha Wei" (Fraud and Forgery), "Qing Qiu" (Asking for Bribery), "Gao Yan" (Prosecution), "Tao Wang" (Fleeing), "Xi Xun" (Interrogation) and "Duan Yu" (Trials and Punishments). The law consisted of totally 1537 articles.

Although there was not such category as "Zhong Zui Shi Tiao" (Ten Felonies) in *Bei Zhou Lv* (*The Penal Code of the Northern Zhou Dynasty*), its basic contents were absorbed. It was recorded in "Xing Fa Zhi" (The Record of the Criminal Law) in *Sui Shu* (*The History of Sui Dynasty*) that, "in March of the 3rd year of Baoding (563 A. D.), the twenty-five chapters of laws called *Da Lv* (*The Great Code*) were completed... with no articles of 'Shi E' (The Ten Abominations) included, but such crimes as 'E Ni' (abusing or murdering the elders), 'Bu Dao' (depravity), 'Da Bu Jing' (being greatly irreverent), 'Bu Xiao' (being unfilial), 'Bu Yi' (injustice), 'Nei Luan' (committing incest) were stressed. So anyone who had committed 'E Ni' (abusing or murdering the elders) would be executed with his body displayed in public for three days;...anyone who had committed the crime of 'Dao Zei' (Theft), "Mou Fan" (plotting rebellion or plotting to endanger the country), 'Da Ni' (great sedition), 'Xiang' (surrender), "Pan" (treason), 'E Ni' (abusing or murdering the elders) which were punishable by 'Liu' (exile) would be punished by having his household registered as 'Za Hu' (people lower than ordinary citizens but higher than servants)."

Yu Wen, the ruler of Northern Zhou Dynasty, "was very keen on learning from the customs of Hua (Han nationality)",[69] so laws were made by intentionally following the ancient people. For example, they not only copied *Zhou Li* (*The Rites of Zhou*) and drew from both *Zhou Guan* (*The Official System of Zhou Dynasty*) and *Shang Shu* (*The Book of Historical Document*) in contents, they also imitated *Zhou Li* (*The Rites of Zhou Dynasty*) and *Da Gao* (*The Great Imperial Mandate*) in form. Just as what was commented in "Xing Fa Zhi" (The Record of the Criminal Law) in *Sui Shu* (*The History of Sui Dynasty*), "compared with the laws of Qi Dynasty, there are more chapters in the new law with more complicated and overloaded contents, but with fewer important points." Therefore, although the new nation was founded by Sui Dynasty after Zhou Dynasty, the laws of Zhou Dynasty were rejected, but *Bei Qi Lv* (*The Penal Code of the Northern Qi Dynasty*) was adopted instead. Indeed, legal development is rooted in society, so it is a scientific summary that "laws should be changed in accordance with times." Therefore, it will definitely lead to ambiguity and contradiction between the past and the present to blindly copy and imitate the ancient people without taking into the consideration of reality. In the lawmaking, the legal forms and contents of "San Dai" (the three dynasties: Xia, Shang, and Zhou) were applied to adapt to the society

---

[69]Cheng Shude, "Latter Zhou Lv Kao" (A Textual Research of the Laws in Han Dynasty) in *Jiu Chao Lv Kao* (*A Textual Research of the Laws of the Nine Dynasties from Han to Sui*).

of Northern Zhou society established 1000 years later, it was certain that the laws made were just products of "unnatural" subjective imagination, so it would inevitably lead to their elimination.

As for the legal system of Northern Dynasty, after long time of exploration, to the time of Northern Qi Dynasty, it had entered a new stage, with the layout, chapters, names of crimes, penalties and precedents all tended to be finalized. Thus, it was on this basis that more mature feudal legal systems were made in Sui and Tang dynasties.

In conclusion, it can be seen that Wei, Jin and the Northern and Southern Dynasty are the important periods of development in Chinese legal history.

First, frequent drafting and revision of legal codes and the diversity of legal forms. During the period, each dynasty was very active in lawmaking, which is quite rare in Chinese history. Moreover, the forms of laws were diversified. Besides "Lv" (criminal law) and "Ling" (decree), the other forms of laws such as "Ke" (rule), "Bi" (analogy), "Gu Shi" (old rules for handling things), "Ge" (injunction), and "Shi" (standard) were also made, which had become a tight legal network by mutual complementation. Thus, it is on this basis that the finalized legal forms of "Lv" (criminal law), "Ling" (decree), "Ge" (injunction), and "Shi" (standard) in the Sui and Tang dynasties are developed.

The difference between "Lv" (criminal law) and "Ling" (decree) is as follows: "'Lv' (criminal law) is made to punish the crimes, while 'Ling' (decree) is made to set the standards"[70]; so those that could not be included in law "would be regulated by 'Ling' (decree);... anyone who has violated 'Ling' (decree) would be punished by law."[71]

The original meaning of "Ke" was "to levy tax." It was explained in *Shi Ming* (*The Origin of the Word Meaning*) that, "anyone who is not punishable by law shall be punished by 'Ke'; anyone who has violated 'Ke' (rule) shall be punished by law." Although "Ke" (rule) is part of criminal law, it is attached to law in form to provide supplementary details of law enforcement. In Liang and Chen of the Southern Dynasty, thirty chapters of "Ke" (rule) were made respectively. In Northern Dynasty, "Ke" (rule) was also made besides law. After Sui and Tang dynasties, "Ke" (rule) was no longer an independent form of law, and it was incorporated in "Ge" (injunction) and "Lv" (criminal law).

"Bi" (analogy), also called "Bi Fu Yuan Yin," started to be used since Western Zhou Dynasty. It was widely used in Qin and Han dynasties because it could be conveniently used at any time and under any circumstances. Moreover, it was not restrained by the established laws. During the time of Northern Qi Dynasty, "'Bi Fu' (legal analogy) was often used in trials, but if the judge wanted to intentionally sentence a guilty person innocent or a felony misdemeanor, the rules for lenient punishment would be used, if the judge wanted to intentionally sentence an innocent person guilty or a misdemeanor felony, the rules for severe punishment would be

---

[70]"Xing Fa Bu" (The Section of Penal Law) in *Yi Wen Lei Ju* (*Collection of Classics*), vol. 54.

[71]"Xing Fa Zhi" (The Record of the Criminal Law) in *Jin Shu* (*The History of Jin Dynasty*).

used, so it was often used by evil officials to play favoritism."[72] It can be seen that "Bi" (analogy) has become an important basis of judicial judgment. "Bi" (analogy) is different from "Li" (precedent) in that "Bi" (analogy) means choosing the laws which are similar in contents, while "Li" (precedent) is based on the established precedents. In the six dynasties in the period of Han and Wei, "Bi" (analogy) was emphasized but no special provisions were made for "Li"(precedent). "Li"(precedent) became popular in the period of Tang and "Wu Dai" (the Five Dynasties), and it tended to replace "Chi" (instruction) in Song Dynasty. However, in Ming and Qing dynasties it has begun to be considered as important as law.

As a law, "Gu Shi" (old rules for handling things) originated from the early Eastern Han Dynasty. According to "Pei Xiu Zhuan" (The Biography of Pei Xiu) in *Jin Shu (The History of Jin Dynasty)*, "the system of 'Chao Yi' (imperial court consultation) was established by Liu Xiu to discuss judicial affairs, which was called 'Gu Shi' (old rules for handling things) and was widely utilized in later times." In Northern Wei Dynasty, "most judgments were made according to 'Gu Shi' (old rules for handling things),"[73] which showed that as a case law, "Gu Shi" (old rules for handling things) was used concurrently with other laws and codes.

"Ge" (injunction) originated from "Ke" (rule) in Han Dynasty and it replaced "Ke" (rule) in Northern Wei as a supplement to "Lv" (criminal law). It was recorded in "Xing Fa Zhi" (The Record of the Criminal Law) in *Sui Shu (The History of Sui Dynasty)* that "since no appropriate provisions of 'Lv' (criminal Law) could be applied, 'Ge' (injunction) was made for temporary application." By Eastern Wei Dynasty, *Lin Zhi Ge (Lin Zhi Injunction)* was made. Thus, it became an independent law and it was revised and renamed *Bei Qi Lin Zhi Ge (Bei Qi Lin Zhi Injunction)* in Northern Qi Dynasty.

"Shi" (standard) originated from "Pin Shi Zhang Cheng" (the procedure for activities and standard formula of document of administrative organizations) in Han Dynasty. In the Western Wei Dynasty, Su Chuo drafted *Da Tong Shi (Da Tong Standard)*, which was the earliest "Shi" (standard) that was accepted as a form of law. In the Northern and Southern Dynasty, "Ge" (injunction) and "Shi" (standard) were used concurrently with "Lv" (criminal law) and "Ling" (decree), which was an important development since Qin and Han dynasties and which had exerted great influence on the later generations. The laws of Tang and Song dynasties included "Lv"(criminal law), "Ling"(decree), "Ge" (injunction), and "Shi"(standard), and it was not until in Ming and Qing dynasties that "Ge" (injunction) and "Shi' (Standard) lost their independent position.

Second, the basic contents of feudal law were formed by the integration of the legal cultures of Northern and Southern Dynasty. As the chief contents of Chinese feudal law, it was in this period that "Ba Yi" (Eight Deliberations) and "Shi E" (Ten Abominations) were made, "Liu" (exile) and "Xi" (the penalty of banishing the

---

[72]"Xing Fa Zhi" (The Record of the Criminal Law) in *Sui Shu (The History of Sui Dynasty)*.
[73]"Guo Zuo Zhuan" (The Biography of Guo Zuo) in *Wei Shu (The History of Northern Wei Dynasty)*.

criminals to do forced labor in remote areas) were begun to be used as criminal punishment and death penalties were begun to be divided into "Jiao" (hanging) and "Zhan" (beheading).

After the rulers of Northern Dynasty entered the central plains, they attached great importance to the function of law, so it became a custom for "the children of the families of scholars to study law." The legal culture of Han, Wei and Jin dynasties exerted a great influence on those of Northern Dynasty, which were characterized by the mixture of the laws of different ethnic groups. Just as Engels said that, "under most circumstances, if the conquerors are more barbaric, they have to adapt to a more advanced 'economic situation' and be assimilated by those whom they have conquered. So most of them even have to use the languages of the conquered."[74] Indeed, historical facts had testified that the rulers of the Northern Dynasty had to adopt the laws of Han nationality and accept its legal culture to stabilize their governance in the central plains.

Then, private clan laws were rigorously maintained to adapt to the needs of society under the structure of the political power of aristocratic families. In Wei, Jin, Northern and Southern Dynasty, some aristocratic families became more and more powerful, so aristocratic politics came into being. In Eastern Jin Dynasty, Wang, Xie, Yu, Huan became the four most powerful families and even the emperor had to show respect to them. In Southern Dynasty, although the ordinary people could take part in politics, aristocratic politics was still very powerful. Against this background, the political and ethical morals of prioritizing family status over that of the state were set up, so the centre of feudal hierarchy shifted not only from state to family, but also from loyalty to filial piety, so that the scholars no longer felt ashamed of becoming the officials of the new dynasty. In law, this change was manifested in the strict maintenance of the private clan law, so even the Northern Dynasty were also influenced by this social moral.

In Northern Dynasty, to overcome the old customs of nomadic people, laws were employed to maintain "Li Jiao" (feudal ethical code) and "Lun Chang" (feudal order of importance) to curb the separatist trend of some powerful families. Thereby, the relationship between family and state was coordinated and the authoritarian centralization was consolidated.

Finally, a new legal system was formed based on mutual assimilation. After Jin Dynasty, China was split into Northern and Southern Dynasty. Though the laws in both dynasties were based on *Han Lv* (*Han Code*), they accordingly belonged to different systems. In Song, Qi, Liang, Chen of Southern Dynasty, *Jin Lv* (*Jin Code*) was applied for over 200 years. It was not until Chen was overthrown by Sui Dynasty that the southern legal system was terminated.

---

[74] *Ma Ke Si En Ge Si Xuan Ji* (*The Selected Works of Marx and Engels*), The People's Publishing House, 1972, p. 222.

6.1 The Legislative Achievements in Wei, Jin, Southern and Northern Dynasty

The legal system of Northern Dynasty was beginning to be set up with the making of *Wei Lv* (*Wei Code*) and it had reached to a very high level when *Bei Qi Lv* (*The Penal Code of the Northern Qi Dynasty*) was made. During the time, the new legal forms of "Ge" (injunction) and "Shi" (standard) were also created. The legalization of "Ba Yi" (Eight Deliberations) and "Zhong Zui Shi Tiao" (Ten Felonies) and the institutionalization of "Wu Xing" (five penalties) had all laid a solid foundation for the lawmaking of Sui and Tang dynasties and for the development of the feudal laws in later times. The legal systems of Northern Dynasty can be regarded as the origin of the legal development in the middle of the feudal society of our country. Therefore, it is not by coincidence that the laws of the Northern Dynasty are superior to those of the Southern Dynasty. On the one hand, under the ruling of the corrupted and decadent nobles, the rulers of Southern Dynasty were keen on metaphysics and Buddhism but were contemptuous of the study of criminal laws and legal cases, so the legal system became more conservative and "Lv Xue" (the study of statutory laws) began to decline; on the other hand, after the minority groups entered the central plains, they were full of entrepreneurial spirit and completed the transformation quickly from the nomadic to feudal agricultural culture. Thus, they demonstrated great initiative either in economy or in politics or in ideology and culture. To make full use of the weapon of law, the renowned Confucianists and legal experts of Han nationality such as Cui Hao, Gao Yun and Xiong Ansheng were appointed, who had not only done a great deal to publicize the advanced Han culture, but also summarized the legal experience since Wei and Jin dynasties and made great achievement in the legal system of Northern Dynasty. To take *Bei Qi Lv* (*The Penal Code of the Northern Qi Dynasty*) as an example, under the host of Cui Ang, many other legal experts such as Feng Shu, Zhao Yanshen, Wei Zheng, Yang Xiuzhi, Ma Jingde had jointly taken part in the lawmaking and spent more than ten years completing the code. In *Bei Qi Lv* (*The Penal Code of the Northern Qi Dynasty*), the complexity of the laws of Southern Dynasty was avoided, the combination of "Li" (rites) and "Fa" (law) was emphasized and some innovations were made in crimes and punishment. Therefore, *Bei Qi Lv* (*The Penal Code of the Northern Qi Dynasty*), which was described as "clear in law and decree and concise and explicit in rule and article," was an important achievement of the integration of different legal culture, so it had constituted a splendid page in Chinese legal civilization.

Cheng Shude had once described the historical development of law in *Jiu Chao Lv Kao (A Textual Research of the Laws of the Nine Dynasties form Han to Sui)*, which is listed as follows:

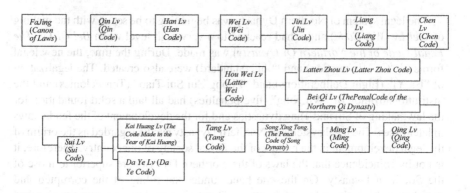

6.2 The Basic Contents of the Laws in Different Dynasties

6.2.1 The Strengthening of the Tendency of the Codification of Administrative Law

Seen from nationwide, though the period of Wei, Jin, Southern and Northern Dynasty was one of feudal separation, within each dynasty the regime of government was still autocratic where the emperor had the supreme sovereignty. The administrative legislation in this period was developing towards codification.

Zhuge Liang, "Cheng Xiang" (the prime minister) of the Kingdom of Shu Han wrote *Ba Wu* (*Eight Things that Must be Done*), *Qi Jie* (*Seven Commandments*), *Liu Kong* (*Six Kinds of Worries*), and *Wu Ju* (*Five Kinds of Fears*) to eliminate the corruptive bureaucracy and to strengthen the law enforcement. Qi and Liang of the Southern Dynasty had made their own codes called *Dian* by collecting the rules and regulations of the previous dynasties. In Northern Dynasty, great achievements were also made in the administrative law. Emperor Fei of the Northern Wei "had made laws of 'Jiu Ming' (nine ranks) to assess the work of the officials both in and out of the capital."[75] In the 10th year of Datong during the reign of Western Wei Dynasty (544 A.D.), a book called *Da Tong Shi* (*Da Tong Standard*) was compiled, and comments were made in "Wen Di Ji" (The Records of Emperor Wen) in *Zhou Shu* (*The History of Zhou Dynasty*) as follows:

In March of the 1st year of Datong (535 A.D.), because many civilians had served in the army and corvée, which had made both the civilians and officials exhausted, Taizu (Yuwen Tai) ordered the relevant departments to change the laws to adapt to the times by learning from history. Thus, the twenty-four articles were drafted and presented to the emperor for approval.

---

[75]"Xing Fa Zhi" (The Record of the Criminal Law) in *Sui Shu* (*The History Sui Dynasty*).

6.2 The Basic Contents of the Laws in Different Dynasties

In the winter (November) of the 7th year of Datong (541 A.D.), Taizu issued another twelve articles of law. He worried that the officials did not perform their duties well, so another order was issued.

In July of the 10th year of Datong (544 A.D.), "the thirty six provisions and the twelve newly made provisions were taken by Emperor Wei as 'Zhong Xing Yong Shi'. So Su Chuo, 'Shang Shu' (minister) was ordered to have them revised and collected in five volumes (called *Da Tong Shi*) to be enforced throughout the country." The emperor also recruited the talented and virtuous and appointed them as "Mu Shou'" (feudal provincial or prefectural governor), "Ling Zhang" (magistrate of a county) under the new system. Thus, the people got used to the new law within a few years.

Da Tong Shi (*Da Tong Standard*) not only included the administrative rules, standards, and detailed catalogues of the state organs, but also the punishment for the duty-related crimes of the officials, so it was a law characteristic of the administrative law in separate edition.

Emperor Wen of Northern Zhou Dynasty also ordered Lu Bian to "establish 'Liu Guan' (six ministers) and the official position of 'Gong' (duke), 'Qing' (minister), 'Da Fu' (senior officials in ancient China) and 'Shi' (scholars) according to 'Li' (rites) of Zhou Dynasty. In addition, the rules for "Chao Yi" (imperial court consultation) was compiled to regulate carriages, clothes and utensils in accordance with ancient 'Li' (rites), with the laws of Han and Wei Dynasty abolished."[76] The emperor also ordered Liu Min, Su Chuo, etc. to "make new laws to be used as 'Dian' (code) in the imperial court."[77]

The making of "Dian" (code) and "Shi" (standard) showed that ancient China's administrative law had entered a new stage, meanwhile, it also indicated the tendency of the historical development of the separation of "Dian" (code) and "Lv" (criminal law) in the Tang Dynasty.

6.2.1.1 From the laws of this period we can see that the system of "San Sheng" (the three departments) of the central government was already set up. "Shang Shu Tai" (Imperial Secretariat), which was already the highest administrative organ in the Eastern Han Dynasty, was independent of "Shao Fu" (in charge of emperor's income and royal affairs) since Cao Wei Dynasty and became the highest administrative organ directly under the leadership of the emperor. The trusted followers and senior officials were appointed by the emperor as "Lu Shang Shu Shi" (ancient official in charge of assisting emperors) to be "in charge of military and state affairs."[78] So he was the most powerful official under the emperor and he was officially called "Zai Xiang" (the prime minister). However, "Lu Shang Shu Shi" (ancient official in charge of assisting emperors) was only a temporary post, and the permanent one was "Shang Shu Ling" (ancient official equivalent to prime minister), who was also

---

[76]"Lu Bian Zhuan" (The Biography of Lu Bian) in *Zhou Shu* (*The History of Zhou Dynasty*).

[77]"Liu Min Zhuan" (The Biography of Liu Min) in *Zhou Shu* (*The History of Zhou Dynasty*).

[78]"Bei Hai Wang Xiang Zhuan" (The Biography of Xiang, the Vassal of Beihai) in *Wei Shu* (*The History of Northern Wei Dynasty*).

called "Zai Xiang" (the prime minister). Under "Shang Shu Ling" (ancient official equivalent to prime minister), there were also many kinds of assistant officials, such as "Zuo You Pu She" (the chief and deputy supervisor of other officials) "Zuo You Cheng" (the left and right vice prime minister) and "Shang Shu" (the minister) of various "Cao" (department) who were in charge of carrying out the specific affairs of the government. The various "Cao" (department) were important administrative organs of the central government, among which "Zuo Min Cao" was in charge of land and household register; "Du Zhi Cao" was in charge of financial revenue and expenditure; "Ke Cao" was in charge of diplomacy; "Wu Bing Cao" was in charge of military affairs; "San Gong Cao" (the office of the three councilors) and "Du Guan Cao" (in charge of military prisons and penalty) were in charge of judicature, and "Dian Zhong Cao" was in charge of court affairs. Besides, "Shang Shu" (the minister) was the head of each "Cao" (department) and "Xiao Cao" (vice minister) was established under "Shang Shu" (the minister), with "Lang Zhong" (head of a subministry department) as the head. As for the importance of "Shang Shu Tai" (Imperial Secretariat), Emperor Xiaowen of Northern Wei Dynasty had commented that "the officials in 'Shang Shu Tai' (Imperial Secretariat) are in charge of so many important affairs that the success and failure all depend on their work."[79]

With its expansion, the organization of "Shang Shu Tai" (Imperial Secretariat) was changed to "Shang Shu Sheng" (The Department of Secretary) in South Liang Dynasty, below which various "Cao" (department) were set up, so they were called "Liu Cao" (the six departments). The change of "Shang Shu Tai" (Imperial Secretariat) to "Shang Shu Sheng" (The Department of Secretary) reflected the busyness of the state affairs and the strengthening of the bureaucratic organs.

After Cao Pi became the emperor of Cao Wei Dynasty, to maintain the emperor's authority and constrain the increasing power of "Shang Shu Ling" (ancient official equivalent to prime minister), "Mi Shu Jian" (the official in charge of the national collection and compilation work) was replaced by "Zhong Shu Sheng" (the supreme organization in charge of the state affairs), which was headed by "Zhong Shu Jian" (equivalent to the head of the secretariat) and "Zhong Shu Ling" (head of the secretariat). In Qin and Han dynasties, the position of "Zhong Shu Jian" (equivalent to the head of the secretariat) and "Zhong Shu Ling" (head of the secretariat) was often taken up by junior officials, such as eunuchs. But now, because they stayed close to the emperor to be in charge of reviewing the reports submitted to the emperors, drafting the imperial edict, and handling important and confidential affairs, their power was continuously increased. Ma Duanlin wrote in *Wen Xian Tong Kao* (*A General Textual Research of the Documents*) that "the position of 'Zhong Shu Jian' (equivalent to the head of the secretariat) and 'Zhong Shu Ling' (head of the secretariat) was often taken up by 'Zai Xiang' (the prime minister)." Thus, "Zhong Shu Jian" (equivalent to the head of the secretariat) and "Zhong Shu Ling" (head of the secretariat) were often taken up by scholars, under which the

---

[79]"Guang Ling Wang Yu Zhuan" (The Biography of Yu, the Vassal of Guangling) in *Wei Shu* (*The History of Northern Wei Dynasty*).

6.2 The Basic Contents of the Laws in Different Dynasties

official positions like "Zhong Shu Shi Lang" (Vice Director of Secretariat), "Zhong Shu She Ren" (the official in charge of drafting imperial edicts in "Zhong Shu Sheng"), "Zhu Shu" (chief of clerical assistant) and "Zhu Shi" (junior officials) were set up. The power of "Shang Shu Sheng" (The Department of Secretary) was gradually seized by "Zhong Shu Sheng" (the supreme organization in charge of the state affairs) because it often participated in deciding the military and state affairs. In Jin Dynasty, "Zhong Shu Sheng" (the supreme organization in charge of the state affairs) was called "Feng Huang Chi" (the pool of phoenix, the legendary bird in Chinese culture). Xun Xu, after being demoted from "Zhong Shu Ling" (head of the secretariat) to "Shang Shu Ling" (ancient official equivalent to prime minister), was very upset and had said: "My 'Feng Huang Chi' has been taken away." In late Southern Dynasty, "Zhong Shu Sheng" (the supreme organization in charge of the state affairs) became the pivot of administrative organs.

However, the emperor also feared that the increasing influence of "Zhong Shu Sheng" (the supreme organization in charge of the state affairs) might threaten the royal power. Thus, to curb the power of "Zhong Shu Sheng" (the supreme organization in charge of the state affairs), in Wei and Jin periods, the emperor invited "Shi Zhong" (the assistant official) to join in the decision-making, so a new department, namely, "Men Xia Sheng" (the organization in charge of examining the imperial edicts in ancient China) was gradually set up. The emperor often consulted with "Shi Zhong" (the assistant official) on some important political issues. Because "'Shi Zhong' (assistant official) often put forward some useful suggestions to redress the wrongdoing," he was accordingly favored by the emperor. When Ren Kai was "Shi Zhong" (the assistant official) in Western Jin Dynasty, he was "often consulted about the political issues, so his power was even greater than that of Jia Chong, who was "Shang Shu Ling" (ancient official equivalent to prime minister) at the time."[80] "Men Xia Sheng" (the organization in charge of examining the imperial edicts in ancient China) not only had the power to impeach other officials, but also to reject the imperial decrees issued. Thus, "Shi Zhong" (the assistant official) was also called "Zai Xiang" (prime minister). Under "Shi Zhong" (the assistant official), the assistant officials like "Huang Men Shi Lang" (ancient official helping emperor to deal with court affairs), and "Ji Shi Zhong" (the senior assistant of the emperor and the supervisor of officials) were appointed. In Northern Wei Dynasty, the position of "Shi Zhong" (the assistant official) was also established to assist the rulers to govern the country.

As the highest administrative organ, "San Sheng" (The Three Departments) was responsible for law drafting and policy making, the heads of "San Sheng" (The Three Departments) usually were chosen from the gentry clans. In Eastern Jin Dynasty, an aristocrat named Wang Dao who was "Si Tu" (the minister of civil affairs) held the concurrent post of the head of "Zhong Shu Jian" (equivalent to the head of the secretariat) and "Lu Shang Shu Shi" (ancient official in charge of assisting emperors) for decades. The head of "San Sheng" (The Three Departments)

---

[80]"Ren Kai Zhuan" (The Biography of Ren Kai) in *Jin Shu* (*The History of Jin Dynasty*).

was "Zai Xiang" (the prime ministers) who had the real power to settle the state affairs, so a kind of check and balance mechanism was constituted. Du You said in *Tong Dian* (*The General Codes*) that "great stress has been laid on "Zhong Shu" (the prime minister) since Wei and Jin dynasties, because has acted as the mouthpiece of the state, while "Shang Shu" (the minister) became less important. In Jin, Liang, and Chen dynasties, all the important affairs were handled by "Zhong Shu" (the prime minister) and the task of offering suggestions was undertaken by "Men Xia" (the official in charge of examining the imperial edicts in ancient China), while "Shang Shu" (the minister) was only in charge of doing things according to orders." This was not only beneficial to the maintaining of autocratic ruling centered by imperial power, but also beneficial to the strengthening of the ruling of the country and to the joint decision making on state and military affairs. Hence, the system of "San Sheng" (The Three Departments) was a great development of the feudal administration with a far-reaching influence.

Besides the system of "San Sheng" (The Three Departments), the organization of "Jiu Qing" (the nine high-rank officials in ancient times) was either merged or renamed. For example, it was called "Jiu Si" in Northern Qi Dynasty, but in Liang Dynasty it was called "Chun Xia Qiu Dong Shi Er Qing" (twelve ministers of spring, summer, autumn and winter), namely, the minister of spring: "Tai Chang" (the Minister of Sacrificial Worship), "Zong Zheng" (official in charge of the royal affairs) and "Si Nong" (Minister of National Treasury); the minister of summer: "Tai Fu" (Minister of National Financial Affairs), "Tai Pu" (official in charge of emperor's carriages and horses) and "Shao Fu" (in charge of emperor's income and royal affairs); the minister of winter: "Wei Wei"(official in charge of emperor's personal safety), "Ting Wei" (the supreme official in charge of judicature) and "Da Jiang" (great master); the minister of winter: "Guang Lu" (in charge of banqueting), "Hong Lu" (the court of state ceremonial) and "Tai Zhou" (ancient official). From then on, the state organs were no longer named after the officials' titles, which was a great progress in the history of the development of the state organizations.

6.2.1.2 "Yu Shi Tai" (The Censorate), a supervisory organ in the central government, was no longer affiliated to "Shao Fu" (in charge of emperor's income and royal affairs), and it had become an independent supervisory organ directly under the control of the emperor. The head of "Yu Shi Tai" (The Censorate) was called "Yu Shi Zhong Cheng" (Grand Censor), which was called "Nan Si" and "Nan Tai" in Southern Dynasty and "Yu Shi Zhong Wei" (palace commandant of censors) and "Xian Si"(constitutional office) in Northern Dynasty. "Yu Shi Zhong Wei" (palace commandant of censors) was very powerful because he had an authority to "supervise all the other officials," as was recorded in history books: "Roads had to be cleared in advance for him to pass by. Besides, he had the right to share the road with the crown prince, so even the nobles and vassals showed respect to him. When other officials met him on the street, they had to get off their horses or carriages and wait for his passing. Those who were slow in action or who failed to do so would be flogged."[81] In Wei and Jin dynasties, it was allowed that report should be made by "Yu Shi" (the censor) to the emperor about the wrong doings of the other officials, so if "Yu Shi Zhong Cheng" (Grand Censor) failed to discover the wrongdoings of other officials, he would be dismissed. In the meantime, it was forbidden for the people of noble and upper class to be chosen as "Yu Shi Zhong Cheng" (Grand Censor) to prevent them from playing favoritism or committing irregularities. After Jin Dynasty, the organizations like "Dian Zhong Shi Yu Shi" (the attendant censor in palace), "Jian Xiao Yu Shi" (the inspection censor), "Du Yun Yu Shi" (the censor in charge of water transportation) and "Jian Jun Yu Shi" (the army inspection censor) were established below "Yu Shi Tai" (The Censorate). Thus, the names of state organs were many and varied and the number is large, which had made it more redundant. Besides, many of the official positions were established for temporary missions, so their function and power were also not unified.

For local areas, no more fixed supervisory positions were established, so "Chu Xun Yu Shi" (patrol censor) was irregularly sent by the central government to supervise the local officials. "Si Li Xiao Wei" (local censor) was retained at the beginning of Wei and Jin dynasties to conduct the supervision of officials together with "Yu Shi Zhong Cheng" (Grand Censor),[82] but their duties sometimes overlapped. Because "Si Li Xiao Wei" (local censor) began to be mainly in charge of the administrative work, up to the time of East Jin Dynasty, it was officially abolished with its supervision power transferred to "Yu Shi Tai" (The Censorate) and his administrative power transferred to "Ci Shi" (a supervisor assigned by the central government to a local area) of Yangzhou (the capital of Eastern Jin Dynasty).

So the improvement of the power of the supervisory organs, the expansion of the organizational agencies and the strictness of the selection of supervisory officials had all reflected the rulers' awareness of the function of the supervisory organs in impeaching the officials' dereliction of duty, in punishing the corrupted officials, and in increasing the effectiveness of the ruling of the state. However, under the situation that the state affairs was controlled by the nobility and the powerful gentry clans, even the emperor was like a puppet in their hands, let alone "Yu Shi Zhong Cheng" (Grand Censor). Thus, in the later years of Cao Wei, it was no longer possible for "Yu Shi Tai" (The Censorate) to play its roles normally. In the period of Western and Eastern Jin dynasties, although there were many organizations in charge of supervision, the unbridled behavior of the powerful gentry clans and the disorder of the court and the commonalty were not changed. Even the emperor dared not offend the powerful families, so the influence of the supervisory organs was further weakened. In Southern Dynasty, with the decrease of the ranks of "Yu Shi" (the censor), "Yu Shi Tai" (The Censorate), the position and power of procuratorates further declined.

---

[81]"Zhi Guan" (State Officials) (Part 6) in *Tong Dian* (*The General Codes*), Vol. 24.

[82]"Zhi Guan" (State Officials) (Part 6) in *Tong Dian* (*The General Codes*), Vol. 24.

However, the supervisory laws and regulations were developed to some extent during this period compared with those of Qin and Han dynasties. In Cao Wei Kingdom, *Liu Tiao Cha Li* (*Six Articles for Official Supervision*) was made and its main contents included "checking the injustice and hardships of the people, checking the delinquency of the officials, checking the administrative achievements of the officials above county magistrates, checking criminal acts of the bandits and the treacherous people, checking the violators the rule of 'Si Shi Jin' (in the season of regulation, it is forbidden to go into the mountains and cut down trees) in *Tian Lv* (*Statutes on Farming and Forest Protection*), checking the gifted people who are filial, righteous and talented, and checking the officials who fail to register the population and to record the grain harvest and the income properly."[83] *Liu Tiao Cha Li* (*Six Articles for Official Supervision*) was different from *Han Liu Tiao* (*Six Articles of Han Dynasty*) made in Han Dynasty, with the former on focused more on the administrative supervision, security, and finance. However, as Emperor Wen of Wei Dynasty was not as enterprising as Emperor Wu of Western Han Dynasty, and the power of "Zhou Mu" (governor) was much greater than that of "Ci Shi" (a supervisor assigned by the central government to a local area) in Han Dynasty, so that in the period of Cao Wei, there lacked the authority to effectively carry out the law.

In the 2nd year of Taishi in Jin Dynasty (266 A.D.), five imperial edicts about the supervision of vassal states were successively issued, which in fact were five laws to supervise the vassal states: "The first one is called 'Zheng Shen' (being righteous and setting a good example); the second one is called 'Qin Bai Xing' (working hard for people); the third one is called 'Fu Gu Gua' (consoling the orphans and the widowed); the fourth one is called 'Dun Ben Xi Mo' (prioritizing agriculture over business) and the fifth one is called 'Qu Ren Shi' (simplifying inter-personal relationships)."[84] In the 4th year of Taishi (268 A.D.), *Cha Chang Li* (*Shi Tiao*) (*Ten Articles about the Administration of Local Officials*) and *Cha Chang Li* (*Ba Tiao*) (*Eight Articles about the Administration of Local Officials*) were issued by Emperor Wu, among which the articles like "the cultivation of land, improvement of people's livelihood, establishment of 'Li Jiao' (feudal ethical code), and implementation of prohibition" were regarded as the achievements of the competent officials, while "the poverty of the people, the failure of agriculture, the occurrence of rebellion, frequent holding of trials and enforcement of punishments, overriding of the superiors by inferiors and the declining of 'Li' (rites)" were regarded as the failure of incompetent officials.[85] It would be checked carefully whether the local officials were "just, unselfish, righteous and honest" or "greedy, flattering, and keen

---

[83]Cheng Shude, "Wei Lv Kao" (An Investigation of the Laws of Wei Dynasty) in *Jiu Chao Lv Kao* (*A Textual Research of the Laws of the Nine Dynasties from Han to Sui*), quoted from "Qi Gu An Lu Zhao Wang Bei Wen" (Tablet Inscription of King Lu Zhao in Qiuuan) in "Han Shu Yin Yi" (The Interpretation of the History of Han Dynasty) in *Wen Xuan* (*Selected Readings*).

[84]"Wu Di Ji" (The Record of Emperor Wu) in *Jin Shu* (*The History of Jin Dynasty*).

[85]"Wu Di Ji" (The Record of Emperor Wu) in *Jin Shu* (*The History of Jin Dynasty*).

6.2 The Basic Contents of the Laws in Different Dynasties

on obtaining personal gains without making much contribution to the public"[86] so that "the good officials would be encouraged and rewarded while the bad ones would be impeached and punished." Although the supervisory rules mentioned above covered a wide range, they lacked focus, so it was very hard to put them into practice under the condition that the gentry clan was very powerful at that time.

As for the supervisory laws of the Southern and Northern Dynasty, it was represented by "Nine Articles Issued by the Emperor on Sending Ambassadors to Make an Inspection Tour to the Various States," enacted by Emperor Wu in Northern Zhou Dynasty, which was called "Nine Articles." The "Nine Articles" are as the following: "first, verdicts should be made according to law; second, marriage with a person outside 'Wu Fu' (relatives within the five degrees of mourning) is allowed if the mother's relatives have all died; third, punishments should be executed by 'Zhang'(flogging with heavy sticks) and orders must be carried out under the law; fourth, the official of 'Jun' (shire) and 'Xian' (county) who fail to arrest the robbers in his jurisdiction shall be reported to the emperor; fifth, certificates of merit should be posted on the gates of families whose children are filial and spouses are respectful to each other; if members of such families are talented and capable, they should be recommended by the officials to the emperor; sixth, there might be people who have made great contribution but have no fame or position, and people who are poor but talented, so the local officials should visit them and make report to the emperor; seventh, if officials above 'Qi Pin' (the seventh rank) in the Northern Qi Dynasty have received the imperial recruitment edict or officials below 'Ba Pin' (the eighth rank) in Northern Qi want to be appointed as an official, they shall be appointed two ranks lower than their original position; eighth, the learned people like 'Xiu Cai' (one who passed the imperial examination at the county level) shall be recommend by 'Zhou' (subprefecture) and the righteous people who are expert at the Confucian classics like 'Xiao Lian' (being filial to parents, and impartial in dealing with things) should be recommended by 'Jun' (shire), with 'Shang Zhou' and 'Shang Jun' (administrative regions with biggest population) recommending one person each year, while 'Xia Zhou' and 'Xia Jun' (administrative regions with smallest population) one person in three years; ninth, people over seventy years old can still be appointed as officials in accordance with law, the widower, the widow and the people who cannot support themselves shall get relief from the government."[87] Among the nine articles, the most important one was making convictions according to law, which not only showedthat the spirit of "Fa Zhi" (the rule of law) was much stressed by Northern Dynasty, but also showedthat the malpractice and corruption of the local officials were very serious.

In a word, as far as the supervisory regulations of Wei, Jin, Southern and Northern Dynasty are concerned, generally speaking "Liu Tiao" (six articles) made by Emperor Wu in Han Dynasty was inherited, but "Cha" (supervision) and "Ju"

---

[86]"Wu Di Ji" (The Record of Emperor Wu) in *Jin Shu* (*The History of Jin Dynasty*).

[87]"Xuan Di Ji" (The Record of Emperor Xuan) in *Zhou Shu* (*The History of Zhou Dynasty*).

(to recommend talented people to the emperor by officials) were combined, so it had reflected the feature of the times.

6.2.1.3 As for the local administrative system, the three-level system of "Zhou" (subprefecture), "Jun" (shire), and "Xian" (county), which was formed in the late Eastern Han Dynasty, was followed. However, at the beginning of Jin Dynasty, twenty-seven members of the royal family were appointed by Emperor Wu to be the kings of different states which had the same status as "Jun" (shire). These states were relatively independent in administration and finance. "Xiang Zuo Wang" (minister) whose rank was equivalent to that of "Jun Shou" (governor) was appointed to assist the kings. In the 10th year of Taikang during the reign of Emperor Wu (289 A.D.), "Xiang Zuo Wang" (minister) was replaced by "Nei Shi" (official in charge of passing and reading the orders from the king) who were appointed by the kings. Besides, different military systems were set up in accordance with the population of a state, the bigger states were allowed to have three armies, including "Shang" (upper), "Zhong" (intermediate) and "Xia" (lower), which had about 5000 soldiers. The states with fewer people were allowed to have two armies, namely, "Shang" (upper) and "Xia" (lower), which had about 3000 soldiers, and the states with fewer population were allowed to have an army of 1500 soldiers. Moreover, the military power was controlled by the kings themselves. However, consequently, these states, which were originally set up to maintain the royal power and to suppress the local separatists, had ended up to become the cradle of separatist forces, which had aggravated the struggle for central power and throne and finally led to "Ba Wang Zhi Luan" (The Rebellion of Eight Princes) that occurred during the political turmoil of Empress Jia with the succession of the throne by Emperor Hui after the death of Emperor Wu.

In early Jin Dynasty, "Gong Hou Guo" (vassal state) was also set up to meet the gentry's demand to participate in the administrative and political affairs. After "Ba Wang Zhi Luan" (The Rebellion of Eight Princes), based on clan system, the powerful families in the locality had recruited more "Bu Qu" (the private army) and tenants, built fortresses, set up their own army, at the same time, they had also become officials directly in separatist areas or become the real political and military ruler by controlling the local elections. Because "Ci Shi"(a supervisor assigned by the central government to a local area) in the local place was also concurrently the military commander, who also held the post of "Du Du Zhu Zhou Jun Shi" (commanding the military affairs in the subprefectures) with the military title of a general and who even had the power to kill the officials below 2000 *dan*, the emperors usually appointed people from the royal family or the people whom he deeply trusted to be "Ci Shi" (a supervisor assigned by the central government to a local area) to prevent him from becoming over powerful to threaten the central government. At times the position of "Ci Shi" (a supervisor assigned by the central government to a local area) was not established and its work was replaced by the officials affiliated; or at some other times, "Dian Qian" was set up to below "Ci Shi" (a supervisor assigned by the central government to a local area) to supervise and share his power, as was recorded in the saying that "'Dian Qian' is in charge of delivering the emperor's edicts, supervising 'Ci Shi' (a supervisor assigned by the central government to a local area), and preventing him from abusing power."[88] For those states that had fallen into the enemy's hands, a nominal "Ci Shi" (a supervisor assigned by the central government to a local area) called "Yao Ling" was set up.

As was stated before, under "Zhou" (subprefecture), "Jun" (shire) was set up. The head of "Jun" in the capital area was called "Yin," while those of the areas other than the capital area were called "Jun Tai Shou" (head of prefecture) who also had some military power. In Jin Dynasty, "Jun Tai Shou" (head of prefecture) was also called "Jiang Jun" (the general), who had more assistants in Jin Dynasty than in Han Dynasty.

Under "Jun," "Xian" (county) was set up, and "Ling" (magistrate) was set up in bigger counties while "Zhang" (executive officer) was set up in smaller counties. In addition, there were also more subordinate officials under "Xian Ling" (county magistrate) than before.

The increase of political organs in "Jun" (shire) and "Xian" (county) was a reflection of the complexity of the local affairs and the strengthening of the local government.

The basic organizations below "Xian" (county) remained almost the same as those in the Han Dynasty.

In the Northern Dynasty, after north China was unified by the Northern Wei Dynasty, government organizations were set up by imitating that of the Han Dynasty. However, for the local official positions of "Ci Shi" (a supervisor assigned by the central government to a local area), "Tai Shou" (governor of a prefecture) and "Xian Ling" (county magistrate), three official positions were usually set up, one from the royal family of Tuoba, one from other families of Xian Bei ethnic group, and one from Han nationality, which had reflected the characteristics of politics in the Northern Dynasty featured by the joint governance of the upper-class of all the ethnic groups centered by Tuoba nobility.

As for the grassroots organization, "Zong Zhu Du Hu Zhi" (local grassroots organization headed by Suzerain) was carried out in Northern Wei Dynasty, and based on "Wu Bao" (a civilian defense system), large landowners from powerful families were appointed the patriarch to be in charge of the government in the Northern Wei Dynasty. However, "Zong Zhu Du Hu Zhi" (local grassroots organization headed by Suzerain) was a temporary grassroot government set up by clans. During Emperor Xiaowen's reform, "Zong Zhu Du Hu Zhi" (local grassroots organization headed by Suzerain) was abolished and a new system called "San Zhang Zhi" (the system headed by three seniors of a neighborhood) was set up. In this system, five households constituted a "Lin" (neighborhood) with its head called "Lin Zhang" (head of neighborhood); five "Lin" (neighborhood) constituted a "Li" (a basic resident organization consisting of five neighborhoods), with its head called "Li Zhang"; five "Zhang" constituted a "Dang," with its head called "Dang Zhang." Therefore, it was very similar to the system of "Shi Wu" (a basic level organization

---

[88] *Zi Zhi Tong Jian* (*History as a Mirror*), Vol. 128.

grouped by five or ten households), which had been carried out in feudal China for a long time. The three local officials were in charge of checking people's registration, collecting tax, allocating corvée, and recruiting soldiers. The implementation of "San Zhang Zhi" (the system headed by three seniors of a neighborhood) was an important development of the grassroots organizations of North dynasties.

To strengthen the rule over the Han and other people, in the 3rd year of Yanxing in Northern Wei Dynasty (473 A.D.), it was stipulated that if a "Xian Ling" (county magistrate) could eliminate the robbers in one county, he would be entrusted with two; if he could eliminate the robbers in two counties, he would be entrusted with three and he would be promoted to "Jun Tai Shou" (head of prefecture) after three years. If a "Jun Tai Shou" (head of prefecture) could eliminate the robbers in two "Jun" (shire), he would be entrusted with three and be promoted to "Zhou Ci Shi" (feudal provincial or prefectural governor) three years later. However, these measures had led to people's rebellion all over the country to fight against oppression, which had taught the rulers of the Northern Dynasty a lesson. During the reign of Emperor Xiaowen, laws were made to award those good local officials to let them stay in their position for a longer time, while the officials with poor performance were dismissed even if their term of office had not terminated.

6.2.1.4 In the later years of Eastern Han Dynasty, frequent wars and the migration of people had made it impossible to carry on with the system of appointing officials according to the recommendation of villagers. After the foundation of Cao Wei Dynasty, Cao Cao, the emperor, put forward the slogan of "selecting officials according to their ability," so he appointed the prestigious local people to be "Zhong Zheng Guan" (official responsible for the assessment of local talents) and ranked the local people into nine grades (nine ranks) according to their talents, from whom the officials were chosen according to their ranks by the government. In 220 A.D., after Emperor Cao Pi of Wei Dynasty replaced Han Dynasty, to further win the support of the nobilities, "Jiu Pin Zhong Zheng Zhi" (The Nine Rank System, an important election system in Wei, Jin, Southern and Northern Dynasty) was established according to the suggestion of Chen Qun, who was "Li Bu Shang Shu" (the minister of the department of personnel). That is to say, the current officials who were "talented and who capable of finding able and virtuous people" would be appointed by the court as "Zhong Zheng" (supervisor) of a "Jun" (shire) or "Zhou" (subprefecture) where he was born, those of "Jun" (shire) were called "Xiao Zhong Zheng Guan" and those of "Zhou" (subprefecture) were called "Da Zhong Zheng Guan." Their duties were to rank people into nine grades according to their family background, ability, and virtue. The nine grades include: "Shang Shang" (the most excellent), "Shang Zhong" (very excellent), "Shang Xia" (not very excellent), "Zhong Shang" (above the average), "Zhong Zhong" (average), "Zhong Xia" (below the average), "Xia Shang" (not very poor), "Xia Zhong" (very poor), "Xia Xia" (the poorest). After the assessment was made by "Xiao Zhong Zheng," it would be reported to "Da Zhong Zheng," who would report to "Si Tu" (the minister of civil affairs) and finally they would be appointed by the imperial court in accordance with their degrees. "Jiu Pin Zhong Zheng Zhi" (The Nine Rank System, an important

6.2 The Basic Contents of the Laws in Different Dynasties

election system in Wei, Jin, Southern and Northern Dynasty) was the official appointment system established during the special period when political power was dominated solely by the gentry class.

When "Jiu Pin Zhong Zheng Zhi" (The Nine Rank System, an important election system in Wei, Jin, Southern and Northern Dynasty) was first established, although the government declared that "the officials are selected according to their ability rather than their social status",[89] yet because all "Zhong Zheng Guan" (official responsible for the assessment of local talents) were in fact from the gentry class, the first standard they employed to evaluate people was social status, so ability would come in the second place. In Western Jin Dynasty, family background became the sole standard to choose officials, so the first two ranks were all filled by people from the gentry class, which not only gave the gentry class greater political privileges, but also led to the phenomenon that "no people from poor families were appointed as officials of 'Shang Pin' (the grades of 'Shang Shang', 'Shang Zhong' and 'Shang Xia') and no people from gentry class were appointed as officials of 'Xia Pin' (the grades of 'Xia Shang', 'Xia Zhong' and 'Xia Xia')." Since then, the official appointment was closely linked with gentry class. In Eastern Jin Dynasty, "Men Fa Zhi Du" (The System of Dominant Family) entered its heyday and the whole country was dominated in turn by Wang family, Xie family, Yu family, Huan family, and so on. Thus, their family members were all appointed senior officials for generations and their descendants could even start their political career at the age of twenty as "Mi Shu Lang" (an official in charge of book collection) and they had the priority of being promoted, as was illustrated in the statement that "the mediocre from the gentry class could even be promoted to the position of ministers merely because of their eminent family background."[90] However, for children of "Shu Zu" (humble background) and "Han Men" (humble and ordinary families), they could only be appointed as minor officials at the age of thirty, from which we can see that there was a huge gap between the gentry class and the common people.[91] The practice of "Jiu Pin Zhong Zheng Zhi" (The Nine Rank System, an important election system in Wei, Jin, Southern and Northern Dynasty) reinforced the system of gentry class based on land ownership and institutionalized the political privilege of the monopoly of the state power by the gentry class. The officials selected by this means "do not do their jobs but just spend their time drinking, eating and idling all day long,"[92] and "their luxury and waste have done more harm to the society than natural disasters," which had aggravated the political corruption.

---

[89]"En Xing Zhuan" (The Biography of En Xing) in *Song Shu* (*The History of Song Dynasty*).

[90]"Chu Yuan Wang Jian Zhuan" (The Biographies of Chu Yuan and Wang Jian) in *Nan Qi Shu* (*The History of Southern Qi Dynasty*).

[91]"Wang Hong Zhuan" (The Biography of Wang Hong) in *Song Shu* (*The History of Song Dynasty*).

[92]"Mian Xue Pian" (On Encouraging Study) in *Yan Shi Jia Xun* (*The Instruction of the Family of Yan*).

In the later years of the Southern and Northern Dynasty, the uprisings that frequently took place all over the country had weakened the power of the gentry class; meanwhile, the landlords from the lower class had gained momentum, which had in turn destroyed the basis of "Jiu Pin Zhong Zheng Zhi" (The Nine Rank System, an important election system in Wei, Jin, Southern and Northern Dynasty).

In Northern Dynasty, although no definite official appointment system was established, the gentry class still enjoyed great privileges. The officials were assessed every three years at the beginning of the reign of Cao Wei to decide whether they should be dismissed or promoted. During the reign of Emperor Ming, to have a better management of the officials, *Du Guan Kao Ke Fa Qi Shi Er Tiao* (*Seventy-Two Rules for Supervising Officials*) was made by Liu Shao, who was "San Qi Chang Shi" (ancient official helping emperor to deal with court affairs) at the time. The process was described by Liu Shao in his memorial to the emperor: "The official assessment is one of the most important aspects of administration, however, no job has been done so far for the lack of relevant laws, so the competent and the incompetent officials are muddled together. Your majesty is ambitious with grand plans like the saints in history, and often conduct self-examination and worry about the insufficiency of the disciplines among the officials, so imperial edicts were issued to make the law. For your gratitude and inspiration, according to your order, I have drafted *Du Guan Kao Ke Fa Qi Shi Er Tiao* (*Seventy-Two Rules for Supervising Officials*) and one chapter of explanation. Indeed, I am really not so learned and gifted as to express your Majesty's great intension. So the law is made in the end."[93] *Kao Ke Fa Qi Shi Er Tiao* (*Seventy-Two Rules for Supervising Officials*) had already been lost, but from some comments made by Du Shu, who was "San Qi Huang Men Shi Lang" (ancient official helping emperor to deal with court affairs) at the time, it can be seen that it covered wide range of contents: "The officials who are diligent with their duties day and night, who are just, righteous, who are not flattery to the nobilities, who enforce law without working for personal gains, and who have given advice and warning to the imperial court should be made known to the emperor; while those who earn a high salary but fail to put forward their opinions, who evade their responsibilities while in office, who make use of their official positions to serve their own interests, who have never given any useful advice for fear of making mistakes should also be made known to the emperor."[94]

In Jin Dynasty, Du Yu had criticized that *Du Guan Kao Ke Fa Qi Shi Er Tiao* (*Seventy-Two Rules for Supervising Officials*) was harsh and cumbersome because it was difficult to be implemented. He said, "It is true that the contents of the law are strict in logic, however, it is so cumbersome that it is against its original intention, so it is difficult to be put into practice."[95] Therefore, the principle of "eliminating what

---

[93]"Liu Shao Zhuan" (The Biography of Liu Shao) in "Wei Shu" (The History of Northern Wei Dynasty) in *San Guo Zhi* (*The Record of the Three Kingdoms*).

[94]"Du Ji Zhuan" (The Biography of Du Ji) in "Wei Shu" (The History of Northern Wei Dynast) in *San Guo Zhi* (*The Record of the Three Kingdoms*).

[95]"Du Yu Zhuan" (The Biography of Du Yu) in *Jin Shu* (*The History of Jin Dynasty*).

6.2 The Basic Contents of the Laws in Different Dynasties

is complicated, adopting what is simple, absorbing what is concise and easy" was adopted,[96] when he was ordered to draft the rules on official evaluation, and his proposal was approved by Emperor Wu of Jin Dynasty. In June of the 4th year of Taishi (268 A.D.), the law on official assessment was released in the form of an imperial decree:

> The ministers of 'Jun Guo' (vassal state) must make an inspection tour of 'Xian' (county) once in every three years in spring, which was an ancient custom to propagate ethical morality and to promote justice. The ministers have to meet the local officials, observe the customs, coordinate the ritual and law, examine the weight and measurement tools, and visit the elderly and centenarians in person. Besides, they also have to interrogate the prisoners, rectify wrong cases, check carefully the gain and loss of administration and get to know the sufferings of the people. Whether far or near, it would be just as if I myself were there; they should promote the education of 'Wu Jiao' (five moral principles: righteousness of father, kindness of mother, friendliness of elder brother, respect of the younger brother, filial piety of children), urge farming, encourage the study of Confucian classics and oppose other schools of thoughts to make greater achievements in the future. Those scholars and common people who are industrious, virtuous, filial, worthy, honest and excellent should be recommended and encouraged; while those who are unfilial to their parents, disrespectful to the clan elders, opposed to 'Li' (rites) and disobedient to ethic customs and laws should be impeached and punished. The cultivation of land, improvement of people's livelihood, establishment of 'Li Jiao' (feudal ethical code), and implementation of prohibition are regarded as the achievements of the competent officials, while the poverty of the people, the failure of agriculture, the occurrence of rebellion, frequent holding of trials and enforcement of punishments, overriding of the superiors by inferiors and the declining of 'Li' (rites) are regarded as the failure of incompetent officials. It will be checked carefully whether the local officials are just, unselfish, righteous and honest or greedy, flattering, and keen on obtaining personal gains without making much contribution to the public so that the good officials will be encouraged and rewarded while the bad ones will be impeached and punished. This is the reason for me to make the outline and order Yu Liang, who is 'Er Qian Dan' (the ancient official with a monthly salary of 2000 *dan*), to have the law drafted to be issued.[97]

In the 5th year of Taishi (269 A.D.), another decree was issued and it was stipulated that "in ancient times, officials' performance was assessed every year, with rewards and punishments conducted every three years. But only the bad officials are recorded and dismissed, while no measures have been taken to encourage the good ones, which is harmful to the promotion and demotion of officials. So it should be made a routine for the hard-working and competent officials to be recorded once a year. So I shall reward them according to their achievements."[98]

At the beginning of Southern Dynasty, the officials were examined every six years. Later, "it was considered too long a period, so it was decided that officials should be examined every three years, which was called 'Xiao Man'."[99] The

---

[96]"Du Yu Zhuan" (The Biography of Du Yu) in *Jin Shu* (*The History of Jin Dynasty*).

[97]"Wu Di Ji" (The Record of Emperor Wu) in *Jin Shu* (*The History of Jin Dynasty*).

[98]"Wu Di Ji" (The Record of Emperor Wu) in *Jin Shu* (*The History of Jin Dynasty*).

[99]"Xuan Ju Kao" (An Examination of Election) (Part 12) in *Wen Xian Tong Kao* (*A General Examination of Documents*), Vol. 39.

contents of assessment can be seen from the imperial edicts issued in the 20th year of Yuanjia during the reign of Emperor Wen of Song Dynasty (443 A.D.): "to check whether the farmland is cultivated, sericulture is promoted or the land is wasted; to make assessment of the work of local officials and to check whether have used the out-dated regulations; to award and punish officials according to whether they are diligent or lazy; to promote and demote officials in accordance with their ability."[100] In the 7th year of Daming during the reign of Emperor Xiaowu of Song Dynasty (463 A.D.), another decree was issued: "The local officials who are diligent and conscientious will be rewarded; while those who disturb the people with unnecessary service and heavy tax and corvée shall be punished. So careful investigation should be made by the chief officials to make report to the central government."[101]

In Southern Qi Dynasty, the general official assessment conducted once in three years was changed to once a year. In the 3rd year of Yongming (485 A.D.), the criteria for the assessment of local officials was released by Emperor Wu: "In investigation, the most important thing that 'Shou Zai' (the local governor) should do is to show care to the people; the primary task of 'Ci Shi' (feudal provincial or prefectural governor) is to make sure whether faming and sericulture tax is strictly collected and whether the land is cultivated. Those who are performing well in faming and sericulture or who are effective in controlling the deteriorate and impetuous people will be rewarded; those who are arrogant or who have interfered with agriculture by causing trouble shall be punished to encourage people to work diligently. The assessment shall be made once a year to decide whether the local officials shall be promoted or demoted."[102] It was reaffirmed in the imperial decree issued in the 2nd year of Jianwu in the reign of Emperor Ming of Southern Qi (495 A.D.) that "in investigation, the most important thing that 'Shou Zai' (the local governor) should do is to show care to the people and the primary task of 'Mu Bo' (head of prefecture and subprefecture) is to make sure whether faming and sericulture tax is strictly collected, whether the land is cultivated, whether the diligent people are encouraged, whether the deteriorate and impetuous people are punished or whether dams are built. The officials' work will be assessed, those who have made achievements in faming and sericulture will be awarded and those who are lazy and impetuous will be impeached and punished, and detailed rules should be made by those in charge."[103]

In the 15th year of Tianjian during the reign of Emperor Wu in Southern Liang Dynasty (516 A.D.), an imperial edict was issued about the outline of the assessment of the achievements of officials:

> Investigations shall be conducted as to whether 'Shou Zai' (the local governor) is honest and righteous, or whether he has obtained personal gains by encroaching upon others' property,

---

[100]"Wen Di Ji" (The Record of Emperor Wen) in *Song Shu* (*The History of Song Dynasty*).
[101]"Xiao Wu Di Ji" (The Record of Emperor Xiao Wu) in *Song Shu* (*The History of Song Dynasty*).
[102]"Wu Di Ji" (The Record of Emperor Wu) in *Nan Qi Shu* (*The History of Southern Qi Dynasty*).
[103]"Ming Di Ji" (The Record of Emperor Ming) in *Nan Qi Shu* (*The History of Southern Qi Dynasty*).

6.2 The Basic Contents of the Laws in Different Dynasties

if so, they shall be reported to the emperor to decide whether they will be promoted or demoted. Besides, the superior officials should be strict in tax collection and carry out the task of dam building personally to avoid causing trouble to farming. If the collection of market tax is inappropriate, the out-dated rules must be revised by the officials in charge according to the circumstances.[104]

He also pointed out that "if the officials in small counties are competent, they will be promoted to be officials in bigger counties; if the magistrates of bigger counties perform well, they will be promoted to the position of 'Er Qian Dan' (the ancient official with a monthly salary of 2000 *dan*)."[105]

In the 4th year of Taijian during the reign of Emperor Xuan in Southern Chen Dynasty (572 A.D.), it was stated in an imperial edict that it should be the yardstick of official assessment "whether they are honest or corrupt, or whether they are competent or incompetent."[106] Besides, the principal of "Zui" (excellent) and "Dian" (poor) was also made by the emperor. Yet, few emperors of Southern Chen Dynasty were competent and politically ambitious, so the official appraisal system was hardly put into practice.

Compared with the Southern Dynasty, in the Northern Wei Dynasty, the people were more enthusiastic about reforms, so a strict official appraisal system was set up. *San Deng Chu Zhi Fa (Law for Three-Level Promotion and Dismissal)* made in the 18th year of Taihe during the reign of Emperor Xiaowen in Northern Wei Dynasty (494 A.D.) was the most representative law of the period:

> It is a time-honored system to have officials' performance assessed every three years, and one's promotion or demotion should be decided after three times of assessment. However, if the tradition is followed, then the incompetent people will stay too long in office, so the more competent talents will have to wait for too long for promotion. Therefore, from now on, the decisions must be made immediately after the assessment in order to clear the way for the promotion of competent officials. In addition, some officials will specially be appointed to be in charge of the assessment and all the officials will be classified into three levels. Those officials who are of or below 'Liu Pin' (the sixth rank) will be re-examined by 'Shang Shu' (ministers); those senior officials who are of or above 'Wu Pin' (the fifth rank) will be examined by me and other ministers. Those whose performance is evaluated as 'Shang Shang' (the most excellent) will be promoted; those whose performance is evaluated as 'Xia Xia' (the poorest) will be demoted; those whose performance is evaluated as 'Zhong Zhong' (average) will retain their posts.[107]

To ensure the implementation of this system, the officials who were of or above "Wu Pin" (the fifth rank) and the officials in "Shang Shu Sheng" (The Department of Secretary) were examined by the emperor himself in the imperial court; the officials like "Shang Shu Ling" (ancient official equivalent to prime minister) and "Pu She" (the supervisor of other officials) or the official below these ranks would be demoted or removed from their offices or deprived of salaries if they were found guilty or

---

[104]"Wu Di Ji" (The Record of Emperor Wu) in *Liang Shu* (*The History of Liang Dynasty*).

[105]"Liang Li Zhuan" (The Biographies of Good Officials) in *Liang Shu* (*The History of Liang Dynasty*).

[106]"Xuan Di Ji" (The Record of Emperor Xuan) in *Chen Shu* (*The History of Chen Dynasty*).

[107]"Gao Zu Ji" (The Record of Emperor Gaozu) in *Wei Shu* (*The History of Northern Wei Dynasty*).

dereliction of duty or violation of "Li" (rites). Thus, "more than twenty people are removed from their offices."[108] In the 19th year of Taihe (495 A.D.), another imperial edict was issued by the emperor: "The work of their subordinates should be examined carefully by 'Zhou Mu' (governor) and classified into three grades. The result should be presented to the emperor, who will determine their promotion or demotion by himself."[109] In addition, because "'Ting Wei' (the supreme official in charge of judicature) has the right to decide the life and death of the ordinary people," Emperor Xiaowen was even stricter with the assessment of judicial officials, so it was stipulated that "only those who are honest and righteous and those who are merciful to the common people or brave enough to punish the bigwigs and the nobility can be considered as good judges." At the same time, he had conducted careful examination of the work of judicial officials and "Si Zhi" (official in charge of supervising the officials in capital) who were subordinate to "Ting Wei" (the supreme official in charge of judicature) by himself; moreover, he "usually thinks it over before making decisions" to show his prudence and cautiousness.[110]

During the period of Taihe, the focus of assessment shifted from impeaching the illegal activities of the local officials to examine the officials' competence and their administrative efficiency. Therefore, a new prevailing custom was formed and it was generally held that "laws and disciplines should be strictly enforced, awards and punishments should be fairly carried out, the old systems should be thoroughly reformed and the country should be ruled by law,"[111] which was highly praised in history books.

During the reign of Emperor Xuanwu in Northern Wei Dynasty, the law for official assessment was further revised, so the official assessment was classified into two types: "Ren Shi Guan" (the current official with specific duties) was examined every three years and "San Guan" (ancient honorary officials title) was examined every four years to determine the officials' promotion and demotion. In the 1st year of Xiaochang during the reign of Emperor Ming in Northern Wei Dynasty (525 A. D.), the policy was revised, so assessment was conducted annually rather than once in every three years. Moreover, all officials of "Jun" (shire) were required to "award the good and punish the evil and to rule the country according to law. 'Jun Shou' (governor) is in charge of supervising 'Ling Zhang' (magistrate of a county), and 'Ci Shi' (feudal provincial or prefectural governor) is in charge of supervising 'Shou Xiang' (deputy prime minister) to assess his performance annually to decide whether they are qualified or not. Should there be anything wrong, they will be convicted of

---

[108] "Kao Ji" (Assessment) in "Xuan Ju" (Election) (Part 3) in *Tong Dian* (*The General Codes*).

[109] "Gao Zu Ji" (The Record of Emperor Gaozu) in *Wei Shu* (*The History of Northern Wei Dynasty*).

[110] "Guang Ling Wang Yu Zhuan" (The Biography of Yu, the Vassal of Guangling) in *Wei Shu* (*The History of Northern Wei Dynasty*).

[111] "Liang Li Zhuan" (The Biographies of Good Officials) in *Wei Shu* (*The History of Northern Wei Dynasty*).

6.2 The Basic Contents of the Laws in Different Dynasties

misconducting assessment."[112] Thus, they tried to guarantee the implementation of the assessment system by law.

In summary, although laws and regulations were made about official assessment and their contents were constantly revised in Wei, Jin, Southern and Northern Dynasty, the assessment was hard to be carried out because of the occurrence of frequent wars, the turmoil of politics and the rapid change of the duties of officials. Especially under the circumstance that the political power was controlled by the aristocrats and powerful families, serious formalism existed in the assessment system, so "the real and false cannot be distinguished and facts and fiction are muddled together."[113]

Besides, the salary and retirement systems were also improved and institutionalized. During the Cao Wei period, the official position was decided by "Jiu Pin Zhong Zheng Zhi" (The Nine Rank System, an important election system in Wei, Jin, Southern and Northern Dynasty), which had no doubt initiated the legalized official rank system of feudal society. Therefore, the system was applied until the end of Qing Dynasty without any changes. In the period of Liang and Chen in Southern Dynasty, the officials rank system and grading system were applied simultaneously. In Wei and Qi states in Northern Dynasty the system of "Jiu Pin" (the ninth rank) was further divided into "Zheng" (the principal) and "Cong" (the accessory), so the system was developed to altogether eighteen grades.

As for the salary system, the practice of Han Dynasty was adopted in Cao Wei period and the practice of Jin Dynasty was adopted in the Southern Dynasty. During the Jin Dynasty, land was given to officials as salaries based on their ranks: fifty *qing* to the officials of "Yi Pin" (the first-rank), forty-five to "Er Pin" (the second-rank), and ten to the officials to "Shi Pin" (the tenth-rank) successively. Besides land, the other salaries included grain and silk.

In early Northern Wei Dynasty, neither central nor local officials got paid. "Shou Zai" (the local governor) only needed to hand in a certain amount of rent to the government, then he could plunder people's property unscrupulously, as was described in a saying that "when an official assumes the office, he had nothing but only a horse, but when he leaves his office, he is with hundreds of loads of goods," which had led to people's violent protest. In the 8th year of Taihe during the reign of Emperor Xiaowen (484 A.D.), with the establishment and development of feudal bureaucracy, the salary system began to be carried out and "different amount of silk and grain were given to officials with different ranks."

As for the retirement of officials, it was recorded in "Tian Yu Zhuan" (The Biography of Tian Yu) in "Wei Shu"(The History of Northern Wei Dynasty) in *San Guo Zhi (The Record of the Three Kingdoms)* that Yu demanded retirement for his old age but he was rejected several times by 'Tai Fu' (Minister of National Financial Affairs) Sima Yi. Yu explained that, "I'm over seventy years old but still in

---

[112]"Su Zong Ji" (The Record of Su Zong) in *Wei Shu* (*The History of Northern Wei Dynasty*).

[113]"Lu Yu Zhuan" (The Biography of Lu Yu) in "Wei Shu" (The History of Northern Wei Dynast) in *San Guo Zhi* (*The Record of the Three Kingdoms*).

office. So I am in my declining years, just like the bell ceasing ringing, the clepsydra running out, or one still walking at night without rest. So it's a crime." According to the record, the retirement age was seventy years old. In Jin Dynasty this retirement system was also adopted, yet the retired was often recalled to office by the emperor. For example, General Chen Qian "was awarded by the emperor for his contribution and old age," so he was still in office after retirement age.[114] In the year of Yongming in Southern Qi Dynasty, "Yu Shi" (the censor) Shen Yuan proposed to Emperor Ming that "all officials should be allowed to retire at the age of seventy years old,"[115] which had become a rule ever since.

The rules for retirement in Northern Wei Dynasty were more flexible; though the retirement age was seventy, considering their merits and contributions, "the officials were persuaded to stay." Thus, "the officials still held office after reaching the age of seventy." In the 4th year of Zhengguang in the reign of Emperor Xiaoming in Northern Wei Dynasty (523 A.D.), it was provided in an imperial edict that "those brilliant, meritorious, and virtuous old officials who are well-known to the people could retain their office with exception."[116]

Officials' salary after retirement was determined by their posts. Generally speaking, "if they are not exceptionally excellent, all officials will have half of the salary after their retirement."[117] The meritorious senior officials could have full salary as before and some would even be awarded with houses, money and "Ji Zhang" (chairs and canes given to the elderly as a sign of respect) as a sign of honor and glory.

6.2.2 The Tendency of Applying Severe Punishments and the Drafting of "Zhong Zui Shi Tiao" (Ten Felonies)

6.2.2.1 "Zhong Zui Shi Tiao" (Ten Felonies) included "Fan Ni" (treachery), "Da Ni" (great sedition), "Pan" (treason), "Xiang" (surrender), "E Ni" (abusing or murdering the elders), "Bu Dao" (depravity), "Bu Jing" (being irreverent), "Bu Xiao" (being unfilial), "Bu Yi" (injustice) and "Nei Luan" (committing incest). Therefore, "none of these felonies would be absolved by 'Ba Yi' (The Eight Deliberations) and 'Lun Shu' (ransom)."[118] Besides, in Han Dynasty, the crimes of "Mou Fan" (plotting rebellion or plotting to endanger the country), "Da Ni" (great sedition), "Pan" (treason), "Xiang" (surrender) and the others were separated from the felony of "Bu Dao" (depravity) and were listed as independent accusations

---

[114] "Chen Qian Zhuan" (The Biography of Chen Qian) in *Jin Shu* (*The History of Jin Dynasty*).

[115] "Ming Di Ji" (The Record of Emperor Ming) in *Nan Qi Shu* (*The History of Southern Qi Dynasty*).

[116] "Su Zong Ji" (The Record of Su Zong) in *Wei Shu* (*The History of Northern Wei Dynasty*).

[117] "Su Zong Ji" (The Record of Su Zong) in *Wei Shu* (*The History of Northern Wei Dynasty*).

[118] "Xing Fa Zhi" (The Record of the Criminal Law) in *Sui Shu* (*The History Sui Dynasty*).

ranking on the top of "Zhong Zui Shi Tiao" (Ten Felonies), which had shown the priorities of fighting against crimes. As early as during the period of the Kingdom of Cao Wei, the crime of "Fan Ni" (treachery) that endangered the state was punished by "Zu Xing" (killing of the whole clan of a criminal), so in Jin Dynasty this practice was continued except that women were not punished by "Lian Zuo" (being punished for being related to somebody who committed an offence). It was recorded in "Yan Zuan Zuan" (The Biography of Yan Zuan) in *Jin Shu* (*The History of Jin Dynasty*) that "since the beginning of Jin Dynasty, the penalties were so severe that capital punishment was frequently enforced. Although it was acceptable to punish the criminal himself by death penalty, it was not acceptable to kill all the family members of the guilty."

The penalty system of Jin was continued in the Southern Dynasty and it was provided in *Nan Liang Lv* (*The Code of Southern Liang*) that "the crimes severer than 'Mou Fan' (plotting rebellion or plotting to endanger the country), 'Da Ni' (great sedition), 'Pan' (treason) and 'Xiang' (surrender) shall be punished by "Qi Shi" (exposing the executed body publicly at markets). The male family members, young or old, shall all be executed, while female members shall be reduced to servants with all the property confiscated."[119]

In Northern Dynasty, class and national oppression intertwined, so the punishment of "Fan Ni" (treachery) grew harsher. It was recorded in "Xing Fa Zhi" (The Record of the Criminal Law) in *Wei Shu* (*The History of Northern Wei Dynasty*) that "in the 2nd year of Zhao Cheng, anyone who has committed the crime of "Da Ni" (great sedition) will be executed along with his family members, whether young or old, and male or female." During the years of Shenjia, a law was made by Cui Hao in which it was stipulated that "those who has committed 'Da Ni' (great sedition) or 'Bu Dao' (depravity) shall be punished by 'Yao Zhan' (cutting in two at the waist) with his family members punished, among whom the males under fourteen will be punished by 'Gong' (castration) and the females will be punished by serving as servants in the government."

Among "Zhong Zui Shi Tiao" (Ten Felonies), "Mou Fan" (plotting rebellion or plotting to endanger the country), "Da Ni" (great sedition), "Pan" (treason), "Xiang" (surrender) were the summarization and legalization of the experience of the suppression of the crimes of endangering the state, which had become the core part of the feudal criminal law and which had reflected the feature of emphasizing the public rights in ancient Chinese law.

To prevent powerful local officials from betraying the central government, the so-called system of "Zhi Ren" (hostage system), which was established at the end of Eastern Han Dynasty, was continued by other dynasties. According to this system, the local official's family members were held hostage. During the Cao Wei period, "Tai Shou" (governor of a prefecture) of important frontier fortresses must send their

---

[119]"Xing Fa Zhi" (The Record of the Criminal Law) in *Sui Shu* (*The History Sui Dynasty*).

sons to the city of Ye (the capital city).[120] In an imperial edict issued in the 1st year of Taishi in Jin Dynasty (265 A.D.), it was mentioned by emperor Wu that ..., the practice of "'Zhi Ren' (hostage system) is abolished for those below 'Bu Qu' (the private army),"[121] which indicated that "Zhi Ren" (hostage system) in Jin Dynasty was applied not only to the local magistrates of "Jun" (shire) and "Xian" (county), but also to the intermediate-level officials. The implementation of "Zhi Ren" (hostage system) also fully exposed the emperor's suspicion of and precaution against the local officials and army generals.

"Bu Jing" (being irreverent) in "Zhong Zui Shi Tiao" (Ten Felonies) referred to the crime of offending the royal power. During the periods of "San Guo" (Three Kingdoms), the Western and Eastern Jin dynasties, and the Southern and Northern Dynasty, as far as the whole country was concerned, it was in a situation of feudal fragmentation, but for the specific dynasties, they were still autocratic centralized regimes headed by the emperors. To maintain the supremacy of monarchs, to uniformly maneuver all forces of the country and to ensure the functioning of state apparatus, the offenses of the throne such as the falsification of edicts, the curse pray, the slandering, the collision with colleagues, the cheating of the emperor and the false accusation of other people would all be severely punished. In Southern Qi Dynasty, "Tai Shou" (governor of a prefecture) Wang Zhan in Yongjia county was "sentenced to death," because "he had knelt before the emperor inappropriately."[122] To guarantee the emperor's control of death penalty, "nobody shall be killed without authorization unless on the battlefield"; otherwise, "the violators will be charged with murder."[123] In Northern Wei Dynasty, to prevent the imperial harem from interfering in politics and to prevent "Wai Qi" (relatives of an emperor on the side of his mother or wife) from usurping power, it was even stipulated that "the imperial harem will be forced to commit suicide after giving birth to a son who will become the crown prince."[124]

Among "Zhong Zui Shi Tiao" (Ten Felonies), "E Ni" (abusing or murdering the elders), "Bu Xiao" (being unfilial) and "Nei Luan" (committing incest) referred to severe crimes against the feudal code of ethics. It had been a time-honored practice dated back to Xia Dynasty to kill those who were involved in "Bu Xiao" (being unfilial). During the Cao Wei period, it was clearly stipulated that ""Bu Xiao" (being unfilial) was the most serious crime among 'Wu Xing' (Five Penalties)."[125] Thus, it was a capital crime which was as serious as killing one's own mother to kill one's

---

[120]"Wang Guan Zhuan" (The Biography of Wang Guan) in *San Guo Zhi* (*The Record of the Three Kingdoms*).

[121]"Wu Di Ji" (The Record of Emperor Wu) in *Jin Shu* (*The History of Jin Dynasty*).

[122]"Wang Xuan Zai Zhuan" (The Biography of Wang Xuanzai) in *Nan Qi Shu* (*The History of Southern Qi*).

[123]"Xiao Wu Di Ji" (The Record Emperor Xiao Wu) in *Song Shu* (*The History of Song Dynasty*).

[124]"Liu Huang Hou Zhuan" (The Biography of Queen Liu) in *Wei Shu* (*The History of Northern Wei Dynasty*).

[125]"San Shao Di Ji" (The Biography of Three Young Kings) in "Wei Shu" (The History of Northern Wei Dynasty) in *San Guo Zhi* (*The Record of the Three Kingdoms*).

step-mother. In Jin Dynasty, the process of the Confucianization of law was accelerated, so "Gang Chang Ming Jiao" (feudal cardinal guides and constant virtues) which was advocated by Confucianism was reaffirmed by law. For example, in *Jin Lv* (*Jin Code*), the crime of "Bu Xiao" (being unfilial) was punished by "Qi Shi" (exposing the executed body publicly at markets), while in *Song Lv* (*Song Code*), it was ruled that "those who hurt and beat their parents shall be punished by 'Xiao Shou' (the penalty of hanging the head of the criminal on top of a pole for public display); those who curse their parents or murder the parents-in-law will be sentenced to 'Qi Shi' (exposing the executed body publicly at markets)."[126] During the reign of Emperor Ming in Song Dynasty, an amnesty was offered, but "those who have murdered their parents, grandparents or elder brothers are not included in the amnesty."[127] Before the reign of Liu family in Song Dynasty, if parents and grandparents were convicted, the offspring must express their agreement at court according to procedure. However, during the reign of Liu family in Song Dynasty, the law was considered "most unceremonious and immoral,"[128] so it was abolished. In *Liang Lv* (*Liang Code*) and *Chen Lv* (*Chen Code*), "Qing Yi Jin Gu" (people would be confined to their native town if they have offended feudal ethics) was added to the law and it was stipulated that for the gentry and scholars, if they had violated "Gang Chang Ming Jiao" (feudal cardinal guides and constant virtues), "Bu Xiao" (being unfilial), "Nei Luan" (committing incest), corruption, adultery and robbery, then they had committed the crime of "Xiang Lun Qing Yi" (the crime against Confucian ethic morality and public opinion), so they would be held in "lifelong contempt" and be deprived of their election rights in the village, which had shown the great influence that feudal ethics had exerted on law.

In the 11th year of Taihe in Northern Wei Dynasty (487 A.D.), when Emperor Xiaowen called together all officials to make *Xing Dian* (*Criminal Code*), "Bu Xiao" (being unfilial) was considered as the most severe crime among the three thousand crimes, so it should be punished severely. Even the careless behavior in the mourning of one's parents would be regarded as one of the reasons for the officials to be dismissed. According to the record in "Ren Cheng Wang Yun Zhuan Fu Cheng Zhuan" (The Biography of Wang Yun in Ren Cheng and the Biography of Fu Cheng) in *Wei Shu* (*The History of Northern Wei Dynasty*), Yuan Song's uncle died, but he did not cry over his uncle's death and went on safari. Thus, Emperor Xiaowen got furious and reprimanded that "Yuan Song has not followed the principle of 'Ke Ji Fu Li' (subduing one's self and recovering the rites) and is contemptuous of laws and regulations,.... Although it is as sad as to lose one's father to lose an uncle, yet he is not as painful as a son should be. Moreover, he even enjoys himself. How short a time has he mourned! So he shall be dismissed." During the period of Northern Zhou and Northern Qi Dynasty, "Bu Xiao" (being unfilial) was even listed among "Zhong

---

[126]"Kong Ji Gong Zhuan" (The Biography of Kong Jigong) in *Song Shu* (*The History of Song Dynasty*).
[127]"Suo Lu Zhuan" (The Biography of Suo Lu) in *Song Shu* (*The History of Song Dynasty*).
[128]"Cai Kuo Zhuan" (The Biography of Cai Kuo) in *Song Shu* (*The History of Song Dynasty*).

Zui Shi Tiao" (Ten Felonies), so although categorized in "Ba Yi" (The Eight Deliberations), it was not pardoned.

Seen from above, the making of "Zhong Zui Shi Tiao" (Ten Felonies) was not only closely related with the growing authority of the emperor in Northern Dynasty, but also with the increasing emphasis on the ruling of "Li" (rites), "Gang Chang" (the Chinese ethical tradition) and "Lun Li" (ethics), the improvement of the techniques of criminal legislation and the long-time accumulation of the experience of judicial practice. Seen from the origin of the development, the crimes of "Bu Dao" (depravity) and "Bu Jing" (being irreverent) in the Han Dynasty had become the historical origin of "Zhong Zui Shi Tiao" (Ten Felonies). It was stated in *Tang Lv Shu Yi* (*The Comments on Tang Code*) that "although the *Jiu Zhang Lv* (*The Code in Nine Chapters*) of Han Dynasty was lost, the crimes of 'Bu Dao' (depravity) and 'Bu Jing' (being irreverent) was retained." These rules were adopted in *Jin Lv* (*Jin Code*) and a further explanation was made by Zhang Fei on these concepts: "'Bu Jing' (being irreverent) means lacking of 'Li' (rites) and violation of etiquette," while "'Bu Dao' (depravity) means being heartless and unsympathetic."[129] Besides, "the offense of 'Gu Du Yan Mei' (to agitate and mislead people by demagogy) also belonged to 'Bu Dao' (depravity)," so "all the family members involved shall be beheaded with their houses burnt."[130] Seen from the internal relationship of the development of criminal law between Northern Qi and Northern Zhou, even before "Zhong Zui Shi Tiao" (Ten Felonies) was made in Northern Qi state, ten kinds of felonies had already been included in *Bei Zhou Lv* (*The Penal Code of the Northern Zhou Dynasty*), and what was different was that the expression of "Mou Fan" in *Bei Zhou Lv* (*The Penal Code of the Northern Zhou Dynasty*) was changed to "Fan Ni" (treachery) in *Bei Qi Lv* (*The Penal Code of the Northern Qi Dynasty*); while "Da Bu Jing" (being greatly irreverent) in *Bei Zhou Lv* (*The Penal Code of the Northern Zhou Dynasty*) was changed to "Bu Jing" (being irreverent) in *Bei Qi Lv* (*The Penal Code of the Northern Qi Dynasty*) and the rest were all the same, which had indicated that lawmakers in Northern Zhou and Northern Qi dynasties held similar views on felonies.

"Zhong Zui Shi Tiao" (Ten Felonies) was also the predecessor of "Shi E" (ten abominations) in the feudal codes of Sui, Tang, Ming and Qing dynasties.

Besides "Zhong Zui Shi Tiao" (Ten Felonies), in the laws of all dynasties in this period, the crime of property violation, namely, the crime of "Qiang Dao" (robbery) was severely punished without exception, and "Dao Lv" (Statutes on Theft) and "Jie Lue Lv" (Statutes on Robbery) were listed in parallel in the eighteen chapters of *Wei Lv* (*Wei Code*). In addition, the boundary of the crime of violence and non-violence was differentiated in the annotation of *Jin Lv* (*Jin Code*) according to the criminal methods, so the crime of "Dao" (robbery) was further divided into "Dao" (theft) and "Qiang Dao" (robbery). "'Dao' (theft)" refers to stealing others' property, while

---

[129]"Xing Fa Zhi" (The Record of the Criminal Law) in *Jin Shu* (*The History of Jin Dynasty*).

[130]"Xing Fa Zhi" (The Record of the Criminal Law) in *Wei Shu* (*The History of Northern Wei Dynasty*).

6.2 The Basic Contents of the Laws in Different Dynasties

"'Qiang Dao' (robbery) refers to taking others' property by force."[131] For the crime of "Qiang Dao" (robbery), the criminal would be beheaded with his families forced to do military service. It was further stipulated in *Song Lv* (*Song Code*) that "all robbers shall be beheaded with their family members sentenced to 'Qi Shi' (exposing the executed body publicly at markets)."[132] Besides, in Northern Wei Dynasty it was also stipulated in the law that "the people who have committed the crime of 'Qiang Dao' (robbery) will be sentenced to 'Qi Shi' (exposing the executed body publicly at markets)." In Western Zhou Dynasty, "Qun Dao" (gang robbery) was divided into robbing with weapon and robbing without weapon, as was stipulated that "if those who are involved in gang robbery have robbed more than one *pi* with weapon and more than five *pi* without weapon, they will be punished by death penalty...".[133] "If the bandits have attacked the fellow townsmen or broken into people's houses," "the victim can kill them for justifiable defense without being found guilty."[134] As for the crime of stealing royal and official property, cows or horses, those involved would be punished by death penalty. In Southern Qi Dynasty, a ten-year-old child was "sent to jail" for stealing a bunch of rice in his neighbor's land.[135] Thus, it can be seen that the penalty for the crime of infringement on private property was very severe. Furthermore, under the principle of subsequent accomplices, it was even regulated in *Wei Lv* (*Wei Code*) that "if people have intentionally bought the stolen goods, they would be regarded as the accessories."[136]

Besides the crime of property violation, the crime of assaulting human body was divided into "Zei Sha" (premeditated murder), "Mou Sha" (murder) and "Gu Sha" (intentional killing) in Han Dynasty. According to Zhang Fei's annotation of *Jin Lv* (*Jin Code*), there were seven kinds of killing: "Zei Sha" (premeditated murder), "Mou Sha" (murder), "Gu Sha" (intentional killing), "Dou Sha" (killing during fighting), "Xi Sha" (killing during playing), "Wu Sha" (manslaughter), and "Guo Shi Sha Ren" (involuntary killing). Besides, sentences were also different according to circumstances. For example, "those involved in 'Wu Sha' (manslaughter) would be sentenced to three years of imprisonment."[137] In the period of Emperor Wen in the Northern Wei Dynasty, killing for revenge was prohibited, as was stipulated in the rule that "the people who dares to revenge for personal grudge will be sentenced

---

[131]"Xing Fa Zhi" (The Record of Criminal Law) in *Jin Shu* (*The History of Jin Dynasty*).

[132]"He Shang Zhi Zhuan" (The Biography of He Shangzhi) in *Song Shu* (*The History of Song Dynasty*).

[133]"Xing Fa Zhi" (The Record of the Criminal Law) in *Sui Shu* (*The History of Sui Dynasty*).

[134]"Xing Fa Zhi" (The Record of the Criminal Law) in *Sui Shu* (*The History of Sui Dynasty*).

[135]"Liang Zheng Zhuan" (The Biography of Liang Zheng) in *Nan Qi Shu* (*The History of Southern Qi Dynasty*).

[136]"Xing Kao" (A Textual Research of the Criminal Penalties) (Part 8) in *Wen Xian Tong Kao* (*A General Examination of Documents*), Vol. 169.

[137]"He Cheng Tian Zhuan" (The Biography of He Chengtian) in *Song Shu* (*The History of Song Dynasty*).

to the punishment of 'Zu' (killing of the whole clan of a criminal)."[138] Besides, in Western Wei Dynasty, "the prime culprit and accomplice in crime of homicide were distinguished," as was stipulated that "in the circumstance that the victim recovered after a lethal injury, the prime culprit will be sentenced to death and the accomplice would be exiled; if the victim had died, they would be beheaded.[139] Under the influence of Confucian spirit of ruling by "Li" (rites), the penalties for homicide among superior and inferior were very different. For example, "the grandparents or parents who had killed their offspring with weapons out of anger would be sentenced to five years of imprisonment," while "the people who had killed their parents would be sentenced to the punishment of 'Huan' (the criminal being pulled by five carts and broken into six pieces)."[140]

To punish the corrupted officials, among the eighteen chapters of *Wei Lv* (*Wei Code*), there were two special chapters entitled "Qing Qiu" (Asking for Bribery) and "Chang Zang" (Accepting Bribes). Besides, a "Ling" (decree) called "He Ren Shou Qai" (getting money from the convicted by threatening them) and a "Ke" (rule) called "Shi Zhe Yan Lu" (obtaining bribes when checking goods) were also made, which showed that the law for the punishment of corruption tended to be more elaborate. In Jin Dynasty, law annotation was popular, so the concept of taking bribery was more standardized. For example, "the bribes obtained in the form of goods or money is called 'Zang' (booty)"; "the bribes obtained by threatening with criminal methods is called 'Shou Qiu'"; "the bribes obtained by threatening the convicted is called 'Liu Nan'; the bribes stored in the office is called 'Shan Fu'."[141]

In the period of Cao Wei, the penalty for corruption was extremely severe, and the people involved would be sentenced to "Qi Shi" (exposing the executed body publicly at markets). According to *Jin Lv* (*Jin Code*), for the officials who committed the crime of corruption and who did not deserve to be punished by death penalty, they were forbidden to hold office for their lifetime even in the case of amnesties; for the officials who committed the crime of misdemeanor, they were forbidden to hold office for twenty years. In the period of Southern Chen Dynasty, the provision of accepting bribes without perverting the law was added, and its penalty was the same as that for "Dao" (robbery). In the period of Xianzu in Northern Wei Dynasty, a series of separately edited penal regulations were successively enacted in the form of imperial edicts to punish corruption. The following are some of the best examples: It was stipulated in the imperial edict issued on 5th of September in the 5th year of Taian (459 A.D.) that "if a 'Mu Shou' (feudal provincial or prefectural governor) has violated people's property to keep it as his own, which has resulted in the loss of

---

[138]"Wen Di Ji" (The Record of Emperor Wen) in "Wei Shu" (The History of Northern Wei Dynasty) in *San Guo Zhi* (*The Record of the Three Kingdoms*).

[139]"Xing Fa Zhi" (The Record of the Criminal Law) in *Wei Shu* (*The History of Northern Wei Dynasty*).

[140]"Xing Fa Zhi" (The Record of the Criminal Law) in *Wei Shu* (*The History of Northern Wei Dynasty*).

[141]"Xing Fa Zhi" (The Record of the Criminal Law) in *Jin Shu* (*The History of Jin Dynasty*).

6.2 The Basic Contents of the Laws in Different Dynasties

national revenue, he shall be convicted even after he has been transferred from the position"[142]; "for those supervisory officials, if they have accepted one goat or one *hu* (a unit of measurement, one *hu* is about five *dou*) of wine, they shall be sentenced to capital punishment and the briber shall be punished as an accessory."[143] In the 8th year of Taihe (484 A.D.), Emperor Xiaowen of Northern Wei sent an official to make an inspection tour around the whole country to investigate and punish the local officials who broke the law. Consequently, forty people were punished by death penalty for taking bribes. Xin Xiong, the famous judicial official even put forward evidence theory for the incrimination of the crime of corruption. He said: "If it requires that the evidence is tenable only after three people have witnessed the suspect's acceptance of bribes, it will be too loose, but if hearsay is also taken as evidence, it will be too harsh. So I suggest that if three people have witnessed the bribery and the evidence is quite obvious, the accused shall be convicted." Xin Xiong's proposal was approved by the emperor, so an imperial edict was issued: "Please do as what Xin Xiong has suggested."[144]

In Northern Qi Dynasty, the crime of "Wang Fa" (taking bribes by bending the law) was also punished by death penalty. According to "Zu Ting Zhuan" (The Biography of Zu Ting) in *Bei Shi* (*History of the Northern Dynasty*), "Ting planned to recruit more than ten 'Ling Shi' (official responsible for clerical affairs), who all had bribed him....It was found out afterwards.... So he was arrested and sent to 'Ting Wei' (the supreme judicial officer). Finally, he was sentenced to 'Jiao' (hanging) for 'Wang Fa' (taking bribes by bending the law)." It can be seen that all crimes of corruption were severely punished in Wei, Jin, Southern, and Northern Dynasty.

The rulers of Northern Dynasty were very suspicious of "Shi Da Fu" (literati and officials) from Han nationality whom they had employed and depended, so they often punished them on the excuse of the crime of literary inquisition. For example, in the 11th year of Taiping Zhenjun (450 A.D.), Cui Hao, the scholar from Han nationality and "Si Tu" (the minister of civil affairs) at the time, was put into prison for the crime of "improper recording" of national history. Emperor Taiwu of Northern Wei Dynasty interrogated him in person and ordered that "all the one hundred and twenty-eight officials below him and above servants would be sentenced to 'Yi Wu Zu' (the law of killing the five generations of a family)." After Gao Yun's interference, only Cui Hao's clan was exterminated, and "the other officials were all executed with their clans exempted."[145] This was a major case of convicting people by literary inquisition. However, literary punishment was just an excuse, and the real reason was that Cui Hao was so talented and influential that he had formed a

---

[142]"Gao Zong Ji" (The Record of Emperor Gao) in *Wei Shu* (*The History of Northern Wei Dynasty*).

[143]"Zhang Gun Zhuan" (The Biography of Zhang Gun) in *Wei Shu* (*The History of Northern Wei Dynasty*).

[144]"Xin Xiong Zhuan" (The Biography of Xin Xiong) in *Wei Shu* (*The History of Northern Wei Dynasty*).

[145]"Gao Yun Zhuan" (The Biography of Gao Yun) in *Bei Shi* (*History of the Northern Dynasty*).

serious threat to the Northern Dynasty headed by Xian Bei nationality (an ancient nationality of China), so he was punished for the crime of "improper recording" of national history.

During this period, slavery system was prevalent, so there were great numbers of slaves, which not only seriously affected social production and national income tax, but was become a potential factor that had led to social disorder. Therefore, in *Jin Lv* (*Jin Code*), the provision of "Bu Wang" (arresting) and "reducing the escaped prisons to official slaves" were abolished."[146]

In the laws of the Southern Dynasty, it was forbidden to force "Liang Min" (the decent people) to become "Jian Min" (rabbles or people of lower social status) so as to show the impassability of "Liang" (common citizens) and "Jian" (rabbles or people with lower social status). In Northern Dynasty, the increasing number of private slaves had done great harm to national interest, so it was restated in *Dao Lv* (*Statutes on Theft*) in Northern Wei Dynasty that "those who are involved in kidnapping, or kidnapping and trafficking people, or selling people into slavery would be sentenced to death".[147] It was reiterated in the laws of Northern Zhou Dynasty that "those who bully and oppress 'Liang Min' (the decent people) shall be killed with his wife and children punished by 'Ji Mo' (the cancellation of a household registration)".[148] Furthermore, in late Northern Dynasty, slaves were set free on a large scale.

6.2.2.2 The penalty system tended to be much severer. During the Cao Wei period, there were three kinds of death penalties, four kinds of penalties for "Kun" (having the criminal's long hair cut short), three kinds of penalties for "Wan" (forced labor), and eleven kinds of penalties for "Zuo" (imprisonment and labor service), six kinds of penalties for "Fa Jin" (fines), and seven miscellaneous penalties for "Shu" (atonement). Moreover, "Zu Xing" (killing of the whole clan of a criminal) was restored. Although without being written in the criminal law, for the crime of "Da Ni Bu Dao" (against all the heavenly laws of morality and filial love), the criminal would be punished by "Yao Zhan" (cutting in two at the waist) with all their family members implicated except "their grandparents and grandsons."

At the beginning of Jin Dynasty, to ease class contradiction, the punishments like "Xiao Shou" (the penalty of hanging the head of the criminal on top of a pole for public display), "Yao Zhan" (cutting in two at the waist), "Zu Zhu" (killing of the whole clan of a criminal) and "Cong Zuo" (the innocent people in connection with the offender are punished for the offender's crimes) were abolished, and the punishment of "Lian Zuo" (being punished for being related to somebody who committed an offence) and "Fu Mu Qi Shi" (exposing the executed body of parents publicly) were not enforced except for the crime of "Mou Fan" (plotting rebellion or

---

[146]"Xing Fa Zhi" (The Record of the Criminal Law) in *Jin Shu* (*The History of Jin Dynasty*).
[147]"Xing Fa Zhi" (The Record of the Criminal Law) in *Jin Shu* (*The History of Jin Dynasty*).
[148]"Hou Mo Chen Ying Zhuan" (The Biography of Hou Mo and Chen Ying) in *Sui Shu* (*The History Sui Dynasty*).

6.2 The Basic Contents of the Laws in Different Dynasties

plotting to endanger the country), divorcing foster mother and marrying daughter.[149] In the 1st year of Yongjia during the reign of Emperor Huai of Jin Dynasty (307 A. D.), the penalty of "Yi San Zu" (the law of killing the three generations of a family) was abolished. "However it was reestablished in the 3rd year of Taining (324 A.D.) during the reign of Emperor Ming of Eastern Jin Dynasty, but it was not applied to females."[150]

The penalty system in Jin Dynasty was divided into five categories: "Si Xing" (death penalties), "Kun" (having the criminal's long hair cut short), "Shu" (atonement), the miscellaneous compensation penalties and "Fa Jin" (fines). Thus, "the death penalty symbolizes severe winter; the penalty of 'Kun' (having the criminal's long hair cut short) symbolizes withered autumn; the penalties of 'Shu' (atonement) symbolizes the remorseful spring."[151] There were three kinds of death penalties: "'Xiao Shou' (the penalty of hanging the head of the criminal on top of a pole for public display), 'Yao Zhan' (cutting in two at the waist) and 'Qi Shi' (exposing the executed body publicly at markets)." "'Xiao Shou' was applied to the most evil crimes; 'Yao Zhan' was applied to the serious crimes; 'Qi Shi' was applied to crimes less serious than death penalty."[152] There were four levels of penalties for "Kun" (having the criminal's long hair cut short): "'Kun Qian' (the punishment of having the criminal's hair cut with an iron ring tied on his neck) for five years with the punishment of 'Chi' (flogging with light sticks) for two hundred strokes; 'Kun Qian' for four years, 'Kun Qian' for three years, 'Kun Qian' for two years, and 'Kun Qian' for fewer than three years." The penalty of "Kun" (having the criminal's long hair cut short) was often combined with "Zuo" (imprisonment and labor service), hence "Kun Zuo" was enforced together "to show the dignity of the criminal law." For those delinquents with good intention, redemption was allowed to give them a warning for their behaviors. There were five levels of penalties for "Shu" (atonement): two *jin* of gold for the atonement of death penalty, 1.75 *jin* of gold for the atonement of five years' imprisonment, with each reducing 0.25 *jin* of gold for the atonement of four years, three years and two years imprisonment.[153] According to annotation of *Tang Liu Dian* (*The Six Statutes of Tang Dynasty*), "silk could be used for redemption in Jin Dynasty." Thus, it can be seen that both gold and silk can be used for redemption during Jin Dynasty. "Za Di Zui" (miscellaneous compensation penalties) in Wei Jin dynasties was a general name for canceling of the titles, removal of the names off the roll and dismissal from the official posts, which could be regarded as the prototype of "Guan Dang" (giving up one's official position for the atonement for a crime). There were five levels for "Za Di Zui" (miscellaneous

---

[149]"Hou Mo Chen Ying Zhuan" (The Biography of Hou Mo and Chen Ying) in *Sui Shu* (*The History Sui Dynasty*).

[150]Ming Di Zhuan" (The Biography of Emperor Ming) in *Jin Shu* (*The History of Jin Dynasty*).

[151]"Xing Fa Zhi" (The Record of the Criminal Law) in *Jin Shu* (*The History of Jin Dynasty*).

[152]"Xing Fa Zhi" (The Record of the Criminal Law) in *Jin Shu* (*The History of Jin Dynasty*).

[153]"Shang Shu Xing Bu" (The Minister of the Department of Punishment) in *Tang Liu Dian* (*The Six Statutes of Tang Dynasty*) ,Vol. 6.

compensation penalties), with each imposed a fine of twelve, eight, four, two and one *liang* of gold.

To distinguish from "Si Xing" (death penalties), there were altogether fourteen kinds of penalties that were summarized as "Sheng Zui" (penalties alive), including four levels of the penalty of "Kun" (having the criminal's long hair cut short), five levels of the penalties of "Shu" (atonement) and five levels of "Za Di Zui" (miscellaneous compensation penalties). According to *Tang Liu Dian* (*The Six Statutes of Tang Dynasty*), the five kinds of penalties were established to protect "Jun Zi" (gentlemen) and punish "Xiao Ren" (common people), which had shown the target of the punishment of criminal law.

In *Liang Lv* (*Liang Code*) made in Southern Dynasty, two kinds of death penalties were made, as was stipulated that "the most serious crimes are punished by 'Xiao Shou' (the penalty of hanging the head of the criminal on top of a pole for public display) and the less serious crimes are punished by 'Qi Shi' (exposing the executed body publicly at markets)",[154] but "Yao Zhan" (cutting in two at the waist) was not included. Emperor Liangwu restored the penalty of "Shu" (atonement) in the 11th year of Datong (545 A.D.). Besides, there were four levels of "Kun Qian" (the punishment of having the criminal's hair cut with an iron ring tied on his neck) with the punishment of "Chi" (flogging with light sticks) for two hundred strokes. One major change of penalty system in Liang Dynasty was that the penalty of "Jiu Deng Zhi Cha" (nine levels of difference), ranging from the punishment below one year of imprisonment to ten strokes of whipping, and "Ba Deng Zhi Cha" (eight levels of difference), ranging from the punishment which was lighter than being removed from their official posts after being punished by "Zhang" (flogging with heavy sticks) for ten strokes to the punishment which was heavier than being removed from their official posts with one hundred more strokes added. It was also clearly stipulated that silk can be used for redemption. In Chen Dynasty, the laws of Liang Dynasty were followed, except that "Shu Xing" (atonement) could only be applied to officials.

In Northern Wei Dynasty, "Jiao" (hanging) was added to "Si Xing" (death penalties) in the law revision undertaken by Cui Hao. Thus, "Si Xing" (death penalties) was divided into "Zhan" (beheading), "Jiao" (hanging), "Che Lie" (tearing a person asunder with carts), "Yao Zhan" (cutting in two at the waist), and "Chen Yuan" (drown in water), etc. Those who were accused of "Da Ni Bu Dao" (against all the heavenly laws of morality and filial love) or patricide would be punished with "Che Lie" (tearing a person asunder with carts); those who were accused of less serious crimes would be punished by "Yao Zhan" (cutting in two at the waist); those who were accused of harming other people by "Gu Du Yan Mei" (to agitate and mislead people by demagogy) or stealing horses would be punished by "Zhan" (beheading); those who were accused of adultery would be punished with "Jiao" (hanging); those who were accused of hurting people with witchcraft would be punished with "Chen Yuan" (drown in water). In addition, in the Northern Wei Dynasty, a penalty called "Men Zhu" (killing of whole family) was adopted.

---

[154]"Xing Fa Zhi" (The Record of the Criminal Law) in *Sui Shu* (*The History of Sui Dynasty*).

6.2 The Basic Contents of the Laws in Different Dynasties

Although in the 4th year of Yanxing, an imperial decree was issued to stipulate that only the criminal himself would be punished for his crime except the crime of "Da Ni" (great sedition), there were still sixteen chapters concerning the punishment of "Men Zhu" (killing of whole family) when the law was amended in Taihe Period. Obviously, the penalty of "Men Zhu" (killing of whole family) was not abolished in Northern Wei Dynasty. Thus, the main criminal penalties in Northern Qi Dynasty included "Si" (death penalty), "Liu" (exile), "Nai" (having the criminal's beard shaven for two years), "Bian" (whipping), and "Pu" (corporal punishment including "Chi," "Bian" and "Zhang"). As for the death penalties, "Zhan" (beheading), "Yao Zhan" (cutting in to two at the waist), and "Qi Shi" (exposing the executed body publicly at markets) were retained, with "Jiao" (hanging) added as the fourth penalty. The punishment of "Qian" and "Xi" (the penalty of banishing the criminals to do forced labor in remote areas) was combined with "Liu" (exile), which was next to death penalty in harshness. The distance for the penalty of "Liu" (exile) varied, so in most cases, the criminals were sent to the border regions as soldiers, but for those who could not travel afar, the male would be punished by "Tu" (imprisonment), while the female would be punished by "Chong" (the punishment of women thrashing rice for lifetime) for six years respectively. In fact, "Liu" (exile) was originally a penalty of Xian Bei nationality, and it was listed as the main penalty to supply soldiers to the north border towns and to adjust malpractice of the imbalance of the criminal penalty system, which was a great reform of the feudal criminal penalty system. Therefore, from what was mentioned above, we can see the innovation made by the small minorities from absorbing the legal culture of Han nationality.

In early Northern Dynasty, the penalty of "Yi Xing" (servitude) was enforced with the term ranging from one to five years, which was also called "Nian Xing." "Nian Xing" was called "Nai Zui" in Northern Qi Dynasty, and it was classified into five levels, with each of them punished by "Bian" (whipping) for one hundred strokes and various strokes of "Chi" (flogging with light sticks). The penalty of "Nian Xing" was changed into the penalty of "Tu Xing" (penal servitude) in Northern Zhou Dynasty. "All criminals serving the punishment of "Tu Xing" (penal servitude) were forced to do labor work in accordance with their ability."[155] The punishment of "Tu Xing" (penal servitude), which aimed at restricting the freedom of the criminals and forcing them to work, was also classified into five levels. In addition, there were five levels of "Bian" (whipping) and two levels of "Zhang" (flogging with heavy sticks), both of which were corporal punishments. Thus, the system of five penalties, which was mainly made up of "Zhang" (flogging with heavy sticks), "Bian" (whipping), "Tu" (imprisonment), "Liu" (exile), and "Si" (death penalty), was formed. The punishment of "Zhang" (flogging with heavy sticks) varied from ten to fifty strokes and "Bian" (whipping) from sixty to one hundred strokes, each of which was divided into five levels. "Liu" (exile) was also divided into five levels, starting from 2000 *li*, with 500 *li* added for each level of more serious crimes. "Tu Xing" (penal servitude) was combined with "Bian"

---

[155]"Xing Fa Zhi" (The Record of the Criminal Law) in *Sui Shu* (*The History of Sui Dynasty*).

(whipping). As for "Si Xing" (death penalties), it consisted of "Jiao" (hanging), "Zhan" (beheading), 'Xiao' (the penalty of hanging the head of the criminal on top of a piece of wood), "Lie" (tearing a person asunder with carts), and "Pan" (Strangling). Besides the main penalties, punishments relevant to property, which were used as supplementary means, were also made. This penalty mainly consisted of "Fa Jin" (fines), "Shu" (atonement), and "Za Di Zui" (miscellaneous compensation penalties).

"Bu Bing," another penalty in Northern Dynasty, referred to sending the criminals to serve in the army in remote areas, which not only acted as a punishment to the criminals, but also served as a very important method to defend and stabilize the border regions.

In Wei and Jin dynasties, because of the frequent peasant uprising, there was an increasing demand for the restoration of corporal punishment to suppress the rebels. For example, Chen Qun and Zhong You (two officials) had advocated the reestablishment of corporal punishment to prevent crimes. Chen Qun believed that "if ancient penalties are enforced, with the adulterers punished by 'Gong' (castration) (also called 'Can Shi'), and thieves punished by 'Yue' (to amputate the feet), then there will be neither adultery nor theft."[156] Afterwards, Li Sheng stressed that corporal punishment was an essential way to warn the bad people, so he said that "the corporal penalty imposed on one person may give a warning to the rest."[157] However, Wang Lang, Xia Houxuan and others opposed this opinion. Xia Houxuan said that "even death penalty cannot prevent the people who are suffering cold and hunger from committing crimes, let alone the corporal punishment."[158]

In Jin Dynasty, Liu Song also submitted a memorial to the emperor to require that corporal punishment should be restored, because it not only could save the criminal's life and "get rid of the means of crime,"[159] but also "is helpful to eradicate the roots of evildoing."[160] After several rounds of debating, corporal punishment was not restored in Wei and Jin dynasties in the end, but this was not out of the "benevolence" of the rulers, but out of their fear of the people's rebellion. General Wang Dun in the reign of Emperor Yuan in Jin Dynasty had directly pointed out that "the people have got used to living without corporal punishments, so it will bring panic if they are restored. Moreover, the rebellious people have not been wiped out, so it is inappropriate to hear the screams of brutal punishments."[161] During the Southern and Northern Dynasty, concerns about resuming corporal penalty were expressed occasionally, but they were fewer debates. However, in practice, the application of

---

[156]"Chen Qun Zhuan" (The Biography of Chen Qun) in "Wei Shu" (The History of Northern Wei Dynasty) in *San Guo Zhi* (*The Record of the Three Kingdoms*).

[157]*Tong Dian* (*The General Codes*), Vol. 168.

[158]*Tong Dian* (*The General Codes*), Vol. 168.

[159]"Xing Fa Zhi" (The Record of the Criminal Law) in *Jin Shu* (*The History of Jin Dynasty*).

[160]"Xing Fa Zhi" (The Record of the Criminal Law) in *Jin Shu* (*The History of Jin Dynasty*).

[161]"Xing Fa Zhi" (The Record of the Criminal Law) in *Jin Shu* (*The History of Jin Dynasty*).

the penalties such as "Yi" (to cut down the nose), "Yue" (to amputate the feet), and "Qing" (to tattoo on the face) had never been stopped.

As for the reformation of criminal system, it is noteworthy that the penalty of "Gong" (castration) was abolished. In the 13th year of Datong during the reign of Emperor Wen of Western Wei Dynasty (547A.D.), an imperial edict was issued and it was stated that "those who should have been punished by 'Gong' (castration) shall be punished by having their property confiscated instead."[162] In the 5th year of Tiantong (569 A.D.), a similar edict was issued by the last emperor of Northern Qi state and it was stipulated that "those who should have been punished by 'Gong' (castration) shall be made official slaves."[163] So the penalty of "Gong" (castration) was no longer a legalized punishment. Furthermore, the penalty system of "Cong Zuo" (the innocent people in connection with the offender are punished for the offender's crimes) for women was also reformed. Since Han and Wei dynasties, married women would be sentenced to death if her father or the members of her husband's family committed crimes punishable by the penalty of "Zu" (killing of the whole clan of a criminal). So it was not fair for a woman to suffer from death penalty for the crimes committed by both sides of the family. The regulation was changed by Gaoguixianggong (Cao Mao, the 4th emperor of Cao Wei), and it was stipulated that "the unmarried women would be punished for the crimes committed by her parents and the married women would be punished for the crimes committed by her husband's family,"[164] which was followed by later generations.

As for the absolution of crimes, the regulations of Western and Eastern Han dynasties were followed by most of the dynasties and amnesties were offered frequently for various reasons. For example amnesties were offered for hunting rare animals and birds and for having seals carved with authorization, which was of no use to the legal order, but had led to the abuse of law and social disorder instead. However, only Zhuge Liang was an exception, so he pursued the policy of "governing the country with great 'De' (virtue) instead of petty favor"[165] and was strict with amnesties.

To sum up, the criminal principles of this period are as follows:

First, "Ba Yi" (The Eight Deliberations) was included in law. The system of "Ba Yi" originated from "Ba Bi" (the eight conditions for mitigating punishments) in *Zhou Li* (*The Rites of Zhou Dynasty*). Although there were cases applicable by "Ba Yi" (The Eight Deliberations) in the codes and records of Han Dynasty, it was not written in law. Thus, in Cao Wei period, "Ba Yi" (The Eight Deliberations) was first included in law as a criminal principle. It was annotated in *Tang Liu Dian* (*The Six*

---

[162] "Xi Wei Wen Di Ji" (The Record of Emperor Wen of Western Wei) in *Bei Shi* (*The History of North Dynasties*).

[163] "Hou Zhu Ji" (The Record of the Last Monarch) in *Bei Qi Shu* (*The History of Northern Qi Dynasty*).

[164] "Xing Fa Zhi" (The Record of the Criminal Law) in *Jin Shu* (*The History of Jin Dynasty*).

[165] "Hou Zhu Zhuan" (The Biography of the Last Monarch) in "Shu Shu" (The History of Shu State) in *San Guo Zhi* (*The Record of the Three Kingdoms*), quoted from *Hua Yang Guo Zhi* (*The History of Southwest China*).

Statutes of Tang Dynasty) that "'Ba Yi' (The Eight Deliberations) was first included in the laws of Wei Dynasty." The so-called "Ba Yi" (The Eight Deliberations) included the following cases: "Yi Qin" (the cases that involved "Huang Qin": the relatives of the emperor), "Yi Gu" (the old retainers of the emperor: including those who had been in the emperor's service for a long period), "Yi Xian" (the morally worthy: including worthy men or superior men whose speech and conduct were greatly virtuous and may be taken as a model for the country), "Yi Neng" (the great ability: including people of great talent), "Yi Gong" (the great achievement: including those of great achievement and glory), "Yi Gui" (the high position: including all active duty officials of the third rank and above), "Yi Qin" (the diligent: including military and civil officials who have displayed great diligence in their work through thorough occupation of public affairs), and "Yi Bin" (the guests of the state: to treat the descendants of previous dynasties as guests of the state who could enjoy a legal privilege). People belonging to these eight groups enjoyed the privilege of penalty reduction or exemption. The system of "Ba Yi" (The Eight Deliberations) was continued from the period of Cao Wei to the end of Qing Dynasty and lasted for more than 1600 years.

The inclusion of "Ba Yi" (The Eight Deliberations) in law had provided legal protection for officials and nobles to oppress the common people without worrying about corresponding punishment. During Jin Dynasty, Yang Dan, "Tai Shou" (governor of a prefecture) of Luling was impeached by the judicial officials to be punished by death penalty because he had killed more than 200 people by mistake, however, he escaped death penalty because he belonged to one of the cases of "Yi Qin" (the cases that involved "Huang Qin": the relatives of the emperor). During the reign of Liu family in Song Dynasty, Zhang Shao, "Ci Shi" (feudal provincial or prefectural governor) of Yongzhou should have been sentenced to death for taking bribes and exploiting the people, but Xie Shu, who was "Zuo Wei Jiang Jun" (left general of the guards) at the time, had defended him and said that "Zhang Shao has served the late emperor, so he should be better treated."[166] So in the end, Zhang Shao was only punished by being removed from his post. During Southern Qi Dynasty, a prince of Badong had killed his assistant official, but Dai Sengjing defended him and said that "the prince has killed people by mistake, so it is not a serious crime."[167] Especially in the law of Liang Dynasty, the privileges of nobles were more protected, so it was ruled that all members of the royal families would be exempted from penalty. Consequently, "the children of noble families are so arrogant that they have violated the law wantonly."[168] An old man of Moling county said to Emperor Wu of Liang Dynasty when the emperor was making an inspection tour of the county, "Your Majesty is eager to apply the law to the ordinary people, but slow to apply it to the nobles, which should not be the long-term strategy. If Your Majesty can do it

---

[166] *Zi Zhi Tong Jian* (*History as a Mirror*) ,Vol. 122.

[167] "Dai Jing Seng Zhuan" (The Biography of Dai Jingseng) in *Nan Qi Shu* (*The History of Southern Qi Dynasty*).

[168] "Xing Fa Zhi" (The Record of the Criminal Law) in *Sui Shu* (*The History of Sui Dynasty*).

otherwise, then it will be a great fortune to the country."[169] In feudal society, nobody dared to blame the emperor in person unless he had prepared to risk his life. Thus, the old man had expressed people's piled-up grievances of long standing.

During the reign of Liu Song in Southern Dynasty, to protect the nobility and the officials, it was stipulated that if the rebellious commoners had hurt the nobility and the officials, they would be severely punished even in case of general amnesty. Moreover, their family members would be forced to be "Nu Bi" (the slave girls and maidservants) or "Bu Bing" (sending the criminals to serve in the army in remote areas).

The principle of "Ba Yi" (The Eight Deliberations) was also affirmed in the laws of Northern Dynasty. The nobilities and officials belonged to "Ba Yi" (The Eight Deliberations) would be "forgiven" or "declared innocent" even if they had committed crimes.

Because the crimes committed by the nobilities and their family members were indulged by "Ba Yi" (The Eight Deliberations), it had finally not only led to the discontent of the people, but also endangered the stability of the state. Therefore, the insightful people at that time realized that "the act of pardoning the privileged class is as dangerous as freeing the pernicious animals like hogs and snakes in the territory."[170]

In Northern Qi Dynasty, because of the sharp contradiction of the society and to protect the interest of the state, the scope of the application of "Ba Yi" (The Eight Deliberations) was limited. Thus, "the crimes that were seriously harmful to the state "would be excluded from the privileges stipulated in 'Ba Yi' (The Eight Deliberations)."

Second, the principle of "Mian Guan" (dismissal) and "Guan Dang" (giving up one's official position for the atonement for a crime). As early as the Han Dynasty, the deprivation of the nobility title and dismissal from official position could be used to atone for one's legal punishments. However, these methods only served as expedient rather than formal rules. Thus, for the first time, it was made clear in the law of Jin Dynasty that "the three-year imprisonment can be atoned for by the removal of one's official position" and that "the officials found guilty shall be removed from their official positions. Besides, those civil and military officials who have committed crimes should all be removed from their official posts."[171] Under the laws of Liang Dynasty, official dismission was classified into two levels: "first, the removal of official positions with additional punishment of 'Zhang' (flogging with heavy sticks) for one hundred strokes; second, the removal of official positions."[172] In Southern Chen Dynasty, the principle of "Guan Dang" (giving up

---

[169]"Xing Fa Zhi" (The Record of the Criminal Law) in *Sui Shu* (*The History of Sui Dynasty*).

[170]"Xing Fa Bu" (The Section of Penal Law) (Part 18) in *Tai Ping Yu Lan* (*Imperial Readings of the Taiping Era*) (Chapter 652).

[171]"Xing Fa Bu" (The Section of Penal Law) (Part 17) in *Tai Ping Yu Lan* (*Imperial Readings of the Taiping Era*), Vol. 651.

[172]"Xing Fa Zhi" (The Record of the Criminal Law) in *Sui Shu* (*The History of Sui Dynasty*).

one's official position for the atonement for a crime) was established, according to which the sentences can be redeemed by depriving the convicts of their official positions or tiles of nobility. It was stated in the law that "if one is sentenced to four or five years of imprisonment, his punishment can be reduced by two years by giving up his official position with the rest of the sentences served; if one is sentenced to three years of imprisonment, his punishment can also be reduced by giving up his official position with the rest of the sentences served. Nevertheless, if one has committed crimes unintentionally, he shall only be imposed with a fine; if one is sentenced to two years of imprisonment, the sentence can be atoned for by giving up his official position."[173]

In Northern Dynasty, a law called *Shen Jia Lv* (*Shen Jia Code*) was enacted by Cui Hao, in which it was provided that "if the officials of 'Jiu Pin' (the ninth rank) have committed crimes, they can be exempted from punishment by giving up their official positions." In *Fa Li Lv* (*Law on Precedents*), which was made later, it was explicitly stipulated that "the people with the top five noble titles (duke, marquis, earl, viscount, baron) and the officials of 'Wu Pin' (the fifth rank) can have their term of punishment reduced by two years by the deprivation of their titles or official positions, and those who have been removed from official positions could be appointed at posts one rank lower than their previous ones three years later,"[174] which had made it possible for the convicted officials to resume their political career.

At the end of Northern Wei Dynasty, the rule of "Guan Dang" (giving up one's official position for the atonement for a crime) was even applied to the junior officials who had made certain achievements but who had neither official positions nor salaries, such as "Zhong Zheng" (supervisor), the guards of the palace and so on.

In summary, this policy had enabled the privileged class to escape punishment, which had not only damaged the fairness and authority of law, but also finally led to bureaucratic corruption. Despite these disadvantages, "Guan Dang" (giving up one's official position for the atonement for a crime), which originated from Southern Chen Dynasty, had been existent till the end of the feudal society, so it had shown the privileged nature of the feudal legal system.

Third, the crime of "Qin Shu Xiang Fan" (infringement among relatives) was punished according to "Lun Chang" (feudal order of importance), and the sentence was made according to the blood relation of the two parties, which was a general principle employed in Wei, Jin and Southern Dynasty. After being influenced by the legal culture of Han nationality, the Northern Dynasty also took it as one of their criminal legal principles. Therefore, under the laws of Northern Wei Dynasty, the penalty of the crime of "Qin Shu Xiang Fan" (infringement among relatives) was decided according to the relationship between the criminal and the victim, so the punishment would be aggravated if the crime was committed by the young or the inferior. It was stated that "those who killed their parents or grandparents would be

---

[173]"Xing Fa Zhi" (The Record of the Criminal Law) in *Sui Shu* (*The History of Sui Dynasty*).
[174]"Xing Fa Zhi" (The Record of the Criminal Law) in *Wei Shu* (*The History of Northern Wei Dynasty*).

punished by 'Huan' (the criminal being pulled by five carts and broken into six pieces)."[175] On the contrary, the punishment would be mitigated if the crime was committed by the elder or the superior. In Northern Wei Dynasty, it was prescribed in *Dou Lv* (*Statutes on Fighting*) that "if grandparents and parents kill their children in anger with weapons, they will be sentenced to five years of imprisonment; if grandparents and parents beat their children to death, they will be sentenced to four years of imprisonment; if they have harbored hatred and killed their children or grandchildren on purpose, they will be punished one level severer."[176] However, if there was no blood relationship between the two parties, the criminal would be sentenced to death for murder. According to law, "if the common people have kidnapped, or kidnapped and trafficked people, or sold people into slavery, they would be sentenced to death,"[177] but if people sold their own children, they would only be sentenced to one year in prison. Those who sold their superiors within "Wu Fu" (relatives within the five degrees of mourning) would be sentenced to death, while those who sold other relatives would be sentenced to the punishment of "Liu" (exile). Thus, the indent and ethical relationship of the criminal played a pivotal role in the conviction and punishment of crimes.

Especially after the establishment of the principle of "preventing crimes by applying 'Li Jiao' (feudal ethical code) and making sentences under the rules of 'Wu Fu'" (relatives within the five degrees of mourning) in *Jin Lv* (*Jin Code*), the custom of making convicts and passing sentences in accordance with ethical relationship was further institutionalized and legalized. "Wu Fu" (relatives within the five degrees of mourning) was a mourning apparel system which was classified into five categories according to the blood relationship between the dead and the living, namely, "Zhan Cui" (mourning apparel made out of the crudest cloth, with the seaming places untrimmed, mourning three years), "Qi Cui" (mourning apparel made out of the crudest cloth, with the seaming places trimmed, mourning three years to three months), "Da Gong" (the person wearing the mourning apparel of soft sackcloth in the third mourning degree), "Xiao Gong" (the person wearing the mourning apparel of soft sackcloth in the fourth mourning degree) and "Si Ma" (the person wearing the mourning apparel of soft sackcloth in the fifth mourning degree). Thus, it had increased the proportion of "Li" (rites) in the criminal law to make convicts and pass sentences according to "Wu Fu" (relatives within the five degrees of mourning), which had reflected the ethical color of the Chinese legal system. Until the law was revised in the end of Qing Dynasty, the principle of "making sentences in accordance with the rules of 'Wu Fu'" (relatives within the five degrees of mourning) was not only applicable to criminal offences, but also to civil

---

[175]"Xing Fa Zhi" (The Record of the Criminal Law) in *Wei Shu* (*The History of Northern Wei Dynasty*).

[176]"Xing Fa Zhi" (The Record of the Criminal Law) in *Wei Shu* (*The History of Northern Wei Dynasty*).

[177]"Xing Fa Zhi" (The Record of the Criminal Law) in *Wei Shu* (*The History of Northern Wei Dynasty*).

disputes among the relatives. Therefore, "Fu Zhi" (mourning apparel system) became the necessary knowledge of judges, so the pictures of mourning apparel were listed at the front pages of the laws of Ming and Qing dynasties.

Finally, the punishment for the negligent offenses by the old, the young and the female were mitigated. According to *Jin Lv* (*Jin Code*), "the punishment of 'Zhang' (flogging with heavy sticks) and "Shu" (atonement) for the old, the young and the female who commit crimes by negligence shall be reduced by half."[178] As this principle was applicable to those who posed less danger to the society and who had committed offenses out of negligence, the mitigation would not affect social order, what' more, it could also show the intention of "Xu Xing" (penalty reduction).

6.2.3 The Civil Law Under the Privileged System of "Shi Zu" (the Gentry)

Compared with the Western and the Eastern Han dynasties, the civil law in Wei, Jin and Southern and Northern Dynasty were more developed. Moreover, because the social wealth was monopolized by gentry but the social status of gentry and civilians was restricted, a distinctive feature of the civil law was formed.

6.2.3.1 "Shi Zu"(the gentry), who topped the class of landlords and owned large pieces of land, were entitled to complete rights of civil law. The ordinary landlords, named "Shu Zu" (the common people) or "Han Men" (humble and ordinary families), were also entitled to complete rights of civil law, though their rights to participate in government and political affairs were less than that of "Shu Zu" (the common people). The class of peasants, however, was sharply divided under the historical conditions of great turbulence, brutal tangled warfare and unbridled plundering. Consequently, except that the land-holding peasants were given civil legal rights, the peasants, who had depended themselves on big gentry families, were lowered to "Bu Qu" (the private army) and "Dian Ke" (tenant) in social ranks with the result that they had lost their social status of independent civil legal subjects. During the period of Cao Wei, a gentry named Li Dian owned 3000 "Bu Qu" (the private army) in his clan, and other gentry named Sun Wu and Zhu Heng even owned more than 10,000 "Bu Qu" (the private army). The title of "Bu Qu" (the private army) was inheritable, and the farmland that "Bu Qu" (the private army) rented could be rented continuously by their descendents or by other people, but it was not allowed to be sold. If permitted by the owners, "Bu Qu" (the private army) could therefore have the status of civilians.

"Dian Ke" (tenant), which developed from the system of "Zhan Tian" (owning and opening up wasteland), also referred to the peasants depending on big gentry families. During the period of Cao Wei, a law about "applying different regulations

---

[178]"Xing Fa Zhi" (The Record of the Criminal Law) in *Jin Shu* (*The History of Jin Dynasty*).

6.2 The Basic Contents of the Laws in Different Dynasties

to the peasants who rent cattle from 'Gong Qing' (councilors and ministers) or the petty officials" was enacted. Based on this law, the system of "Zhan Tian" (owning and opening up wasteland) was further established in Western Jin Dynasty, so it was stipulated that the owning of farmland and peasants and the protection of the owners' relatives should be regulated in accordance with official ranks. Thus, by this law, the economic privilege of big gentry families was systematized, which had provided a legal basis for their plundering of peasants' farmland, to own peasants personally and to exploit them mercilessly. According to the regulations in Eastern and Western Jin dynasties, based on official ranks, the pieces of farmland that the officials were allowed to hold varied from ten to fifty *qing*, the numbers of "Dian Ke" (tenant) they were allowed to own varied from one to fifty households, and the numbers of servants or relatives that they were allowed to shelter ["Bi Yin" (put their relatives under their protection)] varied from three to nine generations. Except the bureaucratic families and "Shi Zu" (the gentry), the royal relatives, state guests, the descendants of the scholars of the past, and the descendants of gentry were all allowed to shelter their relatives by "Bi Yin" (put their relatives under their protection) according to their official ranks. In fact, the rules of "Bi Yin" (put their relatives under their protection) allowed aristocracies and "Shi Zu" (the gentry) to legally possess the dependent peasants. As they were "protected," "Dian Ke" (tenant) did not have his own household registration, so he had to follow the strict rules to depend personally on their masters. In the period of Cao Wei, "Dian Ke" (tenant), just like land, money and bolts of silk, could also be bestowed as rewards. In fact, at that time, the pieces of farmland and the numbers of peasants possessed by aristocracy and "Shi Zu" (the gentry) were far more than what were regulated by law.

"Nu Bi" (the slave girls and maidservants) were at the bottom of social ranks, and they were the subjects to be traded, granted and awarded, so they did not have any civil legal rights at all. Even if "Nu Bi" (the slave girls and maidservants) were killed by their masters, their masters wouldn't be punished. Because "Nu Bi" (the slave girls and maidservants) were the property of their masters, it was forbidden by law to "lure or harbor the escaped 'Nu Bi' (the slave girls and maidservants)." Most of people became "Nu Bi" (the slave girls and maidservants) because they "had sold themselves due to poverty." As it was legalized by the state for the "notable families, great clans" and "Shi Zu" (the gentry) to own and enslave "Nu Bi" (the slave girls and maidservants), and the policy of changing war captives and criminals to "Nu Bi" (the slave girls and maidservants) were carried out to provide service to government, the aristocratic families and "Shi Zu" (the gentry) vied with each other to own "Nu Bi" (the slave girls and maidservants). For example, in Eastern Jin Dynasty, a gentry named Diao Kui "had possessed more than 10,000 *qing* of fertile farmland and thousands of 'Nu Bi' (the slave girls and maidservants)."[179] As "Nu Bi" (the slave girls and maidservants) were at the bottom of social rank, in feudal hierarchical system, it was strictly forbidden to "change 'Liang Ren' (the decent people) into 'Nu Bi' (the slave girls and maidservants)," so those involved would be severely

---

[179]"Diao Gao Zuan" (The Biography of Diao Gao) in *Jin Shu* (*The History of Jin Dynasty*).

punished by law. However, such stipulations showed that the social position of the land-holding peasants were significantly reduced and that the conflicts between state and the gentry class over labor force and tax were more intensified.

In Eastern and Western Jin dynasties, the males between "sixteen and sixty years old were ruled as adults" who had full capacity for civil conduct. In Southern Dynasty, the males between "fifteen and sixteen years old were regulated as minors," who had only limited capacity of civil conduct. In the Northern Dynasty, the males between eighteen and sixty-five years old were ruled as adults who had full capacity of civil conduct.

6.2.3.2 The core of ownership was the ownership of farmland. There were two kinds of farmland: the official farmland owned by the state and the private farmland owned by the landlords and peasants. The system of "Tun Tian" (wasteland opened up by garrison troops or peasants) in the period of Cao Wei and the system of "Zhan Tian" (owning and opening up wasteland) in the Western Jin Dynasty were both about the allotment and management of the state-owned farmland. During that time, "Shi Zu" (the gentry) and local despots backed up by the state power had been doing their utmost to increase and enlarge the pieces of farmland that they had already held. Therefore, they had sharp conflicts over the system of land ownership of the state. In Eastern Jin Dynasty, to safeguard the system of state ownership, it was stipulated by law that "those who encroach upon the state-owned lakes and marshes ... if the occupied area is more than one *zhang* (a unit of length equal to 3.3 meters), he shall be punished by 'Qi Shi' (exposing the executed body publicly at markets)."[180] Although this rule did deter the common peasants, it never stopped the gentry's unbridled plundering of land. On the contrary, the hierarchical ownership of land by "Shi Zu"(the gentry), the aristocracy and the local despots was actually legalized by the system of "Zhan Tian" (owning and opening up wasteland), which in turn promoted the development of the system of large-scale land ownership.

In the Southern Dynasty, in the reign of Liu Song, the system of "Zhan Tian" (owning and opening up wasteland), which was practiced in Jin Dynasty, was followed and the officials and local despots were allowed to occupy one to three *qing* of mountain land, which had provided a legal basis for "Shi Zu"(the gentry) and local despots to plunder land by force. During this period, the state-owned "mountain forests, rivers, and marshes" which were with great economic value, were changed into privately-owned property of the gentry class, which had become an outstanding feature of the system of land occupation. Under the chaotic circumstance that "the powerful families merge with each other and the stronger bullied the weaker," "the common people became homeless, so they were unable to protect their own property."[181] For this reason, during the reign of Xiao Wu, five regulations were issued successively about "mountain land occupation," in which it was stipulated

---

[180]"Yang Xuan Bao Zhuan" (The Biography of Yang Xuanbao) in *Song Shu* (*The History of Song Dynasty*).

[181]"Wu Di Ji" (The Record of Emperor Wu) in *Song Shu* (*The History of Song Dynasty*).

that if the mountain rivers or lakes had been occupied, "they will not be confiscated by the government" and that "if the mountain land has already been occupied, the occupied areas will not been changed; if the occupied areas are smaller than the areas regulated in law, the shortfall will be made up." At the same time, it was also stipulated that "the officials of 'Yi Pin' (the first-rank) and 'Er Pin' (the second-rank) are allowed to occupy three *qing* of mountain land" and that "the officials of 'Jiu Pin' (the ninth-rank) are allowed to occupy one *qing* of mountain land."[182] From what is mentioned above, we can see clearly that "the regulation on the occupation of mountain land" was not only a transplantation of the regulations on farmland occupation of the Western Jin Dynasty, but also a legal recognition of the illegal conduct of "occupying the mountain land and lakes" by "Shi Zu"(the gentry).

The law of the Northern Dynasty was similar to that of the Southern Dynasty in the protection and development of feudal land ownership. For example, "Jun Tian Zhi" (The System of Land Equalization) was established in the Northern Dynasty, according to which, land could also be allocated to "Nu Bi" (the slave girls and maidservants) according to household registration so that the bureaucrats and landlords who possessed a large number of "Nu Bi" (the slave girls and maidservants) could occupy large pieces of farmland under the precondition of ensuring the land ownership of the feudal state. In the Northern Wei Dynasty, after summing up the experience of the system of land equalization, "Jun Tian Ling" (Decree of Land Equalization) was issued, and it was stipulated that one male adult could receive twenty *mu* of land for planting mulberry trees (for silkworms). Besides, the land "shall be the family property without being confiscated by the state even after the owner has died"[183] and be inherited by the owner's children and grandchildren. This had shown a great change in land system. Although the policy of "dividing equally the land to individual families" had enabled the peasants to obtain a certain amount of land, it was still the bureaucrats and the gentry class who were greatly benefited. In Northern Qi Dynasty, "Yong Ye Tian" (family farmland), which was owned by the officials, were included in the laws and decrees.

During the time of the Northern Qi Dynasty, many people in the central plains started to move to the south of country, but they "were homeless and stayed in the strange land for decades." Therefore, once they returned to their former hometown, it was more likely that they would be involved in conflicts with the people who were holding the land. Since "years had passed and the fellow-townsmen were all confused about the original owners, although there were many testimonies from people, none of them were reliable. So both parties provided more testimonies given by their relatives, but still there was something confusing in their testimonies." In this regard, the legal actions were prolonged, and sometimes they could even last for years." Consequently, "the fertile land was wasted without being plowed, the tender

---

[182]"Yang Xuan Bao Zhuan" (The Biography of Yang Xuanbao) in *Song Shu* (*The History of Song Dynasty*).

[183]"Shi Huo Zhi" (The Records of National Finance and Economy) in *Wei Shu* (*The History of the Northern Wei Dynasty*).

leaves of mulberry trees became withered without being picked, so many people would like to try their chances to seek private gains, which had brought about numerous cases of lawsuits."[184] To solve the problem, Emperor Xiaowen accepted the proposals put forward by his ministers and began to set a time schedule for the settlement of the lawsuits of land: "A time schedule should be set for the settlement of the lawsuits of land. If the period for the settlement of lawsuit has expired, but the lawsuit still has not been settled, the land in dispute shall be given to the current owner"[185] to show the emphasis on the ownership of current land holders.

During the reign of Emperor Xiaowen, temples were extensively built up all over the country because of the prevalence of Buddhism. For this reason, temples were not only the places of the religious activities, but also the owners of large pieces of land and the masters of numerous depending peasants. Consequently, the temple became a special civil subject.

The changes of taxation system were closely related to those of land system. The military expedition, national defense and the increase of the state fiscal spending had promoted tax legislation. Therefore, the major achievement of legislation was the enactment of law of "Zu Diao." "Zu" referred to farm rent, "Diao" referred to "household" and it was a method of tax collection applicable to small-peasant economy. The law of "Zu Diao" was made according to "Hu Diao Ling" (the rule of household taxation) issued in the 9th year of Jian'an (204 A.D.) in the period of Cao Wei, according to which, the poll taxation system of "Kou Fu" (poll tax) and "Suan Fu" (capitation tax) in Han Dynasty was changed into a household taxation system. It was regulated that "for every *mu* of farmland, four *sheng* of rice should be paid for tax, and for every household, two *pi* of rough silk and two *pi* of cloth should be paid for tax."[186] The purpose of issuing "Hu Diao Ling" (the rule of household taxation) was to prevent the local despots from plundering the peasants mercilessly, to recover the fragile economy and to stabilize the social order. In the 19th year of Jian'an (208 A.D.), in the State of Shu, "the tax was adjusted in order to cover the military expenses."[187] It was also recorded that in the 5th year of Huangwu (226 A. D.) that in the State of Wu "the tax was reduced and the taxation of household was abolished."[188]

In the 1st year of Taikang (280 A.D.) in the Western Jin Dynasty, *Zhan Tian Ling* (*The Decree of Farmland Occupation*) was made, and in the meantime *Hu Diao Shi* (*The Rule of Household Tax*) was issued, according to which every male adult

---

[184]"Li Xiao Bo Zhuan" (The Biography of Li Xiao Bo) in *Wei Shu* (*The History of the Northern Wei Dynasty*).

[185]"Li Xiao Bo Zhuan" (The Biography of Li Xiao Bo) in *Wei Shu* (*The History of the Northern Wei Dynasty*).

[186]"Wu Di Ji" (The Record of Emperor Wu) in "Wei Shu" (The History of the Northern Wei Dynasty) in *San Guo Zhi* (*The Record of the Three Kingdoms*).

[187]"Zhuge Liang Zhuan" (The Biography of Zhuge Liang) in "Wu Shu" (The History of Wu State) in *San Guo Zhi* (*The Record of the Three Kingdoms*).

[188]"Wu Zhu Zhuan" (The Biography of the King of Wu) in "Wu Shu" (The History of Wu State) in *San Guo Zhi* (*The Record of the Three Kingdoms*).

6.2 The Basic Contents of the Laws in Different Dynasties

should pay four *hu* of rice for every fifty *mu* of farmland that he owned. In other words, every male adult should pay eight *sheng* of rice for every *mu* of farmland that he owned. Apart from farm rent, "Hu Diao" (household tax) was also collected, so if a male adult was the head of a household, he should pay three *pi* of rough silk and three *jin* of cotton for tax every year; if a female adult was the head of a household, she should pay half of the tax paid by a male every year. In Zhaojun, Zhongshan, and Changshan where fine silk was taken as the substitute for rough silk for paying tax and in other places where rough cotton cloth was taken as substitutes for fine cotton cloth for paying tax, one *pi* of fine silk could substitute for six *zhang* of rough silk, one *pi* of rough cotton cloth could substitute for one *pi* of rough silk, and one *pi* of rough silk could substitute for three *jin* of cotton."[189] So it can be clearly seen that taxation in the Western Jin Dynasty was obviously higher than that in the period of Wei.

At the beginning of Southern Dynasty, "other things were allowed to be used as household tax,"[190] and it was also regulated that "two thirds of the tax can be paid by money, one third by cloth." However, in the period Liang and Chen (the late periods of the Southern Dynasty), it was stipulated that "the male adults should pay two *zhang* of cloth and rough silk, three *liang* of silk thread and eight *liang* of cotton for tax"; they should also pay "eight *chi* of rough silk (which would be later paid as a part of officials' salary) and three *liang* and two *fen* of cotton (which would be later paid as a part of officials' salary) . . . the female adults should pay half of the tax paid by male adults."[191] The "rice, rough silk and cotton that were paid to officials as salary" were originally additional tax for the salaries of "Ci Shi" (a supervisor assigned by the central government to a local area), "Shou" (prefecture chiefs) and "Ling" (magistrate) and for army rations, but later they became regular tax. Additionally, there were other sundry tax, such as "Kou Qian" (poll tax) and "Tang Ding Shui" (irrigation tax), etc., some of which were collected temporarily for war expenses. In Southern Dynasty, tax was collected in accordance with the number of male or female adults because the household registration was in great confusion so that it was difficult to collect tax according to households.

After entering central plains, Emperor Daowu of Tuoba nationality in Northern Wei Dynasty changed the nomadic life of his people, carried out the policy of "making them settle down by giving them land" and collected tax from the peasants according to "Hu Diao Fa" (The Law of Household Taxation). Later on, besides "Jun Tian Ling" (Decree of Land Equalization), "Zu Diao Fa" (the law on farm rent) was also issued, according to which "every couple of a household should pay one *pi* of

---

[189] Xu Jian (Tang Dynasty), *Chu Xue Ji* (*The Collection of Writings*) (Part 27), quoted from "Jin Ling" (Orders and Decrees in Jin Dynasty).
[190] "Xiao Wu Di Ji" (The Record of Emperor Xiao Wu) in *Song Shu* (*The History of Song Dynasty*).
[191] "Shi Huo Zhi" (The Records of National Finance and Economy) in *Sui Shu* (*The History of Sui Dynasty*).

silk and two *dan* of millet."[192] This taxation system was not only adaptable to the social conditions of the time, but also was able to meet the demands of the state; therefore, it was adopted by the later Sui and Tang dynasties.

In summary, the economic law, represented by "Jun Tian Fa" (the law on land equalization) and "Hu Diao Fa" (The Law of Household Taxation), was greatly developed based on the laws of the Eastern and Western Han dynasties, which not only promoted social economy, but also met the financial demands of the country.

6.2.3.3 The primary form of debt was the debt of contract, in which the sale and loan contracts were the most popular. According to the laws of Eastern and Western Jin dynasties, "contracts" should be signed in farmland, house, cattle and horse transaction, and the volume of business should be clearly recorded on those documents with four percent of the volume paid for deed tax by the parties in the proportion of three to one. For the transaction of other products (personal property), although it was unnecessary to sign documents, tax should still be paid, so if there were any disputes over the business, the receipts of deed tax would be provided as evidence. The system of deed tax originated from the Eastern Jin Dynasty. A bond about "Yang Shao's purchasing of floor tiles" signed in the 5th year of Taikang in Western Jin Dynasty (284 A.D.) was newly discovered, on which it was written that "this contract is as effective as a law." Thus, it showed that the contracts signed privately by people in farmland business were very common and that the legal effect of those contract were recognized by the state. In Southern Dynasty, the laws of Jin Dynasty were usually followed by the various states.

During this historic time, debtor-creditor relationship was so widely spread that even the nobility was involved in usury practice. It was recorded in "Cai Kuo Zhuan" (The Biography of Cai Kuo) in *Song Shu* (*The History of Song Dynasty*) that as a result of usury business by the princess and prince, "the rate of interest kept rising, so more cases needed to be supervised and settled." According to "Gu Kai Zhi Zhuan" (The Biography of Gu Kaizhi) in *Song Shu* (*The History of Song Dynasty*), when Gu Kaizhi was the magistrate of Wujun, his son, named Chuo, "had obtained so much personal wealth that many gentry in the county owed him debts." At that time, even "Ci Shi" (a supervisor assigned by the central government to a local area) of the local place also "forced the common people to loan money," which not only showed the special feature of debtor-creditor relationship in ancient China, but also reflected the greediness of the nobility and bureaucrats and the corruption of law. The nobility and bureaucrats were so corrupted and greedy that they even vied with each other in loaning money and earning interest, not to mention the wealthy businessmen, landlords and local despots. It was recorded that "the interest rate could even be increased ten times within ten days."[193] Since the social situation of Northern Wei

---

[192]"Shi Huo Zhi" (The Records of National Finance and Economy) in *Wei Shu* (*The History of the Northern Wei Dynasty*).

[193]"Gao Zong Ji" (The Record of Emperor Gao Zong) in *Wei Shu* (*The History of the Northern Wei Dynasty*).

6.2 The Basic Contents of the Laws in Different Dynasties

Dynasty was unchanged, imperial decrees were issued by Emperor Wen Cheng to forbid officials to be engaged in usury business. In his view, the usury business in which the officials of herdsmen and wealthy businessmen were engaged was "the most serious malpractice in politics." Therefore, an order was issued and it was stipulated that "all usury practices are forbidden, so those who earn interest as much as ten bolts of cloth by violating the law shall all be punished by death penalty. This prohibition should be publicized nationwide and made known to all the people."[194]

The popularity of debtor-creditor relationship had fostered the development of loan contracts. Usually, in the loan contracts, the issues about loan interest and debt guarantee were stipulated. Because of the exploit by usury in money lending, for example, after crop harvest in autumn, a creditor had to pay three times as much as the rice he had borrowed, a large number of land-holding peasants went bankrupt. To pay off their debts, some of them even had to sell their children and some had to work as laborers.

As to the guarantee of debt payment, in Han Dynasty, there was already the guarantee of using objects as pledges. In Jin Dynasty, there were records like "people being used as pledges." In "Heng Chong Zhuan" (The Biography of Heng Chong) in *Jin Shu (The History of Jin Dynasty)*, it was recorded that "... the family was extremely poor and the mother was ill. Moreover, they had to get a sheep to treat her disease, but they had no money, so the elder brother named Wen had to make his younger brother a pledge."

During the period of Wei, Jin and Southern and Northern Dynasty, the contract system was well developed and established. Generally speaking, the contents of a contract included the two parties, the date of signing the contract, the object of the contract and its condition, the contract guarantee, the liquidated damages, the guarantors and witnesses and so on. Moreover, the words that "no one should go back on his words and the fine should be doubled if violated" are written in almost all the contracts that have been discovered so far. With the adoption of the system of property guarantee, joint liability of relatives and guarantors and the implementation of the system of deed tax, the probative force of contract was strengthened, which showed that the legal effect of contract had been strengthened. In addition, from the stipulation that "contracts are signed after agreement being made between two parties" and that "the contracts are signed between people according to the provisions of law," we can see that integrity had become one of the most important factors in entering into a contract.

Under the influence of the principle of "taking and giving things according to documents" and "getting relief from government according to documents" in Wei and Jin dynasties, the agreement form of contract had appeared in the Western Jin Dynasty. For example, on the upper end of "the agreement of Qu Jiangnv's purchasing of a coffin at Gaochang in the 9th year of Taishi in the Western Jin Dynasty," the right part of Chinese character "同" was written in rapid cursive style. In the

---

[194]"Gao Zong Ji" (The Record of Emperor Gao Zong) in *Wei Shu (The History of the Northern Wei Dynasty)*.

period of "Shi Liu Guo" (The Sixteen Kingdoms) in the Northern Dynasty, contracts were already widely used in business, loan, and employment. For instance, in "the contract for Zhao Ming'er's purchase of servants at Gaochang in the 4th year of Yan Shou," the words that "both parties have agreed on the contract" were recorded and in "the contract for Zhao Shanzhong's purchasing of land for building houses in the 5th year of Yanshou at Gaochang," the words that "three parties have agreed on the contract" were recorded; and in "the contract for Shu'er's harvest of millet for wine tax in summer at Gaochang," the words that "both of the parties have '和同'" (joined in agreement) so this agreement is made for both parties" were recorded. In Chinese, "合同" (contract) is the homonym of "和同," which showed that consensual agreement was the precondition of signing a contract. Therefore, this is what should be paid attention to when doing research on ancient contracts.

6.2.3.4 In the period of Wei, Jin and Southern and Northern Dynasty, *Hu Hun Lv* (*Statutes on Marriage, Tax and Household Registration*) were exclusively issued for adjusting marriage and family relationship. To solve the problem of the shortage of the sources of troops caused by wars and to increase the poll tax, early marriage was encouraged by the government in the period. It was stipulated in the 9th year of Taishi in the reign of Emperor Wu in Jin Dynasty (973 A.D.) that "if a 17-year-old daughter has not been married off in a family, the chief local official shall choose a husband for her."[195] The legally marriageable age in the Southern Dynasty was younger than that of the Jin Dynasty: "if a 15-year-old girl has not been married off, her family members should be implicated."[196] In Northern Wei Dynasty, the marriageable age was even younger than that in the Southern Dynasty. According to historical records, when crown prince Huang was fifteen years old, his son was already given birth; when the son of Emperor Xianwen was given birth, he was only thirteen years old. From these records, we can see the situation of the early marriage among the common people. It was stipulated in Northern Qi Dynasty that "all the unmarried women between fourteen and twenty years old shall be gathered in the province. If anyone has concealed the fact, her family shall be punished by death penalty."[197] So it was not because of social convention but the national interest that the people were forced to get married early by severe punishment.

"Liu Li" (six kinds of etiquette in feudal marriage), as one of the most important condition for marriage, was still continued. According to the stipulations of the Jin Dynasty, "betrothal presents are the most important thing in marriage, regardless of private promises."[198] Under the influence of upholding "Li" (rites) in Northern Dynasty, "Liu Li" (six kinds of etiquette in feudal marriage) was also followed. Moreover, to "strictly carry out the codes of 'Li Jiao' (feudal ethical code), it was

---

[195]"Wu Di Ji" (The Record of Emperor Wu) in *Jin Shu* (*The History of Jin Dynasty*).
[196]"Zhou Lang Zhuan" (The Biography of Zhou Lang) in *Song Shu* (*The History of Song Dynasty*).
[197]"Hou Zhu Ji" (The Record of the Last Monarch) in *Bei Qi Shu* (*The History of the Northern Qi Dynasty*).
[198]"Xing Fa Zhi" (The Record of the Criminal Law) in *Jin Shu* (*The History of Jin Dynasty*).

stipulated in the law of the Northern Wei Dynasty that "the men and women who have close contact with each other without performing 'Liu Li' (six kinds of etiquette in feudal marriage) shall be punished by death penalty."[199] In the meantime, the restrictive force of the private promise was also acknowledged.

Since the system of hereditary aristocracy was prevalent, family status and background were valued in marital relationship. If a family of "Shi Zu"(the gentry) was connected with a family of "Shu Zu" (the common people) through marriage, the family of "Shi Zu"(the gentry) would be regarded as "heterogeneous," so would be ridiculed and accused. In Northern Liang Dynasty, after a "Shi Zu"(the gentry) named Wang Yuan married her daughter to a family of "Shu Zu" (the common people) in Fuyang named Man, he was accused by "Yu Shi Zhong Cheng" (Grand Censor) named Shen Yue, because "this is the worst thing that has been done. He is only interested in his personal gains, but he has brought humiliation to the people of his class." Therefore, "please consider what he has done, remove him from his position and sentence him to life imprisonment."[200] After learning that the General-in-Chief named Latter Jing wished to establish relationship with the great clans of Wang and Xie through marriage, Emperor Wu of Liang Dynasty said, "The family status of Wang and Xie is much higher than yours. So you can establish relationship with the families of lower status like Zhu and Zhang."[201] From this, we can clearly see the rigid hierarchy of family status.

The marriage system based on family status was also carried out in Northern Dynasty and it was forbidden for the families with different social status to have marriage relationship by violating the system. In the 4th year of Heping (463 A.D.) of the Northern Wei Dynasty, a decree was issued by Emperor Wencheng: "Because of the different social status and the different application of 'Li' (rites) . . . from today forward, it is forbidden for royal families, Grand Tutors, princes, dukes and gentry families to have marriage relationship with craftsmen, artisans and the families with humble surnames, so the violators should be punished."[202] In the 2nd year of Taihe (478 A.D.), another decree was issued by Emperor Xiaowen, and it was stipulated that "all the families, including the royal, the noble or the gentry, no matter whether their social status is high or low, if they marry those from the families of different status," "they shall be punished for violating the relevant regulations."[203]

Influenced by the feudal hierarchy system, for a long time, the families of "Liang" (the common people) were not allowed to have relationship with the families of "Jian" (people of a lower social status than common people) through marriage.

---

[199]"Xing Fa Zhi" (The Record of the Criminal Law) in *Jin Shu* (*The History of Jin Dynasty*).

[200]"Zou Tan Wang Yuan" (Accusing Wang Yuan) in *Zhao Ming Wen Xuan* (*Collections of Zhao Ming*),Vol. 40.

[201]"Latter Jing Zhuan" (The Biography of Latter Jing) in *Nan Shi* (*The History of the Southern Dynasty*).

[202]"Gao Zong Ji" (The Record of Emperor Gao Zong) in *Wei Shu* (*The History of the Northern Wei Dynasty*).

[203]"Gao Zong Ji" (The Record of Emperor Gao Zong) in *Wei Shu* (*The History of the Northern Wei Dynasty*).

However, in the periods when the hereditary aristocracy was prevailing, the hierarchical marriage was carried to extremes. Therefore, through marriage relationship, it was possible for "Shi Zu" (the gentry) to maintain their special social status, to strengthen the relationship and unity between themselves and to consolidate their control over the state. In addition, the royal families also established relationship with the noble families and great clans through marriage to win their support.

As "Nu Bi" (the slave girls and maidservants) did not have independent legal entity, their marriage depended on their masters' decision. According to stipulations, the marriages between "Liang" (the common people) and "Jian" (people of a lower social status than common people) were forbidden, so if a slave married a woman of "Liang" (the common people) by the master, or if the slave took the advantage of the master's power to marry a woman of "Liang" (the common people), the master should be punished. In "Jing Zhao Wang Zhuan" (The Biography of King Jing Zhao) in the chapter of "Dao Wu Qi Wang Lie Zhuan" (The Collected Biographies of the Seven Kings of Dao Wu) in *Wei Shu* (*The History of Wei Dynasty*), it was recorded that "when Ji was in Qingzhou, the people were suffering from poverty. So he married a daughter of common family to his servant as a concubine and enslaved the people of "Liang" (the common people) as maidservants. Consequently, he was accused by 'Yu Shi' (the censor) and was imprisoned with his official position and title removed."

There was no prohibition for the marriages between people with the same surnames at beginning of the Northern Dynasty. In the reign of Emperor Xiaowen, "Li" (rites) was upheld, so the marriages between people of the same surnames were harshly punished for "being immoral." In Western Wei Dynasty, "the marriages between paternal or maternal cousins or mother's sisters" were further forbidden by Emperor Wen. Until Emperor Wu in Zhou Dynasty, the marriages between people with the same surnames were still prohibited, so it was stipulated that if engagement had already been approved, it should be canceled and new engagement should be arranged. In Northern Dynasty, laws were made successively to prohibit marriages between people with the same surnames, which showed that the Confucianization of law was further developed.

Influenced by the Confucian doctrine of "men guiding women and women being obedient to men," in Southern Dynasty wives enjoyed no rights in the family. Whether for the disposal of family property or children's education, women should follow their husband's decisions. According to the tradition of Xian Bei nationality, women were the supporters of families, so the social position of women in the Northern Dynasty was higher than that of the Southern Dynasty. In "Zhi Jia" (Regulating Families) in *Yan Shi Jia Xun* (*Family Instructions of Yan*), it was recorded that "according to the tradition of Ye Xia, women are the supporters of families. So they file lawsuits to tell the right from wrong, welcome guests and visitors, drive carriages in streets and avenues and handle business in government offices. Moreover, they appeal to the officials on behalf of their sons and redress the wrongs of their husbands. This is a custom left by the previous dynasties of Heng and Dai (Xian Bei nationality)."

In terms of divorce, in Southern Dynasty, "Qi Chu" (the seven possible reasons for divorcing one's wife), namely, "being unfilial to parents-in-law," "failing to bear a male offspring," "being lascivious," "being jealous," "having severe illness," "gossiping" and "committing theft"), which was recorded in *Da Dai Li Ji* (*The Rites of Da Dai*) became the legal basis for divorce. However, it was rare in Northern Dynasty that women were forced to divorce for giving birth to no children.

During this period, it was legal to take concubines. Therefore, it was clearly stipulated in the laws of Jin Dynasty that the number of concubines that bureaucrats could take varied from one to four according to their official ranks. It was also recorded in *Yan Shi Jia Xun* (*Family Instructions of Yan*) that "Jiang Zuo was not afraid of mentioning 'Shu Nie' (the children of the concubines). After his wife's death, all the family affairs were dealt with by his concubines."

To keep the order of the family, to further stabilize the domination of the state, and especially to fulfill the role the patriarchs played in a family, the system of the domination of feudal family by patriarchs was legalized and the strict rules of unfair family hierarchies were maintained. In the meantime, patriarchs were also asked to shoulder a greater responsibility to their country and it was regulated in Jin Dynasty that "if the members of a family have escaped, the patriarchs shall be punished by 'Zhan' (beheading)."[204]

As far as inheritance is concerned, because family status and the pedigree of the clan are the bases of the privilege, lineal and concubine descent are clearly differentiated. Only "Di Zi" (the eldest son of the legal wife) was entitled to the right of inheritance, while "Shu Zi" (the son born of a concubine) was only allowed to inherited parts of family property. In the 10th year of Taishi (274 A.D.), an imperial decree was issued by Emperor Wu of the Western Jin Dynasty, according to which, "the differentiation of 'Di Zi' (the eldest son of the legal wife) and 'Shu Zi' (the son born of a concubine) is to decide the social status of the upper and the low and the noble and the humble."[205] To maintain the continuity of lineal blood, it was regulated that "if the wife has sons, the eldest son shall be appointed as the heir; if she has no sons, the son of the same lineage shall be appointed as the heir." As the heir should be chosen from the same lineage and the same generation of the family, the females and the males out of the linage were denied the rights of inheritance. It was written in *Wei Lv* (*Wei Code*) that "it is to prevent the family property from being divided to exclude 'Yi Zi' (adopted son) from inheritance."[206]

In Northern Dynasty, the lineal primogeniture system was also accepted. In this regard, "Shu Zi" (the son born of a concubine) was unfairly discriminated. In the law of the Northern Dynasty it was regulated that "the legal wife and her sons should be the lineal descents," but actually in one family more than one woman were entitled the status of wife, so consequently, it had caused the confusion in inheritance relationship. Originally, the lineal primogeniture system was protected by law to

---

[204]"Xing Fa Zhi" (The Record of the Criminal Law) in *Jin Shu* (*The History of Jin Dynasty*).
[205]"Wu Di Ji" (The Record of Emperor Wu) in *Jin Shu* (*The History of Jin Dynasty*).
[206]"Xing Fa Zhi" (The Record of the Criminal Law) in *Jin Shu* (*The History of Jin Dynasty*).

prevent the ruling right from being weakened and the family property from being divided. Because it was the actual power and right that would be inherited, there were always bloody struggles in a family for the right of inheritance, which had torn up the veil that was labeled as blood ties and family affection. In "Hou Qu Pian" (Remarriages) in *Yan Shi Jia Xun (Family Instructions of Yan)*, it is recorded that after Jiang Zuo, the patriarch, died, "the lawsuits that his family members filed against each other filled the government office and the defamatory and insulting words that they said to each other could have filled the streets. The sons of late wife accused their step-mother of a concubine; the sons of the step-mother denounced the late wife's sons as slaves. In order to prove themselves, they showed their father's testament and handwriting and blamed their father for his faults, which occurred almost every day."

6.3 Inheriting the Judicial System of Han Dynasty

In the periods of Wei, Jin and Southern and Northern Dynasty, the central judicial office was still named "Ting Wei" (the Supreme Court) by following the system of Han Dynasty. In the reign of Emperor Ming in the period of Cao Wei, after accepting Wei Kai's proposal, "Lv Bo Shi" (Scholar of Law) was entitled to teach law to improve the quality of judges. In Northern Qi Dynasty, "Ting Wei" (the Supreme Court) was expanded to "Da Li Si" (The Bureau of Judicial Review) to meet the need of judicial activities. Based on the system, below "Zheng Qing" (the minister), the subordinate posts of "Shao Qing" (the vice president), "Zheng" (director), "Jian" (ancient supervisory official) and "Ping" (ancient official) and so on were established. Besides, the number of "Lv Bo Shi" (Scholar of Law) was increased to four, and new official posts were also set up, including "Ming Fa Chuan" (chief law specialists), which was made up of twenty-four people, "Jian Che Du" (supervisor of cart for prisoners), which was made up of two people, and "Chuan" (clerks), "Si Zhi" (official in charge of supervising the officials in capital) and "Ming Fa" (law official) consisting of ten people, respectively, etc. To the Northern Zhou Dynasty, the central judicial office was named "Qiu Guan Da Si Kou" (minister of criminal justice in charge of penalty) to follow the ancient customs. With the primary establishment of "San Sheng" (The Three Departments), departments in charge of judicial, administrative and judgment were also established in the various sections of "Shang Shu Tai" (Imperial Secretariat). At the beginning of Cao Wei, besides "San Gong Cao" (the office of the three councilors) and "Er Qiang Dan Cao" (ancient officials or head of prefecture), which were inherited from the Han Dynasty, one office called "Bi Bu" (ancient government office in charge of in charge of prison and penalty) was added to be "put in the charge of prison and penalty" and "the post of

6.3 Inheriting the Judicial System of Han Dynasty

'Du Guan' was set up to be put in the charge of military prisons and penalty."[207] At the beginning of Jin Dynasty, "San Gong Shang Shu" (Three Ducal Ministers and Imperial Secretariat) was "put in the charge of prison and penalty," but later on "Li Bu Shang Shu" (the minister of the department of personnel) was set up to be jointly "put in the charge of prison and penalty." During the reign of Liu in Song Dynasty, which was the first dynasty of the Southern Dynasty, "Du Guan Shang Shu" (senior minister of imperial court) was appointed to be put in the charge of "the legal disputes in capital" and "prison and penalty."[208] At the beginning of Northern Wei Dynasty, "San Du Da Guan" was put in the charge of judicial affairs, and till the Northern Qi Dynasty, "Dian Zhong Shang Shu" (Imperial Secretariat of Court) was put in the charge of "San Gong Cao" (the office of the three councilors) to "issue orders on seasonal and agricultural affairs, to convict criminals, to manage prisons, and to prepare for the guard of honor on the day of amnesty and so forth"[209]; "Du Guan Shang Shu" (senior minister of imperial court) was put in the charge of "Bi Bu" (ancient government office in charge of in charge of prison and penalty) and the affairs like drafting "imperial decrees, laws and the management of supervisory work," and so on. Therefore, the judicial affairs were jointly managed by the central administrative offices, which showed that the administrative intervention of judicature was much more strengthened; on the other hand, the expansion of judicial agencies also reflected the increase of legal actions and the important role they played in the maintenance of the ruling of state.

The trial levels of the local judicial office were the same as those of local administrative offices, which meant that the local judicial power was still controlled by the local administrative officials. Before the reigning of Liu Song in Southern Dynasty, all legal decisions made by "Xian" (county) would be examined by the investigators appointed by "Jun" (shire) before being carried out. In Song Dynasty, the process was changed so that both legal records and prisoners would be handed over to "Jun" (shire) after the legal decisions were made by "Xian" (county) and that the cases should be reviewed and decided by "Jun Tai Shou" (head of prefecture) afterwards. If cases were difficult for "Jun Tai Shou" (head of prefecture) to decide, they would be further handed over to "Zhou Ci Shi" (feudal provincial or prefectural governor); if doubts still existed, the cases would be handed over to "Ting Wei" (the supreme official in charge of judicature). Generally speaking, the local officials had greater judicial power so that the ordinary cases were all settled by "Zhou" (subprefecture) and "Jun" (shire). As to the cases in "Jing Shi" (the capital city), they should be settled together by "Shang Shu" (the minister) and "Shou Zai" (the local governor) who were directly responsible to Emperor. At the beginning of

---

[207]"Bai Guan Zhi" (The Record of the Officials of all Ranks) in *Song Shu* (*The History of Song Dynasty*) (Book 1).

[208]"Shang Shu Xing Bu" (The Minister of the Department of Punishment) in *Tang Liu Dian* (*The Six Statutes of Tang Dynasty*), Vol. 6.

[209]"Bai Guan Zhi" (The Record of the Officials of all Ranks) in *Sui Shu* (*The History of Sui Dynasty*) (Book 2).

Northern Wei Dynasty, most of "Shou Zai" (the local governor) were military commanders, so they often took advantage of their power to kill people indiscriminately. With the consolidation of dictatorial system, to control the execution of death penalty, it was officially stipulated in *Shen Jia Lv* (*Shen Jia Code*) that "the cases of death penalty in all country shall be reported to the central government to be reviewed before being executed."[210]

As for the prosecution at that time, the system of Han Dynasty was followed, so private prosecution was restricted. During the period of Cao Wei, *Xin Lv* (*New Laws*) were divided into *Gao He Lv* (*Statutes on Prosecution*), *Xi Xun Lv* (*Statutes on Interrogation*), and *Duan Yu Lv* (*Statutes on Trials and Punishments*), according to which the laws on litigation and trial were separately edited, which was a innovation in legislation and judicature. According to the law, children and grandchildren were forbidden to accuse their parents and grandparents; otherwise, they would be punished by death penalty. Moreover, the criminals in custody were also forbidden to accuse other people. However, in the 1st year of Yuankang (291 A.D.) in Jin Dynasty, "Deng Wen Gu" (Deng Wen Drum, one of the most important ways of direct appeal in ancient China) was set up to inform about the conditions of the lower levels. In the reign of Emperor Shi Zu in Northern Wei Dynasty, "Deng Wen Gu" was also set up, so "if people had complaints and petitions, they can presented them to the Emperor by beating the drums or submit memorials by stopping the carriage of the emperor."[211] To strengthen the supervision over local courts by imperial court, direct appeals were encouraged to report the offenders to the government, but it was stipulated that "if false accusation is lodged, the prosecutor will be punished according to the crimes which he has falsely accused."[212]

As for the trial system, it was greatly developed because of the long time accumulation of the judicial experience and the serious summary made in the law revision in Wei and Jin dynasties. Especially, many legal concepts were clarified through legal annotation and explanation, which had made it easy for judges to enforce appropriate punishments. However, as politics was corrupted and many judges took bribes by bending the law, it was difficult to establish a perfect legal system in practice. According to historical records, in Western Jin Dynasty, "punishments were enforced randomly," and "it even became a custom for judges to settle cases arbitrarily." Therefore, in Southern Dynasty, if nobility and aristocrats had committed crimes, "they were always punished without strictly following the law." According to "Kong Zhi Zhuan" (The Biography of Kong Zhi) in *Nan Qi Shu* (*The History of Southern Qi Dynasty*), the judicial officials were often "muddle-headed, wicked and merciless, so they had cruelly exploited the people, embezzled their

---

[210]"Xing Fa Zhi" (The Record of the Criminal Law) in *Wei Shu* (*The History of Northern Wei Dynasty*).

[211]"Xing Fa Zhi" (The Record of the Criminal Law) in *Wei Shu* (*The History of Northern Wei Dynasty*).

[212]"Han Qilin Zhuan" (The Biography of Han Qilin) in *Wei Shu* (*The History of Northern Wei Dynasty*).

6.3 Inheriting the Judicial System of Han Dynasty

property and killed them illegally by filing many fabricated charges against them." According to records in "Xing Fa Zhi" (The Record of the Criminal Law) in *Jin Shu* (*The History of Jin Dynasty*), "the wicked officials often played with literary skills in interpreting the law and took bribes by making use of their power, which had led to great injustice in the end." This could be regarded as a general description of the judicial condition in this period.

In terms of interrogation, inquisition by torture was widely used. In Southern Liang Dynasty, "Ce Qiu," a method of cutting off food supplies to prisoners, was even used to force prisoners to confess their crimes. The brutality of torture and the injustice it had brought about were reflected in the writings of the people at that time. For example, Zhou Hongzheng, "Du Guan Shang Shu" (senior minister of imperial court) in the Southern Chen Dynasty said, "... under cruel torture and intimidation, nobody could bear the pain, so most of them pleaded guilty. That's why many people were wrongly executed."[213]

To control the supreme judicial power, the emperor sometimes also heard cases in person. In the 3rd year of Taihe (229 A.D.), Emperor Ming of Wei Dynasty changed "Ping Wang Guan" (The Temple of Level Land) into "Ting Song Guan" (The Temple of Hearing Cases), and the emperor himself "frequently went to the temple to hear the important cases."[214] Emperor Wu of the Northern Zhou Dynasty often "tried cases in Zheng Wu Palace from morning to night, sometimes candles had to be lit up."[215] In Northern Wei Dynasty, the right of executing death penalty was controlled by the emperor himself, as was stated in the saying that "the cases of death penalty shall be reported and reviewed by the emperor before execution."[216] Thus, this system, which was established to strengthen the autocratic centralization of state power, was accepted and followed by the later dynasties.

In Northern Wei Dynasty, it was advocated that "law is the key factor in administration," so the officials were demanded to hear cases according to law. However, at the same time, "Li" (rites) was stressed, the principle of "Chun Qiu Jue Yu" (Settling Lawsuits by Chun Qiu or Confucianism Classics), which had been used since Han Dynasty, was followed in settling cases, and the current laws were revised and cases were settled according to the spirit and principles of *Chun Qiu Gong Yang Zhuan* (*Annotation to Chun Qiu by Master Gong Yang*). In the imperial decree issued in the 6th year of Taiping Zhenjun recorded in "Shi Zu Ji" (The Record of Emperor Shi Zu) in *Wei Shu* (*The History of Northern Wei Dynasty*), it was stipulated that "all the doubtful cases shall be reported to 'Zhong Shu' (the prime minister) and shall be decided according to Confucian classics." It was recorded in "Xing Fa Zhi" (The Record of the Criminal Law) in *Wei Shu* (*The History of*

---

[213] "Shen Zhu Zhuan" (The Biography of Shen Zhu) in *Chen Shu* (*The History of Chen Dynasty*).

[214] "Ming Di Ji" (The Record of Emperor Ming) in "Wei Shu" (The History of the Northern Wei Dynasty) in *San Guo Zhi* (*The History of the Three Kingdoms*).

[215] "Wu Di Ji" (The Record of Emperor Wu) in *Zhou Shu* (*The Book of Zhou Dynasty*).

[216] "Xing Fa Zhi" (The Record of the Criminal Law) in *Wei Shu* (*The History of Northern Wei Dynasty*).

Northern Wei Dynasty) that "the difficult and doubtful cases shall be reported to 'Zhong Shu' (the prime minister) to be decided according to the ancient Confusion classics." In practice, Cui Ting, one of the officials, submitted a memorial to the emperor and stated that the provision that "if one is arrested for his crime, all his family members shall be implicated to serve forced labor" was inappropriate, because he believed the principle that "if one is benevolent, even his descendants shall be rewarded, while if one is evil, only he himself shall be punished," which was stipulated in *Chun Qiu (Spring and Autumn Annuals)* should be upheld. "So his ideas were accepted by Emperor Gaozu."[217]

According to stipulation, if a criminal refused to accept the verdict made by court, he was allowed to lodge an appeal, or his family members could do it on behalf of him: "When the sentence is made, the judge should meet the prisoner and read the judgment. If the prisoner claims that he is wronged and asks for an appeal, he is allowed to do so."[218] However, in the period of Cao Wei, "this regulation was inapplicable to the cases punishable by two years of imprisonment or above" to "simplify the over-elaborate legal proceedings."[219]

In summary, the time of Wei, Jin and Southern and Northern dynasties was an important period of development in both Chinese legal history and the history of "Lv Xue" (the study of statutory laws). Besides, it was also a time of great integration of Chinese legal culture. *Bei Qi Lv (The Penal Code of the Northern Qi Dynasty)* was made from the laws of Han Dynasty by absorbing the laws of Wei, Jin and Southern dynasties, so in both system structure and basic contents, it not only set a model for the lawmaking of Sui and Tang dynasties, but also reflected the great contribution the ethnic nationalities had made to Chinese legal system and the overall improvement of legal civilization.

---

[217]"Cui Ting Zhuan" (The Biography of Cui Ting) in *Wei Shu (The History of Northern Wei Dynasty).*

[218]"Suo Yin" (Index) in "Xiao Hou Ying Lie Zhuan" (The Collected Biographies of Xia Houying) in *Shi Ji (The Record of the Grand Historian).*

[219]"Xing Fa Zhi" (The Record of the Criminal Law) in *Jin Shu (The History of Jin Dynasty).*

Chapter 7
The Legal Systems of Sui and Tang Dynasties: The Finalization of the Forms of Chinese Legal Civilization

(581 A.D.–907 A.D.)

7.1 The Legal System of Sui Dynasty Made by Adopting the Strong Points of the Laws of Southern and Northern Dynasties

Sui Dynasty was a famous but a short-lived state in ancient China. The role of the legal system of Sui Dynasty was very important because it had formed a connection between the legal systems of the preceding and the later dynasties, so it had continued the legal systems of Wei and Jin dynasties and initiated those of Tang and Song dynasties.

The legislators in the early period of Sui Dynasty, rather than rigidly adhering to the discriminatory policy against any individual state or nationality, emphasized "making changes according to times." Thus, *Kai Huang Lv* (*The Code Made in the Year of Kai Huang*) was made by adopting the strong points of the legislation of Southern and Northern dynasties and absorbing the quintessence of the legal culture of other nationalities, so the value of *Kai Huang Lv* (*The Code Made in the Year of Kai Huang*) was of historical importance in history. Its enactment symbolized that the basic Chinese feudal legal principle and system were gradually finalized.

However, there were only two crowned emperors in Sui Dynasty and their reigning merely lasted for about thirty years. One of the reasons for such a short-lived dynasty was that the law was not only made in accordance with the will of the upper class, but also was wantonly trampled on by them, which had consequently caused the social disorder and turbulence and the downfall of the dynasty. When laws were made during the reign of Emperor Wen, a group of judicial officials, such as Su Wei, Zhao Zhuo, Liang Pi, and Liu Xingben, etc. had had enough courage to argue face to face with the emperor based on law. Consequently, there emerged a flourishing age in which "the gentlemen lived a happy life, the common people lived and worked in peace and contentment, the strong did not bully the weak, and the majority did not show prejudice to the minority. So population increased, the country was rich and prosperous, and both the rulers and the common people were in great harmony. Within twenty years, the whole country was in peace with no troubles in the local places."[1] Nevertheless, once law was trampled on by the upper class, the country would be defeated and the home would be lost. This is a natural law of historical development, which is applicable to both past and present, from which a lesson must be learned. In fact, the rise and fall of the legal systems of the Sui Dynasty also reflected the prosperity and decline of the history of the Sui Dynasty.

7.1.1 Legislation in the Early Period of Sui Dynasty and the Historical Role of Kai Huang Lv (The Code Made in the Year of Kai Huang)

Under the hundreds of years of ruling of "San Guo" (Three Kingdoms), the Western and Eastern Jin and the Southern and Northern dynasties, although China was ruled by separatist regimes and different states were confronting each other, the close business relationship between the northern and southern China, the strengthening of the integration between different nationalities, and the declining of the power of despots and nobility caused by peasant uprisings had provided an important condition for the reestablishment of a united feudal state.

In 581 A.D., Yang Jian, who was one of the representatives of big landlords and bureaucrats in Guanlong District and who had controlled the real the administrative and military power of the Northern Zhou Dynasty, crowned himself as Emperor Wen and founded the Sui Dynasty after overthrowing the imperial ruling of Northern Zhou Dynasty. In 589 A.D., with the annexation of the Southern Chen Dynasty, the two hundred and seventy years of separation and confrontation of northern and southern China, which had started from the end of Western Jin Dynasty, was ended, and China was finally reunited, which had greatly accelerated the development of Chinese feudal society.

The Sui Dynasty was a feudal regime consisted mainly of the landlords of Han nationality with the absorption of some of the nobilities of Xian Bei nationality and the upper classes of other nationalities. In the early period of Sui Dynasty, to consolidate the unification of the state, a series of reforms were carried out, among which, legal reform had become one of the most important parts.

7.1.1.1 The Enactment of *Kai Huang Lv* (*The Code Made in the Year of Kai Huang*)

Emperor Wen, named Yang Jian, was once not only a relative but also an important minister of the emperor of Northern Zhou Dynasty. He once presented a memorial to the emperor of the Northern Zhou Dynasty suggesting, "it is not the way to rule the

---

[1] "Gao Zu Ji" (The Record of Emperor Gaozu) in *Sui Shu* (*The History of Sui Dynasty*) (Book 2).

country to merely make numerous laws and decrees."[2] He also said, "(Emperor Xuan) likes to make complicated and strict laws but prefers to indulge himself in women and pleasures instead, ... so he will not live a long life."[3] After the death of Emperor Xuan, Yang Jian, who assumed the arbitrary power of administration as "Cheng Xiang" (the prime minister), "started to replace the cruel and strict laws of Emperor Xuan with lenient ones. So he abolished the old codes, made, and enacted *Xing Shu Yao Zhi* (*Penal Codes and Important Systems*) immediately after submitting it to the emperor."[4] These measures showed that legal system reform had always been the major task of his administration. After crowning himself as Emperor Wen, Yang Jian drew a lesson from the downfall of the Northern Zhou Dynasty and put the legal system reform on his urgent work agenda. Thus, he ordered a group of officials and Confucianists, such as Pei Zheng, Su Wei, Gao Ying, Zheng Ze, Yang Su, Chang Ming, Han Rui, Li E, and Liu Xiongliang, etc., to make a new legal code in accordance with the principle of "taking the legal codes of Wei, Jin, Qi, and Liang dynasties as the essence and continuing to execute the penalties by mediating the lenience and severity of punishments."[5] However, after the enactment of the new code, "because the regulations of the code were too strict, many people were convicted," which had consequently led to more than 10,000 trials every year. Therefore, in the 3rd year of Kaihuang (583 A.D.), the officials such as Su Wei, Niu Hong, and so on, were ordered to have the new code revised, so eighty-one provisions of death penalty, one hundred and fifty-four provisions of "Liu" (exile) and more than one thousand provisions of "Zhang" (flogging with heavy sticks) were abolished. The revision of *Kai Huang Lv* (*The Code Made in the Year of Kai Huang*) was finally completed with "only five hundred provisions retained."[6]

As for the chapters of *Kai Huang Lv* (*The Code Made in the Year of Kai Huang*), they were made based on the twelve chapters of *Bei Qi Lv* (*The Penal Code of the Northern Qi Dynasty*), so "Jin Wei" (Palace Guards) was changed into "Wei Jin"; "Hun Hu" (Marriage, Tax and Household Registration) into "Hu Hun"; "Wei Zhi" (Punishing Officials' Dereliction of Duty), into "Zhi Zhi" (The State Office System), and "Jiu Mu" (Statutes on Farming and Husbandry) into "Jiu Ku." Additionally, "Bu Duan" (Statutes on Arresting) was divided into "Bu Wang" (Statutes on Arresting) and "Duan Yu" (Statutes on Trials and Punishments) and "Sun Hui" (Statutes on Defacement and Damages) was abolished. Consequently, *Kai Huang Lv* (*The Code Made in the Year of Kai Huang*) contained altogether twelve chapters, including "Ming Li" (The Categories of Penalties and General Principles), "Wei Jin" (Statutes on Palace Guards), "Zhi Zhi" (Statutes on the State Office System), "Hu Hun" (Statutes on Marriage, Tax and Household Registration), "Jiu Ku" (Statutes on Stables), "Shan Xing" (Statutes on Sending Troops without Authorization), "Dao

---

[2]"Gao Zu Ji" (The Record of Emperor Gaozu) in *Sui Shu* (*The History of Sui Dynasty*)(Book1).
[3]"Yu Wen Qing Zhuan" (The Biography of Yu Wenqing) in *Sui Shu* (*The History of Sui Dynasty*).
[4]*Zi Zhi Tong Jian* (*History as a Mirror*), Vol. 174.
[5]"Pei Zheng Zhuan" (The Biography of Pei Zheng) in *Sui Shu* (*The History of Sui Dynasty*).
[6]"Xing Fa Zhi" (The Record of the Criminal Law) in *Sui Shu* (*The History of Sui Dynasty*).

Zei" (Statutes on Robbing and Theft), "Dou Song" (Statutes on Litigation), "Zha Wei" (Statutes on Fraud and Forgery), "Za" (Miscellaneous Laws), "Bu Wang" (Statutes on Arresting), and "Duan Yu" (Statutes on Trials and Punishments).

To illustrate the guiding principles and the major changes of *Kai Huang Lv* (*The Code Made in the Year of Kai Huang*), a special decree was issued by Emperor Wen:

> When emperors make legal codes, they continue and adopt different laws in accordance with the concrete situations. Therefore, some laws have been added and some have been abolished. The penalty of 'Jiao' (hanging) is applied to kill people and 'Zhan' (beheading) is applied in special cases. For the wicked and the evil, such penalties are the severest. The punishment of 'Xiao Shou' (the penalty of hanging the head of the criminal on top of a pole for public display) is not justified because it is not helpful to prevent the crimes by using severe penalties. 'Jiao' (hanging) and 'Zhan' (beheading) which were applied in the previous dynasties are no longer suitable to be used to show righteousness, because they are applied not to punish or eliminate crimes but only to show cruelty and severity. The penalty of 'Bian' (whipping) hurts prisoners' bodies and causes them great pain, so it is as cruel as cutting the prisoners' bodies with knives. Although the penalties of 'Xiao Shou' (the penalty of hanging the head of the criminal on top of a pole for public display) and "Bian" (whipping) have been used since ancient times, they are not the penalties that a benevolent emperor should apply, therefore, they have all been abolished. Additionally, it has already been written into the new code that the great and meritorious statesmen should be respected and should not be imprisoned, and that special consideration should be given to the senior officials and the nobility, who are entitled to the privileges of taking carriages, wearing official robes and sheltering their relatives. The six-year penalty of 'Liu' (exile) executed in the previous dynasties has been changed into five years and the five-year-imprisonment has been changed into three years. In the new code, many lenient provisions are made to replace the severe ones and death penalties are replaced by life imprisonments. Besides, there are many provisions which are written on bamboo writing slips. Other old miscellaneous and strict regulations have all been abolished in order to make it easier for them to be enforced nationwide and to set a standard. The rules are made to warn people to give up the intention of violating the law and punishments are enforced to prevent the abuse of death penalty in the country. So the penalties are made but will never be executed in the near future. Hopefully, my thoughts will be understood by the officials all over the country.[7]

The decree had shown Emperor Wen's own understanding and pursuit of legal civilization.

Compared with *Bei Zhou Lv* (*The Penal Code of the Northern Zhou Dynasty*), although the chapter titles, penalty system and the names of crimes of the latter Qi Dynasty "were mainly followed" in *Kai Huang Lv* (*The Code Made in the Year of Kai Huang*),[8] the remaining provisions of *Bei Zhou Lv* (*The Penal Code of the Northern Zhou Dynasty*) were also included because of the inheritance relationship between *Bei Zhou Lv* (*The Penal Code of the Northern Zhou Dynasty*) and *Bei Qi Lv* (*The Penal Code of the Northern Qi Dynasty*). Therefore, what was recorded in "Xing Fa Zhi" (The Record of the Criminal Law) in *Jiu Tang Shu* (*The Old Book of Tang Dynasty*) was believed to be true: "In order to show magnanimity and justice, Emperor Wen made codes by following the old administrative principles of the latter

---

[7]"Xing Fa Zhi" (The Record of the Criminal Law) in *Sui Shu* (*The History of Sui Dynasty*).

[8]"Xing Fa Zhi" (The Record of the Criminal Law) in *Sui Shu* (*The History of Sui Dynasty*).

Qi Dynasty with the cruel and strict laws abolished." Additionally, most of the drafters of *Kai Huang Lv* (*The Code Made in the Year of Kai Huang*) were once the senior ministers of the Northern Zhou Dynasty. Especially, Pei Zheng, who had been "Shi Lang" (vice minister) of "Xing Bu" (The Department of Punishment) in Northern Zhou Dynasty and who had been ordered to "participate in making the law of Zhou Dynasty" because he "knew the issues very well," had played an important role in the process of making *Kai Huang Lv* (*The Code Made in the Year of Kai Huang*). It was recorded that "whenever there are difficulties in drafting, Pei Zheng will be consulted."[9] Thus, it is possible that "Pei Zheng may have made the new code by making reference to the old administrative principles," while the other opinion that there is no relationship between "*Kai Huang Lv* (*The Code Made in the Year of Kai Huang*) and *Bei Zhou Lv* (*The Penal Code of the Northern Zhou Dynasty*)" may not be historically true.

Emperor Wen knew very well that *Bei Zhou Lv* (*The Penal Code of the Northern Zhou Dynasty*), which was made by deliberately imitating the ancient law, was difficult to be implemented because it was not only redundant and brutal but also divorced with social reality. Nevertheless, *Bei Qi Lv* (*The Penal Code of the Northern Qi Dynasty*) was clear and concise, so it had epitomized the legal system construction of the Southern and Northern dynasties. For this reason, *Kai Huang Lv* (*The Code Made in the Year of Kai Huang*) was completed within less than three years after the foundation of the country based on the *Bei Qi Lv* (*The Penal Code of the Northern Qi Dynasty*).

As for the lawmaking in the early period of Sui Dynasty, it became an established principle to abandon the prejudice against any individual state or nationality, to absorb the essence and the greatness of those states and nationalities and to assimilate things of diverse nature. That is why *Kai Huang Lv* (*The Code Made in the Year of Kai Huang*), which was considered as a milestone in the history of Chinese legal civilization, was able to be finally made.

7.1.1.2 The Historical Status of *Kai Huang Lv* (*The Code Made in the Year of Kai Huang*)

Kai Huang Lv (*The Code Made in the Year of Kai Huang*) was a comprehensive summary of the successful experience of legal system construction throughout the Wei and Jin dynasties. In this law, the tradition of emphasizing "clear stipulation and concise provision" of *Bei Qi Lv* (*The Penal Code of the Northern Qi Dynasty*) was inherited,[10] and the new achievements of legislative technology made in the periods of Wei and Jin dynasties were synthesized. Although the same number of chapters was retained, half of its provisions were simplified. In *Wei Lv* (*Wei Code*), "Ju Lv" (the general principle) was changed to "Xing Ming" (name of punishment) and was

---

[9] "Pei Zheng Zhuan" (The Biography of Pei Zheng) in *Sui Shu* (*The History of Sui Dynasty*).
[10] "Xing Fa Zhi" (The Record of the Criminal Law) in *Sui Shu* (*The History of Sui Dynasty*).

listed at the beginning of the code; in *Jin Lv (Jin Code)*, the whole text was linked up by "Xing Ming" (name of punishment) and "Fa Li" (legislation); while in *Kai Huang Lv (The Code Made in the Year of Kai Huang)*, "Ming Li" (categories of penalties and general principles) were used as the general principle, so the layout of chapters became more reasonable and a fixed style of Chinese feudal legal code was finally formed. Moreover, in *Kai Huang Lv (The Code Made in the Year of Kai Huang)*, the achievements of "Lv Xue" (the study of statutory laws) in Wei and Jin dynasties were absorbed and new progress was made either in the confirmation of the concept of crimes, or in the integration between "Li" (rites) and "Xing" (punishment), or in the coordination of "Zhi Fa Yuan Qing" (executing law according to the concrete situation of specific issues), which could be proved by the records in "Xing Fa Zhi" (The Record of the Criminal Law) in *Sui Shu (The History of Sui Dynasty)* and in *Tang Lv Shu Yi (The Comments on Tang Code)*. In *Kai Huang Lv (The Code Made in the Year of Kai Huang)*, some cruel penalties which had been applied throughout Wei and Jin dynasties were also abolished and the Chinese feudal statutory penalty system represented by "Wu Xing" (Five Penalties), namely, "Chi" (flogging with light sticks), "Zhang" (flogging with heavy sticks), "Tu" (imprisonment), "Liu" (exile), and "Si" (death penalty), was established, which reflected the progress of the time and legal civilization. Because Emperor Wen attached great importance to the construction of judicial system and advocated that sentences should be made according to law, the general practice of hearing cases by employing Confucian classics, which had been continued ever since Wei and Jin dynasties suffered heavy losses.

Kai Huang Lv (The Code Made in the Year of Kai Huang) further standardized the legal adjustment of the state and society, so the targets of the adjustment in each chapter were clear and the contents were specific. For example, "Ming Li Lv" (Statutes and Terms) was like a general principle; "Wei Jin Pian" (The Chapter of Palace Guards) was about guarding the imperial court; "Zhi Zhi Pian" (The Chapter of the State Office System) was about the requirement for civil officials and the punishment for the crime of dereliction of duty; "Hu Hun Pian" (The Chapter of Marriage, Tax and Household Registration) was about household registration, farmland, and marriage; "Dao Zei Pian" (The Chapter of Robbing and Theft) was about the punishment for the crime of infringing upon property and personal safety and the crime of endangering social order; "Duan Yu Pian" (The Chapter of Trials and Punishments) was about the stipulation for judicial trials. Generally, *Kai Huang Lv (The Code Made in the Year of Kai Huang)* had not only met the needs of the legal adjustment of economy, politics, military, judicature, family, and individuals, but also successfully guaranteed the implementation of "Jun Tian Zhi" (The System of Land Equalization) and the new tax system by making use of coercive punitive measures. Thus, overall, *Kai Huang Lv (The Code Made in the Year of Kai Huang)*, whether in the degrees of complexity of provisions, the appropriateness of punishment, the aggravation and mitigation of crimes, or the definitions of specific charges, was a serious summary of the historical experience and it had reached a new level of the historic development of Chinese legal system.

7.1 The Legal System of Sui Dynasty Made by Adopting the Strong Points...

The enactment of *Kai Huang Lv* (*The Code Made in the Year of Kai Huang*) provided an important foundation for the making of *Tang Lv Shu Yi* (*The Comments on Tang Code*) and for the development of feudal legal system after Tang Dynasty. Tang Dynasty was a flourishing age in Chinese feudal society and *Tang Lv Shu Yi* (*The Comments on Tang Code*), which was made based on the *Kai Huang Lv* (*The Code Made in the Year of Kai Huang*), had become a model of Chinese feudal legal codes. It was recorded in historical books that when *Tang Lv* (*Tang Code*) was revised in the early period of Tang Dynasty, "the addition and deletion of provisions and the abolishment of severe stipulations were all made according to *Kai Huang Lv* (*The Code Made in the Year of Kai Huang*)." Therefore, "*Kai Huang Lv* (*The Code Made in the Year of Kai Huang*) had become the criterion for making great policies."[11] It was also written in the preface of *Tang Lv Shu Yi* (*The Comments on Tang Code*) that "*Tang Lv* (*Tang Code*) is made according to *Sui Lv* (*Sui Code*), so the layout of chapters remains unchanged." In *Tang Lv Shu Yi* (*The Comments on Tang Code*), the traces of *Kai Huang Lv* (*The Code Made in the Year of Kai Huang*) can still be easily found in the layout of chapters, provisions, penalties, and stipulations, as is the saying goes that "even though Sui Dynasty was overthrown, its law had never been abandoned."[12]

In summary, *Kai Huang Lv* (*The Code Made in the Year of Kai Huang*) made in Sui Dynasty had played a great historical role of acting as a connection between the past and future in the Chinese feudal legal history, and it had significantly influenced the legal progress of Tang Dynasty and the dynasties ever since with its compilation style, its rich contents of the integration of different laws and its stipulations for system construction.

After the reign of Emperor Wen and in the 3rd year of Da Ye (607 A.D.), *Da Ye Lv* (*Da Ye Code*) was made by Emperor Yang based on the revision of *Kai Huang Lv* (*The Code Made in the Year of Kai Huang*). In contents, *Da Ye Lv* (*Da Ye Code*) was the same as *Kai Huang Lv* (*The Code Made in the Year of Kai Huang*) with chapters increased to eighteen. To be more specific, the three chapters of "Zei Dao" (Stealing and Robbery), "Hu Hun" (Marriage, Tax and Household Registration), and "Jiu Ku" (Stables) in *Kai Huang Lv* (*The Code Made in the Year of Kai Huang*) were divided into six chapters: "Zei" (Banditry), "Dao" (Robbery), "Hu" (Household), "Hun" (Marriage), "Cang Ku" (Warehouse), and "Jiu Mu" (Farming and Husbandry), with another three chapters added, namely, "Qing Qiu" (Asking for Bribery), "Gao He" (Prosecution), and "Guan Shi" (Border Market).

Although Emperor Yang had boasted of "treating people with sincerity and ruling with benevolence" and advocated "abolishing the provisions of 'Shi E' (The Ten Abominations) abolished"[13] and "retaining only eight of the original ten

---

[11]"Xing Fa Zhi" (The Record of the Criminal Law) in *Jiu Tang Shu* (*The Old Book of Tang Dynasty*).

[12]Wang Fuzhi (Ming Dynasty), "Sui Wen Di" (Emperor Wen of Sui Dynasty) in *Du Tong Jian Lun* (*Comments on Reading the History as a Mirror*).

[13]"Xing Fa Zhi" (The Record of the Criminal Law) in *Sui Shu* (*The History of Sui Dynasty*).

provisions,"[14] according to what was truly recorded in historical books, he was actually "pretending to show benevolence to cover up his deeds and to fish undeserved reputation."[15] With more increasing demand for forced labor, "the officials tried to coerce people into doing forced labor by using harsh punishments whenever it was needed and bribery was publically taken against law...",[16] which showed that *Da Ye Lv* (*Da Ye Code*) had become a mere formality soon after its enactment. The legal revision and reform undertaken by Emperor Yang was also disrupted and ruined by the corrupted officials who had unscrupulously trampled on people like mud and ashes and who had bent the law to suit their own purposes, just like the tax and corvée law reform which was carried out to "reduce corvée and tax" was disrupted by a large-scale architectural work.

In Sui Dynasty, except for the enactment of *Sui Lv* (*Sui Code*), *Kai Huang Ling* (*Kai Huang Decrees*) was also revised and made by Gao Jiong and other people. *Kai Huang Ling* (*Kai Huang Decrees*) consisted of thirty chapters, including official rank, province, temple, guard, "Dong Gong" (Eastern Palace), local administration, "Zhou" (subprefecture), ancestral temple, household, school, election, "Kao Ke" (according to certain standards on the performance of the official assessment to determine the reward and punishment), clothes, "Guan Shi" (Border Market) and funeral, etc. Its contents were very completed and it had covered almost all aspects of administration, farmland system, judicature, and so on. During the reign of Emperor Yang, *Da Ye Ling* (*Da Ye Decrees*) with 30 volumes was also made and implemented. According to "Xue Dao Heng Zhuan" (The Biography of Xue Daoheng) in *Sui Shu* (*The History of Sui Dynasty*), there were many difficulties in the making of *Da Ye Ling* (*Da Ye Decrees*): "long time discussion was held about the making of new decrees but it is difficult to make specific decisions. Then Xue Daoheng said to other officials: 'If Gao Jiong has not died, then the new decrees should have been made and implemented long time ago.'" However, he then was punished by death penalty for such remarks, with his wife and sons punished by "Liu" (exile).

The legal forms of "Ge" (injunction) and "Shi" (standard) were continuously used in Sui Dynasty, as was recorded in "Li De Lin Zhuan" (The Biography of Li Delin) in *Sui Shu* (The History of Sui Dynasty) that "after the enactment of 'Ge' (injunctions) and 'Ling' (decree), Su Wei also wanted to change some of the provisions. However, according to Delin, once 'Ge' (injunction) and 'Ling' (decree) were enacted, they must be consistent with each other. Even though there were some flaws, they should not be changed unless they were harmful to the administration or the people." Additionally, according to "Yang Di Ji" (The Record of Emperor Yang) in *Sui Shu* (*The History of Sui Dynasty*), in the 4th year of the reign of Emperor Yang, "new 'Shi' (standard) was enacted and publicized to people all over the

---

[14]*Tang Lv Shu Yi* (*The Comments on Tang Code*).

[15]"Yang Di Ji" (The Record of Emperor Yang) (Part 2) in *Sui Shu* (*The History of Sui Dynasty*).

[16]"Xing Fa Zhi" (The Record of the Criminal Law) in *Sui Shu* (*The History of Sui Dynasty*).

country."[17] Moreover, in "Su Wei Zhuan" (The Biography of Su Wei) in *Sui Shu* (*The History of Sui Dynasty*), it was also recorded that "most of 'Lv' (criminal law), 'Ling' (decree), 'Ge' (injunction), and 'Shi' (standard) were made by Su Wei."

From the aforementioned words, we can see that, after carefully chosen, there were a variety of legal forms in Sui Dynasty, which had provided the historical foundation for the making "Lv" (criminal law), "Ling" (decree), "Ge" (injunction), and "Shi" (standard) in Tang Dynasty.

7.1.2 The Management System and the System of "Kai Ke Qu Shi" (To Recruit Talents Through Imperial Examination) in Sui Dynasty

Although some stipulations of administrative law in Sui Dynasty could be found in *Kai Huang Lv* (*The Code Made in the Year of Kai Huang*), most of them were included in *Kai Huang Ling* (*Kai Huang Decrees*). *Kai Huang Ling* (*Kai Huang Decrees*) was with the nature of administrative law, according to which the aspects such as the central and local administrative organs, the official management system, "Guan Shi" (border market), and the ritual ceremonies, etc., were regulated.

In Sui Dynasty, the system of "San Sheng" (The Three Departments) was continued, and "San Sheng" (The Three Departments) was in charge of the management the central administrative affairs. Specifically speaking, "Shang Shu Ling" (ancient official equivalent to prime minister), the chief minister of "Shang Shu Sheng" (The Department of Secretary), "Na Yan," the chief minister of "Meng Xia Sheng" (the Department of Chancellery), and "Nei Shi Ling," the chief minister of "Nei Shi Sheng," [for avoiding a taboo, "Zhong Shu Sheng" (the supreme organization in charge of the state affairs) was changed into "Nei Shi Sheng" (the office in charge of the internal affairs of the palace) and "Zhong Shu Ling" (head of the secretariat) into "Nei Shi Ling" in the Sui Dynasty] were all recognized as "Zai Xiang" (the prime minister), who were in charge of imperial administrative affairs and who shared equal political status. Under "Shang Shu Sheng" (The Department of Secretary), "Liu Bu" (The Six Departments) were established, including "Li Bu" (The Department of Personnel), "Min Bu" (The Department of Civil Affairs), "Li Bu" (The Department of Rites), "Bing Bu" (The Department of Defense), "Xing Bu" (The Department of Punishment), and "Gong Bu" (The Department of Works), which were executive organs which were put the charge of administration, economy, military, judicature, and culture, etc. Four "Si" (bureau) were established under each department, so altogether there were twenty-four "Si" (bureau). The administrative management system, or the system of "San Sheng" (The Three Departments), "Liu Bu" (The Six Departments), and twenty-four "Si" (bureau), created in Sui Dynasty, was proved to be a great development in the seven hundred years ever since the Qin

---

[17]"Yang Di Ji" (The Record of Emperor Yang) in *Sui Shu* (*The History of Sui Dynasty*) (Book 2).

and Han dynasties, which had demonstrated that the feudal rulers' experience had become much more mature in the management of the state affairs and in giving play to the function of the administrative organs.

As to the local administrative system, a three-level-system, namely, "Zhou" (subprefecture), "Jun" (shire), and "Xian" (county) was adopted in the early period of Sui Dynasty. In the 3rd year of Kaihuang (583 A.D.), because of the wars frequently occurred since Wei and Jin dynasties, the administrative regions were often changed and the areas of the regions were reduced, so the area of one "Zhou" (subprefecture) was only as big as that of one "Jun" (shire) in the Han Dynasty, and the three-level-system of "Zhou" (subprefecture), "Jun" (shire), and "Xian" (county) was changed into a two-level-system consisting of "Zhou" (subprefecture) and "Xian" (county) ("Zhou" was changed into "Jun" in the reign of Emperor Yang) in accordance with the principle of "retaining what is the important, eliminating what is outdated and integrating what is small"[18] to strengthen the control of the local authorities by the central government and to adjust the new divisions of administrative regions. Consequently, the level of local administration was reduced, the number of local officials was decreased, and their power was weakened. Before the founding of Sui Dynasty, although the system of centralized despotism was adopted, the great power was still grasped by the local chief officials who not only held the authority over the military, penalty, financial, and agricultural affairs in the areas under their administration, but also the power to appoint and to remove the subordinate officials from their offices, or "to employ subordinate officials" by themselves, as was so described later, which had not only given them the chance to set up the separatist regimes but also prevented the implementation of the administrative orders of the central government. Therefore, the rulers of the Sui Dynasty centralized the power of appointing and removing important subordinate officials at the time of adjusting the local administrative system. Consequently, the officials with or above the rank of "Jiu Pin" (the ninth rank) should all be appointed and dismissed by "Li Bu" (The Department of Personnel) and be evaluated by "Li Bu" (The Department of Personnel) annually. Later, it was stipulated that the local officials below the rank of "Ci Shi" (a supervisor assigned by the central government to a local area) and "Xian Ling" (county magistrate) should be changed every three years without being appointed again and they were not allowed to be appointed in the prefectures where they were born, which had made it difficult for the local despots to control over the administrative affairs. Additionally, the system of "Chao Ji" (imperial meeting) was established in Sui Dynasty, according to which the local officials must accept the supervision of the imperial government and go to the capital to report on their work at the end of year. Especially, in Sui Dynasty, the power of executing death penalty was taken back from the local officials by following the example of Northern Wei Dynasty, so it was clearly stipulated in the imperial decree issued by Emperor Wen that "the local officials of 'Zhou'

---

[18]"Yang Shangxi Zhuan" (The Biography of Yang Shangxi) in *Sui Shu* (*The History of Sui Dynasty*) (Book 1).

(subprefecture) have no rights to settle the cases punishable by death penalty, and they must be transferred to 'Da Li Si' (The Bureau of Judicial Review) and be further reported to the Emperor for final decision."[19]

The local administrative system reform implemented in Sui Dynasty was not only conducive to the elimination of the separatist regimes, but also to the changing of the phenomenon that "there were more officials than civilians, and there were more shepherds than sheep"[20] and to the promotion of the executive efficiency of the administrative offices. At this point, the feudal local administrative system had developed into a new stage.

During the periods of the Wei, Jin, and the Southern and Northern dynasties, the special appointment system, namely, "Jiu Pin Zhong Zheng Zhi" (The Nine Rank System, an important election system in Wei, Jin, Southern and Northern Dynasty), which was once established for consolidating the privileges of gentry, had become a barrier in expanding the basis of ruling class and strengthening the centralization of authority because of the declining of gentry and uprising of landlords. Consequently, after the country was united in Sui Dynasty, the system of "Jiu Pin Zhong Zheng Zhi" (The Nine Rank System, an important election system in Wei, Jin, Southern and Northern Dynasty) was abolished, and the system of "Ke Ju" (the imperial examination) was established instead.

The so-called system of "Ke Ju" (the imperial examination) referred to the standardized examination which was held regularly. Thus, the subjects of the examination were chosen by the government and the candidates who passed the exams would be appointed as officials. This was called "Kai Ke Qu Shi" (to recruit talents through imperial examination) and "Fen Ke Ju Ren" (to recommend officials through the examination of different subjects). During the reign of Emperor Wen, "Xiu Cai Ke" (one of the subjects of selecting officials in ancient China) was established, and the candidates of the examination were asked to register their names by themselves and then further examined by the imperial court if they could pass the examination. From this time on, it became a very important content in the Chinese feudal civil official system to recruit officials through "Ke Ju" (the imperial examination). During the reign of Emperor Yang in Sui Dynasty, "Jin Shi Ke" (the most difficult examination in the imperial examination: usually Confucian classics and poetry would be examined) was additionally set up, by which the channel for enlisting talents was broadened. By the implementation of the system of "Ke Ju" (the imperial examination), the power of recruiting state officials was taken back from the local gentry and centralized by the central government, which was not only beneficial to the extension of the scope of political participation, but also to the selection of more talents and to the strengthening of the centralization of authority. Therefore, the examination system established in the early period of Sui Dynasty had been adopted by the later dynasties.

---

[19] "Xing Fa Zhi" (The Record of the Criminal Law) in *Sui Shu* (*The History of Sui Dynasty*).
[20] "Yang Shang Xi Zhuan" (The Biography of Yang Shangxi) in *Sui Shu* (*The History of Sui Dynasty*).

As to the official assessment in Sui Dynasty, there are very few records. According to "Bai Guan Zhi" (The Record of the Officials of all Ranks) in *Sui Shu* (*The History of Sui Dynasty*), "'Dian Zui' (official assessment) is held annually. The promotion or demotion of 'Ci Shi' (a supervisor assigned by the central government to a local area) and 'Xian Ling' (county magistrate) is decided by the result of the assessment conducted every three years and the promotion or demotion of 'Zuo Guan' (deputies) is decided by the results of the assessments conducted every four years." Additionally, according to the regulations issued in Gengshen in July of the 2nd year of Daye (606 A.D.), during the reign Emperor Yang in Sui Dynasty, "the officials should be promoted not only according to their assessment results, but also to their meritorious performance and virtue."[21]

7.1.3 The Establishment of the Basic Framework of Feudal Criminal Law

Kai Huang Lv (*The Code Made in the Year of Kai Huang*) consisting of twelve chapters was an important legal code which was mainly made up of criminal laws with an integration of other laws. Up to Sui Dynasty, the basic framework of feudal criminal law, which numerous lawmakers and legal scholars had been working hard to improve ever since Wei and Jin dynasties had already been successfully established in the end. By the time, the system of criminal punishment and the principles of criminal law, which were relevant to this framework, were becoming increasingly mature.

Based on "Zhong Zui Shi Tiao" (Ten Felonies) issued in the Northern Qi Dynasty, the crime of "Xiang" (surrender) was abolished and the crime of "Bu Mu" (inharmonious) was added in *Kai Huang Lv* (*The Code Made in the Year of Kai Huang*), so the provisions of "Shi E" (The Ten Abominations) were basically formed, which included: "Mou Fan" (plotting rebellion or plotting to endanger the country), "Mou Da Ni" (great sedition), "Mou Pan" (treason), "E Ni" (abusing or murdering the elders), "Bu Dao" (depravity), "Da Bu Jing" (being greatly irreverent), "Bu Xiao" (being unfilial), "Bu Mu" (inharmonious), "Bu Yi" (injustice), and "Nei Luan" (committing incest). In Sui Dynasty, "Shi E" (Ten Abominations) began to be officially written into law, and it had become the most important part of criminal law in feudal times ever since, so the violators of these crimes would be harshly punished. It was recorded in "Xing Fa Zhi" (The Record of the Criminal Law) in *Sui Shu* (*The History of Sui Dynasty*) that "the fathers and brothers of those who have committed the offenses of 'Mou Da Ni' (great sedition) and 'Mou Pan' (treason) shall all be punished by 'Zhan' (beheading) with their family members punished by serving as official slaves." It was also stipulated that "'Shi E' (The Ten Abominations) was not included in the regulations on redemption in 'Ba Yi' (The

---

[21]"Yang Di Ji" (The Record of Emperor Yang) in *Sui Shu* (*The History of Sui Dynasty*) (Book 1).

Eight Deliberations)," which meant that the violators would not be exempted from punishment even if they were offered an amnesty.

Because Emperor Wen had seized state power through coup d'état, under the historical circumstances where the Confucian views of loyalty and filial piety were widely accepted, to guard against the gossiping of the officials and to prevent them from endangering of the regime seized, he also tried to dominate people's minds and control public opinion apart from threatening them with the penalty of felonies like "Mou Da Ni" (great sedition), "Mou Pan" (treason) and "Mou Fan" (plotting rebellion or plotting to endanger the country). If people had talked about him behind his back or spoken ill of him, they would be punished for defaming the emperor without being forgiven although they were as respectable as the meritorious founding fathers. For instances, an important minister, Gao Jiong, who was called "Zhen Zai Xiang" (a real prime minister), was ordered to be removed from his office by Emperor Wen just for being suspected of gossiping[22]; another minister of "Guang Lu" (bureau in charge of banqueting) named Li Min was executed by death penalty for "whispering with someone behind the creen."[23] Emperor Yang was always suspicious of other people. For example, Gao Jiong, who was ordered to resume his former official position of "Tai Chang" (the Minister of Sacrificial Worship) by Emperor Yang, was reported to have secretly criticized the imperial court for its "lack of social order and law," so he was punished by death penalty with "his sons exiled to border regions."[24]

To prevent people from defaming the emperor by the form of recording national history, in the 13th year of Kaihuang (593 A.D.), an imperial decree was issued, according to which "it is forbidden for people to write national history privately and to make negative comments on people."[25] It was also recorded in history books that Emperor Wen "was born a suspicious man," and that "he was not benevolent and tolerant, but was acerb and mean."[26] In fact, this was not a problem of the defects of his character, but the hidden sharp struggle for power.

As prophecy divination of mystical belief was prevalent in the country since the Western and Eastern dynasties, for the purpose of stopping people from making use of auguries to rebel against the imperial government, an imperial decree was issued by Emperor Wen in the 13th year of Kaihuang (593 A.D.), and it was ordered that, "auguries and the books of prophecies are forbidden to be kept at home."[27] During the reign of Emperor Yang, "officials were sent everywhere to conduct supervision. The books about auguries and prophecies which were discovered were all burnt up, and the people who had argued with officials over the books were all killed."[28] So

---

[22]"Gao Jiong Zhuan" (The Biography of Gao Jiong) in *Sui Shu* (*The History of Sui Dynasty*).
[23]"Li Min Zhuan" (The Biography of Li Min) in *Sui Shu* (*The History of Sui Dynasty*).
[24]"Gao Jiong Zhuan" (The Biography of Gao Jiong) in *Sui Shu* (*The History of Sui Dynasty*).
[25]"Gao Zu Ji" (The Record of Emperor Gaozu) in *Sui Shu* (*The History of Sui Dynasty*) (Book 2).
[26]"Gao Zu Ji" (The Record of Emperor Gaozu) in *Sui Shu* (*The History of Sui Dynasty*) (Book 2).
[27]"Gao Zu Ji" (The Record of Emperor Gaozu) in *Sui Shu* (*The History of Sui Dynasty*) (Book 2).
[28]"Jing Ji Zhi" (The Record of Classic Books) in *Sui Shu* (*The History of Sui Dynasty*).

many ministers and noblemen who were involved in prophetic remarks such as Wang Yi, He Song, Yang Xiu, and Zhang Zhongrang, etc. were all punished. It needs to be pointed out that the rulers opposed auguries and prophecies in Sui Dynasty not because they wanted to fight against fetishes and superstitions or to show respect to science, but because they wanted to take precautions to prevent people from gathering together to making trouble and to endanger the Sui government by making use of auguries and prophecies. Additionally, to restrict people's ideology, Buddhism and Taoism were forced to be established by using harsh punishments, as was stipulated that "those who destroy or steal the images of the Buddha, or celestial beings, or the images of holy ceremonies, shall all be punished for depravity. If Buddhist monks destroy the images of Buddha, or Taoist priests destroy the images of celestial beings, they shall be punished for contumacy."[29]

With the development of absolutism, it was considered a serious crime to join and organize cliquish groups. During the reign of Emperor Wen, an official named Lang Mao "was removed from his office and exiled to Mojun" for the crime of "organizing cliques, being partial to subordinates, and deceiving the emperor."[30] Another official, named Li Hun, was punished by death penalty with rest of his clansmen, "young or old, all exiled to Linwai"[31] for the crime of joining cliques with other clansmen.

To take strict precautions against peasants' uprising, civilians were forbidden to make or hide weapons. It was ordered in the 3rd year of Kaihuang (583 A.D.) in Sui Dynasty that "civilians are forbidden to possess broadswords and long-spears"[32]; it was ordered in another decree issued in the 9th year of Kaihuang (589 A.D.) that "the armors and weapons which the civilians possess shall all be destroyed"[33]; in the 15th year of Kaihuang (595 A.D.) it was again ordered that "all weapons of the civilians should be confiscated, and those who make weapons secretly shall be imprisoned with their relatives."[34] During the reign of Emperor Yang, because of the successive peasant uprising, the making of forks, hooks and the ironware for peasants' daily usage were also ridiculously regarded as weapons and were all banned. It was recorded in "Yang Di Ji" (The Record of Emperor Yang) in *Sui Shu* (*The History of Sui Dynasty*) that "in January of the 5th year, ... all the forks, hooks, long-spears, and swords were confiscated and destroyed."

Additionally, in the 18th year of Kaihuang (598 A.D.) during the reign of Emperor Wen, an order was issued to "have all the civilian boats with the length of three *zhang* in the states of the southern Yangtze River confiscated" just because

---

[29]"Gao Zu Ji" (The Record of Emperor Gaozu) in *Sui Shu* (*The History of Sui Dynasty*) (Book 2).
[30]"Lang Mao Zhuan" (The Biography of Lang Mao) in *Sui Shu* (*The History of Sui Dynasty*).
[31]"Li Hun Zhuan" (The Biography of Li Hun) in *Sui Shu* (*The History of Sui Dynasty*).
[32]"Gao Zu Ji" (The Record of Emperor Gaozu) in *Sui Shu* (*The History of Sui Dynasty*) (Book 1).
[33]"Gao Zu Ji" (The Record of Emperor Gaozu) in *Sui Shu* (*The History of Sui Dynasty*) (Book 2).
[34]"Gao Zu Ji" (The Record of Emperor Gaozu) in *Sui Shu* (*The History of Sui Dynasty*) (Book 2).

7.1 The Legal System of Sui Dynasty Made by Adopting the Strong Points... 485

"people in these areas had gathered together and made large ships privately, which might have led to violence and trouble."[35]

The infringement upon private and official property had always been regarded as the most serious crime that ought to be punished according to criminal law throughout history. After the issuing of *Kai Huang Lv* (*The Code Made in the Year of Kai Huang*), "because the crimes of stealing and robbery could not yet be prevented, the emperor decided to apply much harsher punishments." However, the chief minister of "Xing Bu" (The Department of Punishment), named Zhao Zhuo, advised the emperor and said, "Your majesty has treated people with benevolence and forgiveness by following the ancient sages like Yao and Shun. Since law symbolizes the credibility of the state, how can it be destroyed?"[36] Zhao Zhuo's advice was accepted by the emperor, but severe punishment for the crimes against private and official property was still enforced because of the increasing crimes of robbery and stealing. For example, in the 16th year of Kaihuang (596 A.D.), because seven thousand *dan* of millet stored in Hechuan were stolen, the chief official in charge of the storehouse was executed by death penalty with "all of his family members punished to serve as official servants and the millet which he had stored for his family sold to make up for the loss of the stolen millet."[37] After this, a stipulation about stealing was made: "From today forward, those who steal more than one *sheng* of grain will be punished by death penalty with their family members all punished by serving as 'Nu Bi' (the slave girls and maidservants)."[38] Meanwhile, it was stipulated that "those who steal more than one *qian* of money shall be punished by 'Qi Shi' (exposing the executed body publicly at markets);...if the administrative official has stolen more than one *qian* of money, but if the witness has failed to report, he will be punished by life-long imprisonment for being involved in the crime;... if four people have conspired to steal one square rafter or three people have conspired to steal one melon, they shall all be punished by death penalty as soon as they are caught."[39] Definitely, such extremely strict stipulations about theft were strongly opposed by people. In the end, the provision that "those who steal one *qian* of money will be punished by 'Qi Shi' (exposing the executed body publicly at markets)" was forced to be abolished.[40] However, when it came to the reign of Emperor Yang, "the poor people had nowhere to speak of their suffering so they had to gather together to become robbers. Consequently, even harsher punishments were enforced. So it was ordered that those who had committed crimes more serious than stealing should be beheaded whether they had actually committed the crimes or not, without needing to report to the emperor. ...all the property of the thieves shall be confiscated."[41] However, the

---

[35] "Gao Zu Ji" (The Record of Emperor Gaozu) in *Sui Shu* (*The History of Sui Dynasty*) (Book 2)..

[36] "Zhao Zhuo Zhuan" (The Biography of Zhao Zhuo) in *Sui Shu* (*The History of Sui Dynasty*).

[37] "Xing Fa Zhi" (The Record of the Criminal Law) in *Sui Shu* (*The History of Sui Dynasty*).

[38] "Xing Fa Zhi" (The Record of the Criminal Law) in *Sui Shu* (*The History of Sui Dynasty*).

[39] "Xing Fa Zhi" (The Record of the Criminal Law) in *Sui Shu* (*The History of Sui Dynasty*).

[40] "Xing Fa Zhi" (The Record of the Criminal Law) in *Sui Shu* (*The History of Sui Dynasty*).

[41] "Xing Fa Zhi" (The Record of the Criminal Law) in *Sui Shu* (*The History of Sui Dynasty*).

crimes of stealing were not eliminated by imposing harsh punishment upon the thieves, on the contrary, the imperial government was more isolated, so it was finally overthrown by the great uprising of those "thieves."

As for the penalty system of Sui Dynasty, the old tradition was continued and a new way was opened up for future. Until the Sui Dynasty, the penalty system became finalized. From the lesson of the perishing of Northern Zhou Dynasty caused by "the disintegration of people because of the cruel punishments and strict administrative rules,"[42] imperial decrees were issued by Emperor Wen to abolish the brutal punishments, such as "Gong" (castration), "Bian" (whipping), "Xiao Shou" (the penalty of hanging the head of the criminal on top of a pole for public display), "Nu Lu" (being punished for being the children or grandchildren of offenders), and "Xiang Zuo" (being punished for being related to or friendly with offenders), etc. Thus, five statutory penalties, namely, "Si" (death penalty), "Liu" (exile), "Tu" (imprisonment), "Zhang" (flogging with heavy sticks), and "Chi" (flogging with light sticks) were finally established, with only two kinds of death penalties, namely, "Zhan" (beheading) and "Jiao" (hanging) retained. The penalty of "Liu" (exile) for 1000 *li* was changed to 3000 *li* with two years, two and a half years, and three years of labor work respectively. The penalty of "Tu" (imprisonment) was changed from one to three years; the penalty of "Zhang" (flogging with heavy sticks) was increased from sixty strokes to one hundred strokes and the penalty of "Chi" (flogging with light sticks) was increased from ten strokes to fifty strokes. Generally speaking, the penalty system of Sui Dynasty was fruit of the penalty system reform of the early period of Han Dynasty after the abolishment of corporal punishment, which had reflected function of the progress of the times in the promotion of legal civilization. However, in the later years of Emperor Wen, "many brutal penalties were enforced".[43] The old rule that the families of the criminal would be exempted from punishment unless they had committed the crime of "Mou Pan" (plotting treason) was abolished, the laws on "Ji Mo" (the cancellation of a household registration) and the punishment of "Jiu Zu" (the nine generations of the clan) were restored: "(the offenders) shall either be punished by 'Che Lie' (tearing a person asunder with carts), or 'Xiao Shou' (the penalty of hanging the head of the criminal on top of a pole for public display), or killed by arrows after their arms and legs were cut off."[44]

---

[42]"Gao Zu Ji" (The Record of Emperor Gaozu) in *Sui Shu* (*The History of Sui Dynasty*) (Book 1).
[43]"Xing Fa Zhi" (The Record of the Criminal Law) in *Sui Shu* (*The History of Sui Dynasty*).
[44]"Xing Fa Zhi" (The Record of the Criminal Law) in *Sui Shu* (*The History of Sui Dynasty*).

7.1.4 The Civil and Economic Laws Centered on "Jun Tian Zhi" (The System of Land Equalization) and "Zu Yong Diao Fa" (Law on Farmland Rent, Handicraft Tax, and Corvée)

In Sui Dynasty, "Jun Tian Zhi" (The System of Land Equalization) was inherited from the Northern Qi Dynasty and was implemented nationwide. According to "Jun Tian Zhi" (The System of Land Equalization), farmland was distributed to peasants according to the number of people in a family, so first the age limit of adults was stipulated by law. According to "Shi Huo Zhi" (The Records of National Finance and Economy) in *Wei Shu* (*The History of Northern Wei Dynasty*), the male and female under three years old were referred to as "Huang" (ignorant youth), under ten years old were "Xiao" (youth), under seventeen years old were "Zhong" (middler), above eighteen and under sixty years old (it was changed into twenty-one years old in the 3rd year of Kaihuang) were "Ding" (adult), and above sixty years old were "Lao" (elder). When people became adults, they were distributed farmland. Hence, the people who were eighteen years old were also called "Ding Nian" (the year of manhood).

One adult male could be allocated eighty *mu* of "Lu Tian" (state-owned farmland) or "Kou Fen Tian" (assigned according to members of one family) and twenty *mu* of "Sang Tian" (farmland for planting mulberry trees for silkworms) or "Yong Ye Tian" (family farmland), while one adult female could be allocated forty *mu* of "Lu Tian" (state-owned farmland). However, the farmland allocated to bureaucrats and nobilities were much more than that allocated to peasants. For example, the princes could be allocated thirty to one hundred *qing* of family farmland. Additionally, they could also be allocated "Zhi Fen Tian" (the farmland allocated according to their official ranks) and "Gong Xie Tian" (the farmland allocated for government offices, whose rent was for office expenses). Especially, "Nu Bi" (slave girls and maidservants) of bureaucrats and nobilities were also entitled to farmland according to the number of adults in their families. Thus, the farmland that bureaucrats and nobilities owned was much more than what was regulated by "Jun Tian Zhi" (The System of Land Equalization). However, the implementation of "Jun Tian Zhi" (The System of Land Equalization) had made it possible for the central government to control most of the peasants in the country, to ensure the tax revenue of the imperial government, and to open up the state-owned wasteland. For instance, the wasteland opened up in the 9th year of Kaihuang (589 A.D.) was only 1,944,267 *qing*, but during the period of Daye (605 A.D.–618 A.D.), it was increased to 55,840,040 *qing*, which had greatly contributed to the prosperity and national power of the Sui Dynasty, just as Du You had once commented that "this had indeed led to the prosperity of Sui Dynasty."[45] Because of the implementation of "Jun Tian Zhi" (The System of Land

---

[45]"Shi Huo" (National Finance and Economy) in *Tong Dian* (*The General Codes*) (Book 7).

Equalization), the peasants were allocated small pieces of farmland, which had, to some extent, not only improved their lives but also stabilized the society.

In feudal times, the individual peasants were the basic units to pay tax and serve corvée, so the more peasants the local government could directly control, the more stable and powerful the centralized administration would be. Therefore, in the early period of Sui Dynasty, with the implementation of "Jun Tian Zhi" (The System of Land Equalization), household registration was also established by the centralized government to increase the number of peasants who can perform their duties of tax and corvée under the direct control of central government. In 583 A.D., Emperor Wen ordered that "Da Suo Mao Yue" should be carried out nationwide, which meant that the chief officials of "Zhou" (subprefecture) and "Xian" (county) should be in charge of checking whether members had been left out in the household registration and whether the information of household registration was consistent with people's postures and facial features,[46] if there were any mistakes, the local officials who were in charge of registration would be exiled to remote places. From the general survey, it was discovered that there were altogether 443,000 adult men, and 1,640,000 people were newly registered. To prevent the common people from evading tax, to prevent officials from playing favoritism and committing irregularities and to make the burden of tax collection consistent with the changes of the levels of household registration, "Shu Ji Fa" (law on tax and household register) was carried out by Emperor Wen according to Gao Jiong's suggestion.[47] According to this law, on the 5th day of January of every lunar year, inspections should be conducted by "Xian Ling" (county magistrate) and the people should be organized into one "Tuan" based on three or five "Dang" (one "Dang" consisted of 500 families) to decide the ranks of household and the amount of tax which they should pay.

The implementation of "Da Suo Mao Yue" (checking out registration information, recording the postures and facial features of people) and "Shu Ji Fa" (law on tax and household register) had not only enabled the imperial government to have a more effective control of the peasants to prevent them from escaping to other places to evade revenue, but also guaranteed the tax and corvée needs of the state, weakened the power of local separatist regimes and consolidated the central government's control of the country.

In the early period of Sui Dynasty, to recover the state economy, the policy of tax and corvée reduction was implemented, so according to this law, one couple was obliged to pay three *dan* of millet for tax; the age for male adults to do corvée labor was changed from "eighteen to twenty-one years old"; the time for male adults to do annual corvée labor was reduced from one month to twenty days; the amount of rough silk which they were obliged to pay for tax was reduce from four *zhang* to two *zhang*. This law was also called "Zu Yong Diao Fa" (Law on Farmland Rent,

---

[46]"Shi Huo Zhi" (The Records of National Finance and Economy) in *Sui Shu* (*The History of Sui Dynasty*).

[47]"Shi Huo Zhi" (The Records of National Finance and Economy) in *Sui Shu* (*The History of Sui Dynasty*).

Handicraft Tax, and Corvée). Its implementation had not only reduced the peasants' burden of tax and corvée, but also made it possible for peasants to be engaged in reproduction, which had finally led to the economic prosperity of the early Sui Dynasty.

As there was no unified and standard official monetary system in the Southern and Northern dynasties, the problem of illegal minting became so serious that the whole monetary system was thrown into disorder, so Emperor Wen ordered that the power of minting should be controlled by the central government. In September of the 1st year of Kaihuang (581 A.D.), "the illegal and private minting of old coins was forbidden"; at the same time, "Wu Zhu Qian" (Wu Zhu Coin) was ordered to be minted.[48] Additionally, it was also ordered that "notices should be put up on the walls of roadhouses in the capital and in each 'Zhou' (subprefecture) with standard coins made and shown to the public. So it is forbidden for the non-standard coins to be used at markets."[49] In the 4th year of Kaihuang (584 A.D.), another imperial decree was issued, according to which, "if illegal minting of coins cannot be stopped, 'Xian Ling' (county magistrate) of the county shall be punished with his half a year of salary suspended"[50] and "if illegal coins are used in trading," the offenders would be severely punished. It was recorded in "Zhao Zhuo Zhuan" (The Biography of Zhao Zhuo) in *Sui Shu* (*The History of Sui Dynasty*) that in the capital, someone had violated the laws by trading with illegal coins, so Emperor Wen was very angry and wanted to punish him by death penalty, but the minister of 'Da Li Si' (The Bureau of Judicial Review) named Zhao Zhuo advised him: "It is not lawful to execute this offender because he should be punished by 'Zhang' (flogging with heavy sticks) instead."

In addition, because of the development of industry and commerce, the business exchanges and the close trade relationship between China and the countries in the western regions, a chapter entitled "Guan Shi" (Border Market) was particularly included into *Da Ye Lv* (*Da Ye Code*) to cope with the situation.

Therefore, the civil and economic laws of Sui Dynasty had effectively protected the civil legal activities and promoted the restoration and development of overall social economy based on agriculture.

7.1.5 *The Judicial System of the Centralized Government*

As to the central judicial organs of the Sui Dynasty, "Du Guan Sheng" (in charge of judicial administration) was in charge of judicial administration; "Da Li Si" (The

---

[48] *Zi Zhi Tong Jian* (*History as a Mirror*), Vol. 175.

[49] "Shi Huo Zhi" (The Records of National Finance and Economy) in *Sui Shu* (*The History of Sui Dynasty*).

[50] "Shi Huo Zhi" (The Records of National Finance and Economy) in *Sui Shu* (*The History of Sui Dynasty*).

Bureau of Judicial Review) was in charge of trial, and "Yu Shi Tai" (The Censorate) was in charge of judicial supervision and trial of important cases. The reform of local judicial office was in agreement with that of local government, so the local judicial office of "Zhou" (subprefecture) and "Xian" (county) was concurrently headed by the magistrates of the local government.

As to litigation, the lawsuits either were filed to court by officials and supervisory offices or by the parties in action, but false accusations were forbidden. If cases were settled unjustly, or if they would not be accepted by the court of local county, they could be transferred to "Shang Shu Sheng" (The Department of Secretary) gradually by "Zhou" (subprefecture) and "Jun" (shire). Besides, the plaintiffs even could go to imperial court themselves to file lawsuits by "Wo Deng Wen Gu" (beat the drum and deliver the complaints, it is one of the important direct complaints in ancient China). It was stipulated in *Kai Huang Lv* (*The Code Made in the Year of Kai Huang*) that "if cases are settled unjustly but are rejected by the local county courts, they shall be transferred to higher court by 'Zhou' (subprefecture) and 'Jun' (shire); if cases are still unacceptable by the provincial court, the plaintiffs can express their grievance by "Wo Deng Wen Gu" (beat the drum and deliver the complaints, it is one of the important direct complaints in ancient China). Then their complaints will be recorded and reported to emperor afterwards."[51] Such step-by-step appeal system had reflected the protection of the rights of parties in action at the beginning of Sui Dynasty.

To strengthen the construction of the judicial personnel and to improve the quality and efficiency of court, Emperor Wen attached much weight to the training of judicial officials. After the enactment of *Kai Huang Lv* (*The Code Made in the Year of Kai Huang*), eight "Lv Bo Shi" (Scholar of Law) and twenty "Ming Fa" (law official) were appointed in "Da Li Si" (The Bureau of Judicial Review) to be in charge of hearing important legal cases and teaching law, as was described that "in hearing important cases, law specialists are often consulted first before judgment is made."[52] Apart from those posts, "Lv Bo Shi" (Scholar of Law) in "Zhou" (subprefecture) and "Jun" (shire) were often allowed to recruit students to "study and do researches on law." It was also regulated that all officials in "Zhou" (subprefecture) whose ranks were lower than "Zhang Shi" (Junior Official) but higher than "Xing Can Jun" (Military Staff Officer) must study law and take exams in the capital. Under the guarantee of this system, most officials in Sui government were well equipped with legal knowledge, so "Lv Xue" (the study of statutory laws) was full of vitality again. However, in the 5th year of Kaihuang, a law student in Wuping county had made a false charge against an official named Murong Tianyuan by playing with literary skills, so Emperor Wen was outraged by the case and said, "the important matter of life-and-death is decided by law, so the law is made clearly for people to understand easily. Besides, meritorious officials are

---

[51]"Shi Huo Zhi" (The Records of National Finance and Economy) in *Sui Shu* (*The History of Sui Dynasty*).

[52]"Xing Fa Zhi" (The Record of the Criminal Law) in *Sui Shu* (*The History of Sui Dynasty*).

always selected and appointed to take their responsibilities, so there should be no doubtful points in the judgment of minor or serious offenses. By following the systems of the previous dynasties, legal officials are especially appointed to make legal decisions. However, such an important job of deciding the life-and-death of the people is always in the charge of villainous people. This is the particular reason for enforcement of unjust punishments and the tyrannically abuse of legal power, which is the greatest malpractice in politics." Therefore, an imperial decree was issued, so "'Lv Bo Shi' (Scholar of Law) in 'Da Li Si' (The Bureau of Judicial Review) and 'Ming Fa' (law official) in 'Shang Shu Sheng' (The Department of Secretary) and 'Xing Bu' (The Department of Punishment) were abolished."[53] However, as the officials were required to "make sentence according to legal provisions," the officials who were ignorant of the law were incompetent in the legal work. Thus, in the 6th year of Kaihuang (586 A.D.), an imperial decree was issued by Emperor Wen: "All officials in "Zhou" (subprefecture) below the rank of 'Zhang Shi' (Junior Official) and above the rank of 'Xing Can Jun' (Military Staff Officer) shall study law and then take exams held in the capital."[54]

In judicial trials, in the early years of Kaihuang, the judicial officials were strictly ordered to hear cases according to statutory provisions, as was described in the saying that "cases should be judged according to the written statutory provisions."[55] It was recorded in "Quan Wu Zhuan" (The Biography of Quan Wu) in *Su Shu* (*The History of Sui Dynasty*) that an official named Quan Wu "often heard cases without applying the legal stipulations, because he thought that Nanyue was an outlying area and it should be governed according to local conventions and measures suitable to local conditions." It should be mentioned that Quan Wu's view was to some extent reasonable because it was in accordance with the local conditions. However, "since the emperor had ordered all officials to hear cases according to law without exception, so (after knowing what he had done) the emperor was furious and ordered to have him punished by death penalty." To encourage officials to hear cases according to statutory provisions, Emperor Wen "even often interrogated the prisoners by himself."[56]

As to the interrogation of prisoners, "the brutal measures were abolished and it was stipulated that the strokes for punishment of 'Zhang' (flogging with heavy sticks) should not exceed two hundred, the length and the width of the sticks and the size of cangues should all be standardized and the staff executing the punishment of 'Zhang' (flogging with heavy sticks) should not be changed during the process of the punishment".[57] Additionally, the measure of extorting confession by starvation was abolished.

---

[53]"Xing Fa Zhi" (The Record of the Criminal Law) in *Sui Shu* (*The History of Sui Dynasty*).
[54]"Xing Fa Zhi" (The Record of the Criminal Law) in *Sui Shu* (*The History of Sui Dynasty*).
[55]"Xing Fa Zhi" (The Record of the Criminal Law) in *Sui Shu* (*The History of Sui Dynasty*).
[56]"Xing Fa Zhi" (The Record of the Criminal Law) in *Sui Shu* (*The History of Sui Dynasty*).
[57]"Xing Fa Zhi" (The Record of the Criminal Law) in *Sui Shu* (*The History of Sui Dynasty*).

With respect to the cases of death penalty in each "Zhou" (subprefecture), strict instructions were given: "As to the cases of death penalty, they should not be executed by the local courts of 'Zhou' (subprefecture) without authorization, so all the cases shall be reported to and reviewed by 'Da Li Yuan' (The Supreme Court) first and then be reported to the emperor for final decision".[58] It was also stipulated that three memorials about the cases of the death penalty should be submitted to the emperor before the death penalty was executed. In Sui Dynasty, the power of executing death penalty was controlled by the central government, which had effectively avoided the malpractice of killing people arbitrarily by local officials. At the same time, the practice of submitting three memorials to the emperor had reflected the spirit of prudent punishment. However, the reviewing system of death penalty was abolished in the later period of the reign of Emperor Yang, so it had resulted in more indiscriminate killings.

In Sui Dynasty, the time for executing death penalty was arranged in autumn and winter by following the system of Han Dynasty. However, during the reign of Emperor Wen, "some of the convicts were killed by 'Zhang' (flogging with heavy sticks) in June," although it was disapproved by the chief minister of 'Da Li Yuan' (The Supreme Court) named Zhao Zhuo, because he thought, "in summer all things on earth are growing, so it is not a season for killing." Nevertheless, emperor Wen argued, "it is true that June is the season for everything to grow, but sometimes there are still thunderbolts at this time, which is a symbol of the anger of 'Tian' (Heaven). Now I am following 'Tian Dao' (The Way of Heaven), what is wrong with it?" "The convicts were then killed."[59]

In summary, although Sui Dynasty was a very short-lived dynasty which had lasted for only thirty-seven years, it was still a very great important dynasty, especially in the area of legal system construction. Thus, the law of Sui Dynasty, either in system, chapter, or category of punishment, had laid a solid foundation for the legal system construction in the later feudal society.

In Sui Dynasty, not only great efforts were made to carry out legal system reform, positive measures were also taken to conduct legal revision and laws were strictly enforced. For example, the son of Emperor Wen, named Yang Jun, was "compelled to go back home" to be punished by house confinement for building houses and palaces without permission. Although memorials were presented to the emperor by the ministers of imperial court to persuade him that the punishment given to his son was too severe, Emperor Wen refused and replied, "laws should not be violated." Because "I have five sons, would it be better if I follow the ministers' suggestions to make a law particularly for my own sons? Zhou Gong (Duke of Zhou) is a man of decency, so he once has sentenced the brothers of the King Wu of Zhou Dynasty named Guan and Cai to death penalty. I'm not as meritorious as Zhou Gong, so how can I violate the law?"[60] Another example: Wang Yi was an old friend of Emperor

---

[58]*Zi Zhi Tong Jian* (*History as a Mirror*), Vol. 178.

[59]"Xing Fa Zhi" (The Record of the Criminal Law) in *Sui Shu* (*The History of Sui Dynasty*).

[60]"Yang Jun Zhuan" (The Biography of Yang Jun) in *Sui Shu* (*The History of Sui Dynasty*).

Wen, and he was a meritorious statesman who had been the assistance of the emperor for a long time. Besides, his son had married the fifth daughter of Emperor Wen. However, years later, "the ministers of imperial court admonished Emperor Wen that Wang Yi had committed serious crimes, so should be punished by death penalty." Emperor called in the ministers and sadly told them, "the Duke (Wang Yi) and I used to study together and I am very sorry for him. But what can I do before the law?" "Then emperor's order was issued to Wang Yi, so he killed himself in his own house."[61]

To enforce law fairly, Emperor Wen paid much attention to the selection and appointment of judicial officials. He appointed Xue Zhou as "Da Li Qing" (the president of the supreme court of justice) and Zhao Zhuo as "Shao Qing" (the vice president). According to history books, the two people "were praised for their generosity, kindness and benevolence and both of them were good and competent officials because Xue Zhou had always enforced laws in accordance with the concrete situations of specific cases and Zhao Zhuo had always handled cases in accordance with legal provisions."[62] The successor of the post of "Da Li Qing" (the president of the supreme court of justice), named Liang Pi, was also "respected by others because he was able to handle cases impartially."[63] In terms of judicial supervision, Emperor Wen appointed Liu Yu as "Zhi Shu Chi Yu Shi" (Imperial Censor of Inspection). According to records, "he had inspected fifty-two 'Zhou' (subprefecture) in Hebei Province and more than two hundred incompetent officials were dismissed from their posts for taking bribery upon his memorial to the emperor. So the officials of 'Zhou' (subprefecture) and 'Xian' (county) were all shocked and frightened."[64] In the feudal society, though law was a primary means to govern people, it was actually applied to people according to their social status. In the early period of Sui Dynasty, qualified officials were highly valued by Emperor Wen so that the virtuous people were promoted and talented people were recommended. Consequently, the official groups became upright, righteous and intelligent, which had played a positive role in maintaining the legal system of Kaihuang, in stabilizing the social order and in promoting economy.

Therefore, it could be commented then that it was the guarantee of the maintenance of the legal system of Kaihuang to show respect to law and to stress law in the early years of the reign of Emperor Wen, but in the later years of the reign of Emperor Wen, the initial intention of the legislation to "replace severe punishments with lenient ones, to change the death penalty to life imprisonment" and "to abolish the provisions of 'Lian Zuo' (being punished for being related to somebody who committed an offense)" was totally ignored.[65] Consequently, "much more severe penalties were implemented and more people were killed due to the emperor's

---

[61] "Wang Yi Zhuan" (The Biography of Wang Yi) in *Sui Shu* (*The History of Sui Dynasty*).

[62] "Zhao Zhuo Zhuan" (The Biography of Zhao Zhuo) in *Sui Shu* (*The History of Sui Dynasty*).

[63] "Liang Pi Zhuan" (The Biography of Liang Pi) in *Sui Shu* (*The History of Sui Dynasty*).

[64] "Liu Yu Zhuan" (The Biography of Liu Yu) in *Sui Shu* (*The History of Sui Dynasty*).

[65] "Xing Fa Zhi" (The Record of the Criminal Law) in *Sui Shu* (*The History of Sui Dynasty*).

changeable moods."⁶⁶ As the emperor had supreme authority over the law and had always wantonly enforced punishments beyond law, the officials also tried to conjecture the emperor's will to persecute people by throwing them into prisons or to make false charges against the innocents. According to history books, "whenever crimes were committed by senior officials, their cases would be reported to Emperor Hou by judicial officials for final decision when he was bad-tempered so that the offenders would be severely punished. Consequently, numerous people were sentenced to death penalty just for minor crimes," "and those who were about to be executed all shouted in tears that they had been treated unjustly."⁶⁷

In Emperor Wen's life, he had made great contribution to the making and enforcement of law, but at the same time, he had also violated and bent the law by playing with the legal rules, which was determined by the autocratic system under which all the laws were made by the monarch and the monarchal power always overtopped the law. When Emperor Wen was on his deathbed, he regretted profoundly for his own actions and explored the true reason for the rise and fall of the state. He finally realized the importance of the establishment of legal system, so in his imperial testamentary edict, he emphasized that the legal system must "be reformed in accordance with real situation . . . and must be taken as an essence of administration." However, although Emperor Wen stressed the importance of legal system construction, he still insisted on the legislative power of the monarch. He stated, "the wise monarchs make laws according to their own needs ever since the ancient times . . . if 'Lv' (criminal law), 'Ling' (decree), 'Ge' (injunction), and 'Shi' (standard) are not applicable any more, they must all be revised based on the old ones which are applied in the previous dynasties."⁶⁸ What he said had clearly shown the emperor's way of thinking under the autocratic system.

During his early years of reigning, Emperor Yang was very active in law revision and he had always boasted of his lenient administration, because he thought that "the penalties during the reign of Emperor Gaozu are too severe."⁶⁹ However, his policy of "serving onerous corvée and levying heavy tax"⁷⁰ had intensified the already sharp social contradiction in the later years of Emperor Wen. Consequently, "there were more thieves and robbers in the country, while in the cities, the official houses were looted and people slaughtered wantonly."⁷¹ Under such social circumstances, Emperor Yang finally gave up his pretended benevolence and generosity, so "the trouble makers were brutally suppressed by enacting urgent and strict rules, applying severe punishments, and using military means." Consequently, "riots spread throughout the country and people were living in misery."⁷² In the 9th year of

---

⁶⁶"Gao Zu Ji" (The Record of Emperor Gaozu) in *Sui Shu* (*The History of Sui Dynasty*) (Book 2).
⁶⁷"Xing Fa Zhi" (The Record of the Criminal Law) in *Sui Shu* (*The History of Sui Dynasty*).
⁶⁸"Gao Zu Ji" (The Record of Emperor Gaozu) (Part 2) in *Sui Shu* (*The History of Sui Dynasty*).
⁶⁹"Xing Fa Zhi" (The Record of the Criminal Law) in *Sui Shu* (*The History of Sui Dynasty*).
⁷⁰"Yang Di Ji" (The Record of Emperor Yang) (Part 2) in *Sui Shu* (*The History of Sui Dynasty*)
⁷¹"Yang Di Ji" (The Record of Emperor Yang) (Part 2) in *Sui Shu* (*The History of Sui Dynasty*).
⁷²"Yang Di Ji" (The Record of Emperor Yang) (Part 2) in *Sui Shu* (*The History of Sui Dynasty*).

Daye (613 A.D.), after suppressing the uprising led by Yang Xuangan, Emperor Yang told Pei Yun, who was then "Yu Shi Da Fu" (Grand Censor), that "more than 100,000 people have responded to Xuangan's call, so I think that we shouldn't have so many people in the country, because if so, they would always get together to rebel in groups; if they are not killed, it is impossible to warn the future generations." Therefore, "strict laws were enacted, and more than 30,000 people were sentenced to death, with all their families punished by 'Ji Mo' (the cancellation of a household registration). Among the people killed, almost half of them were wronged. Additionally, as many as 6,000 people were punished by 'Liu' (exile)",[73] which had finally led to the rapid downfall of Sui Dynasty. In Chinese history, both Qin and Sui dynasties had once been prosperous and strong, but both of them quickly collapsed when the second emperor was on the throne. Thus, many historical lessons can be drawn from such facts. Especially, one objective natural law has been proved by historical facts, namely, it is only when the legal system has been established that it is possible for a state to be strong and prosperous, but the state will be in danger if its legal system is destroyed.

7.2 The Legal System of Tang Dynasty Symbolizing the Establishment of Chinese Legal System

Tang Dynasty was an age of peace and prosperity in Chinese feudal society, with the recovery and fast development of its economy, the unification, and stability of the state and the booming and flourishing of its culture, which had made ancient China one of the strongest countries in the ancient world of civilization. In his book, *The Outline of History: Being a Plain History of Life and Mankind*, the British scholar, Herbert George Wells stated that Tang Dynasty had won its "leading position" in the history of world civilization and had maintained that position for "about 1,000 years."

The social and historical situation of Tang Dynasty had provided the essential condition for the glorious age of the civilization of Chinese legal system. At this historical moment, a large number of wise politicians and legalists emerged, such as Li Shimin, Wei Zheng, Fang Xuanling, Du Ruhui, Zhangsun Wuji, Dai Zhou and so on, who had greatly promoted the development of the legal civilization of Tang Dynasty.

The legal system of Tang Dynasty, represented by *Tang Lv Shu Yi* (*The Comments on Tang Code*), not only symbolized of the formation, but also the peak of the Chinese legal system. It was written in the abstract of *"Tang Lv Shu Yi"* (*The Comments on Tang Code*) in *Si Ku Quan Shu Zong Mu Ti Yao* (*Descriptive Catalogue to Si Ku Quan Shu*) that *"Tang Lv* (*Tang Code*), complying with the principles of 'Li' (rites), is the best legal code of both ancient and modern times." In

---

[73]*Zi Zhi Tong Jian* (*History as a Mirror*), Vol. 182.

this sense, on the one hand, *Tang Lv* (*Tang Code*) had shown its aboriginality deeply rooted in the soil of Chinese culture; on the other hand, it had shown the cosmopolitan characteristics as well, because the neighboring countries, such as Japan, Vietnam, and Liuqiu (an ancient country used to be located between Taiwan and Japan), had all established their own legal systems mainly based on *Tang Lv* (*Tang Code*), so that their legal systems had become the branches of the Chinese legal system. Except that those neighboring countries had shared similar national conditions with Tang Dynasty, this was also because of the ethicality, scientificity, and completeness reflected in *Tang Lv* (*Tang Code*). In *Tang Lv* (*Tang Code*), the five hundred and two legal provisions covered every field of Tang Dynasty such as politics, economy, military, diplomacy, marriage, family, and individual and had an overall adjustment of the social relationship and the state activities. For the purpose of clarifying the points and simplifying the application, comments and explanations were added to the legal provisions to explain the meaning of each legal provision. Such combination of legal provisions and comments was a great innovation in statute law. Thus, the Chinese law, although having experienced thousands of years of development after Tang Dynasty, had never gone beyond the principles of *Tang Lv* (*Tang Code*). This was the exact why *Da Ming Lv* (*The Great Ming Code*), which was made based on the *Tang Lv* (*Tang Code*), could continuously exert a great influence on the lawmaking of the countries like Japan and Korea. It was agreeable in the conclusion drawn by Niida Noboru, a Japanese scholar of legal history, that "ancient China, like the periods of Tang and Ming dynasties, had had a great influence on the area of East Asia through its Confucian culture as well as its legal codes."[74]

7.2.1 The Legislative Ideology Drawn from the Lessons of the Extinction of Sui Dynasty

The national peasant uprising broken out in 611 A.D. in the later period of Sui Dynasty had quickly swept through the whole country like a violent storm, which had not only overthrown the government of Sui Dynasty, but also greatly affected the newly built imperial government of Tang Dynasty. The bureaucratic group, headed by Li Yuan and his son who settled in the area of Shaanxi and Gansu, had witnessed the decline of the imperial government of Sui Dynasty when uprisings were spreading like a raging fire, so they had taken the chance to call on the people to "fight against the Sui Dynasty." On the one hand, with the help of strong military forces, they occupied the regions of the central Shaanxi plain and began to suppress the peasant uprisings ruthlessly; on the other hand, to disintegrate the military forces of the armed peasants with political means, they not only abolished the severe laws

---

[74]Niida Noboru (Japan), *The History of the Chinese Legal System*, translated by Mo Fasong, Shanghai Classics Publishing House, 2010, p 52.

7.2 The Legal System of Tang Dynasty Symbolizing the Establishment...

of Sui Dynasty and the civil law consisting of twelve provisions, but also enforced the military rules more strictly. Suppressed by the military forces of Li Yuan and his group and attacked by their political offensives, the peasant uprising soon ended up in failure. Consequently, a new feudal dynasty, Tang Dynasty, was founded in 618 A.D. Tang Dynasty, which had lasted for about two hundred and ninety years, was not only a famous, strong, and prosperous dynasty in Chinese history, but also a dynasty in which the Chinese legal civilization was highly developed and the Chinese legal system was finalized. Therefore, it had exerted a great influence on the development of domestic and foreign legal systems.

In the early period of Tang Dynasty, the ruling class was both "shocked and alerted" after they witnessed the sudden collapse of Sui Dynasty although it was armed with a strong military force and a powerful state machine. Emperor Taizong (Li Shimin) told his ministers, "it is fearful to think that if 'Tian Zi' (the son of Heaven)... is immoral and brutal, he will be overthrown and cast aside by people."[75] To rebuild the state, to consolidate the feudal power, to recover the declining economy, and to change the situation where "thousands of houses of the towns were empty and smoke and fire for cooking could hardly be seen within the area of thousands of *li*,"[76] a series of policies concerning people's lives were carried out. For example, in the 7th year of Wude (624 A.D.), "Jun Tian Ling" (Decree of Land Equalization) was issued to grant peasants some small pieces of farmland and "Zu Yong Diao Fa" (Law on Farmland Rent, Handicraft Tax, and Corvée) was made to reduce the burden of hard labor and tax. Additionally, severe punishments were mitigated, official management was stressed, corrupt officials were punished, farming was encouraged and awarded, water conservancy projects were built and agricultural production was emphasized, all of which had played a positive role in bringing about "Zhen Guan Zhi Zhi" (Excellent Governance during the Reign of Zhen Guan).

It needs to be pointed out that the ruling class of Tang Dynasty attached much attention to the function of legal system in social control, so they not only actively encouraged legislation but also put forward some brand new legal ideology.

7.2.1.1 Advocating Law, Inflicting Penalty with Prudence and Governing the State with Benevolence and Generosity

As Emperor Taizong (Li Shimin) and his assistant ministers, such as Wei Zheng, Wang Gui, Fang Xuanling, Tu Mahui, Ma Zhou, and Dai Zhou, etc., had all witnessed the decline and collapse of Sui Dynasty in spite of its previous prosperity, they realized that "the collapse of Sui Dynasty should be remembered and be taken

---

[75]"Zheng Ti" (The Political System) in *Zhen Guan Zheng Yao* (*The Essentials about Politics during the Reign of Zhen Guan*), Vol. 1.

[76]"Li Mi Zhuan" (The Biography of Li Mi) in *Jiu Tang Shu* (*The Old Book of Tang Dynasty*).

as a warning when they make decisions."[77] They had learned from the lessons of the extinction of Sui Dynasty that the most important reason which led to "the great pain and suffering of the people and the extinction of Sui Dynasty"[78] was that "the legal codes of Sui Dynasty were abandoned,"[79] "the officials who committed crimes were not punished"[80] while "the legal provisions were too rigorous."[81] Thus, after the founding of Tang Dynasty, to recover the legal order, much attention was paid to the construction of legal system and the restoration of legal order. Wei Zheng once advised Emperor Taizong and said, "the law is just like the weights and measures of the state and the yardstick of the times. Weights and measures are applied to determine the weight (the order of priority) and the yardstick is applied to determine evenness (right and wrong)." "If 'the great master' 'abandons the law willfully'," it is the same as "determining the evenness (right and wrong) without using yardstick, or determining weight (the order of priority) without using weights and measures. Wouldn't it lead to confusion?"[82] Wei Zheng's expostulations were approved by Emperor Taizong who had repeatedly said, "the law is not made for me, it is made for people all over the country," so nobody should "interfere with law enforcement"[83] for his own private interests. Apparently, the principle of making and enforcing laws strictly and impartially had been taken as "the first priority both in providing security for the people and in establishing a government,"[84] which had obviously become a common view shared by both the emperor and the ministers in the early period of Tang Dynasty. Thus, laws should be publicized and enforced to "stop violence, to punish the wickedness, to maintain and carryout 'Gang Chang Ming Jiao' (feudal cardinal guides and constant virtues)",[85] to stabilize social order, and to prevent the recurrence of peasant uprisings which took place during the later period of the Sui Dynasty because of the degrading of laws and disciplines.

During the reign of Emperor Taizong, he not only attached great importance to promoting laws, but also to inflicting penalties with prudence. Thus, he put forward the idea of "governing the country with benevolence and enforcing penalties with

---

[77]"Xing Fa" (The Criminal Law) in *Zhen Guan Zheng Yao* (*The Essentials about Politics during the Reign of Zhen Guan*), Vol. 8.

[78]"Xing Fa Zhi" (The Record of the Criminal Law) in *Jiu Tang Shu* (*The Old Book of Tang Dynasty*).

[79]"Xing Fa Zhi" (The Record of the Criminal Law) in *Sui Shu* (*The History of Sui Dynasty*).

[80]*Wei Zheng Gong Jian Lu* (*Collection of Master Wei Zheng's Expostulation*), Vol. 3.

[81]"Xing Fa Zhi" (The Record of the Criminal Law) in *Jiu Tang Shu* (*The Old Book of Tang Dynasty*).

[82]"Gong Ping" (Impartiality) in *Zhen Guan Zheng Yao* (*The Essentials about Politics during the Reign of Zhen Guan*), Vol. 5.

[83]"Gong Ping" (Impartiality) in *Zhen Guan Zheng Yao* (*The Essentials about Politics during the Reign of Zhen Guan*), Vol. 5.

[84]"Xing Fa Zhi" (The Record of the Criminal Law) in *Jiu Tang Shu* (*The Old Book of Tang Dynasty*).

[85]"Xing Fa Zhi" (The Record of the Criminal Law) in *Jiu Tang Shu* (*The Old Book of Tang Dynasty*).

prudence,"[86] In the early period of Tang Dynasty, a minister named Feng Deyi had suggested that "severe penalties should be enforced to make the people obedient." He said, "The people have become frivolous, false, and hypocritical ever since the early three dynasties (Xia, Shang, and Zhou), therefore, severe penalties were applied in Qin Dynasty and harsh rules were employed in Han Dynasty. Wouldn't it be wrong to say that those monarchs do not want to have people moralized? Perhaps the truth is that they are unable to do so." He criticized Wei Zheng for his suggestion of benevolent government and said, "Wei Zheng is just a bookish man who does not understand the situation of the times. So if his impractical theory is accepted and believed, the state would end up in failure."[87] On the contrary, Wei Zheng advocated ruling the country with benevolence, so he argued, "'Ren' (benevolence) and 'Yi' (righteousness) are "Ben" (the essential) of the truth, while 'Xing' (penalty) and 'Fa' (fine) are "Mo" (the inessential). It is like riding a horse with a whip to apply penalties to attain truth. So if people are moralized, there is no need to inflict penalties; if a horse can run as fast as he can, there is no need to use the whip." In conclusion, he said, "The sages have always attached importance to the teaching of morality and rites instead of the application of penalty."[88] In responding to Feng Deyi's criticism, Wei Zheng argued, "'San Huang Wu Di' (three emperors and five kings) had tried to make their people moralized but ended in failure instead. In ancient times, 'Huang Di' (Yellow Emperor) had waged a punitive expedition against Chi You; Emperor Zhuan Xu had killed Jiu Li; King Tang of Shang had exiled King Jie of Xia; King Wu had sent a punitive expedition against King Zhou, but those countries had all enjoyed a time of peace and prosperity. Isn't it the result of employing wise rules to end serious chaos?"[89] In the debate, Emperor Taizong accepted Wei Zheng's ideas, because he realized that in the later period of Sui Dynasty, Emperor Wen had lost his people's support because he had "neglected Confucian doctrines but focused on using harsh penalties to punish the people for their minor wrong doings"[90] and that Emperor Yang's "random infliction of penalties on people" had led to the tragedy of "the sudden extinction of the state." Emperor Taizong said, "As far as I know, the emperors who had governed their countries with benevolence and tolerance had reigned over their countries for a longer time, while those who had controlled their people by applying severe laws had often ended up in failure, even though severe laws could help them temporarily. The success of the previous rulers can be viewed as the lessons to the ruling of a

---

[86] "Xing Fa Zhi" (The Record of the Criminal Law) in *Xin Tang Shu* (*The New Book of Tang Dynasty*).

[87] *Zi Zhi Tong Jian* (*History as a Mirror*), Vol. 193.

[88] "Gong Ping" (Impartiality) in *Zhen Guan Zheng Yao* (*The Essentials about Politics during the Reign of Zhen Guan*), Vol. 5.

[89] *Zi Zhi Tong Jian* (*History as a Mirror*), Vol. 193.

[90] "Ru Lin Zhuan" (The Biography of the Confucian Scholars) in *Sui Shu* (*The History of Sui Dynasty*).

country."⁹¹ To put the theory of "governing the country with benevolence and enforcing penalties with prudence"⁹² into practice, Emperor Taizong demanded that judicial officials pay much attention to evidence and that cases should not be settled without sufficient evidence. If the judicial officials failed to settle the cases appropriately, they would be punished according to their misconducts; if they had misused penalties, they would be punished by "Zhang" (flogging with heavy sticks).

Emperor Taizong had made a rule by himself: "From today forward, the cases of 'Da Bi' (capital punishment) should be reviewed by officials with or above the rank of 'Si Pin' (the fourth rank) in 'Zhong Shu Men Xia' (the supreme state organization) and 'Jiu Qing' (nine high-rank officials in ancient times) in 'Shang Shu Sheng' (The Department of Secretary)."⁹³ Thus, the prototype of the system of "Jiu Qing Hui Shen" (joint hearing by nine high-rank officials in ancient times) was set up. Additionally, a judicial review system for death penalty was also carried out, according to which "three memorials" should be presented consecutively to the emperor for final decision. However, because "three memorials are consecutively presented to the emperor within a very short period, quite often there is not enough time for deliberation before making decisions. So, what is the point of presenting those memories?" For this reason, the system of "three memorials" was changed into "five memorials."

Considering that "lenient punishment should be enforced because one cannot come back to life if he is punished by death penalty,"⁹⁴ the legal provisions for death penalty were reduced, and more severe punishments were changed into lenient ones. It was recorded in history books that, compared with *Zhen Guan Lv* (*Zhen Guan Code*), "ninety-two legal provisions about the punishment of 'Da Bi' (capital punishment) and seventy-one legal provisions about the punishment of 'Liu' (exile)" were reduced. Moreover, the provision that "the brother of those who have committed crimes should all be punished by death penalty" was deleted. Consequently, "half of the provisions for death penalty were abolished compared with the ones in ancient laws" and "legal revisions were made to change the complex provisions to simple ones and to change the severe punishments to lenient ones."⁹⁵ During this time, Emperor Taizong had especially pointed out that "people become thieves and robbers because they have heavy burdens of tax and corvée and they have been severely exploited by the corrupted officials... so they have no sense of shame (of committing crimes). As an emperor, I shall reduce the expenses of

---

⁹¹"Ren Yi" (Benevolence and Justice) in *Zhen Guan Zheng Yao* (*The Essentials about Politics during the Reign of Zhen Guan*), Vol. 5.

⁹²"Xing Fa Zhi" (The Record of the Criminal Law) in *Xin Tang Shu* (*The New Book of Tang Dynasty*).

⁹³"Xing Fa" (The Criminal Law) in *Zhen Guan Zheng Yao* (*The Essentials about Politics during the Reign of Zhen Guan*), Vol. 8.

⁹⁴"Xing Fa" (The Criminal Law) in *Zhen Guan Zheng Yao* (*The Essentials about Politics during the Reign of Zhen Guan*), Vol. 8.

⁹⁵"Xing Fa Zhi" (The Record of the Criminal Law) in *Jiu Tang Shu* (*The Old Book of Tang Dynasty*).

luxuries, cut down tax and corvée, employ more honest officials and give people enough food, so that they do not want to be thieves and robbers any more. If so, what is the use of applying severe punishments?"[96]

Emperor Taizong's understanding of the roots of crimes and the measures which he had taken in dealing with the crimes were not only very useful in practice but also very creative in the theory of criminal law in ancient China.

As the theory of "governing the country with benevolence and enforcing penalties with prudence" was carried out in practice, it had become a general mood of society to observe laws and disciplines. According to history books, in the 4th year of Zhenguan, "only twenty-nine people were sentenced to death penalty in the whole country, so penalties were almost never used because few people had violated the law."[97]

7.2.1.2 Employing "De" (Virtue) and "Li" (Rites) as "Ben" (the Essence) and "Xing Fa" (Criminal Punishment) as "Yong" (Application)

From Han to Tang dynasties, scholars had been arguing about employing "De" (virtue) and "Li" (rites) as "Ben" (the essence) and "Xing Fa" (criminal punishment) as "Yong" (application) and governing the country by making use of comprehensive measures. Such arguments could be found in the note written by Yan Shigu in "Ku Li Zhuan" (The Biographies of Brutal Officials) in *Han Shu* (*The History of the Former Han Dynasty*): "If people are cultivated by applying the value of 'De' (virtue) and 'Li' (rites), they would have a sense of shame, so it will be a good way to govern the country."

It was recorded in "Si Yi Lie Zhuan" (The Collected Biography of Four Barbarian Tribes) in *Jin Shu* (*The History of Jin Dynasty*) that "it is 'De' (virtue) and 'Li' (rites) that are the principles which should be followed in governing the country; it is 'Xing Fa' (criminal punishment) that is used to save and help people; if the two are used inappropriately, the general principles and law would be in disorder."

In the early period of Tang Dynasty, the following words are recorded in *Zhen Guan Zheng Yao* (*The Essentials about Politics during the Reign of Zhen Guan*):

> Emperors use the principles of 'Li' to moralize people, to cultivate their pure and honest nature and to get to know their needs. If people love and help each other and have a faith in 'Ren' (benevolence) and 'Yi' (righteousness), they will not hurt or mistrust each other. However, such goals cannot be achieved by 'Xing' (punishment) but only by moral teaching. Sages have given more weight to moral teaching and 'Li' (rites) but have thought little of 'Xing' (punishment).[98] So 'Zheng' (government) is the tool for governing a country,

---

[96] *Zi Zhi Tong Jian* (*History as a Mirror*), Vol. 192.

[97] "Xing Fa" (The Criminal Law) in *Zhen Guan Zheng Yao* (*The Essentials about Politics during the Reign of Zhen Guan*), Vol. 8.

[98] "Xiao You" (Filial Piety) in *Zhen Guan Zheng Yao* (*The Essentials about Politics during the Reign of Zhen Guan*).

while 'Xing' (punishment) is its supplementary means; the principles of 'De' (virtue) and 'Li' (rites) are the basic means of governing a country, while 'De' (virtue) is also the origin of 'Li' (rites). But the rulers of later generations do not attach importance to 'De' (virtue), 'Li' (rites) and moral teaching. It is not true that 'De' (virtue) and 'Li' (rites) are useless in making people moralized and in giving them a sense of shame, but it is true that 'Xing' (punishment) does not stop people from committing crimes with a sense of shame. And it may also lead to crimes more serious than 'Shi E' (The Ten Abominations).[99]

Han Yu, a famous scholar in Tang Dynasty, had pointed out in his article "Chao Zhou Qing Zhi Xiang Jiao Die" (Documents for Requiring to Build Local Schools in Chao Zhou) that "Confucius said, 'if people are guided by law and governed by penalty, they will try to avoid punishment but have no sense of shame'. But in my opinion, it is better to fundamentally employ 'De' (virtue) and 'Li' (rites) and take 'Zheng' (government) and 'Xing' (punishment) as the supplementary measures."

In the well-known document, *Tang Lv Shu Yi* (*The Comments on Tang Code*), it was announced in the chapter of "Ming Li" (The Categories of Penalties and General Principles) that "the rules of 'De' (virtue) and 'Li' (rites) are the foundation of politics and moralization, while 'Xing Fa' (criminal punishment) is the supplementary means of politics and moralization." Furthermore, the natural phenomena of "darkness, light, spring, and summer" were used to compare to the close relationship between "De" (virtue), "Li" (rites) and "Xing Fa" (criminal punishment), in which they moved constantly but were correlated with and complementary to each other, as was explained in the expression that "like darkness and light forming one day, spring and autumn forming one year, they will also form a complete unity."

The ideology that employing the principles of "Li" (rites), "Yue" (music), "De" (virtue) and "Li" (rites) as "Ben" (the essence) but "Zheng" (government) and "Xing" (punishment) as "Yong" (application) in governing the country comprehensively was the crystallization of political wisdom which was in accordance with rules of development of the state. Therefore, it is not only helpful to guide the people to move toward kindness and to build a benevolent government, but also to enforce punishment with prudence and to achieve harmony and balance to regard "De" (virtue) and "Li" (rites) as "Ben" (the essence) and "Zheng" (government) and "Xing" (punishment) as "Yong" (application) and to use the four elements comprehensively. Besides, it is also helpful to build a prosperous society and to bring about social harmony and long time stability. Therefore, regarding "De" (virtue) and "Li" (rites) as "Ben" (the essence) has shown the human-oriented spirit of stressing "De" (virtue) and "Li" (rites) in ancient China; while regarding "Xing Fa" (criminal punishment) as "Yong" (application) has indicated "Xing Fa" (criminal punishment) is only the means of governing the country but not the ultimate purpose. These ideas which were formed in the early period of Tang Dynasty had not only rectified the social customs, but also played the role of "Ming Xing Bi Jiao" (integrating punishment with moral teachings). This remarkable guiding ideology of legislation

---

[99]"Xing Fa" (The Criminal Law) in *Zhen Guan Zheng Yao* (*The Essentials about Politics during the Reign of Zhen Guan*), Vol. 8.

7.2 The Legal System of Tang Dynasty Symbolizing the Establishment...

had forcefully created a harmonious and flourishing age of Tang Dynasty characterized by "Fa Zhi" (the ruling of law).

7.2.1.3 The Concise and Consistent Provisions

To avoid the complexity and ambiguity of legal provisions in the law of late Sui Dynasty, it was required that legislations be concise and comprehensible for the common people since the reign of Emperor Gaozu in Tang Dynasty. Emperor Gaozu once instructed his ministers who were in charge of the law revision and said that:

> The initial purpose of enacting law is to make people understand its meaning. However, most of the laws passed down from the previous dynasties are ambiguous in meaning, which has provided opportunities for the corrupted judicial officials to change the penalties wantonly by bending the rules. Therefore, laws must be written to be easily understood.[100]

During the reign of Emperor Taizong in Tang Dynasty, the importance of conciseness, simplicity, and the consistency of legal provisions was further emphasized. Emperor Taizong said that:

> The national laws and regulations should be succinct. Moreover, one crime should not possibly be judged according to several legal provisions. If the legal articles are too complicated for the officials to remember, it may cause unfairness and fraud. So provisions for misdemeanor charges would be possibly applied if an official wants to absolve someone from guilt; but provisions for felonies would be also possibly applied if an official wants to incriminate someone.[101]

In *Wu De Lv* (*Wu De Code*) that was enacted by Emperor Gaozu, he ordered Zhangsu Wuji, Fang Xuanling and other officials who were responsible for the law revision "to abolish the miscellaneous and impractical parts by making additions and deletions...."[102] *Zhen Guan Lv* (*Zhen Guan Code*) which was made according to Emperor Taizong's instruction was a legal code characterized by its conciseness, leniency, clarity and accessibility among feudal codes. In addition, in January of the 11th year of Zhenguan (637 A.D.), "more than three thousand provisions of 'Chi' (instruction) were deleted and seven hundred provisions of 'Ge' (injunction) were added"[103] in *Zhen Guan Lv* (*Zhen Guan Code*) which was enacted in the reign of Wude.

After the reign of Emperor Taizong, Li Zhi, Emperor Gaozong, who had shown a welcoming attitude towards the laws made in Zhenguan period, clearly stated in *Ban*

---

[100]"Liu Wen Jing Zhuan" (The Biography of Liu Wenjing) in *Jiu Tang Shu* (*The Old Book of Tang Dynasty*).

[101]"She Ling" (The Decrees of Amnesty) in *Zhen Guan Zheng Yao* (*The Essentials about Politics during the Reign of Zhen Guan*), Vol. 8.

[102]"Xing Fa Zhi" (The Record of the Criminal Law) in *Jiu Tang Shu* (*The Old Book of Tang Dynasty*).

[103]"Xing Fa Zhi" (The Record of the Criminal Law) in *Xin Tang Shu* (*The New Book of Tang Dynasty*).

Xing Xin Lv Zhao (*Decrees of the Enactment of New Code*) in September of the 2nd year of Yonghui that it should be the principle which *Xin Lv* (*The New Legal Code*) should follow "to adopt one unified system, to be concise and to be easier to understand; furthermore, the provisions of the law should be simple but comprehensive."[104] *Yong Hui Lv* (*Yong Hui Code*), as the typical legal code of Tang Dynasty, is highly praised because "it has deleted the miscellaneous provisions of penalties and included the simple and concise provisions."[105]

Emperor Taizong not only required that the laws should be simple and comprehensible, but also stressed that they should be consistent. Thus, he demanded that if any legal provision needs to be changed, it must be done "prudently."[106] He said, "Laws should not be changed frequently, because if they are done so, it would be difficult for the officials to remember the provisions so that different charges would be petitioned for the same crime and that officials would play favoritism and commit irregularities by taking the advantage of their power."[107] He also said that "if 'Zhao' (decree), 'Ling' (decree), 'Ge' (injunction) and 'Shi' (standard) are not consistent, they would cause great confusion, unfairness and fraud." Thus, "laws must be examined and decided for the purpose of a permanent application."[108] Under the guidance of such ideology, "'Lv' (criminal law), 'Ling' (decree), 'Ge' (injunction), and 'Shi' (standard) which were revised by ministers such as Fang Xuanling, etc. had never been changed throughout the whole period of the reigning of Emperor Taizong."[109] Additionally, in *Yong Hui Lv* (*Yong Hui Code*) which was made in the reign of Emperor Gaozong, a strict regulation was made as far as the procedure was concerned. Therefore, it was stipulated that "if any provisions of 'Lv' (criminal law), 'Ling' (decree) and 'Shi' (standard) are not suitable for application, they should be reported to 'Shang Shu Sheng' (The Department of Secretary) for discussion; if they are not reported, the official who has changed the provision without authorization shall be punished by two years of imprisonment."[110]

In the particular social environment after great social turmoil, it was very important to the recovery of economy, to the sustaining of the political stability and to the maintaining of the authority of law to keep the consistency of law, and in fact it had received some effect. From the perspective of summarizing historical experience, Wang Fuzhi, the remarkable thinker in the period of late Ming and early Qing

---

[104]"Da Tang Ji Gong Song" (Ode to Great Achievements of Great Tang) in *Quan Tang Wen* (*Anthology of Essays in Tang Dynasty*), Vol. 1.

[105]"Ci Gong Chen Xi Feng Ci Shi Biao" (Memorial to Emperor about Declining Meritorious Statesman's Succession of the Title of Inspector) in *Quan Tang Wen* (*Anthology of Essays in Tang Dynasty*), Vol. 136.

[106]*Zi Zhi Tong Jian* (*History as a Mirror*), Vol 194.

[107]*Zi Zhi Tong Jian* (*History as a Mirror*), Vol 194.

[108]"She Ling" (The Decrees of Amnesty) in *Zhen Guan Zheng Yao* (*The Essentials about Politics during the Reign of Zhen Guan*), Vol. 8.

[109]"Xing Fa Zhi" (The Record of the Criminal Law) in *Xin Tang Shu* (*The New Book of Tang Dynasty*).

[110]"Zhi Zhi" (The State Office System) in *Tang Lv Shu Yi* (*The Comments on Tang Code*).

Dynasty, had pointed out that "laws were strict and "Jing Tian Zhi" (the "nine squares" system of land ownership in China) was established in the reign of Emperor Taizong."[111] One of the reasons was that the law was relatively consistent.

7.2.1.4 All Criminal Offenses Being Punished According to Law

The consequences of trampling on laws in Sui Dynasty had made Emperor Taizong of Tang Dynasty realize the importance of observing and abiding by law by both officials and civilians. In the 1st year of Zhenguan (627 A.D.), he seriously pointed out that although laws and regulations have been enacted, "they are often violated by some of the officials in and out of the capital, so their behaviors are often against the law."[112] Emperor Taizong, who knew very well about the feudal politics, was aware that "the law is not thoroughly carried out because they are violated by the people from the upper class." Thus, he often exhorted his ministers and said: "I know Emperor Yang of Sui Dynasty has always been suspicious and worried that the people would rebel against him, but he has turned a blind eye to his officials' random violation of law. However, I'm not like him. What I worry most is your violation of law and the unjust, false and erroneous cases which it may bring about."[113] To have all criminals punished according to law, he paid much attention to making officials observe and abide by law. In addition, supervisory organs were set up in the central and local government to be in charge of supervising law enforcement. He said, "Anyone who has served his country heart and soul, no matter whether he is an enemy or friend, shall be rewarded; anyone who has violated the law, no matter whether he is a relative of mine or not, shall be punished."[114] Gao Zengsheng, "Du Fu" (the viceroys and procurators) of Minzhou, should have been punished by death penalty in accordance with law because he had falsely accused Li Jing of rebellion. But considering that he was once Emperor Taizong's old subordinate, some officials suggested that he should be forgiven, yet they were sharply criticized by Emperor Taizong and he said that, "Zengsheng has disobeyed the orders issued by Li Jing, 'Jie Du Shi' (military governor) and then lodged a false accusation against him. If I have pardoned him, how can the law be enforced? From the time when we revolted in Jinyang to the establishment of the empire, there are numerous meritorious statesmen in this country. If Zengsheng is forgiven by what he has done, how can I punish those who break the law in future? It is true that he is a subordinate of mine and he has performed meritorious service and I can never forget all of that, but it is also the reason why I cannot pardon him." Consequently, although he was exempted

---

[111]Wang Fuzhi (Ming Dynasty), *Du Tong Jian Lun* (*Comments on Reading the History as a Mirror*), Vol. 20.

[112]*Ce Fu Yuan Gui* (*The Record of the Great Events*), Vol. 151.

[113]*Wei Zheng Gong Jian Lu* (*Collection of Master Wei Zheng's Expostulation*), Vol. 3.

[114]"Gong Ping" (Impartiality) in *Zhen Guan Zheng Yao* (*The Essentials about Politics during the Reign of Zhen Guan*), Vol. 5.

from the punishment of "Lian Zuo" (being punished for being related to somebody who committed an offense) "still he was punished by 'Liu' (exile) to the border areas."[115] As for the officials who had accepted bribes by bending the law to suit their private interests, they were ordered to "be more severely punished."[116] The King of Jiangxia, the uncle of Emperor Taizong, was also "removed from his office with his fiefs reduced" for "accepting bribes and persecuting other people."[117]

In feudal times, it was a very important condition to maintain the feudal legal system for the officials who were entitled to certain statutory privileges to observe law, and it was especially the key of the problem whether the emperor, who was "the lawmaker himself," could respect, carry out and observe law. During the period of Zhenguan, the successful establishment of feudal legal system was inseparable from the exemplary role that Emperor Taizong had played. For example, in the early period of Tang Dynasty, because some of the appointed officials had faked their qualifications and records of service, a particular decree was issued by Emperor Taizong, in which it was stipulated that if the officials were not willing to voluntarily surrender themselves within the given period, they would be punished by death penalty. Soon the faked documents of a military official named Liu Xiong were discovered in Wenzhou, "so he was punished by "Liu" (exile) in accordance with the law" by Dai Zhou who was "Shao Qing" (the vice president) in "Da Li Si" (The Bureau of Judicial Review). "Emperor Taizong said:

> 'I have issued 'Chi' (instruction) to tell the people that if the offenders have not voluntarily surrendered themselves, they shall be punished by death penalty. Now you have changed the punishment to 'Liu' (exile), which will make people lose faith in me'. Dai Zhou then replied, 'I could do nothing if Your Majesty wants to kill that man immediately. However, the case now is being dealt with by the judicial institution and I dare not violate the law.' The emperor then said, 'You are telling people that you are observing the law, but are you trying to let people lose faith in me?' In reply, Dai Zhou said, 'The law is the publicized regulation of the state, and it is made to win the trust of people. What Your Majesty has said is out of your joy or anger. It is not right if people are killed because Your Majesty is angry. Now if Your Majesty permits the case to be judged in accordance with the law, it will be the right way to restrain Your Majesty's 'little' anger and to win the 'great' trust of the people. But if Your Majesty yields to your own 'little' anger but loses the 'great' trust of people, I will feel sorry for Your Majesty.

Finally, Emperor Taizong was convinced and said, "I am wrong in law enforcement, but I have you who can rectify those mistakes. What else should I worry about?"[118] Another example: after learning that a supervisor named Pei Rengui had enslaved some people as his doormen without permission, Emperor Taizong was angry and ordered to have him punished by death penalty. However, the offense he

---

[115] *Zi Zhi Tong Jian* (*History as a Mirror*), Vol 194.

[116] "Zheng Ti" (The Political System) in *Zhen Guan Zheng Yao* (*The Essentials about Politics during the Reign of Zhen Guan*), Vol. 1.

[117] "Zong Shi Zhuan" (The Biography of Royal Families) in *Jiu Tang Shu* (*The Old Book of Tang Dynasty*).

[118] "Gong Ping" (Impartiality) in *Zhen Guan Zheng Yao* (*The Essentials about Politics during the Reign of Zhen Guan*).

had committed was not as serious as that punishable by death penalty in accordance with the provision of law, because it was stipulated that "if the supervisors enslave the people in their supervisory areas without permission ... they shall be punished for the crime of accepting people's property in their supervisory area." Therefore, "Jian Cha Yu Shi" (the supervisory censor), named Li Qianyou, strongly argued that "the law is made for both Your Majesty and your subjects, but not merely for Your Majesty at all. Today, Rengui has committed a minor crime, but he will be severely punished instead. So I'm afraid that such severe punishment will shock the people and make them bewildered."[119] Finally, Emperor Taizong was convinced, so the order was recalled. Later on, Li Qianyou was even promoted to be "Shi Yu Shi" (subordinate of Grand Censor). The third example: "Du Du" (military viceroys and procurators) of Guangzhou named Dang Renhong was punishable by death penalty according to law, but Emperor Taizong (Li Shemin) exempted him from death penalty in consideration of "his old age and his contribution to his country."[120] However, after that, Emperor Taizong issued an imperial edict of self-criticism and asked "'Tian' (Heaven) to have him punished" for bending the law to practice favoritism for a particular person. He said, "In law enforcement... it is wrong to make people lose faith by my selfishness. Now, I have violated the law by pardoning my associate, Renhong. What I have done has violated 'Tian Li' (heavenly principles). So I ... will hold a ceremony for three days to express my apology for the offense I have committed."[121] In the meanwhile, he had also confessed that he had committed three kinds of crimes:

> I have indulged myself, followed my own inclination and let the evil behaviors of the officials go unchecked, so I have deceived the public, which is the first crime I have perpetrated; I have chosen the officials unwisely so that some corrupted officials have been appointed, which is the second crime I have perpetrated; I have not rewarded the meritorious, nor have I punished the guilty, which is the third crime I have perpetrated.[122]

Emperor Taizong had set a good example for his people, so his stories were widely told and spread by the folks. Consequently, "most officials were well-disciplined, honest, upright and cautious about their behaviors. The families of princes, dukes, princesses and wealthy people, who had regarded the emperor with reverence, all restrained themselves and never dared to ride roughshod over the common people."[123] Besides, the ministers of the imperial court also had the courage to argue with the emperor according to law although he was the embodiment of absolute power. In the 11th year of Zhenguan period (637 A.D.), when Emperor

---

[119]*Zi Zhi Tong Jian* (*History as a Mirror*), Vol. 192.

[120]"Xing Fa Zhi" (The Record of the Criminal Law) in *Xin Tang Shu* (*The New Book of Tang Dynasty*).

[121]*Zi Zhi Tong Jian* (*History as a Mirror*), Vol. 196.

[122]*Ce Fu Yuan Gui* (*The Record of the Great Events*), Vol. 150.

[123]"Zheng Ti" (The Political System) in *Zhen Guan Zheng Yao* (*The Essentials about Politics during the Reign of Zhen Guan*), Vol. 1.

Taizong asked Liu Dewei "why so many people are so severely punished recently," Liu, the minister of "Da Li Si" (The Bureau of Judicial Review), answered that:

> The matters like penalty are determined by Your Majesty, but not by the ministers. If Your Majesty is benevolent, penalties would be lenient; if Your Majesty is mean, the penalties would be severe. ...While at the present, many innocent people are incriminated by erroneous judgments, and those who have been released will be punished more severely if they are discovered again. The reason for officials to apply severe penalties now is that they want to evade their liabilities because they are afraid of being punished, so it is not because they are ordered to do so. If Your Majesty insist on enforcing punishment according to law, this situation will surely be changed.[124]

Wei Zheng then pointed out directly that "if the senior officials are correct, even if orders are not issued, the people will carry them out; if the senior officials are incorrect, even if orders are issued, the people will not obey them."[125] What he said had really reflected the crucial problems in the feudal legal system.

However, the nature of feudal autocracy had decided that it was impossible for the enlightened monarchs to uphold or observe law during the whole period of their reigning, so even Emperor Taizong was not an exception. With the development and prosperity of the imperial government, the emperor had lost his usual ways of doing things, such as being strict with himself or accepting people's criticism open-mindedly, which was shown in Wei Zheng's memorial to the emperor submitted in the 11th year of Zhenguan period (637 A.D.):

> The essential point of giving reward and imposing penalty is to persuade people to do good deeds and to penalize the vicious. Therefore, in penalty enforcement, an emperor should not show the difference of leniency and severity just because people are his close or distant relatives or just because they are in superior or inferior positions. Nowadays the ways of giving reward and enforcing penalties are not the same as before, because they are all determined by officials' likes or dislikes. It all depends on the officials' happiness or anger whether to enforce lenient or severe penalties, so when they are happy, they will wantonly involve their personal happiness in the law enforcement; when they are angry, they will incriminate people with no reason. If the officials like someone, they would vigorously praise that person and it seems that they want to split a bird's skin to show the beauty of its feathers, no matter how deep the feather are in the skin; if those officials dislike someone, they would criticize the person severely and it seems that they want to find out the tiny dirt after it has been washed away. Tiny dirt can be found out, but penalty is abused; the beauty of feathers can be shown, but the reason for awarding is wrong. So the abuse of penalty will promote evil intention of the villains; the wrong rewards will damage the credit of the gentlemen. I have never heard that the order of a country can still be maintained if the wickedness of the mean people is not punished and the good deeds of the gentlemen are not rewarded.[126]

Especially, in the later period of Zhenguan, Emperor Taizong also followed the ways of the feudal emperors to "impose lenient or severe penalties upon people

---

[124] *Zi Zhi Tong Jian* (*History as a Mirror*), Vol. 196.

[125] *Wei Zheng Gong Jian Lu* (*Collection of Master Wei Zheng's Expostulation*), Vol. 5.

[126] "Xing Fa" (The Criminal Law) in *Zhen Guan Zheng Yao* (*The Essentials about Politics during the Reign of Zhen Guan*), Vol. 8.

randomly," which had ruined the legal order established with difficulty in the early period of Tang Dynasty.

In summary, the goal of the guiding ideology of the legislation in the early period of Tang Dynasty was to maintain the legal order and to restrain the unruly acts of the privileged. It was not only the direct consequence of the changes of relationship between different classes after the turbulent days in the later period of Sui Dynasty, but also the general demand of people. Thus, it had a profound social background. The improvement of legal environment had provided a favorable condition for the economic and cultural development, which had led to the emergence of a harmonious society in which "people were obedient" and "peaceful."[127] According to the records in history books:

> When the companies of travelling merchants rested in open fields, they were never bothered by thieves. Besides, prisons were empty; horses and cattle could be seen everywhere in fields; doors were not bolted at night. During the time, there were consecutive years of bumper harvest, so the price of rice was only three or four *qian* for one *dou*. When the companies of travelling merchants traveled on the way from the capital to the Five Ridges, or from Shandong to the seaside, they did not have to carry food for themselves, because all the food was given by people along the way. When arriving at the villages in Shandong, the passages were treated kindly and generously, and they were even given presents before leaving ....[128]

The history of "Zhen Guan Zhi Zhi" (Excellent Governance during the Reign of Zhen Guan) had eloquently proved the relationship between flourishing age and "Fa Zhi" (the ruling of law). As one of the embodiment of feudal "Fa Zhi" (the ruling of law), it was a kind of restriction of power, especially royal power. No doubt, its emergence had its own complex social and political reasons, but it was also inseparable from the emperors' personal character and moral value. Therefore, it can be said that "Fa Zhi" (the ruling of law) in the feudal times was hard-won, rare and unstable.

7.2.2 The Legislative Activities and the Major Legislative Achievements

7.2.2.1 The Making of Legal Codes in the Four Periods of Reigning Represented by *Yong Hui Lv* (*Yong Hui Code*)

The legal system of Tang Dynasty was the advanced form of Chinese feudal legal system and major legislative activities were carried out in the four periods of the reigning by Wude, Zhenguan, Yonghui and Kaiyuan. Even at the time of revolting,

---

[127]"She Zong" (Extravagance and Indulgence) in *Zhen Guan Zheng Yao* (*The Essentials about Politics during the Reign of Zhen Guan*), Vol. 6.
[128]"Zheng Ti" (The Political System) in *Zhen Guan Zhen Yao* (*Essentials about Politics from Zhen Guan Reign*), Vol. 1.

Emperor Gaozu, Li Yuan, had already advocated "abolishing all of the severe penalties of Sui Dynasty." Consequently, all the penalties in "Yue Fa Shi Er Tiao" (twelve-article covenant) were abolished except the death penalty for the crimes of murder, stealing and treason. After the founding of Tang Dynasty, in the 2nd year of Wude, Pei Ji, Liu Wenjing and others were ordered to work with "the knowledgeable scholars of the imperial court" to have the code amended,so finally fifty-three articles of "Ge" (injunction) were made, which had begun the prelude to the legislation of Tang Dynasty. Soon after that, another fifteen officials, including Pei Ji, "Shang Shu Zuo Pu She" (the chief supervisor of other officials), Xiao Yu, "You Pu She" (the deputy supervisor of other officials), Cui Shanwei, "Da Li Si Qing" (equivalent to president of the Supreme Court), and Wang Jingye, "Ji Shi Zhong" (the senior assistant of the emperor and the supervisor of officials) and so on were ordered to draw up a legal code according to the social conditions of the early Tang Dynasty by referring to the codes of Sui Dynasty. In the 7th year of Wude period, *Wu De Lv* (*Wu De Code*) consisting of twelve chapters and five hundred articles was enacted. Additionally, "Wu De Ling" (Orders of Wu De), "Wu De Ge" (Injunctions of Wu De) and "Wu De Shi" (Standards of Wu De), etc. were also made and issued.

After ascending the throne, Emperor Taizong ordered Fang Xuanling and Zhangsu Wuji to begin the revision of Wu *De Lv* (*Wu De Code*). The revision work lasted for ten years (from the 1st year to the 11th year of Zhenguan period) and finally *Zhen Guan Lv* (*Zhen Guan Code*) which consisted of twelve chapters and five hundred articles was completed and enacted. In addition, "about 1,546 decrees were made and categorized as 'Ling' (Orders or Ordinances); the original three thousand 'Chi' (instruction) made since the reign of Wude were reduced to seven hundred and categorized as 'Ge' (Injunction); the regulations for the registration of the offices of 'Shang Shu Sheng' (The Department of Secretary) (including 'Lie Cao': different departments, 'Si': bureau, 'Jian': ancient supervisory office and 'Shi Liu Wei': ancient Chinese imperial guard system) were adopted and categorized as 'Shi' (standard)."[129]

During the reign of Emperor Gaozong, based on the codes of Wude and Zhenguan, *Yong Hui Lv* (*Yong Hui Code*) consisting of twelve chapters and five hundred articles was made by Zhangsun Wuji, "Tai Wei" (the minister of defense), Li Ji, "Si Kong" (the minister of public works), and Yu Zhining, "Zuo Pu She" (the chief supervisor of other officials) and others and was enacted in the 2nd year of Yonghui (651 A.D.). In the next year, considering that "there are no authoritative commentaries on the law and that there are not any standards in the examination of law every year," a decree was issued by Emperor Gaozong to "recruit more annotators to begin the work of law interpretation and to make report to the emperor."[130] So the task was ordered to be undertaken by Zhangsu Wuji, Li Ji, Yu Zhining and

---

[129]"Xing Fa Zhi" (The Record of the Criminal Law) in *Xin Tang Shu* (*The New Book of Tang Dynasty*).
[130]"Xing Fa Zhi" (The Record of the Criminal Law) in *Jiu Tang Shu* (*The Old Book of Tang Dynasty*).

other people. According to the principle of "investigating and collecting the injunctions and imperial mandates and studying and examining the ancient books and records,"[131] annotations were added to each article of *Yong Hui Lv* (*Yong Hui Code*). They not only explained the meaning of the codes and shown the origins of the legal texts, but also provided authoritative explanations to the theoretical principles and concepts. Such unified annotation of the code was called *Lv Shu* (*The Comments on Law*), which was enacted in the 4th year of Yonghui (652 A.D.) after being approved by the emperor. The comments were attached to the end of each legal text and were regarded the same as legal texts, so "they were often used by the judges in analyzing the legal texts."[132] The comments and legal texts were compiled into *Yong Hui Lv Shu* (also named *Tang Lv Shu Yi*) and later was entitled *Tang Lv Shu Yi* (*The Comments on Tang Code*). The making of *Lv Shu* (*The Comments on Law*) not only played an important role in the unified application of law, but also promoted the development of "Lv Xue" (the study of statutory laws). The combination of "Lv" (criminal law) and *Lv Shu* (*The Comments on Law*) had also shown the improvement of legislative technology, so it had exerted great influence on some foreign countries.

After Emperor Gaozong, Empress Wu Zetian ascended the throne. During her reign, two volumes of *Chui Gong Xin Ge* (*New Injunctions in Chui Gong Period*), six volumes of *Chui Gong Liu Si Ge* (*Injunctions for Government Offices in Chui Gong Period*), and thirty volumes of *Chui Gong Shi* (*Standards in Chui Gong Period*) were drafted. It is recorded in "Xing Fa Zhi" (The Record of the Criminal Law) in *Jiu Tang Shu* (*The Old Book of Tang Dynasty*) that "only twenty-four articles of criminal laws and decrees were amended, and the articles which were difficult to be revised remain unchanged."

When it came to the reign of Emperor Xuanzong, the emperor ordered Song Jing, who was "Zai Xiang" (the prime minister) at the time and Lin Fu to carry out the task of the revision of "Lv" (statutes), "Ling" (orders or ordinance), "Ge" (injunction) and "Shi" (standard) and other legal provisions mainly by checking and proofreading *Yong Hui Lv Shu* (also named *Tang Lv Shu Yi*). They also compiled thirty volumes of administrative regulations called *Tang Liu Dian* (*The Six Statutes of Tang Dynasty*).

In short, the legal texts of Tang Dynasty were categorized as "Lv" (criminal law), "Ling" (decree), "Ge" (injunction) and "Shi" (standard). According to the interpretation of *Tang Liu Dian* (*The Six Statutes of Tang Dynasty*), "'Lv' was made for making judgments and enforcing penalties, 'Ling' was made for establishing models and systems, 'Ge' was made for preventing the violation of prohibitions and rectifying the wickedness and 'Shi' was made for establishing standards and procedures." Similar explanation could also be found in "Xing Fa Zhi" (The Record of the Criminal Law) in *Xin Tang Shu* (*The New Book of Tang Dynasty*): "'Ling'

---

[131]"Jin Lv Shu Yi Biao" (A Memorial to Emperor about Commentaries on Law) in *Quan Tang Wen* (*Anthology of Essays in Tang Dynasty*), Vol. 136.

[132]"Xing Fa Zhi" (The Record of the Criminal Law) in *Jiu Tang Shu* (*The Old Book of Tang Dynasty*).

referred to the rules for the superior, the inferior, the noble and the humble and the regulations for the nation; 'Ge' referred to the principles for officials and the government offices and 'Shi' referred to the common law that should be observed. So these three kinds of laws should be followed in the administration of the state, and any offenders, evildoers and criminals should be punished in accordance with these laws." From the explanations in history books, it can be seen that "Lv" referred to the basic criminal legal code. Although *Yong Hui Lv* (*Yong Hui Code*) was basically a criminal code, it had included the provisions of civil, administrative, and procedural law in its structure of "Zhu Fa He Ti" (the integration of various laws). Tang Dynasty was a prosperous age in Chinese feudal times and the science of law in the period had also reached an unprecedented degree, but it was still impossible to make a criminal law in the modern sense because of the overall social development, the level of criminal theory, or the legislative technology at that time. Therefore, it was not strange to find some non-criminal provisions in the code of Tang Dynasty. Thus, even in "*Da Qing Lv Li*" (*The Laws and Precedents of Great Qing*), which was the very last legal code of the feudal times, the mode of "Zhu Fa He Ti" (the integration of various laws) used in *Tang Lv Shu Yi* (*The Comments on Tang Code*) was still retained.

Besides "Lv" (criminal law), "Ling" (decree) referred to the legal regulations of the state organizational system and the activities of administrative management. It covered a larger scope, including "the making of criteria and regulations" and the implementation of financial and economic systems. According to the record in *Tang Liu Dian* (*The Six Statutes of Tang Dynasty*), during the period of Kaiyuan, "twenty-seven collections of 'Ling' (decree) were made."

"Ge" (injunction) referred to the separate orders issued temporarily by the emperor. They were about the official and government routines and they became law and were regarded as "permanent legal provisions" after being collected together. During Tang Dynasty, when there were special events or important cases, emperors always made decisions by issuing "Zhi" (imperial decree) or "Chi" (instruction), but they could not be applied as legal provisions. "If they are wrongly applied to have led to unjust verdicts, the officials in charge shall be punished for the crime of the negligence of their duties."[133] Besides, the "Zhi" (imperial decree) and "Chi" (instruction) could not be used as "Yong Ge" (permanent injunctions) or formal legal provisions until they were sorted out and compiled. In terms of the contents of "Ge" (injunction), besides some criminal ones, the main provisions were administrative, whose target of adjustment was both specific and general. The provisions of "Ge" (injunction) were important supplementary documents to the formal codes. Because the provisions of "Ge" (injunction) were compiled based on the imperial "Zhi" (imperial decree) or "Chi" (instruction), they had achieved great legal effect. When the contents of the provisions of "Ge" (injunction) were in conflict with the law, "Ge" (injunction) would be considered authoritative. From *Wu De Xin Ge* (*The New Injunctions in Wu De Period*) to *Kai*

---

[133]"Duan Yu" (Trials and Punishments) in *Tang Lv Shu Yi* (*The Comments on Tang Code*).

Yuan Ge (*Kai Yuan Injunctions*), a large number of "Ge" (injunction) was enacted in the different periods of the times. For example, just in the period of Kaiyuan, as many as twenty-four chapters of "Ge" (injunction) were the enacted.

"Shi" (standard) referred to the rules of the official documents and the specific activities of the government offices, which had the feature of administrative regulations. From the period of Wude when "Shi" (standard) was drafted to the period of Kaiyuan, altogether thirty-three chapters of "Shi" were made.

7.2.2.2 The Making of *Tang Liu Dian* (*The Six Statutes of Tang Dynasty*)

In the 10th year of Kaiyuan (722 A.D.), a decree was issued by Emperor Xuanzong to order the ministers to begin the revision work of "Zheng Dian" (the statute of administration) made in Tang Dynasty by following model of the six statutes of *Zhou Li* (*The Rites of Zhou Dynasty*). In addition, he wrote the six statutes by himself, including, "Li Dian" (the statute of Confucian classics), "Jiao Dian" (the statute of education), "Li Dian" (the statute of rites), "Zheng Dian" (the statute of administration), "Xing Dian" (the statute of penalty) and "Shi Dian" (the statute of daily affairs) and he ordered the ministers to use them as the outlines of the statute and required that "the contents should be collected and compiled in accordance with the titles."[134] However, Xu Jian, who was in charge of the compilation of the statute "was unable to make up his mind for years," and "he did not even know what to do after thinking it over for years."[135] Later on, Wu Jiong, Yu Xin, Xian Yi, Sun Jiliang, Wei Shu, and others joined in the work of compilation. They "examined the work of the judicial officials in the previous dynasties, "Ling" (decree) and "Shi" (standard) were used to regulate the six bureaus and finally completed the six statutes by following those of Zhou Dynasty." Years later, more people joined in the work. "After many years of hard work and after overcoming many difficulties," the statute was finally completed in the 26th year of Kaiyuan (738 A.D.) and then "it was reported to the emperor and was issued nationwide."[136] In *Tang Liu Dian* (*The Six Statutes of Tang Dynasty*), the following stylistic rules and layout are adopted: "The statutes are made according to official titles; 'Ling' (decree) and 'Shi' (standard) are used to regulate the six bureaus with all the additions and deletions recorded in notes."[137] So accordingly, "the junior officials were headed by the senior officials with each of them in charge of their own affairs." Besides, the administrative regulations were integrated with the relevant administrative departments.

---

[134]"Jing Ji Kao" (A Textual Research of Classic Works) (Part 28) in *Wen Xian Tong Kao* (*A General Textual Research of the Documents*), Vol. 220.

[135]"Zhu Shu" (Works) in *Da Tang Xin Yu* (*New Anecdotes of the Great Tang*), Vol. 9.

[136]"Zhu Shu" (Works) in *Da Tang Xin Yu* (*New Anecdotes of the Great Tang*), Vol. 9.

[137]"Shi Bu" (The Section of History) (Part 35) in *Si Ku Quan Shu Zong Mu Lu Ti Yao* (*Descriptive Catalogue to Si Ku Quan Shu*), Vol. 79.

In *Tang Liu Dian* (*The Six Statutes of Tang Dynasty*), the regulations on the ranks of government officials were used as the outline and the government organs were discussed in different volumes, such as "Zhong Yang San Shi" (three officials in charge of important governmental affairs); "San Gong" (the three councilors); "Liu Bu" (The Six Departments), namely, "Li Bu" (The Department of Personnel), "Hu Bu" (The Department of Revenue), "Li Bu" (The Department of Rites), "Bing Bu" (The Department of Defense), "Xing Bu" (The Department of Punishment) and "Gong Bu" (The Department of Works); the five departments such as "Men Xia Sheng" (the organization in charge of examining the imperial edicts in ancient China), "Zhong Shu Sheng" (the supreme organization in charge of the state affairs), "Mi Shu Sheng" (the central body that specialized in the administration of the national library), "Dian Zhong Sheng" (the organization in charge of palace affairs), "Nei Si Sheng" (the organization in charge of emperor's daily service, and the internal affairs of the court); "Yu Shi Tai"(The Censorate); "Jiu Si" (nine bureaus), such as "Tai Chang" (bureau in charge of sacrificial worship), "Guang Lu" (bureau in charge of banqueting), "Wei Wei" (bureau in charge of emperor's personal safety), "Zong Zheng" (bureau in charge of the royal affairs), "Tai Pu" (bureau in charge of emperor's carriages and horses), "Da Li Si" (The Bureau of Judicial Review), "Hong Lu" (the court of state ceremonial), "Si Nong" (bureau in charge of national treasury), and "Tai Fu" (bureau in charge of national financial affairs); "Wu Jian" (five supervisory offices), such as "Guo Zi Jian" (the highest educational body in ancient China), "Shao Fu Jian" (in charge of the handicraft production and royal affairs), "Jun Qi Jian" (in charge of weaponry), "Jiang Zuo Jian" (in charge of imperial architecture), and "Du Shui Jian" (in charge of irrigation works); "Shi Liu Wei" (ancient Chinese imperial guard system); "Tai Zi Dong Gong Fu Shuai" (Affairs of Crown Prince); "Zhu Wang Gong Zhu Fu Yi" (Affairs of Princes and Dukes); the three local administrative organs, "Fu" (ancient administrative district between province and county), "Du Hu" (military viceroys and procurators), "Zhou" (subprefecture) and "Xian" (county). Besides, in *Tang Liu Dian* (*The Six Statutes of Tang Dynasty*), the duties of ministries and departments, the official ranks, the authorized organization of the governmental offices, the scope of the officials' responsibilities, the basic principles, methods, and procedures of administrative management, the relationship between administrative offices, and the historical continuation and changes of the names of departments, ministries and official titles were also regulated.

Tang Liu Dian (*The Six Statutes of Tang Dynasty*) was a collection of officially revised administrative regulations with the current "Ling" (decree) and "Shi" (standard) as the main contents, so it legal effect came from the current administrative regulations which were included. As a collection of administrative regulation, it did not need to be carried out according to the general legislative process. However, because *Tang Liu Dian* (*The Six Statutes of Tang Dynasty*) was easy to be applied in legal practice by the administrative departments, during the reign of Emperor Xianzhong, Zheng Zeng, who was "Zai Xiang" (the prime minister) at the time suggested that "three or five knowledgeable and reasonable people should be selected from among the officials to carry out the revision work of *Tang Liu Dian* (*The Six Statutes of Tang Dynasty*)" so that it might be issued and implemented.[138]

As a collection of officially revised administrative regulation, *Tang Liu Dian* (*The Six Statutes of Tang Dynasty*) reflected the progress of legislative technology and the value of easy application. This was just the reason why it was possible for *Da Ming Hui Dian* (*Collected Statutes of the Great Ming*) and *Da Qing Hui Dian* (*Collected Statutes of the Great Qing*) which were with nature of administrative statutes to be made and issued in Ming and Qing dynasties based on the *Tang Liu Dian* (*The Six Statutes of Tang Dynasty*).

In summary, in the four famous periods of reigning in the early years of Tang Dynasty, namely, during the reign of Wude, Zhenguan, Yonghui and Kaiyuan, intensive and large scale law revision were carried out to "solve the problems completely, to clarify the ambiguity, to uphold the principles of constitution and to set up examples for later generations."[139] However, among the laws made in those periods, only *Yong Hui Lv Shu* (also named *Tang Lv Shu Yi*) and *Tang Liu Dian* (*The Six Statutes of Tang Dynasty*) were well preserved. Now the existing *Yong Hui Lv Shu* (also named *Tang Lv Shu Yi*) is one of the most representative legal codes made during the feudal times, in which the legal provisions for the protection of feudal states and social norms were elaborated in detail, so it was in conformity with the social and national situation of ancient China. Indeed, it was the most influential legal code in the history of the development of Chinese law. The enactment of *Yong Hui Lv Shu* (also named *Tang Lv Shu Yi*) was not incidental; it was not only the product of the stage of prosperity of Chinese feudal society, but also a summary of the legislative and judicial experience accumulated ever since Qin and Han dynasties and a summary of experience in strengthening the centralized authority after a long-term disruption of the state and the ruling of feudal separatists. In the implementation of *Yong Hui Lv Shu* (also named *Tang Lv Shu Yi*), apart from rectifying the meaning of the words in the articles, more work was done in the compilation of *Ge Hou Chi* (*A Collection of Imperial Instructions*) based on the collections of "Chi" (instruction). For example, in the 7th year of Kaiyuan (729 A.D.), "Shi Zhong" (the assistant official) named Pei Guangting and "Zhong Shu Ling" (head of the secretariat) named Xiao Song "had presented a memorial to the emperor and asked the emperor to order the relevant departments to draft the six volumes of *Ge Hou Chang Xing Chi* (*A Collection of the Most Commonly Used Imperial Instructions*) to be issued in the country."[140] *Ge Hou Chi* (*A Collection of Imperial Instructions*) was a collection of "Chi" (instruction) issued over the years. Before being included in the collection, they were revised according to classifications and categories, and then "were

---

[138]"Dai Zheng Xiang Gong Qing Shan Shi Xing Liu Dian Kai Yuan Li Zhuang" (Zheng Xianggong's Memorial to Emperor about Requiring to Stop the Implementation of Liu Dian and the Rites of Kaiyuan) in *Quan Tang Wen* (*Anthology of Essays in Tang Dynasty*), Vol. 627.

[139]"Xing Fa Zhi" (The Record of the Criminal Law) in *Jiu Tang Shu* (*The Old Book of Tang Dynasty*).

[140]"Xing Fa Zhi" (The Record of the Criminal Law) in *Jiu Tang Shu* (*The Old Book of Tang Dynasty*).

organized in a proper order"[141] with the contradictory and repeated parts deleted. In the 25th year of Kaiyuan (737 A.D.), Li Linfu presented a memorial to the emperor and suggested that "'Chi' (instruction) which is issued before the 30th of May and which is not included in the new 'Ge' (instruction) and 'Shi' (standard) should be applied without time limits."[142] The actual meaning of his memorial was that the new collection of "Chi" (instruction) should take the place of *Ge Hou Chang Xing Chi*" (*A Collection of the Most Commonly Used Imperial Instructions*) which was enacted in the 17th year of Kaiyuan.

7.2.2.3 The Main Legislative Activities in the Middle of Tang Dynasty

After the middle period of Tang Dynasty when the government was gradually losing its power, the collection and compilation "Ge Hou Chi" (*A Collection of Imperial Instructions*) became the main legislative activities to increase the imperial power and meet the emergency. For example, in the 1st year of Zhenyuan during the reign of Emperor Dezong (785 A.D.), the thirty volumes of *Zhen Yuan Ding Ge Hou Chi* (*A Collection of Imperial Instructions in the Period of Zhenyuan*) was completed by "Shang Shu Sheng" (The Department of Secretary); in the 10th year of Yuanhe during the reign of Emperor Xianzong (815 A.D.), Xu Mengrong and others in "Xing Bu" (The Department of Punishment) were ordered to complete thirty volumes of *Kai Yuan Ge Hou Chi* (*A Collection of Imperial Instructions in the Period of Kai Yuan*); in the 13th year of Yuanhe (818 A.D.), Zhen Yuqing and other officials completed thirty volumes of *Yuan He Ge Hou Chi* (*A Collection of Imperial Instructions in the Period of Yuan He*); in the 7th year of Taihe during the reign of Emperor Wenzong (833 A.D.), fifty volumes of *Tai He Ge Hou Chi* (*A Collection of Imperial Instructions in the Period of Yuan He*) was completed by "Xing Bu" (The Department of Punishment); in the 4th year of Kaicheng (839 A.D.), ten volumes of *Kai Cheng Xiang Ding Ge* (*A Collection of Elaborate Imperial Instructions in the Period of Kai Cheng*) was made by Di Jianmo and others in "Xing Bu" (The Department of Punishment); in the 5th year of Dazhong during the reign of Emperor Xuanzong (851 A.D.), Liu Zhuo and other officials were ordered to complete sixty volumes of *Da Zhong Xing Fa Zong Yao Ge Hou Chi* (*A General Collection of Imperial Instructions of Penal Law in the Period of Da Zhong*); in the 7th year of Dazhong (853 A.D.), twelve volumes of *Da Zhong Xing Lv Tong Lei* (*Catalogue of the Penal Law in the Period of Da Zhong*) was completed by an official named Zhang Kui.

As "Chi" (instruction) was the authoritative regulation, the legal effect of "Chi" (instruction) was greater and its scope of application was much broader than that of

---

[141]"Ding Ge Ling" (Making Injunctions and Decrees) in *Tang Hui Yao* (*Collections of Historical Records of Tang Dynasty*).

[142]"Ding Ge Ling" (Making Injunctions and Decrees) in *Tang Hui Yao* (*Collections of Historical Records of Tang Dynasty*).

7.2 The Legal System of Tang Dynasty Symbolizing the Establishment...

"Lv" (criminal law), "Ling" (decree), "Ge" (injunction), and "Shi" (standard). This could be proved by the instructions issued on December 23rd in the 3rd year of Changqing (823 A.D.) recorded in "Duan Yu Lv" (Statutes on Trials and Punishments) in *Song Xing Tong* (*The Penal Code of Song Dynasty*): "'Yu Shi Tai' (The Censorate) presented a memorial to the emperor to require that whenever cases were heard, collections of 'Chi' (instruction) should be consulted and decisions should be made accordingly. If relevant articles could not be found in the collection of 'Chi', the articles in 'Ge' (injunction) and 'Lv' (criminal law) should be applied." In the legal system of the middle period of the Tang Dynasty, more weight was given to "Chi" (instruction) than to "Lv" (criminal law), "Ling" (decree), "Ge" (injunction), and "Shi" (standard). For example, in *Da Zhong Xing Fa Zong Yao Ge Hou Chi* (*A General Collection of Imperial Instructions of Penal Law in the Period of Da Zhong*), altogether 60 volumes of "Chi" (instruction) were collected, among which "the miscellaneous instructions with 646 categories and 2,165 articles made in the 224 years" from June 20th in the 2nd year of Zhenguan period to April 13th day in the 5th year of Dazhong were recorded.[143]

In the 7th year of Dazhong (853 A.D.), "Zuo Wei Shuai Fu Cang Cao Can Jun" (the military staff in charge of warehouses) named Zhang Kui divided the provisions of the legal codes of Tang Dynasty into 121 categories, attached 1250 articles of "Ling" (decree), "Ge" (injunction) and "Shi" (standard) "in similar forms" to the end of legal texts and named it *Xing Lv Tong Lei* (*Collections of Criminal Laws*). Thus, *Xing Lv Tong Lei* (*Collections of Criminal Laws*), which was compiled by the combination of "Lv" (criminal law), "Ling" (decree), "Ge" (injunction), and "Shi" (standard) with "Chi" (instruction), had changed the traditional style of law revision, which were helpful for the judges to refer to and to apply the articles, therefore, after *Xing Lv Tong Lei* (*Collections of Criminal Laws*) was submitted to Emperor Xuanzong, it was approved to be issued nationwide. Historically, *Da Zhong Xing Lv Tong Lei* (*Collections of Criminal Laws in Da Zhong Period*) was the predecessor of *Song Xing Tong* (*The Penal Code of Song Dynasty*) made in Song Dynasty.

In the later period of Tang Dynasty, the great social, economic and political changes caused by "An Shi Zhi Luan" (the Rebellion of An Lushan and Shi Siming) had greatly impacted the existing legal order. Additionally, because the emperors at that time were inclined to stick to the laws made by their ancestors, their ideology was more likely to be conservative; therefore they had lost the courage and the enterprising spirit which their emperors had in the early period of Tang Dynasty. The main legal form of the compilation of "Chi" (instruction) had clearly shown the relaxing of legal principles.

---

[143]"Xing Fa Zhi" (The Record of the Criminal Law) in *Jiu Tang Shu* (*The Old Book of Tang Dynasty*).

7.2.3 The Organic Law of the Administrative Organs and the Official Administration Law

Tang Dynasty had experienced a great development in feudal economy, politics and culture; therefore the laws which it had made on administrative management were so elaborate that it was incomparable in the previous dynasties. The administrative law of Tang Dynasty was composed of "Lv" (criminal law), "Ling" (decree), "Ge" (injunction) and "Shi" (standard). It was recorded in *Tang Liu Dian* (*The Six Statutes of Tang Dynasty*) that the "Ling" (decree) made in the period of Kaiyuan during the reign of Emperor Xuanzong consisted of twenty-seven chapters and thirty volumes: chapter one consisted of two parts and it was about the official ranks; chapter two was about the rules for "San Shi" (three officials in charge of important governmental affairs: "Tai Shi," "Tai Fu" and "Tai Bao"), "San Gong" (the three councilors) and the officials in other departments and offices; chapter three was about the rules for the staff in "Si" (bureau) and "Jian" (ancient supervisory office); chapter four was about the rules for the staff of guards; chapter five was about the rules for the staff of Eastern Palace and royal palaces; chapter six was about the rules for the officials who were in charge of "Zhou" (subprefecture), "Xian" (county), and those guarding strategically important places, mountain and frontier passes and rivers ports; chapter seven was about the rules for the mandated women of emperor and ministers; chapter eight was about the rules for the ancestral halls; chapter nine was about the rules for households; chapter ten was about the rules for the selection and appointment of officials; chapter eleven was about the rules for "Kao Ke" (according to certain standards on the performance of the official assessment to determine its reward and punishment); chapter twelve was about the rules for the security and guards of palace; chapter thirteen was about the rules for military defense; chapter fourteen was about the rules for clothing; chapter fifteen was about the rules for sacrificial ceremonies; chapter sixteen consisted of two parts and it was about the rules for "Lu Bu" (the official system for many largely ceremonial duties of the major state affairs); chapter seventeen consisted of two parts and it was about the rules for "Gong Shi" (Formula); chapter eighteen was about the rules for land; chapter nineteen was about the rules for tax and corvée; chapter twenty was about the rules for warehouses; chapter twenty-one was about the rules for "Jiu Mu" (farming and husbandry); chapter twenty-two was about the rules for "Guan Shi" (border market); chapter twenty-three was about the rules for medicare and illnesses; chapter twenty-four was about the rules for "Yu Guan" (warden); chapter twenty-five was about the rules for "Ying Shan" (construction); chapter twenty-six was about the rules for "Sang Zang" (funeral) and chapter twenty-seven was about the rules for "Za Ling" (miscellaneous orders). There were altogether 1540 articles in *Tang Liu Dian* (*The Six Statutes of Tang Dynasty*). Unfortunately, "Ling" (decree) made in Tang Dynasty was lost in history. In *Tang Ling Shi Yi* (*An Interpretation of the Orders of Tang Dynasty*), the Japanese scholar, Niida Noboru, restored 715 articles of "Ling" (decree) of the Tang Dynasty, which was approximately half of the original ones.

"Ge" (injunction) originated from "Chi" (instruction), the purpose of which was to adjust "the principles of the official and government routines." For this reason, in the twenty-four chapters of *Kai Yuan Ge* (*Kai Yuan Injunctions*) included in *Tang Liu Dian* (*The Six Statutes of Tang Dynasty*), "the names of twenty-four 'Si' (bureau) under 'Shang Shu Sheng' (The Department of Secretary) were used as the titles of the chapters": "Li Bu" (The Department of Personnel), "Si Feng" (The Department of Conferment), "Si Xun" (The Department of Reward), "Kao Gong" (The Department of Performance Evaluation), "Hu Bu" (The Department of Revenue), "Du Zhi" (The Department of Finance), "Jin Bu" (The Department of Currency and Measurement), "Cang Bu" (The Department of Storage), "Li Bu" (The Department of Rites), "Ci Bu" (The Department of Sacrificial Ceremony), "Shan Bu" (The Department of Construction), "Zhu Ke" (The Department of Foreign Affairs), "Bing Bu" (The Department of Defense), "Zhi Fang" (The Department of Geographical Maps), "Jia Bu" (The Department of Carriages), "Ku Bu" (The Department of Weaponry), "Xing Bu" (The Department of Punishment), "Du Guan" (ancient government office in charge of military prisons and penalty), "Bi Bu" (ancient government office in charge of in charge of prison and penalty), "Si Men" (The Department of Customs), "Gong Bu" (The Department of Works), "Tun Tian" (The Department of Fields and Land), "Yu Bu" (The Department of City Management), and "Shui Bu" (The Department of Irrigation). With the development of administrative affairs and consolidation of dictatorial system, it was recorded in history books that numerous "Ge" (injunction) had been compiled, such as "Wu De Xing Ge" (The New Injunctions in Wu De Period), "Zhen Guan Ge" (Zhenguan Injunctions), "Yonghui Ge" (Yong Hui Injunctions), "Chui Gong Ge" (Chui Gong Injunctions), "Shen Long Ge" (Shen Long Injunctions), "Tai Ji Ge" (Tai Ji Injunctions), "Kai Yuan Ge" (Kai Yuan Injunctions), "Zhen Yuan Ge" (Zhen Yuan Injunctions), "Yuan He Ge" (Yuan He Injunctions), "Tai He Ge" (Tai He Injunctions), and "Kai Cheng Ge" (Kai Cheng Injunctions), etc.

Basically, "Ge" (injunction) was the administrative law, and only *Xing Bu Ge* (*Injunctions of the Department of Punishment*) involved the contents of legal norms of penal law. For example, "the behaviors such as sleeping on roadside at night and men and women staying together are forbidden; if this rule is violated, the neighbors of the offenders shall be punishable by 'Tu' (imprisonment) for one year and 'Li Zheng' (head of 'Li': the basic resident organization in ancient China) shall be punished by 'Zhang' (flogging with heavy sticks) for one hundred strokes."[144]

"Shi" (standard) referred to the detailed rules and regulations of the administrative management and the work detail made by central administrative organs. In the twenty-four chapters of *Kai Yuan Ge* (*Kaiyuan Injunctions*) included in *Tang Liu Dian* (*The Six Statutes of Tang Dynasty*), "the names of thirty-three 'Cao'

---

[144]The incomplete manuscript of "Shen Long San Ban Xing Bu Ge" (The Individual Instructions of the Department of Punishment of Shenlong), quoted from Liu Junwen, *Dun Huang Tu Lu Fan Tang Dai Fa Zhi Wen Shu Kao Shi* (*Explanation of the Legal Documents of Tang Dynasty Unearthed from Dunhuang and Turpa*), Zhonghua Book Company, 1989, p. 252.

(department) under 'Shang Shu Sheng' (The Department of Secretary) were used as the titles of the chapters": "Li Bu" (The Department of Personnel), "Si Feng" (The Department of Conferment), "Si Xun" (The Department of Reward), "Kao Gong" (The Department of Performance Evaluation), "Hu Bu" (The Department of Revenue), "Du Zhi" (The Department of Finance), "Jin Bu" (The Department of Currency and Measurement), "Cang Bu" (The Department of Storage), "Li Bu" (The Department of Rites), "Ci Bu" (The Department of Sacrificial Ceremony), "Shan Bu" (The Department of Construction), "Zhu Ke" (The Department of Foreign Affairs), "Bing Bu" (The Department of Defense), "Zhi Fang" (The Department of Geographical Maps), "Jia Bu" (The Department of Carriages), "Ku Bu" (The Department of Weaponry), "Xing Bu" (The Department of Punishment), "Du Guan" (ancient government office in charge of military prisons and penalty), "Bi Bu" (ancient government office in charge of in charge of prison and penalty), "Si Men" (The Department of Customs), "Gong Bu" (The Department of Works), "Tun Tian" (The Department of Fields and Land), "Yu Bu" (The Department of City Management), and "Shui Bu" (The Department of Irrigation), "Mi Shu" (The central body that specialized in the administration of the national library), "Tai Chang" (bureau in charge of sacrificial worship), "Si Nong" (The Department of National Treasury), "Guang Lu" (bureau in charge of banqueting), "Tai Pu" (the department in charge of emperor's carriages and horses), "Tai Fu" (the department in charge of national financial affairs), "Shao Fu" (the department in charge of emperor's income and royal affairs), "Jian Men Su Wei" (the department in charge of gate keeping and palace guarding), and "Ji Zhang" (the department in charge of census registration). Obviously, "Shi" (standard) was the administrative regulation made by the imperial court for the official department, which referred to "the general regulations that officials and departments should observe," but in *Xing Bu Shi* (*Standards of the Department of Punishment*), regulations of penal law were also included.

In summary, the administrative laws of the Tang Dynasty were much elaborated and complete. In addition to the rules for the establishment of the national institutions, the authorized personnel of governmental officials, the regulated jurisdiction of officials, the official ranks and salaries, the relationship between different departments, the selection, appointment, evaluation, punishment and reward, inspection and the retirement of governmental officials, the administrative laws also included the land tax, household registration, tax and corvée, taxation, official purchase of grain, storage, national handicraft, national business, construction works, irrigation, science and technology, education, religion and temple, management of clergymen and the administrative management of the residence areas of national minorities and so on. Therefore, it was unprecedented that the law was made with broad scopes, detailed regulations and norms, elaborate systems and technical methods for legal coordination. It can be said that, as a collection of administrative laws, *Tang Liu Dian* (*The Six Statutes of Tang Dynasty*) had reached the primary level of administrative legal code. Therefore, the national activities and the management of government officials were further included in the tracks of legal system, which had played an important role in the achievement of the great prosperity in the early period of Tang Dynasty. Consequently, it had exerted a great influence not only on the eastern neighboring countries, but also on the western countries far away, because the civil official system in the western countries was believed to be originated from Tang Dynasty.

7.2.3.1 The Management System of the Finalized Autocratic Centralization of Authority

The feudal administrative law was the organic law of governmental departments, so its main task was to establish the system of administrative management of the central and local government.

In the system of national institutions of Tang Dynasty, the emperor was in a supreme dominating position, so he assumed an overall authority. Under the emperor, there were "San Shi" (three officials in charge of important governmental affairs: "Tai Shi," "Tai Fu" and "Tai Bao") and "San Gong" (the three councilors), who assisted the emperor in governing the country as the consultants of the affairs of national defense and administration. They had high official ranks in the government, but did not have real power, nor did they have any offices or subordinates. In this case, their official titles were actually only the honorable titles granted them, as was recorded in *Tang Liu Dian* (*The Six Statutes of Tang Dynasty*) that "'San Shi' (three officials in charge of important governmental affairs: "Tai Shi," "Tai Fu" and "Tai Bao") was in charge of tutoring" and "'San Gong' (the three councilors) was in charge of discussing the doctrines of ruling" but "they were all senior officials just in name only" and "had no real power." In the imperial court, the top level administrative organs which had real power were "San Sheng Liu Bu" (Three Departments and Six Ministries). As early as in Sui Dynasty, a system had been adopted, in which the power was shared by three departments. In other words, "Zhong Shu Sheng" (the supreme organization in charge of the state affairs) was responsible for proposing and drafting all imperial decrees and edicts; "Men Xia Sheng" (the organization in charge of examining the imperial edicts in ancient China) was responsible for reviewing and rejecting the decrees and edicts and "Shang Shu Sheng" (The Department of Secretary) was the executive institution of the imperial government.

In Tang Dynasty, "Zhong Shu Sheng" (the supreme organization in charge of the state affairs) which was headed by "Zhong Shu Ling" (head of the secretariat) was the central and the supreme agency for making policies. "Zhong Shu Sheng" (the supreme organization in charge of the state affairs) was in charge of dealing with the affairs of national defense and administration and handling the memorials and documents presented to the emperor by "Shang Shu Sheng" (The Department of Secretary) and other departments. Moreover, it was responsible for proposing and drafting all imperial decrees and edicts and delivering them to "Men Xia Sheng" (the organization in charge of examining the imperial edicts in ancient China) for reviewing, verifying and implementation. This department was described as "the department that assisted the emperor to handle the national affairs and to rule the country."¹⁴⁵ Because of the important position of "Zhong Shu Sheng" (the supreme organization in charge of the state affairs), its institutional organization was also extended. Under "Zhong Shu Ling" (head of the secretariat), the officials like "Zhong Shu Shi Lang" (Vice Director of Secretariat), "Zhong Shu She Ren" (the official in charge of drafting imperial edicts in "Zhong Shu Sheng"), "You San Ji Chang Shi" (ancient deputy official, assistant attendants of Emperor), "You Bu Que" (ancient deputy official in charge of giving advice to emperor) and "You Shi Yi" (ancient deputy official in charge of picking up what is missing or rectifying mistakes in policy made by emperor), etc. were appointed.

"Men Xia Sheng" (the organization in charge of examining the imperial edicts in ancient China) was an agency for reviewing and verifying the administrative orders issued by "Zhong Shu Sheng" (the supreme organization in charge of the state affairs). The chief official of this department was called "Shi Zhong" (the assistant official) and his position was equivalent to "Zhong Shu Ling" (head of the secretariat). "Men Xia Sheng" (the organization in charge of examining the imperial edicts in ancient China) was authorized to "deal with the state affairs" and was responsible for examining and verifying the imperial decrees and edicts, correcting the errors of imperial court, reviewing the documents that were about to be issued to the junior officials and giving advice to the emperor in make decisions. Therefore, "Men Xia Sheng" (the organization in charge of examining the imperial edicts in ancient China) was like an important adviser to the emperor, so it was described as "the department that assisted the emperor to rule the country."¹⁴⁶ As far as "Men Xia Sheng" (the organization in charge of examining the imperial edicts in ancient China) was concerned, if the decrees and edicts drafted by "Zhong Shu Sheng" (the supreme organization in charge of the state affairs) to be issued to the junior officials were improper for implementation, it had the rights to refuse to accept them. To some extent, such system of rejection and dismissal had balanced the exercise of imperial power and become an important link in the strengthening of the ruling of autocracy, because its purpose was to ensure that the imperial decrees could effectively meet the national needs and serve the national interests. Once emperor Taizong told "Huang Men Shi Lang" (Attendant Official in Palace) Wang Gui that: "the initial purpose of establishing 'Zhong Shu Sheng' (the supreme organization in charge of the state affairs) and 'Men Xia Sheng' (the organization in charge of examining the imperial edicts in ancient China) is to let the two departments supervise each other. 'Zhong Shu Sheng' is in charge of proposing and drafting imperial decrees and edicts, so if there are errors, 'Men Xia Sheng' (the organization in charge of examining the imperial edicts in ancient China) is responsible for rejecting and rectifying those decrees and edicts. Although different people have different views and sometimes it is even difficult for them to exchange their views with each other. So it would be better if they can put forward reasonable and appropriate suggestions, give up their own opinions and accept others' advice

---

¹⁴⁵ *Tang Liu Dian* (*The Six Statutes of Tang Dynasty*), Vol. 9.
¹⁴⁶ *Tang Liu Dian* (*The Six Statutes of Tang Dynasty*), Vol. 8.

when they are having discussion. However, recently, some people tend to conceal their mistakes, so they have grudges against each other and have fomented feelings of estrangement from each other. Even though some of them are aware of their mistakes, they do nothing to correct them or to avoid causing personal resentment. So it is the administration which may bring destruction to a nation to show consideration to one person by bringing great disasters to thousands of people."[147] In "Men Xia Sheng" (the organization in charge of examining the imperial edicts in ancient China), except "Shi Zhong" (the assistant official), the official positions such as "Men Xia Shi Lang" (Attendant Official in Palace), "Ji Shi Zhong" (the senior assistant of the emperor and the supervisor of officials), "Zuo San Ji Chang Shi" (ancient chief official, attendants of Emperor), "Jian Yi Da Fu" (ancient official, in charge of having discussions on national matters), "Zuo Bu Que" (ancient chief official in charge of giving advice to emperor), "Zuo Shi Yi" (ancient chief official in charge of picking up what is missing or rectifying mistakes in policy made by emperor), etc. were established.

"Shang Shu Sheng" (The Department of Secretary) was the supreme administrative agency, and its head was called "Shang Shu Ling" (ancient official equivalent to prime minister). Because the King of Qin (became Emperor Taizong in later years) used to be in the position of "Shang Shu Ling" (ancient official equivalent to prime minister) in the early period of Tang Dynasty, this official title was not conferred upon people any more in later time, but instead "Shang Shu Sheng" (The Department of Secretary) was managed by "Zuo Pu She" (the chief supervisor of other officials) and "You Pu She" (the deputy supervisor of other officials) and under the two officials positions, "Zuo Cheng" (left vice prime minister) and "You Cheng" (right vice prime minister) were installed. The senior officials of "Shang Shu Sheng" (The Department of Secretary) were authorized to deal with the national affairs such as defense and administration, moreover, they were in charge of the execution of the imperial decrees and edicts delivered by "Zhong Shu Sheng" (the supreme organization in charge of the state affairs) and "Men Xia Sheng" (the organization in charge of examining the imperial edicts in ancient China). As national affairs became more complicated, the official organization of "Shang Shu Sheng" (The Department of Secretary) was greatly expanded, and a complete system was formed, so it had become an important governmental institution for performing the state function. Emperor Taizong once said: "'Shang Shu Sheng' (The Department of Secretary) is not only in charge of making the guiding principle for the country but also in charge of hundreds of bureaus in the government. So if a mistake was made, it would bring disaster to all the people in the country."[148]

"Shang Shu Sheng" (The Department of Secretary) was made up of six departments, including "Li Bu" (The Department of Personnel), "Hu Bu" (The Department of Revenue), "Li Bu" (The Department of Rites), "Bing Bu" (The Department of

---

[147] *Zi Zhi Tong Jian* (*History as a Mirror*).Vol. 192.

[148] "Dai Zhou Zhuan" (The Biography of Dai Zhou) in *Jiu Tang Shu* (*The Old Book of Tang Dynasty*).

Defense), "Xing Bu" (The Department of Punishment) and "Gong Bu" (The Department of Works). Moreover, there were four "Si" (bureau) in each department, so altogether there were twenty-four "Si" (bureau). The administrative organizational system of "Liu Bu" (The Six Departments) and twenty-four "Si" (bureau) was continued for more than 1000 years from its establishment in Sui Dynasty to the Ming and Qing dynasties, so it showed that this organization was suitable to the tasks and requirements of the administrative management of feudal state and that it had played an important role. The specific function of "Liu Bu" (The Six Departments) are as follows:

"Li Bu" (The Department of Personnel) was responsible for appointing, dismissing, promoting, demoting, inspecting, evaluating, rewarding and punishing the civil officials in the country. Under "Li Bu" (The Department of Personnel), four "Si" (bureau) were set up, including "Li" (Personnel), "Si Feng" (Conferment), "Si Xun" (Reward), and "Kao Gong" (Performance Evaluation).

"Hu Bu" (The Department of Revenue) was responsible for the household registration, land, taxation, money, agriculture, financial income and expenses of the country. Under "Hu Bu," four "Si" (bureau) were set up, including "Hu Bu" (Revenue), "Du Zhi" (Finance), "Jin Bu" (Currency and Measurement), and "Cang Bu" (Storage).

"Li Bu" (The Department of Rites) was in charge of the ritual ceremonies, sacrifices, "Ke Ju" (the imperial examination), and school education of the country. Under "Li Bu" (The Department of Rites), four "Si" (bureau) were set up, including "Li Bu" (Rites), "Ci Bu" (Sacrificial Ceremony), "Shang Bu" (Sacrificial Instrument), and "Zhu Ke" (Foreign Affairs).

"Bing Bu" (The Department of Defense) was in charge of appointing and dismissing, promoting, demoting, inspecting, evaluating, rewarding and punishing the military officials in the country. Under "Bing Bu" four "Si" (bureau) were set up, including "Bing Bu" (Defense), "Zhi Fang" (Geographical Maps), "Jia Bu" (Carriages), and "Ku Bu" (Weaponry).

"Xing Bu" (The Department of Punishment) was responsible for the judicial and administrative affairs and the hearings of important cases of the country. Under "Xing Bu" (The Department of Punishment), four "Si" (bureau) were set up, including "Xing Bu" (Punishment), "Du Guan" (ancient government office in charge of military prisons and penalty), "Bi Bu" (ancient government office in charge of in charge of prison and penalty), and "Si Men" (Bureau of Customs).

"Gong Bu" (The Department of Works) was responsible for agriculture, forestry, water conservancy, construction projects and the management of craftsmen. Under "Gong Bu" (Works), four "Si" (bureau) were set up, including "Tun Tian" (Wasteland Opened up by Garrison Troops or Peasants), "Yu Bu" (City Management), and "Shui Bu" (Irrigation).

In "Liu Bu" (The Six Departments), "Shang Shu" (the minister) and "Shi Lang" (vice minister) were the head and deputy of the department respectively. In each bureau, "Lang Zhong" was the head and "Yuan Wai Lang" (deputy head of a subministry department) was the deputy, and staff were recruited in each bureau to deal with the concrete affairs.

7.2 The Legal System of Tang Dynasty Symbolizing the Establishment...

After the establishment of "Liu Bu" (The Six Departments), the system of "Zhu Qing" (ministers: "Jiu Qing": the nine high-rank officials in ancient times or "Lie Qing") which was set up since the period of Warring States and Qin and Han dynasties was still retained, but its power was reduced so that the ministers of the bureaus had just become the chief stewards of the departments.

In summary, the system of "San Sheng" (The Three Departments) has the following characteristics:

The function and power of "San Sheng" (The Three Departments) and their relationship of sharing out the work and cooperating with one another were further systematized and legalized.

Before Tang Dynasty, although the system of "San Sheng" (The Three Departments) had been set up, the division of the responsibilities of each department was not clearly drawn and the three departments were not well-organized. Until the Tang Dynasty, the responsibilities for each department were clearly defined. During this period, on the one hand, "San Sheng" (The Three Departments) had the rights to jointly participate in the administration and discussion of state affairs and they were actually the central institution under the emperor which were in charge of "governing all the officials and administering the state affairs"; on the other hand, to reinforce the administrative management of the country, a relationship of sharing out the work and cooperating with one another was set up in the system. In other words, "Zhong Shu Sheng" (the supreme organization in charge of the state affairs) was responsible for proposing and drafting all imperial decrees and edicts, "Men Xia Sheng" (the organization in charge of examining the imperial edicts in ancient China) was responsible for reviewing and rejecting the decrees and edicts and "Shang Shu Sheng" (The Department of Secretary) was responsible for implementing the decisions made by the imperial government.

The heads of the three departments shared the power of "Zai Xiang" (the prime minister).

After the Qin and Han dynasties, the agency of "Zai Xiang" (the prime minister) was divided into three parts, which not only promoted the governing efficiency of each department, divided and weakened the power of "Zai Xiang" (the prime minister), but also strengthened the monarchical power. In the feudal political history, the competition for power by the monarchs and "Zai Xiang" (the prime minister) was sometimes fiercer and sometimes more peaceful, but it was the major conflict existing among the ruling class.

After "Zhong Shu Ling" (head of the secretariat) and "Men Xia Shi Zhong" (head of "Men Xia Sheng") were both officially acknowledged as "Zai Xiang" (the prime minister), because of their different responsibilities, disputes sometimes arose between them so that the exchanging of documents between the two departments were often delayed and the administrative efficiency were greatly affected. For this reason, a government organization system was set up, in which the chief official of "Zhong Shu Sheng" (the supreme organization in charge of the state affairs) and "Men Xia Sheng" (the organization in charge of examining the imperial edicts in ancient China), could jointly participated in the discussion of the state affairs. In "Zhi Guan" (State Officials) (Part 4) in *Wen Xian Tong Kao* (*A General Textual Research of the Documents*) (volume 50), there were the following records: "'Zheng Shi Tang' (The Chamber of Meeting) was initially established for 'Zhong Shu Sheng' (the supreme organization in charge of the state affairs) to propose and draft imperial decrees and edicts and 'Men Xia Sheng' (the organization in charge of examining the imperial edicts in ancient China), to review and check the decrees and edicts, but the two departments always had disputes; therefore, 'Zhong Shu Sheng' (the supreme organization in charge of the state affairs) and 'Men Xia Sheng' (the organization in charge of examining the imperial edicts in ancient China) were ordered to have a discussion together and to make decisions in 'Zheng Shi Tang' (The Chamber of Meeting) and to present a memorial to the emperor afterward." "Zheng Shi Tang" (The Chamber of Meeting) was initially set up in "Men Xia Sheng" (the organization in charge of examining the imperial edicts in ancient China), but in the middle period of the Tang Dynasty, it was moved to 'Zhong Shu Sheng' (the supreme organization in charge of the state affairs) because of the greater power possessed by "Zhong Shu Ling" (head of the secretariat). In the 11th year of Kaiyuan (723 A.D.), an official seal engraved with "Zhong Shu Men Xia" (the supreme state organization) was made, which meant that "Zhong Shu Sheng" (the supreme organization in charge of the state affairs) became a joint official organization of "Zai Xiang" (the prime minister). Because "Zhong Shu" (the prime minister) and "Men Xia" (the official in charge of examining the imperial edicts in ancient China) were working together, the reviewing procedures of "Men Xia Sheng" (the organization in charge of examining the imperial edicts in ancient China) were usually completed during the joint discussion.

In the early period of Tang Dynasty, the post of the minister of "San Sheng" (The Three Departments) was not installed intentionally just because the emperors thought that its power was too great. Therefore, the department affairs were all managed by the deputies and other officials. For example, during the reign of Emperor Taizong, Du Yan took part in the administration and management of the state affairs with the title of "Li Bu Shang Shu" (the minister of the Department of Personnel) and Wei Zheng did so with the title of "Mi Shu Jian" (the official in charge of the national collection and compilation work). After the period of Emperor Gaozong, the officials who were permitted to discuss state affairs in "Zheng Shi Tang" (The Chamber of Meeting) were entitled to "Tong Zhong Shu Men Xia San Pin" (an official title in ancient China), [it was changed to "Er Pin" (the second rank) in the later period] or "Tong Zhong Shu Men Xia Ping Zhang Shi" (an official title in ancient China), who were both referred to as "Zai Xiang" (the prime minister) to undertake due responsibilities. For this reason, in Tang Dynasty, usually four or five officials, even more than ten officials at most, were given the title of "Zai Xiang" (the prime minister) to undertake due responsibilities, which was helpful in unifying the ideology of the bureaucrats in ruling the country, strengthening the management of the state, balancing the power of "Zai Xiang" (the prime minister) from each other and preventing them from grabbing all the power; which at the same time was also helpful for the emperor to dismiss them or to change their position at any moment when he thought it necessary.

7.2 The Legal System of Tang Dynasty Symbolizing the Establishment...

Among those "Zai Xiang" (the prime minister) who discussed state affairs in "Zheng Shi Tang" (The Chamber of Meeting), the one who chaired the meetings was referred to as "Zhi Zheng Shi Bi" or "Zhi Bi." It was this person who was responsible to sort out the resolutions of meeting, compiled them into imperial commands and decrees and presented them to emperor to be approved and delivered to "Shang Shu Sheng" (The Department of Secretary) for implementation. During the period of Kaiyuan, Li Linfu and Yang Guozhong were "Zai Xiang" (the prime minister), but they had usurped the position of "Zhi Zheng Shi Bi" and grabbed the power for a long time. For this reason, when Emperor Xiaozong ascended the throne, a decree was issued in the 2nd year of Zhide and it was ordered that "'Zai Xiang' (the prime minister) should take turns to hold the post of 'Zhi Zheng Shi Bi', and every "Zai Xiang" (the prime minister) should hold the post for only ten days." During the reign of Emperor Dezong, on May 8th in the 10th year of Zhenyuan (794 A.D.), a decree was issued that "every 'Zai Xiang' (the prime minister) should hold the post of 'Zhi Bi' for only one day"[149] and that five offices, namely, "Li" (personnel), "Shu Ji" (the confidential departments or positions of the central government), "Bing" (defense), "Hu" (Revenue) and "Xing" (punishment), should be set up "to be in charge of the affairs in each bureau."[150] It can be imagined how important the position of "Zheng Shi Tang" (The Chamber of Meeting) was, because all the fundamental policies were made by it.

In Tang Dynasty, the further division of the power of "Zai Xiang" (the prime minister) was reflected by the establishment of "Han Lin Yuan" (The Hanlin Academy) in the middle period. At the beginning, "Han Lin Yuan" (The Hanlin Academy) was set up in the imperial palace and it was composed of intellectuals who just acted as imperial consultants without involving any political affairs. In the period of Emperor Gaozong, the post of "Han Lin Dai Zhao" (members of the Hanlin Academy providing service to the Emperor) was set up to be in charge of drafting imperial decrees and edicts. In the 26th year of Kaiyuan (738 A.D.), Emperor Xuanzong ordered that "Han Lin Xue Shi Yuan" (Hanlin Academic Institute) be set up to be in charge of drafting "Nei Ming" (imperial orders), including the secrete decrees and edicts such as "appointing or dismissing generals and prime ministers and issuing orders for a punitive expedition."[151] Hence, the scholars of "Han Lin Xue Shi Yuan" (Hanlin Academic Institute) were referred to as "Nei Xiang" (Imperial Chancellor). The scholars of "Han Lin Xue Shi Yuan" (Hanlin Academic Institute) were private secretaries of the emperor and they were appointed by the emperor randomly, so the number was not fixed. To the reign of Emperor Xianzong, "Han Lin Xue Shi Cheng Zhi" (Chief Imperial Scholar) was set

---

[149]"Zhong Shu Ling" (Head of the Secretariat) in *Tang Hui Yao* (*Collections of Historical Records of Tang Dynasty*), Vol. 51.

[150]"Bai Guan Zhi" (The Record of the Officials of all Ranks) in *Xin Tang Shu* (*The New Book of Tang Dynasty*) (Book 1).

[151]"Bai Guan Zhi" (The Record of the Officials of all Ranks) in *Xin Tang Shu* (*The New Book of Tang Dynasty*) (Book 1).

up for the scholars of "Han Lin Xue Shi Yuan" (Hanlin Academic Institute) to be in charge of drafting imperial decrees and edicts according to emperor's will. In this sense, it had become a very important post in "Han Lin Xue Shi Yuan" (Han Lin Academic Institute). The establishment "Han Lin Xue Shi Yuan" (Han Lin Academic Institute) and the transferring of confidential power had demonstrated the strengthening of the monarchical power and the division of the power of "Zai Xiang" (the prime minister).

In the 1st year of Yongtai (765 A.D.) during the reign of Emperor Daizong, the post of "Nei Shu Mi Shi" (official in charge of the affairs of the court) exclusively held by eunuchs was set up to be in charge of the confidential memorials to the emperor and delivering imperial decrees and edicts. Those eunuch officials not only participated in the administration and management of the state affairs, but also held military power. Therefore, this official post provided a favorable condition for the eunuchs to seize the power of the imperial court in the later period of Tang Dynasty, which had also further divided the power of "Zai Xiang" (the prime minister).

In Tang Dynasty, other departments were also set up by the central government, such as "Jiu Si" (nine bureaus) and "Wu Jian" (five supervisory offices) and so on, to be in charge of administrative affairs. "Jiu Si" (nine bureaus) included "Tai Chang" (bureau in charge of sacrificial worship), "Guang Lu" (bureau in charge of banqueting), "Wei Wei" (bureau in charge of emperor's personal safety), "Zong Zheng" (bureau in charge of the royal affairs), "Tai Pu" (bureau in charge of emperor's carriages and horses), "Da Li" (The Bureau of Judicial Review), "Hong Lu" (the court of state ceremonial), "Si Nong" (bureau in charge of national treasury) and "Tai Fu" (bureau in charge of national financial affairs). "Jiu Si" (nine bureaus) originated from "Jiu Qing" (the nine high-rank officials in ancient times) in the Qin and Han dynasties, but during the Northern Qi Dynasty, "Qing" was changed to "Si" (bureau) and in Sui and Tang dynasties the old system of Northern Qi Dynasty was succeeded. However, after the establishment of the system of "Liu Bu" (The Six Departments), the position of "Jiu Si" (nine bureaus) in the imperial court of Tang Dynasty became lower than that in the Qin and Han dynasties and "Jiu Si" (nine bureaus) was assigned to be in charge of specific affairs, just as was recorded that "'Sheng' (the departments) was responsible for managing all officials and 'Si' (bureau) was responsible for the specific affairs."[152] In "Jiu Si" (nine bureaus), "Qing" referred to the chief officials and "Shao Qing" (the vice president) referred to the deputies.

As far as "Wu Jian" (five supervisory offices) was concerned, the first one was "Guo Zi Jian" (the highest educational body in ancient China), which was responsible for the affairs of school education. Among the feudal government institutions, it was from Sui Dynasty that special institutions were set up for the management of school education, and it was called "Guo Zi Si" (the highest educational body in ancient China), but in Tang Dynasty, "Si" was changed to "Jian." The establishment

---

[152]"Yang Mu Zhuan" (The Biography of Yang Mu) in *Xin Tang Shu* (*The New Book of Tang Dynasty*).

of "Guo Zi Jian" (the highest educational body in ancient China) reflected that the feudal government had attached great importance to the cultivation of talents; the second one was "Shao Fu Jian" (in charge of the handicraft production and royal affairs), which was responsible for the handicraft production of the state and the palace; the third one was "Jiang Zuo Jian" (in charge of imperial architecture), which was responsible for the construction of palaces, imperial temples, cities, and governmental offices; the fourth one was "Jun Qi Jian" (in charge of weaponry), which was responsible for the making of weapons. After Han Dynasty, the production of weapons was managed by "Kao Gong" (The Department of Performance Evaluation) and "Shang Fang" (government office in charge of making utensils used by emperor) under "Shao Fu Jian" (in charge of the handicraft production and royal affairs). When it came to Tang Dynasty, to adapt to the large scale expedition, the two institutions were expanded and combined to become an independent department to be in charge of military production. The fifth one was "Du Shui Jian" (in charge of irrigation works), which was responsible for managing water conservancy, shipping and navigation, embankment and the building of bridges. Although they had no formal affiliation with the system of "Liu Bu" (The Six Departments), the institution of "Jiu Si" (nine bureaus) and "Wu Jian" (five supervisory offices) actually became the subordinate institutions of "Shang Shu Sheng" (The Department of Secretary), just because it was hard to divide the scope of responsibilities between them.

As to the local government, the system of Sui Dynasty was followed in Tang dynasty, and the local government was divided into two levels, namely, "Zhou" (subprefecture) and "Xian" (county). During the reign of Emperor Xuanzong, "Zhou" (subprefecture) was changed to "Jun" (shire), but soon after it was changed back to "Zhou" (subprefecture). In "Zhou" (subprefecture), the chief official (the chief official was named "Tai Shou" when "Jun" was used) was called "Ci Shi" (a supervisor assigned by the central government to a local area). "Zhou" (subprefecture) where the capital or "Pei Du" (the second capital) was located was referred to as "Fu" (ancient administrative district between province and county) and the chief official was called "Fu Yin." As "Zhou" (subprefecture) was the most important level of local administration, Emperor Taizong attached much attention to the selection of "Ci Shi" (a supervisor assigned by the central government to a local area). According to his view, "nothing is more important than the post of 'Ci Shi' (a supervisor assigned by the central government to a local area), because it is fundamental to personnel management."[153] He even copied the names of "Ci Shi" (a supervisor assigned by the central government to a local area) on his screen for him to "read when he is sitting or lying down" to make it convenient for him to award or punish them according to their achievements.[154]

---

[153]"Xun Li Zhuan" (The Biography of Excellent Officials) in *Xin Tang Shu* (*The New Book of Tang Dynasty*).

[154]"Ze Guan" (The Selection of Officials) in *Zhen Guan Zheng Yao* (*The Essentials about Politics during the Reign of Zhen Guan*), Vol. 1.

Under "Zhou" (subprefecture) "Xian" (county) was set up, and the chief of "Xian" (county) was referred to as "Xian Ling" (county magistrate). The chief officials and important officials of "Zhou" (subprefecture) and "Xian" (county) were appointed or dismissed by the central government in the Tang Dynasty, which showed an important development of the autocratic centralization of the authority. Additionally, at the same time, it was clearly stated that special merits and heroic actions, good harvests or crop failure, the increase and decrease of households, tax and corvée, the numbers of thieves and brigands were all employed as the standard to assess the work of local officials by "Li Bu" (The Department of Personnel).

During the reign of Emperor Taizong, to strengthen the control over the local government, the whole country was divided into ten "Dao" (the administration district below the province) (it was changed into fifteen in later period) as supervisory areas, and "Xun An Shi" (official assigned to supervise the local officials) were appointed temporarily by Emperor Taizong to inspect the officials of "Zhou" (subprefecture) and "Xian" (county) in each "Dao" (the administration district below the province). Sometimes "Xun An Shi" (official assigned to supervise the local officials) was also referred to as "Cai Fang Chu Zhi Shi," which was later changed into "Guan Cha Shi." Additionally, other official posts such as "Ying Tian Shi" (official in charge of opening up wasteland and agriculture), "Zhuan Yun Shi" (official in charge of transportation), and "Zu Yong Shi" (official in charge of the country's tax administration) and so on were also set up to be in charge of financial and economic affairs. Gradually, "Dao" (the administration district below the province) became a government institution whose level was higher than that of "Zhou" (subprefecture).

In the early period of Tang Dynasty, military areas were designated in "Zhou" (subprefecture) which was located in the border regions, and "Zong Guan" (The General Governor) was set up to prevent the aliens from invading the country and to suppress the subjugated people of all nationalities in the Northwestern regions. Later on, the military areas were expanded to "Du Du Fu" (Offices of Military Affairs), and the governor was referred to as "Du Du" (military viceroys and procurators) to be in charge of the military affairs of several "Zhou" (subprefecture) with his subordinate staff similar to those of "Zhou" (subprefecture). Among "Du Du" (military viceroys and procurators), some governors had the word "Da" (great) before their titles, which meant that they belonged to "Qin Wang Yao Ling" (princes who only had the official titles but never worked in office), so their actual affairs were taken care of by other senior officials in the relevant departments. During the reign of Emperor Gaozong, the governors with the title of "Shi Chi Jie" were referred to as "Jie Du Shi" (military governor). During the reign of Emperor Huizong, "Jie Du Shi" (military governor) was specially set up to be charge of the military affairs of several "Zhou" (subprefecture) without interfering with the administrative affairs. In the middle period of Kaiyuan, in the towns of Shuofang, Longyou, Hedong, and Hexi, "Jie Du Shi" (military governor) was also set up. Because several "Zhou" (subprefecture) consisted of one town, "Zhou Ci Shi" (feudal provincial or prefectural governor) became the subordinate of "Jie Du Shi" (military governor). As "Jie

7.2 The Legal System of Tang Dynasty Symbolizing the Establishment...

Du Shi" (military governor) had the titles of "Jing Guan" (the official in the capital) and "Yu Shi Da Fu" (Grand Censor) and he also had the mission of "An Cha" (judicial commission), "An Fu" (dispatched by the central government to deal with local affairs) and "Du Zhi" (finance), etc., he could control the military, civil administration, financial, and supervisory affairs, so that he had a higher position and carried greater responsibilities and the institutions under his control were also expanded. After "An Shi Zhi Luan" (the Rebellion of An Lushan and Shi Siming), the title of "Jie Du Shi" (military governor) was given to most of the meritorious generals and the post was also set up inland to be in charge of three or four or even more than ten "Zhou" (subprefecture), so the officials holding the post of "Jie Du Shi" (military governor) gradually turned into separatist forces who had not only land but also people, army and financial revenue.

Under "Xian" (county), the grassroots administrative organization like "Xiang" (townships) and "Li" (a basic resident organization consisting of five neighborhoods) were set up. "one hundred households form one 'Li' (a basic resident organization consisting of five neighborhoods), and five 'Li' form one 'Xiang' (townships)." Within the capital, "Pei Du" (the second capital), "Zhou" (subprefecture) and "Xian" (county), "the downtown areas were divided into 'Fang' (lanes), and the suburban areas were divided into 'Cun' (villages)."[155] Obviously, the administrative structures of urban and suburban areas were different, which meant that "Cun" (village) was used as an unit in rural areas and "Fang" (neighborhood) was used as an unit in urban areas. "Xiang Zhang" (chief official in townships) was set up in "Xiang" (townships), "Li Zheng" (head of "Li": the basic resident organization in ancient China) was set up in "Li" and "Cun Zheng" (chief official in village) was set up in "Cun" (villages). Additionally, compact organizations like "Lin Bao" were set up for neighbors to keep a lookout for each other. According to the statistics kept in the 1st year of Tianbao (742 A.D.), there were 16,829 "Xiang" (townships) in the country.[156] "Li Zheng" (head of "Li": the basic resident organization in ancient China) and "Cun Zheng" (chief official in village) (according to the law on equalization of field) referred to the officials at the grassroots level who were responsible for collecting and distributing land, supervising and inspecting farming and sericulture, collecting tax, allocating military service and corvée, etc.

As to "Fang" (neighborhood), taking the residential and commercial areas in Chang'an city for example, the areas were divided into one hundred and ten "Fang" (neighborhood). The affairs within "Fang" (neighborhood) and the keys to the gates of "Fang" (neighborhood) were all controlled by "Fang Zheng" (chief official of neighborhood).

In Tang Dynasty, the system of "Yi" (courier station) was set up to strengthen the link between the central and local government. Along the communication lines, one

---

[155]"Zhi Guan Zhi" (The Record of State Officials) in *Jiu Tang Shu* (*The Old Book of Tang Dynasty*).
[156]"Xuan Zong Ji" (The Record of Emperor Xuanzong) in *Jiu Tang Shu* (*The Old Book of Tang Dynasty*) (Book 2).

"Yi" (courier station) was set up for every thirty *li*. After the middle period, there were one thousand two hundred and ninety-seven "Yi" (courier station) on land, two hundred and sixty "Yi" (courier station) along riverside and eighty-six dual-purpose "Yi" (courier station) in the country, and in each "Yi" (courier station) there were buildings and post-horses. The post-horses were used when issuing important imperial decrees from the capital Chang'an to other places or delivering urgent documents to the capital. Before sending courier solders, the relevant institution should give a clear indication of the days that the courier may need on the way on the tally in accordance with the degrees of the urgency of the documents. If the couriers delayed the mission and failed to arrive at the destination within the prescribed time limit, they would be punished according to the days they delayed or according to the degrees of urgency of the documents. It can be seen from such regulations that the administrative law was elaborate and the contact between the central and local government was strengthened.

7.2.3.2 The Law on Official Management Adaptable to the Needs of Bureaucratic Politics

7.2.3.2.1 (1) The Establishment of the Civil Official Examination System

According to "Xuan Ju Zhi" (The Record of Election) in *Xin Tang Shu* (*The New Book of Tang Dynasty*):

> Generally speaking, in Tang Dynasty, the system of 'Ke Ju' (the imperial examination) of Sui Dynasty was followed, but specifically, it mainly included three aspects: the students who took the examination from schools were called 'Sheng Tu'; the students who took the examination from 'Zhou' (subprefecture) and 'Xian' (county) were called 'Xiang Gong'; moreover, it would be determined by the officials in certain department whether all of them could pass the examination. The subjects of the examination included 'Xiu Cai' (one of the subjects of selecting officials in ancient China), 'Ming Jing' (Confucian classics studies), 'Jun Shi' (those who entered 'Tai Xue': The Imperial College), 'Jin Shi' (the most difficult examination in the imperial examination: usually Confucian classics and poetry would be examined), 'Ming Fa' (law), 'Ming Zi' (calligraphy), 'Ming Suan' (natural science), 'Yi Shi' (history), 'San Shi' (referring to *The Records of the Grand Historian*, *The History of Han Dynasty* and *The History of Latter Han Dynasty*), 'Kaiyuan Li'(Rites in Kaiyuan Period), 'Dao Ju' (referring to *Lao Zi, Wen Zi, Lie Zi, Zhuang Zi*), and 'Tong Zi' (the examination for children). The examination of the subjects of Confucian classics included 'Wu Jing' (Five Classics), 'San Jing' (Three Classics or New Interpretation of Three Classics), 'Er Jing' (Two Classics: the classics of Confucianism and Buddhism), and 'Xue Jiu Yi Jing' (learning one classics thoroughly). Other subjects of the examination also included 'San Li' (three rites), 'San Zhuan' (three biographies) and 'Shi Ke' (history). These were the ordinary subjects examined annually. The examination that was conducted according to imperial decrees was called 'Zhi Ju' (an examination subject set up temporarily), which was held for selecting special talents.

Clearly, there were two kinds of systems for "Ke Ju" (the imperial examination) in Tang Dynasty, namely, "Chang Xuan" (ordinary examination) and "Zhi Ju" (an examination subject set up temporarily). "Chang Xuan" (ordinary examination) was held every year, and the people who took the examination were mostly students from "Guo Zi Jian" (the highest educational body in ancient China), "Zhou" (subprefecture) and "Xian" (county) who registered for examination voluntarily. If they had passed "Chang Xuan" (ordinary examination), they would be recommended by "Zhou" (subprefecture) and "Xian" (county) where they came from to take "Sheng Shi" (provincial examination) held by "Li Bu" (The Department of Rites) in "Shang Shu Sheng" (The Department of Secretary). The date and subjects of "Zhi Ke" (an examination subject set up temporarily) that was held to select special talents according to imperial decrees were decided temporarily. The people who took the exam should be examined to see whether they were virtuous and honest, whether they could give advice to the emperor honestly, whether they could organize and write articles excellently, whether they had a good knowledge of Confucian classics, whether they could put what they had learned from those classics into practice or whether they were far-sighted in military strategies, etc. The people who passed these examinations would be granted high-ranking positions with high salaries, so it was a means of recruiting the so-called special talents in Tang Dynasty. However, it was not considered to be a right way to achieve success to pass the examination of "Zhi Ke" (an examination subject set up temporarily). For example, among the eight brothers of Zhang Gui, seven had the background of "Jin Shi" (those who passed the imperial examination at the national level in ancient China), but only one had the background of "Zhi Ke," thus he was viewed as a "freak." Among the subjects of "Chang Xuan" (ordinary examination), "Ming Jing" (Confucian classics studies) and "Jin Shi" (the most difficult examination in the imperial examination: usually Confucian classics and poetry would be examined) were the most popular, and "Jin Shi" was especially so, because the passing of the examination was regarded as the most important identity to enter the official circles. Therefore, the passing of "Jin Shi" (the most difficult examination in the imperial examination: usually Confucian classics and poetry would be examined) was described as "an entrance ticket to the Dragon's Gate," as was described in the saying that "it is too late for one to pass 'Ming Jing' (Confucian classics studies) in his 30s but it is too early for one to pass 'Jin Shi' in his 50s."

In Tang Dynasty, if one had passed all the examinations, it meant that he was only qualified for being an official, but it did not mean that he would be granted an official title immediately. Besides, he should take "Quan Shi" (selection examination) held by "Li Bu" (The Department of Personnel). If he had passed this examination, he would be granted an official title; otherwise, it would be the only way to have the chance to be appointed as an official to be a senior official's advisor. The well-known litterateur Han Yu was such a case in point. After he passed the examination of "Jin Shi" (the most difficult examination in the imperial examination: usually Confucian classics and poetry would be examined), he failed the examination of "Sheng Shi" (provincial examination) for three times. Thus, he finally went into politics after he had served as a military commissioner's advisor.

According to "Xuan Ju" (Election) (Part 3) in *Tong Dian* (*The General Codes*), there were four requirements for "Quan Shi" (selection examination) held by "Li Bu" (The Department of Personnel):

The selected officials shall meet four requirements: first, health, so those who are healthy and strong shall be selected; second, language, so those who have clear enunciation and who are eloquent shall be selected; third, calligraphy, so those who can write with beautiful strokes in calligraphy shall be selected; fourth, the ability of analytical judgment, so those who can argue reasonably and who are coherent in their arguments shall be selected. Among those who meet the four requirements, the virtuous ones will be given priority in the selection; among the virtuous people, the talented ones will be given priority in the selection; among the talented people, the ones who have made more merits and accomplishments will be given priority in the selection.

And also in *Gu Jin Tu Shu Ji Cheng* (*A Complete Collection of Ancient and Modern Books*), it was recorded that:

> Among the four requirements for the candidates examined by 'Li Bu' (The Department of Personnel), the ability of analytical judgment is most strictly demanded, because it is most important in dealing with political affairs and governing people, meanwhile, it can also show whether the officials have a good master of the knowledge of the world, whether they are expert at law, whether they are able to tell the right from the wrong or whether they are able to discover the hidden trouble.[157]

Since after passing the examination held by "Li Bu" (The Department of Personnel), the candidates would become formally appointed officials, this examination was also referred to as "Shi He Shi," which meant that the candidates would take off their coarse cotton garments and put on official uniforms.

The officials below "Liu Pin" (the sixth rank) should also take exams regularly, and they would be appointed according to their scores in the examination, their virtue, talent, merits and accomplishments. Then they would be reported to "Zhong Shu Sheng" (the supreme organization in charge of the state affairs) and "Men Xia Sheng" (the organization in charge of examining the imperial edicts in ancient China) for reviewing. Finally, their appointment would be decided by the emperor. The appointment of judicial officials was jointly discussed and decided by "Li Bu" (The Department of Personnel) and "Xing Bu Shang Shu" (the minister of the Department of Punishment) and then was reported to the relevant offices.

During the reign of Wu Zetian, to expand the class foundation of the government and to make an utmost effort to select supporters from the middle and lower landlords, the system of "Ke Ju" (the imperial examination) was further developed. Wu Zetian once ordered that the officials of low ranks and the common people could all take the imperial examination, and she also created "Dian Shi" (the final imperial examination) that was presided by her. In February of the 1st year of Zaichu, "the candidates were examined by the Empress in Luo Cheng Palace for several days, which had initiated the examination of candidates in palace."[158] In addition, the examination of military subjects were also added, and those who passed the examination would be granted military titles. In Tang Dynasty, the subjects of "Ke Ju" (the imperial examination) were very complicated, but the main subjects, namely,

---

[157]"Quan Heng Dian" (Law on Official Selection) in *Gu Jin Tu Shu Ji Cheng* (*A Complete Collection of Ancient and Modern Books*), Vol. 22.
[158]"Xuan Ju" (Election) (Part 3) in *Tong Dian* (*The General Codes*), Vol. 15.

the subject of "Tie Jing" (the recitation of ancient classics) in 'Ming Jing' (Confucian classics studies) and the subject of "Shi Fu" (poetry and rhymed prose) in "Jin Shi" (the most difficult examination in the imperial examination: usually Confucian classics and poetry would be examined) were the most important, that was why there were so many poets in Tang Dynasty.

The further systematization and legalization of selecting officials through "Ke Ju" (the imperial examination) were inseparable from the economic and political development. After the implementation of "Jun Tian Zhi" (The System of Land Equalization), the economic situation of landlords was obviously improved, and the number of middle and lower landlords also increased greatly. Thus, those people claimed to share the political power to protect the economic interests and to strengthen their political positions. Besides, the ruling classes also hoped to select more talents through "Ke Ju" (the imperial examination) so that the positions of the national institutions could be filled, the power of centralization of authority could be strengthened and vitality would be restored in bureaucratic politics. Therefore, the implementation of the system of "Ke Ju" (the imperial examination) had not only paved the way for the middle and small landlords to share political power but also helped to recruited some "Shi Da Fu" (literati and officials) with the background of "Han Su" (lower class), such as Ma Zhou, Sun Fujia, Zhang Xuansu, and others in the reign of Emperor Taizong. All those people had held important posts in the imperial court and Li Yifu was even promoted to "Zai Xiang" (the prime minister) through "Ke Ju" (the imperial examination), although "no one had an official rank in his family."

Since Tang Dynasty, most of the officials were promoted according to the "essays" which they had written. "Shi Da Fu" (literati and officials) of the feudal times held the political power through "Ke Ju" (the imperial examination), which further reduced the power of the gentry and the powerful and influential families so that the power of selecting and appointing officials was tightly controlled by the central government and that a special relationship was formed between the imperial government and "Shi Da Fu" (literati and officials). In this way, attending school, taking imperial examination and being appointed as an official was closely connected, which had become an effective method to win over the feudal "Shi Da Fu" (literati and officials). When Emperor Taizong "secretly went to the Gate of Duan of his palace" one day and saw "Jin Shi" (those who passed the imperial examination at the national level in ancient China) who were newly-selected in the imperial examination filing out of the Gate, he was greatly pleased and said, "The talents in this country are all held in the palm of my hands."[159] As Confucian classics were used as the criteria of "Ke Ju" (the imperial examination), the knowledge of Confucian classics not only became a stepping-stone to success, but also was used as a very important means to maintain the dictatorial control over ideology. The system of selecting officials through "Ke Ju" (the imperial examination) was continued all the way from Sui and Tang dynasties to Qing dynasty.

---

[159]Wang Dingbao, *Tang Zhi Yan* (*Collected Stories from Tang Dynasty*), Vol. 1.

Compared with the selection system of "Jiu Pin Zhong Zheng Zhi" (The Nine Rank System, an important election system in Wei, Jin, Southern and Northern Dynasty), the system of "Ke Ju" (the imperial examination) was more "democratic," because in this system all the common people were given the chance to pursue their own scholarly honor and official ranks through the examination. However, the wealthy and privileged class could still be selected and appointed without following the normal routines, but the common people could not afford much money and time to read books and take examinations. Therefore, the system of "Ke Ju" (the imperial examination) had opened up the way for "Shi Da Fu" (literati and officials) to obtain political power and adjusted the power distribution among all social stratums within the ruling classes.

In Tang Dynasty, schools began to boom because of the demand of the cultivation of the bureaucratic reserve forces and the implementation of the system of "Ke Ju" (the imperial examination). During the reign of Emperor Xuanzong, the laws on education and school system were both included in *Tang Liu Dian* (*The Six Statutes of Tang Dynasty*).

In addition, much attention was attached to law in Tang Dynasty, so accordingly, the subject of "Ming Fa" (law) was included in "Ke Ju" (the imperial examination), which was one of the compulsory subjects that ought to be examined. The contents of the examination included "Lv Ba Tiao" (eight provisions of the statutes) and "Ling San Tiao" (three provisions of ordinances). Moreover, the course of "Lv Xue" (the study of statutory laws) was set up in "Guo Zi Jian" (the highest educational body in ancient China) and it became one of the six studies specially set for legal education. Compared with the subjects of "Ming Jing" (Confucian classics studies) and "Jin Shi" (the most difficult examination in the imperial examination: usually Confucian classics and poetry would be examined), the subject of "Ming Fa" (law) was next in importance, which had fully reflected the guiding ideology of regarding "De" (virtue) and "Li" (rites) as "Ben" (the essence) and "Xing Fa" (criminal punishment) as "Yong" (application).

Apart from selecting officials through "Ke Ju" (the imperial examination), the officials above "Wu Pin" (the fifth rank) in the capital and the local officials below "Ci Shi" (a supervisor assigned by the central government to a local area) all had the responsibility to recommend talents. But the officials would be punished if "they do not make recommendation as is required" or "recommend someone who should not be recommended." Besides, special process was stipulated for selecting professional officials. For example, the judicial officials should not be appointed until they were jointly discussed and decided by "Li Bu" (The Department of Personnel) and "Xing Bu Shang Shu" (the minister of the department of punishment).

7.2.3.2.2 (2) The Procedure and Standard for Civil Official Assessment

In Tang Dynasty, the system of assessment was strictly carried out and the contents and procedures of the assessment were all improved to increase the administrative efficiency and to enroll competent officials. "Kao Gong Si" (Bureau of Performance

7.2 The Legal System of Tang Dynasty Symbolizing the Establishment...

Evaluation) in "Li Bu" (The Department of Personnel) took charge of the civil official assessment. It was recorded in *Tang Liu Dian* (*The Six Statutes of Tang Dynasty*) that "'Lang Zhong' (head of a subministry department) and 'Yuan Wai Lang' (deputy head of a subministry department or an honorary title) in 'Kao Gong Si' (Bureau of Performance Evaluation) are charge of civil and military official assessment inside and outside of imperial court."[160] However, the officials assessed by "Li Bu" (The Department of Personnel) were only the ones below "Si Pin" (the fourth rank), because the officials above "San Pin" (the third rank) were assessed by the emperor himself, as was described in the record that "the promotion of officials is not determined solely by 'You Si' (official)."[161] In terms of the period of assessment, a quiz was usually held every year, which was called "Sui Ke" and which was presided over by the directors of the bureau or the senior officials of "Zhou" (subprefecture). The final assessment was taken every four years, which was called "Ding Ke."

The criterion for the official assessment in Tang Dynasty was standardized, and a method called "Si Shan Er Shi Qi Zui" (the criteria for official assessment in Tang Dynasty) was used. The so-called "Si Shan" (the four excellent moral standards) referred to "'De Yi' (virtue and righteousness), 'Qing Sheng' (honesty and prudence), 'Gong Ping' (impartiality), 'Qin Ge' (diligence and hard working)"; the so-called "Er Shi Qi Zui" (Twenty-seven Best Behaviors: specific criteria in terms of competence) includes the following aspects: the best for close attendants: to present the good, to get rid of the bad and to make up for the things left out; the best for the bureau of personnel: to evaluate the candidates impartially and to recruit the talents; the best for the officials of evaluation: to praise the honest, to criticize the dishonest and to pass appropriate judgment on others; the best for judicial officials: to make timely and proper judgments in accordance with Confucian classics; the best for judges: to handle the affairs in a decisive manner and to settle the cases impartially; the best for supervisors: to make thorough investigation and to impeach properly; the best for military generals and commanders: to award and punish strictly and to be victorious in war, etc. After the assessment, the scores of the officials were given according to three levels [including "Shang" (excellent) "Zhong" (average) and "Xia" (poor)] with nine degrees that were set as criteria. For example, those who had four kinds of excellent moral quality and more than one best behavior would be given a score of "Shang Shang" (the most excellent); those who had three kinds of excellent moral quality and more than one best behavior would be given a score of "Shang Zhong" (very excellent); those who had two kinds of excellent moral quality and more than one best behavior would be given a score of "Shang Xia" (not very excellent), those who had no excellent moral quality but two best behaviors would be give a score of "Zhong Shang" (above the average); those who had no excellent moral quality but one good behavior would be give a score of "Zhong Zhong"

---

[160]"Shang Shu Li Bu" (The Minister of the Department of Personnel) in *Tang Liu Dian* (*The Six Statutes of Tang Dynasty*), Vol. 2.

[161]"Li Bo Zhuan" (The Biography of Li Bo) in *Xin Tang Shu* (*The New Book of Tang Dynasty*).

(average); those who did not work carefully and had neither excellent moral quality nor best behaviors would be give a score of "Zhong Xia" (below the average); those who showed their likes and dislikes unrestrainedly and made decisions unreasonably would be given a score of "Xia Shang" (not very poor); those who went against public interests, played favoritism to get private interests and did not fulfill their responsibilities properly would be give a score of "Xia Zhong" (very poor); those who made false charges against others and had fraudulent conducts would be given a score of "Xia Xia" (the poorest).[162]

As to the assessment of local officials, in addition to "Si Shan Er Shi Qi Zui" (the criteria for official assessment in Tang Dynasty), the specific contents of official assessment also included the increase or decrease of households, the cultivation of land and the harvest of crops.

As to the government staff, they were divided into four degrees in the assessment:

> Those who are honest, diligent and conscientious and who hear the cases impartially will be given a score of 'Shang' (excellent); those who is painstaking with their work and handle affairs impartially will be given a score of 'Zhong' (average); those who are lazy and had misconducts will be given a score of 'Xia' (poor); those who go against public interests and obtain private gains by playing favoritism and those who proved to be corrupted by evidence will be give a score of 'Xia Xia' (the poorest).[163]

Meanwhile, a rewarding system that was relevant to the assessment was set up. To guarantee the quality of the officials and the staff, the imperial government of Tang required that "the number of the officials who are assessed should be limited, so if they do not have merits, they should not be assessed to make up the number."[164] According to regulation, higher salary would be rewarded to those who were considered qualified in the annual assessment, but the salary of those unqualified would be reduced; at the same time, those qualified in the final assessment would be promoted to higher ranks, but those unqualified officials would be demoted, or even be removed from their offices or punished. If an official was once demoted because of his misconducts, but he made greater achievements in his later official career and performed well in his assessment, he still had the chance to be promoted. According to "Kao Ke Ling" (Edicts of Assessments), the officials who had a score of "Zhong Shang" (above the average) or above in their assessment would be rewarded with higher salaries, the officials who had a score of "Zhong Zhong" (average) in their assessment would not be rewarded and that the officials who had a score of "Zhong Xia" (below the average) or lower in their assessment would be "punished by having their salaries reduced."

---

[162]"Zhi Guan Zhi" (The Record of State Officials) in *Jiu Tang Shu* (*The Old Book of Tang Dynasty*) (Book 2).

[163]"Shang Shu Li Bu" (The Minister of the Department of Personnel) in *Tang Liu Dian* (*The Six Statutes of Tang Dynasty*), Vol. 2.

[164]"Zhi Guan Zhi" (The Record of State Officials) in *Jiu Tang Shu* (*The Old Book of Tang Dynasty*) (Book 2).

7.2 The Legal System of Tang Dynasty Symbolizing the Establishment...

In Tang Dynasty, not only laws were made on the assessment, for a long period the assessment was conducted according law. For example, during the reign of Emperor Gaozong, when the King of Teng named Yuan Yin was the "Ci Shi" (a supervisor assigned by the central government to a local area) of Quanzhou, he was given a score of "Xia Xia" (the poorest) in his assessment because of his poor performance. Therefore, if the judges in charge of assessment had acted wrongly out of personal consideration and "did not give the right scores according to the real performance of the officials," they would be punished for the crime of "recommending the wrong person," but the punishment would be reduced by one level. As the most reverent person, the emperor often wrote the comments for the senior ministers or conducted the assessment of the senior ministers by himself, so the emperor was the real chief examiner of the assessment. The following comment was written by Emperor Xuanzong for Zhang Shuo who was "Zhong Shu Ling" (head of the secretariat) at that time:

> You can scrupulously abide by the moral principles, and I have heard that you often give honest, frank and sincere advice and your admonishment was strategic and well-planned. So accordingly, government decrees have to be revised for your suggestion and books and manuscripts have to be checked or proofread for your opinion. You have both great talents and reputation, so you shall be highly praised and promoted. Your performance in this assessment is 'Zhong Shang' (above the average).[165]

However, after "Tian Bao Zhi Luan" (Tian Bao Rebellion), the country was on the decline, which had led to great chaos in politics, therefore, the official assessment just became a matter of formality.

In the early period of Zhenguan, it was regulated that "all official who are seventy years old shall retire voluntarily. The retirement of those whose official ranks are above 'Wu Pin' (the 5th rank) shall be reported to His Majesty and the retirement of those whose official ranks are below 'Liu Pin' (the 6th rank) shall be reported to the apartment which they belong to, and then be reported to His Majesty." It was also stipulated that "those who have not reached the age of retirement but who look old shall also retire voluntarily."[166] The officials who have reached the age of retirement could apply in person first, which was called "Qi Hai Gu," and the process of the approval their retirement was different for different people with official ranks. For example, the retirement of those whose official ranks were above "Wu Pin" (the 5th rank) should be reported to the emperor; those whose official ranks were above "Wu Pin" (the 5th rank) should be reported to the emperor for approval by "Shang Shu Sheng" (The Department of Secretary). Because of economic prosperity and political stability, the treatment for the officials who reached the age of retirement was improved and the political and economic treatment were separately provided. In the 2nd year of Zhenguan (628 A.D.) it was stipulated that the civil and military officials who reached the age of retirement could still attend to imperial court but

---

[165]"Zhang Shuo Zhuan" (The Biography of Zhang Shuo) in *Jiu Tang Shu* (*The Old Book of Tang Dynasty*).
[166]"Zhi Guan" (State Officials) in *Tong Dian* (*The General Codes*), Vol. 33.

their positions were "higher than the current officials with the same rank" to show the honors granted them. Those officials were also permitted to attend "Chao Shuo Wang" (only attend to the imperial court on the 1st and the 15th day of the lunar month). When officials retired, they had the privilege to take "Gong Cheng" (public carriage) to go back to their hometown to show the solemnity of their retirement. In the 3rd year of Tianbao (744 A.D.), when "Tai Zi Bin Ke" (an senior official in the crown prince palace, ranking in the third grade) named He Zhizhang retired and returned to his hometown, Emperor Xuanzong attended his farewell dinner in person and even wrote a poem for him as a farewell gift. The emperor also ordered his six ministers and other hundreds of officials to hold farewell dinner at Qingmen Gate of Chang'an and hoped that this would become a common practice.

With respect to the economic treatment of the retired officials, "Zai Xiang" (the prime minister) was offered the full salary. For example, Fang Xuanling and Song Jing were specially permitted to be given the full salary by the emperor. The officials above "Wu Pin" (the fifth rank) could have half of their salary and "the salary would be paid to them until after they died." Those who were meritorious could also have the full salary with the approval of the emperor. Besides, the salary was calculated according to the amount of grain, and sometimes the officials were also granted silk or monthly salary by the emperor. The officials in the capital lower than "Liu Pin" (the sixth rank) or the officials of local government would be granted "Yong Ye Tian" (family farmland) to live out their lives in retirement. The retired officials, no matter whether in their hometown or in other "Zhou" (subprefecture), could receive their salaries paid in grain at the places where they lived according to the order of the imperial government.

After the middle period of Tang Dynasty, because of political corruption and the reluctance of the officials to give up their official posts, it was impossible to implement the system of "Zhi Shi" (retirement) according to law. Bai Juyi wrote a poem entitled "Bu Zhi Shi" (Not Obeying the Retirement System) collected in *Qin Zhong Yin* (*Verses in Qin*), which was a true description of the official circles:

> Officials should retire when they are seventy years old, which is prescribed in law, but why those people who are greedy for high positions and great wealth have turned a deaf ear to this? Those poor old people are already eighty or ninety years old and they have lost their teeth and do not have good eyesight. Even though the periods of time which they have in future are as short as the time of morning dews, they are still hankering after fame and wealth; even though their lives are as weak as the dim light before dusk, they are still worrying about the fortune of their descendants, so even though they have reached age of retirement, they could not take their eyes of the decorations on their official hats. They should have returned their carriages to the government, but they are reluctant to part with their red wheels; they are so old that they cannot stand straight to hold the gold badges on their waists, but they still work in office with their stooped shoulders. Who would not have a strong desire for high positions and great wealth? Who would not want to be bestowed upon by His Majesty? They should retire when they are old and they should be removed from their posts after they have achieved success and won reputation. When they were young, they used to mock at the aged people who were reluctant to retire, but when they are old, they just follow suit. There were two sages named Shu (Su Guang and Su Shou) in Han Dynasty who had voluntarily retired. So how wise and sagacious they are! Now the East Gate is in solitude

7.2 The Legal System of Tang Dynasty Symbolizing the Establishment... 541

because no one wants to follow them to go through it (it is the gate the two sages go through when they resign from office and go back to their native town).

In addition to the retirement of officials, their holidays were also regulated and it was stipulated in *Jia Ning Ling* (*Order for Holidays*) that the officials could have one day off every ten days, which was called "Xun Jia"; the other holidays for "Zhong Qiu" (Medium-Autumn), "Qi Xi" (the seventh day of the July), "Chong Yang" (the ninth day of the September), "Dong Zhi" (The Winter Solstice) were called "Jie Ling Jia" (festive holidays); the days they asked for leave because of illness or other business were called "Shi Gu Jia" and the days off for weddings and funerals were called "Hun Sang Jia"(holidays for wedding or funeral). Besides, time limits were also regulated for holidays, so the offenders who overstayed their leave would be punished by having their salaries reduced; if any officials had repeatedly asked for leave for more than one hundred days, they would be removed from the office.

7.2.3.2.3 (3) The Establishment of the Independent Supervisory System

In Tang Dynasty when autocratic centralization of authority was apparently strengthened, the supervisory system was established as an independent system, by which an elaborate network which covered almost all activities of the country was formed.

"Yu Shi Tai" (The Censorate) was the central supervisory institution, which consisted of one "Yu Shi Da Fu" (Grand Censor) who acted as the chief official and two "Yu Shi Zhong Cheng" (Grand Censor) who acted as the assistants to "be in charge of issuing imperial edicts about the legal provisions of the country and rectifying the orders of imperial court"[167] and "the evil doings of the officials according to law."[168] The inspectors had the rights to impeach officials, to hear the trials, to inspect the ritual ceremonies, to give advice to officials and to present memorials to the emperor, so they were very important officials in the imperial court and were often called "the eyes and ears of the emperor." It was recorded in "Zhi Guan" (State Officials) in *Wen Xian Tong Kao* (*A General Textual Research of the Documents*) (Book 7) that "from Zhenguan period, the country was ruled by law, so the position of judicial official was very important and the position of 'Yu Shi' (the censor) was especially important." In "Ci Shi Xian Ling Zhao" (Imperial Decree for Governors and the Magistrate of County) in *Chi Yu Shi* (*The Reorganization of Censors*), Emperor Xuanzong had once stated that "'Yu Shi' (the censor) is in charge of the supervision of law enforcement, which is important to the social order of the state."[169] Emperor Ruizong once also said, "It was what 'Yu Shi' (the censor) should do to encourage the good, to punish the evil, to praise the honest and to crack down

---

[167] *Tang Liu Dian* (*The Six Statutes of Tang Dynasty*), Vol. 13.

[168] "Bai Guan Zhi" (The Record of the Officials of all Ranks) in *Xin Tang Shu* (*The New Book of Tang Dynasty*) (Book 1).

[169] *Quan Tang Wen* (*Anthology of Essays in Tang Dynasty*), Vol. 29.

on the corruption. So 'Yu Shi' (the censor) is responsible for getting rid of the political chaos."[170]

Under "Yu Shi Tai" (The Censorate), other institutions, such as "Tai Yuan," "Dian Yuan" and "Cha Yuan" were established. In "Tai Yuan" there were six "Zhi Shu Shi Yu Shi" (official in charge of impeaching the other officials in central government), who was in charge of handling the cases which were transferred by other departments according to the orders of the Emperor and making final decisions on miscellaneous affairs. "Shi Yu Shi" (subordinate of Grand Censor) carried special weight because he had greater power and responsibilities and his rank was the highest among all "Yu Shi" (the censor). "Shi Yu Shi" was directly appointed by the emperor or was appointed by "Li Bu" (The Department of Personnel) after being approved by "Zai Xiang" (the prime minister) or "Yu Shi Da Fu" (Grand Censor).

In "Dian Yuan," there were four "Dian Zhong Shi Yu Shi" (the attendant censor in palace); in "Cha Yuan," there were fifteen "Jian Cha Yu Shi" (the supervisory censor), three of whom were responsible for "Liu Bu" (The Six Departments). It was recorded in history books that "they were responsible for inspecting the six departments of 'Shang Shu' (The Department of Secretary) and rectifying the wrong doings,"[171] which was called "Bu Cha" (the inspections by departments). The other twelve censors were responsible for making inspection tours to local "Zhou" (subprefecture) and "Xian" (county). In Tang Dynasty, the inspection areas were divided into "Dao" (the administration district below the province), so the inspection of these areas was called "Dao Cha" (circuit inspection), which was either carried out temporarily by "Jian Chan Yu Shi" (the supervisory censor) who was appointed by "Cha Yuan" and who was somehow like a special envoy sent according to imperial order or was carried out regularly. Although "Jian Chan Yu Shi" (the supervisory censor) in "Yu Shi Tai" (The Censorate) had a lower official rank (under the eighth rank), they could impeach other officials directly to the emperor without needing to be approved by the senior officials of "Yu Shi Tai" (The Censorate). In the 8th year of Zhenguan period, *Qian Shi Xun Xing Tian Xia Zhao* (*Imperial Decree of Sending Inspectors to Inspect the Country*) was issued and it was stated that:

> It is to let people know my concern to send inspectors to make inspection tours to the country. The inspectors shall investigate the weal and woe of the people, observe the gain and loss of the customs and inspect the malpractice of penal and administrative institutions on their way. The people who are old, who show filial obedience, who work hard on their farm land, or the people whose husbands are righteous or whose wives are virtuous shall all be praised and awarded financially; the people who are disabled or who have become widows or widowers shall be given the goods from state warehouse; the inspectors shall inquire about the specially gifted people who have not been recruited by the government, and inquire about the hermits and sages and intelligent people who are now engaged in humble business. So, the inspectors shall visit all of the people and treat them with special courtesy and they shall try their best to do their work as if I am visiting them in person.[172]

---

[170] *Quan Tang Wen* (*Anthology of Essays in Tang Dynasty*), Vol. 19.

[171] *Tang Liu Dian* (*The Six Statutes of Tang Dynasty*), Vol. 13.

[172] *Quan Tang Wen* (*Anthology of Essays in Tang Dynasty*), Vol. 5.

7.2 The Legal System of Tang Dynasty Symbolizing the Establishment...

In February of the 2nd year of Shenlong (706 A.D.), an imperial command was issued:

> Twenty officials should be chosen to inspect ten 'Dao' (the administration district below the province) with a two-year work shift in order to ensure a fair and honest administration of 'Zhou' (subprefecture). They should inspect the officials and rectify their misconduct, console the common people, discuss legal cases, execute lenient punishments and help those in difficulties with the goods stored in warehouses. If they can put forward their views frankly and make reports according to facts without caring about the powerful and influential people, or if they are compassionate and benevolent and can manage official promotion and demotion properly, they shall not only be specially praised and promoted, but also shall be treated as outstanding talents. However, if they curry favor with the powerful by flattering or sailing with the wind, or if they are overcautious and indecisive, or if they attach themselves to people in power, they shall all be demoted, or removed from their positions, or punished according to law.[173]

In August of the 8th year of Kaiyuan (720 A.D.), when Emperor Xuanzong sent "Yu Shi Da Fu" (Grand Censor) named Wang Deng to conduct an inspection tour of "Dao" (the administration district below the province) in the country, he said that "in the inspection area, some senior officials are corrupt and troublesome, so they hear cases unjustly so that people's grievance is never to be redressed; they are timid and weak in character; although they receive salary from government, they never fulfill their responsibilities. Moreover, they are harsh and cruel to other officials. Now I hope the inspectors could have a thorough investigation of the lawsuits filed by others, rectify the malpractice and make judgments by complying with regulations so that the accused can be brought to justice. Reports should be made to me then."[174]

Sometimes "Yu Shi Zhuan Cha" (censor commissioners) was sent to handle the special matters. For example, in July of the 4th year of Kaiyuan (716 A.D.), when inspectors were making the tour of inspection to "Dao" (the administration district below the province), they focused on the judicial inspection and it was recorded that "if the prisoners in the country have grievances, they shall be handled by 'Da Li Si' (The Bureau of Judicial Review) and the inspectors sent by the central government. If there are testimonies for the offenses, or if the offenses are less serious than those punishable by 'Liu' (exile), or if the offenses do not involve the violation of 'Ming Jiao' (Confucian ethical code) or if the offenses do not involve the taking and receiving of bribery from junior officials, those involved shall be punished by 'Shou Shu' (to atone for one's crime with money) one level lighter; if there are no testimonies, but they are suspected of the offenses less serious than those punishable by 'Zhang' (flogging with heavy sticks), they shall be released."[175] During the reign of Taihe, "Yu Shi" (the censor) was specially sent to inspect rice price because of the high prices caused by natural disasters.

---

[173]"An Cha" (On Judicial Commission) (Part 1) in *Tang Da Zhao Ling Ji* (*Collected Grand Edicts and Decrees of Tang Dynasty*), Vol. 130.

[174]"An Cha" (On Judicial Commission) (Part 2) in *Tang Da Zhao Ling Ji* (*Collected Grand Edicts and Decrees of Tang Dynasty*), Vol. 140.

[175]*Quan Tang Wen* (*Anthology of Essays in Tang Dynasty*), Vol. 5.

When "Yu Shi" (the censor) was sent to make tours of inspection, especially when the special envoy was sent out to conduct inspection, their activities were all under the control of the emperor, which can be found in the records of history books: "When the inspectors make tours of inspection, they inspect all kinds of matters. No matter how important or trivial the things are, they shall be reported to the emperor when they return to the imperial court. What they have done has helped the emperors to have a thorough and comprehensive mastery of the situation."[176] This was the reason why "Yu Shi" (the censor) had great power though they had low ranks. The inspection of "Yu Shi" (the censor) had helped to portray the emperor as a monarch who showed great care to the common people's suffering, at the same time, it had also helped to solve the problems in official management and strengthened the autocratic system.

During the early period of Tang Dynasty when the imperial government tried to establish the legal order, the importance of handling political affairs according to law was emphasized. In *Jiu He Wei Lv Xing Shi Zhao* (*The Imperial Decree on the Impeachment of the Violations of Law*), Emperor Taizong said, "From today forward, any official who violates the law shall be impeached by the institutions where he works and shall be reported to me without delay."[177] Initially, the officials were impeached by "Jian Cha Yu Shi" (the supervisory censor) according to "Liu Tiao Wen Shi" (the six articles for handling matters). During the reign of Wu Zetian, the forty-eight legal provisions which were used in inspecting "Zhou" (subprefecture) and "Xian" (county) under the imperial order were revised by "Shang Shu Shi Lang" (the deputy minister of the department of secretary) Wei Fangzhi, as was recorded that "forty-eight provisions were applied to inspect the 'Zhou' (subprefecture) and 'Xian' (county)."[178] After being applied for ten years, the provisions were abolished because of the difficulties in implementation caused by the complicated contents. In the period of Kaiyuan in the reign of Emperor Xuanzong, *Liu Cha Fa* (*Law on Inspections of Six Aspects*) was made, and the details are as follows:

> To inspect whether the officials are kind or wicked; or whether there are loopholes in registration of population or mistakes in the registration of households, or whether there are unfairness in the collection of tax; to inspect whether people are lazy in farming and sericulture and whether there are waste and damages of the goods kept in warehouses; to inspect whether there are cunning and evil people as well as thieves and brigands who do not work for a living but bring harm to people's lives and property; to inspect whether there are people who are virtuous for filial piety and fraternal duty, or whether there are people who have extraordinary talents and abilities and who should be recruited to provide service to imperial government, but who refuse to do so by covering up their abilities and concealing their tracks; to inspect whether there are cunning officials who colluding with wealthy and

---

[176] "Yan Zhen Qing Zhuan" (The Biography of Yan Zhenqing) in *Jiu Tang Shu* (*The Old Book of Tang Dynasty*).

[177] *Tang Da Zhao Ling Ji* (*Collected Grand Edicts and Decrees of Tang Dynasty*), Vol. 82.

[178] "Bai Guan Zhi" (The Record of the Officials of all Ranks) in *Xin Tang Shu* (*The New Book of Tang Dynasty*).

7.2 The Legal System of Tang Dynasty Symbolizing the Establishment... 545

influential clans to indulge themselves in brutalities, and who make the poor and vulnerable unable to file their grievances.[179]

Although *Liu Cha Fa* (*Law on Inspections of Six Aspects*) was based on *Ci Shi Liu Tiao* (*Six Provisions for Supervision*) made in Han Dynasty, it was further developed under the different historical background of Tang Dynasty. This point was clearly pointed out by Emperor Xuanzong in *Zhi Shi Dao Cai Fang Shi Chi* (*Imperial Instruction for Setting up Ten Circuit Supervisors*) issued on the 29th of the February of the 22nd year of Kaiyuan (734 A.D.):

> The region is divided into ten 'Dao' (the administration district below the province) which will be managed by *Liu Cha Fa* (*Law on Inspections of Six Aspects*). Since Zhou and Han dynasties, this rule has been followed and amended, but the imperial system should be changed with times. So it is better to appoint supervisors and to set up 'Cai Fang Shi' (supervisor from 'Dao': the administration district below the province) to take charge of the 'Dao' (the administration district below the province) of the country by following the old system. If the chief officials of 'Zhou' (subprefecture) and 'Xian' (county) do not fulfill their responsibilities, it is impossible to rule the areas effectively; if other ordinary officials embezzle public property and make profits for their own by taking advantage of their duties, human relationships cannot be well handled. So tax should be levied on people reasonably. These things should be handled by 'Yu Shi' (the censor) quickly and properly according to what I have instructed. They shall not wantonly interfere with other miscellaneous matters.[180]

In Han Dynasty, thirteen supervisory areas were set up to have a supervision of the powerful families, wealthy clans, the officials of 2000 *dan* and their children to carry out the policy of "Qiang Gan Ruo Zhi" (strengthen the central forces and weaken the local ones). In Tang Dynasty, both ordinary official staff and the chief officials of "Zhou" (subprefecture) and "Xian" (county) were the focus of the inspection, which had shown the development of the system of local bureaucracy and the importance which the imperial government attached to local officials. After Han, Wei and Jin dynasties, the powerful families, wealthy and influential clans gradually fell into decline after heavily hit by the peasants' uprising in the later period of Sui Dynasty so that they were not considered as a threat to the centralization of authority any more. Therefore, those families were the last to be inspected according to *Liu Cha Fa* (*Law on Inspections of Six Aspects*).

Ultimately, the prosperity of Tang Dynasty led to the agricultural development based on "Jun Tian Zhi" (The System of Land Equalization). Therefore, the economic matters were taken as the priority in the inspection of the local officials, such as the registered permanent residence, the registration of households, tax and corvée, agriculture and sericulture and warehouses.

Additionally, as to official selection, the system of "Cha Ju" (election system of Han Dynasty: the talents are recommended by the dukes, heads of different ministry, provincial governors and appointed by the court) and "Zheng Bi" (recommended by

---

[179]"Bai Guan Zhi" (The Record of the Officials of all Ranks) in *Xin Tang Shu* (*The New Book of Tang Dynasty*).

[180]*Tang Da Zhao Ling Ji* (*Collected Grand Edicts and Decrees of Tang Dynasty*), Vol. 100.

the emperor is called "Zheng" and recommended by the government is called "Bi") which had been carried out since Han Dynasty were replaced by "Ke Ju" (the imperial examination). As the malpractice in selecting local officials was not in the scope of inspection, efforts were made to recruit "the talents among the common people who are serviceable for the imperial government were."

Liu Cha Fa (*Law on Inspections of Six Aspects*) not only included officials' merits and accomplishments, but also their morality, knowledge and competence, which reflected the basic condition of civil official appointment in Tang Dynasty.

Because the objects, requirements, scopes and methods of inspection were elaborately regulated in *Liu Cha Fa* (*Law on Inspections of Six Aspects*), it not only provided the basic rules which should be followed by "Yu Shi" (the censor) in their tours of inspection, but also restricted the power of "Yu Shi" (the censor) with lower ranks and prevented them from abusing the power of inspection. In the imperial instruction made in April of the 10th year of Zhenyuan (794 A.D.), an order was issued to "Yu Shi" (the censor) who were about to make the tour of inspection: "From today forward, if the joint recommendation of officials has not been made according to *Liu Cha Fa* (*Law on Inspections of Six Aspects*) by the relevant bureaus, memorials should be sent to me by 'Yu Shi' (the censor). But other miscellaneous matters shall not be interfered by 'Yu Shi' (the censor)."[181] If "Yu Shi" (the censor) "are not sent to inspect the interrogation of prisoners, they are not allowed to dispatch the judges randomly," and "they are not allowed to act arrogantly, to make the people of 'Zhou' (subprefecture) and 'Xian' (county) stand along the roads to welcome them or to make the chief officials of 'Zhou' (subprefecture) and 'Xian' (county) wait upon them like servants."[182]

To avoid the negative consequences brought about by "Feng Wen Tan Ren" (impeaching the officials according to rumors), a decree was issued by Emperor Zhongzong and it was stipulated that "before an impeachment is made, memorials shall be presented to the emperor for approval by 'Yu Shi' (the censor),"[183] which had then gradually become a regular rule. Additionally, to prevent "Yu Shi" (the censor) from organizing cliques, in March of the 1st year of Zhenyuan (785 A.D.), an imperial decree was issued to the imperial advisors and "Yu Shi" (the censor): "From today forward, memorials about impeachment shall be presented individually by the officials to avoid being suspected of organizing cliques."[184] In April of the 1st year of Dazhong, because of the increasing number of civil law suits were directly filed to "Yu Shi Tai" (The Censorate), a memorial was specially approved and issued by the Emperor, according to which cases were not allowed to be directly filed to "Yu Shi Tai" (The Censorate) without being tried by the other bureaus to ensure the primary function of "Yu Shi Tai" (The Censorate) in "supervising officials and rectifying the

---

[181] *Tang Hui Yao* (*Collections of Historical Records of Tang Dynasty*), Vol. 60.

[182] *Tang Hui Yao* (*Collections of Historical Records of Tang Dynasty*), Vol. 62.

[183] Liu Su (Tang Dynasty), *Sui Tang Jia Hua* (*Praise for Sui and Tang Dynasties*) (Book 2).

[184] *Tang Hui Yao* (*Collections of Historical Records of Tang Dynasty*), Vol. 61.

7.2 The Legal System of Tang Dynasty Symbolizing the Establishment...

illegal matters" and to prevent people from acting beyond the authority. The memorial approved by the emperor is as follows:

> 'Yu Shi Tai' (The Censorate) is set up for supervising the various bureaus and rectifying the illegal matters. If its official duty is simple, the laws and disciplines will naturally be enforced strictly; however, if its official duty is complicated, the laws and disciplines will be neglected and underestimated. The cases involving disputes over marriage and land or the cases involving monetary matters shall be initially filed to and handled by the bureaus of 'Fu' (ancient administrative district between province and county) or 'Xian' (county); if the cases involve military affairs, they shall also be heard by 'Fu' (ancient administrative district between province and county) or 'Xian' (county). But recently, many cases are directly sent to 'Yu Shi Tai' (The Censorate), which has brought overloaded work and caused much trouble. So from today forward, we require that the cases involving private or public debts and disputes over marriage and land shall be filed to and heard by the bureaus of 'Zhou' (subprefecture) and 'Xian' (county) without being sent to 'Yu Shi Tai' (The Censorate). If the cases have been sent to 'Yu Shi Tai' (The Censorate) or have been transferred to 'Yu Shi Tai' (The Censorate) with the approval of 'Zai Xiang' (the prime minister) without being heard by the bureaus where they ought to be sent, they shall be sent back; if a case has been heard by the relevant bureau but the verdict is considered to be unjust, then the case shall be transferred to 'Yu Shi Tai' (The Censorate); if 'Yu Shi Tai' (The Censorate) decides that the unfair settlement of the case is true, the judge of the case in the bureau of 'Zhou' (subprefecture) shall come to 'Yu Shi Tai' (The Censorate) for reviewing and shall take the responsibility for the settlement of the case according to law; if the offense of the judge is minor, he shall be directly given a low score in his official assessment; if the offense is serious, he shall be removed from his office or be demoted. It is for the purpose of taking disciplinary action against officials' incompetency that the judges involved in the case are punished.[185]

In Tang Dynasty, the supervisory censors "held great power though their ranks were low." Although they only ranked "Ba Pin" (the eighth rank), which was lower than that of "Xian Ling" (county magistrate), the officials whom they had the right to investigate ranged from the chief officials of various bureaus to local senior officials. Their ranks were low, so it was easier for the emperor to control them, but at the same time they had great power because the emperor had attached great importance to them. Therefore, it was largely determined by the personal morality of the emperor whether the supervisory censors could bring their role into full play. During the period of Zhenguan, after "Shi Yu Shi" (subordinate of Grand Censor) named Liu Fan impeached the King of Wu named Luo (Emperor Taizong's son) for wantonly trampling upon other's crops when he was on a hunting trip, Emperor Taizong told his servant that "it is Quan Wanji (the tutor of the King of Wu) who has the responsibility to teach my son, since his dereliction of duty has led to my son's misdeed, he shall be punished by death penalty."[186]

In the early period of Tang Dynasty, after learning a lesson from the destruction of Sui Dynasty, the imperial monarchs gave much weight to taking advice from the officials. Especially, Emperor Taizong had set a good example in accepting other

---

[185] *Tang Hui Yao* (*Collections of Historical Records of Tang Dynasty*), Vol. 60.
[186] "Zhi Guan Kao" (An Examination of State Officials) (Book 7) in *Wen Xian Tong Kao* (*A General Textual Research of the Documents*), Vol. 53.

people's advice, which had become an important reason for his success. Because much importance was attached to taking advice from the officials, the institutions for collecting advice were expanded, and the official positions for giving advice to the emperor which were headed by "Zhong Shu Sheng" (the supreme organization in charge of the state affairs) and "Men Xia Sheng" (the organization in charge of examining the imperial edicts in ancient China), such as "Zuo You San Ji Chang Shi" (the chief and deputy officials, attendants of Emperor), "Zuo You Jian Yi Da Fu" (the chief and deputy officials in charge of having discussions on national matters), "Zuo You Bu Que," (the chief and deputy officials in charge of giving advice to emperor) and "Zuo You Shi Yi" (the chief and deputy officials in charge of picking up what is missing or rectifying mistakes in policy made by emperor), etc. were set up. Thus, it was the responsibility of 'Jian Yi' (ancient official, in charge of having discussions on national matters) to carry on researches on state policy, law, and some important measures and systems. If those officials had discovered any malpractice in the above-mentioned aspects, they were responsible for giving advice to the emperor, which was encouraged because it was not only helpful to the exercise of the imperial power, but also helpful to the governing of the country. In the later years of Emperor Taizong, *Ling Qun Chen Zhi Yan Zhao* (*Decree for Officials to State Outright*) was issued and it was stated that "ever since I ascended the throne and began the administration, I have been worrying that my character flaws might have caused improprieties and my carelessness have caused trouble. ... In the past, Wei Zhi is the only person who has always pointed out my mistakes, but after his death, though I have made mistakes, no one has had any courage to point them out. From today forward, you shall spare no effort to act sincerely and faithfully and to speak frankly without reservation whenever I make mistakes."[187] In April of the 12th year of Kanyuan (724 A.D.), a "Chi" (instruction) was issued by Emperor Taizong:

> From today forward, the sealed memorials written by 'Jian Yi' (ancient official, in charge of having discussions on national matters) shall be presented to me at any time without being delayed by any officials in charge of palace gates. If anything needs to be reported, memorials should be submitted immediately so that they can be handled in time. If there are malpractices in removal or promotion of officials, inappropriateness of the carrying out of the decrees or orders, mishandling of punishments and awards, over levying of tax, grievances and complaints, they should be reported and discussed without reservation. So the order is issued.[188]

Later, many such instructions were issued in the following dynasties. For example, in April of the 2nd year of Qianyuan (759 A.D.), the following imperial instruction is given:

> 'Jian Yi' (ancient official, in charge of having discussions on national matters) in the two departments (namely, 'Zhong Shu Sheng' and 'Men Xia Sheng') shall present sealed memorials every ten days to report the gains and loss of the matters. Moreover, the language

---

[187] *Tang Da Zhao Ling Ji* (*Collected Grand Edicts and Decrees of Tang Dynasty*), Vol. 150.
[188] *Tang Hui Yao* (*Collections of Historical Records of Tang Dynasty*), Vol. 55.

7.2 The Legal System of Tang Dynasty Symbolizing the Establishment...

of the memorials should be concise and direct and I hope that it will become a way of 'Dian Zui' (official assessment) and will be employed to prevent evil deeds and to encourage good deeds.[189]

Another imperial instruction was issued on the 21st of September of the 2nd year of Guangde (764 A.D.): "This instruction is to order 'Jian Yi' (ancient official, in charge of having discussions on national matters) to present one sealed memorial every month to discuss the matters of administration."[190] On the 23rd day of the January of the 1st year of Yongtai (765 A.D.), the following imperial instruction was issued: "Every month on the day of presenting remonstrance, one official shall do the oral presentation of memorial to the emperor without following the order of official ranks." On the 12th day of the April of 12th year of Dali (777 A.D.), another imperial instruction was issued: "From today forward, the sealed memorials written by 'Jian Yi' (ancient official, in charge of having discussions on national matters) shall be presented to me anytime."[191]

So it is true that 'Jian Yi' (ancient official, in charge of having discussions on national matters) do help to rectify the mistakes of the emperors. For example, on the 1st day of the September of 2nd year of Yonghe (651 A.D.), "Zuo Wu Hou Yin Jia" (ancient imperial guards) named Lu Wencao had stolen the goods from the state warehouse. After Emperor Gaozong ordered to sentence Lu Wencao to death, "Jian Yi Da Fu" (ancient official, in charge of having discussions on national matters) named Xiao Jun advised that:

> Lu Wencao's offense should not be pardoned. However, his offense is not punishable by death penalty according to the provisions of law. If he is punished by the death penalty, the people of this country will surely know it, so they must say Your Majesty have have only made decisions according to Your Majesty's own moods and cared much about material things by ignoring the law and neglecting people's lives. My responsibility is to give Your Majesty advice, so this is what I think and I dare not keep silent.

The emperor accepted his advice and said, "'Since your job is to give me advice, today you have fulfilled your responsibility, and I will specially exempt Lu Wencao from death penalty just for your advice." Then the emperor turned to his assistant and said, "Su Jun is a competent 'Jian Yi' (ancient official, in charge of having discussions on national matters)."[192]

As "Yu Shi" (the censor) and "Jian Yi" (ancient official, in charge of having discussions on national matters) had the function of self-rectifying in the feudal state, their personal qualities were highly stressed by the imperial government. Thus, it was stipulated that "before rectifying the mistakes of other officials, 'Yu Shi' (the censor) must correct his own misconducts. So he is charge of appointing the upright officials and removing the crooked ones without considering whether they are his relatives or enemies. Moreover, he will solve the problems and correct the mistakes

---

[189] *Tang Hui Yao* (*Collections of Historical Records of Tang Dynasty*), Vol. 55.
[190] *Tang Hui Yao* (*Collections of Historical Records of Tang Dynasty*), Vol. 56.
[191] *Tang Hui Yao* (*Collections of Historical Records of Tang Dynasty*), Vol. 56.
[192] *Tang Hui Yao* (*Collections of Historical Records of Tang Dynasty*), Vol. 55.

impartially. If 'Yu Shi' (the censor) has heard that some officials have made mistakes but instigated others to conceal the fact or if he shows his private favor to things randomly, but if I still entrust tasks to him, how can he act properly as my eyes and ears to fulfill his duty of punishing the cruel and evil people? If any 'Yu Shi' (the censor) has completed his tasks in this way, I will be greatly disappointed, because I have placed great hope in him. So he will be removed from his office from today forward."[193]

In summary, the supervisory institutions of Tang Dynasty were expanded greatly and at the same time they were given greater supervisory power. Moreover, the supervisory laws were further enriched in contents, which had not only made it possible for the supervisory institutions to conduct supervision according to law, but also to exercise their supervisory power and to fulfill the function of enforcing laws and disciplines and supervising officials properly. The legalization of the supervisory activities had shown the continuing improvement of the feudal administrative management.

7.2.4 The Finalized Criminal Law

Although the previous compilation style of "Zhu Fa He Ti" (the integration of various laws) was inherited in the well-known *Tang Lv Shu Yi* (*The Comments on Tang Code*), it actually was a typical criminal legal code as far as its basic nature was concerned. In *Tang Lv Shu Yi* (*The Comments on Tang Code*), "Shi E" (The Ten Abominations) and "Ba Yi" (The Eight Deliberations) were formally written in law, and the laws on "Qi Sha" (the Seven Killings) and "Liu Zang" (The Six Crimes of Obtaining Private or Public Property Illegally) were also established and finalized. Besides, the finalized regulations for "Wu Xing" (Five Penalties) had a significant influence. Within the twelve chapters of *Tang Lv* (*Tang Code*), "Ming Li Lv" (Statutes and Terms) could be regarded as its general principle as well as the epitome of the basic principles of *Xing Fa* (*The Criminal Law*), as was explained in *Shu Yi* (*Tang Lv Shu Yi*), "the titles of the statutes are used as the names of offenses of 'Wu Xing' (Five Penalties) and the precedents are used as its stylistic rules and layout."

The names of the offenses included in *Tang Lv Shu Yi* (*The Comments on Tang Code*) are mainly as follows:

"Shi E" (The Ten Abominations). "Shi E" (The Ten Abominations) originated from the ten felonies in *Bei Qi Lv* (*The Penal Code of the Northern Qi Dynasty*) and the terms were changed to "Shi E" (The Ten Abominations) in Sui and Tang dynasties, which referred to the most serious crimes. "Shi E" (The Ten Abominations) included: "Mou Fan," namely, plotting rebellion or plotting to overthrow the country; "Mou Da Ni," namely, great sedition or plotting to destroy imperial ancestral temples, mausoleums, or palaces; "Mou Pan," namely, treason or plotting

---

[193] *Tang Da Zhao Ling Ji* (*Collected Grand Edicts and Decrees of Tang Dynasty*), Vol. 100.

to commit treason against the state; "E Ni," namely, abusing or murdering the elders, or murdering one's own parents and grandparents, uncles, aunts or one's husband's parents, grandparents or other relatives; "Bu Dao," namely, depravity or to murder three or more innocent people, to disembowel a victim's body after committing a murder; "Da Bu Jing," namely, being greatly irreverent, or stealing the objects for the sacrifices to the spirits or the clothing or the personal belongings of the emperor; stealing or counterfeiting the imperial seals, violating the correct prescriptions when preparing imperial medicine or making a mistake in writing or tagging the labels, unwittingly violating the dietary prescriptions when preparing the imperial food, or unwittingly failing to make imperial boats sturdy; "Bu Xiao," namely, being unfilial or suing or cursing paternal grandparents or parents, or establishing separate household registers and dividing the family property when paternal grandparents or parents are still alive, or failing to take care of one's aged paternal grandparents or parents, or fraudulently claiming that one's parents have died, or failing to mourn for the death of paternal grandparents or parents, or entertaining oneself during the periods of mourning; "Bu Mu," namely, inharmonious or murdering one's elder relatives above "Si Ma," striking or suing one's husband's elder relatives above "Da Gong" or "Xiao Gong"; "Bu Yi," namely, injustice or the official murdering the chief official of his bureau or "Ci Shi" or "Xian Ling" (county magistrate), or an official staff or a soldier murdering his chief official above "Wu Pin," or murdering his own tutor, or showing on mourning for the death of one's husband or having entertainment or marry other person during the periods of mourning; "Nei Luan," namely, committing incest or raping one's elder relative above "Xiao Gong" or having affairs with the concubine of one's father or grandfather, or fornicating the concubine of one's father or grandfather, etc.

The reason why the crimes of "Shi E" (The Ten Abominations) were regarded as the most serious felonies was that they had directly endangered the ruling of the country and the supreme imperial power, violated the principle of "Gang Chang Ming Jiao" (feudal cardinal guides and constant virtues) and the order of the superior and the inferior, the noble and the humble, as was written in *Shu Yi* (*Tang Lv Shu Yi*): "Among the offenses of 'Wu Xing' (Five Penalties), 'Shi E' (The Ten Abominations) are the most serious because they have ruined 'Ming Jiao' (Confucian ethical code) and endangered royal power, that is why they are arranged in the first chapter to give warnings." Because "Shi E" (The Ten Abominations) referred to the serious offenses that "would never be pardoned even in ordinary amnesties," the offenders should be punished by death penalty, "Liu" (exile) or "Tu" (imprisonment). Besides, the punishments above "Tu" (imprisonment) were not allowed to be pardoned or atoned for with money. Among the offenses of "Shi E" (The Ten Abominations), "Mou Fan" (plotting rebellion or plotting to endanger the country), "Mou Da Ni" (great sedition) and "Mou Pan" (treason) were the most serious. In *Tang Lv* (*Tang Code*) it was stipulated that for the offenses of "Mou Fan" (plotting rebellion or plotting to endanger the country) and "Mou Da Ni" (great sedition), whether the offenders were the principal or accessories of the crime, they should all be punished by "Zhan" (beheading) with the offenders' fathers and sons who were sixteen years old or older all strangulated; with the offenders' children who were fifteen years old or younger and the offender's mother, wife, concubines (their sons' wives and concubines), grandfather and grandchildren, brothers, sisters, and "Bu Qu" (the private army) all punished to be servants in official departments; with their personal property, land and houses all confiscated; with the offender's uncles and the sons of brothers all punished by "Liu" (exile) to a distance of 3000 *li*. Thus, a great number of people were punished. The offender's grandfather, uncles, brothers, female family members, and children who were fifteen years old or younger were exempted from death penalty, because the rulers were afraid that it might cause more violent rebellion to kill too many people. Additionally, the rulers would like to give those children and women a way out just because they had learned from experience that those people had posed less threat to the society. However, the most important reason for exempting those people from death penalty was that they had not actively participated in the rebellion or insurrection; otherwise, they should have been punished by "Zhan" (beheading). In *Tang Lv* (*Tang Code*), only for the offenses of "Mou Fan" (plotting rebellion or plotting to endanger the country) and "Mou Da Ni" (great sedition) were the offenders' relatives implicated in punishment, which had shown the focal point of punishment. Moreover, for the offenses of "Mou Fan" (plotting rebellion or plotting to endanger the country), although "the offenders' failed to instigate people to follow them through propaganda or they were not powerful enough to lead an army," all the principal and accessories would be punished by "Zhan" (beheading) with their parents and wives and children exiled to places 3000 *li* away. Even if someone "had spoken of a rebellion without the real intention to do so, or no evidence was found for the so-called rebellion," he would still be exiled to places 2000 *li* away, which actually aimed to have people punished just for their ideology. However, if the young or the humble sued the elderly or the noble for the crimes of "Mou Fan" (plotting rebellion or plotting to endanger the country) and "Mou Da Ni" (great sedition), they would not be found guilty; on the contrary, if anyone had concealed such crimes, they would be punished by "Jiao" (hanging).

The offenders who committed the crime of "Mou Pan" (treason) would be punished by "Jiao" (hanging) or "Zhan" (beheading), and their wives and children would be punished by "Liu" (exile) to a distance of 2000 *li*. If they had incited more than one hundred people to follow them, their parents, wives, children would be punished by "Liu" (exile) to a distance of 3000 *li*, and the people who concealed the crime of "Mou Pan" (treason) would also be punished by "Liu" (exile) to a distance of 2000 *li*. In *Shu Yi* (*Tang Lv Shu Yi*), an explanation was given to this offense: "Such crazy plot may endanger the safety of the country, so it shall be regarded as "Mou Pan" (treason) even though the plan has not been carried out. Therefore, the offenders shall still be punished by death penalty." In other words, although the plan of "Mou Pan" (treason) was not accomplished, it still constituted a crime. The word "plotting" in *Tang Lv* (*Tang Code*) meant to collude with more than one person, but for the offense of plotting "Mou Pan" (treason), "even though evidence shows that only one person is involved in the crime, the others will also be punished." Obviously, this regulation had gone beyond the criminal principles regulated in *Tang Lv* (*Tang Code*). In fact, the cruel suppression of rebellion was beyond the restriction of law. For example, in the later period of Tang Dynasty, when Pang Xun instigated the soldiers in Guilin to rise in rebellion, more than 10,000 soldiers were killed with "their relatives caught and decapitated. Consequently, several thousand people were killed."[194]

As the central issue of strengthening the autocratic centralization authority was to consolidate the imperial power, the regulation of "Shi E" (The Ten Abominations) had reflected intention to maintain the "sacred and majestic" authority of the imperial power. In *Shu Yi (Tang Lv Shu Yi)*, it was declared that the emperor "was the mandate of 'Tian' (Heaven)" and "was destined to be the parents of the common people." Besides, the emperor was the supreme leader who had incorporated the monarchical power, the divine power and the paternal power. For this reason, if any person had "the intention to go against the emperor's wishes," he shall be severely punished for "violating the heavenly regulations and human principles." The other offense of "Da Bu Jing" (being greatly irreverent) which involved blaspheming against the emperor's dignity or endangering the emperor's personal safety had covered a much larger scope. For example, the offenses such as stealing the objects for the sacrifices to the spirits or the clothing or the personal belongings of the emperor, stealing or counterfeiting the imperial seals, violating the correct prescriptions when preparing imperial medicine or making a mistake in writing or tagging the labels, unwittingly violating the dietary prescriptions when preparing the imperial food, or unwittingly failing to make imperial boats sturdy, slandering the imperial court when delivering a speech and disobeying the orders of the inspectors specially sent by the emperor and so on were all included in "Da Bu Jing" (being greatly irreverent). Thus, any offenders would be punished by "Si Xing" (death penalties) or the punishment of "Liu" (exile). Additionally, in *Wei Jin Lv (Statutes on Palace Guards)* and *Zhi Zhi Lv (Statutes on the State Office System)*, a series of regulations which were made to maintain the imperial power and autocratic ruling could also be found.

As the feudal order of importance or seniority in human relationships had embodied concretely the feudal order of ruling and provided a social foundation for paternity, the authority of husband and the authority of clan, it was rigidly maintained in *Tang Lv (Tang Code)* so that half of the contents of "Shi E" (The Ten Abominations) involved the regulations for the punishment of the misbehaviors of endangering the harmony of family and the violation of the principles of "Li" (rites). The misbehaviors, such as the humble offending the noble, neglecting the care of one's aged paternal grandparents or parents, the establishment of the separate household registration or dividing family property when the paternal grandparents or parents were still alive, the entertainment or marriage during the periods of the mourning of one's parents, the beating, cursing or prosecuting one's close relatives, were all included in the crimes of "E Ni" (abusing or murdering the elders), "Bu Xiao" (being unfilial) and "Bu Mu" (inharmonious), so those involved would consequently be severely punished. It was one of the characteristics of Chinese

---

[194]*Zi Zhi Tong Jian (History as a Mirror)*.Vol. 251.

legal system that the violation of ritual principles was regarded as the evidence of criminal responsibilities and that the offenders who committed the same crime were punished differently according to their humble or noble social status in the hierarchical order.

"Qi Sha" (The Seven Killings). "Qi Sha" (The Seven Killings) included "Mou Sha" (murder), "Gu Sha" (intentional killing), "Dou Sha" (killing during fighting), "Wu Sha" (manslaughter), "Guo Shi Sha" (involuntary killing), "Xi Sha" (killing during playing), and "Jie Sha" (killing in robbing prisoners). As for the regulation on the offense of "Mou Sha" (murder), it was stipulated in *Shu Yi (Tang Lv Shu Yi)* that "the offender who plots murder shall be punished by 'Tu' (imprisonment) for three years; the offender who causes injury shall be punished by 'Jiao' (hanging), and the offender who causes death shall be punished by 'Zhan' (beheading). The person who assists the murdering shall be punished by 'Jiao' (hanging); the person who does not assist the murdering shall be punished by 'Liu' (exile) to a distance of 2000 *li*; the person who has an intention but does not carry out the murdering is also considered the principal of the crime."[195] It was explained in *Shu Yi (Tang Lv Shu Yi)* that "when there are more than two offenders committing the murder," the principal and the accessory offenders would be treated differently. Thus, if the person had intended to murder, although he "does not carry out the murder in person, the murder is committed, he will still be considered the principal offender and will be punished by 'Zhan' (beheading)." Because murder was a crime committed together with other person, it was the most serious, and its influence on society were especially harmful, it was listed as the first crime among the seven killings. The offenders who had committed the attempted murder would be punished, but the level of punishment would be reduced. However, if a "Nu Bi" (the slave girls and maidservants) had murdered his or her master or a grandchild had murdered his or her close elder relatives, they would all be sentenced to death, which had shown the intention to maintain "Gang Chang Ming Jiao"(feudal cardinal guides and constant virtues). As for "Gu Sha" (intentional killing), it was stipulated in *Shu Yi (Tang Lv Shu Yi)* that "it shows an intention of harming others with knives, and it refers to intentional killing of someone without fighting or for no reason." Usually, the offenders would be punished by "Zhan" (beheading), but if a master killed his "Nu Bi" (the slave girls and maidservants), he should only be punished by "Tu" (imprisonment) for one year. Besides, those committing both "Dou Sha" (killing during fighting) and "Wu Sha" (manslaughter) should be punished one level lighter than that for murder; the punishment for "Xi Sha" (killing during playing) would be reduced by two levels than that for "Dou Sha" (killing during fighting) and the crime of "Guo Shi Sha" (involuntary killing) would be punished by "Shou Shu" (to atone for one's crime with money). However, if any "Nu Bi" (the slave girls and maidservants) or any member of "Bu Qu" (the private army) killed their masters involuntarily, they would be punished by "Jiao" (hanging). "Jie Sha" referred to the killing in robbing, and the offenders of this offense would all be punished by "Zhan" (beheading). The law on

---

[195]"Zei Dao" (Stealing and Robbery) in *Tang Lv Shu Yi (The Comments on Tang Code)*.

7.2 The Legal System of Tang Dynasty Symbolizing the Establishment... 555

"Qi Sha" (the Seven Killing) had reflected the great development of the feudal criminal theory, because it had summarized the circumstances of the offenses of killing and thoroughly examined the motives and effects before measuring the levels of penalties to crack down on the most harmful crimes.

"Liu Zang" (The Six Crimes of Obtaining Private or Public Property Illegally) referred to "Qiang Dao" (robbery), "Qie Dao" (robbing and theft), "Wang Fa" (taking bribes by bending the law), "Bu Wang Fa" (taking bribes without bending the law), "Shou Suo Jian Lin" (illegally accepting the people's money and property in one's supervisory area), and "Zuo Zang" (embezzlement). It was stipulated in *Shu Yi* (*Tang Lv Shu Yi*) that "Qiang Dao" referred to "robbing somebody of his property by force." The penalty for "Qiang Dao" was very severe, so although one offender did not gain anything in the robbing, he would still be punished by "Tu" (imprisonment) for two years. If he had robbed one *chi* of cotton cloth, he would be punishable by "Tu" (imprisonment) for three years; if he had robbed ten *pi* of cotton cloth and caused injury, he would be punished by "Jiao" (hanging); if he had caused the death of others, he would be punished by "Zhan" (beheading); if the robber had a weapon, although he failed to rob anything, he would also be punished by "Liu" (exile) to a distance of 3000 *li*; if the robber had robbed five *pi* of cotton cloth with a weapon, he would be punished by "Jiao" (hanging); if he had caused the injury of others, he would be punished by "Zhan" (beheading). Within the area of "Zhou" (subprefecture), "Xian" (county), "Xiang" (townships) or "Cun" (village), if there was one robber or one was found to accommodate any robbers, "Li Zheng" (head of "Li": the basic resident organization in ancient China) would be punished by "Chi" (flogging with light sticks) for fifty strokes; if three robbers were found, the penalty would be increased by one level, and the chief officials of "Zhou" (subprefecture) and "Xian" (county) would be punished by "Chi" (flogging with light sticks) or by two years of "Tu" (imprisonment) according to the particular circumstances. Because "Nu Bi" (the slave girls and maidservants) belonged to private property, the offense of plundering and selling other person's "Nu Bi" (the slave girls and maidservants) or luring other person's "Nu Bi" (the slave girls and maidservants) away from their masters was considered as committing the same crime of the infringement upon the other's property, so any offenders would be punished by the same penalty for robbing by force. For the crime of robbery, if it was committed in collusion, both the principal and accessory offenders would be punished; if the person initially plotted robbery but did not participate in the crime in the end, or if his followers also did not carry out the robbery, they should be punished according to their principal and accessory identities.

In *Shu Yi* (*Tang Lv Shu Yi*), "Qie Dao" (robbing and theft) was defined as "robbing something secretly by masking one's face." If the offender had conducted robbing but obtained nothing, he would be punished by "Chi" (flogging with light sticks) for fifty strokes; if the offender had robbed one *chi* of cotton cloth, he would be punished by "Zhang" (flogging with heavy sticks) for sixty strokes; if he had robbed one *pi* of cotton cloth, the penalty for him would be increased by one level; if he had robbed five *pi* of cotton cloth, he would be punished by "Tu" (imprisonment) for one year; if he had robbed fifty *pi* of cotton cloth, he would be punished by "Liu" (exile) to serve as a laborer; if he had stolen the emperor's imperial seal, he would be punished by "Jiao" (hanging); if he had stolen the objects for the great sacrifices to the spirits, or had committed the crime of blasphemy which was stipulated in "Shi E" (The Ten Abominations), he would be punished by "Liu" (exile) to a distance of 2500 *li*; if he had stolen and destroyed the statue of a god or Buddha, he would be punished by "Tu" (imprisonment) for three years. For other offenses of stealing, such as "stealing the clothing or the personal belongings of the emperor," stealing the tallies of the palace gates and stealing the forbidden weapons, the offenders would all be punished by "Liu" (exile) to a distance of 2000 *li* or 2500 *li*; if one had stolen the plants from other person's cemetery, or stolen things from official departments, or stolen other person's cows or horses and killed them, he would be punished by "Tu" (imprisonment); if one had broken into other person's houses at night for no reason, he would be punished by "Chi" (flogging with light sticks) for forty strokes; however, if the master of the house found the intruder and killed him, he would be exempted from punishment; if one official staff had stolen what was entrusted to his care, or incited other people to steal something, or caused death involuntarily in the process of stealing, the penalty for him would be aggravated. Nevertheless, if one had stolen something from his relative or from his own family, the penalty for him would be reduced. In addition, the offenses such as luring "Nu Bi" (the slave girls and maidservants) away from their masters, conniving at the escaping of "Nu Bi" (the slave girls and maidservants), lending the official belongings entrusted to one's care without permission, misappropriating and concealing the collected tax, would all be punished the same as that for "Qie Dao" (robbing and theft). After the middle period of Tang Dynasty, because of the sharp conflicts between different classes, the penalties for the crime of "Qie Dao" (robbing and theft) were aggravated. For example, it was stipulated that "if the amount of money that one has stolen is more than 1,000 *qian*, he will be sentenced to death." Moreover, it was even stipulated that "...if one has stolen less than 100 *qian*, he will be punished by 'Si' (death penalty)."[196]

"Tan Zang Wang Fa" (taking bribes by bending the law). Official corruption is a basic attribute of the feudal bureaucratic system, so it is also a common social phenomenon. The officials' excessive plundering and corruption have become one of the reasons for the breaking out of peasant uprising. For this reason, in the early period of Tang Dynasty, very harsh penalties were imposed upon the corrupt and evil officials. For example, if a chief official had taken bribes by bending the law in his supervisory area, he would be punished by "Zhang" (flogging with heavy sticks) for one hundred strokes for each *chi* of cotton cloth he had taken; if he had taken one *pi* of cotton cloth, his penalty would be reduced by one level; if he had taken fifteen *pi* of cotton cloth, he would be punished by "Jiao" (hanging); if he had taken bribes without bending the law, he would be punished by "Zhang" (flogging with heavy sticks) for ninety strokes for each *chi* of cotton cloth he had taken; if he had taken two *pi* of cotton cloth, his penalty would be aggravated by one level; if he had taken

---

[196]*Tang Hui Yao* (*Collections of Historical Records of Tang Dynasty*), Vol. 39.

thirty *pi* of cotton cloth, he would be punished by "Liu" (exile) and serving hard labor work. Additionally, if one official had accepted the property or the gifts like pigs or sheep from the people in his supervisory area, or had enslaved the people in his supervisory area without permission, or had borrowed money or objects or "Nu Bi" (the slave girls and maidservants) from the people, he would be punished for the crime of corruption, which had reflected the detailedness of the regulation and the severity of the punishment. During the period of Zhenguan, Emperor Taizong "hated the evilness and corruption of the officials so much that he never pardoned the corrupt officials who had taken bribes by bending the law. If any officials were involved in corruption, no matter whether they were in capital or local areas, their crimes would be recorded in memorials and be presented to the emperor to be severely punished."[197] However, after the period of Zhenguan, the punishment for corrupted officials was not so severe as before, so when bureaucrats and senior officials embezzled money and engaged in corruption, measures were specially taken to exempt them from punishment. During the reign of Xuanzong, the magistrate of Wujiang named Pei Jingxian should have been punished by death penalty for taking the bribes of 5000 *pi* of silk, but his penalty was reduced just because "his grandfather used to be meritorious in helping the emperor to establish the country."[198]

In *Shu Yi* (*Tang Lv Shu Yi*), the offense of "Zuo Zang" (embezzlement) was defined as the following:

> If the official who is not the chief supervisor of one area has taken bribes for doing things for others, he is then guilty, which is called 'Zuo Zang Zhi Zui' (the crime of embezzlement). If the offender has taken one *chi* of cotton cloth, he shall be punished by 'Chi' (flogging with light sticks) for twenty strokes; if the offender has taken one *pi* of cotton cloth, his punishment shall be aggravated by one level; if the offender has taken ten *pi* of cotton cloth, he shall be punished by 'Tu' (imprisonment) for one year; if the offender has taken another ten *pi* of cotton cloth, his punishment shall be aggravated by one level, with the maximum punishment of 'Tu' (imprisonment) for three years.

As the monarchs of Tang Dynasty had learned a lesson from Sui Dynasty that the large scale architectural work would finally lead to rebellion, regulations were additionally made to forbid the construction of architectural work without authorization. It was stipulated in "Shan Xing Lv" (Statutes on Sending Troops without Authorization) in *Tang Lv* (*Tang Code*) that any important construction, such as the building of cities and river dams, should be reported to "Shang Shu Sheng" (The Department of Secretary) for approval. If an official had started the construction and increased tax and corvée without permission, or if he had used more than ten laborers in the construction, he would be punished for the crime of corruption. If an official had failed to accurately report the amount of money or the number of laborers used or employed in construction, he would be punished by "Chi" (flogging with light

---

[197]"Zheng Ti" (The Political System) in *Zhen Guan Zheng Yao* (*The Essentials about Politics during the Reign of Zhen Guan*), Vol. 1.

[198]"Li Chao Yin Zhuan" (The Biography of Li Chaoyin) in *Jiu Tang Shu* (*The Old Book of Tang Dynasty*).

sticks) for fifty strokes; if the circumstances were serious, he would be punished for the crime of corruption with the punishment reduced by one level; if the official had employed laborers without observing the regulations on labor dispatching, or if he had employed laborers or craftsmen without permission, or if he had privately kept the laborers or craftsmen, he would be severely punished.

In Tang Dynasty, because of the implementation of "Jun Tian Zhi" (The System of Land Equalization) and "Zu Yong Diao Fa" (Law on Farmland Rent, Handicraft Tax, and Corvée), household registration was strictly managed, so if any households failed to be registered, those in charge would be severely punished. According to *Shu Yi* (*Tang Lv Shu Yi*), if the registered households or if the number of registered people were inconsistent with facts, it would be regarded as a dereliction of duty; if there were unregistered households, the head of the family would be punished by "Tu" (imprisonment) for three years; if the head of the family told lies about the number of people in one household or one's age in the household to evade tax, he would be punished by "Tu" (imprisonment) for one to three years. Moreover, "Li Zheng" (head of "Li": the basic resident organization in ancient China) or the magistrates of "Zhou" (subprefecture) and "Xian" (county) would also be punished by "Chi" (flogging with light sticks) or 'Tu' (imprisonment) according to the number of people who were not registered in the supervisory areas. If "Li Zheng" (head of "Li": the basic resident organization in ancient China) had tried to get private gains by concealing some of the households in registration, he would be punished by 'Tu' (imprisonment), "Liu" (exile) or "Yi Liu" (exile with labor service) for the crime of corruption.

Among the penalties of Tang Dynasty, the provisions for cruel torture were abolished and the five penalties of "Chi" (flogging with light sticks), "Zhang" (flogging with heavy sticks), "Tu" (imprisonment), "Liu" (exile) and "Si" (death penalty) were used as statutory punishments, which not only showed a great change of ancient Chinese criminal system, but also reflected the development of society and the progress of legal civilization.

"Chi" (flogging with light sticks): it was divided into five levels ranging from ten to fifty strokes with ten strokes of flogging added for each level of punishment. According to *Shu Yi* (*Tang Lv Shu Yi*), "'Chi' means beating, which is used for making people humiliated. If people have committed minor crimes, they shall be punished, so beating is used to make them humiliated. In Han Dynasty, bamboo sticks were used, but now sticks made of 'Chu' (a kind of plant) are used." In the punishment of "Chi" (flogging with light sticks), the offenders' legs and bottoms should be beaten, so it was the most lenient punishment in "Wu Xing" (Five Penalties).

"Zhang" (flogging with heavy sticks): it was divided into five levels ranging from sixty strokes to one hundred strokes with ten strokes of flogging added for each level of punishment. According to *Shu Yi* (*Tang Lv Shu Yi*), "the sticks can be held in hand for beating." The bamboo sticks with the length of "San Chi Wu Cun" (three *chi* and five *cun*) were called "Fa Zhang" (wand), which was used to beat the offenders' back, bottoms and legs.

7.2 The Legal System of Tang Dynasty Symbolizing the Establishment... 559

"Tu" (imprisonment): it was divided into five levels ranging from one to three years with a half year of 'Tu' (imprisonment) added for each level of punishment. According to *Shu Yi* (*Tang Lv Shu Yi*), "'Tu' means to enslave, so it means making people humiliated by having him enslaved." This punishment was a combination of penal and enslaving punishment. Therefore, the offenders should do labor work with chains and shackles, with the serious offenders sent to "Jiang Zuo Jian" (in charge of imperial architecture), the women offenders sent to "Shao Fu Jian" (in charge of the handicraft production and royal affairs) and the local offenders sent to work in the handcraft workshops or sent to do miscellaneous things as laborers.

"Liu" (exile): it was divided into three levels with the distance ranging from 2000 to 2500 *li*, with a distance of 500 *li* added for each one level of punishment. It was explained in *Shu Yi* (*Tang Lv Shu Yi*) that "since it is too cruel to punish the offenders by death penalty, they are pardoned by being sent to a place far away." Although there were three different levels for the distance of exile, all offenders were subject to laborious work for one year no matter which level of punishment they were given, which was referred to as "Chang Liu" (common exile). Later on, "Yi Liu" (exile with labor service) was added, according to which the offenders were subject to laborious work for three years.

"Si Xing" (death penalty): it was divided into two levels, namely, "Jiao" (hanging) and "Zhan" (beheading).

As to the execution of penalty, in Tang Dynasty, one penalty was used for one particular offense, which was different from Qin and Han dynasties when several penalties were applied for one offense. Moreover, in Tang Dynasty, there were strict regulations for the mitigation or aggravation of penalties. For example, "the level of punishment shall not be aggravated when it comes to the maximum punishment." Moreover "it is forbidden for the punishment to be directly added up to 'Si' (death penalty)" and "it is also forbidden for the punishment to be further added up to 'Zhan' (beheading) when the offender is already punished by 'Jiao' (hanging)." Additionally, except for the most serious offenses included in "Shi E" (the Ten Abominations), the penalties ranging from "Chi" (flogging with light sticks) with ten strokes to "Si" (death penalty) were allowed to be exempted by paying one *Jin* to one hundred and twenty *Jin* of copper as ransom money. From these regulations, it can be seen clearly that it is the poor and helpless laboring people who are often punished by "Wu Xing" (Five Penalties).

Although some cruel penalties were abolished in *Tang Lv* (*Tang Code*), the penalty of "Zhang" (flogging with heavy sticks) was still frequently used. The offenders were often found to be beaten to death before they could bear the full numbers of the strokes of flogging, as was recorded in books that "although death penalty was not imposed on offenders, most of them died anyway."[199] Until the later period of Tang Dynasty, because of increasing violent class struggle, the penalties,

---

[199]"Jian Di Zui Ren Jue Zhang Fa Zhao" (An Imperial Decree on Reducing the Flogging of Offenders) in *Tang Da Zhao Ling Ji* (*Collected Grand Edicts and Decrees of Tang Dynasty*), Vol. 82.

such as "Yao Zhan" (cutting at waist), "Xiao Shou" (the penalty of hanging the head of the criminal on top of a pole for public display), and "Yi San Zu" (the law of killing the three generations of a family) were occasionally used. In the later period of Tang Dynasty, the relatives of offenders, "including young children, would all be killed, no matter whether they were close or remote relatives of the offenders." Such severe punishments showed that the principle of "Qing Xing Shen Fa" (employing lenient punishments and imposing punishments with prudence) established in the early period of Tang Dynasty was only a policy which was applied under some special circumstances, so it was impossible to be continuously applied for a long time. Anyway, its application could not change the real nature of feudal penalties.

In *Tang Lv* (*Tang Code*), the principle of criminal law application was further standardized. Especially, the laws on penalty reduction or penalty exemption for the privileged, such as "Yi" (deliberation: cases involving eight privileged groups were not to be tried directly by judicial organs, but to be reported to and decided by the emperor, thus the accused would usually be pardoned or remitted), "Qing" (petition: cases involving officials above the 5th rank shall be reported to and decided by the emperor, the punishment other than death penalty would be remitted by one degree), "Jian" (mitigation: except for death penalty, other punishments on officials above the 7th rank and their families could be remitted by one degree), "Shu" (atonement) and "Guan Dang" (giving up one's official position for the atonement for a crime) were elaborately regulated.

"Ba Yi" (The Eight Deliberations) included "Yi Qin" (the cases which involved "Huang Qin": the relatives of the emperor), "Yi Gu" (the old retainers of the emperor: including those who had been in the emperor's service for a long time), "Yi Xian" (the morally worthy: including worthy men or superior men whose speech and conduct were greatly virtuous and may be taken as a model for the country), "Yi Neng" (the great ability: including people of great talent), "Yi Gong" (the great achievement: including those of great achievement and glory), "Yi Gui" (the high position: including all active duty officials of the third rank and above), "Yi Qin" (the diligent: including military and civil officials who have displayed great diligence in their work through thorough occupation of public affairs), and "Yi Bin" (the guests of the state: to treat the descendants of previous dynasties as guests of the state who could enjoy a legal privilege). If the aristocrats and bureaucrats enjoying the privilege of "Ba Yi" (The Eight Deliberations) had committed crimes which were not included in "Shi E" (The Ten Abominations), or if their punishment was lighter than that of "Liu" (exile), their penalties might be enforced one level lighter than that for the commoners; if their crimes were punishable by death, the penalty reduction and the crimes which they had committed should be discussed by a groups of officials in accordance with their status and should be reported to the emperor for final decision later on. The system of "Ba Yi" (The Eight Deliberations) originated from *Zhou Li* (*The Rites of Zhou Dynasty*), so in *Shu Yi* (*Tang Lv Shu Yi*) the following is recorded:

> What we call 'Ba Yi' (The Eight Deliberations) today was called 'Ba Bi' (the eight conditions for mitigating punishments) in the Zhou Dynasty. It was regulated in *Zhou Li* (*The Rites of Zhou Dynasty*) that 'the penal statutes should not be applied to high-ranking

officials'. If the senior officials have committed crimes, the cases shall be discussed according to the rules of 'Ba Yi' (The Eight Deliberations) and the severity or leniency of penalties shall not be determined according to the legal codes. The people enjoying the privileges of 'Ba Yi' (The Eight Deliberations) are usually the relatives of the emperor, or the people who have been in the emperor's service for a long time, or who are of great talents, or who are of great achievements and glory, or who are favored by the emperor, or who have made great contribution to the glory of the emperor's family. So if these people have committed felonies, their cases shall be deliberated and reported in memorials to the emperor for final decision. Therefore, the officials of judicial institutions dare not carry out the punishment without authorization. Such regulations are made by the emperor to pay respect to his relatives and the people of great virtue to show his admiration for the honored guests of the state and to show the high praise to the people of great talents.

However, it was also stipulated that "'Ba Yi' (The Eight Deliberations) was not applicable to those who had committed the crimes of "Shi E" (The Ten Abominations). Thus, it can be seen from these regulations that when "Ba Yi" (The Eight Deliberations) was in conflict with the state interests, the former should be subordinated to the latter. In addition to "Ba Yi" (The Eight Deliberations), in *Tang Lv* (*Tang Code*), other regulations on penalty reduction or exemption for the noble officials or their relatives were also made, such as "Yi" (deliberation: cases involving 8 privileged groups were not to be tried directly by judicial organs, but to be reported to and decided by the emperor, thus the accused would usually be pardoned or remitted), "Qing" (petition: cases involving officials above the 5th rank shall be reported to and decided by the emperor, the punishment other than death penalty would be remitted by one degree), "Jian" (mitigation: except for death penalty, other punishments on officials above the 7th rank and their families could be remitted by one degree), "Shu" (atonement), "Guan Dang" (giving up one's official position for the atonement for a crime) and "Mian Guan" (dismissing from official position).

"Qing" (petition): the people who enjoyed the privilege of "Qing" (petition) included the relatives above "Da Gong" (the person wearing the mourning apparel of soft sackcloth in the third mourning degree) of the crown prince's dauphines or the relatives and grandchildren of "Qi Qin" (relatives being in mourn for one year), and all current officials of "Wu Pin" (the fifth rank) or above. If these people had committed crimes punishable by "Liu" (exile) or the punishment lighter, their punishment could be reduced by one level; if they had committed crimes punishable by death penalty, their cases should be presented in memorials to the emperor for the final decision. As the social status of those who enjoyed "Qing" (petition) were lower than those enjoying "'Ba Yi' (The Eight Deliberations), the scope of applying "Qing" (petition) was relatively narrower, so it was stipulated that "the law is not applicable to those who have committed the crimes of 'Shi E' (the Ten Abominations), who are the relatives of the offenders punished for 'Fan Ni' (treachery), 'Yuan Zuo' (the penalty of punishing somebody for being related to or friendly with someone who has committed a crime), 'Sha Ren' (murder), 'Jian Shou Nei Jian' (who have stolen what is entrusted to their care), 'Dao' (who have committed the offenses of stealing) and 'Lue Ren' (who have plundered people), or who have taken bribes by bending the law."

"Jian" (mitigation): it was applicable to officials above "Qi Pin" (the seventh rank) and the relatives of those who enjoyed the privilege of "Qing" (petition). If these people had committed crimes punishable by "Liu" (exile) or the punishment lighter, their punishment could be reduced by one level.

"Shu" (atonement): applicable to the officials of "Jiu Pin" (the ninth rank) and the relatives of the officials of "Qi Pin" (the seventh rank). If these people had committed crimes punishable by "Liu" (exile) or the punishment lighter, their punishment could be redeemed. In fact, the death penalty could be redeemed as well. In *Tang Lv* (*Tang Code*), the amount of ransom money for the redemption of each crime was clearly stipulated: the punishment of "Zhang" (flogging with heavy sticks) for fifty strokes could be redeemed by paying five *jin* of copper; the punishment of "Zhang" (flogging with heavy sticks) for one hundred strokes could be redeemed by paying ten *jin* of copper; the punishment of three-year-penal-servitude could be redeemed by paying sixty *jin* of copper; the punishment of "Si" (death penalty) could be redeemed by paying one hundred and twenty *jin* of copper. Thus, the legalization of "Shu" (atonement) had opened the door for the rich people to be exempted from punishment.

"Guan Dang" (giving up one's official position for the atonement for a crime): applicable to ordinary officials. In other words, the officials could use the ranks of their official titles to atone for their crimes. For example, an official above "Wu Pin" (the fifth rank) could use his official title to atone for his "private crime" punishable by a two-year punishment of "Tu" (imprisonment), or to atone for his "public crime" punishable by a three-year punishment of "Tu" (imprisonment). An official above "Jiu Pin" (the ninth rank) could use his official title to atone for his "private crime" punishable by a one-year punishment of "Tu" (imprisonment), or "public crime" punishable by a two-year punishment of "Tu" (imprisonment). If the official had a concurrent post, he should first use his higher ranking title to atone for the crime, and then the lower one; if the official in a higher rank had committed a minor offense, he could keep the position but should pay the redemption; if the official in a lower rank had committed a serious felony, he should give his title up and pay the redemption; if a person had lost his title because of the atonement, he could be again employed as an official ranking one level lower than his previous one, one year later. From these regulations, it can be seen that although the ordinary officials were not able to enjoy the privileges of "Yi" (Deliberations) and "Qing" (petition), they could still use their official titles to atone for their crimes to reduce or be exempted from punishments.

"Mian Guan" (dismissing from official position): it could be used to "atone for a two-year punishment of 'Tu' (imprisonment). If one official was dismissed from his office but he had kept his official position, his crime punishable by a one-year punishment of 'Tu' (imprisonment) could be atoned." However, this law "is not applicable to the staff with no titles in offices." The officials who were dismissed from their offices but still retained their official positions could be again employed as officials one level lower one year later. In Qing Dynasty, a man named Xue Yunsheng wrote in *Tang Ming Lv He Bian* (*A Collection of Laws in Tang and Ming Dynasties*) that "*Tang Lv* (*Tang Code*) has given preferential treatment and meticulous care to the officials."

7.2 The Legal System of Tang Dynasty Symbolizing the Establishment...

The series of regulations from "Ba Yi" (The Eight Deliberations) to "Mian Guan" (dismissing from official position) had shown that *Tang Lv* (*Tang Code*) was made just to protect the privileges of those aristocrats and bureaucrats.

In addition, the crimes were divided into public and private crimes. In *Qin Lv* (*Qin Code*), the crimes were initially divided into "public crimes" and "private crimes." It was stipulated in *Tang Lv* (*Tang Code*) that public crimes "referred to the crimes committed by officials when handling public affairs rather than private affairs"; while the private crimes referred to "the crimes committed by officials when doing private business rather than public business," or "the crimes committed by the officials who handled public affairs for private interests ...or bent the law for someone... or made a plea for someone by violating the laws." Generally speaking, because private crimes were deliberately committed by officials when they abused their power for personal gains, they were always harshly punished. However, these crimes, whether "public" or "private," were permitted to be redeemed by the method of "Guan Dang" (giving up one's official position for the atonement for a crime).

"Zi Shou Jian Zui" (reducing penalties for those who have surrendered themselves). It was stipulated in *Tang Lv* (*Tang Code*) that if one could surrender himself before he committed the crime, he would be exempted from punishment; if one was accused of a minor crime, but if he could confess his serious crime which he had committed before, he should be exempted from a severe punishment. "So in interrogation, if one makes a confession of another crime," his punishment would be reduced for surrendering himself. It was also provided that one could make a confession on behalf of another person. If one could confess his own crime after being prosecuted, his penalty could be reduced by two levels. However, if one had lied or concealed some facts during the interrogation, he would be punished for the crime of telling lies. Besides, the offender could surrender himself to officials or to victims, if "one offender had confessed his crime to the owner of the property that he had stolen or the money or property he had defrauded, it was the same as making confessions to the officials." In *Tang Lv* (*Tang Code*), to disintegrate the organized crime, it was also stipulated that if one offender who had committed minor crimes could help to arrest other offenders who had committed more serious crimes or could voluntarily surrender himself, he would be exempted from punishment, but this regulation was not applicable to the circumstances where "the stealing has been reported," or where "the crimes of intentional killing and injuring have been committed." From the regulation on penalty reduction and exemption made for those who had surrendered themselves, it can be seen that the chief criminals were targeted in the criminal law enforcement to narrow down the scope of attack and to stabilize the social order.

The offenders were divided into accomplices, chief offenders, and recidivists. In *Tang Lv* (*Tang Code*), in a joint offense, the offenders were divided into principal or accessory offenders and they were punished according to the crimes which they had committed individually. In a joint offense, the person who had the initial idea of committing a crime, or who was the chief instigator was viewed as the principal offender and would be punished severely; while his followers were viewed as the accessory offenders, whose penalties would be reduced by one level. As to the accomplices in the cases of affrays and batteries, the one who had caused the most serious harm would be severely punished. If it was impossible to identify who had caused the most serious harm, the chief instigator should be severely punished; if a family committed a joint offense, the elder of the family should be punished. However, in the cases of serious crimes, such as "Mou Fan" (plotting rebellion or plotting to endanger the country) and "Mou Da Ni" (great sedition), it was not necessary to identify the principal or accessory offenders, because all of the offenders would be severely punished. Moreover, the penalties for recidivists would be aggravated. In *Shu Yi (Tang Lv Shu Yi)*, it was explain that "if one has been put in prison for three times," "then he is truly incorrigible" so "strict rules shall be applied in order to punish him for what he has done." For example, if "one has committed the crime of robbery for three times, he shall be punished by 'Liu' (exile) to a distance of 2,000 *li*; if one has been punished by 'Liu' (exile) for three times, he shall be punished by 'Jiao' (hanging)."

Penalty reduction for "Lao" (elder), "You" (young) and "Fei Ji" (the disabled, including mentally disabled and mute, fractured lumbar vertebra, one crippled arm or leg, etc). Those who were seventy years old or older, or fifteen years old or younger, or "Fei Ji" (disabled, including mentally disabled and mute, fractured lumbar vertebra, one crippled arm or leg, etc.) and those who were punishable by "Liu" (exile) or the penalties lighter could have their punishments redeemed. However, this regulation was not applicable to those who were punishable by "Liu" (exile) with labor work, or those who were punishable by "Liu" (exile) or "Yuan Zuo" (the penalty of punishing somebody for being related to or friendly with someone who has committed a crime) for the crime of "Fan Ni" (treachery), or those who were punishable by "Liu" (exile) after being pardoned for an amnesty. If those who were eighty years old or older, or ten years old or younger or disabled had committed crimes punishable by "Si" (death penalty), they could petition to the emperor for remission; if they had committed the crime of "Dao" (robbery) or had caused injuries, they were permitted to redeem their punishment and to be exempted from the punishment of other offenses. However, those who were ninety years old or older, or seven years old or younger should not be punished, although they were punishable by "Si" (death penalty). If people were healthy and young when committing crimes, but were aged and sick when the crimes were discovered, they would be punished according to the provisions on the aged or sick; if people were young when committing crimes, but became grown-ups when crimes were discovered, they would be punished according to the provisions on the young. It was proved by experience that such groups of people would not do any serious harm to society, so even if they were punished leniently, it would not influence the stability of the country and the society, on the contrary, it could be used to propagandize the doctrine of "Xu Xing" (penalty reduction) as well as the rulers' benevolence.

"Tong Ju Xiang Yin" (The concealment of the crimes committed by the people living together). The principle of "Qin Qin De Xiang Shou Ni" (a law in Han Dynasty which ruled that crimes committed among the kinfolks should be concealed and not reported to the government) was initially made in *Han Lv* (*Han Code*), but in *Tang Lv* (*Tang Code*) it was further stipulated:

7.2 The Legal System of Tang Dynasty Symbolizing the Establishment... 565

> If those who are living under one roof have concealed the crimes committed by their relatives above 'Da Gong' (the person wearing the mourning apparel of soft sackcloth in the third mourning degree) or by their maternal parents, their maternal grandchildren, their wives of grandchildren, their husbands' brothers and their husbands' wives, they shall all be exempted from punishment; if 'Bu Qu' (the private army) and 'Nu Bi' (the slave girls and maidservants) have concealed the crimes committed by their masters, they shall also be exempted from punishment;... if people have concealed the crimes committed by their relatives of 'Xiao Gong' (the person wearing the mourning apparel of soft sackcloth in the fourth mourning degree), their penalties shall be three levels lighter than that for the common people. However, this regulation is not applicable to the cases where the relatives have committed the crimes of 'Mou Pan' (treason) and other felonies.

Obviously, the relatives within the fourth generation were all permitted to conceal the crimes for each other, but some different regulations were made for the relatives of "Da Gong" (the person wearing the mourning apparel of soft sackcloth in the third mourning degree) and "Xiao Gong" (the person wearing the mourning apparel of soft sackcloth in the fourth mourning degree). Additionally, "Bu Qu" (the private army) and "Nu Bi" (the slave girls and maidservants) were also permitted to conceal the crimes committed by their masters. However, the crimes that were permitted to be concealed were just within the scope of ordinary crimes, as to the crimes seriously harmful to the government of the country, they were forbidden to be concealed; on the contrary, it was permitted for the grandchildren to report the serious crimes committed by grandparents and it was also permitted for 'Bu Qu' (the private army) and 'Nu Bi' (the slave girls and maidservants) to report the crimes committed by masters.

"Bing He Long Zui Cong Zhong" (when several crimes are committed concurrently, punishment will be enforced according to the most serious one). It was stipulated in *Tang Lv (Tang Code)* that "when two or more crimes are committed, penalties shall be enforced on the most serious one; so when the crimes are committed repeatedly, penalties shall also be enforced on the most serious one." If one crime was committed first and the sentence had already been made, then the other crimes were committed subsequently, but if the subsequent crimes were less serious or as serious as the first one, the original sentence should be retained. Nevertheless, if the subsequent crimes were more serious, the criminal should be tried again and be more severely punished. Therefore, this regulation was made to crack down on more serious crimes.

"Lei Tui Shi Yong" (the principle of analogy). It was stipulated that "as for the crimes which are not regulated in the law, if they should be punished more leniently, the principle of "Ju Zhong Ming Qing" (where there are no legal provisions to be applied for the judgment of certain illegal conducts, if there are provisions which are much severer on similar conducts, then lighter punishments shall be implemented) should be applied; and if they should be punished more severely, the principle of "Ju Qing Ming Zhong" (where there are no legal provisions to be applied for the judgment of certain illegal conducts, if there are provisions which are much lenient on similar conducts, then severer punishments shall be implemented) should be applied." And it was also clearly stipulated that "this regulation of 'Bi Fu' (legal analogy) is applicable to more complicated cases." The application of "Lei Tui Yuan

Ze" (the principle of analogy) was determined by the legal awareness and the pursuit of interest of the legal officials. To prevent the officials from abusing this principle, a regulation was specially made in *Tang Lv* (*Tang Code*): "if 'Zhi' (imperial decree) and 'Chi' (instruction) cannot be used as 'Yong Ge' (permanent injunctions), they shall not be used as the analogies in the enforcement of penalties; if anyone has used them to make inappropriate judgment, he shall be punished for the crime of intentional negligence." Therefore, the principle of analogy had made the provisions of law more elaborate.

The crimes committed by "Hua Wai Ren" (foreigners). Because there were frequent trade and business relationship between the imperial government of Tang Dynasty and the neighboring countries, there were about 100,000 foreigners living or doing business in China, including Indians, Persians, the people from Central Asia, the people from Southeast Asia, and Jews. To solve the disputes in trade or among the people, it was stipulated in *Tang Lv* (*Tang Code*) that "in the cases where disputes arose between 'Hua Wai Ren' (foreigners) themselves, penalties shall be enforced according to the laws of foreign countries; in the cases where disputes arose between 'Hua Wai Ren' and the native people, penalties shall be enforced according to the native law." According to the explanation of *Shu Yi* (*Tang Lv Shu Yi*), the so-called "Hua Wai Ren" referred to the people who came from "Fan Yi Zhi Guo" (vassal states and foreign countries), which showed that the imperial government of Tang Dynasty had considered itself to be a Celestial Empire. According to the provisions of *Tang Lv* (*Tang Code*), if the litigation only involved foreigners, the cases should be judged in accordance with the laws of foreign countries, but if the litigation involved people with different nationalities (including Chinese people), the cases should be judged in accordance with the codes of Tang Dynasty. This provision not only reflected the respect shown to the laws of foreign countries, but also maintained the independent judicial power from the perspective of trials, so this provision was used until the Qing Dynasty.

In summary, the penalties for different crimes were regulated in *Tang Lv* (*Tang Code*), at the same time, great importance was paid to the prevention of crimes. For example, in *Dao Zei Lv* (*Statutes on Robbing and Theft*), it was stipulated that "if the offenders are pardoned under the general amnesty, their families shall be moved to a place 1,000 *li* away." This was explained in *Shu Yi* (*Tang Lv Shu Yi*): "Those who have committed homicide shall be punished by 'Si' (death penalty); however, if the criminals are pardoned under the general amnesty, or if the victims still have relatives of 'Qi Qin' (relatives being in mourn for one year), the criminals' families shall be moved to a place 1,000 *li* away." This regulation was made to prevent the relatives of the victims from taking revenge on the criminals, which in fact showed that it was the society that had shouldered the responsibility of crime prevention. Because of the limitation of the contents of law code, it was impossible for all crimes to be included in *Tang Lv* (*Tang Code*), so at the end of *Za Lv* (*Miscellaneous Laws*), it was stipulated that "if one has engaged in a behavior that should not be conducted (that is, though it is not an offense included in the provision of law, it is still forbidden to be done), the person shall be punished by 'Chi' (flogging with light sticks) for forty strokes; if the behavior is seriously harmful, the person shall be punished by 'Zhang' (flogging with heavy sticks) for eighty strokes." This rule was helpful for the officials to punish the illegal acts beyond the regulations of law.

7.2.5 The More Complicated Civil Law

In Tang Dynasty, although the legal system was well developed, under the influence of the principle of stressing the public rights and neglecting the private rights, the tendency of "Zhong Xing Qing Min" (stressing the criminal law and neglecting the civil law) was not changed, so that although criminal law had already been developed to its maturity and was well establishment, the civil law was only separately collected in "Lv" (criminal law), "Ling" (orders or ordinances), "Ge" (injunction) and "Chi" (instruction). It can be learned from some unearthed documents that, in reality, customs and tradition still played a very important role in handling the civil affairs. However, it needs to be pointed out that the development of feudal commercial economy and property relationship which was becoming gradually more complicated in Tang Dynasty did provide a solid foundation for the development of civil law. Thus, seen from the process of the overall development of Chinese civil law, it was evident that the civil law of Tang Dynasty had reached a new stage.

7.2.5.1 The Civil Legal Capacity and the Disposing Capacity

In Tang Dynasty, when there lacked a "personal equality" in the relationship between rights and obligations, the legal and disposing capacity of the subject of civil rights was different for different people with different identities. The noblemen and bureaucrats were the privileged class with noble blood lineage who governed and ruled the common people, and who enjoyed the statutory privileges granted to them by the imperial government, so the civil rights were just of the secondary importance for the privileged people. The common people were referred to as "Liang Ren" (the decent people) and "Fan Ren" (the ordinary people) in *Tang Lv* (*Tang Code*), including military personnel, peasants, laborers, and businessmen. In "Hu Bu Lang Zhong Yuan Wai Lang" (head and deputy of a subministry department of The Department of Revenue) in *Tang Liu Dian* (*The Six Statutes of Tang Dynasty*), the following is stipulated:

> The people are divided into four groups and they are engaged in their own work. Those who are well-educated and trained in military skills belong to 'Shi' (scholars); those who make a living on farming and sericulture belong to 'Nong' (peasant); those who make handcrafts belong to 'Gong' (artisan); those who butcher cattle and sell liquor belong to 'Shang' (businessmen). The people from 'Gong' (artisan) and 'Shang' (businessmen) shall not interfere with the work of 'Shi' (scholars), and the people who earn salaries from the government shall not submit themselves to work of 'Shang' (businessmen).

Therefore, it can be learned from this provision that "Shi" (scholars) was on top of the four groups of people, so once they entered the official circle, as the subjects of the complete civil legal and disposing capacity, they could enjoy the statutory privileges according to their official ranks. The people from "Nong" (peasant), "Gong" (artisan), "Shang" (businessmen) also had civil legal and disposing capacity, but the people from "Gong" (artisan), "Shang" (businessmen) were not permitted to enter the official circle.

The so-called "Jian Min" (rabbles or people of lower social status) was divided into two groups, namely, "Guan Jian Min" and "Si Jian Min." "Guan Jian Min" included "Guan Nu Bi" (the slave girls and maidservants working in government offices), "Guan Hu" (criminals and their relatives who became servants of officials), "Gong Yue Hu" (criminals and their families registered as musicians), "Za Hu" (families registered as workers) and "Tai Chang Yin Sheng" (musicians serving in Tai Chang Bureau). "Si Jian Min" (slave girls and maidservants working in private houses) included "Nu Bi" (the slave girls and maidservants), "Bu Qu" (the private army), "Ke Nv" (women having higher social status than that of maidservants) and "Sui Shen" (personal servants or maids) ("Lin Ren" worked as personal servants or maids and they gave up their identity of "Jian Min" and become "Liang Ren" after their employment came to an end), etc. Among "Jian Min" (rabbles or people of lower social status), "Nu Bi" (the slave girls and maidservants) working in government offices and private houses had the lowest social status, who "were treated like animals and who were the property owned by their masters," so that they had neither legal and disposing capacity nor household registration of their own. Thus, it was clear that in the civil legal relationship, one party referred to the people who were granted privileges, such as noblemen, bureaucrats, landlords and the major part of the four groups of people; the other party referred to the people who were at the bottom of the society, and who were granted no legal capacity or just part of legal capacity. In the legal regulations, it was forbidden for "Liang Ren" (the decent people) to become "Jian Min" (rabbles or people of lower social status) by breaking down their barriers to maintain the ruling order and the relationship of rights and obligations manifested in the form of social hierarchy.

With the development of economy and foreign trade, a large quantity of foreign businessmen came to China and went into business in Tang Dynasty. It was acknowledged in the law of Tang Dynasty that those foreign businessmen were the subjects of civil legal capacity, so they "were permitted to open shops." Besides, "Hua Wai Ren" (foreigners) were even permitted to marry Chinese, but the wives of those foreigners were not permitted to leave China.

In terms of disposing capacity, there were no specific concepts nor unified regulations on the ages of people, but generally, the age of "Ding Nian" (the year of manhood) which was stipulated by the law for serving corvée and paying tax was regarded as the age to enjoy disposing capacity. In the early period of Sui Dynasty, those who were above eighteen years old were called "Ding" (adult), but the age was changed into twenty-one years old in the 3rd year of Kaihuang (583 A.D.) and into twenty-two years old during the reign of Emperor Yang. In Tang Dynasty, the regulations of Sui Dynasty were followed. According to a decree issued in April of the 7th year of Emperor Wude (624 A.D.), "the newly born boys and girls are referred to as 'Xiao' (youth), the children who are four years old are referred to as

'Huang' (ignorant youth), the teenagers who are sixteen years old are referred to as 'Zhong' (middler), the youngsters who are twenty-one years old are referred to as 'Ding' (adult), and the people who are sixty years old are referred to as 'Lao' (elder)."[200] In the 3rd year of Yianbao during the reign of Emperor Xuanzong (744 A.D.), a decree was issued and it was ordered that the people who were eighteen years old were referred to as 'Zhong' (middler) and the people who were twenty-two years old were referred to as "Ding" (adult). It was stipulated in another imperial edict issued in July of the 1st year of Guande (763 A.D.) that "the male who are twenty-three years old are referred to as 'Ding' (adult) and the male who are fifty-eight years old are referred to as 'Lao' (elder)."[201] The different regulations for "Ding Nian" (the year of manhood) in different dynasties was mainly determined by the number of population and the needs of corvée.

Moreover, much importance was attached to the management of household registration, because tax was collected according to the number of population. It was recorded in "Shi Huo Zhi" (The Records of National Finance and Economy) in *Jiu Tang Shu* (*The Old Book of Tang Dynasty*) that "the regulation was initially made in the 7th year of Wude... and the households shall be registered every three years." Besides, "the property of each household shall be figured up and registered every year" and then be reported to "Zhou" (subprefecture), "Xian" (county) and "Hu Bu" (The Department of Revenue). Meanwhile, the households of the nation were divided into nine levels according to their property, as was stipulated that "the property of the small minorities who had pledged allegiance to the imperial government of Tang Dynasty should also be divided into nine levels,"[202] and "the households of the female and male Taoist priests and the Buddhist monks and nuns shall be registered every three years."[203] If the household registration was mishandled, or if it had caused the loss of tax collection, the persons in charge would be punished. It was recorded in "Hu Hun Lv" (Statutes on Marriage, Tax and Household Registration) in *Tang Lv* (*Tang Code*) that if a head of a family had made mistakes in household registration, he would be punished by "Tu" (imprisonment) for three years; if the head of a family had left out one person in household registration or lied about the age or the physical condition of a person for the purpose of evading tax, he would be punished by "Tu" (imprisonment) for one year, and the penalty would be aggravated by one level for every two people left out unregistered with the maximum penalty of "Tu" (imprisonment) for three years. If "Li Zheng" (head of "Li": the basic resident organization in ancient China) had carelessly left out or added one person in household registration, he would be punished by "Chi" (flogging with light

---

[200]"Shi Huo Zhi" (The Records of National Finance and Economy) in *Jiu Tang Shu* (*The Old Book of Tang Dynasty*).

[201]"Shi Huo Zhi" (The Records of National Finance and Economy) in *Jiu Tang Shu* (*The Old Book of Tang Dynasty*).

[202]"Hu Bu Lang Zhong Yuan Wai Lang" (The Chief and Deputy Minister of The Department of Revenue) in *Tang Liu Dian* (*The Six Statutes of Tang Dynasty*), Vol. 3.

[203]Niida Noboru (Japan), "Za Ling" (Miscellaneous Orders) in *Tang Ling Shi Yi* (*An Interpretation of the Orders of Tang Dynasty*), in the 7th year of Kaiyuan.

sticks) for forty strokes; if he had left out three persons in household registration, his penalty would be aggravated by one level; if he had already been punished by "Zhang" (flogging with heavy sticks) for one hundred strokes, his penalty would be aggravated by one level for every ten people left out in registration with the maximum penalty of "Tu" (imprisonment) for three years; if one chief official of "Zhou" (subprefecture) and "Xian" (county) had carelessly left out or added ten people in household registration, he would be punished by "Chi" (flogging with light sticks) for thirty strokes and his penalty would be aggravated by one level for every thirty people left out or added in household registration with the maximum penalty of "Tu" (imprisonment) for three years.

7.2.5.2 The Rights of Estate Under "Jun Tian Zhi" (The System of Land Equalization)

The personal property and real estate were called "Chan," "Ye," or "Chan Ye," which are called the property rights nowadays. The real estate mainly referred to farmland and houses, in other words, "farmland refers to a place which is associated with people's residence, so it is necessary to differentiate it from personal belongs."[204] The owner of the real estate was called "Ye Zhu" or "Chan Zhu." The real estate included personal belongs, cattle, and "Nu Bi" (the slave girls and maidservants), which were called "Cai" or "Wu," and the owner was called "Cai Zhu" or "Wu Zhu."

The protection of property rights provided by *Tang Lv* (*Tang Code*) included the prohibition of fraudulent claim for land, the restitution of illegal gains and the offering of compensation. If the property did not belong to a person but was fraudulently claimed, it was called fraudulent claim, which was different from mistaken claim. But whether fraudulent claim or mistaken claim, the aggrieved party could require the confirmation of property right. As to the illegally gained property, both the original property and the interests produced herein should be returned to the owner, as was written in volume four of *Tang Lv Shu Yi* (*The Comments on Tang Code*): "One asks: if the objects of others are stolen and used for making profits or lenting for collecting interest, will the money made herein be viewed as the same interest that shall be paid back to the owners? If the stolen objects are persons or cattle that have been passed down by different people and from different places in trade, or if the buyers know or do not know they are stolen objects, how the interest produced by the objects should be dealt with? The answer is: it is stipulated in law that the produced interest is the interest that is produced by the original product. So if the interest is made from a business at a later time, it is the interest made by other people in later business but not by the original owners. Since such interest is neither produced by the original owner, nor is included in the concept

---

[204]"Hu Hun" (Marriage, Tax and Household Registration) in *Tang Lv Shu Yi* (*The Comments on Tang Code*).

of the produced interest, it shall be given to the people in later business. If the buyers know the objects are stolen and that they have been sold by different people, both the stolen objects and the interest should be returned to their original owner; if the buyers do not know they are stolen objects, the objects and the interest should be given to the people who buy them in later business."

Moreover, the property obtained in controversy, or obtained by threatening, or by fraudulent methods, or by robbery or forcible measures was all illegal, so they should be returned to the original owner. In *Tang Lv* (*Tang Code*), the compensation for the damage of the property was also stipulated.

The categories of property rights in Tang Dynasty mainly included "Suo You Quan" (ownership), "Dian Quan" (tenancy rights), "Zhi Quan" (pledge rights) and "Dian Quan" (pawn rights).

7.2.5.2.1 (1) The Obtaining and Protection of Ownership

"Suo You Quan" (ownership) of land was obtained by land equalization, and the object of ownership was the farmland. Thus, the people from all walks of life had extensively obtained farmland according to "Jun Tian Ling" (Decree of Land Equalization). In the 7th year of Wude (624 A.D.), "Jun Tian Ling" (Decree of Land Equalization) was issued and the details are as follows:

> Each 'Ding Nan' (adult man) and 'Zhong Nan' (middler) shall be assigned one *qing* of family farmland; each 'Du Ji' (the incapacitated) and 'Fei Ji' (the disabled) shall be assigned forty *mu* of farmland, each wife or concubine whose husband has died shall be assigned thirty *mu* of farmland. If these people are the heads of the households, the farmland assigned to them shall be increased by one *mu*. Twenty percent of the assigned farmland is 'Kou Fen Tian' (state-owned farmland) and eighty percent is "Shi Ye Tian" (family farmland, which could be passed to next generation) which is allowed to be passed down to next generation after the current owner dies, while 'Kou Fen Tian' (state-owned farmland) shall be returned to the government and assigned to other person after the current owner dies. The amount of farmland which is assigned in the places with small territory and dense population shall be half of that which is assigned in the places with vast territory and sparse population. If the pieces of farmland are different in natural condition, or if some people would like to alternatively cultivate them every year, the farmland assigned to them shall be doubled; if the people in the places with vast territory and sparse population have alternatively cultivated the land three times, the farmland assigned to them shall not be increased.[205]

Until the 25th year of Kaiyuan (737 A.D.), "Jun Tian Ling" (Decree of Land Equalization) was further amended based on the experience of the implementation of the system. The decree is as follows:

> Each 'Ding Nan' (adult man) shall be assigned twenty *mu* of 'Yong Ye Tian' (family farmland, which could be passed to next generation) and eighty *mu* of 'Kou Fen Tian' (state-owned farmland); 'Zhong Nan' (middler) who is eighteen three years old or older shall be assigned farmland as a 'Ding Nan' (adult man). Each 'Lao Nan' (the old man), 'Du Ji'

---

[205]Niida Noboru (Japan), "Tian Ling" (Decrees on Farmland) in *Tang Ling Shi Yi* (*An Interpretation of the Orders of Tang Dynasty*), in the 7th year of Wude.

(incapacitated) and 'Fei Ji' (disabled) shall be assigned 40 *mu* of 'Kou Fen Tian' (state-owned farmland); each wife or concubine whose husband has died shall be assigned 30 *mu* of 'Kou Fen Tian' (state-owned farmland). Those who have been given 'Yong Ye Tian' (family farmland, which could be passed to next generation) previously shall also be assigned 'Kou Fen Tian' (state-owned farmland). The heads of the households who are 'Huang' (ignorant youth), Xiao' (youth), 'Zhong' (middler), 'Ding Nan' (adult man), women, 'Lao Nan' (the old man), 'Du Ji' (the incapacitated) or 'Fei Ji' (the disabled), or wives or concubines whose husbands have died shall be assigned twenty *mu* of 'Yong Ye Tian' (family farmland, which could be passed to next generation) and twenty *mu* of 'Kou Fen Tian' (state-owned farmland). In the places with vast territory and sparse population, the amount of farmland shall be assigned according to regulation. In the places with small territory and dense population, the amount of land assigned should be half as much as the amount of 'Kou Fen Tian' (state-owned farmland) which was assigned in the places with vast territory and sparse population. If those who are granted 'Kou Fen Tian' (state-owned farmland) would like to alternatively cultivate the land in different natural conditions each year, the farmland assigned to them shall be doubled (if the people in the places with vast territory and sparse population have alternatively cultivated the land three times, they shall be assigned farmland according to the rules of the town).[206]

"Yong Ye Tian" (family farmland, which could be passed to next generation) could be passed down on to the next generation, and "it shall not be returned to the imperial government, even if any successor of the land has committed crimes or has been punished by removing his name from his family," while "'Kou Fen Tian' (state-owned farmland) shall be returned to the imperial government after the owner has died. Within 'Zhou' (subprefecture) and 'Xian' (county), the places with vast territory and sparse population are referred to as 'Kuan Xiang'; the places with small territory and dense population are referred to as 'Xia Xiang'."[207]

Moreover, it was also stipulated that "'Kou Fen Tian" (state-owned farmland) and "Yong Ye Tian" (family farmland, which could be passed to next generation) which are given to the businessmen should be reduced by half and no land is given to them if they are in 'Xia Xiang'."[208] In addition, "each Taoist priest shall be given thirty *mu* of land, each female Taoist shall be given twenty *mu* of land" and "the amount of land given to each Buddhist monk and nun is the same."[209] Moreover, "'Za Hu' (families registered as workers) shall be given land according to regulation, while those who are old or childless shall be given land according to the rules for the common people. The amount of land given to officials is half as much as that assigned to the common people."[210]

---

[206] Niida Noboru (Japan), "Tian Ling" (Decrees on Farmland) in *Tang Ling Shi Yi* (*An Interpretation of the Orders of Tang Dynasty*), in the 25th year of Kaiyuan.

[207] Niida Noboru (Japan), "Tian Ling" (Decrees on Farmland) in *Tang Ling Shi Yi* (*An Interpretation of the Orders of Tang Dynasty*), in the 25th year of Kaiyuan.

[208] Niida Noboru (Japan), "Tian Ling" (Decrees on Farmland) in *Tang Ling Shi Yi* (*An Interpretation of the Orders of Tang Dynasty*), in the 25th year of Kaiyuan.

[209] Niida Noboru (Japan), "Tian Ling" (Decrees on Farmland) in *Tang Ling Shi Yi* (*An Interpretation of the Orders of Tang Dynasty*), in the 25th year of Kaiyuan.

[210] Niida Noboru (Japan), "Tian Ling" (Decrees on Farmland) in *Tang Ling Shi Yi* (*An Interpretation of the Orders of Tang Dynasty*) in the 25th year of Kaiyuan.

7.2 The Legal System of Tang Dynasty Symbolizing the Establishment...

The date of granting and returning land was fixed, and it was stipulated that "every year on the 1st day of October, 'Li Zheng' (head of "Li": the basic resident organization in ancient China) should begin to check and register the households; in November, 'Xian Ling' (county magistrate) should collect the names of the people who should be given or who should return their land; in December, the work of giving and returning land should be completed."[211]

Apart from "Yong Ye Tian" (family farmland, which could be passed to next generation) and "Kou Fen Tian" (state-owned farmland), "Liang Kou" (the decent people) could also get gardens and crofts. According to law, "each family with three family members shall be granted one *mu* of land with each *mu* of land added for every three more family members. For 'Jian Kou' (rabbles or people of lower social status), each family with five members shall be granted one *mu* of land with each *mu* of land added for every five more family members. However, the regulation on 'Yong Ye Tian' (family farmland) and 'Kou Fen Tian' (state-owned farmland) is not applicable to 'Jian Kou' (rabbles or people of lower social status)."[212]

The noblemen and senior officials could get "Yong Ye Tian" (family farmland, which could be passed to next generation) according to their official ranks, as was stipulated that "'Yong Ye Tian' (family farmland, which could be passed to next generation) shall be given to the officials, nobleman and the meritorious family." The specific amount of land given is regulated as follows:

> The princess shall be given 100 *qing* of land; the chief ministry officials of 'Yi Pin' (the first rank) shall be given 60 *qing* of land; the king of vassal states and vice ministry officials of 'Yi Pin' (the first rank) shall be respectively given 50 *qing* of land; the chief officials of 'Er Pin' (the second rank) with the title of 'Guo Gong' (the rank of nobleman lower than that of duke) shall be given 40 *qing* of land; the vice ministry officials of 'Er Pin' (the second rank) with the title of 'Jun Gong' (the rank of nobleman lower than that of 'Guo Gong') shall be given 35 *qing* of land; the chief ministry officials of 'San Pin' (the third rank) with the title of duke shall be given 25 *qing* of land; the vice ministry officials of 'San Pin' (the third rank) shall be given 20 *qing* of land; the chief ministry officials of 'Si Pin' (the fourth rank) with the title of marquis shall be given 14 *qing* of land; the vice ministry officials of 'Si Pin' (the fourth rank) with the title of earl shall be respectively given 11 qing of land; the chief ministry officials of 'Wu Pin' (the fifth rank) with the title of viscount shall be respectively given 8 *qing* of land; the vice ministry officials of 'Wu Pin' (the fifth rank) with the title of Baron shall be respectively given 5 *qing* of land. 'Shang Zhu Guo' (one of 'Xun Guan': ancient senior official with highest honorary title, ranked 12) shall be given 30 *qing* of land; 'Zhu Guo' (one of 'Xun Guan': ancient senior official with honorary title, ranked 11) shall be given 25 *qing* of land; 'Shang Hu Jun' (one of 'Xun Guan': ancient senior official with honorary title, ranked 10) shall be given 20 *qing* of land; 'Hu Jun' (one of 'Xun Guan': ancient senior official with honorary title, ranked 9) shall be given 15 *qing* of land; 'Shang Qing Che Du Wei' (one of 'Xun Guan': ancient senior official with honorary title, ranked 8) shall be given 10 *qing* of land; 'Qing Che Du Wei' (one of 'Xun Guan': ancient senior official with honorary title) shall be given 7 *qing* of land; 'Shang Qi Du Wei' (one of 'Xun Guan': ancient senior official with honorary title, ranked 6) shall be given 6 *qing* of land; 'Qi

---

[211] Niida Noboru (Japan), "Tian Ling" (Decrees on Farmland) in *Tang Ling Shi Yi* (*An Interpretation of the Orders of Tang Dynasty*) in the 25th year of Kaiyuan.

[212] Niida Noboru (Japan), "Tian Ling" (Decrees on Farmland) in *Tang Ling Shi Yi* (*An Interpretation of the Orders of Tang Dynasty*) in the 25th year of Kaiyuan.

Du Wei' (one of 'Xun Guan': ancient senior official with honorary title, ranked 5) shall be given 4 *qing* of land; 'Xiao Qi Wei' (one of 'Xun Guan': ancient senior official with honorary title, ranked 4) shall be given 4 *qing* of land; 'Fei Qi Wei' (one of 'Xun Guan': ancient senior official with honorary title, ranked 3) shall be given 80 *mu* of land; 'Yun Qi Wei' (one of 'Xun Guan': ancient senior official with honorary title, ranked 2) and 'Wu Qi Wei' (one of 'Xun Guan': ancient senior official with lowest honorary title, ranked 1) shall be given 60 *mu* of land respectively.

In addition, those people could also obtain the land bestowed by the emperor.

Not only that, the civil and military officials in the capital could also be given land around the capital within one hundred *li* according to their official ranks. Specifically, "officials of 'Yi Pin' (the first rank) shall be given twelve *qing* of land; officials of 'Er Pin' (the second rank) shall be given ten *qing* of land; officials of 'San Pin' (the third rank) shall be given nine *qing* of land;... officials of 'Jiu Pin' (the ninth rank) shall be given two *qing* of land."[213]

As to the officials in "Zhou" (subprefecture), "Du Hu Fu" (the administrative organs set up by Han Dynasty in the western region: now Xinjiang region) and prince palaces, "the officials of 'Er Pin' (the second rank) shall be given twelve *qing* of land; the officials of 'San Pin' (the third rank) shall be given ten *qing* of land; the officials of 'Si Pin' (the fourth rank) shall be given eight *qing* of land;...the officials of 'Jiu Pin' (the ninth rank) shall be given two *qing* and fifty *mu* of land."[214]

As to "Gong Xie Tian," which was used for the administrative expenses of different levels of government offices, the official departments in the capital were given two to twenty-six *qing* of land, while those outside the capital were given one to forty *qing* of land.[215]

"Nu Bi" (the slave girls and maidservants) could also obtain land according to the number of adults in the family. However, the amount of land given to the noblemen and bureaucrats was far more than that given to the common people. As forcible occupation of peasants' land often occurred in the process of land distribution, it was regulated in *Tang Lv* (*Tang Code*) that each prince could be given "one *qing* of land which can be used as their gardens. If no land within the city is available, the land near the city shall be given; if no official land is available, the land of the common people shall be given."[216]

In the early period of Tang Dynasty, "Ju Tian Zhi" (the system of land equalization) was completely implemented in the country; therefore, it was not a coincidence that "the records of given land" and "the records of returned land" were discovered in the documents unearthed in Dunhuang, which had clearly reflected the situation of

---

[213]Niida Noboru (Japan), "Tian Ling" (Decrees on Farmland) in *Tang Ling Shi Yi* (*An Interpretation of the Orders of Tang Dynasty*), in the 25th year of Kaiyuan.

[214]Niida Noboru (Japan), "Tian Ling" (Decrees on Farmland) in *Tang Ling Shi Yi* (*An Interpretation of the Orders of Tang Dynasty*), in the 25th year of Kaiyuan.

[215]Niida Noboru (Japan), "Tian Ling" (Decrees on Farmland) in *Tang Ling Shi Yi* (*An Interpretation of the Orders of Tang Dynasty*), in the 25th year of Kaiyuan.

[216]Niida Noboru (Japan), "Tian Ling" (Decrees on Farmland) in *Tang Ling Shi Yi* (*An Interpretation of the Orders of Tang Dynasty*), in the 25th year of Kaiyuan.

the implementation of "Ju Tian Zhi" (the system of land equalization) at the time. Because of the long-term massive wars at the end of Sui Dynasty, many people died or were forced to leave their native land (in the 1st year of Zhenguan there were fewer than three million families in the country, which was less than one third of the population in Sui Dynasty), the imperial government owned a large amount of farmland which were without owners, so it created a favorable condition for the implementation of "Ju Tian Zhi" (the system of land equalization). One fact that could not be denied by the rulers of Tang Dynasty was that some of the land which was finally occupied by the imperial government was actually the land obtained from the landlords by the peasants during the peasant uprising in the later period of Sui Dynasty. Because of the implementation of "Jun Tian Zhi" (The System of Land Equalization), the income tax of the imperial government was increased, which had eased the conflicts between the different classes, sped up the recovery and development of social production and strengthened the centralization of authority.

Apart from what is mentioned above, the other methods of obtaining property rights are as follows:

The occupation of the unclaimed property. The preemption of unclaimed property was stipulated in *Tang Lv* (*Tang Code*): "If one person has already done some work in cultivating, plowing, harvesting or collecting the objects in the mountainous areas or open fields, but if another person claims for those mountainous areas or open fields fraudulently, the latter shall be found guilty of larceny."[217] According to the explanation of *Shu Yi* (*Tang Lv Shu Yi*), the so-called "objects in the mountainous areas or open fields" referred to "the grass, trees, herbs, and stones." Therefore, if some people had cultivated the land, harvested or collected the products, it was forbidden for others to claim for them; otherwise, they would be punished for larceny.

The discovery of buried objects. In *Tang Lv* (*Tang Code*), "Su Cang Wu" referred to the buried objects. It was explained in *Shu Yi* (*Tang Lv Shu Yi*) that "if one has discovered some objects buried in other people's fields, the objects shall be divided equally with the owner of the land; if the person who has discovered the objects has concealed the truth, in addition to dividing the objects with the landlord, he shall also be punished for fraud property, but his penalty shall be reduced by three levels; if he has discovered an antique in a special form without reporting to officials, ... he shall be punished for the same offense"; "if he has reported it and handed it over to the official department," he would be awarded; if one had discovered some objects buried underneath the land or the house he had rented from other people or government, he "shall divide the objects with the owner"; "if there are already owners for the private land and houses, or if the tenant has not done any work, or if the worker has found the buried objects, then he shall divide the objects and share them with the owner. However, because the tenant is not the owner and because he

---

[217]"Zei Dao" (Stealing and Robbery) in *Tang Lv Shu Yi* (*The Comments on Tang Code*), Vol. 20.

has done no work on the land or the houses, he shall not share the discovered objects."[218]

The picking up of "Lan Yi Wu." "Lan Yi Wu" referred to the lost property, which, according to *Shu Yi* (*Tang Lv Shu Yi*), included "treasures, seals, tallies, and the miscellaneous objects." It was stipulated that "if one has picked up the lost property from the ground and has kept it for five days without delivering it to government, he shall be punished for the offense of 'Wang Shi' (having lost things); if the lost property is more valuable, he shall be punished for the offense of 'Zuo Zang' (embezzlement); if the lost property belongs to a person, he shall still be punished for the offense of 'Zuo Zang', but the punishment shall be reduced by two levels."[219] Moreover, "a notice of the lost property should be posted up on the door outside the office to inform people, if the property is not claimed by anyone within one year, it shall be confiscated by the government."[220] In other word, if nobody went to the government office to claim for the property within one year, the property would be confiscated.

Collecting flotsam. According to article eleven in "Za Ling" (Miscellaneous Orders) in *Tang Ling Shi Yi* (*An Interpretation of the Orders of Tang Dynasty*):

> In the case where pieces of wood or bamboo are drifting away by flood, if a person collects them and puts them on the bank of a river and posts a notice beside them and then reports them to the government, he shall be rewarded after the owner claims for them. If he collects the drifting objects from a river, he shall be awarded by two fifth of the object; if he collects the drifting objects from water in other places, he shall be awarded by one fifth of the object; if the drifting objects are not claimed for by anyone within thirty days, they shall be given to the person who collects them.

The ownership of "Sheng Chan Fan Xi" (the interest of production). The so-called "Sheng Chan Fan Xi" (interest of production) referred to the legal rights generated in the reproduction of the objects because of the natural law, such as "a maid giving birth to a baby or a horse foaling." In *Tang Lv* (*Tang Code*), "Nu Bi" (the slave girls and maidservants) were regarded as the property of their masters. In other words, "they are the property of their masters like the cattle," therefore, the child of a maid and a foal of a horse were all regarded as "the interest of production" and their ownership was also clearly stipulated: "The child and the foal all belong to their masters together with their mothers in accordance with the law."

Additionally, as to the ownership in Tang Dynasty, it was divided into joint ownership and partnership ownership. The joint ownership mainly included the natural products such as mountains, rivers, pools, and lakes, etc., while the things such as the ancestors' tombs of the clan, etc. belonged to partnership ownership.

In *Tang Lv* (*Tang Code*), the property rights was strictly protected. For example, it was stipulated that "it is forbidden to occupy land beyond quota" or to infringe

---

[218]"Za Lv" (Miscellaneous Laws) in *Tang Lv Shu Yi* (*The Comments on Tang Code*), Vol. 27.

[219]"Za Lv" (Miscellaneous Laws) in *Tang Lv Shu Yi* (*The Comments on Tang Code*), Vol. 27.

[220]"Bai Guan Zhi" (The Record of the Officials of all Ranks) in *Xin Tang Shu* (*The New Book of Tang Dynasty*) (Book 1).

upon other people's rights of property. Thus, "if one occupies land beyond quota, he shall be punished by 'Chi' (flogging with light sticks) for ten strokes for every ten *mu* of land with his penalty aggravated by one level for every ten *mu* of land which he occupies; if he has been punished by 'Zhang' (flogging with heavy sticks) for sixty strokes, his penalty shall be aggravated by one level for every twenty *mu* of land which he occupies with the maximum penalty of 'Tu' (imprisonment) for one year." However, this regulation was not applicable to "Kuan Xiang" where there was vast land and sparse people to encourage people to cultivate the wasteland. According to *Tang Lv* (*Tang Code*), "one is not found guilty if he occupies the land in places where there is vast wasteland."[221]

Moreover, regulations were made in *Tang Lv* (*Tang Code*) to punish the illegal acts such as "occupying and cultivating the public or private land," "fraudulently claiming for and selling the public or private land" and "occupying and cultivating the tomb land of other people." Besides, "the illegal grant of land by 'Li Zheng' (head of 'Li': the basic resident organization in ancient China)" was also forbidden, and the punishment for such offenses varied from "Chi" (flogging with light sticks) for thirty strokes to "Tu" (imprisonment) for two years according to the specific circumstances. To prevent officials from taking advantage of their power to occupy the land of the common people to avoid the intensification of social contradiction, it was stipulated in *Tang Lv* (*Tang Code*) that "if one official occupies the private land of another person, he shall be punished by 'Zhang' (flogging with heavy sticks) for sixty strokes for every *mu* of land or less.... with the maximum punishment of 'Tu' (imprisonment) for two and a half years. If the official occupies the private garden of another person, his penalty shall be aggravated by one level."[222]

To protect the ownership of land obtained by land equalization, it was forbidden for "Kou Fen Tian" (state-owned farmland) to be sold, rent or mortgaged. It was recorded in "Hu Hun Lv" (*Statutes on Marriage, Tax and Household Registration*) that "Kou Fen Tian" (state-owned farmland) was not allowed to be sold unless "it is used to build houses and mills for threshing and grinding grain or to build road houses"; or unless someone had moved from "Xia Xiang" (the places with small territory and dense population) to "Kuan Xiang" (the places with vast territory and sparse population); or unless someone was too poor to afford his tomb after his own death. Additionally, "the offender who sells one *mu* of 'Kou Fen Tian' (state-owned farmland) shall be punished by 'Chi' (flogging with light sticks) for ten strokes, and the punishment shall be aggravated by one level for every twenty *mu* of land with the maximum punishment of 'Zhang' (flogging with heavy sticks) for one hundred

---

[221]"Hu Hun" (Marriage, Tax and Household Registration) in *Tang Lv Shu Yi* (*The Comments on Tang Code*), Vol. 13.

[222]"Hu Hun" (Marriage, Tax and Household Registration) in *Tang Lv Shu Yi* (*The Comments on Tang Code*), Vol. 13.

strokes. Then the land shall be returned to the owner with the profits made confiscated by the government, but the buyer shall not be punished."[223]

Moreover, the one who had the intention to sell the land "shall apply to the local government for approval," and "transference of ownership shall be dealt with by both the buyer and the seller at the end of year. If one has no written approval from the government, the profits made in the trade shall be confiscated by the government. Then the land shall be returned to the owner, but the buyer shall not be punished."[224] Until the middle period of Tang Dynasty, "Jun Tian Zhi" (The System of Land Equalization) came to a crisis because of the large scale land annexation. During the reign of Empress Wu Zetian, the situation turned out to be more serious, so the peasants were forced to flee away after they had lost their land. Because "half of the households are forced to leave where they have once lived,"[225] "tax collection declined and state revenue was insufficient." Thus, in September of the 23rd year of Kaiyuan, a decree was issued to prohibit the trade of "Kou Fen Tian" (state-owned farmland) and "Yong Ye Tian" (family farmland, which could be passed to next generation):

> The transaction of 'Kou Fen Tian' (state-owned farmland) and 'Yong Ye Tian' (family farmland) are frequently conducted, so from now on the land is forbidden to be sold, pawned and mortgaged. If I have heard that the trade has not been stopped, or if it has caused the loss of the poor but brought wealth to the rich, the penalties should be restated. So the trade is forbidden and the offenders shall be severely punished.[226]

After "An Shi Zhi Luan" (the Rebellion of An Lushan and Shi Siming), because of the decline of the imperial government, no measures were taken to stop the noblemen, bureaucrats and landlords from annexing the land viciously. What was worse, the act of annexation was even legalized through the signing of contracts. Consequently, "Jun Tian Zhi" (The System of Land Equalization) was completely destroyed.

As for "Tie Lin" (rent) and "Zhi" (pledge) of "Kou Fen Tian" (state-owned farmland), they were also forbidden by law, so they were allowed to be carried out unless under special conditions. In the 25th year of Kaiyuan, a *Tian Ling* (*Decrees on Farmland*) was promulgated:

> The land is forbidden to be rented or mortgaged, and the profits the offender has made shall be confiscated by the government with no punishment imposed upon the buyer, but the land should be returned to its original owner. However, if the land owner has to go to a distant place to render compulsory service or to take up an official post with no other person taking care of the land, the owner is allowed to rent or mortgage his land. The sale, rent and

---

[223]"Hu Hun" (Marriage, Tax and Household Registration) in *Tang Lv Shu Yi* (*The Comments on Tang Code*), Vol. 13.

[224]Niida Noboru (Japan), "Tian Ling" (Decrees on Farmland) in *Tang Ling Shi Yi* (*An Interpretation of the Orders of Tang Dynasty*), in the 25th year of Kaiyuan.

[225]"Wei Si Li Zhuan" (The Biography of Wei Sili) in *Jiu Tang Shu* (*The Old Book of Tang Dynasty*).

[226]*Ce Fu Yuan Gui* (*The Record of the Great Events*), Vol. 495, in the 23rd year of Kiyuan.

7.2 The Legal System of Tang Dynasty Symbolizing the Establishment...

mortgage of 'Yong Ye Tian' (family farmland) and the land which is rewarded are not prohibited.[227]

The protection of the ownership of personal property. In addition to the strict protection provided by *Tang Lv* (*Tang Code*) for the real estate, such as farmland and houses, various protection was also conducted for the ownership of personal property. It was even stipulated by the law that it was forbidden to pick up the vegetables and fruits in the official or private gardens. According to *Tang Lv* (*Tang Code*), "if people have picked up melons or fruits in official or private gardens, they shall be punished for the crime of 'Zuo Zang' (embezzlement); if they have abandoned or destroyed the melons or fruits, they shall also be punished for the same offense; if they take the melons or fruits away, they shall be punished for the offense of stealing." Thus, "the penalty for the principal offender who gives the fruits to others shall be aggravated by one level."[228] For another example, it was forbidden to use the property received in deposit, "if the property received in deposit is used without authorization, the offenders shall be punished for 'Zuo Zang' (embezzlement) with their penalties reduced by one level"; "if the objects are announced dead or lost by deception, the offenders shall be punished for obtaining property by defrauding with their penalties reduced by one level." However, if the animals deposited had died anyway or if the property "is stolen, the trustees do not have to take the responsibility of making compensation."[229]

7.2.5.2.2 (2) The Adjustment of Tenancy Relationship and the Protection of "Dian Quan" (Tenancy Rights)

"Dian Quan" (tenancy rights) refers to the rights of tenants to occupy, cultivate and make profits from the farmland after he has paid the rent. The forms of contract for renting farmland and the regulations on the protection of "Dian Quan" (tenancy rights) in Sui and Tang dynasties could be learned from the documents unearthed in Turpan and Dunhuang. For example, three contracts of land renting signed in the period of Yanshou in Gangchang country were unearthed in the north district of Astana, and one contract entitled *Dan Ren Zhi Jia Xia Tian Qi* (*The Contract of A Taoist Priest Named Zhi Jia for Renting Summer Land*) was signed in the 24th year of Yanshou (584 A.D.), which had shown clearly that the tenancy relationship had already existed and the relevant legal documents were already commonly used at the place in the early period of Sui Dynasty. In Astana, some contracts for land renting signed in Tang Dynasty were unearthed, such as *Gao Chang Zhao Huai Man Xia Tian Quan* (*The Bond of Zhao Huaiman for Renting Summer Land in Gaochang*) signed in the 17th year of Zhenguan (634 A.D.), *Zhao E Huan Ren Yu Zhang Hai*

---

[227]Niida Noboru (Japan), "Tian Ling" (Decrees on Farmland) in *Tang Ling Shi Yi* (*An Interpretation of the Orders of Tang Dynasty*), in the 25th year of Kaiyuan.

[228]"Za Lv" (Miscellaneous Laws) in *Tang Lv Shu Yi* (*The Comments on Tang Code*), Vol. 27.

[229]"Za Lv" (Miscellaneous Laws) in *Tang Lv Shu Yi* (*The Comments on Tang Code*), Vol. 26.

Long Zu Dian Chang Tian Qi (*The Contract Signed between Zhao E Huanren and Zhang Hailong for Tenanting Regular Land*) signed in the 3rd year of Longshuo (663 A.D.), *Zhang Wen Xin Zu Tian Qi* (*The Contract of Zhang Weixin for Tenanting Land*) signed in the years of Tianshou; *Lv Cai Yi Chu Zu Tian Qi* (*The Contract of Lv Caiyi for Renting Land*) signed in the years of Tianbao, *Dun Hong Liu Jia Xing Chu Zu Tian Qi* (*The Contract of Liu Jiaxing for Renting Land in Dunhuang*) signed in the 2nd year of Tianfu (902 A.D.), *Dun Huang Ling Hu Fa Xing Chu Zu Di Qi* (*The Contract of Linghu Faxing for Renting Land in Dunhuang*).[230]

In the unearthed land contracts of Tang Dynasty, it had fully reflected that "Dian Quan" (tenancy rights) was protected. For example, it was written in *"Fan Cao Zi Zu Di Qi"* (*The Contract of Fan Caizi for Renting Land*) that "the land and objects shall be paid and received on the day respectively. After the contract is signed and the two parties have stamped on the contract, the contract should not be breached. The one who breaches the contract shall be punished for □ (words are missing in the original text)." Here is another example: it was written in *"Jian Yuan Zi Zu Di Qi"* (*The Contract of Jia Yuanzi for Renting Land*) that "after the contract is signed and the two parties have stamped on the contract, the contract should not be breached. The one who breaches the contract shall be punished for □□□ (words are missing in the original text), and will be confiscated by the government. Oral promise being no guarantee, a written statement is hereby given." Besides, the unearthed contracts also showed that the interests of landlords were protected, so if the tenants were unable to pay the rent on time, their property was allowed to be taken away by the landlords. For example, it was recorded in *"Zhao Huai Man Zu Di Qi"* (*The Contract of Zhao Huaiman for Renting Land*) that "if the rent cannot be paid, the family property shall be confiscated by the government to make compensation."[231] In Tang Dynasty, the land tax recorded in the unearthed contract was as high as 50% of the rent income, so the burden of land tax was very heavy. In the article of "Jun Jie Fu Shui Xu Bai Xing" (Reducing Tax and Corvée to Show Sympathy to the Common People), the rent of the private land described by Li Zhi was surprising: "Within the area of capital, the official tax for each *mu* of farmland is 5,000 *qian*, but the rent of private land is about one *dan* of grain for each *mu* of land, which is twenty times higher than the official tax; so even the rent is reduced moderately, or reduced by half, it is still ten times higher than the official tax."

The adjustment of the tenancy relationship and the protection of "Dian Quan" (tenancy rights) stipulated by *Tang Lv* (*Tang Code*) had fully demonstrated the important development of civil legal relationship, which was inseparable from the fact that peasants had obtained small pieces of farmland because of the

---

[230]Zhang Chuanxi, *Zhong Guo Li Dai Qi Yue Hui Bian Kao Shi* (*A Textual Research and Interpretation of the Collected Contracts of the Past Dynasties of China*) (Book 1), Peking University Press, 1995.

[231]Zhang Chuanxi, *Zhong Guo Li Dai Qi Yue Hui Bian Kao Shi* (*A Textual Research and Interpretation of the Collected Contracts of the Past Dynasties of China*) (Book 1), Peking University Press, 1995.

7.2 The Legal System of Tang Dynasty Symbolizing the Establishment...

implementation of "Jun Tian Zhi" (The System of Land Equalization). Additionally, after the abolishing of the right of landlords to shelter their privileged relatives, the attachment relationship between landlords and tenants was weakened. Therefore, it was possible for tenants to make use of farmland and to make profits by signing contracts. Although restrictions were made on "Dian Quan" (tenancy rights), the legalization of tenancy relationship had promoted the development of the agricultural economy.

7.2.5.2.3 (3) "Zhi Quan" (Pledge Rights) and "Dian Quan" (Pawn Rights)

Today we regard "Zhi Quan" (pledge rights) as the real rights for security, and it refers to the rights which the creditors have to occupy the property of the debtor or the property transferred by the third party to pay off debts in advance with the money earned in selling the property because of the guaranteed credit. As early as in Han Dynasty, objects or persons were used as the guarantees for credits. "Zhi Quan" (pledge rights) was greatly developed in Tang Dynasty because of the prosperous commodity economy; therefore, "whether the people are officials ... or the common people," they all "have privately built storehouses for holding pledges."[232] To make profits from "Zhi Quan" (pledge rights), the storehouses for holding pledges were even built in temples with the names of "Chang She Ku" and "Wu Jin Ku." "Zhi Ku Zhang" (The Account of Pledge House) unearthed in the tomb of No. 206 at Astana in Turpan was the account of a pledge house located in Xinchangfang in Chang'an or near Chang'an, which had provided a precious evidence for the understanding of the system of "pledge house." In the account, the circumstances of basic mortgage, the value estimation of the real objects and the pledge of money were all recorded: the pledge of a white unlined upper garment of Ma Siniang was forty-five *qian* and the pledge of □ (words in the original text are missing) a white unlined upper garment of Asi was fifty *qian*. The value of objects estimated by pledge house was always lower than that at the market. When redeeming the objects, the mortgagor not only had to pay back the money he had obtained for the mortgage, but also had to pay the interest. This was the way by which the pledge house made profits by lending money to the poor people at usurious rates. Therefore, a provision was specially made for restricting the dealing. In volume six of *Tang Liu Dian* (*The Six Statutes of Tang Dynasty*), an annotation was made on the provision of "Bi Bu Lang Zhong Yuan Wai Lang" (head and deputy of a subministry department in charge of prison and penalty): "The interest made from pledge shall not be higher than 5%." Moreover, in addition to the interest stipulated by the contract of pledge, "the interest of the original capital shall not be changed and increased, and the interest made shall not be added to the capital."

---

[232]"Jia Zun Hao Hou Xiao Wu She Wen" (No Pardoning after Bing Awarded the Honorable Titles) in *Quan Tang Wen* (*Anthology of Essays in Tang Dynasty*), Vol. 78.

The time limit for the redemption of the pledged objects was also stipulated. If the redemption went beyond the time limit, the pledge house would take back the property right of the pledged objects.

Although "Liang Qing He Tong" (the agreement between two parties) was accepted by the imperial government as the condition of making a pledge contract,[233] as was stated in the regulation that "the cases involving the contracts signed between people will not be heard by the government,"[234] "if the head of a clan is living near the place ('living near' refers to a distance within 300 li and a place without being cut off by any passes), it is forbidden for his brothers or nephews or other people to sell their farmland or to mortgage their 'Nu Bi' (the slave girls and maidservants), cattle, farmland, houses or other property privately. (This provision is also applicable to the cases in which no real objects are mortgaged)."[235]

In debt relationship, although in law "compulsory service was permitted to be used as the compensation for debts," it was forbidden for creditors to keep people as pledges for making profits. It was stipulated in "Zei Dao" (Stealing and Robbery) in *Tang Lv Shu Yi* (*The Comments on Tang Code*) that "if people have privately kept others as pledges, they shall be punished by 'Zhan' (beheading)," but it was legal for "Nu Bi" (the slave girls and maidservants) to be kept as pledges. Clearly, the nature of feudal exploitation and the social relationship protected by the pledge rights were reflected by the provisions.

"Dian Quan" (pawn rights) today refers to the usufructuary rights, and it is the rights which the pawn holders have to pay for the value of pawn, to occupy the real estate of the person who has pawned the property and to use the real estate to make profits. The pawn holders have the rights to use, to make profits from, or to rent or transfer the pawn to other people. The person who has pawned the property has the rights to pay off the money he has made in pawning within a time limit and to redeem the pawn without paying interest. If the pawn holder has destroyed the pawn intentionally or negligently, he is responsible for the compensation; but if the pawn is destroyed or lost by force majeure, such as natural disasters, the pawn holder is not responsible for the compensation.

In ancient China, the words "Dian" (pawn) and "Mai" (sell) were always used together in the expression of "Dian Mai" or "Tie Mai." The rules for "Tie Mai" were made as early as in the Northern Qi Dynasty. It was written in "Song Xiao Wang Guan Dong Feng Su Zhuan" (The Records of the Costumes in Northeast by Song Xiaowang) in *Tong Dian* (*The General Codes*) that "the one who pawns off the wasteland for seven years and the farmland for five years shall have the land returned after he has paid off the pawn according to the law." The rules for pawning were

---

[233]Niida Noboru (Japan), "Tian Ling" (Decrees on Farmland) in *Tang Ling Shi Yi* (*An Interpretation of the Orders of Tang Dynasty*), in 25th year of Kaiyuan.

[234]Niida Noboru (Japan), "Tian Ling" (Decrees on Farmland) in *Tang Ling Shi Yi* (*An Interpretation of the Orders of Tang Dynasty*), in the 25th year of Kaiyuan.

[235]Niida Noboru (Japan), "Tian Ling" (Decrees on Farmland) in *Tang Ling Shi Yi* (*An Interpretation of the Orders of Tang Dynasty*), in the 25th year of Kaiyuan.

developed in Tang Dynasty, as was stated in "Xian Zong Ben Ji" (The Biography of Emperor Xianzong) (Part 2) in *Jiu Tang Shu* (*The Old Book of Tang Dynasty*) that in December of the 8th year of Yuanhe (807 A.D.) "the following 'Chi' (instruction) was made in 'the year of Xinsi': It is allowed for the places, such as the houses, mills, shops, the places for buying and renting carts, and gardens etc., that have been bestowed on princes, dukes, princess, and officials to be pawned, and the relevant matters of these places such as service and tax shall be managed by the local government of 'Zhou' (subprefecture) and 'Xian' (county)."

In "Lu Qun Zhuan" (The Biography of Lu Qun) in *Jiu Tang Shu* (*The Old Book of Tang Dynasty*), there were the records such as "pawning several *mu* of fertile farmland." However, it needs to be noted there was no clear distinction between "Dian" (pawn) and "Zhi" (pledge) in Tang Dynasty. In Du Fu's poem, the word "Dian" in "Chao Hui Ri Ri Dian Chun Yi" (Every day coming back from the imperial court, I go to pawn my spring clothes to liquor) actually means "Zhi" (pledge).

In Tang Dynasty, houses were allowed to be pawned, which could be proven by the contract of "He Nan Xian Huan De Cong Xian Qi Tui Huan Dian Zhai Qian Qi" (The Contract of Huan Decong for Returning the Money of the Pawned House Within the Time Limit in Henan) signed in the 22nd year of Zhenguan (648 A. D.).[236] In the early period of Tang Dynasty when "Jun Tian Zhi" (The System of Land Equalization) was implemented, the establishment of "Dian Quan" (pawn rights) was restricted by the specific circumstances at the time, so "Kou Fen Tian" (state-owned farmland) was forbidden to be pawned. The abolishment of "Jun Tian Zhi" (The System of Land Equalization) had made the circulation of land a reality, so the pawning of farmland was irresistible. Moreover, the contracts about pawning oneself and one's own son signed during the period of "Wu Dai" (the Five Dynasties) have also been unearthed, such as "Dun Huang Wu Qing Shun Dian Shen Qi" (The Contract of Wu Qingshun in Dunhuang for Pawning Himself) signed in the 8th year of Tianfu in the later period of Jin Dynasty (943 A.D.), "Du Huang Zhao Seng Zi Dian Er Qi" (The Contract of Zhao Sengzi for Pawning His Son) signed in the 2nd year of Qingtai (935 A.D.).[237]

It was required that "Dian Quan" (pawn rights) should be established in written form and be signed by the relevant parties, such as the officials, the parties themselves, the owners, and the neighbors; otherwise, their "Dian Quan" (pawn rights) would be considered invalid.

---

[236]Zhang Chuanxi, *Zhong Guo Li Dai Qi Yue Hui Bian Kao Shi* (*A Textual Research and Interpretation of the Collected Contracts of the Past Dynasties of China*) (Book 1), Peking University Press, 1995.

[237]Zhang Chuanxi, *Zhong Guo Li Dai Qi Yue Hui Bian Kao Shi* (*A Textual Research and Interpretation of the Collected Contracts of the Past Dynasties of China*) (Book 1), Peking University Press, 1995.

7.2.5.3 The Expansion of the Legal Adjustment of Debt

In ancient China, "Zhai" (debt) was referred to as "Ze," which basically meant that "one has not paid back a loan." In addition, the debtor was referred to as "Zhai Ren," "Ze Ren" or "Fu Ren," while the creditor was referred to as "Zhai Zhu," "Ze Zhu" or "Qian Zhu"; the failure of paying off debts was referred to as "Wei Fu" or "Bu Chang"; the act of paying debts was referred to as "Chang" or "Huan." In *Tang Lv* (*Tang Code*), the concept of "Zhai" (or "Ze") was narrowly defined, and it mainly referred to the act of incurring debts or owing somebody some money. It was stipulated that if one person's property had been damaged by the other persons illegally, he could ask for "Bei Chang" (compensation). However, in *Tang Lv* (*Tang Code*), there were no such regulations on making compensation for the infringement upon other people's freedom or reputation.

In Tang Dynasty, contracts were very important evidence for the creation of obligation. Whether in the transference of personal property or real estate, all contracts should be concluded in written form, which were referred to as "Quan" or "Wen Quan." Besides, there were also oral contracts. If there were disputes over debts, the contract should be used as evidence and the intermediary should be asked by the government to give testimonies. Therefore, if no contract was signed, the buyer, the seller and the chief official in charge of the market would all be punished. It was stipulated in "Za Lv" (Miscellaneous Laws) in *Tang Lv* (*Tang Code*) that "in the transaction of 'Nu Bi' (the slave girls and maidservants), horses, cows, camels, mules or donkeys, if contracts are not signed after money has been paid for three days, the buyers shall be punished by Chi' (flogging with light sticks) for thirty strokes, and the punishment for sellers shall be reduced by one level"; "if the transaction has been conducted but the chief official in charge of the market has not signed the contract, he shall be punished by 'Chi' (flogging with light sticks) for thirty strokes for a delaying of one day, and his punishment shall be aggravated by one level for each delaying, with the maximum punishment of 'Zhang' (flogging with heavy sticks) for one hundred strokes."

To guarantee the payment of debt, the person who breached the contract would be punished, so "if the debt is one *pi* of cotton cloth or more, the offender shall be punished by 'Chi' (flogging with light sticks) for twenty strokes for a delay of twenty days, and his penalty shall be aggravated by one level for each delay of twenty days with the maximum penalty of 'Zhang' (flogging with heavy sticks) for sixty strokes; if the debt is thirty *pi* of cotton cloth, his punishment shall be aggravated by two levels; if the debt is one hundred *pi*, his punishment shall be aggravated by three levels; if he has failed to pay the debt within one hundred days, he shall be punished by 'Tu' (imprisonment) for one year with the payment of compensation." Meanwhile, the creditors were permitted to get the compensation from debtors by "self-help" when the debtors breached the contract and refused to pay off the debt.

"Qian Che": the creditor was permitted to seize the property of debtor by force if the latter breached the contract and failed to pay off the debt, but the value of the property should not exceed that prescribed in the contract and the creditor should report the seized property to officials; otherwise, he would be punished. In "Za Lv" (Miscellaneous Laws) in *Tang Lv* (*Tang Code*), it was stipulated that "for the cases of debts, if the value of the property seized by creditors by force exceeds that which is prescribed in the contract without reporting to the government, the creditors shall be punished for the offense of 'Zuo Zang' (embezzlement)." Furthermore, it was specifically regulated that "for the cases of public or private debts, if the creditors have seized the property of those who have breached the contact, they shall make reports to the officials to be judged. If any of case is not reported, or if the value of the property seized by the creditor by force, such as 'Nu Bi' (the slave girls and maidservants) and animal products, has exceeded that which is prescribed in the contract, the creditor shall be punished for the offense of 'Zuo Zang' (embezzlement)."

"Yi Shen Zhe Chou": it is also called "Ren Shen Zhe Chou" (offering compulsory service as compensation for debts) and it means that an creditor can order an debtor or the males of the debtor's family to render the compulsory service, which can be regarded as a compensation for the debt if the debtor has lost his family fortune and is unable to pay the debt. According to the regulation in "Za Ling" (Miscellaneous Orders) in *Tang Ling Shi Yi* (*An Interpretation of the Orders of Tang Dynasty*) which was issued in the 25th year of Kaiyuan (735 A.D.), "the cases involving mortgages on the public or private property should be handled according to contracts, and they should not be accepted by the government offices.... and those who have lost their family fortune are permitted to offer compulsory service to compensate for the debts. The males of the debtors' families are permitted to be sent to provide the compulsory service ...."

From what is mentioned above, it can be seen that in *Tang Lv* (*Tang Code*) not only the debtors were forced to pay off the debts according to law, the acts of "Qian Che" and "Yi Shen Zhe Chou" were also legalized to ensure the creditors' compensation.

Because of complicated property relationship, some new types of contracts were used in Tang Dynasty, such as the sales contract, lease contract, employment contract, loan contract, depositing property contract, and the contract of hired works, etc. The following are the main characteristics of each of those contracts:

Sales contract: most contracts in Tang Dynasty were sales contracts. In *Tang Lv* (*Tang Code*) the principle regulations for buy-seller relationships, such as the agreement principles, the responsibilities for the defects of products, the deposit systems, and the priorities for the buying of real estate were all stipulated in detail. In the transaction of farmland, houses and important personal property, contracts must be signed; otherwise, it would be considered invalid. According to the rules on farmland, "for the cases of buying and selling of farmland, if one has an intention to trade a piece of land, he shall first send an application to the local government to obtain the permit, and both the buyer and the seller shall work on the transference of ownership at the end of the year. If one has no written approval from the government, the profits made in the trade shall be confiscated by the government. Besides, no punishment shall be enforced upon the buyer and the land shall be returned to its original owner."[238] Although the implementation of "Jun Tian Zhi" (The System of Land Equalization) had restricted the transaction of farmland, the sales of "Yong Ye Tian" (family farmland) was still permitted by law under special circumstances. Especially, according to the law, it was allowed for "Kou Fen Tian" (state-owned farmland) owned by noblemen and the bureaucrats and the farmland given them "to be sold and rented." Additionally, "it is permitted for landlords who run business to sell their farmland to be used in building houses, opening road shops and building mills for threshing and grinding grain, though the landlords are forbidden to move about from one place to another." To the common people, "if they are about to move to other places or if they are too poor to afford their own funerals, they are permitted to sell their 'Yong Ye Tian' (family farmland)." Moreover, for the people "who move from 'Xia Xiang' (the places with small territory and dense population) to 'Kuan Xiang' (the places with vast territory and sparse population), they are permitted to sell both their 'Yong Ye Tian' (family farmland) and 'Kou Fen Tian' (state-owned farmland)." Therefore, the farmland sale contract was still the primary type of contract at that time. Based on the practical experience, the regulations on contract became more and more strict. For example, in "Dun Huang Seng Zhang Yue Guang Bo Yuan Tian Qi" (The Contract of A Monk Named Zhang Yueguang for Selling the Farmland of Boyuan in Dunhuang) signed in the 6th year of Dazhong (852 A.D.) and "Dun Huang Chen Du Zhi Mai Di Qi" (The Contract of Chen Duzhi for Selling Farmland in Dunhuang) signed in the 2nd year of Qianfu (875 A.D.),[239] the items such as the names of the parties agreeing to sign the contracts, the amount of the farmland, the location of the farmland, the value of each *mu* of land and the names of the intermediaries, etc. were required to be clearly recorded.

In the transaction of personal property, such as "Nu Bi" (the slave girls and maidservants) and cattle, the transaction would be invalid if contracts were not signed. It was stipulated in "Guan Shi Ling" (Orders on Border Market) which was issued in the 25th year of Kaiyuan (737 A.D.) that "for the transaction of 'Nu Bi' (the slave girls and maidservants), cows, horses, camels, mules and donkeys, contracts should be made and checked by the market bureaus or departments." It was also recorded in "Zhang You Xin Zhuan" (The Biography of Zhang Youxin) in *Xin Tang Shu* (*The New Book of Tang Dynasty*) that Zhang Youxin, "who was one of the those nicknamed 'Ba Guan Shi Liu Zi'(sixteen gifted men around the eight Passes)," was "searched and insulted" even by a 'Ya Ren' (middleman) just because he had bought a maidservant without signing a contract. Later, he was even impeached by a "Yu Shi" (the censor) for his act. In the existing "Gao Chang Zuo Tong Xi Mai Nu Qi" (The Contract of Zuo Tongxi for Buying Slave Girls in Gaochang) signed in the 1st year of Longshuo, the dates, price, names and ages of the slave girls and the cooling-off period of three days after the transaction were all

---

[238]Niida Noboru (Japan), "Tian Ling" (Decrees on Farmland) in *Tang Ling Shi Yi* (*An Interpretation of the Orders of Tang Dynasty*), in the 25th year of Kaiyuan.

[239]Zhang Chuanxi, *Zhong Guo Li Dai Qi Yue Hui Bian Kao Shi* (*A Textual Research and Interpretation of the Collected Contracts of the Past Dynasties of China*) (Book 1).

clearly recorded. Here is another example: it was noted in "Xi Zhou Kang Si Li Mai Ma Qi" (The Contract of Kang Sili for Selling the Horse in Xizhou) that "in the days afterward, if anyone shows up and claims that the horse is stolen from another person, the owner should be liable for the matter, but not the buyer."[240]

In sales contracts, the buyer's guarantee liability was systematized. There were two types of guarantees: the defect guarantee of the subject matter and default guarantee. It was regulated in "Za Lv" (Miscellaneous Laws) in *Tang Lv Shu Yi* (*The Comments on Tang Code*) that "in the transaction of 'Nu Bi' (the slave girls and maidservants), horses, cows, camels, mules, and donkeys, after signing the contracts, if the objects they have bought are found to have been ill, ...the buyers are allowed to breach the contract within three days. However, if the buyers are fraudulent, they shall be punished by 'Chi' (flogging with light sticks) for forty strokes"[241] Obviously, this provision was for the defect guarantee. As to default guarantee, most of the sales contracts unearthed in Dunhuang included the penalties for the initiative breach of contracts. The main method of penalty was to pay the fine of the objects. For example, in some contracts, it was agreed that "anyone who breaches the contract initiatively shall be imposed with a fine of five *pi* of silk" and the fine would be paid to the person who abided by the contract or be confiscated by the government. In some contracts, the civil punishment was combined with criminal punishment. For example, in "Dun Huang Seng Zhang Yue Guang Bo Yuan Tian Qi" (The Contract of the Monk Named Zhang Yueguang for Selling the Farmland of Boyuan in Dunhuang), it was recorded that "if anyone breaches the contract, he shall be imposed with a fine of as much as twenty loads of wheat for the army and be punished by 'Chi' (flogging with light sticks) for thirty strokes"[242] In a contract of buying bricks signed in the years of Yuanhe in the reign of Emperor Xianzong, it was even stipulated: "If you breach the contract, you will be flogged for 9,000 strokes and you will become a 'Nu Bi' (the slave girls and maidservants)."[243]

In the system of guarantee liability, the guarantors were liable for assuming debts. In accordance with social customs, the relatives of a seller were often the guarantors. Thus, in the sale contract, if the buyers and middlemen were brothers or relatives in marriage, it should be noted in the contracts. In some contracts it was even clearly stipulated that "the debtor's liability in this contract should not be exempted even if an amnesty is offered,"[244] from which we can see that guarantee liability was greatly stressed in *Tang Lv* (*Tang Code*).

---

[240]Zhang Chuanxi, *Zhong Guo Li Dai Qi Yue Hui Bian Kao Shi* (*A Textual Research and Interpretation of the Collected Contracts of the Past Dynasties of China*) (Book 1).

[241]"Za Lv" (Miscellaneous Laws) in *Tang Lv Shu Yi* (*The Comments on Tang Code*), Vol. 26.

[242]Zhang Chuanxi, *Zhong Guo Li Dai Qi Yue Hui Bian Kao Shi* (*A Textual Research and Interpretation of the Collected Contracts of the Past Dynasties of China*) (Book 1).

[243]Zhang Chuanxi, *Zhong Guo Li Dai Qi Yue Hui Bian Kao Shi* (*A Textual Research and Interpretation of the Collected Contracts of the Past Dynasties of China*) (Book 1).

[244]Zhang Chuanxi, *Zhong Guo Li Dai Qi Yue Hui Bian Kao Shi* (*A Textual Research and Interpretation of the Collected Contracts of the Past Dynasties of China*) (Book 1).

Loan Contract: the words "Jie" and "Dai" had special meanings in Tang Dynasty, and "Jie" generally referred to the act of "loaning for use." For example, in *Zhi Zhi Lv* (*Statutes on the State Office System*), the words such as "privately loaning official property of 'Nu Bi' (the slave girls and maidservants) or animal products" and "loaning 'Nu Bi' (the slave girls and maidservants), horses, cows, camels, mules, carriages, boats, mills or road houses" were recorded. In these cases the subject matters were "Nu Bi" (the slave girls and maidservants), animal products, carriages or boats, etc. "Dai" generally referred to "loaning for consumption," as was expressed in the words like "loaning the property from one's supervisory area" and "privately loaning official property" which were recorded in *Zhi Zhi Lv* (*Statutes on the State Office System*). In these cases, the subject matters were silver, money, grain, and silk, etc. The difference between loaning for use and loaning for consumption was that the former often referred to a specific matter. For example, if a slave girl named "A" was loaned, it was "A" that should be returned; while the latter was not a specific matter. In other words, after being used, the original matters that have been loaned could not be returned.

There were two types of loan contracts: interest-earning contract and interest-free contract. Interest-earning contract referred to "Chu Ju" and interest-free contract referred to "Fu Zhai." Among the contracts, interest-earning contract was the main form of contract and the interest earned in these contracts was always high. In history books, it was recorded that "in the early period of Tang Dynasty, the officials' salary was paid with the interest earned in the business of loaning money by the wealthy families. But when the interest doubled, many people went broken."[245] Therefore, in the 16th year of Kaiyuan (728 A.D.), an imperial edict was issued: "From today forward, the loan interest should not exceed 4%, and the interest on official loans should not exceed 5%."[246] In the 25th year of Kaiyuan (728 A.D.), another edict was issued: "In the cases of earning interest by loaning private or official property, the monthly interest should not exceed 6%, and the total interest should not be more than double of the capital." As to the business of earning interest by loaning grain, it was regulated that the interest should be paid annually and that "the interest of the original capital shall not be changed and increased and the earned interest shall not be added to the capital."[247] "If anyone earns interest beyond contracts or earns interest from interest-free loans by breaking the law, the profits he has made shall be confiscated by the government." Moreover, if a debtor defaulted on the debt or delayed paying off the debt, the creditor could charge a crime upon the debtor or petition for the payment of the debt. The debtor should be investigated for legal responsibility to pay off the debt according to the law. It was stipulated in "Za Lv" (Miscellaneous Laws) in *Tang Lv Shu Yi* (*The Comments on Tang Code*) that "in all cases where the debts are defaulted, if the debt is one *pi* of cotton cloth or more, or if

---

[245] *Zi Zhi Tong Jian* (*History as a Mirror*).Vol. 212.

[246] *Tang Hui Yao* (*Collections of Historical Records of Tang Dynasty*).

[247] Niida Noboru (Japan), "Tian Ling" (Decrees on Farmland) in *Tang Ling Shi Yi* (*An Interpretation of the Orders of Tang Dynasty*), in the 25th year of Kaiyuan.

it is delayed to be paid for over twenty days, the debtor shall be punished by 'Chi' (flogging with light sticks) for twenty strokes; the punishment shall be aggravated by one level for each delaying of twenty days, with the maximum punishment of 'Zhang'(flogging with heavy sticks) for sixty strokes; if the debt is thirty *pi* of cotton cloth, the punishment shall be aggravated by two levels; if the debt is one hundred *pi* of cotton cloth, the punishment shall be aggravated by three levels. So the debtor shall fulfill his obligations accordingly."

After personal objects were borrowed, they should be taken good care of; if one delayed returning them, the owner could charge a crime upon him and petition for their returning.

It needs to be noted that the imperial government of Tang Dynasty also loaned out money to people, and the loan interest was always higher than that of private loaning to pay officials' salary, as was recorded in volume nine of *Tang Hui Yao* (*Collections of Historical Records of Tang Dynasty*): "After the reign of Wude, the national treasury was almost empty, so the imperial government gave the officials money as the capital for loaning and then the earned interest was distributed among the officials for their food allowances." Such phenomenon was very common in Tang Dynasty.

Although the creditor-debtor relationship was established in the contracts signed privately, the humble and the young were forbidden to loan out money to others and the officials were also forbidden to do such business in their supervisory areas. The records in the contracts unearthed in Dunhuang were consistent with the regulations on the contracts in *Tang Lv* (*Tang Code*). For example, the following words were written in "Tian Shan Xian Zhang Li Fu Ju Qian Qi" (The Contract of Zhang Lifu for Loaning Money in Tianshan County) signed in the 5th year of Xianqing (660 A.D.): Zhang Lifu took out a loan of ten *qian* and the monthly interest on the loan was one *qian*, so both of the interest and the capital should be paid back on the day agreed in the contract. If Zhang Lifu was absent, the money should be paid back by his wife or son; if the loan was defaulted, the family property should be left to the discretion of the creditor. The agreement was signed and approved by both parties with their fingerprints pressed.[248]

To guarantee the debtors' performance of debt contract, objects should be pledged whether in private or official loaning. Among the contracts unearthed in Dunhuang, some debtors even pledged their whole family property, as was recorded that "if the loans are defaulted, the family property, miscellaneous objects and cows and cattle shall all be confiscated." Moreover, the system of "guarantor" was established, according to which, when a debtor failed to fulfill his obligation or did not completely fulfill his obligation, the creditor had the rights to force the guarantor to fulfill the obligation or to make compensation. For example, in the case where the debtor had fled away, the guarantor should pay the debt instead. Guarantees were often provided by the family members or relatives. For example, in "Zhang

---

[248]Zhang Chuanxi, *Zhong Guo Li Dai Qi Yue Hui Bian Kao Shi* (*A Textual Research and Interpretation of the Collected Contracts of the Past Dynasties of China*) (Book 1).

Hai Huan Bai Huai Luo Dai Yin Qian Qi" (The Contract of Zhang Haihuan and Bai Huailuo for Loaning Money) signed in the 2nd year of Linde (665 A.D.), the following words were recorded: "if the payback is delayed … or if Zhang flees away, his wife and son and the guarantor are liable for the payment." In this contract, there were five guarantors, including Zhang Haihuan's wife, named Guo Rulian, his mother and his eldest daughter, etc.[249] Therefore, it was a common phenomenon that the debt guarantee for the creditors was often assumed by the main family members or even by the whole family, which also showed that the property was shared by the whole family. The guarantor system had guaranteed the debtor's fulfillment of his obligation, which not only promoted the development of creditor-debtor relationship, but also sped up the circulation of money and objects.

In the cases of loaning for use, the public property was always used. If one person had borrowed the object from government and delayed its returning for ten days, he should be punished. It was stipulated in "Jiu Ku Lv" (Statutes on Stables) in *Tang Lv Shu Yi* (*The Comments on Tang Code*) that "in the case of borrowing object from government, if a person delays its returning for ten days, he shall be punished by 'Chi' (flogging with light sticks) for thirty strokes and the punishment shall be aggravated by one level for every ten days of delaying with the maximum punishment of 'Zhang' (flogging with heavy sticks) for one hundred strokes; if a person has privately used the official uniform, his punishment shall be aggravated by one level."

Additionally, the official staff and the chief officials were forbidden to privately loan out the objects entrusted to their care. The following provisions were included in "Jiu Ku Lv" (Statutes on Stables) in *Tang Lv Shu Yi* (*The Comments on Tang Code*):

> If a chief official has privately borrowed or loaned out the official 'Nu Bi' (the slave girls and maidservants) or animal products entrusted to his care, he and the person who loans them out shall be punishable by 'Chi' (flogging with light sticks) for fifty strokes; if the loans are large in amount, he shall be punished for the offense of 'Zuo Zang' (embezzlement) in his supervisory area; if he loans out a donkey in a courier station, his punishment shall be aggravated by one level"; "if a chief official privately takes out a loan or loans out the objects belonging to the government entrusted to his care, or if the loans are not recorded, he and the person who loans the objects shall be punished for the offense of robbery; if the loans are recorded, he and the person who loans the objects shall be punished for the offense of quasi-robbery"; "if a chief official privately takes out a loan or loans out the objects belonging to the government entrusted to his care, he and the person who loans the objects shall be punished by 'Chi' (flogging with light sticks) for fifty strokes; if the objects are delayed to be returned, he and the person who loans the objects out shall be punished for the offense of 'Zuo Zang' (embezzlement), but the punishment shall be reduced by two levels.

To obtain long-term interest and to stress the power of the government in solving the disputes over debts, the creditors were prohibited from infringing upon the rights of debtors according to the provisions of *Tang Lv* (*Tang Code*), so the limitation of

---

[249]Zhang Chuanxi, *Zhong Guo Li Dai Qi Yue Hui Bian Kao Shi* (*A Textual Research and Interpretation of the Collected Contracts of the Past Dynasties of China*) (Book 1).

7.2 The Legal System of Tang Dynasty Symbolizing the Establishment...

lawsuit actions was established for the first time in the resolution of civil debt disputes, which is of great significance in Chinese civil legal history.

"Lin Yong Qi Yue" (lease and employment contract): as early as in Han Dynasty, "Lin Tian" (the lease of field) and "Lin Geng" (the lease of farmland) were recorded in legal codes. According to the note in "Guang Ya" (the first encyclopedia in ancient China), "'Yong' means employment, or being hired to work." However, before Tang Dynasty, there was no difference between leasing and employment so that they were generally referred to as "Lin" (hired person) and "Yong" (employment of labor). Thus, it was in *Tang Lv (Tang Code)* that the concept of "Lin Yong" was initially included and the two words were differentiated for the first time. In "Ming Li" (The Categories of Penalties and General Principles) in *Tang Lv (Tang Code)*, it was stipulated that "if 'Lin' (hired person) and 'Yong' (employment of labor) are illegally obtained, they shall be confiscated," although "'Lin' (hired person) and 'Yong' (employment of labor) are allowed, the profit shall not exceed their own value." It was further explained in *Shu Yi (Tang Lv Shu Yi)* that "'Yong' refers to the act of privately borrowing and using the horses and carriages that are entrusted to one's care"; "'Lin' refers to the act of leasing out mills, roadside houses or boats; so the punishment is enforced according to the value of what has been leased out." Clearly, the act of using and employing the labor of others were referred to as "Yong"; the act of using the roadside houses or other objects were referred to as "Lin." Moreover, the profits made by "Lin" were called "Lin Jia" and "Lin Zhi." The relationship of rights and obligations can be seen from the remaining employment contracts of Tang Dynasty which were unearthed in Dunhuang. For example, the payment which the employees received from the employers were mainly cash, but they also included clothes and grain. The first part of the payment would be given to the employees as soon as they started to work, and the rest of it would be paid off when the contract was terminated. The term for the contract could be as long as one year, or as short as a few months. If the employees were lazy, they should be imposed with a fine; if they had destroyed the farm tools or lost the animals, they should pay for the compensation; if they had escaped, the guarantors should pay for the compensation. Therefore, both the employer and the employee should be imposed with a fine if they had breached the contracts (usually a sheep would be paid as the fine). Moreover, in the documents of Tang Dynasty, there were also the contracts of hiring cows, donkeys and camels, etc., in which the specific prices, terms, punishment for breaching the contracts, the measures of handling the sick and dead animals, and the costs of guarantees, etc. were also clearly recorded. The following is a contract entitled "Dun Huang Wa Jiang Si Ying Zhen Shou Gu Qi" (The Contract for the Employment of the Bricklayer Named Si Yingzhen in Dunhuang) signed in the year of Yin during the reign of Tufan (the 2nd year of Changqing, 822 A.D.):

> A Buddhist monk named Cideng will build a hall for worshipping Buddha at Donghe village on the 7th of August in the year of Yin... Si Yingzhen will build the hall and plaster it with soft mud. The hall will be in use on the 15th of August... shall pay one *pi* of cloth which is amounted to four *dan* and two *dou* of wheat. Subtracting two *dan* and one *dou* of wheat owed to Cideng before, now one *dan* and seven *dou* of wheat is owed to Si Yingzhen, which

will be paid on the day when the building is accomplished. Once it is agreed, nobody should breach the contract. The one who initially breaches the contract will be imposed with a fine and he will pay three loads of wheat to the person who abides by the contract. Oral promise being no guarantee, a written statement is hereby given. The personal stamps of the two parties are hereby printed.[250]

Indemnity contract: it was stipulated that if a person's property was infringed upon or his body was injured by other person, he should be compensated, which was referred to as the debt for compensation for damages. To guarantee the rights of the aggrieved parties to claim for indemnity, sometimes indemnity contracts were made. For example, in "Dun Huang Li Tiao Shun Pei Chang Qi" (The Compensation Contract of Li Tiaoshun in Dunhuang) signed in the year of Yin in Turpan (the 2nd year of Changqing), the following is recorded:

> On the 19th of August in the year of Yin, Yang Qianrang is in dispute with Li Tiaoshun and then Yang injuries Li. The case is later decided by Jie'er (a title of a subprefecture official) and he orders that Li has to stay in bed for recovery. Before the 26th of August, the senior fellow apprentices and relatives of Tiaoshun should send a doctor to treat Yang and look after him. From the day forward till the recovery of Yang, the cost of medicine and the necessities for Yang's recovery shall be paid by Li's family.... The government is ruled by law, so the contract should be abided by everyone. This contract is hereby made to be a proof offered in days to come.[251]

As to the contracts in Tang Dynasty, there are also the forms like "Dian Mai Qi Yue" (pawn contract) and "Ji Cun Qi Yue" (deposit contract), but it is unnecessary to go into details in this chapter.

7.2.5.4 The Full Approval and Protection of the Systems of Feudal Marriage, Family and Inheritance

7.2.5.4.1 (1) The Arrangement and Dissolution of Marriage

According to *Tang Lv* (*Tang Code*), marriages should be arranged by "marriage contract" or private agreement, both of which had legal effect. It was stipulated that "if a person breaks off an engagement for no reason, he should be punished by 'Zhang' (flogging with heavy sticks) for sixty strokes; if the head of a woman's family marries her off again to another man, the head of the woman's family should be punished by 'Zhang' (flogging with heavy sticks) for one hundred strokes; if she has already got married, the head of the family shall be punished by 'Tu' (imprisonment) for one and a half year. As for the man who agrees to take the married woman, if he knows the truth, his the punishment should be reduced by one level. So

---

[250]Zhang Chuanxi, *Zhong Guo Li Dai Qi Yue Hui Bian Kao Shi* (*A Textual Research and Interpretation of the Collected Contracts of the Past Dynasties of China*) (Book 1).

[251]Zhang Chuanxi, *Zhong Guo Li Dai Qi Yue Hui Bian Kao Shi* (*A Textual Research and Interpretation of the Collected Contracts of the Past Dynasties of China*) (Book 1).

the woman will return to her first husband; if her first husband does not want to take her, she should return the wedding presents and marry her second husband."

The marriage of the inferior and the young should be arranged by the paternal grandparents or parents or the superior and the elder of the households; if anyone violated the rule, he should be punished by "Zhang" (flogging with heavy sticks) for one hundred strokes, which showed that marriages were always arranged by the elders without considering the will of their children. However, "if the superior and elder relatives of an inferior or young arrange a marriage for him after he has already married a woman of his own free will while he is away from home, the previous marriage is valid; but if he has not married the woman, he should accept the marriage that they have arranged for him by obeying his superior and elder relatives. If he does not accept the arranged marriage, he shall be punished by 'Zhang' (flogging with heavy sticks) for one hundred strokes."

The arrangement of match-makers was also one of the most important requirements of legal marriage. It was stipulated in *Shu Yi* (*Tang Lv Shu Yi*) that "marriages should be arranged by match-makers" and that "the arrangements of match-makers are necessary in marriage." Besides, six ceremonies, namely, "Na Cai" (men and women giving gifts to each other), "Wen Ming" (the inquiry of the woman's name, the date of birth and the eight characters of a horoscope), "Na Ji" (the divination of the man and woman's the dates of birth and the eight characters of a horoscope), "Na Zheng" (sending wedding presents to the woman's family), "Qing Qi" (the arrangement of the date of wedding), and "Qin Ying" (holding the wedding ceremony) should be conducted for legal marriage. It was stipulated in *Shu Yi* (*Tang Lv Shu Yi*) that "a wife refers to a woman who carries on the family line, who offers sacrifices to gods or family ancestors and who is married by following the six ceremonies and the ceremony of worshipping 'Tian' (heaven) and 'Di' (Earth)"; "if the woman has been given wedding presents, though no marriage contract is signed," the marriage was still legal. Influenced by the social customs of "families selling their daughters for profits and buying wives by paying silk" which was prevalent in Wei, Jin and Southern and Northern dynasties, some people "haggled over the value of wedding presents and often hoped to get more money but to pay back less, so it was like bargaining at markets." "Emperor Taizong once said that the gentlemen in Shandong valued family background and social status, although it was on the decline, the descendants were afraid of failing to live up to their ancestors' expectation, so they asked for as many as betrothal gifts as possible in marriage. That is why their marriages were referred to as 'Mai Hun' (collecting money by marriage)."[252] In Tang dynasty, the social morality of asking for betrothal gifts featured by "charging more money and obtaining bribes" was not changed despite repeated prohibition.

In the 1st year of Zhenguan, the legal age for marriage was "twenty years old for male and fifteen years old for female." In the 25th year of Kaiyuan (737 A.D.), to increase population, the legal age for marriage was reduced. Thus, it was stipulated

---

[252]"Gao Jian Zhuan" (The Biography of Gao Jian) in *Xin Tang Shu* (*The New Book of Tang Dynasty*).

by the imperial decree issued in the 25th year of Kaiyuan (737 A.D.) that "if a male is fifteen years old and a female is thirteen years old or older, marriages should be arranged." If the time for wedding has been arranged, it should not be changed on any excuses; if the man's family had no intention to arrange the wedding ceremony to marry the woman within three years, the woman should be arranged to marry another man by "You Si" (official) who was in charge of the affairs; if it was not yet the time agreed for wedding, it was forbidden for the woman to be taken to the man's family by force, but wedding ceremony was forbidden to be held during the mourning period of one's parents or one's husband, or during the period when one's paternal grandparents or parents were imprisoned; if it was violated, the violators should be punished by "Zhang" (flogging with heavy sticks) or "Tu" (imprisonment).

As for marriage restrictions, there are the following regulations:

The marriage between "Liang" (the decent people) and "Jian" (people of a lower social status than common people) was prohibited, and it was stipulated in the 25th year of Kaiyuan (737 A.D.) that "the people from the families of 'Gong Yue Hu' (criminals and their families registered as musicians), 'Za Hu' (families registered as workers), 'Guan Hu' (criminals and their relatives registered as slave girls in official households), 'Bu Qu' (the private army), 'Ke Nv' (women having higher social status than that of maidservants), 'Gong Si Nu Bi' (official or private slave girls and maidservants) should marry the people of the same social status."[253] If a man of "Jian Ren" (people of a lower social status than common people) married a woman of "Liang Ren" (the decent people), they should be punished by "Tu" (imprisonment) for one year and a half. Thus, it was annotated in *Shu Yi* (*Tang Lv Shu Yi*) that "it is natural that people should have get married, but they should marry those whose social status is the same as theirs; 'Liang' (the decent people) and 'Jian' (people of a lower social status than common people) are different from each other, so it is unsuitable for them to get married."

The marriage between two people with the same surnames was prohibited. In *Shu Yi* (*Tang Lv Shu Yi*), it was explained that "it is forbidden to marry someone with the same surname or from the same clan," so the offenders should be punished by "Tu" (imprisonment) for two years. If one married some elder relatives above "Si Ma" (the person wearing the mourning apparel of soft sackcloth in the fifth mourning degree), he should be punished for fornication; however the law was not applicable to the cases where the two people had the same surnames but were from different clans.

The marriage between paternal and maternal cousins was prohibited. In *Shu Yi* (*Tang Lv Shu Yi*) it was explained that "as for paternal and maternal cousins, though they do not have mourning degrees, if their parents are the relatives of "Si Ma" (the person wearing the mourning apparel of soft sackcloth in the 5th mourning degree) or are elders, marriage is not suitable"; if it was violated, the offenders would be

---

[253]Niida Noboru (Japan), "Tian Ling" (Decrees on Farmland) in *Tang Ling Shi Yi* (*An Interpretation of the Orders of Tang Dynasty*), in the 25th year of Kaiyuan.

7.2 The Legal System of Tang Dynasty Symbolizing the Establishment...

punished by "Zhang" (flogging with heavy sticks) for one hundred strokes, with the marriage cancelled.

As to the inferior and the superior, though they did not have the same surnames, if they had blood ties, the marriage between them was still prohibited, if it was violated, the offenders would be punished for fornication.

It was forbidden to take an escaped woman as a wife or concubine, the violators would be punished for the same crime as that for the woman.

Lastly, it was forbidden for a supervisory official to take a woman in his supervisory area as a wife or concubine; otherwise, he would be punished by "Zhang" (flogging with heavy sticks) for one hundred strokes.

If marriages were against the law, "the paternal grandparents or parents who have arranged the marriage shall be punished." "If the superior and elder people of the close relatives have arranged the marriage, they are the principal offenders and the two in marriage are the accessory; if the elders of distant relatives have arranged the marriage by violating the law, they are the principal offenders and the two in marriage are the accessory; if the two people in marriage have violated the law, they are the principle offenders and the relatives who have arranged the marriage are the accessory."[254] The punishment should be enforced in accordance with the offenses which the superior and elder relatives had committed. The severer the superior and elder relatives were punished, the severer the two people involved in marriages would be punished. As for the condition for exemption, if the man married the woman according to the order of his paternal parents or parents, he would be exempted from punishment.

In Tang Dynasty, widows were permitted to marry again. According to the imperial edict issued on the 4th of February of the 1st year of Zhenguan, "if the mourning period for a widow's deceased husband has ended, or if she has applied for remarriage, she is allowed to do so." But the remarriage could be arranged only after it was approved by the woman's parents or paternal parents. Besides, a woman who did not want to remarry again should not be forced to do so by other people; otherwise, those people who had arranged the marriage "should be punished by 'Tu' (imprisonment) for one year; but if they are the close relatives of the woman, their penalties shall be reduced by two levels. So accordingly, the marriage should be dissolved and the woman should go back to her first husband, but the man who is to take the woman as his wife should not be punished."

It was legal for a man to take a married woman as a concubine. "If a 'Nu Bi' (the slave girl and maidservant) has given birth to a child or her social status is raised to that of 'Liang Ren' (the decent people) by her master, she can be taken as a concubine." It was explained in *Shu Yi* (*Tang Lv Shu Yi*) that "if a 'Nu Bi' (the slave girl and maidservant) has sexual relationship with her master, or if she has given birth to a child, or even if she has no child but if her social status was raised to

---

[254]"Hu Hun" (Marriage, Tax and Household Registration) in *Tang Lv Shu Yi* (*The Comments on Tang Code*), Vol. 14.

that of 'Liang Ren' (the decent people), she can be taken her as a concubine," but marriage contract should be signed before she was taken as a wife or concubine.

There were two kinds of divorce, namely, compulsory divorce and divorce by agreement. Compulsory divorce was divided into official compulsory divorce and the compulsory divorce by her husband. If marriages were against the law, or if a husband who wanted to break off the relationship "has beat his wife's paternal grandparents or parents or killed his wife's maternal grandparents, parents, father's brothers, brothers, aunts or sisters," or if a wife who wanted to break off the relationship "has beat her husband's paternal parents, parents, or killed her husband maternal grandparents, parents, father's brothers, brothers, aunts or sisters or the relatives of 'Si Ma' (the person wearing the mourning apparel of soft sackcloth in the fifth mourning degree) or above," the marriage should be dissolved by officials. Under such circumstances, the one who refused to divorce should be punished by "Tu" (imprisonment) for one year. If a wife was considered to have committed the offense of "Qi Chu" (seven reasons to repudiate the wife: "being unfilial to parents-in-law," "failing to bear a male offspring," "being lascivious," "being jealous," "having severe illness," "gossiping" and "committing theft"), she should be compelled to dissolve the marriage. The seven reasons of repudiating the wife originated from "Ben Ming Pian" (Sexagenary Cycle of One's Birth) in *Da Dai Li Ji* (*The Rites of Da Dai*):

> There are seven reasons for women to be repudiated ...it is the violation of virtue to show no filial obedience to parents; it is the violation of the taboo of having no offspring to give birth to no children; it is the violation of clan order to be lascivious; it is the violation of family order to be jealous; it is impossible to enjoy 'Zi Sheng'(millet placed in a sacrificial vessel) to be seriously ill; it is driving a wedge between relatives to be gossipy; it is against justice to commit theft.

Although there were seven reasons for women to be repudiated, there were also three conditions under which women should not be divorced, which was called "San Bu Qu." According to the explanation in *Shu Yi* (*Tang Lv Shu Yi*), "the three conditions under which women should not be divorced include: the wife has been in mourning for the death of the husband's parents for three years; the husband has become rich after taking the woman in marriage; the woman is homeless if she is repudiated." Thus, "if the husband repudiated his wife who has not violated the seven taboos or who never shows the intention of breaking off the relationship, he shall be punished by 'Tu' (imprisonment) for one and a half years; if the wife has committed one of the seven taboos, or if she meets one of the three conditions for not being repudiated, but if the husband insists on the wife's divorce, he shall be punished by 'Zhang'(flogging with heavy sticks) for one hundred strokes and the wife should go back to her husband." The regulation of "San Bu Qu" (the three conditions under which women should not be divorced) showed the influence which "Li" (rites) had exerted on law and the continuation of the validity of the will of the deceased elders who had arranged the marriage. However, if the wife had serious illness or had committed the taboo of being lascivious, she was not protected by the regulations of "San Bu Qu" (the three conditions under which women should not be divorced). In fact, a husband could divorce his wife at will, but if a wife left her

7.2 The Legal System of Tang Dynasty Symbolizing the Establishment...

husband without permission, she would be punished by "Tu" (imprisonment) for two years; if a woman remarried afterward, her punishment should be aggravated by two levels.

If the marriage was dissolved voluntarily by the husband and the wife, it was referred to as "He Li" (peaceful dissolution of marriage). According to the regulation in "Hu Hun Lv" (Statutes on Marriage, Tax and Household Registration) in *Tang Lv* (*Tang Code*): "if the marriage is dissolved for disharmony, the husband and wife will not be punished," which was significant in alleviating the suffering of the women caused by marital relationship.

7.2.5.4.2 (2) The Legalization of the Patriarchal System

The patriarchal system was confirmed in the form of law in *Tang Lv* (*Tang Code*), according to which "among the people who live together, there must be the elder" and "the head of a household is held by the patriarch." The patriarch should be the most respected man in a family, so only when there was no male in a family could a female be the patriarch. Under the patriarchal system, a patriarch had the right to possess the family property, to instruct the children, to punish the family members, to send the children to the government to be punished, and to arrange the children's marriage. No doubt, the children's legitimate rights and interests all depended on the patriarch, so they should obey the patriarch's orders; otherwise, they would be considered unfilial, which was one of the felonies in "Shi E" (The Ten Abominations). Moreover, if one person's paternal parents or parents were still alive, but if he had established separate household registration or divided the family property, he should be punished by "Tu" (imprisonment) for three years. If the inferior or the young had made use of the family property without authorization, he should be punished by "Chi" (flogging with light sticks) and "Zhang" (flogging with heavy sticks) for ten to one hundred strokes. If the children or grandchildren had violated the instructions or did not fulfill the obligations of supporting their parents or paternal grandparents, they should be punished by "Tu" (imprisonment) for three years. According to the explanation in *Shu Yi* (*Tang Lv Shu Yi*), "if paternal grandparents or parents have given instructions which are useful in dealing with daily affairs, they should be obeyed by the grandchildren and children faithfully without violation... but if the instructions are against the law, it is guilty to follow them; if the family is poor and cannot afford to support (the paternal grandparents or parents) properly, the person is considered guilty, so he should also be punished." This provision was very different from that in *Jin Lv* (*Jin Code*), so it was a great improvement of the traditional "Li" (rites) and "Fa" (law).

For the cases of affray and fighting between the inferior and superior, different penalties were enforced because of their different social status. If a grandchild or child beat his paternal grandparents or parents, he would be punished by "Jiao" (hanging); however, if grandchildren or children were killed by their paternal grandparents or parents for violating the instructions, their paternal grandparents or parents would only be punished by "Tu" (imprisonment) for one and a half years;

if the paternal grandparents or parents killed their grandchildren or children involuntarily, they would not be exempted from punishment; if grandchildren or children prosecuted their paternal grandparents or parents, they would be considered "stonehearted or disobedient," so they had violated the principles of "Li" (rites), therefore, they should be punished by "Jiao" (hanging).

The patriarch of the household not only had the right to manage his family, but also the obligation to pay tax, to render the corvée service and to register the household; if there was any offender, he would be punished by "Chi" (flogging with light sticks) for forty strokes or "Tu" (imprisonment) for three years.

As to the family status of the husband and wife, the tradition of the authority of husband featured by "Nan Zun Nv Bei" (man is superior to woman) was upheld. Therefore, the family status of the husband and the wife were unequal, as long as the husband was alive, it was impossible for the wife to exercise her rights either in managing family property or instructing children. If there were physical injuries between the husband and wife, their punishments were very different: if the husband beat and injured the wife, his penalty was two levels lighter than that for the common people; if the husband beat and injured a concubine, his penalty was two levels lighter than that which was enforced for injuring wife (reduced by four levels than that for the common people). Thus, "if he was accused by his wife or concubine," he would be punished. In contrast, if the wife beat and injured the husband, she should be punished by 'Tu' (imprisonment) for one year; if "Teng" (a maid that had accompanied the legal wife to her husband's house) or a concubine beat her husband, their penalties should be one level severer than that for the wife.

In summary, in *Tang Lv* (*Tang Code*) the feudal marriage and family system was completely acknowledged, which had demonstrated the legal inequality between the superior and the inferior, the noble and the humble, and the male and the female. Such inequality was a reflection of the relationship of personal attachment in the feudal times, and it was also the requirement of the hierarchical and ethical society to maintain such unequal relationship.

7.2.5.4.3 (3) Identity Inheritance Is the Core of Inheritance Law

The identity inheritance is the most important element in the inheritance system, so the inheritance system of "Di Zhang Zi" (the eldest son born of the legal wife) was carried out; if "Di Zhang Zi" (the eldest son born of the legal wife) has died, "Di Zhang Sun" (the eldest grandson of the legal wife) would become "Zong Tiao" (the succession to the headship) of the family. If there was no "Di Zhang Zi" (the eldest son born of the legal wife), "Shu Zi" (the son born of a concubine) would be the heir. In accordance with *Tang Lv* (*Tang Code*), the legal wife's eldest son is called "Di Zi" (the son born of the legal wife). "If this principle is violated, it will be 'considered unlawful'. So the offenders will be punished by 'Tu' (imprisonment) for one year." If the wife's son died after she was fifty years old or older, "it is permitted for 'Shu Zi' (the son born of a concubine) to become 'Di Zi' (the son born of the legal wife)," but "the eldest son should be chosen; if this principle is violated, the offender shall be punished by 'Tu' (imprisonment) for one year." In addition, according to *Tang Lv* (*Tang Code*), "if the wife has no 'Di Zi' (the son born of the legal wife), or her son has committed crimes or is ill, her 'Di Sun' (the grandson of the legal wife) should be chosen as the heir; if the wife has no 'Di Sun' (the grandson of the legal wife), his brother born of the same mother should be the heir; if there is no brother born of the same mother, 'Shu Zi' (the son born of a concubine) should be the heir; if there is no 'Shu Zi' (the son born of a concubine), the brother of 'Shu Zi' (the son born of a concubine) born of the same mother should be the heir; if there is on brother of 'Shu Zi' (the son born of a concubine) born of the same mother, 'Shu Sun' (the grandson born of a concubine) should be the heir, and the inheritance of the great-grandsons or the great-great-grandson should all follow this principle." Thus, it can be seen that, the inheritance of a clan is limited to male and to the lineal relatives of the next generation. If there was no male in the next generation of the family, "Li Si" (to adopt a son as the heir for the succession of family line) should be conducted. According to law, "if there are no sons in a family, it is permitted to adopt a son of the same lineage of 'Zhao Mu' (the patriarchal system of arranged order and order of generation in the temple or cemetery) as the heir."[255] "So in order to continue the family line, separate households should not be registered until the they are eighteen years old or older."[256] The statutory inheritance system above-mentioned was strictly protected by law, so if "Shu Zi" (the son born of a concubine) had pretended to be "Di Zi" (the son born of the legal wife) to inherit the family property, he would be punished by "Tu" (imprisonment) for two years; if he defrauded the inheritance in somebody else's name, he would be punished by "Liu" (exile) to a distance of 2000 *li*.

The inheritance of hereditary titles was different from identity inheritance. In the system of the inheritance of hereditary titles, the heirs were the children and grandchildren of the lineal relatives but not the brothers of collateral lines. If there were no sons or grandsons, the hereditary title should be taken away.

As to the inheritance of the family property, generally the family property should be shared equally by children. According to "Hu Ling" (Decrees on Household) which was quoted in "Hu Hun Lv" (Statutes on Marriage, Tax and Household Registration) in *Tang Lv* (*Tang Code*) issued in the 25th of Kaiyuan (737 A.D.), "farmland, houses and family property should be shared equally by those who had the right to inherit;... if the brothers have died, their parts should be inherited by their sons; if no brothers are alive, the family property should be inherited and shared equally by their sons. Among the sons, if one has not married, he should be given extra money for wedding presents; if the husband' sisters or female cousins have not married, they should be given half of the money as their sons' wedding presents; if a widow has no sons, she should inherit the property of her deceased husband; ...

---

[255]Niida Noboru (Japan), "Tian Ling" (Decrees on Farmland) in *Tang Ling Shi Yi* (*An Interpretation of the Orders of Tang Dynasty*), in 25th year of Kaiyuan.

[256]Niida Noboru (Japan), "Tian Ling" (Decrees on Farmland) in *Tang Ling Shi Yi* (*An Interpretation of the Orders of Tang Dynasty*), in 25th year of Kaiyuan.

however, if the widow has remarried, she was not allowed to inherit any 'Bu Qu' (the private army), 'Nu Bi' (the slave girls and maidservants), farmland or houses of her deceased husband."

If there were no sons in a family, the property should be inherited by the daughters of the family, as was stipulated in a "Chi" (instruction) issued on the 5th of July of the 1st year of Kaicheng period (836 A.D.) which was quoted in the provision of "Hu Jue Zi Chan" (no male heirs to succeed the household property) in "Hu Hun" (Marriage, Tax and Household Registration) in *Song Xing Tong (The Penal Code of Song Dynasty)*: "from today forward, if the common people and people of other social status have no sons but only married daughters, they can inherit and share the family property."

7.2.6 The Strengthening of the Legal Adjustment of Economic Relationships

7.2.6.1 The Implementation of "Zu Yong Diao Fa" (Law on Farmland Rent, Handicraft Tax, and Corvée) Based on the "Jun Tian Zhi" (The System of Land Equalization)

It was stipulated in "Zu Yong Diao Fa" (Law on Farmland Rent, Handicraft Tax, and Corvée) which was issued in the 7th year of Wude (624 A.D.) that the people who were assigned farmland should pay two *dan* of millet or three *hu* (a dry measure used in ancient times) of rice, which was referred to as "Zu" (farmland rent) or "Tian Fu" (Land Tax). Every year, each male adult should serve corvée for twenty days, with two more days added in a leap year; if the male adult did not want to serve corvée, they could pay tough silk or cotton cloth; one day accounted for three *chi* of tough silk or 3.75 *chi* of cotton cloth, which was referred to as "Yong" (employment of labor). Thus, it meant the corvée which the people should serve for the country. Besides, people should also pay two *zhang* of tough silk or damask silk and three *liang* of silk floss every year. For those who lived in the places where silk was not produced, they should pay 2.5 *chi* of cotton cloth and three *jin* of linen, which was referred to as "Diao" (handicraft tax). Therefore, it meant the handicraft tax which the state collected from people or household tax simply. In addition to the compulsory service, there was also extra service. If people had rendered fifteen days of extra service, they could be exempted from the payment of "Diao" (handicraft tax); if they had rendered thirty days of extra service, they could be exempted from the payments of "Zu" and "Diao." From "Zu Yong Diao Fa" (Law on Farmland Rent, Handicraft Tax, and Corvée), it can be seen that tax collection was based on farmland, households and people, the three of which were closely connected, as was stated in the saying that "where there is farmland, there is rent; where there are households, there is 'Diao' (handicraft tax), where there are people, there is 'Yong' (employment of labor). In this country people are living in a big family, so the law should be applied impartially. Even though some people have planned to move to other places

7.2 The Legal System of Tang Dynasty Symbolizing the Establishment...

(in order to evade tax), fraudulency is forbidden. Therefore, people are all united, and everything is regulated by the established rules."[257] The implementation of "Jun Tian Zhi" (The System of Land Equalization) and "Zu Yong Diao Fa" (Law on Farmland Rent, Handicraft Tax, and Corvée) not only put the peasants under the control of the imperial government, but also fettered them on the farmland; at the same time, it had met the demand of the maximum exploitation of the imperial government and made it possible for the peasants to afford to live within the scope of law.

According to "Shi Huo" (National Finance and Economy) in *Tong Dian Tong Dian* (*The General Codes*), "Zu" (farmland rent), "Yong" (employment of labor) and "Diao" (handicraft tax) should be paid within certain days: "'Yong' (employment of labor) and 'Diao' (handicraft tax) should be started to be paid during the first ten days of August every year and completed within thirty days. Then the collection will be transferred to 'Zhou' (subprefecture) in September." "'Zu' should be collected according to the harvest time of each 'Zhou' (subprefecture), the degree of difficulty and the distance of transportation. After the collection has been completed within each 'Zhou' (subprefecture), they will be transported in November and the transportation will be completed within thirty days."

In addition to the regulation on the time of paying "Zu" (farmland rent) and "Diao" (handicraft tax), regulations on the amounts that officials and landlords should pay on time was also stipulated; if it was violated, the offenders should be punished. According to regulation, "the tax payment of the official departments is divided into ten grades. if the payment is overdue for one grade, those involved will be punished by 'Chi' (flogging with light sticks) for forty strokes with his penalty aggravated by one level for each grade." "In a village where one hundred *dan* of grain should be collected, if one fails to pay ten *hu* (one *dan*) of grain, he shall be punished by 'Chi' (flogging with light sticks) for forty strokes with his penalty aggravated by one level for each ten *hu*; if all his payment is overdue, he shall be punished by 'Tu' (imprisonment) for two years"; "if the head of a household delays the payment, he shall be punished by 'Chi' (flogging with light sticks) for forty strokes." Besides, he would also be ordered to pay the whole amount after the flogging.[258] From these regulations, it can clearly be seen that "Li Zheng" (head of "Li": the basic resident organization in ancient China) and the head of a household had played an important role in tax collection.

According to *Tang Lv* (*Tang Code*), "if a person ought to pay tax (referred to as "Ke Kou") in a family, it is referred to as 'Ke Hu'."[259] "Ke Hu" was the household mainly responsible for paying tax. However, the households of princes, dukes, or the

---

[257]Lu Zhi (Ming Dynasty), *Lu Xuan Gong Zou Yi* (*Lu Xuangong's Memorials to the Emperor*), Vol. 14.

[258]"Hu Hun" (Marriage, Tax and Household Registration) in *Tang Lv Shu Yi* (*The Comments on Tang Code*) *Tang Code*.

[259]"Shi Huo Zhi" (The Records of National Finance and Economy) in *Xin Tang Shu* (*The New Book of Tang Dynasty*) (Book 2).

nobleman and bureaucrats with lower ranks were not treated as "Ke Hu." Therefore, in Tang Dynasty, the tax payers were mainly peasants, which had reflected the nature of the taxation system of Tang Dynasty.

Because "Zu" (farmland rent), "Yong" (employment of labor) and "Diao" (handicraft tax) were collected uniformly, the amount of tax was relatively fixed. Moreover, the regulation on the increase and decrease of tax was elaborate and detailed, and all of them were confirmed by law, so it can be said that the taxation system of Tang Dynasty was a summary of the successful historical experience.

In the later period of Tang Dynasty, "Jun Tian Zhi" (The System of Land Equalization) was destroyed, so the basis for the existence of "Zu Yong Diao Fa" (Law on Farmland Rent, Handicraft Tax, and Corvée) was lost, which had led to "the insufficiency of the revenue income of the imperial government."[260] After Emperor Dezong ascended the throne, to solve the economic problem, "Zai Xiang" (the prime minister) named Yang Yan presented a memorial to the emperor to require that "Zu Yong Diao Fa" (Law on Farmland Rent, Handicraft Tax, and Corvée) which "was made mainly on the basis of compulsory service and tax" be abolished and an alternative tax law which was based on family property and farmland should be made instead. Yang Yan's suggestion was approved by the emperor, so "Liang Shui Fa" (two-tax law) was enacted in the 1st year of Jianzhong. The main contentsare as follows:

"Liang Chu Zhi Ren," which meant that the total amount of the tax was determined by the amount of fiscal expenditure, according to which the quota of tax was allocated to each place in the country.

All households, whether "Zhu Hu" (households having real estate), "Ke Hu" (households having no real estate but renting other people's farmland), native or non-native, should be registered in the places where they lived. Thus, "there are no distinctions between 'Zhu Hu' (households having real estate) and 'Ke Hu' (households having no real estate but renting other people's farmland), they should all have their households registered in the places of residence."[261]

The amount of the tax of the household was determined by their family property, so the tax should be paid in the places where the households lived. If businessmen did not have permanent residence, they should pay one thirtieth of their income as tax to "Zhou" (subprefecture) and "Xian" (county) where they lived.

"Zu" (farmland rent), "Yong" (employment of labor) and "Diao" (handicraft tax) and other miscellaneous tax and corvée were all abolished but "the tax paid by male adults" and the registration book of male adults of each household were still retained.

---

[260]"Yang Yan Zhuan" (The Biography of Yang Yan) in *Jiu Tang Shu* (*The Old Book of Tang Dynasty*).
[261]"Shi Huo Zhi" (The Records of National Finance and Economy) in *Xin Tang Shu* (*The New Book of Tang Dynasty*) (Book 2).

The tax was paid twice each year, so "'Liang Shui Shi' was established for tax collection."[262] The collection of summer tax should be completed in June of each year, and the collection of autumn tax should be completed in November of each year; tax was collected in the form of cash, but objects could also be used to compensate for tax.

The numbers of households and the increase or decrease of tax were used as the basis for evaluating the officials' merits and accomplishments each year.

In summary, "Liang Shui Fa" (two-tax law) simplified the tax collection by unifying all kinds of tax. At the same time, the traditional "Ji Ding Er Shui" (tax was collected according to the numbers of the male adults in one household) was changed, and "Ji Zi Er Shui" (tax was collected according to the family property) was extensively implemented, which not only was in accordance with the tax principle of "collecting tax according to people's ability," but also changed the unfair tax collection system in which the charges and donations were mainly imposed upon the peasants, and solved the financial crisis of the imperial government in time. However, the measure of using objects to compensate for tax and collecting extra tax beyond the law which was caused by "Liang Shui Fa" (two-tax law) became another insurmountable malpractice.

7.2.6.2 The Legal Adjustment of Handicraft Industries

In Tang Dynasty, the handicraft production management organization was not only huge but also elaborate in labor division. Thus, the organizations such as "Gong Bu" (The Department of Works), "Shao Fu Jian" (in charge of the handicraft production and royal affairs), "Jun Qi Jian" (in charge of weaponry), and "Jiang Zuo Jian" (in charge of imperial architecture) were established. It was recorded in history books that there were 19,850 craftsmen under "Shao Fu Jian" (in charge of the handicraft production and royal affairs) and there were 15,000 craftsmen under "Jiang Zuo Jian." These craftsmen were recruited from all over the country because "they were strong and highly skilled." To guarantee that there were qualified successors in each handicraft industry, it was regulated by the law that the children of the craftsmen "are not allowed to work in any other professions."[263]

As for the management of craftsmen, a strict organizational system was set up. For example, to make sure that the craftsmen could take turns to work, "the craftsmen in 'Zhou' (subprefecture) and 'Xian' (county) are organized into 'Tuan' (regiment); every five craftsmen are organized into one 'Huo' (military unit) and in

---

[262]"Shi Huo Zhi" (The Records of National Finance and Economy) in *Xin Tang Shu* (*The New Book of Tang Dynasty*) (Book 2).

[263]"Shang Shu Gong Bu" (The Minister of the Department of Works) in *Tang Liu Dian* (*The Six Statutes of Tang Dynasty*), Vol. 7.

every five 'Huo' one headman is appointed."[264] As to the identity of the craftsmen, it was divided into three types: first, "Guan Nu Bi" (the slave girls and maidservants working in government offices) who "are the relatives of the offenders punished for 'Fan Ni' (treachery) and who therefore have to serve in official departments with their family property confiscated." These craftsmen "worked all year long from generation to generation without having a day off."[265] Second, the craftsmen who took turns to work. "'Fan Hu' (official slaves once pardoned) worked three times every year and 'Za Hu' (families registered as workers) worked five times in every two years."[266] The time for each round was one month, hence, "Fan Hu" (official slaves once pardoned) worked for three months each year, and "Za Hu" (families registered as workers) for two and a half months each year. Both "Fan Hu" and "Za Hu" were referred to as "Jian Min" (rabbles or people of lower social status). Third, hired craftsmen. Most of them were free craftsmen and were hired temporarily. Those people were paid equally according to the days they had worked whether they were highly skillful or not. It was required in *Tang Lv* (*Tang Code*) that the male adults and craftsmen should render service on time: "For the service delayed, if one delays for one day, he shall be punished by 'Chi'(flogging with light sticks) for thirty strokes; if one delays for three days, his punishment shall be aggravated by one level with the maximum punishment of 'Zhang' (flogging with heavy sticks) for one hundred strokes." Meanwhile, the craftsmen's skill, medical care and production safety were also stipulated in *Tang Lv* (*Tang Code*): "If the official has not made full use of laborers, he should be punished by 'Zuo Zang' (embezzlement) according to the amount of money paid to the laborers with the penalty reduced by one level." In *Shu Yi* (*Tang Lv Shu Yi*), an explanation was given: "This refers to the cases of wasting the work of officially hired laborers. For example, the hired laborers are sent to collect medicinal herbs or to cut trees. If the official has made all the laborers do what they should not, he shall be charged of a complete dereliction of his duty; if he has made part of the laborers do what they should not, he shall be charged of a part dereliction of his duty and be punished for the offense of 'Zuo Zang' (embezzlement) with the penalty reduced by one level."[267] "In the cases of hiring artisans ... if one is sick in the place where he is hired, or if the manager does not send for a physician to have him treated, the manager shall be punished by 'Chi'(flogging with light sticks) for forty strokes; if, as a result, the laborer dies, he shall be punished by 'Tu' (imprisonment) for one year."[268] "If there are damages in the construction work and no proper measures are taken, or someone has been killed as a result of

---

[264]"Shi Huo Zhi" (The Records of National Finance and Economy) in *Xin Tang Shu* (*The New Book of Tang Dynasty*) (Book 1).

[265]"Shang Shu Xing Bu" (The Minister of the Department of Punishment) in *Tang Liu Dian* (*The Six Statutes of Tang Dynasty*), Vol. 6.

[266]"Shang Shu Xing Bu" (The Minister of the Department of Punishment) in *Tang Liu Dian* (*The Six Statutes of Tang Dynasty*), Vol. 6.

[267]"Shan Xing" (Sending Troops without Authorization) in *Tang Lv Shu Yi* (*The Comments on Tang Code*), Vol. 16.

[268]"Za Lv" (Miscellaneous Laws) in *Tang Lv Shu Yi* (*The Comments on Tang Code*), Vol. 26.

7.2 The Legal System of Tang Dynasty Symbolizing the Establishment... 605

carelessness, the official in charge and the laborers shall be punished by 'Tu' (imprisonment) for one and half years for the crime of 'Wu Sha' (manslaughter)." According to the explanation in *Shu Yi* (*Tang Lv Shu Yi*), "in the construction work, if damages are caused, which has led to the death of workers just because improper measures or precautions are taken, the official in charge shall be punished by 'Tu' (imprisonment) for one and a half years for the crime of 'Wu Sha' (manslaughter). The artisans and the supervisory officials shall be punished for what they are responsible for or what they have ordered others to do. Besides, it is not permitted to extend excessive liability to those who are not directly responsible. Since the punishment is imposed upon those who have caused the death of others, those who have caused injuries will be exempted from punishment."[269]

As to production management, first, it was emphasized that work should be done in accordance with law. If "one does not work according to law," for example, "if one does not follow the designs in the construction of an official building,... he shall be punished by 'Chi' (flogging with light sticks) for forty strokes and be dismissed from his post;... if an official changes the building designers personally, he shall be punished for the offense of 'Zuo Zang' (embezzlement) according to the salary he has paid to the designers whom he has hired personally with the punishment reduced by one level, while the designers he has hired personally shall be punished for the offense of 'Zuo Zang' (embezzlement) with the punishment aggravated by two levels. In addition, each artisan involved in the work shall be punished for what they have constructed with their punishment and the punishment for the officials in charge reduced by three levels."[270] Second, the size of the products was clearly required. For example, one *pi* of brocade, satin, silk and cotton cloth should have a width of one *chi* and eight *cun* and a length of four *zhang*; one *pi* of cotton cloth should have five *zhang*. To guarantee the quality of the product, it was stipulated that "if the wares or cotton or silk cloth for daily use are made in poor quality or carelessly or if they do not meet the standard or are damaged, but they are still sold to the consumers, the manufacturers shall be punished by 'Zhang' (flogging with heavy sticks) for sixty strokes.""If the wares are not strong enough, they are called 'Xing'; if they are not genuine, they are called 'Lan'"; "if the length of one *pi* of silk is less than forty *chi*, or the length of one *pi* of cotton cloth is less than fifty *chi* and its width is less than one *chi* and eight *cun*," the silk and the cotton cloth are considered "short and narrow" (poor quality); so "the poor quality and shoddy wares will be confiscated by the government, and the "short and narrow" (poor quality) wares shall be returned to the manufacturer." If the unqualified wares were sold, "the amount of illegally gained profits should be calculated; if the amount is large, the person who has made the profit shall be punished for the crime of theft and the seller shall also be punished for the same offense. If the officials of cities, 'Zhou'

---

[269]"Shan Xing" (Sending Troops without Authorization) in *Tang Lv Shu Yi* (*The Comments on Tang Code*), Vol. 16.
[270]"Shan Xing" (Sending Troops without Authorization) in *Tang Lv Shu Yi* (*The Comments on Tang Code*), Vol. 16.

(subprefecture) and 'Xian' (county) know (the unqualified wares are being sold) but do not make a report, they will receive the same penalty as the offenders; if the official fails to discover the dealing, his penalty shall be reduced by two levels."[271] Lastly, the clear-cut responsibilities of production were regulated, namely, the makers were required to inscribe their names on the products, as was recorded in "Guan Shi Ling" (Order on Border Market) in *Tang Ling Shi Yi* (*An Interpretation of the Orders of Tang Dynasty*): "The bows, arrows, and revolving knives should be made according to the government rules, so the artisans who make them should inscribe their names on the products before the sale, so the making of other wares should also follow suit." Moreover, "the dates and the names of the makers should all be inscribed on the weaponry."[272]

7.2.6.3 The Legal Adjustment of Business

In Tang Dynasty, business was prosperous so that there were many famous markets all over the capital and other places, at which "Nu Bi" (the slave girls and maidservants), cattle, horses, camels, mules, donkeys and other products were sold. Therefore, business management was an important part in *Tang Lv* (*Tang Code*), and it involved many aspects, such as markets, merchandise price and weights and measures. To maintain normal business order and to prevent people from buying or selling by force, dominating markets, and forcing up prices, it was stipulated in *Tang Lv* (*Tang Code*) that "in the cases of the purchase and sale of products, if one party monopolizes the market and takes all the profit by himself without the permission of the other, or if a trader makes an arrangement with a commission agent and jointly formulates an illegal criminal plot to sell (their own) cheap goods as valuable ones, or to buy the valuable goods (of others) at a low price, they shall be punished by 'Zhang' (flogging with heavy sticks) for eighty strokes." If the profit made was huge, it would be calculated, and the violator should be punished for the crime of theft. The so-called "Mai Mai Bui He" referred to buying and selling "without the agreement of the two parties," or buying and selling by force; the so-called "Er Jiao Gu Qu Zhe" referred to "dominating the market and forbidding others to sell"; the so-called "Geng Kai Chu Bi" referred to the collusion of seller and buyer in "selling the cheap goods at high price and buying the expansive goods at lower price"; the so-called "Can Shi" referred to the collusion of peddlers in cheating others. In the four cases mentioned above, the offenders would all be punished by "Zhang" (flogging with heavy sticks) for eighty strokes. If "one has made profit, then the amount of the illegally made profit should be calculated; if he is punishable by "Zhang" (flogging with heavy sticks) for eighty strokes for the amount of the profit

---

[271]"Shan Xing" (Sending Troops without Authorization) in *Tang Lv Shu Yi* (*The Comments on Tang Code*), Vol. 16.
[272]"Bai Guan Zhi" (The Record of the Officials of all Ranks) in *Xin Tang Shu* (*The New Book of Tang Dynasty y*) (Book 3).

made, he shall be punished for the crime of theft. "Since the profit is gained by theft, it should be confiscated and returned to the owner."

As to the price management, as the price of merchandise concerned the lives of thousands of people, they were also the key element in market control. Thus, officials were often sent to "investigate and set" the prices of product "in the official and private business" according to the production, supply, demand and quality of the merchandise. If the official set a higher price for the merchandise which was cheap or set a lower price for the merchandise which was expensive, he should be punished. According to "Za Lv" (Miscellaneous Laws) in *Tang Lv* (*Tang Code*), "if one official has set an unjust price, he should be punished for 'Zuo Zang' (embezzlement) according to the price which he set unjustly; if he takes it for his own use, he shall be punished for theft." The officials were required to set fair price. Moreover, they were also given authority to inspect the qualities of the merchandise and to punish those who sold the shoddy products which did not meet the market requirement according to law. It was stipulated that "the amount of illegally gained profits should be calculated, if the amount of the illegally made profits is large, the party shall be punished for the crime of theft"; "if the officials of a city, 'Zhou' (subprefecture) and 'Xian' (county) know (the unqualified articles are being sold) and do not report, they will be punished the same as the offenders; if the official fails to discover the dealing, his penalty shall be reduced by two levels."

With respect to the management of weights and measures, the unified system of weights and measures was established in the country. "Jin Bu" (The Department of Finance) in "Hu Bu" (The Department of Revenue) under "Shang Shu Sheng" (The Department of Secretary) was in charge of "setting the standards of weights and measures." Although individuals were permitted to make the instruments of weights and measures, they should be inspected, approved and stamped before being used. "Tai Fu Si Jiao Yin Shu" (The Office of Financial Accounting Bureau) and the local institutions of "Zhou" (subprefecture) and "Xian" (county) were responsible for the checking of the instruments of weights and measures. According to "Guan Shi Ling" (Order on Border Market), "'Hu' (a dry measure used in ancient times), 'Dou' (a measure for grain), scales, and linear measures should be inspected every year and should be put to use only after they are checked and stamped by the government." The weights and measurements should be checked in August of each year. If the privately-made weights and measures did not meet the standard but were still used in markets, the makers should be punished by 'Chi' (flogging with light sticks) for fifty strokes; although the weights and measures met the standards, if it had not been checked and stamped by the government, the one who used it should be punished by 'Chi' (flogging with light sticks) for forty strokes. If the items of weights and measures were increased or decreased, which had caused the losses of others, the losses should be calculated and the offenders should be punished for the offense of theft; if the official who was responsible for the weights and measures conducted illegally out of personal reason, he should still be punished. It was stipulated in "Za Lv" (Miscellaneous Laws) in *Tang Lv* (*Tang Code*) that "if measures which are not made in accordance with the rules are issued by the government, the officials in charge shall be punished by 'Zhang' (flogging with heavy sticks) for seventy strokes; if the inspecting official is negligent in his inspection, his penalty shall be reduced by one level; if he knows the circumstances, he shall be punished the same."

The law on foreign trade administration was an important part of the economic law and it also reflected the characteristics of times.

In Tang Dynasty, the development of commodity economy and the stability of the united country had provided a favorable condition for foreign trade, so the trade between the imperial government and the European and Asian countries and the nations along the border regions became unprecedentedly prosperous. According to records in "Di Li Zhi" (The Record of Geography) (Part 2) in *Xin Tang Shu* (*The New Book of Tang Dynasty*), there were seven roads leading to domestic and foreign markets: "the first, from Yingzhou to Andongdao; the second, from Haihang of Dengzhou to Ancient Korea and the Bohai Sea; the third, from the northern-frontier of Xiazhou (Shannxi and Shanxi today) to Yunzhong of Datong; the fourth, from Zhongshoujian City (Baotou City of Inner Mongolia Autonomous Region) to Hugu; the fifth, from Anxi to Xiyu; the sixth, from Annan to Ancient India; the seventh, from Guangzou to Haiyi."

As trading with foreign countries had a great influence on economy and politics, the foreign trade was all monopolized by the imperial government through many measures, such as setting up "Hu Shi Jian" (ancient government office taking the charge of the foreign trade on land road and the trade of horses with ethnic minorities) to take charge of the trade on land, setting up "Shi Bo Si" (the office in charge of the management of foreign trade) to take the charge of the trade on water, sending officials to go to the border areas to take the charge of commodity exchanges between the peoples of different nationalities along the border and the neighboring countries, and setting up fixed markets for commodity exchanges. According to "Guan Shi Ling" (Order on Border Market), "when setting up foreign trade markets or markets along the border areas, the markets should be inspected by the trade officials. In addition, the markets should be walled up by fences with trenches on each side and the gates of the markets should be guarded. On the market day, the goods and animal products should be transported to the market after sunrise and the officials in charge should check and set the prices of the products with the foreign businessmen before the markets open."[273]

Because of the development of foreign trade, the resident population of the foreign businessmen and their families in China kept increasing. To strengthen the management of the living areas of the foreign businessmen, "Fan Chang" was specially set up to protect the property rights of those foreigners. For example, a decree was issued on the 23rd of August of the 8th year of Dahe during the reign of Emperor Wenzong, according to which after the people who came from Persia or any other countries to do business in China died, their property should be returned to

---

[273] Niida Noboru (Japan), "Za Ling" (Miscellaneous Orders) in *Tang Ling Shi Yi* (*An Interpretation of the Orders of Tang Dynasty*), in the 7th year of Kaiyuan.

their relatives who were with them, such as their parents, wives, sons, daughters or brothers.

The individuals should have certificates, which were called "Guo Suo," before they crossed the border to do business. The individuals who had crossed the border and done business without authorization would be punished. It was stipulated in "Wei Jin Lv" (Statutes on Palace Guards) in *Tang Lv* (*Tang Code*) that "anyone who crosses the border and the pass without authorization should be punished by 'Tu' (imprisonment) for two years; if he has secretly bought something from or sold something to any foreigners, or if it is one *pi* of cloth, he shall be punished by 'Tu' (imprisonment) for two years; if it is three *pi* of cloth, his penalty shall be aggravated by one level; if it is fifteen *pi* of cloth, he shall be punished by 'Liu' (exile) with labor service." Besides, was it was also prohibited to exchange goods without authorization.

Out of the consideration of the state interests, some products were prohibited to be exported. For example, "the following products should not be sold across the western borders, northern passes and in "Zhou" (subprefecture) alongside the border areas: brocade, satin, damask silk, satin, bourette silk, silk floss, tough silk, silk, cotton, the tails of yaks, pearls, gold, silver, iron, etc."[274]; "if one person secretly takes the prohibited products across the border, he shall be punished for the offense 'Zuo Zang' (embezzlement); if the amount of the product is small, he shall be punished for the offense of secretly making and keeping prohibited objects"; "if he crosses the border with prohibited products and is caught by someone, his products shall be divided into three parts, among which two parts will be given to the person who catches him as a award, and one part will be confiscated by the government."[275]

In summary, it can be inferred from what is mentioned above that the legal adjustment which had led to the prosperity of the commodity economy in Tang Dynasty was mainly carried out through the enforcement of criminal punishment and economic sanctions, which had shown a mixture of economic and criminal law. Thus, this was an important feature of feudal economic law.

7.2.7 The Judicial System Tending To Be Perfect

In Tang Dynasty, rich experience was accumulated through its long legal practice, which had made it possible for its judicial system to become more perfect.

---

[274]Niida Noboru (Japan), "Za Ling" (Miscellaneous Orders) in *Tang Ling Shi Yi* (*An Interpretation of the Orders of Tang Dynasty*), in the 7th year of Kaiyuan.

[275]"Wei Jin Lv" (Statutes on Palace Guards) in *Tang Lv Shu Yi* (*The Comments on Tang Code*).

7.2.7.1 The Judicial System of "San Si Tui Shi" (The Joint Trial by Three Departments)

"Da Li Si" (The Bureau of Judicial Review) was the supreme judicial organ responsible for hearing the cases involving the offenses committed by government officials, the cases involving the punishment of "Tu" (imprisonment) or "Liu" (exile) and the cases involving more serious punishments in the capital area. The punishments of "Tu" (imprisonment) and "Liu" (exile) should be reviewed by "Xing Bu" (The Department of Punishment), while the death penalties should be directly presented to the emperor for his approval. Additionally, the emperor was also responsible for reviewing the doubtful cases involving death penalty which were transferred by "Xing Bu" (The Department of Punishment) from local areas. As to the organization, the old systems of "San Guo" (Three Kingdoms) and Jin dynasties were followed by "Da Li Si" (The Bureau of Judicial Review), so the official positions, such as "Qing" (minister), "Shao Qing" (the vice president), "Zheng" (director), "Cheng" (the assistant of county magistrate), "Si Zhi" (official in charge of supervising the officials in capital) and "Ping Shi" (junior official in "Da Li Si") and many other subordinate official positions were set up. Emperor Taizong attached great importance to the selection of the ministers of "Da Li Si" (The Bureau of Judicial Review), so he once said that "the official position of 'Da Li' directly concerns human life, therefore the minister of 'Da Li' (The Bureau of Judicial Review) must be extremely carefully selected."[276]

"Xing Bu" (The Department of Punishment) was the supreme administrative organ, which included the following official positions: "Shang Shu" (the minister), "Shi Lang" (vice minister), "Lang Zhong" (head of a subministry department) and "Yuan Wai Lang" (deputy head of a subministry department or an honorary title), etc. Besides, there were four subordinate bureaus in "Xing Bu" (The Department of Punishment), namely "Xing Bu" (The Bureau of Punishment), "Du Guan" (ancient government office in charge of military prisons and penalty), "Bi Bu" (ancient government office in charge of in charge of prison and penalty) and "Si Men" (The Bureau of Customs), which were in charge of "making criminal laws and issuing government decrees concerning the administration of prisoners and the settlement and reviewing of major cases."[277] In addition, it was also in charge of reviewing the cases heard by "Da Li Si" (The Bureau of Judicial Review), the cases involving the punishment lighter than "Liu" (exile) and the cases involving the punishment of "Tu" (imprisonment) or more severe punishments transferred by "Zhou" (subprefecture) and "Xian" (county). If there were any doubtful points in these cases, those involving the punishment of "Tu" (imprisonment) and "Liu" (exile) should be sent back to the original trial organs to be tried again, while

---

[276]"Da Li Si" (The Bureau of Judicial Review) in *Tang Hui Yao* (*Collections of Historical Records of Tang Dynasty*), Vol. 66.

[277]"Zhi Guan Zhi" (The Record of State Officials) in *Jiu Tang Shu* (*The Old Book of Tang Dynasty*).

7.2 The Legal System of Tang Dynasty Symbolizing the Establishment... 611

those involving "Si Xing" (death penalties) should be transferred to "Da Li Si" for reviewing.

"Yu Shi Tai" (The Censorate) was the supreme supervisory organ, and "Yu Shi Da Fu" (Grand Censor) and "Yu Shi Zhong Cheng" (Grand Censor) were appointed as the director and deputy director respectively. It was mainly in charge of impeaching the government officials and "purifying the impropriety from the imperial court"[278]; meanwhile, it was also in charge of supervising the trial activities of "Da Li Si" and "Xing Bu" (The Department of Punishment).

In Tang Dynasty, the major cases were often jointly tried by the minister of "Da Li Si," "Shang Shu" (the minister) in "Xing Bu" (The Department of Punishment) and "Yu Shi Zhong Cheng" (Grand Censor) in "Yu Shi Tai" (The Censorate), which was referred to as "San Si Tui Shi" (the joint trial by three departments). Thus, it had set an example for the joint trial system of "San Fa Si" (Three Judicial Departments) in later dynasties. Moreover, the emperor often ordered the non-judicial organs to participate in case trials according to the specific circumstances of the cases. For example, the cases involving "Si Xing" (death penalties) should be jointly reviewed by "Xing Bu" (The Department of Punishment), "Zhong Shu Sheng" (the supreme organization in charge of the state affairs) and "Men Xia Sheng" (the organization in charge of examining the imperial edicts in ancient China) to show that penalties were prudently enforced upon the offenders. For the important cases in local places which had not yet been transferred to the central government, they were jointly heard by "San Si Shi" (Inspectors of the Three Departments), namely, "Jian Cha Yu Shi" (the supervisory censor), "Xing Bu Yuan Wai Lang" (deputy of the department of punishment) and "Da Li Ping Shi" (junior official in "Da Li Si"). Sometimes "Ji Shi Zhong" (the senior assistant of the emperor and the supervisor of officials) in "Men Xia Sheng" (the organization in charge of examining the imperial edicts in ancient China), "Zhong Shu She Ren" (the official in charge of drafting imperial edicts in "Zhong Shu Sheng") in "Zhong Shu Sheng" (the supreme organization in charge of the state affairs) and "Yu Shi" (the censor) in "Yu Shi Tai" (The Censorate) would jointly form a special tribunal, which was called "Xiao San Si" (Small Three Departments) to be in charge of settling the cases of appeal.

Until the Tang Dynasty, it had already become an established model to divide the central judicial organ into three sections to conduct mutual check and balance and to improve judicial efficiency. However, in the system of autocratic monarchy, it was the emperor who had the supreme power of trial, referendum and absolution, which had reflected the strengthening of the royal power over the control of judiciary.

The local judicial organs were still concurrently controlled by the administrative offices. The heads of "Zhou" (subprefecture) and "Xian" (county) were also the supreme judicial officials at the level and more assistant officials were appointed to handle the lawsuits directly than those of the previous dynasties. For example, "Si Hu Can Jun Shi" (local government offices hearing civil and criminal cases) and "Hu Cao Can Jun Shi" (local government offices in charge of household registration)

---

[278]*Tang Liu Dian* (*The Six Statutes of Tang Dynasty*), Vol. 13.

were set up respectively in "Zhou" (subprefecture) and "Du Du Fu" (Offices of Military Affairs) to be "in charge of analysing and settling the civil cases: for the cases concerning marriage, they should clarify family names of bridegroom and bride and decide whether the marriage was legal; for the cases concerning farmland, they should make decisions and make sure that their decisions be followed by the interested parties." "Fa Cao Can Jun Shi" (local government offices in charge of judicature) and "Si Fa Can Jun Shi" (local government offices in charge of passing sentences) were also set up respectively in "Zhou" (subprefecture) and "Du Du Fu" (Offices of Military Affairs) to be in charge of hearing the criminal cases, "carrying out 'Lv' (criminal law), 'Ling' (decree), 'Ge' (injunction), 'Shi' (standard), enforcing punishments, supervising the arresting of robbers, correcting the misconducts, investigating the truth of the cases, making relevant laws, pardoning those who have committed serious crimes unintentionally, mitigating the punishment for those if there is not enough evidence so that people can learn what to do, do good deeds and avoid evildoing."[279]

At the level of "Xian" (county), "Si Fa Zuo" (judicial assistance) and "Si Fa Shi" (official in charge of judicial affairs) were in charge of the judicial affairs. Under the level of "Xian" (county), the heads of "Li" (a basic resident organization consisting of five neighborhoods), "Fang" (neighborhood) and "Cun" (village) had certain power of mediating and settling the cases of civil litigation over marriage, farmland, and so on. If the parties refused to accept the decisions, they could appeal to the judicial organs of "Xian" (county). The criminal cases were heard directly by the judicial organs of "Xian" (county) without being heard by the officials of "Xiang" (townships). To improve the qualification of judicial officials, all senior judicial officials must sit and pass imperial examinations. During the reign of Emperor Taizong, the office of "Lv Xue" (the study of statutory laws) was set up in "Guo Zi Jian" (the highest educational body in ancient China) to promote the education of the reserve forces of judicial officials.

In the early period of Tang Dynasty, the criminal law was famous for its "leniency and simplicity," however, malpractice still existed, as was described in the records that "nowadays, as for the reviewing of criminal cases, severe punishment is often enforced by the judicial officials in order to achieve a better performance evaluation."[280] In the 11th year of Zhenguan (637 A.D.), Wei Zheng had particularly criticized the abuse of judicial power by Emperor Taizong. Wei Zheng said:

> In recent years, I have realized that although the nets are closely cast, however, whether a fish which is discovered in deep water should be caught or not is always determined by people's love or hatred, and the severity and the leniency of the penalty is always determined according to the mood of judges. When a person whom the judges like commits a serious offense, he is defended by the prestigious people with sophistry; when a person whom the judges dislike commits a minor offense, his criminal motive is always deeply explored.[281]

---

[279]*Tang Liu Dian (The Six Statutes of Tang Dynasty)*, Vol. 30.

[280]*Tang Hui Yao (Collections of Historical Records of Tang Dynasty)*, Vol. 40.

[281]"Gong Ping" (Impartiality) in *Zhen Guan Zheng Yao (The Essentials about Politics during the Reign of Zhen Guan)*, Vol. 5.

After the middle period of Tang Dynasty, the judicial practice had gradually deorbited the track required by the feudal legal system.

7.2.7.2 Prosecution and Jurisdiction

There were two types of prosecution in Tang Dynasty: one was reporting the offenses by supervision organs or officials at different levels to the governmental authorities, which was called "Ju He" (impeachment by listing offenses), which is similar to "Gong Su" (public prosecution) in modern times. Therefore, those who should make reports but failed to do so should bear criminal liability; the other was the prosecution filed by the party interested or his relatives to the government authorities, which was similar to "Zi Su" (private prosecution) in modern times.

In Tang Dynasty, an indictment which was called "Ci Die" was used for prosecution, and the person who was unable to write could ask the officials or to employ others to write for him. However, the person who wrote indictments for others should not "add the contents of prosecution by himself. If the prosecution does not agree with facts, he shall be punished by 'Chi' (flogging with light sticks) for fifty strokes; if more made-up offenses are added randomly which lead to more severe penalties, he should be punished for the offense of 'Wu Gao' (false accusation) with one level reduced."[282] Oral prosecution had the same legal effect as written prosecution. However, except for offenses of "Mou Fan" (plotting rebellion or plotting to endanger the country), "Mou Da Ni" (great sedition) and "Mou Pan" (treason), it was forbidden for the inferior and the young to accuse the superior and the elder, and it was also forbidden for "Nu Bi" (the slave girls and maidservants) to accuse their owners; otherwise, they would be severely punished. It was stipulated in an imperial edict issued in the 2nd year of Zhenguan (628 A.D.) that "from today forward, a slave who accuses his owner of an offense shall be punished by 'Zhan' (beheading)." It was also stipulated in "Dou Song" (Litigation) in *Tang Lv Shu Yi* (*The Comments on Tang Code*) that "'Bu Qu' (the private army) or 'Nu Bi' (the slave girls and maidservants) shall be punished by 'Jiao' (hanging) if he or she accuses his or her owner of an offense other than 'Mou Fan' (plotting rebellion or plotting to endanger the country), 'Mou Da Ni' (great sedition) and 'Mou Pan' (treason)." Generally speaking, the prisoner, the man over eighty years old, and the children under ten years old or 'Du Ji' (the incapacitated) had no rights to initiate "Zi Su" (private prosecution). Therefore, the lawsuits filed by those who had no rights to initiate "Zi Su" (private prosecution) were unacceptable; otherwise the officials who had accepted and heard such cases "should be punished three levels lighter than that for the offender himself."

However, mandatory obligation of accusation was stipulated for certain offenses. For example, "if one person knows of the offense of 'Mou Fan' (plotting rebellion or plotting to endanger the country) and 'Mou Da Ni' (great sedition), he shall secretly

---

[282]"Dou Song" (Litigation) in *Tang Lv Shu Yi* (*The Comments on Tang Code*).

report the offense to the government authority nearby; if he does not do so, he or she shall be punished by 'Jiao' (hanging)." If the offense was reported by his relatives, they shall be exempted from the punishment of "Lian Zuo" (being punished for being related to somebody who committed an offense); "if a person knows of an offense committed by someone within 'Wu Bao' (the same neighborhood of five families) and knows that this person still hides himself in this neighborhood, but does not report to the government authority, he shall be punished by 'Tu' (imprisonment) for one year if the offense involves death penalty; he shall be punished by 'Zhang' (flogging with heavy sticks) for one hundred strokes if the offense involves 'Liu' (exile); he shall be punished by 'Zhang' (flogging with heavy sticks) for seventy strokes if the offense involves 'Tu' (imprisonment). However, the female or the male under fifteen years old in the family shall be exempted from punishment."[283] "The person shall be punished by 'Liu' (exile) to a distance of 2,000 *li*, if his or her paternal grandparents, parents or husband are murdered, or if he or she has made private agreement with the murderer; if his or her 'Qi Qin' (relatives being in mourn for one year) have been murdered, but he or she has made private agreement with the murderer, he or she shall be punished by 'Tu' (imprisonment) for two and a half years"; "even though the person does not make private agreement with the murderer, but if he or she does not make reports about the killing within thirty days, he or she will be punished two levels lighter."[284] Besides, provisions on voluntary surrender were also regulated in "Ming Li Lv" (Statutes and Terms) in *Tang Lv Shu Yi* (*The Comments on Tang Code*): a criminal suspect could surrender himself to the government, he could also "ask somebody else to make a confession on behalf of himself. For the cases of "Xiang Rong Yin" (prohibiting indictment or testifying each other between relatives), if one made report to the government or turned his relatives in, the informant would be punished according to the provisions on 'Zi Shou' (an offender surrendering himself)."

To ensure the truthfulness of the accusation, it was stipulated in "Dou Song" (Litigation) in *Tang Lv Shu Yi* (*The Comments on Tang Code*) that "the accusation shall be dated and shall contain statements on criminal facts. Besides, no doubtful points shall be contained in the report. If accusation does not agree with the provision, the person concerned shall be punished by 'Chi' (flogging with light sticks) for fifty strokes." When one asked somebody else to report an offense on his behalf, "if the accusation is not true, he shall be punished the same as that which he intends to inflict upon the accused, and he shall be rewarded if the accusation is true"; "if one stops the carriage of the authority or accuses somebody of an offense by 'Wo Deng Wen Gu' (beat the drum and deliver the complaints, it is one of the important direct complaints in ancient China), he shall be considered as a private accuser. If accusation is false, he shall be punished by 'Zhang' (flogging with heavy sticks) for eighty strokes."[285] "If a person accuses someone of an offense

---

[283]"Dou Song" (Litigation) in *Tang Lv Shu Yi* (*The Comments on Tang Code*).
[284]"Zei Dao" (Stealing and Robbery) in *Tang Lv Shu Yi* (*The Comments on Tang Code*).
[285]"Zei Dao" (Stealing and Robbery) in *Tang Lv Shu Yi* (*The Comments on Tang Code*).

7.2 The Legal System of Tang Dynasty Symbolizing the Establishment... 615

anonymously, he shall be punished by 'Liu' (exile) to a distance of 2,000 *li*"; if the person had made a false accusation, he shall be punished the same as that which he intended to inflict upon the accused.

In Tang Dynasty, the authority at the level of "Xian" (county) was the trial organ of first instance which had the jurisdiction over the cases involving the punishment lighter than "Zhang" (flogging with heavy sticks). The authority at the level of "Zhou" (subprefecture) was the trial organ of second instance which had the jurisdiction over appeal. For the cases involving the punishment severer than "Tu" (imprisonment) and "Liu" (exile), they should be reported and transferred to "Xing Bu" (The Department of Punishment) for settlement, as was stated in the provisions that "all offenses shall be tried at the level of 'Zhou' (subprefecture) and 'Xian' (county),"[286] and "Yue Su" (overstepping indictment) was forbidden. "If one appeals by overstepping indictment, both the plaintiff and the official who accepts and hear the cases shall be punished by 'Chi' (flogging with light sticks) for forty strokes." It was noted in *Shu Yi* (*Tang Lv Shu Yi*) that "according to law, all lawsuits shall be filed from bottom-up. So the cases should be first handled at the level of 'Xian' (county) and then handled at the levels of 'Zhou' (subprefectures), 'Fu' (ancient administrative district between province and county) and 'Sheng' (departments) successively. If one appeals by overstepping indictment, the plaintiff and the official who accepts and hears the case shall be punished by 'Chi' (flogging with light sticks) for forty strokes respectively"[287]

The government authorities at the level of "Xian" (county) were courts of first instance for civil cases. The following is documented in volume fifty-five of "Sheng Hao" and "Yu Shi Tai" (The Censorate) (Part 1) in *Tang Hui Yao* (*Collections of Historical Records of Tang Dynasty*) about the institutionalization of complaints and acceptance of civil cases:

> In July of 14th year of Dali (779 A.D.), Cui Zao, the counsellor of "Li Gui Shi" (ancient government office in charge of collecting the opinions of officials and conveying them to the emperor) submitted a memorial to the emperor. According to his explanation, "when there are complaints about dereliction of duty by a deceased official, or disputes over marriages and farmland or claims to property, etc., they shall all be filed to the local bureaus of 'Xian' (county) by which the cases should be heard first; if they are not accepted by the local bureaus of 'Xian' (county), they should be filed to the provincial bureaus; if they are not accepted by the provincial bureaus, they should be filed to 'San Si' (The Three Departments); if they are not accepted by 'San Si' (The Three Departments), they should be filed to "Li Gui Shi" (ancient government office in charge of collecting the opinions of officials and conveying them to the emperor). However, this rule is not applicable to the cases which are filed directly to this bureau without being heard by 'San Si' (The Three Departments) or the cases which are not fairly heard. This rule is also not applicable to the cases in which there is something urgent to be reported to the emperor. The person who submits a petition with no evidence shall be s handled by 'Tai Fu' (bureau in charge of national financial affairs)." So an imperial edict of approval was issued later on according to his memorial.

---

[286]Niida Noboru (Japan), "Za Ling" (Miscellaneous Orders) in *Tang Ling Shi Yi* (*An Interpretation of the Orders of Tang Dynasty*), in the 7th year of Kaiyuan.

[287]"Dou Song" (Litigation) in *Tang Lv Shu Yi* (*The Comments on Tang Code*).

In April of the 1st year of Dazhong (847 A.D.), a memorial was presented by "Yu Shi Tai" (The Censorate) to the emperor:

"... the cases involving the disputes over marriage and farmland or the cases involving rent and interest shall be initially sent to and handled by the bureaus of 'Zhou' (subprefecture) and 'Xian' (county); if the cases involve military affairs, they shall also be heard by 'Zhou' (subprefecture) and 'Xian' (county). However, recently, many cases are directly sent to 'Yu Shi Tai' (The Censorate), which has brought overloaded work and caused much trouble. So from today forward, we require that the cases involving private or public debts and the disputes over marriage and farmland be sent and heard by the bureaus of 'Zhou' (subprefecture) and 'Xian' (county) without being sent to 'Yu Shi Tai' (The Censorate) anymore. If the cases have been sent to 'Yu Shi Tai' (The Censorate) or have been transferred to 'Yu Shi Tai' (The Censorate) with the approval of 'Zai Xiang' (the prime minister) without being heard by the bureaus where they ought to be sent, they shall be sent back to the local bureaus. If a case has been heard by a bureau but the court trial is considered to be unjust, the case shall be transferred to 'Yu Shi Tai' (The Censorate). If the case is considered truly unjust by 'Yu Shi Tai' (The Censorate), the judicial official in charge of the case in the local bureau of 'Zhou' (subprefecture) and 'Xian' (county) shall come to 'Yu Shi Tai' (The Censorate) to make decision according to the situation of the cases. If the offense of the judge is minor, he shall be directly scored a low grade in his official assessment; if the offense is serious, he shall be removed from office or demoted. So the purpose of enforcing punishment on the judges is to take disciplinary action against their incompetency. I have presented an oral memorial to Your Majesty in Yanying Hall on the 3rd of this month and this is the written form of the memorial which Your Majesty order me to write." So an imperial decree of approval was issued later on according to this memorial.[288]

The above-mentioned record shows that since the middle period of Tang Dynasty, with the increase of the number of civil cases, the rulers paid great attention to civil proceedings. In judicial practice, the majority of civil cases were settled after the trial at the level of "Xian" (county), so only a small number of cases were continued to be appealed, and some even were appealed to the emperor. For example, the case of "the concubine of Lu Yue vs. the wife of Lu Yue" about family property inheritance documented in volume 163 of "Mu Ning Fu Mu Zan Zhuan" (The Biography of Mu Ning and Mu Zan) in *Xin Tang Shu* (*The New Book of Tang Dynasty*) and the case of the private debt wrongfully judged by Lai Junchen documented in volume 110 of "Xue Na Zhuan" (The Biography of Xue Na) in *Xin Tang Shu* (*The New Book of Tang Dynasty*) were all historical evidence of the civil cases being appealed directly to the central judicial organs.

As to regional jurisdiction, when two or more judicial organs at the same level had jurisdiction over a case within one hundred, the principles of jurisdiction are as follows: "Qing Cong Zhong," namely, when both misdemeanors and serious offenses were charged, the punishment should be enforced according to the serious offenses which the criminal had committed; "Shao Cong Duo," namely, when criminal charges were similar in two 'Xian' (county), the case should be tried by the judicial organ of the 'Xian' (county) where more cases had been handled; "Hou Cong Xian," namely, when the suspects were arrested because they had committed

---

[288]"Yu Shi Tai (Shang)" (The Censorate: Book 1) of *Tang Hui Yao* (*Collections of Historical Records of Tang Dynasty*) Vol. 60.

7.2 The Legal System of Tang Dynasty Symbolizing the Establishment...

more crimes, they should be tried by the judicial organ of the place where the suspects were first arrested. However, when it was beyond one hundred *li*, the suspects should be tried by the judicial organ of the place where the crimes were actually committed.

7.2.7.3 The Trial System of "Yi Zhuang Ju Yu" (Interrogating the Suspect in Accordance with the Facts Alleged in the Complaint)

After the lawsuit was accepted by the local government, the parties of the case should be summoned for interrogation, and the offenders should be arrested and imprisoned immediately.

To ensure the fairness of trial, the avoidance system in trial proceedings, namely, "Huan Tui Zhi Du" (avoidance system) was further improved. If a judicial official had kinship or teacher-student relationship with the party of the case, or a judicial official felt resentful towards the party of the case, or if a judicial official ever served as a "Ci Li" (feudal provincial or prefectural governor) or "Xian Ling" (county magistrate) in the place, he should withdraw himself from the trial. It was stipulated in "Xing Bu" (The Department of Punishment) in *Tang Liu Dian* (*The Six Statutes of Tang Dynasty*) that "if a judge has kinship with or if he is resentful towards the accused, he shall withdraw himself from the settlement of the case."

In interrogation, "Pan Guan Qin Wen" (judges shall try the cases by themselves) and "Yi Zhuang Ju Yu" (interrogating the suspect in accordance with the facts alleged in the complaint) were required and that the affairs beyond the complaint should not be investigated. In "Duan Yu" (Trials and Punishments) in *Tang Lv Shu Yi* (*The Comments on Tang Code*), it was stipulated that "in interrogation, it is necessary to conduct the investigation in accordance with what is alleged in the complaint. If the official has inquired about other instances which is not included in the complaint, he should be punished for the crime of 'Ru Zui' (to intentionally sentence an innocent person guilty or a misdemeanor felony)." Wei Zheng ever pointed out that "as for the matters of trial, judgment should be mainly made on the basis the offense committed without using torture, without inquiring about what is not included in the complaint and without interfering with irrelevant matters to show the intelligence of the magistrate."[289] However, it was not limited to the offenses accused by others or the offenses which were discovered later.

To ascertain the truth, the requirements for evidence were further specified. For example, the confession of the accused was regarded as the basis of conviction; however, "if the illegally obtained property is found or if there are not any doubtful points, even if the accused does not plead guilty, the judge can still render a

---

[289] "Gong Ping" (Impartiality) in *Zhen Guan Zheng Yao* (*The Essentials about Politics during the Reign of Zhen Guan*), Vol. 5.

judgment based upon the property illegally obtained."²⁹⁰ So in this aspect, material evidence played a decisive role, but besides confession and material evidence, witness was also required in certain cases. For example, it was stated in *Shu Yi* (*Tang Lv Shu Yi*) that "only when three or more people could corroborate the facts without doubts may the accused be convicted." However, to prevent partiality, the family members of the accused were not allowed to testify against each other (namely, the elder or the young of family members may conceal the crime committed by each other). Moreover, "the person who is over eighty years old or older or under ten years old or younger, or who is 'Du Ji' (the incapacitated), shall not be ordered to testify in court," this was because they lacked the competence to testify. A witness who had made false statements should be punished, as was stated in the regulation that "if a witness does not state facts…which has thus led to wrongful judgments, he shall be punished two levels lighter."²⁹¹ Moreover, if a person had made a false examination of injury, he should also be punished, as was stated in the regulation that "if a false illness, death or injury is claimed, which thus has led to a false examination, the person shall be punished for the crime of cheating for his fraudulent claims, but the penalty shall be reduced by one level; if the claimed illness, death or injury is true, but no proper authentication is made, the person who has conducted the examination shall be punished for intentional incrimination."²⁹²

Because "Zui Cong Gong Ding" (enforcing punishments in accordance with the convicts' confessions) was a general practice in the feudal trial practice, it was legal to obtain confession by making use of torture. However, in Tang Dynasty, some restrictions were stipulated to prevent extorting confessions by torture. For example, "the magistrate who is in charge of interrogating the accused must make careful and repeated investigation about the facts and statements according to specific circumstances. If he still cannot decide on the case or if the cases need to be further investigated, he shall place the case on file for investigation or hear it jointly with the judges before making use of torture."²⁹³ The so-called "Li An Tong Pan" (hearing the cases jointly) meant that the doubtful cases should be tried jointly by the judge with his supervisors before the accused was tortured. Thus, only the person who was seventy years old or older, or fifteen years old or younger, or "Fei Ji" (the disabled), or the pregnant could be exempted from torture. However, according to rules, "torture" could only be used for no more than three times with twenty days of interval between each of them and the total strokes should be no more than 200. If the accused was tortured to death within this limit, the case should not be investigated anymore; if the accused was tortured to death beyond this limit, the magistrate should be punished by a maximum penalty of "Tu" (imprisonment) for two years. Since the reign of Emperor Taizong, the body parts of the accused that should be tortured was changed from back to buttocks. Therefore, the torture system in Tang

---

[290] "Duan Yu" (Trials and Punishments) in *Tang Lv Shu Yi* (*The Comments on Tang Code*).
[291] "Za Wei" (Rules for False Accusations) in *Tang Lv Shu Yi* (*The Comments on Tang Code*).
[292] "Za Wei" (Rules for False Accusations) in *Tang Lv Shu Yi* (*The Comments on Tang Code*).
[293] "Duan Yu" (Trials and Punishments) in *Tang Lv Shu Yi* (*The Comments on Tang Code*).

Dynasty was a restraint of the judge's unlimited power, however, with the corruption of feudal legal system, this kind of restraint gradually became a formality, so even the emperor himself also admitted that "torture has become so cruel that I was also shocked" and that "if so much pain was inflicted upon the accused, one can obtain any confession from him."[294] However, torture was applied only to the ordinary people, the people who had the privileges of "Yi" (deliberation), "Qing" (petition), "Jian" (mitigation) were never to be tortured. Thus, if torture was misused against them, the judicial officials concerned would be punished.

To ensure that the confession obtained through torture would not be overturned by the accused, the accused was required to write his confession by himself, as was stated that "if an accused is unable to write, the official registrar shall write for him and read the confession to the judicial officials,"[295] who then made the judgment according to the written confession.

For the case trials concerning foreigners, official translators were usually engaged. The translators should translate accurately without making false statements; otherwise, he would bear criminal responsibility.

While making judgments, convictions and punishments should be enforced according to law, as was stated that "in hearing cases, the magistrate shall follow 'Lv' (criminal law), 'Ling' (orders or ordinances), 'Ge' (injunction), and 'Shi' (standard); if he does not follow this provision, he shall be punished by 'Chi' (flogging with light sticks) for thirty strokes; if there are many rules included in one article of the law, it is permitted that for the official to refer to the ones which are relevant to the actual offense that is committed,"[296] which had fully demonstrated the spirit of "Fa Zhi" (the ruling of law) and won due respect in the world history of legal civilization. In Tang Dynasty the rule of law was much stressed, so only under this historical condition could "Fa Zhi" (the ruling of law) be carried out and implemented seriously. Since the principle of "Zui Xing Fa Ding" (a legally prescribed punishment for a specified crime) was emphasized and the authority of law was established, which in turn guaranteed that judicial activities were completely carried out in accordance with the national interest. Moreover, the magistrates' judicial liability was more seriously stressed, the abuse of power was effectively prevented and the extra-judicial persecution of the parties was greatly reduced. Not only that, according to the rules in "Duan Yu" (Trials and Punishments) in *Tang Lv Shu Yi* (*The Comments on Tang Code*), "the imperial instructions, the punishments made according to specific circumstances, the rules which are not included in 'Yong Ge' (permanent injunctions) should not be used as precedents in future," which was actually a restraint of the random application of 'Ren Zhu Quan Duan' (sentences made according to circumstances)."

---

[294]*Tang Da Zhao Ling Ji (Collected Grand Edicts and Decrees of Tang Dynasty)*, Vol. 82.

[295]Niida Noboru (Japan), "Tian Ling" (Decrees on Farmland) in *Tang Ling Shi Yi (An Interpretation of the Orders of Tang Dynasty)*, in the 25th year of Kaiyuan.

[296]"Duan Yu" (Trials and Punishments) in *Tang Lv Shu Yi (The Comments on Tang Code)*.

Nonetheless, in feudal society, the principles like "Yuan Fa Duan Zui" (making judgments in accordance with the law) and "Zui Xing Fa Ding" (a legally prescribed punishment for a specified crime) were seriously impacted in two aspects. First, judicial power was dominated by the emperor. It was stipulated in *Tang Lv* (*Tang Code*) that if a magistrate had rendered a judgment over a case that should "be reported to his supervisors" or "submitted to be approved by his supervisors" without authorization, he should be punished "three levels lighter than that for intentional violation of law or dereliction of duty. Second, the application of "Lei Tui Shi Yong" (the principle of analogy). It was stipulated in "Ming Li Lv" (Statutes and Terms) in *Tang Lv Shu Yi* (*The Comments on Tang Code*) that "as for the crimes which are not regulated in the law, if there are the cases of 'Chu Zui' (to intentionally sentence a guilty person innocent or a felony misdemeanor), the principle of "Ju Zhong Ming Qing" (where there are no legal provisions to be applied for the judgment of certain illegal conducts, if there are provisions which are much severer on similar conducts, then lighter punishments shall be implemented) should be applied; if there are the cases of 'Ru Zui' (to intentionally sentence an innocent person guilty or a misdemeanor felony), the principle of 'Ju Qing Ming Zhong' (where there are no legal provisions to be applied for the judgment of certain illegal conducts, if there are provisions which are much lenient on similar conducts, then severer punishments shall be implemented) should be applied. Moreover, the provision like "doing what ought not to be done though without prohibited by law" was made, which covered many acts which were not legally specified. However, generally speaking, compared with ancient dynasties, it was more strictly required that magistrates should enforce laws accurately in Tang Dynasty. For example, as for the offense of "Gu Chu Ru Ren Zui" (to deliberately increase or reduce the punishment when making sentences), it was stipulated that "if an official has unjustly treated the accused," or "if an official has aggravated the penalty of the accused," or "if an official has mitigated the penalty of the accused, he should be punished by the same penalty which he had enforced upon the accused according to law." However, the punishment should be reduced by three to five levels according to different circumstances.

To ensure the impartiality of the judgment, for the more serious cases punishable by "Tu" (imprisonment) or other major cases, it was required that "they should be jointly heard by the supervisory officials with their joint signatures" to bear joint responsibility. It was stipulated in the article of "Tong Zhi Fan Gong Zuo" (officials bearing the same responsibility for the cases they jointly hear) in "Ming Li Lv" (Statutes and Terms) in *Tang Lv Shu Yi* (*The Comments on Tang Code*) that "the officials of joint signatures are divided into four levels, and they should bear the same responsibility for the cases they jointly hear. The first level includes the directors of the institutions, the second level includes 'Tong Pan Guan' (official in charge of agriculture, water conservancy and litigation under prefecture and subprefecture), the third level includes 'Pan Guan' (assistants of local magistrates), the fourth level includes 'Zhu Dian' (the official in charge mainly of dealing with official documents). Therefore, in trial, "those officials should summon the accused and their relatives to the court and make public the crimes which the accused have committed." The officials should also require the accused to write confession by himself, namely, they should "require the accused to make confession" to avoid their overturning of the confession later on. Besides, the convicted may submit an appeal against the judgment if he did not accept it. If the convicted did not accept the judgment made by a magistrate at the level of "Xian" (county), he could submit the appeal to "Zhou" (subprefecture); if he did not accept the judgment made by a magistrate at the level of "Zhou" (subprefecture), he could submit the appeal to "Shang Shu Sheng" (The Department of Secretary), so his case would "be reviewed carefully by 'Zuo You Cheng Xiang' (the prime minister and deputy prime minister)." If he did not accept the judgment made by "Shang Shu Sheng," he could "submit the petition to 'San Si' (The Three Departments)."[297] But generally speaking, "Yue Su" (overstepping indictment) was not allowed. The judicial organs which accepted the appeal must "review the case more accurately." If the magistrate who reviewed the appeal violated this provision, he would be punished by "Chi" (flogging with light sticks) for fifty strokes; if the case being reviewed involved "Si Xing" (death penalties), he should be punished by "Zhang" (flogging with heavy sticks) for one hundred strokes. Nonetheless, under the influence of the ideology of "Guan Wu Hui Pan" (Once a sentence is made, it cannot be changed), fewer judgments had ever been changed in court. Consequently, many cases were delayed in the procedure and the parties involved in the cases had to bear high procedural risk or costs. Thus, emperor Gaozong once pointed out in one of his decrees that "when an accused is taken into custody, many people who are related to him are also involved in the trouble; when they are kept in custody, they are exposed to coldness in winter and heat in summer, and they suffer from wind and dew all year long so that they are both ill and painful"[298] Emperor Wenzong also criticized in one of his decrees that "even some extremely trivial cases cannot be settled in months."[299]

As to the cases which involved the punishment severer than "Tu" (imprisonment), they must "be tried by the supervising officials jointly." Additionally, the convicted offenses of these cases must be announced to the defendants and his family members, and "the accused shall be brought to the court to make his confession." If the accused "refused to do so," he was allowed to submit an appeal not only to the courts of different levels, but also to the imperial court directly, which was called "Zhi Su" (direct appeal). "Zhi Su" (direct appeal) could be submitted through three channels: first, "Wo Deng Wen Gu" (beat the drum and deliver the complaints, it is one of the important direct complaints in ancient China). Therefore, an official complaint drum was placed outside the imperial court and the complainant who wanted to appeal for the redressing of the wrongly made judgment might beat the drum to have his complaint heard. The word "Deng Wen" first appeared in

---

[297]Niida Noboru (Japan), "Tian Ling" (Decrees on Farmland) in *Tang Ling Shi Yi (An Interpretation of the Orders of Tang Dynasty)*, in the 25th year of Kaiyuan.
[298]"Jin Liu Yu Zhao" (An Imperial Edict about No Delaying of the Settlement of Lawsuits) in *Quan Tang Wen (Anthology of Essays in Tang Dynasty)*, Vol. 1.
[299]*Tang Hui Yao (Collections of Historical Records of Tang Dynasty)*, Vol. 40.

the codes of Han Dynasty. Thus, according to "Dou Song" (Litigation) in *Tang Lv Shu Yi* (*The Comments on Tang Code*), "if the complainant beats 'Deng Wen Gu' (beat the drum and delivers the complaints, it is one of the important direct complaints in ancient China) and makes a false denunciation, he shall be punished by 'Zhang' (flogging with heavy sticks) for eighty strokes; if the official in charge does not accept and hear the case immediately, he shall be punished one level lighter." Second, submitting "Gui Han" (petition letters). In the period of Wuzhou in Tang Dynasty, four bronze boxes named "Gui" were set up in the imperial court, among which, the one named "Complaint Box" contained the complaints put in by the complainant, and an inspector was especially put in charge of handling those complaints. Third, stopping an imperial carriages, namely, to stop the carriages of the emperor when the carriage passed by and then to cry out one's grievances. It was stipulated in "Dou Song" (Litigation) in *Tang Lv Shu Yi* (*The Comments on Tang Code*) that "if one stops the imperial carriage… and makes a false complaints, he shall be punished by 'Zhang' (flogging with heavy sticks) for eighty strokes"; "if the official in charge does not accept and hear the case immediately, he shall be punished one level severer." However, extraordinary appeal procedures were always restricted in each dynasty. In Tang Dynasty, if a complainant stopped the imperial carriage to submit his complaint, he could only do so by kneeling down in front of the guards of honor. If a complainant rushed into the guards of honor, he would be punished by "Zhang" (flogging with heavy sticks) for sixty strokes.

In terms of the execution of the judgment, the punishment of "Chi" (flogging with light sticks) and "Zhang" (flogging with heavy sticks) were enforced at the level of "Xian" (county). If the person punished by "Zhang" (flogging with heavy sticks) was a pregnant woman, the enforcement should be suspended within the period of one hundred days after her childbirth. As to the enforcement of "Tu" (imprisonment), if it was in the capital region, the male prisoners should be sent to "Jiang Zuo Jian" (in charge of imperial architecture), the female prisoners should be sent to "Shao Fu Jian" (in charge of the handicraft production and royal affairs) to do labor work. At the level of "Zhou" (subprefecture) and "Xian" (county), the prisoners should be sent to local government to do labor work. The prisoner who was sentenced to the punishment of "Liu" (exile) should be immediately sent to the penal colony, if the prisoner was detained, for one day of delaying, the official in charge would be punished by "Chi" (flogging with light sticks) for thirty strokes and his punishment would be aggravated by one level for every three days' delaying. In addition, as to the execution of "Si Xing" (death penalties), it should be presented to the emperor for reviewing. In the capital region, "the cases of 'Si Xing' (death penalties) shall be presented to the emperor in five consecutive memorials for reviewing," while in local regions, they "shall be presented to the emperor in three consecutive memorials for reviewing." If "Si Xing" (death penalties) was executed before the reviewing results were publicized, the executor would be punished by "Liu" (exile) for 2000 *li*. As the inappropriateness of the punishment of "Si Xing" (death penalties) might lead to social disturbance, the rulers of Tang Dynasty were very cautious about its execution. If someone was sentenced to thepunishment of "Jiao" (hanging), but he was executed by "Zhan" (beheading) instead, or vice versa, the executor would be punished by "Tu" (imprisonment) for one year; if the death penalty was executed during the period between the beginning of spring and the autumnal equinox when all living things were breeding and growing, the executor should be punished by "Tu" (imprisonment) for one year. However, for the crimes of "Mou Fan" (plotting rebellion or plotting to endanger the country), "Mou Da Ni" (great sedition), "Mou Pan" (treason), "E Ni" (abusing or murdering the elders) or the crime of "Bu Qu" (the private army) or "Nu Bi" (the slave girls and maidservants) killing their masters, it only needed to be presented once for reviewing before the execution was carried out. The reviewing system was not only a demonstration of prudent punishment, but also an important measure to consolidate the power of the centralized authority and to guarantee the uniform practice of judicial power. Generally, "Si Xing" (death penalties) was executed "at a public market, but the officials above 'Wu Pin' (the fifth rank) are allowed to commit suicide at home if they have committed the crime of contumacy or more serious crimes. As to the officials above 'Qi Pin' (the seventh rank), or the members of royal family or the women, if they are not punishable by 'Zhan' (beheading), they shall be punished by 'Jiao' (hanging) in private places."[300]

In Tang Dynasty, from the punishment of "Chi" (flogging with light sticks) to "Si Xing" (death penalties), all the punishments could be redeemed by paying copper money, but the redemption should be paid within certain periods: "the redemption of 'Si Xing' (death penalties) shall be paid within eighty days, 'Liu' (exile), sixty days, 'Tu' (imprisonment), forty days, 'Zhang' (flogging with heavy sticks), forty days and 'Chi'(flogging with light sticks), thirty days. If the redemption is not paid within the limited time periods for no reason, the crimes may not be pardoned even when amnesty is offered."[301]

With regard to civil litigation, the system of "Wu Xian" (limitation of litigation) was established for the protection of agricultural production. According to *Za Ling* (*Miscellaneous Orders*) made in Tang Dynasty, "the litigation concerning land, house, marriage and debt may only be handled between the 1st day in October and the 30th day in March, and any litigation handled beyond this period is against the rule. However, this provision is not applicable to the cases if case files have already been submitted."[302] With regard to civil trial (including minor criminal cases), mediation was always conducted before the trial. "Xiang Lao" (the elders in townships), "Li Zheng" (head of "Li": the basic resident organization in ancient China), "Cun Zheng" (chief official in village) and "Fang Zheng" (chief official of neighborhood) were responsible for mediating the civil litigation in their neighborhoods in order that they could be solved before being brought to trial. The magistrates at the level of "Xian" (county), after accepting the cases, may also have the cases settled by mediation.

---

[300]Niida Noboru (Japan), "Tian Ling" (Decrees on Farmland) in *Tang Ling Shi Yi* (*An Interpretation of the Orders of Tang Dynasty*), in the 7th year of Kaiyuan.

[301]Niida Noboru (Japan), "Tian Ling" (Decrees on Farmland) in *Tang Ling Shi Yi* (*An Interpretation of the Orders of Tang Dynasty*), in the 25th year of Kaiyuan.

[302]*Song Xing Tong* (*The Penal Code of Song Dynasty*), Vol. 13.

In civil cases, the one who caused financial losses by misconducts only bore civil liability. For example, according to the comments on the provision of "damaging the public or private goods by livestock" in "Jiu Ku" (Statutes on Stables) in *Tang Lv Shu Yi* (*The Comments on Tang Code*), "if a person kills or injures livestock by negligence, he shall not be prosecuted, but he must pay for the damage caused." It was stipulated in "Za Lv" (Miscellaneous Laws) in *Tang Lv Shu Yi* (*The Comments on Tang Code*) that "if one causes damage by fire or water intentionally, he shall pay for the damage caused, however if the damage is caused by negligence, it shall not be compensated." If one destroyed "an object that is built with effort by negligence," "he shall be ordered to rebuild the object but shall not be prosecuted"; "if one abandons, destroys, loses or destroys public or private goods by negligence, he shall be ordered to compensate." The above-mentioned provisions showed that independent civil liabilities had already existed in Tang Dynasty and that the provisions were a reflection of the continuous improvement of the civil litigation system.

As for the civil judgment, besides "Lv" (criminal law), "Ling" (decree), "Ge" (injunctions), and "Shi" (standard), judgments may also be made according to the generally accepted social customs, habits, village rules and regulations, but the statutory laws of the state should not be violated. Besides, private contract also had the validity of proof. It was stipulated in *Za Ling* (*Miscellaneous Orders*) that "the magistrate shall not accept and hear the cases about the contracts involving the mortgage of the public or private property signed among people.... However, if interests are collected beyond legal limits, or a creditor seizes property of his debtor without authorization, the case shall be accepted and heard by the magistrates." The losing party would be ordered to carry out the civil verdict already taken effect.

Generally speaking, the main characteristics of moral education and non-litigation run through the judicial system of Tang Dynasty. In the civil litigation and trials, "De" (virtue) and "Li" (rites) were taken as the fundamental principles and the ruling with the combination of "Fa" (law) and "Qing" (human relationships) was stressed. Taken the civil case in Turpan case files as an example, the following judgment is made:

> A eunuch of the royal court married a woman named Mao. After three years of marriage, Mao gave birth to a boy. After another five years, an amnesty was declared by the emperor. Song Yu, one of their neighbors, came to declare that he committed adultery with Mao and the boy was his son. However, Mao insisted that she did not commit adultery with Song Yu. The boy looked much like the eunuch, so from the circumstances it could be presumed that Song Yu committed adultery with Mao. To whom should the boy belong? Mao was the wife of a eunuch. As a normal young woman, it was very common for her to feel sentiments of love, and at her age, how could she keep herself from having resentments? When she heard a melody at night, she might fall in love with Xiangru; when she looked out of the wall during the day, she might keep an eye on Song Yu. So there was no doubt that she could have had such feelings. Moreover, (Song) Yu lived to the west of her house, the roof of their houses were linked together, so it was normal that they had contacts with each other. With the lapse of time, it was also normal that they had more contacts. In the house of the eunuch, Mao was not forbidden to have contacts with the others ever since. So Song Yu was determined to please Mao and Mao was also determined to devote herself to Song Yu. They wanted to stay together with each other, so nobody could have stopped them.

But they denied to have committed adultery because they were afraid of other people's gossip. Mao was afraid of getting bad reputation, thus the government did not reveal the facts, too. This was the reason why they insisted that they had not committed adultery. However, it was very clear that they had sexual relations with each other. Since the eunuch was a eunuch, he was unable to have sex, it was also crystal clear that the boy that his wife gave birth to was not his son. Although the boy looked much like him, the same conclusion could be made. Today, if the resemblance between people is used as a criterion to judge whether a boy is the son of a man or not, it would be possible to see that there would be a father at every home and every child could be his son. Many men may seek to bring lawsuits in order to get a son, so many disputes may arise. It was a fact that Song Yu had confessed that he had committed adultery, it could be deduced without doubt that Mao had also committed adultery. The offense of adultery may be pardoned and the boy should be returned to his biological father. Thus, the son should be returned to Song Yu, but Mao should go back to the eunuch. And all the contacts between Mao's family and Song Yu's family should be cut off.[303]

In Tang Dynasty, a central prison was set up in "Da Li Si" (The Bureau of Judicial Review) and was managed by "Yu Cheng" (prison director) and "Yu Li" (prison wards). In both the capital region and "Zhou" (subprefecture) and "Xian" (county), local prisons were also set up and were managed by "Dian Yu" (wardens).

In Tang Dynasty, the prisons were well-administered. When the criminals were imprisoned, "they were arranged in different cells according to their social ranks and gender," and the instruments of torture such as cangue, tongs, handcuffs or shackles were also used according to the concrete circumstances of the cases. According to *Tang Lv* (*Tang Code*), the prison directors or wards who were in charge of prison would be punished by "Chi" (flogging with light sticks) or "Zhang" (flogging with heavy sticks) if the instruments of torture, such as cangue, handcuffs or shackles which should be used were actually not used, or were taken off, or were changed without authorization. To prevent prisoners from exchanging information with each other or escaping from prisons, paper, writing brushes, alcohol and sticks were forbidden to be taken into prisons. If a ward gave a rope, saw or other instrument to a prisoner or if the latter used it to commit suicide or to escape from the prison, he would be punished by "Zhang" (flogging with heavy sticks) for one hundred strokes; if the prisoner used it to escape from the prison or injure himself or somebody else, he would be punished by "Tu" (imprisonment) for one year; if the prisoner used it to commit suicide or commit murder, he would be punished by "Tu" (imprisonment) for two years; if he failed to provide prisoners with clothes, food or medicine or failed to inform a prisoner's family members of visiting the prisoner or failed to take off the cangue, handcuffs or shackles from the prisoner, he should be punished by "Zhang" (flogging with heavy sticks) for sixty strokes; if a prisoner died because cangue, the handcuffs or shackles were failed to be removed, those in charge should be punished by "Tu" (imprisonment) for one year; if he reduced the food supply of a

---

[303]Line 101 to 114 in "Wen Ming Pan Ji Can Juan" (The Remnant Volumes of the Civilized Judgment), quoted from Liu Junwen, *Dun Huang Tu Lufan Tang Dai Fa Zhi Wen Shu Kao Shi* (*Explanation to the Legal Documents of Tang Dynasty Unearthed from Dunhuang and Turpa*), Zhonghua Book Company, 1989, pp. 443-444.

prisoner, he should be punished by "Zhang" (flogging with heavy sticks) for fifty strokes; if a prisoner died because he had deliberately reduced the food supply, he would be punished by "Jiao" (hanging).

The prisoner interrogation system which was applied in Han Dynasty was also followed in Tang Dynasty. Sometimes, the emperor even "interrogated the prisoners in person." Moreover, the government officials were also ordered to interrogate the prisoners themselves. Therefore, the officials such as "Xun Cha Shi" (inspector), "An Cha Shi" (head of judicial commission), "Lian Cha Shi" (special envoy from "Yu Shi Tai": The Censorate), and "Cai Fang Shi" (supervisor from 'Dao': the administration district below the province) often conducted temporary interrogation according to imperial order. It was stipulated that "a prisoner can submit a petition if the prison provision about cangue, lock, bed, medicine or food were violated."[304] In January every year, inspectors would be sent by "Xing Bu" (The Department of Punishment) to interrogate the prisoners in local prisons. Meanwhile, judicial supervision was conducted by "Yu Shi Tai" (The Censorate) through prisoner interrogation, and "Du Du" (military viceroys and procurators) and "Ci Shi (a supervisor assigned by the central government to a local area) were also sent to local places to conduct prisoner interrogation at county level.

However, as the saying goes, "the law cannot be established by itself, if there are gifted men, the law will be effectively carried out; if there are not such men, the law will be openly violated." In the early period of Tang Dynasty, the judicial officials were very carefully selected, therefore, there appeared many upright and honest magistrates who were very strict in law enforcement, such as Dai Zhou, Zhang Wenguan, Xu Yougong, and Yuan Renjing. However, during the reign of Empress Wu Zetian, brutal officials such as Suo Yuanli, Zhou Xing, and Lai Junchen were highly appreciated. Each time before an order of amnesty was issued, "Lai Juncheng always ordered prison wards to kill almost all prisoners who had committed serious crimes," so the prison law was thus turned into mere formality. Consequently, even Emperor Zhongzong admitted that "the cries of complaints and grievances could be heard everywhere."[305] Bai Juyi, a famous poet, also lamented that "even though the laws of Zhenguan are retained, there are not any officials who are as upright as those in Zhanguan period, wouldn't it be difficult to show mercy and justice?"[306]

---

[304]Niida Noboru (Japan), "Tian Ling" (Decrees on Farmland) in *Tang Ling Shi Yi (An Interpretation of the Orders of Tang Dynasty)*, in the 7th year of Kaiyuan.

[305]*Ku Li Zhuan (The Biographies of Brutal Officials)* (Book 1).

[306]Bai Juyi (Tang Dynasty), "Chang Qing Ji" (Collection of Works in the Year of Changqing) in *Si Bu Cong Kan (Series of Four Essential Classics)* (edition of Song Dynasty in large Chinese characters, reprinted in Japan).

7.2.8 The Characteristics of **Tang Lv** *(***Tang Code***) and Its World Position*

Tang Lv (*Tang Code*) was a complete legal system consisted of various legal forms such as "Lv" (criminal law), "Ling" (decree), "Ge" (injunctions), "Shi" (standard), "Dian" (code), "Chi" (instruction), and "Li" (precedent) which were centered on "Lv" (criminal law). Here is an analysis of the characteristics of *Tang Lv* (*Tang Code*) and its world position the based on *Tang Lv Shu Yi* (*The Comments on Tang Code*):

First, "judgments are made according to the principles of 'Li' (rites)." Through the introduction of "Li" (rites) into "Fa" (law) in the Western and Eastern Han dynasties and the Confucianization of law in the Wei and Jin dynasties, the combination of "Li" (rites) and "Fa" (law) had come to a new stage in Tang Dynasty. In the early period of Tang Dynasty, to create a mainstream ideology, the definitive edition of the five Confucian classics and the newly made "Wu Li" (five rites) were established and the order of "San Jiao" (the three doctrines of Confucianism, Buddhism, Taoism) was determined by the rulers, which had further promoted the integration of "Li" (rites) with "Fa" (law). However, the so-called integration did not mean that "Li" (rites) was simply equal to "Fa" (law), but that "Li" (rites) and "Fa" (law) were interconnected, interpenetrated and inseparable, just as was recorded in *Shu Yi* (*Tang Lv Shu Yi*) that "'De' (virtue) and 'Li' (rites) are 'Ben' (the essence), while 'Xing Fa' (criminal punishment) is 'Yong' (application) in the administration, and they are interdependent and complementary with each other just like morning and evening and spring and autumn." Montesquieu, a French jurist, said insightfully when he commented on Chinese legal spirit: "The general national spirit is formed by 'Li' (rites)..... So the life of Chinese people is absolutely guided by 'Li' (rites)."[307] Thus, "Li" (rites) is fully expressed in the legislation. The details are as follows:

7.2.8.1 Lawmaking Guided by "Gang Chang" (The Chinese Ethical Tradition)

Emperor Taizong once clearly stated that "what is the prohibited by 'Li' (rites) is all included in penal code." Wei Zheng also pointed out that "'Li' (rites) is 'Gang Ji' (social order and law)..... while penalties are clarified to be the complementary means."[308] As "San Gang" (three cardinal guides) promoted by the Confucianists was the core element of "Li" (rites), the principal line of ideology in *Tang Lv* (*Tang Code*) was to maintain "San Gang" (three cardinal guides). The reason for "Shi E" (The Ten Abominations) to be regarded as the felony that "should never be pardoned

---

[307]Montesquieu (France), *The Spirit of the Laws* (Book One), translated by Zhang Yan, The Commercial Press, 2005, pp. 377-378.
[308]"Xing Fa Zhi" (The Record of the Criminal Law) in *Sui Shu* (*The History of Sui Dynasty*).

even in general amnesty" was that they had violated the doctrines of "Li" (rites), by which the principle of ruler guiding subjects, father guiding son and husband guiding wife was advocated.

In *Tang Lv* (*Tang Code*) which was guided by the doctrine of "Gang Chang" (the Chinese ethical tradition), the moral principles of patriarchal ethics were placed above the law, and were at the same time included into the law. Hence, *Tang Lv* (*Tang Code*) was a law code with a strong color of "Li Jiao" (feudal ethical code). In addition, "Ren Zheng" (benevolent administration) and "De Zhi" (the ruling of virtue), as the embodiment of "Li" (rites), were not only the governing strategy in the early period of Tang Dynasty, but also an important basis of legislation in the period of Zhenguan. Consequently, a number of legal provisions which were characterized by "Shen Xing" (prudent punishment) and "Xu Xing" (penalty reduction) were enacted. If it is the Confucianists who have integrated "Li" (rites) and "Gang Chang" (the Chinese ethical tradition) with the system of Confucianism, which has made it lasting for thousands of years, then it is the integration of "Gang Chang" (the Chinese ethical tradition) and "Li Jiao" (feudal ethical code) into the legal system that has made the Chinese legal system unique among the various legal systems of the world.

7.2.8.2 The Legalization of the Basic Norms of "Li" (Rites)

The five hundred and two articles in *Tang Lv* (*Tang Code*) originated either directly or indirectly from "Li" (rites). Especially, the system of "Ba Yi" (The Eight Deliberations) which was modeled on "Ba Bi" (the eight conditions for mitigating punishments) in *Zhou Li* (*The Rites of Zhou Dynasty*) was finalized and included in *Tang Lv* (*Tang Code*) after it was confirmed in the Southern and Northern dynasties, and became the cornerstone of *Tang Lv* (*Tang Code*) which was a law with typical feudal hierarchal privilege.

In addition, the crime of the violation of patriarchal ethics which was centered by the main contents of "Bu Xiao" (being unfilial) was completely included in the provisions of *Tang Lv* (*Tang Code*). Moreover, it was stipulated in "Za Lv" (Miscellaneous Laws) in *Tang Lv Shu Yi* (*The Comments on Tang Code*) that "if one has done what is forbidden to do, he shall be punished by 'Chi' (flogging with light sticks) for forty strokes; if the circumstance is serious, he shall be punished by 'Zhang' (flogging with heavy sticks) for eighty strokes." It was specifically pointed out in the comments that "even though it is not provided in statues and laws, no one should do what is forbidden." According to Guan Zi, "'Li' (rites) means 'being reasonable'."[309] Therefore, "the acts which are forbidden by reason" actually were also "the acts which are forbidden by 'Li' (rites)." Clearly, according to this principle, all acts that were against "Li" (rites) were included in the orbit of legal punishment. In other words, the basic norms of "Li Jiao" (feudal ethical code) were

---

[309] "Xin Shu" (Of Principles of Mind) in *Guan Zi* (*The Book of Master Guan*).

endowed with legal effect, which had become a great impassable defensive line. Consequently, the traditional perception that what was forbidden by law was also prohibited by "Li" (rites) and that what "Li" (rites) allowed was also acceptable by law was further implemented.

The introduction of ethical codes into law and the combination of "Li" (rites) and "Fa" (law) were not only reflected in legal provisions, but also in *Shu Yi* (*Tang Lv Shu Yi*) in which the legal provisions were interpreted. In *Shu Yi* (*Tang Lv Shu Yi*), the interpretation of legal provisions which was made based on "Li" (rites) could be found everywhere. Thus, through *Lv Shu* (*The Comments on Law*), the ethical contents of legal provisions were elaborated, the ethical value of legal provisions was proved, the national and social circumstances upon which *Tang Lv* (*Tang Code*) was based and the rich Chinese cultural deposits was fully expressed.

As the basic norms of "Li" (rites) were reflected by the forcible enforcement of law which was backed up by penal punishment, the principles of "Gang Chang" (the Chinese ethical tradition) were therefore reinforced, and patriarchal familism, male domination, obligation orientation, and status system had constituted the unshakable pillars of society. Under the double influence of both "Li" (rites) and "Fa" (law), the rights and values of individuals were ignored.

7.2.8.3 The Leniency and Severity of Punishment Determined by the Principle of "Li" (Rites) in Judicial Practice

As a great unified and powerful feudal state with a highly centralized government, a uniform application of law in judicial practice in Tang Dynasty was required to avoid injustice in judicial process which might be caused by the different understanding of the legal provisions by different local judicial officials, so *Lv Shu* (*The Comments on Law*) was written. With the help of *Lv Shu* (*The Comments on Law*), the local magistrates' different understanding of the legal provisions was unified and their judicial practice was guided. In a certain sense, *Tang Lv* (*Tang Code*) was a great code of "Li Jiao" (feudal ethical code), and the strict application of *Tang Lv* (*Tang Code*) itself had reflected the requirements that punishments must be enforced by following the principles of "Li" (rites).

The crimes and punishments stipulated in *Tang Lv* (*Tang Code*) reflected the classification of the hierarchical ranks of "Liang" (the common people) and "Jian" (people of a lower social status than common people) and the superior and inferior, showed the relationship of rights and obligations standardized by the principles of "Li" (rites) which were suitable to their social status, maintained the social structure in which the social status of the superior and inferior, the noble and the humble were clearly differentiated and emphasized. Taking the crime of "Dou Ou" (fighting) for example, generally speaking, "if a person engages in 'Dou Ou' (fighting) and assaults another person, he shall be punished by 'Chi' (flogging with light sticks) for forty strokes." However, "if the person assaults his brother or sister of 'Si Ma' (the person wearing the mourning apparel of soft sackcloth in the fifth mourning degree), he shall be punished by 'Zhang'(flogging with heavy sticks) for one hundred strokes; if he assaults his relative of 'Xiao Gong' (the person wearing the mourning apparel of soft sackcloth in the fourth mourning degree) or 'Da Gong' (the person wearing the mourning apparel of soft sackcloth in the third mourning degree), his penalty shall be aggravated by one level respectively; if the person assaults the superior or the elder relatives in his family, his penalty shall be aggravated by another level"; "if a person assaults his elder brother or sister, he shall be punished by 'Tu' (imprisonment) for two and a half years; if he assaults his uncles, parents, aunts, maternal grandparents, his penalty shall be aggravated by one level respectively; if he assaults his paternal grandparents and parents, he shall be punished by 'Zhan' (beheading)."[310] To sum up, if "Dou Ou" (fighting) occurred between "Liang" (the common people) and "Jian" (people of a lower social status than common people) and the superior and inferior, their punishments should be either aggravated or mitigated according to their social status, which was not only required by the principles of "Li" (rites), but also was stipulated in the law as well.

Although it was required in *Tang Lv* (*Tang Code*) that a judicial official should follow "Lv" (criminal law), "Ling" (decree), "Ge" (injunction), and "Shi" (standard) when hearing cases, the judicial officials were allowed to enforce the law according to both specific circumstances and "Li" (rites). Emperor Taizong once stated that:

> Recently the judicial officials have adjudicated the cases by applying legal provisions. Although some cases belong to 'Ke Jin' (worthy of compassion), the judicial officials in charge just make sentences by strictly observing the law for fear that the accused should be convicted wrongfully. So from today forward, 'Men Xia Sheng' (the organization in charge of examining the imperial edicts in ancient China) should conduct an investigation of the crimes punishable by death penalty to see whether any of them belong to 'Ke Jin' (worthy of compassion); if there are, the cases should be recorded and reported to me.[311]

In the judicial practice of Tang Dynasty, there were many instances that the cases were judged according to the principles of "Li" (rites) and "Fa" (law). For example, during the reign of Chang Qing, a woman who had whipped her daughter-in-law to death was sentenced to death penalty by "Jing Bei Fu" (Jing Bei Prefecture). However, the judgment was changed by Liu Gongzhuo, who was then "Xing Bu Shang Shu" (the minister of the department of punishment) in the light of "Li" (rites). It was recorded in *Ce Fu Yuan Gui* (*The Record of the Great Events*) that "When Liu Gongzhuo was 'Xing Bu Shang Shu' (the minister of the department of punishment), a woman in Jingzhao district had whipped her daughter-in-law to death for a trivial thing. After the case was presented to 'Jing Bei Fu' (Jing Bei Prefecture), the woman was sentenced to death penalty by an official named Dou. Then Gongzhuo said, 'this is a case where the senior has whipped the junior, so it is not the case of 'Dou Ou' (fighting). Besides, the woman's son is still alive, so it is

---

[310] "Dou Song" (Litigation) in *Tang Lv Shu Yi* (*The Comments on Tang Code*).
[311] Quoted from *A Collection of Political and Economic Materials in Quan Tang Wen* (*Anthology of Essays in Tang Dynasty*), edited by Li Jiping, San Qin Publishing House, 1992, p. 110.

immoral to kill his mother just because of his daughter-in-law's death'. So the decision was changed according to Liu Gongzhou's opinion."[312]

It can be seen that among all of the recorded judicial cases of Tang Dynasty, almost all punishments for the crimes against "Li" (rites) were aggravated.

Because it is a judicial principle which is protected by the state to enforce punishment in accordance with the principles of "Li," it has reflected the publicly-accepted value of measurement that morality overtops law, so the judicial officials would rather break the law than violate the principle of "Li" (rites). Indeed, if a judicial official had broken the law, he might lose his official title, but if he had violated "Li" (rites), he might be considered to be immoral. Indeed, it meant observing "Li" (rites) to observe "Fa" (law), however, at any rate, it was impossible to cover all the norms of "Li" (rites) by the five hundred and two articles included in *Tang Lv* (*Tang Code*), and it was also impossible to reflect the whole spirit of "Li" (rites) absolutely. Therefore, the judicial officials were required to give their subjective initiative into full play. Because it was the understanding of Confucian classics that was considered the most important criterion for the selection of officials through "Ke Ju" (the imperial examination), those selected judicial officials were familiar with both law and the norms of "Li" (rites) and it was not difficult for them to settle the cases according to "Li" (rites). In each dynasty, it was regarded as the source of turmoil to abuse the punishment and it was regarded as the most important method of ruling the country to observe "Li" (rites), so it was advocated by the people of the later generations to make judgments according to the principle of "Li" (rites).

Second, the structure of the integration of codes and comments and the new achievements of "Lv Xue" (the study of statutory laws). In the reign of Emperor Gaozong, *Yong Hui Lv* (*Yong Hui Code*) was enacted in the 2nd year of Yonghui (651 A.D.) and *Tang Lv Shu Yi* (*The Comments on Tang Code*) which was annexed to the legal provisions with the same legal effect was enacted in the 4th year (653 A.D.). Thus, a new form of legislative structure was created through the compilation of legal provisions and comments. *Tang Lv Shu Yi* (*The Comments on Tang Code*) also demonstrated the new achievements of "Lv Xue" (the study of statutory laws) in Tang Dynasty. As the accurate interpretation of the meaning of the codes and legal terms and the detailed analysis of the historical origins of laws and legal principles were regarded as its basic contents, and the enforcement and practice of the law were regarded as its goal, it had a very high theoretical and practical value.

In Tang Dynasty, the famous scholars of "Lv Xue" (the study of statutory laws), namely, Fang Xuanling, Zhangsun Wuji, Li Ji, Song Jing, Yu Zhining, etc, not only had a good knowledge of both Confucian classics and law, they were also very important officials who assisted the emperor in the imperial court and participated in a series of legislative activities. In *Tang Lv Shu Yi* (*The Comments on Tang Code*), which was completed by those scholars, the advantages and disadvantages and the gains and losses of the laws of the previous dynasties and the achievements in "Lv

---

[312]"Xing Fa Bu" (The Section of Penal Law) in *Ce Fu Yuan Gui* (*The Record of the Great Events*), Vol. 616.

Xue" (the study of statutory laws) were all summarized by the method of historical comparison. Moreover, it had also further promoted the integration of "Li" (rites) and "Fa" (law) by carrying out the orthodox feudal legal and moral consciousness through interpreting the law according to the principle of "Li" (rites) under the guidance of the Confucian ideology of "Gang Chang" (the Chinese ethical tradition) and "Li Zhi" (the system of "Li"). The social status and authority of these scholars had also made the interpretation of *Tang Lv Shu Yi* (*The Comments on Tang Code*) more authoritative.

The provisions of *Lv Shu* (*The Comments on Law*) were based on extensive materials, as was described in the records that "the materials which it includes are extensive, ranging from the imperial decrees issued in the previous dynasties and the posthumous laws made by the people like Jia Chong, by which the sources and the origins of the laws were thoroughly investigated and explored. Besides, its contents are comprehensive and its style of compilation is simple."[313] As to the interpretation of legal provision in *Lv Shu* (*The Comments on Law*), it not only explained the meaning of the legal provision, but also analyzed the connotation, given the definitions of the terms, introduced the concepts, investigated the historical origins of the principles and systems, put forward the questions and given answers, and discussed the doubtful points of the legal provisions through differentiation and analysis. The methods it used not only reflected the latest development of criminal jurisprudence and litigation, but also demonstrated the great achievements in the areas of jurisprudence, historical jurisprudence, and glossators. Because comments had the same legal effect as legal provisions, it had become a very important basis in practice for the judicial officials to convict the accused and enforce punishment. Therefore, it had really played the role of "measuring the weights by rectifying the yard stick and determining the circumference by employing the gauge and carpenter's square."[314]

In *Lv Shu* (*The Comments on Law*), the word meaning was explained. For example, for the meaning of the word "Chi" (flogging with light sticks), it was explained that "'Chi' means beating and it is used for humiliation. If people have committed minor crimes, they shall be punished, so beating is used to have them humiliated."

In addition, some concepts were also explained. For example, as for the concept of "Hua Wai Ren" (foreigners), it was explained that "'Hua Wai Ren' refers to the people coming from 'Fan Yi Zhi Guo' (vassal states and foreign countries), who have their own kings and different customs and laws." This explanation had a far-reaching influence.

In *Lv Shu* (*The Comments on Law*), explanations were made to the historical resources of some provisions. For example, as for "Wei Jin Lv" (Statutes on Palace Guards), it was explained that "*Wei Jin Lv* (*Statutes on Palace Guards*) was once not

---

[313]"Ming Li" (The Categories of Penalties and General Principles) in *Tang Lv Shu Yi* (*The Comments on Tang Code*).

[314]"Ming Li" (The Categories of Penalties and General Principles) in *Tang Lv Shu Yi* (*The Comments on Tang Code*).

included in the laws of Qin, Han and the later period of Wei dynasties, so it was drafted by the people like Jia Chong, who was 'Zai Xiang' (the prime minister) in Jin Dynasty by adding and deleting some provisions according to the laws of Han and Wei dynasties, and was entitled *Wei Gong Lv*. It was then applied from Song Dynasty until the latter Zhou Dynasty without any changes. When it came to Northern Qi Dynasty, the provisions of strategic passes were added and then the law was changed into 'Jin Wei Lv'. During the reign of Kaihuang, it was changed into *Wei Jin Lv (Statutes on Palace Guards)*."

In *Lv Shu (The Comments on Law)*, explanations were also made by quoting Confucian classics. For example, the punishment of "Liu" (exile) is explained as follows:

> It is recorded in classic books that 'Liu' is one of the penalties for those who have committed the crimes punishable by 'Wu Xing' (Five Penalties). Since it is unbearable to impose death penalty on the offenders, they were pardoned by being sent to a place far away. So it is also recorded that 'there are different places for the exile, and the five places are located in three different directions'. The offenders who have committed felonies shall be exiled to 'Si Yi' (the remote places) or to places overseas; the offenders who committed less serious offenses shall be exiled to places out of 'Jiu Zhou' (the nine states); the offenders who committed minor offenses shall be exiled to places out of China, which probably started from the periods of Tang Yao and Shun Yu.

Besides, explanations were also made to the application of the provisions. For example, "as for the crimes which are not regulated in the law, if the punishments should be mitigated, the principle of 'Ju Zhong Ming Qing' (where there are no legal provisions to be applied for the judgment of certain illegal conducts, if there are provisions which are much severer on similar conducts, then lighter punishments shall be implemented) should be applied. In *Lv Shu (The Comments on Law)*, it was explained that: "if there are no specific legal provisions for particular 'cases of exoneration' in the law, *Zei Dao Lv (Statutes on Stealing and Robbery)* should be used as a reference for inflicting punishments: 'if one person enters other person's house at night for no reason, or if he is killed by the master on the spot, the master shall not be punished'; if the person who enters the house illegally is injured by the master, the master shall not be punished either."

In summary, "Lv Xue" (the study of statutory laws) in Tang Dynasty represented by *Lv Shu (The Comments on Law)* was an official study of statutory law, and its purpose, as was required by the unified centralization of authority of the feudal empire, was to conduct a unified application of law. The basic characteristic of the traditional "Lv Xue" (the study of statutory laws) was "Zhong Xing Qing Min" (stressing the criminal law and neglecting the civil law), which had reflected the strong influence of Confusion classics. The experiences summarized by "Lv Xue" (the study of statutory laws) in legal practice enriched the legislators' legal consciousness, offered very important guidance to state legislation, improved the accuracy of law application by these judicial officials, and provided a model for people to interpret the legal provisions.

The Chinese traditional "Lv Xue" (the study of statutory laws) was a special jurisprudence developed in a self-enclosed circumstance, so it was also tightly controlled by the state. Because it was not influenced by the jurisprudence of the foreign countries, during its process of evolution, there was only longitudinal inheritance but no lateral absorbing or comparison. Such independent feature was also its special characteristic and its isolating nature. As scholars of "Lv Xue" (the study of statutory laws), whether bureaucrats or so-called private schools, the security of their social status and the roles which they could play were all determined by the trust and support of the emperor, so there were few chances for them to fully make use of their advantages. That was why "Lv Xue" (the study of statutory laws) could only exist in the form of glossators under the system of feudal autocracy.

Third, the relative completeness of *Tang Lv (Tang Code)*. *Tang Lv (Tang Code)* was composed of provisions written in the forms of "Lv" (criminal law), "Ling" (decree), "Ge" (injunctions), and "Shi" (standard), "Dian" (code), "Chi" (instruction), and "Li" (precedent), by which a relatively completed legal system was formed. In *Tang Lv (Tang Code)*, the legal norms for adjusting the economic, political, military, judicial, social, and family relationships were elaborately made to meet the interests of the ruling class and the central government based on the summarization of the experiences of the legal construction in Qin and Han dynasties. As the objects which they aimed to adjust were different, there were different focal points for the different forms of *Tang Lv (Tang Code)*, but they coordinated with each other by integrating the diversity with uniformity, so a complete and stable legal system was formed. In this system, the criminal law was used as the main body, the civil was combined with criminal law, the administrative was integrated with judiciary law, morality was mixed with law, the substantial law was mingled with procedural law, based on which the structure of the feudal codes was successfully constructed. Indeed, the structure fitted in with the economic basis dominated by natural economy, reflected the special Chinese national conditions which was completely controlled by the patriarchal moral principles, and showed the legal cultural accumulation of feudal autocracy. Therefore, it was not accidental that it was finalized and inherited by the later generations.

Moreover, the national system of the autocratic centralization of authority was also confirmed and strengthened in *Tang Lv (Tang Code)*. First, imperial power was greatly reinforced and it was acknowledged that the emperor had the overall authority in administration, military, and judiciary, so any acts against the emperor's will or challenging the emperor's sacred authority or infringing upon the emperor's safety were considered to be felonies "against heavenly principles and human ethics," so the violators would be severely punished. It would also be punished to mention the emperor's name unintentionally: "If the officials have accidentally broken the taboo and mention the imperial ancestors' names when making reports or presenting memorials to the emperor, they shall be punished by 'Zhang' (flogging with heavy sticks) for eighty strokes; if they have broken the taboo by a slip of the tongue when discussing affairs with the emperor in the imperial court or by mistake when writing other official documents, they shall be punished by 'Zhang' (flogging with heavy sticks) for fifty strokes; if anyone has deliberately referred to the names

7.2 The Legal System of Tang Dynasty Symbolizing the Establishment...

of the imperial ancestors, he shall be punished by 'Tu' (imprisonment) for three years."[315]

Furthermore, in *Tang Lv* (*Tang Code*), the power distribution in the central and local government was adjusted according to law. Thus, for a long time, the centralized authority of the royal power was successfully maintained. Lastly, in *Tang Lv* (*Tang Code*), the state monopoly of farmland and water sources, the intervention in industry and commerce, and major construction works were all confirmed by written law, which had successfully strengthened the autocratic ruling in the economic area.

In the judicial area, whether in legal process, judicial procedure, or in the system of evidence, interrogation, avoidance, agency, mediation, review, appeal or execution, a complete and perfect degree which could be reached in the seventh century A.D. had been achieved.

Therefore, the perfectness which *Tang Lv* (*Tang Code*) had achieved was inseparable from the historical condition of Tang Dynasty under which the feudal society had entered a period of great prosperity. Moreover, the perfectness was also the result of the accumulation of the rich experience of the rulers on how to consolidate the system of the autocratic centralization of authority and how to enforce law after the long and repeated separation of the state. However, the completeness of *Tang Lv* (*Tang Code*) was only relative as far as its position in the development of feudal legal system was concerned. As for its nature, such completeness was nothing more than a elaborate and strict regulation to maintain the feudal ruling order.

Fourth, in *Tang Lv* (*Tang Code*) a certain scientificity was reflected. As an important part of the legal system of Tang Dynasty, "Lv" (criminal law), "Ling" (decree), "Ge" (injunctions), and "Shi" (standard) were clearly differentiated to perform different functions, as was stated in *Tang Liu Dian* (*The Six Statutes of Tang Dynasty*) that "'Lv' is for executing penalties for punishment; 'Ling' is for establishing standards and regulations; 'Ge' is for preventing violations and wickedness, and 'Shi' is for establishing routines and disciplines." Those four forms were not only interconnected but also unified as a whole. It was stipulated that "these three forms ('Ling', 'Ge' and 'Shi') must be used in administration, so any illegal acts or any evildoing of the people should be punished according to law."[316]

As for its text structure, *Tang Lv* (*Tang Code*) consisted of chapters, volumes and articles with totally five hundred and two legal provisions. It was compiled by listing the general articles first and the detailed divisions next. Moreover, the provisions were categorized according to their contents, so it was not only logical in legal theories, but also easier for the judicial officials to make use of the provisions.

Moreover, according to *ting Lv* (*Tang Code*), "if the punishment for a case is not accurately prescribed in the law, the principle of 'Qing Zhong Xiang Ju' (the punishment can be executed by analogy: for crimes that should be dealt with leniently, the law enumerates a heavy penalty to justify their crimes; for crimes

---

[315]"Zhi Zhi" (The State Office System) in *Tang Lv Shu Yi* (*The Comments on Tang Code*).
[316]"Xing Fa Zhi" (The Record of the Criminal Law) in *Xin Tang Shu* (*The New Book of Tang Dynasty*),

that should be dealt with severely, the law enumerates a light penalty to justify their crimes) could be used"; but at the same time, it was stipulated that "not all cases should be heard by following 'Lv' (criminal law), 'Ling' (decree), 'Ge' (injunctions), and 'Shi' (standard)." When discussing whether the principles mentioned above are contradictory to each other, Dong Kang pointed out that:

> The real intention of this provision in *Tang Lv* (*Tang Code*) is to decide whether the misconduct is punishable or whether it should be used as the criterion for punishment. Its meaning is similar to the supplementary provisions of 'Ci Song Bi'(The Precedents Compiled according to Judicial Experiences) and 'Jue Shi Bi' (the precedents in lawsuit settlements) in "Chen Chong Zhuan" (The Biography of Chen Chong) in *Latter Han Shu* (*The Book of Later Han Dynasty*), so it belongs to the measurement of the punishment... In *Ming Lv* (*Ming Code*), they are changed into mitigation or aggravation of penalties according to 'Bi Fu' (legal analogy), which has covered a larger scope, so the original intention of *Tang Lv* (*Tang Code*) is lost. That is why it has become an obstacle to the legal development of our country.[317]

By comparison, Dong Kang had discovered the subtle difference of this problem in *Tang Lv* (*Tang Code*), which had further shown the scientificity of *Tang Lv* (*Tang Code*).

From the above brief analysis of the characteristics of *Tang Lv* (*Tang Code*), it can be seen that it is not accidental that *Tang Lv* (*Tang Code*) has been praised by the later dynasties as an excellent example of the legal code.

The world position of *Tang Lv* (*Tang Code*) and its influence on the neighboring countries:

The law in Tang Dynasty, represented by *Tang Lv Shu Yi* (*The Comments on Tang Code*), is the earliest and the most completed feudal legal code that has been preserved so far. *Tang Lv* (*Tang Code*) was made in Tang Dynasty when feudal economy, politics and culture were developing rapidly by summarizing the experience of legal construction in the previous dynasties, so "it was finally completed with new provisions added and the unnecessary ones deleted by the scholars through careful work."[318] Therefore, *Tang Lv* (*Tang Code*) was a typical and great legal code which had served as a link between the past and future, so it had exerted a great influence on other legal codes. For example, the laws implemented in the period of "Wu Dai Shi Guo" (Five Dynasties and Ten Kingdoms) (907 A.D.–960 A.D.) were all adopted from Tang Dynasty without any changes. In Song Dynasty, "the laws were revised on the basis of 'Lv' (criminal law), 'Ling' (decree), 'Ge' (injunctions), and 'Shi' (standard) of Tang Dynasty according to new situations. Besides, 'Chi' (instruction) was added with its contents adjusted according to different 'Si' (bureau), 'Lu' (ancient administrative region), 'Zhou' (subprefectures), and 'Xian'

---

[317] Dong Kang, "Ke Xue De Tang Lv" (The Scientific Tang Lv) in *Dong Kang Fa Xu Wen Ji* (*A Collection of Dong Kang's Legal Essays*), edited by He Qinhua and Wei Qiong, China University of Political Science and Law Press, 2005, p. 315.

[318] Xue Yunsheng (Qing Dynasty), "Li Yan" (Introductory Remarks) in *Tang Ming Lv He Bian* (*A Collection of Laws in Tang and Ming Dynasties*).

(counties)."[319] In the 4th year of Taiding in Yuan Dynasty (327 A.D.), Liu Shi wrote in his book *Tang Lv Shu Yi Xu* (*Preface to the Comments on Tang Code*) that:

> If there was no constancy, there would not be the period of ancient times; if there were no changes, there would not be the current law. However, the arrangement and compilation of *Tang Lv* (*Tang Code*) are just appropriate; if more provisions are added to it, it will become redundant, if some provisions are deleted from it, it will become incomplete, so both redundancy and incompleteness may cause its imbalance.

In Song Dynasty, *Zhi Yuan Xin Ge* (*The New Injunctions in the Reign of Zhiyuan*) was made. Among its twenty chapters, nine chapters were adopted from *Tang Lv* (*Tang Code*). For example, the provisions for "Bai Yi" (The Eight Deliberations), "Shi E" (The Ten Abominations) and "Guan Dang" (giving up one's official position for the atonement for a crime) were all adopted from Tang Dynasty. In the early period of Ming Dynasty, the people like Li Shanchang who was "Zai Xiang" (the prime minister) at the time had said that "the laws implemented in the previous dynasties are all adopted from the nine chapters of the law in Han Dynasty. Until the Tang Dynasty, those laws are collected and compiled, on the basis of which the current laws are all made. So his opinion is accepted by Emperor Taizu."[320] Therefore, four civil officials were ordered to work with the judicial officials to teach twenty provisions of *Tang Lv* (*Tang Code*) every day. In addition, *Da Qing Lv Li* (*The Laws and Precedents of Great Qing*) was also influenced by *Tang Lv* (*Tang Code*), and it was recorded in *Si Ku Quan Shu Zong Mu Ti Yao* (*Descriptive Catalogue to Si Ku Quan Shu*) that "the chapters of *Tang Lv* (*Tang Code*) which are still applied today include: 'Ming Li' (Categories of Penalties and General Principles), 'Zhi Zhi' (The State Office System), 'Zei Dao' (Stealing and Robbery), 'Zha Wei' (Fraud and Forgery), 'Za Fan' (Miscellaneous Crimes), 'Bu Wang' (Arresting) and 'Duan Yu' (Trials and Punishments). Some of them used to be independent chapters in *Tang Lv* (*Tang Code*), but now they are divided into several parts in the code. For example, 'Hu Hun' (*Marriage, Tax and Household Registration*) is divided into 'Hu Yi' (households) and 'Hun' (marriage); 'Jiu Ku' (Stables) is divided into 'Cang Ku' (warehouse) and 'Jiu Mu' (farming and husbandry) and 'Dou Song' (Litigation) is divided into 'Dou Ou' (fighting) and 'Su Song' (litigation). Some of the titles of the original chapters are slightly changed, but they contain the same contents. For example, 'Wei Jin' (Palace Guards) is changed into 'Gong Wei' and 'Shan Xing' (Sending Troops without Authorization) is changed into 'Jun Zheng' (Army and Military)...." Thus, the study of *Tang Lv* (*Tang Code*) can help people to understand both the changes and the origins of the provisions. Just as Sun Xingyan, a scholar in Qing Dynasty, once said: "No one can get to know how the laws are changed in the successive dynasties in the pre-Qin era without reading *Tang Lv* (*Tang Code*)."

Because Tang Dynasty was a country with advanced civilization in the world at the time, there were frequent trade contacts and friendly exchanges between the

---

[319]"Xing Fa Zhi" (The Record of the Criminal Law) in *Song Shi* (*The History of Song Dynasty*).

[320]"Xing Fa Zhi" (The Record of the Criminal Law) in *Ming Shi* (*The History of Ming Dynasty*).

imperial government and the neighboring countries. Consequently, many countries, especially the countries in Eastern Asia, had sent numerous envoys and overseas students to China to study the advanced Chinese culture, legal codes and regulations. Therefore, *Tang Lv (Tang Code)* was the embodiment of Chinese legal system and it had reached the peak of the legal civilization in world at that time. *Tang Lv Shu Yi (The Comments on Tang Code)* was all-inclusive with elaborate, concise and clear provisions and the integration of laws and comments. Besides, history was incorporated with reality, the principles of "Li" (rites), "Fa" (law) and "Qing" (human relationships) were complementary with each other, and the family, state and society were uniformly adjusted. Therefore, *Tang Lv Shu Yi (The Comments on Tang Code)* had exerted a great influence on the laws of the neighboring countries, such as Korea, Japan, Vietnam and Liuqiu. During the periods of Sui and Tang dynasties, Japan had sent many envoys and scholars to China to study laws, which was called "the ancestral teaching" or "ancestral law" in Japan.[321] From their own experience, the Japanese people had realized that "the Great Tang is a great country with complete laws."[322] They, therefore, suggested transplanting the laws of Sui and Tang dynasties to Japan to build its own legal system. The scholars, such as Kibi Makibi, Nagaoka Yamato, Saga Asakuni, and others not only studied "Lv" (criminal law), "Ling" (decree), "Ge" (injunction), and "Shi" (standard) in Tang Dynasty and discussed legal questions, but also initiatively made Japanese laws based on the laws of Tang Dynasty. From the later period of the seventh year of A.D. to the periods of Nara and Heian in Japan, based on *Tang Lv (Tang Code)* and the relevant regulations, a series of legal codes were made and enacted successively by the Mikadoes (the emperors of Japan) to strengthen the ruling of feudal autocracy. The codes and regulations are as follows:

In the 7th year of Tenji in Japan (668 A.D.), the overseas students from Japan, such as Kuromasa and Monk Min, etc. had presided over the enactment of twenty-two volumes of *Jin Jiang Ling (The Ōmi Code)*, which was the first statute law in Japanese history. According to *A Comparison between Tang Ling (The Orders of Tang Dynasty) and Japanese Code* written by Nakata Kaoru, *Jin Jiang Ling (The Ōmi Code)* was made on the bases of "Ling" (decree) issued during the reign of Wude, Zhenguan, Yonghui, Linde, Qianfeng, Yifeng, and Chuigong. However, *Jin Jiang Ling (The Ōmi Code)* was lost in the period of Nara in Japan.[323]

In the 13th year of Tenmu in Japan (686 A.D.), the overseas students from Japan, such as Iki no Hakatoko, etc. had presided over the compilation of *The Law of Tianwu*, which was also made according to the laws enacted during the reign of Zhenguan and Yonghui.

---

[321] Yu Yousun, *Sui Tang Wu Dai Zhong Ri Guan Xi Shi (The History of Sino-Japanese Relationship in the Sui, Tang and Five Dynasties)*, The Commercial Press, 1964, p. 99.

[322] "Tui Gu Tian Huang San Shi Yi Tiao" (Thirty-One Articles in Empress Suiko Period) in *Ri Ben Shu Ji (The Record of Japan)*.

[323] Nakata Kaoru (Japan), *Ri Ben Si Fa Fa Zhi Shi Jiang Yi (The Teaching Materials of the Legal History of the Japanese Private Law)*.

7.2 The Legal System of Tang Dynasty Symbolizing the Establishment...

In the 1st year of Taihō during the reign of Emperor Monmu in Japan (701 A.D.), the epoch-making codes, namely, the six volumes of *Taihō Lv* and eleven volumes of *Taihō Ling* were enacted. The people who participated in the making of *Taihō Lv Ling* (*Taihō Code*) included the overseas students from Japan, such as Iki no Hakatoko, Hanibe Ikuo, and the descendents of Chinese immigrants, such as Huang Wenbei, Duan Dajiao, etc. According to *Lv Ling Kao* (*A Textual Research on Laws and Orders*) written by Satoh Seiji, "*Taihō Lv Ling* (*Taihō Code*) was made on the basis of *Jin Jiang Ling* (*The Ōmi Code*), in which the decrees issued during the reign of Wude, Zhenguan and Yonghui were mainly followed with most part of the decrees adopted from those of Yonghui." It was also recorded in "Xing Fa Zhi" (The Record of the Criminal Law) in *Ri Ben Guo Shi* (*The History of Japan*) that "during the reign of Kotoku, the system of Tang Dynasty was adopted. So 'Xing Bu' (The Department of Punishment) was first established, which was made up of two departments: one was in charge of returning the stolen goods, the other one was in charge of imprisonment. Thereafter, the penal code consisting of twelve chapters was made, including 'Ming Li (Categories of Penalties and General Principles), 'Wei Jin' (Palace Guards), 'Zhi Zhi' (The State Office System), 'Hu Hun' (Marriage, Tax and Household Registration), 'Jiu Ku' (Stables), 'Shan Xing' (Sending Troops without Authorization), 'Dao Zei' (Stealing and Robbery), "Dou Song" (Litigation), 'Zha Wei' (Fraud and Forgery), 'Za' (Miscellaneous Affairs), 'Bu Wang' (Arresting), and 'Duan Yu' (Trials and Punishments). Additionally, it also included provisions for 'Wu Xing' (Five Penalties), 'Ba Nue' (The Eight Cruelties) and 'Liu Yi' (The Six Deliberations) which were similar to *Tang Lv* (*Tang Code*). At that time, after studying law in China, many of the overseas students from Japan went back to their country to teach law, so the laws which they made later on were all complete, detailed and elaborate."

The Japanese scholar Kuwabara Jitsuzoh wrote in his book *On the History of Chinese Legal System*: "Generally speaking, the provisions of *Tang Lv* (*Tang Code*) were adopted in *Taihō Lv Ling* (*Taihō Code*), but they were changed according to the national situations in our country." For example, in *Taihō Lv Ling* (*Taihō Code*), the provisions of "Bai Yi" (The Eight Deliberations) in *Tang Lv* (*Tang Code*) were simplified and changed to "Liu Yi" (The Six Deliberations) by deleting "Yi Qin" (the cases which involved "Huang Qin": the relatives of the emperor) and "Yi Bin" (the Guests of the State: to treat the descendants of previous dynasties as guests of the state who could enjoy a legal privilege); "Shi E" (The Ten Abominations) was changed into "Ba Nue" (The Eight Cruelties) by deleting "Bu Mu" (inharmonious) and "Nei Luan" (committing incest). As to the names of offenses, in *Taihō Lv Ling* (*Taihō Code*), "Wu Xing" (Five Penalties) in *Tang Lv* (*Tang Code*), namely, "Chi" (flogging with light sticks), "Zhang" (flogging with heavy sticks), "Tu" (imprisonment), "Liu" (exile) and "Si" (death penalty) were inherited. The only difference was that for the punishment of "Liu" (exile), accurate distance was not stipulated, with three levels, namely, the exile of short, medium and long distances added. As to the names of offenses, such as "entering the palace without authorization," "blundering against the emperor's carriages," "cursing the emperor," "crossing the border passes without authorization," etc. were exactly the same as those in *Tang Lv* (*Tang Code*).

Taihō Lv Ling (*Taihō Code*) was made during "Taika-Reform." Although it was lost, it was very influential in Japan.

In the 4th year of Yōrō during the reign of Mikado Gensho (718 A.D.), the most completed codes in the history of Japan, namely *Yanglao Lv* (*Yoro Code*) and *Yanglao Ling* (*Yoro Oder*), which consisted of 10 volumes respectively were enacted. *Yanglao Lv* (*Yoro Code*) and *Yanglao Ling* (*Yoro Oder*) were the amendments of *Taihō Lv Ling* (*Taihō Code*) which were made according to *Yong Hui Lv Shu* (also named *Tang Lv Shu Yi*) with a reference to *Kai Yuan Lv Ling* (*Laws and Orders of Kaiyuan*). The codes were ordered to be amended by Kibi no Makibi who used to be an envoy sent by the imperial government of Japan to China and who "had studied and done research on Confucian classics, history and arts in China."[324] The number of articles, titles, and the contents of the chapters were all similar to those of *Tang Lv* (*Tang Code*), so the only difference was that it had fewer provisions.

Apart from "Lv" (criminal law) and "Ling" (decree), the other legal forms of "Ge" (injunction) and "Shi" (standard) in *Tang Lv* (*Tang Code*) also exerted a great influence on the development of legal system in Japan. For example, *Shan Ding Ling Ge* (*Revised Orders and Injunctions*) was issued during the reign of Emperor Kanmu, *Hongren Ge Shi* (*Hongren Injunctions and Standards*) during the reign of Emperor Saga, *Zhen Guan Ge Shi* (*Zhenguan Injunctions and Standards*) during the reign of Emperor Seiwa, and *Yan Xi Ge Shi* (*Yanxi Injunctions and Standards*) during the reign of Emperor Daigo, as was recorded in "Xing Fa Zhi" (The Record of the Criminal Law) in *Da Ri Ben Shi* (*The History of Japan*) that, "the code is perfect, because the imperial court has shown respect to gods, followed the legal system of Tang Dynasty and revised the codes of 'Wu Dai' (the Five Dynasties)." Until the 6th year of Meiji (1873 A.D.), before making *Gai Ding Lv Li* (*The Revised Laws and Precedents*) by "referring to the laws of other countries," the spirit and the basic contents of *Tang Lv* (*Tang Code*) were fully adopted into the Japanese laws, which had surely influenced the development of Japanese legal culture.

Gao Li Lv (*The Law of Korea*) was also made based on the *Tang Lv* (*Tang Code*). According to "Xing Fa Zhi" (The Record of the Criminal Law) in *Gao Li Shi* (*The History of Korea*), which was written by Zheng Linzhi, the minister during the reign of Sejong, "*Gao Li Lv* (*The Law of Korea*) was also based on *Tang Lv* (*Tang Code*). The penal law was also made based on the *Tang Lv* (*Tang Code*) with changes made according to concrete circumstances. The penal code included two articles of 'Yu Guan Ling' (Order of Warden), twelve articles of 'Ming Li' (Categories of Penalties and General Principles), four articles of 'Wei Jin' (Palace Guards), fourteen articles of 'Zhi Zhi' (The State Office System), four articles of 'Hu Hun' (Laws on Marriage, Tax and Household Registration), three articles of 'Jiu Ku' (Stables), three articles of 'Shan Xing' (Sending Troops without Authorization), six articles of 'Dao Zei' (Stealing and Robbery), seven articles of "Dou Song" (Litigation), two articles of 'Zha Wei' (Fraud and Forgery), two articles of 'Za' (Miscellaneous Affairs), eight

---

[324]"Tian Ping Qi Nian Tiao" (The Article Made In the Seventh Year of Emperor Mommu) in *Xu Ri Ben Ji* (*Shoku Nihongi*).

7.2 The Legal System of Tang Dynasty Symbolizing the Establishment...

articles of 'Bu Wang' (Arresting), and four articles of 'Duan Yu' (Trials and Punishments), with totally seventy-one articles. The complicated ones were deleted and the simple ones were retained. So the codes were implemented and applied for some time and what was recorded was authentic." In *Gao Li Lv* (*The Law of Korea*), not only the arrangement of the chapters, but also the names of crimes, the preferential rules for the privileged and the rules on other aspects were all very similar to those in *Tang Lv* (*Tang Code*).

The laws of Li Dynasty (The Lý Dynasty) and Chen Dynasty (Trần Dynasty) in Vietnam were also influenced by *Tang Lv* (*Tang Code*). According to the records in "Xing Fa Zhi" (The Record of the Criminal Law) in *Li Chao Xian Zhang Lei Zhi* (*Records of Laws and Regulations of the Past Dynasties*), most of *Xing Shu* (*Penal Code*) which was consisted of three volumes enacted in the 1st year of Mingdao during the reign of Emperor Lý Thái Tông (1042 A.D.) and *Guo Chao Xing Lv* (*The Penal Code of Guochao*) enacted in the 6th year of Jianzhong during the reign of Emperor Trần Thái Tông were written based on the *Tang Lv* (*Tang Code*). It was recorded that "in lawmaking at that time, efforts were made to follow the old laws of Tang and Song dynasties, with severity and leniency of the provisions taken into consideration." In *Hong De Xing Lv* (*The Penal Law of Hongde*) made in the 1st year of Lê Dynasty (1401 A.D.) "the articles and criteria in the laws of Tang Dynasty were also adopted. The code was implemented in the following dynasties and was finally adapted into the constitution." This penal law not only included the provisions of "Shi E" (The Ten Abominations) and "Ba Yi" (The Eight Deliberations), but also other provisions, such as "Wei Jin" (palace guards), "Jun Zheng" (military administration), "Hu Hun" (marriage, tax and household registration), "Dao Zei" (stealing and robbery), "Jian Ying" (adultery), "Ou Song" (affrays and accusation), "Zha Wei" (fraud and forgery), "Wei Zhi" (punishing officials' dereliction of duty), "Za Fan" (miscellaneous crimes), "Bu Wang" (arresting) and "Duan Yu" (trials and punishments), which were all similar to those in *Tang Lv* (*Tang Code*).

Except for the special characteristics of *Tang Lv* (*Tang Code*), the other reason why the Chinese legal system was accepted by Japan, Korea, Vietnam, and Liuqiu as their mother legal system was that those countries had similar national condition to Tang Dynasty. Besides, the economy of all of the above-mentioned countries was agriculture-based, and great importance was attached to patriarchal ethics and the political system of autocracy. Moreover, they were all under the influence of Confucian ideology. Thus, the national condition had provided an important material basis for the acceptance of Chinese legal system. However, for those countries, in accepting the Chinese legal system, they did not simply copy it without making any changes, actually many changes were made according to the specific circumstances of their own countries. For example, In *Taihō Lv Ling* (*Taihō Code*), the crime of "Shi E" (The Ten Abominations) included in *Tang Lv* (*Tang Code*) was changed into "Ba Nue" (The Eight Cruelties), namely, "Mou Fan" (plotting rebellion or plotting to endanger the country), "Mou Da Ni" (great sedition), "Mou Pan" (treason), "E Ni" (abusing or murdering the elders), "Bu Dao" (depravity), "Da Bu Jing" (being greatly irreverent), "Bu Xiao" (being unfilial), and "Bu Yi" (injustice), with the provision of "Bu Mu" (inharmonious) combined with "Bu Dao" (depravity) and with the provision of "Nei Luan" (committing incest) abolished. Moreover, the courtesies and etiquettes listed in *Tang Lv (Tang Code)* were also reduced in *Taihō Lv Ling (Taihō Code)*. Therefore, it can be inferred that as an independent legal system, it should not only have its own unique characteristics, but also be accepted and adopted by other countries and regions; otherwise, it would not be considered as an independent system. The Chinese legal civilization is longstanding, so the Chinese legal system has already been completely formed and established in Tang Dynasty, which could be proved by the basic characteristics of *Tang Lv (Tang Code)* and its impacts abroad. Therefore, *Tang Lv (Tang Code)* not only occupied a very important historical position in the history of the development of Chinese legal system, but also was a glorious page in the history of the development of the world legal system.

7.3 The Legal Systems of "Wu Dai Shi Guo" (Five Dynasties and Ten Kingdoms)

In the late period of Tang Dynasty, though the peasant uprising led by Huang Chao was cruelly suppressed, the ruling of the imperial government of Tang Dynasty was also on the brink of collapse. The military governors of the vassal states separated themselves from the central government by taking the advantage of the uprising, held sway over their regions and fought wars against each other. Thus, finally in 907 A.D., a general named Zhu Wen, who turned traitor to insurrectionary army, subverted the imperial government of Tang Dynasty, proclaimed himself emperor and established a country named Hou Liang. Later on, other four imperial governments were successively set up in the central plains of China, namely Latter Tang, Latter Jin, Latter Han, and Latter Zhou. The five imperial governments altogether were referred to as "Wu Dai" (the Five Dynasties). In the same period, some powerful "Jie Du Shi" (military governor) in the country successively proclaimed themselves emperors by setting up ten separatist ruling regions, which were referred to as "Shi Guo" (the Ten Kingdoms) in history. The emergence of "Wu Dai Shi Guo" (Five Dynasties and Ten Kingdoms) was the continuing and malignant development of the separatist regimes of "Fan Zhen" (local regimes) by military governors in late Tang Dynasty.

During the administration of "Wu Dai Shi Guo" (Five Dynasties and Ten Kingdoms), a separatist country of Qidan (Khitan) located in Liaohe River Basin in Northeast of China began to spring up. Gradually, it had seized sixteen "Zhou" (subprefecture) of Yanyun and then established a new country named Liao and made Yanjin (Beijing today) the capital. Liao finally became a powerful country in northern China. Until then, China again was entrapped in the split situation of northern and southern China.

Basically, the laws implemented during the period of "Wu Dai Shi Guo" (Five Dynasties and Ten Kingdoms) included "Lv" (criminal law), "Ling" (decree), "Ge" (injunction) and "Shi" (standard) and "Chi" (instruction) which were applied in the later period of Tang Dynasty, but "Chi" (instruction) was used as the major form of law, which could be proved by what was recorded in a book: "The conviction is made by 'Chi' (instruction)."[325] Therefore, the compilation of "Chi" (instruction) became the major legislative activity.

In September of the 3rd year of Kaiping (909 A.D.), a decree was issued by Zhu Wen, Emperor Taizu of Hou Liang to have "Lv" (criminal law), "Ling" (decree), "Ge" (injunction) and "Shi" (standard) revised. In December of the following year, the newly-made law was presented to him by his ministers. The law consisted of thirty volumes of "Lv Ling" (Laws and Orders), twenty volumes of "Shi" (standard), eleven volumes of "Ge" (injunction), thirteen volumes of catalogue and thirty volumes of *Lv Shu* (*The Comments on Law*) with totally five parts, eleven sections, one hundred and thirty volumes, which was called *Da Liang Xin Ding Ge Shi Lv Ling* (*The Newly-Made "Ge" "Shi" "Lv" "Ling" of the Great Liang*).

In the 3rd year of Tongguang during the reign of Emperor Zhuangsong in Latter Tang (925 A.D.), based on *Da Zhong Xing Lv Tong Lei* (*Collections of Criminal Laws in Dazhong Period*), which was implemented during the reign of Emperor Xuanzong in Tang Dynasty, the thirteen volume *Tong Guang Xing Lv Tong Lei* (*The Catalogue of the Penal Code of Tonggang*) was enacted. In the 2nd year of Qingtai (935 A.D.), "'Chi' (instruction) which was issued within the eleven years before the 1st year of Qingtai and which could be permanently implemented, were compiled into thirteen volumes with totally three hundred and ninety-four articles,"[326] which was collectively called *Qing Tai Bian Chi* (*Collection of Imperial Instructions*).

In the 3rd year of Tianfu in Latter Jin (938 A.D.), *Tian Fu Za Chi* (*Collection of Imperial Instructions on Miscellaneous Affairs*) was made.

In the 1st year of Guangshun in Latter Zhou (951 A.D.), "'Chi' (instruction) about the penal law which was implemented in Jin and Han dynasties and the early period of Latter Zhou was collected together and divided into two volumes. Later, they were included the collection of imperial instructions entitled *Da Zhou Xu Bian Chi* (*The Sequel of the Imperial Instructions of the Great Zhou*) and were implemented in the various departments and bureaus according to orders."[327] In the 4th year of Xiande during the reign of Emperor Shizong in Zhou Dynasty (957 A.D.), "because the laws are outdated, the expressions are old-fashioned, the articles and items are complicated and misleading, and the provisions of 'Chi' (instruction) and 'Ge' (injunction) were repetitive and difficult to be applied," Zhang Shi, who was "Shi Yu Shi" (subordinate of Grand Censor) at the time and some other people were ordered to make a new penal law. In the next year, *Da Zhou Xing Tong* (*The United Penal Code*

---

[325]"Yi Yu" (On Prison) in "Xing Fa Bu" (The Section of Penal Law) in *Ce Fu Yuan Gui* (*The Record of the Great Events*) (Book 3).

[326]"Ding Lv Ling" (The Making of Laws and Decrees) in "Xing Fa Bu" (The Section of Penal Law) in *Ce Fu Yuan Gui* (*The Record of the Great Events*) (Book 3).

[327]"Xing Fa Zhi" (The Record of the Criminal Law) in *Jiu Wu Dai Shi* (*The Old History of the Five Dynasties*).

of the Great Zhou) consisting of twenty-one volumes was completed and "enacted nationwide together with *Tang Lv Shu Yi* (*The Comments on Tang Code*), *Ling* (*Decree*) and *Shi* (*Standard*)."[328] *Da Zhou Xing Tong* (*The United Penal Code of the Great Zhou*) was compiled based on the *Da Zhong Xing Lv Tong Lei* (*Catalogue of the Penal Law in the Period of Dazhong*), in which the laws were divided into different categories to which "Lv" (criminal law), "Ling" (decree), "Ge" (injunction), "Shi" (standard), and "Chi" (instruction) with similar contents were attached. *Da Zhou Xing Tong* (*The United Penal Code of the Great Zhou*) was carefully made, so a new stylistic rule and layout was created. It was recorded that "in the code, the provisions are considered as the major texts; when the words or the meaning of the provisions are difficult to understand, the comments and interpretation are made; when the words and provisions are easy to understand, the comments and interpretation are omitted; the rules and orders with similar contents are arranged after the main text of the provisions which was followed by the abolished imperial instructions; when it is not appropriate to give interpretations for the provisions or the interpretations are not complete, a new article is arranged after the provision; when the provisions are misleading for archaic and doubtful expressions, explanations which are printed in red color are given. The imperial prohibition and common rules in 'Zhou' (subprefecture) and 'Xian' (county) are all collected, classified and attached to the code according to their names."[329] Those changes had had a great impact on the later legislation in Song Dynasty.

As to the laws implemented in the period of "Shi Guo" (the Ten Kingdoms), Emperor Taizu of Wu, who came to power from a common person, had undertaken the task of law revision and made *Ge Ling* (*Injunctions and Orders*) consisting of fifty volumes. As early as when he was "Zai Xiang" (the prime minister) of Wu state, Li Sheng had always devoted himself to promoting what was beneficial and abolishing what was harmful to the country. Meanwhile, "he had committed himself to the revision of old laws. So after he succeeded to the throne in Nan Tang, he ordered the judicial officials and imperial ministers to begin the work of law revision. So finally the thirty-volume *Sheng Yuan Tiao* (*The Articles of Shengyuan*) was completed."[330] According to "Yi Wen Zhi" (Books and Records) in *Song Shi* (*The History of Song Dynasty*), the following laws were also implemented in Nan Tang: *Jiang Nan Xing Lv Tong Lei* (*The United Catalogue of the Penal Code of Jiangnan*), *Jiang Nan Ge Ling Tiao* (*The Articles of Jiangnan*), and *Shu Za Zhi Chi* (*The Imperial Instructions on Miscellaneous Affairs*). However, all the laws and codes made in the period of "Wu Dai Shi Guo" (Five Dynasties and Ten Kingdoms) were unfortunately lost.

---

[328]"Xing Fa Zhi" (The Record of the Criminal Law) in *Jiu Wu Dai Shi* (*The Old History of the Five Dynasties*).
[329]"Xing Fa Zhi" (The Record of the Criminal Law) in *Jiu Wu Dai Shi* (*The Old History of the Five Dynasties*).
[330]*Zi Zhi Tong Jian* (*History as a Mirror*), Vol. 283.

7.3 The Legal Systems of "Wu Dai Shi Guo" (Five Dynasties and Ten Kingdoms)

As to the civil and economic law, considering the social and economic changes and the complication of civil disputes in the later period of "Wu Dai Shi Guo" (Five Dynasties and Ten Kingdoms), specific legal provisions were enacted on acquisitive prescription of property rights, "Dian Quan" (pawn rights) and "Zhai Quan" (creditor's rights). For example, in December of the 1st year of Guangshun during the reign of Emperor Taizong in Zhou Dynasty (951 A.D.), in a reply of the documents presented by Kaifeng Fu (Kaifeng prefecture), the system of contracts and "Ya Bao" (intermediary agent) wascomprehensively regulated:

> During the transaction of 'Ya Ren' (middleman) and shop owners, money should be paid and goods should be taken away immediately; if the money cannot be paid in full, 'Ya Ren' (middleman) and the shop owners should schedule a time limit for the rest of the payment of the goods and sign contracts with the buyers as guarantees. If a 'Ya Ren' (middleman) escapes or the time limit is exceeded but buyer still cannot afford to pay, the other people who have signed the contract should help to pay for it. If some 'Ya Ren' (middleman) is poor or dishonest, and someone is worried that it will be difficult to pay back the money, the contract can be used as evidence by the people who have signed it.[331]

In the 2nd year of Guangshun (952 A.D.), a complete code of *Jin Si Yan Qu Fa* (*Law on the Prohibition of Secret Making of Salt and Distiller's Yeast*) was enacted, in which the making and trading of salt and distiller's yeast were regulated in detail, which had exerted a great influence on the evolution of salt law in later dynasties.

As to the criminal law, according to the records in "Ding Lv Ling" (The Making of Laws and Decrees) in "Xing Fa Bu" (The Section of Penal Law) in *Ce Fu Yuan Gui* (*The Record of the Great Events*), in the 2nd year of Changxing during the reign of Emperor Mingzong of Latter Tang Dynasty (931 A.D.) it was regulated in *Kai Cheng Ge* (*Kaicheng Injunctions*) that "the accused should be punished after the evidence of his illegal encroachment of property has been discovered. If the accused is tortured to death in interrogation, those involved shall be punished for intentional killing." In the period of "Wu Dai" (the Five Dynasties) when interrogation was misused, it was undoubtedly a protection of the accused to investigate the judge's responsibility for the death of the accused in interrogation. In an imperial instruction issued in the 1st year of Tiancheng (926 A.D.), for the judge's willful acts of implicating the innocent people in punishment, it was stipulated that "from today forward, the principal offender who has committed the crime of theft shall be punished after he is caught and after the evidence of his illegal encroachment of property is discovered. However, the relevant witnesses shall not be implicated in the punishment and their residence should not be searched."[332]

In the 2nd year of Changxing of Latter Tang (931 A.D.), an official of "Lu Shi Can Jun" (the local supervisor) in Puzhou presented a memorial about prison administration to the emperor, in which he stated that "in the prisons of 'Dao' (the administration district below the province), the prisoners are tortured illegally, so

---

[331]"Ding Lv Ling" (The Making of Laws and Decrees) in "Xing Fa Bu" (The Section of Penal Law) in *Ce Fu Yuan Gui* (*The Record of the Great Events*) (Book 5).

[332]"Xing Fa Za Lu" (The Record of Miscellaneous Criminal Affairs) in *Wu Dai Hui Yao* (*Collections of Historical Records of the Five Dynasties*).

many of them cannot bear the pain of torture. Some of them are ill, and some even have died. Please issue an order to set up hospitals in prison to provide medical treatment for and to give medicine to the prisoners."[333] His memorial was approved by Emperor Mingzong, so an edict was issued: "Hospitals should be set up in the prisons of 'Dao' (the administration district below the province), 'Zhou' (subprefecture) and 'Fu' (prefecture)." Therefore, "if prisoners are sick, doctors should be sent to have them treated. The prisoners shall be retried after the treatment according to their criminal offenses." Besides, "wooden shackles should be washed every five days."[334] Later on, the regulations on prison administration which were included in *Yu Guan Ling* (*Order of Warden*) made in Tang Dynasty were emphasized. For example, "if the prisoners died without relatives, they shall be given coffins by the government and shall be buried in the land of government. Moreover, the tombs shall be separated from the open fields with bricks, and gravestones shall be set up with their names engraved on."[335] In addition, decrees were issued by Emperor Taizu of Latter Zhou Dynasty to order the officials of "Dao" (the administration district below the province), "Zhou" (subprefecture) and "Fu" (ancient administrative district between province and county) to "hear the cases timely without delay and to inflict lenient punishments on the accused. Besides, the warders should clean the cells and wash the prisoners' shackles frequently to get rid of fleas and louses; the prisoners should not suffer from hunger and thirst and they should be supplied with water and porridge; if prisoners are sick, they should be allowed to be looked after and visited by their families; if they do not have families, the prison warden should send doctors to look after them to rescue the dying." It was also recorded that "wardens were often sent to clean the cells and the wooden shackles of the prisoners. If the prisoners were hungry or thirsty, water and porridge were supplied; if some of them were sick, their families were allowed to look after them; if some of them did not have families, the doctors would be sent to look after them in order to avoid unreasonable death and to bring damage to harmony."[336] Another decree was issued in the 2nd year of Xiande during the reign of Emperor Shizong of Zhou (955 A.D.):

> If the prisoners in the prisons of 'Dao' (the administration district below the province) do not have families to give them food, they should be given two *Sheng* of rice everyday by the government. Besides, it is forbidden for wardens to reduce their food and water supply at

---

[333]"Xing Fa Zhi" (The Record of the Criminal Law) in *Jiu Wu Dai Shi* (*The Old History of the Five Dynasties*).

[334]"Xing Fa Za Lu" (The Record of Miscellaneous Criminal Affairs) in *Wu Dai Hui Yao* (*Collections of Historical Records of the Five Dynasties*).

[335]"Xing Fa Za Lu" (The Record of Miscellaneous Criminal Affairs) in *Wu Dai Hui Yao* (*Collections of Historical Records of the Five Dynasties*).

[336]"Xing Fa Zhi" (The Record of the Criminal Law) in *Jiu Wu Dai Shi* (*The Old History of the Five Dynasties*).

will. Their cells and shackles should be cleaned with water every five days. If prisoners are sick, the doctors shall be sent during the daytime.[337]

As Emperor Shizong attached much importance to prison administration and he even often "heard the cases in his palace," "the other officials all inspected prisons and heard the cases in person by following his example."[338] So the construction of prison administration during the reign of emperor Shizong was very valuable in the history of prison administration in China. However, the fact that great importance was attached to prison administration by the successful monarchs in the period of "Wu Dai" (the Five Dynasties) had just shown the darkness of prison administration and the cruelty of the officials and warden in this period.

The main characteristics of the legal system in "Wu Dai Shi Guo" (Five Dynasties and Ten Kingdoms) were the misuse of punishment, which was inseparable from the situation where rebels arose in the land like swarms of wasps and despotic ruling was adopted by almost all rulers. In Song Dynasty, Wen Yanbo once pointed out that "in the later period of Tang and 'Wu Dai' (the Five Dynasties), severe punishments were implemented to solve the social problems. Therefore, beyond the regulation of law, the penalties of 'Tu' (imprisonment) and 'Liu' (exile) could be randomly aggravated to that of 'Si' (death penalty)."[339] According to *Tang Lv* (*Tang Code*), the maximum penalty for theft was "Liu" (exile) with labor service. However, in the later period of Tang Dynasty, if the stolen property amounted to three *pi* of cloth, the thieves could be punished by death penalty in public. This punishment was continued in the period of Latter Tang. In the early period of Tianfu in Latter Jin, "if the stolen property accounts to five *pi* of cloth, the thieves will be sentenced to death; if the stolen property amounts to three *pi* of cloth, the thieves will be punished by 'Liu' (exile) with the punishment of 'Zhang' (flogging with heavy sticks)." An imperial decree was issued in the 12th year of Tianfu in Han Dynasty: "As long as the thieves are caught and the evidence of illegally obtained property is certain, no matter how much the property is, they shall be sentenced to death."[340] During the period of Latter Han, "if a thief has stolen one *qian* of money, he shall be sentenced to death penalty."

In Latter Zhou Dynasty, lenient punishments were adopted by Emperor Taizu and it was stipulated that "if the stolen property amounts to three *pi* of silk cloth, the thieves should be executed in public."[341]

Generally speaking, during the period of "Wu Dai" (the Five Dynasties), the crime of "Qiang Dao" (robbery) was severely punished by "Zu Zhu" (killing of the whole clan of a criminal). For the crime of fornication, the man and woman involved

---

[337]"Xing Fa Za Lu" (The Record of Miscellaneous Criminal Affairs) in *Wu Dai Hui Yao* (*Collections of Historical Records of the Five Dynasties*).

[338]*Zi Zhi Tong Jian* (*History as a Mirror*), Vol. 292.

[339]"Xing Fa Zhi" (The Record of the Criminal Law) in *Song Shi* (*The History of Song Dynasty*).

[340]"Xing Kao" (A Textual Research of the Criminal Penalties) (Part 5) in *Wen Xian Tong Kao* (*A General Textual Research of the Documents*), Vol. 166.

[341]"Ding Zang" (To Verify the Stolen Goods) in *Wu Dai Hui Yao* (*Collections of Historical Records of the Five Dynasties*).

should be sentenced to death. The offenders who secretly sold salt or made distiller's yeast would all be punished severely. In the period of Latter Tang, if one person had secretly sold salt as much as ten *jin* or more, he should be sentenced to death; if one had secretly made salt, he should be punished by death penalty without considering how much he had made. Moreover, the person who reported the case to the government would be rewarded. In the period of Latter Han, the people who secretly made salt and distiller's yeast should be punished by death penalty without considering how much they had made. In Latter Zhou Dynasty, this regulation was changed: If people have secretly made salt and distiller's yeast which "amounts to five *jin* or more, they shall be punished by death penalty after being punished by 'Zhang' (flogging with heavy sticks)."[342]

In the aspect of "Xing Fa" (criminal punishment), it fully reflected the characteristics of the times featured by the malpractice of penalty. Zhao Yi in Qing Dynasty had pointed out in "Er Shi Er Shi Zha Ji" (Reading Notes of the Twenty-Two Official Histories) in *Wu Dai Lan Xing* (*The Abuse of Punishment in the Five Dynasties*) that "during the troubled times of 'Wu Dai' (the Five Dynasties), there were no fixed regulations in law, so the common people were all trampled like mud and ashes. If one had committed crimes, it would be common to see his whole clan was punished by 'Si Xing' (death penalties)." The cruelest penalty, "Ling Chi" (the punishment of dismemberment and the lingering death), was created in the period of "Wu Dai" (the Five Dynasties). Thus, it was stated by the famous poet Lu You in Song Dynasty in "Tiao Dui Zhuang" (Statement to the Emperor) in *Wei Nan Wen Ji* (*The Collection of Lu You's Poems in Weinan*):

> It was troubled time in 'Wu Dai' (the Five Dynasties), so it was difficult to prevent people from committing crimes by enforcing the common penalties. Then the penalty of 'Ling Chi' (the punishment of dismemberment and the lingering death) was specially enforced beyond the law. During the execution of this penalty, though the muscles of accused had all been dismembered, the accused could still breathe; their livers and hearts were still functioning and they were still able to see and hear.

In judicial adjudication, it was a common phenomenon that "harsh penalties were applied for minor crimes," or "the accused were imprisoned overtime," or "the accused were granted amnesty after having been executed."[343]

Because of social turmoil caused by the long-lasting brutal wars and the continuous rebellion of people, the rulers felt that their power was under great threat. Therefore, they tried to intimidate the common people with harsh punishments and to get through the troubled political situation. However, the autocratic administration of warlords sustained by military forces and harsh punishments could not last long. Consequently, these dynasties were overthrown by Song Dynasty, so the separated China was unified again.

---

[342]"Shi Huo Zhi" (The Records of National Finance and Economy) in *Jiu Wu Dai Shi* (*The Old History of the Five Dynasties*).
[343]"Xing Fa Za Lu" (The Record of Miscellaneous Criminal Affairs) in *Wu Dai Hui Yao* (*Collections of Historical Records of the Five Dynasties*).